Greek for Reading

Preliminary Edition

Greek for Reading

Gerda M. Seligson
with
Susan Shelmerdine
and
Ariel Loftus

Ann Arbor
THE UNIVERSITY OF MICHIGAN PRESS

ISBN 0-472-08266-3
Library of Congress Catalog Card No. 94-78343
Published in the United States of America by
The University of Michigan Press
Manufactured in the United States of America

2001 2000 1999 1998 7 6 5 4

Note on the Preliminary Edition

In this edition of *Greek for Reading* we note where the original Greek of the Basic Sentences has been adapted. The most frequent adaptations have been omissions, but in the earlier lessons some sentences have been more thoroughly rewritten. Sentences without attributions are inspired by Greek originals but do not reflect the originals' vocabulary or syntax. For more practice sentences, we suggest T.B. Harbottle's *Anthology of Classical Quotations* (re-issued, San Antonio, 1984).

In future editions of *Greek for Reading* we plan to include more materials for reading. Meanwhile we would recommend Hillard and Botting's hundred-year old *Elementary Greek Translation* (re-issued, Duckworth 1982). The instructor will not find it too difficult to compensate for the differences in the order of presentation. The vocabulary in Hillard and Botting prepares the student well for reading Plato or Euripides in the third semester.

Acknowledgments

Greek for Reading in its present form is a companion volume to *Latin For Reading* (Knudsvig, Seligson, Craig, Ann Arbor, 1986). It was originally my intention to revise J. T. Allen's *The First Year of Greek* according to the principles found productive in *Latin for Reading*. I received permission to do so from the Macmillan Company. However the order in which concepts are introduced is an integral feature of both *Latin for Reading* and of *Greek for Reading*. Allen's *The First Year of Greek* has wonderful selections from Greek prose and poetry, but the order of chapters was too different and it proved impossible for me to carry out my intention. In his preface Allen says of his selections, "They have been chosen for their intrinsic merit and graded with greatest care, and deserve to be read and reread many times." With the permission of Macmillan I have included the Euclid passage and the Plato passages. I regret that more selections could not be included into *Greek for Reading,* but, for example, the Euclid passages which Allen placed at the beginning of his textbook, could only be placed at the end of *Greek for Reading*. Nevertheless, following in Allen's footsteps, I hope that some of the "old wine" has been preserved in this "new bottle."

Like Allen, I am grateful to all who have helped in bringing this textbook to the form it has now. Over the years instructors at the University of Michigan, Virginia Polytechnic, the University of North Carolina at Greensboro, and Wabash College have relayed their suggestions and observations. In particular I am grateful to Andrew Becker who learned his Latin from *Latin for Reading* as an undergraduate and continued his support for the method into his teaching career. Among the many people who have encouraged me, I owe a special debt of gratitude to James Boyd White, Roger Hornsby, Donald McClosky and most recently Gregory Dobrov. In addition Ann Hanson has done much more than proofreading, and William Brehm much more than formatting. Finally the reactions both positive and negative of my students at Lawrence University, the University of Iowa, and the University of Michigan have been invaluable for the genesis and development of this book.

Gerda M. Seligson
Ann Arbor, Michigan

Table of Contents

Introduction

To the Instructor

Greek for Reading begins with the simple sentence, and progresses through a series of expansions, substitutions and transformations, which, like the expanding landscapes seen through the windows of a spiraling staircase, gradually encompass the full possibilities of the complex sentence.

Greek for Reading is built on the same conviction as *Latin for Reading*, namely, that learning to read a language is different from learning to write a language, and that it must be taught differently. Our ability to read is the result of our ability to expect and recognize complete structures. In our own language we do this without much trouble, in a foreign language we must learn to expect and recognize complete structures.

With reading rather than writing being the goal, there will be a change in priority among the areas to be mastered by the students. Traditionally morphology and vocabulary have claimed the first places, as indeed necessary for correct writing. These places will now be given to syntax and semantics. I personally consider that providing an outline of morphology stressing the morpheme rather than the allomorphs (see Glossary) will allow time in the classroom to be spent on acquiring correct syntactic expectations. Likewise emphasis on sense-groups and stems rather than on single items will allow a qualitative rather than a quantitative attitude towards the frightening number of items in the dictionary. Of course, morphology and vocabulary should be included in tests, but with moderation. Both will naturally receive their due as the students begin to read connected passages. Being in command of syntax and semantics they will perhaps adopt some useful shortcuts or they will simply cram vocabulary with rather better results than I did at their age. Ideally they will read Greek as they do English.

On the elementary level, at which this book aims, the fully complete structure is the sentence. On subsequent levels complete structures will be paragraphs, chapters, books, where reading with comprehension will depend on attention to the signals of cohesion and on discourse analysis. Some of these signals will naturally occur on the elementary level also, but the purpose of this book will be accomplished when the student can handle the sentence.

Looking at the table of contents you will notice that the Lessons proper, twenty-six plus the Reviews, are preceded and followed by unnumbered sections with various purposes.

Before the Lessons

The Glossary has been put in front of the book so it will be easy to find and use. It aims at giving simple working definitions, not technically refined ones. More terms will be listed in the Reviews, where the students are asked to write their own definitions. Even gifted students at first find it very difficult to describe the antecedent and to distinguish between the subject of a governing clause and the antecedent of a relative clause contained in that governing clause. In saving as much time as possible from rote learning tasks, the instructor can focus on critical thinking skills.

The **Pre-view** deals with items seen on the printed page other than those treated in the lessons: the alphabet, sound changes, breathings and accents. The Pre-view is meant to serve as a guide for you to use whenever it is appropriate. The alphabet must, of course, be learned immediately. An early acquaintance with the concept and the principles of sound changes can ease future memorization and recognition of paradigms. While students learn to spell and observe other visible signals, they might as well hear about elision, *etc.*. For students, the section may also serve as a reference summary of individual topics to be consulted as they are introduced throughout the book. However many instructors may wish to direct students only to the alphabet page and use the rest of the section sparingly, if at all.

In contrast to the Pre-view, **Speechacts** should be taken seriously. The concept of the speechact is basic to language and to this course. Time spent on it is always well spent. It is also an opportunity to discuss differences between the students' speech habits and changes in acceptable English. This will help loosening some monolingual prejudices.

After the Lessons

The **Re-view** is just that, a review of the concepts and principles basic to this course. It is also to be used for reference.

The list of **Basic Sentences** can be utilized for all sorts of tasks, e.g., morphological, syntactic and semantic analysis, transformations, expansions, substitutions, even English comprehension question and translations.

The section on **Verbforms** will allow practice in the vital and difficult skill of locating a word in the Greek dictionary.

The **Morphology** lists complete paradigms of all parts of speech for reference, synopsis, observations on allomorphs or memorization.

The **Stem List** lists the most common Greek stems and should be integrated into vocabulary learning early on.

The Lessons

The **Lessons** are all built on a similar format:

Titles	
Basic Sentences	model
Morphology	explanation
Syntax	explanation
Semantics	explanation
Exercises	practice
Readings	application
Vocabulary	

The core of the lessons are the **exercises**, designed to be done as homework assignments. Because understanding the explanations is a precondition for doing the exercises, students soon learn that they must read and reread the explanations and instructions. They can do so without the instructor necessarily pre-teaching the new material. The instructor can, however, orient students by going over contents of the lessons with them, separating old from new information. For example, in Lesson Six the syntactic term 'kernel' is familiar, whereas the notion of 'voice' and the morphology of the passive and the middle voice are new items. The syntactic concept of adverbial modifier is old, so is the morphology of the dative and the genitive. But the semantics of these cases open a new view on the possibilities of the sentence. The instructor can then reinforce what has already been learned, while leaving the new picture to be scrutinized by the students themselves.

Like Caesar's commentaries (*si parva licet componere magnis*), the explanations are kept sparse and lean, yet hopefully clear enough to be understood and applied by the average student. I comment on them only after I have seen the mistakes in the students' homework. I insist that this be in my hands some time before class. (I am fortunate, because I teach four times a week at the eleventh hour.) While I study the work that has been handed in, some students with fears and learning difficulties are encouraged to do their homework in my office rather than struggling unsuccessfully alone. Obviously they do not do so every day, but often enough to save class time for reading. Translation should not be a means of learning, but a reward for understanding.

Pre-view

Note to Instructor

This section is not intended as a first lesson either in part or as a whole. It is included as an overview and guide for the instructor's presentation of punctuation, alphabet and the rules of Greek spelling. The Lessons direct students to this section as needed. As suggested in To The Instructor, some instructors may wish to use only the alphabet page.

How to make the best of the printed page

Originally ancient Greek texts were handwritten, not printed. There were no divisions between words, let alone punctuation marks, accents, breathing marks or deletion signals. All of these were added gradually as Greek became the *lingua franca* of the Hellenistic world.

A printed page in a modern edition of an ancient Greek text shows the following signs:

- Punctuation marks
- Word divisions
- Letters
- Breathing marks
- Accents
- Apostrophe

Some Punctuation Marks

1. The period [.] indicates that all syntactic expectations have been fulfilled.
2. The question mark [;] looks like the English semicolon. It also indicates that all syntactic expectations have been fulfilled. In addition it indicates the speech act question.
3. The comma [,] indicates that a present chain of expectations has been fulfilled or is being interrupted or is being duplicated.
4. A raised period [·]indicates an English colon and semicolon.

Word divisions

Words are surrounded by spaces.

Preview

Letters

The standard Greek alphabet has twenty-four **letters**.

Form	*Name*	*Transliterated*	*Sound*	*Greek example*
Α α	alpha	A a	drama	δρᾶμα
Β β	beta	B b	bible	βιβλίον
Γ γ	gamma	G g	ganglion	γάγγλιον
Δ δ	delta	D d	decade	δέκα
Ε ε	epsilon	E e	epic	ἔπος
Ζ ζ	zeta	Z z	adds, zone	ζώνη
Η η	eta	E e	they	ἤδη
Θ θ	theta	Th th	atheist	θεός
Ι ι	iota	I i	intrigue	ἐπιπίπτω
Κ κ	kappa	K k	kind	καιρός
Λ λ	lambda	L l	logic	λόγος
Μ μ	mu	M m	meter	μέτρον
Ν ν	nu	N n	noon	νῦν
Ξ ξ	xi	X x	axiom	νύξ
Ο ο	omicron	O o	obstacle	ἀπό
Π π	pi	P p	poet	ποιητής
Ρ ρ	rho	R r	rhinoceros	ἔρως
Σ σ, ς	sigma	S s	symbol	σοφός
Τ τ	tau	T t	topography	τόπος
Υ υ	upsilon	U u	put, boot	γυμναστική, Κῦρος
Φ φ	phi	Ph ph	philosophy	φιλοσοφία
Χ χ	chi	Ch ch	cat	χορός
Ψ ψ	psi	Ps ps	eclipse	ψυχή
Ω ω	omega	O o	ode	ἄνθρωπος

The form ς is used only and always at the end of a word. Elsewhere σ is used.

The ancients used only capital letters; the small letters came into use during the Middle Ages.

Diacritical marks

There are two **breathing marks**: rough breathing ‘, which corresponds to English h and smooth breathing ’, the latter signaling the absence of rough breathing. All initial vowels and diphthongs show breathing signs and so does the letter ῥ. Accents and breathings appear on the second vowel of a diphthong.

PREVIEW

There are three **accent marks**: the acute ʹ, the circumflex ˜ and the grave .
The **apostrophe** signals a zero, the absence of a sound or sounds that must be understood as being there.

Sounds

Greek was not only a written language but also a spoken language. Learning to pronounce the sounds is often useful. The letters represent sounds and the sounds are customarily arranged into **vowels** and **consonants**. The vowels are **α, ε, η, ι, ο, υ, ω,** the rest of the letters are consonants.

Vowels

Vowels are long or short. ε, ο are always short; η, ω are always long. α, ι, υ are sometimes long and sometimes short .

Two vowels united in one syllable are called **Diphthongs.** Diphthongs are always long. The second vowel is either ι or υ, as follows: αι, ει, οι, αυ, ευ, ου. If the first vowel is long ᾱ or η or ω, an ι is written under it instead of next to it: ᾳ, ῃ, ῳ. This iota is called **iota subscript** and it is not pronounced.

Diphthongs	*Sound*	*Greek Examples*
αι	**ai**sle	κ**αι**ρός
ει	fr**ei**ght	λύ**ει**
οι	t**oi**l	καλ**οί**
υι	**we**	**υἱ**ός
αυ	n**ow**	π**αύ**ει
ευ	**eh - oo**	**εὐ**τύχει
ηυ	**ei - oo**	**ηὕ**ρηκα
ου	b**oo**t	λύκ**ου**

All initial Vowels and Diphthongs are spelled with a breathing sign {᾿} {῾}. ἕν is pronounced "hen," but ἐν is pronounced "en."

The rough breathing affects the pronunciation and spelling of some preceding stops. See Elision.

Hiatus Avoidance

The Greeks, especially the Athenians, disliked the immediate succession of two vowel-sounds between two words. This is called **hiatus** and was avoided. The four ways to avoid hiatus are by **elision**, **contraction**, **movable ν** and **crasis.**

PREVIEW

Elision

An apostrophe followed by an empty space indicates the dropping of a short vowel at the end of a word when the next word begins with a vowel. The two words are printed as two separate words. For example, ἀπὸ ἐμοῦ is printed as ἀπ' ἐμοῦ. This process is called **elision**. In a compound word elision is not indicated by an apostrophe.

When, because of elision, the letters τ and π precede a rough breathing, they become aspirated themselves. Thus τ appears as θ; μεθ' οὗ ← μετ ὰ οὗ. π appears as φ; ἀφ' οὗ ← ἀπὸ οὗ. The title for the five overseers in Sparta, the Ephors, comes from ἐπὶ and ὁράω. It is written ἔφοροι.

Contraction

The Greeks also disliked the immediate succession of certain vowel-sounds within the same word. They avoided this by uniting or contracting the two sounds into a diphthong. There is no special sign in print to indicate **contraction**. Contraction can be learned by mastering as many paradigms of nouns, adjectives and verbs as possible. But note especially the following patterns:

$$\alpha + \varepsilon \rightarrow \bar{\alpha}$$
$$\alpha + o \rightarrow \omega$$
$$\varepsilon + \begin{Bmatrix} \varepsilon \\ \iota \\ \varepsilon\iota \end{Bmatrix} \rightarrow \varepsilon\iota$$
$$\varepsilon + \begin{Bmatrix} o \\ o\upsilon \end{Bmatrix} \rightarrow o\upsilon$$
$$\varepsilon o + \iota \rightarrow o\iota$$
$$\varepsilon + \alpha \rightarrow \eta$$
$$o + \begin{Bmatrix} \varepsilon \\ o \\ o\upsilon \end{Bmatrix} \rightarrow o\upsilon$$

Movable ν.

Another way of avoiding hiatus is the addition of ν to a limited number of words. This ν is called '**movable ν**.' Movable ν often appears at the end of the word ἐστί. See S10.2 Λύπης ἰατρός ἐστιν ὁ χρηστὸς φίλος.

Preview

Crasis

A fourth process, called **crasis** (mixture) occurs frequently in poetry. It is the combination of a vowel or diphthong at the end of a word with one at the beginning of the following word. The two words are then printed as one word. In S4.2 κἀν is the result of crasis between καί and ἐν.

Consonants

Consonants are grouped according to their sounds. Consonants are either continuants or stops. The continuants are:

nasals	μ ν γ (This γ pronounced /N/, called agma.)
liquids	λ ρ
sibilants	σ , written ς at the end of a word

The stops are:

labials	π β φ
dentals	τ δ θ
palatals	κ γ χ

There are also three double consonants which represent combinations of a dental, labial or palatal with σ:

ψ ← labial + σ

ζ ← dental + σ

ξ ← palatal + σ

See the section Spelling, Pronunciation and Sound Changes.

Syllable and Accent Marks

Syllable

Although scholars disagree on details regarding the division of words into syllables, the notion of 'syllable' is indispensable for the description of word accentuation and of metric rhythm.

In Greek, every vowel or diphthong makes a distinct syllable. A syllable may consist of a vowel, or a consonant + vowel, or a consonant + vowel +consonant. For example, ἐρωτα is divided into three syllables: ἐ-ρω-τα.

PREVIEW

♦ Exercise

Count the number of syllables.

ἀνθρωπος　　παιδαγωγος　　παυει　　και　　ἀρετη

Accent Marks

After Alexander the Great, king of the Macedonian Greeks, had conquered the kingdoms of the east, such as Egypt and Persia, Greek became the common language of commerce, administration and culture, much as today's English. Many of the non-native speakers included in the Greek world at that time were unable to pronounce Greek correctly. Therefore during the Third century B.C., scholars of the famous library in Alexandria in Egypt began marking one of the last three syllables of Greek words with either an **Acute**, **Circumflex** or **Grave** accent.

The **Acute accent** ´ probably indicates a high tone. It occurs on long or short vowels and on diphthongs.

The **Circumflex accent** ˆ probably indicates a high tone followed by a low tone. It occurs on long vowels and on diphthongs.

The **Grave** sign ` replaces the acute accent on the last syllable of a word except at the end of a clause or a sentence. For the reader the grave signals continuance of clause or sentence.

Almost every Greek word has one accent.

The last three syllables are named as follows:

The last syllable is called **Ultima**.
The last-but-one syllable is called **Penultima**.
The last-but -two syllable is called **Antepenultima**.

Words are named according to their accent as follows:

A word with an acute on the ultima is called **Oxytonon.**
A word with an acute on the penultima is called **Paroxytonon.**
A word with an acute on the antepenultima is called **Proparoxytonon.**
A word with a circumflex on the ultima is called **Perispomenon**.
A word with a circumflex on the penultima is called **Properispomenon**.

♦ Exercise

Copy every word of Basic Sentences 5.1–5.4 and name it according to accent. Grave accents occur only in continuous text, and some words have no accent.

The position of an accent in a given vocabulary item cannot be predicted, it must be learned. Within the paradigm of nouns and adjectives certain changes in the position and nature of the accent can be predicted; if the vowel of the last syllable is long, a proparoxytonon and a properispomenon become a paroxytonon:

> φιλόσοφον but φιλοσόφου
> πλοῦτον but πλούτου
> λέγω but ἔλεγον

Otherwise the accent on nouns and adjectives is *persistent*: the accent remains on the same syllable, if possible. The accent of verbs is generally *recessive*: the accent occurs as far from the end as possible.

♦ Exercise
Given the proparoxytonon κίνδυνος, put the proper accent on these forms.

κινδυνου κινδυνῳ κινδυνων κινδυνοις κινδυνους κινδυνον

♦ Exercise
Given the properispomenon μῦθος, put the proper accent on these forms.

μυθον μυθῳ μυθοις μυθους μυθου μυθων

♦ Exercise
Given the oxytone ἰατρός, supply the proper accent for the following forms.

ἰατρον ἰατρῳ ἰατροις ἰατρους ἰατρου ἰατρων

Enclitics and Proclitics

Some words do not appear to have any accent. They are so closely attached to the preceding word as to become virtually a part of it. Such words are called **enclitics**, literally 'leaners.' Compare what happens to the English word 'not,' when it combines with 'is' into 'isn't.'
Examples of frequently occurring **enclitics** are:

the indefinite pronoun	τις, in all its forms
the personal pronouns	μου, μοι, με
	σου, σοι, σε
the conjunction	τε
the particle	γε
the verb	ἐστί

An accented syllable cannot be followed by more than two unaccented syllables, so the following changes occur when an enclitic 'leans' onto a word:

PREVIEW

1. A perispomenon (τοῦ) preceding a one-syllable enclitic keeps its accent. The enclitic loses its accent: τοῦ γε. An oxytonon also preserves its own accent and never changes its final acute to the grave sign: ἀδελφός τις.
2. When a paroxytonon (φίλος) is followed by a two-syllable enclitic, the enclitic retains its accent: φίλος ἐστίν, φίλον τινά. A monosyllabic enclitic loses its accent: φίλος τις.
3. A proparoxytonon (φιλόσοφος) or a properispomenon (δοῦλος) adds an acute on the last syllable: φιλόσοφός ἐστιν, φιλόκαλός γε, ἄνθρωπόν τινα, δοῦλός τε.

On the other hand, a few very frequent words of one syllable never have an accent of their own, but attach themselves closely to a following word. Such words are called **proclitics**.

Examples of **proclitics** are:

articles	ὁ, ἡ, οἱ, αἱ
negatives	οὐ, οὐκ, οὐχ
prepositions	ἐν, εἰς, ἐκ

Spelling, Pronunciation and Sound Changes

The Vocal Apparatus

We produce sounds by means of our vocal apparatus which consists of the mouth, the nasal cavity and the vocal chords. The pronunciation and spelling of Greek consonant sounds (also called **stops**) are determined by two criteria, **manner of articulation** and **place of articulation.**

Here is a chart showing manner and place of articulation both for stops (labials, dentals, palatals) and for nasals.

		manner		
place	*unvoiced*	*voiced*	*+h (aspirate)*	*nasal*
labial	π	β	φ	μ
dental	τ	δ	θ	ν
palatal	κ	γ	χ	γγ, γκ, γχ

Pre-view

Manner
Voiced sounds involve an approximation of the two vocal chords, unvoiced sounds involve a clear separation. Aspirates involve an h-like sound after the con-sonant. Nasals are produced by the air passing through the open nasal passage.

Place
Labials involve the two lips; dentals involve the tongue tip and teeth or gums. Palatals involve the tongue and palate.

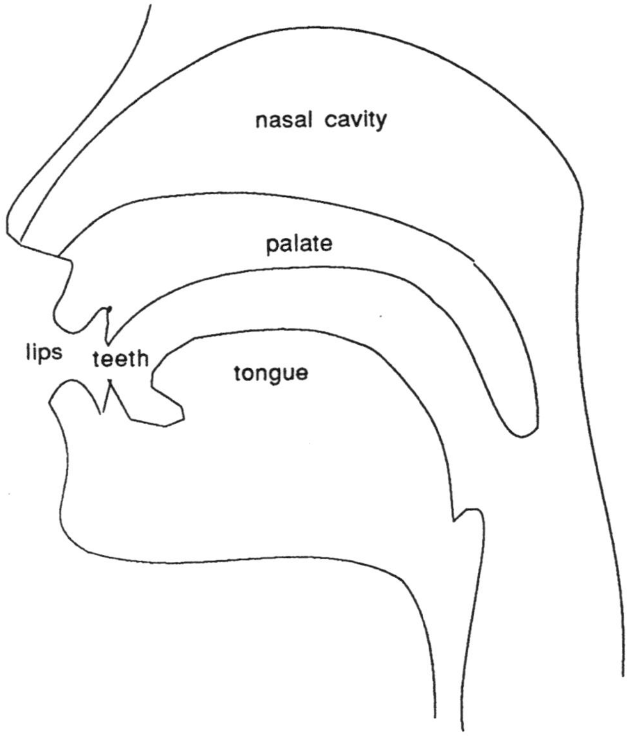

Consonant Changes

While the English spelling of compound words often preserves the pronunciation of the original elements, Greek spelling reflects the pronunciation of the whole word rather than that of its parts. When two parts are combined in a Greek word, the final consonant of the first part is affected by the beginning sound of the second. Since these **consonant changes** are governed by rules, they are predictable. Being aware of these sound changes allows us to find words in the dictionary and to identify forms more easily.

Rule 1 concerns the sound changes of stops before σ.

The letter ψ (English ps) represents labials before σ.

ψ ← π + σ
← πτ + σ
← β + σ
← φ + σ

The letter ξ represents palatals before σ.

ξ ← κ + σ
← γ + σ
← χ + σ

Dentals before σ disappear.

PREVIEW

♦ Exercise

In the vocabulary find the dictionary entry for:
βλάψω, γράψω, λείψω, νίψω, πείσομαι

Rule 2 concerns the sound changes of nasals before stops.

Nasals assimilate to **the place of articulation** of the following consonant.

μ ← ν + π
← ν + β
← ν + φ

γ (called agma) ← ν + κ
← ν + γ
← ν + χ

The letter ν remains ν before the dentals τ, δ, θ because the place of articulation is the same.

♦ Exercise

All the words below are compounds of the Greek word σύν plus another word. Explain the spelling of each:

σύμβολον
συγγενής
σύνδεσμος

Rule 3

All stops assimilate to **the manner of articulation** of the following stop.

φ ← π + aspirate
← β + aspirate

θ ← τ + aspirate
← δ + aspirate

χ ← κ + aspirate
← γ + aspirate

Stops before nasals and unvoiced stops also are subject to sound changes. These sound changes can be introduced later. Although sound changes are liable to interference, it pays to be aware of those presented here.

Preview

Metrical Rhythm

The rhythm of all classical Greek depends upon the weight/quantity of the syllable, not upon the accent or the length of the vowel. The weight/quantity of the syllable is a factor of great importance in the pronunciation of ancient Greek poetry and artistic prose. Greek poetry is based, not on rhyme, but on different sequences of heavy and light syllables.
A syllable is considered heavy under two conditions:

1. if its vowel is long by nature, such as all diphthongs and ᾱ, η and ω
2. if its short vowel is followed by two consonants,
   but: a syllable containing a short vowel followed by stop + liquid may be considered either heavy or light.

GLOSSARY

Glossary

This short glossary is intended as a summary. It does not replace the explanation of terms in the Lessons.

Articular power is a term of syntax that refers to the power of the article to nominalize.

Expectations
Expectations allow the reader to read with understanding. The lowest-level expectation is the expectation of a kernel. The highest-level expectation is the expectation of sense. In reading a foreign language expectations must be tested against the constraints of foreign morphology, syntax, semantics and pragmatics.

Morphological expectations
Morphological expectations allow the reader to predict ambiguity. Since many Greek forms are ambiguous, it is necessary to for the reader to rely on syntactic expectations in order to resolve the ambiguity.

Syntactic expectations
Syntactic expectations sum up the reader's feel for the completeness of a kernel.

Semantic expectations
Semantic expectations make use of ordinary notions of compatibility. Sunshine is golden or warm but not blue or icy. The sun rises or shines or sets, it does not swim or shout or jump. After a verb meaning to invite, the reader should not expect a statement. After a verb meaning to hear or to see, the reader should not expect a command.

Pragmatic expectations
Pragmatic expectations are of two kinds. The first kind consist of universal assumptions about the world: a person who is alive cannot be spoken of as dead, unless the statement is potential or contrary to fact. The second kind consist of culture and text specific facts: an adjective describing a beautiful woman's skin cannot mean "tanned" in a fifth century B.C. drama because being tanned was not fashionable in fifth century Greece.

Finite verb is a term of morphology denoting a verb form marked for person.

Gap or Ø
Gap is a term of syntax designating the fact that a syntactically necessary item is not in the text where it is expected, and must therefore be supplied. Awareness of a gap results from the ability of the reader to form expectations.

Head of construction is a term of syntax identifying the item that is modified.

Indeclinable is a term of morphology. Indeclinables are words that never change form.

Kernel
Kernel is a term of syntax sometimes called the skeleton or minimum framework of a sentence. For the reader it means the indispensable items which must be expected in the sentence, though one or more of these items may be gapped.

Morpheme and allomorph
Morpheme and allomorph are terms of morphology. They are minimum units with the same meaning.

Glossary

Nominalization
Nominalization is a term of syntax. Nominalization devices can change the status of an item from any part of speech to a noun. The most important nominalization device in Greek is the article.

Noun (nominal) clause is a term of syntax identifying a clause that functions as a noun.

Sames
Sames is a term of syntax used to denote two or more items that are syntactically equivalent. Sames are marked by the presence of a co-ordinating connector.

Speech Act is a term of functional grammar, distinguishing statements from questions, commands, etc.

Syntax
Syntax is the study of how words combine to form sentences and the study of the patterns of those sentences.

Speech Acts

Whenever we wish to communicate, we commit a speech act. We speak for several purposes. The following are among our most frequent purposes:

1. to give information
2. to get information
3. to demand an action by an addressee
4. to suggest an action by ourselves or others
5. to wish for something
6. to ask for advice

The following are the names of the speech acts we commit in order to accomplish our purpose:

1. to give information we make a **statement**
2. to get information we ask a **question**
3. to demand an action from an addressee we give a **command**
4. to suggest an action we utter an **exhortation**
5. to wish for something we utter a **wish**
6. to ask for advice we utter a **deliberative question**

♦Exercise 1

With the help of your native competence, label the sentences below as statements, questions, commands, exhortations, wishes or deliberative questions.

1. Should I read the new book
2. Let them read the new book
3. Is she reading the new book
4. Would that I were reading the new book
5. Read the new book
6. We read the new book

♦Exercise 2

Add punctuation marks to the above sentences.

In statements and questions we may also choose to communicate our view on the probability of the information by differentiating statements and questions as either factual (plain), or possible (potential), or impossible (contrary to fact).

♦ Exercise 3

Label the following as statements or questions and as plain, potential or contrary-to-fact.

1. They are reading the new book.
2. Are they reading the new book?
3. May / might they be reading the new book?
4. They may / might be reading the new book.
5. They would be reading the new book but...
6. Would they be reading the new book if...?

♦ Exercise 4

List the linguistic devices by means of which English seems to signal the different speech acts:

Expectation and Completeness

The two single most important items for learning to read are the **expectation** of a complete sentence and a feeling for the **completeness** or incompleteness of a given sentence. Both come naturally to the native speakers of any language because they react to the regular patterns of their language.

♦ Exercise 5

Instructions: Label the following English utterances as complete or incomplete. Complete the incomplete sentences following your own speech habits.

1. sees the philosopher
2. the philosopher finds
3. the philosopher seems
4. the philosopher is
5. in the marketplace there is

Readers of a foreign language cannot rely on their instincts because they do not understand the patterns of the foreign language. They must learn to test expectations by observing form rather than meaning. Luckily the number of grammatical expectations is limited. Expectations concern three groups:

kernel: every sentence has a **kernel.**
modifiers: the parts of the kernel may or may not be modified or expanded.
connectors: each item in the sentence may be single or multiple.

The Kernel

The kernel of a sentence consists of a combination of '**functions**,' called **subject** and **predicate**. In English the subject is generally the first noun in a simple sentence. The predicate consists of a verb and sometimes a second noun as **direct object** or **complement**.

♦ Exercise 6

Underline the subjects in the following sentences.

1. The beginning is half of the whole.
2. The farmer loves peace.
3. Peace nourishes the farmer.
4. Thieves steal treasures.
5. Ignorance causes trouble.
6. Time flies.
7. There is a marketplace in the center of Athens.

♦ Exercise 7

Copy all the verbs from the above sentences.

♦ Exercise 8

Circle the second noun in each sentence in Exercise 6.

Modern languages such as French, Italian, Dutch or German are relatively easy for speakers of English to read because the words are often put together in a way similar to that of English. In the following French sentences the noun *le fermier* functions as subject or object according to its position. So does *la paix*.

le fermier aime la paix	*la paix aide le fermier*
the farmer loves peace	peace helps the farmer

Languages which operate by word order are called analytic languages. Classical Greek is not an analytic language; it is a so-called synthetic language, because most functions in the sentence are signaled not by word order, but by **morphology**. For example, the function of a noun in the sentence is signaled by **case**. A Greek noun has 4 (5) cases, each with its different ending. A set of these cases is called the **paradigm**. The names of the cases are:

Nominative
Genitive
Dative
Accusative
Vocative.

Lesson 1

Introduction to the Greek Sentence

Introduction to Greek Nouns, Verbs and Articles

Syntax: The Complete Sentence

Metaphrasing: A Technique for Learning to Read Greek

All texts consist of interacting speech acts, which are represented by sentences. The sentence is the unit for the initial processing of words, and therefore words must be understood within the sentence before they can be understood within the paragraph and text. So, from the first lesson to the last, the **sentence**, rather than the word or the paragraph, is the focus of *Greek for Reading*. The goal of Lesson 1 is to enable the beginner both to understand how the words in Basic Sentences 1.1 – 1.6 mean what they mean and to read and translate other sentences of the same kind.

Basic Sentences

1.1 κρίνει τὸν φίλον ὁ καιρός.

The crisis tests a friend. Menander
A crisis tests a friend.

1.2 χεὶρ χεῖρα νίπτει.

A hand washes a hand = one hand washes the other/another. Menander

1.3 ἡ χεὶρ τὴν χεῖρα νίζει.

The hand washes the hand = one hand washes the other/another. Epicharmus (adapted)

1.4 ἔρωτα παύει λιμός.

Hunger stops love / a (feeling of) love. Menander

1.5 ὁ χρόνος τρέχει.

Time runs (= flies). Greek Anthology

1.6 ἀρετὴ μένει.

Excellence endures. Anonymous

LESSON 1

Introduction to the Greek Sentence

In order to begin to understand how the Basic Sentences mean what they mean and to read other sentences of the same kind, it is necessary to know that **sentences** are put together from **words** and that words, as indicated in dictionaries, are **nouns** or **verbs** or some other part of speech. **Parts of speech** were described and named by the ancient Greeks because of their interest in describing language. The Greeks thought about the structure of language as they thought about other fields such as mathematics, astronomy, logic, etc. They distinguished groups of words according to several criteria. One of the criteria was meaning,for example, **nouns** are words for names of persons, places, things, ideas, etc., **verbs** are words for actions or states of being or events, **adjectives** are words describing nouns. The Romans took over the Greek terminology and with some adaptations this terminology is still used today.

Until about 200 years ago language was described in the terms set by the scholars of ancient Greece, Protagoras, Plato and the Stoics, who concentrated on meaning. Only around 200 years ago under the influence of the Sanscrit scholar Panini, whose methods are used by what we now call structural linguistics, attention began to be concentrated on the form of utterances. In this textbook both approaches are combined. We want you to learn how to read, to learn how to determine *meaning* by observing *form.*

Lesson 1 introduces Greek sentences consisting of **nouns** and **verbs** and **articles**.

♦Exercise 1

From the English translations of the Basic Sentences, copy five English words that are nouns and five words that are verbs.

Each of the words in the Greek Basic Sentences is either a verb, a noun, or an article. In order to find out what part of speech a Greek word may be, it is helpful to look at its ending. For example, the ending **-ει** indicates a verb.

♦Exercise 2

Copy 6 verbs from the Greek Basic Sentences.

Nouns in these Basic Sentences appear with a variety of endings. However, these endings fall into two groups: those that end in **ν** or **α**, and those that do not end in **ν** or **α**. τόν and τήν, ὁ and ἡ are articles.

♦Exercise 3

Copy the Greek nouns and articles ending in **ν** or **α**. Next copy those nouns and articles not ending in **ν** or **α**.

*Ending in -***ν** *or -***α** (6) *Not ending in -***ν** *or -***α** (9)

In these sentences, the nouns function as **subjects** or as **direct objects**. In English, **function** is indicated by the **word order**. In an English statement the noun before the verb functions as **subject**, the noun after the verb as **direct object**. In an English question the word order is different!

♦ Exercise 4

From the English translations of the Basic Sentences, copy five English nouns that function as subjects and three nouns that function as direct objects.

In contrast to English, which uses word order to indicate function, Greek does *not* use word order to indicate function. In Greek word ***endings*** indicate function. Nouns in these Basic Sentences that do not end in -ν or -α function as subjects, those that end in -ν or -α function as direct objects. A trace of this older Greek system is preserved in English pronouns. For example, the English pronouns *him* and *she* each retain their same function whether they occur in a sentence using regular English word order, "she likes him," or in the unusual order "him she likes." *She* is the subject and *him* is the direct object in both word orders. *Him* is never subject, *he* is never direct object. The contrast between such pronoun forms as *he* and *him* or *they* and *them* is the closest thing in English to the Greek system of word endings. In the Greek language not only pronouns, but also articles, nouns and adjectives have different endings, indicating different functions in the sentence. These different forms are called **cases**.

Introduction to Greek Nouns, Verbs and Articles

The Paradigm of the Greek Noun

The Greek noun has four **cases** and the vocative. Only two cases, **nominative** and **accusative,** occur in the Basic Sentences for Lessons 1 and 2. The remaining cases are called **genitive** and **dative**. Lesson 4 will introduce the dative case, Lesson 9 the genitive case. However, the genitive will appear in all chapters as part of the dictionary listing of nouns.

Greek nouns, like English nouns, have different forms for singular and plural number, for example, in English, "opportunity/opportunities" and "success/successes." Since Greek has four cases, Greek nouns therefore have eight forms. The eight forms together are called the **paradigm** of the noun.

Lesson 1

Here is the paradigm for λιμός (hunger), a noun in S1.4, and φίλος (friend), a noun in S1.1.

Singular		
Nominative	λιμός	φίλος
Genitive	λιμοῦ	φίλου
Dative	λιμῷ	φίλῳ
Accusative	λιμόν	φίλον
Plural		
Nominative	λιμοί	φίλοι
Genitive	λιμῶν	φίλων
Dative	λιμοῖς	φίλοις
Accusative	λιμούς	φίλους

♦ Exercise 5

On the model of λιμός, write the paradigm of καιρός,
on the model of φίλος write the paradigm of χρόνος. Write out the names of the cases.

nominative	καιρός	χρόνος

In addition to the set of endings used above, there are two other sets of endings for nouns. All nouns that have the same set of endings are said to belong to the same **declension**. A noun belongs to one and only one declension. For example, ἀρετή, μνήμη, and δίκη all belong to the First Declension. Here are the nominative and accusative of nouns from each of the three declensions. The differences among sets of endings do not always appear in these two cases. See Morphology in the Reference section in the back of the book.

Case	*First declension*	*Second declension*	*Third declension*
Singular			
Nominative	ἀρετή	λιμός	χείρ
Accusative	ἀρετήν	λιμόν	χεῖρα
Singular			
Nominative	μνήμη	φίλος	νύξ
Accusative	μνήμην	φίλον	νύκτα
Singular			
Nominative	δίκη	χρόνος	θρίξ
Accusative	δίκην	χρόνον	τρίχα

Lesson 1

♦Exercise 6

Examine the paradigms above and copy those case endings that seem to be recurrent or predictable in each declension.

		Declension	
Case	*First*	*Second*	*Third*
Nominative	_____	______	______
Accusative	_____	______	______

Technical Terms Used to Describe Parts of Words

χείρ and χεῖρα in S1.3 are forms of the same noun. It is clear that they are somewhat similar and somewhat different. Part of each of these words is the same, {χειρ}, and part, {Ø},[1] {α}, is different. Each of these parts contributes to the meaning. The technical term for parts of a word that carry meaning is **morpheme**. The study of morphemes is **morphology**. Consider the following English words in terms of morphology:

English Noun
truth has one morpheme, {truth}.
truths has two morphemes, {truth} and {s}.
truth's has two morphemes, {truth} and {'s}.

English Verb
learn has one morpheme, {learn}.
learns has two morphemes, {learn} and {s}.
learned has two morphemes, {learn} and {ed}.

In the noun *truths*, {truth} is called the **stem morpheme** and {s} is called the **inflectional morpheme**. In the verb *learns*, {learn} is the stem morpheme and {s} is the inflectional morpheme.

Note:

In linguistic terminology /final α / and /final ν/ are **allomorphs** for the same **morpheme**, and thus final /α/ and final /ν/ are said to be in complementary distribution. They signal the same function, but they never occur in the same environment. Compare the three allomorphs for the plural of English nouns: /s/ as in pots, /z/ as in dogs and /´z/ as in churches. Final /s/, final /z/ and final /´z/ are allomorphs. Likewise in Greek final /ς/ and /Ø/ are allomorphs for the nominative singular; final /α/ and final /ν/ are allomorphs for the accusative singular. Linguists more or less arbitrarily declare one allomorph the morpheme and speak of the other(s) as allomorphs.

---

[1]Ø means the absence of a visible signal, here a signal for the nominative.

Lesson 1

Morphology of the Greek Noun

Inasmuch as the Greek word χείρ contrasts with the Greek word χεῖρα in S1.3, it appears that each of these words has two morphemes:

> the stem morpheme {χειρ} and the inflectional morpheme {Ø} in χείρ,
> the stem morpheme {χειρ} and the inflectional morpheme {α} in χεῖρα.

The accusative singular of all but a few nouns ends in {α}or the allomorph /ν/. Some of the nominatives have the inflectional morpheme {Ø}, others have the allomorph /ς/.

All cases singular and plural of one noun from each declension are provided below as an overview of noun morphology. See Morphology.

Noun Paradigm

		First declension	*Second declension*	*Third declension*
Singular				
	Nominative	ἀρετή	φίλος	χείρ
	Genitive	ἀρετῆς	φίλου	χειρός
	Dative	ἀρετῇ	φίλῳ	χειρί
	Accusative	ἀρετήν	φίλον	χεῖρα
Plural				
	Nominative	ἀρεταί	φίλοι	χεῖρες
	Genitive	ἀρετῶν	φίλων	χειρῶν
	Dative	ἀρεταῖς	φίλοις	χερσί
	Accusative	ἀρετάς	φίλους	χεῖρας

Morphology of the Greek Verb

Greek verbs have many different forms. In this lesson the morpheme {**ει**} is the only inflectional morpheme that indicates a Greek verb. The {**ει**} indicates that the subject of the verb is third person and singular. Allomorphs of (**ει**) will be met later.

Verb Morphology

	Singular		*Plural*	
first person	κρίνω	I am testing	κρίνομεν	we are testing
second person	κρίνεις	you are testing	κρίνετε	you (all) are testing
third person	κρίνει	he, she, it or ____ is testing	κρίνουσι(ν)	they or ____ are testing

Lesson 1

All verbs in the sentences in Lessons 1 through 6 are in the third person singular. Later lessons will introduce the other persons and the plural number of the verb.

♦ Exercise 7

Name the part of speech and the form of each word in these Basic Sentences.
For verbs, give person and number. κρίνει: verb; third person, singular.
For nouns, give case and number. ἔρωτα: noun; accusative, singular.

S1.2 χεὶρ χεῖρα νίπτει.
S1.4 ἔρωτα παύει λιμός.
S1.6 ἀρετὴ μένει.

1. χεὶρ
2. χεῖρα
3. νίπτει
4. ἔρωτα
5. παύει
6. λιμός
7. ἀρετή
8. μένει

Morphology of the Greek Article

Like the Greek noun, the Greek article has case and number. It also has three different sets, called genders, to agree with the three different genders of nouns. For additional information on the article see Lesson 5.

		Singular			*Plural*	
	Masculine	*Feminine*	*Neuter*	*Masculine*	*Feminine*	*Neuter*
Nominative	ὁ	ἡ	τό	οἱ	αἱ	τά
Genitive	τοῦ	τῆς	τοῦ	τῶν	τῶν	τῶν
Dative	τῷ	τῇ	τῷ	τοῖς	ταῖς	τοῖς
Accusative	τόν	τήν	τό	τούς	τάς	τά

All the articles in Lessons 1 through 4 are either nominative or accusative, and either masculine or feminine singular.

♦ Exercise 8

Name the part of speech and the form of each word in these Basic Sentences. For nouns give case and number. χεῖρα: accusative singular. For articles give case, number and gender. ὁ: nominative, singular, masculine. For verbs give person and number. τρέχει: third singular.

S1.1 κρίνει τὸν φίλον ὁ καιρός
S1.3 ἡ χεὶρ τὴν χεῖρα νίζει
S1.4 ἔρωτα παύει λιμός

1. κρίνει
2. νίζει
3. χεὶρ
4. φίλον
5. λιμός
6. χεῖρα
7. ἡ
8. τὸν
9. ἔρωτα
10. τὴν
11. ὁ
12. καιρός

Lesson 1

♦ Exercise 9

On the basis of morphology alone, name the part of speech and the form of each word in sentences from the readings section of this lesson.

R1.1 ὁ φόβος μνήμην ἐκπλήσσει.
R1.2 τὴν ἀλήθειαν εὑρίσκει πόνος.
R1.3 λύει λύπην λόγος.

1. φόβος
2. μνήμην
3. ἐκπλήσσει
4. τὴν
5. ἀλήθειαν
6. εὑρίσκει
7. πόνος
8. λύει
9. λύπην
10. λόγος

Introduction to the Article

A reader of English may expect a definite article, an indefinite article, or no article with a noun: the truth, a truth, truth. A reader of Greek, on the other hand, may expect a definite article or no article. Greek has no indefinite article. The definite article in Lessons 1–2 indicates the presence of a noun, with which the article agrees in case, number, and gender. The syntactic power of the Greek article is very great. Where Greek may use an article, English may not and vice versa. Additional information on the article will be presented in future lessons under the heading, **the power of the article.**

Syntax: The Complete Sentence

Syntax

Syntax is the study of how words combine to form sentences and the study of the patterns of those sentences.

The Complete Sentence

In order to read a language it is not enough to know the morphology of the language or the meaning of its words. If this were so, all that one would need would be a summary of morphology and a dictionary. To be a successful reader, one must have a feeling for whether or not a string of words forms a complete sentence. Few people would maintain that the following are complete sentences in English: "dog and," "dog chases," "chases." This feeling for completeness enables one to read a single word or phrase at a time, setting up **expectations** about what is to come in the sentence, and drawing on **'respectations'** about relevant information from a previous part of the text. However only in one's own language is this feeling for completeness instinctive. In learning to read a foreign language, where rules for completeness of a sentence may be different or where a sentence may be put together differently, the non-native reader needs to acquire a conscious knowledge of how words form a complete sentence in that language.

The Kernel of the Sentence

The one requirement for a complete sentence is that there be a minimum framework or skeleton. In this text the minimum framework is called the **kernel**. As one reads, one must expect kernels, because every sentence has one or more kernels. Most sentences also have one or more words that are not part of the kernel. These are either modifiers or connectors and they will be presented in later lessons. In the English sentence,"Dogs chase cats." each word is part of the kernel. In the sentence "Most *dogs* happily *chase* frightened *cats*." three words, *most, happily*, and *frightened* are modifiers. In the sentence "*Dogs chase cats* happily and confidently." two words, *happily* and *confidently*, are modifiers and one word, *and*, is a connector.

Each Basic Sentence in this lesson has only one kernel. There are no modifiers or connectors. Each word or item in the kernel has one of the following functions:

subject
verb
direct object

This book describes six types of kernels. Two types occur in this lesson.

A **transitive** kernel has items filling these three functions:

verb
subject
direct object

An **intransitive** kernel has items filling these two functions:

verb
subject

In English, an analytic language, the items that are part of a kernel usually occur in the following order: subject, verb, direct object (if present).

♦Exercise 10

Name the kernel type of the translations of the Basic Sentences from this lesson.

1. A crisis tests a friend.
2. One hand washes the other.
3. Hunger stops love.
4. Time flies.
5. Excellence endures.

LESSON 1

In Greek, a synthetic language, the items that are part of the kernel may occur in any order. The function of a noun in a sentence is indicated by case, not by its position in the sentence. For example, in S1.1 καιρός is subject signaled by the nominative case, and τὸν φίλον is direct object signaled by the accusative case.

♦Exercise 11

Write S1.4 ἔρωτα παύει λιμός in five different word orders. All five sentences have the same syntax. Why?

The items in the kernel of a Greek sentence, as well as the kernel type, will be entered on a kernel chart such as the one below. The kernel chart may be filled out in two steps. First, copy out all the kernel parts as they occur from left to right in the Greek sentence: ἡ χεὶρ τὴν χεῖρα νίζει

	Item: Function	*Item: Function*	*Item: Function*	*Kernel Type*
1.	ἡ χεὶρ	τὴν χεῖρα	νίζει	

Next go back and label the function of each kernel part on the chart, and name the kernel type.

	Item: Function	*Item: Function*	*Item: Function*	*Kernel Type*
1.	ἡ χεὶρ: Subject	τὴν χεῖρα: Direct object	νίζει: Verb	Transitive

Note:
The word 'noun' names a part of speech only and does not correspond to a specific function within a sentence, e.g., subject. On the other hand, the word 'verb' is the name of both a part of speech and a function within the kernel. This double use of the word 'verb' is unfortunate, but corresponds to current practice.

Reacting to the kernel will gradually become automatic.

♦Exercise 12

Using a kernel chart, copy each kernel item in the order in which it appears in the Greek sentence (together with its article, if any), and then name its function. Name the kernel type.

1. ἀρετὴ μένει.
2. ὁ χρόνος τρέχει.
3. ἔρωτα παύει λιμός.
4. κρίνει τὸν φίλον ὁ καιρός.

Lesson 1

♦ Exercise 13

From the Readings (R) section at the end of the lesson copy each kernel item onto a kernel chart and name its function. All nouns in these sentences are either nominative case or accusative case. R1.4 is given as an example.

	Item: Function	*Item: Function*	*Item: Function*	*Kernel Type*
R1.4	μουσικὴν: Direct Object	ἔρως: Subject	διδάσκει: Verb	Transitive

Metaphrasing: A Technique for Learning to Read Greek

Reading a sentence is primarily a linear activity. The reader processes one word or group of words after another in the sequence in which they appear in the sentence. This is so in Greek, as well as in English or any other language. Because the sequence in which Greek words appear is rarely the same as the sequence of English words in the equivalent clause or sentence, a person learning to read or translate Greek must develop a special technique in order to relate the Greek system of morphology and syntax to English word order patterns. Thus this book introduces the technique of **metaphrasing**. While metaphrasing, the reader proceeds through a sentence, item by item, simulating in slow-motion the manner in which a proficient reader might process information from Greek and express it in English.

Every metaphrase begins with a basic framework for English kernels:

[subject] [verb] ± [direct object].

This is to be read as "blank" "blanks" "plus or minus" "blank." The symbol ± (plus or minus) allows for a transitive or an intransitive kernel. It is retained in the metaphrase until one is certain whether there is or is not a direct object.

Metaphrasing a Greek Noun

Upon seeing the word ἔρωτα in S1.4 ἔρωτα παύει λιμός, it is not enough to process only vocabulary information,namely that the word ἔρωτα means "love." It is just as important to process the morphological and syntactic information and to relate that information to the English word order patterns. Thus, ἔρωτα, a noun in the accusative case, is to a reader of Greek what the word "love" in the pattern "________ ________s love" ("blank blanks love") is to a reader of English. The *form* of the word ἔρωτα in Greek conveys the same syntactic information about its function as the *position* of the word "love" conveys in English. In both languages the word has raised the expectation of a subject and a verb. Likewise, the *form* of the word λιμός tells the reader that λιμός is to a reader of Greek what "hunger ________s ± ________" is to a reader of English. Both raise the expectation at least of a verb, and possibly of a direct object.

LESSON 1

Metaphrasing a Greek Article

In classical Greek the article is always definite. Quite often it corresponds to the English possessive pronoun when there is no doubt as to the possessor. For example, S2.5 ὁ λύκος τὴν τρίχα, οὐ τὴν γνώμην ἀλλάττει, "The wolf changes his hide, not his attitude." At other times the article is best left untranslated, as in S1.5. The Greek way of expressing indefiniteness will be discussed in Lesson 3.

Metaphrasing a Greek Verb

Greek does not distinguish, as English does, between the simple, the progressive, and the emphatic forms of the verb. Therefore κρίνει can mean "tests," "is testing," or "does test," according to the context.

Metaphrasing does not yield a polished translation; it yields what is called a structural translation. It is a most useful technique for beginners, but, if carried to extremes, becomes cumbersome and should be modified as the reader becomes more adept.

The metaphrasing guidelines to be learned in this book cover some of the most common problems of English speakers learning to read Greek. They will be introduced as needed. The first two guidelines are as follows.

> In English a subject precedes a verb.
> In English a direct object, if present, follows the verb.

Here are examples of how to metaphrase Greek words in isolation (where the words listed are not part of a complete sentence.)

Item	*Syntactic Information*	*Metaphrase*
κρίνει	verb	______ tests ____.
ἡ χεὶρ	subject	The hand _____s ± ______.
τὸν φίλον	direct object	______ _____s the friend.
χεῖρα	direct object	______ _____s hand.
ὁ καιρὸς	subject	The crisis _____s ± _____.

A metaphrase of a complete sentence is called a **cumulative** metaphrase (where the words form a complete sentence). A cumulative metaphrase of the sentence ἔρωτα παύει λιμός is as follows.

Item	*Syntactic Information*	*Metaphrase*
ἔρωτα	direct object	______ ______s love.
ἔρωτα παύει	verb	______ stops love.
ἔρωτα παύει λιμός	subject	Hunger stops love.

LESSON 1

Summary

Metaphrasing shows how the morphology of a Greek word relates to English word order. It also shows how the information obtained from one word *raises expectations* of other words with specific functions.

The presence of a direct object raises the expectation of a verb and of a subject.

The presence of a verb raises the expectation of a subject, and possibly a direct object.

The presence of a subject raises the expectation of a verb, and possibly a direct object

While metaphrasing is a useful technique for learning to read Greek, the notion of **expectation** (and **respectation**) is central to the reading process at all levels of reading in all languages. To use syntactic expectations one need not know the 'dictionary meaning' of words. But since reading means comprehension of the text, not only syntactic analysis, the would-be-reader should learn as much of the vocabulary as possible and as soon as possible.

♦Exercise 14

Complete the following metaphrase chart for the words given in isolation. Metaphrase each in the structural context of a complete kernel.

Item	*Part of Speech Identification*	*Syntactic Information*	*Metaphrase*
1. ὁ χρόνος			
2. τὴν χεῖρα			
3. νίζει			
4. μουσικὴν			
5. τὴν ἀλήθειαν			
6. εὑρίσκει			

♦Exercise 15

Using a chart like the one below, write a cumulative metaphrase of the sentence μουσικὴν ἔρως διδάσκει. Use lesson vocabulary.

Item	*Part of Speech and Identification*	*Syntactic Information*	*Cumulative Metaphrase*
1. μουσικὴν	noun: acc. sing.	direct object	____ ____s music

Lesson 1

Readings

At this stage do not worry too much about the article. The rules for the use of the article differ in different languages.

1.1 ὁ φόβος μνήμην διαφθείρει. Thucydides

1.2 τὴν ἀλήθειαν εὑρίσκει πόνος. Anonymous

1.3 λύει λύπην λόγος. Menander

1.4 μουσικὴν ἔρως διδάσκει. Euripides

1.5 δίκην δίκη τίκτει. Zenobius

1.6 ἀνάγκη οὐκ ἔχει νόμον. Anonymous

Practice Sentences

Lesson 1:

1. χρόνος μνήμην παύει.
2. ἀλήθεια μένει.
3. τίκτει νόμον λόγος.
4. πόνον πόνος τίκτει.
5. φίλος φίλον διδάσκει.
6. λύπην λύει μουσική.

Lesson Vocabulary

The standard practice for listing a **noun** in Greek dictionaries is to give the nominative and one other case, because the nominative does not always show the stem morpheme. *This is especially true of third declension nouns.* This book follows the practice of most Greek dictionaries which give the nominative and genitive cases.

The standard practice for listing a **verb** in Greek dictionaries is to give the principal parts of the verb; all principal parts are the first person singular, the "I ______" form, but the English equivalent is given in the "to" form. From Lesson 1 to 13 all Greek verbs will be listed with three principle parts; from Lesson 13 on all six parts will be listed. The 2nd and 3rd principal parts indicate future and past time. These will appear in Lessons 8 and 9.

LESSON 1

The English word(s) given with a Greek word in the Lesson Vocabulary represent the word's basic meaning, and are not always the same as those used in the translation of the Basic Sentences. The main reason for the difference is that the translations of the Basic Sentences are often literary, specialized, or idiomatic. Using the Stem List in the Reference section, the learner should acquire early on the habit of grouping Greek words according to the basic meaning of their stems. Just as, in the English, the words "handle," "mishandle," "handy," "underhanded" can be grouped under the stem "hand," in Greek the words φόβος and φοβέω can be grouped under the stem φοβ.

Nouns

ἡ ἀλήθεια, τῆς ἀληθείας	truth
ἡ ἀνάγκη, τῆς ἀνάγκης	necessity
ἡ ἀρετή, τῆς ἀρετῆς	virtue
ἡ δίκη, τῆς δίκης	right, justice
ὁ ἔρως, τοῦ ἔρωτος	love
ἡ θρίξ, τῆς τριχός	hair, hide
ὁ καιρός, τοῦ καιροῦ	moment
ὁ λιμός, τοῦ λιμοῦ	hunger
ὁ λόγος, τοῦ λόγου	word, speech, thought, consideration
ἡ λύπη, τῆς λύπης	grief
ἡ μνήμη, τῆς μνήμης	memory
ἡ μουσική, τῆς μουσικῆς	music
ὁ νόμος, τοῦ νόμου	law
ἡ νύξ, τῆς νυκτός	night
ὁ πόνος, τοῦ πόνου	toil, trouble
ὁ φίλος, τοῦ φίλου	friend
ὁ φόβος, τοῦ φόβου	fear
ἡ χείρ, τῆς χειρός	hand
ὁ χρόνος, τοῦ χρόνου	time

Verbs

διαφθείρω, διαφθερῶ, διέφθειρα	to destroy
διδάσκω, διδάξω, ἐδίδαξα	to teach
ἐκπλήσσω, ἐκπλήξω, ἐξέπληξα	to destroy
εὑρίσκω, εὑρήσω, ηὗρον	to find
ἔχω, ἕξω/σχήσω, ἔσχον	to have
κρίνω, κρινῶ, ἔκρινα	to judge
λύω, λύσω, ἔλυσα	to dissolve, release, destroy
μένω, μενῶ, ἔμεινα	to remain
νίπτω, νίψω, ἔνιψα	to wash
νίζω, νίψω, ἔνιψα	to wash

παύω, παύσω, ἔπαυσα	to cause to stop, stop
τίκτω, τέξω, ἔτεκον	to produce
τρέχω, θρέξομαι, ἔθρεξα/ἔδραμον	to run

Adverbs

οὐ, οὐκ, οὐχ	not

Lesson 2

Connection

The Gap

Morphology: More on Noun Paradigms

Lesson 1 introduced kernels and functional items within kernels. This lesson introduces **connection** through **coordinating conjunctions,** commas or **gaps**. Gaps occur in sentences in which words that are expected are not present.

Basic Sentences

2.1 ἡ δὲ χεὶρ τὴν χεῖρα νίζει.

One hand washes the other. Epicharmus (adapted)

2.2 χεὶρ χεῖρα νίπτει, δάκτυλον δὲ δάκτυλος.

One hand washes the other, and one finger the other finger. Menander (adapted)

2.3 δίκη δίκην τίκτει, βλάβην δὲ βλάβη.

Justice brings forth justice and injury injury. Zenobius

2.4 νὺξ μὲν ἀναπαύει, ἡμέρα δὲ ἔργον ποιεῖ.

Night relieves toil, but day brings it. Menander

2.5 ὁ λύκος τὴν τρίχα, οὐ τὴν γνώμην ἀλλάττει.

The wolf changes his hide, not his attitude. Apostolius

Lesson 2

Connection

In Lesson 1 all sentences consisted of one kernel, and all parts of the kernel consisted of one item, one subject, one verb or one direct object. Through the use of connection any number of sentences or items having the same function can appear in both Greek and English sentences. In the sentence "I like math, physics and geography," the items "math," "physics" and "geography" are all direct objects connected by either a comma or "and." Commas and words like *and*, a **coordinating conjunction,** function as connectors.

Part of Speech: Coordinating Conjunction

In contrast to nouns and verbs, conjunctions have only one form. Words that have only one form are sometimes called **indeclinables**. Connection is expressed in this lesson by a single coordinating conjunction, such as καί or τε "and" and, δέ or ἀλλά "but." There are also double conjunctions, such as μέν ... δέ "on the one hand ... on the other hand." Additional coordinating conjunctions will occur in other lessons.

Connection is also expressed by the use of the comma, especially by the comma followed by a negative such as οὐ not, which expresses contrast. Some conjunctions, especially δέ but, and γάρ for, often appear in the opening sentence of a passage or a paragraph. In this book they are then called clause connectors. The importance of conjunctions for comprehending what one reads is enormous, as you will see when you read connected texts.

Syntax

Coordinating conjunctions indicate that two "**sames**" — items with the same syntactic function — are connected to each other:

a subject to a subject,
a direct object to a direct object,
a kernel to a kernel, etc.

In English connectors usually appear between the two items connected:

sooner or later
in and out
slowly but surely
"Give me liberty or give me death."
men and women
"to be or not to be"
"Twas brillig and the slithy toves did gyre and gimble in the wabe."

In Greek connectors do not always appear between the two items connected. τε and δέ appear regularly after the first word of the second "same," as in S2.2 χεὶρ χεῖρα νίπτει,

LESSON 2

δάκτυλον δὲ δάκτυλος. μέν usually follows the first word of the first "same" as in S2.4 νὺξ μὲν ἀναπαύει, ἡμέρα δὲ ἔργον ποιεῖ.

A connector never connects a subject to a verb, or a whole kernel to a direct object, although it may seem to. Note that in S2.3 (δίκη δίκην τίκτει, βλάβην δὲ βλάβη) the δέ connects two kernels.

♦ Exercise 1

Copy each of the sames that are connected and name them by function within the kernel or as kernels.

Example: *He ran* and *the dog followed.* *two kernels*

1. I hear the saxophone and the trombone.
2. The man writes and paints.
3. He lost the money yesterday and she found it today.
4. Once upon a time there were knights and ladies.
5. My sister skates and her husband swims.

The Gap, Ø

The ability to read rests on a person's sense of completeness of expression. Everybody makes use of this sense. The one-kernel sentences of Lesson 1 are easy to read, because all expected items are present. Sentences, however, of two or more kernels are more difficult, because identical items can be left out or gapped "Ø" according to patterns specific to the particular language. The symbol Ø indicates a gapped item.

Syntax

According to the gapping patterns in Greek, any kernel item may be gapped in the first or second of two kernels. When an item is gapped in the first kernel, it must be understood from the second. This is called respectation. In S2.5 the verb is gapped in the first kernel and the subject is gapped in the second.

S2.5 ὁ λύκος τὴν τρίχα Ø = ἀλλάττει, **οὐ τὴν γνώμην ἀλλάττει** Ø = ὁ λύκος.

In English subjects and verbs are gapped only in the second of two connected kernels. The metaphrase of the first kernel in S2.5 ὁ λύκος τὴν τρίχα would be "the wolf _____s the hide" or "the wolf Ø = changes the hide". The metaphrase of the second kernel would be " ______ does not change its nature" or "Ø = the wolf does not change its nature." Notice that the second kernel of this sentence could be completed by substituting the pronoun *it* for "the wolf."

Lesson 2

In contrast to English, in Greek, an identical direct object of two or more kernels can be gapped in any of the kernels. For example, in R2.1 the direct object is gapped in the second kernel

R2.1 βίον τίκτει γῆ, πάλιν δὲ λαμβάνει Ø = βίον Ø = γῆ.

In English an identical direct object of two or more kernels can be gapped only in the first kernel: "Adam likes — but Ben dislikes — rhubarb." is grammatical, but "Adam likes rhubarb, but Ben dislikes" is not grammatical. The metaphrase of the second kernel in R2.1 πάλιν δὲ λαμβάνει Ø = βίον Ø = γῆ. would be "________ takes ________" or "Ø = the earth takes Ø = life."

Summary

Connection in Greek is accomplished in three different ways:

1. The presence of coordinating conjunctions (δὲ, καὶ, μέν . . . δὲ)
2. The presence of punctuation, commas *etc.*
3. The presence of a gap.

All three ways are used to connect sames and to form a cohesive text. For example, the coordinating conjunction, δέ, can be used within a sentence to connect two kernels, as in S2.2. δέ can also be used to connect sentences within a longer text, as in S4.7 τὴν δὲ ὀρθότητα καὶ τὴν ὠφέλειαν καὶ τὸ εὖ καὶ τὸ καλῶς ἡ ἀλήθεια ἀποτελεῖ. In this text (*Laws* 667C) the philosopher, Plato, is discussing the roles of pleasure and truth in learning. Here δέ helps to contrast the role of pleasure, mentioned just previously, and that of truth. Connection of this sort signals cohesion in a text (see Re-view).

♦ Exercise 2

Enter and label all kernel items from S2.2, S2.3 and S2.4 on a kernel chart. Include all Ø items (example: Ø = ἀλλάττει).

	Clause Connector	*Item: Function*	*Item: Function*	*Item: Function*	*Kernel Type*
S2.2		χεὶρ: Subject	χεῖρα: Direct Object	νίπτει: Verb	Transitive

♦ Exercise 3

Complete a connector chart, like the one below, for S2.2 through S2.5. Include Ø items.

	Connector	*First same*	*Second same*
S2.2	δὲ	χεὶρ χεῖρα νίπτει	δάκτυλον δάκτυλος Ø = νίπτει

Lesson 2

♦ Exercise 4

Rewrite the following Greek sentences supplying all gapped items. Follow the example: δίκη δίκην τίκτει καὶ βλάβην βλάβη = δίκη δίκην τίκτει καὶ βλάβην βλάβη (∅ = τίκτει)

1. ἀνὴρ γὰρ ἄνδρα καὶ πόλις πόλιν σώζει.
2. ξίφος τιτρώσκει σῶμα, τὸν δὲ νοῦν λόγος.
3. ἀνδριάντα μὲν εἶδος, ἄνδρα δὲ ἡ πρᾶξις κοσμεῖ.

♦ Exercise 5

Metaphrase each item in the structural context of a complete kernel. Watch the inflectional morphemes.

1. τὸν λύκον
2. νὺξ ἡμέραν
3. λιμὸν τίκτει
4. τὴν γνώμην ὁ φίλος
5. ποιεῖ καὶ ἀλλάττει

More on noun paradigms

So far, nouns with the inflectional morpheme -α have been accusative singular. From now on, nouns ending in -α can also be nominative singular of the first declension. There are two groups:

Nouns ending in "**pure**" **α** preceded by ε, ι, ρ retain the α throughout the paradigm.

Singular							
Nominative	ἡ	ἡμέρα	ἡ	ἀλήθεια	ὁ	νεανίας
Genitive	τῆς	ἡμέρας	τῆς	ἀληθείας	τοῦ	νεανίου
Dative	τῇ	ἡμέρᾳ	τῇ	ἀληθείᾳ	τῷ	νεανίᾳ
Accusative	τὴν	ἡμέραν	τὴν	ἀλήθειαν	τὸν	νεανίαν
Plural							
Nominative	αἱ	ἡμέραι	αἱ	ἀλήθειαι	οἱ	νεανίαι
Genitive	τῶν	ἡμερῶν	τῶν	ἀληθειῶν	τῶν	νεανιῶν
Dative	ταῖς	ἡμέραις	ταῖς	ἀληθείαις	τοῖς	νεανίαις
Accusative	τὰς	ἡμέρας	τὰς	ἀληθείας	τοὺς	νεανίας

Lesson 2

Nouns ending in **"impure" α**. The α appears in the nominative and accusative only.

Singular

Nominative	ἡ	θάλαττα
Genitive	τῆς	θαλάττης
Dative	τῇ	θαλάττῃ
Accusative	τὴν	θάλατταν

Plural

Nominative	αἱ	θάλατται
Genitive	τῶν	θαλαττῶν
Dative	ταῖς	θαλάτταις
Accusative	τὰς	θαλάττας

Readings

2.1 βίον τίκτει γῆ, πάλιν δὲ λαμβάνει. — Euripides

2.2 ἔρωτα παύει λιμὸς ἢ πενία. — Menander

2.3 οὐ μὲν ἀδικίαν θεὸς τίει ἀλλὰ δίκην. — Homer

2.4 οὐχ ἡ μορφὴ, ἀλλ' ἡ ἀρετὴ τέρπει τὸν φίλον. — Euripides

2.5 δίκη δίκην τίκτει καὶ φόνος φόνον.

Practice Sentences

Lesson 2:

1. χρόνος μὲν παύει, ἔρως δὲ μνήμην τίκτει.
2. φίλον φίλος, νεανίας νεανίαν τέρπει.
3. οὐ τὴν γνώμην τίει ὁ θεός, ἀλλὰ τὴν ὀρθότητα.
4. ὁ μὲν ἔρως τὸν ἔρωτα, ὁ δὲ φίλος τὸν φίλον διδάσκει.
5. ἀνάγκη ἢ φόβον ἢ ἀρετὴν ποιεῖ.
6. οὐχ ἡ γνώμη λύει τὸν φόβον, ἀλλ' ἡ ἀλήθεια.
7. ἡ γὰρ γῆ τὸν νεανίαν τέρπει.

Lesson 2

Lesson Vocabulary

Nouns	
ἡ ἀδικία, τῆς ἀδικίας	injustice, wrong
ὁ βίος, τοῦ βίου	life
ἡ βλάβη, τῆς βλάβης	harm
ἡ γῆ, τῆς γῆς	earth
ἡ γνώμη, τῆς γνώμης	opinion, attitude
ὁ δάκτυλος, τοῦ δακτύλου	finger
τό ἔργον, τοῦ ἔργου	labor, work
ἡ ἡμέρα, τῆς ἡμέρας	day
ἡ θάλαττα, τῆς θαλάττης	sea
ὁ θεός, τοῦ θεοῦ	god
ὁ λύκος, τοῦ λύκου	wolf
ἡ μορφή, τῆς μορφῆς	shape, form
ὁ νεανίας, τοῦ νεανίου	young man
ἡ πενία, τῆς πενίας	poverty
ὁ φόνος, τοῦ φόνου	killing, murder
Verbs	
ἀλλάττω, ἀλλάξω, ἤλλαξα	to change
ἀναπαύω, ἀναπαύσω, ἀνέπαυσα	to cause to stop
λαμβάνω, λήψομαι, ἔλαβον	to take, seize
ποιέω, ποιήσω, ἐποίησα	to make, do, cause to be
τέρπω, τέρψω, ἔτερψα	to please
τιτρώσκω, τρώσω, ἔτρωσα	to wound
τίω, τίσω, ἔτισα	to honor, value
Adverbs	
πάλιν	again
Coordinating Conjunctions	
ἀλλά	but, however
γάρ	for
δέ	but, and
ἤ	or
ἤ...ἤ	either...or
καί, τε	and
μέν...δέ, ἀλλά	on one hand...on the other

Lesson 3

Another Speech Act: Questions

Interrogative and Indefinite Pronouns

This lesson introduces sentences that are questions rather than statements. It also introduces the interrogative and indefinite pronouns.

Basic Sentences

3.1 τίς τὴν τρίχα ἀλλάττει;

Who changes his hide?

3.2 τί ὁ λύκος ἀλλάττει;

What does the wolf change?

3.3 ἆρα ὁ λύκος τὴν τρίχα ἀλλάττει;

Does the wolf change his hide?

3.4 ἀλλάττει τις τὴν τρίχα.

Somebody changes his hide.

3.5 ἀλλάττει ὁ λύκος τι.

The wolf changes something.

Another Speech Act: Questions

The Basic Sentences in Lessons 1 and 2 are statements. This section introduces another speech act: questions such as S3.1, S3.2, and S3.3. Both questions and statements use the same kernel types and syntax.

Lesson 3

A question can be distinguished from a statement in three different ways.

1. by the presence of an **interrogative pronoun.** These are *wh-* words in English (who, what, etc.) and the equivalent τ/π- words in Greek (τίς, πότε). Such question words seek a specific word or words as answers. Example: S3.1 **τίς** τὴν τρίχα ἀλλάττει; ὁ λύκος. = Who changes his hide? The wolf.
2. by the presence of **interrogative particles.** An English question of the yes/no type is generally signaled by word order: "Does the wolf change his hide?" A Greek question of this type is signalled by particles (e.g. μὴ οὖν = μῶν; or ἆρα;) as in S3.3.ἆρα ὁ λύκος τὴν τρίχα ἀλλάττει;
3. by the presence of a **question mark.** In both English and Greek the above signals can be omitted and the question indicated instead by intonation alone. On the printed page this intonation is signaled by punctuation. The question mark on a page of Greek looks like an English semi-colon (;).

Interrogative and Indefinite Pronouns

Morphology: Interrogative Pronouns

Compare the English **interrogative pronoun** with the Greek interrogative pronoun:

Animate	*Non-animate*		*Animate*	*Non-animate*
who?	what?	*Nominative*	τίς;	τί;
whose?	whose?	*Genitive*	τίνος;	τίνος;
to whom?	to what?	*Dative*	τίνι;	τίνι;
whom?	what?	*Accusative*	τίνα;	τί;

Morphology: Indefinite Pronouns

The **indefinite pronoun** has the same forms as the interrogative pronoun except for the accent. The pronoun τίς; when accented with an acute accent on the first syllable is interrogative: "who?" "what?" When unaccented or with a grave on the second syllable it is indefinite: "some," "any." See Pre-View on Enclitics and Proclitics.

Lesson 3

Indefinite Pronouns

	Animate	*Non-animate*
Nominative	τις	τι
Genitive	τινός	τινός
Dative	τινί	τινί
Accusative	τινὰ	τι

Syntax

Most Greek **pronouns** are used both as nouns and adjectives. In this lesson the pronoun is used only as a noun. See Lessons 5 and 10.

Semantics: Animate versus Non-animate

Both Greek and English discriminate between nouns with the *semantic feature* **animate** or **non-animate**. The distinction between animate and non-animate is built into the interrogative pronouns of both languages.

> A *who?* question calls for an answer such as "thief," "friend," "wolf," or "lamb," each of which has the feature **animate**.
>
> A *what?* question calls for an answer such as "hope," "success," "clothing," or "truth," each of which has the feature **non-animate**.

The distinction between the features animate/non-animate will be a very important semantic distinction to be considered in reading and interpretation. For example, the figure of speech, personification, means that the feature, animate, is added to a word that does not have it naturally. The noun, χρόνος, "time," is not in itself animate, but it is personified in S1.5 ὁ χρόνος τρέχει, "time runs," because τρέχει, "runs," raises the semantic expectation of a subject with the feature, animate.

♦ Exercise 1

Rewrite the following statements as questions, replacing the first noun with the equivalent interrogative pronoun. Be careful to observe the semantic difference between nouns with the semantic feature **animate** and those with the semantic feature **non-animate**. S1.4 is given as an example.

ἔρωτα παύει λιμός — τί παύει λιμός;

1. κρίνει τὸν φίλον ὁ καιρός
2. χεὶρ χεῖρα νίπτει
3. λύκος τὴν τρίχα ἀλλάττει
4. δίκην δίκη τίκτει
5. τίκτει δίκη δίκην

LESSON 3

♦ Exercise 2

Answer the following questions on Basic Sentences (S) and Readings (R). S1.1 is given as an example.

τί κρίνει τὸν φίλον; ὁ καιρός.

S1.5 τί τρέχει;
R1.1 τί ὁ φόβος διαφθείρει;
R1.2 τί τὴν ἀλήθειαν εὑρίσκει;
S2.5 τίς τὴν τρίχα ἀλλάττει;
R2.3 τίς δίκην τίει;
R2.4 τίνα ἡ ἀρετὴ τέρπει;

♦ Exercise 3

Enter the kernels of the following sentences into a kernel chart, like the one below. In the last column indicate whether the speech act is a statement or question.

1. χρόνος τρέχει.
2. τί τρέχει;
3. ἔρως μουσικὴν διδάσκει.
4. τίς μουσικὴν διδάσκει;
5. τίνα ἡ ἀρετὴ τέρπει;

	Item: Function	*Item: Function*	*Item: Function*	*Kernel Type*	*Label*
1.	χρόνος: Subject	τρέχει: Verb		Intransitive	Statement

Lesson Vocabulary

Pronouns

τίς;	who? which...?
τί;	what? which?
τις	somebody, anybody; some, any...
τι	something, anything; some, any...

Particles

ἆρα	with any answer expected
ἆρα οὐ	with positive answer expected
οὐκοῦν	with positive answer expected
μὴ οὖν (= μῶν)	with negative answer expected
ἆρα μή	with negative answer expected

Lesson 4

Morphology: Adverbs and Prepositions

Syntax: Adverbial Modification

Semantics: Adverbial Modification

The Greek sentences in the previous lessons introduced the kernel of the sentence and the connectors. This lesson introduces the modifiers, adverbs and prepositional phrases.

Basic Sentences

4.1 ἀεὶ γὰρ καλῶς βάλλει τὸν κύβον Ζεύς.

For Zeus always throws the die successfully/well.

4.2 εἰρήνη μὲν γεωργὸν κἀν (=καὶ ἐν) πέτρᾳ τρέφει καλῶς, πόλεμος δὲ κἀν πεδίῳ κακῶς.

Peace feeds the farmer well even on a rocky hill but war feeds him badly even in the plain. Menander

4.3 πρὸς γὰρ τὸν πλοῦτον ὁ φθόνος ἕρπει.

For envy creeps upon wealth. Sophocles (adapted)

4.4 σὺν θεῷ.

With God (Ø = let us walk) Motto

4.5 ἄνευ δὲ εὐψυχίας τέχνη πρὸς τὸν κίνδυνον οὐκ ἰσχύει.

Without good spirit skill is of no avail in time of danger. Thucydides (adapted)

4.6 σὺν δίκῃ.

With justice Motto

4.7 τὴν δὲ ὀρθότητα καὶ τὴν ὠφέλιαν καὶ τὸ εὖ καὶ τὸ καλῶς ἡ ἀλήθεια ἀποτελεῖ.

But truth brings about uprightness and usefulness and goodness and nobility.
Plato (adapted)

Lesson 4

Morphology: Adverbs and Prepositions

Part of Speech: Adverb

Most words ending in the morpheme {**ως**} are adverbs. Examples are καλῶς in S4.1 and 4.2. There are also many adverbs, such as ἀεί in S4.1 that cannot be recognized by their form. Adverbs are indeclinables.

Part of Speech: Preposition

Prepositions are indeclinable words such as ἐν, πρός, σύν and ἄνευ. A Greek preposition patterns with a noun to form a prepositional phrase. Examples are **ἐν** πέτρᾳ "**on** the rock" in S4.2, **πρὸς** τὸν πλοῦτον "**towards** wealth" in S4.3 and S4.5, **σύν** θεῷ "**with** God" in S4.4, and **ἄνευ** εὐψυχίας, "**without** good spirit" in S4.5 Some prepositions appear with one case only, others with two or three.

The Dative Case

Some of the prepositions in this lesson pattern with nouns in the **dative case**. This is the first of several uses of the dative case. The inflectional morpheme for the dative singular is final {ι}. If the stem ends in the vowels α/η or ο/ω, the ι appears *under* the vowel. This is called **iota subscript**. Examples are S4.2 πέτρᾳ and πεδίῳ, S4.4 θεῷ, S4.6 δίκῃ. See Pre-view.

The Genitive Case

Some prepositions also pattern with nouns in the **genitive case**. There is no single inflectional morpheme for the genitive singular. It is the second item in a dictionary listing for nouns. In S4.5 εὐψυχίας is a genitive. The preposition ἄνευ always appears with a genitive.

♦Exercise 1

Identify each word by part of speech and, if a noun or pronoun, by case and number.

1. τρίχα
2. ἰσχυρῶς
3. ἀεί
4. σύν
5. γεωργόν
6. τίς;
7. ἄνευ
8. γνώμη
9. εὐψυχίᾳ
10. σοφῶς

Lesson 4

Syntax: Adverbial Modification

The words in the sentences of the previous lessons have all functioned as kernel items or connectors. This lesson introduces a third function, **modifier**. Modifiers are neither kernel items nor connectors. They may modify any kernel item or another modifier. The item that is modified is called the **head of construction. A modifier raises the expectation of a head.** Modifiers are of two kinds:

1. **adverbial modifiers**: the head of construction is a verb, adjective, or adverb, *but not a noun.*
2. **adjectival modifiers**: the head of construction is a noun.

In this lesson all modifiers are adverbial. They are of two types:

1. **adverbs**, e.g., καλῶς, ἀεί
2. **prepositional phrases** consisting of a preposition and a noun in the genitive, dative or accusative.
   In R4.2 σὺν τῷ φίλῳ εὐτυχεῖ ὁ ἀγαθὸς ἀεί, σὺν τῷ φίλῳ modifies the head εὐτυχεῖ. ἀεί is an adverb which also modifies εὐτυχεῖ. These adverbial phrases describe with whom and how long the action takes place. They do not describe ὁ ἀγαθὸς.

Note:
In Greek, prepositional phrases can also function as adjectival modifiers modifying noun phrases, as they frequently do in English, e.g., "the man in the moon," "her father-in-law." Uses of the prepositional phrase as adjectival modifier will occur in the next lesson.

Modifiers are **not** part of the kernel. Therefore, modifiers can be entered into a modifier chart like the one below which shows selected modifiers from S4.1, S4.2 and S4.4.

	Item	*Descriptive Information*	*Syntactic Information*	*Head of Construction*
4.1	ἀεὶ	adverb	adverbial modifier	βάλλει
4.2	ἐν πέτρᾳ	prepositional phrase		
4.4	σὺν θεῷ	prepositional phrase		not expressed

Remember a prepositional phrase constitutes a single item.

LESSON 4

♦ Exercise 2

Enter the remaining modifiers of S4.1 through S4.5 into a modifier chart, like the one below.

Item		*Descriptive Information*	*Syntactic Information*	*Head of Construction*
4.1	ἀεὶ	adverb	adverbial modifier	βάλλει

♦ Exercise 3

Enter the kernels only of S4.1, S4.2, and S4.3 into a kernel chart, like the one below.

Clause Connector	*Item: Function*	*Item: Function*	*Item: Function*	*Kernel Type*	*Label*

The Power of the Article: the articular adverb

In contrast to English, the Greek article together with an adverb or a prepositional phrase (S7.7) functions as a noun phrase. In S4.7 τὸ εὖ and τὸ καλῶς are syntactic equivalents of τὴν ὀρθότητα and τὴν ὠφέλειαν. More on the power of the article is presented in Lessons 5, 7 and 9.

Semantics: Adverbial Modification

Accompaniment, Manner, Frequency

A summary of common semantic categories, including accompaniment, manner and frequency occurs at the end of this section. In Greek distinguishing between accompaniment and manner depends on making the distinction between the semantic features animate and non-anmiate. S4.4 the prepositional phrase σὺν θεῷ, "with God," answers the question "with whom?" because the noun θεός has the semantic feature **animate**. However in S4.6 σὺν δίκῃ, "with justice," the prepositional phrase answers the question "in what manner?" because the noun δίκη has the semantic feature **non-animate**. Therefore σὺν θεῷ indicates the semantic category **accompaniment** and σὺν δίκῃ indicates the semantic category **manner**. The adverb ἀεί, "always," has the semantic feature **frequency**. For more categories see Lesson 6.

LESSON 4

Place

In Greek, as in English, some nouns have the semantic feature **place**: Λιβύη "Libya," πεδίον "plain," πέτρα "rock." When such a noun occurs in a prepositional phrase, the case of the noun determines the meaning of the phrase.

The accusative indicates motion towards a place, the dative indicates the place where an action occurs, the genitive indicates motion away from a place. In S4.3 πρὸς + πλοῦτον indicates the semantic category place to which, because πλοῦτον, an abstract noun, is thought of metaphorically as a place. The same is true for κίνδυνον in S4.5.

Semantics: Summary

Greek Question Word	*Semantic Category*	*English Question Word*
πῶς;	Manner	In what manner?
ποῦ;	Place Where	In what place? Where?
πόθεν;	Place from Which	From what place?
ποῖ;	Place to Which	Whereto?
σὺν τίνι;	Accompaniment	With whom?
ποσάκις;	Frequency	How often?
πόσος;	Size	How large?
πόσοι;	Quantity	How many?
διὰ τί;	Cause	Why?

♦Exercise 4

Copy any item that is a *semantically possible* answer to the question provided.

1. πῶς ὁ θεὸς τὸν κύβον βάλλει;	σὺν εὐψυχίᾳ, σὺν τῷ φίλῳ, ἀεὶ
2. ποῦ ἡ εἰρήνη τὸν γεωργὸν τρέφει;	σὺν δὶκῃ, ἄνευ τέχνης ἐν τῷ πεδίῳ
3. σὺν τίνι ὁ σοφὸς μένει;	σὺν δίκῃ, καλῶς, σὺν τῷ φίλῳ
4. ποῖ ὁ λύκος τρέχει;	πρὸς τὴν θάλατταν, πρὸς τῆς πέτρας, ἐν τῷ πεδίῳ

Lesson 4

Metaphrasing: Adverbial Modifiers

Adverbs may be metaphrased before the verb or after the kernel. Prepositional phrases are best metaphrased after the kernel. Any adverbial modifier may be moved elsewhere in a final translation.

♦ Exercise 5

Metaphrase in isolation each of the following. Remember that every metaphrase must show a complete kernel.

ἄνευ δὲ εὐψυχίας __________ __________s ± _______ without good spirit.

1. σὺν τῷ γεωργῷ	4. ἄνευ τέχνης
2. τὸν πόλεμον ἀεί	5. ἀεὶ ἰσχύει
3. τίς σὺν φθόνῳ βάλλει;	6. ἐν πέτρᾳ

Readings

4.1 ἄγει ὁ θεὸς τὸν κακὸν πρὸς δίκην.	Menander
4.2 σὺν τῷ φίλῳ εὐτυχεῖ ὁ ἀγαθὸς ἀεί.	Menander
4.3 τέχνη οὐκ ὠφελεῖ ἄνευ ἀλκῆς.	Thucydides
4.4 οὐ φέρει ἐν μνήμῃ τὴν ἀτυχίαν ὁ σοφός.	Menander
4.5 ἀεὶ Λιβύη φέρει αἴσθησιν.	Aristotle

Practice Sentences

1. σὺν μὲν δίκῃ τρέφει τὴν πόλιν ὁ πολίτης, σὺν δὲ ἀδικίᾳ οὐ.
2. ἄγει ὁ νόμος τὸν ἀγαθὸν πρὸς εἰρήνην, καὶ ὁ φθόνος τὸν κακὸν πρὸς φόνον.
3. ὁ μὲν φθόνος τὸν γεωργὸν πρὸς πόλεμον ἄγει, ὁ θεὸς ἐν δὲ καιρῷ λύει τὸν κίνδυνον.

Lesson 4

Lesson Vocabulary

Nouns

ὁ ἀγαθός, τοῦ ἀγαθοῦ	good person
ἡ αἴσθησις, τῆς αἰσθήσεως	observation
ἡ ἀλκή, τῆς ἀλκῆς	strength
ἡ ἀτυχία, τῆς ἀτυχίας	misfortune
ὁ γεωργός, τοῦ γεωργοῦ	farmer
ἡ εἰρήνη, τῆς εἰρήνης	peace
ἡ εὐψυχία, τῆς εὐψυχίας	good spirit
ὁ Ζεύς, τοῦ Διός	Zeus
ὁ κακός, τοῦ κακοῦ	bad person
ὁ κίνδυνος, τοῦ κινδύνου	danger
ὁ κύβος, τοῦ κύβου	die, pl. dice
ἡ Λιβύη, τῆς Λιβύης	Libya
ἡ ὀρθότης, τῆς ὀρθότητος	uprightness
τὸ πεδίον, τοῦ πεδίου	plain
ἡ πέτρα, τῆς πέτρας	rock
ὁ πλοῦτος, τοῦ πλούτου	wealth
ὁ πόλεμος, τοῦ πολέμου	war
ὁ σοφός, τοῦ σοφοῦ	wise person
ἡ τέχνη, τῆς τέχνης	skill
ὁ φθόνος, τοῦ φθόνου	envy
ἡ ὠφέλια, τῆς ὠφελίας	usefulness

Verbs

ἄγω, ἄξω, ἤγαγον	to do, drive, lead
ἀποτελέω, ἀποτελήσω, ἀπετέλεσα	to produce, accomplish
βάλλω, βαλῶ, ἔβαλον	to throw
ἕρπω, ἕρψω, εἵρπυσα	to creep
εὐτυχέω, εὐτυχήσω, εὐτύχησα	to be happy
ἰσχύω, ἰσχύσω, ἴσχυσα	be strong, prevail
τρέφω, θρέψω, ἔθρεψα	to feed
φέρω, οἴσω, ἤνεγκα/ἤνεγκον	to bring, carry, endure
ὠφελέω, ὠφελήσω, ὠφέλησα	to be useful

Adverbs

ἀεί	always
εὖ	good, well
ἰσχυρῶς	well
καί (when not connecting two things)	even, also (See S11.3.)

Lesson 4

κακῶς	badly
καλῶς	beautifully, well
σοφῶς	wisely

Question words

πόθεν;	From what place?
ποῖ;	Whereto?
ποσάκις;	How often?
πόσοι;	How many?
πόσος;	How large?
ποῦ;	In what place? Where?
πῶς;	In what manner? How?

Prepositions

ἄνευ + genitive	without
διά + accusative	because of
διά + genitive	through
ἐν + dative	in, on
πρός + accusative	to, towards, against
πρός + dative	near, in addition to
πρός + genitive	from
σύν + dative	with, together with, in accordance with

Lesson 5

Gender

Morphology:

More on First Declension Nouns

Neuter Nouns

Adjectives

Syntax: Adjectival Modification

Semantics: More on Adverbial Modification

The last lesson introduced two parts of speech, prepositions and adverbs. This lesson introduces one new part of speech, the **adjective**. This lesson also introduces a new type of modification, namely, **adjectival modification**.

Basic Sentences

5.1 ἡ γὰρ παράκαιρος ἡδονὴ τίκτει βλάβην.

Untimely pleasure produces damage. — Menander (adapted)

5.2 τὸ ῥόδον ἀκμάζει βαιὸν χρόνον.

The rose blooms a short time. — Greek Anthology

5.3 ὁ γὰρ ἐν καιρῷ μόχθος εὐδαιμονίαν τίκτει.

Toil at the right time produces well-being. — Euripides (adapted)

5.4 ὁ σοφὸς περιφέρει τὴν οὐσίαν.

The wise man carries his fortune (with him). — Menander (adapted)

5.5 πρὸς υἱὸν ὀργὴν οὐκ ἔχει χρηστὸς πατήρ.

A good father does not hold a grudge against his son. — Menander

Lesson 5

Gender

Every noun belongs to one of three gender classes: **masculine**, **feminine**, or **neuter**. The full dictionary entry for a noun consists of the article, its nominative singular, its genitive singular, and the article which signals its **gender**:

πατήρ, πατρός, ὁ
ἡδονή, ἡδονῆς, ἡ
ῥόδον, ῥόδου, τό

The gender of a noun must be memorized, but there are some helpful generalizations. Gender can sometimes be deduced from declension. For example, most nouns in the first declension are feminine, most nouns of the second declension are masculine or neuter. Gender is sometimes predictable from meaning. For example, nouns denoting males and females or their cultural roles are masculine or feminine, respectively. Neuter, derived from the Latin adjective *neuter, neutra, neutrum* "neither of two," means literally that a noun is neither masculine nor feminine; some objects are neuter. Most abstract nouns are feminine. However the gender of many nouns cannot be predicted from their meaning. For example, a Greek word for earth, γῆ, is feminine, ἀήρ, a word for air, is masculine, and a word for water, ὕδωρ, is neuter.

Morphology: More on First Declension and Neuter Nouns

More First Declension Nouns

Most nouns of the first declension are feminine, but there are some that are masculine, ending in -ης or -ας. See Lesson 2.

Nominative	ὁ πολίτης	ὁ νεανίας
Genitive	τοῦ πολίτου	τοῦ νεανίου
Dative	τῷ πολίτῃ	τῷ νεανίᾳ
Accusative	τὸν πολίτην	τόν νεανίαν

The plural of these nouns is the same as that of the first declension feminine nouns. See Morphology.

Many of these masculine first declension nouns end in the morpheme {της} and share the semantic feature **practitioner**.

♦Exercise 1

ὁ πολίτης means the "man of the city, the citizen". Guess the meaning of:

ὁ ἀθλητής	ὁ κριτής	ὁ μαθητής
ὁ ναύτης	ὁ ποιητής	ὁ σοφιστής
ὁ στρατιώτης	ὁ ὑποκριτής	

Lesson 5

Neuter Nouns

Neuter nouns are grouped in the second and third declensions. The **nominative** and the **accusative** of neuter nouns are *always alike*. Neuter nouns of the second declension end in -ον in both cases. Neuter nouns of the third declension have many different endings in the nominative singular, and, therefore, in the accusative singular also. This morphological ambiguity is usually resolved within the syntax of the sentence. If not, the meaning of the sentence depends on the context.

Paradigm for Nouns in the Neuter Gender

	Second Declension	*Third Declension*	*Third Declension*
Singular			
Nominative	ῥόδον	ῥῆμα	κέρδος
Genitive	ῥόδου	ῥήματος	κέρδους
Dative	ῥόδῳ	ῥήματι	κέρδει
Accusative	ῥόδον	ῥῆμα	κέρδος
Plural			
Nominative	ῥόδα	ῥήματα	κέρδη
Genitive	ῥόδων	ῥημάτων	κερδῶν
Dative	ῥόδοις	ῥήμασι(ν)	κέρδεσι(ν)
Accusative	ῥόδα	ῥήματα	κέρδη

Notice that the genitive plural always ends in -ων and the nominative and accusative plurals end in -α.

Nouns of the type κέρδος have an -ε in the stem; the declension of these nouns follows the rules for vowel contraction. See Pre-view.

κέρδους = κέρδε + ος
κέρδει = κέρδε + ι
κέρδη = κέρδε + α

Nouns of type ῥῆμα form the dative plural ῥήμασι(ν) following the rules for consonant changes. See Pre-view.

♦Exercise 2

Using the dictionary listings provided, identify the following nouns by case, number and gender.

γένος, γένους, τό
ἥβη, ἥβης, ἡ
δαίμων, δαίμονος, ὁ
βιβλίον, βιβλίου, τό

1. τὸν δαίμονα	3. τὸ γένος	5. ἡ ἥβη	7. τὸ βιβλίον
2. τὸ γένος	4. τοῦ γένους	6. τῇ ἥβῃ	8. τὸ βιβλίον

Lesson 5

Morphology: Adjectives

Adjectives look like nouns and have nearly the same morphemes for case and number. One group of adjectives looks like nouns of the first and second declensions. The other group looks like nouns of the third declension. The full dictionary entry for an adjective consists of the nominative singular, masculine, feminine, and neuter. The endings of Greek adjectives indicate three grammatical categories: case, number, and **gender**. Some of the forms of adjectives are ambiguous with regard to gender. Compound adjectives like φιλάνθρωπος look the same whether they modify a masculine or a feminine noun. There are even adjectives with one ending in the nominative singular for all three genders.

Paradigm for First and Second Declension Adjectives

καλός, καλή, καλόν (good, noble, attractive) represents the group of adjectives called **first** and **second declension adjectives**.

	Masculine	*Feminine*	*Neuter*
Singular			
Nominative	καλός	καλή	καλόν
Genitive	καλοῦ	καλῆς	καλοῦ
Dative	καλῷ	καλῇ	καλῷ
Accusative	καλόν	καλήν	καλόν
Plural			
Nominative	καλοί	καλαί	καλά
Genitive	καλῶν	καλῶν	καλῶν
Dative	καλοῖς	καλαῖς	καλοῖς
Accusative	καλούς	καλάς	καλά

Note the following comparisons with the morphology of nouns of the first and second declensions.

The first column is on the model of the second declension masculine noun λιμός.
The second column is on the model of the first declension noun ἀρετή.
The third column is on the model of the second declension neuter noun τὸ ῥόδον.

Other common adjectives with this paradigm include:

σοφός, σοφή, σοφόν wise
κακός, κακή, κακόν evil, bad
ἀγαθός, ἀγαθή, ἀγαθόν good
δίκαιος, δικαία, δίκαιον just, fair
μακρός, μακρά, μακρόν big, large, great
μικρός, μικρά, μικρόν small

Lesson 5

Paradigm for Third Declension Adjectives

ψευδής, ψευδές (false) represents the group of adjectives with **third declension** endings. These adjectives use the same forms for the masculine and feminine genders. The dictionary entry for this groups shows two forms ψευδής, ψευδές.

	Masculine /Feminine	*Neuter*
Singular		
Nominative	ψευδής	ψευδές
Genitive	ψευδοῦς	ψευδοῦς
Dative	ψευδεῖ	ψευδεῖ
Accusative	ψευδῆ	ψευδές
Plural		
Nominative	ψευδεῖς	ψευδῆ
Genitive	ψευδῶν	ψευδῶν
Dative	ψευδέσι	ψευδέσι
Accusative	ψευδεῖς	ψευδῆ

Note that adjectives of the type ψευδής, ψευδές have an -ε in the stem and form their endings by contraction. See the noun κέρδος above. Another common form of third declension adjectives is εὐδαίμων. See Morphology for paradigm.

♦ Exercise 3

Identify the following adjectives by case, number (singular), and gender. Give all possibilities for ambiguous forms.

1. καλόν
2. ψευδές
3. μικρῷ
4. ψευδῆ
5. ἀγαθή
6. ψευδεῖ
7. μικροῦ
8. μακρά

Syntax: Adjectival Modification

Adjectival modifiers modify nouns. The noun that is modified is called the **nounhead**. In Greek the adjective as modifier has the same case, number and gender as its nounhead. This is called **agreement**.

Any adjective can modify a noun of any declension, although their endings do not always look the same (see on allomorphs under Technical Terms in Lesson 1). In S5.5 πρὸς υἱὸν ὀργὴν οὐκ ἔχει **χρηστὸς πατήρ**, the adjective χρηστός is in agreement

Lesson 5

with its nounhead πατήρ: both have the same case, number and gender, although, because they belong to different declensions, they have different endings.

The Adjective as Adjectival Modifier

In contrast to the adverbial modifier, an adjectival modifier can often be recognized by **word order**. When its nounhead has an article, the adjectival modifier regularly occurs in one of two positions:

In the **attributive** position the modifier appears between the article and the nounhead:

ὁ ἀγαθὸς πολίτης "the good citizen ______s ± ________"

In the **appositional** position the modifier follows the noun and a repetition of the article:

ὁ πολίτης ὁ ἀγαθός "the good citizen ______s ± ________"

In the absence of an article, the adjectival modifier may occur before or after its nounhead:

S5.2 βαιὸν χρόνον
R5.4 νύμφη ἄπροικος

In either case the adjective can always be recognized by agreement with the nounhead. See Lesson 10 for another function of the adjective without the article.

The Prepositional Phrase as Adjectival Modifier

In Greek as well as in English a prepositional phrase can function both as **an adverbial** and as **an adjectival modifier**. "We have been on the moon, but the man in the moon didn't show. Where was the man in the moon? Was he on earth?" Just like an adjective, a prepositional phrase functions as an adjectival modifier when it is in the **attributive** or **appositional** position:

ὁ ἐν τῇ πόλει ἀνὴρ "the man in the city ______s ± ________"
ὁ ἀνὴρ ὁ ἐν τῇ πόλει "the man in the city ______s ± ________"

In the absence of an article a prepositional phrase usually functions as an adverbial modifier:

τὸ ῥόδον ἀκμάζει ἄνευ μόχθου. "the rose blooms without toil"

Lesson 5

♦ Exercise 4

In English a prepositional phrase as adjectival modifier follows its nounhead directly, while a prepositional phrase as adverbial modifier does not:

The man *from Marathon* arrived.
The man arrived *from Marathon.*

Write three examples of a prepositional phrase as adjectival modifier, and three examples of a prepositional phrase as adverbial modifier in English.

The Power of the Article: The Articular Adjective

While English has a definite article "the" and an indefinite article "a," Greek has only a definite article (see Lesson One). The Greek definite article is derived from a pronoun and retains number, gender and case but no longer occurs by itself.* Most commonly it occurs with nouns, as in S5.1 ἡ ἡδονή, S5.2 τὸ ῥόδον, S5.3 ὁ μόχθος. The article combines with whatever follows to form noun phrases in a process called **nominalization**. In S5.4, where the **power of the article** is apparent, σοφός, an adjective, has by nominalization become ὁ σοφός, a noun phrase meaning "the wise man." This kind of nominalization, as in Dryden's "Alexander's Feast": "happy, happy pair, only the brave deserves the fair" is very rare in English. Such a phrase is termed **articular adjective.** ἡ σοφή stands for "the wise woman" (girl, maid *etc.*). τὸ σοφόν for "the wise thing" (idea, thought *etc.*).

The Pronoun as Adjectival Modifier

Most Greek pronouns are used both as nouns and as adjectives modifying a nounhead (see Lesson 3). τίς; (the interrogative pronoun) as adjective usually precedes the nounhead as in τίς ἀνήρ; "which man?" As a noun τίς; is translated into English as "who?," but as an adjective τίς is translated as "which?" or "what?" τὶς, the indefinite pronoun, on the other hand usually follows the noun as an enclitic keeping or losing its accent according to the rules on enclitics: ἀνήρ τις "some man," "a certain man." See Pre-View.

Metaphrasing: The Adjective as Adjectival Modifier

According to the principle that a modifier raises the syntactic expectation of a head, an adjective raises the expectation of a nounhead. It has the basic metaphrase (**adjective**) (**nounhead**). In S5.1 ἡ γὰρ παράκαιρος ἡδονὴ τίκτει βλάβην, the words ἡ γὰρ παράκαιρος must be metaphrased, "For, ill-timed _____ _______s ± _____."

---

* The Greek indefinite pronoun τις (see Lesson 3) has retained its pronomial character when it occurs by itself. It is the equivalent of "somebody," "something," "anybody," "anything." Otherwise it is almost the equivalent of the English indefinite article "a." See S7.8

LESSON 5

♦ Exercise 5

Identify each adjective by case, number and gender and copy any noun with which it agrees. Refer to the lesson vocabulary as needed.

Each of these adjectives agrees in **number** and **gender** with the nouns listed on the same line. Copy those nouns which agree also in **case**.

Adjective	*Identification*		*Nouns*	
μικρόν		χρόνῳ	ἔρως	υἱόν
καλὴ		χεῖρα	ἡδονὴν	νύξ
χρηστῷ		πόνος	βίῳ	καιρόν

Each of these adjectives agrees in **case** and **number** with the nouns. Copy those nouns which agree also in **gender**.

Adjective	*Identification*		*Nouns*	
ἀγαθὴν		ἄνδρα	εὐψυχίαν	ἔργον
μακρῷ		δίκῃ	ῥόδῳ	νυκτί
κακός		γῆ	βίος	ἡμέρα

♦ Exercise 6

Give all possible identifications for the adjectives in the left column. Then copy any of the four following nouns with which the adjective could agree.

κακή	βλάβην	ψυχῇ	ἀνήρ	ἀρετή
χρηστός	χρόνῳ	μόχθος	ὀργήν	ἀνήρ
δειλόν	ἔργον	ἄνδρα	ῥήματι	ἡδονῇ

♦ Exercise 7

Metaphrase the following items in isolation. Remember that every metaphrase must show a complete kernel.

σοφὴν: ____ _____s wise _________.

1. καλὴ
2. καλὴν
3. καλὸν
4. καλὸν

Lesson 5

♦ Exercise 8

Using the chart below, write a cumulative metaphrase of the sentences given.

1. πρὸς υἱὸν ὀργὴν οὐκ ἔχει χρηστὸς πατήρ.
2. τὸ δειλὸν κέρδος βλάβην ποιεῖ.

Item	*Part of Speech and Form*	*Syntactic Information*	*Cumulative Metaphrase*
πρὸς υἱὸν	prepositional phrase	adverbial modifier	________ ______s + _____ against a son
ὀργὴν	noun in the accusative case	direct object	________ ______s a grudge against a son

Semantics: More on Adverbial Modification

Time

Just as Greek uses adverbial modification to indicate the semantic catagory place, it also uses adverbial modifiers to indicate **time**. Time can be expressed by a prepositional phrase or by a noun in the accusative, dative or genitive without a preposition. The accusative case indicates **length of time**, the dative **time when** and the genitive **time within which**:

Compare the examples below:

βαιὸν χρόνον	"for a short time"	→	παρὰ πάντα τὸν χρόνον	"for the whole time"
νυκτί	"at night"	→	ἐν νυκτί	"in the night"
νυκτός	"during the night"	→	διὰ νυκτός	"throughout the night"

When an expression of time occurs without a preposition, special attention must be paid to the kernel. For example, in S5.2 τὸ ῥόδον ἀκμάζει is a complete kernel. βαιὸν χρόνον does not function as direct object. There are many more accusatives of this kind with various semantic features.

Lesson 5

♦ Exercise 9

Enter all modifiers from the Basic Sentences of this lesson into a modifier chart like the one below. Include both adverbial and adjectival modifiers.

		Syntactic Information		
Modifier	*Description*	*Adverbial*	*Adjectival*	*Head*
5.1 παράκαιρος	Adjective		X	ἡδονή

♦ Exercise 10

Identify the boldface adjectives as part of noun phrases or as modifiers.

1. ὁ **σοφὸς** ἀνήρ
2. τὸ **ἀγαθόν**
3. ἐν τῷ **ἀληθεῖ**
4. ἐκ τῆς **ἀληθοῦς** δόξας

Metaphrasing: The Prepositional Phrase as Adjectival Modifier

Prepositional phrases in the attributive position must be metaphrased after their nounhead. In S5.3 ἐν καιρῷ is in the attributive position between ὁ and μόχθος: "toil at the right time." Of course this is the equivalent of: "well-timed toil!"

Readings

5.1. ῥῆμα παράκαιρον τὸν ὅλον ἀνατρέπει βίον. Menander

5.2. τὸ δ' ὄργανον πρὸς τὸ ἔργον ἡ φύσις ποιεῖ, ἀλλ' οὐ τὸ ἔργον πρὸς τὸ ὄργανον.

Aristotle

5.3. τὸ δειλὸν κέρδος πημονὴν ποιεῖ/τίκτει. Sophocles

5.4. νύμφη δ' ἄπροικος οὐκ ἔχει παρρησίαν. Menander

5.5. ψευδὴς διαβολὴ τὸν βίον βλάπτει.

5.6. οὐκ ἰσχύει ἄνευ δίκης ἡ πόλις οὐδὲ ὁ πολίτης.

Lesson 5

Practice Sentences

1. σὺν μὲν δίκῃ τὴν πόλιν τρέφει ὁ σόφος πολίτης, σὺν δὲ ἀδικίᾳ ὁ κακὸς πολίτης διαφθείρει.
2. πρὸς νύμφην ὀργὴν οὐκ ἔχει ὁ χρηστός.
3. οὐκ ἀλλάττει τὴν δικαίαν γνώμην ὁ δίκαιος.
4. ὁ ἐν πόλει γεωργὸς κέρδος οὐ τίκτει.
5. οὐ τίκτει κέρδος ἐν πόλει ὁ γεωργός.
6. εἰρήνη μὲν παύει, πόλεμος δὲ ποιεῖ ἀδικίαν.
7. πῶς τὴν γῆν διαφθείρει ὁ κακός γεωργός;
8. τί γὰρ ἐν πέτρᾳ τρέφει τόν γεωργόν; εἰρήνη.
9. οὐδέ ὠφελεῖ τὴν ψύχην τὸ κακὸν κέρδος.
10. ἐν δὲ τῇ ψυχῇ ἡ σοφὴ ἡδονὴν εὑρίσκει.
11. ἆρα βάλλει κακῶς τὸν κύβον Ζεύς;
12. ἆρα οὐ λαμβάνει τὸν μικρὸν λύκον ὁ ἀνὴρ ὁ μακρός;

Lesson Vocabulary

Nouns

ἀήρ, ἀέρος, ὁ	air
ἀθλητής, ἀθλητοῦ, ὁ	athlete
ἀνήρ, ἀνδρός, ὁ	man, husband
βιβλίον, βιβλίου, τό	book
γένος, γένους, τό	race, kind
δαίμων, δαίμονος, ὁ, ἡ	daimon, deity, destiny
διαβολή, διαβολῆς, ἡ	slander
δόξα, δόξης, ἡ	opinion, reputation, glory
εὐδαιμονία, εὐδαιμονίας, ἡ	happiness
ἥβη, ἥβης, ἡ	youth
ἡδονή, ἡδονῆς, ἡ	pleasure
κέρδος, κέρδους, τό	gain
κριτής, κριτοῦ, ὁ	judge
μαθητής, μαθητοῦ, ὁ	student
μόχθος, μόχθου, ὁ	toil, effort
ναύτης, ναύτου, ὁ	sailor
νύμφη, νύμφης, ἡ	bride
ὄργανον, ὀργάνου, τό	tool, instrument

LESSON 5

ὀργή, ὀργῆς, ἡ	anger
οὐσία, οὐσίας, ἡ	possession, substance, property
παρρησία, παρρησίας, ἡ	freedom of speech
πατήρ, πατρός, ὁ	father
πημονή, πημονῆς, ἡ	pain
ποιητής, ποιητοῦ, ὁ	poet
πόλις, πόλεως, ἡ	city
πολίτης, πολίτου, ὁ	citizen
ῥῆμα, ῥήματος, τό	word, thing
ῥόδον, ῥόδου, τό	rose
σοφιστής, σοφιστοῦ, ὁ	sophist
σῶμα, σώματος, τό	body
ὕδωρ, ὕδατος, τό	water
υἱός, υἱοῦ, ὁ	son
ὑποκριτής, ὑποκριτοῦ, ὁ	actor
φύσις, φύσεως, ἡ	nature
ψυχή, ψυχῆς, ἡ	soul

Verbs

ἀκμάζω, ἀκμάσω, ἤκμασα	to bloom
ἀνατρέπω, ἀνατρέψω, ἀνέτρεψα	to overturn
βλάπτω, βλάψω, ἔβλαψα	to hurt, harm, damage
περιφέρω, περιοίσω, περιήνεγκα	to carry around

Adjectives

ἀγαθός, ἀγαθή, ἀγαθόν	good
ἀληθής, ἀληθές	true
ἄπροικος, ἄπροικον	without a dowry
βαιός, βαιά, βαιόν	short
δειλός, δειλή, δειλόν	vile, wretched
δίκαιος, δικαία, δίκαιον	just
εὐδαίμων, εὐδαῖμον	happy, lucky
κακός, κακή, κακόν	bad, evil, ugly
καλός, καλή, καλόν	good, noble, attractive
μακρός, μακρά, μακρόν	large, big, great
μικρός, μικρά, μικρόν	small
ὅλος, ὅλη, ὅλον	whole
παράκαιρος, παράκαιρον	ill-timed
σοφός, σοφή, σοφόν	wise
φιλάνθρωπος, φιλάνθρωπον	kind, humane
χρηστός, χρηστή, χρηστόν	good, useful

ψευδής, ψευδές	false
Coordinating Conjunctions	
οὐδέ	and not, but not, nor
Prepositions	
παρά + *acc.*	to the side of, towards
παρά + *dat.*	by the side of, beside
παρά + *gen.*	from (the side of)

Review 1

♦ Exercise 1

Define each of the terms below in your own words. Give a Greek example where appropriate.

Lesson 1

- allomorph
- expectation
- inflectional morpheme
- intransitive kernel
- kernel
- metaphrase
- morpheme
- morphology
- stem morpheme
- syntax
- transitive kernel

Lesson 2

- coordinating conjunction
- gap
- indeclinable

Lesson 3

- animate
- indefinite
- interrogative
- non-animate
- pronoun

Lesson 4

- adjectival
- adverbial
- head of construction
- modifier

Lesson 5

- agreement (noun-adjective)
- nounhead

♦ Exercise 2

Translate into Greek on the model provided. For vocabulary see the English to Greek Vocabulary in the Reference section.

S2.4 νὺξ μὲν παύει, ἡμέρα δὲ ἔργον ποιεῖ.

2.1 Peace nourishes the farmer, but war hurts him.

2.2 Time flies, excellence endures.

S3.1 τίς τὴν τρίχα ἀλλάττει;

3.1 Who always throws dice sucessfully?

3.2 What does Zeus throw successfully?

S4.5 ἄνευ δὲ εὐψυχίας* τέχνη πρὸς τὸν κίνδυνον οὐκ ἰσχύει.

4.1 Without wealth justice does not always prevail.

4.2 With peace the farmer produces wealth well.

S5.3 ὁ γὰρ ἐν καιρῷ μόχθος εὐδαιμονίαν τίκτει.

5.1 For the farmer in the city does not produce well-being.

5.2 But the farmer does not produce well-being.

Roots

Many English words contain Greek roots, which are sometimes recognizable without much difficulty. Learning to recognize Greek roots can aid in acquiring vocabulary. See Stem List in the Reference Section.

♦ Exercise

In the English words below, the segments in bold are Greek roots. With the help of a dictionary suggest a meaning for these roots. Then copy them in small Greek letters and surround them with curly braces. Note that letter y reflects Greek υ.

English word	*meaning of Greek root*	*Greek spelling*
1. tele**graph**	write	{γραφ}
2. apo**crypha**		
3. **log**ical		
4. **charit**able		
5. el**lip**tical		

* εὐψυχίας is a genitive. The preposition ἄνευ always appears with a genitive.

REVIEW 1

Required Vocabulary

Lesson 1

Nouns

ἡ ἀλήθεια, τῆς ἀληθείας	truth
ἡ ἀνάγκη, τῆς ἀνάγκης	necessity
ἡ ἀρετή, τῆς ἀρετῆς	virtue
ἡ δίκη, τῆς δίκης	right, justice
ὁ ἔρως, τοῦ ἔρωτος	love
ὁ καιρός, τοῦ καιροῦ	moment
ὁ λιμός, τοῦ λιμοῦ	hunger
ὁ λόγος, τοῦ λόγου	word, speech, thought, consideration
ἡ λύπη, τῆς λύπης	grief
ἡ μνήμη, τῆς μνήμης	memory
ἡ μουσική, τῆς μουσικῆς	music
ὁ νόμος, τοῦ νόμου	law
ἡ νύξ, τῆς νυκτός	night
ὁ πόνος, τοῦ πόνου	toil, trouble
ὁ φίλος, τοῦ φίλου	friend
ὁ φόβος, τοῦ φόβου	fear
ἡ χείρ, τῆς χειρός	hand
ὁ χρόνος, τοῦ χρόνου	time

Verbs

διδάσκω, διδάξω, ἐδίδαξα	to teach
εὑρίσκω, εὑρήσω, ηὗρον	to find
ἔχω, ἕξω/σχήσω, ἔσχον	to have
κρίνω, κρινῶ, ἔκρινα	to judge
λύω, λύσω, ἔλυσα	to dissolve, release, destroy
μένω, μενῶ, ἔμεινα	to remain
παύω, παύσω, ἔπαυσα	to cause to stop, stop

Adverbs

οὐ, οὐκ, οὐχ	not

Lesson 2

Nouns

ἡ ἀδικία, τῆς ἀδικίας	injustice, wrong
ὁ βίος, τοῦ βίου	life
ἡ βλάβη, τῆς βλάβης	harm
ἡ γῆ, τῆς γῆς	earth

Review 1

ἡ γνώμη, τῆς γνώμης	opinion, attitude
τό ἔργον, τοῦ ἔργου	labor, work
ἡ ἡμέρα, τῆς ἡμέρας	day
ἡ θάλαττα, τῆς θαλάττης	sea
ὁ θεός, τοῦ θεοῦ	god
ὁ λύκος, τοῦ λύκου	wolf
ὁ νεανίας, τοῦ νεανίου	young man

Verbs

ἀλλάττω, ἀλλάξω, ἤλλαξα	to change
λαμβάνω, λήψομαι, ἔλαβον	to take, seize
ποιέω, ποιήσω, ἐποίησα	to make, do, cause to be
τέρπω, τέρψω, ἔτερψα	to please

Adverbs

πάλιν	again

Coordinating Conjunctions

ἀλλά	but, however
γάρ (never in first position)	for
δέ	but, and
ἤ	or
ἤ...ἤ	either...or
καί, τε	and
μέν...δέ, ἀλλά	on one hand...on the other

Lesson 3

Pronouns

τίς;	who? which...?
τί;	what? which?
τις	somebody, anybody; some, any...
τι	something, anything; some, any...

Particles

ἆρα	with any answer expected
ἆρα οὐ	with positive answer expected
οὐκοῦν	with positive answer expected

Review 1

Lesson 4

Nouns

ἡ ἀτυχία, τῆς ἀτυχίας	misfortune
ὁ γεωργός, τοῦ γεωργοῦ	farmer
ἡ εἰρήνη, τῆς εἰρήνης	peace
ὁ κίνδυνος, τοῦ κινδύνου	danger
τὸ πεδίον, τοῦ πεδίου	plain
ὁ πόλεμος, τοῦ πολέμου	war
ἡ πέτρα τῆς πέτρας	rock
ἡ τέχνη, τῆς τέχνης	skill
ὁ φθόνος, τοῦ φθόνου	envy

Verbs

ἄγω, ἄξω, ἤγαγον	to do, drive, lead
βάλλω, βαλῶ, ἔβαλον	to throw
τρέφω, θρέψω, ἔθρεψα	to feed
φέρω, οἴσω, ἤνεγκα/ἤνεγκον	to bring, carry, endure
ὠφελέω, ὠφελήσω, ὠφέλησα	to be useful

Adverbs

ἀεί	always
καί (when it is not connecting two things)	even, also (See S11.3.)
κακῶς	badly
καλῶς	beautifully, well
σοφῶς	wisely

Prepositions

διά + accusative	because of
διά + genitive	through
ἐν + dative	in
πρός + accusative	to, towards, against
πρός + dative	near, in addition to
πρός + genitive	from
σύν + dative	with, together with, in accordance with
ἄνευ + genitive	without

Lesson 5

Nouns

ἀνήρ, ἀνδρός, ὁ	man, husband
γένος, γένους, τό	race, kind

Review 1

δαίμων, δαίμονος, ὁ	daimon, deity, destiny
δόξα, δόξης, ἡ	opinion, reputation, glory
εὐδαιμονία, εὐδαιμονίας, ἡ	happiness
ἥβη, ἥβης	youth
ἡδονή, ἡδονῆς, ἡ	pleasure
κέρδος, κέρδους, τό	gain
νύμφη, νύμφης, ἡ	bride
ὀργή, ὀργῆς, ἡ	anger
πατήρ, πατρός, ὁ	father
πόλις, πόλεως ἡ	city
πολίτης, πολίτου,ὁ	citizen
ῥόδον, ῥόδου, τό	rose
σῶμα, σώματος, τό	body
φύσις, φύσεως, ἡ	nature
ψυχή, ψυχῆς, ἡ	soul
Adjectives	
ἀγαθός, ἀγαθή, ἀγαθόν	good
δίκαιος, δικαία, δίκαιον	just
κακός, κακή, κακόν	bad, evil
καλός, καλή, καλόν	good, noble, attractive
μακρός, μακρά, μακρόν	large
μικρός, μικρά, μικρόν	small
ὅλος, ὅλη, ὅλον	whole
σοφός, σοφή, σοφόν	wise
χρηστός, χρηστή, χρηστόν	worthy, good
ψευδής, ψευδές	false
Verbs	
βλάπτω, βλάψω, ἔβλαψα	to hurt, harm, damage
Coordinating Conjunctions	
οὐδὲ	and not, but not, nor
Prepositions	
παρά + *acc.*	to the side of, towards
παρά + *dat.*	by the side of, beside
παρά + *gen.*	from (the side of)

Review 1

ANSWER KEY

Lesson 1:

1. Time puts a stop to memory.
2. Truth remains.
3. Reason produces law.
4. Work produces work.
5. A friend teaches a friend.
6. Music relieves sorrow.

Lesson 2:

1. On the one hand time stops, but love produces, memory.
2. A friend pleases a friend, a young man pleases a young man.
3. The god does not honor opinion, but he honors uprightness.
4. Love teaches love, and a friend, a friend.
5. Necessity causes either fear or virtue.
6. Mere opinion does not remove fear, but truth does.
7. For the earth makes the young man happy.

Lesson 4:

1. The citizen nourishes the city in accordance with justice, but not in accordance with injustice.
2. The law leads a good man to peace, and envy leads an evil man to destruction.
3. Envy pushes the farmer toward war, but at the right moment god removes the danger.

Lesson 5:

1. The wise citizen nourishes the city in accordance with justice, but the bad citizen destroys the city in accordance with injustice.
2. A good man does not carry a grudge against his bride.
3. A just man does not change a just opinion.
4. The farmer in the city does not produce a profit.
5. The farmer does not produce a profit in the city.
6. Peace puts a stop to injustice, but war makes it.

7. How does the bad farmer ruin the land?
8. For what keeps the farmer alive on rocky soil? Peace does.
9. Unjust gain does not benefit the soul.
10. A wise woman finds pleasure in her soul.
11. Does Zeus throw dice unsuccessfully?
12. Does the tall man not catch the little wolf?

Lesson 6

The Passive Kernel: A New Kernel Type

The Middle Voice: A Variant Verb Form

Semantics:

More on Adverbial Modification

Semantic Categories Expressed by Case

All verbs in previous kernels have been **active** in **voice**. This lesson introduces a new kernel type that has a verb in the **passive** voice. In addition, this lesson introduces two other types of adverbial modifier, a noun in the dative without a preposition and a prepositional phrase with the genitive.

Basic Sentences

6.1 ὁ πένης ἐλεεῖται, ὁ δὲ πλούσιος φθονεῖται.

The poor person is pitied, the rich person is envied. — Sotades (adapted)

6.2 οὐκ ἀμελεῖται ὑπὸ θεοῦ ὁ δίκαιος.

The just person is not neglected by God. — Plato (adapted)

6.3 χρηστὸς πονηρῷ οὐ τιτρώσκεται λόγῳ.

A fine person is not wounded by a mean word.

6.4 τάχα γάρ σε παρέρχεται ἥβη.

Youth passes you by swiftly. — Theocritus (adapted)

6.5 ψευδὴς διαβολὴ τὸν βίον λυμαίνεται.

A false slander destroys life. — Menander

6.6. οὐδεὶς μετ' ὀργῆς ἀσφαλῶς βουλεύεται.

No one makes safe plans for himself when angry. — Menander

Lesson 6

Morphology: εἷς, μία, ἕν

Here is the paradigm of the number εἷς, μία, ἕν, "one":

	Masculine	*Feminine*	*Neuter*
Nominative	εἷς	μία	ἕν
Genitive	ἑνός	μιᾶς	ἑνός
Dative	ἑνί	μιᾷ	ἑνί
Accusative	ἕνα	μίαν	ἕν

This number combines with the negatives (οὐ, μή) to form other adjectives or pronouns, for example οὐδείς (R6.4) and μήδεις (Lesson 22).

The Passive Kernel: A New Kernel Type

Morphology: The Verb in the Active, Passive and Middle Voice

Verb forms such as κρίνει, τρέφει, and ἀλλάττει have so far been identified as third person singular. In addition to person and number, verbs are also identified by tense (about which more in Lesson 13) and **voice**. Greek has three voices, active, passive and middle. English has only two, active and passive. The inflectional morpheme {ει} indicates third person, singular, **active** voice. The inflectional morpheme {ται} indicates third person, singular, **passive or middle** voice. The morpheme {ται} is attached to the stem morpheme with a so-called thematic vowel, {ε } or {ο}. This situation may be obscured as in φθονεῖται, ἀμελεῖται, τιμᾶται. See Pre-view on contraction.

♦ Exercise 1

Identify the possible voice of the following verb forms. You do not need to know the meaning of the verb.

1. ἀναπαύεται	4. ἔχει
2. ἕρπει	5. βάλλεται
3. ποιεῖ	6. ἀκμάζει

Not all verbs have a complete set of active, middle, and passive verb forms. There is a group of verbs that have middle/passive forms only. These are known as **deponent verbs.** They can be recognized from their dictionary listing; the first principle part will have the ending -μαι instead of -ω. Deponent verbs are either transitive, such as λυμαίνεται in S6.5, or intransitive, such as βουλεύεται in S6.6. Therefore S6.5 has a transitive kernel and S6.4 an intransitive kernel.

Some verbs have only middle/passive forms in certain tenses; these are called defective verbs. See Principle Parts in Reference section.

LESSON 6

Syntax: The Passive Kernel

So far there have been two kernel types. The verb in both these kernels may be active, middle or deponent.

A **transitive** kernel has items filling the three syntactic functions of:

Verb
Subject
Direct Object

A **intransitive** kernel has words filling the two functions of:

Verb
Subject

There is now a third kernel type, the passive kernel. Note that the verb in the passive kernel is in the passive voice.

The **passive** kernel has items filling the two functions:

Verb
Subject

The intransitive active kernel and the passive kernel each has only a subject and a verb.

♦Exercise 2

Name the possible kernel type of the following sentences.

1. ὁ πλούσιος φθονεῖται.
2. ἔρωτα παύει λιμός.
3. ὁ χρόνος τρέχει.
4. ἀρετὴ μένει.
5. τὸν κακὸν ὁ σοφὸς λυμαίνεται.

♦Exercise 3

Enter S6.2 and S6.3 into a kernel chart like the one below. The example given is S6.1 ὁ πένης ἐλεεῖται, ὁ δὲ πλούσιος φθονεῖται. The adverbial modifier section of this lesson describes the modifiers in these sentences.

	Clause Connector	*Item: Function*	*Item: Function*	*Item: Function*	*Kernel Type*	*Label*
S6.1		ὁ πένης: Subject	ἐλεεῖται: Verb		Passive	Statement
S6.1	δὲ	ὁ πλούσιος: Subject	φθονεῖται: Verb		Passive	Statement

LESSON 6

Semantic Roles: Agent, Patient and Beneficiary

The subject of an active verb plays the role of **agent**. The direct object of an active verb plays the role of **patient**. The subject of a passive verb also functions as the patient. However it is not easy to make a unified statement about the role played by the subject of a middle verb. The subject of a middle verb seems to play two roles simultaneously, either the roles of agent and beneficiary, or the roles of agent and patient.

In the first case, the subject both acts and benefits by the action of the verb:

Active		*Middle*	
φέρει	____ carries	φέρεται	____ wins (for his/her own)
φυλάττει	____ guards	φυλάττεται	____ guards against

In the second, the middle voice may seem simply reflexive:

Active		*Middle*	
κοσμεῖ	____ adorns	κοσμεῖται	____ adorns him/herself
φαίνει	____ shows	φαίνεται	____ shows him/herself, seems

Middle verbs occur in either transitive or intransitive kernels; there is no separate middle kernel.

Metaphrasing

All of the verbs in Lessons 1 through 5 have been in the active voice with the metaphrase "_______ _______s +/- _______." The verb in a passive kernel is metaphrased "_______ is _______-ed +/- by _______" or "_______ is being _______-ed +/- by _______." Thus, the metaphrase of κρίνεται is "_______ is tested" or "_______ is being tested."

Many speakers of English confuse the term *passive* with other terms describing verbs, especially the term *past*. For example, "the thief is being recognized" and "the thief is recognized," both in the passive voice, are *not the same* as "the thief recognized" or "has recognized" or "had recognized," all of which express *past time* and are in the *active voice*.

♦Exercise 4

Metaphrase the following active verb forms in an appropriate kernel following the example.

νίζει: (The servant) washes (Odysseus' foot).

1. τρέφει
2. τιτρώσκει
3. κρίνει
4. παύει

Lesson 6

Metaphrase the following as passive verb forms.

νίζεται: (Odysseus' foot) is washed.

1. τρέφεται
2. τιτρώσκεται
3. κρίνεται
4. παύεται

Metaphrase the following as middle verb forms. Give both possibilities as indicated by the example.

νίζεται: (The servant) washes (him/herself)

1. τρέφεται
2. τιτρώσκεται
3. κρίνεται
4. παύεται

Semantics: More on Adverbial Modification

The Prepositional Phrase with ὑπό + Genitive

There frequently occurs with the passive kernel a prepositional phrase with ὑπό plus a noun that has the semantic feature **animate**. Usually this prepositional phrase indicates "by whom" the action is done. Such a passive kernel is metaphrased "(**subject**) is (**passive verb**)-ed by (**animate noun in genitive**)."

This prepositional phrase answers the Greek question ὑπὸ τίνος? = "by whom?" and is traditionally called **genitive of agent**. The information as to the "agent" is here expressed by a modifier, and not by a kernel item. In the previous sentences the subject of the kernel played the role of agent. In the examples below, the agent is printed in bold type:

"**The boy** watches the dog."
"The boy is watched **by the dog**."

In S6.2. the agent is θεοῦ:

οὐκ ἀμελεῖται **ὑπὸ θεοῦ** ὁ ἀγαθός.
"The good person is not neglected by God."

The following sentence is an active transformation of S6.2: ὁ θεὸς still functions as the agent, but it is now the subject of the active verb.

οὐκ ἀμελεῖ **ὁ θεὸς** τὸν ἀγαθόν.
"God does not neglect the good person."

Lesson 6

Noun in the Dative without a Preposition

In S6.3 the noun λόγῳ is in the dative case without a preposition:

χρηστὸς πονηρῷ οὐ τιτρώσκεται **λόγῳ**.
"A fine person is not wounded by a mean word."

λόγος has the semantic feature **non-animate**. Traditionally this use of the dative is called **dative of means** or **dative of instrument**. This dative is metaphrased with the English prepositions "by/by means of" or "with." (For other uses of the dative, see Lesson 8.)

Although both genitive of agent and dative of means are metaphrased in English as a prepositional phrase with the preposition "by." The semantic roles of these two prepositional phrases are different: one noun is animate (agent) and the other is non-animate (instrument).

Semantic Categories Expressed by Case

It is customary to speak of **case uses** with names derived from semantic categories. The following list of names for semantic categories covers the uses of the nominative, accusative, genitive and dative introduced so far; it includes uses both with and without prepositions. Other uses of the dative and genitive without a preposition will be introduced in later lessons.

Semantic Categories Expressed by Case with and without a Preposition

Greek Construction	*Semantic Category*	*Question Answered*
σύν + dative of animate noun	accompaniment	with whom?
μετά + genitive of animate noun	accompaniment	with whom?
nominative + verb in the active voice	agent	who, what?
nominative + verb in the middle voice	agent + patient	who, what?
nominative + verb in the middle voice	agent + beneficiary	who, what?
ὑπό + genitive of animate noun	agent	by whom?
accusative + verb in the active voice	patient	whom, what?
nominative + verb in the passive voice	patient	who, what?
dative without preposition	means or instrument	by what means?
σύν + dative of non-animate noun	manner	in what manner?

LESSON 6

More Semantic Categories Expressed by Case

μετά + genitive of non-animate noun	manner	in what manner?
ἀπό/ἐξ + genitive	place from where	from where?
εἰς/πρός + accusative	place to which	where to?
ἐν + dative	place where	where?
ἐν + dative	time when	when?
accusative	time how long	how long?
διὰ + accusative	cause	why?

Note

Adverbs also belong to semantic categories, of which *manner* and *place* are the most common.

♦Exercise 5

Give the semantic category most nearly describing the italicized phrase.

1. The doctor treats the patient *with a new medicine.*
2. The doctor treats the patient *with gentleness.*
3. The doctor comes *with an assistant.*
4. The doctor treats the patient *in the home.*
5. The doctor comes *to the home.*
6. The doctor treats the patient *at night.*
7. The doctor comes *from the office.*
8. The doctor is aided *by the computer.*
9. The doctor is aided *by the assistant.*
10. The *baby* is treated in the home.
11. The *doctor* treats the baby in the home.

♦Exercise 6

Which of the English prepositional phrases in Exercise 5 would be expressed in Greek by a noun in the dative *without* a preposition? (3)

Which of the English prepositional phrases in Exercise 5 would be expressed in Greek by a prepositional phrase? And what would be the preposition for each? (6)

LESSON 6

♦ Exercise 7

Enter all modifiers from the Basic Sentences of this lesson into a modifier chart like the one below. Name the semantic category of adverbial modifiers in the semantic information column.

Syntactic Information					*Semantic Information*
Modifier	*Description*	*Adverbial*	*Adjectival*	*Head*	*Semantic category*
ὑπὸ θεοῦ	*prepositional phrase*	*X*		ἀμελεῖται	*agent*

♦ Exercise 8

The following sentences are Passive transformations of earlier Basic Sentences and Readings. Translate them as they are now:

1. λιμῷ ἔρως παύεται.
2. κρίνεται ὁ φίλος τῷ καιρῷ.
3. χειρὶ χεὶρ νίζεται.
4. φόβῳ μνήμη ἐκπλήσσεται.
5. εὑρίσκεται πόνῳ ἡ ἀλήθεια.
6. θρίξ ὑπὸ τοῦ λύκου ἀλλάττεται.
7. ἀεὶ γὰρ καλῶς βάλλεται ὁ κύβος ὑπὸ τοῦ θεοῦ.

♦ Exercise 9

Transform the kernel of the following sentences and readings from the transitive active into the passive kernel. You must change the former subject into an adverbial modifier, and watch its semantic features.

1. λύει λύπην λόγος. λύεται λύπη λόγῳ.
2. μουσικὴν ἔρως διδάσκει.
3. νὺξ ἔργον ἀναπαύει.
4. ῥῆμα παράκαιρον τὸν ὅλον ἀνατρέπει βίον.
5. τὸ δ' ὄργανον πρὸς τὸ ἔργον ἡ φύσις ποιεῖ, ἀλλ' οὐ τὸ ἔργον πρὸς τὸ ὄργανον.
6. οὐ μὲν ἀδικίαν θεὸς τίει, ἀλλὰ δίκην.
7. οὐχ ἡ μορφή, ἀλλ' ἡ ἀρετὴ τέρπει τὸν φίλον.
8. ἄγει ὁ θεὸς τὸν κακὸν πρὸς δίκην.

LESSON 6

♦ Exercise 10

Name the semantic category of the items in bold letters (see chart above).

1. εἰρήνη μὲν γεωργὸν καὶ **ἐν πέτρᾳ** τρέφει **καλῶς**, πόλεμος δὲ καὶ **ἐν πεδίῳ κακῶς**.
2. οὐ φέρει **ἐν μνήμῃ** τὴν ἀτυχίαν ὁ σοφός.
3. ὁ γὰρ **ἐν καιρῷ** μόχθος εὐδαιμονίαν τίκτει.
4. οὐδεὶς **μετ' ὀργῆς ἀσφαλῶς** βουλεύεται.

♦ Exercise 11

For extra reading try the following made-up sentences without looking up words. Use ___________ for unknown words.

1. ὀργὴ ὀργὴν τίκτει καὶ διαβολὴ διαβολήν.
2. οὐ τιτρώσκει ἡ ψευδὴς διαβολὴ τὸν δίκαιον.
3. τῷ χρόνῳ λύεται ἡ λύπη.
4. τῇ διαβολῇ ὁ πονηρὸς τιτρώσκει τὸν νεανίαν.
5. πόνῳ ἢ ξίφει σῴζεται ἡ πόλις.
6. τίνα οὐ τέρπει ὁ ἔρως, τίνα οὐ τὸ κέρδος;
7. τίς οὐκ ἐκπλήσσεται τῇ ἀδικίᾳ;
8. λυμαίνεται ἡ κακὴ ἡδονὴ τὸ σῶμα καὶ τὴν ψυχήν.
9. τῷ ὀργάνῳ τῷ μικρῷ ὁ ἀνὴρ ὁ μακρὸς ἀνατρέπεται.
10. ἡ ἐν τῇ πόλει δικαιοσύνη τὴν εὐδαιμονίαν τίκτει.
11. ἄνευ ὀργάνου οὐκ ἰσχύει ἡ ἀλκή.
12. ὑπὸ τοῦ δειλοῦ φθονεῖται ὁ χρηστός.
13. ἐλεεῖται ὁ πονηρὸς ὑπὸ τοῦ σοφοῦ.
14. ἐν πολέμῳ οὐ τιμᾶται ὁ νόμος.
15. οὐ τιτρώσκεται ὁ δίκαιος τῇ διαβολῇ.
16. τῇ ἐν πόλει δικαιοσύνῃ ἡ εὐδαιμονία τίκτεται.
17. τὸν χρηστὸν φθονεῖ ὁ δειλός.

Lesson 6

Readings

6.1. ὁ μέσος δὲ βίος τιμᾶται.

6.2. ὑφ' ἡδονῆς* ὁ φρόνιμος οὐχ ἁλίσκεται. — Menander

6.3. ἀνὴρ ἄβουλος ἡδονῇ θηρεύεται. — Menander

6.4. χθὼν βίον κομίζει καὶ πάλιν κομίζεται. — Menander

6.5 ὁ Μέλων ... ἔρχεται πρῶτον εἰς τὴν χώραν νυκτός. — Xenophon

Practice Sentences

1. ὑπὸ τοῦ πένητος ὁ νεανίας ὁ πλούσιος φθονεῖται.
2. παρέρχεται βίος.
3. ψευδεῖ διαβολῇ νικᾶται ἡ ἀλήθεια.
4. τῷ ἐν καίρῳ μόχθῳ εὐδαιμονία τίκτεται.
5. ὑπὸ τοῦ σοφοῦ οὐ φέρεται ἐν μνήμῃ ἡ ἀτυχία.
6. ἐν νυκτὶ πόνος ἀναπαύεται.
7. ἆρα λύεται ἡ φιλία τῇ ὀργῇ;

Lesson Vocabulary

Nouns

δικαιοσύνη, δικαιοσύνης, ἡ	justice
Μέλων, Μέλωνος, ὁ	Melon
πένης, πένητος, ὁ	poor man
τρόπος, τρόπου, ὁ	character, behavior, kind
χθών, χθόνος, ἡ	earth

Verbs

ἀδικέω, ἀδικήσω, ἠδίκησα	to do wrong
ἁλίσκομαι, ἁλώσομαι, ἥλων	to be caught
ἀμελέω, ἀμελήσω, ἠμέλησα	to neglect
βουλεύω, βουλεύσω, ἐβούλευσα	to plan, devise
βουλεύομαι, βουλεύσομαι, ἐβουλευσάμην	to take counsel, deliberate

* Note that in R6.2 the word ἡδονῆς is treated like an animate noun. It is used metaphorically. This metaphorical use is called **personification**. In R6.3 ἡδονῇ is not personified.

Lesson 6

ἐλεέω, ἐλεήσω, ἠλέησα	to pity
ἔρχομαι, ἐλεύσομαι, ἦλθον	to come, go
θηρεύω, θηρεύσω, ἐθήρευσα	to catch, hunt
κομίζομαι, κομιέομαι, ἐκομισάμην	to take, receive
κομίζω, κομιῶ, ἐκόμισα,	to give, supply, carry away
λυμαίνομαι, λυμανοῦμαι, ἐλυμηνάμην	to destroy
παρέρχομαι, παρελεύσομαι, παρῆλθον	to pass
σώζω, σώσω, ἔσωσα	to save
τιμάω, τιμήσω, ἐτίμησα	to honor
φαίνω, φανῶ, ἔφηνα	to show, cause to appear
φθονέω, φθονήσω, ἐφθόνησα	to envy

Adjectives

ἄβουλος, ἄβουλον	ill-advised
εἷς, μία, ἕν	one
μέσος, μέση, μέσον	middle, middle of, moderate
πλούσιος, πλουσία, πλούσιον	rich
πένης, πένες	poor
πονηρός, πονηρά, πονηρόν	bad
φρόνιμος, φρόνιμον	sensible, prudent

Pronoun

οὐδείς, οὐδεμία, οὐδέν	no one, nothing
σε (accusative case)	you (See Lesson 7.)

Adverbs

ἀσφαλῶς	safely
πρῶτον	first
τάχα	quickly, swiftly

Prepositions

ἀπό + genitive	away from, from
εἰς + accusative	into, against
ἐκ, ἐξ + genitive	out of, from
μετά + accusative	after
μετά + genitive of animate noun	with
μετά + genitive of inanimate noun	in, with, through, etc.
ὑπό + accusative	(motion towards and) under
ὑπό + dative	under, beneath, at the foot of
ὑπό + genitive of animate noun	by
ὑπό + genitive of inanimate noun	from under

Lesson 7

Number of Nouns and Verbs

Person of Pronouns and Verbs

Semantics: More on Connection

All nouns and verbs in previous lessons have been singular. This lesson introduces the plural of nouns, articles, adjectives and verbs.

Basic Sentences

7.1 νύκτες μὲν ἀναπαύουσιν, ἡμέραι δὲ ἔργα ποιοῦσιν.

Nights relieve, but days bring toils.

7.2 οἱ λύκοι τὰς τρίχας, οὐ τὴν γνώμην ἀλλάττουσιν.

Wolves change their hides, not their nature.

7.3 ἀεὶ γὰρ καλῶς βάλλει τοὺς κύβους Ζεύς.

For Zeus always throws the dice successfully.

7.4 τὰ ῥόδα ἀκμάζει βαιὸν χρόνον.

The roses bloom a short time only.

7.5 ψευδεῖς διαβολαὶ τόν βίον λυμαίνονται.

False slanders destroy life.

7.6 ἀνήρ τις δύο ἔσχεν ἑταίρας, τὴν μὲν γραῦν, τὴν δὲ νέαν.[1]

A man had two girlfriends, the one an old woman, the other a young girl.

7.7 τὰ περὶ δρόμους[2] **ἀνδράσι τε καὶ γυναιξὶ ταῦτά ἐστιν.**[3]

These are the rules concerning races for men and women. Plato

7.8 οἱ μὲν φεύγουσι, οἱ δὲ μένουσιν.

Some are fleeing, others are staying.

---

[1] ἔσχεν is a past of ἔχω.
[2] In S7.7 the article τά together with the prepositional phrase περὶ δρόμους also functions as a noun phrase. See the articular adverb in Lesson 4.
[3] For kernel type see Lesson 10.

LESSON 7

Number

So far this book has described the inflectional morphemes of nouns, including articles, pronouns and adjectives, in terms of syntactic functions as subjects, direct objects or modifiers in the sentence.

These functions are signaled by case. However, the inflectional morphemes of nouns do not only express case, but also **number**. English distinguishes between two numbers: **singular** and **plural**. Singular indicates the number one and Plural any other number. Greek has a third number, the **dual**, which indicates the number two, but it is infrequent and will not occur in this book.

Morphology of Plural Nouns, Articles and Adjectives

The following inflectional final morphemes (among others) may indicate plural number.

	First &Second declension		*Third declension*	
	Masculine/Feminine	*Neuter*	*Masculine/Feminine*	*Neuter*
Nominative	-ι	- α	-ες	- α
Genitive	-ων	-ων	- ων	- ων
Dative	-ις	-ις	-σι	-σι
Accusative	-νς 〉 -ας, ους	- α	-νς 〉 -ας	- α

The charts below show the forms of the article + adjective + noun.

	Singular			*Plural*		
Nominative	ὁ	ψευδὴς	λόγος	**οἱ**	ψευδ**εῖς**[1]	λόγο**ι**
Genitive	τοῦ	ψευδοῦς	λόγου	**τῶν**	ψευδ**ῶν**	λόγ**ων**
Dative	τῷ	ψευδεῖ	λόγῳ	**τοῖς**	ψευδέ**σι**	λόγο**ις**
Accusative	τὸν	ψευδῆ	λόγον	**τοὺς**	ψευδ**εῖς**[2]	λόγο**υς**

	Singular			*Plural*		
Nominative	ἡ	καλὴ	νύξ	**αἱ**	καλαί	νύκτ**ες**
Genitive	τῆς	καλῆς	νυκτός	**τῶν**	καλ**ῶν**	νυκτ**ῶν**
Dative	τῇ	καλῇ	νυκτί	**ταῖς**	καλ**αῖς**	νυ**ξί**†
Accusative	τὴν	καλὴν	νύκτα	**τὰς**	καλ**άς**	νύκτ**ας**

---

[1] Observe the predictable sound changes, as stems combine with inflectional morphemes (See Pre-View)
νυξί 〈 νυκτσι: the dental τ is dropped before σ, the palatal κ combines with σ into ξ
κέρδη 〈 κερδεσα: intervocalic σ is dropped, ε plus α contract into η
ψευδεῖς 〈 ψευδεσες: intervocalic σ is dropped, ε plus ε contract into ει

[2] This accusative looks like the nominative, probably because of a very strong tendency in languages to eliminate redundant distinctions. This is called paradigmatic analogy or leveling out.

Lesson 7

	Singular			*Plural*		
Nominative	τὸ	κακὸν	κέρδος	τὰ	κακὰ	κέρδη†
Genitive	τοῦ	κακοῦ	κέρδους	τῶν	κακῶν	κερδῶν
Dative	τῷ	κακῷ	κέρδει	τοῖς	κακοῖς	κέρδεσι
Accusative	τὸ	κακὸν	κέρδος	τὰ	κακὰ	κέρδη

♦Exercise 1

On the model of these charts, generate the full paradigm of the noun-adjective pair, τὸ ῥόδον + ψευδής, ψευδές.

♦Exercise 2

Copy all Basic Sentences from S8.1–11.5 and underline articles, adjectives and nouns that could be plural forms based on the above paradigms.

♦Exercise 3

Identify each of the words you underlined by case. If ambiguous, give both possibilities.

Morphology of Plural Verbs

Verbs too indicate the difference between one and more than one by different inflectional morphemes. The full paradigms will be presented in Lessons 13 and 14.

The following morphemes indicate plural:

Active	*Passive*
-μεν	-μεθα
-τε	-σθε
-σι(ν)	-νται
-ν/σαν	-ντο

Syntax: Agreement in Number

Verbs and subjects agree in number. The one exception to this pattern is that neuter plural subjects pattern with singular verbs, as in S7.4 τὰ ῥόδα ἀκμάζει βαιὸν χρόνον.

♦Exercise 4

Using the list of Basic Sentences in the Reference section, copy all words that could be plural verbs together with their subjects from S15.9, S18.4, S18.5 and S18.6. The subject may or may not be expressed.

Lesson 7

Person

While number and case are characteristic for nouns, number, case and **person** are characteristic for **pronouns**.

It is customary to speak of three 'persons': the first person for the speaker(s), the second person for the addressee(s), the third person for everything else.

Currently used English pronoun forms referring to the speaker (first person) are:

singular	*plural*
I	we
me	us

There is only one currently used pronoun referring to the addressee (second person):

you

Currently used pronoun forms referring to the person or thing spoken of (third person) are:

singular	*plural*
he, she, it	they
his, her, its	their
him, her, it	them

Morphologically speaking, there is a great deal of ambiguity, which is usually resolved in context.

Morphology of the Greek Personal Pronouns

Greek personal pronouns have complete case paradigms.

	First Person		*Second Person*	
	singular	*plural*	*singular*	*plural*
Nominative	ἐγώ	ἡμεῖς	σύ	ὑμεῖς
Genitive	ἐμοῦ / μου	ἡμῶν	σοῦ / σου	ὑμῶν
Dative	ἐμοί / μοι	ἡμῖν	σοί / σοι	ὑμῖν
Accusative	ἐμέ / με	ἡμᾶς	σέ / σε	ὑμᾶς

It may be argued that in Attic Greek there is no personal pronoun corresponding to the English pronoun of the third person. Instead of the third person pronoun, Greek uses demonstrative pronouns which will be introduced in Lesson 10. Note that the genitive, dative and accusative of ἐγώ and σύ have alternative enclitic forms with the same meaning.

Lesson 7

Syntax: Agreement of Verbs in Person

Verb forms that agree with their subject in person are called **finite**. Not all verb forms show this agreement, as will become clear in future lessons. Finite Greek verbs show agreement with their subjects by their personal endings. These endings are obligatory. The presence of subject pronouns in Greek is not obligatory but is a matter of a particular text and gives additional meaning, as does emphasis in English. Compare: "we speak" to "*we* speak."

English verbs only express agreement with their subjects in the third person singular: in the sentence "she runs," the presence of /s/, the third person singular morpheme, shows agreement between the verb "runs" and the subject "she." The presence of subject pronouns in English is obligatory.

♦ Exercise 5

With the help of the morphology in Lessons 13 and 14 identify the person and number of the following verb forms taken from Basic Sentences. Then supply the appropriate Greek personal pronoun as the subject. Disregard voice.

17.1 θέλομεν	18.2 δείξω
17.1 δυνάμεθα	18.4 ἤκουσατε
17.5 βούλομαι	19.2 ἠρωτᾶτε
18.1 παύσω	19.4 ποιήσω

♦ Exercise 6

Beginning with S22.1 copy ten words that could be verbs in the first or second person singular or plural. Supply the appropriate personal pronoun in Greek and English. For example:

22.1 τέμω ἐγώ

Semantics: More on Connection

Greek texts use connectors more frequently than English texts. In Greek connectors indicate semantic relationships. They are a great help to comprehension, because they often make the relationship between two ideas or actions more obvious. For example, γάρ indicates **cause**, ἀλλά indicates sharp **contrast**, δέ may indicate parallelism.

♦ Exercise 7

Compose English sentences that could precede the sentences below.

S4.5 ἄνευ δὲ εὐψυχίας τέχνη πρὸς τὸν κίνδυνον οὐκ ἰσχύει.
S5.1 ἡ γὰρ παράκαιρος ἡδονὴ τίκτει βλάβην.
S5.3 ὁ γὰρ ἐν καιρῷ μόχθος εὐδαιμονίαν τίκτει.

Lesson 7

Note

The connectors μέν and δέ are frequently employed with forms of the article: ὁ μέν...ὁ δε "(the) one...the other," οἱ μέν...οἱ δε "some...others." In this special usage the article returns to its original demonstrative force (see Lesson 10): 7.6 ἀνήρ τις δύο ἔσχεν ἑταίρας, τὴν μὲν γραῦν, τὴν δὲ νέαν. "A man had two girlfriends, the one, an old woman, the other, a young girl."

Practice Sentences

1. κρίνει τοὺς φίλους ὁ καιρός.
2. οἱ μὲν ἐν τῇ ψυχῇ τὴν οὐσίαν περιφέρουσιν, οἱ δὲ οὐδέν.
3. ἀνήρ τις δύο ἔχει ἑταίρας, τὴν μὲν νέαν, τὴν δὲ γραῦν. ἡ μὲν γέροντας φιλεῖ, ἡ δὲ νεανίας.
4. οἱ ἀγαθοὶ ὑπὸ θεῶν οὐκ ἀμελοῦνται.
5. ἆρα τοὺς ἀγαθοὺς ψευδεῖς λόγοι βλάπτουσιν;
6 τί ἀλλάττεται ὑπὸ τῶν λύκων;
7. οὐκ ἀμελοῦνται ὑπὸ τοῦ θεοῦ οἱ χρηστοί. ὁ γὰρ θεὸς τὴν ἀρετὴν φιλεῖ.

Lesson Vocabulary

Nouns

γραῦς, γραός, ἡ	old woman
γυνή, γυναικός, ἡ	woman, wife
δρόμος, δρόμου, ὁ	race
ἑταίρα, ἑταίρας, ἡ	girlfriend, companion, hetaira

Verbs

ἀκούω, ἀκούσομαι, ἤκουσα	to hear
δείκνυμι, δείξω, ἔδειξα	to show
φεύγω, φεύξομαι, ἔφυγον	to flee

Adjectives

δύο	two
νέος, νέα, νέον	new, young

Pronouns

ἐγώ	I, me
σύ	you
ἡμείς	we
ὑμεῖς	you

Lesson 8

Syntax:

The Dative Case

The Special Intransitive Kernel

Semantics: Non-Kernel Uses of the Dative Case

Morphology:

Πολύς, Πολλή, Πολύ

Future Tense

Nouns in the dative case can be expected as kernel items in a new kernel type that is introduced in this lesson. Most nouns in the dative case, however, are not kernel items. These non-kernel datives can theoretically be expected in any sentence and have a variety of semantic roles.

Many prepositions pattern with a dative to form a prepositional phrase. See Lesson 6 for semantic categories.

Basic Sentences

8.1 οἱ μὲν οἰκέται τοῖς δεσπόταις, οἱ δὲ φαῦλοι ταῖς ἐπιθυμίαις δουλεύουσιν.

Servants serve their masters, weak men their passions. — Diogenes (adapted)

8.2 ἐκ τῶν πόνων γὰρ τἀγαθὰ[1] αὔξεται[2] βροτοῖς.

From their toils men's blessings will grow. — Menander

8.3 χρηστὸς πονηροῖς οὐ τιτρώσκεται λόγοις.

A good man is not wounded by wicked words. — Menander

8.4 ἀβουλίᾳ πολλοὶ βλάπτονται.

Many people are hurt because of thoughtlessness. — Anonymous

---

[1] See Pre-View on Hiatus Avoidance; τἀγαθὰ = τὰ ἀγαθά.
[2] Review Lesson 7 on Syntax: Agreement in Number.

Lesson 8

Syntax: The Dative Case

All datives have an **iota** in the singular, which may show as an iota subscript. See Lesson 4.

The Special Intransitive Kernel

A dative in the environment of certain intransitive verbs is the equivalent of the accusative object of transitive verbs. This kernel type is called a **special intransitive kernel.**

In the examples below, the dative τοῖς δεσπόταις in the first sentence is equivalent to the accusative τοὺς δεσπότας in the second.

> οἱ μὲν οἰκέται **τοῖς δεσπόταις** δουλεύουσιν (S8.1)
> "Servants serve their masters"
>
> οἱ μὲν οἰκέται **τοὺς δεσπότας** θεραπεύουσιν
> "Servants serve their masters."

It is practical, therefore, to consider this dative as a kernel item with the same function as an object in the accusative. The label direct object is traditionally reserved for the accusative with transitive verbs. Use the label **dative object** for datives in special intransitive kernels. Semantically the dative in this kernel is an animate noun, less often an abstract noun standing metaphorically for a person.

Here is a list of special intransitive verbs which regularly raise the expectation of a dative object.

ἀρέσκω	please
βοηθέω	help
δουλεύω	serve
ἔοικα	be like
πείθομαι	obey
πιστεύω	trust

Note:

So far four kernel types have been introduced:

- transitive
- intransitive
- passive
- special intransitive

LESSON 8

♦ Exercise 1

On the model of S8.1 below, enter all kernel items from S8.2 and S8.3 into a kernel chart.

Clause Connector	*Item: Function*	*Item: Function*	*Item: Function*	*Kernel Type*	*Label*
8.1	οἱ οἰκέται: Subject	τοῖς δεσπόταις: Dative Object	Ø = δουλεύουσιν: Verb	Special Intransitive	Statement
8.1	οἱ φαῦλοι: Subject	ταῖς ἐπιθυμίαις: Dative Object	δουλεύουσιν: Verb	Special Intransitive	Statement

Semantics: Non-Kernel Uses of the Dative Case

A non-kernel dative that occurs without any special signal in the environment might suggest **person interested** or **means/manner** or **instrument** or **cause. It may also suggest** one or more other semantic categories, according to the semantic features of the noun and the verb in the sentence. In S8.4 ἀβουλίᾳ seems to belong to the semantic category **cause**, but it also might suggest **means.** νόμῳ in R8.6 might be translated "by means of the law," "according to the law," or "in consequence of the law."

If the noun in the dative has the feature non-animate, it often bears the semantic information **means/manner**. In S8.3, for example, the non-animate λόγοις shows the means by which good men are not harmed. See Lesson 6 for manner expressed by a noun with a preposition.

If the noun in the dative has the feature animate, it bears the semantic information person interested. This is so with βρότοις in S8.2, which may be metaphrased: "from their toils good things grow for mortals." The dative designates the person, less often the thing, to whom the sentence refers or is of interest. The name commonly used to describe it is **dative of interest**, or **dative of reference**, or **indirect object.** Its semantic role is **recipient** or **beneficiary**.

If the noun in the dative with or without a preposition has the semantic feature **time**, it often designates the time at which an action took place. See Lesson 5.

For the purposes of the beginning student of Greek it is convenient to consider datives of the types described above as adverbial modifiers.

LESSON 8

♦Exercise 2

Enter all adverbial modifiers from S8.2 and S8.3 into a modifier chart.

Syntactic Information					*Semantic Information*
Modifier	*Description*	*Adverbial*	*Adjectival*	*Head*	*Semantic category*

Morphology: Πολύς, Πολλή, Πολύ

The adjective πολύς, πολλή, πολύ, "much, many" is very common. Because the forms of this adjective vary from the usual adjective endings, it must be learned separately. The nominative and accusative singular masculine forms are πολύς, πολύν and the nominative singular neuter form is πολύ. For the full paradigm see Morphology.

Morphology: Future Tense

So far verb forms have been identified for person, number and voice. Verbs also signal time: an action occurs either in past, present or future time. Since Lesson 1 verbs have been listed in three forms, indicating present, future and past. The morpheme for the future is an infix sigma {-σ-}, which appears between the root and the ending.

Verb Morphology: Future Active

	Singular		*Plural*	
first person	λύσω	I will release	λύσομεν	we will release
second person	λύσεις	you will release	λύσετε	you (all) will release
third person	λύσει	he, she, it or ____ will release	λύσουσι(ν)	they or ____ will release

Verb Morphology: Future Middle

	Singular		*Plural*	
first person	λύσομαι	I will ransom	λυσόμεθα	we will ransom
second person	λύσει	you will ransom	λύσεσθε	you (all) will ransom
third person	λύσεται	he, she, it or____ will ransom	λύσονται	they or ____ will ransom

Lesson 8

However {-σ-} is not always overtly visible. When the root of the verb ends in a stop, the {-σ-} regularly combines with this final consonant in the following predictable pattern.

		manner		
place	*unvoiced*	*voiced*	*+h (aspirate)*	*nasal*
labial	π	β	φ	μ
dental	τ	δ	θ	ν
palatal	κ	γ	χ	γ=ng

Rule 1

σ combines with labials to be spelled ψ (English ps).
σ causes dentals to be dropped (Compare the American pronunciation of facts as /facs/.)
σ combines with palatals to be spelled ξ (English x).

♦ Exercise 3

According to the rule above, generate the future for following third person singular present verb forms.

1. ἄγει
2. πλέκει
3. βρέχει
4. λείπει
5. λείβει
6. τρέφει
7. σπεύδει
8. ψεύδει
9. κλέπτει

Readings

8.1 ἄνδρες ἄβουλοι ἡδοναῖς θηρεύονται.

8.2 ἡ μωρία ἀνθρώποις ἀτυχίαν τίκτει.

8.3 λῦπαι γὰρ ἀνθρώποις ἀτυχίαν τίκτουσι.

8.4 γέρων γέροντι καλὴν γλῶττην ἔχει.

8.5 ὁ σοφὸς τῷ σοφῷ πείθεται.

8.6 νόμῳ ὁ βίος κρίνεται ὑπὸ τῶν πολιτῶν.

8.7 ἐν νυκτὶ βουλαὶ τοῖς σοφοῖς γίγνονται.

8.8 τοῖς ξίφεσι οἱ στρατιῶται μάχονται.

Lesson 8

More Readings

8.9 αἱ γυναῖκες σιγῇ τὸ πάθος φέρουσιν.

8.10 Θράσυλος δὲ τῇ τρίτῃ ἡμέρᾳ μετὰ τὴν εἰσβολὴν εἰς Ἔφεσον ἀποπλεῖ.

♦Exercise 4

Copy each dative from the above and identify it as part of a prepositional phrase, kernel item, means/manner, reference/interest or time. (11)

♦Exercise 5

Write a final metaphrase for the above readings, making educated guesses about the semantic role of the non-kernel datives. For example the first reading might be metaphrased: "Thoughtless men are caught by means of pleasures," or "Thoughtless men are caught because of pleasures."

♦Exercise 6

For the verb διαφέρω write the first and second person singular and plural in the active voice. Add the appropriate personal pronoun as subject and give an English equivalent. Do the same for αἰσθάνομαι. Use the Morphology for reference if necessary.

Practice Sentences

1. ταῖς μὲν ἀρέσκουσι οἱ νεανίαι, ταῖς δὲ οἱ γέροντες.
2. τἀγαθὰ τῷ πόνῳ γίγνεται τοῖς πολίταις.
3. ταῖς ἡδοναῖς βλάπτονται οἱ πονηροί.
4. οἱ μὲν κακοὶ τοῖς κακοῖς, οἱ δὲ σοφοὶ τοῖς σοφοῖς πείθονται.

Lesson Vocabulary

Nouns

ἀβουλία, ἀβουλίας, ἡ	bad advice, thoughtlessness
ἄνθρωπος, ἀνθρώπου, ὁ	man, mankind
βουλή, βουλῆς, ἡ	thought, counsel, idea
βροτοί, βροτῶν, οἱ	mortals
γέρων, γέροντος, ὁ	old man
γλῶττα, γλώττης, ἡ	tongue, speech
δεσπότης, δεσπότου, ὁ	master
εἰσβολή, εἰσβολῆς, ἡ	attack, invasion

LESSON 8

ἐπιθυμία, ἐπιθυμίας, ἡ	desire
Ἔφεσος, Ἐφέσου, ὁ	Ephesus
Θράσυλος, Θρασύλου, ὁ	Thrasylus
μωρία, μωρίας, ἡ	stupidity, foolishness
ξίφος, ξίφους, τό	sword
οἰκέτης, οἰκέτου, ὁ	servant
πάθος, πάθους, τό	suffering
σιγή, σιγῆς, ἡ	silence
στρατιώτης, στρατιώτου, ὁ	soldier

Verbs

ἀποπλέω, ἀποπλεύσω, ἀπέπλευσα	to sail away
ἀρέσκω, ἀρέσω, ἤρεσα (+ dat.)	to please
αὐξάνω/αὔξω, αὐξήσω, ηὔξησα	to increase
βοηθέω, βοηθήσω (+ dat.)	to help
γίγνομαι, γενήσομαι, ἐγενόμην	to become, happen, be, be born
δουλεύω, δουλεύσω, ἐδούλευσα (+ dat.)	to be a slave, serve
ἔοικα perfect form with present meaning (+ dat.)	to be like, resemble
μάχομαι, μαχοῦμαι, ἐμαχεσάμην	to fight
πείθομαι, πείσομαι, ἐπιθόμην (+ dat.)	to obey
πιστεύω, πιστεύσω, ἐπίστευσα (+ dat.)	to trust

Adjectives

πολύς, πολλή, πολύ	much, many
τρίτος, τρίτη, τρίτον	third
φαῦλος, φαύλη, φαῦλον	weak, mean

Review 2

♦ Exercise 1

Define each of the terms below in your own words. Give a Greek example where appropriate.

Lesson 6

contraction

deponent verb

thematic vowel

Lesson 7

agreement (verb)

demonstrative pronoun

finite (verb)

Lesson 8

dative object

non-kernel dative

recipient

special intransitive kernel

♦ Exercise 2

Translate into Greek.

6.1 Wealth is carried by the wise person in his soul.

6.2 The evil person is not wounded by an evil word, but the good one is.

7.1 Sticks and stones will break my bones but words will never hurt me.

Hint: I am wounded by stones, but not by words.

λίθος, λίθου ὁ
stone

Write the above sentence using first person plural and second person singular and plural. (We are wounded...; you are wounded...)

7. 2 Some change their opinions, others do not.

8.1 Our deeds are judged by the citizens.

8.2 Thoughtlessness produces harm for men and women.

REVIEW 2

Required Vocabulary

Lesson 6

Nouns

τρόπος, τρόπου, ὁ	character, behavior, kind
χθών, χθόνος, ἡ	earth

Verbs

ἁλίσκομαι, ἁλώσομαι, ἥλων	to be caught
ἀμελέω, ἀμελήσω, ἠμέλησα (+ gen.)	to neglect
βουλεύω, βουλεύσω, ἐβούλευσα	to plan, devise
βουλεύομαι, βουλεύσομαι, ἐβουλευσάμην	to take counsel, deliberate
ἔρχομαι, ἐλεύσομαι, ἦλθον	to come, go
τιμάω, τιμήσω, ἐτίμησα	to honor
φαίνω, φανῶ, ἔφηνα	to show, cause to appear
φθονέω, φθονήσω, ἐφθόνησα	to envy

Adjectives

ἄβουλος, ἄβουλον	ill-advised
εἷς, μία, ἕν	one
μέσος, μέση, μέσον	middle, middle of, moderate
οὐδείς, οὐδεμία, οὐδέν	no one, nothing
πένης, πένης, πένες	poor
πλούσιος, πλουσία, πλούσιον	rich
πονηρός, πονηρά, πονηρόν	bad

Adverbs

ἀσφαλῶς	safely
πρῶτον	first

Prepositions

ἀπό + genitive	away from, from
εἰς + accusative	into, against
ἐκ, ἐξ + genitive	out of, from
μετά + accusative	after
μετά + genitive of animate noun	with
μετά + genitive of inanimate noun	in, with, through, etc.
ὑπό + accusative	(motion towards and) under
ὑπό + dative	under, beneath, at the foot of
ὑπό + genitive of animate noun	by
ὑπό + genitive of inanimate noun	from under

Review 2

Lesson 7

Nouns

γυνή, γυναικός ἡ	woman, wife

Verbs

ἀκούω, ἀκούσομαι, ἤκουσα	to hear
δείκνυμι, δείξω, ἔδειξα	to show
φεύγω, φεύξομαι, ἔφυγον	to flee

Pronouns

ἐγώ	I, me
σύ	you
ἡμεῖς	we
ὑμεῖς	you

Lesson 8

Nouns

ἀβουλία, ἀβουλίας, ἡ	bad advice, thoughtlessness
ἄνθρωπος, ἀνθρώπου, ὁ	man, mankind
βουλή, βουλῆς, ἡ	thought, counsel, idea
βροτοί, βροτῶν, οἱ	mortals
γέρων, γέροντος, ὁ	old man
γλῶττα, γλώττης, ἡ	tongue, speech
δεσπότης, δεσπότου, ὁ	master
ἐπιθυμία, ἐπιθυμίας, ἡ	desire
οἰκέτης, οἰκέτου, ὁ	servant
σιγή, σιγῆς, ἡ	silence
στρατιώτης, στρατιώτου, ὁ	soldier

Verbs

ἀρέσκω, ἀρέσω, ἤρεσα (+ dat.)	to please
αὐξάνω/αὔξω, αὐξήσω, ηὔξησα	to increase
βοηθέω, βοηθήσω (+ dat.)	to help
γίγνομαι, γενήσομαι, ἐγενόμην	to become, happen, be
δουλεύω, δουλεύσω, ἐδούλευσα (+ dat.)	to be a slave, serve
ἔοικα (+ dat.)	to be like, be similar to
μάχομαι, μαχοῦμαι, ἐμαχεσάμην	to fight
πείθομαι, πείσομαι, ἐπιθόμην (+ dat.)	to obey
πιστεύω, πιστεύσω, ἐπίστευσα (+ dat.)	to trust

REVIEW 2

Adjectives

πολύς, πολλή, πολύ	much, many
φαῦλος, φαύλη, φαῦλον	weak, mean

ANSWER KEY

Lesson 6:

1. The rich young man is envied by the poor man.
2. Life passes.
3. The truth is overcome by false slander.
4. Happiness is produced by effort at the right time.
5. Misfortune is not stored in memory by a wise man.
6. Work stops at night.
7. Is friendship ruined because of anger?

Lesson 7:

1. A crisis tests friends.
2. Some people carry their fortune in their soul, but others carry nothing.
3. A certain man has two girlfriends, one young, and the other old. The young one loves old men, and the old one loves young men.
4. Good men are not neglected by the gods.
5. Do false rumors harm good people?
6. What is being changed by the wolves?
7. Good people are not neglected by god. For god loves virtue.

Lesson 8:

1. Young men are pleasing to some women, and old men are pleasing to others.
2. Good things come to the citizens because of their labor.
3. Bad people are harmed by pleasures.
4. Evil people obey evil people, but wise people obey the wise.

Lesson 9

Syntax:

The Genitive Case

More on The Special Intransitive Kernel

The Power of the Article: The Articular Genitive

More on Adjectival Modification

More on Adjectives: Πᾶς, Πᾶσα, Πᾶν

Morphology: Past Tense

It should be clear by now that the same case has different roles according to syntactic or semantic variables. This is true also of the genitive case that is introduced in this lesson.

Just like the dative, the genitive may be a kernel part, because there are special intransitive verbs that pattern with an object in the genitive. Most genitives are not kernel parts but are adjectival modifiers.

Basic Sentences

9.1 πάντες γὰρ τῶν ἀγαθῶν ἐπιθυμοῦσιν.

For all people desire what is good. Plato (adapted)

9.2 ψυχῆς πόνοι γὰρ ὑπὸ λόγου κουφίζονται.

For the troubles of the soul are eased by talk.

9.3 ὁ ἀγαθὸς πολίτης καὶ τοῦ σώματος καὶ τῆς οὐσίας προνοεῖται· ὁ τοιοῦτος καὶ[1] τὰ τῆς πόλεως βούλεται ὀρθοῦσθαι.[2]

The good citizens takes care both of his body and his property. Such a man also wants the affairs of the city to be put straight. Thucydides (adapted)

9.4 ὁ χρόνος λύπης ἰατρός.

Time (is) a healer of grief. Menander (adapted)

---

[1] καὶ here means "even." See note on S11.3.

[2] ὀρθοῦσθαι is an infinitive. see Lesson 17.

Lesson 9

Syntax: The Genitive Case

Nouns are listed in the dictionary in the nominative and in the genitive singular, so that one can recognize the base of a noun by taking off the inflectional morpheme for the genitive singular.

All genitives end in **-ων** in the plural.

More on The Special Intransitive Kernel

Just as there are some intransitive verbs that pattern with a dative object as a kernel part, so there are verbs with which one should expect a genitive. In S9.1 ἐπιθυμοῦσιν is such a verb, here in a kernel with τῶν ἀγαθῶν. Use the label **genitive object** for genitives in special intransitive kernels.

Here is a partial list of special intransitive verbs which regularly raise the expectation of an object in the genitive case.

αἰσθάνομαι	perceive
ἀπέχω	be distant
ἅπτομαι	grab on
ἄρχομαι	begin
ἄρχω	rule
βασιλεύω	rule
δέομαι	lack, need
διαφέρω	be different from
ἐπιθυμέω	desire
ἐπιλανθάνομαι	forget
μεταλαμβάνω	share

You will learn more of these verbs later. Many have the semantic notion of "being without or away from."

The Power of the Article: The Articular Genitive

Syntax

In contrast to English, the article together with a genitive may function as a noun phrase. In S9.3 the genitive τῆς πόλεως is preceded by the article τά where, as often, the neuter article means "the affair/condition/power/possession of ____." A feminine or masculine article mostly indicates the child-parent relationship, with the noun in the genitive referring to the parent or the relationship of dependent person to superior. The particular relationship depends on the context.

♦ Exercise 1

Find a suitable English noun to precede the articular genitive. For example, ἡ τοῦ πολίτου the daughter of the citizen; ὁ τοῦ πολίτου the slave of the citizen.

1. τὸ τῶν τυράννων	the ____	of the tyrants
2. τὰ φίλων	the ____	of friends
3. τὰ τῆς πόλεως	the ____	of the city
4. ὁ 'Ολόρου	the ____	of Oloros
5. ἡ Οἰδίπου	the ____	of Oedipus
6. οἱ 'Αλεξάνδρου	the ____	of Alexander

More on Adjectival Modification

Syntax

The most common role of the genitive is to modify another noun. The syntactic information conveyed by this genitive is adjectival modifier. The usual position for this genitive is the attributive position: ἡ τῶν πατέρων τιμή "the honor of the fathers." In the absence of an article, there may be syntactic ambiguity as to which of two nounheads is the nounhead for the genitive. S9.4 χρόνος λύπης ἰατρός, means "time is a healer of grief," but it could mean "A doctor is a time of grief." The reader should assume the genitive modifies the nearest noun with which it makes a sense: "time is the physician for grief," not "the physician is time for grief!" In the spoken language, there would be a pause after χρόνος, not after λύπης.

Semantics

There is a variety of possible semantic relationships between nounhead and noun in the genitive. For example, in the phrase "the portrait of Adam," Adam may be the owner of the painting, the painter or the person painted. Traditionally, the following labels have been used to describe the semantic relationships between the genitive and its nounhead.

Possessive: "the portrait of Adam" = Adam owns the portrait.

Subjective/Agent: "the portrait of Adam" = Adam painted the portrait.

Objective/Patient: "the portrait of Adam" = someone painted Adam's portrait.

Partitive: "some of the portraits" = some part of the whole number of paintings.

LESSON 9

♦ Exercise 2

Enter all modifiers from S9.2 into a modifier chart.

Metaphrasing

In metaphrasing the genitive, the noun in the genitive case can be placed either before or after its nounhead. The genitive may appear before its nounhead as a noun with an apostrophe: "time is grief's physician." More commonly the genitive is placed after its nounhead and is preceded by the English preposition "of" as in "time is the physician of grief."

♦ Exercise 3

Which of the following prepositional phrases can be expressed with an English -'s form?

1. lots of candy
2. love of truth
3. truth of love
4. property of the people
5. people of property
6. writer of a story
7. story of a writer
8. the oldest of the sisters

More on Adjectives: Πᾶς, Πᾶσα, Πᾶν

Morphology

The adjective πᾶς, πᾶσα, πᾶν is very common. Learn the full paradigm:

Singular		*Masculine*	*Feminine*	*Neuter*
	Nominative	πᾶς	πᾶσα	πᾶν
	Genitive	παντός	πάσης	παντός
	Dative	παντί	πάσῃ	παντί
	Accusative	πάντα	πᾶσαν	πᾶν

Plural		*Masculine*	*Feminine*	*Neuter*
	Nominative	πάντες	πᾶσαι	πάντα
	Genitve	πάντων	πασῶν	πάντων
	Dative	πᾶσι	πάσαις	πᾶσι
	Accusative	πάντας	πάσας	πάντα

Lesson 9

Syntax

The adjective πᾶς, πᾶσα, πᾶν occurs in the attributive and appositional positions where it means "entire": μυριοπλάσια πάντα ἔχει **ἡ πᾶσα πόλις.** "Our entire city provides all things in a great variety.". Outside the attributive or appositional position πᾶς, πᾶσα, πᾶν means "every, all": **πᾶσα ἡ πόλις** ἑνὶ ἑκάστῳ βοηθεῖ τῶν ἰδιωτῶν. "Every city helps each of its private citizens."

Morphology: Past Tense

The morpheme for the past aorist consists of the prefix {ε-} and the infix {-σ-}. The same consonant changes occur in the past aorist as in the future.

Past Aorist Active

	Singular		*Plural*	
first person	ἔλυσα	I released	ἐλύσαμεν	we released
second person	ἔλυσας	you released	ἐλύσατε	you (all) released
third person	ἔλυσε	he, she, it or ____ released	ἔλυσαν	they or ____ released

Past Aorist Middle

	Singular		*Plural*	
first person	ἐλυσάμην	I ransomed	ἐλυσάμεθα	we ransomed
second person	ἐλύσω	you ransomed	ἐλύσασθε	you (all) ransomed
third person	ἐλύσατο	he, she, it or ____ ransomed	ἐλύσαντο	they or ____ ransomed

♦Exercise 4

Using the rules of consonant change, generate the past aorist for the following third person singular present verb forms.

1. λέγει	4. σπεύδει	7. λείβει
2. πλέκει	5. ψεύδει	8. βλάπτει
3. βρέχει	6. πέμπει	9. κλέπτει

Lesson 9

Readings

9.1. δοῦλοι γὰρ τὰ δεσπότων ἐπίστανται καλὰ καὶ αἰσχρά. Lucian

9.2. πόνος πόνον πόνῳ φέρει. Sophocles

9.3. τίς ἐστι οἰκίας δοῦλος; ὁ δεσπότης. Menander

9.4. ὁ ἄνευ καιροῦ λόγος ἀτυχίαν τίκτει.

9.5. τὸ ἀνθρώπινον γένος μεταλαμβάνει τῆς ἀθανασίας. Plato

9.6. ὁ Κῦρος ὧδε ἄρχεται τοῦ λόγου. Xenophon

9.7. πολλοὶ δὲ ἡδονῇ τοῦ νόστου ἐπιλανθάνονται.

9.8. οἱ δὲ τοῦ Κύρου στρατιῶται τοῖς Πέρσαις οὐ πιστεύουσιν. Lucian

9.9. ὦτα καὶ ὀφθαλμοὶ πολλοὶ βασιλέως. Herodotus

♦ Exercise 5

Enter all kernel items from R9.2, R9.4, R9.6 and R9.8 into a kernel chart.

♦ Exercise 6

Enter all modifiers from R9.1, R9.3, R9.4, R9.5 and R9.7 into a modifier chart.

♦ Exercise7

Translate the Readings.

♦ Exercise 8

Compose three new sentences by changing the noun subjects of three Basic Sentences or Readings to personal pronouns. Translate.

Lesson 9

Practice Sentences

1. ταῖς μὲν ἡμῶν ἀρέσκουσιν οἱ νεανίαι, ταῖς δὲ οἱ γέροντες.
2. τῷ τῶν πολιτῶν πόνῳ τὰ τῆς πόλεως ἰσχύει.
3. οἱ μὲν τοῦ κέρδους ἐπιθυμοῦσιν, οἱ δὲ τῆς εὐδαιμονίας.
4. καὶ ὁ Κῦρος καὶ ὁ Ἀλέξανδρος τοὺς στρατιώτας ἐκ τῆς Ἑλλάδος εἰς τὴν Ἀσίαν ἄξουσιν.
5. πολλοὶ ἄνθρωποι τῷ αἰσχρῷ κέρδει ἁλίσκονται.

Lesson Vocabulary

Nouns

ἀθανασία, ἀθανασίας, ἡ	immortality
Ἀλέξανδρος, Ἀλεξάνδρου, ὁ	Alexander
Ἀσία, Ἀσίας, ἡ	Asia
βασιλεύς, βασιλέως, ὁ	king
δοῦλος, δούλου, ὁ	slave
Ἑλλάς, Ἑλλάδος, ἡ	Greece
ἰατρός, ἰατροῦ, ὁ	healer, doctor, physician
ἰδιώτης, ἰδιώτου, ὁ	private citizen
Κῦρος, Κύρου, ὁ	Cyrus
νόστος, νόστου, ὁ	return
οἰκία, οἰκίας, ἡ	house
οὖς, ὠτός, τό	ear
ὀφθαλμός, ὀφθαλμοῦ, ὁ	eye
Πέρσαι, Περσῶν, οἱ	Persians
τύραννος, τυράννου, ὁ	tyrant, ruler

Verbs

ἅπτομαι, ἅψομαι, ἡψάμην (+ gen.)	to grab on, fasten onto
ἄρχομαι, ἄρξομαι ἠρξάμην (+ gen.)	to begin
ἄρχω, ἄρξω, ἦρξα (+ gen.)	to rule
βασιλεύω, βασιλεύσω, ἐβασίλευσα (+ gen.)	to rule, be king
βούλομαι, βουλήσομαι, ἐβουλήθην (+ inf.)	to want to
δέομαι, δεήσομαι (+ gen.)	to lack, need, want
διαφέρω, διοίσω, διένηγκον (+ gen.)	be different from
ἐπιθυμέω, ἐπιθυμήσω, ἐπεθύμησα (+ gen.)	to desire

LESSON 9

ἐπιλανθάνομαι, ἐπιλήσομαι, ἐπελαθόμην (+ gen.)	to forget
ἐπίσταμαι, ἐπιστήσομαι, ἠπιστήθην	to know something
ἐστί (3rd singular of εἰμί)	____ is
κουφίζω, κουφιῶ, ἐκούφισα	to make easy
μεταλαμβάνω, μεταλήψομαι, μετέλαβον (+ gen.)	to share
ὀρθόω, ὀρθώσω, ὤρθωσα	to put straight
προνοέομαι, προνοήσομαι, προυνοησάμην (+ gen.)	to take care of, take thought for

Adjectives

αἰσχρός, αἰσχρά, αἰσχρόν	shameful
ἀνθρώπινος, ἀνθρωπίνη, ἀνθρώπινον	human
ἕκαστος, ἑκάστη, ἕκαστον	each
μυθοπλάσιος, μυθοπλάσιον	multiform
πᾶς, πᾶσα, πᾶν	every, all, entire
τοιοῦτος, τοιαύτη, τοιοῦτο	such

Adverbs

ὧδε	thus, in the following manner

Connectors

καί...καί	both...and

Lesson 10

The Linking Kernel and the Verb εἰμί

Predicative Position

The Factitive Kernel

Part of Speech:

Demonstrative Pronouns

αὐτός, αὐτή, αὐτό

The number and nature of kernel types vary according to the theories of the person offering the description of a given language. The description in this book has been adopted with the practical needs of the reader in mind. It teaches the reader to expect one of six kernel types, four of which have been studied so far. They are:

transitive :	subject + active/middle verb + direct object
intransitive:	subject + active/middle verb
passive:	subject + passive verb
special intransitive:	subject + active/middle verb + dative/genitive object

This lesson introduces the **linking** and the **factitive** kernels. Because an understanding of **predicative** position will help the reader master all the elements of the lesson, predicative position is introduced early in the lesson.

Basic Sentences

10.1 τό τε γὰρ ἀγαθὸν ἁπλοῦν, τὸ δὲ κακὸν πολύμορφον.

For good is single, evil has many shapes. — Aristotle

10.2 λύπης ἰατρός ἐστιν ὁ χρηστὸς φίλος.

The good friend is a healer for grief. — Menander

10.3 ἰδίας νόμιζε[1] τῶν φίλων τὰς συμφοράς.

Consider the misfortunes of your friends your own! — Menander

---

[1] νόμιζε is the command form of νομίζει: "Consider!" See Lesson 21 on commands.

LESSON 10

10.4 ὁ δὲ πλοῦτος ἡμᾶς πάντας τυφλοὺς ποιεῖ.

And wealth makes us all blind. — Antiphanes (adapted)

10.5 φασὶν κακίστους οἱ πονηροὶ τοὺς κακούς.

Evil people call bad people outrageously bad. — Anonymous

The Linking Kernel

Morphology: εἰμί

In Greek, as in many languages, the verb "to be," εἰμί, is irregular and must be learned carefully. The present progressive personal endings of this irregular verb differ from the personal endings of -ω verbs like κρίνω. Other -μι verbs will be presented in Lesson 14. Here are the progressive forms of εἰμί.

		past	**present**
Singular			
	first person	ἦν, ἦ	εἰμί
	second person	ἦσθα	εἶ
	third person	ἦν	ἐστί
Plural			
	first person	ἦμεν	ἐσμέν
	second person	ἦτε, ἦστε	ἐστέ
	third person	ἦσαν	εἰσί

Syntax

Most kernels have a subject, a verb and either an accusative direct object in a transitive kernel, or a genitive or dative object in a special intransitive kernel. In a linking kernel, the third kernel item is in the nominative case and is called a **subject complement** because it refers to the subject. Therefore, a linking kernel has items with these functions: subject + linking verb + subject complement (nominative).

The list of verbs that occur in a linking kernel is short. The most frequently occurring are:

καλεῖται	is named, is called
ἐστίν	is
γίγνεται	is, becomes
φύεται	is, grows to be
ποιεῖται	is made, becomes
νομίζεται	is considered
φαίνεται	seems

Lesson 10

Note: Some of these linking verbs have different meanings in the active voice. Three of the verbs, καλεῖται, νομίζεται and ποιεῖται are passive in form and meaning. γίγνεται is a deponent verb, passive in form and active in meaning.

In a linking kernel the subject may or may not appear with an article; the subject complement mostly appears without an article. In S10.2 the presence of the article before φίλος marks ὁ φίλος as the subject, while ἰατρός is the subject complement. The subject complement in a linking kernel may be either a noun or an adjective. For example, in S10.1 ἁπλοῦν, an adjective without an article, is the subject complement.

Predicative Position

The meaning of a phrase or a kernel is sometimes dependent on word order. The adjective, πᾶς, πᾶσα, πᾶν, in Lesson 9, was metaphrased "every" or "entire" depending on its position.

μυριοπλάσια πάντα ἔχει **ἡ πᾶσα πόλις.**
"The entire city provides all things in a great variety."

πᾶσα ἡ πόλις ἑνὶ ἑκάστῳ βοηθεῖ τῶν ἰδιωτῶν.
"Every city helps each of its private citizens."

πᾶσα in the phrase **πᾶσα ἡ πόλις** is in the **Predicative position**. A word in the predicative position is not preceded by an article and must be carefully distinguished from the attributive (ὁ σοφός ἀδελφὸς) or appositional (ὁ ἀδελφὸς ὁ σοφός) positions.

Recognizing a word in the predicative position helps the reader to fulfill his or her expectations of completeness in a linking kernel when the linking verb is gapped. Although sentences of this type, without verbs, are very rare in English, they occur frequently in Latin, Hebrew, Arabic and Greek. For example, S9.4 ὁ χρόνος λύπης ἰατρός lacks the verb, ἐστί, but recognizing that ἰατρός is in the predicative position allows the reader to understand that it is a complete sentence: "Time is a healer of grief." See also R10.1.

♦Exercise 1

Review the Adjective as Adjectival Modifier, Lesson 5. Label the following constructions as examples of attributive, appositional or predicative position.

1. ὁ ἀδελφὸς σοφός
2. ὁ σοφὸς ἀδελφός
3. ὁ ἀδελφὸς ὁ σοφὸς
4. σοφὸς ὁ ἀδελφός
5. ὁ ἐν καιρῷ μόχθος
6. ὁ μόχθος ὁ ἐν καιρῷ

♦ Exercise 2

From Exercise 1 copy the two constructions that are complete kernels.

♦ Exercise 3

In S10.2 replace the linking verb ἐστιν by three other linking verbs, keeping ὁ χρηστὸς φίλος as subject and ἰατρός as subject complement.

Metaphrasing

In order to indicate that a linking verb is expected, it is convenient to show an equal sign (=) in the verb slot. The verb "to be" can occur in two kernel types: the enclitic ἐστί occurs in a linking kernel, "_____ is _____;" ἔστι with the accent on the first syllable occurs in an intransitive kernel, "______ is/exists" or "there is _____."

The Factitive Kernel

Syntax

The factitive kernel uses the active forms of the same verbs as the linking kernel (except ἐστίν, γίγνεται and φύει):

καλεῖ	name, call
ποιεῖ	makes
νομίζει	considers
φαίνει	shows.

Factitive verbs pattern with two accusatives that are in the semantic relationship of X is Y or X becomes Y, as in the following English examples.

They made a teacher treasurer. (the teacher "is/becomes" treasurer.)
They consider the water pure. (the water "is/seems" pure.)
They call the agreement a fraud. (the agreement "is/is called" a fraud.)

A factitive kernel has items with these functions:

subject + verb + direct object + **object complement**.

In a factitive kernel the presence of the article with one accusative can help to distinguish the direct object from the object complement. S10.3 has two items in the accusative, ἰδίας and συμφοράς. It also has a factitive verb, νόμιζε. ἰδίας has no article, while συμφοράς has the article τάς. Therefore ἰδίας must be the object complement in the factitive kernel, and συμφοράς the direct object: "consider the misfortunes... your own." In R10.7 υἱόν has the article τόν. Therefore ἱππέα is the object complement. What is the object complement in S10.5?

Lesson 10

Metaphrasing

It is useful to metaphrase the two accusatives in a factitive kernel as "_______ (to be/become) _______." For example, ἰδίας τὰς συμφοράς can be metaphrased "_____ _____s misfortunes (to be) your own."

Kernel Information

S10.2 λύπης ἰατρός ἐστιν ὁ χρηστὸς φίλος.

Item:Function	*Item:Function*	*Item:Function*	*Kernel Type*	*Label*
ἰατρός: Subject Complement	ἐστιν: Verb	ὁ φίλος: Subject	Linking	Statement

S10.4 ὁ δὲ πλοῦτος ἡμᾶς πάντας τυφλοὺς ποιεῖ.

Cl.Marker	*Item:function*	*Item:function*	*Item:function*	*Kernel Type*	*Label*
δὲ	ὁ πλοῦτος: Subject	ἡμᾶς: Direct Object τυφλοὺς: Object Complement	ποιεῖ: Verb	Factitive	Statement

◆Exercise 4

Metaphrase each of the following sets of items and label the kernel type. Signal a linking verb by the word *equals* or the = sign.

	Kernel Type	*Metaphrase*
ὁ φίλος ἰατρός	linking	the friend = doctor the friend is a doctor

1. ἄνθρωπος ὁ λύκος
2. ὁ ἄνθρωπος λύκος
3. ὁ υἱὸς ἱππεύς
4. τὸν υἱὸν ἱππέα
5. πενία δ' ἄτιμος
6. πενία δ' ἄτιμον τὸν εὐγενῆ
7. ῥόδον κάλλιστον
8. ῥόδον κάλλιστον

Lesson 10

♦ Exercise 5

Identify the kernels as transitive or factitive.

1. ὁ πατὴρ τὸν παῖδα καλεῖ.
2. ὁ πατὴρ τὸν παῖδα σοφὸν καλεῖ.
3. ὁ πλοῦτος φθόνον ποιεῖ.
4. ὁ πλοῦτος ἄνθρωπον τυφλὸν ποιεῖ.
5. μωρὸς λόγον παρ' ἐχθροῦ φίλον νομίζει.

Part of Speech: Demonstrative Pronouns

In Lessons 3, 5 and 7 the interrogative, indefinite and personal pronouns of the first and second person were introduced. This lesson introduces the three demonstrative pronouns.

ὅδε, ἥδε, τόδε
οὗτος, αὕτη, τοῦτο
ἐκεῖνος, ἐκείνη, ἐκεῖνο

As adjectival modifiers ὅδε and οὗτος are the equivalent of "this _______" or "these _______" and ἐκεῖνος is the equivalent of "that______" or "those ______."

οὗτος, αὕτη, τοῦτο

		Masculine	*Feminine*	*Neuter*
Singular				
	Nominative	οὗτος	αὕτη	τοῦτο
	Genitive	τούτου	ταύτης	τούτου
	Dative	τούτῳ	ταύτῃ	τούτῳ
	Accusative	τοῦτον	ταύτην	τοῦτο
Plural				
	Nominative	οὗτοι	αὗται	ταῦτα
	Genitive	τούτων	τούτων	τούτων
	Dative	τούτοις	ταύταις	τούτοις
	Accusative	τούτους	ταύτας	ταῦτα

See Morphology for the paradigm of ὅδε, ἥδε, τόδε and ἐκεῖνος, ἐκείνη, ἐκεῖνο.

Syntax

These pronouns, like τις, may function as nounheads or as adjectival modifiers. As nounheads ὅδε, οὗτος, ἐκεῖνος are used as the third person personal pronouns "he, she, it, they." As adjectival modifiers all three stand in the **predicative position**:

ὅδε ὁ ἀδελφός	this brother
αὕτη ἡ πόλις	this city
ἐκεῖνο τό γένος	that kind

Lesson 10

◆Exercise 6

Identify the demonstratives in the isolated items as nounheads or modifiers and metaphrase. Remember that you must add "things" when metaphrasing a neuter plural: ταῦτα = these *things*, ≠ these.

	modifier	*nounhead*	*metaphrase*
1. οὗτος ὁ ἀνὴρ			
2. οὗτος			
3. τήνδε τὴν πόλιν			
4. ἐκείνους τοὺς ἄνδρας			
5. ἐκείνη ἡ γυνή			
6. τάδε			
7. ὁ ἀνὴρ οὗτος			

αὐτός

This lesson also introduces αὐτός, αὐτή, αὐτό. It is especially important not to confuse these forms with those of οὗτος, αὕτη, τοῦτο.

αὐτός, αὐτή, αὐτό

		Masculine	*Feminine*	*Neuter*
Singular				
	Nominative	αὐτός	αὐτή	αὐτό
	Genitive	αὐτοῦ	αὐτῆς	αὐτοῦ
	Dative	αὐτῷ	αὐτῇ	αὐτῷ
	Accusative	αὐτόν	αὐτήν	αὐτό
Plural				
	Nominative	αὐτοί	αὐταί	αὐτά
	Genitive	αὐτῶν	αὐτῶν	αὐτῶν
	Dative	αὐτοῖς	αὐταῖς	αὐτοῖς
	Accusative	αὐτούς	αὐτάς	αὐτά

As a nounhead αὐτός like ὅδε, οὗτος and ἐκεῖνος, functions as the personal pronoun "he, she, it, they." As an adjectival modifier αὐτός has two meanings depending on its position: *same* and *self*.

In the **attributive** or **appositional** position αὐτός means *same*:
ὁ αὐτὸς ἀνήρ or ὁ ἀνήρ ὁ αὐτὸς "the same man."

In the **predicative** position, αὐτός means *himself*:
ὁ ἀνὴρ αὐτός, αὐτὸς ὁ ἀνήρ "the man himself."

Lesson 10

♦ Exercise 7

Identify each of the following forms as personal pronoun or modifier in the attributive position or predicative position and metaphrase.

	pronoun/ modifier	attributive	predicative	metaphrase
1. τὸν βασιλέα αὐτὸν	modifier		X	______ ______s the king himself.
2. αὐτὴ				
3. αὕτη				
4. τὸ αὐτὸ βιβλίον				
5. τὸ αὐτὸ βιβλίον				
6. τὰ δράματα αὐτά				
7. αὐτὰ τὰ δράματα				

Readings

10.1. μέγα βιβλίον μέγα κακόν. — Callimachus

10.2. τὸ ἦθος ἐστὶ ἔθος πολυχρόνιον. — Plutarch

10.3. κάλλιστον ἐν κήποις φύεται ῥόδον. — Menander

10.4. πενία δ' ἄτιμον καὶ[1] τὸν εὐγενῆ ποιεῖ. — Menander

10.5. πλούσιον νόμιζε[2] τὸν σοφόν! — Plato

10.6. μὴ νόμιζε[3] λόγον παρ' ἐχθροῦ φίλον! — Menander

10.7. Θεμιστοκλῆς τὸν υἱὸν ἱππέα διδάσκεται ἀγαθόν.

10.8. ὁ γὰρ ἄνθρωπος οὐ μόνον πολιτικὸν, ἀλλὰ καὶ οἰκονομικὸν ζῷον. — Aristotle

---

[1] See note on S11.3.
[2] See Lesson 21 on commands.
[3] See Lesson 21 on negative commands.

Lesson 10

Practice Sentences

1. πολλοὺς ὁ πλοῦτος τυφλοὺς ποιεῖ. Οὗτοι οὐ μόνον τὰ τῆς οἰκίας, ἀλλὰ καὶ τὰ τῆς πόλεως διαφθείρουσιν.
2. μεγάλη ἐστιν ἡ τοῦ Θεμιστοκλέους δόξα.
3. ἀλλὰ οὐχ ὑπὸ πάντων ὁ Θεμιστοκλῆς τιμᾶται. πολλοὶ γὰρ αὐτὸν φθονοῦσιν.

Lesson Vocabulary

Nouns

ἀδελφός, ἀδελφοῦ, ὁ	brother
δρᾶμα, δράματος, τό	drama
ἔθος, ἔθους, τό	habit
ἐχθρός, ἐχθροῦ, ὁ	enemy
ζῷον, ζῴου, τό	living being
ἦθος, ἤθους, τό	character
Θεμιστοκλῆς, Θεμιστοκλοῦς, ὁ	Themistokles
θησαυρός, θησαυροῦ, ὁ	treasure
ἱππεύς, ἱππέως, ὁ	horseman
κῆπος, κήπου, τό	garden
παῖς, παιδός ὁ, ἡ	child, boy, slave
συμφορά, συμφορᾶς, ἡ	disaster, calamity

Pronouns

αὐτός, αὐτή, αὐτό	same; self; he, she, it
ἐκεῖνος, ἐκείνη, ἐκεῖνο	that, those; he, she, it
ὅδε, ἥδε, τόδε	this, these; he, she, it
οὗτος, αὕτη, τοῦτο	this, these; he, she, it

Verbs

διδάσκομαι (+ 2 accusatives)	to train somebody as
εἰμί, ἔσομαι, ἐγενόμην	to be
καλέω, καλέσω, ἐκάλεσα	to call
νομίζω, νομιῶ, ἐνόμισα	to consider, think
φαίνομαι, φανοῦμαι, ἐφηνάμην	to seem, appear
φημί, φήσω, ἔφησα	to declare, say, tell
φύομαι, φύσομαι, ἔφυν	to grow

Adjectives

ἁπλοῦς, ἁπλῆ, ἁπλοῦν	simple, single

Lesson 10

ἄτιμος, ἄτιμον	dishonored
εὐγενής, εὐγενές	well-born
ἴδιος, ἰδία, ἴδιον	one's own
κάκιστος, κακίστη, κάκιστον	very bad
κάλλιστος, καλλίστη, κάλλιστον	very beautiful
μέγας, μεγάλη, μέγα	great
μωρός, μωρά, μωρόν	stupid, foolish
οἰκονομικός, οἰκονομική, οἰκονομικόν	private
πολιτικός, πολιτική, πολιτικόν	public
πολύμορφος, πολύμορφον	many-shaped
πολυχρόνιος, πολυχρόνιον	long-lasting
τυφλός, τυφλή, τυφλόν	blind

Coordinating Conjunctions

οὐ μόνον...ἀλλὰ καὶ	not only...but also

Lesson 11

Dependent Clauses

Dependent Clauses as Adverbial Modifiers

So far, whenever there has been a sentence with more than one clause, the clauses have been connected to each other in one of three ways:

1. by a connector such as καὶ, as in R2.5 δίκη δίκην τίκτει καὶ φόνος φόνον.
2. by a comma, as in S2.2 χεὶρ χεῖρα νίπτει, δάκτυλον δὲ δάκτυλος.
3. by a gap, as in S2.5 ὁ λύκος τὴν τρίχα, οὐ τὴν γνώμην ἀλλάττει.

In sentences such as these, the clauses are **coordinate clauses**, that is, they are on the same syntactic level. This lesson introduces sentences in which the clauses are not on the same level; one is a **main clause**, the other is a **dependent clause**.

Basic Sentences

11.1 **ἐκ τῶν πόνων γὰρ τἀγαθὰ αὔξεται βροτοῖς, ἐπεὶ ὁ ἐν καιρῷ μόχθος εὐδαιμονίαν τίκτει.**

For from toil good things will come to mortals, since well-timed effort brings prosperity.

11.2 **Κλέαρχος ὧδε ἄρχεται λόγου, ὅτε οἱ στρατιῶται τοῖς Πέρσαις οὐ πιστεύουσιν.**

Clearchus begins his speech in the following manner, when his soldiers do not trust the Persians.

11.3 **ὁ πένης ἐλεεῖται, ὡς ἡ πενία ἄτιμον καὶ[1] τὸν εὐγενῆ ποιεῖ.**

The poor person is pitied, because poverty causes even the well-born to be without status.

---

[1] *Caution*
καὶ does not always connect two sames. In S11.3 it does not connect ἄτιμον and τὸν εὐγενῆ. And it does not connect S11.5 to anything previous. If it does not connect two sames, καὶ is best translated by the particle, "even, also." This is often so at the beginning of a sentence. See S9.3, R10.4, R12.2.

Lesson 11

11.4 ὁ ἀγαθὸς πολίτης τὰ τῆς πόλεως βούλεται ὀρθοῦσθαι ἕως ὁ ἄνθρωπος οἰκονομικὸν ζῷον.

The good citizen wishes the affairs of the city to be put straight, as long as man is a householding being.

11.5 καὶ εἰ κάλλιστον ἐν κήποις φύεται ῥόδον, βαιὸν ἀκμάζει χρόνον.

Even if it is most beautiful in the gardens, the rose blooms a short time only.

Dependent Clauses

Each of the above sentences has a **main clause** and one or more **dependent clauses**. An understanding of the different semantic and syntactic roles and relationships of clauses is as important for the reader as an understanding of the basic kernel. Only with this understanding, among other skills, can one learn to read the works of the great ancient authors. This lesson introduces dependent clauses that function as adverbial modifiers. These clauses are marked by **subordinating conjunctions**. In English they come first in the dependent clause. In Greek, however, they do not always come first in the clause. One or more words of the clause may precede them. In this book, because of their role in marking clauses, subordinating conjunctions will be referred to as **clause markers**.

Clause Markers

The number of clause markers is not very large. Several of the most common clause markers, ὡς, ὅτι have more than one English equivalent, and therefore set up a variety of semantic expectations for the dependent clause. Here follows a partial list of clause markers. Additional English equivalents for these as well as a few more clause markers will be introduced in later lessons.

Greek	*English Equivalent*
ὅτε	when (at a time when)
ἕως	as long as, while, until
ἐπεί	after, since (causal), when
ὅτι, διότι	because
εἰ	if
καὶ εἰ	even if, although, granted that
ὅπου	where
ὡς τάχιστα	as soon as
ὥσπερ	just as
ὡς	when, as, because

Lesson 11

Note:

When ὡς... appears in a main clause, it may mean "how...!" See Lesson 25.

♦ Exercise 1

Identify all clause markers and copy the dependent clauses in this paragraph describing the Persian attack on Greece.

Although the Persians had been badly defeated in the battle of Marathon, Darius continued to plan attacks against the Greeks. He had to postpone them, however, because the Egyptians, who at this time were his subjects, had revolted against the Persian rule. While Darius was on his way to Egypt, he died. If he had lived, he would have made another attempt to incorporate the Greeks into the Persian empire. When Darius was dead, his son, Xerxes, became king. After he had subdued the Egyptians, he decided to undertake a campaign against the mainland Greeks, as he wished to avenge the defeat at Marathon, where his father had been beaten. He built a pontoon bridge across the straits of the Dardanelles, but as soon as the bridge was ready, the cables with which the ships had been fastened together broke. Although Xerxes is said to have been so angry about this, that in his hybris he ordered the sea to be flogged, because she had defied the King of Kings, he built another bridge. Then he marched south, until he came to Thermopylae. But after he managed to overwhelm the small band of 300 Spartans who guarded the pass, he was defeated at Salamis, as his father had been at Marathon.

Dependent Clauses as Adverbial Modifiers

Syntax

The Basic Sentences and Readings in this lesson consist of a main clause and one or more dependent clauses, each with a clause marker. These dependent clauses have a kernel of their own. *The main kernel is complete without them.* They are syntactically equivalent to other adverbial modifiers such as prepositional phrases or adverbs. The dependent clause in the sentence "although it is most beautiful in the garden, the rose blooms a short time only," corresponds syntactically to a prepositional phrase such as "in spite of its beauty," or "with all its beauty."

Note:

The term **complex sentence** is often used in contrast with the term, simple sentence, for a sentence that has dependent clauses.

The position of the **adverbial clause** within the sentence is relatively free. It may come before or after the main clause or it may interrupt the main clause. Moreover, it may interrupt another dependent clause. There is, however, one restriction common to all languages: *the interrupting adverbial clause must be completed before the interrupted clause continues to its own completion.* Try this on the English paragraph above.

♦ Exercise 2

Rewrite the description of the Persian invasion of Greece so that adverbial clauses interrupt the main kernel. You might use the following sentence as a model: *Darius, although the Persians had been badly defeated in the battle of Marathon, continued to plan attacks against the Greeks.* Is there a difference in meaning between the two versions of the story?

♦ Exercise 3

Rewrite S11.2-11.5, putting the dependent clauses in a different position. S11.1 is given as an example.

S11.1 ἐπεὶ ὁ ἐν καιρῷ μόχθος εὐδαιμονίαν τίκτει, ἐκ τῶν πόνων τἀγαθὰ αὔξεται βροτοῖς.

Semantics

The semantic categories of adverbial clauses correspond to those of the other kinds of adverbial modifiers. Some of the clause markers clearly indicate one category only, others have several possible interpretations. A clause marked by ὡς can indicate **comparison**, time or cause, as it does in S11.3 ὁ πένης ἐλεεῖται, ὡς ἡ πενία ἄτιμον καὶ τὸν εὐγενῆ ποιεῖ. Traditionally such a clause is called a **causal clause**. A clause marked by ἐπεὶ or ὅτι can also indicate a causal clause, as it does in S11.1. Elsewhere clauses marked by ἐπεὶ may indicate "time after," and are traditionally called a **temporal adverbial clauses**. A clause marked by εἰ "if" is called a **conditional clause**. καὶ εἰ "even if" in S11.5 marks a **concessive clause,** ὅπου "where" a **clause of place**.

Greek	*English Equivalent*	*Semantic category*
ὅτε	when (at a time when)	time
ἕως	as long as, while, until	time
ἐπεί	after, since (causal), when	time, cause
ὅτι, διότι	because	cause
εἰ	if	condition
καὶ εἰ	even if, although, granted that	concession
ὅπου	where	place
ὡς τάχιστα	as soon as	time
ὥσπερ	just as	comparison
ὡς	when	time
ὡς	as	comparison
ὡς	because	cause

Lesson 11

♦ Exercise 4

Label the semantic categories of the clauses in Exercise 1.

Ø or the Gap

Any item, whether kernel part or modifier, may be gapped across clause boundaries. For example, καὶ εἰ κάλλιστον ἐν κήποις φύεται ῥόδον, βαιὸν ἀκμάζει χρόνον Ø=τὸ ῥόδον.

Kernel Information

Dependent clauses may be entered in the following way on a kernel chart. M/D stands for a main clause or dependent clause. The label column identifies the dependent clause as causal, temporal, conditional, etc.

Clause Marker	*Item: Function*	*Item: Function*	*Item: Function*	*KT*	*M/D*	*Label*
καὶ εἰ	κάλλιστον: Subject Complement	φύεται: Verb	ῥόδον: Subject	Linking	D	Concessive
—	ἀκμάζει: Verb	Ø = τὸ ῥόδον: Subject		Intransitive	M	Statement

♦ Exercise 5

Enter the kernel items of all dependent clauses in the Basic Sentences into a kernel chart.

♦ Exercise 6

Enter all dependent clauses from the Basic Sentences into a modifier chart. All dependent clauses in these sentences are adverbial modifiers. Include semantic information.

	Item	*ID*	*Syntactic information*	*Semantic information*	*Head*
S11.1	ἐπεὶ…τίκτει	Dependent Clause	Adverbial Modifier	Causal	αὔξεται

Metaphrasing

A clause marker stands at the beginning of a clause in English, but in Greek it may be preceded by one or more words. It will not, however, be the last word in a clause.

LESSON 11

In a structural translation the reader's expectation for a main kernel can be fulfilled by placing the main kernel first and putting adverbial clauses after the main clause. The position of the adverbial clause in the final translation depends on other considerations, such as emphasis, style, context, cohesion of discourse.

♦ Exercise 7

Form four or more complex sentences from any Basic Sentences or Readings in the previous lessons. Translate them.

Readings

The readings in this and some of the following lessons have been combined and adapted from previous sentences and readings.

11.1 νύμφη δ' ἄπροικος οὐκ ἔχει παρρησίαν, ἐπεὶ ἔρωτα παύει λιμός.

11.2 εἰ ἀνὴρ ἄβουλος ἡδονῇ θηρεύεται, ὑφ' ἡδονῆς ὁ φρόνιμος οὐχ ἁλίσκεται.

11.3 νὺξ μὲν ἀναπαύει, ἡμέρα δὲ πόνον ποιεῖ, χθὼν ὡς βίον κομίζει καὶ πάλιν κομίζεται.

11.4 ἀβουλίᾳ πολλοὶ βλάπτονται, ὡς ἀνὴρ ἄβουλος ἡδοναῖς θηρεύεται.

11.5 λῦπαι ἀνθρώποις ὅτε τίκτουσιν νόσους, λυπῶν ἰατρὸς λόγος.

11.6 ἀνδρὸς πονηροῦ καρδία οὐ μαλάσσεται, εἰ οἱ φαῦλοι ταῖς ἐπιθυμίαις δουλεύουσιν.

11.7 ἄνευ δ' εὐψυχίας ὡς πρὸς τὸν κίνδυνον οὐκ ἰσχύει τέχνη, ὁ ἄνευ καιροῦ λόγος ἀτυχίαν τίκτει.

11.8 ὡς γὰρ ἐν σώματι ὄψις, ἐν ψυχῇ νοῦς.

11.9 ὥσπερ ὁ ἰὸς σίδηρον, οὕτως ὁ φθόνος τὴν ψυχὴν κατεσθίεται. Stobaeus

Practice Sentences

1. ἐκ μὲν τοῦ ἐν καιρῷ μόχθου τὰ ἀγαθὰ τοῖς ἀνθρώποις τίκτεται, ἐκ δὲ ἀβουλίας τὰ κακά.
2. οἱ πλούσιοι οὐκ ἀεὶ εὐδαίμονες ἐπεί πρὸς τὸν πλοῦτον ὁ φθόνος ἕρπει.

Lesson 11

More Practice Sentences

3. ὁ φαῦλος τῇ ἐπιθυμίᾳ δουλεύει ὥσπερ ὁ δοῦλος τῷ δεσπότῃ.
4. Ὥς γὰρ νυκτὸς ἡ σελήνη, οὕτως ὁ ἥλιος ἡμέρας ἄρχει ἐν τῷ οὐρανῷ.
5. ἀεὶ γὰρ καλῶς βάλλει τοὺς κύβους Ζεύς, ἐπεὶ βασιλεύς ἐστιν τῶν θεῶν.

Lesson Vocabulary

Nouns

ἰός, ἰοῦ, ὁ	rust
Κλέαρχος, Κλεάρχου, ὁ	Clearchus
νοῦς, νοῦ, ὁ	mind, sense
νόσος, νόσου, ἡ	sickness, disease
ὄψις, ὄψεως, ἡ	the ability to see
σίδηρον, σιδήρου, τό	iron

Verbs

κατεσθίομαι, κατέδομαι, κατέφαγον	to devour
μαλάσσω, μαλάξω, ἐμάλαξα	to soften

Correlatives (See Lesson 16)

ὥσπερ...οὕτως	just as...thus, so

Clause Markers

εἰ	if
ἐπεί	after, since (causal), when
ἕως	as long as, while, until
καὶ εἰ	even if, although
ὅπου	where
ὅτε	when (at a time when)
ὅτι, διότι	because
ὡς	when
ὡς	as
ὡς	because
ὥσπερ	just as
ὡς τάχιστα	as soon as

Lesson 12

Morphology: Relative Pronoun

Syntax:

Relative Clauses as Adjectival Modifiers

Relative Clauses as Noun Equivalents

There are three types of dependent clauses: adverbial, adjectival and nominal, (nominal clauses are more commonly called **noun clauses**). Lesson 11 introduced adverbial clauses, which function as adverbial modifiers. This lesson introduces **relative clauses.** Most relative clauses function as **adjectival modifiers**; however, some relative clauses function as noun clauses. It is very important to learn how to distinguish between the two. Relative clauses are marked by **relative pronouns**.

Basic Sentences

12.1 [Δαρεῖος] Κῦρον δὲ μεταπέμπεται ἀπὸ τῆς ἀρχῆς, ἧς αὐτὸν σατράπην ἐποίησεν.[1]

And [Darius] sends for (recalls) Cyrus from the province, over which he had appointed him as satrap. Xenophon

12.2 ἔστιν δίκης ὀφθαλμός,[2] ὃς τὰ πάνθ' ὁρᾷ[3].

Justice has an eye which sees all things. Menander

12.3 μακάριος, ὅστις οὐσίαν καὶ νοῦν ἔχει.

Blessed is he who has money and good sense. Menander

12.4 ὃν οἱ θεοὶ φιλοῦσιν, ἀποθνῄσκει νέος.

Whomever the gods love dies young. Menander

12.5 ὅστις τῶν Μουσῶν ἐπιλανθάνεται, οὗτος βίον διαφθείρει.

Whoever forgets the Muses, this man destroys his own life.

---

[1] ἐποίησε from ποιέω 3rd singular past aorist active. See next lesson.
[2] Literally, "There is an eye of justice."
[3] ὁρᾷ = ὁράει

Lesson 12

Morphology: Relative Pronoun

The relative pronoun in English has the following forms: "who, whom, whose, which, that." In Greek the relative pronouns are ὅς, ἥ, ὅ, "who" and ὅστις, ἥτις, ὅ τι, "whoever," etc. They are declined as follows:

ὅς, ἥ, ὅ

Singular	*Masculine*	*Feminine*	*Neuter*
Nominative	ὅς	ἥ	ὅ
Genitive	οὗ	ἧς	οὗ
Dative	ᾧ	ᾗ	ᾧ
Accusative	ὅν	ἥν	ὅ
Plural			
Nominative	οἵ	αἵ	ἅ
Genitive	ὧν	ὧν	ὧν
Dative	οἷς	αἷς	οἷς
Accusative	οὕς	ἅς	ἅ

ὅστις, ἥτις, ὅ τι

Singular	*Masculine*	*Feminine*	*Neuter*
Nominative	ὅστις	ἥτις	ὅ τι
Genitive	οὗτινος, ὅτου	ἧστινος	οὗτινος, ὅτου
Dative	ᾧτινι, ὅτῳ	ᾗτινι	ᾧτινι, ὅτῳ
Accusative	ὅντινα	ἥντινα	ὅ τι
Plural			
Nominative	οἵτινες	αἵτινες	ἅτινα, ἅττα
Genitive	ὧντινων	ὧντινων	ὧντινων
Dative	οἷστισι(ν)	αἷστισι(ν)	οἷστισι(ν)
Accusative	οὕστινας	ἅστινας	ἅτινα, ἅττα

Note:
ὅστις is compounded of the relative ὅς and the indefinite τις, and is called the *indefinite* relative. Notice that both parts of the indefinite relative are declined.

Lesson 12

Syntax: Relative Clauses as Adjectival Modifiers

Most relative clauses are syntactic equivalents of adjectives in that they both modify nounheads. For example the two-kernel complex sentence "the engineer needs a fuse which is smaller" corresponds to the one-kernel simple sentence, "the engineer needs a smaller fuse." The relative clause "which is smaller" and the adjective "smaller" both modify the noun "fuse."

♦ Exercise 1

Rewrite the following sentences with a relative clause.

1. I love bitter chocolate.
2. Bitter chocolate is satisfactory.
3. They vote for bitter chocolate.
4. The virtues of bitter chocolate are many.

Like other adjectival modifiers, the adjectival relative clause has a nounhead. In Greek this nounhead usually stands outside the relative clause. The nounhead of the relative clause is called the **antecedent**. *The case of the relative pronoun indicates the function of the relative pronoun in its own clause.* The relative pronoun may be either a kernel item, as in sentences 1 and 2 below or a modifier, as in sentence 3.

1. ὁ ἀνὴρ, **ὃν** ᾽Ατόσσα θεραπεύει, Δαρεῖός ἐστιν.

   Darius is the man *whom* Atossa cares for.

2. ὁ ἀνὴρ, **ὃς** ὑπ᾽ ᾽Ατόσσης θεραπεύεται, Δαρεῖός ἐστιν.

   Darius is the man, *who* is cared for by Atossa.

3. ἡ γυνή, **ὑφ᾽ ἧς** θεραπεύεται Δαρεῖός, ᾽Ατόσσα ἐστιν.

   Atossa is the woman *by whom Darius is cared for.*

Relative pronouns, like all pronouns, take their gender and number from the noun that they replace. For the reader, this means that the relative pronoun in an adjectival relative clause shows the same number and gender as the antecedent. The case of the antecedent and the case of the relative pronoun need not be the same, although in both S12.1 and S12.2 this happens to be so.

Kernel Information

The relative pronoun is a kernel item of its own clause if it is the subject or direct object. Whether or not it is a kernel item, a **relative pronoun** is *always* a **clause marker**.

Lesson 12

ὁ ἀνὴρ, ὃν ᾿Ατόσσα θεραπεύει, Δαρεῖός ἐστιν.

Clause Marker	*Item: Function*	*Item: Function*	*Item: Function*	*KT*	*M/D*	*Adj Adv. Noun*	*Label*
	ἀνὴρ: Subject	Δαρεῖός: Subject Complement	ἐστιν: Verb	Linking	M		Statement
ὃν	ὃν: Direct Object	᾿Ατόσσα: Subject	θεραπεύει: Verb	Transitive	D	Adj.	Relative Clause

♦Exercise 2

Using the model provided, enter all kernel items from S12.1–2 into a kernel chart like the one above. Fill the new column by indicating whether a dependent clause is an adverbial, adjectival, or noun clause.

Metaphrasing

In contrast to adverbial clauses, the position of adjectival relative clauses within the sentence is not free, but restricted by the rules of English word order. Within the main kernel, the adjectival relative clause immediately follows its antecedent. Within the relative clause, the English relative pronoun comes first, even if it is a direct object in that clause, for example, "the woman, whom I love, loves the man, whom I detest." This is a notable exception to the regular English subject + verb + object word order.

Note:

Although the metaphrase for the sentence ὁ ἀνὴρ ὃν ᾿Ατόσσα θεραπεύει Δαρεῖός ἐστιν is "The man whom Atossa cares for is Dareios," idiomatic English prefers "The man Atossa cares for is Dareios." English can delete the relative pronoun if it is the direct object of its own clause. Greek cannot.

♦Exercise 3

Metaphrase these items in the context of a complete sentence. Treat each preceding noun or noun phrase as the antecedent of the relative pronoun.

ὁ στρατηγὸς ὃν
the general, (whom *subject* + *verb*), ______s + _______

1. ὑπὸ τοῦ στρατηγοῦ ᾧ
2. τὸν στρατηγὸν ὑφ᾿οὗ
3. πρὸς τὴν οἰκίαν ἐν ᾗ
4. τὰ τῆς πόλεως ἃ
5. τὸ ῥόδον ὃ
6. τὸ ῥόδον ὃ

LESSON 12

Syntax: Relative Clauses as Noun Equivalents

Not all relative clauses function as adjectival modifiers. Like adjectives, some of them have no definite nounhead, either expressed or understood, and thus function as the syntactic equivalents of nouns. Therefore they are called **noun relative clauses**. Semantically the absence of a nounhead in the main kernel means the absence of definiteness. For this reason these clauses are sometimes called **indefinite relative clauses**. Consider these English sentences.

Whoever helped the children will get the reward.
The girl who helped the children will get the reward.

In the first sentence, the clause "whoever helped the children" is a noun relative clause that functions as the subject of "will get the reward." On the other hand, in the second sentence, the clause "who helped the children" is not a kernel item, but an adjectival modifier of the nounhead "girl."

To the question "Who will get the reward?" the answer for sentence 1 is "whoever helped the children." The answer to the same question for sentence 2 is "the girl who helped the children." Semantically, the answer for the first sentence has the feature **indefiniteness**, and the answer for the second has the feature **definiteness**. Compare these sentences.

S12.5 ὅστις τῶν Μουσῶν ἐπιλανθάνεται, τὸν βίον διαφθείρει.
Whoever forgets the Muses destroys life.

The relative clause in this sentence functions as the subject of the governing kernel, just as the *wh-* clause does in English.

ὁ νεανίας, ὃς τῶν Μουσῶν ἐπιλανθάνεται, τὸν βίον διαφθείρει.
The young man who forgets the Muses destroys his own life.

The relative clause in this sentence is an adjectival relative clause modifying the nounhead ὁ νεανίας.

Indefinite Pronouns

Morphemes such as {soever} and {ever} on the English pronouns *whosoever* and *whatsoever* overtly indicate indefiniteness. In Greek {τις} usually indicates indefiniteness, as in the pronoun ὅστις. Sometimes a demonstrative pronoun in the governing clause also raises the expectation of an indefinite noun relative clause, as in S12.5:

ὅστις τῶν Μουσῶν ἐπιλανθάνεται, οὗτος τὸν βίον διαφθείρει.
Whoever forgets the Muses destroys life.

In some cases, however, ὅστις can appear in adjectival clauses and ὅς in noun relative clauses.

Lesson 12

Negatives

In any context of **indefiniteness** the negative is μή, not οὐ.

♦Exercise 4

Copy the noun relative clause in each English sentence. Identify the clause as subject or object of the main kernel.

1. Who steals my purse steals trash. = He who... Shakespeare's Iago
2. Many people dislike what they don't understand.
3. Whoever wins will be praised.
4. I will take my boots and whatever I need for hiking.

♦Exercise 5

From the Readings in this lesson copy the relative clauses which are kernel parts.

Kernel Information

Since the noun relative clause is the syntactic equivalent of a noun, the clause is to be treated as a single item on a kernel chart. When the governing kernel is incomplete, the noun relative clause functions as a kernel part. When the governing kernel is complete, the noun clause functions either as an adverbial modifier as the object of a preposition, or as an adjectival modifier, just as a noun can function as an adjectival modifier when it appears in the genitive case or in apposition to another noun. R12.2 is given as an example in the chart below.

Clause Marker	*Item: Function*	*Item: Function*	*Item: Function*	*KT*	*M/D*	*Adj Adv. Noun*	*Label*
	[ὃν...φιλ οῦσιν]: Subject	φιλεῖται: Verb		Passive	M		Statement
ὃν	ὃν: Direct Object	Μοῦσαι: Subject	φιλοῦσιν: Verb	Transitive	D	Noun	Indefinite Relative Clause

Readings

12.1 ὁ νεανίας ὃν αἱ μοῦσαι φιλοῦσιν καὶ ὑπ' ἀνθρώπων φιλεῖται.

12.2 ὃν αἱ Μοῦσαι φιλοῦσιν, καὶ ὑπ' ἀνθρώπων φιλεῖται.

LESSON 12

12.3 ὁ νεανίας ὅστις φοβεῖται τὸν πατέρα οὗτος πολίτης ἀγαθός ἐστιν.

12.4 ὅστις στρατηγεῖ ἄνευ τέχνης, αὐτὸς ἑκατόμβην ἐξάγει τοῖς πολεμίοις.

12.5 τὸν νεανίαν ὃς τὸν πατέρα καὶ τὴν μητέρα τιμᾷ φιλοῦσιν οἱ θεοί.

12.6 ᾧτινι οἱ θεοὶ βοηθοῦσιν νικᾷ.

♦ Exercise 6

Enter the adjectival relative clauses from the Readings into a kernel chart.

♦ Exercise 7

Enter the adjectival relative clauses only into a modifier chart.

Practice Sentences

1. Κῦρον ᾧ οἱ στρατιῶται πιστεύουσιν, μεταπέμπεται ὁ Δαρεῖος.
2. ὅντινα οἱ θεοὶ φιλοῦσιν οὐκ ἀμελεῖται ὑπὸ τῶν σοφῶν.
3. καὶ εἰ ὁ υἱὸς ἀμελεῖ τῆς μητρὸς τοῦ τε πατρός, ὀργὴν οὐκ ἔχουσι πρὸς αὐτόν.
4. ὃν αἱ μοῦσαι φιλοῦσιν καὶ τοῖς ἀνθρώποις ἀρέσκει.
5. καὶ οἱ οἰκέται, οἳ τοῖς δεσποταῖς, καὶ φαῦλοι, οἳ ταῖς ἐπιθυμίαις πείθονται, δουλεύουσιν.

Lesson Vocabulary

Nouns

ἀρχή, ἀρχῆς, ἡ	rule, province, beginning
Ἀτόσσα, Ἀτόσσης, ἡ	Atossa
Δαρεῖος, Δαρείου, ὁ	Dareus
μήτηρ, μητρός, ἡ	mother
ἑκατόμβη, ἑκατόμβης, ἡ	a public sacrifice, hecatomb
Μοῦσα, Μούσης, ἡ	Muse
πολέμιος, πολεμίου, ὁ	enemy; pl. the enemy, public enemy
σατράπης, σατράπου, ὁ	satrap
στρατήγος, στρατήγου, ὁ	general

Verbs

ἀποθνῄσκω, ἀποθανοῦμαι, ἀπέθανον	to die
ἐξάγω, ἐξάξω, ἐξήγαγον	to lead out, bring out

Lesson 12

μεταπέμπομαι, μεταπέμψομαι, μετεπεμψάμην	to send for, recall
νικάω, νικήσω, ἐνίκησα	to conquer, win
ὁράω, ὄψομαι, εἶδον	to see
στρατηγέω, στρατηγήσω, ἐστρατήγησα	to be a general, command
φιλέω, φιλήσω, ἐφίλησα	to love
φοβέομαι, φοβήσομαι, ἐφοβησάμην	to fear, revere

Adjectives

μακάριος, μακαρία, μακάριον	blessed, happy

Adverbs

μή	not

Relative Pronouns

ὅς, ἥ, ὅ	who, which
ὅστις, ἥτις, ὅ τι	whoever, whichever

Lesson 13

Aspect + Time = Tense

Morphology: Active Voice of -ω Verbs

Synopsis: A Tool for Producing Verb Forms

This lesson has no Basic Sentences or Readings. It should help in identifying and handling Greek verb forms, but it does not claim to be exhaustive.

So far all verbs in the Basic Sentences and Readings have been third person, singular or plural, active, middle or passive voice. The remarks on the morphology of the Greek verb in Lesson 1 describe {ει} as indicating that the subject of the verb is third person singular. The morpheme {s} in English is one of only three morphemes that combine with the verb stem to form one word. Most English verb forms consist of more than one word because English uses free morphemes to express grammatical categories associated with verbs. Greek uses bound morphemes, so most Greek verb forms consist of one word.

The following grammatical categories for verbs have already been introduced: **person**, **number**, **voice**. Review Lesson 6 for voice and Lesson 7 for person and number.

♦ Exercise 1

Identify the Greek verb forms by person, number and voice.

1. τρέφει
2. πιστεύουσιν
3. ποιεῖ
4. τιμῶσι

This lesson introduces two more categories: **aspect** and **time**.

Aspect

In Greek and English an action can be regarded in one of three ways:

an action can be thought of as *being in progress*: to be writing *or* ____ is writing.

an action can be regarded *merely as an occurrence* : to write *or* ____ writes *or* ____ wrote.

an action can be thought of as *completed*: to have written *or* ____ has written.

To express these three different ways of regarding an action, English places auxiliary verbs (be, have, etc.) before the stem morphemes and adds the suffixes {ing} or {ed}; active English verb forms expressing neutral aspect consist of one word.

Lesson 13

♦ Exercise 2

Identify the following English verb forms by aspect and voice.

1. ___ was teaching
2. ___ is being taught
3. ___ were learning
4. ___ are being taught
5. ___ taught
6. ___ is taught
7. ___ learns
8. ___ has been taught
9. ___ had been taught
10. ___ has taught

Greek verbs have three different forms of the stem morpheme called **aspect stems**. This is not unlike the difference between the English forms "take, took and taken."

The first of these **aspect stems** is called the **progressive** aspect stem. It appears in the first **principal part**. For the verb κρίνω the progressive aspect stem is κριν. For the verb δίδωμι it is διδω or διδο. For the verb ἵστημι it is ἱστη or ἱστα. A verb form showing the progressive stem is a sign its action is in progress.

The second aspect stem merely names the action and is called the **aorist or neutral aspect**. The term ἀ-όριστος, coined by the ancient Greek grammarians, means *undefined*. Its active form appears as the **third principal part.** For the verb κρίνω it is ἔκρινα; for δίδωμι it is ἔδωκα; for λύω it is ἔλυσα.

The third aspect views the action as completed and is called the **perfective**. It appears in the **fourth and fifth principal parts** of a Greek verb. For the verb λύω, the perfective active stem is λελυκ.

♦ Exercise 3

Identify the following verb forms by aspect, given the contrast between the progressive aspect and the aorist aspect in the pairs below.

Progressive Stem	{φευγ}	{λυο/ε}	{λαμβαν}	{πεμπο/ε}
Aorist Stem	{φυγ}	{λυσ}	{λαβ}	{πεμψ}

1. φεύγομεν
2. φύγωμεν
3. ἔφυγε
4. λύσωσιν
5. φυγών
6. λύεις
7. πέμψετε
8. πέμπεις
9. ἔλυσα
10. ἔλυον
11. λαβοῦσα
12. λαμβάνοντες
13. ἔπεμπον
14. ἔπεμψα
15. λάβοις

Lesson 13

Time

In addition to aspect, Greek verbs are also marked for **time**: an action occurs either in the past, present or future. The following explanation is intended only to lighten the reader's task in identifying verb forms. The Greek verb system is complicated by the laws of sound change, holes in the system and allomorphs.

Aspect occurs in past, present and future. Here is a simplified chart of English active verb forms, illustrating aspect and time expressed together.

		Aspect	
Time	*Progressive*	*Aorist-Neutral*	*Perfective*
past	was teaching	taught	had taught
present	is teaching	teaches	has taught
future	will be teaching	will teach	will have taught

Tense

Aspect and **Time** together are spoken of as **tense**.

♦Exercise 4

Identify the tense and voice.

1. took	4. is taking
2. was taking	5. has taken
3. takes	6. had taken

When used to identify verb forms, verbal categories are customarily presented in the order **person, number, tense (= aspect + time), voice**. This is, however, not the order in which their morphemes are "put together" in the Greek verb. Moreover, some morphemes signal more than one category, and some categories are signaled by more than one morpheme.

Greek being a synthetic language, morphemes for Greek verbs are put together in the following order:

Time: **past** time is marked by a prefix customarily called the **augment**. The augment immediately precedes the verb stem. Absence of the **augment** means present or future time. Verb stems beginning with a consonant use the prefix {ε}; those beginning with a vowel lengthen the vowel.

ο ⇒ ω,

ᾰ, α and ε ⇒ η

Lesson 13

ι ⇒ ῑ

υ ⇒ ῡ.

The ι- diphthongs subscribe the ι:

οἴομαι has the aorist ᾠήθην.

αἰτιάομαι has the aorist ᾐτιασάμην.

If the verb has another prefix, the augment appears *after* the prefix: ἀπολύω has the aorist ἀπέλυσα.

Aspect: one of the three aspect stems (progressive, aorist, or perfective).

Personal Ending: English expresses person with a noun or pronoun (I, you, he, she, it, we, they); Greek also has personal pronouns, but uses them mostly for rhetorical effect. Greek must express person in the ending of the verb itself. Note the {s} in the English verb form "he writes." Personal endings do more than mark person; they also indicate number; they contrast present/future time with past time and active voice with middle/passive voice. Thus there are four sets of personal endings. Present/future endings are called **primary** endings; Past endings are called **secondary** endings.

Thematic Vowel

Between the aspect stem and the personal endings some verb forms show a **thematic vowel**. The thematic vowel is -ε- except before the nasal consonants μ and ν where the thematic vowel is -ο-.

λυ + ε + τε = λύετε
λυ + ο + μεν = λύομεν

Morphology: Active Voice of -ν Verbs

Primary Endings + Thematic Vowel
Active

Singular:

first person	**-ω**
second person	**-εις**
third person	**-ει**

Plural:

first person	**-ομεν**
second person	**-ετε**
third person	**-ουσι**

LESSON 13

Present and Future Progressive Verb Forms

Here are the present and future active forms of λ ύω:

Singular		*Present*	*Future*
	first person	λύω	λύσω
	second person	λύεις	λύσεις
	third person	λύει	λύσει
Plural			
	first person	λύομεν	λύσομεν
	second person	λύετε	λύσετε
	third person	λύουσι	λύσουσι

Present and future progressive verb forms have **primary endings** and are **thematic**.

- Verbs like ποιέω whose stem ends in the vowels α, ε, or ο often **contract** with the thematic vowel:

  ποιῶ ← ποιέ-ω
  ποιεῖς ← ποιέ-εις
  ποιεῖ ← ποιέ-ει

  ποιοῦμεν ← ποιέ-ομεν
  ποιεῖτε ← ποιέ-ετε
  ποιοῦσι ← ποιέ-ουσι

  See Pre-view for the rules of contraction and see Morphology for other paradigms of **contract verbs**.

- Verbs whose root ends in a liquid (λ, ρ) or a nasal (μ, ν) do not have a *sigma* on the future stem. Their future forms will look like the contract forms of ποιέω. Most futures have a *sigma* **-σ-** following the aspect stem. *Sigma* combines with the preceding consonant according to regular sound changes. See Pre-view for spelling rules.

♦Exercise 5

Using regular sound changes generate the correct spellings for first person singular future progressive active of the following present progressive verb forms. See Pre-View if needed.

1. λείπω	5. πλέκω
2. γράφω	6. ἔχω
3. κλέπτω	7. σπε ύδω
4. ἄγω	8. στασιάζω

Lesson 13

Secondary Endings

Singular		
	first person	-ν, α
	second person	-ς
	third person	—
Plural		
	first person	-μεν
	second person	-τε
	third person	-ν

Past Progessive and Aorist Verb Forms

Here are the forms of the past progressive and aorist active of the four main groups of secondary verb forms:

	Past Progressive	*Second Aorist Thematic*
Singular		
first person	ἔφευγον	ἔφυγον
second person	ἔφευγες	ἔφυγες
third person	ἔφευγε	ἔφυγε
Plural		
first person	ἐφεύγομεν	ἐφύγομεν
second person	ἐφεύγετε	ἐφύγετε
third person	ἔφευγον	ἔφυγον

	Past Progressive	*Second Aorist Athematic*
Singular		
first person	ἐγίγνωσκον	ἔγνων
second person	ἐγίγνωσκες	ἔγνως
third person	ἐγίγνωσκε	ἔγνω
Plural		
first person	ἐγιγνώσκομεν	ἔγνωμεν
second person	ἐγιγνώσκετε	ἔγνωτε
third person	ἐγίγνωσκον	ἔγνωσαν

Lesson 13

	Past Progressive	*First Aorist Sigmatic*
Singular		
first person	ἔλυον	ἔλυσα
second person	ἔλυες	ἔλυσας
third person	ἔλυε	ἔλυσε
Plural		
first person	ἐλύομεν	ἐλύσαμεν
second person	ἐλύετε	ἐλύσατε
third person	ἔλυον	ἔλυσαν

	Past Progressive	*First Aorist Asigmatic*
Singular		
first person	ἔμενον	ἔμεινα
second person	ἔμενες	ἔμεινας
third person	ἔμενε	ἔμεινε
Plural		
first person	ἐμένομεν	ἐμείναμεν
second person	ἐμένετε	ἐμείνατε
third person	ἔμενον	ἔμειναν

Note: The past progressive is given the traditional label ***imperfect*** *in the Morphology.*

Past progressive and aorist verb forms have an augment (**ἔ**-φυγον) and secondary endings. Past progressive and most second aorists are **thematic**. First aorists are **athematic**: they lack the thematic vowel ο/ε.

- Secondary person endings indicate past time. The past progressive shows the thematic vowel, ο/ε before the endings. The first person singular has the -ν ending.
- There are four different forms of the past aorist stem. These first two groups are called **first aorists**.

1. The verb root + σα, e.g, ἔλυσα.
2. The verb root ending in a liquid or nasal consonant, λ, μ, ν, ρ + α. The vowel of the root lengthens, e.g., ἔμ**ει**να ← μ**έ**νω.

These second two groups are called **second aorists**.

3. The verb root plus the thematic vowel ο/ε. The vowel of the root is shortened, and the first person has the **-ν** ending, e.g. ἔφυγον ← φ**εύ**γω.
4. The verb root without the thematic vowel. The first person has the **-ν** ending, e.g., ἔγνων.

Lesson 13

♦ Exercise 6

Using the principle parts given below, identify the following verb forms by person, number, time/aspect and voice. Some verb forms are ambiguous; indicate all possibilities:

γράφω, γράψω, ἔγραψα
λέγω, λέξω, ἔλεξα
ποιέω, ποιήσω, ἐποίησα
τρίβω, τρίψω, ἔτριψα

1. λέξετε
2. ἐλέγετε
3. λέγετε
4. ποιεῖ
5. ποιήσει
6. ἐποιοῦμεν
7. ἔτριβον
8. τρίψεις
9. τρίβουσι
10. ἐγράφετε
11. ἔγραφον
12. γράψεις

Synopsis: A Tool for Producing Verb Forms

One tool for mastering Greek verb forms is a synopsis. A **synopsis** is a chart producing verb forms in a given person and number, in all times/aspects and voices, as in the following example:

second person plural active of πιστεύω:

	Progressive	*Aorist*	*Perfective*
Past	ἐπιστεύετε	ἐπιστεύσατε	ἐπεπιστεύετε
Present	πιστεύετε	________	πεπιστεύκατε
Future	πιστεύσετε	________	________

♦ Exercise 7

Write a synopsis in the progressive active for the following verbs.
λύω, λύσω 3rd pl. is given as an example.

γράφω, γράψω 2nd sing.
φιλέω, φιλήσω 1st pl.
κρίνω, κρινῶ 2nd pl.

	Progressive	*Aorist*	*Perfective*
Past	ἔλυον	________	________
Present	λύουσι	________	________
Future	λύσουσι	________	________

Lesson 13

♦Exercise 8

Using regular sound changes generate the correct spelling of the first person singular first (sigmatic) aorist active of the following present progressive verb forms.

1. τρίβω	4. λέγω
2. γράφω	5. ἐλέγχω
3. λείβω	6. σπεύδω

♦Exercise 9

Identify the following past aorists by person and number.

1. ἐλέξατε
2. ἐκρίναμεν
3. ἔφησας
4. ἔγραψε
5. ἐνόμισαν
6. ἤγγειλα

♦Exercise 10

Using the first and third principal parts given below, identify the aspect of the following verb forms as progressive or second aorist. Then metaphrase each form.

τυγχάνω,______, ἔτυχον	to happen
λείπω, ______, ἔλιπον	to leave
βαίνω, ______, ἔβην	to step, go
λανθάνω, ______, ἔλαθον	to escape notice

1. ἐτύγχανε	5. ἔβητε
2. ἔτυχες	6. ἐλείπετε
3. ἔβαινον	7. ἐλίπετε
4. ἐλάθομεν	8. ἐλάνθανε

♦Exercise 11

On the model of λύω below, write a synopsis of the regular verb πιστεύω 1st singular, including the progressive and aorist forms.

	Progressive	*Aorist*	*Perfective*
Past	ἔλυες	ἔλυσας	______
Present	λύεις	________	______
Future	λύσεις	________	______

LESSON 13

Tenses of The Perfective Aspect

The **Perfective Aspect** occurs in past, present and future. The perfect active stem must be learned as the fourth principal part. Perfect tenses are easily recognized because they often show a doubling of the initial sound called **reduplication** (e.g. **λέλυκα**). The present perfect active has endings which look like those of the aorist active except in the third person plural. The past perfect adds the augment to the reduplicated stem.

Note: The past perfective is given the traditional label ***pluperfect*** *in the Morphology.*

		Present Perfect	*Past Perfect*
Singular:			
	first person	λέλυκα	ἐλελύκη
	second person	λέλυκας	ἐλελύκης
	third person	λέλυκε	ἐλελύκει
Plural:			
	first person	λελύκαμεν	ἐλελύκεμεν
	second person	λελύκατε	ἐλελύκετε
	third person	λελύκασι	ἐλελύκεσαν

The future perfect and the past perfect are less common than the present perfect. The future perfect is not included in this book.

♦Exercise 12

On the model of λύω (2nd pl.) below, write a synopsis of the regular verb πιστεύω 3rd plural, including the progressive, aorist and perfective forms.

	Progressive	*Aorist*	*Perfective*
Past	ἐλύετε	ἐλύσατε	ἐλελύκετε
Present	λύετε	________	λελύκατε
Future	λύσετε	________	________

♦Exercise 13

Translate the following sentence.

ὁ κόσμος σκηνή, ὁ βίος πάροδος. ἦλθες, εἶδες, ἀπῆλθες.

Lesson 13

Lesson Vocabulary

Verbs

ἀγγέλλω, ἀγγελῶ, ἤγγειλα, ἤγγελκα, ἤγγελμαι, ἠγγέλθην	to report, announce
ἀμύνω, ἀμυνῶ, ἤμυνα	to defend, ward off
βαίνω, βήσομαι, ἔβην, βέβηκα	to go, walk
γράφω, γράψω, ἔγραψα, γέγραφα, γέγραμμαι, ἐγράφην	to write
δέχομαι, δέξομαι, ἐδεξάμην, δέδεγμαι, ἐδέχθην	to receive
κλέπτω, κλέψω, ἔκλεψα, κέκλοφα, κέκλεμμαι, ἐκλάπην	to steal
λανθάνω, λήσω, ἔλαθον, λέληθα, λέλησμαι, ἐλήσθην	to hide, escape the notice of
λέγω, ἐρῶ/λέξω, εἶπον/ ἔλεξα, εἴρηκα, λέλεγμαι, ἐλέχθην	to say, speak, tell
λείβω, λείψω, ἔλειψα	to pour
μανθάνω, μαθήσομαι, ἔμαθον, μεμάθηκα (+ inf.)	to learn (to)
πλέκω, πλέξω, ἔπλεξα, πέπλοχα, πέπλεγμαι, ἐπλέχθην	to weave, twist
σπεύδω, σπεύσω, ἔσπευσα, ἔσπευκα, ἔσπευσμαι	to hasten, hurry
στασιάζω, στασιάσω	to rebel
τρίβω, τρίψω, ἔτριψα, τέτριφα, τέτριμμαι, ἐτρίφθην/ἐτρίβην	to rub
τυγχάνω, τεύξομαι, ἔτυχον, τετύχηκα	to happen to ..., meet

Lesson 14

Morphology: Active Voice of -μι Verbs

More on Verb Forms:

Middle Voice

Passive Voice

Greek verbs are customarily divided into two types: **-ω** verbs and **-μι** verbs. This lesson presents the present progressive active forms of -μι verbs, and the Middle and Passive forms of both -ω verbs and -μι verbs.

Morphology: Active Voice of -μι Verbs

The endings of most -μι verbs differ from those of -ω verbs *only* on forms built on the **present progressive stem**. Verbs in -μι do not have the thematic vowel {ο/ε} before the personal ending. Personal endings attach directly to the vowel of the stem, either ω/ο as in δίδωμι, or η/α as in ἵστημι, or η/ε as in τίθημι. It is advisable to learn the personal endings separately.

Primary Endings: Active

Singular:

first person	-μι
second person	-ς
third person	-σι

Plural:

first person	-μεν
second person	-τε
third person	-ασι

Lesson 14

Learn the following forms of the present progressive of δίδωμι, ἵστημι, and τίθημι:

	Present Active		
Singular			
first person	δίδω**μι**	ἵστη**μι**	τίθη**μι**
second person	δίδως	ἵστης	τίθης
third person	δίδω**σι**	ἵστη**σι**	τίθη**σι**
Plural			
first person	δίδο**μεν**	ἵστα**μεν**	τίθε**μεν**
second person	δίδο**τε**	ἵστατε	τίθετε
third person	διδό**ασι**	ἱστ**ᾶσι**	τιθέ**ασι**

- The endings of most -μι verbs differ from those of -ω verbs *only* on forms built on the **progressive stem.** Notice that the stem ends in a long vowel in the singular and ends in a short vowel in the plural. The **secondary endings** of -μι verbs are identical to those of -ω verbs. See Morphology for paradigms.
- The **future** of some -μι verbs is formed on a so-called future stem which must be learned. The endings are identical to those of -ω verbs.
  ἵστημι στ ήσω
  δίδωμι δ ώσω
  τ ίθημι θ ήσω
- In addition to lacking the thematic vowel in the progressive forms, some -μι verbs have a **second aorist** without the thematic vowel: ἵστημι has the form ἔστην. (See the paradigm of ἔγνων in Lesson 13 and the Morphology for other -μι verbs) Note that δίδωμι, τίθημι and ἵστημι have first aorist forms ending in -κα.

♦Exercise 1

Learn the following principle parts for -μι verbs. Then identify and metaphrase each of the following verb forms.

δίδωμι, δώσω, ἔδωκα, δέδωκα	to give
ἵστημι, στήσω, ἔστην/ἔστησα, ἕστηκα	to stand
τίθημι, θήσω, ἔθηκα, τέθηκα	to place

1. διδόασιν	5. ἱστᾶσιν	9. κατέθηκα
2. ἵστης	6. ἔδωκα	10. ἀποδίδοτε
3. ἐδίδοσαν	7. ἵστην	11. δίδως
4. ἔστης	8. ἐδίδουν	12. ἀπεδίδοτε

♦Exercise 2

Write a synopsis in the progressive active for:

τίθημι, θήσω 3rd sing.

Lesson 14

More on Verb Forms: Middle and Passive Voice

Morphology: -ω Verbs

The middle voice of -ω verbs is formed in exactly the same way as the active voice, but it uses a different set of personal endings:

Verb Stem + Thematic Vowel (**ο** or **ε**) + Personal Ending:

λυ + ε + σθε ⇒ λυέσθε
λυ + ο + μεθα ⇒ λυόμεθα

Middle/Passive Primary Endings

Singular:

first person	**-μαι**
second person	**-σαι**
third person	**-ται**

Plural:

first person	**-μεθα**
second person	**-σθε**
third person	**-νται**

Here are the present and future middle forms of λ ύω.

	Present	*Future*
Singular		
first person	λύο**μαι**	λύσο**μαι**
second person	λύ**ει**, λύ**ῃ**	λύσ**ει**, λύσ**ῃ**
third person	λύε**ται**	λύσε**ται**
Plural		
first person	λυό**μεθα**	λυσό**μεθα**
second person	λύε**σθε**	λύσε**σθε**
third person	λύο**νται**	λύσο**νται**

- In the 2nd singular middle/passive of -ω verbs, the **-σ-** of the ending drops out and the thematic vowel (-**ε**-) combines with the rest of the ending (-αι) to form the diphthong -ει (or sometimes -ῃ). λύε**σαι** 〉 **λύει, λύῃ**. See Pre-view.
- As in the active voice, the middle/passive voice of **contract verbs** like ποιέω whose stem ends in the vowels α, ε, or ο often contract with the thematic vowel of the personal endings:

  ποιοῦμαι ← ποιέ-ο-μαι

  ποιεῖ ← ποιέ-ε-σαι

  ποιεῖται ← ποιέ-ε-ται

ποιούμεθα ← ποιε-ό-μεθα
ποιεῖσθε ← ποιέ-ε-σθε
ποιοῦνται ← ποιέ-ο-νται

See Morphology for paradigms of other contract verbs.

Middle/Passive Secondary Endings

Singular

first person	**-μην**
second person	**-σο**
third person	**-το**

Plural

first person	**-μεθα**
second person	**-σθε**
third person	**-ντο**

Here are the forms of the past progressive and aorist middle of λ ύω:

		Imperfect	*Aorist*
Singular			
	first person	ἐλυό**μην**	ἐλυσά**μην**
	second person	ἐλύ**ου**	ἐλύσ**ω**
	third person	ἐλύε**το**	ἐλύσα**το**
Plural			
	first person	ἐλυό**μεθα**	ἐλυσά**μεθα**
	second person	ἐλύε**σθε**	ἐλύσα**σθε**
	third person	ἐλύο**ντο**	ἐλύσα**ντο**

- In the 2nd singular middle/passive of -ω verbs, the **-σ-** of the ending drops out and the thematic vowel (**-ε-**) combines with the rest of the ending (-ο or -α) to form the contracted endings shown above. ἐλύ**σο** > ἐλύ**ου**; ἐλύσα**σο** > ἐλύσ**ω**. See Pre-view.
- The second aorist middle forms in the same way as the second aorist active. Here are the second aorist middle forms of γίγνομαι.

Singular

first person	ἐγενόμην
second person	ἐγένου
third person	ἐγένετο

Plural

first person	ἐγενόμεθα
second person	ἐγένεσθε
third person	ἐγένοντο

Lesson 14

♦Exercise 3

Identify the following middle verb forms by person, number and tense.

1. λέξεσθε	7. ἐλέξω
2. ἐτριβόμην	8. ἐγραψάμεθα
3. ἐλέγεσθε	9. ἐλέγετο
4. τρίψει	10. ἐγράφοντο
5. λέγεται	11. λέξεται
6. τρίβονται	12. ἐγράψατο

♦Exercise 4

Write a synopsis in the progressive middle for:

γράφω, γράψω	2nd sing.
φιλέω, φιλήσω	1st pl.
κρίνω, κρινῶ	2nd pl.

Write a synopsis in the progressive and aorist middle for:

λύω, λύσω, ἔλυσα	3rd pl.
γράφω, γράψω, ἔγραψα	2nd pl.
φιλέω, φιλήσω, ἐφίλησα	1st sing.
κρίνω, κρινῶ, ἔκρινα	2nd sing.

♦Exercise 5

Identify the following past aorists by person, number, mood (always indicative so far) and voice. Then metaphrase each form.

1. ἐλέξατε	5. ἐγράψατο
2. ἐτρίψαμεν	6. ἤγγειλα
3. ἀπεκρίναντο	7. ἐπαιδεύσασθε
4. ἐνέγκατε	8. ἠμύνατο

♦Exercise 6

Using the first three principal parts listed below, identify the aspect of the following verb forms as progressive or aorist. Then metaphrase each form.

τυγχάνω, τεύξομαι, ἔτυχον	to happen
πυνθάνομαι, πεύσομαι, ἐπυθόμην	to find out
βαίνω, βήσομαι, ἔβην	to step, go
λανθάνω, λήσω, ἔλαθον	to escape notice

1. ἐτύγχανομεν	5. ἔβητε
2. ἔτυχετο	6. ἐπυνθάνεσθε
3. ἔπυθον	7. ἐπύθεσθε
4. ἐλάθομεν	

Lesson 14

The Perfect Middle

The **perfective middle** stem must be learned as the fifth principal part. Perfect middle verb forms are easily recognized because, like the perfect active forms, they often show reduplication (**λέλυμαι**). The present perfect middle uses primary middle endings *without the variable vowels (ο/ε).* The past perfect middle uses secondary middle endings *without the variable vowels.*

		Present Perfect	*Past Perfect*
Singular:			
	first person	λέλυ**μαι**	ἐλελύ**μην**
	second person	λέλυ**σαι**	ἐλέλυ**σο**
	third person	λέλυ**ται**	ἐλέλυ**το**
Plural:			
	first person	λελύ**μεθα**	ἐλελύ**μεθα**
	second person	λέλυ**σθε**	ἐλέλυ**σθε**
	third person	λέλυ**νται**	ἐλέλυ**ντο**

♦ Exercise 7

On the model of λύω (2nd pl.) below, write a synopsis of the regular verb πιστεύω 3rd plural, middle, including the progressive, aorist and perfective forms.

	Progressive	*Aorist*	*Perfective*
Past	ἐλύεσθε	ἐλύσασθε	ἐλέλυσθε
Present	λύεσθε		λέλυσθε
Future	λύσεσθε		

Passive Voice

The forms of the passive voice of -**ω** verbs are identical to those of the middle voice in the present and past progressive:

Verb Stem + Thematic Vowel (**ο** or **ε**) + Personal Ending:

λυ	+	**ε**	+	σθε	⇒	λύεσθε
λυ	+	**ο**	+	μεθα	⇒	λυόμεθα

The present perfect and past perfect have endings added directly to the stem without a thematic vowel.

Lesson 14

The Aorist Passive

The **aorist passive** has both a past and a future. The morpheme for both is {θη} with an allomorph {η}. The past aorist uses secondary active endings. The future aorist uses middle primary endings. The aorist passive stem must be learned as the sixth principal part; λύω → ἐλύθην.

Here are the aorist passive forms of λ ύω:

		Past	*Future*
Singular			
	first person	ἐλύθην	λυθήσομαι
	second person	ἐλύθης	λυθήσει/λυθήσῃ
	third person	ἐλύθη	λυθήσεται
Plural			
	first person	ἐλύθημεν	λυθησόμεθα
	second person	ἐλύθητε	λυθήσεσθε
	third person	ἐλύθησαν	λυθήσονται

♦Exercise 8

Write a synopsis for the aorist aspect of the regular verb πιστεύω 1st singular past active and middle, and past and future passive.

The Perfect Passive

The **perfect passive** forms are identical to the middle forms in all three tenses, past, present and future. See Pre-view and Morphology.

Here are all principal parts of λύω.

λύω, λύσω, ἔλυσα, λέλυκα, λέλυμαι, ἐλύθην.

Morphology: -μι Verbs

Middle/ Passive Primary Endings

Singular		
	first person	-μαι
	second person	-σαι
	third person	-ται
Plural		
	first person	-μεθα
	second person	-σθε
	third person	-νται

Here are the forms of the present progressive of ἵστημι and δίδωμι:

LESSON 14

Present Progressive Middle/Passive

Singular

first person	ἵσταμαι	δίδομαι
second person	ἵστασαι	δίδοσαι
third person	ἵσταται	δίδοται

Plural

first person	ἱστάμεθα	διδόμεθα
second person	ἵστασθε	δίδοσθε
third person	ἵστανται	δίδονται

- As in the plural forms of the active, the stem of the middle/passive forms ends in the short vowel. This is true both in the singular and plural.

♦Exercise 9

Learn the paradigms for -μι verbs in the morphology, then identify the following verb forms.

1. δίδονται	7. ἱστάμεθα
2. ἱστᾶσι	8. ἐτίθεσθε
3. ἐδίδοσαν	9. στήσεται
4. ἵστανται	10. ἀποδίδομεθα
5. ἐδίδοντο	11. ἵσταται
6. ἔδιδοσθε	12. ἀπεδίδομεθα

♦Exercise 10

Write a synopsis in the active voice for:

τίθημι, θήσω 3rd sing.

	Progressive	*Aorist*	*Perfective*
Past			
Present			
Future			

Lesson Vocabulary

Verbs

δίδωμι, δώσω, ἔδωκα, δέδωκα, δέδομαι, ἐδόθην	to give
εἰμί, ἔσομαι, ἦν (imperfect)	to be
ἵστημι, στήσω, ἔστησα/ἔστην, ἕστηκα, ἕσταμαι, ἐστάθην	to stand, make to stand

Lesson 14

παιδεύω, παιδεύσω, ἐπαίδευσα, πεπαίδευκα, πεπαίδευμαι, ἐπαιδεύθην	to educate
πυνθάνομαι, πεύσομαι, ἐπυθόμην, πέπυσμαι	to learn by inquiry, ask
τίθημι, θήσω, ἔθηκα,τέθηκα, τέθειμαι, ἐτέθην	to place, put

Lesson 15

The Participle: A Non-finite Verb Form

Verb forms that are marked for person are called finite. So far, all verbs with the exception of infinitives have been marked for person. For example, νικῶ, "I conquer" is first person, but νικᾷ, "he, she, it conquers" is third person. (See Lesson 7.) Infinitives (from the Latin word for "non-finite") and participles are non-finite verb forms. They are not identified for person. They do, however, have such verbal properties as **voice** and **aspect**. Participles also have the adjectival properties **case, number** and **gender.** They are therefore usually described as verbal adjectives.

Greek and English participles compared

Both English and Greek mark participles by adding special morphemes, but they differ in how they add these morphemes. English participles can be recognized by one of two endings called **suffix morphemes**: {-ing} and {-ed}, as in "learning" and "learned." Most Greek participles can be recognized by one of two **infix morphemes** {-ντ-} for the active and {-**μεν**-} for the middle and passive; an infix morpheme appears between the verb stem and the ending. Case, number and gender are indicated by the regular adjective endings.

Greek and English participles also differ in function. English participles combine freely with auxiliaries to form many other complex verbal expressions ("to be jumping," "to have jumped," "to have been jumped," etc.), while Greek participles rarely combine with auxiliaries. However, where English has only two forms of participle, Greek has more than ten participial verb forms representing various aspects, tenses and voices.

Morphology

The progressive active participle shows the progressive aspect stem followed by the thematic vowel (ο/ω) and the {-ντ-} infix. The aorist active participle shows the aorist aspect stem followed by the thematic vowel (α) and the {-ντ-} infix. The masculine and neuter forms show the third declension endings; the feminine forms use a special infix and show the first declension endings.

λυ + ο/ω + {-ντ-} + ος = λύοντος
λυ + σ + α + {-ντ-} + ος = λύσαντος

LESSON 15

Progressive Active

		Masculine	*Feminine*	*Neuter*
Singular				
	Nominative	λύων	λύουσα	λύον
	Genitive	λύοντος	λυούσης	λύοντος
	Dative	λύοντι	λυούσῃ	λύοντι
	Accusative	λύοντα	λύουσαν	λύον
Plural				
	Nominative.	λύοντες	λύουσαι	λύοντα
	Genitive.	λυόντων	λυουσῶν	λυόντων
	Dative.	λύουσι	λυούσαις	λύουσι
	Accusative.	λύοντας	λυούσας	λύοντα

Aorist Active

		Masculine	*Feminine*	*Neuter*
Singular				
	Nominative	λύσας	λύσασα	λύσαν
	Genitive	λύσαντος	λυσάσης	λύσαντος
	Dative	λύσαντι	λυσάσῃ	λύσαντι
	Accusative	λύσαντα	λύσασαν	λύσαν
Plural				
	Nominative	λύσαντες	λύσασαι	λύσαντα
	Genitive	λυσάντων	λυσασῶν	λυσάντων
	Dative	λύσασι	λυσάσαις	λύσασι
	Accusative	λύσαντας	λυσάσας	λύσαντα

The middle participles show the aspect stem followed by the thematic vowel and the {-μεν} infix. All genders show the endings of the first and second declensions.

λυ + ο + {-μεν-} + ος = λυόμενος
λυ + σ + α + {-μεν-} + ος = λυσάμενος

Masculine forms of the participle are given in the chart below as an example. For the full paradigm of the future and perfect active participles and middle/passive participles see Morphology.

	Active	*Middle*	*Passive*
future	λύσων, λύσοντος	λυσόμενος	λυθησόμενος
aorist	λύσας, λύσαντος	λυσάμενος	λυθείς, λυθέντος
perfective	λελυκώς, λελυκότος	λελυμένος	λελυμένος

Lesson 15

♦ Exercise 1

Not all words ending in {-ing} or {-ed} are participles. Copy those you think are *not* participles.

1. spring
2. springing
3. offspring
4. embed
5. said
6. headed

♦ Exercise 2

Write the participles for the following English verbs on the model of cook, cooking, cooked.

1. change
2. turn
3. speak
4. take
5. make
6. fake

♦ Exercise 3

Copy all forms that could be progressive participles.

1. προσιόντα
2. πόντον
3. φιλῶν
4. φίλων
5. ποιοῦντες
6. οὖσα
7. ὄντες
8. λαβών
9. λαβόντες
10. ἀστραγαλίζοντες

♦ Exercise 4

Copy all verb forms that could be {-μεν-} participles. Remember the {-μεν-} must follow a verb stem and be followed by first or second declension endings.

1. δυναμένῳ
2. ποιμένος
3. ποιούμενος
4. φρόνιμοι
5. ᾠκοδομημένη
6. κεκοσμημένους
7. προαιρούμενοι
8. ἐρόμενον
9. κόσμους
10. ἀνεῳγμένην

♦ Exercise 5

Copy all participles in the following paragraph from the *Life of Euripides*.

ἐτελεύτησε δὲ τὸν τρόπον τοῦτον. ἐν τῇ Μακεδονίᾳ κώμη ἐστὶ καλουμένη Θρᾳκῶν διὰ τό ποτε κατῳκηκέναι ἐνταῦθα Θρᾷκας. ἐν ταύτῃ ποτὲ τοῦ Ἀρχελάου Μολοττικὴ κύων ἦλθεν ἀποπλανηθεῖσα. ταύτην Θρᾷκες, ὡς ἔθος, θύσαντες ἔφαγον. καὶ δὴ ὁ Ἀρχέλαος ἐζημίωσεν αὐτοὺς ταλάντῳ. ἐπεὶ οὖν οὐκ εἶχον, Εὐριπίδου ἐδεήθησαν ἀπολύσεως τυχεῖν δεηθέντος τοῦ βασιλέως. χρόνῳ δὲ ὕστερον Εὐριπίδης ἐν ἄλσει τινὶ πρὸ τῆς πόλεως ἠρέμει, Ἀρχελάου δὲ ἐπὶ κυνηγέσιον ἐξελθόντος, τῶν σκυλάκων ἀπολυθέντων ὑπὸ τῶν κυνηγῶν καὶ περιτυχόντων Εὐριπίδῃ, διεσπαράχθη καταβρωθεὶς ὁ ποιητής. ἦσαν δὲ ἔκγονοι οἱ σκύλακες τῆς ὑπὸ Θρᾳκῶν ἀναιρεθείσης κυνός, ὅθεν καὶ παροιμία ἐστὶ παρὰ τοῖς Μακεδόσι 'κυνὸς δίκη'.

Lesson 15

Basic Sentences

15.1 ὁ μὴ[1] γαμῶν ἄνθρωπος οὐκ ἔχει κακά.

An unmarried man has no troubles. Menander
Any unmarried man is free of trouble.
A man who is unmarried is free of trouble.

15.2 ὁ ἄνθρωπος μὴ γαμῶν οὐκ ἔχει κακά. Menander (adapted)

A man has no troubles, if he doesn't marry.

15.3 συμβουλεύω σοι καίπερ νέος ὤν.

I give you advice, though I am young. Xenophon (adapted)

15.4 ὁ Κῦρος ἅτε παῖς ὢν καὶ φιλόκαλος καὶ φιλότιμος ἥδετο τῇ στολῇ.

Cyrus kept enjoying the garment being, after all, a child and fond of pretty things and attention. Xenophon (adapted)

15.5 οἶδα σοφὸς ὤν.

I am wise and aware of it.

15.6 στυγεῖ δὲ τοὺς τεκόντας, αὐτὸς οὐ θέλων θανεῖν.[2]

He (= Admetos) hates his parents, though he himself is not willing to die.
Euripides

15.7 πατὴρ οὐχ ὁ γεννήσας, ἀλλ' ὁ θρέψας σε.

Not the man who has begotten you is your father, but the one who has brought you up.

15.8 ἡδὺ τῷ μισοῦντι τοὺς φαύλους τρόπους ἐρημία.

Solitude is a sweet thing to the man who hates bad behavior. Menander

15.9 οἱ δὲ Λυδοί τε καὶ οἱ Μῆδοι, ἔπειτε εἶδον νύκτα ἀντὶ ἡμέρας γενομένην ἐπαύσοντο μαχόμενοι.

The Lydians and the Persians stopped fighting because they saw night happening in place of day. Herodotus (adapted)

---

[1] Review Lesson 12 for Negatives.
[2] θανεῖν is an infinitive used to complete the meaning of the participle θέλων "willing to die." See Lesson 17.

Lesson 15

Form Identification

From now on you should identify all finite verb forms as they occur with the help of the Morphology and the Principal Parts:

Finite verbs forms are identified by the following properties:

person
number
time
aspect
mood (thus far indicative)
voice

Non-finite verb forms are identified by the following properties

case
number
gender
aspect
voice

Participles as Modifiers

The Participle in the Attributive or Appositional Position: Attributive Use

Syntax

In S15.1 γαμῶν is in the attributive position between the article ὁ and the noun ἄνθρωπος. This position is the syntactic equivalent of the appositional position, where the article and the participle follow the noun, as in ὁ ἄνθρωπος ὁ μὴ γαμῶν. In either the attributive or appositional position the participle is the equivalent of an adjectival relative clause.

♦Exercise 6

In the following sentences copy the adjectival relative clauses from Lesson 12.

1. Δαρεῖος Κῦρον μεταπέμπεται ἀπὸ τῆς ἀρχῆς ἧς αὐτὸν σατράπην ἐποίησεν.
2. ἔστιν δίκης ὀφθαλμὸς ὃς τὰ πάντ᾽ ὁρᾷ.
3. ὁ νεανίας ὃν αἱ Μοῦσαι φιλοῦσι, καὶ ὑπ᾽ἀνθρώπων φιλεῖται.

♦Exercise 7

Transform the adjectival participles into adjectival relative clauses.

1. the singing bird
2. the sinking ship
3. the laughing children

Lesson 15

Metaphrase

The participle in the attributive or appositional position is metaphrased between the article and the noun, except when the English participle has an object or an adverb. Then the English participle must follow the noun.

ὁ γράφων ποιητής	"the writing poet..."
ὁ ταῦτα γράφων ποιητής	"the poet writing these things..."

It is often useful to metaphrase such participles as relative clauses.

ὁ ταῦτα γράφων ποιητής	"the poet who is writing these things..."

♦ Exercise 8

Translate the following sentences into English, using relative clauses.

1. ὁ ταῦτα ποιῶν ἀθλητὴς οὐ φιλόσοφός ἐστι.
2. ἡ γυνὴ ἡ ταῦτα ποιοῦσα πλουτεῖ.
3. οἱ μαθηταὶ οἱ τοῦτο τὸ μάθημα μανθάνοντες σοφοὶ γίγνονται.
4. οἱ τοῦτο τὸ μάθημα διδάσκοντες διδάσκαλοι οὐ πλουτοῦσιν.
5. ἡ ἐκεῖνο τὸ μάθημα διδάσκουσα γυνὴ οὐ πλουτήσει.

♦ Exercise 9

Rewrite the following sentences substituting a participial clause for the relative clause.

1. ὁ νεανίας ὅστις φοβεῖται τὸν πατέρα οὗτος πολίτης ἀγαθός ἐστιν.
2. τὸν νεανίαν ὃς τὸν πατέρα καὶ τὴν μητέρα τιμᾷ φιλοῦσιν οἱ θεοί.

The Participle in the Predicative Position: Circumstantial Use

Participles can also stand in the predicative position, as in S15.2, where the participle, γαμῶν, does not follow an article. The participle in the predicative position modifies the governing verb like an adverbial clause.

Participles in the predicative position express the same semantic categories as adverbs, prepositional phrases or adverbial clauses. They can express time, manner, cause, purpose, concession, condition — in short any attendant circumstances. Thus the participial clause ὁ ποιητὴς ταῦτα γράψας may be the syntactic and semantic equivalent of any of the following finite adverbial clauses:

ἐπεὶ ὁ ποιητὴς ἔγραψε ταῦτα	"when the poet wrote those things"
εἰ ὁ ποιητὴς ἔγραψε ταῦτα	"if the poet wrote those things"
ὅτι ὁ ποιητὴς ἔγραψε ταῦτα	"because the poet wrote those things"
καὶ εἰ ὁ ποιητὴς ἔγραψε ταῦτα	"although the poet wrote those things"

For this reason the participle in the predicative position is sometimes called the **circumstantial** participle.

♦ Exercise 10

From the text in Exercise 5 copy five examples of the circumstantial participle. If applicable, copy the nounhead also.

Kernel Information

It is recommended that attributive participles be entered into modifier charts and that circumstantial participles be entered into kernel charts, with P in the clause marker column. This practice is open to debate, but it seems practical at this time.

♦ Exercise 11

In the following sentences identify the participles as attributive or circumstantial. Then enter them into a modifier or kernel chart.

1. ἀνήρ τις μέσην ἔχων ἥβην δύο εἶχεν ἑταίρας.
2. ἐχθρὰ γὰρ ἡ ἐπιοῦσα μητρυιὰ τέκνοις τοῖς πρόσθεν.
3. ὁ μὴ δαρεὶς ἄνθρωπος οὐ παιδεύεται.

Participial Clause Markers

Most circumstantial participles appear without a clause marker, so that their individual meaning depends on one's own semantic interpretation of the context. There are, however, some particles with which one may expect a circumstantial participial clause, and which are therefore called **participial clause markers**. In S15.3 καίπερ is such a participial clause marker with the semantic category, concession; in R15.9, ὡς signals purpose. Caution is needed because some of these participial clause markers can occur in several different semantic categories. Here is a partial list:

Clause marker	*English equivalent*	*Semantic category*
ἅμα	at the same time, while =	time
εἰ	if =	condition
καίπερ	although =	concession
ἅτε/οἷα	as, since, because, in as much as =	cause
ὡς/ὥσπερ	as if, just as =	concession or comparison
ὡς	because =	cause
ὡς	in order to (future participle) =	purpose

Lesson 15

Metaphrase

Circumstantial participial clauses can be metaphrased by English participles. However, because participial clause markers, such as "while, though" are rather rare in English, it is usually easier to metaphrase the participial clause with a finite adverbial clause. The sentence ἅμα ταῦτ' εἰπὼν ἀνέστη can be translated as "while saying this, he stood up" or as "while he said this, he stood up."

♦ Exercise 12

In the Basic Sentences find two examples of participial clauses with participial clause markers. Translate them by means of adverbial finite clauses. Adverbial clause markers are introduced in Lesson 11.

♦ Exercise 13

Translate the following sentences into English.

1. ταῦτα γράφων πολλὰ μανθάνω.
2. ὁ φιλόσοφος, ταῦτα ποιῶν, οὐ φιλόσοφός ἐστιν.
3. ἡ γυνὴ ταῦτα ποιοῦσα οὐ πλουτήσει.
4. οἱ μαθηταὶ τοῦτο μανθάνοντες σοφοὶ γίγνονται.

The Participle as Part of a Finite Verb Phrase: Supplementary Use

The participle combines with a limited number of verbs to fill the function of verb in a kernel. In S15.5 οἶδα ὤν functions as the verb in the kernel, not οἶδα by itself. In the sentence, οἱ μαθηταὶ ἥδονται ἀκούοντες τοῦ φιλοσόφου, the kernel verb is ἥδονται ἀκούοντες, not ἥδονται. Notice that the supplementary participle agrees with the subject, οἱ μαθήται, in case, number, and gender. The supplementary participle supplies specific meaning and governs the case of the object or complement of the kernel. The verb ἄκουω governs the genitive, so τοῦ φιλοσόφου is in the genitive case. While participles are not defined for person, person is indicated by the verb with which they combine. ἥδονται is third person plural. In a kernel chart both the supplementary participle and the verb with which it combines are listed as the item, verb.

Here is a partial list of verbs with which one may expect a supplementary participle. The list is grouped by sense, and an example is given for each group.

παύεται τούτων ἐπιθυμῶν	*"He ceases desiring these things."*
ἄρχομαι	begin
παύομαι	cease, stop
οἴχομαι	go away
ἥδεται ταῦτα μανθάνουσα	*"She enjoys learning these things."*

Lesson 15

ἥδομαι	rejoice, enjoy
χαίρω	rejoice, enjoy
λυπέω	grieve
εὖ ἔχω	do well, be well
κακῶς ἔχω	do badly, fare badly
οἶδα τούτου αἴτιος ὤν	*"I am aware of being the cause of this."*
οἶδα	know, be aware of
λανθάνομεν πένητες ὄντες	*"We hide being poor."*
τυγχάνω	chance
λανθάνω	escape observation, hide
φαίνεται ἀποθανών	*"He is obviously dead."*
φαίνομαι	seem, appear

Metaphrase

While a metaphrase is always advisable to begin with, it is often more idiomatic to translate the Greek supplementary participle as the main verb and the main verb as an adverb. οἱ μαθηταὶ ἥδονται ἀκούοντες τοῦ φιλοσόφου may be translated as "the students listen joyfully to the philosopher." παύεται τούτων ἐπιθυμῶν may be translated as, "he no longer desires those things."

♦Exercise 14
In the readings find two examples of a verb phrase containing a supplementary participle and metaphrase them. Then give an idiomatic translation.

♦Exercise 15
Enter the kernel items from the above examples into a kernel chart.

The Power of the Article: The Articular Participle

Like adjectives, prepositional phrases, adverbs and genitives, the participle may be nominalized. When appearing with an article, it is often called **articular participle.** The nominalized participle functions as a noun phrase. In the kernel ὁ σοφὸς γιγνόμενος ______s ______, ὁ σοφὸς γιγνόμενος, "the one/ man/ person becoming wise," functions as the subject of the kernel. Notice that in the English equivalent, "the person becoming wise," the participle needs a nounhead. This use of the participle may occasionally also appear without the article. See Lesson 16.

Lesson 15

♦Exercise 16

From the Basic Sentences and Readings copy three examples of an articular participle.

There is one more use of the participle which will be taught in Lesson 16.

Readings

Pre-Reading Exercises

From this chapter on you should perform the following set of tasks before translating assigned readings:

Mark all words which belong to a finite kernel.
Mark all words which belong to a participial kernel.
Identify all participles as:
- articular
- attributive
- circumstantial
- supplementary

Draw arrows from the participle to the nounhead. If necessary supply gapped nounheads.

15.1 ἐχθρὰ γὰρ ἡ ἐπιοῦσα μητρυιὰ τέκνοις τοῖς πρόσθεν. — Euripides

15.2 ἀνήρ τις, μέσην ἔχων ἥβην, δύο ἔσχεν ἑταίρας. — Aesop

15.3 κύων τις, λαγὼν διώξας,[1] ἐκράτησεν. — Aesop

15.4 λέαινα ὀνειδιζομένη ὑπὸ ἀλώπεκος, ἐπεὶ ἕνα τίκτει, "Ἕνα," ἔφη, "ἀλλὰ λέοντα." — Aesop

15.5 πολλοὺς ὁ καιρὸς οὐκ ὄντας ποιεῖ φίλους. — Menander

15.6 οὐκ ἠθέλησα ζῆν ἀποσπασθεῖσα σου. — Euripides

15.7 ψευδόμενος οὐδεὶς λανθάνει πολὺν χρόνον. — Menander

---

[1] The aorist participle indicates either an act occuring without reference to time or duration, or an act prior in time to that of the governing verb. The reader must use his or her own judgement in choosing between the two in a given context.

15.8 τί σὺ πρὸς μελάθροις; τί σὺ τῇδε πολεῖς;
Φοῖβ', ἀδικεῖς αὖ τιμὰς ἐνέρων
ἀφοριζόμενος καὶ καταπαύων. Euripides

15.9 Θράσυλλος δὲ ἐξαγαγὼν Ἀθηναίους καὶ τοὺς ἄλλους ἅπαντας παρέταξε παρὰ τὸ Λύκεον, ὡς μαχούμενος. Xenophon

15.10 ἄρξομαι ἀπὸ τῆς ἰατρικῆς λέγων. Plato

Practice Sentences

1. ὁ Σωκράτης καίπερ γέρων ὢν ἥδετο τοῖς τῶν νέων λόγοις.
2. οὐ παύσομαι μανθάνων.
3. τῶν γεννησάντων οὐκ ἀμελοῦσιν οἱ ἀγαθοί.
4. ὁ μὴ γαμῶν πατὴρ τιμὴν οὐκ ἔχει.
5. ὁ ἀνὴρ μὴ γαμῶν οὐ μὸνον κακά, ἀλλὰ καὶ τιμὴν οὐκ ἔχει.
6. ὁ τοὺς φαύλους τρόπους μισῶν ἐν τῇ ἐρημίᾳ εὖ ἕξει.

Lesson Vocabulary

Nouns

ἀλώπηξ, ἀλώπεκος, ἡ — fox
διδάσκαλος, διδασκάλου, ὁ — teacher
ἔνεροι, ἐνέρων, οἱ — gods of the underworld, the dead
ἐρημία, ἐρημίας, ἡ — solitude
κόσμος, κόσμου, ὁ — order, world
κύων, κυνός, ὁ — dog
λαγώς, λαγώ, ὁ — hare, rabbit
λέαινα, λεαίνης, ἡ — lioness
λέων, λέοντος, ὁ — lion
Λύδος, Λύδου, ὁ — a Lydian
Λύκειον, Λυκείου, τό — the Lyceum (a gymnasium in Athens)
μέλαθρον, μελάθρου, τό — ceiling; pl. house
Μῆδος, Μήδου, ὁ — a Persian
μητρυιά, μητρυιᾶς, ἡ — step-mother
παῖς, παιδός, ὁ — child, boy, slave
ποιμήν, ποιμένος, ὁ — shepherd
πόντος, πόντου, ὁ — sea
στολή, στολῆς, ἡ — garment
τέκνον, τέκνου, τό — child

τεκόντες, τεκόντων, οἱ	parents
τιμή, τιμῆς, ἡ	honor
φιλόσοφος, φιλοσόφου, ὁ	philosopher
Φοῖβος, Φοίβου, ὁ	Phoebus Apollo

Verbs

ἀνοίγνυμι, ἀνοίξω, ἀνέῳξα, ἀνέῳχα, ἀνέοιγμαι, ἀνεῴχθην	to open
ἀποσπάω, ἀποσπάσω, ἀπέσπασα, ἀπέσπακα, ἀπέσπασμαι, ἀπεσπάσθην (+ gen.)	to sever, separate from
ἀφορίζομαι, ἀφορίσομαι, ἀφωρισάμην, ἀφῴρισμαι, ἀφωρίσθην	to appropriate, limit
γαμέω, γαμῶ, ἔγημα, γεγάμηκα, γεγάμημαι, ἐγαμήθην	to marry
γεννάω, γεννήσομαι, ἐγέννησα	to beget, bring forth
δέρω, δερῶ, ἔδειρα, δέδαρμαι, ἔδαρην	to flay
διώκω, διώξω, ἐδίωξα, δεδίωχα, δεδίωγμαι, ἐδιώχθην	to pursue
ἐθέλω/θέλω, θελήσω, ἠθέλησα, ἠθέληκα (+ inf.)	to be willing (to)
ἔχω εὖ (*see* ἔχω)	to do well
ἔχω κακῶς	to do badly
ἔπειμι, ἐπιών (participle)	to come upon, approach, follow
ζάω, ζήσω	to live
ἥδομαι, ἡσθήσομαι, ἡσάμην, ἥσθην (+ dat.)	to enjoy
θνῄσκω, θανοῦμαι, ἔθανον, τέθηνκα	to die
καταπαύω, καταπαύσω, κατέπαυσα	to cause to stop
κρατέω, κρατήσω, ἐκράτησα	to be strong(er)
λυπέω, λυπήσω, ἐλύπησα	to grieve
μισέω, μισήσω, ἐμίσησα, μεμίσηκα, μεμίσημαι, ἐμισήθην	to hate
οἶδα, εἴσομαι (+ part.)	to know, to be aware
οἰκοδομέω, οἰκοδομήσω, ᾠκοδόμησα, ᾠκοδομήθην	to build
οἴχομαι, οἰχήσομαι	to go
ὀνειδίζω, ὀνειδιῶ, ὠνείδισα, ὠνείδηκα, ὠνειδίσθην	to scold
παρατάττω, παρατάξω, παρέταξε	to draw up a battle line

παύομαι, παύσομαι, ἐπαυσάμην, πεπαύσμαι, ἐπαύσθην (+ part.)	to stop from doing
πλουτέω, πλουτήσω, ἐπλούτησα, πεπλούτηκα	to be rich
πολέω, πολήσω, ἐπόλησα	to go about, range, hunt
πορεύομαι, πορεύσομαι, ἐπορεύθην	to walk, march, travel
προαιρέω, προαιρήσω, προεῖλον	produce
στυγέω, στυγήσω, ἐστύγησα, ἐστύγηκα, ἐστύγημαι, ἐστυγήθην	to hate
συμβουλεύω, συμβουλεύσω, συνεβούλευσα, συμβεβούλευκα, συμβεβούλευμαι, συνεβουλεύθην (+ dat.)	to counsel, give advice
χαίρω, χαιρήσω, κεχάρκα, ἐχάρην	to rejoice, be glad
ψεύδομαι, ψεύσομαι, ἐψευσάμην, ἔψευσμαι, ἐψεύσθην	to lie

Adjectives

ἐχθρός, ἐχθρά, ἐχθρόν	hostile
ἡδύς, ἡδεῖα, ἡδύ	sweet
ἰατρικός, ἰατρική, ἰατρικόν	of healing, skilled in medicine
ἡ ἰατρική (subst.)	the art of healing
φιλόκαλος, φιλόκαλον	loving the beautiful
φιλότιμος, φιλότιμον	loving honor, ambitious

Adverbs

αὖ	again
πρόσθεν	earlier
τῇδε	in this place, here

Prepositions

ἀντί + genitive	in place of, instead of

Clause Markers

ἅμα	at the same time, while
ἅτε/οἷα	as, since, because, in as much as
εἰ	if
ἔπειτε	because, since
καίπερ	although
ὡς (+ future part.)	in order to
ὡς/ὥσπερ	as if, just as
ὡς	because

Review 3

♦ Exercise 1

Define each of the terms below in your own words. Give a Greek example where appropriate.

Lesson 9

genitive object

Lesson 10

factitive kernel

linking kernel

predicative position

subject complement

Lesson 11

clause marker

subordinating conjunction

Lesson 12

antecedent

nominal clause

Lesson 13

bound morpheme

free morpheme

morpheme

aspect

neutral

progressive

second aorist

sigmatic aorist

Lesson 15

circumstantial participle

nominalized

participial clause marker

participle

supplementary participle

♦ Exercise 2

Translate into Greek.

9.1 All people desire gain without toil.

9.2 Both young men and old men often forget the affairs of the city. πολλάκις: often

10.1 A friendly word from an enemy is either thoughtless or false.

10.2 Gain makes both slaves and masters blind.

11.1 Bad men are slaves to their desires because desire for wealth makes men blind.

11.2 Even if youth passes, virtue remains.

12.1 Whomsoever the Muses love is happy, even if he is neglected by men.

12.2 Many people who desire wealth are harmed by thoughtlessness.

15.1 We are foolish and aware of it.

15.2 Although we are poor, we do not forget the Muses.

15.3 We saw Cyrus rejoicing over the robe.

15.4 Everybody, married or unmarried, has troubles.

Hint: the one who marries or the one who does not marry.

Required Vocabulary

Lesson 9

Nouns

βασιλεύς, βασιλέως, ὁ	king
Ἑλλάς, Ἑλλάδος, ἡ	Greece
ἰατρός, ἰατροῦ, ὁ	healer, physician, doctor
τύραννος, τυράννου ὁ	tyrant, king

Verbs

ἅπτομαι, ἅψομαι, ἡψάμην (+ gen.)	to grab on, fasten onto
ἄρχομαι, ἄρξομαι ἠρξάμην (+ gen.)	to begin
ἄρχω, ἄρξω, ἦρξα (+ gen.)	to rule
βασιλεύω, βασιλεύσω, ἐβασίλευσα (+ gen.)	to rule, be king
βούλομαι, βουλήσομαι, βεβούλημαι, ἐβουλήθην (+ inf.)	to want to
δέομαι, δεήσομαι (+ gen.)	to lack, need, want
ἐπιθυμέω, ἐπιθυμήσω, ἐπεθύμησα (+ gen.)	to desire
ἐπιλανθάνομαι, ἐπιλήσομαι, ἐπελαθόμην (+ gen.)	to forget

Review 3

ἐπίσταμαι, ἐπιστήσομαι, ἠπιστήθην	to know something
εἰμί, ἔσομαι	to be
ὀρθόω, ὀρθώσω, ὤρθωσα	to put straight

Adjectives

αἰσχρός, αἰσχρά, αἰσχρόν	shameful
πᾶς, πᾶσα, πᾶν	every, all, entire
τοιοῦτος, τοιαύτη, τοιοῦτο	such

Adverbs

ὧδε	thus, in the following manner

Connectors

καὶ...καὶ	both ... and

Lesson 10

Nouns

ἀδελφός, ἀδελφοῦ, ὁ	brother
ἔθος, ἔθους, τό	habit
ἐχθρός, ἐχθροῦ, ὁ	enemy
ζῷον, ζῴου, τό	living being
ἦθος, ἤθους, τό	character
ἱππεύς, ἱππέως, ὁ	horseman
παῖς, παιδός, ὁ	child, boy, slave

Pronouns

αὐτός, αὐτή, αὐτό	same; self; he, she, it
ἐκεῖνος, ἐκείνη, ἐκεῖνο	that; he, she, it
ὅδε, ἥδε, τόδε	this; he, she, it
οὗτος, αὕτη, τοῦτο	this; he, she, it

Verbs

ἐστίν	_____ exists
καλέω, καλέσω, ἐκάλεσα	to call
νομίζω, νομίσω, ἐνόμισα	to consider, think
φημί, φήσω, ἔφησα	to declare, say, tell
φύομαι, φύσομαι, ἔφυν	to grow

Adjectives

ἄτιμος, ἄτιμον	dishonored
εὐγενής, εὐγενές	well-born
κάκιστος, κακίστη, κάκιστον	very bad
κάλλιστος, καλλίστη, κάλλιστον	very beautiful

μέγας, μεγάλη, μέγα	great
πολιτικός, πολιτική, πολιτικόν	public
πολύμορφος, πολύμορφον	many-shaped
πολυχρόνιος, πολυχρόνιον	long-lasting
τυφλός, τυφλή, τυφλόν	blind

Coordinating Conjunctions

οὐ μόνον...ἀλλὰ καὶ	not only ... but also

Lesson 11

Nouns

νοῦς, νοῦ, ὁ	mind, sense
σίδηρον, σιδήρου, τό	iron

Correlatives (See Lesson 15)

ὥσπερ...οὕτως	just as ... thus, so

Clause Markers

εἰ	if
ἐπεί	after, since (causal), when
ἕως	as long as, while, until
καὶ εἰ	even if, although, granted that
ὅπου	where
ὅτε	when (at a time when)
ὅτι, διότι	because
ὡς	when
ὡς	as
ὥσπερ	just as
ὡς τάχιστα	as soon as

Lesson 12

Nouns

ἀρχή, ἀρχῆς, ἡ	rule; province; beginning
Μοῦσα, Μούσης, ἡ	Muse
πολέμιος, πολεμίουν, ὁ	enemy; pl. the enemy
στρατηγός, στρατηγοῦ, ὁ	general

Verbs

ἀποθνήσκω, ἀποθανοῦμαι, ἀπέθανον	to die
ἐξάγω, ἐξάξω, ἐξήγαγον	to lead out, bring out
νικάω, νικήσω, ἐνίκησα, νενίκηκα	to conquer, win
ὁράω, ὄψομαι, ὤφθην	to see

Review 3

στρατηγέω, στρατηγήσω, ἐστρατήγησα	to be a general, command
φιλέω, φιλήσω, ἐφίλησα	to love
φοβοῦμαι, φοβήσομαι, ἐφοβησάμην	to fear, revere

Adjectives

μακάριος, μακαρία, μακάριον	blessed, happy

Adverbs

μή	not

Relative Pronouns

ὅς, ἥ, ὅ	who, which
ὅστις, ἥτις, ὅ τι	whoever, whichever

Lesson 13 & 14

Verbs

ἄγγελλω, ἀγγελῶ, ἤγγειλα, ἤγγελκα, ἤγγελμαι, ἠγγέλθην	to report, announce
ἀμύνω, ἀμυνῶ, ἤμυνα	to defend, ward off
βαίνω, βήσομαι, ἔβην, βέβηκα	to go, walk
γράφω, γράψω, ἔγραψα, γέγραφα, γέγραμμαι, ἐγράφην	to write
δέχομαι, δέξομαι, ἐδεξάμην, δέδεγμαι, ἐδέχθην	to receive
δίδωμι, δώσω, ἔδωκα, δέδωκα, δέδομαι, ἐδόθην	to give
εἰμί, ἔσομαι	to be
ἵστημι, στήσω, ἔστησα/ἔστην, ἕστηκα, ἕσταμαι, ἐστάθην	to stand
κλέπτω, κλέψω, ἔκλεψα, κέκλοφα, κέκλεμμαι, ἐκλάπην	to steal
λανθάνω, λήσω, ἔλαθον, λέληθα	to hide, escape notice of
λέγω, ἐρῶ/λέξω, εἶπον/ ἔλεξα, εἴρηκα, λέλεγμαι, ἐλέχθην	to say, speak, tell
λείβω, λείψω, ἔλειψα	to pour
μανθάνω, μαθήσομαι, ἔμαθον, μεμάθηκα	to learn
παιδεύω, παιδεύσω, ἐπαίδευσα, πεπαίδευκα, πεπαίδευμαι, ἐπαιδεύθην	to educate

πλέκω, πλέξω, ἔπλεξα, πέπλοχα, πέπλεγμαι, ἐπλέχθην	to weave, twist
πυνθάνω, πεύσομαι, ἐπυθόμην, πέπυσμαι	to learn by inquiry, ask
σπεύδω, σπεύσω, ἔσπευσα, ἔσπευκα, ἔσπευσμαι	to hasten, hurry
στασιάζω, στασιάσω	to rebel
τίθημι, θήσω, ἔθηκα, τέθηκα, τέθειμαι, ἐτέθην	to place, put
τρίβω, τρίψω, ἔτριψα, τέτριφα, τέτριμμαι, ἐτρίφθην/ἐτρίβην	to rub
τυγχάνω, τεύξομαι, ἔτυχον, τετύχηκα	to happen to, meet

Lesson 15

Nouns

κόσμος, κόσμου, ὁ	order, world
κύων, κυνός, ὁ	dog
ποιμήν, ποιμένος, ὁ	shepherd
πόντος, πόντου, ὁ	sea
τέκνον, τέκνου, τό	child
τιμή, τιμῆς, ἡ	honor

Verbs

γαμέω, γαμήσω, ἔγημα, γεγάμηκα, γεγάμημαι, ἐγαμήθην	to marry
διώκω, διώξω, ἐδίωξα, δεδίωχα, δεδίωγμαι, ἐδιώχθην	to pursue
ἐθέλω/θέλω, θελήσω, ἐθέλησα, ἠθέληκα (+ inf.)	to be willing
ἥδομαι, ἡσθήσομαι, ἡσάμην, ἥσθην (+ dat.)	to enjoy
κρατέω, κρατήσω, ἐκράτησα	to be strong(er)
οἶδα, εἴσομαι (+ participle)	to know, to be aware
στυγέω, στυγήσω, ἐστύγησα, ἐστύγηκα, ἐστύγημαι, ἐστυγήθην	to hate
συμβουλεύω, συμβουλεύσω, συνεβούλησα, συμβεβούλευκα, συμβεβούλευμαι, συνεβουλεύθην (+ dat.)	to counsel, give advice
χαίρω, χαιρήσω, κεχάρκα, ἐχάρην	to rejoice, be glad

Review 3

Adjectives

ἐχθρός, ἐχθρά, ἐχθρόν	hostile
ἡδύς, ἡδεῖα, ἡδύ	sweet

Adverbs

αὖ	again
πρόσθεν	earlier
τῇδε	in this place, here
τί;	why?

Prepositions

ἀντί + genitive	in place of, instead of

Participial Clause Markers

ἅμα	at the same time, while
ἅτε/οἷα	as, since, because, in as much as
εἰ	if
ὡς	because
καίπερ	although
ὡς	in order to (future participle)
ὡς/ὥσπερ	as if, just as

ANSWER KEY

Lesson 9:

1. Young men are pleasing to some of us, and old men are pleasing to others.
2. The affairs of the city grow strong because of the labor of the citizens.
3. Some people desire gain, but others desire happiness.
4. Both Cyrus and Alexander will lead their soldiers from Greece into Asia.
5. Many men are caught by shameful profit.

Lesson 10:

1. Wealth makes many people blind. These people destroy not only the affairs/possessions of their house, but also the affairs of the city.
2. The reputation of Themistocles is great.
3. But Themistocles is not honored by all people, for many people envy him.

Lesson 11:

Review 3

1. Good things happen to people from effort at the right moment, but bad things from thoughtlessness.
2. Rich people are not always happy because envy creeps up on wealth.
3. A bad person is a slave to his desire just as a slave is to his master.
4. For just as the moon rules in the sky at night, so the sun rules during the day.
5. For Zeus always throws the dice sucessfully since he is the king of the gods.

Lesson 12:

1. Darius sends for Cyrus, whom the soldiers trust.
2. Whomever the gods love is not neglected by the wise.
3. Even if a son neglects his mother and his father, they do not harbor anger against him.
4. Whomever the Muses love is pleasing also to men.
5. Both the servants who obey their masters and the evil people who obey their desires are slaves.

Lesson 15:

1. Although he was an old man, Socrates enjoyed conversations with the young.
2. I will not stop learning.
3. Good people do not neglect their parents.
4. An unmarried father does not have honor.
5. A person, if he does not marry, not only does not have troubles, but he also does not have honor.
6. A person who hates bad manners will be happy in solitude.

Lesson 16

Comparison in Terms of Unequalness
Comparison in Terms of Equalness

So far adjectives in this book have all appeared in the **positive** form, "big," "good," etc.. This lesson introduces the **comparative** and **superlative** forms of the adjective.

Basic Sentences

16.1. ἰσχυρότερον δέ γ' οὐδέν ἐστιν τοῦ λόγου.

Nothing is *more* powerful than reason. Menander

16.2. καὶ παρ' ἡμῖν πειθαρχεῖν[1] δεῖ θεῷ μᾶλλον ἢ ἀνθρώποις.

With us it is necessary to obey God more than men. Eusebius

16.3. ἀνδρειότερος εἶναί μοι δοκεῖ ὁ τῶν ἐπιθυμιῶν ἢ τῶν πολεμίων κρατῶν; καὶ γὰρ χαλεπώτατόν ἐστι τὸ ἑαυτὸν νικῆσαι.

The person who conquers his desires, seems to me to be braver than the person who conquers the enemy; for to overcome oneself is most difficult.

16.4. οὗτος σοφώτατός ἐστιν ἀνθρώπων, ὅστις, ὥσπερ Σωκράτης, ἔγνωκεν οὐδενὸς ἄξιος ὢν πρὸς σοφίαν.

This person is the wisest of people, who, like Socrates, has become aware of being worth nothing with regard to knowledge. Plato (adapted)

16.5. ἔστιν γὰρ οὕτως ὥσπερ οὗτος λέγει.

For it is so/thus as this person says. Sophocles

Comparison in Terms of Unequalness

This part of the lesson introduces comparison in terms of the unequalness of items as expressed through adjectives and adverbs. Many adjectives and adverbs in Greek and in English are inflected to show degree. "Big" is said to show positive degree, "bigger" comparative degree and "biggest" superlative degree.

[1] The forms πειθαρχεῖν and εἶναι νικῆσαι (in S16.3) are Infinitives. See Lesson 17.

LESSON 16

Morphology

Greek adjectives express comparison by adding different **infix morphemes** to the positive degree. The comparative may have either first and second declension endings or third declension endings. The superlative degree adds first and second declension endings. The adverbs μᾶλλον "more," μάλιστα "most," combined with the positive degree of the adjective can also express unequal comparison, for example, μᾶλλον φίλος "dearer," μάλιστα φίλος "dearest."

Adjectives Using -τερος, -τατος

Most adjectives form the comparative using the infix morpheme {**-τερ-**} or the allomorph {**-εστερ-**}. These adjectives form the superlative using the infix morpheme {**-τατ-**} or {**-εστατ**}:

Positive	*Comparative*	*Superlative*
δεινο-	δεινό**τερ**ος	δεινό**τατ**ος
σοφο-	σοφώτερος	σοοώτατος
ἀληθεσ-	ἀληθέ**στερ**ος	ἀληθέ**στατ**ος
σωφρον-	σωφρον**έστερ**ος	σωφρον**έστατ**ος

Note that adjectives in **-ος** with a *short penultima* lengthen the ο to ω, as in σοφός above.

Adjectives Using -ιων, -ιστος

A few adjectives form the comparative by adding the endings **-ιων**, **-ιον** to the root. These adjectives form the superlative by adding the endings **-ιστος**, **-η**, **-ον** to the root:

Positive	*Comparative*	*Superlative*
ἡδύς (ἡδ-)	ἡδ**ίων**	ἥδ**ιστος**

Comparatives in **-ιων** are declined as follows:

		Masculine / Feminine	*Neuter*
Singular			
	Nominative	βελτίων	βέλτιον
	Genitive	βελτίονος	βελτίονος
	Dative	βελτίονι	βελτίονι
	Accusative	βελτίονα/βελτίω	βέλτιον
Plural			
	Nominative	βελτίονες/βελτίους	βελτίονα/βελτίω
	Genitive	βελτιόνων	βελτιόνων
	Dative	βελτίοσι(ν)	βελτίοσι(ν)
	Accusative	βελτίονας/βελτίους	βελτίονα/βελτίω

Lesson 16

Note that the accent is recessive in the forms such as βέλτιον, ἄμεινον, ἔλαττον.

Some common adjectives form the comparative and superlative from alternative or syncopated stems. The following forms should be learned separately:

ἀγαθός	ἀμείνων βελτίων κρείττων	ἄριστος βέλτιστος κράτιστος
μικρός	μικρότερος ἐλάττων (for *ἐλαχιων) ἥττων	μικρότατος ἐλάχιστος ἥκιστος
κακός	κακίων χείρων	κάκιστος χείριστος
πολύς	πλείων (πλέων)	πλεῖστος
καλός	καλλίων	κάλλιστος
αἰσχρός (αἰσχ-)	αἰσχίων	αἴσχιστος
μέγας (μεγ-)	μείζων (for *μεγ-ιων)	μέγιστος
ταχύς (θαχ-)	θάττων (for *θαχ-ιων)	τάχιστος

Note: Some variant forms have different meanings. See the vocabulary at the end of the lesson.

Comparison of Adverbs

The comparative of those **adverbs** derived from adjectives usually looks like the neuter accusative *singular* of the comparative form of the adjective.

The superlative adverb usually looks like the neuter accusative *plural* form of the superlative adjective:

σοφῶς	σοφώτερον	σοφώτατα
καλῶς	κάλλιον	κάλλιστα

Lesson 16

Learn the following adverbs separately:

μάλα	μᾶλλον	μάλιστα
"very"	"more"	"most"
ἧττον	ἥκιστα	
"more"	"least"	

♦ Exercise 1

Copy all forms that could be comparative adverbs or adjectives.

1. εὐδαίμονες	8. ἀξιοῦται
6. προτέρων	4. ἀληθέσι
2. δεύτερος	9. κουφότερα
7. ἀζιώτατοι	5. ἀληθέστερον
3. ἀνδρειότεροι	10. βέλτιον

♦ Exercise 2

Write the paradigm, singular and plural, of the following noun plus comparative adjective pairs.

τὸ μεῖζον κέρδος ἡ κρείττων πόλις

♦ Exercise 3

Write the paradigm, singular and plural, of the following noun plus superlative adjective pairs.

ὁ σοφώτατος πολίτης ὁ ἐλάχιστος παῖς

Syntax of the Comparative

An adjective or adverb in the comparative degree raises the expectation of two items being compared. Thus, in the English translation of S16.1 the comparative phrase "more powerful" sets up a comparison between "nothing" and "reason." In Greek, the item to which comparison is being made can be in the genitive, as λόγου is in S16.1. This genitive in the environment of a comparative is labeled **genitive of comparison**.

In place of a genitive of comparison the reader may find instead a clause starting with ἤ containing the item to which comparison is being made. ἤ in this environment is a connector meaning "than." The compared word in the ἤ clause is in the same case as the other compared word. S16.1 can therefore be expressed also as ἰσχυρότερον δὲ γ' οὐδέν ἐστιν ἢ ὁ λόγος (ø = ἰσχυρός ἐστιν). There is extensive gapping in both Greek and English in such comparative clauses. For example, the adjective is almost always gapped.

In Greek, comparatives and superlatives sometimes appear without genitives. It seems that Greek readers automatically supplied the compared item; they gapped it. In English, too, the superlative is often found without a point of comparison: "water is best."

♦ Exercise 4

Rewrite each sentence showing the comparison without using ἤ. Write a final metaphrase of each sentence.

1. οὐδέν ἐστιν κάκιον ἢ ἀναρχία
2. οἱ νεανίαι μείζονές εἰσιν ἢ οἱ γέροντες
3. ἰσχυρότερον δέ γ'οὐδέν ἐστιν ἢ ὁ λόγος
4. ἅπαντες ἥττονες ἢ κέρδος

Syntax of the Superlative

An adjective or adverb in the superlative degree raises the expectation of a noun in the genitive denoting the whole with which a part is being compared. For example, in S16.4 ἀνθρώπων is the whole of which Socrates is the wisest part. This use of the genitive case is called the **partitive genitive**.

In the absence of a noun, adverbs like "rather" and "very" are used in translating comparatives and superlatives. In S16.3 χαλεπώτατον may be translated as "most difficult," or as "very difficult." ὡς followed by a superlative is the same as English "as ______ as possible." For example, ὡς τάχιστα, "as quickly as possible."

Comparison in Terms of Equalness

Comparison in term of equalness is signaled in English by so-called **correlative pairs**, such as:

as great	as
as many	as
as/so	as
as often	as
such	as
so	(just) as

LESSON 16

♦ Exercise 5

Copy the correlative pairs where the item on the left raises the expectation of the item on the right.

1. He comes here as often as he can.
2. She has as many friends as anyone I know.
3. Their courage was such as to inspire us all.
4. He is as great as he is famous.

♦ Exercise 6

For the sentences below, supply a second clause to fulfill the expectation of unequalness raised by the first clause.

1. He spends more...
2. She has less money...
3. I believe this more firmly...

♦ Exercise 7

For the sentences supply a second clause to fulfill the expectation of equalness raised by the first.

1. He spends as much...
2. She has as little money...
3. I do believe this as firmly...

♦ Exercise 8

Construct a first clause.

1.	...than he can.
2.	...as he can.
3.	...just as the winter brings snow.
4.	...just as I love music.

A frequent correlative pair in Greek is οὕτως ... ὥσ(περ) "so ... (just) as." In S16.5 οὕτως is correlative to ὥσπερ οὗτος λέγει.

♦ Exercise 9

Enter all adverbial modifiers from S16.5 into a modifier chart.

Lesson 16

Readings

16.1 σοφὸς Σοφοκλῆς, σοφώτερος δ'Εὐριπίδης, ἀνδρῶν δὲ πάντων Σωκράτης σοφώτατος — ancient oracle

16.2 Σωκράτης ἀδικεῖ, ζητῶν τά τε ὑπὸ γῆς καὶ οὐρανία καὶ τὸν ἥττω λόγον κρείττω ποιῶν καὶ ἄλλους ταὐτὰ ταῦτα διδάσκων. — Plato

16.3 φίλος μοι Σωκράτης, ἀλλὰ φιλτέρα ἡ ἀλήθεια. — Ammonius

16.4 ἔστι γὰρ τὸ ἔλαττον κακὸν μᾶλλον αἱρετὸν τοῦ μείζονος. — Aristotle

16.5 ὁ πλεῖστα πράττων πλεῖσθ' ἁμαρτάνει. — Euripides

16.6 ἀλλ' εἰσὶ τοῦ κέρδους ἅπαντες ἥττονες. — Aristophanes

16.7 οὐ καλῶς εἰρημένον[1] τὸ "γνῶθι σεαυτόν." χρησιμώτερον γὰρ ἦν τὸ "γνῶθι τοὺς ἄλλους." — Menander

16.8 ὅσον αἱ κατὰ τὸ σῶμα ἡδοναὶ ἀπομαραίνονται, τοσοῦτον αὔξονται αἱ περὶ τοὺς λόγους ἐπιθυμίαι. — Plato

Practice Sentences

1. οὐδὲν κρεῖττον τῆς φιλοσοφίας.
2. οὐδεὶς σοφώτερος Σωκράτους.
3. πάντες βρότοι ὄντες ἴσμεν.[2]
4. οὐ παύσονται μανθάνοντες σοφοί.
5. αὕτη ἡ γυνὴ πασῶν ἐστι καλλίστη.

Lesson Vocabulary

Nouns

ἀναρχία, ἀναρχίας, ἡ	anarchy
Εὐριπίδης, Εὐριπίδου, ὁ	Euripides
Πυθία, Πυθίας, ἡ	the Pythia, the medium uttering the prophecies in the oracle of Apollo at Delphi

---

[1] εἰρημένον is from the perfective participle of λέγω.

[2] ἴσμεν is first person plural of the verb οἶδα. See Lesson 17.

Lesson 16

σοφία, σοφίας, ἡ	wisdom, knowledge
Σοφοκλῆς, Σοφοκλοῦς, ὁ	Sophocles
Σωκράτης, Σωκράτους, ὁ	Socrates

Verbs

ἀξιόω, ἀξιώσω, ἠξίωσα, ἠξίωκα, ἠξίωμαι, ἠξιώθην	to think worthy
ἁμαρτάνω, ἁμαρτήσομαι, ἥμαρτον, ἡμάρτηκα, ἡμάρτημαι, ἡμαρτήθην	to do wrong
ἀπομαραίνομαι, ἀπεμαρηνάμην, ἀπεμαράνθην	to dry up, wither away
γιγνώσκω, γνώσομαι, ἔγνων, ἔγνωκα, ἔγνωσμαι, ἐγνώσθην	to become aware, recognize
γνῶθι	aorist imperative of γιγνώσκω
δεῖ, δεήσει, ἐδέησε (+ inf.)	it is necessary to
δοκέω, δόξω, ἔδοξα, δέδογμαι	to seem, think
ζητέω ζητήσομαι, ἐζήτησα, ἐζήτηκα	to seek
οἶδα, part. εἰδώς	to know
πειθαρχέω, πειθαρχήσω (+ dat.)	to obey, be obedient to
πράττω, πράξω, ἔπραξα, πέπραχα, πέπραγμαι, ἐπράχθην	to do, achieve, manage

Adjectives

ἀγαθός, ἀγαθή, ἀγαθόν	good
ἀμείνων, ἄμεινον	better (in courage)
ἄριστος, ἀρίστη, ἄριστον	best (in courage)
βελτίων, βέλτιον	better (morally)
βέλτιστος, βελτίστη, βέλτιστον	best (morally)
κρείττων, κρεῖττον	better (physically)
κράτιστος, κρατίστη, κράτιστον	best (physically)
αἱρετός, αἱρετή, αἱρετόν	preferable
αἰσχρός, αἰσχρά, αἰσχρόν	shameful
αἰσχίων, αἴσχιον	more shameful
αἴσχιστος, αἰσχίστη, αἰσχίστον	most shameful
ἀνδρεῖος, ἀνδρεία, ἀνδρεῖον	brave
ἄξιος, ἀξία, ἄξιον (+ gen.)	worthy of, guilty of
ἅπας, ἅπασα, ἅπαν	every, all, entire
δεῖνος, δείνη, δεῖνος	terrible, marvellous
δεύτερος, δεύτερα, δεύτερον	second
ἰσχυρός, ἰσχυρά, ἰσχυρόν	strong
κακός, κακή, κακόν	bad
κακίων, κάκιον	worse

Lesson 16

κάκιστος, κακίστη, κάκιστον	worst
χείρων, χεῖρον	weaker
χείριστος, χειρίστη, χείριστον	weakest
μέγας, μεγάλη, μέγα	great
μείζων, μεῖζον	greater
μέγιστος, μεγίστη, μέγιστον	greatest
μικρός, μικρά, μικρόν	small
μικρότερος, μικροτέρα, μικρότερον	smaller
μικρότατος, μικροτάτη, μικρότατον	smallest
ἐλάττων, ἔλαττον	less, weaker
ἐλάχιστος, ἐλαχίστη, ἐλάχιστον	least, weakest
ἥττων, ἧττον	less, weaker
ἥκιστος, ἡκίστη, ἥκιστον	least, weakest
οὐράνιος οὐρανία, οὐράνιον	heavenly
πολύς, πολλή, πολύ	much, many
πλείων (πλέων), πλεῖον	more
πλεῖστος, πλείστη, πλεῖστον	most
πρότερος, προτέρα, πρότερον	first
ταχύς, ταχεῖα, ταχύ	swift
θάττων, θάττον	swifter
τάχιστος, ταχίστη, τάχιστον	swiftest
χαλεπός, χαλεπή, χαλεπόν	hard, difficult
χρήσιμος, χρησίμη, χρήσιμον	useful

Adverbs

μάλιστα	most
μᾶλλον	more
ὡς + superlative	as…as possible

Pronouns

ἑαυτοῦ, ἑαυτῆς, ἑαυτοῦ	himself, herself, itself (reflexive)

Connector

ἤ	than

Correlatives

ὅσον…τόσον/τοσοῦτον	as much…as
οὕτως…ὥσπερ	thus/so…as
τοιοῦτος…ὅς/ὅστις/οἷος	such…as

Particles

γε	emphatic particle, often not translated in English; sometimes equivalent to "at least"

Lesson 17

The Infinitive: Another Non-finite Verb Form
Irregular Verb: οἶδα

This lesson introduces another non-finite verb form and two of its uses. This form has already appeared in S9.3, S11.4, S15.6, S16.2, and S16.3.

Basic Sentences

17.1 θέλομεν καλῶς ζῆν[1] πάντες, ἀλλ' οὐ δυνάμεθα.

We all want to live a good life, but we are not all able to do it. — Menander

17.2 δύναται τὸ πλουτεῖν καὶ φιλανθρώπους ποιεῖν.

Being rich can even produce a social conscience. — Menander

17.3 φύσιν πονηρὰν μεταβαλεῖν οὐ ῥάδιον.

To alter an evil nature is not easy. — Menander

17.4 πιστεύειν δεῖ τοὺς μανθάνοντας.

For students it is necessary to have faith.

17.5 καὶ δὴ καὶ νῦν ἔξεστιν ἡμῖν τὸ βέλτιστον σκοπεῖν περὶ νόμων.

Now we can study the best form of the laws. — Plato (adapted)

The Infinitive: Another Non-finite Verb Form

Like the participle the infinitive is a verb form that is not finite. It is not marked for person, but it does have such verbal properties as voice and aspect. In addition it has the noun properties of gender, always neuter, and of number, always singular.

---

[1] ζῆν is the infinitive of ζάω = ζά-ειν. See Morphology for contract verbs.

Lesson 17

Greek and English infinitives compared

Greek has only one verbal noun, the infinitive. A regular verb may have up to eleven infinitives with different morphemes for aspect and voice. The infinitive is not always easily recognized, because one of its suffix morphemes {-**αι**} is also a morpheme for the nominative plural of the first declension. The morphemes {-**ειν**} and {-**σθαι**} are easier to recognize. English on the other hand has two verbal nouns, the infinitive and the gerund. The English infinitive is often but not always preceded by "to," the gerund has the suffix morpheme {-ing-}. Because the English participle has the same suffix morpheme, the gerund and the participle are easily confused. Remember that the participle is an adjective, and the gerund is a noun.

♦Exercise 1

Underline those words in {-ing-} that are gerunds.

1. Go while the going is good.
2. Going slowly you will arrive safely.
3. One learns to dance by dancing.
4. There will be dancing in the streets.
5. Did you see the people dancing?

Morphology: the Greek Infinitive

	Progressive	*Future*	*Aorist*	*Perfective*
Active	λύειν	λύσειν	λῦσαι	λελυκέναι
Middle	λύεσθαι	λύσεσθαι	λύσασθαι	λελῦσθαι
Passive	λύεσθαι	λυθήσεσθαι	λυθῆναι	λελῦσθαι

For the infinitive forms of -μι and contract verbs see Morphology.

Lesson 17

Syntax

The Infinitive as Part of a Finite Verb Phrase: Complementary Infinitive

Like the participle, the infinitive without article combines with a limited number of verbs (some of which rarely appear without it) to fill the function, verb, in a finite kernel. In S17.1 the two complete verbs are θέλομεν ζῆν and δυνάμεθα ζῆν, not θέλομεν and δυνάμεθα. Just like the supplementary participle, this infinitive also supplies meaning and determines the kernel type. Logically, this infinitive should be called the supplementary infinitive to be parallel to the supplementary participle, but by tradition it is called the **complementary infinitive**.

Here is a partial list of verbs with which one may expect a complementary infinitive. The list is grouped by sense, and an example is given for each group.

δοκοῦσι ἀκούειν τούτων *"They seem to be listening to these things."*
δοκέω seem to

βουλόμεθα πιστεύειν αὐτῷ *"We want to trust him."*
βούλομαι want, wish to
ἐθέλω, θέλω want, be willing to
ἐπιθυμέω desire to
δύναμαι be able to
οἷός τε εἰμί be able to
πειράομαι try to
παύομαι stop, cease to

οἶδα ποιεῖν ταύτα *"I know how to do these things."*
γιγνώσκω understand how to
ἐπίσταμαι know how to
οἶδα know how to
μανθάνω learn to
νομίζω consider, believe to
οἶμαι consider, believe to
φημί declare to, admit to
εὔχομαι vow to

Note
When not combined with a complementary infinitive, these verbs may have other meanings! See Lesson 18.

Lesson 17

♦ Exercise 2

Rewrite the finite verbs in S1.2-6 and S6.1-3 and S8.1-3, changing them into a complementary infinitive and adding an appropriate verb from the list above. A rewritten version of S1.1 is given as an example

S1.1 κρίνειν τὸν φίλον ὁ καιρὸς οἷός τε ἐστίν.

♦ Exercise 3

From the Readings copy two sentences with a complementary infinitive and underline all items belonging to the kernel.

The Power of the Article (even when Ø) The Articular Infinitive

Like adjectives, prepositional phrases, adverbs, genitives and participles the infinitive may be nominalized. It may appear with or without the article. When appearing with an article it is often called the **articular infinitive**. In S17.2 τὸ πλουτεῖν, an articular infinitive, is the subject of the kernel. Like any other noun, the articular infinitive may appear in all four cases. In the absence of an article, the nominalized infinitive can be recognized by means of kernel analysis. In S17.3 φύσιν πονηρὰν μεταβαλεῖν is needed as subject of the linking kernel. A nominalized infinitive together with all the words it governs may fill any function in the kernel except the function, "verb."

♦ Exercise 4

Identify the syntactic function of the infinitives in R17.7.

Often the nominalized infinitive, mostly without an article, has a subject of its own. This subject is usually in the accusative case. In addition, the nominalized infinitive, with or without its own subject, may be expected as the subject in a linking kernel and in a number of impersonal expressions. For example, in S17.4 τοὺς μανθάνοντας is the accusative subject of πιστεύειν, and the phrase, πιστεύειν τοὺς μανθάνοντας, is the subject of the impersonal verb δεῖ. Here is a partial list of impersonal expressions with which one may expect a nominalized infinitive:

ἀνάγκη ø ἐστίν	There is a need to
νόμος ἐστιν	is lawful
δυνατόν ἐστιν	is possible
χαλεπόν ἐστιν	is difficult
ἔξεστιν (+ dat.)	is allowed
χρή	is necessary
δεῖ	is necessary
δοκεῖ	seems (good)

LESSON 17

Kernel Information

Clause Marker	*Item: Function*	*Item: Function*	*Item: Function*	*KT*	*M/ D*	*F/ N*	*Adv. Adj. Noun*	*Label*
	φύσιν πονηρὰν μεταβάλλειν: Subject	ῥάδιον: Subject Complement	Ø=Verb	*Linking*	*M*	*F*		*Statement*

♦ Exercise 5

Using the above example of S17.3, enter the kernels for the following sentences into a kernel chart.

1. ἄριστόν ἐστι πάντ' ἐπίστασθαι καλά. Menander

2. θυμοῦ κρατῆσαι καὶ ἐπιθυμίας καλόν. Menander

♦ Exercise 6

Write the Greek for "It is necessary to try to win, but it is not necessary to win."

Irregular Verb: οἶδα

This lesson introduces the first in a series of verbs whose forms are less predictable than the verb forms introduced in Lessons 13 and 14. οἶδα, "to know," is a defective verb which has only perfective forms.

		Perfect	*Pluperfect*
Singular			
	first	οἶδα	ᾔδη, ᾔδειν
	second	οἶσθα	ᾔδησθα, ᾔδεις
	third	οἶδε	ᾔδει, ᾔδειν
Plural			
	first	ἴσμεν	ᾖσμεν, ᾔδεμεν
	second	ἴστε	ᾖστε, ᾔδετε
	third	ἴσασι	ᾖσαν, ᾔδεσαν

Infinitive

εἰδέναι

Participle

εἰδώς, εἰδυῖα, εἰδός

For the full paradigm see Morphology.

LESSON 17

Readings

17.1 βουλόμεθα πλουτεῖν πάντες ἀλλ' οὐ δυνάμεθα.

17.2 λύπην γὰρ εὔνους οἶδεν ἰᾶσθαι λόγος. Menander

17.3 ἡ γὰρ σιωπὴ μαρτυρεῖ τὸ μὴ θέλειν. Menander

17.4 δίκαιος ἀδικεῖν οὐκ ἐπίσταται τρόπος. Menander

17.5 χαλεπὸν τὸ ποιεῖν, τὸ δὲ κελεῦσαι ῥάδιον. Philemon

17.6 γράμματα μαθεῖν δεῖ καὶ μαθόντα νοῦν ἔχειν. Menander

17.7 τὸ ζῆν γὰρ ἴσμεν, τοῦ θανεῖν δ' ἀπειρίᾳ
πᾶς τις φοβεῖται φῶς λιπεῖν τοῦ ἡλίου. Euripides

17.8 μοχθεῖν ἀνάγκη τούς θέλοντας εὐτυχεῖν. Menander

17.9 ἥδιστόν ἐστι εὐτυχοῦντα νοῦν ἔχειν. Menander

17.10 ὥσπερ οὖν οὐκ οἶδα, οὐδὲ οἴομαι εἰδέναι. Plato

17.11 ἀνὴρ δικαιός ἐστιν οὐχ ὁ μὴ ἀδικῶν Philemon
ἀλλ' ὅστις ἀδικεῖν δυνάμενος οὐ βούλεται.

1712 χαλεπὸν τὸ μὴ φιλῆσαι,
χαλεπὸν δὲ καὶ φιλῆσαι.
χαλεπώτατον δὲ πάντων
ἀποτυγχάνειν φιλοῦντα.

Practice Sentences

1. τὴν γνώμην ἀλλάττειν χαλεπώτερόν ἐστιν ἢ τὴν τρίχα.

2. πείθεσθαι δεῖ τοῖς τῆς πόλεως νόμοις μᾶλλον ἢ τοῖς τοῦ τυράννου λόγοις.

3. οὐκ ἔξεστιν τοὺς πολίτας ἀμελεῖν τὰ τῆς πόλεως.

4. τοὺς ἀγαθοὺς πολίτας καὶ τὰ τῆς οἰκίας καὶ τὰ τῆς πόλεως δεῖ θεραπεύειν.

Lesson 17

5. ἀδύνατον ἐφαίνετο τοῖς Πέρσαι εἰσβάλλειν εἰς τὴν Ἀττικὴν, ἐπεὶ πολλοὶ αὐτῶν ἀπέθανον ἐν τῇ μάχῃ. ἔδοξε οὖν τῷ στρατηγῷ οἴκαδε ἀπιέναι.

6. οὐ πάντα δυνάμεθα ἔχειν ἃ βουλόμεθα.

7. οὔ μοι ἔξεστιν ποιεῖν ἃ βούλομαι.

Lesson Vocabulary

Nouns

ἀπειρία, ἀπειρίας, ἡ — inexperience
Ἀττική, Ἀττικῆς, ἡ (γῆ) — Attica
γράμμα, γράμματος, τό — letter of the alphabet
ἥλιος, ἡλίου, ὁ — sun
θυμός, θυμοῦ, ὁ — will, will power
σιωπή, σιωπῆς, ἡ — silence
φῶς, φωτός, τό — light

Verbs

ἀνάγκη (ἐστιν) — is a need
ἀποτυγχάνω, ἀποτεύξομαι, ἀπέτυχον, ἀποτετύχηκα (+ gen.) — to fail
δύναμαι, δυνήσομαι, δεδύνημαι, ἐδυνήθην (+ inf.) — to be able (to)
εἰδέναι — infinitive of οἶδα
ἔξεστιν (+ dat.) — is allowed
ἐπίσταμαι, ἐπιστήσομαι (+ inf.) — to know how to
εὔχομαι, εὔξομαι, ηὐξάμην, ηὖγμαι — to pray, boast
ἰάομαι, ἰάσομαι, ἰασάμην, ἴαμαι, ἰάθην — to heal
κελεύω, κελεύσω, ἐκέλευσα, κεκέλευκα, κεκέλευσμαι, ἐκελεύσθην — to command, order
λείπω, λείψω, ἔλιπον, λέλοιπα, λέλειμμαι, ἐλείφθην — to leave
μανθάνω, μαθήσομαι, ἔμαθον, μεμάθηκα (+ inf.) — to learn to
μαρτυρέω, μαρτυρήσω, ἐμαρτύρησα, μεμαρτύρημαι, ἐμαρτυρήθην — to witness, attest
μεταβάλλω, μεταβαλῶ, μετέβαλον, μεταβέβληκα, μεταβέβλημαι, μετεβλήθην — to change, alter

Lesson 17

μοχθέω, μοχθήσω, ἐμόχθησα, ἐμόχθην	to work hard, toil
οἴομαι/οἶμαι, οἰήσομαι, ᾠήθην	to think, suppose, believe, consider
οἷός τε εἰμί	"I am able"
πειράω, πειράσω, ἐπείρασα, πεπείρακα, πεπείραμαι, ἐπειράθην	to try
σκοπέω, σκέψομαι, ἐσκεψάμην, ἔσκεμμαι	to look at, consider
χρή, χρήσει, ἐχρῆν (+ inf.)	it is necessary to

Adjectives

ἀδυνατός, ἀδυνατόν	impossible
δυνατός, δυνάτη, δυνατόν	possible
εὔνους, εὔνουν	kind, well-disposed
οἷος, οἷα, οἷον	such
ῥᾴδιος, ῥᾴδια, ῥᾴδιον	easy

Adverbs

δή	indeed
καὶ δή καὶ	and especially
νῦν	now

Lesson 18

Non-finite Noun Clauses:

Indirect Perception

Indirect Command and Indirect Statement

Irregular Verb: φημί

The Greek dependent clauses introduced so far have functioned as adverbial or adjectival modifiers, with one exception, the indefinite relative clause, which functions as the syntactic equivalent of a noun. Other noun clauses introduced in this lesson are speech acts changed from **direct** into **indirect** form. For example, in S18.3, "Clearchus was riding through" is changed to "Clearchus riding through." The noun clauses introduced in this lesson are non-finite. In the following lesson finite dependent noun clauses will be introduced.

The clauses introduced in this lesson are the **participial noun clause**, whose verb is a participle, and the **infinitive noun clause**, whose verb is in the form of an infinitive. These noun clauses *always* have a subject different from that of the governing kernel; the subject of these noun clauses is *never* in the nominative. It is mostly in the accusative case, but may be in the dative or genitive case.

Basic Sentences

18.1 ἀλλ' ἐγὼ παύσω τοῦτο γιγνόμενον.

But I will stop this from happening. — Plato

18.2 καὶ δείξω αὐτὸν πολλῶν θανάτων οὐχ ἑνὸς ὄντ' ἄξιον.

I will show him worthy of dying many times, not just once. — Demosthenes

18.3 τῶν δὲ Μένωνος στρατιωτῶν τις εἶδε Κλέαρχον διελαύνοντα.

One of Menon's soldiers saw Clearchus riding through. — Xenophon (adapted)

18.4 ἤκουσαν αὐτοῦ φωνήσαντος.

They heard him speak. — Xenophon

Lesson 18

18.5 δοῦλον ἐῶσι ποιεῖν ἃ βούλεται, σὲ δὲ διακωλύουσιν;

(The parents) allow a slave to do what he wants, but do they prevent you ∅ from doing what you want? Plato (adapted)

18.6 καὶ οἱ ἀγαθοὶ πάντα τὰ κέρδη βούλονται ἔχειν;

Don't good men, too, want to have every advantage? Plato (adapted)

18.7 νόμιζε δ' εἰ σὺ φιλεῖς τὴν ψυχήν, φιλεῖν ἅπαντας.

Consider that, if you love your life, everyone loves ∅ theirs.

18.8 χαίρεις ὁρῶν τὸ φῶς; πατέρα δ'οὐ χαίρειν δοκεῖς;

You rejoice seeing the daylight? Don't you think that your father also rejoices ∅ seeing it? Euripides

18.9 ἐκ τούτου ἀντιστάμενοι πάντες ἔλεγον τοὺς τούτων ἄρξαντας δίκην δοῦναι.

Rising up at this, all demanded that the ringleaders should suffer punishment. Xenophon (adapted)

Indirect Perception

Semantically a clause consisting of a governing verb of knowing or perceiving and a participial noun clause expresses **indirect perception**. Here is a partial list of verbs that raise the expectation of a clause of indirect perception:

αἰσθάνομαι	notice
ἀκούω (+ gen.)	hear (as in S18.4)
ὁράω	see (as in S18.3)
γιγνώσκω	recognize, become aware
εὑρίσκω	find
οἶδα	know
ἐπίσταμαι	understand
μέμνημαι	remember
πυνθάνομαι	find out, learn

Lesson 18

A participial noun clause may also be expected as direct object of a few governing verbs with the semantic feature "cause."

παύω	cause to stop (as in S18.1)
δείκνυμι	show, cause to appear (as in S18.2)
φαίνω	show, cause to appear

Without a participial noun clause, these verbs may have a different meaning.

Kernel Information

S18.1 has been entered into the kernel chart below as an example.

Clause Markers	*Item: function*	*Item: function*	*Item: function*	*KT*	*M D*	*F/ N*	*Adj Adv. Noun*	*Label*
	ἐγώ: Subject	παύσω: Verb	τοῦτο γιγνόμενον: Direct Object	*Transitive*	*M*			*Statement*
P	τοῦτο: Subject	γιγνόμενον: Verb		*Intrans.*	*D*	*N*	*Noun*	

♦Exercise 1

Copy the principal parts of the following verbs from the Principle Parts in the Reference section.

1. δείκνυμι
2. ὁράω
3. εὑρίσκω
4. οἶδα
5. πυνθάνομαι
6. ἐπίσταμαι

♦Exercise 2

Copy the participial kernels from S18.1–4.

♦Exercise 3

Copy three participial kernels from the Readings.

Lesson 18

♦ Exercise 4

Enter both the governing and the participial kernels for your sentences into a kernel chart. For the participial kernels put P in the clause marker column.

Indirect Command and Indirect Statement

Semantically sentences consisting of a verb of desiring, ordering, preventing, etc. and an infinitive noun clause express **indirect command**. Here is a partial list of verbs that raise the expectation of an indirect command:

βούλομαι	wish (as in S18.6)
θέλω, ἐθέλω	wish
ἐπιθυμέω	desire
ἐάω	allow (as in S18.5)
κελεύω	order
κωλύω	prevent
ἀναγκάζω	force, compel
λέγω	demand (as in S18.9)

Semantically sentences consisting of a verb of saying, thinking, etc. and an infinitive noun clause express **indirect statement**. Here is a partial list of verbs that raise the expectation of an indirect statment:

νομίζω	hold as customary, suppose, consider (S18.7)
δοκέω	think (S18.8)
οἴομαι	think
ἡγέομαι	believe, hold, suppose
λέγω	say, tell that
φημί	say, tell that
ἀγγέλλω	announce

Lesson 18

Kernel Information

Indirect commands and indirect statements are syntactic equivalents, distinguished only by the semantic range of their governing verbs. For this reason their kernel structures will look identical. R18.7 has been entered into the kernel chart below as an example.

Clause Markers	*Item: function*	*Item: function*	*Item: function*	*KT*	*M/D*	*F/ N*	*Adj Adv. Noun*	*Label*
	νομίζω: Verb	ὑμᾶς ἐμοὶ εἶναι καὶ φίλους καί συμμάχους: Direct Object		*TA*	*M*			*Statement*
I	ὑμᾶς: Subject	εἶναι:Verb	φίλους, συμμάχους: Subject Complement	*L*	*D*	*N*	*Noun*	*Indirect Statement*

♦ Exercise 5

Copy the principal parts of all of the above verbs from the Vocabulary.

♦ Exercise 6

Copy the infinitive clauses from S18.5–8. Remember that the subject of an infinitive is in the accusative case. It may, of course, be Ø.

♦ Exercise 7

Copy two infinitive kernels from the Readings.

♦ Exercise 8

Enter both the governing and the infinitive kernel for your sentences into a kernel chart. For infinitive kernels put I in the clause marker column.

Lesson 18

Metaphrasing and Semantics

At this advanced stage, semantics and **pragmatics** (see Re-view) must be taken more and more into consideration when reading.

1. Semantically Greek sentences consisting of a verb of knowing or perceiving and a participial clause express **Indirect Perception**. English indirect perceptions appear either as **finite** clauses, "They see that he is coming," or as **non-finite** participial clauses, "They see him coming."
2. Semantically Greek sentences consisting of a verb of ordering or desiring and an infinitive noun clause express **Indirect Commands**. English indirect commands appear likewise as **non-finite** infinitive clauses, "They want him to come."
3. Semantically Greek sentences consisting of a verb of saying or thinking and an infinitive noun clause express **Indirect Statements**. English indirect statements, however, usually appear as **finite** clauses with the optional clause marker "that," "They say (that) he is coming," or with backshift "They said that he was coming."

Irregular Verb: φῆμι

		Present	*Imperfect*
Singular			
	First	φημί	ἔφην
	Second	φῄς, φής	ἔφης/ ἔφησθα
	Third	φησί	ἔφη
Plural			
	First	φαμέν	ἔφαμεν
	Second	φατέ	ἔφατε
	Third	φασί	ἔφασαν

Infinitive

φάναι

Participle

φάσκων, φάσκουσα, φάσκον

Lesson 18

Readings

Remember to watch for non-finite noun clauses. Underline participial clauses. Double underline infinitive clauses.

18.1 ὁρῶμεν τὸν δοῦλον τρέχοντα.

18.2 ὁρῶμεν τὸν δοῦλον τὸν τρέχοντα.

18.3 οἱ Ἕλληνες οὐκ ᾔδεσαν Κῦρον τεθνηκότα.[1] Xenophon

18.4 Περικλῆς ἔγνω τὴν εἰσβολὴν ἐσομένην. Thucydides

18.5 ἐπιδείξω τοῦτον μάρτυρας ψευδεῖς παρεχόμενον. Demosthenes

18.6 τοὺς φυγάδας ἐκέλευσε σὺν αὐτῷ στρατεύεσθαι. Xenophon

18.7 νομίζω ὑμᾶς ἐμοὶ εἶναι καὶ φίλους καὶ συμμάχους. Xenophon

Practice Sentences

1. δεικνύναι βουλόμεθα Σωκράτην τῆς μεγίστης τιμῆς ἄξιον ὄντα.
2. οἱ πολλοὶ νομίζουσι τοὺς θεοὺς τὰ μὲν εἰδέναι, τὰ δὲ οὐκ εἰδέναι.
3. οἱ μὲν δικαίοι οὐκ ἀδικεῖν, οἱ δὲ ἄδικοι ἐπίστανται.
4. ἃ δ' ἐν δόμοις ἔδρασε, θαυμάσει κλύων. ἐπεὶ γὰρ ᾖσθε θ' ἡμέραν τὴν κυρίαν ἤκουσαν, ... ἤκουσα αὐτῆς φωνησάσης.

Lesson Vocabulary

Nouns

Ἕλληνες, Ἑλλήνων, οἱ — Greeks
θάνατος, θανάτου, ὁ — death.
μάρτυς, μάρτυρος, ὁ — witness
Μένων, Μένωνος, ὁ — Menon
Περικλῆς, Περικλοῦς, ὁ — Pericles
σύμμαχος, συμμάχου, ὁ — ally
φυγάς, φυγάδος, ὁ — fugitive, exile

---

[1] τεθνηκότα is accusative singular masculine of the perfective participle of (ἀπο)θνῄσκω.

Lesson 18

Verbs

ἀναγκάζω, ἀναγκάσω, ἠνάγκασα, ἠνάγκακα, ἠνάγνκασμαι, ἠναγκάσθην	to force, compel
ἀνίστημι, ἀναστήσω, ἀνέστησα/ἀνέστην, ἀνέστηκα	to make to stand up, stir up; Mid. to stand up, rise
διακωλύω, διακωλύσω, διεκώλυσα, διακεκώλυκα, διακεκώλυμαι, διεκωλύθην	to hinder, forbid, stop from
διελαύνω, διελῶ, διήλασα, διελήλακα, διελήλαμαι, διηλάθην	to ride through
ἐάω, ἐάσω, εἴασα, εἴακα, εἴαμαι, εἰάθην	to let, allow
ἐπιδείκνυμι, ἐπιδείξω, ἐπέδειξα, ἐπιδέδειγμαι, ἐπεδείχθην	to exhibit
ἡγέομαι, ἡγήσομαι, ἡγησάμην, ἥγημαι, ἡγήθην	to believe
μιμνήσκομαι, μνήσομαι, ἐμνησάμην, μέμνημαι, ἐμνήσθην	to remember (μέμνημαι is used for the present)
παρέχω/παρέχομαι, παρασχήσω, παρέσχον, παρέεσχηκα, παρέσχημαι,	to produce, present
στρατεύω, στρατεύσομαι, ἐστράτευσα, ἐστράτευμαι, ἐστρατεύθην	to serve in war
φωνέω, φωνήσω, ἐφώνησα, πεφώνηκα, ἐφωνήθην	to speak

Lesson 19

More on Finite Noun Clauses:

Indirect Question

Indirect Perception

Indirect Statement and Indirect Command

More on Adverbial Modification

Irregular Verb: εἶμι

The noun clauses introduced in Lesson 18 were non-finite clauses: their verbs were participles or infinitives. Greek, like English, also has finite noun clauses. This lesson introduces the finite clause, **indirect question**. This lesson also introduces finite variants of the **indirect perception, indirect statement** and **indirect command.**

Basic Sentences

19.1 **ἠρώτων ὅ τι ἐστὶν τὸ πρᾶγμα.**

I kept asking what the matter was. Xenophon

19.2 **ᾔδει δὲ οὐδεὶς ὅποι στρατεύουσιν.**

Nobody knew where they were marching to. Thucydides

19.3 **Ἆγις ὁ Ἀρχιδάμου ἐρωτηθεὶς τί μάλιστα μάθημα ἐν Σπάρτῃ ἀσκεῖται "Τὸ γιγνώσκειν," ἔφη, "ἄρχειν τε καὶ ἄρχεσθαι."**

Agis, son of Achidamos, when he was asked what lesson was especially drilled in Sparta, said, "To know how to rule and how to be ruled." Plutarch

19.4 **εἰ μὲν δὴ δίκαια ποιήσω οὐκ οἶδα.**

I don't know whether I shall do just deeds. Xenophon

19.5 **διηρώτα τὸν Κῦρον πότερον βούλεται μένειν ἢ ἀπιέναι.**

She kept asking Cyrus whether he wanted to stay or to go away. Xenophon (adapted)

Lesson 19

19.6 Συέννεσις ᾔσθετο ὅτι τὸ Μένωνος στράτευμα ἤδη ἐν Κιλικίᾳ ἦν.

Syennesis realized that Menon's army was already in Cilicia. Xenophon (adapted)

19.7 οὗτοι ἔλεγον ὅτι Κῦρος τέθνηκε.

These men continued to say that Cyrus was dead. Xenophon

19.8 μέμνησο[1] νέος ὢν ὡς γέρων ἔσῃ ποτέ.

Remember when you are young, that you will be old at some time. Menander

The Indirect Question

Syntax

A finite clause marked by a question-word as clause marker is called an **indirect question**. Like other noun clauses the indirect question may be expected as either the subject or object of verbs meaning "to ask", such as ἐρωτάω. Other verbs meaning to "say", "think", "know", or "perceive" may also raise the expectation of an indirect question. See the lists of Greek verbs in Lessons 17 and 18.

Here is a partial list of question-words. Those in the left column signal direct or indirect questions; those in the right column signal only indirect questions.

	Direct / Indirect	*Indirect*
Pronouns/Adjectives	who?	τίς, ὅστις
	what?	τί, ὅ τι
	which of two?	πότερος, ὁπότερος
	how much/many?	πόσος, ὁπόσος/ὅσος
	what sort of?	ποῖος, ὁποῖος/ποῖος
Adverbs	where?	ποῦ/πόθι, ὅπου/ὁπόθι
	from where	πόθεν, ὁπόθεν
	to where?	ποῖ, ὅποι
	when?	πότε, ὁπότε
	why?	διὰ τί, δι' ὅτι
	how?	πῶς, ὅπως

[1] μέμνησο is command. See Lesson 21.

Lesson 19

Introducing yes-or-no questions	expecting yes	οὐ, ἆρ’οὐ, οὐκοῦν, ἄλλο τι ἤ
	expecting no	μη, μὴ οὖν, μῶν, μῶν μή
	whether? if?	εἰ
	whether? or?	πότερον...ἢ, εἴτε...εἴτε, εἰ...ἤ,

Note:

Occasionally a relative pronoun seems to introduce an indirect question. Plato, in *Protagoras* 312B, uses the relative pronoun ὅ where the reader might expect ὅ τι: οἶσθα ὃ μέλλεις...πράττειν; "Do you know what you are about to do?"

Metaphrasing

Indirect questions do not pose any special problems for metaphrasing. When the governing verb is in a past tense, it is helpful to metaphrase with the English backshift as, in S19.1, "I kept on asking what **was** the matter." This sentence could also be metaphrased without backshift as, "I kept on asking, 'What **is** the matter?'"

♦ Exercise 1

Copy the indirect questions from the Basic Sentences. Indicate whether they function as subject or as object in the main kernel.

Indirect Perception and Statement

A finite noun clause marked by ὅτι or ὡς is called **indirect perception** or **indirect statement**. This construction corresponds exactly to English noun clauses marked by "that." These clauses function syntactically as the subject or object of verbs meaning to "say,", "think," "know," or perceive." They also function as the subject of impersonal expressions such as δῆλόν ἐστι "it is clear that." See the lists of Greek verbs and impersonal expressions in Lessons 17 and 18. Note that if the governing kernel is complete, **ὅτι** may introduce an adverbial causal clause.

Indirect Command

A finite noun clause marked by **ὅπως (μὴ)** is called an **indirect command**. Such clauses may function as either the subject or object of verbs meaning to "desire," or "command." See the list of Greek verbs in Lesson 18.

Lesson 19

♦Exercise 2

Write four Greek sentences. Choose a governing verb from the lists in Lessons 17 and 18, and combine it with a Basic Sentence from Lessons 1-6, in order to make an indirect statement or indirect perception. Then translate each sentence. For example:

οἶδα ὅτι ἀεὶ καλῶς βάλλει τὸν κύβον Ζεύς.
I know that Zeus always throws the die successfully.

♦Exercise 3

Replace the finite noun clauses in each of your sentences with a non-finite clause. Be careful about the difference between participial and infinitive noun clauses in regard to the semantics of the governing verb. For example:

οἶδα ἀεὶ καλῶς βάλλοντα τὸν κύβον Δία.
I know that Zeus always throws the die successfully.

♦Exercise 4

Enter all kernels from S19.1-19.5 into a kernel chart.

♦Exercise 5

Identify the governing verbs from S19.1-19.5 by person, number, tense (= aspect + time) and voice.

♦Exercise 6

Identify the verbs of the indirect questions in S19.1-19.5 by person, number, tense (= aspect + time) and voice.

♦Exercise 7

Enter both finite and non-finite kernels from the following passage from Plato's *Lysis* into a kernel chart. Then translate. Socrates is speaking:

νῦν μὲν καταγέλαστοι γεγόναμεν, ἐγώ τε γέρων ὤν καὶ ὑμεῖς.
ἐροῦσι γὰρ οἵδε ἀπιόντες ὅτι οἰόμεθα ἡμεῖς ἀλλήλων φίλοι εἶναι·
οὔπω δὲ ὅ τι ἔστιν ὁ φίλος οἷοί τε ἐσμὲν ἐξευρεῖν.

καταγέλαστος, καταγέλαστον	ridiculous
ἀλλήλων	of each other
ἐξ-ευρίσκω, ἐξ-ευρήσω, ἐξ-ηῦρον	discover

LESSON 19

More on Adverbial Modification

Adverbial Accusative

In addition to the semantic categories of place and time, the adverbial accusative may also express a general limitation, especially on adjectives and certain verbs. This adverbial accusative is often called the **accusative of respect**. Words describing an emotion or physical or mental quality and words with the semantic features good/bad and like/unlike raise the expectation of an accusative of respect. For example, ὁ ἄνθρωπος τὸν δάκτυλον ἀλγεῖ, "the person hurts in (respect to) his finger," πάντα κακός, "(he is) evil in all respects."

Irregular Verb εἶμι

The irregular verb εἶμι, "go" occurs only in the present and imperfect tenses.

		Present	*Imperfect*
Singular			
	First person	εἶμι	ᾖα, ᾔειν
	Second person	εἶ	ᾔεις, ᾔειθα
	Third person	εἶσι	ᾔει, ᾔειν
Plural			
	First person	ἴμεν	ᾖμεν
	Second person	ἴτε	ᾖτε
	Third person	ἴασι	ᾖσαν, ᾔεσαν

Infinitive

ἰέναι

Participle

ἰών, ἰοῦσα, ἰόν

Readings

19.1 εἶπόν τινες ὅτι νῆες ἐπιπλέουσιν. Thucydides

19.2 καὶ Σωκράτης "Ἐγὼ" ἔφη, "ἐπιμελεῖσθαι Θεοὺς νομίζω ἀνθρώπων οὐχ ὃν τρόπον οἱ πολλοὶ νομίζουσιν. οὗτοι μὲν γὰρ οἴονται τοὺς Θεοὺς τὰ μὲν εἰδέναι, τὰ δὲ οὐκ εἰδέναι. ἐγὼ δὲ πάντα μὲν οἶμαι Θεοὺς εἰδέναι, τά τε λεγόμενα καὶ πραττόμενα καὶ τὰ σιγῇ βουλευόμενα, πανταχοῦ δὲ παρεῖναι

Lesson 19

καὶ σημαίνειν τοῖς ἀνθρώποις περὶ τῶν ἀνθρωπείων πάντων."

Xenophon

19.3 ὅ τι μὲν ὑμεῖς, ὦ ἄνδρες Ἀθηναῖοι,[1] πεπόνθατε ὑπὸ τῶν ἐμῶν κατηγόρων οὐκ οἶδα. Plato

19.4 ἐρωτηθεὶς ὑπὸ Διονυσίου διὰ τί οἱ μὲν φιλόσοφοι ἐπὶ τὰς τῶν πλουσίων θύρας ἔρχονται, οἱ δὲ πλούσιοι ἐπὶ τὰς τῶν φιλοσόφων οὐκέτι, ἔφη ὅτι οἱ μὲν ἴσασιν ὧν δέονται, οἱ δ' οὐκ ἴσασιν. Aristippus

19.5 τίς δ' οἶδεν εἰ τὸ ζῆν μὲν ἔστι κατθανεῖν, τὸ κατθανεῖν δὲ ζῆν νομίζεται βρότοις; Euripides

19.6 πολλάκις ἀκήκοά σου λέγοντος ὅτι ταῦτα ἀγαθὸς ἕκαστος ἡμῶν, ἅπερ σοφός, ἃ δὲ ἀμαθής, ταῦτα δὲ κακός. Plato

19.7 τίς πόθεν εἷς[2] ἀνδρῶν, πόθι τοι πόλις ἠδὲ τοκῆες,
ὁπποίης τ' ἐπὶ νηὸς ἀφίκεο, πῶς δέ σε ναῦται
ἤγαγον εἰς Ἰθάκην, τίνες ἔμμεναι εὐχετόωντο; Homer

Practice Sentences

1. ἠρώτησέ τις τὸν Ἀρέστιππον διὰ τί οἱ μὲν φιλόσοφοι ἐπὶ τὰς τῶν πλουσίων οἰκίας ἔρχονται, οἱ δὲ πλούσιοι ἐπί τὰς φιλοσόφων οὐκέτι. "ὅτι," ἔφη, "οἱ μὲν ἴσασι ὧν δέονται, οἱ δὲ οὔ."
2. οὔπω δῆλον ἦν τί ποιήσουσιν οἱ ἄλλοι.

Lesson Vocabulary

Nouns

Ἆγις, Ἄγεως, ὁ	Agis
Ἀρχιδᾶμος, Ἀρχιδάμου, ὁ	Archidamus
Διονύσιος, Διονυσίου, ὁ	Dionysius
θύρα, θύρας, ἡ	door
Ἰθάκη, Ἰθάκης, ἡ	Ithaca
κατήγορος, κατηγόρου, ὁ	accuser

---

[1] ὦ ἄνδρες Ἀθηναῖοι is in the vocative case. The vocative is used for direct address. See Lesson 21.
[2] εἷς is a second person singular form of εἰμί.

LESSON 19

Κιλικία, Κιλικίας, ἡ	Cilicia
μάθημα, μάθηματος, τό	lesson, subject
ναῦς, νεώς, ἡ (*plural*: αἱ νῆες)	ship
πρᾶγμα, πράγματος, τό	thing, matter
Σπάρτη, Σπάρτης, ἡ	Sparta
στράτευμα, στρατεύματος, τό	army, campaign
Συέννεσις, Συέννεσεως, ὁ	Suennesis
τοκῆες, τοκήων, οἱ (Attic form = τοκεῖς)	parents

Verbs

αἰσθάνομαι, αἰσθήσομαι, ᾐσθόμην, ᾔσθημαι	to perceive, notice
ἄπειμι, ἀπέσομαι, ἀπῆν	to go away
ἀσκέω, ἀσκήσω, ἤσκησα, ἤσκηκα, ἤσκημαι	to train, drill
ἀφικνέομαι, ἀφίξομαι, ἀφικόμην, ἀφῖγμαι; ἀφίκεο command form	to have come, arrive
δῆλον ἐστι	is clear
ἔμμεναι, Attic εἶναι infinitve	to be
ἐπιμελέομαι, ἐπιμελήσομαι, ἐπιμελησάμην, ἐπιμεμέλημαι, ἐπεμελήθην (+ gen.)	to take care of
ἐπιπλέω, ἐπιπλεύσομαι, ἐπέπλευσα	to approach, to sail upon
ἐρωτάω, ἐρωτήσω, ἠρώτησα, ἠρώτηκα, εὐχετάομαι	to ask
εὐχετόωντο, Attic εὐχετάοντο	"they boasted"
καταθνῄσκω, καταθανέομαι, κατέθανον, κατατέθνηκα	to die
μέμνησο, command form of, μέμνημαι,	to remember
πάρειμι, παρέσομαι, παρῆν	to be present
πάσχω, πείσομαι, ἔπαθον, πέπονθα	to suffer, experience
σημαίνω, σημανῶ, ἐσήμηνα, σεσήμασμαι, ἐσημάνθην	to give signals

Adjectives

ἄλλος, ἄλλη, ἄλλο	other, another
ἀνθρώπειος, ἀνθρωπεία, ἀνθρώπειον	human
ἀμαθής, ἀμαθές	ignorant
δῆλος, δήλη, δῆλον	clear
ἐμός, ἐμή, ἐμόν	mine, my
ὅσπερ, ἥπερ, ὅπερ	which

Lesson 19

Adverbs	
ἤδη	already, now
ὃν τρόπον	in which manner = in the manner in which
ὅποι	where
οὐκέτι	no longer
οὔπω	not yet
πανταχοῦ	everywhere
πόθι	where?
πολλάκις	often, many times
ποτέ	at some time
πότερον ...ἤ	whether...or
Prepositions	
ἐπί + accusative	to
ἐπί + dative	in addition to, near
ἐπί + genitive	on
Connectors	
ἠδέ	and
Clause Markers	
ὅτι	that
Indeclinables	
τοι	indeed

Lesson 20

The Genitive Absolute: A Non-Finite Adverbial Clause

Adverbial clauses introduced in Lesson 11 were dependent clauses with finite verbs. This lesson introduces a non-finite adverbial clause called the **genitive absolute**, which uses a circumstantial participle and a noun, both in the genitive case.

Basic Sentences

20.1 **Κῦρος δ' οὖν ἀνέβη ἐπὶ τὰ ὄρη οὐδενὸς κωλύοντος.**

So Cyrus went up to the mountains with no one hindering him. Xenophon

20.2 **πολλοὶ γὰρ κατέβησαν καὶ ἅτε θεωμένων τῶν ἑταίρων πολλὴ φιλονικία ἐγίγνετο.**

For many came and, because their comrades were watching, much competition was going on. Xenophon

20.3 **παρήγγειλε τοῖς φρουράρχοις λαμβάνειν ἄνδρας Πελοποννησίους ὡς ἐπιβουλεύοντος Τισσαφέρνους ταῖς πόλεσιν.**

He ordered the captains to hire men from the Peloponnesus, on the grounds that Tissaphernes was plotting against the cities. Xenophon

20.4 **καὶ χρήματα πολλὰ προσλαβὼν οὕτως, ἀποπλεῖ οἴκαδε καίπερ μέσου χειμῶνος ὄντος.**

And, having acquired much money in this way, he sailed home even though it was mid-winter. Xenophon (adapted)

The Genitive Absolute: A Non-Finite Adverbial Clause

The word "genitive" in the name genitive absolute is descriptive in that both the subject of the participle and the participle are in the genitive case. As in adjectival participial clauses, the subject functions as the nounhead of the participle. For example, in S20.1 οὐδενός κωλύοντος, the genitive οὐδενός is the subject of the genitive participle κωλύοντος.

Lesson 20

Like any kernel the genitive absolute can be transitive, intransitive, linking, factitive, passive or special intransitive.

Genitive absolutes are the syntactic equivalents of finite adverbial clauses and have the same semantic interpretations. Thus οὐδενὸς κωλύοντος can be interpreted as:

ἐπεὶ οὐδεὶς ἐκώλυε ∅=αὐτόν	"when no one hindered ∅=him"
εἰ οὐδεὶς ἐκώλυε ∅=αὐτόν	"if no one hindered ∅=him"
ὅτι οὐδεὶς ἐκώλυε ∅=αὐτόν	"because no one hindered ∅=him"
καὶ εἰ οὐδεὶς ἐκώλυε ∅=αὐτόν	"although no one hindered ∅=him"

The correct interpretation depends on comprehension of the context. As the name "absolute" (meaning "detached") indicates, this construction is a separate clause. The genitive absolute and the governing clause do not, as a rule, have a noun in common. The subject of the genitive absolute is almost always expressed, and the participle is usually found nearby. Greek also has another similar construction called the accusative absolute which will be introduced briefly in Lesson 26.

Notice that the exact nature of the relationship between the genitive absolute and the governing clause is sometimes overtly indicated by means of particles. ἅτε in S20.2 indicates cause, καίπερ in S20.4 indicates concession, and ὡς in S20.3 indicates an assumption. However, ὡς can also signal many other relationships. See Lesson 26.

Without a special clause marker a genitive absolute containing a progressive participle usually indicates *time during which,* and a genitive absolute containing an aorist participle indicates *time after which.*

Note: The Genitive Absolute is *never* the object of a preposition.

♦ Exercise 1

Enter the genitive absolutes from the Basic Sentences into a kernel chart. Under Clause Marker put the participial clause marker P.

♦ Exercise 2

Copy the genitive absolutes from the R20.1-7 and name their kernel types.

♦ Exercise 3

Metaphrase the above genitive absolutes from the Readings.

Lesson 20

Readings

20.1 θεοῦ θέλοντος δύνατα ταῦτα γίγνεται.

20.2 καὶ Πολυφόντους κελεύοντος ἐκχωρεῖν...Οἰδίπους Πολυφόντην καὶ Λάιον ἀπέκτεινε. Apollodorus

20.3 πῶς δίκης οὔσης ὁ Ζεὺς οὐκ ἀπόλωλεν;

20.4 Ἀστερίου δὲ ἀποθανόντος Μίνως βασιλεύειν θέλων Κρήτης ἐκωλύετο.

Apollodorus

20.5 μιᾶς γὰρ κοπτομένης κεφαλῆς δύο ἀνεφύοντο. Apollodorus

20.6 ἀποτμηθείσης δὲ τῆς κεφαλῆς, ἐκ τῆς Γοργοῦ ἐξέθορε Πήγασος.

20.7 (Θάνατος ἔφη) νέων φθινόντων μεῖζον ἄρνυμαι γέρας. Euripides

20.8 ἦ μὴν σὺ παύσῃ καίπερ ὠμὸς ὢν ἄγαν.
τοῖος Φέρητος εἶσι πρὸς δόμους ἀνὴρ,
Εὐρυσθέως πέμψαντος ἵππειον μέτα
ὄχημα Θρῄκης ἐκ τόπων δυσχειμερίων
ὃς δὴ ξενωθεὶς τοῖς δ' ἐν' Αδμήτου δόμοις
βίᾳ γυναῖκα τήνδε σ' ἐξαιρήσεται. Euripides

Practice Sentences

1. εἰρήνης οὔσης, ὁ γεωργὸς κἀν πέτρᾳ καλῶς τρέφεται.
2. τί δὲ βίος, τί δὲ τερπνὸν, παρελθούσης ἥβης;
3. ταῦτα οὖν ἡμῶν λεγόντων ἀφίκετο ὁ Κτήσιππος.

LESSON 20

Lesson Vocabulary

Nouns

Ἄδμητος, Ἀδμήτου, ὁ	Admetus
Ἀστέριος, Ἀστερίου, ὁ	Asterius
βία, βίας, ἡ	force
γέρας, γέραος, τό	prize, honor
Γοργώ, Γοργοῦς, ἡ	Gorgon
δόμος, δόμου, ὁ	house; pl. palace
Εὐρυσθεύς, Εὐρυσθέως, ὁ	Eurystheus
Θρῄκη, Θρῄκης, ἡ	Thrace
κεφαλή, κεφαλῆς, ἡ	head
Κρήτη, Κρήτης, ἡ	Crete
Λάιος, Λάιου, ὁ	Laius
Μίνως, Μίνωος, ὁ	Minos
Οἰδίπους, Οἰδίποδος, ὁ	Oedipus
ὄρος, ὄρους, τό	mountain
ὄχημα, ὀχήματος, τό	chariot
Πελοποννήσιος, Πελοποννησίου, ὁ	a Peloponnesian
Πήγασος, Πηγάσου, ὁ	Pegasus
Πολυφόντης, Πολυφόντους, ὁ	Polyphontes
Τισσαφέρνης, Τισσαφέρνους, ὁ	Tissaphernes
τόπος, τόπου, ὁ	place
Φέρης, Φέρους, ὁ	Pheres
φιλονικία, φιλονικίας, ἡ	competition
φρούραρχος, φρουράρχου, ὁ	captain
χειμών, χειμῶνος, ὁ	winter, stormy weather
χρῆμα, χρήματος τό	goods, money

Verbs

ἀναβαίνω, ἀναβήσομαι, ἀνέβην, ἀναβέβηκα	to go up
ἀναφύομαι, ἀνέφυν	to grow again, back
ἀποκτείνω, ἀποκτενῶ, ἀπέκτεινα, ἀπέκτονα	to kill
ἀπόλλυμαι, ἀπολοῦμαι, ἀπωλόμην, ἀπόλωλα	to perish
ἀποτέμνω, ἀποτεμῶ, ἀπέτεμον, ἀποτέτμηκα, ἀπετμήθην	to cut off, slay
ἄρνυμαι, ἀροῦμαι, ἀρόμην,	(defective verb) to win, gain, receive
ἐκθρώσκω, ἐκθοροῦμαι, ἐξέθορον	to jump out

Lesson 20

ἐκχωρέω, ἐξεχωρήσω, ἐξεχώρησα	to depart
ἐξαιρέομαι, ἐξελοῦμαι, ἐξειλόμην, ἐξῄρημαι, ἐξῃρέθην (+ 2 acc.)	to rob somebody of something
ἐπιβουλεύω, ἐπιβουλεύσω, ἐπεβούλευσα, ἐπεβουλεύκα, ἐπεβούλευμαι, ἐπεβουλεύθην (+ dat.)	to plot against
θεάομαι, θεάσομαι, ἐθεασάμην, τεθέαμαι, ἐθεάθην	to view, watch
καταβαίνω, καταβήσομαι, κατέβην, καταβέβηκα	to go down
κόπτω, κόψω, ἔκοψα, κέκοφα, κέκομμαι, ἐκόπην	to strike, hit
κωλύω, κωλύσω, ἐκώλυσα, κεκώλυκα, κεκώλυμαι, ἐκωλύθην	to prevent, hinder
ξενόω, ξενώσω, ἐξένωμαι, ἐξενώθην	to host
πέμπω, πέμψω, ἔπεμψα, πέπομφα, πέπεμμαι, ἐπέμφθην	to send
προσλαμβάνω, προσλήψομαι, προσέλαβον, προσείληφα, προσλελάβηκα	to take/receive in addition, to make gains
φθίνω, φθίσομαι, ἐφθίμην, ἔφθιμαι	to waste away, wither, decline

Adjectives

δυσχείμερος, δυσχείμερον	disagreeably cold, wintry
ἵππειος, ἱππεία, ἵππειον	of a horse
ὠμός, ὠμή, ὠμόν	cruel

Adverbs

ἄγαν	too much, too
ἦ μήν	surely
οἴκαδε	homeward

Review 4

♦ Exercise 1

Define each of the terms below in your own words. Give a Greek example where appropriate.

Lesson 16

- Comparative
- Correlative pairs
- Degree
- Positive
- Superlative

Lesson 17

- Articular infinitive
- Complementary infinitive
- Gerund
- Impersonal expression
- Mode

Lesson 18

- Indirect Command
- Indirect Perception
- Indirect Statement
- Noun clause

Lesson 19

- Indirect Question

Lesson 20

- Genitive absolute

♦ Exercise 2

Translate into Greek.

16.1 Nothing is better than a true friend.

16.2 Socrates is the wisest because he is aware that he knows nothing.

17.1 For teachers it is necessary to understand the concerns of those who learn.

17.2 If you are trying to do what you want, you will often do what you don't want.

19.1 Did you yourself hear Socrates speak?

19.2 Do your parents want to prevent you from doing what you want?

20.1 The soldiers do not realize what Cyrus will do.

20.2 We want to know from where you have come, who your parents are and what you intend to do.

20.3 The Eleven ordered Socrates to drink the poison since the boat had arrived.

"Ενδεκα, οἱ· the eleven

Required Vocabulary

Lesson 16

Nouns

ἀναρχία, ἀναρχίας, ἡ	disorder
Πυθία, Πυθίας, ἡ	the Pythia, the medium uttering the prophecies in the oracle of Apollo at Delphi

Verbs

ἁμαρτάνω, ἁμαρτήσομαι, ἥμαρτον, ἡμάρτηκα, ἡμάρτημαι, ἡμαρτήθην	to do wrong
γιγνώσκω, γνώσομαι, ἔγνων, ἔγνωκα, ἔγνωσμαι, ἐγνώσθην	to become aware, recognize
γνῶθι	aorist imperative of γιγνώσκω
δεῖ, δεήσει, ἐδέησε (+ inf.)	it is necessary (to)
δοκέω, δόξω, ἔδοξα, δέδογμαι	to seem, think
εἰδέναι	infinitive of οἶδα (to know)
εἰδώς	part. of οἶδα (to know)
οἴομαι, οἰήσομαι, ᾠήθην	to think, suppose, believe
πράττω, πράξω, ἔπραξα, πέπραχα, πέπραγμαι, ἐπράχθην	to do, achieve, manage

Adjectives

ἀμείνων, ἄμεινον	better (in courage)
ἄξιος, ἀξία, ἄξιον (+ gen.)	worthy of, guilty of
ἅπας, ἅπασα, ἅπαν	every, all, entire
ἄριστος, ἀρίστη, ἄριστον	best (in courage)
βελτίων, βέλτιον	better (morally)
βέλτιστος, βελτίστη, βέλτιστον	best (morally)
κρείττων, κρεῖττον	better (physically)
κράτιστος, κρατίστη, κράτιστον	best (physically)
αἰσχίων, αἴσχιον	more shameful

αἴσχιστος, αἰσχίστη, αἴσχιστον	most shameful
κακίων, κάκιον	worse
κάκιστος, κακίστη, κάκιστον	worst
χείρων, χεῖρον	weaker
χείριστος, χειρίστη, χείριστον	weakest
μείζων, μεῖζον	greater
μέγιστος, μεγίστη, μέγιστον	greatest
ἐλάττων, ἔλαττον	less, weaker
ἐλάχιστος, ἐλαχίστη, ἐλάχιστον	least, weakest
ἥττων, ἧττον	less, weaker
ἥκιστος, ἡκίστη, ἥκιστον	least, weakest
πλείων (πλέων), πλεῖον	more
πλεῖστος, πλείστη, πλεῖστον	most
θάττων, θάττον	swifter
τάχιστος, ταχίστη, τάχιστον	swiftest

Adverbs

μάλιστα	most
μᾶλλον	more

Pronouns

ἑαυτόν -ήν -όν	himself, herself, itself (reflexive)

Connector

ἤ	than

Correlatives

ὅσον...τόσον/τοσοῦτον	as much...as
οὕτως...ὥσπερ	thus/so...as
τοιοῦτος...ὅς/ὅστις/οἷος	such...as

Lesson 17

Nouns

ἥλιος, ἡλίου, ὁ	sun
θυμός, θυμοῦ, ὁ	will, will power
σιωπή, σιωπῆς, ἡ	silence
φῶς, φωτός, τό	light

Verbs

ἀνάγκη (ἐστιν)	is a need
δύναμαι, δυνήσομαι, ἐδυνησάμην, δεδύνημαι, ἐδυνήθην (+ inf.)	to be able to

ἔξεστιν (+ dat.)	is allowed
εὔχομαι, εὔξομαι, ηὐξάμην, ηὖγμαι,	to pray, boast
κελεύω, κελεύσω, ἐκέλευσα, κεκέλευκα, κεκέλευσμαι, ἐκελεύσθην	to command, to order
λείπω, λείψω, ἔλιπον, λέλοιπα, λέλειμμαι, ἐλείφθην	to leave
μανθάνω, μαθήσομαι, ἔμαθον, μεμάθηκα (+ inf.)	to learn to
μαρτυρέω, μαρτυρήσω, ἐμαρτύρησα, μεμαρτύρημαι, ἐμαρτυρήθην	to witness, to attest
οἶδα (+ inf.)	to know how to
πειράω, πειράσω, ἐπείρασα, πεπείρακα, πεπείραμαι, ἐπειράθην	to try
χρή, χρήσει, ἐχρῆν (+ inf.)	it is necessary to

Adjectives

εὔνους, εὔνουν	kind, well-being
ῥάδιος, ῥαδία, ῥάδιον	easy

Adverbs

νῦν	now

Lesson 18

Nouns

Ἕλληνες, Ἑλλήνων, οἱ	Greeks
μάρτυς, μάρτυρος, ὁ	witness
σύμμαχος, συμμάχου, ὁ	ally
φυγάς, φυγάδος, ὁ	fugitive, exile

Verbs

ἀναγκάζω, ἀναγκάσω, ἠνάγκασα, ἠνάγκακα, ἠνάγκασμαι, ἠναγκάσθην	to force, compel
διακωλύσω, διεκώλυσα, διακεκώλυκα, διακεκώλυμαι, διεκωλύθην	to hinder, forbid, stop from
διελαύνω, διελῶ, διήλασα, διελήλακα, διελήλαμαι, διηλάθην	to ride through
ἐάω, ἐάσω, εἴασα	to let, to allow
ἡγέομαι, ἡγήσομαι, ἡγησάμην, ἥγημαι, ἡγήθην	to believe

REVIEW 4

μιμνῄσκομαι, μνήσομαι, ἐμνησάμην, μέμνημαι, ἐμνήσθην	to remember
παρέχω/παρέχομαι, παρασχήσω, παρέσχον, παρέσχηκα, παρέσχημαι	to produce, present
φωνέω, φωνήσω, ἐφώνησα	to speak

Lesson 19

Nouns

θύρα, θύρας, ἡ	door
κατήγορος, κατηγόρου, ὁ	accuser
ναῦς, νεώς, ἡ pl. αἱ νῆες	ship
πρᾶγμα, πράγματος, τό	thing, matter

Verbs

αἰσθάνομαι, αἰσθήσομαι, ᾐσθόμην, ᾔσθημαι	to perceive, notice
ἄπειμι, ἀπέσομαι, ἀπῆν	to go away
ἐρωτάω/διερωτάω, ἐρωτήσω, ἠρώτησα	to ask
πάρειμι, παρέσομαι, παρῆν	to be present
πάσχω, πείσομαι, ἔπαθον, πέπονθα	to suffer, experience
σημαίνω, σημανῶ, ἐσήμηνα, σεσήμασκα, σεσήμασμαι, ἐσημάνθην	to give signals

Adjectives

ἄλλος, ἄλλη, ἄλλο	another
ἀμαθής, ἀμαθές	ignorant
ἐμός, ἐμή, ἐμόν	mine, my
ὅσπερ, ἥπερ, ὅπερ	which

Adverbs

ὃν τρόπον	in which manner = in the manner in which
οὐκέτι	no longer
οὔπω	not yet
πανταχοῦ	everywhere
πόθι;	where?
πολλάκις	often, many times
ποτέ	at some time

Prepositions

ἐπί + accusative	to

Review 4

ἐπί + dative	in addition to, near
ἐπί + genitive	on

Connectors

ἠδέ	and

Clause Markers

ὅτι	that

Lesson 20

Nouns

βία, βίας, ἡ	force
γέρας, γέραος, τό	prize, honor
δόμος, δόμου, ὁ	house; pl. palace
κεφαλή, κεφαλῆς, ἡ	head
ὄρος, ὄρους, τό	mountain
τόπος, τόπου, ὁ	place
χειμών, χειμῶνος, ἡ	winter, stormy weather
χρῆμα, χρήματος τό	goods, money

Verbs

ἀναβαίνω, ἀναβήσομαι, ἀνέβην, ἀναβέβηκα	to go up
ἀποκτείνω, ἀποκτενῶ, ἀπέκτεινα, ἀπέκτονα	to kill
ἀπόλλυμαι, ἀπολοῦμαι, ἀπωλόμην, ἀπόλωλα	to perish
ἀποτέμνω, ἀποτεμῶ, ἀπέτεμον, ἀποτέτμηκα, ἀπετμήθην	to cut off, slay
ἐξαιρέομαι, ἐξελοῦμαι, ἐξειλόμην, ἐξῄρημαι, ἐξῃρέθην (+ 2 accusatives)	to rob somebody of something
καταβαίνω, καταβήσομαι, κατέβην, καταβέβηκα	to go down
κόπτω, κόψω, ἔκοψα, κέκοφα, κέκομμαι, ἐκόπην	to strike, hit
θεάομαι, θεάσομαι, ἐθεασάμην, τεθέαμαι, ἐθεάθην	to view, watch
κωλύω, κωλύσω, ἐκώλυσα, κεκώλυκα, κεκώλυμαι, ἐκωλύθην	to prevent, hinder
ξενόω, ξενώσω, ἐξένωμαι, ἐξενώθην	to host
πέμπω, πέμψω, ἔπεμψα, πέπομφα, πέπεμμαι, ἐπέμφθην	to send

Review 4

προσλαμβάνω, προσλήψομαι, προσέλαβον, προσείληφα, προσλελάβηκα	to take/receive in addition, make gains

Adverbs

ἄγαν	too much, too

Answer Key

Lesson 16:

1. Nothing is stronger than philosophy.
2. No one is wiser than Socrates.
3. We all know that we are mortal.
4. Intelligent people do not stop learning.
5. This woman is the loveliest of all.

Lesson 17:

1. It is harder to change one's mind than one's appearance.
2. It is necessary to obey the laws of the city rather than the words of the tyrant.
3. Citizens are not allowed to neglect the concerns of the city.
4. It is necessary for good citizens to take care both of the affairs of their household and of the affairs of the city.
5. It seemed impossible to the Persians to invade Attica because many of them had died in the battle. Therefore it seemed good to the general to return home.
6. We cannot have everything that we want.
7. It is not possible for me to do what I want.

Lesson 18:

1. We want to show that Socrates was worthy of the greatest honor.
2. Most people believe that the gods know some things but not other things.
3. Just people do not know how to do wrong, but unjust people do.
4. But you will be astonished to hear what (Alcestis) did in the palace. For when she realized that the appointed date had come … I heard her saying ….

Review 4

Lesson 19:

1. Someone asked Aristippus why the philosophers go to the houses of the rich, but the rich no longer go to the houses of the philosophers. "Because," said he, "some know what they need and others do not."
2. It was not yet clear what the others would do.

Lesson 20:

1. When there is peace the farmer is well fed even on a rocky hill.
2. What is life, what is pleasure, when youth has passed?
3. While we were discussing these things, Ktesippos arrived.

Lesson 21

A New Mood: The Imperative

A Third Speech Act: Command

So far, speech acts have been statements and questions. This lesson introduces **commands**. The command given in "Annie, get your gun!" is "get your gun!" So far finite verb forms were in the **indicative mood**. Verb forms expressing a command are in the **imperative mood**. Two more moods will be introduced in the next lessons.

Basic Sentences

21.1 εἰ βούλει καλῶς ἀκούειν, μάνθανε καλῶς λέγειν.

If you want to be well spoken of, learn to speak well — Epictetus

21.2 μαθὼν δὲ καλῶς λέγειν πειρῶ καλῶς πράττειν, καὶ καρπώσῃ τὸ καλῶς ἀκούειν.

And having learned to speak well, strive also to act well; thus, you will succeed in being well spoken of. — Epictetus

21.3 εἰς Μύνδον ἐλθὼν καὶ θεασάμενος μεγάλας τὰς πύλας, (μικρὰν δὲ τὴν πόλιν), "ἄνδρες Μύνδιοι," ἔφη, "κλείσατε τὰς πύλας· πόλις ὑμῶν ἐξ·εῖσιν."

Arriving in Myndos and noticing that the gates were large, (but the city small), Diogenes said, "Men of Myndos, close the gates; your city is walking out!" — Diogenes (adapted)

21.4 ἴστω[1] νῦν εὐκλεής γε κατθανουμένη
γυνή τ'ἀρίστη τῶν ὑφ'ἡλίῳ μακρῷ.

Let Alcestis be aware (that she is going to) die with fair fame and as the best wife of those under the broad sun! — Euripides

21.5 ἃ μὴ προσήκει μήτ' ἄκουε μήθ' ὅρα.

Neither hear nor see things which are not fitting! — Menander

---

[1] ἴστω is a 3rd person singular imperative of the verb οἶδα. Third person imperatives will be learned in the second year.

Lesson 21

A New Mood: The Imperative

Morphology: The Imperative

In Greek the imperative has active, middle and passive forms, in the second and third person, singular and plural. However, commands to the third person are rare and they are not given in this book. The imperative may also occur in all three aspects: progressive, aorist and perfective.

Active			
Progressive			
	singular	λῦε	ποίει
	plural	λύετε	ποιεῖτε
Aorist			
	singular	λῦσον	ποίησον
	plural	λύσατε	ποιήσατε
Middle			
Progressive			
	singular	λύου	ποιοῦ
	plural	λύεσθε	ποιεῖσθε
Aorist			
	singular	λῦσαι	ποίησαι
	plural	λύσασθε	ποιήσασθε
Passive			
Progressive			
	singular	λύου	ποιοῦ
	plural	λύεσθε	ποιεῖσθε
Aorist			
	singular	λύθητι	ποιήθητι
	plural	λύθητε	ποιήθητε

For the aorist and perfective imperatives of -ω verbs, and the imperatives of -μι verbs, see Morphology.

Morphology: The Vocative Case

Most vocatives look like nominatives, often preceded by ὦ = English "oh." However, first declension singular masculine nouns end in {-α}, as in ὁ νεανίας: ὦ νεανίᾱ, and second declension singular masculine nouns end in {-ε}, as in ὁ ἄνθρωπος: ὦ ἄνθρωπε.

Lesson 21

A Third Speech Act: Command

Syntax

Sentences with a verb in the imperative mood express a command; negative commands use the particle μή, not οὐ. There is no other difference in kernel type or in syntax between statements, questions and commands. The subject of an imperative, mostly "*you*," or more rarely "*he, she, or it*'," is not usually expressed

All speech acts may be expanded by naming the person to whom the speech act is directed. The person named occurs in Greek in the **vocative case**. In "Annie, get your gun!" "Annie" is the person to whom the speech act is directed. A vocative may be expected more often with a command or a question than with a statement.

♦Exercise 1

Copy all the second person imperatives from the Basic Sentences. Identify them by number, aspect and voice.

♦Exercise 2

Enter the commands from S21.1-5 into a kernel chart.

♦Exercise 3

With the help of the Morphology write the second person singular imperatives for παιδεύω, "to educate."

♦Exercise 4

Copy the imperatives from the Readings.

Readings

21.1 λυποῦντα λύπει, καὶ φιλοῦνθ' ὑπερφίλει. — Menander

21.2 εὔφραινε σαυτόν, πῖνε, τὸν καθ' ἡμέραν
βίον λογίζου σόν, τὰ δ' ἄλλα τῆς τύχης. — Euripides

21.3 πάρεστε καὶ μένοντες ἀντηχήσατε
παιᾶνα τῷ κάτωθεν ἀσπόνδῳ θεῷ. — Euripides

21.4 δέχου νῦν εἴσω τήνδε γενναίων δόμων. — Euripides

21.5 δός[1] μοι ποῦ στῶ[2] καὶ κινήσω τὴν γῆν. Archimedes

21.6 μὴ μόνον ἐπαινεῖτε τοὺς ἀγαθούς, ἀλλὰ καὶ μιμεῖσθε. Isocrates

21.7 ῏Ωναξ Παιάν, ἔξευρε μηχανάν τιν' Ἀδμήτῳ κακῶν,
πόριζε δὴ πόριζε·
καὶ πάρος γὰρ τοῦδ' ἐφηῦρες, (τοῦδ' ∅ = χρόνου)
καὶ νῦν λυτήριος ἐκ θανάτου γένου, φόνιον δ'
ἀπόπαισον Ἅιδαν. Euripides

Practice Sentences

1. ὡς μανθάνοντες, πιστεύετε τῷ χρηστῷ διδασκάλῳ!
2. ὦ ἄνδρες Ἀθήναιοι, εἰς τὴν πόλιν σπεύσατε!

Lesson Vocabulary

Nouns

Ἀίδης, Ἀίδου, ὁ	Hades
λυτήριος, λυτηρίου, ὁ	redeemer
μηχανή, μηχανῆς, ἡ	instrument, means, cure
Μύνδος, Μύνδου, ἡ	Myndus
παιάν, παιᾶνος, ὁ	hymn, praise, Paean
πύλη, πύλης, ἡ	gate
τύχη, τύχης, ἡ	fortune, luck

Verbs

ἀντηχέω, ἀντηχήσω, ἀντήχησα	to resound
ἀποπαίω, ἀποπαίσω, ἀπέπαισα, ἀποπέπαικα, ἀποπέπαισμαι, ἀπεπαίσθην	to drive away
ἐξευρίσκω, ἐξευρήσω, ἐξηῦρον, ἐξηύρηκα, ἐξηύρημαι, ἐξηυρέθην	to find
ἐξέρχομαι, ἐξελεύσομαι, ἐξῆλθον, ἐξελήλυθα	to come, to go
ἐπαινέω, ἐπαινέσω, ἐπῄνεσα, ἐπῄνεκα	to praise

[1] 2nd singular aorist imperative active of δίδωμι.
[2] Aorist subjunctive of ἵστημι

Lesson 21

εὐφραίνω, εὐφρανῶ/ηὐφρανῶ, εὔφρανα, εὐφράνθην/ηὐφράνθην	to cheer, gladden
καρπόω, καρπώσω, ἐκάρπωσα, ἐκάρπώθην	to reap
κινέω, κινήσω, ἐκίνησα, κεκίνημαι, ἐκινήθην	to move
κλείω, κλείσω, ἔκλεισα, κέκλεικα, κέκλειμαι, ἐκλείσθην	to shut
λογίζομαι, λογιοῦμαι, ἐλογισάμην, λελόγισμαι, ἐλογίσθην (+ two acc.)	to count as, to consider as
μιμέομαι, μιμήσομαι, ἐμιμησάμην, μεμίμημαι, ἐμιμήθην	to imitate
πίνω, πίομαι, ἔπιον, πέπωκα, πέπομαι, ἐπόθην	to drink
πορίζω, πορίσω, ἐπόρισα, πεπόρικα, πεπόρισμαι, ἐπορίσθην	to furnish
προσήκει	it concerns, befits
ὑπερφιλέω, ὑπερφιλήσω, ὑπερεφίλησα, -εφίληκα, -εφίλημαι, -εφιλήθην	to love beyond measure

Adjectives

ἄσπονδος, ἄσπονδον	implacable
γενναῖος, γενναία, γενναῖον	noble
εὐκλεής, εὐκλεές	noble, of good reputation
σός, σή, σόν	your, yours
φόνιος, φονία, φόνιον	bloody, murderous

Pronouns

σαυτοῦ, σαυτῆς reflexive pronoun	yourself (see αὐτός in Morphology)

Adverbs

κάτωθεν	from below, below
μήτε... μήτε	neither...nor
πάρος + genitive	before, earlier than

Prepositions

εἴσω + accusative	into
εἴσω + genitive	inside, within
κατά + accusative	in accordance with
κατά + genitive	down from, against

Lesson 22

Three More Speech Acts:

Exhortation

Negative Command

Deliberative Question

A New Mood: The Subjunctive

Speech acts in Greek like speech acts in English must have been signalled by intonation. We have no direct experience of how it worked, although word order seems to have played a limited part. The main signal in Greek for the different speech acts are different forms of the verb, called **moods**, plus the presence or absence of the **particle ἄν**. The mood of a verb form is indicated by suffix morphemes as in the imperative, or by **mood morphemes,** infixes, which precede the personal endings. The mood morpheme for the subjunctive mood is the *length of the vowel* preceding primary personal endings. See Morphology for the complete paradigm.

Subjunctive Mood: Active and Middle Voice

		Present	*Aorist*
Active			
Singular			
	First	λύω	λύσω
	Second	λύῃς	λύσῃς
	Third	λύῃ	λύσῃ
Plural			
	First	λύωμεν	λύσωμεν
	Second	λύητε	λύσητε
	Third	λύωσι	λύσωσι
Middle			
Singular			
	First	λύωμαι	λύσωμαι
	Second	λύῃ	λύσῃ
	Third	λύηται	λύσηται
Plural			
	First	λυώμεθα	λυσώμεθα
	Second	λύησθε	λύσησθε
	Third	λύωνται	λύσωνται

Lesson 22

Subjunctive Mood: Passive Voice

Passive

Singular

First	λύωμαι	λυθῶ
Second	λύῃ	λυθῇς
Third	λύηται	λυθῇ

Plural

First	λυώμεθα	λυθῶμεν
Second	λύησθε	λυθῆτε
Third	λύωνται	λυθῶσι

For the subjunctive forms of the contract verbs and -μι verbs see Morphology.

♦Exercise 1

List all verb forms that could be subjunctives. λύωμαι is subjunctive because of the ω; λύομαι is indicative. Remember that the augment *always* indicates the **indicative** mood.

1. δεχόμεθα	11. ἀπεστήσαντο	21. ἐκφυγῶσι
2. φεύγωμεν	12. δοκῶσι	22 ἦτε
3. τιμωρήσεσθε	13. ποιησώμεθα	23. δοκῇ
4. δέχηται	14. ἔρχωμαι	24. ᾠκοδόμησαν
5. βουλῆσθε	15. ἀποχωρήσετε	25. ὦσιν
6. τιμωρεῖσθε	16. ᾖ	26. δοκεῖ
7. νομίσῃς	17. ἀνέγνω	27. ἐποιήσαντο
8. ἐβούλεσθε	18. ἀποχωρῆτε	28. ἀφῆτε
9. ὦμεν	19. εἴασαν	29. ἐδοκοῦμεν
10 ἐνόμιζε	20. ἐπολιόρκησαν	30. οἰκοδομῇς

♦Exercise 2

With the help of the Morphology write a synopsis of φεύγω, φεύξομαι, ἔφυγον in the first person plural progressive and aorist, indicative and subjunctive.

Lesson 22

Basic Sentences

22.1 τέμω τρίχα

καὶ μέλανα στολμὸν πέπλων ἀμφιβαλώμεθ' ἤδη;

δῆλα μὲν, φίλοι, δῆλά γε, ἀλλ' ὅμως

θεοῖσιν[1] εὐχώμεθα! θεῶν γὰρ δύναμις μεγίστη.

Should I cut my hair and should we already put on the black raiment of robes? Things are clear, friends, surely clear, but all the same, let us pray to the gods! For the power of the gods is very great. Euripides

22.2 ἴωμεν εἰς Σαλαμῖνα, μαχησόμενοι περὶ νήσου!

Let us go to Salamis, ready to fight for the island! Solon

22.3 λόγον παρ' ἐχθροῦ μήποθ' ἡγήσῃ φίλον!

Never consider a word from an enemy friendly! Menander

Syntax

In the main clause, a verb in the subjunctive mood raises the expectation of several distinct speech acts.

When the verb in the subjunctive mood is in the first person plural, the speech act is often an **exhortation**. εὐχώμεθα in S22.1, ἴωμεν in S22.2 are examples.

When the subjunctive verb occurs in the environment of a question word or question mark, the speech act is a **deliberative question**. τέμω and ἀμφιβαλλώμεθα in S22.1 are examples.

When the subjunctive verb occurs in the aorist aspect with μή, or a compound of μή such as μήποτε, μήπω, μηδείς, the speech act is a **negative command**. μήποθ' ἡγήσῃ in S22.3 is an example.

♦ Exercise 3

Enter the seven kernels of the Basic Sentences into a kernel chart. In the last column name the speech act.

---

[1]θεοῖσιν is a dative plural.

Lesson 22

♦ Exercise 4

Identify the subjunctives from the Readings by person, number, aspect and vqice.

♦ Exercise 5

Copy one exhortation, one deliberative question and one negative command from the Readings.

Readings

22.1 μή, πρὸς θεῶν,[1] μαινώμεθα μηδ' αἰσχρῶς ἀπολώμεθα! Xenophon

22.2 εἴπωμεν ἢ σιγῶμεν; ἢ τί δράσωμεν; Euripides

22.3 μήπω μέγ' εἴπῃς, πρὶν τελευτήσαντ' ἴδῃς! Sophocles

22.4 πῶς λέγεις; μὴ ἀποκρίνωμαι; Plato

22.5 μήτε παυσώμεθα δρῶντες εὖ βρότους! Plutarch

22.6 ὡς τάχιστα πρὸς πόλιν σπεύσωμεν! Aristophanes

22.7 μήτ' ἄναρκτον βίον
μήτε δεσποτούμενον αἰνέσῃς!
παντὶ μέσῳ τὸ κράτος θεὸς ὤπασεν. Aeschylos

22.8 σπονδὰς ἢ πόλεμον ἀγγείλω; Xenophon

22.9 καὶ μηδεὶς ὑμῶν προσδοκησάτω[2] ἄλλως. Plato

Practice Sentences

1. παρερχομένης ἡμᾶς ἥβης, χαίρωμεν.
2. μήποτε ἔχθρον φίλον νόμιζε!
3. τί δράσω;

[1] πρὸς θεῶν signals an oath, "by the gods ...!"
[2] προσδοκησάτω is a third person singular aorist imperative.

LESSON 22

Lesson Vocabulary

Nouns

δύναμις, δυνάμεως, ἡ	power, ability
κράτος, κράτους, τό	strength, power
νῆσος, νήσου, ἡ	island
πέπλος, πέπλου, ὁ	robe
Σαλαμίς, Σαλαμῖνος, ἡ	Salamis
σπονδαί, σπονδῶν, αἱ	treaty; truce
στολμός, στολμοῦ, ὁ	clothing

Verbs

αἰνέω, αἴνεσω, ᾔνεσα, ᾔνεκα, ᾔνημαι, ᾐνέθην	to praise
ἀμφιβάλλομαι, ἀμφιβαλοῦμαι, ἀμφεβαλόμην, ἀμφιβέβλημαι, ἀμφεβλήθην	to throw/wrap around
ἀναγίγνωσκω, ἀναγνώσομαι, ἀνέγνων, ἀνέγνωκα, ἀνέγνωσμαι, ἀνεγνώσθην	to read aloud
ἀποκρίνομαι, ἀποκρινοῦμαι, ἀπεκρινάμην, ἀποκέκριμαι, ἀπεκρίθην	to answer
δεσποτέω, δεσποτήσω	to be despotically ruled (in passive)
δράω, δράσω, ἔδρασα, δέδρακα, δέδραμαι, ἐδράσθην	to do
δράω εὖ	to benefit
εἶμι	to go
ἐκφεύγω, ἐκφεύξομαι, ἐξέφυγον, ἐκπέφευγα	to escape
ἴδῃς = subjunctive of οἶδα	to know
μαίνομαι, μανήσομαι, ἐμηνάμην, μέμηνα, μεμάνημαι, ἐμάνην	to rage
ὀπάζω, ὀπάσω, ὤπασα	to make to follow, to give
πολιορκέω, πολιορκήσω, ἐπολιόρκησα, πεπολιόρκηκα, πεπολιόρκημαι, ἐπολιορκήθην	to beseige
προσδοκάω, προσδοκήσω, προσεδόκησα, προσδεδόκηκα, προσεδοκήθην	to expect, look for

Lesson 22

σιγάω, σιγήσομαι, ἐσίγησα, σεσίγηκα, σεσίγημαι, ἐσιγήθην	to be silent
τελευτάω, τελευτήσω, ἐτελεύτησα, τετελεύτηκα, τετελεύτημαι, ἐτελευτήθην	to bring to an end, to die
τέμνω, τεμῶ, ἔτεμον, τέτμηκα, τέτμημαι, ἐτμήθην	to cut

Adjectives

ἄναρκτος, ἄναρκτον	not governed
μέλας, μέλαινα, μέλαν	black
μηδείς, μηδεμία, μηδέν	no one, nothing

Adverbs

ἄλλως	otherwise
μήπω	not yet
μήποτε	never

Prepositions

περί + accusative	around
περί + dative	around
περί + genitive	about, concerning

Coordinating Connectors/Clause Markers

μηδέ	and not, but not
μήτε	and not, nor
ὅμως	but still, nevertheless
πρίν clause-marker	before + subjunctive or infinitive

Lesson 23

Two More Speech Acts:

Hopeful Wishes

Hopeless Wishes

A New Mood: The Optative

Lesson 22 presented three distinct speech acts all signaled by the subjunctive mood. This lesson introduces two additional speech acts: the hopeful wish is signaled by a verb in the optative mood; the hopeless wish by a verb in the indicative mood. In English a "hopeful" wish may be indicated by *may* as in "long may she reign!" A "hopeless" wish may be indicated by *if only* as in "if only I had known!"

The mood morpheme for the **optative** is ι or ιη, preceding **secondary personal endings** (except -μι).

Optative Mood: Active and Middle Voice

		Present	*Aorist*
Active			
Singular	*First*	λύοιμι	λύσαιμι
	Second	λύοις	λύσειας/λύσαις
	Third	λύοι	λύσειε/λύσαι
Plural	*First*	λύοιμεν	λύσαιμεν
	Second	λύοιτε	λύσαιτε
	Third	λύοιεν	λύσειαν/λύσαιεν
Middle			
Singular	*First*	λυοίμην	λυσαίμην
	Second	λύοιο	λύσαιο
	Third	λύοιτο	λύσαιτο
Plural	*First*	λυοίμεθα	λυσαίμεθα
	Second	λύοισθε	λύσαισθε
	Third	λύοιντο	λύσαιντο

LESSON 23

Optative Mood: Passive Voice

Passive			
Singular	*First*	λυοίμην	λυθείην
	Second	λύοιο	λυθείης
	Third	λύοιτο	λυθείη
Plural			
	First	λυοίμεθα	λυθεῖμεν/λυθείημεν
	Second	λύοισθε	λυθεῖτε/λύθείητε
	Third	λύοιντο	λυθεῖεν/λυθείησαν

For the full paradigm of the future and perfect optatives see Morphology. For the optative of the contract verbs and -μι verbs see Morphology.

♦Exercise 1

List all verb forms that could be optative. Be careful about contract verbs: ποιοῖμεν is an optative but not ποιῶμεν or ποιοῦμεν.

1. βούλοιο
2. βουλοίμην
3. εἴη
4. ἕλοιτο
5. γένοιντο
6. ἔχῃ
7. λῦσαι
8. λύσαι
9. βούληται
10. φίλοιεν
11. εὐδαιμονοίης
12. ἡγήσεται
13. ἡγήσηται
14. ἡγήσαιτο
15. ἁπτοίμην
16. κωλύοιεν
17. ἐπιθυμῇς
18. ὑφαίνοιμι
19. ποιήσωμεν
20. πώλει
21. αἰσθάνωνται
22. ἐπιστήσειν
23. ἔσῃ
24. ᾖς
25. διαφέρει
26. ποιεῖ
27. βούλει
28. λύσαις
29. θείη
30. δοῖμεν

♦Exercise 2

With the help of the Morphology write a synopsis of γράφω, γράψω, ἔγραψα, γέγραφα, γέγραμμαι, ἐγράφην in the first person singular in all moods and voices.

LESSON 23

Basic Sentences

23.1 **χαίροιτε ... ἥρωες! ἡ λύρη γὰρ μόνους ἔρωτας ἀίδει.**

Farewell, heroes! For our lyre sings only of love. Anacreon

23.2 **ὦ φίλε Πάν τε καὶ ἄλλοι ὅσοι τῇδε θεοί! δοίητέ μοι καλῷ γενέσθαι τἄνδοθεν![1] ἔξωθεν δ' ὅσα ἔχω, τοῖς ἐντὸς εἶναί μοι φίλια! πλούσιον δὲ νομίζοιμι τὸν σοφόν!**

Dear Pan and the other gods here! May you grant me to become beautiful inside! Such outward advantages as I possess, may be friendly to the inward advantages! May I consider the wise man rich! Socrates in Plato's *Phaedrus*

23.3 **εἴθε τοὺς νεκροὺς ἤσθιες καὶ μὴ τοὺς ζῶντας!**

If only you would eat corpses and stop eating those who are alive! Aesop: the fox to the bear

23.4 **εἴθ' ηὕρομέν σ', Ἄδμητε, μὴ λυπούμενον!**

If only we had found you, Admetos, not being in mourning! Euripides

Syntax

A speech act whose verb is in the **optative mood** and which often begins with εἰ, εἰ γάρ, εἴθε is a **hopeful wish**. χαίροιτε in S23.1 and δοίητε and νομίζοιμι in S23.2 are examples.

A speech act whose verb is in the **indicative** mood, regularly signaled by εἴθε, εἰ, εἰ γάρ, is a **hopeless wish**. Aspect, not tense, determines whether the "hopeless" wish refers to the present or past time. The imperfect tense, built on the stem in the progressive aspect, expresses **continuity**. The aorist, built on the stem in the aorist aspect expresses **non-continuity**. Therefore the imperfect tense signals a hopeless wish continuing into the present time, while the aorist signals a hopeless wish that is no longer continuing. ἤσθιες in S23.3 is an example of a hopeless wish referring to the present time. ηὕρομεν in S23.4 is an example of a hopeless wish referring to past time.

---

[1]τἄνδοθεν = τὰ ἔνδοθεν. See Preview for crasis.

Lesson 23

♦ Exercise 3

Name the speech acts in the following.

1.	ὦ γενναία καὶ μεγ' ἀρίστη, χαῖρε!	Euripides
2.	πρόφρων σε χθόνιος θ' Ἑρμῆς Ἀίδης τε δέχοιτο!	Euripides
3.	εἰ γὰρ τοσαύτην δύναμιν εἶχον ὥστε σὴν εἰς φῶς πορεῦσαι γυναῖκα!	Euripides
4.	τί δράσωμεν;	
5.	νῦν ἴωμεν καὶ ἀκούσωμεν τοῦ ἀνδρός!	Plato

Practice Sentences

1. εἴθε ἔφυγε Σωκράτης!
2. μή μοι γένοιτο ἃ βούλομαι, ἀλλ' ἅ μοι ὠφελεῖ.

Lesson Vocabulary

Nouns

Ἑρμῆς, Ἑρμοῦ, ὁ	Hermes
ἥρως, ἥρωος, ὁ	hero
λύρη, λύρης, ἡ	lyre
νεκρός, νεκροῦ, ὁ	corpse

Verbs

ᾄδω/ἀείδω, ᾄσομαι/ἀείσομαι, ἤεισα	to sing, sing of
ἐσθίω, ἔδομαι, ἔφαγον, ἐδήδοκα, ἐδήδεσμαι, ἠδέσθην	to eat

Adjectives

μόνος, μόνη, μόνον	alone, only
ὅσος, ὅση, ὅσον	as, as great/much/many/long as
πρόφρων, πρόφρονος	eager
φίλιος, φιλία, φίλιον	friendly
χθόνιος, χθονία, χθόνιον	earthly

Adverbs

ἔνδοθεν	inside, from within
ἐντός	inward, within
ἔξωθεν	outside, from without

Lesson 24

The Particle ἄν: Part 1

Speech Acts:

Potential Statements and Questions

Contrary-to-Fact Statements and Questions

This lesson introduces two variations on speech acts you have already learned. We may choose to communicate our view on the **probability of information** by differentiating statements and questions as:

plain
potential
contrary-to-fact.

♦ Exercise 1

Label the following as statements or questions and as plain, potential or contrary-to-fact.

1. They are reading the new book.
2. Are they reading the new book?
3. May they, perhaps, be reading the new book?
4. They might, perhaps, be reading the new book.
5. They would be reading the new book but...
6. Would they be reading the new book if...?

♦ Exercise 2

Name some linguistic devices by means of which English seems to signal the speech act variations.

Basic Sentences

24.1 σοῦ γὰρ φθιμένης, οὐκέτ' ἂν εἴην.

With you gone, I don't think I would exist any longer. Euripides

24.2 οὐ τοι ἂν φθιμένης γ' (ø = αὐτῆς) ἐσιώπων.

For indeed they would not be silent, if she were gone. Euripides

24.3 τίς γὰρ ἂν ᾠήθη ταῦτα γενέσθαι;

Who would have thought this would happen? Demosthenes

Lesson 24

Syntax

Both potential and contrary-to-fact speech acts are signaled in Greek by the presence of the particle **ἄν**. The difference between the two is signaled by the mood of the verb.

Speech Acts: Potential Statements and Questions

A speech act whose verb is in the **optative mood** and which appears with the particle **ἄν** is a potential statement or potential question. ἂν εἴην in S24.1 is an example.

Speech Acts: Contrary-to-Fact Statements and Questions

A speech act whose verb is in a **past** tense of the **indicative** mood and which appears with the particle ἄν, is a contrary-to-fact statement or question. Aspect, not tense, determines whether the contrary-to-fact speech act refers to past or present time. The imperfect tense, built on the stem in its progressive aspect, expresses **continuity**. The aorist, built on the stem in its aorist aspect, expresses **non-continuity**. (See Syntax on wishes in Lesson 23.) ἂν...ἐσιώπων in S24.2 is an example of a contrary-to-fact speech act referring to the present or future time. ἂν...ᾠήθη in S24.3 is an example of a contrary-to-fact speech act referring to past time.

♦Exercise 3

Identify the time of each speech act. Note that it can be difficult to distinguish between potential and contrary-to-fact speech acts in English. For the purposes of this exercise consider the sentences as contrary-to-fact speech acts.

1. No one would come.
2. Who would come?
3. Who could have come?
4. No one would have come.
5. Who wouldn't be charmed by you?
6. Who wouldn't have been charmed?
7. We wouldn't be invited.
8. We wouldn't have been invited.

♦Exercise 4

Translate, being careful to react to the aspects and to the presence or absence of ἄν.

1. τί εἶπες;
2. τίς ἂν ἀπέθανε;
3. τί ἂν εἶπες;
4. οὐδεὶς ἀφικνεῖτο.
5. τί ἔλεγες;
6. οὐδεὶς ἂν ἀφικνεῖτο

7. τί ἂν ἔλεγες;
8. οὐδεὶς ἀφίκετο
9. τίς ἀπέθανε;
10. οὐδεὶς ἂν ἀφίκετο
11. οὐκ ἂν τὰ τῶν φαύλων ἐφρόνησας
12. οὐκ ἂν τὰ τῶν φαύλων ἐφρόνεις

♦ Exercise 5

Identify the speech act.

1. μὴ θάψῃς τούσδε τοὺς νεκρούς!
2. τὸν φρατέρα θάπτωμεν!
3. τίνι διδῶ τόδε τὸ βιβλίον;
4. εἴποι ἄν τις τάδε
5. σμικροῖς πόνοις τὰ μεγάλα πῶς ἕλοι τις ἄν;
6. εἰ γὰρ ἔρχοιτό τις!
7. εἴθε ἀπέλθοιεν!
8. ἀφικόμην ἔγωγ' ἄν.
9. μή μοι γένοιθ' ἃ βούλομαι!
10. τιμῶμεν τοὺς ὑπὲρ τῆς πατρίδος μαχομένους!
11. διὰ τί λύσωμεν τοὺς δούλους;
12. ὦ παῖ, γένοιο πατρὸς εὐτυχέστερος!
13. ἤκουον ἄν.
14. ἤκουσα ἄν.
15. ἔλθοι!
16. τί βουλευώμεθα;

The Oblique Optative

In a finite clause governed by a verb in the past, the optative without ἄν may replace an indicative and be translated as an indicative. It may also replace a subjunctive.

> ἔλεγεν ὅτι ἕτοιμος εἴη ἡγεῖσθαι αὐτοὺς εἰς τὸ Δέλτα.
> He said that he *was* ready to lead them into the Delta. Xenophon

> ἐπεχείρουν ἐρωτᾶν ὁπότερος σοφώτερος αὐτῶν εἴη.
> I was just on the point of asking which of them *was* the wiser. Plato

LESSON 24

διηγοῦντο οἱ στρατηγοὶ περὶ τῆς ναυμαχίας ὅτι αὐτοὶ μὲν ἐπὶ τοὺς πολεμίους πλέοιεν, τὴν δὲ ἀναίρεσιν τῶν ναυαγῶν προστάξαιεν ἄνδρασιν ἱκανοῖς.

The admirals set out in detail regarding the naval battle that they themselves *were* sailing against the enemy, but that they *had* assigned the rescue of the shipwrecks to able men. Xenophon

♦ Exercise 6

Review Lessons 18 and 19 for non-finite and finite noun clauses. Then determine the semantic groups to which the verbs in the governing speech acts belong in sentences 18.5
18.6, 19.2, 19.3, 19.6, 19.7. Copy the verbs and the name of the group; e.g. in S8.3 the verb εἶδε belongs to the semantic group, perception.

♦ Exercise 7

Reconstruct the original speech acts embedded in the above sentences. Be sure to identify statements, questions, commands and wishes. Be careful about possible change in person, e.g. the original speech act in S18.3 would have been the statement, Κλέαρχος διελάυνει.

Lesson 24

Summary of Speech Acts

Speech Act	*Mood*	*Particle*	*Greek*	*English*	*Neg.*
statement					
plain	ind.	–	γράφομεν	we write	οὐ
				we do write	
				we are writing	
potential	opt.	ἄν	γράφοιμεν	we may, perhaps, write	οὐ
contrary-to-fact	ind.	ἄν	ἐγράφομεν	we would write but	οὐ
		ἄν	ἐγράψαμεν	we would have written but	οὐ
question					
plain	ind.	–	(ἆρα) γράφομεν	are we writing?	οὐ
				do we write?	
potential	opt.	ἄν	(ἆρα) γράφοιμεν	would we, perhaps, write?	οὐ
contrary-to-fact	ind.	ἄν	(ἆρα) ἐγράφομεν;	would we write if?	οὐ
		ἄν	(ἆρα) ἐγράψαμεν;	would we have written if?	οὐ
deliberative	subj.	–	(ἆρα) γράφωμεν;	should we write?	οὐ
command					
direct	imp.	–	γράφε!	write!	μή
negative	subj.	–	μὴ γράψῃς!	do not write!	μή
	imp.		μὴ γράφε!		
exhortation					
	subj.	–	γράφωμεν!	let us write!	μή
wish					
hopeful	opt.	εἰ, εἰ γὰρ, εἴθε	γράφοιμεν!	we would (really) like to write!	μή
hopeless	ind.	εἴθε	ἐγράφομεν!	if only we might write	μή
		εἴθε	ἐγράψαμεν!	if only we would have written	μή

Lesson 24

Lesson Vocabulary

Nouns

ἀναίρεσις, ἀναιρέσεως, ἡ	taking up (of dead bodies)
ναυμαχία, ναυμαχίας, ἡ	shipwreck
πατρίς, πατρίδος, ἡ	fatherland
φράτηρ, φράτερος, ὁ	clansman

Verbs

αἱρέω, αἱρήσω, εἷλον, ᾕρηκα, ᾕρημαι, ᾑρέθην	to take; mid. choose
διηγέομαι, διηγήσομαι, διηγησάμην	to set out, explain
ἐπιχειρέω, ἐπιχειρήσω, ἐπεχείρησα	to put one's hand upon a thing, attempt
ἡγέομαι, ἡγήσομαι, ἡγησάμην (+ dat. or acc.)	to lead
θάπτω, θάψω, ἔθαψα, τέθαμμαι, ἐθάφθην/ἐτάφην	to bury
πλέω, πλεύσομαι, ἔπλευσα, πέπλευκα, πέπλευσμαι	to sail
προστάττω, προστάξω, προσέταξα, προστέταχα, προστέταγμαι, προσετάχθην	to assign
σιωπάω, σιωπησομαι, ἐσώπησα, σεσιώπηκα, σεσιώπημαι, ἐσιωπήθην	to be silent, to keep silence, to keep in silence, to keep secret
φρονέω, φρονήσω, ἐφρόνησα, πεφόνηκα	to think, to understand, to mean, intend, to heed

Adjectives

ἕτοιμος, ἕτοιμον	ready, prepared
ἱκανός, ἱκανή, ἱκανόν	sufficient, competent, able
ναυαγός, ναυαγόν	shipwrecked

Prepositions

ὑπέρ + genitive	on behalf of

Lesson 25

Mood in Dependent Clauses: Conditions
The Particle ἄν: Part 2

This lesson treats a few indispensable topics out of the many topics which are included in comprehensive grammars. So far finite verbs in dependent clauses have been in the indicative mood. We will also examine dependent clauses where the verb is in the subjunctive or in the optative mood.

Basic Sentences

25.1 οὐκ ἂν ἐποίησε Ἀγασίας ταῦτα, εἰ μὴ ἐγὼ αὐτὸν ἐκέλευσα.

Agasias would not have done this, if I had not ordered him. Xenophon

25.2 εἰ ἀλγεῖν συνέβαινε τὴν κεφαλὴν πρὸ τοῦ πιεῖν, ἡμῶν οὐδὲ εἷς ἔπινεν ἄν.

If the headache came before drinking, not one of us would drink. Clearchus (adapted)

25.3 εἴ τις ὑπερβάλλοι τὸ μέτριον, τὰ ἐπιτερπέστατα ἀτερπέστατα ἂν γίγνοιτο.

If one oversteps the bonds of moderation, the greatest pleasures would cease to please. Epictetus

25.4 ἢν δ' ἔγγυς ἔλθῃ θάνατος, οὐδεὶς βούλεται θνῄσκειν.

If death is approaching, nobody wants to die. Euripides

25.5 ὅστις οἴεται κακόν τι πράσσων τοὺς θεοὺς
λεληθέναι, δοκεῖ πονηρὰ καὶ δοκῶν ἁλίσκεται,
ὅταν σχολὴν ἄγουσα τυγχάνῃ δίκη.

Whoever believes he has escaped the notice of the gods while doing something evil, thinks evil thoughts and, thinking them, is caught whenever justice happens to have leisure ø = to catch him. Euripides (adapted)

LESSON 25

Mood in Dependent Clauses: Conditions

Indicative

An adverbial dependent clause marked by εἰ with a verb in the **indicative mood** sometimes appears with a contrary-to-fact speech act. Because different speakers of English have different habits, these clauses must be translated with special care. ἐκέλευσα, a verb with **aorist aspect**, in S25.1 indicates a contrary-to-fact condition in the past. This clause may be translated as

> "if I had not ordered him, ..."
> "if I would not have ordered him, ..."
> "if I should not have ordered him,...."

συνέβαινε, a verb in a past tense with **progressive aspect**, in S25.2 indicates a contrary-to-fact condition in the present. This clause may be translated as

> "if the headache came before the drinking, ..."
> "if the headache would come before the drinking..."
> "if the headache might come before the drinking...."

The combination of a dependent clause marked by εἰ with a contrary-to-fact speech act is traditionally called a **contrary-to-fact conditional sentence**.

♦Exercise 1

Translate the following according to your own speech habit:

1. τί εἶπες;
2. τί ἂν εἶπες;
3. εἰ τοῦτ' ἠρόμην, τί ἂν εἶπες;
4. τί ἂν ἀπεκρίνω;
5. εἰ ταῦτ' ἠρόμεθα, τί ἂν ἀπεκρίνω;
6. τίνες ἀπέθανον;
7. τίνες ἂν ἀπέθανον;
8. οὐδεὶς ἂν ἀπέθανεν.
9. οὐδεὶς ἀφίκετο.
10. οὐδεὶς ἂν ἀφίκετο.
11. εἰ μὴ σὺ ἀφίκου, πάντες ἀπέθανον ἄν.
12. εἰ τοῦτ' ἐπίομεν, πάντες ἂν ἀπεθνῄσκομεν.
13. εἰ μηδεὶς ἀφίκετο, ταῦτ' ἂν ἤρεσθε;
14. εἰ μὴ ἀφικόμην, ἆρ' ἂν οἴκαδ' ἀπήλθετε;
15. εἰ χρήματ' εἴχομεν, φίλους ἂν εἴχομεν.
16. μέγ' ἂν ἐνομίζομεν κέρδος, εἰ ἀλλήλοις ὠφέλιμοι ἐγιγνόμεθα.
17. ἰ καλῶς ζῆν ἤθελες, οὐκ ἂν τὰ τῶν φαύλων ἐφρόνεις·

18. εἴ τις καλῶς ἀκούειν ἐβούλετο, ἐμάνθανεν ἂν καλῶς λέγειν.
19. εἰ λίαν ἐφίλεις σεαυτόν, οὐκ ἂν φίλον εἶχες·
20. εἰ ἐβούλου λαβὼν τὴν μάστιγα τύπτειν τοὺς ἵππους, οὐκ ἂν σ' ἐκώλυεν ὁ πατήρ;
21. εἴ τίς σε ταῦτ' ἤρετο, τί ἂν ἀπεκρίνω;

Optative

A verb in the **optative mood** in a dependent clause marked by εἰ must also be translated with special care, when it appears with a potential speech act. In S25.3 ὑπερβάλλοι, a verb in the **optative**, may be translated as:

"if one oversteps, ..."
"if one should overstep, ..."
"if one might overstep, ..."

The combination of a potential condition with a potential speech act is traditionally called a **future less vivid conditional sentence**.

♦ Exercise 2
Translate.

εἰ ἀναγκαῖον εἴη ἀδικεῖν ἢ ἀδικεῖσθαι, ἑλοίμην ἂν μᾶλλον ἀδικεῖσθαι ἢ ἀδικεῖν.

Plato, *Gorgias*

Subjunctive

A verb in the **subjunctive mood** in a dependent clause, marked by ἐάν ἄν, ἤν, when it appears with a plain speech act in the present or future, may usually be translated by what looks like an English indicative. Thus, ἐγγὺς ἔλθῃ in S25.4 may be translated as, "if death is approaching." However, one could also use the English form of the subjunctive, rarely used now, and translate, "if death be approaching."

The combination of such a clause with a plain present or future speech act is traditionally called a **future more vivid conditional sentence**.

♦ Exercise 3

Translate the following passage from Matthew.

ὁ λύχνος τοῦ σώματός ἐστιν ὁ ὀφθαλμός. ἐὰν οὖν ᾖ ὁ ὀφθαλμός σου ἁπλοῦς, ὅλον τὸ σῶμά σου φωτεινὸν ἔσται. ἐὰν δὲ ὁ ὀφθαλμός σου πονηρὸς ᾖ, ὅλον τὸ σῶμά σου σκοτεινὸν ἔσται. εἰ οὖν τὸ φῶς τὸ ἐν σοὶ σκότος ἐστί, τὸ σκότος ὅσον.

— Ἐκ τοῦ εὐαγγελίου τοῦ κατὰ Μαθθαῖον, ϛ΄, κβ΄-κγ΄

♦ Exercise 4

Translate the following passage from Euclid.

KOINAI ENNOIAI[1]

Axioms (Gr. *Common Notions*) of Euclid

α΄. Τὰ τοῦ αὐτοῦ ἴσα καὶ ἀλλήλοις ἐστὶν ἴσα.

β΄. Καὶ ἐὰν ἴσοις ἴσα προστεθῇ (*be added*), τὰ ὅλα ἐστὶν ἴσα.

γ΄. Καὶ ἐὰν ἀπ' ἴσων ἴσα ἀφ-αιρεθῇ, (*be taken away*), τὰ λοιπά ἐστιν ἴσα

δ΄. Καὶ ἐὰν ἀνίσοις ἴσα προστεθῇ, τὰ ὅλα εστὶν ἄνισα.

ε΄. Καὶ ἐὰν ἀπ' ἀνίσων ἴσα ἀφ-αιρεθῇ, τὰ λοιπά ἐστιν ἄνισα.

ϛ΄. Καὶ τὰ τοῦ αὐτοῦ διπλάσια ἴσα ἀλλήλοις ἐστίν.

ζ΄. Καὶ τὰ τοῦ αὐτοῦ ἡμίση ἴσα ἀλλήλοις ἐστίν.

η΄. Καὶ τὸ ὅλον μεῖζον τοῦ μέρους ἐστίν.

ONOMATA KAI PHMATA

ἄνισος ἄνισον *unequal*[1] (ἴσος).
ὅλος ὅλη ὅλον *whole, entire.*
διπλάσιος -ον *double*
ἔμπροσθεν *earlier, before.*
ἡμίση (τά) *the halves* (ἥμισυ).
ἴσος ἴση ἴσον *equal. Cf.* isothermal (ἄνισος).
μέρος (τό) *part.* Gen. *μέρους*, 117 b
πολλάκις *many times* (πολλοί).

---

[1]This and the following passages from Euclid are reprinted and revised with permission of the Macmillan Company from *The First Year of Greek* by J. T. Allen. Copyright 1931 by Macmillan Publishing Company. Renewed 1959 by Lois H. Allen.

LESSON 25

♦ Exercise 5

Translate the following passage from Euclid Book I Proposition XXV.

ΤΟΥ ΠΡΩΤΟΥ ΒΙΒΛΙΟΥ ΕΥΚΛΕΙΔΟΥ ΠΡΟΤΑΣΙΣ ΚΕ΄

Ἐὰν δύο τρίγωνα τὰς δύο πλευρὰς ταῖς δυοῖν πλευραῖς ἴσᾱς ἔχῃ, ἑκατέρᾱν ἑκατέρᾳ, τὴν δὲ βάσιν τῆς βάσεως μείζονα ἔχῃ, καὶ τὴν γωνίᾱν τῆς γωνίᾱς μείζονα ἕξει, τὴν ὑπὸ τῶν ἴσων εὐθειῶν περι-εχομένην

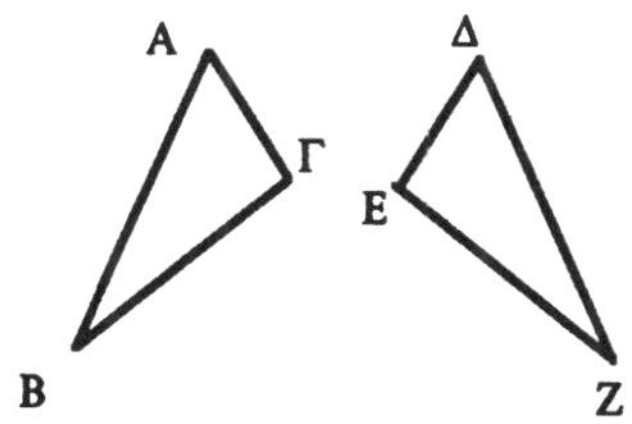

Ἔστω δύο τρίγωνα τὰ ΑΒΓ, ΔΕΖ, τὰς δύο πλευρὰς τὰς ΑΒ, ΑΓ ταῖς δυοῖν πλευραῖς ταῖς ΔΕ, ΔΖ ἴσᾱς ἔχοντα, ἑκατέραν ἑκατέρᾳ, τὴν μὲν ΑΒ τῇ ΔΕ, τὴν δὲ ΑΓ τῇ ΔΖ· βάσις δὲ ἡ ΒΓ βάσεως τῆς ΕΖ μείζων ἔστω. λέγω ὅτι καὶ γωνίᾱ ἡ ὑπὸ ΒΑΓ γωνίᾱς τῆς ὑπὸ ΕΔΖ μείζων ἐστίν. Εἰ γὰρ μή, ἴση ἐστὶν αὐτῇ, ἢ ἐλάττων. ἴση μὲν οὖν οὐκ ἔστιν ἡ ὑπὸ ΒΑΓ τῇ ὑπὸ ΕΔΖ, ἴση γὰρ ἂν ἦν καὶ ἡ βάσις ἡ ΒΓ βάσει τῇ ΕΖ. οὐκ ἔστι δέ. οὐκ ἄρα ἴση ἐστὶ γωνίᾱ ἡ ὑπὸ ΒΑΓ τῆς ὑπὸ ΕΔΖ. οὐδὲ μὴν ἐλάττων ἐστὶν ἡ ὑπὸ ΒΑΓ τῆς ὑπὸ ΕΔΖ, ἐλάττων γὰρ ἂν ἦν καὶ βάσις ἡ ΒΓ βάσεως τῆς ΕΖ. οὐκ ἔστι δέ. οὐκ ἄρα ἐλάττων ἐστὶν ἡ ὑπὸ ΒΑΓ γωνίᾱ τῆς ὑπὸ ΕΔΖ. ἐδείχθη δὲ ὅτι οὐδ' ἴση· μείζων ἄρα ἐστὶν ἡ ὑπὸ ΒΑΓ τῆς ὑπὸ ΕΔΖ,

Ἐὰν ἄρα δύο τρίγωνα τὰς δύο πλευρὰς ταῖς δυοῖν πλευραῖς ἴσᾱς ἔχῃ, ἑκατέρᾱν ἑκατέρᾳ, τὴν δὲ βάσιν τῆς βάσεως μείζονα ἔχῃ, καὶ τὴν γωνίᾱν τῆς γωνίᾱς μείζονα ἕξει, τὴν ὑπὸ τῶν ἴσων εὐθειῶν περι-εχομένην. ὅπερ ἔδει δεῖξαι

ΟΝΟΜΑΤΑ ΚΑΙ ΣΧΟΛΙΑ

βάσις (ἡ) *step, base.* Gen. *βάσεως,* Dat. *βάσει,* Acc. *βάσιν.*

ἑκάτερος -α -ον *each* (of two).

ἑκατέραν ἑκατέρᾳ *each to each.*

εὐθεῖα, εὐθείας ἡ a straight line, side

γωνία, γωνίας ἡ angle

πλευρ ά, πλευρᾶς ἡ side

τρίγωνον, τριγώνου τό triangle

Lesson 25

The Particle ἄν: Part 2

The particle ἄν does not function in the same way in a speech act and in a dependent clause, unless the dependent clause *is* an embedded speech act.

The particle ἄν helps to mark the action of the governing verb as contingent on circumstances outside the main clause. When those circumstances are expressed in an adverbial clause marked by εἰ, the result is a contrary-to-fact or future less vivid conditional sentence. See S25.1, S25.2, S25.5.

In a dependent clause with a subjunctive verb, however, ἄν signals that the action of the verb is general. Sometimes ἄν combines with a clause marker like the English "ever," in "if ever," "whoever," "whenever," as in S25.5 ὅταν. Here is a partial list of these clause markers:

εἰ	plus ἄν = ἐάν, ἤν, ἄν	if
ἕως		until, while, as long as
πρίν		before
οὐ πρίν		not before
ὅπου		where
ἐπεί	plus ἄν = ἐπειδάν	when, since
ὅτε	plus ἄν = ὅταν	when
ὡς		in order that
ὅπως		in order that

Note:

In past sequence the **optative *without* ἄν** may replace the **subjunctive *with* ἄν**. See Lesson 23: The Oblique Optative.

♦ Exercise 6

Translate the following.

εἶπεν ὅτι ἐπιτίθεσθαι μέλλοιεν αὐτῷ, ὁπότε ἀπάγοι τὸ στράτευμα = μέλλουσιν ἐπιτίθεσθαι, ὁπόταν ἀπάγῃ. Xenophon, *Cyr.*

Lesson 25

Lesson Vocabulary

Nouns

Ἀγασίας, Ἀγασίου, ὁ	Agasias
ἵππος, ἵππου, ὁ	horse
λύχνος, λύχνου, ὁ	lamp
μάστιξ, μάστιγος, ἡ	whip
σκότος, σκότου, ὁ, τό	shadow, darkness
σχολή, σχολῆς, ἡ	leisure, free time

Verbs

ἀλγέω, ἀλγήσω, ἤλγησα	to feel pain
ἔρομαι, ἐρήσομαι, ἠρόμην	to ask
συμβαίνω, συμβήσομαι, συνέβην, συμβέβηκα	to happen, occur
τύπτω, τύψω, ἔτυψα, τέτυμμαι, ἐτύφθην	to hit

Adjectives

ἀλλήλων (oblique cases only)	each other
ἀναγκαῖος, ἀναγκαία, ἀναγκαῖον	necessary
ἀτερπής, ἀτερπές	unpleasant
ἐπιτερπής, ἐπιτερπές	pleasant, delightful
μέτριος, μετρία, μέτριον	moderate
σκοτεινός, σκοτεινή, σκοτεινόν	dark
φωτεινός, φωτεινή, φωτεινόν	giving light, shining
ὠφέλιμος, ὠφέλιμον	useful

Adverbs

ἐγγύς	near
λίαν	too much, exceedingly, very

Prepositions

πρό + genitive	before

Clause Markers

ὅταν	whenever

Review 5

♦ Exercise 1

Define each of the terms below in your own words. Give a Greek example where appropriate.

Lesson 21

Imperative

Vocative

Lesson 22

Deliberative question

Infix

Mood morpheme

Lesson 23

Hopeful wish

Hopeless wish

Lesson 24

Contrary-to-fact speech act

Oblique optative

Plain (factual) speech act

Potential speech act

Probability of information

Lesson 25

Conditional sentences

contrary-to-fact

future less vivid

future more vivid

General statements

♦ Exercise 2

Translate into Greek.

21.1 Do not ask, friend, what will be. What will be, will be.

21.2 Do not only learn, friends, to speak well, but also to act well.

22.1 Shall I stay or shall I go?

22.2 Let us not drink too much.

23.1 May we delight in good friends!

Review 5

23.2 They may delight in horses.

24.1 With Cyrus being dead, the soldiers might flee.

24.2 With Cyrus being dead, the soldiers might have fled.

Hint: Κύρου τεθνηκότος

24.1 If Cyrus would die, the soldiers might flee.

25.2 If Cyrus had died, the soldiers would have fled.

25.3 If the soldiers flee, Cyrus will die.

Required Vocabulary

Lesson 21

Nouns

μηχανή, μηχανῆς, ἡ	instrument, means, cure
πύλη, πύλης, ἡ	gate
τύχη, τύχης, ἡ	fortune, luck

Verbs

ἐξευρίσκω, ἐξευρήσω, ἐξηῦρον, ἐξηύρηκα, ἐξηύρημαι, ἐξηυρέθην	to find
ἐπαινέω, ἐπαινέσω, ἐπῄνεσα, ἐπῄνεκα	to praise
κινέω, κινήσω, ἐκίνησα, κεκίνημαι, ἐκινήθην	to move
λυπέω, λυπήσω, ἐλύπησα	to grieve
πίνω, πίομαι, ἔπιον, πέπωκα, πέπομαι, ἐπόθην	to drink
πορίζω, πορίσω, ἐπόρισα, πεπόρικα, πεπόρισμαι, ἐπορίσθην	to furnish
προσήκει	it concerns, befits

Adjectives

γενναῖος, γενναία, γενναῖον	noble
εὐκλεής, εὐκλεές	noble, of good reputation
σός, σή, σόν	your, yours

Adverbs

κάτωθεν	from below, below
πάρος + genitive	before, earlier than

Review 5

Prepositions

κατά + accusative	in accordance with
κατά + genitive	down from, against

Lesson 22

Nouns

δύναμις, δυνάμεως, ἡ	power, ability
κράτος, κράτους, τό	strength, power
νῆσος, νήσου, ἡ	island
πέπλος, πέπλου, ὁ	robe
σπονδαί, σπονδῶν, αἱ	treaty, truce

Verbs

ἀποκρίνομαι, ἀποκρινοῦμαι, ἀπεκρινάμην, ἀποκέκριμαι, ἀπεκρίθην	to answer
δράω, δράσω, ἔδρασα, δέδρακα, δέδραμαι, ἐδράσθην	to do
εἶμι	to go
ἐκφεύγω, ἐκφεύξομαι, ἐξέφυγον, ἐκπέφευγα	to escape
μαίνομαι, μανήσομαι, ἐμηνάμην, μέμηνα, μεμάνημαι, ἐμάνην	to rage
σιγάω, σιγήσω, ἐσίγησα, σεσίγηκα, σεσίγημαι, ἐσιγήθην	to be silent
τελευτάω, τελευτήσω, ἐτελεύτησα, τετελεύτηκα, τετελεύτημαι, ἐτελευτήθην	to bring to an end, to die

Adjectives

μέλας, μέλαινα, μέλαν	black
μηδείς, μηδεμία, μηδέν	none

Prepositions

περί + accusative	around
περί + dative	around
περί + genitive	about, concerning

Connectors/Clause Markers

μήδε	and not/but not
μήτε	nor
μήτε...μήτε	neither...nor
ὅμως	but still, nevertheless

Review 5

πρίν clause-marker + subjunctive or infinitive	before
πρίν clause-marker + past indicative	until

Lesson 23

Nouns

ἥρως, ἥρωος, ὁ	hero
νεκρός, νεκροῦ, ὁ	corpse

Verbs

ἐσθίω, ἔδομαι, ἔφαγον ἐδήδοκα, ἐδήδεσμαι, ἠδέσθην	to eat

Adjectives

μόνος, μόνη, μόνον	alone, only
ὅσος, ὅση, ὅσον	as, as great/much/many/long as

Adverbs

ἔνδοθεν	inside, from within
ἐντός	inward, within
ἔξωθεν	outside, from without

Lesson 24

Nouns

πατρίς, πατρίδος, ἡ	fatherland

Verbs

αἱρέω, αἱρήσω, εἷλον, ᾕρηκα, ᾕρημαι, ᾑρέθην	to take
ἡγέομαι, ἡγήσομαι, ἡγησάμην (+ dative or accusative)	to lead
θάπτω, θάψω, ἔθαψα, τέθαμμαι, ἐθάφθην/ἐτάφην	to bury
πλέω, πλεύσομαι, ἔπλευσα, πέπλευκα, πέπλευσμαι	to sail

Adjectives

ἕτοιμος, ἕτοιμον	ready, prepared
ἱκανός, ἱκανή, ἱκανόν	sufficient, competent, able

Prepositions

ὑπέρ + genitive	on behalf of

Lesson 25

Nouns

σχολή, σχολῆς, ἡ	leisure, free time

Review 5

Verbs

ἔρομαι, ἐρήσομαι, ἠρόμην	to ask
συμβαίνω, συμβήσομαι, συνέβην, συμβέβηκα	to happen, occur

Adverbs

ἐγγύς	near

Clause Markers

ὅταν	whenever

ANSWER KEY

Lesson 21

1. While you are a learner, trust a good teacher!
2. Men of Athens, hurry into the city!

Lesson 22

1. Let us rejoice, since youth is passing us by.
2. Never think an enemy a friend!
3. What should I do?

Lesson 23

1. If only Socrates had gone into exile!
2. May I not receive what I want, but rather what is useful to me.

Lesson 26

More on the Particle ὡς

There are several more variations of conditional and other clauses.

Instructors and students tend to be fascinated and overawed by these variations which are perhaps more important for understanding logic than for beginning to read. If you continue with the study of Greek you will want to master these variations. At your present level, it seems necessary to strengthen your mastery of the procedures you have already learned in order to help with another difficulty not limited to Greek.

While the meaning range of a word in one language is never exactly the same as that of a word in another language, this is especially true of clause markers. εἰ does not always mark a conditional clause, nor does ὅτι always mean *because*, nor does ὡς always correspond to English *as*. A wrong assumption may lead to trouble. Here are some guide lines for ὡς based on what you have learned so far.

I. Decide whether ὡς functions as a clause marker. Remember that for a word to function as clause marker there must be more than one kernel. Try to identify the kernel(s).

If there is only one kernel you have about five possibilities:

1. ὡς at the beginning of any sentence signals the speech act exclamation
   ὡς ἀστεῖος ὁ ἄνθρωπος
   How charming the man is! Plato

2. ὡς plus an accusative of a noun with the semantic feature animate is a preposition
   Τισσαφέρνης πορεύεται ὡς τὸν βασιλέα.
   Tissaphernes sets out towards the king. Xenophon

3. ὡς plus a superlative modifies the superlative
   οὐκοῦν βούλονταί σε ὡς εὐδαιμονέστατον γενέσθαι;
   Don't they want you to be as happy as possible? S18.6

4. ὡς as a comparative connector
   ἔξεστι χρῆσθαι τούτῳ ὡς ἀνδραπόδῳ.
   It is allowed to treat this person as a slave. Xenophon

5. μήτε σωμάτων ἐπιμελεῖσθαι μήτε χρημάτων πρότερον μηδὲ οὕτω σφόδρα ὡς τῆς ψυχῆς....
   (It is necessary) to take care neither of body nor of money as seriously as of the soul.... Plato, *Apology*

LESSON 26

II. If ὡς marks a clause, decide whether the clause is **finite** or **non-finite**. If the clause is **finite**, decide whether it is a noun-clause or an adverbial clause. Remember: if the governing kernel is not complete, the dependent clause is a noun clause. If so:

1. After a governing verb of saying/thinking/perceiving ὡς marks an indirect statement or an indirect perception.
   μέμνησο νέος ὢν **ὡς** γέρων ἔσει ποτέ.
   Remember while you are young, *that* you will be old some day. S19.8
2. After a governing verb of asking or informing ὡς marks an indirect question
   οἱ δὲ ἐν Σαλαμῖνι Ἕλληνες ὡς ἐξηγγέλθη **ὡς** ἔσχε τὰ περὶ τὴν Ἀθηναίων Ἀκρόπολιν.
   But the Greeks in Salamis when it was reported *how* things stood about the Acropolis of the Athenians... Herodotus

If the governing kernel is complete, ὡς marks a variety of adverbial clauses, among them are the following:

3. in any environment a temporal clause
   οἱ δὲ ἐν Σαλαμῖνι Ἕλληνες **ὡς** ἐξηγγέλθη ὡς ἔσχε τὰ περὶ τὴν Ἀθηναίων Ἀκρόπολιν...
   But the Greeks in Salamis *when* it was reported how things stood about the Akropolis of the Athenians...
4. in any environment a causal clause
   ὁ πένης ἐλεεῖται, **ὡς** ἡ πενία ἄτιμον καὶ τὸν εὐγενῆ ποιεῖ.
   The poor man is pitied *because* poverty makes even the well-born person dishonored. S11.3
5. with a signboard word a comparative clause
   ἐκέλευσε τοὺς Ἕλληνας, **ὡς** νόμος αὐτοῖς εἰς μάχην, **οὕτω** ταχθῆναι.
   He ordered the Greeks to establish the battle line *thus as* was their custom.
   Xenophon
6. after a signboard word a result clause
   οἱ δὲ ἐν Σαλαμῖνι Ἕλληνες ὡς ἐξηγγέλθη ὡς ἔσχε τὰ περὶ τὴν Ἀθηναίων Ἀκρόπολιν, εἰς **τοσοῦτον** θόρυβον ἀφίκοντο **ὡς**...ἱστία ἀείροντο
   But the Greeks in Salamis when it was reported how things stood about the Acropolis of the Athenians, fell into *such* a confusion *that*....they set sail.
7. followed by a subjunctive or a oblique optative
   ὡς, ὅπως or ἵνα may signal a purpose clause.
   παρακαλεῖς ἰατροὺς ὅπως μὴ ἀποθάνῃ.
   You are calling in doctors in order that he may not die. Xenophon

   βασιλεὺς αἱρεῖται οὐχ ἵνα ἑαυτοῦ καλῶς ἐπιμελῆται, ἀλλ᾽ ἵνα καὶ οἱ ἑλόμενοι δι᾽ αὐτὸν εὖ πράττωσι.

A king is chosen not that he may care for his own interest, however nobly, but that those who chose him may prosper through him. Xenophon

If the clause is **non-finite**

1. ὡς with a future participle signals purpose
οἱ δὲ ἐν Σαλιμῖνι Ἕλληνες ὡς ἐξηγγέλθη ὡς ἔσχε τὰ περὶ τὴν ᾿Αθηναίων Ακρόπολιν, εἰς τοσοῦτον θόρυβον ἀφίκοντο ὡς...ἱστία ἀείροντο **ὡς ἀποθευσόμενοι**.
But the Greeks in Salamis when it was reported how things stood about the Acropolis of the Athenians, fell into such a confusion that...they set sail *in order to* run away.

2. & 3. ὡς plus a circumstantial participle may signal a clause of comparison or a clause of cause. Which one it does signal, depends on the context and the comprehension of the pragmatic situation. When Xenophon *An*.4.2.5 writes ἐνταῦθ' ἔμενον **ὡς** τὸ ἄκρον κατέχοντες, it can mean "there they remained *since* they were occupying the summit," or it can mean "there they remained *as if* they were occupying the summit." In light of the following sentence "οἱ δ'οὐ κατεῖχον," "but they didn't occupy it," it must mean the latter. See Smyth 3001. The same holds for the genitive absolute. In S20.3 **ὡς** ἐπιβουλεύοντος Τισσαφέρνους can mean either '*because* Tissaphernes was plotting' or '*on the grounds that* Tissaphernes was plotting' or '*as if* Tissaphernes was plotting.'

You will perhaps now appreciate what a learner of English must learn so as to understand sentences containing *as*

She cooks a turkey exactly as my mother did..
I regard him as my best friend
Students should take notes so as to make revision easier.
Naked as I was I braved the storm.
Buy your tickets as soon as you reach the station.
As the strength of the defenders failed, so their courage grew.
As I am unaccustomed to public speaking, I beg your indulgence.
Quirk, *et al., A Comprehensive Grammar of The English Language*

Lesson 26

Readings

Now test your understanding of ὡς with some passages from Herodotus, appended by Allen to his *First Year of Greek:*

King Croesus of Lydia addresses Adrastus who needs purification, having accidentally killed his own brother:

> ἄνδρων τε φίλων τυγχάνεις ἔκγονος ὢν καὶ ἐλήλυθας ὡς φίλους. ἔνθα δεήσῃ χρήματος οὐδενὸς μένων ἐν ἡμῶν, τήν τε ταύτην ὡς κουφώτατα φέρων συμφορὰν κερδανεῖς πλεῖστον.

He entrusts Adrastus with his only son as the son, for whose life Croesus fears, insists on going on a dangerous hunt. These are his last words to his son

> ὡς οὖν νενικημένος ὑπὸ σοῦ μεταγιγνώσκω καὶ ἐῶ σε ἰέναι ἐπὶ τὴν ἄγραν.

As is to be expected the son is killed by the very Adrastus, who then gives himself up to Croesus.

> στὰς δ'οὗτος πρὸ τοῦ νεκροῦ παρεδίδου ἑαυτὸν Κροίσῳ...λέγων τὴν προτέραν συμφορὰν καὶ ὡς οὐκέτι αὐτῷ βιώσιμον.

Reading Vocabulary

βιώσιμον	life worth living
δεήσῃ	you will need
ἔκγονος	son
ἔνθα	there
κερδανεῖς	you will gain
κουφός, κουφή, κουφόν	easy
μεταγιγνώσκω	I change my mind
νεκροῦ (gen. of νεκρός)	of the corpse

Re-view

Speech Acts

All speech consists of speech acts. The main speech acts are

statement
question
command.

Text

A number of interactive speech acts following each other is called **text**. A good text is cohesive, it hangs together. How text coheres is one of the subjects of a new field of study called **pragmatics**.

Words and Word Classes: Parts of Speech

All speech acts and text consist of words put together according to phonetic, morphological, syntactic, semantic and pragmatic constraints. Words are commonly understood as belonging to word classes, also called **Parts of Speech**, that are morphologically and semantically defined. In this textbook the main **parts of speech** are: words that inflect for any of the following:

	case	number	gender	degree	person	tense	aspect	mood	voice
pronouns	•	•	•		•				
nouns	•	•							
article	•	•	•						
adjectives	•	•	•	•					
verbs		•			•	•	•	•	•
adverbs				•					

Words that do not inflect, also called indeclinables:

conjunctions
prepositions
particles

Words are subject to predictable **sound changes** which must be expected when looking for a word in the dictionary. Some of these have been treated in Pre-view.

Linguistic Devices

There are four linguistic devices

- word order
- function words
- agreement
- inflection

• **Word order**
Word order is the main syntactical device of English. This is not so in Greek, where word order mostly works as a pragmatic device involving text cohesiveness and functional sentence perspective. However, there are some fixed word order patterns, e.g. for enclitics or for the position of an adjectival modifier.

• **Function words**
Function words, primarily prepositions, another frequent syntactical device in English, become more frequent in ancient languages as case morphology weakens.

• **Agreement**
Compared to Greek there is little agreement in English. For the would-be writer the rules of agreement are very important. For the reader it is helpful to expect a plural subject, if the verb is plural, and something similar for the noun adjective relationship. See also sequence of mood.

• **Inflection**
The description of all possible forms in which the parts of speech that inflect appear is called **morphology**. Each of the parts of speech has its own morphology. Greek has a large morphology, English has a small one. See Morphology.

The Sentence and Syntactic Analysis

Speech acts appear in the form of sentences. A reader must always expect a complete **sentence**, at a minimum Plato's "Πρωταγόρας ἥκει." = "Protagoras is coming." (Plato *Protagoras* 310 B), no matter which speech act is involved. (And no matter how many items are Ø!) There are no restrictions on the length of a sentence; a sentence could be indefinitely long. The description of a sentence is called **syntax**. To be complete a sentence must have at least one complete framework or skeleton called the **kernel**. In addition there may be **modifiers** for each kernel part and **connectors** by means of which any item may be multiplied. The function an item fulfills on the level of kernel, modifier or connector is expressed by means of the linguistic devices.

The Kernel

The finite kernel of the Greek Sentence appears in the following forms, each part of which raises the expectation of the whole.

verb function	*subject*	*complement*
transitive active	•	accusative direct object
transitive passive	•	
intransitive active	•	
linking	•	nominative complement
factitive	•	2 accusatives
special	•	dative or genitive complement

Verbs are finite or non-finite:

Finite verbs are in the indicative, subjunctive, optative or imperative mood.
Non-finite verbs are infinitives or participles.
A finite verb raises the expectation of a subject in the nominative case, with which it agrees in person and number.

An infinitive raises the expectation of a subject in the accusative case.
The subject of a participle will be in the case required by text. The subject and the participle agree in case, number, gender.

Each part of the kernel may be Ø.

The kernel is expanded by **modifiers** or by **connection.**

The Modifiers

Modifiers modify any part of the kernel or each other.
Whatever is modified is the head of the modification construction.
A modifier raises the expectation of a head. The reverse is not true.

Modification constructions are of two kinds:

The **adjectival** modifier, where the head of the construction is a noun or noun equivalent.

The **adverbial** modifier, where the head of the construction is a verb, adjective, adverb or equivalent.

Connection

Connectors connect syntactical **sames**.

A connector raises the expectation of two **sames**.

Connectors are of two kinds:

The **coordinating** connection, where both sames play the same syntactic role.
The **subordinating** connection, where one same loses its independent character.

Syntactic Equivalents

For the purposes of syntactic analysis, the following are equivalents:

noun	=	pronoun, articular phrases consisting of article plus adjective, participle, genitive, prepositional phrase, infinitive phrase, participial phrase, dependent clause
adjective	=	pronoun, participle, a noun in a particular case, dependent clause
adverb	=	a noun in any case except nominative or vocative, with or without a preposition, dependent clause

Semantics

Semantics is the study of the structures of meaning. It cannot be described with the definiteness of syntax or morphology. But for the reader, certain semantic expectations, raised by certain parts of speech or syntactic functions can be helpful.

Semantic Roles:

Greek employs case inflection not only to indicate syntactic functions, but also to indicate semantic roles. These do not necessarily coincide.

The most frequent role for a subject, (never mind in what case), is **agent**, especially if the word in the subject slot has the semantic feature animate and the verb is in the active voice. The object most likely has the role of **patient**. However, if the verb is in the **passive voice**, the subject does not play the role of agent, but of **patient**. The subject may play other semantic roles, and the role of agent can be expressed in other ways, for example, by ὑπό with a genitive if the sentence verb is passive. The object of the preposition ὑπό may be assumed to have the semantic feature animate. In a sentence like "John loves dogs and baseball," *dogs* has the feature animate and *baseball* doesn't. "Dogs" and "baseball" are syntactic equivalents, but they are not semantic equivalents. One might argue that baseball here stands for people that play baseball or that dogs stand for games that dogs play. Such considerations are the subject matter of **pragmatics**, i.e. the interpretation of text by means of other considerations in addition to syntax and semantics.

For the reader semantic considerations are very useful in making acceptable inferences about the meaning of unknown words rather than relying on the dictionary. Semantic categories also help in learning vocabulary.

For example, in common language one expects an animate agent and a perceptable patient if the **verb** means to perceive or see, *e.g.* the elephant sees the mouse.

Most **nouns** in the genitive case raise the syntactic expectation of a nounhead of which the genitive is an adjectival modifier. Semantically a genitive raises the expectation of an agent, a patient, an owner or a whole.

Sense

It used to be said that one must expect a text to make sense (as opposed to no sense, not nonsense). Inasmuch as the sense structure of a language is like a network, in which the senses of all elements are directly or indirectly related to all other elements, this is good advice. Sense here means the kind of meaning associated with words and sentences by the language system, and not the individual speaker's meaning. If a verb means 'to give birth,' an agent will include the semantic features 'female' and 'alive,' even though pragmatically the agent might be 'sentiment/emotion, etc.' The referent of 'square' basically will have four equal sides and four right angles, although metaphorically and pragmatically it might mean a staid, conventional person. Learning to operate within the network of language, enables us to read, but learning to comprehend means going outside of the sentence. This is the arena of **Pragmatics**.

Pragmatics

"Pragmatics is sometimes contrasted with Semantics, which deals with meaning without reference to the user and communicative functions of sentences." "It is the study of the use of language in communication, particularly the relationship between sentences and the contexts and situations in which they are used." It recommends attention to tense, person, voice as signals for textual cohesion rather than as a means of syntax alone. It also recommends attention to the deictic dynamics of pronouns which can help with forming expectations and respectations. Attention to the meaning of word-order is another concern of pragmatics. The minimal sentence Πρωταγόρας ἥκει appears a few lines later as ἥκει Πρωταγόρας. Does this difference have any meaning? In terms of pragmatics one would examine the immediate and the larger context of the two speech acts for possible comprehension differences. The immediate context would include attention to the speakers and the hearers of the two sentences. A larger context would note that Plato had already previously told the reader about the arrival of Protagoras. An even larger context would possibly enquire about the intentions of Plato or the importance of sophists like Protagoras in Greek culture, and many other points. In short, pragmatics would look very much like 'Interpretation.' And like interpretation it might be wrong or right, but in any case interesting.

Socrates

Τὸ Μεμνῆσθαι Σωκράτους Ἥδιστον

Read, find, and copy as fully as necessary examples of:
1. καὶ, καὶ....καὶ, τε...καὶ, οὔτε...οὔτε
2. adjective in the attributive position
3. genitive in the attributive position
4. circumstantial participle
5. nominalized participle
6. non-finite participial noun-clause
7. non-finite infinitive noun-clause
8. finite noun-clause in kernel with a verb of perception
9. interrogative pronoun
10. indefinite pronoun
11. dative of time
12. genitive of indefinite time
13. dative of animate noun
14. nominalized prepostional phrase
15. nominalized genitive
16. kernel whose verb contains a supplementary participle
17. kernel whose verb contains a complementary infinitive
18. non-finite adverbial kernel
19. finite adjectival clause
20. speech act: command

SOCRATES

Τὸ Μεμνῆσθαι Σωκράτους Ἥδιστον Α'

The Phaedo of Plato describes the death of Socrates. The dialogue begins with a conversation between Phaedo, a devoted friend of Socrates and a certain Echecrates of Philiasia, a district near Corinth.

θαυμάζω, θαυμάσομαι wonder
παρα-γίγνομαι, παρα-γενήσομαι, παρ-εγενόμην be with (dat.)
πυνθάνομαι, πεύσομαι, ἐπυθόμην, πέπυσμαι learn (by inquiry, etc.)
τελευτάω -ήσω -ησα -ηκα bring to an end; die
φαίνομαι appear
δεσμωτήριον (τό) prison
δίκη (ἡ) right, justice, lawsuit, trial
ἐκεῖθεν from there
ἡδέως gladly
ξένος (ὁ) stranger, foreigner
οὐδεὶς πάνυ τι no one at all
πάλαι long ago
πλήν except
πολλῷ ὕστερον much later
σαφής σαφές clear (**σαφῶς**)
συχνός = πολύς
τρόπος (ὁ) turn, way, manner
ὃν τρόπον in what way
φάρμακον (τό) drug, poison

Αὐτός, ὦ Φαίδων, παρεγένου Σωκράτει ἐκείνῃ τῇ ἡμέρᾳ ᾗ τὸ φάρμακον ἔπιεν ἐν τῷ δεσμωτηρίῳ, ἢ ἄλλου του ἤκουσας;

Αὐτός. ὦ Ἐχέκρατες.

Τί οὖν δή ἐστιν ἅττα εἶπεν ὁ ἀνὴρ πρὸ τοῦ θανάτου; καὶ πῶς ἐτελεύτα; ἡδέως γὰρ ἂν ἐγὼ ἀκούσαιμι. καὶ γὰρ οὔτε τῶν πολιτῶν Φλειασίων οὐδεὶς πάνυ τι ἐπι-χωριάζει τὰ νῦν Ἀθήναζε, οὔτε τις ξένος ἀφ-ῖκται χρόνου συχνοῦ ἐκεῖθεν, ὅστις ἂν ἡμῖν σαφές τι ἀγγεῖλαι οἷός τ' ἦν περὶ τούτων, πλήν γε δὴ ὅτι φάρμακον πιὼν ἀπο-θάνοι· τῶν δὲ ἄλλων οὐδὲν εἶχεν φράζειν.

Οὐδὲ τὰ περὶ τῆς δίκης ἄρα ἐπύθεσθε ὃν τρόπον ἐγένετο;

Ναί, ταῦτα μὲν ἡμῖν ἤγγειλέ τις, καὶ ἐθαυμάζομέν γε ὅτι πάλαι γενομένης αὐτῆς πολλῷ ὕστερον φαίνεται ἀπο-θανών. Τί οὖν ἦν τοῦτο, ὦ Φαίδων;

Σχόλια

2 φάρμακον hemlock, poison
5 ἅττα = ἅτινα
7 Φλειαίων Philiasians In apposition with πολιτῶν

Τὸ Μεμνῆσθαι Σωκράτους Ἥδιστον Β'

ἄγω, ἄξω, ἤγαγον, ἦχα lead
ἀπάγω lead away, conduct
ἀποκτείνω, ἀποκτενῶ, ἀπέκτεινα kill
ἄρχομαι, ἄρξομαι, ἠρξάμην begin (gen.)
εὔχομαι, εὔξομαι, ηὐξάμην pray, vow
οἴχομαι + supplementary participle to go away
πέμπω, -ψω, ψα, πέπομφα send, conduct
σῴζω, σώσω, ἔσωσα, σέσωκα save
τυγχάνω, τεύξομαι, ἔτυχον (+ supplementary participle to chance)
ἄνεμος (ὁ) wind
'Απόλλων (ὁ) -ωνος Apollo
δίς twice
ἐνιαυτός (ὁ) year=ἔτος
κατ' ἐνιαυτόν each year
ἐνίοτε sometimes
ἔτος (τό) year
ἑκάστου ἔτους each year
πλοῖον (τό) boat
προτεραίᾳ on the day before
πρύμνα (ἡ) stern (of a boat)
τύχη (ἡ) chance, luck, fortune

Τύχη τις αὐτῷ, ὦ Ἐχέκρατες, συν-έβη· ἔτυχεν γὰρ τῇ προτεραίᾳ τῆς δίκης ἡ πρύμνα ἐστεμμένη τοῦ πλοίου, ὃ εἰς Δῆλον Ἀθηναῖοι πέμπουσιν.
Τοῦτο δὲ δὴ τί ἐστιν;
Τοῦτ' ἔστι τὸ πλοῖον, ὥς φασιν Ἀθηναῖοι, ἐν ᾧ Θησεύς ποτε εἰς Κρήτην τοὺς δὶς ἑπτὰ ἐκείνους ᾤχετο ἄγων καὶ ἔσωσέ τε καὶ αὐτὸς ἐσώθη. τῷ οὖν Ἀπόλλωνι ηὔξαντο, ὡς λέγεται, τότε, εἰ σωθεῖεν, ἑκάστου ἔτους θεωρίαν ἀπ-άξειν εἰς Δῆλον· ἣν δὴ ἀεὶ καὶ νῦν ἔτι ἐξ ἐκείνου κατ' ἐνιαυτὸν τῷ Θεῷ πέμπουσιν. ἐπειδὰν οὖν ἄρξωνται τῆς θεωρίας, νόμος ἐστὶν αὐτοῖς ἐν τῷ χρόνῳ τούτῳ δημοσίᾳ μηδένα ἀπο-κτεῖναι, πρὶν ἂν εἰς Δῆλον τε ἀφ-ίκηται τὸ πλοῖον καὶ πάλιν δεῦρο. τοῦτο δ' ἐνίοτε ἐν πολλῷ χρόνῳ γίγνεται, ὅταν τύχωσιν ἄνεμοι ἀπο-λαβόντες αὐτούς.

Σχόλια

18 τύχη τις...συν ἔβη a piece of luck befell
18 ἔτυχε...ἐστεμμένη chanced to have been wreathed (with wreaths of laurel) This indicated the beginning of the festival.
23 Θησεύς The legend was that the Athenians had agreed to send every ninth year to Minos, king of Crete, seven youths and seven maidens to be offered as a sacrifice to the Minotaur.
24 ᾤχετο ἄγων he had gone leading. Trans. conducted.
ἐσώθη escaped (was saved)
27 ἐξ ἐκείνου (τοῦ χρόνου)
32 ὅταν τύχωσιν...ἀπο-λαβόντες αὐτούς whenever they chance to delay them (ἀπο-λαμβάνω -λήψομαι, -έλαβον cut off, intercept, etc.)

Τὸ Μεμνῆσθαι Σωκράτους Ἥδιστον Γ'

στέφω, -ψω, -ψα, wreathe **ἐστεμμένη**
διηγέομαι, διηγήσομαι, διηγησάμην to narrate (+ gen.)
σχολάζω be at leisure
ἀσχολία (ἡ) business, engagement
ἐπιτήδειος (ὁ) intimate friend
ἔρημος -ον destitute of
ἥδιστος -η -ον most pleasant
ἱερεύς (ὁ) priest
μεταξύ between
ὡς σαφέστατα as clearly as possible
σχολή (ἡ) leisure

Ἀρχὴ δ' ἐστὶ τῆς θεωρίας, ἐπειδὰν ὁ ἱερεὺς τοῦ Ἀπόλλωνος στέψῃ τὴν πρύμναν τοῦ πλοίου. τοῦτο δ' ἔτυχεν, ὥσπερ λέγω, τῇ προτεραίᾳ τῆς δίκης γεγονός. διὰ ταῦτα καὶ πολὺς χρόνος ἐγένετο τῷ Σωκράτει ἐν τῷ δεσμωτηρίῳ ὁ μεταξὺ τῆς δίκης καὶ τοῦ θανάτου.

Τί δὲ δὴ τὰ περὶ αὐτὸν τὸν θάνατον, ὦ Φαίδων; Τί ἦν τὰ λεχθέντα καὶ πραχθέντα, καὶ τίνες οἱ παρα-γενόμενοι τῶν ἐπιτηδείων τῷ ἀνδρί; ἢ οὐκ εἴων οἱ ἄρχοντες παρ-εῖναι, ἀλλ' ἔρημος ἐτελεύτα φίλων;

Οὐδαμῶς, ἀλλὰ παρ-ῆσάν τινες, καὶ πολλοί γε. Ταῦτα δὴ πάντα πειρῶ ὡς σαφέστατα ἡμῖν ἀπαγγεῖλαι, εἰ μή τίς σοι ἀσχολία τυγχάνει οὖσα. Ἀλλὰ σχολάζω γε καὶ πειράσομαι ὑμῖν δι-ηγήσασθαι. καὶ γὰρ τὸ μεμνῆσθαι Σωκράτους καὶ αὐτὸν λέγοντα καὶ ἄλλου ἀκούοντα ἔμοιγε ἀεὶ πάντων ἥδιστον.

Σχόλια

38 ὁ μεταξύ, i.e. ὁ χρόνος μεταξύ
41 τὰ λεχθέντα καὶ (τὰ) πραχθέντα the things that were said and done
42 οἱ παρα-γενόμενοι those who were present with
43 οἱ ἄρχοντες the officials These were a board of police commissioners known as The Eleven. They had jurisdiction over malefactors and authority over the servants of the prison.
45 καὶ πολλοί γε yes, many.

Το Μεμνησθαι Σωκρατους Ηδιστον Δ'

ἀν-οίγω, ἀν-οίξω, ἀν-έῳξα, ἀν-εῴχθην open
δι-ημερεύω spend the day
ἥκω have come, be present
κρίνω, κρινῶ, ἔκρινα, ἐκρίθην distinguish, judge, condemn
περι-μένω wait (around), await
συλ-λέγω, -ξω, -ξα, -συν-ελέγην gather, collect M/P come together
σωφρονέω be of sound mind
φοιτάω, -ήσω come (go) frequently
ἀκριβέστατα most accurately
δικαστήριον (τὸ) court of justice
ἑκάστοτε each time
ἑσπέρας in the evening
ἕωθεν early in the morning
ἕως until
ὅπως ποτέ how in the world
πλησίον near
πρῴ early Comp. πρῳαίτερον, Super. πρωάιτατα

Ἀλλὰ μήν, ὦ Φαίδων, καὶ τοὺς ἀκουσομένους γε τοιούτους ἑτέρους ἔχεις· ἀλλὰ πειρῶ ὡς ἂν δύνῃ ἀκριβέστατα δι-εξ-ελθεῖν πάντα...

Ἐγώ σοι, ὦ Ἐχέκρατες, ἐξ ἀρχῆς πάντα πειράσομαι δι-ηγήσασθαι. ἀεὶ γὰρ δὴ καὶ τὰς πρόσθεν ἡμέρας εἰώθεμεν φοιτᾶν καὶ ἐγὼ καὶ οἱ ἄλλοι παρὰ τὸν Σωκράτη, συλ-λεγόμενοι ἕωθεν εἰς τὸ δικαστήριον, ἐν ᾧ καὶ ἡ δίκη ἐγένετο· πλησίον γὰρ ἦν τοῦ δεσμωτηρίου. περι-εμένομεν οὖν ἑκάστοτε, ἕως ἀν-οιχθείη τὸ δεσμωτήριον, δια-τρίβοντες μετ' ἀλλήλων· ἀν-εῴγετο γὰρ οὐ πρῴ. ἐπειδὴ δὲ ἀν-οιχθείη, εἰσ-ῆμεν παρὰ τὸν Σωκράτη καὶ τὰ πολλὰ δι-ημερεύομεν μετ' αὐτοῦ. καὶ δὴ καὶ τότε πρῳαίτερον συν-ελέγημεν. τῇ γὰρ προτεραίᾳ ἡμέρᾳ ἐπειδὴ ἐξ-ήλθομεν ἐκ τοῦ δεσμωτηρίου ἑσπέρας, ἐπυθόμεθα ὅτι τὸ πλοῖον ἐκ Δήλου ἀφ-ιγμένον εἴη. παρ-ηγγείλαμεν οὖν ἀλλήλοις ἥκειν ὡς πρῳαίτατα εἰς τὸ εἰωθός.

Σχολια

52 τοὺς ἀκουσομένους those who are about to hear. Transl. you have (in) your listeners others of like disposition
57 εἰώθεμεν it was our custom (we were accustomed). A past form of εἴωθα
60 ἕως ἀν-οιχθεί τό δ. until the prison should be opened.

Το Μεμνησθαι Σωκρατους Ηδιστον Ε'

ἀν-ευφημέω cry aloud, shriek
βοάω, βοήσομαι shout, bawl
γιγνώσκω, γνώσομαι recognize, know
κατα-λαμβάνω seize, catch, come upon, find
κόπτομαι strike oneself, beat one's breast
προσ-αγορεύω προσ-ερῶ, προσεῖπονaddress
ὑπ-ακούω listen, hearken to, answer (a knock at the door)
ἄρτι just now
ἀρτι λελυμένον just released (from his shackles)
θυρωρός (ὁ) doorkeeper
Κρίτων (ὁ) -ωνος Criton, a friend of Socrates
Ξανθίππη (ἡ) Xanthippe, the wife of Socrates
τοιαῦτα ἄττα (some) such things
ὕστατον δή for the very last time

καὶ ἥκομεν καὶ ἡμῖν ἐξ-ελθὼν ὁ θυρωρός, ὅσπερ εἰώθει ὑπ-ακούειν, εἶπεν περι-μένειν καὶ μὴ πρότερον παρ-ιέναι, ἕως ἂν αὐτὸς κελεύσῃ· "Λύουσι γάρ," ἔφη, "οἱ ἕνδεκα Σωκράτη καὶ παρ-αγγέλλουσιν ὅπως ἂν τῇδε τῇ ἡμέρᾳ τελευτήσῃ." οὐ πολὺν δ' οὖν χρόνον ἐπι-σχὼν ἧκεν καὶ ἐκέλευεν ἡμᾶς εἰσ-ιέναι. εἰς-ελθόντες οὖν κατ-ελαμβάνομεν τὸν μὲν Σωκράτη ἄρτι λελυμένον, τὴν δὲ Ξανθίππην (γιγνώσκεις γάρ) ἔχουσάν τε τὸ παιδίον αὐτοῦ καὶ παρα-καθ-ημένην. ὡς οὖν εἶδεν ἡμᾶς ἡ Ξανθίππη, ἀν-ηυφήμησέ τε καὶ τοιαῦτ' ἄττα εἶπεν, οἷα δὴ εἰώθασιν αἱ γυναῖκες, ὅτι "Ὦ Σώκρατες, ὕστατον δή σε προσ-εροῦσι νῦν οἱ ἐπιτήδειοι καὶ σὺ τούτους." καὶ ὁ Σωκράτης βλέψας εἰς τὸν Κρίτωνα· "Ὦ Κρίτων," ἔφη, "ἀπ-αγέτω τις αὐτὴν οἴκαδε." καὶ ἐκείνην μὲν ἀπ-ῆγόν τινες τῶν τοῦ Κρίτωνος βοῶσάν τε καὶ κοπτομένην...

Σχολια

71 εἶπεν = ἐκελευσεν
73 οἱ ἕνδεκα The Eleven
75 ἐπι-σχών delaying Aorist participle of ἐπ-έχω check, restrain, used intransitively: check oneself, wait, pause
78 τὸ παιδίον this was probably Socrates' youngest son
79 παρα-καθ-ημενην sitting beside (Socrates)
85 τῶν τοῦ Κρίτωνος (ἀκολούθων) attendants)

Το Μεμνησθαι Σωκρατους Ηδιστον Σ

ἐκφεύγω flee away, escape
ἡγέομαι think
θάπτω bury
θαρρέω take heart, be of good cheer
φάναι to say. Infinitive of φνμί
φεύγω φεύξομαι, ἔφυγον, πέφευγα flee
ἐάνπερ if
ἡσχυῇ quietly
νεκρός (ὁ) corpse
νόμιμος, -η, -ον customary

After Xanthippe had been haled away Socrates and his companions discussed at great length the subject of immortality. At the conclusion of the dialogue Crito asked Socrates: how are we to bury you?

"Ὅπως ἄν," ἀπ-εκρίνατο Σωκράτης, "βούλησθε, ἐάνπερ γε λάβητέ με καὶ μὴ ἐκ-φύγω ὑμᾶς."

γελάσας δὲ ἅμα ἡσυχῇ καὶ πρὸς ἡμᾶς ἀπο-βλέψας εἶπεν· "Οὐ πείθω, ὦ ἄνδρες, Κρίτωνα, ὡς ἐγὼ εἰμι οὗτος ὁ Σωκράτης, ὁ νῦν δια-λεγόμενος καὶ δια-τάττων ἕκαστον τῶν λεγομένων, ἀλλ' οἴεταί με ἐκεῖνον εἶναι, ὃν ὄψεται ὀλίγον ὕστερον νεκρόν, καὶ ἐρωτᾷ δή, πῶς με θάπτῃ."...

"Ἀλλ', ὦ ἄριστε Κρίτων, θαρρεῖν τε χρὴ καὶ φάναι τοὐμὸν σῶμα θάπτειν, καὶ θάπτειν οὕτως ὅπως ἄν σοι φίλον ᾖ καὶ μάλιστα ἡγῇ νόμιμον εἶναι."

Σχολια

92 δια-τάττων... λεγομένων duly arranging every part of his discourse
94 πῶς με θάπτῃ indirect for of the deliberative question
96 With the second θάπτειν supply χρή.

Το Μεμνησθαι Σωκρατους Ηδιστον Ζ

δια-λέγομαι converse
δια-τρίβω, -τρίψω, -έτριψα spend (time)
ἐπι-στέλλω, -στελῶ, -έστειλα order, command
ἅττα = ἅτινα
δυσμαί, (αἱ) setting
ἐγγύς near (+gen.)
ἐναντίον in the presence of (+gen.)
ἔνδον within
οἰκεῖος, -α, -ον belonging to the household
οἴκημα (τό) room, chamber
υἱεῖς (οἱ) sons
ἕπτομαι, past imperf.εἰπόμην follow (+dat.)
λούομαι, -σομαι, -σάμην, λέλουμαι take a bath
φέρω, οἴσω, ἤνεγκα/ἤνεγκον, aor. pass. **ἠνέχθην** bear, bring

ταῦτ᾽ εἰπὼν ἐκεῖνος μὲν ἀν-ίστατο εἰς οἴκημά τι ὡς λουσόμενος, καὶ ὁ Κρίτων εἵπετο αὐτῷ, ἡμας δ᾽ ἐκέλευε περι-μένειν … ἐπειδὴ δὲ ἐλούσατο καὶ ἠνέχθη παρ᾽ αὐτὸν τὰ παιδία – δύο γὰρ αὐτῷ υἱεῖς σμικροὶ ἦσαν, εἷς δὲ μέγας - καὶ αἱ οἰκεῖαι γυναῖκες ἀφ-ίκοντο, ἐκείναι ἐναντίον τοῦ Κρίτωνος δια-λεχθείς τε καὶ ἐπι-στείλας ἅττα ἐβούλετο, τὰς μὲν γυναῖκας καὶ τὰ παιδία ἀπ-ιέναι ἐκέλευσεν, αὐτὸς δὲ ἧκε παρ᾽ ἡμᾶς. καὶ ἦν ἤδη ἐγγὺς ἡλίου δυσμῶν· χρόνον γὰρ πολὺν δι-έτριψεν ἔνδον. ἐλθὼν δ᾽ ἐκαθέζετο λελουμένος, καὶ οὐ πολλὰ μετὰ ταῦτα δι-ελέχθη.

Σχολια

98 ἀν-ίστατο εἰς οἴκημά τι arose and went into a room

Το Μεμνησθαι Σωκρατους Ηδιστον Η’

Socrates as seen by an ordinary person.
Instructions: Read and translate, continuing the speech
The servant of the Eleven came and standing near him, said “Oh Socrates, I shall not accuse you of that of which I accuse other men, namely that...

χαλεπαίνω be angry with
ἀναγκάζω to force
ἄλλως on other occasions
πώποτε ever yet
ἀναγκαῖος -α-ον necessary
μεταστρέφομαι to turn around
καταράομαι to curse
γιγνώσκω to come to know
πρᾶος -ον gentle
αἴτιος -α -ον guilty
δακρυω to cry

“...ὅτι μοι χαλεπαίνουσι καὶ κατ-αρῶνται, ἐπειδὰν αὐτοῖς παρ-αγγείλω πίνειν τὸ φάρμακον ἀναγκαζόντων τῶν ἀρχόντων. σὲ δὲ ἐγὼ καὶ ἄλλως ἔγνωκα ἐν τούτῳ τῷ χρόνῳ γενναιότατον καὶ πραότατον καὶ ἄριστον ἄνδρα ὄντα τῶν πώποτε δεῦρο ἀφ-ικομένων, καὶ δὴ καὶ νῦν εὖ οἶδ’ ὅτι οὐκ ἐμοὶ χαλεπαίνεις (γιγνώσκεις γὰρ τοὺς αἰτίους) ἀλλὰ ἐκείνοις. νῦν οὖν, οἶσθα γὰρ ἃ ἦλθον ἀγγέλλων, χαῖρέ τε καὶ πειρῶ ὡς ῥᾷστα φέρειν τὰ ἀναγκαῖα.” καὶ ἅμα δακρύσας μεταστρεφόμενος ἀπ-ῄει.

Basic Sentences

1.1 κρίνει τὸν φίλον ὁ καιρός.

1.2 χεὶρ χεῖρα νίπτει.

1.3 ἡ χεὶρ τὴν χεῖρα νίζει.

1.4 ἔρωτα παύει λιμός.

1.5 ὁ χρόνος τρέχει.

1.6 ἀρετὴ μένει.

2.1 ἡ δὲ χεὶρ τὴν χεῖρα νίζει.

2.2 χεὶρ χεῖρα νίπτει, δάκτυλον δὲ δάκτυλος.

2.3 δίκη δίκην τίκτει, βλάβην δὲ βλάβη.

2.4 νὺξ μὲν ἀναπαύει, ἡμέρα δὲ ἔργον ποιεῖ.

2.5 ὁ λύκος τὴν τρίχα, οὐ τὴν γνώμην ἀλλάττει.

3.1 τίς τὴν τρίχα ἀλλάττει;

3.2 τί ὁ λύκος ἀλλάττει;

3.3 ἆρα ὁ λύκος τὴν τρίχα ἀλλάττει;

3.4 ἀλλάττει τις τὴν τρίχα.

3.5 ἀλλάττει ὁ λύκος τι.

4.1 ἀεὶ γὰρ καλῶς βάλλει τὸν κύβον Ζεύς.

4.2 εἰρήνη μὲν γεωργὸν κἀν (=καὶ ἐν) πέτρᾳ τρέφει καλῶς, πόλεμος δὲ κἀν πεδίῳ κακῶς.

4.3 πρὸς γὰρ τὸν πλοῦτον ὁ φθόνος ἕρπει.

4.4 σὺν θεῷ.

4.5 ἄνευ δὲ εὐψυχίας τέχνη πρὸς τὸν κίνδυνον οὐκ ἰσχύει.

4.6 σὺν δίκῃ.

4.7 τὴν δὲ ὀρθότητα καὶ τὴν ὠφέλιαν καὶ τὸ εὖ καὶ τὸ καλῶς ἡ ἀλήθεια ἀποτελεῖ.

5.1 ἡ γὰρ παράκαιρος ἡδονὴ τίκτει βλάβην.

5.2 τὸ ῥόδον ἀκμάζει βαιὸν χρόνον.

5.3 ὁ γὰρ ἐν καιρῷ μόχθος εὐδαιμονίαν τίκτει.

5.4 ὁ σοφὸς περιφέρει τὴν οὐσίαν.

5.5 πρὸς υἱὸν ὀργὴν οὐκ ἔχει χρηστὸς πατήρ.

6.1 ὁ πένης ἐλεεῖται, ὁ δὲ πλούσιος φθονεῖται.

6.2 οὐκ ἀμελεῖται ὑπὸ θεοῦ ὁ δίκαιος.

6.3 χρηστὸς πονηρῷ οὐ τιτρώσκεται λόγῳ.

6.4 τάχα γάρ σε παρέρχεται ἥβη.

6.5 ψευδὴς διαβολὴ τὸν βίον λυμαίνεται.

Basic Sentences

6.6. οὐδεὶς μετ' ὀργῆς ἀσφαλῶς βουλεύεται.

7.1 νύκτες μὲν ἀναπαύουσιν, ἡμέραι δὲ ἔργα ποιοῦσιν.

7.2 οἱ λύκοι τὰς τρίχας, οὐ τὴν γνώμην ἀλλάττουσιν.

7.3 ἀεὶ γὰρ καλῶς βάλλει τοὺς κύβους Ζεύς.

7.4 τὰ ῥόδα ἀκμάζει βαιὸν χρόνον.

7.5 ψευδεῖς διαβολαὶ τόν βίον λυμαίνονται.

7.6 ἀνὴρ τις δύο ἔσχεν ἑταίρας, τὴν μὲν γραῦν, τὴν δὲ νέαν.

7.7 τὰ περὶ δρόμους ἀνδράσι τε καὶ γυναιξὶ ταῦτά ἐστιν.

7.8 οἱ μὲν φεύγουσι, οἱ δὲ μένουσιν.

8.1 οἱ μὲν οἰκέται τοῖς δεσπόταις, οἱ δὲ φαῦλοι ταῖς ἐπιθυμίαις δουλεύουσιν.

8.2 ἐκ τῶν πόνων γὰρ τἀγαθὰ αὔξεται βροτοῖς.

8.3 χρηστὸς πονηροῖς οὐ τιτρώσκεται λόγοις.

8.4 ἀβουλίᾳ πολλοὶ βλάπτονται.

9.1 πάντες τῶν ἀγαθῶν ἐπιθυμοῦσιν.

9.2 ψυχῆς πόνοι γὰρ ὑπὸ λόγου κουφίζονται.

9.3 ὁ ἀγαθὸς πολίτης καὶ τοῦ σώματος καὶ τῆς οὐσίας προνοεῖται· ὁ τοιοῦτος καὶ τὰ τῆς πόλεως βούλεται ὀρθοῦσθαι.

9.4 ὁ χρόνος λύπης ἰατρός.

10.1 τό τε γὰρ ἀγαθὸν ἁπλοῦν, τὸ δὲ κακὸν πολύμορφον.

10.2 λύπης ἰατρός ἐστιν ὁ χρηστὸς φίλος.

10.3 ἰδίας νόμιζε τῶν φίλων τὰς συμφοράς.

10.4 ὁ δὲ πλοῦτος ἡμᾶς πάντας τυφλοὺς ποιεῖ.

10.5 φασὶν κακίστους οἱ πονηροὶ τοὺς κακούς.

11.1 ἐκ τῶν πόνων γὰρ τἀγαθὰ αὔξεται βροτοῖς, ἐπεὶ ὁ ἐν καιρῷ μόχθος εὐδαιμονίαν τίκτει.

11.2 Κλέαρχος ὧδε ἄρχεται λόγου, ὅτε οἱ στρατιῶται τοῖς Πέρσαις οὐ πιστεύουσιν.

11.3 ὁ πένης ἐλεεῖται, ὡς ἡ πενία ἄτιμον καὶ τὸν εὐγενῆ ποιεῖ.

11.4 ὁ ἀγαθὸς πολίτης τὰ τῆς πόλεως βούλεται ὀρθοῦσθαι ἕως ὁ ἄνθρωπος οἰκονομικὸν ζῷον.

11.5 καὶ εἰ κάλλιστον ἐν κήποις φύεται ῥόδον, βαιὸν ἀκμάζει χρόνον.

Basic Sentences

12.1 [Δαρεῖος] Κῦρον δὲ μεταπέμπεται ἀπὸ τῆς ἀρχῆς, ἧς αὐτὸν σατράπην ἐποίησεν.

12.2 ἔστιν δίκης ὀφθαλμός, ὃς τὰ πάνθ' ὁρᾷ.

12.3 μακάριος, ὅστις οὐσίαν καὶ νοῦν ἔχει.

12.4 ὃν οἱ θεοὶ φιλοῦσιν, ἀποθνῄσκει νέος.

12.5 ὅστις τῶν Μουσῶν ἐπιλανθάνεται, οὗτος βίον διαφθείρει.

15.1 ὁ μὴ γαμῶν ἄνθρωπος οὐκ ἔχει κακά.

15.2 ὁ ἄνθρωπος μὴ γαμῶν οὐκ ἔχει κακά.

15.3 συμβουλεύω σοι καίπερ νέος ὤν.

15.4 ὁ Κῦρος ἅτε παῖς ὢν καὶ φιλόκαλος καὶ φιλότιμος ἥδετο τῇ στολῇ.

15.5 οἶδα σοφὸς ὤν.

15.6 στυγεῖ δὲ τοὺς τεκόντας, αὐτὸς οὐ θέλων θανεῖν.

15.7 πατὴρ οὐχ ὁ γεννήσας, ἀλλ' ὁ θρέψας σε.

15.8 ἡδὺ τῷ μισοῦντι τοὺς φαύλους τρόπους ἐρημία.

15.9 οἱ δὲ Λυδοί τε καὶ οἱ Μῆδοι, ἔπειτε εἶδον νύκτα ἀντὶ ἡμέρας γενομένην ἐπαύσαντο μαχόμενοι.

16.1. ἰσχυρότερον δέ γ' οὐδέν ἐστιν τοῦ λόγου.

16.2. καὶ παρ' ἡμῖν πειθαρχεῖν δεῖ θεῷ μᾶλλον ἢ ἀνθρώποις

16.3. ἀνδρειότερος εἶναί μοι δοκεῖ ὁ τῶν ἐπιθυμίων ἢ τῶν πολεμίων κρατῶν; καὶ γὰρ χαλεπώτατόν ἐστι τὸ ἑαυτὸν νικῆσαι.

16.4. οὗτος σοφώτατός ἐστιν ἀνθρώπων, ὅστις, ὥσπερ Σωκράτης, ἔγνωκεν οὐδενὸς ἄξιος ὢν πρὸς σοφίαν.

16.5. ἔστιν γὰρ οὕτως ὥσπερ οὗτος λέγει.

17.1 θέλομεν καλῶς ζῆν πάντες, ἀλλ' οὐ δυνάμεθα.

17.2 δύναται τὸ πλουτεῖν καὶ φιλανθρώπους ποιεῖν.

17.3 φύσιν πονηρὰν μεταβαλεῖν οὐ ῥάδιον.

17.4 πιστεύειν δεῖ τοὺς μανθάνοντας.

17.5 οὔ μοι ἔξεστιν ποιεῖν ἃ βούλομαι.

18.1 ἀλλ' ἐγὼ παύσω τοῦτο γιγνόμενον.

18.2 καὶ δείξω αὐτὸν πολλῶν θανάτων οὐχ ἑνὸς ὄντ' ἄξιον.

18.3 τῶν δὲ Μένωνος στρατιωτῶν τις εἶδε Κλέαρχον διελαύνοντα.

18.4 ἤκουσαν αὐτοῦ φωνήσαντος.

18.5 δοῦλον ἐῶσι ποιεῖν ἃ βούλεται, σὲ δὲ διακωλύουσιν;

18.6 οὐκοῦν βούλονταί σε ὡς εὐδαιμονέστατον γενέσθαι;

18.7 νόμιζε δ' εἰ σὺ φιλεῖς τὴν ψυχήν, φιλεῖν ἅπαντας.

Basic Sentences

18.8 χαίρεις ὁρῶν τὸ φῶς; πατέρα δ'οὐ χαίρειν δοκείς;

18.9 πάντες ἔλεγον τοὺς τούτων ἄρξαντας δίκην δοῦναι.

19.1 οὔπω δῆλον ἦν τί ποιήσουσιν οἱ ἄλλοι.

19.2 ἠρώτων ὅ τι ἐστὶν τὸ πρᾶγμα.

19.3 ᾔδει δὲ οὐδεὶς ὅποι στρατεύουσιν.

19.4 εἰ μὲν δὴ δίκαια ποιήσω οὐκ οἶδα.

19.5 διηρώτα τὸν Κῦρον πότερον βούλεται μένειν ἢ ἀπιέναι.

19.6 Συέννεσις ᾔσθετο ὅτι τὸ Μένωνος στράτευμα ἤδη ἐν Κιλικίᾳ ἦν.

19.7 οἱ ἄνδρες ἔλεγον ὅτι Κῦρος τέθνηκε.

19.8 μέμνησο νέος ὢν ὡς γέρων ἔσει ποτέ.

20.1 Κῦρος δ' οὖν ἀνέβη ἐπὶ τὰ ὄρη οὐδενὸς κωλύοντος.

20.2 πολλοὶ γὰρ κατέβησαν καὶ ἅτε θεωμένων τῶν ἑταίρων πολλὴ φιλονικία ἐγίγνετο.

20.3 παρήγγειλε τοῖς φρουράρχοις λαμβάνειν ἄνδρας Πελοποννησίους ὡς ἐπιβουλεύοντος Τισσαφέρνους ταῖς πόλεσιν.

20.4 καὶ χρήματα πολλὰ προσλαβὼν οὕτως, ἀποπλεῖ οἴκαδε καίπερ μέσου χειμῶνος ὄντος.

21.1 εἰ βούλει καλῶς ἀκούειν, μάνθανε καλῶς λέγειν· μαθὼν δὲ καλῶς λέγειν πειρῶ καλῶς πράττειν, καὶ καρπώσῃ τὸ καλῶς ἀκούειν.

21.2 μαθὼν δὲ καλῶς λέγειν πειρῶ καλῶς πράττειν, καὶ καρπώσῃ τὸ καλῶς ἀκούειν.

21.3 εἰς Μύνδον ἐλθὼν καὶ θεασάμενος μεγάλας τὰς πύλας, μικρὰν δὲ τὴν πόλιν "ἄνδρες Μύνδιοι," ἔφη, "κλείσατε τὰς πύλας, μὴ ἡ πόλις ὑμῶν ἐξέλθῃ."

21.4 ἴστω νῦν εὐκλεής γε κατθανουμένη
γυνή τ'ἀρίστη τῶν ὑφ'ἡλίῳ μακρῷ.

21.5 ἃ μὴ προσήκει μήτ'ἄκουε μήθ'ὅρα.

22.1 τέμω τρίχα / καὶ μέλανα στολμὸν πέπλων ἀμφιβαλώμεθ'ἤδη; / δῆλα μὲν, φίλοι, δῆλά γε, ἀλλ'ὅμως / θεοῖσιν εὐχώμεθα! θεῶν γὰρ δύναμις μεγίστη.

22.2 ἴωμεν εἰς Σαλαμῖνα, μαχησόμενοι περὶ νήσου!

22.3 λόγον παρ'ἐχθροῦ μήποθ' ἡγήσῃ φίλον!

23.1 χαίροιτε ... ἥρωες! ἡ λύρη γὰρ μόνους ἔρωτας ᾄδει.

23.2 ὦ φίλε Πάν τε καὶ ἄλλοι ὅσοι τῇδε θεοί! δοίητέ μοι καλῷ γενέσθαι τἄνδοθεν! ἔξωθεν δ' ὅσα ἔχω, τοῖς ἐντὸς εἶναί μοι φίλια! πλούσιον δὲ νομίζοιμι τὸν σοφόν!

23.3 εἴθε τοὺς νεκροὺς ᾔσθιες καὶ μὴ τοὺς ζῶντας!

Basic Sentences

23.4 εἴθ'ηὕρομέν σ',"Αδμητε, μὴ λυπούμενον!

24.1 σοῦ γὰρ φθιμένης, οὐκέτ'ἂν εἴην.

24.2 οὐ τοι ἂν φθιμένης γ' (ø = αὐτῆς) ἐσιώπων.

24.3 τίς γὰρ ἂν ᾠήθη ταῦτα γενέσθαι;

25.1 οὐκ ἂν ἐποίησε 'Αγασίας ταῦτα, εἰ μὴ ἐγὼ αὐτὸν ἐκέλευσα.

25.2 εἰ ἀλγεῖν συνέβαινε τὴν κεφαλὴν πρὸ τοῦ πιεῖν, ἡμῶν οὐδὲ εἷς ἔπινεν ἄν.

25.3 εἴ τις ὑπερβάλλοι τὸ μέτριον,
τὰ ἐπιτερπέστατα ἀτερπέστατα ἂν γίγνοιτο.

25.4 ἢν δ'ἔγγυς ἔλθῃ θάνατος, οὐδεὶς βούλεται θνῄσκειν.

25.5 ὅστις οἴεται κακόν τι πράσσων τοὺς θεοὺς
λεληθέναι, δοκεῖ πονηρὰ καὶ δοκῶν ἁλίσκεται,
ὅταν σχολὴν ἄγουσα τυγχάνῃ δίκη.

Morphology

The Definite Article

	masculine	*feminine*	*neuter*
nominative	ὁ	ἡ	τὸ
genitive	τοῦ	τῆς	τοῦ
dative	τῷ	τῇ	τῷ
accusative	τὸν	τὴν	τὸ
nominative	οἱ	αἱ	τὰ
genitive	τῶν	τῶν	τῶν
dative	τοῖς	ταῖς	τοῖς
accusative	τοὺς	τὰς	τὰ

Nouns

First Declension

α and η stems

	feminine			
nominative	τιμή	μνήμη	θάλαττα	σοφία
genitive	τιμῆς	μνήμης	θαλάττης	σοφίας
dative	τιμῇ	μνήμῃ	θαλάττῃ	σοφίᾳ
accusative	τιμήν	μνήμην	θάλατταν	σοφίαν
nominative	τιμαί	μνῆμαι	θάλατται	σοφίαι
genitive	τιμῶν	μνημῶν	θαλαττῶν	σοφιῶν
dative	τιμαῖς	μνήμαις	θαλάτταις	σοφίαις
accusative	τιμάς	μνήμας	θαλάττας	σοφίας

	masculine	
nominative	πολίτης	νεανίας
genitive	πολίτου	νεανίου
dative	πολίτῃ	νεανίᾳ
accusative	πολίτην	νεανίαν
nominative	πολῖται	νεανίαι
genitive	πολιτῶν	νεανιῶν
dative	πολίταις	νεανίαις
accusative	πολίτας	νεανίας

Morphology

Second Declension
o and ω stems

	masculine	neuter	contract noun (masc.)
nominative	ἄνθρωπος	ἔργον	νοῦς
genitive	ἀνθρώπου	ἔργου	νοῦ
dative	ἀνθρώπῳ	ἔργῳ	νῷ
accusative	ἄνθρωπον	ἔργον	νοῦν
nominative	ἄνθρωποι	ἔργα	νοῖ
genitive	ἀνθρώπων	ἔργων	νῶν
dative	ἀνθρώποις	ἔργοις	νοῖς
accusative	ἀνθρώπους	ἔργα	νοῦς

Third Declension
Consonant stems

	Π/K mute	T mute	-σ	-ι
nominative	ὁ κῆρυξ	ὁ ἄρχων	τό γένος	ἡ πόλις
genitive	κήρυκος	ἄρχοντος	γένους	πόλεως
dative	κήρυκι	ἄρχοντι	γένει	πόλει
accusative	κήρυκα	ἄρχοντα	γένος	πόλιν
nominative	κήρυκες	ἄρχοντες	γένη	πόλεις
genitive	κηρύκων	ἀρχόντων	γενῶν	πόλεων
dative	κήρυξι	ἄρχουσι	γένεσι	πόλεσι
accusative	κήρυκας	ἄρχοντας	γένη	πόλεις

	liquid	syncopated liquid	diphthong	-υ
nominative	δαίμων	ἀνήρ	βασιλεύς	ἄστυ
genitive	δαίμονος	ἀνδρός	βασιλέως	ἄστεως
dative	δαίμονι	ἀνδρί	βασιλεῖ	ἄστει
accusative	δαίμονα	ἄνδρα	βασιλέα	ἄστυ
nominative	δαίμονες	ἄνδρες	βασιλεῖς	ἄστη
genitive	δαιμόνων	ἀνδρῶν	βασιλέων	ἄστεων
dative	δαίμοσι	ἀνδράσι	βασιλεῦσι	ἄστεσι
accusative	δαίμονας	ἄνδρας	βασιλέας	ἄστη

Morphology

Adjectives

Three endings

A- and O- stems

	masculine	*feminine*	*neuter*
nominative	ἀγαθός	ἀγαθή	ἀγαθόν
genitive	ἀγαθοῦ	ἀγαθῆς	ἀγαθοῦ
dative	ἀγαθῷ	ἀγαθῇ	ἀγαθῷ
accusative	ἀγαθόν	ἀγαθήν	ἀγαθόν
nominative	ἀγαθοί	ἀγαθαί	ἀγαθά
genitive	ἀγαθῶν	ἀγαθῶν	ἀγαθῶν
dative	ἀγαθοῖς	ἀγαθαῖς	ἀγαθοῖς
accusative	ἀγαθούς	ἀγαθάς	ἀγαθά

Contract O- stem

masculine	*feminine*	*neuter*
χρυσοῦς	χρυσῆ	χρυσοῦν
χρυσοῦ	χρυσῆς	χρυσοῦ
χρυσῷ	χρυσῇ	χρυσῷ
χρυσοῦν	χρυσῆν	χρυσοῦν
χρυσοῖ	χρυσαῖ	χρυσᾶ
χρυσῶν	χρυσῶν	χρυσῶν
χρυσοῖς	χρυσαῖς	χρυσοῖς
χρυσοῦς	χρυσᾶς	χρυσᾶ

Consonant declensions

	masculine	*feminine*	*neuter*	*masculine*	*feminine*	*neuter*
nominative	ἑκών	ἑκοῦσα	ἑκόν	ἡδύς	ἡδεῖα	ἡδύ
genitive	ἑκόντος	ἑκούσης	ἑκόντος	ἡδέος	ἡδείας	ἡδέος
dative	ἑκόντι	ἑκούσῃ	ἑκόντι	ἡδεῖ	ἡδείᾳ	ἡδεῖ
accusative	ἑκόντα	ἑκοῦσαν	ἑκόν	ἡδύν	ἡδεῖαν	ἡδύ
nominative	ἑκόντες	ἑκοῦσαι	ἑκόντα	ἡδεῖς	ἡδεῖαι	ἡδέα
genitive	ἑκόντων	ἑκουσῶν	ἑκόντων	ἡδέων	ἡδειῶν	ἡδέων
dative	ἑκοῦσι	ἑκούσαις	ἑκοῦσι	ἡδέσι	ἡδείαις	ἡδέσι
accusative	ἑκόντας	ἑκούσας	ἑκόντα	ἡδεῖς	ἡδείας	ἡδέα

A- declensions

masculine	*feminine*	*neuter*	*masculine*	*feminine*	*neuter*
πᾶς	πᾶσα	πᾶν	μέλας	μέλαινα	μέλαν
παντός	πάσης	παντός	μέλανος	μελαίνης	μέλανος
παντί	πάσῃ	παντί	μέλανι	μελαίνῃ	μέλανι
πάντα	πᾶσαν	πᾶν	μέλανα	μέλαινα	μέλαν
πάντες	πᾶσαι	πάντα	μέλανες	μέλαιναι	μέλανα
πάντων	πασῶν	πάντων	μελάνων	μελαινῶν	μελάνων
πᾶσι	πάσαις	πᾶσι	μέλασι	μελαίναις	μέλασι
πάντας	πάσας	πάντα	μέλανας	μελαίνας	μέλανα

MORPHOLOGY

Two endings

	masculine/ feminine	*neuter*	*masculine/ feminine*	*neuter*
nominative	ἀληθής	ἀληθές	εὐδαίμων	εὔδαιμον
genitive	ἀληθοῦς	ἀληθοῦς	εὐδαίμονος	εὐδαίμονος
dative	ἀληθεῖ	ἀληθεῖ	εὐδαίμονι	εὐδαίμονι
accusative	ἀληθῆ	ἀληθές	εὐδαίμονα	εὔδαιμον
nominative	ἀληθεῖς	ἀληθῆ	εὐδαίμονες	εὐδαίμονα
genitive	ἀληθῶν	ἀληθῶν	εὐδαιμόνων	εὐδαιμόνων
dative	ἀληθέσι	ἀληθέσι	εὐδαίμοσι	εὐδαίμοσι
accusative	ἀληθεῖς	ἀληθῆ	εὐδαίμονας	εὐδαίμονα

Irregular declensions

	masculine	*feminine*	*neuter*	*masculine*	*feminine*	*neuter*
nominative	πολύς	πολλή	πολύ	μέγας	μεγάλη	μέγα
genitive	πολλοῦ	πολλῆς	πολλοῦ	μεγάλου	μεγάλης	μεγάλου
dative	πολλῷ	πολλῇ	πολλῷ	μεγάλῳ	μεγάλῃ	μεγάλῳ
accusative	πολύν	πολλήν	πολύ	μέγαν	μεγάλην	μέγα
nominative	πολλοί	πολλαί	πολλά	μεγάλοι	μεγάλαι	μεγάλα
genitive	πολλῶν	πολλῶν	πολλῶν	μεγάλων	μεγάλων	μεγάλων
dative	πολλοῖς	πολλαῖς	πολλοῖς	μεγάλοις	μεγάλαις	μεγάλοις
accusative	πολλούς	πολλάς	πολλά	μεγάλους	μεγάλας	μεγάλα

Comparatives

	masculine/feminine	*neuter*
nominative	ἡδίων	ἥδιον
genitive	ἡδίονος	ἡδίονος
dative	ἡδίονι	ἡδίονι
accusative	ἡδίονα, ἡδίω	ἥδιον
nominative	ἡδίονες, ἡδίους	ἡδίονα, ἡδίω
genitive	ἡδιόνων	ἡδιόνων
dative	ἡδίοσι	ἡδίοσι
accusative	ἡδίονας, ἡδίους	ἡδίονα, ἡδίω

Superlatives

	masculine	*feminine*	*neuter*
nominative	ἥδιστος	ἡδίστη	ἥδιστον
genitive	ἡδίστου	ἡδίστης	ἡδίστου
dative	ἡδίστῳ	ἡδίστῃ	ἡδίστῳ
accusative	ἥδιστον	ἡδίστην	ἥδιστον
nominative	ἥδιστοι	ἥδισται	ἥδιστα
genitive	ἡδίστων	ἡδίστων	ἡδίστων
dative	ἡδίστοις	ἡδίσταις	ἡδίστοις
accusative	ἡδίστους	ἡδίστας	ἥδιστα

Morphology

Pronouns

Interrogative / Indefinite

	Interrogative *masculine/ feminine*	Interrogative *neuter*	Indefinite *masculine/ feminine*	Indefinite *neuter*
nominative	τίς	τί	τις	τι
genitive	τίνος, τοῦ	τίνος, τοῦ	τινός, του	τινός, του
dative	τίνι, τῷ	τίνι, τῷ	τινί, τῳ	τινί, τῳ
accusative	τίνα	τί	τινά	τι
nominative	τίνες	τίνα	τινές	τινά
genitive	τίνων	τίνων	τινῶν	τινῶν
dative	τίσι	τίσι	τισί	τισί
accusative	τίνας	τίνα	τινάς	τινά

Personal

	first person	*second person*
nominative	ἐγώ	σύ
genitive	ἐμοῦ, μου	σοῦ
dative	ἐμοί, μοι	σοί
accusative	ἐμέ, με	σέ
nominative	ἡμεῖς	ὑμεῖς
genitive	ἡμῶν	ὑμῶν
dative	ἡμῖν	ὑμῖν
accusative	ἡμᾶς	ὑμᾶς

Intensive

	masculine	*feminine*	*neuter*
nominative	αὐτός	αὐτή	αὐτό
genitive	αὐτοῦ	αὐτῆς	αὐτοῦ
dative	αὐτῷ	αὐτῇ	αὐτῷ
accusative	αὐτόν	αὐτήν	αὐτό
nominative	αὐτοί	αὐταί	αὐτά
genitive	αὐτῶν	αὐτῶν	αὐτῶν
dative	αὐτοῖς	αὐταῖς	αὐτοῖς
accusative	αὐτούς	αὐτάς	αὐτά

Demonstrative

	masculine	*feminine*	*neuter*
nominative	οὗτος	αὕτη	τοῦτο
genitive	τούτου	ταύτης	τούτου
dative	τούτῳ	ταύτῃ	τούτῳ
accusative	τοῦτον	ταύτην	τοῦτο
nominative	οὗτοι	αὗται	ταῦτα
genitive	τούτων	τούτων	τούτων
dative	τούτοις	ταύταις	τούτοις
accusative	τούτους	ταύτας	ταῦτα

Morphology

Demonstratives continued

	masculine	*feminine*	*neuter*
nominative	ὅδε	ἥδε	τόδε
genitive	τοῦδε	τῆσδε	τοῦδε
dative	τῷδε	τῇδε	τῷδε
accusative	τόνδε	τήνδε	τόδε
nominative	οἵδε	αἵδε	τάδε
genitive	τῶνδε	τῶνδε	τῶνδε
dative	τοῖσδε	ταῖσδε	τοῖσδε
accusative	τούσδε	τάσδε	τάδε

	masculine	*feminine*	*neuter*
nominative	ἐκεῖνος	ἐκείνη	ἐκεῖνο
genitive	ἐκείνου	ἐκείνης	ἐκείνου
dative	ἐκείνῳ	ἐκείνῃ	ἐκείνῳ
accusative	ἐκεῖνον	ἐκείνην	ἐκεῖνο
nominative	ἐκεῖνοι	ἐκεῖναι	ἐκεῖνα
genitive	ἐκείνων	ἐκείνων	ἐκείνων
dative	ἐκείνοις	ἐκείναις	ἐκείνοις
accusative	ἐκείνους	ἐκείνας	ἐκεῖνα

Relative

	masculine	*feminine*	*neuter*	*masculine*	*feminine*	*neuter*
nominative	ὅς	ἥ	ὅ	ὅστις	ἥτις	ὅ τι
genitive	οὗ	ἧς	οὗ	οὗτινος, ὅτου	ἧστινος	οὗτινος, ὅτου
dative	ᾧ	ᾗ	ᾧ	ᾧτινι, ὅτῳ	ᾗτινι	ᾧτινι, ὅτῳ
accusative	ὅν	ἥν	ὅ	ὅντινα	ἥντινα	ὅ τι
nominative	οἵ	αἵ	ἅ	οἵτινες	αἵτινες	ἅτινα, ἅττα
genitive	ὧν	ὧν	ὧν	ὧντινων, ὅτων	ὧντινων	ὧντινων, ὅτων
dative	οἷς	αἷς	οἷς	οἷστισι, ὅτοις	αἷστισι	οἷστισι, ὅτοις
accusative	οὕς	ἅς	ἅ	οὕστινας	ἅστινας	ἅτινα, ἅττα

Morphology

Verbs

ω Verbs - active

Indicative

	Present	*Imperfect*	*Future*	*Aorist*	*Perfect*	*Pluperfect*
First	λύω	ἔλυον	λύσω	ἔλυσα	λέλυκα	ἐλελύκη
Second	λύεις	ἔλυες	λύσεις	ἔλυσας	λέλυκας	ἐλελύκης
Third	λύει	ἔλυε	λύσει	ἔλυσε	λέλυκε	ἐλελύκει
First	λύομεν	ἐλύομεν	λύσομεν	ἐλύσαμεν	λελύκαμεν	ἐλελύκεμεν
Second	λύετε	ἐλύετε	λύσετε	ἐλύσατε	λελύκατε	ἐλελύκετε
Third	λύουσι	ἔλυον	λύσουσι	ἔλυσαν	λελύκασι	ἐλελύκεσαν

Subjunctive

	Present	*Imperfect*	*Future*	*Aorist*	*Perfect*
First	λύω			λύσω	λελύκω
Second	λύῃς			λύσῃς	λελύκῃς
Third	λύῃ			λύσῃ	λελύκῃ
First	λύωμεν			λύσωμεν	λελύκωμεν
Second	λύητε			λύσητε	λελύκητε
Third	λύωσι			λύσωσι	λελύκωσι

Optative

	Present	*Imperfect*	*Future*	*Aorist*	*Perfect*
First	λύοιμι		λύσοιμι	λύσαιμι	λελύκοιμι
Second	λύοις		λύσοις	λύσειας	λελύκοις
Third	λύοι		λύσοι	λύσειε	λελύκοι
First	λύοιμεν		λύσοιμεν	λύσαιμεν	λελύκοιμεν
Second	λύοιτε		λύσοιτε	λύσαιτε	λελύκοιτε
Third	λύοιεν		λύσοιεν	λύσειαν	λελύκοιεν

Imperative

	Present	*Aorist*
Second	λῦε	λῦσον
Third	λυέτω	λυσάτω
Second	λύετε	λύσατε
Third	λυόντων	λυσάντων

Infinitive

Present	*Future*	*Aorist*	*Perfect*
λύειν	λύσειν	λῦσαι	λελυκέναι

Participle

Present	*Future*	*Aorist*	*Perfect*
λύων, -ουσα, -ον	λύσων, -ουσα, -ον	λῦσας, -ασα, -αν	λελυκώς, -υῖα, -ός

Morphology

ω -Verbs - middle

Indicative

	present.	*imperfect*	*future*	*aorist*	*perfect*	*pluperfect*
First	λύομαι	ἐλυόμην	λύσομαι	ἐλυσάμην	λέλυμαι	ἐλελύμην
Second	λύει	ἐλύου	λύσει	ἐλύσω	λέλυσαι	ἐλέλυσο
Third	λύεται	ἐλύετο	λύσεται	ἐλύσατο	λέλυται	ἐλέλυτο
First	λυόμεθα	ἐλυόμεθα	λυσόμεθα	ἐλυσάμεθα	λελύμεθα	ἐλελύμεθα
Second	λύεσθε	ἐλύεσθε	λύσεσθε	ἐλύσασθε	λέλυσθε	ἐλέλυσθε
Third	λύονται	ἐλύοντο	λύσονται	ἐλύσαντο	λέλυνται	ἐλέλυντο

Subjunctive

present	aorist	perfect
λύωμαι	λύσωμαι	λελυμένος ὦ
λύῃ	λύσῃ	λελυμένος ᾖς
λύηται	λύσηται	λελυμένος ᾖ
λυώμεθα	λυσώμεθα	λελυμένοι ὦμεν
λύησθε	λύσησθε	λελυμένοι ἦτε
λύωνται	λύσωνται	λελυμένοι ὦσι

Optative

present	future	aorist	perfect
λυοίμην	λυσοίμην	λυσαίμην	λελυμένος εἴην
λύοιο	λύσοιο	λύσαιο	λελυμένος εἴης
λύοιτο	λύσοιτο	λύσαιτο	λελυμένος εἴη
λυοίμεθα	λυσοίμεθα	λυσαίμεθα	λελυμένοι εἴημεν/εἶμεν
λύοισθε	λύσοισθε	λύσαισθε	λελυμένοι εἴητε/εἶτε
λύοιντο	λύσοιντο	λυσαιντο	λελυμένοι εἴησαν/εἶεν

Imperative

present	aorist
λύου	λῦσαι
λυέσθω	λυσάσθω
λύεσθε	λύσασθε
λυέσθων	λυσάσθων

Participle

present	future	aorist	perfect
λυόμενος, -μένη, -μενον	λυσόμενος, -μένη, -μενον	λυσάμενος -μένη, -μενον	λελυμένος, -μένη, -μενον

Infinitive

present	future	aorist	perfect
λύεσθαι	λύσεσθαι	λύσασθαι	λελῦσθαι

Morphology

ω -Verbs - passive

Indicative

	present.	*imperfect*	*future*	*aorist*	*perfect*	*pluperfect*
First	λύομαι	ἐλυόμην	λυθήσομαι	ἐλύθην	λέλυμαι	ἐλελύμην
Second	λύει	ἐλύου	λυθήσει	ἐλύθης	λέλυσαι	ἐλέλυσο
Third	λύεται	ἐλύετο	λυθήσεται	ἐλύθη	λέλυται	ἐλέλυτο
First	λυόμεθα	ἐλυόμεθα	λυθησόμεθα	ἐλύθημεν	λελύμεθα	ἐλελύμεθα
Second	λύεσθε	ἐλύεσθε	λυθήσεσθε	ἐλύθητε	λέλυσθε	ἐλέλυσθε
Third	λύονται	ἐλύοντο	λυθήσονται	ἐλύθησαν	λέλυνται	ἐλέλυντο

Subjunctive

present	aorist	perfect
λύωμαι	λυθῶ	λελυμένος ὦ
λύῃ	λυθῇς	λελυμένος ᾖς
λύηται	λυθῇ	λελυμένος ᾖ
λυώμεθα	λυθῶμεν	λελυμένοι ὦμεν
λύησθε	λυθῆτε	λελυμένοι ἦτε
λύωνται	λυθῶσι	λελυμένοι ὦσι

Optative

present	future	aorist	perfect
λυοίμην	λυθησοίμην	λυθείην	λελυμένος εἴην
λύοιο	λυθήσοιο	λυθείης	λελυμένος εἴης
λύοιτο	λυθήσοιτο	λυθείη	λελυμένος εἴη
λυοίμεθα	λυθησοίμεθα	λυθεῖμεν	λελυμένοι εἴημεν/εἶμεν
λύοισθε	λυθήσοισθε	λυθεῖτε	λελυμένοι εἴητε/εἶτε
λύοιντο	λυθήσοιντο	λυθεῖεν	λελυμένοι εἴησαν/εἶεν

Imperative

present	aorist
λύου	λύθητι
λυέσθω	λυθήτω
λύεσθε	λύθητε
λυέσθων	λυθέντων

Participle

present	future	aorist	perfect
λυόμενος, -μένη, -μενον	λυθησόμενος, -μένη,-μενον	λυθείς, -εῖσα, έν	λελυμένος, -μένη, -μενον

Infinitive

present	future	aorist	perfect
λύεσθαι	λυθήσεσθαι	λυθῆναι	λελῦσθαι

Morphology

-μι Verbs

Progressive stem - Active Voice

Present Indicative

First	ἵστημι	τίθημι	δίδωμι	δείκνυμι
Second	ἵστης	τίθης	δίδως	δείκνυς
Third	ἵστησι	τίθησι	δίδωσι	δείκνυσι
First	ἵσταμεν	τίθεμεν	δίδομεν	δείκνυμεν
Second	ἵστατε	τίθετε	δίδοτε	δείκνυτε
Third	ἱστᾶσι	τιθέασι	διδόασι	δεικνύασι

Imperfect Indicative

First	ἵστην	ἐτίθην	ἐδίδουν	ἐδείκνυν
Second	ἵστης	ἐτίθεις	ἐδίδους	ἐδείκνυς
Third	ἵστη	ἐτίθει	ἐδίδου	ἐδείκνυ
First	ἵσταμεν	ἐτίθεμεν	ἐδίδομεν	ἐδείκνυμεν
Second	ἵστατε	ἐτίθετε	ἐδίδοτε	ἐδείκνυτε
Third	ἵστασαν	ἐτίθεσαν	ἐδίδοσαν	ἐδείκνυσαν

Present Subjunctive

First	ἱστῶ	τιθῶ	διδῶ	δεικνύω
Second	ἱστῇς	τιθῇς	διδῷς	δεικνύῃς
Third	ἱστῇ	τιθῇ	διδῷ	δεικνύῃ
First	ἱστῶμεν	τιθῶμεν	διδῶμεν	δεικνύωμεν
Second	ἱστῆτε	τιθῆτε	διδῶτε	δεικνύητε
Third	ἱστῶσι	τιθῶσι	διδῶσι	δεικνύωσι

Present Optative

First	ἱσταίην	τιθείην	διδοίην	δεικνύοιμι
Second	ἱσταίης	τιθείης	διδοίης	δεικνύοις
Third	ἱσταίη	τιθείη	διδοίη	δεικνύοι
First	ἱσταῖμεν	τιθεῖμεν	διδοῖμεν	δεικνύοιμεν
Second	ἱσταῖτε	τιθεῖτε	διδοῖτε	δεικνύοιτε
Third	ἱσταῖεν	τιθεῖεν	διδοῖεν	δεικνύοιεν

Imperative

Second	ἵστη	τίθει	δίδου	δείκνυ
Third	ἱστάτω	τιθέτω	διδότω	δεικνύτω
Second	ἵστατε	τίθετε	δίδοτε	δείκνυτε
Third	ἱστάντων	τιθέντων	διδόντων	δεικύντων

Participle

ἱστάς, ἱστᾶσα, ἱστάν	τιθείς, τιθεῖσα, τιθέν	διδούς, διδοῦσα, διδόν	δεικνύς, δεικνῦσα, δεικνύν

Infinitive

στάναι	τιθέναι	διδόναι	δεικνύναι

Second Aorist- active voice

Indicative

First	ἔστην	ἔθηκα	ἔδωκα
Second	ἔστης	ἔθηκας	ἔδωκας
Third	ἔστη	ἔθηκε	ἔδωκε
First	ἔστημεν	ἔθεμεν	ἔδομεν
Second	ἔστητε	ἔθετε	ἔδοτε
Third	ἔστησαν	ἔθεσαν	ἔδοσαν

Subjunctive

First	στῶ	θῶ	δῶ
Second	στῇς	θῇς	δῷς
Third	στῇ	θῇ	δῷ
First	στῶμεν	θῶμεν	δῶμεν
Second	στῆτε	θῆτε	δῆτε
Third	στῶσι	θῶσι	δῶσι

Optative

σταίην	θείην	δοίην
σταίης	θείης	δοίης
σταίη	θείη	δοίη
σταῖμεν	θεῖμεν	δοῖμεν
σταῖτε	θεῖτε	δοῖτε
σταῖεν	θεῖεν	δοῖεν

Imperative

Second	στῆθι	θές	δός
Third	στήτω	θέτω	δότω
Second	στῆτε	θέτε	δότε
Third	στάντων	θέντων	δόντων

Infinitive

στῆναι	θεῖναι	δοῦναι

Participle

στάς, στᾶσα, στάν	θείς, θεῖσα, θέν	δούς, δοῦσα, δόν

Morphology

Perfect of ἵστημι

	Indicative.	*Subjunctive*	*Optative*	*Imper.ative*
First	(ἕστηκα)	ἑστῶ	ἑσταίην	
Second	(ἕστηκας)	ἑστῇς	ἑσταίης	ἕσταθι
Third	(ἕστηκε)	ἑστῇ	ἑσταίη	ἑστάτω
First	ἕσταμεν	ἑστῶμεν	ἑσταῖμεν	
Second	ἕστατε	ἑστῆτε	ἑσταῖτε	ἕστατε
Third	ἑστᾶσι	ἑστῶσι	ἑσταῖεν	ἑστάντων

	Infinitive	*Participle*
	ἑστάναι	ἑστώς, ἑστῶσα, ἑστός

μι-Verbs Progressive Middle / Passive

Present Indicative

First	ἵσταμαι	τίθεμαι	δίδομαι	δείκνυμαι
Second	ἵστασαι	τίθεσαι	δίδοσαι	δείκνυσαι
Third	ἵσταται	τίθεται	δίδοται	δείκνυται
First	ἱστάμεθα	τιθέμεθα	διδόμεθα	δεικνύμεθα
Second	ἵστασθε	τίθεσθε	δίδοσθε	δείκνυσθε
Third	ἵστανται	τιθένται	δίδονται	δείκνυνται

Imperfect Indicative

First	ἱστάμην	ἐτιθέμην	ἐδιδόμην	ἐδεικνύμην
Second	ἵστασο	ἐτίθεσο	ἐδίδοσο	ἐδείκνυσο
Third	ἵστατο	ἐτίθετο	ἐδίδοτο	ἐδείκνυτο
First	ἱστάμεθα	ἐτιθέμεθα	ἐδιδόμεθα	ἐδεικνύμεθα
Second	ἵστασθε	ἐτίθεσθε	ἐδίδοσθε	ἐδείκνυσθε
Third	ἵσταντο	ἐτίθεντο	ἐδίδοντο	ἐδείκνυντο

Subjunctive

First	ἱστῶμαι	τιθῶμαι	διδῶμαι	δεικνύωμαι
Second	ἱστῇ	τιθῇ	διδῷ	δεικνύῃ
Third	ἱστῆται	τιθῆται	διδῶται	δεικνύηται
First	ἱστώμεθα	τιθώμεθα	διδώμεθα	δεικνυώμεθα
Second	ἱστῆσθε	τιθῆσθε	διδῶσθε	δεικνύησθε
Third	ἱστῶνται	τιθῶνται	διδῶνται	δεικνύωνται

Optative

First	ἱσταίμην	τιθείμην	διδοίμην	δεικνυοίμην
Second	ἱσταῖο	τιθεῖο	διδοῖο	δεικνύοιο
Third	ἱσταῖτο	τιθεῖτο	διδοῖτο	δεικνύοιτο
First	ἱσταίμεθα	τιθείμεθα	διδοίμεθα	δεικνυοίμεθα
Second	ἱσταῖσθε	τιθεῖσθε	διδοῖσθε	δεικνύοισθε
Third	ἱσταῖντο	τιθεῖντο	διδοῖντο	δεικνύοιντο

Imperative

Second	ἵστασο	τίθεσο	δίδοσο	δείκνυσο
Third	ἱστάσθω	τιθέσθω	διδόσθω	δεικνύσθω
Second	ἵστασθε	τίθεσθε	δίδοσθε	δείκνυσθε
Third	ἱστάσθων	τιθέσθων	διδόσθων	δεικύσθων

Infinitive

ἵστασθαι	τίθεσθαι	δίδοσθαι	δείκνυσθαι

Participle

ἱστάμενος, -μένη, -μενον	τίθέμενος, -μένη, -μενον	διδόμενος, -μένη, μενον	δεικν ύμενος, -μένη, μενον

-μι Verbs Aorist Middle

Indicative

First	ἐθέμην	ἐδόμην
Second	ἔθου	ἔδου
Third	ἔθετο	ἔδοτο
First	ἐθέμεθα	ἐδόμεθα
Second	ἔθεσθε	ἔδοσθε
Third	ἔθεντο	ἔδοντο

Subjunctive

First	θῶμαι	δῶμαι
Second	θῇ	δῷ
Third	θῆται	δῶται
First	θώμεθα	δώμεθα
Second	θῆσθε	δῶσθε
Third	θῶνται	δῶνται

Morphology

Optative

First	θείμην	δοίμην
Second	θεῖο	δοῖο
Third	θεῖτο	δοῖτο
First	θείμεθα	δοίμεθα
Second	θεῖσθε	δοῖσθε
Third	θεῖντο	δοῖντο

Imperative

Second	θοῦ	δοῦ
Third	θέσθω	δόσθω
Second	θέσθε	δόσθε
Third	θέσθων	δόσθων

Infinitive

	θέσθαι	δόσθαι

Participle

	θέμενος, -μένη, -μενον	δόμενος, -μένη,-μενον

Contract Verbs Progressive stem

Active Voice

Present Indicative

First	τιμῶ	ποιῶ	δηλῶ
Second	τιμᾷς	ποιεῖς	δηλοῖς
Third	τιμᾷ	ποιεῖ	δηλοῖ
First	τιμῶμεν	ποιοῦμεν	δηλοῦμεν
Second	τιμᾶτε	ποιεῖτε	δηλοῦτε
Third	τιμῶσι	ποιοῦσι	δηλοῦσι

Imperfect Indicative

First	ἐτίμων	ἐποίουν	ἐδήλουν
Second	ἐτίμας	ἐποίεις	ἐδήλους
Third	ἐτίμα	ἐποίει	ἐδήλου
First	ἐτιμῶμεν	ἐποιοῦμεν	ἐδηλοῦμεν
Second	ἐτιμᾶτε	ἐποιεῖτε	ἐδηλοῦτε
Third	ἐτίμων	ἐποίουν	ἐδήλουν

MORPHOLOGY

Subjunctive

First	τιμῶ	ποιῶ	δηλῶ
Second	τιμᾷς	ποιῇς	δηλοῖς
Third	τιμᾷ	ποιῇ	δηλοῖ
First	τιμῶμεν	ποιῶμεν	δηλῶμεν
Second	τιμᾶτε	ποιῆτε	δηλῶτε
Third	τιμῶσι	ποιῶσι	δηλῶσι

Optative

First	τιμῷμι	ποιοῖμι	δηλοῖμι
Second	τιμῷς	ποιοῖς	δηλοῖς
Third	τιμῷ	ποιοῖ	δηλοῖ
First	τιμῷμεν	ποιοῖμεν	δηλοῖμεν
Second	τιμῷτε	ποιοῖτε	δηλοῖτε
Third	τιμῷεν	ποιοῖεν	δηλοῖεν

*alternate form, more common in singular

First	τιμῴην	ποιοίην	δηλοίην
Second	τιμῴης	ποιοίης	δηλοίης
Third	τιμῴη	ποιοίη	δηλοίη
First	τιμῴημεν	ποιοίημεν	δηλοίημεν
Second	τιμῴητε	ποιοίητε	δηλοίητε
Third	τιμῴησαν	ποιοίησαν	δηλοίησαν

Imperative

Second	τίμα	φίλει	δήλου
Third	τιμάτω	ποιείτω	δηλούτω
Second	τιμᾶτε	ποιεῖτε	δηλοῦτε
Third	τιμώντων	ποιούντων	δηλούντων

Infinitive

	τιμᾶν	ποιεῖν	δηλοῦν

Participle

	τιμῶν, τιμῶσα,τιμῶν	ποιῶν, ποιοῦσα, ποιοῦν	δηλῶν, δηλοῦσα, δηλοῦν

Morphology

Contract Verbs Progressive stem

Middle / Passive Voice

Present Indicative

First	τιμῶμαι	ποιοῦμαι	δηλοῦμαι
Second	τιμᾷ	ποιεῖ	δηλοῖ
Third	τιμᾶται	ποιεῖται	δηλοῦται
First	τιμώμεθα	ποιούμεθα	δηλούμεθα
Second	τιμᾶσθε	ποιεῖσθε	δηλοῦσθε
Third	τιμῶνται	ποιοῦνται	δηλοῦνται

Imperfect Indicative

First	ἐτιμώμην	ἐποιούμην	ἐδηλούμην
Second	ἐτιμῶ	ἐποιοῦ	ἐδηλοῦ
Third	ἐτιμᾶτο	ἐποιεῖτο	ἐδηλοῦτο
First	ἐτιμώμεθα	ἐποιούμεθα	ἐδηλούμεθα
Second	ἐτιμᾶσθε	ἐποιεῖσθε	ἐδηλοῦσθε
Third	ἐτιμῶντο	ἐποιοῦντο	ἐδηλοῦντο

Subjunctive

First	τιμῶμαι	ποιῶμαι	δηλῶμαι
Second	τιμᾷ	ποιῇ	δηλοῖ
Third	τιμᾶται	ποιῆται	δηλῶται
First	τιμώμεθα	ποιώμεθα	δηλώμεθα
Second	τιμᾶσθε	ποιῆσθε	δηλῶσθε
Third	τιμῶνται	ποιῶνται	δηλῶνται

Optative

First	τιμῴμην	ποιοίμην	δηλοίμην
Second	τιμῷο	ποιοῖο	δηλοῖο
Third	τιμῷτο	ποιοῖτο	δηλοῖτο
First	τιμῴμεθα	ποιοίμεθα	δηλοίμεθα
Second	τιμῷσθε	ποιοῖσθε	δηλοῖσθε
Third	τιμῷντο	ποιοῖντο	δηλοῖντο

Imperative

Second	τιμῶ	ποιοῦ	δηλοῦ
Third	τιμάσθω	ποιείσθω	δηλούσθω
Second	τιμᾶσθε	ποιεῖσθε	δηλοῦσθε
Third	τιμάσθων	ποιείσθων	δηλούσθων

Infinitive

	τιμᾶσθαι	ποιεῖσθαι	δηλοῦσθαι

Morphology

Participle

τιμώμενος, -μένη, -μενον	ποιούμενος, -μένη, -μενον	δηλούμενος, -μένη.-μενον.

Common Irregular Verbs

Active Voice

Present Indicative

First	εἰμί	εἶμι	φημί
Second	εἶ	εἶ	φῄς, φής
Third	ἐστί	εἶσι	φησί
First	ἐσμέν	ἴμεν	φαμέν
Second	ἐστέ	ἴτε	φατέ
Third	εἰσί	ἴασι	φασί

Imperfect Indicative

First	ἦν, ἦ	ᾖα, ᾔειν	ἔφην
Second	ἦσθα	ᾔεις, ᾔεισθα	ἔφης
Third	ἦν	ᾔει, ᾔειν	ἔφη
First	ἦμεν	ᾖμεν	ἔφαμεν
Second	ἦτε, ἦστε	ᾖτε	ἔφατε
Third	ἦσαν	ᾖσαν, ᾖεσαν	ἔφασαν

Subjunctive

First	ὦ	ἴω	φῶ
Second	ᾖς	ἴῃς	φῇς
Third	ᾖ	ἴῃ	φῇ
First	ὦμεν	ἴωμεν	φῶμεν
Second	ἦτε	ἴητε	φῆτε
Third	ὦσι	ἴωσι	φῶσι

Optative

First	εἴην	ἴοιμι, ἰοίην	φαίην
Second	εἴης	ἴοις	φαίης
Third	εἴη	ἴοι	φαίη
First	εἶμεν	ἴοιμεν	φαῖμεν
Second	εἶτε	ἴοιτε	φαῖτε
Third	εἶεν	ἴοιεν	φαῖεν

Imperative

Second	ἴσθι	ἴθι	φαθί, φάθι
Third	ἔστω	ἴτω	φάτω
Second	ἔστε	ἴτε	φάτε
Third	ἔστων	ἰόντων	φάντων

MORPHOLOGY

Infinitive

εἶναι	ἰέναι	φάναι

Participle

ὤν, οὖσα, ὄν	ἰών, ἰοῦσα, ἰόν	φάσκων, -ουσα, -ον

ἵημι
Active
Progressive Active

	Present	Imperfect	Subjunctive	Optative	Imperative
First	ἵημι	ἵην	ἱῶ	ἱείην	
Second	ἵης, ἱεῖς	ἵεις	ἱῇς	ἱείης	ἵει
Third	ἵησι	ἵει	ἱῇ	ἱείη	ἱέτω
First	ἵεμεν	ἵεμεν	ἱῶμεν	ἱεῖμεν	
Second	ἵετε	ἵετε	ἱῆτε	ἱεῖτε	ἵετε
Third	ἱᾶσι	ἵεσαν	ἱῶσι	ἱεῖεν	ἱέντων

Infinitive	Participle
ἱέναι	ἱείς, ἱεῖσα, ἱέν

Aorist Active

	Indicative	Subjunctive	Optative	Imperative
First	ἧκα	ὧ	εἵην	
Second	ἧκας	ἧς	εἵης	ἕς
Third	ἧκε	ἧ	εἵη	ἕτω
First	εἷμεν	ὧμεν	εἷμεν	
Second	εἷτε	ἧτε	εἷτε	ἕτε
Third	εἷσαν	ὧσι	εἷεν	ἕντων

Infinitive	Participle
εἷναι	εἵς, εἷσα, ἕν

Middle
Indicative

	Present	*Imperfect*	*Aorist*
First	ἵεμαι	ἱέμην	εἵμην
Second	ἵεσαι	ἵεσο	εἷσο
Third	ἵεται	ἵετο	εἷτο
First	ἱέμεθα	ἱέμεθα	εἵμεθα
Second	ἵεσθε	ἵεσθε	εἷσθε
Third	ἵενται	ἵεντο	εἷντο

MORPHOLOGY

Subjunctive

	Present	*Aorist*
First	ἱῶμαι	ὧμαι
Second	ἱῇσαι	ἧσαι
Third	ἱῆται	ἧται
First	ἱώμεθα	ὥμεθα
Second	ἱῆσθε	ἧσθε
Third	ἱῶνται	ὧνται

Optative

	Present	*Aorist*
First	ἱείμην	εἵμην
Second	ἱεῖο	εἷο
Third	ἱεῖτο	εἷτο
First	ἱείμεθα	εἵμεθα
Second	ἱεῖσθε	εἷσθε
Third	ἱεῖντο	εἷντο

Imperative

	Present	*Aorist*
Second	ἵεσο	οὗ
Third	ἱέσθω	ἕσθω
Second	ἵεσθε	ἕσθε
Third	ἱέσθων	ἕσθων

Infinitive

Present	*Aorsist*
ἵεσθαι	ἕσθαι

Participle

Present	*Aorist*
ἱέμενος, -μένη, -μενον	ἕμενος, -μένη, -μενον

Irregular verb: οἶδα

Indicative

	Perfect	*Pluperfect*
First	οἶδα	ᾔδη, ᾔδειν
Second	οἶσθα	ᾔδησθα, ᾔδεισθα
Third	οἶδε	ᾔδει, ᾔδειν
First	ἴσμεν	ᾖσμεν
Second	ἴστε	ᾖστε
Third	ἴσασι	ᾖσαν, ᾔδεσαν

Subjunctive

Perfect
εἰδῶ
εἰδῇς
εἰδῇ
εἰδῶμεν
εἰδῆτε
εἰδῶσι

Optative

Perfectg
εἰδείην
εἰδείης
εἰδείη
εἰδεῖμεν, εἰδείημεν
εἰδεῖτε, εἰδείητε
εἰδεῖεν, εἰδείησαν

Imperative

Second	ἴσθι
Third	ἴστω
Second	ἴστε
Third	ἴστων

Infinitive

εἰδέναι

Participle

εἰδώς, εἰδυῖα, εἰδός

MORPHOLOGY

Irregular verb: γιγνώσκω

Indicative		**Subjunctive**	**Optative**
First	ἔγνων	γνῶ	γνοίην
Second	ἔγνως	γνῷς	γνοίης
Third	ἔγνω	γνῷ	γνοίη
First	ἔγνωμεν	γνῶμεν	γνοῖμεν
Second	ἔγνωτε	γνῶτε	γνοῖτε
Third	ἔγνωσαν	γνῶσι	γνοῖεν

Imperative	**Infinitive**	**Participle**
γνῶθι	γνῶναι	γνούς, γνοῦσα, γνόν,
γνώτω		
γνῶτε		
γνώντων		

Participles

λύω
Progressive Active

nominative	λύων	λύουσα	λῦον
genitive	λύοντος	λυούσης	λύοντος
dative	λύοντι	λυούσῃ	λύοντι
accusative	λύοντα	λύουσαν	λῦον
nominative	λύοντες	λύουσαι	λύοντα
genitive	λυόντων	λυουσῶν	λυόντων
dative	λύουσι	λυούσαις	λύουσι
accusative	λύοντας	λυούσας	λύοντα

Future Active

nominative	λύσων	λύσουσα	λῦσον
genitive	λύσοντος	λυσούσης	λύσοντος
dative	λύσοντι	λυσούσῃ	λύσοντι
accusative	λύσοντα	λυσούσαν	λῦσον
nominative	λύσοντες	λύσουσαι	λύσοντα
genitive	λυσόντων	λυσουσῶν	λυσόντων
dative	λύσουσι	λυσούσαις	λύσουσι
accusative	λύσοντας	λυσούσας	λύσοντα

Morphology

Aorist Active

nominative	λύσας	λύσασα	λύσαν
genitive	λύσαντος	λυσάσης	λύσαντος
dative	λύσαντι	λυσάσῃ	λύσαντι
accusative	λύσαντα	λύσασαν	λύσαν
nominative	λύσαντες	λύσασαι	λύσαντα
genitive	λυσάντων	λυσασῶν	λυσάντων
dative	λύσασι	λυσάσαις	λύσασι
accusative	λύσαντας	λυσάσας	λύσαντα

Progressive Middle/Passive

nominative	λυόμενος	λυομένη	λυόμενον
genitive	λυομένου	λυομένης	λυομένου
dative	λυομένῳ	λυομένῃ	λυομένῳ
accusative	λυόμενον	λυομένην	λυόμενον
nominative	λυόμενοι	λυόμεναι	λυόμενα
genitive	λυομένων	λυομενῶν	λυομένων
dative	λυομένοις	λυομέναις	λυόμενοις
accusative	λυομένους	λυομένας	λυόμενα

Future Middle

nominative	λυσόμενος	λυσομένη	λυσόμενον
genitive	λυσομένου	λυσομένης	λυσομένου
dative	λυσομένῳ	λυσομένῃ	λυσομένῳ
accusative	λυσόμενον	λυσομένην	λυσόμενον
nominative	λυσόμενοι	λυσόμεναι	λυσόμενα
genitive	λυσομένων	λυσομενῶν	λυσομένων
dative	λυσομένοις	λυσομέναις	λυσόμενοις
accusative	λυσομένους	λυσομένας	λυσόμενα

Aorist Middle

nominative	λυσάμενος	λυσαμένη	λυσάμενον
genitive	λυσαμένου	λυσαμένης	λυσαμένου
dative	λυσαμένῳ	λυσαμένῃ	λυσαμένῳ
accusative	λυσάμενον	λυσαμένην	λυσάμενον
nominative	λυσάμενοι	λυσάμεναι	λυσάμενα
genitive	λυσαμένων	λυσαμενῶν	λυσαμένων
dative	λυσομένοις	λυσαμέναις	λυσάμενοις
accusative	λυσαμένους	λυσαμένας	λυσάμενα

Perfect Active

nominative	λελυκώς	λελυκυῖα	λελυκός
genitive	λελυκότος	λελυκυίας	λελυκότος
dative	λελυκότι	λελυκυίᾳ	λελυκότι
accusative	λελυκότα	λελυκυῖαν	λελυκός
nominative	λελυκότες	λελυκυῖαι	λελυκότα
genitive	λελυκότων	λελυκυιῶν	λελυκότων
dative	λελυκόσι	λελυκυίαις	λελυκόσι
accusative	λελυκότας	λελυκυίας	λελυκότα

Perfect Middle/Passive

nominative	λελυμένος	λελυμένη	λελυμένον
genitive	λελυμένου	λελυμένης	λελυμένου
dative	λελυμένῳ	λελμένῃ	λελυμένῳ
accusative	λελυμένον	λελυμένην	λελυμένον
nominative	λελυμένοι	λελυμέναι	λελυμένα
genitive	λελυμένων	λελυμενῶν	λελυμένων
dative	λελυμένοις	λελυμέναις	λελυμένοις
accusative	λελυμένους	λελυμένας	λελυμένα

Future Passive

nominative	λυθησόμενος	λυθησομένη	λυθησόμενον
genitive	λυθησομένου	λυθησομένης	λυθησόμενου
dative	λυθησομένῳ	λυθησομένη	λυθησόμενῳ
accusative	λυθησόμενον	λυθησομένην	λυθησόμενον
nominative	λυθησόμενοι	λυθησόμεναι	λυθησόμενα
genitive	λυθησομένων	λυθησομενῶν	λυθησομένων
dative	λυθηομένοις	λυθησομέναις	λυθησομένοις
accusative	λυθησομένους	λυθησομένας	λυθησόμενα

Aorist Passive

nominative	λυθείς	λυθεῖσα	λυθέν
genitive	λυθέντος	λυθείσης	λυθέντος
dative	λυθέντι	λυθείσῃ	λυθέντι
accusative	λυθέντα	λυθεῖσαν	λυθέν
nominative	λυθέντες	λυθεῖσαι	λυθέντα
genitive	λυθέντων	λυθεισῶν	λυθέντων
dative	λυθεῖσι	λυθείσαις	λυθεῖσι
accusative	λυθέντας	λυθείσας	λυθέντα

MORPHOLOGY

Progressive Active of -*μι* Verbs

ἵστημι

nominative	ἱστάς	ἱστᾶσα	ἱστάν
genitive	ἱστάντος	ἱστάσης	ἱστάντος
dative	ἱστάντι	ἱστάσῃ	ἱστάντι
accusative	ἱστάντα	ἱστᾶσαν	ἱστάν
nominative	ἱστάντες	ἱστᾶσαι	ἱστάντα
genitive	ἱστάντων	ἱστασῶν	ἱστάντων
dative	ἱστᾶσι	ἱστάσαις	ἱστᾶσι
accusative	ἱστάντας	ἱστάσας	ἱστάντα

δίδωμι

nominative	διδούς	διδοῦσα	διδόν
genitive	διδόντος	διδούσης	διδόντος
dative	διδόντι	διδούσῃ	διδόντι
accusative	διδόντα	διδοῦσαν	διδόν
nominative	διδόντες	διδοῦσαι	διδόντα
genitive	διδόντων	διδουσῶν	διδόντων
dative	διδοῦσι	διδούσαις	διδοῦσι
accusative	διδόντας	διδούσας	διδόντα

τίθημι

nominative	τιθείς	τιθεῖσα	τιθέν
genitive	τιθέντος	τιθείσης	τιθέντος
dative	τιθέντι	τιθείσῃ	τιθέντι
accusative	τιθέντα	τιθεῖσαν	τιθέν
nominative	τιθέντες	τιθεῖσαι	τιθέντα
genitive	τιθέντων	τιθεισῶν	τιθέντων
dative	τιθεῖσι	τιθείσαις	τιθεῖσι
accusative	τιθέντας	τιθείσας	τιθέντα

δείκνυμι

nominative	δεικνύς	δεικνῦσα	δεικνύν
genitive	δεικνύντος	δεικνύσης	δεικνύντος
dative	δεικνύντι	δεικνύσῃ	δεικνύντι
accusative	δεικνύντα	δεικνῦσαν	δεικνύν
nominative	δεικνύντες	δεικνῦσαι	δεικνύντα
genitive	δεικνύντων	δεικνυσῶν	δεικνύντων
dative	δεικνῦσι	δεικνύσαις	δεικνῦσι
accusative	δεικνύντας	δεικνύσας	δεικνύντα

Morphology

εἰμί

nominative	ὤν	οὖσα	ὄν
genitive	ὄντος	οὔσης	ὄντος
dative	ὄντι	οὔσῃ	ὄντι
accusative	ὄντα	οὖσαν	ὄν
nominative	ὄντες	οὖσαι	ὄντα
genitive	ὄντων	οὐσῶν	ὄντων
dative	οὖσι	οὔσαις	οὖσι
accusative	ὄντας	οὔσας	ὄντα

Progressive Active of Contract Verbs

τιμάω

nominative	τιμῶν	τιμῶσα	τιμῶν
genitive	τιμῶντος	τιμώσης	τιμῶντος
dative	τιμῶντι	τιμώσῃ	τιμῶντι
accusative	τιμῶντα	τιμῶσαν	τιμῶν
nominative	τιμῶντες	τιμῶσαι	τιμῶντα
genitive	τιμώντων	τιμωσῶν	τιμώντων
dative	τιμῶσι	τιμώσαις	τιμῶσι
accusative	τιμῶντας	τιμώσας	τιμῶντα

ποιέω

nominative	ποιῶν	ποιοῦσα	ποιοῦν
genitive	ποιοῦντος	ποιούσης	ποιοῦντος
dative	ποιοῦντι	ποιούσῃ	ποιοῦντι
accusative	ποιοῦντα	ποιοῦσαν	ποιοῦν
nominative	ποιοῦντες	ποιοῦσαι	ποιοῦντα
genitive	ποιούντων	ποιουσῶν	ποιούντων
dative	ποιοῦσι	ποιούσαις	ποιοῦσι
accusative	ποιοῦντας	ποιούσας	ποιοῦντα

δηλόω

nominative	δηλῶν	δηλοῦσα	δηλοῦν
genitive	δηλοῦντος	δηλούσης	δηλοῦντος
dative	δηλοῦντι	δηλούσῃ	δηλοῦντι
accusative	δηλοῦντα	δηλοῦσαν	δηλοῦν
nominative	δηλοῦντες	δηλοῦσαι	δηλοῦντα
genitive	δηλούντων	δηλουσῶν	δηλούντων
dative	δηλοῦσι	δηλούσαις	δηλοῦσι
accusative	δηλοῦντας	δηλούσας	δηλοῦντα

Principal Parts

present	future	aorist	perfective	perfective	aorist
ἀγγέλλω	ἀγγελῶ	ἤγγειλα	ἤγγελκα	ἤγγελμαι	ἠγγέλθην
ἄγω	ἄξω	ἤγαγον	ἦχα	ἦγμαι	ἤχθην
αἰνέω	αἰνέσω	ᾔνεσα	ᾔνεκα	ᾔνημαι	ᾐνέθην
αἱρέω	αἱρήσω	εἷλον	ᾕρηκα	ᾕρημαι	ᾑρέθην
αἰσθάνομαι	αἰσθήσομαι	ᾐσθόμην		ᾔσθημαι	
ἀκούω	ἀκούσομαι	ἤκουσα	ἀκήκοα		ἠκούσθην
ἁλίσκομαι	ἁλώσομαι	ἑάλων (ἥλων)	ἑάλωκα		
ἀλλάττω	ἀλλάξω	ἤλλαξα	ἤλλαχα	ἤλλαγμαι	ἠλλάχθην
ἁμαρτάνω	ἁμαρτήσομαι	ἥμαρτον	ἡμάρτηκα	ἡμάρτημαι	ἡμαρτήθην
ἀμελέω	ἀμελήσω	ἠμέλησα	ἠμέληκα		
ἀναγκάζω	ἀναγκάσω	ἠνάγκασα	ἠνάγκακα	ἠνάγκασμαι	ἠναγκάσθην
ἀποθνῄσκω	ἀποθανοῦμαι	ἀπέθανον	ἀποτέθνηκα		
ἀποκτείνω	ἀποκτενῶ	ἀπέκτεινα	ἀπέκτονα		
ἅπτομαι	ἅψομαι	ἡψάμην		ἧμμαι	ἥφθην
ἀρέσκω	ἀρέσω	ἤρεσα	ἀρήρεκα		ἠρέσθην
ἄρχω	ἄρξω	ἦρξα	ἦρχα	ἦργμαι	ἤρχθην
αὐξάνω	αὐξήσω	ηὔξησα	ηὔξηκα	ηὔξημαι	ηὐξήθην
ἀφικνέομαι	ἀφίξομαι	ἀφικόμην		ἀφῖγμαι	
βαίνω	βήσομαι	ἔβην	βέβηκα	βέβαμαι	ἐβάθην
βάλλω	βαλῶ	ἔβαλον	βέβληκα	βέβλημαι	ἐβλήθην
βλάπτω	βλάψω	ἔβλαψα	βέβλαφα	βέβλαμμαι	ἐβλάφθην/ ἐβλάβην
βουλεύω	βουλεύσω	ἐβούλευσα	βεβούλευκα	βεβούλευμαι	ἐβουλεύθην
βούλομαι	βουλήσομαι			βεβούλημαι	ἐβουλήθην
γαμέω	γαμῶ	ἔγημα	γεγάμηκα	γεγάμημαι	ἐγαμήθην

Principal Parts

γίγνομαι	γενήσομαι	ἐγενόμην	γέγονα	γεγένημαι	ἐγενήθην
γιγνώσκω	γνώσομαι	ἔγνων	ἔγνωκα	ἔγνωσμαι	ἐγνώσθην
γράφω	γράψω	ἔγραψα	γέγραφα	γέγραμμαι	ἐγράφθην/ ἐγράφην
δείκνυμι	δείξω	ἔδειξα	δέδειχα,	δέδειγμαι	ἐδείχθην
δέομαι	δεήσομαι			δεδέημαι	ἐδεήθην
δέχομαι	δέξομαι	ἐδεξάμην		δέδεγμαι	ἐδέχθην
διαφθείρω	διαφθερῶ,	διέφθειρα	διέφθαρκα /διέφθορα	διέφθαρμαι	διεφθάρην
διδάσκω	διδάξω	ἐδίδαξα	δεδίδαχα	δεδίδαγμαι	ἐδιδάχθην
δίδωμι	δώσω	ἔδωκα	δέδωκα	δέδομαι	ἐδόθην
διελαύνω	διελῶ (διελάω)	διήλασα	διελήλακα	διελήλαμαι	διηλάθην
διώκω	διώξω	ἐδίωξα	δεδίωχα	δεδίωγμαι	ἐδιώχθην
δράω	δράσω	ἔδρασα	δέδρακα	δέδραμαι	ἐδράσθην
δύναμαι	δυνήσομαι			δεδύνημαι	ἐδυνήθην
ἐάω	ἐάσω	εἴασα	εἴακα	εἴαμαι	εἰάθην
ἐθέλω	ἐθελήσω	ἠθέλησα	ἠθέληκα		
εἰμί	ἔσομαι				
ἐπίσταμαι	ἐπιστήσομαι				ἠπιστήθην
ἔρομαι*	ἐρήσομαι	ἠρόμην			
ἔρχομαι	ἐλεύσομαι	ἦλθον	ἐλήλυθα		
εὑρίσκω	εὑρήσω	ηὗρον	ηὕρηκα	ηὕρημαι	ηὑρέθην
εὐφραίνω	εὐφρανῶ	εὔφρανα/ ηὔφρανα			εὐφράνθην ηὐφράνθην
εὔχομαι	εὔξομαι	ηὐξάμην		ηὖγμαι	
ἔχω	σχήσω/ἕξω	ἔσχον	ἔσχηκα	ἔσχημαι	
ἡγέομαι	ἡγήσομαι	ἡγησάμην		ἥγημαι	ἡγήθην

Principal Parts

ἥδομαι	ἡσθήσομαι	ἡσάμην			ἥσθην
θεάομαι	θεάσομαι	ἐθεασάμην		τεθέαμαι	ἐθεάθην
ἵστημι	στήσω	ἔστησα/ ἔστην	ἕστηκα	ἕστημαι	ἐστάθην
καλέω	καλέσω/καλῶ	ἐκάλεσα	κέκληκα	κέκλημαι	ἐκλήθην
κελεύω	κελεύσω	ἐκέλευσα	κεκέλευκα	κεκέλευσμαι	ἐκελεύσθην
κερδαίνω	κερδανῶ	ἐκέρδανα	κεκέρδηκα		
κλείω	κλείσω	ἔκλεισα	κέκλεικα	κέκλειμαι	ἐκλείσθην
κλέπτω	κλέψω	ἔκλεψα	κέκλοφα	κέκλεμμαι	ἐκλάπην
κόπτω	κόψω	ἔκοψα	κέκοφα	κέκομμαι	ἐκόπην
κρίνω	κρινῶ	ἔκρινα	κέκρικα	κέκριμαι	ἐκρίθην
κωλύω	κωλύσω	ἐκώλυσα	κεκώλυκα	κεκώλυμαι	ἐκωλύθην
λαμβάνω	λήψομαι	ἔλαβον	εἴληφα	εἴλημμαι	ἐλήφθην
λανθάνω	λήσω	ἔλαθον	λέληθα	λέλησμαι	ἐλήσθην
λέγω	λέξω/ἐρῶ	ἔλεξα/εἶπον	εἴρηκα	λέλεγμαι/ εἴρημαι	ἐλέχθην/ ἐρήθην
λείπω	λείψω	ἔλιπον	λέλοιπα	λέλειμμαι	ἐλείφθην
λύω	λύσω	ἔλυσα	λέλυκα	λέλυμαι	ἐλύθην
μανθάνω	μαθήσομαι	ἔμαθον	μεμάθηκα		
μάχομαι	μαχέσομαι/ μαχοῦμαι	ἐμαχεσάμην		μεμάχημαι	
μένω	μενῶ	ἔμεινα	μεμένηκα		
νικάω	νικήσω	ἐνίκησα	νενίκηκα	νενίκημαι	ἐνικήθην
νομίζω	νομιῶ	ἐνόμισα	νενόμικα	νενόμισμαι	ἐνομίσθην
οἴομαι	οἰήσομαι				ᾠήθην
οἴχομαι	οἰχήσομαι		ᾤχηκα	ᾤχημαι	
ὀπάζω	ὀπάσω	ὤπασα			
ὁράω	ὄψομαι	εἶδον	ἑώρακα	ἑώραμαι	ὤφθην
παιδεύω	παιδεύσω	ἐπαίδευσα	πεπαίδευκα	πεπαίδευμαι	ἐπαιδεύθην

Principal Parts

πάσχω	πείσομαι	ἔπαθον	πέπονθα		
παύω	παύσω	ἔπαυσα	πέπαυκα	πέπαυμαι	ἐπαύθην
πείθομαι	πείσομαι	ἐπιθόμην		πέπεισμαι	
πειράω	πειράσω	ἐπείρασα	πεπείρακα	πεπείραμαι	ἐπειράθην
πέμπω	πέμψω	ἔπεμψα	πέπομφα	πέπεμμαι	ἐπέμφθην
πίνω	πίομαι	ἔπιον	πέπωκα	πέπομαι	ἐπόθην
πιστεύω	πιστεύσω	ἐπίστευσα	πεπίστευκα	πεπίστευμαι	ἐπιστεύθην
πλέκω	πλέξω	ἔπλεξα	πέπλοχα	πέπλεγμαι	ἐπλέχθην
ποιέω	ποιήσω	ἐποίησα	πεποίηκα	πεποίημαι	ἐποιήθην
πορεύομαι	πορεύσομαι	ἐπορευσάμην		πεπόρευμαι	ἐπορεύθην
πράττω	πράξω	ἔπραξα	πέπραχα	πέπραγμαι	ἐπράχθην
προσδοκάω	προσδοκήσω	προσεδόκησα	προσδεδόκηκα		προσεδοκήθην
πυνθάνομαι	πεύσομαι	ἐπυθόμην		πέπυσμαι	
σημαίνω	σημανῶ	ἐσήμηνα	σεσήμαγκα	σεσήμασμαι	ἐσημάνθην
σιγάω	σιγήσω	ἐσίγησα	σεσίγηκα	σεσίγημαι	ἐσιγήθην
σπεύδω	σπεύσω	ἔσπευσα	ἔσπευκα	ἔσπευσμαι	
στρατεύω	στρατεύσομαι	ἐστράτευσα		ἐστράτευμαι	ἐστρατεύθην
συμβαίνω	συμβήσομαι	συνέβην	συμβέβηκα		
τελευτάω	τελευτήσω	ἐτελεύτησα	τετελεύτηκα	τετελεύτημαι	ἐτελευτήθην
τέμνω	τεμῶ	ἔτεμον	τέτμηκα	τέτμημαι	ἐτμήθην
τέρπω	τέρψω	ἔτερψα			ἐτέρφθην
τίθημι	θήσω	ἔθηκα	τέθηκα	τέθειμαι	ἐτέθην
τίκτω	τέξω	ἔτεκον	τέτοκα		
τιμάω	τιμήσω	ἐτίμησα	τετίμηκα	τετίμημαι	ἐτιμήθην
τιτρώσκω	τρώσω	ἔτρωσα	τέτρωκα	τέτρωμαι	ἐτρώθην

Principal Parts

τρέφω	θρέψω	ἔθρεψα	τέτροφα	τέθραμμαι	ἐτράφην
τρέχω	δραμοῦμαι	ἔδραμον	δεδράμηκα	δεδράμημαι	
τρίβω	τρίψω	ἔτριψα	τέτριφα	τέτριμμαι	ἐτρίφθην
τυγχάνω	τεύξομαι	ἔτυχον	τετύχηκα		
τύπτω	τύψω	ἔτυψα		τέτυμμαι	ἐτύπην
φαίνομαι	φανοῦμαι	ἐφηνάμην	πέφηνα	πέφασμαι	ἐφάνην
φαίνω	φανῶ	ἔφηνα	πέφηνα	πέφασμαι	ἐφάνην
φέρω	οἴσω	ἤνεγκα /ἤνεγκον	ἐνήνοχα	ἐνήνεγμαι	ἠνέχθην
φεύγω	φεύξομαι	ἔφυγον	πέφευγα	πέφυγμαι	
φημί	φήσω	ἔφησα (ἔφην)			
φθίνω	φθίσομαι			ἔφθιμαι	ἐφθίμην
φθονέω	φθονήσω	ἐφθόνησα			ἐφθονήθην
φιλέω	φιλήσω	ἐφίλησα	πεφίληκα	πεφίλημαι	ἐφιλήθην
φοβέομαι	φοβήσομαι	ἐφοβησάμην		πεφόβημαι	ἐφοβήθην

Verb Roots

Principal Parts According to the Classes of Verb Roots

Verb roots ending on a labial consonant (π, πτ, β, φ)

ἕπομαι	ἕψομαι	ἑσπόμην					follow
θάπτω	θάψω	ἔθαψα	τέθαμμαι	ἐτάφην			bury
κλέπτω	κλέψω	ἔκλεψα	κέκλοφα	κέκλεμμαι	ἐκλάπην		steal
λείπω	λείψω	ἔλιπον	λέλοιπα	λέλοιφα	λέλειμμαι	ἐλείφθην	leave
μέμφομαι	μέμψομαι	ἐμεμψάμην					blame
πέμπω	πέμψω	ἔπεμψα	πέπομφα	πέπεμμαι	ἐπέμφθην		send
τρέπω	τρέψω	ἔτρεψα	τέτροφα	τέτραμμαι	ἐτρέφθην		turn
τρέφω	θρέψω	ἔθρεψα	τέτροφα	τέθραμμαι	ἐτράφην		feed

Verb roots ending on a palatal (guttural) consonant (κ, γ, χ, κτ, σκ)

ἀλάττω	ἀλλάξω	ἤλλαξα	ἤλλαχα	ἤλλαγμαι	ἠλλάχθην	change
δείκνυμι	δείξω	ἔδειξα	δέδειχα	δέδειγμαι	ἐδείχθην	show
δέχομαι	δέξομαι	ἐδεξάμην	δέδεγμαι			receive
διδάσκω	διδάξω	ἐδίδαξα	δεδίδαχα	δεδίδαγμαι	ἐδιδάχθην	teach
δοκέω	δόξω	ἔδοξα	δέδογμαι			seem
διώκω	διώξω	ἐδίωξα				pursue
ἥκω	ἥξω					come
πράττω	πράξω	ἔπραξα	πέπραχα	πέπραγμαι	ἐπράχθην	do
τίκτω	τέξομαι	ἔτεκον				bring forth
τάττω	τάξω	ἔταξα	τέταχα	τέταγμαι	ἐτάχθην	arrange
φεύγω	φεύξομαι	ἔφυγον	πέφευγα			flee

Verb roots ending on a dental consonant (τ, δ, θ)

πείθω	πείσω	ἔπεισα	πέποιθα	πέπεισμαι	ἐπείσθην	persuade
σπεύδω	σπεύσω	ἔσπευσα				hurry
ψεύδω	ψεύσω	ἔψευσα	ἔψευσμαι	ἐψεύσθην		deceive

Verb roots ending on a **liquid** or **nasal consonant** (λ, μ, ν, ρ, γ-nasal)

ἀγγέλλω	ἀγγελῶ	ἤγγειλα	ἤγγελκα	ἤγγελμαι	ἤγγελθην	announce
ἀπόλλυμι	ἀπολῶ	ἀπώλεσα				destroy
βάλλω	βαλῶ	ἔβαλον	βέβληκα	βέβλημαι	ἐβλήθην	throw
γίγνομαι	γενήσομαι	ἐγενόμην	γέγονα	γεγένημαι		become
διαφθείρω	διαφθερῶ	διέφθειρα	διέφθαρκα	διέφθαρμαι	διεφθάρρην	destroy
κρίνω	κρινῶ	ἔκρινα	κέκρικα	κέκριμαι	ἐκρίθην	judge
μένω	μενῶ	ἔμεινα				remain
τέμνω	τεμῶ	ἔτεμον	τέτμηκα	τέτμημαι	ἐτμήθην	cut
φαίνω	φανῶ	ἔφηνα	πέφαγκα πέφηνα	πέφασμαι	ἐφάνθην	show

Verb roots adding -αν- in the progressive aspect

ἁμαρτάνω	ἁμαρτήσομαι	ἥμαρτον	ἡμάρτηκα	ἡμάρτημαι	ἡμαρτήθην	err
ἐπιλάνθάνομαι	ἐπιλαθήσομαι	ἐπελαθόμην				forget
λαμβάνω	λήψομαι	ἔλαβον	εἴληφα	εἴλημμαι	ἐλήφθην	take

Verb Roots

πυνθάνομαι	πεύσομαι	ἐπυθόμην	πέπυσμαι			ascertain find out
τυγχάνω	τεύξομαι	ἔτυχον	τετύχηκα			happen

Verb roots adding -σκ-(inchoative) in the progressive aspect

γιγνώσκω	γνώσομαι	ἔγνων	ἔγνωκα	ἔγνωσμαι	ἐγνώσθην	get to know
εὑρίσκω	εὑρήσω	ηὗρον	ηὕρηκα	εὕρημαι	εὑρέθην	find

Verb roots ending in the vowel -α (contract verbs in -α)

νικάω (= νικῶ) κτλ.	νικήσω	ἐνίκησα	νενίκηκα	νενίκημαι	ἐνικήθην	conquer

Verb roots ending in the vowel -ε (contract verbs in -ε)

ποιέω (= ποιῶ) κτλ.	ποιήσω	ἐποίησα	πεποίηκα	πεποίημαι	ἐποιήθην	make

Verb roots ending in the vowel -ο (contract verbs in -ο)

δηλόω (= δηλῶ) κτλ.	δηλώσω	ἐδήλωσα	δεδήλωκα	δεδήλωμαι	ἐδηλώθην	point out

Verb roots ending in -νυ

δείκνυμι	δείξω	ἔδειξα	δέδειχα	δέδειγμαι	ἐδείχθην	show, point out

Verbs in -μι with reduplication in the progressive aspect

δίδωμι	δώσω	ἔδωκα	δέδωκα	δέδομαι	ἐδόθην		give
ἵστημι	στήσω	ἔστησα	ἔστην	ἕστηκα	ἕσταμαι	ἐστάθην	stand
τίθημι	θήσω	ἔθηκα	τέθηκα	ἐτέθην			put

Verbs, the principal parts of which are for various reasons unpredictable

αἱρέω	αἱρήσω	εἷλον	ᾕρηκα			take
βαίνω	βήσομαι	ἔβην	βέβηκα			go
εἰμί	ἔσομαι	ἦν				be
ἔρχομαι	εἶμι	ἦλθον	ἐλήλυθα			come
ἔχω	ἕξω/σχήσω	ἔσχον	ἔσχηκα			have, hold
οἶδα	εἴσομαι					know
ὁράω	ὄψομαι	εἶδον	ἑόρακα	ἑόραμαι	ὤφθην	see
φέρω	οἴσω	ἤνεγκον	ἐνήνοχα	ἐνήνεγμαι	ἠνέχθην	carry, bring
φημί	ἐρῶ	εἶπον	εἴρηκα	εἴρημαι		say, tell, speak

Stem List

A List of Greek Stems and Roots

Compiled by S. M. Cerutti

While the number of words in the Greek dictionary is large, the number of frequently occurring stems is not. Familiarity with them is one of the best means to enlarge a beginner's vocabulary, especially when used together with a study of prefixes and suffixes. Stems and prefixes undergo, however, certain sound changes according to their environment. Such sound changes have been discussed in the Pre-view, which should be consulted. An * indicates a "weak vowel," that is one that changes or drops out altogether from word to word, such as the first alpha of *thanatos* and its cognates. Alternate stem forms are given when necessary.

ἁβρ soft, delicate, youthful

ἀγαθ good, honorable

ἀγ*λ honor, statue, image

ἀγαν soft, mild, delicate

ἀγγ*λ messenger, message, to announce

ἀγ* to do, act, drive, lead, struggle, contest

ἀδελφ of or pertaining to brothers, brotherhood, clan

αἰσθ to perceive, feel, sense

ἀκου to hear

ἀκρ high, extreme

ἁλ salt, of or pertaining to the sea

ἀλγ pain

ἀλλ other

ἀνδρ man, male, of or belonging to a man

ἀνθ flower, blossom

ἀρχ ancient, primitive, beginning

ἀρθ to join together, articulate

ἀσκ to exercise

αὐτ self(reflexive)

β*λ* (βαλλ, βλη, βολ) throw, put, cast

βαρ weight, pressure

βι life, force

βλαστ bud, formative, substance

βραχ short, small

βραδ slow

Stem List

βου cattle, cow
γαλακ milk
γαμ marriage
γαστ stomach, belly
γε, γα, γη earth, land
γελ laughter
γ*ν to produce, offspring, origin
γερα honor, prize
γερω old age
γλαυκ grey, dusky
γλωττ, γλωσσ tongue, talking
γν* to know, recognize
γραμ, φ that which is drawn or written
γυμν naked
γυναικ woman, female
δακρ tear, sorrow
δακτυ finger
δαιμ spirit, deity
δεκ ten
δεμ, δημ people, man
δενδρ tree, of or like a tree
δερμ skin, hide
δευτερ second (ordinal number)
δι twice, between two
δ*κ to teach, show, opinion
δολ treachery, stealth
δολιχ long
δρ* running, course
δυν force, power, ability
δω to give, gift
εἰδ appearance, form, species
ἑλκ spiral, swirl
ἐργ, εἰργ work, force, energy
ἐρο, ἐρα love, desire

Stem List

ἐθο, ἐθω custom, habit, nature

εὐρ wide, broad

ζευγ, ζευκ, ζευξ, ζυγ to yoke, bind, anything joined together

ζηλ envy, jealousy

ζημι to cause damage, loss fine

ζητ to inquire, seek, search

ζοφ shadow, darkness, gloom

ζοω, ζω life, any living thing

ζων girdle, to gird oneself

ἡβα youth, beauty, happiness

ἡγ (ἀρχ, ἐργ) to rule, command, govern

ἡδ sweetness, pleasure

ἠθ nature, custom, habit

ἡλιο, ἡλ of or pertaining to the sun

ἡμαρ, ἡμερ day, daily

ἡμι half, anything divided

ἡσυχ quiet, calm, still

θ* (θεα, τιθε) to locate, place, view, set

θαλαμ room, bedroom, house

θαλασσ, θαλαττ of or pertaining to the sea

θ*ν (θανα, θνη) mortal, deadly, death

θαρσ (θρας) confidence, good cheer, boldness

θυμ heart, soul, emotions, anger, joy

θαυμ wonder, marvel, astonishment

θελ (εθελ) to be willing, desire, want

θεμισ, θεμιτ lawful, that which is allowed

θε* (θεϝ) divine, of or pertaining to the gods

θερ heat, summer

θεραπ to nurture, nurse

θηρ of or pertaining to wild beasts

θορυβ to make a noise, uproar

ἰατρ physician, medicine, healing

ἰδιο personal, private

Stem List

ἱππ horse

ἰσ equal, equality

ἰσχ _ strength, force, might

ἰχθ of or pertaining to fish

κ*λ to call, summon

κ*ρ (καρ, καρδ, κηρ) head, heart, seat of emotion or intellect

κ*ραν mixture, to mix

κακ evil, bad

καλ good, beauty

καρπ fruit

καυ, καυσ to burn

κεν empty

κεφαλ head

κιν motion

κλα to break

κοσμ to arrange, set in order

κρατ strength, force, might

κρι to judge, decide, separate

κρυπτ secret, hidden

κυαν dark (in color)

κυκλ circular, wheel

κυν dog

κυτ hollow, cell, cavity

λαβ to take, seize

λαμπ to shine, blaze

λατρ to work for hire, to service the gods

λευκ white

λιπ fat, oil, ointment

λιθ stone

λ*γ (λεγ, λογ) to select, reasoning, speech, word

λυ to loosen

μαθ, μανθ, μαντ learning, reckoning, to understand, prophecy

μακαρ happy, blessed, bliss

μακρ large, long

Stem List

μαζ that which is kneaded, bread, breast
μαρτ witness
μεγα large
μελαν black
μεμφ, μεμψ blame, reproach
μερ portion, lot, share
μεσ middle
μι, μ*ν to imitate, mimic
μισ hatred
μνε, μνη memory, to remember
μον one, single
μορφ form, shape
ναι to dwell, inhabit
ναυ, νη ship, sailor, to swim
ναϝ temple
νεκρ dead, corpse
νησ island
νικ victory, conquest
νο, ν*μ to categorize mentally, of or pertaining to the mind
νυξ, νυκτ night, at night, pertaining to the night
ξανθ yellow, blond
ξεν guest, host, visitor, friend
ξιφ of or pertaining to swords
ξυλ wood, anything made of wood, timber
ὀδ song
ὁδ road, way, path
ὀδοντ tooth, teeth
οἰκ house, founder
ὀλιγ few
ὀνομ (cf. ν*μ) name
ὀπ, ὀψ eye, vision
ὁρα to see
ὀρνισ, ὀρνιθ bird

Stem List

ὀρθ straight, erect

παι, παιδ of or pertaining to children

παλαι long ago, old

παντ all, every

παθ to feel, suffer, experience

πατρ, πατρι father, family, clan

πειρ to try, attempt

πετρ rock

πικρ harsh, bitter, pungent

πιστ trust, faith, honesty

πλαγ, πλαν wandering, to roam

πλασ, πλαστ, πλατ to form, mold, anything shaped or flattened

πλ*κ (πλεκ, πλεξ) to weave, intertwine, anything woven

πλε, πλη, πληθ to fill, anything full

ποδ foot, pertaining to feet

ποθ to desire, wish, lust

πολ, πολις city, state

πολη, πολλη many

προτ first, original

πορφ (cf. πυρ) red, purple, anything dyed, exotic

πρεσβ, πρεσβευ, πρεσβυ old age, age

πτε, πτη birds, feathers, anything winged or feathered

πυκ thick, dense, crowded, frequent

πυρ (cf. πορφ) of or pertaining to fire

ῥε, ῥης, ῥητ speech, word, oratory

ῥιγ to shiver, be cold or frightened

ῥιγν, ῥιπ to throw

σαλ toss, stir, shake

σελα, σελη anything bright, shining, the moon

σ*μ sign, signal.token

σεμν holy

σθεν strength

σιγ to be silent, silence

σιδ of or pertaining to iron

Stem List

σιτ food, feed-grain, hunger

σκαπ, σκαπτ, ψ, φ to dig, something used to dig, anything dug out

σκευ equipment, implements, clothing, armor

σκλη rough, harshness, to harden

σκοπ to look, see, watch

σκοτ darkness, shadow, secret

σομ body, corpse

σοφ cleverness, to be wise, to make wise

σπερμ seeds, to sow seeds, to beget, family, race

σπουδ haste, earnest, eagerness

στ* (στασ, στη) uprising, standing, sedition

στεν to groan, moan

στιγ, στιξ to brand, prick, puncture

στ*λ to equip, arm, dress

στ*μ mouth, pertaining to speech, origin

στ*ρ (στερν, στρατ) to deal out, arrange, expedition, command, army

στρεφ, στροφ to turn, bend, twist, revolve

σχεδ near, close by, at hand

σχ* (σχημα) form, shape, anything fashioned

σχισ, σχιζ to cleave, split

σχολ (cf. σχ*) leisure, ease, learning

σ* (σωζω, σωφρον) to preserve, temperate, moderation

τ*τ (ταγ, τασσ, τατт, ταξ) to arrange, order, to command, rule

τ*λ* (ταλας, ταλαι) weight, burden, toil, suffering

τ*ν (ταν, τεμν) to stretch, extend, be thick

ταρα to trouble, disquiet

ταυρ of or pertaining to bulls

ταυτ same

ταχ speed, swiftness

τεγ, τειχ, τοιχ to cover, roof, house, fortify

τελ end, to make an end, finish

τεμ, τεμν - to cut, mark off, portion

τ*ρ (τερ, ταρα) portent, wonder

Stem List

τερπ pleasure, delight

τερσ to dry, wipe up

τ*χ, ν (τεχμα, τεχμη) to esstablish, boundary, goal, end, token, sign

τευχ, τεχν to guild, skill, craft

τιμ, τιμω honor, value, what one deserves, punishment

τλα, τλη, τολ endure, suffer, patience

τοπ place, region

τοξ that which pertains to the bow

τραπεζ table, meal, any flat surface

τρ*γ, χ (τραχ, τριχ) rough, rugged, savage, shaggy

τριβ wear away, rub down, spend time, delay

τρ* (τροπ, τροφ, τροχ) to turn, to roll, to rear

τρυφ delicate, soft, luxury

ὑγι, ὑγια, ὑγιε health, to be well

ὑδωρ, ὑδρ water

ὑλη, ὑλο woods, belonging to woodlands

ὑμην, ὑμνο hymns, songs

ὑψ high, lofty

φ* (φα, φη, φω) utterance, speech

φαϝ (φαα, φαε, φαι, φαο) brilliance, light

φαρμα drug, medicine

φερ, φορ bear, carry, burden

φθι (φθειρ, φθερ, φθον) destroy, waste, perish, ruin, jealousy

φιλ love, friendship

φαυλ, φλαυρ shabby, needy, poor, bad

φοβ fear

φοιν red, ruddy, bloody, anything dyed

φον murder, bloodshed

φραζ, φρασ tell, show, explain

φρην heart, emotions, life, self

φ* (φυ, φυσ) origin, reproduce, to bear or be born, from nature

φυγ to flee, flight, escape, avoid

φυλακ, φυλαξ, φυλατ to watch, keep watch, guard

χαιρ, χαρ to wish one well, say hello, general good will

Stem List

χαλκ of or pertaining to bronze
χαμαι on or belonging to the ground, earth
χειρ the hand, anything done by the hand, to attempt
χθον, χθων of or belonging beneath the surface of the earth
χορ dance, song, chorus
χρει, χρη to be needy, to lack, to be useful
χρον of or pertaining to time
χρυσ gold, anything made of gold
ψαλ to pluck, anything plucked, string instrument
ψευδ, ψευσ to lie, anything false or untrustworthy
ψιλ to strip, anything smooth, bare
ψυχη the soul, belonging to the soul
ὠκ swiftness, speed
ὠμ of or pertaining to the shoulders
ὡρα time, hour, season, youth or any stage of life

Dictionary

Greek to English Vocabulary

A

ἀβουλία, ἀβουλίας, ἡ bad advice, thoughtlessness 8

ἄβουλος, ἄβουλον ill-advised 6

ἀγαθός, ἀγαθή, ἀγαθόν good 5

ἀγαθός, ἀγαθοῦ, ὁ good person 4

ἄγαν too much, too 20

ἀγγέλλω, ἀγγελῶ, ἤγγειλα, ἤγγελκα, ἤγγελμαι, ἠγγέλθην to report, announce 13

Ἀγασίας, Ἀγασίου, ὁ Agasias 25

Ἆγις, Ἄγεως, ὁ Agis, a Spartan king 19

ἄγω, ἄξω, ἤγαγον, ἦχα, ἦγμαι, ἤχθην to do, drive, lead 4

ᾄδω/ἀείδω, ᾄσομαι/ἀείσομαι, ᾖεισα to sing, sing of 23

ἀδελφός, ἀδελφοῦ, ὁ brother 10

ἀδικέω, ἀδικήσω, ἠδίκησα, ἠδίκηκα to do wrong 6

ἀδικία, ἀδικίας, ἡ injustice, wrong 2

Ἄδμητος, Ἀδμήτου ὁ Admetus, king of the Molossians 20

ἀδυνατός, ἀδυνατόν impossible 17

ἀεί always 4

ἀήρ, ἀέρος, ὁ air 5

ἀθανασία, ἀθανασίας, ἡ immortality 9

ἀθλητής, ἀθλητοῦ, ὁ athlete 5

Ἀίδης, Ἀίδου, ὁ Hades 21

αἰνέω, αἰνήσω, ᾔνεσα, ᾔνεκα, ᾔνημαι, ᾐνέθην to praise 22

αἱρετός, αἱρετή, αἱρετόν preferable 16

αἱρέω, αἱρήσω, εἷλον, ᾕρηκα, ᾕρημαι ᾑρέθην to take; *Mid.* to choose 24

αἰσθάνομαι, αἰσθήσομαι, ᾐσθόμην ᾔσθημαι to observe, notice 19

αἴσθησις, αἰσθήσεως, ἡ observation 4

αἰσχρός, αἰσχρά, αἰσχρόν shameful 9

αἰτιάομαι, αἰτιάσομαι, ᾐτιασάμην, ᾐτίαμαι, ᾐτιάθην to accuse

ἀκμάζω, ἀκμάσω, ἤκμασα to bloom 5

ἀκούω, ἀκούσομαι, ἤκουσα, ἀκήκοα, ἠκούσθην to hear 7

ἀλγέω, ἀλγήσω, ἤλγησα to feel pain 25

Ἀλέξανδρος, Ἀλεξάνδρου, ὁ Alexander 9

ἀλήθεια, ἀληθείας, ἡ truth 1

ἀληθής, ἀληθές true 5

ἀληθινός, ἀληθινή, ἀληθινόν true 10

ἁλίσκομαι, ἁλώσομαι, ἑάλων (ἥλων), ἑάλωκα to be caught 6

ἀλκή, ἀλκῆς, ἡ strength 4

ἀλλά but, however 2

ἀλλάττω, ἀλλάξω, ἤλλαξα, ἤλλαχα, ἤλλαγμαι, ἠλλάχθην to change 2

ἀλλήλων (oblique cases only) each other 25

ἄλλος, ἄλλη, ἄλλο other, another 19

ἄλλως otherwise 22

ἀλώπηξ, ἀλώπεκος, ἡ fox 15

ἅμα at the same time, while 15

ἀμαθής, ἀμαθές ignorant 19

ἁμαρτάνω, ἁμαρτήσομαι, ἥμαρτον, ἡμάρτηκα, ἡμάρτημαι, ἡμαρτήθην to do wrong 16

ἀμελέω, ἀμελήσω, ἠμέλησα, ἠμέληκα (+ gen.) to neglect 6

ἀμύνω, ἀμυνῶ, ἤμυνα to defend, ward off 13

ἀμφιβάλλομαι, ἀμφιβαλοῦμαι, ἀμφεβαλόμην, ἀμφιβέβλημαι, ἀμφεβλήθην to throw/wrap around 22

ἀναβαίνω, ἀναβήσομαι, ἀνέβην, ἀναβέβληκα to go up 20

ἀναγιγνώσκω, ἀναγιγνώσομαι, ἀνέγνων, ἀνέγνωκα, ἀνέγνωσμαι, ἀνεγνώσθην to read aloud 22

Dictionary

ἀναγκάζω, ἀναγκάσω, ἠνάγκασα, ἠνάγκακα, ἠνάγκασμαι, ἠναγκάσθην to force, compel 18

ἀναγκαῖος, ἀναγκαία, ἀναγκαῖον necessary 25

ἀνάγκη, ἀνάγκης, ἡ necessity 1

ἀνάγκη (ἐστιν) is a need 17

ἀναίρεσις, ἀναιρέσεως, ἡ taking up (of dead bodies) 24

ἄναξ, ἄνακτος, ὁ lord

ἀναπαύω, ἀναπαύσω, ἀνέπαυσα ἀναπέπαυκα, ἀναπέπαυμαι, ἀνεπαύθην to cause to stop 2

ἄναρκτος, ἄναρκτον not governed 22

ἀναρχία, ἀναρχίας, ἡ anarchy 16

ἀνατρέπω, ἀνατρέψω, ἀνέτρεψα, ἀνατέτροφα, ἀνατετραμμαι, ἀνετράπην to overturn 5

ἀναφύομαι, ἀναφύσομαι, ἀνέφυν, ἀναπέφυκα to grow again, grow back 20

ἀνδρεῖος, ἀνδρεία, ἀνδρεῖον brave 16

ἄνευ prep. + gen. without 4

ἀνήρ, ἀνδρός, ὁ man, husband 5

ἀνθίστημι, ἀντιστήσω, ἀντέστησα to set against

ἀνθρώπειος, ἀνθρωπεία, ἀνθρώπειον human 19

ἀνθρώπινος, ἀνθρωπίνη, ἀνθρώπινον human 9

ἄνθρωπος, ἀνθρώπου, ὁ man, mankind 8

ἀνίστημι, ἀναστήσω, ἀνέστησα/ ἀνέστην, ἀνέστηκα to make to stand up, stir up; Mid. to stand up, rise 18

ἀντηχέω, ἀντηχήσω, ἀντηχήσα to resound 21

ἀντί prep. + gen. in place of, instead of 15

ἄξιος, ἀξία, ἄξιον (+ gen.) worthy of, guilty of 16

ἀξιόω, ἀξιώσω, ἠξίωσα, ἠξίωκα, ἠξίωμαι, ἠξιώθην to think worthy 16

ἅπας, ἅπασα, ἅπαν every, all, entire 16

ἄπειμι, ἀπέσομαι, ἀπῆν to go away 19

ἀπειρία, ἀπειρίας, ἡ inexperience 17

ἀπέχω (+ gen.) to be distant from 9

ἁπλοῦς, ἁπλῆ, ἁπλοῦν simple 10

ἀπό prep. + gen. away from, from 6

ἀποδίδωμι to give back

ἀποθνῄσκω, ἀποθανοῦμαι, ἀπέθανον, ἀποτέθνηκα to die 12

ἀποκρίνομαι, ἀποκρινοῦμαι, ἀπεκρινάμην, ἀποκέκριμαι, ἀπεκρίθην to answer 22

ἀποκτείνω, ἀποκτενῶ, ἀπέκτεινα, ἀπέκτονα to kill 20

ἀπόλλυμαι, ἀπολοῦμαι, ἀπωλόμην, ἀπόλωλα to perish 20

ἀπομαραίνομαι, ἀπεμαρηνάμην, ἀπεμαράνθην to dry up, wither away 16

ἀποπαίω, ἀποπαίσω, ἀπέπαισα, ἀποπέπαικα, ἀποπέπαισμαι, ἀπεπαίσθην to drive away 21

ἀποπλέω, ἀποπλεύσω, ἀπέπλευσα to sail away 8

ἀποσπάω, ἀποσπάσω, ἀπέσπασα (+ gen.) to sever, separate from 15

ἀποτελέω, ἀποτελέσω, ἀπετέλεσα to produce, complete, accomplish 4

ἀποτέμνω, ἀποτεμῶ, ἀπέταμον, ἀποτέτμηκα, ἀπετμήθην to cut off 20

ἀποτυγχάνω, ἀποτεύξομαι, ἀπέτυχον ἀποτετύχηκα (+ gen.) to fail 17

ἄπροικος, ἄπροικον without a dowry 5

ἅπτομαι, ἅψομαι, ἡψάμην, ἧμμαι, ἥφθην to grab on, fasten onto 9

ἆρα; introduces a question 3

ἆρα μὴ ; question,h negative answer expected 3

ἆρα οὐ; question, positive answer expected 3

ἀρέσκω, ἀρέσω, ἤρεσα, ἀρήρεκα, ἠρέσθην (+ dat.) to please 8

ἀρετή, ἀρετῆς, ἡ virtue 1

ἄριστος, ἀρίστη, ἄριστον very good, best 21

ἄρνυμαι (*defective verb*) to win, gain, receive 20

ἀρχή, ἀρχῆς, ἡ rule, beginningr, province 12

Ἀρχιδάμος, Ἀρχιδάμου, ὁ Archidamus 19

ἄρχομαι, ἄρξομαι, ἠρξάμην, ἦργμαι (+ gen.) to begin 9

Dictionary

ἄρχω, ἄρξω, ἦρξα, ἦρχα, ἦργμαι, ἤρχθην (+ gen.) to rule 9

ἀσκέω, ἀσκήσω, ἤσκησα, ἤσκηκα, ἤσκημαι to train, drill 19

ἄσπονδος, ἄσπονδον implacable 21

Ἀστέριος, Ἀστερίου, ὁ Asterius 20

ἀσφαλῶς safely 6

ἅτε as, since, because, in as much as 15

ἀτερπής, ἀτερπές unpleasant 25

ἄτιμος, ἄτιμον dishonored 10

Ἀτόσσα, Ἀτόσσης, ἡ Atossa 12

ἀτυχία, ἀτυχίας, ἡ misfortune 4

Ἀττική, Ἀττικῆς, ἡ (γῆ) Attica 17

αὖ again 15

αὐξάνω/αὔξω, αὐξήσω, ηὔξησα, ηὔξηκα to increase 8

αὐτός, αὐτή, αὐτό same/self/he, she, it 10

ἀφικνέομαι, ἀφίξομαι, ἀφικόμην, ἀφῖγμαι to have come, arrive 19

ἀφορίζομαι, ἀφοροῦμαι, ἀφωρισάμην, ἀφώριμαι to appropriate, limit 15

Β

βαίνω, βήσομαι, ἔβην, βέβηκα, βέβαμαι, ἐβάθην to go, walk 13

βαιός, βαιά, βαιόν short 5

βάλλω, βαλῶ, ἔβαλον, βέβληκα, βέβλημαι, ἐβλήθην to throw 4

βασιλεύς, βασιλέως, ὁ king 9

βασιλεύω, βασιλεύσω, ἐβασίλευσα, βεβασίλευκα, βεβασίλευμαι, ἐβασιλεύθην (+ gen.) to rule, be king 9

βία, βίας, ἡ force 20

βιβλίον, βιβλίου, τό book 5

βίος, βίου, ὁ life 2

βιώσιμος, βιώσιμον worth living 26

βλάβη, βλάβης, ἡ harm 2

βλάπτω, βλάψω, ἔβλαψα, βέβλαφα, βέβλαμμαι, ἐβλάφθην/ἐβλάβην to hurt, harm, damage 5

βοηθέω, βοηθήσω, ἐβοήθησα, βεβοήθηκα, βεβοήθημαι, ἐβοήθην (+ dat.) to help 12

βουλεύω, βουλεύσω, ἐβούλευσα, βεβούλευκα, βεβούλευμαι, ἐβουλεύθην to plan, devise; *Mid.* to take counsel, deliberate 6

βουλή, βουλῆς, ἡ thought, counsel, idea 8

βούλομαι, βουλήσομαι, βεβούλημαι, ἐβουλήθην to want, to wish 9

βροτοί, βροτῶν, οἱ mortals 8

Γ

γαμέω, γαμῶ, ἔγημα, γεγάμηκα, γεγάμημαι, ἐγαμήθην to marry 15

γάρ (*never in first position*) for 2

γε at least 16

γενναῖος, γενναία, γενναῖον noble 21

γεννάω, γεννήσω, ἐγέννησα to beget, bring forth 15

γένος, γένους, τό race, kind 5

γέρας, γέραος, τό prize, honor 20

γέρων, γέροντος, ὁ old man 8

γεωργός, γεωργοῦ, ὁ farmer 4

γῆ, γῆς, ἡ earth 2

γίγνομαι, γενήσομαι, ἐγενόμην, γέγονα, γεγένημαι, ἐγενήθην to be, become, happen, be born 8

γιγνώσκω, γνώσομαι, ἔγνων, ἔγνωκα, ἔγνωσμαι, ἐγνώσθην (+ inf.) to understand how to, become aware, recognize 16

γλῶττα, γλώττης, ἡ tongue, speech 8

γνῶθι aorist imperative of γιγνώσκω, know! 16

γνώμη, γνώμης, ἡ opinion, attitude 2

γονεῖς, γονέων οἱ parents

Γοργώ, Γοργόνος, ἡ Gorgo 20

γράμμα, γράμματος, τό letter 17

γράφω, γράψω, ἔγραψα, γέγραφα, γέγραμμαι, ἐγράφην to write 13

γραῦς, γραός, ἡ old woman 7

γυνή, γυναικός, ἡ woman, wife 7

Δ

δαίμων, δαίμονος, ὁ, ἡ daimon, deity, destiny 5

δάκτυλος, δακτύλου, ὁ finger 2

Dictionary

Δαρεῖος, Δαρείου, ὁ Darius 12

δέ but 2

δεῖ, δεήσει, ἐδέησε (+ inf.) it is necessary 16

δείκνυμι, δείξω, ἔδειξα, δέδειχα, δέδειγμαι, ἐδείχθην to show, make apparent 7

δειλός, δειλή, δειλόν vile, wretched 5

δεινός, δεινή, δεινόν terrible, marvellous 16

δέομαι, δεήσομαι, δεδέημαι, ἐδεήθην (+ gen.) to lack, need, want 9

δεσποτέω, δεσποτήσω to rule despotically 22

δεσπότης, δεσπότου, ὁ master 8

δεύτερος, δευτέρα, δεύτερον second 16

δέχομαι, δέξομαι, ἐδεξάμην, δέδεγμαι, ἐδέχθην to receive 13

δή indeed 17

δῆλος, δήλη, δῆλον clear, visible 19

δῆλον ἐστίν is clear 19

διά prep. + acc. because of 4

διά prep. + gen. through 4

διὰ τί; why 4

διαβολή, διαβολῆς, ἡ slander 5

διακωλύω, διακωλύσω, διεκώλυσα, διακεκώλυκα, διακεκώλυμαι, διεκωλύθην to hinder, forbid, stop from 18

διαφέρω, διοίσω, διήνεγκα, διήνεγμαι, διηνέχθην (+ gen.) to differ from 9

διαφθείρω, διαφθερῶ, διέφθειρα, διέφθαρκα, διέφθαρμαι, διεφθάρην to destroy 1

διδάσκαλος, διδασκάλου, ὁ teacher 15

διδάσκομαι (+ 2 acc.) to train somebody as 10

διδάσκω, διδάξω, ἐδίδαξα, δεδίδαχα, δεδίδαγμαι, ἐδιδάχθην to teach 1

δίδωμι, δώσω, ἔδωκα, δέδωκα, δέδομαι, ἐδόθην to give 14

διελαύνω, διελῶ, διήλασα, διελήλακα, διελήλαμαι, διηλάθην to ride through 18

διερωτάω, διερωτήσω, διηρώτησα, διηρώτηκα to ask 19

διηγέομαι, διηγήσομαι, διηγσάμην to set out, explain 24

δίκαιος, δικαία, δίκαιον just 5

δικαιοσύνη, δικαιοσύνης, ἡ justice 6

δίκη, δίκης, ἡ right, justice 1

Διονύσιος, Διονυσίου, ὁ Dionysius 19

διώκω, διώξω, ἐδίωξα, δεδίωχα, δεδίωγμαι, ἐδιώχθην to pursue 15

δοκέω, δόξω/δοκήσω, ἔδοξα/ἐδόκησα, δεδόκηκα, δέδογμαι/δεδόκημαι, ἐδοκήθην to seem, think 16

δόμος, δόμου, ὁ house; *pl.* palace 20

δόξα, δόξης, ἡ opinion, reputation, glory 5

δουλεύω, δουλεύσω, ἐδούλευσα, δεδούλευκα, δεδούλευμαι, ἐδουλεύθην (+ dat.) to be a slave, serve 8

δοῦλος, δούλου, ὁ slave 9

δρᾶμα, δράματος, τό drama 10

δράω, δράσω, ἔδρασα, δέδρακα, δέδραμαι, ἐδράσθην to do 22

δράω εὖ to benefit 22

δρόμος, δρόμου, ὁ race 7

δύναμαι, δυνήσομαι, δεδύνημαι, ἐδυνήθην (+ inf.) to be able 17

δύναμις, δυνάμεως, ἡ power, ability 22

δυνατός δυνάτη, δυνατόν possible 17

δύο two 7

δυσχείμερος, δυσχείμερον disagreeably cold, wintry 20

Ε

ἑαυτοῦ, ἑαυτῆς, ἑαυτοῦ himself, herself, itself (reflexive) 16

ἐάω, ἐάσω, εἴασα, εἴακα, εἴαμαι, εἰάθην to let, allow 18

ἐγγύς near 25

ἐγώ I 7

ἐθέλω, ἐθελήσω, ἠθέλησα, ἠθέληκα to want, be willing (see θέλω) 15

ἔθος, ἔθους, τό habit 10

εἰ if 11

εἰδέναι *infinitive of* οἶδα 16

εἰμί, ἔσομαι, ἦν (imperfect) to be, to exist 14

DICTIONARY

εἶμι, imperfect ᾖα, subjunctive ἴω, infinitive ἰέναι to go 22

εἶναι *infinitive of* εἰμί 18

εἶπον *see* λέγω

εἰρήνη, εἰρήνης, ἡ peace 4

εἰς prep. + acc. into, against 6

εἷς, μία, ἕν one 6

εἰσβολή, εἰσβολῆς, ἡ attack, invasion 8

εἴσω prep. + acc. into 21

εἴσω prep. + gen. within, inside 21

εἴτε...εἴτε either...or

ἐκ (ἐξ) prep. + gen. out of, from 6

ἕκαστος, ἑκάστη, ἕκαστον each 9

ἑκατόμβη, ἑκατόμβης, ἡ public sacrifice 12

ἔκγονος, ἐκγόνου, ὁ son 26

ἐκεῖνος, ἐκείνη, ἐκεῖνο that/he, she, it 10

ἐκθρῴσκω, ἐκθοροῦμαι, ἐξέθορον to jump out 20

ἐκπλήσσω/ἐκπλήττω, ἐκπλήξω, ἐξέπληξα, ἐκπέπληγα, ἐκπέπλγμαι, ἐξεπλάγην to destroy 1

ἐκφεύγω, ἐκφεύξομαι, ἐκέφυγον, ἐκπέφευγα to escape 22

ἐκχωρέω, ἐκχωρήσω, ἐξεχώρησα, ἐκκεχώρηκα to depart 20

ἐλεέω, ἐλεήσω, ἠλέησα, ἠλέημαι to pity 6

Ἑλλάς, Ἑλλάδος, ἡ Greece 9

Ἕλλήνες, Ἕλλήνων, οἱ Greeks 18

ἔμμεναι = εἶναι, *see* εἰμί to be 19

ἐμός, ἐμή, ἐμόν mine, my 19

ἐν prep. + dat. in, on 4

ἔνδοθεν inside, from within 23

ἔνεροι, ἐνέρων, οἱ the gods of the Underworld, the dead 15

ἔνθα there 26

ἐντός inward, within 23

ἐξάγω, ἐξάξω ἐξήγαγον, ἐξῆχα, ἔξηγμαι, ἐξήχθην to lead out, bring out12

ἐξαιρέομαι, ἐξελοῦμαι, ἐξειλόμην (+ 2 acc.) to rob somebody of something 20

ἐξέρχομαι, ἐξελεύσομαι, ἐξῆλθον to come out, go out 21

ἔξεστιν (+ dat.) is allowed 17

ἐξευρίσκω, ἐξευρήσω, ἐξεῦρον, ἐξηύρηκα, ἐξηύρημαι, ἐξηυρέθην to find 21

ἔξωθεν outside, from without 23

ἔοικα (+ dat.) to be like, resemble 8

ἐπαινέω, ἐπαινέσω, ἐπῄνεσα, ἐπῄνεκα, ἐπῃνέθην to praise 21

ἐπεί after, since (causal), when 11

ἔπειμι, ἐπιέναι to come upon, approach, follow 15

ἔπειτε because, since 15

ἐπί prep. + acc. to 19

ἐπί prep. + dat. in addition to, near 19

ἐπί prep. + gen. on, during 19

ἐπιβουλεύω, ἐπιβουλεύσω, ἐπεβούλευσα, ἐπιβεβούλευκα, ἐπιβεβούλευμαι, ἐπέβουλεύθην (+ dat.) to plot against 20

ἐπιδείκνυμι, ἐπιδείξω, ἐπέδειξα, ἐπιδέδειχα, ἐπιδέδειγμαι, ἐπέδείχθην to exhibit 18

ἐπιθυμέω, ἐπιθυμήσω, ἐπεθύμησα ἐπιτεθύμηκα (+ gen.) to desire 9

ἐπιθυμία, ἐπιθυμίας, ἡ desire 8

ἐπιλανθάνομαι, ἐπιλήσομαι, ἐπελαθόμην, ἐπιλέληθα, ἐπιλέλησμαι, ἐπελήσθην (+ gen.) to forget 9

ἐπιμελέομαι ἐπιμελήσομαι, ἐπιμεμέλημαι, ἐπεμελήθην (+ gen.) to take care of 19

ἐπιπλέω, ἐπιπλεύσομαι, ἐπέπλευσα, ἐπιπέπλευκα, ἐπιπέπλευσμαι to approach, to sail upon 19

ἐπίσταμαι, ἐπιστήσομαι, ἠπιστήθην to know something 9

ἐπίσταμαι + *inf.* to know how to 17

ἐπιτερπής, ἐπιτερπές pleasant, delightful 25

ἐπιχειρέω, ἐπιχειρήσω, ἐπεχείρησα, ἐπιχείρηκα, ἐπιχείρημαι, ἐπεχειρήθην to put one's hand upon a thing, attempt 24

Dictionary

ἔργον, ἔργου, τό labor, work 2

ἐρημία, ἐρημίας, ἡ solitude 15

Ἑρμῆς, Ἑρμοῦ, ὁ Hermes 23

ἔρομαι, ἐρήσομαι, ἠρόμην to ask 25

ἕρπω, ἕρψω, εἵρπυσα to creep 4

ἔρχομαι, ἐλεύσομαι, ἦλθον, ἐλήλυθα to come, to go 6

ἐρῶ I will say (see λέγω) 19

ἔρως, ἔρωτος, ὁ love 1

ἐρωτάω, ἐρωτήσω, ἠρώτησα, ἠρώτηκα to ask 19

ἐσθίω, ἔδομαι, ἔφαγον, ἐδήδοκα, ἐδήδεσμαι, ἠδέσθην to eat 23

ἐστί *3rd singular of* εἰμί 9

ἑταίρα, ἑταίρας, ἡ girlfriend, companion, hetaira 7

ἕτοιμος, ἕτοιμον ready, prepared 24

εὖ good, well 4

εὖ ἔχω to be well 15

εὐγενής, εὐγενές well-born 10

εὐδαιμονία, εὐδαιμονίας, ἡ happiness 5

εὐδαίμων, εὔδαιμον happy, lucky 5

εὐκλεής, εὐκλεές noble, of good reputation 21

εὔνους, εὔνουν kind, well-disposed 17

Εὐριπίδης, Εὐριπίδου, ὁ Euripides 16

εὑρίσκω, εὑρήσω, ηὗρον, ηὕρηκα, ηὕρημαι, ηὑρέθην to find 1

Εὐρυσθεύς, Εὐρυσθεώς, ὁ Eurystheus 20

εὐτυχέω, εὐτυχήσω εὐτύχησα, εὐτύχηκα to be happy, to be well, to be successful 4

εὐφραίνω, εὐφρανῶ, εὔφρανα/ηὔφρανα, εὐφράνθην/ηὐφράνθην to cheer, gladden 21

εὐχετάομαι *Attic* εὐχετάοντο they boasted 19

εὔχομαι, εὔξομαι, ηὐξάμην, ηὖγμαι to pray 17

εὐψυχία, εὐψυχίας, ἡ good spirit 4

ἐφευρίσκω, ἐφευρήσω, ἐφηῦρον, ἐξηύρηκα, ἐξηύρημαι, ἐξηυρέθη to find 21

Ἔφεσος, Ἐφέσου, ὁ Ephesus 8

ἐχθρός, ἐχθρά, ἐχθρόν hostile 15

ἐχθρός, ἐχθροῦ, ὁ enemy 10

ἔχω, σχήσω/ἕξω, ἔσχον, ἔσχηκα, ἔσχημαι, ἐσχήθην to have 1

εὖ ἔχω to be well 15

ἕως as long as, while, until 11

ζ

ζάω, ζήσω, ἔζησα, ἔζηκα (infinitive ζῆν) to live 15

Ζεύς, Διός, ὁ Zeus 4

ζητέω, ζητήσω, ἐζήτησα, ἐζήτηκα to seek 16

ζῷον, ζῴου, τό living being 10

H

ἤ or, than 2, 16

ἤ...ἤ either...or 2

ἦ μήν surely 20

ἥβη, ἥβης, ἡ youth 5

ἡγέομαι, ἡγήσομαι, ἡγησάμην, ἥγημαι, ἡγήθην to believe; (+ 2 acc.) to consider x as y; (+ dat. or acc.) to lead 18, 21, 24

ἠδέ *connector* and 19

ᾔδειν (pastperfect of οἶδα) 18

ἤδη already, now 19

ἥδομαι, ἡσθήσομαι, ἡσάμην, ἥσθην to enjoy 15

ἡδόνη, ἡδονῆς, ἡ pleasure 5

ἡδύς, ἡδεῖα, ἡδύ sweet 15

ἦθος, ἤθους, τό character 10

ἥλιος, ἡλίου, ὁ sun 17

ἡμεῖς we 7

ἡμέρα, ἡμέρας, ἡ day 2

ἡμέτερος, ἡμετέρα, ἡμέτερον our

ἥρως, ἥρωος, ὁ hero 23

Θ

θάλαττα, θαλάττης, ἡ sea 2

θάνατος, θανάτου, ὁ death 18

DICTIONARY

θάπτω, θάψω, ἔθαψα, τέθαμμαι, ἐθάφθην/ἐτάφην to bury 24

θεάομαι, θεάσομαι, ἐθεασάμην, τεθέαμαι, ἐθεάθην to view, to watch 20

θέλω, θελήσω, ἠθέλησα, ἠθέληκα to want, be willing 15

Θεμιστοκλῆς, Θεμιστοκλοῦς, ὁ Themistocles 10

θεός, θεοῦ, ὁ god 2

θεραπεύω, θεραπεύσω, ἐθεράπευσα, ἐθεραπεύθην to care for, attend 9

θηρεύω, θηρεύσω ἐθήρευσα, τεθήρευκα, τεθήρευμαι, ἐθηρεύθην to catch, hunt 6

θησαυρός, θησαυροῦ, ὁ treasure 10

θνῄσκω, θανοῦμαι, ἔθανον, τέθνηκα to die 15

Θράσυλος, Θρασύλου, ὁ Thrasylus 8

Θρῄκη, Θρῄκης, ἡ Thrace 20

θρίξ, τριχός, ἡ hair, hide 1

θυμός, θυμοῦ, ὁ will, will power 17

θύρα, θύρας, ἡ door 19

I

ἰάομαι, ἰάσομαι, ἰασάμην, ἴαμαι, ἰάθην to heal 17

ἰατρικός, ἰατρική, ἰατρικόν of healing, skilled in medicine 15

ἰατρός, ἰατροῦ, ὁ healer, doctor, physician 9

ἴδιος, ἰδία, ἴδιον one's own 10

ἰδιώτης, ἰδιώτου, ὁ private citizen 9

Ἰθάκη, Ἰθάκης, ἡ Ithaca 19

ἱκανός, ἱκανή, ἱκανόν sufficient, competent, able 24

ἰός, ἰοῦ, ὁ rust 11

ἵππειος, ἱππεία, ἵππειον of a horse 20

ἱππεύς, ἱππέως, ὁ horseman 10

ἵππος, ἵππου, ὁ horse 25

ἵστημι, στήσω, ἔστησα/ἔστην, ἕστηκα, ἕσταμαι, ἐστάθην to stand, make to stand 14

ἰσχυρός, ἰσχυρά, ἰσχυρόν strong 16

ἰσχύω, ἰσχύσω, ἴσχυσα, ἴσχυκα to be strong, prevail 4

K

καί even, also 4

καί... καί both...and 9

καί/τε and 2

καί εἰ even if, although 11

καίπερ even if, although 15

καιρός, καιροῦ, ὁ moment 1

κάκιστος, κακίστη, κάκιστον very bad 10

κακός, κακή, κακόν bad, evil, ugly 5

κακός, κακοῦ, ὁ bad person 4

κακῶς badly 4

κακῶς ἔχω to do badly 15

καλέω, καλέσω, ἐκάλεσα, κέκληκα, κέκλημαι, ἐκλήθην to call 10

κάλλιστος, καλλίστη, κάλλιστον very beautiful 10

καλός, καλή, καλόν good, noble, attractive 5

καλῶς beautifully, well 4

καρδία, καρδίας, ἡ heart 9

καρπόω, καρπώσω, ἐκάρπωσα, κεκάρπωκα, κεκάρπωμαι, ἐκαρπώθην to reap 21

κατά prep. + acc. in accordance with 21

κατά prep. + gen. down from, against 21

καταβαίνω, καταβήσομαι, κατέβην, καταβέβηκα to go down 20

καταγέλαστος, καταγελάστη, καταγέλαστον ridiculous 19

καταθνῄσκω, καταθανοῦμαι, κατέθανον, κατατέθνηκα to die 19

καταπαύω, καταπαύσω, κατέπαυσα, καταπέπαυκα, καταπέπαυμαι, κατεπαύθην to cause to stop 15

κατεσθίομαι, κατέδομαι, κατέφαγον to devour 11

κατήγορος, κατηγόρου, ὁ accuser 19

κάτωθεν from below, below 21

κελεύω, κελεύσω ἐκέλευσα, κεκέλευκα, κεκέλευσμαι, ἐκελεύσθην to command, order 17

Dictionary

κερδαίνω, κερδανῶ, ἐκέρδανα, κεκέρδηκα to gain 26

κέρδος, κέρδους, τό gain 5

κεφαλή, κεφαλῆς, ἡ head 20

κῆπος, κήπου, ὁ garden 10

Κιλικία, Κιλικίας, ἡ Cilicia 19

κίνδυνος, κινδύνου, ὁ danger 4

κινέω, κινήσω, ἐκίνησα, κεκίνημαι, ἐκινήθην to move 21

Κλέαρχος, Κλεάρχου, ὁ Clearchus 11

κλείω, κλείσω, ἔκλεισα, κέκλεικα, κέκλειμαι, ἐκλείσθην to shut 21

κλέπτω, κλέψω, ἔκλεψα, κέκλοφα, κέκλεμμαι, ἐκλάπην to steal 13

κομίζομαι, κομιοῦμαι, ἐκομισάμην, κεκόμισμαι, ἐκομίσθην to take, to receive 6

κομίζω, κομιῶ, ἐκόμισα, κεκόμικα, κεκόμισμαι, ἐκομίσθην to give, supply, carry away 6

κόπτω, κόψω, ἔκοψα, κέκοφα, κέκομμαι, ἐκόπην to strike, hit 20

κόσμος, κόσμου, ὁ order, world 15

κουφίζω, κουφιῶ, ἐκούφισα, κεκούφικα, κεκουφισμαι, ἐκουφίσθην to make easy 9

κοῦφος, κούφη, κοῦφον, easy 26

κρατέω κρατήσω ἐκράτησα, κεκράτηκα, κεκράτημαι, ἐκρατήθην (+ gen.) to be strong(er), conquer 15,16

κράτος, κράτους, τό strength, power 22

Κρήτη, Κρήτης, ἡ Crete 20

κρίνω, κρινῶ, ἔκρινα, κέκρικα, κέκριμαι, ἐκρίθην to judge 1

κριτής, κριτοῦ, ὁ judge 5

κύβος, κύβου, ὁ die; *pl.* dice 4

Κῦρος, Κύρου, ὁ Cyrus 9

κύων, κυνός, ὁ dog 15

κωλύω, κωλύσω, ἐκώλυσα, κεκώλυκα, κεκώλυμαι, ἐκωλύθην to prevent, hinder 20

Λ

λαγώς, λαγώ, ὁ hare, rabbit 15

Λαίος, Λαίου, ὁ Laius

λαμβάνω, λήψομαι, ἔλαβον, εἴληφα, εἴλημμαι, ἐλήφθην to take, seize 2

λανθάνω, λήσω, ἔλαθον, λέληθα, λέλησμαι, ἐλήσθην to hide, escape the notice of 13

λέαινα, λεαίνης, ἡ lioness 15

λέγω, λέξω/ἐρῶ, ἔλεξα/εἶπον, εἴρηκα, λέλεγμαι, ἐλέχθην to say, speak, tell 13

λείβω, λείψω, ἐλείψα to pour 13

λείπω, λείψω, ἔλιπον, λέλοιπα, λέλειμμαι, ἐλείφθην to leave 17

λευκαίνω, λελεύκασμαι to whitewash

λέων, λέοντος, ὁ lion 15

λίαν too much, exceedingly, very 25

Λιβύη, Λιβύης, ἡ Africa 4

λιμός, λιμοῦ, ὁ hunger 1

λίθος, λίθου, ὁ stone

λογίζομαι, λογιοῦμαι, ἐλογισάμην, λελόγισμαι, ἐλογίσθην (+ 2 acc.) to count as, consider as 21

λόγος, λόγου, ὁ word, speech, thought, consideration 1

Λυδός, Λυδοῦ, ὁ a Lydian 15

λύκος, λύκου, ὁ wolf 2

λυμαίνομαι, λυμανοῦμαι ἐλυμηνάμην, λελύμασμαι, ἐλυμάνθην to destroy 6

λυπέω, λυπήσω, ἐλύπησα to grieve 15

λύπη, λύπης, ἡ grief 1

λύρη, λύρης, ἡ lyre 23

λυτήριος, λυτηρίου, ὁ redeemer 21

λύχνος, λύχνου, ὁ lamp 25

λύω, λύσω, ἔλυσα, λέλυκα, λέλυμαι, ἐλύθην to dissolve, release, destroy 1

M

μάθημα, μαθήματος, τό lesson, subject 19

μαθητής, μαθητοῦ, ὁ student 5

μαίνομαι, μανοῦμαι, ἐμηνάμην, μέμηνα, μεμάνημαι, ἐμάνην to rage 22

Dictionary

μακάριος, μακαρία, μακάριον blessed, happy 12

μακρός, μακρά, μακρόν large, big, great 5

μαλάσσω/μαλάττω, μαλάξω, ἐμάλαξ, μεμάληκα, μεμάλαγμαι, ἐμαλάχθην to soften 11

μάλιστα most 16

μᾶλλον more 16

μᾶλλον ἤ rather than 16

μανθάνω, μαθήσομαι, ἔμαθον, μεμάθηκα (+ inf.) to learn 13

μάρτυς, μάρτυρος, ὁ witness 18

μαρτυρέω, μαρτυρήσω, ἐμαρτύρησα, μεμαρτύρημαι, ἐμαρτυρήθην to witness, attest 17

μάστιξ, μάστιγος, ἡ whip 25

μάχομαι, μαχοῦμαι, ἐμαχεσάμην, μεμάχημαι to fight 8

μέγας, μεγάλη, μέγα great 10

μέλαθρον, μελάθρου, τό ceiling; *pl.* house 15

μέλας, μέλαινα, μέλαν black 22

Μέλων, Μέλονος, ὁ Melon 6

μέμνημαι, perfect passive of μιμνήσκω to remember 18

μέμνησο *imperative* Remember! 19

μέν...δέ/ἀλλὰ on one hand...on the other 2

μένω, μενῶ, ἔμεινα, μεμένηκα to remain 1

Μένων, Μένονος, ὁ Menon 18

μέσος, μέση, μέσον middle, middle of, moderate 6

μετά prep. + acc. after 6

μετά prep. + gen. (animate) with; (inanimate) in, through, with 6

μεταβάλλω, μεταβαλῶ, μετέβαλον, μεταβέβληκα, μεταβέβλημαι, μετεβλήθην to change, alter 16

μεταλαμβάνω, μεταλήμψομαι, μετέλαβον (+ gen.) to share 9

μεταπέμπομαι, μεταπέμψομαι, μετεπεμψάμην to send for, recall 12

μέτριος, μετρία, μέτριον moderate 25

μή not 12

μὴ οὖν; (= μῶν;) question with negative answer expected 3

μήδε and not, but not 22

μηδείς, μηδεμία, μηδέν no one, nothing 22

Μῆδος, Μήδου, ὁ a Persian 15

μήποτε never 22

μήπω not yet 22

μήτε and not, nor 22

μήτε . . . μήτε neither ... nor 21

μήτηρ, μητρός, ἡ mother 12

μητρυιά, μητρυιᾶς, ἡ stepmother 15

μηχανή, μηχανῆς, ἡ instrument, means 21

μία see εἱς 6

μικρός, μικρά, μικρόν small 5

μιμέομαι, μιμήσομαι, ἐμιμησάμην, μεμίμημαι, ἐμιμήθην to imitate 21

μιμνήσκομαι, μνήσομαι, ἐμνησάμην, μέμνημαι, ἐμνήσθην to remember 18

Μίνως, Μίνωος, ὁ Minos 20

μισέω, μισήσω, ἐμίσησα, μεμίσηκα, μιμίσημαι, ἐμισήθην to hate 15

μνήμη, μνήμης, ἡ memory 1

μοίρα, μοίρας, ἡ fate, destiny 2

μόνος, μόνη, μόνον alone, only 23

μορφή, μορφῆς, ἡ shape, form 2

Μοῦσα, Μούσης, ἡ Muse 12

μουσική, μουσικῆς, ἡ music 1

μοχθέω, μοχθήσω, ἐμόχθησα to work hard, to toil 17

μόχθος, μόχθου, ὁ toil, effort 5

μυθοπλάσιος, μυθοπλάσιον multiform 9

Μύνδος, Μύνδου, ὁ Myndus 21

μῶν; question with negative answer expected 3

μωρία, μωρίας, ἡ stupidity, foolishness 8

μωρός, μωρά, μωρόν stupid, foolish 10

N

ναυαγός, ναυαγή, ναυαγόν shipwrecked 24

ναυμαχία, ναυμαχίας, ἡ shipwreck 24

Dictionary

ναῦς, νεώς, ἡ *pl.* αἱ νῆες ship 19
ναύτης, ναύτου, ὁ sailor 5
νεανίας, νεανίου, ὁ young man, a youth 2
νεκρός, νεκροῦ, ὁ corpse 23
νέος, νέα, νέον new, young 7
νῆσος, νήσου, ἡ island 22
νικάω, νικήσω, ἐνίκησα, νενίκηκα, νενίκημαι, ἐνικήθην to conquer, win 12
νίπτω, νίψω, ἔνιψα, νένιμμαι, ἐνιψάμην to wash 1
νίζω, νίψω, ἔνιψα, νένιμμαι to wash 1
νομίζω, νομιῶ, ἐνόμισα, νενόμικα, νενόμισμαι, ἐνομίσθην to consider, think 10
νόμος, νόμου, ὁ law 1
νόμος ἐστιν is lawful 17
νόσος, νόσου, ἡ sickness, disease 11
νόστος, νόστου, ὁ return 9
νοῦς, νοῦ, ὁ mind, sense 11
νύμφη, νύμφης, ἡ bride 5
νῦν now 17
νύξ, νυκτός, ἡ night 1

Ξ

ξενόω, ξενώσομαι, ἐξενώθην to host 20
ξίφος, ξίφους, τό sword 8

O

ὅδε, ἥδε, τόδε this/he, she, it 10
οἷα as, since, because, in as much as 15
Οἰδίπους, Οἰδίποδος, ὁ Oedipus 20
οἶδα, *inf.* εἰδέναι, ᾔδειν (*past of* οἶδα), *part.* εἰδώς to know; (+ inf.) to know how to 15
οἴκαδε homeward 20
οἰκέτης, οἰκέτου, ὁ servant 8
οἰκία, οἰκίας, ἡ house 9
οἰκονομικός, οἰκονομική, οἰκονομικόν private 10
οἴομαι/οἶμαι, οἰήσομαι, ᾠήθην (+ inf.) to think, suppose, believe, consider 17
οἷος, οἷα, οἷον such 17
οἷός τε εἰμί I am able 17
οἴχομαι, οἰχήσομαι, ᾤχηκα, ᾤχημαι to go 15
ὅλος, ὅλη, ὅλον whole 5
ὅμως but still, nevertheless 22
ὃν τρόπον in which manner = in the manner in which 19
ὀνειδίζω, ὀνειδίσω (ὀνειδιῶ), ὠνείδισα, ὠνείδικα, ὠνείδισμαι, ὠνειδίσθην to scold 15
ὀπάζω, ὀπάσω, ὤπασα to make to follow, to give 22
ὅποι to what place, where 19
ὁποῖος, ὁποῖα, ὁποῖον of what sort 19
ὁπόσος, ὁπόση, ὁπόσον however many 19
ὁπότερος, ὁποτέρα, ὁπότερον which of two 19
ὅπου where 11
ὁράω, ὄψομαι, εἶδον, ἑώρακα, ἑώραμαι, ὤφθην to see 12
ὄργανον, ὀργάνου, τό tool, instrument 5
ὀργή, ὀργῆς, ἡ anger 5
ὀρθότης, ὀρθότητος ἡ uprightness, correctness 4
ὀρθόω, ὀρθώσω, ὤρθωσα, ὤρθωκα, ὤρθωμαι, ὠρθώθην to put straight 9
ὄρος, ὄρους, τό mountain 20
ὅς, ἥ, ὅ who, which; that, what 12
ὅσος, ὅση, ὅσον as, as great/much/many/long as 23
ὅσον...τόσον/τοσοῦτον as much...as 16
ὅσπερ, ἥπερ, ὅπερ which 19
ὅστις, ἥτις, ὅτι whoever, whatever 12
ὅταν whenever 25
ὅτε when 11
ὅτι, διότι because; that 11, 19
ὅ τι which, what 19
οὐ / οὐκ / οὐχ not 1
οὐ μόνον...ἀλλὰ καί not only...but also 10
οὐδέ and not, but not, nor 5
οὐδείς, οὐδεμία, οὐδέν no one, nothing 6
οὐκέτι no longer 19

Dictionary

οὐκοῦν; question with positive answer expected 3
οὖν then, therefore 3
οὔπω not yet 19
οὐράνιος, οὐρανία, οὐράνιον heavenly 16
οὖς, ὠτός, τό ear 9
οὐσία, οὐσίας, ἡ possession, substance, property 5
οὗτος, αὕτη, τοῦτο this/he, she, it 10
οὕτως so, thus, in this way 11
οὕτως...ὥσπερ thus/so...as 16
ὀφθαλμός, ὀφθαλμοῦ, ὁ eye 9
ὄχημα, ὀχήματος, τό chariot 20
ὄψις, ὄψεως, ἡ the ability to see 11

Π

πάθος, πάθους, τό suffering 8
παιάν, παιᾶνος, ὁ hymn, praise, Paean 21
παιδεύω, παιδεύσω, ἐπαίδευσα, πεπαίδευκα, πεπαίδευμαι, ἐπαιδεύθην to educate 14
παῖς, παιδός, ὁ child, boy, slave 10
πάλιν again 2
πανταχοῦ everywhere 19
παρά prep. + acc. to the side of, contrary to, towards 5
παρά prep. + dat. by the side of, beside 5
παρά prep. + gen. from 5
παραγγέλλω, (*see* ἀγγέλλω) to give an order 20
παράκαιρος, παράκαιρον ill-timed 5
παρατάττω, παρατάξω, παρέταξε, to draw up a battle line 15
πάρειμι, *see* εἰμί to be present 19
παρέρχομαι, παρελεύσομαι, παρῆλθον, παρελήλυθα to pass 6
παρέχω/παρέχομαι, παρασχήσω, παρέσχον, παρέσχηκα to produce, present 18
πάρος *adv.* + gen. before, earlier than 21
παρρησία, παρρησίας, ἡ freedom of speech 5
πᾶς, πᾶσα, πᾶν every, all 9
πάσχω, πείσομαι, ἔπαθον, πέπονθα to suffer, experience 19
πατήρ, πατρός, ὁ father 5
πατρίς, πατρίδος, ἡ fatherland 24
παύομαι (+ participle intrans.) to stop from doing 15
παύω, παύσω, ἔπαυσα, πέπαυκα, πέπαυμαι, ἐπαύθην to stop, cause to stop 1
πεδίον, πεδίου, τό plain 4
πειθαρχέω πειθαρχήσω (+ dat.) to obey, be obedient 16
πείθομαι, πείσομαι, ἐπιθόμην, πέπεισμαι (+ dat.) to obey 8
πειράω, πειράσω, ἐπείρασα, πεπείρακα, πεπείραμαι, ἐπειράθην to try 17
Πελοποννήσιοι, Πελοποννησίων, οἱ Peloponnesians
πέμπω, πέμψω, ἔπεμψα, πέπομφα, πέπεμμαι, ἐπέμφθην to send 20
πένης, πένες poor 6
πένης, πενήτος, ὁ a poor man 6
πενία, πενίας, ἡ poverty 2
πέπλος, πέπλου, ὁ robe 22
περί prep. + acc. around 22
περί prep. + dat. around 22
περί prep. + gen. about, concerning 22
Περικλῆς, Περικλοῦς, ὁ Pericles 18
περιφέρω, *see* φέρω to carry around 5
Πέρσαι, Περσῶν, οἱ Persians 9
πέτρα, πέτρας, ἡ rock 4
Πήγασος, Πηγάσου, ὁ Pegasus 20
πημονή, πημονῆς, ἡ pain 5
πίνω, πίομαι, ἔπιον, πέπωκα, πέπομαι, ἐπόθην to drink 21
πιστεύω, πιστεύσω, ἐπίστευσα, πεπίστευκα, πεπίστευμαι, ἐπιστεύθην (+ dat.) to trust, believe 8
πλέκω, πλέξω, ἔπλεξα, πέπλοχα, πέπλεγμαι, ἐπλέχθην to weave, twist 13

Dictionary

πλέω, πλεύσομαι, ἔπλευσα, πέπλευκα, πέπλευμαι to sail 24

πλοῖον, πλοίου, τό boat

πλούσιος, πλουσία, πλούσιον rich 6

πλουτέω, πλουτήσω, ἐπλούτησα, πεπλούτηκα to be rich 15

πλοῦτος, πλούτου, ὁ wealth 4

πόθεν; from what place? 4

πόθι; where? 19

ποῖ; to what place?, whereto? 4

ποιέω, ποιήσω, ἐποίησα, πεποίηκα, πεποίημαι, ἐποιήθην to make, do, cause to be 2

ποιητής, ποιητοῦ, ὁ poet 5

ποιμήν, ποιμένΟς, ὁ shepherd 15

ποῖος, ποία, ποῖον of what sort 19

πολέμιος, πολεμίου, ὁ enemy; *pl.* the enemy 12

πόλεμος, πολέμου, ὁ war 4

πολέω to go about, range, hunt 15

πολιορκέω, πολιορκήσω, ἐπολιόρκησα, πεπολιόρκηκα, πεπολιόρκημαι, ἐπολιορκήθην to beseige 22

πόλις, πόλεως, ἡ city 5

πολίτευω, πολιτεύσω, ἐπολίτευσα, πεπολίτευκα, πεπολίτευμαι, ἐπολιτεύθην to be a citizen

πολίτης, πολίτου, ὁ citizen 5

πολιτικός, πολιτική, πολιτικόν public 10

πολλάκις often, many times 19

πολύμορφος, πολύμορφον many-shaped 10

πολύς, πολλή, πολύ much, many 8

Πολυφόντης, Πολυφόντους, ὁ Polyphontes 20

πολυχρόνιος, πολυχρόνιον long-lasting 10

πονηρός, πονηρά, πονηρόν bad 6

πόνος, πόνου, ὁ toil, trouble 1

πόντος, πόντου, ὁ sea 15

πορεύομαι, πορεύσομαι, ἐπορευσάμην, πεπόρευμαι, ἐπορεύθην to walk, march, travel 15

πορίζω πορίσω, ἐπόρισα, πέπορικα, πεπόρισμαι, ἐπορίσθην to furnish 21

ποσάκις; how often? 4

πόσος, πόση, πόσον; how large?; *pl.* how many? 4

ποτέ at some time 19

πότερον...ἤ whether ... or 19

πότερος, ποτέρα, πότερον which of two?

ποῦ; in what place?, where? 4

πρᾶγμα, πράγματος, τό thing, matter 19

πράττω, πράξω, ἔπραξα, πέπραχα, πέπραγμαι, ἐπράχθην to do, achieve manage 16

πρίν before (*cl. marker*) 22

προνοέομαι, προνοήσομαι, προυνοησάμην, προνενόημαι, προυνήθην (+ gen.) to take care of, take thought for 9

πρόσθεν earlier 15

πρό prep. – gen. before 25

πρός prep. + acc. to, towards, against; with regard to 4, 16

πρός prep. + dat. near, in addition to 4

πρός prep. + gen. from 4

προσδοκάω, προσδοκήσω, προσεδόκησα, προσδεδόκηκα, προσεδοκήθην to expect, look for 22

προσήκει it concerns, it befits 21

πρόσθεν earlier 15

προσλαμβάνω, προσλήψομαι, προσέλαβον, προσείληφα, προσλελάβηκα to take/receive in addition, make gains 20

προστάττω, προστάξω, προσέταξα προστέταχα, προστέταγμαι, προσετάχθην to assign 24

πρότερος, προτέρα, πρότερον first 16

πρόφρων, πρόφρονος eager 23

πρῶτον first 6

Πυθία, Πυθίας, ἡ the Pythia, the medium uttering the prophecies in the oracle of Apollo at Delphi 16

πύλη, πύλης, ἡ gate 21

Dictionary

πυνθάνομαι, πεύσομαι, ἐπυθόμην, πέπυσμαι to learn by inquiry, ask 14

πῶς; in what manner?, how? 4

Ρ

ῥᾴδιος, ῥᾳδία, ῥᾴδιον easy 17

ῥῆμα, ῥήματος, τό word, thing 5

ῥόδον, ῥόδου, τό rose 5

Σ

Σαλαμίς, Σαλαμῖνος, ὁ Salamis 22

σατράπης, σατράπου, ὁ satrap 12

σαυτοῦ, σαυτῆς reflexive pronoun (*contr.* σεαυτόν) yourself 21

σημαίνω σημανῶ, ἐσήμηνα, σεσήμαγκα, σεσήμασμαι, ἐσημάνθην to give signals 19

σιγάω, σιγήσω, ἐσίγησα, σεσίγηκα, σεσίγημαι, ἐσιγήθην to be silent 22

σιγή, σιγῆς, ἡ silence 8

σιδήρος, σιδήρου ὁ iron 11

σιωπάω, σιωπήσομαι, ἐσιώπησα, σεσιώπηκα to keep silent 24

σιωπή, σιωπῆς, ἡ silence 17

σκοπέω, σκέψομαι, ἐσκεψάμην, ἔσκεμμαι to look at, consider 17

σκοτεινός, σκοτεινή, σκοτεινόν dark 25

σκότος, σκότου, ὁ, τό shadow, darkness 25

σός, σή, σόν your yours 21

σοφία, σοφίας, ἡ wisdom, knowledge 16

σοφιστής σοφιστοῦ ὁ expert, Sophist 5

σοφός, σοφή, σοφόν wise 5

σοφός, σοφοῦ, ὁ wise person 4

Σοφωκλῆς, Σοφοκλοῦς, ὁ Sophocles 16

σοφῶς wisely 4

Σπάρτη, Σπάρτης, ἡ Sparta 19

σπεύδω, σπεύσω, ἔσπευσα, ἔσπευκα, ἔσπευσμαι to hasten, hurry 13

σπονδαί, σπονδῶν, αἱ treaty, truce 22

στασιάζω, στασιάσω to rebel 13

στολή, στολῆς, ἡ robe 15

στολμός, στολμοῦ, ὁ clothing 22

στράτευμα, στρατεύματος, τό army, campaign 19

στρατεύω, στρατεύσομαι, ἐστράτευσα, ἐστράτευμαι, ἐστρατεύθην to serve in war 18

στρατηγέω, στρατηγήσω, ἐστρατήγησα to be a general, to command 12

στρατηγός, στρατηγοῦ, ὁ general 12

στρατιώτης, στρατιώτου, ὁ soldier 8

στυγέω, στυγήσω, ἐστύγησα, ἐστύγηκα, ἐστυγήθην to hate 15

σύ you 7

Συέννεσις, Συεννέσεως, ὁ Syennesis 19

συμβαίνω, συμβήσομαι, συνέβην, συμβέβηκα to happen, occur 25

συμβουλεύω, συμβουλεύσω, συνεβούλευσα, συμβεβούλευκα, συμβέβουλεύμαι, συνεβουλεύθην (+ dat.) to counsel, give advice 15

σύμμαχος, συμμάχου, ὁ ally 18

συμφορά, συμφορᾶς, ἡ disaster, calamity 10

σύν prep. + dat. with, in accordance with 4

σχολή, σχολῆς, ἡ leisure, free time 25

σώζω, σώσω, ἔσωσα to save 6

Σωκράτης, Σωκράτους, ὁ Socrates 16

σῶμα, σώματος, τό body 5

σώφρων, σώφρον prudent, sensible 16

Τ

τάχα quickly, swiftly 6

ταχύς, ταχεῖα, ταχύ swift 16

τέκνον, τέκνου, τό child 15

τεκόντες, τεκόντων, οἱ parents 15

τελευτάω, τελευτήσω, ἐτελεύτησα, τετελεύτηκα, τετελεύτημαι, ἐτελευτήθην to bring to an end, to die 22

τέμνω, τεμῶ, ἔτεμον, τέτμηκα, τέτμημαι, ἐτμήθην to cut 22

τέρπω, τέρψω, ἔτερψα, ἐτέρφθην to please 2

τέχνη, τέχνης, ἡ skill 4

τῇδε in this place, here 15

τι something, anything; some, any… 3

DICTIONARY

τί; what?, which?, why? 3

τίθημι, θήσω, ἔθηκα, τέθηκα, τέθειμαι, ἐτέθην to place, put 14

τίκτω, τέξω, ἔτεκον, τέτοκα to produce 1

τιμάω, τιμήσω, ἐτίμησα, τετίμηκα, τετίμημαι, ἐτιμήθην to honor 6

τιμή, τιμῆς, ἡ honor 15

τις somebody, anybody; some, any... 3

τίς; who?, which...? 3

Τισσαφέρνης, Τισσαφέρνους, ὁ Tissaphernes 20

τιτρώσκω, τρώσω, ἔτρωσα, τέτρωκα, τέτρωμαι, ἐτρώθην to wound 6

τίω, τίσω, ἔτισα, τέτιμαι to honor, value 2

τοι indeed 19

τοῖος, τοία, τοῖον such

τοιοῦτος, τοιαύτη, τοιοῦτο such 9

τοιοῦτος...ὅς/ὅστις/οἷος such...as 16

τοκῆες, τοκήων, οἱ parents 19

τόπος, τόπου, ὁ place 20

τρέφω, θρέψω, ἔθρεψα, τέτροφα, τέθραμμαι, ἐτράφην to feed, nourish, bring up 4

τρέχω, δραμοῦμαι, ἔδραμον/ἔθρεξα, δεδράμηκα, δεδράμημαι to run 1

τρίβω, τρίψω, ἔτριψα, τέτριφα, τέτριμμαι, ἐτρίφθην to rub 13

τρίτος, τρίτη, τρίτον third 8

τρόπος, τρόπου, ὁ behavior, manner, kind 6

τυγχάνω, τεύξομαι, ἔτυχον, τετύχηκα (+ part.) to happen to, meet 13

τύραννος, τυράννου, ὁ tyrant, ruler 9

τύπτω, τύψω, ἔτυψα, τέτυμμαι, ἐτύπην to hit 25

τυφλός, τυφλή, τυφλόν blind 10

τύχη, τύχης ἡ fortune, luck 21

Υ

ὕδωρ, ὕδατος, τό water 5

υἱός, υἱοῦ, ὁ son 5

ὑμεῖς you (all) 7

ὑπέρ prep. + gen. on behalf of 24

ὑπερβάλλω (βάλλω) to surpass 25

ὑπερφιλέω, ὑπερφιλήσω, ὑπερεφίλησα, -πεφίληκα, -πεφίλημαι, -ἐφιλήθην to love beyond measure 21

ὑπό prep. + acc. towards and under 6

ὑπό prep. + dat. under, beneath, at the foot of 6

ὑπό prep. + gen. (+ *animate*) by; (+ *inanimate*) from under 6

ὑποκριτής, ὑποκριτοῦ, ὁ interpreter, one who answers 5

Φ

φαίνομαι, φανοῦμαι, ἐφηνάμην, πέφηνα, πέφασμαι, ἐφάνην to seem, appear 10

φαίνω, φανῶ, ἔφηνα, πέφηνα, πέφασμαι, ἐφάνην to show, cause to appear 6

φάρμακον, φαρμάκου, τό poison

φαῦλος, φαύλη, φαῦλον weak, mean 8

Φέρης, Φέρητος, ὁ Pheres 20

φέρω, οἴσω, ἤνεγκα/ἤνεγκον, ἐνήνοχα, ἐνήνεγμαι, ἠνέχθην to bring, carry, endure 4

φεύγω, φεύξομαι, ἔφυγον, πέφευγα, πέφυγμαι to flee 13

φημί, φήσω, ἔφησα (ἔφην) to declare, to say, to tell 10

φθίνω, φθίσομαι, ἔφθιμαι, ἐφθίμην to waste away, wither, decline 20

φθονέω, φθονήσω, ἐφθόνησα, ἐφθονήθην to envy 6

φθόνος, φθόνου, ὁ envy 4

φιλάνθρωπος, φιλάνθρωπον kind, humane 5

φιλέω, φιλήσω, ἐφίλησα, πεφίληκα, πεφίλημαι, ἐφιλήθην to love 12

φίλιος, φιλία, φίλιον friendly 23

φιλόκαλος, φιλόκαλον loving the beautiful 15

φιλότιμος, φιλότιμον loving honor, ambitious 15

φίλος, φίλου, ὁ friend 1

φιλονικία, φιλονικίας, ἡ competition 20

Dictionary

φιλόσοφος, φιλοσόφου, ὁ philosopher 15

φοβέομαι, φοβήσομαι ἐφοβησάμην, πεφόβημαι, ἐφοβήθην to fear, to revere 12

φόβος, φόβου, ὁ fear 1

Φοῖβος, Φοίβου, ὁ Phoebus Apollo 15

φόνιος, φονία, φόνιον bloody, murderous 21

φόνος, φόνου, ὁ killing, murder 2

φράτηρ, φράτερος, ὁ clansman 24

φρονέω, φρονήσω, ἐφρόνησα, πεφρόνηκα to think, understand, mean, intend, heed 24

φρόνιμος, φρόνιμον sensible, prudent 6

φρούραρχος, φρουράρχου, ὁ captain 20

φυγάς, φυγάδος, ὁ, fugitive, exile 18

φύομαι, φύσομαι, ἔφυν, πέφυκα to grow 10

φύσις, φύσεως, ἡ nature 5

φωνέω, φωνήσω, ἐφώνησα, πεφώνηκα, ἐφωνήθην to speak 18

φῶς, φωτός, τό light 17

φῶς, (φάος) φωτός, ὁ man

φωτεινός, φωτεινή, φωτεινόν giving light, shining 25

Χ

χαίρω, χαιρήσω, ἐχάρην, κεχάρηκα, κεχάρημαι to rejoice, be glad 15

χαλεπός, χαλεπή, χαλεπόν hard, difficult 16

χαλεπόν ἐστιν is difficult 17

χειμών, χειμῶνος, ὁ winter, stormy weather 20

χείρ, χειρός, ἡ hand 1

χθόνιος, χθονία, χθόνιον earthly 23

χθών, χθόνος, ἡ earth 6

χρή, χρήσει, ἔχρην (+ inf.) it is necessary 17

χρῆμα, χρήματος, τό goods, money 20

χρήσιμος, χρησίμη, χρήσιμον useful 16

χρηστός, χρηστή, χρηστόν good, useful 5

χρόνος, χρόνου, ὁ time 1

χώρα, χώρας, ἡ land, country 2

Ψ

ψευδής, ψευδές false 5

ψεύδομαι, ψεύσομαι, ἐψευσάμην, ἔψευσμαι, ἐψεύσθην to lie 15

ψυχή, ψυχῆς, ἡ soul 5

Ω

ὧδε in the following manner 9

ὠμός, ὠμή, ὠμόν cruel 20

ὡς as, when 11

ὡς as if, because, in order to 15

ὡς how 26

ὡς + *superlative* as...as possible 16

ὡς τάχιστα as soon as 11

ὥσπερ just as 11

ὥσπερ...οὕτως just as...thus/so 11

ὥστε so that

ὠφέλεια/ὠφέλια, ὠφελείας/ὠφελίας ἡ usefulness 4

ὠφελέω, ὠφελήσω ὠφέλησα, ὠφέληκα, ὠφέλημαι, ὠφελήθην to be useful 4

ὠφέλιμος, ὠφέλιμον useful 25

DICTIONARY

English to Greek Vocabulary

The vocabulary for the English-Greek exercises contains only nouns, verbs, adjectives and a few adverbs. For connectors, prepositions and most adverbs consult the separate lists.

A

to act ἄγω, ἄξω, ἤγαγον, ἦχα, ἦγμαι, ἤχθην
all πᾶς, πᾶσα, πᾶν
always ἀεί
to arrive ἀφικνέομαι, ἀφίξομαι, ἀφικόμην, ἀφῖγμαι
to ask ἐρωτάω, ἐρωτήσω, ἠρώτησα
to become aware γιγνώσκω, γνώσομαι, ἔγνων, ἔγνωκα, ἔγνωσμαι, ἐγνώσθην

B

bad κακός, κακή, κακόν
blind τυφλός, τυφλή, τυφλόν
boat πλοῖον, πλοίου, τό
body σῶμα, σώματος, τό

C

to carry φέρω, οἴσω, ἤνεγκον, ἐνήνοχα, ἐνήνεγμαι, ἠνέχθην
to change ἀλλάττω, ἀλλάξω, ἤλλαξα, ἤλλαχα, ἤλλαγμαι, ἠλλάχθην
citizen πολίτης, πολίτου, ὁ
city πόλις, πόλεως, ἡ
concern πρᾶγμα; ἔργον, ἔργου, τό; πράγματος, τό
Cyrus Κῦρος, Κύρου, ὁ

D

deed ἔργον, ἔργου, τό
to delight ἥδομαι, ἡσθήσομαι, ἥσθην
desire ἐπιθυμία, ἐπιθυμίας, ἡ
to desire ἐπιθυμέω, ἐπιθυμήσω, ἐπεθύμησα ἐπιτεθύμηκα
die (dice) κύβος, κύβου, ὁ
to die ἀποθνήσκω, ἀποθανοῦμαι, ἀπέθανον, ἀποτέθνηκα
to do πράττω; δράω; ἄγω
to drink πίνω, πίομαι, ἔπιον, πέπωκα, ἐπόθην

E

endure φέρω, οἴσω, ἤνεγκον, ἐνήνοχα, ἐνήνεγμαι, ἠνέχθην
enemy ἐχθρός, ἐχθροῦ, ὁ; πολέμιος, πολεμίου, ὁ
evil κακός, κακή, κακόν πονηρός, πονηρά, πονηρόν
excellence ἀρετή, ἀρετῆς, ἡ

F

false ψευδής, ψευδές
farmer γεωργός, γεωργοῦ, ὁ
to flee φεύγω, φεύξομαι, ἔφυγον, πέφυγα, πέφυγμαι
foolish μωρός, μωρά, μωρόν
friendly φίλιος, φιλία, φίλιον
to forget ἐπιλανθάνομαι, ἐπιλήσομαι, ἐπελαθόμην, ἐπιλέληθα, ἐπιλέλησμαι, ἐπελήσθην

G

gain κέρδος, κέρδους, τό
good ἀγαθός, ἀγαθή, ἀγαθόν

H

happy εὐδαίμων, εὐδαῖμον
harm βλάβη, βλάβης, ἡ
to hear ἀκούω, ἀκούσομαι, ἤκουσα, ἀκήκοα, ἠκούσθην
horse ἵππος, ἵππου, ὁ
to hurt βλάπτω, βλάψω, ἔβλαψα, βέβλαφα, βέβλαμμαι, ἐβλάφθην

I

to intend μέλλω, μελλήσω, ἐμέλλησα

K

to know οἶδα; γιγνώσκω,

J

to judge κρίνω, κρινῶ, ἔκρινα, κέκρικα, κέκριμαι, ἐκρίθην
justice δίκη, δίκης, ἡ

L

to learn μανθάνω, μαθήσομαι, ἔμαθον, μεμάθηκα
to love φιλέω, φιλήσω, ἐφίλησα, πεφίληκα, πεφίλημαι, ἐφιλήθην

M

to make, to do ποιέω, ποιήσω, ἐποίησα, πεποίηκα, πεποίημαι, ἐποιήθην
man ἄνθρωπος, ἀνθρώπου, ὁ
man (not woman) ἀνήρ, ἀνδρός, ὁ
man, young νεανίας, νεανίου, ὁ

Dictionary

man, old γέρων, γέροντος, ὁ
many πολλοί, πολλαί, πολλά
to marry γαμέω, γαμέω, ἔγημα, γεγάμηκα, γεγάμημαι, ἐγαμήθην
master δεσπότης, δεσπότου, ὁ
Muse Μοῦσα, Μούσης, ἡ

N

necessary ἀναγκαῖος, ἀναγκαία, ἀναγκαῖον
to neglect ἀμελέω, ἀμελήσω, ἠμέλησα, ἠμέληκα
not οὐ; μή
nothing οὐδέν, οὐδένος
to nourish τρέφω, θρέψω, ἔθρεψα, τέτροφα, τέθραμμαι, ἐτράφην

O

often πολλάκις
opinion γνώμη, γνώμης, ἡ
to order κελεύω, κελεύσω ἐκέλευσα, κεκέλευκα, κεκέλευσμαι ἐκελεύθην
our ἡμέτερος, ἡμετέρα, ἡμέτερον

P

parents γονεῖς, γονέων, οἱ
to pass παρέρχομαι, παρελεύσομαι, παρῆλθον, παρελήλυθα
peace εἰρήνη, εἰρήνης, ἡ
poison φάρμακον, φαρμάκου, τό
to prevail ἰσχύω, ἰσχύσω, ἴσχυσα, ἴσχυκα
to prevent κωλύω, κωλύσω, ἐκώλυσα, κεκώλευκα, κεκώλυμαι, ἐκωλύθην
to produce τίκτω, τίξω, ἔτεκον, τέτοκα
poor πένης, πένες

R

to realize γιγνώσκω, γνώσομαι, ἔγνων, ἔγνωκα, ἔγνωσμαι, ἐγνώσθην
to rejoice ἥδομαι, ἡσθήσομαι, ἥσθην
to remain, stay μένω, μενῶ, ἔμεινα, μεμένηκα
robe στολή, στολῆς, ἡ

S

to see ὁράω, ὄψομαι, εἶδον, ἑώρακα, ἑώραμαι, ὤφθην
slave δοῦλος, δούλου, ὁ
soldier στρατιώτης, στρατιώτου, ὁ
soul ψυχή, ψυχῆς, ἡ
to speak λέγω, ἐρῶ, εἶπον, εἴρηκα, λέλεγμαι, ἐλέχθην
stone λίθος, λίθου, ἡ
successfully εὖ

T

teacher διδάσκαλος, διδασκάλου, ὁ
thoughtless ἄβουλος, ἄβουλον
thoughtlessness ἀβουλία, ἀβουλίας, ἡ
to throw βάλλω, βαλῶ, ἔβαλον, βέβληκα, βέβλημαι, ἐβλήθην
time χρόνος, χρόνου, ὁ
toil, trouble πόνος, πόνου, ὁ
too much ἄγαν
true ἀληθής, ἀληθές
to try πειράω, πειράσω, ἐπείρασα, πεπείρακα, πεπείραμαι, ἐπειράθην

U

to understand γιγνώσκω, γνώσομαι, ἔγνων, ἔγνωκα, ἔγνωσμαι, ἐγνώσθην

V

virtue ἀρετή, ἀρετῆς ἡ

W

to want βούλομαι, βουλήσομαι, βεβούλημαι, ἐβουλήθην
war πόλεμος, πολέμου, ὁ
well εὖ
well-being εὐψυχία, εὐψυχίας, ἡ
wealth πλοῦτος, πλούτου, ὁ
what τί; ὅτι
wise σοφός, σοφή, σοφόν
woman γυνή, γυναικός, ἡ
word λόγος, λόγου, ὁ
to wound τιτρώσκω, τρώσω, ἔτρωσα, τέτρωμαι, ἐτρώθην

Y

you σύ; ὑμεῖς
youth ἥβη, ἥβης, ἡ

Z

Zeus Ζεύς, Διός, ὁ

INDEX

An Extraordinary Journey of Love, Loss & Self Discovery

FINDING YOUR INNER Truth

DISCOVERING PEACE WHEN EVERYTHING CHANGES

NICOLE GABRIEL

AVIVA PUBLISHING
New York

Finding Your Inner Truth
Discovering Peace When Everything Changes

Published by:
Aviva Publishing
Lake Placid, NY
(518) 523-1320
www.AvivaPubs.com

Nicole Gabriel
Telephone (808) 280-5559
email: Nicole@FindingYourInnerTruth.com

www.FindingYourInnerTruth.com
www.Vegan-DogTreats.com
www.AngelDogProductions.com

ISBN: 978-1-940984-18-6
Library of Congress: 2014933181

Editor: Tyler Tichelaar
Cover Design: Angel Dog Productions
Interior Book Design: Angel Dog Productions

Every attempt has been made to source properly all quotes.

Printed in the United States of America

First Edition

2 4 6 8 10 12

Dedication

To my fiancé Patrick Snow: Thank you for supporting me and encouraging me to write this book. You're an awesome coach! (You can find him at www.ThePublishingDoctor.com if you want help writing your book too!) It has been a dream of mine to write this book and you made it come true. I look forward to all of our next steps together in Maui and in life! I love you!

To my parents: Chuck and Merilyn Case: You have always given me freedom to grow and no matter what interesting situation I found myself in you loved and supported me until I figured out a next step. There have been many hurdles and you keep loving me.... Thank you! I love you both!

To my students: Thank you for putting your trust in me and allowing the teachings to flow through, as I have learned more than you know.

To my friend, Jo Rayl for getting me through so much!

To all those I have lost: You have taught me so much in life and in death. In memory of my loving canine companions Shiitake, Tia, Mai Tai, and Sangria. I know you were more than just dogs!

To my Sushi: Thank you for lying by my feet while I wrote this book.

To my readers: Thank you for your support. It means the world to me and I hope you enjoy the book!

To Shar Pei owners everywhere: Thank you for your support, compassion for the breed, shared kind words, learnings, and teachings.

Most of all, this book is dedicated to my Shiitake, as you have become the wise teacher that has finally birthed this book from within me.

Acknowledgments

I would like to recognize and thank the following people for their support, encouragement, and belief in me. I would also like to thank all of those listed here who have helped me with either this book or in my life, as you have touched me more than you know.

Charlee Abrams, Greg Anderson, Sherlynn Black Atp, Kevin Bahula, Tom and Eileen Behnke, Scott Brown, Sylvia Brown, Andrea Cannon, Dolores Cannon, Charlie Case, Lauri Case, the Case Family, the Craton Family, Patrice Donnelly, Dana Duke, Susan Friedmann, Susan Hudson, Lisa Jennings, Aurelia Louise Jones, Ted Josalle, Krishna Kaur, Randall Kotrys, Livjot Kaur, Gurucharan Singh Khalsa, Wendy and Catherine LaCroix, Keith Lawhorn, Lauren Long, Camile Leinbach, Sarma Melngailis, Judith Moore, Ellen and Thane Ostroth, Jeff Papadelis, PeiPeople, Dale Prentiss, Jill Pursell, Jo Rayl, Lisa Ross, Red Lotus Yoga (Brian Granader and Lynn Baum), Shar Pei Savers, Shar Pei rescue groups across the world, Shawn, Isha Singh, Josh Siverson, Susan Smither, South Shore Veterinary Clinic and Dr. Dressler, Kelly Spradlin, Crystal Stalnaker-Mathis, Starbucks staff (Lake Orion and Lapeer, MI), Jeanette Ward-Taber, Hazel Thompson, Margriet Van Der Lelie, Heather Vincent, Valerie Weir, Wake and Kinlen Wheeler, Cheryl Woods, Greg Zallaps, Melissa Zeiman, and all the countless patients, clients and students at the Chiropractic Wellness Center of Metamora and The Maya Center.

I would like to thank the following for their beutiful music, as it helped me heal in so many ways: Snatam Kaur, Jai-Jegdeesh, Guru Ganesha Singh.

I would like to give a special thank you to my editor Tyler Tichelaar. Without his expertise and patience this book would not be what it is today.

SEEK

THE TRUTH

TRUST

IN GOD

BELIEVE

IN YOURSELF

LOVE

UNCONDITIONALLY

Contents

SEEK. TRUST. BELIEVE. LOVE.

INTRODUCTION

STARTING *Over*

"If you look for truth, you may find comfort in the end; if you look for comfort you will not get either comfort or truth, only soft soap and wishful thinking to begin, and in the end, despair."
— C. S. Lewis

You may be hurting inside but you do everything you can do to hide your pain. You are depressed (at times) but may write this off as the norm. Your relationships need work, but it seems like your partner is not a willing participant. You've been different your whole life but now are tired of trying to fit in. All of this has exhausted you but you are still searching for happiness, the real meaning of life and now perhaps your inner truth. You may even be struggling to calm your mind and heal your heart.

Somehow you picked up a copy of this book and are searching for answers. You may be tired of the challenges of day-to-day life, at the end of your rope and looking for solutions for your pain. Your timing couldn't be better because this is where our experiences and stories intersect. It is my hope that, as a result of the many years of my pain and searching, together we can put your mind at ease and bring calmness to your chaos.

Together we will uncover your truth and provide the answers to what the subtitle of this book promises: *Discovering Peace When Everything Changes.*

So let me start by asking you a very important question: How are you going to spend this one unique and precious life you have been given? You may have no power over your circumstances, but you do have control over your mind and how you are going to taste life, enjoy it, and find out the truth about who you are.

What if you worked hard, overachieved to reach your goals, made a good income, loved your spouse and your life, were respected and loved by your family and friends—everything was as near to perfect as you could imagine it being, and then it was all suddenly stripped away? What if everything you ever knew was not what you thought it was? What if each person you knew turned out to be someone different than you thought him or her to be? What if everything you knew was no more? What if all your friends disappeared, you lost your job, lost those you loved the most, lost your home, lost your spouse, lost your career, and had to start all over again? How do you recreate your life (or some semblance of it), and why did it crumble if it was so perfect anyway? Does any of this sound familiar to you?

Imagine that you are pure of heart and seeking something greater than what you already knew to be pretty great. How do you compare? How do you redefine happiness when you thought you were the happiest you could be? Or better yet, how do you find happiness if you never truly knew it to begin with? Do you get caught up in life's monotony, neglect to have moments of appreciation for what you have, and wish for something different? Are you a creature of habit at times—taking for granted the flow of your day, and instead of focusing on it, wandering off to dream—dream of another partner you feel would better complete your needs or harmonize with your life? Do you visualize yourself with a different financial status? How can you be sure, given the choice, that what you would choose would be any better than what you already have? And how do you know whether it is the best spiritual choice? Or do

you even think about spiritual choices? Sure you find moments of pleasure and thankfulness regardless, but what if you are constantly revisiting the same ideas to better yourself? What if your partner, culture, or family isn't along for the ride? What if you are on a path to better yourself when, suddenly, so much changes so quickly that you find yourself gripping at anything left that is familiar? Consider what might happen if, while you were trying to be a better person and connect to something with more meaning, that perfect spouse decided to have an affair, or the person you loved the most died, or that your perfect promotion interview turned into a down-sizing or job loss?

Our world is changing, and many of us have been left asking, "Why?" "How?" and "Who?" Life is sometimes not easy, and just getting through the mundane tasks of eating, paying bills, and caring for loved ones is more than enough to handle. But what if within all that, your spirit is calling? What if something within you says, "This is not right," or "This could be better"? You are now being called to find your truth. The old systems are shutting down, forcing you to figure out your gifts and purpose here on earth. This process may be leading you to seek in ways that some might call "spiritual" in nature. You are being bombarded with "feel good" quotes on Facebook, new healing modalities, and motivational and spiritual technologies popping out of the woodwork. Which if any of these have you connected to? How is it impacting your life? Is it making you feel better or worse about yourself? Do you want to change?

Change happens constantly in life, whether you plan for it or not. And even when you make the effort to change, it can lead to additional changes you did not foresee or necessarily want. For example, divorce usually occurs when one person in the marriage seeks to grow and change while the other tries to hold on to old ways and patterns. Often, the result is pain as well as new growth for both individuals. Similarly, large corporations are failing, forcing you to find new ways to pay your bills. You

can see this change as an opportunity that leads to your working in your true capacity to do what you were meant to on the planet. Are you sure you are doing what you are meant to do in this lifetime?

Maybe it took (or is taking) a great shake up for you to find your truth, or maybe you were one of the lucky ones and gracefully eased into it. When you have a great change occur in your life, it can often be hard to figure out where to start putting the pieces back together. A shift in consciousness is about to take place; you are now a part of what I call "The Great Initiation." Did you know that in the shamanic traditions this great change can sometimes be considered a soul wound, and in other spiritual studies, it's considered a karmic debt from previous lives and the lack of understanding you had then? Some traditions talk of the need to repeat your old stories time and time again in various lifetimes until you learn the lessons you wished for. Yes, the ones you wished for! I believe that one day before you were born and came to earth, you sat down with God and drew up your life's master plan. You were smart and experienced. God called in all the ancient masters, prophets, angels, and guides, and He asked for them to assist you in what would be the greatest plan for this life's experiences.

Because you are now reading this book, it's clear to me that you are searching for a better understanding of the difficulties in your life, and I was included as part of that plan for you. Perhaps you have gone through more strenuous or trying times than I have, but for whatever reason, our master plans have been made to overlap. Now it's my goal to share with you the spiritual and experiential wisdom I've gained along the way. I trust this wisdom will help guide you on your path into your own becoming.

It's hard to imagine when a tragedy occurs that any kind of light at the end of the tunnel can exist. Maybe it's taken you

years to come to believe that the tragic incidents in your life were beneficial for your soul's growth. I actually believed God hated me, wanted to see me suffer and was tempting me with my life. I was angry at God! But anger can serve you by causing you to push forward in ways you never dreamed of doing. What are you angry at, and how has your anger motivated you?

So, if you were at all like me and mad at the world (God in particular), imagine this: You've lost everything, and then you start to see and experience things of the most bizarre nature as you seek to find peace, answers, and truth on your new-found "seeker's path." What if you could draw aside the veil that separates our third-dimensional and heavy earth from all that is included in the universal truth, which may exceed the limits of human wisdom and knowing? Would you be okay with what you would see? I saw the most unimaginable things between the realms of what I knew and what I never could have imagined in my wildest dreams. Everything was a facade. How do you put pieces back together when nothing at all is familiar anymore? Nothing! Could you imagine the crumbling of it all would make you say, "Thank you" and "I had no idea how much better it could be"?

It's taken me a while to understand the value of seeking between the realms on a spiritual path and how doing so can provide balance in life, but I have also learned it's best to know what you are looking for and to develop tools to ground yourself to prepare for all the things you never imagined!

This book will share bizarre incidents and experiences that could not otherwise be had if too much time was spent growing a business, managing staff, raising family, being untruthful with myself, or not listening to that little voice saying, "You must write even if it doesn't make sense to you—it will to others." You may not have the luxury of stepping away from your daily responsibilities to take these kinds of journeys without sacrifice.

In this book, I will share lessons learned following love most of all and also through experiencing death—leading to the path of Peruvian Shamanism—with journeys across Central and South America; the path of yoga (Kundalini in particular). I will also share powerful visual experiences, such as angel visitations, UFO phenomenon, portal openings, conversations, and healings with those who have passed over to the other side; the dances between light and dark and how they serve; depression over loss; visual experiences of the third kind; discussions on what it means to find your truth (and actually seeing lies); surviving the "dark nights of the soul" and coming out clean, grounded, and undisturbed. This book was written so I could share all these things with those beginning to awaken to truth for the benefit of the whole planet.

You may want to know a little more about me before we begin this journey together. I have a Certification in Transpersonal Psychology (at the Master's level), an MBA in Technology Management, a Bachelor's degree in Communications, and more than 500 hours in Kundalini yoga teacher training. I spent the first part of my career in the '90s in advertising, web development, and information technology in executive management in the auto industry in Detroit, Michigan. When my career no longer satisfied my desire for personal growth, I left it to begin a new path opening multiple chiropractic offices with my former husband (a chiropractor). We successfully grew these businesses throughout the 2000s to more than $1 million per year in revenue. I then found that life changes—a divorce, a series of deaths, spiritual visions, and otherworldly experiences—found me seeking a new kind of quest that didn't involve quotas or management of personnel, but instead, tugged at both my heart and sanity as a whirlwind of change turned my life upside-down and inside-out.

During my career and the growth of the offices, I overachieved to obtain all my goals, including attaining a six-figure income

and an MBA by the time I was only twenty-six years old. But the new sandbox I was playing in left my truth in question, and when everyone else walked away, a pure and true relationship with the Divine, the companionship of my Chinese Shar Peis, and a lot of confusion was all I had left. There were no degrees attainable for this training and no measurables to determine how well I was doing at it. I had to learn to rely more on myself than ever before.

In my Kundalini yoga training, I had been taught that to master something was to teach it, and my previous path had been all about achieving mastery. After a series of events, I began to teach Kundalini yoga and Shamanic Healing at my twenty-five-acre retreat in Michigan from 2003-2012. The bizarre occult experiences in my life during those years were not completely new to me since I'd had many experiences as a young child that I had kept to myself my entire life. But this period seemed to be a time for me to experience and understand them more actively and vividly, although it became very hard for me to understand what was going on and to remain grounded. The lessons grew from anger (the death of many loved ones), to curiosity (being a seeker), to searching for something greater, finally calling the search "spiritual," and reading, studying, and experiencing everything metaphysical, making sense of what was practical and useful, adopting concepts and systems that were whole and pure that could be revisited when the visions or outside forces got to be too much, and refresher courses when needed.

I stepped away from my teaching and focused on learning my lessons more internally in 2012 because it was time for more grounding and absorbing of them. In that process, I found great joy in my creative nature—rediscovered from long ago when as a young child I had visions and dreams of being a great artist in the advertising business. I am now ecstatic to be designing book covers, logos, images, and websites with my

fiancé Patrick in Maui, Hawaii. I also am the owner of "Vegan Dog Treats," a vegan treat business for owners looking for healthy, organic, and natural options for their dogs. This business was inspired by one of my true loves—Shiitake, a sassy, lavender Chinese Shar Pei.

I have a diverse background in both education and life experiences, so I understand if you are apprehensive about listening to someone who has taken this odd path, stepped away from her career, and gone an untraditional route. But I have learned over the years that the only thing I can truly offer to anyone is my truth. All of your truths are based on your experiences. What is true for you?

I have wanted to share my stories for many years, but I was worried about what people would think of me. But when I open myself to my truth, I understand I am not alone. There are so many ancient traditions holding universal truths; in fact, many cultures carved these stories onto cave walls so future generations would remember them. If you could carve your truths on a wall, what would they look like? What have you experienced that you are afraid to talk about? It can be scary to go against the way you are programmed and to act or behave in a certain way. But I believe we are so much more similar than we are different, and we are all seeking happiness, contentment, love, grace, and ease.... What are you hiding behind that is keeping you from your light—your truth?

I don't want to tell you what to do, but I do want to show you how I have found my way through my stories and experiences so you can gleam some knowledge for your life's journey. I want to help you step into your becoming and truth and to be your coach and mentor throughout this process. I want to serve you in this way because I believe that to be wounded is to be experienced and to be experienced is to be a great healer! If you change your perception about your experiences and see them

as just simply experiences, you might be able to see them as intended life lessons and serve as a master of them who can teach and help others.

Are you ready to teach your mastery? Are you a Master of Divorce? A Master of Job Loss? A Master of the Paranormal? Please share with me all you have learned, and stop being afraid that you have done something wrong or are out-of-sync with the "norm"! Teach the world your skills! I can almost guarantee you that if you were to teach what you perceived as a wound, you would master that subject! Let's heal this planet together by not being afraid to step out with our stories because they are our truth and our tools for growth, learning, and teaching for others.

Are you ready to step out of your box? To expand your comfort zone? Are you ready to be exposed to things you may not understand or that are different than your current belief systems? Are you ready to heal your grief of your loss? Are you ready to expand your mind, walk between the realms, and discover your inner truth that may have been eluding you for years? If you have answered "Yes" to any of these questions and promise to keep an open mind, then let's begin this journey together!

I sincerely hope that by being open in these pages about my truths and experiences, I will inspire you to be true to you! I encourage you to seek the truth, trust in God, believe in yourself and love unconditionally.

Many blessings and much aloha!

Mahalo,

Nicole Gabriel

SEEK. TRUST. BELIEVE. LOVE.

CHAPTER 1

IDENTIFYING THE Catalyst of Change

"Let him that would move the world
first move himself."
— Socrates

Suppose we were smart enough to set up either obstacles to overcome or lessons to break through for our soul's growth in this life's incarnation. Suppose again that we are masters and creatively designed these challenges (catalysts) well before we came here. We designed the scenarios and all the key players with great thought as to how we would be challenged to respond. Maybe we even picked the timing of these great events and the exact sequences to occur. And maybe if we end up not walking the plan we set in place, we have little reminders pop in that say, "Hey, you're on the wrong path," or "Try this one out." But until you go through many of these challenges and roadblocks, you may be unaware that the results they cause could possibly inflict so much pain...or cause so much growth. They continue to come, and you continue to find ways through them.

Your mind, body, spirit, and soul are going to be challenged to evoke great change. So, if you ask yourself, "In what ways have I not been the same since...?" you will likely find that juicy gift you can thank yourself for later...after you muddle

through it. Or maybe you can shift your mind so you can view these "catalysts" or agents of change as simply experiences needed for your growth. This perspective does take a bit of the pressure off.

AWARENESS

When a loved one dies, the light of the angels fills my awareness. The light only becomes so bright when someone who has touched my soul deeply is passing over. The first time I saw the light of the angels, I was unaware that it would mean someone close to me would be carried over to the other side. The feeling is a bit unsettling—knowing that someone you love is leaving. But the angels do provide some comfort. As much as I have studied death over the last decade, I still cannot find complete peace with it. I know death means that someone I love is leaving and it will be some time before we come together in the physical again. I immediately try to feel whether I can determine who it is before the phone call comes. I know it is someone who has touched me and I have touched him or her. Several days may go by before I know who has passed away, making me think that maybe I have misread the message. Recently, I was out for a run when an email came through on my smartphone telling me that my ex mother-in-law had been carried away. I was touched that my divorce didn't affect our connection, and I was thankful for the unbiased love. I cried the rest of my run home despite not having seen her in years, and I knew the angels had brought her comfort. I cried in happiness, knowing that her love (Joe) waited for her on the other side. I'd never met Joe, but I'd had many conversations with him in spirit. I went home, and with tears in my eyes, during my daily meditation, I prayed that her spirit be released fully to the hands of the angels.

COPING WITH DEATH

Death was never a subject that caught my interest in any way; nor was it a subject I was very familiar with prior to the experiences I'm about to explain, but death would be the largest catalyst of change to spur me on into a whole new way of being. In 2006, the death of my dog, Tia Maria, the one "thing" that meant the most in the whole world to me, would cause a severe "jerk" out of my old ways and cause me to reevaluate everything in my life. I would later learn that, in the shamanic traditions, death is known to be one of life's greatest events that can cause a great shift to occur.

Before we go further, I want you to take a moment and think back to events in your life where you can say without a doubt "I haven't been the same since...." If you have studied shamanism, you will know that time of change is where something called a "soul wound" likely exists. A soul wound is a wound so deep it stays with you (in your soul's "blueprint") until you heal it. I'll explain this a bit more in Chapter 2.

For me, the moment Tia died, my life changed forever. At this time, it was hard for me to understand why people couldn't understand my loss the way I did—I was deeply wounded and shocked. I would later understand this was a "programmed awakening" that I must have previously put in place for this time in my life. Tia was only seven years old and passed away just ten days after she was tested for kidney failure. The day she died, our home was very silent and all the other animals were curled together on the floor in the family room, respecting a kind of mysterious "death space" created on the other side of the back door leading to the small maple tree under which she was breathing heavily in the backyard. I took notice of the other dogs and knew Tia was likely to pass that morning, but my heart wasn't ready for her passing, and I grew confused when I approached her. I didn't know what to do. She had been

on subcutaneous fluids, so my instant reaction was that she needed another dose. As I proceeded to inject her back and squeeze the IV fluid in, I could see very quickly it was not going to help her and that I was invading the space the other animals so instinctively respected, but I didn't know what else to do. In the place of not knowing, I became panicked and confused.

Have you ever experienced death? How did you handle it? How did you prepare for it? How did you walk through it? I had never before been so intimate with death, but now here it was in my face, and it felt like everything I did was a matter of life or death for Tia. I was losing my daughter (not my dog), and I was panicking in trying to figure out how I could save her. I was not prepared for kidney dysfunction to develop so quickly into death. I didn't understand that she wouldn't be with me forever. Despite all my best logical efforts to save her life, there was nothing I could do.

At this time in my life, I didn't believe in God or prayer. I didn't even know there was someone outside of myself or the veterinarian who could help her. I was angry that the veterinarian didn't better prepare me for this moment and tell me what was to come. I was angry that my husband had left me to figure out what to do while he went off to work that morning, and I was just plain confused. The sun was very hot that sunny June day, and as it began to grow warmer, Tia's breathing became more labored. I was so panicked and unable to handle it myself. I called my dad, and he took off work to drive all the way over to be with us. He told me that I could take her to his vet, and she would be put to sleep in the back of the car in her bed. I couldn't even come to grips with the idea that she was leaving, let alone that I would make that choice for her. While I awaited his arrival, I couldn't help but reflect back on my whole life and my time with her. As she faded in and out, I moved from one experience to another.

I would recall how she came into my life—a bit of a mystery really. I had contacted a woman breeder who appeared on the birth certificate of my other dog, Mai Tai. The breeder had acquired Tia as a pup in a trade (often done by breeders). The breeder had been moving and needed to find Tia a home. Now as Tia labored under the maple tree, I began to think of the day Mai Tai and I took that four-hour drive across Michigan to pick her up. When we arrived, dust was in the air from the dirt road under my little BMW convertible and a whole pack of dogs of various breeds greeted us. A woman yelled from a distance, calling all the dogs into the house. When the noise and the dust cleared, there stood a little fawn-colored Shar Pei pup. When she barked quite protectively at us, I was alarmed that she might be aggressive. There was no instant bond that developed—nothing magical that happened between us, but I had just driven all that way so it was likely she was going to go home with me anyway; I often find it hard to say no to any animal. After several minutes, Mai Tai and I determined she was not aggressive and would be a good fit for our home.

We drove home that day in the warm sunlight with the convertible top down. Mai Tai would have his new little "sister." I was gone for long hours in those days, working in executive management in the automotive industry, so I figured he needed the company while I was gone. For many years after Tia arrived in our life, we would await her pedigree in hopes of breeding her. But, after several attempts, she would seem to be from a mysterious no-name breeder. The woman I received her from had moved, and although I checked with every breeder in the Midwest, no one would ever see her again. I will never know any more (logically) about where she came from, but years later, I would run into a shaman healer who gave me a whole different perspective on her appearance in my life. I would find out she was a rare gift from my "lineage" (a term I was unfamiliar with at the time). I was told she was sent from my "spiritual family" to guide me from a place of unconditional

love. Throughout this book, I will explain how I came to understand this more as I sought answers.

As Tia now floated in and out of consciousness there under that maple tree, I sat with her, rubbing lavender oil on her belly (which I think she actually hated) and dropping valerian root and Rescue Remedy flower essences in her mouth in hopes of relaxing her. I had previously needed these "tools" for Mai Tai when he would get stressed, so I figured they might work. I think I was just bothering her, though.

Eventually, my dad arrived, and suddenly, everything became more systematic and grounded and I became less dreamy and more practical-minded, as often inherently happened in his presence. He and I lifted Tia up on her blanket and carried her to the car. As soon as we put her in the backseat, she reached out with her arms, took a deep breath, and, I believe, had a heart attack. Just like that, she was gone. I stared at her and thought it was all a joke and she'd wake back up, but she never did, and I just fell on top of her and bawled like a baby. It was my first intimate loss and the most meaningful.

I had, at a younger age, lost my grandparents, but this loss was much different. My grandparents had lived full lives while Tia was only seven. My parents and funeral homes and hospitals handled everything before, but this was up to me. I don't know why I took precious time away from her dying process, but somewhere in the chaos before I had called my dad, I had gotten on our tractor and proceeded to dig a giant hole in our five-acre yard to place her. I had lined it with blankets and toys and treats, so I guess part of me had decided she was passing that day. I barely remembered digging the hole, but after she passed, my dad and I would carry her over to her grave. We had a huge landscape project going on in the yard that summer, and we were preparing to install twenty-two pallets of grass in a few days. The whole yard was a mess. I placed her

in the hole at the head of the river we were installing; it was a location I could see from my bedroom window each morning as I lay in bed.

I had worked so hard that summer at our home and with our businesses. My husband and I had three chiropractic offices, and I was managing the books, doing massage, working the front desk, and in my free time, remodeling our home basement, painting both the interior and exterior, installing hardscape in the yard, and landscaping it. I didn't even know how exhausted I was until Tia passed. Then it was as if a bomb had gone off. I left the paintbrushes, shovels, and various projects and stopped! I just stopped. I had gone at full pace at 200 percent my whole life—overachieving all my goals, both scholastically and career-wise, but suddenly, everything just stopped! Nothing made sense. I wondered why I was working so hard. I wondered what the point was. Who was I impressing? What was I preparing for? My husband and I always worked so hard and so many long hours and had no friends and no children (during what should have been the most fertile years of my life) so no one was coming over to enjoy it. No one even cared how hard either of us worked.

What has stopped you in your life and made you ask, "Why? For what?"

BEGINNING TO QUESTION

I was in the middle of single-handedly painting the entire exterior of our two-story house. I had been climbing on scaffolding and ladders for a month. I continued moving forward for a bit and hid behind the project so no one could see my pain. There I stood, almost with the paintbrush in my hands mid-stroke, and I just walked away! I was angry and upset and asking big questions now: Why? What is this all about? Why did the one thing that meant the most to me get taken? Who took her? Who

decided it was her time and where did she go? I wanted revenge. I was embarrassed that my dog's death could cause me such pain because other people I knew had lost their children, their parents, their spouses, and this was "just a dog," right?

Then I learned of people who were writing and talking about the passing of animals and the "other side" over the "rainbow bridge." I wanted to know what they knew about this concept and what they knew about where she went. Of course, I realized if I could understand what happened to humans, I could understand what happened to her. I had no idea what I was about to step into. I ended up following one referral to the next. I went on a search for the one person who could tell me what I needed to hear. I had no idea who these people were or what their titles or backgrounds were at the time. But before I knew it I had been to psychics, past life regression therapists, counselors, and energy healers. I didn't care what they did. I just wanted them to tell me where Tia went and how to get there. Now I look back and think of how crazy this all seemed. But within a few months, I ended up sitting in front of the first person who finally made sense to me—a shaman healer. Again not knowing what her background was, I took a chance.

She told me she had a daughter named Nicole and she was going to name her expectant daughter Gabrielle, so she caught my attention. At the point I reached the shaman healer, I was exhausted. I acknowledged that my exhaustion was not just from her death, but from life itself. Her death seemed to force me into understanding this as well as the pain of her death. I kept much of my pain to myself because I was too embarrassed to admit Tia's death had bothered me so much. Not even those close to me knew the pain in my heart. I had a brief consultation with the shaman healer, followed by a session. What I heard that day would change my thinking for the rest of my life.

EXERCISES:

Before I continue, I want to ask you the following questions about your catalyst for reading this book and wanting to find your inner peace:

1. What is the first thing you think of when you ask yourself this question: "What episode in my life has caused me never to be the same again?" ______

2. What emotions did you feel as a result of this event happening? ______

3. Did you seek help from an expert, a friend, or a therapist? What was the result? ______

4. How did this event change you?____________________________

____

____

____

____

5. Who was involved in this event? ____________________________

____

____

____

____

6. Who supported you in this event and who walked away?__

____

____

____

____

7. Is this catalyst a repeat story? Has this situation happened before? Do you notice a pattern? Explain: ________________

____

____

____

BECOMING AWARE

What happened at Tia's death forever changed the way I look at death and medical care. Everything in my life began to click together, and I had more "aha moments" at this stage of my life than any other time. I was beginning to realize that the belief system I had in place and my old ways of doing things were not the best choice. I was breaking out of the "programmed" way of thinking.

Three months after Tia died, I was out walking the other three dogs when I noticed Mai Tai, then nearly ten years old, begin to slow down. I think he was actually heartbroken over Tia's death since they were very close. We were walking in the park when, suddenly, he just lay down. He was very strong-willed, so I had never seen him like that before. As Mai Tai started to slow down, I realized I was awakening to new realizations and everything I had questioned in life was beginning to make sense. I was starting to sense that these were more than just dogs.

Mai Tai first came into my home as a replacement after a "boyfriend gone bad" and served to be a much more reliable and trustworthy companion. But Mai Tai had some health issues that would cause me to look at the pharmaceutical industry differently; I found that homeopathic and natural remedies eased his ailments much better than the medical treatments he had received in the past. For example, at one point he was diagnosed with four different bacteria in his ears, so I was given a medicine to inject in his neck twice daily. The day the bacteria finally cleared up and he no longer needed a shot, he reached around and nearly bit me when I tried to give him another injection, so we never did that again. He just knew it was time to stop. I had to honor that. He would teach me like that for years. As a result of what I learned from observing him, I started doing things differently for my body as well. I had suffered for years with severe stomach aches that would cause me to go into the ER on occasion. I traveled to and from various doctors all over the state in search of a cure / cause. But when I learned about healthier food options for my dogs, I also became aware of healthier options for myself.

Tia's passing would make me more aware of the subtle energies and connection to forces outside myself. This awareness only happened because of her death. It got my attention! Now Mai Tai was slowing down and he had my attention. If Tia could teach me to step out of my old ways and into alternative

worlds, and find healers, and make me curious about all things metaphysical, what would Mai Tai teach me? I knew my animals were in tune with more subtle energies so I started paying attention to all of them, their signs and actions and how they could teach me new ways of being. Suddenly, I would become aware of the most unlikely teachers as I'll explain throughout this book. My questions kept coming and it seemed imperative to get answers. I was awakening a dormant energy within me through the aid of my best and most loyal friends. I began to read and learn as much as I could about countless subjects that I previously had never even heard of—homeopathy, energy healing, quantum physics, psychics, past life regression therapy, EFT tapping, yoga—and now sitting with the shaman healer, I would begin to learn about shamanic healing.

SEARCHING FOR ANSWERS

As I sat with the shaman healer, she asked me many questions, but I almost couldn't hear what she was saying. I was exhausted. I had been crying for countless days and into months. As I woke up spiritually, I was starting to realize that my husband was more concerned about the offices and the unfinished projects around the house than he was with my well-being. I suddenly felt very, very alone and very scared. It felt as if the ground beneath me, which had always been so stable, now was shaking. I began to realize that a power greater than me was taking control over what I thought I owned, managed, and controlled. People would say they were sorry for my loss and ask, "Are you getting another one?" I thought, "If she were my child, would you ask the same question?" Tia was a one-of-a-kind and not replaceable.

However, I sensed that Tia had seemed to die for a reason, and I wanted to understand it. I wanted others to understand that I felt this way, and I wanted to know what that reason was. I wanted to understand answers to questions that the average

person just didn't seem to talk about. I wondered why these matters were kept so quiet and thought inappropriate to talk about in public. I finally began to see that I might be on a spiritual quest for answers, but I couldn't find the institution that taught the kinds of answers I was seeking. Tia had opened up a huge can of worms and I was so overwhelmed and just plain exhausted. I had never spent much time in church, so I didn't know whether the answers I was seeking were written somewhere I could find them. I don't know why a church wasn't the first place I went for answers, but I felt I could find the answers on my own. It felt that was the most logical way to obtain them. First, I had to separate my thoughts from my emotions to frame the questions for which I sought answers. I've listed them below because they may be questions you also have or have been struggling to put into words.

- Why did this event happen? (Why did Tia die?)
- Was I not following the path I should have been?
- Does God not love me? Am I being punished?
- Who is supporting me in my life at this time of need?
- Why do those who have been there all this time not understand my pain?
- What exactly am I seeking? How will I know when I find it?
- Why did the one thing that meant the most to me get taken away?
- How will seeking heal my heart?
- Where do I go to find answers?
- Are there others like me who have suffered a loss? How did they heal?
- Why am I so angry?
- Who or what am I mad at?
- Who conspired to create this tragedy?
- Why wasn't I better prepared for this? Could I have been?
- And now what?

EXERCISES:

Identify a change that has occurred or is occurring and how it has shifted you into a new kind of awareness. Take a moment and just journal. ______________________________

What seemed to make all of this questioning even more interesting was that I would later be enrolled in a transpersonal psychology program, and rather than objectively looking at this situation as an opportunity for growth, my questioning would, on every occasion, define me as being in a "spiritual emergency." As I went deeper down the rabbit hole, what I found most fascinating was that once my situation was classified in psychological terms, it was merely going to be examined or studied, without being seen as an opportunity for healing. I would pay great attention to this fact later and monitor whether the program could actually provide healing for me. Then I would know its likelihood for success in helping others.

HELPING YOU DISCOVER YOUR TRUTH

Sometimes life just doesn't make sense. Loved ones pass on unexpectedly, leaving a hole in your heart. As a result, we are left seeking answers to our questions of "Why me?" and "Why them?" Be grateful for all your blessings because you just never know how long your loved ones will be with you. Just know that it's okay to seek the truth and continuously look for answers; it's part of how you evolve as a human being in the midst of all the changes life sends your way.

SEEK. TRUST. BELIEVE. LOVE.

CHAPTER 2

STEPPING INTO Shamanism

"The best place to find helping hands
is at the end of your own arms."
— Confucious

Shamanism is sometimes said to be the world's oldest spiritual path, but it is not considered a religion. A shaman is responsible for both the physical and spiritual health of people, but he or she bears that responsibility in quite unique ways. The earliest known visual depiction of a Siberian shaman dates back to 1692, although shaman are believed to date back far earlier. The concepts or beliefs of shamanism may be new to you, but the practice is nothing new to humankind. It has been found in indigenous religions in parts of Asia, Africa, Australasia, and the Americas, and it is believed to have played a role in the pre-Christian religions of Europe. Each region has a unique way of practicing shamanism; for example, Celtic Shamanism is a shamanic path based on the Celtic peoples of Western Europe and especially of Britain, Scotland, Wales, and Ireland. What is called the "faery faith" in these areas is based upon the belief that many shaman carry—everything in this and other worlds is alive, and each thing has its own soul or spirit. Before the advent of Christianity, this belief was more prevalent in the Western world.

It's my understanding that a shaman is an intermediary between the human and spirit worlds. Shaman are also able to treat ailments or illnesses by healing a person's soul (or accessing the "soul blueprint"). The blueprint holds "experiences" or "traumas." In more simple terms, the soul is the energy that comes into a physical body to create life, and it is what leaves your physical body at the time of death. The soul can even be called the "light body." It can carry with it wounds that the shaman can help to heal. Breath, on the other hand, is what sustains life.

Wikipedia defines shamanism as:

> *A practice that involves a practitioner reaching altered states of consciousness in order to encounter and interact with the spirit world and channel these transcendental (beyond ordinary) energies into this world. A shaman is a person regarded as having access to, and influence in, the world of benevolent and malevolent spirits, who typically enters into a trance state during a ritual, and practices divination and healing. The term "shamanism" is currently often used as an umbrella term referring to a variety of spiritual practices, although it was first applied to the ancient religion of the Turks and Mongols, as well as those of the neighboring Tungusic and Samoyedic-speaking peoples. The word "shaman" originates from the Evenk language (Tungusic) of North Asia and was introduced to the west after Russian forces conquered the shamanistic Khanate of Kazan in 1552.*

Shamanism is said to be an authentic relationship with spirit. In order to experience that authentic relationship, one must activate altered states to communicate with spirit. And spirit is the source of all things. Whatever your religious affiliation, it is likely that you connect with spirit on some level—sometimes more knowingly than others. In shamanism, it is known that our human suffering exists within the soul. During a healing

event, a shaman will move your energies so you become a new version of yourself—restored and healed. The spirit world will come in any form to get your attention.

It would take me years to learn all of this information about shamanism. (I still don't have all the answers.) And I would know none of it prior to meeting the shaman healer.

MEETING A SHAMAN HEALER

As I sat in my initial interview with the shaman healer, she asked me a variety of questions about why I was there. I was not listening to her because I was more concerned with hiding my emotions and telling myself "Please don't cry; please don't cry" than with what she was saying. In fact, I wasn't even sure why I was trying to find answers again. I wasn't sure what was more exhausting: seeking the why, or experiencing the loss or shifts in my life. I was just exhausted and the shaman healer was likely going to be my last step.

As I sat with the shaman, I took notice of the office furniture gathered around in a square shape with a large cow skin drum glass-topped table in the center. I noticed the strange quietness to the room, yet it was not unwelcoming. I sensed the office wasn't very busy, but it had been prepared for something to come. I observed these things but paid no real attention to them since they were not why I was there. I had noticed two treatment rooms when I came in, and they were set up much like massage rooms. In fact, my bi-weekly massage therapist, Jill, whom I considered well-versed in healing, had referred me there. I counted on Jill quite a bit since she seemed more knowledgeable about healing than me. She had a personal relationship with Jesus, which I was always a bit uneasy about, but I was curious about it nonetheless. We had very connected and meaningful talks during our sessions, and I began to see her more as my friend than my massage therapist. She knew

almost everything about me, and she never judged me; she only provided me with encouragement. Jill was probably the nicest person I had met up to that point in my life, and I deeply trusted her.

So on Jill's trusted advice, I would try once more to find answers to all the questions that had opened up for me as a result of Tia's death. After the shaman healer asked me a string of questions, she asked whether I'd like to do a healing. Of course, I wasn't really there for the small talk, and I already trusted her since Jill had sent me to her. I felt like saying, "I'm exhausted; take my body and give me hope!" So I lay down on the massage table covered in a white sheepskin rug. I figured I didn't have much to lose, and the room felt familiar and comfortable.

At that moment, I had a flashback to a strange sequence of events I'd had with a woman I had contacted after seeing her ad in a local New Age healing magazine. The ad promised she would "shift all blocks and recharge my energy." I didn't know what any of that meant, but when I went, I knew the session didn't feel right. I had a handful of sessions with her, and each time, more and more bizarre events happened post-treatment. For example, after one session, I was driving when a series of rocks hit the passenger side of the windshield and nearly shattered it. During another session, I felt a kind of tugging of energy as if she were taking something out of me from under my skin; it literally pulled me away from the back of my chair. And each time I arrived for a session, I noticed the odd buzzing sound coming out of the radio. Sensing something was not right, I decided not to see her again. When I later talked with the shaman healer about this experience, she said several other people had told her that this woman's sessions did not seem to be performed with the highest and best intentions. I was receiving a lesson in ethical and non-ethical healers before I even really knew what a healer was.

HEALING MY SOUL WOUNDS

Once I was on the shaman healer's table, I lay there watching her swipe feathers around in the room and blow and light things. I began to think how my family would ridicule me for being in this situation. Then within a few minutes, my eyes let loose and I cried harder than I ever had before. I wasn't sure what happened; all I could think was that Tia had left me and nothing else mattered. But then, things came up in the session that made me see that everything else did matter, and that everything else really was connected. I began to see that nothing was separate from anything else. I started to sense a kind of spiritual purpose for her death and that she was meant to pass when she did, as if it had all been scripted. I sensed there were others involved in planning these events and I was walking through each phase just as it had been planned. I can't say how I knew these things. I just did. I would later understand this was a kind of psychic awareness beginning to open up.

Then I asked the shaman to help me understand something that had occurred in my childhood. I wanted to know why, when I was small, I used to talk of a life as Diana. My mom had teased me all of my life that I would say, "When I was Diana, I would…." Years later, my aunt would tell me that I used to go on and on about my kids and husband, and I wanted to know whether they were okay. So I wanted to know whether the shaman could tell me about what seemed to be a past life. She replied that Diana was associated with Diana, the goddess of the moon. I wasn't really aware of what that actually meant, so I was open to it, but I shelved it for later. At that time, I had no reason to doubt the existence of reincarnation. I didn't know that some religions condemned the idea of it, or that I might offend people by discussing it. I had been born asking about another life, so I yearned to understand the topic better.

As the shaman worked above me while I lay on the table in tears, I was too upset to care much about what she was doing.

Time just seemed to fly by, and I felt like something was occurring, but I wasn't sure what. When she completed the session, she barely talked to me or touched me, and I wasn't sure what happened for those two hours. She told me I could just lie there and she would tell me what she had found. She said she saw me as a young girl playing in a glass box with Tia, and all my spiritual family and lineage were surrounding me outside the box. She said everything outside the box was absolutely beautiful, so she couldn't understand why I wouldn't come out of it. I guess she eventually got me out of the box, which was the majority of the healing from what I could tell. She told me Tia meant so much to me because it was rare to receive a gift in physical form from my lineage, and Tia was that gift. Somehow this meant something to me, so I broke down crying some more. The rest of the session seemed to be a kind of blur, but enough of it made sense that I felt I needed to know more, so I immediately scheduled another session before I left. I felt changed as I drove home that night.

A few weeks later, I would return for another session. The shaman healer asked how I had done after the last session. I replied that for the first time in my life I could breathe! "I just noticed (deep breath)...I can breathe!" For the first time ever, I felt understood and as if I had found a kind of home...a kind of family. I finally realized there really was something greater than me. I still didn't know to call this "spirituality," though. I was happy not to label it anything. I was just comforted in a way I had never been before. It was different, yet similar, to the comfort of a mother-daughter bond. It was more than I could comprehend, but nice! Just nice!

The shaman healer lay me down on the table once again, and this time, I was much more at ease and not as emotional. I became very sleepy when she moved me into the darker room across the hallway. I would doze off a bit and come back to, and then I was widely awakened by a very strong burning smell

in the room. I was alarmed and kept looking around to make sure nothing was on fire. There was absolutely no smoke in the room, but the smell was so strong that I could hardly breathe. I was very thankful when she was done so I could get some fresh air, but as the session came to a close, the smell was gone. Later when I asked her about it, she said, "Sometimes in this work there is symbology used to aid in healing," and she explained that she had seen me cutting off and burning my arms and legs over a fire. She said there were bones everywhere and I felt guilty for letting people on horses into the town where I lived because they had killed everyone and left me as a survivor. The guilt was too much for me, so I couldn't live with myself. I didn't understand this statement, but I tried to be open to it nonetheless. I did smell the profound burning smell well before I knew the story. I was both alarmed and amazed at the same time. I was starting to feel stronger and more balanced than I had ever felt in my life.

I left that day with much to think over, and I was excited when the shaman healer told me about an upcoming year-long training program I was welcome to attend. I was very excited to understand the meaning behind my stories and experiences of being Diana, and I couldn't wait to go home and tell my husband all about it! I drove home feeling so excited to be getting answers to questions I'd had most of my life. My body and mind felt so much lighter, and my emotions were calmer than they had been in months.

A FRESH START

I began the year-long training with the shaman healer and her husband soon after. When the training was introduced to the class, we were told that it was brought in from Peru lineage and taught mostly as it was taught by the Four Winds Society and Alberto Villoldo's program. But there were other teachings mixed in from Michael Harner's core shamanism as

well as from other places and people the shaman healer and her husband had traveled with and learned from. I honestly didn't care where it was coming from in the beginning; it was merely my vehicle to find Tia. I hadn't come to grips with where her spirit had gone and the fact that our time together was over. I sensed her spirit was still present even though her body was not. I planned to stick with the training until I found her and / or found a cure for the dreaded kidney diseases so prevalent in the Shar Pei breed. I was dedicating all this work to her, and now Mai Tai was showing signs of slowing down, so I wanted to find a way to ease his pain and discomfort as well. A few times it was more about me, but mostly, it was for them...in the beginning anyway.

I was always so excited to learn new things and come home to share them with my husband, but even when he was there, he lacked interest. The general principles I learned seemed as if they could apply to anyone's life and better it, even if the person wasn't on the path I was. Because my purpose in this book isn't to teach you shamanism, per se, I'll be as brief as I can so you just understand the principles upon which my transformation took place. I also hope these concepts will aid you on your path as they did me. The guiding principles are what are important here because when things went astray for me, they were what got me through. I think they will help you as well—especially if you have not developed your own.

The classes were taught in a medicine wheel style with each direction on a compass having significance. In the first class—the South class—we would learn to understand our wounds and pains and "stuff" we wanted either to heal or learn about ourselves. In the West class, we would talk about death and dying. This class would be extremely useful in my efforts to understand Tia and for my immediate future. Then we moved, nearly six months later, into the North class, in which we learned more about the lineage of great teachers who came before us and

how to leverage that teaching. I now finally started to understand what it meant when Tia was given to me as a gift from my lineage (those who came before me—my great teachers). In the East class, we would come full circle to step into our becoming. The teachings would follow the rich Peruvian culture, and we would learn some of the Quechuan language of the shaman from the Andes. As our teaching continued, all I could think about was actually going to Peru and working directly with the shaman to learn firsthand. But for now, I would absorb as much as I could.

STUDYING SHAMANISM

The medicine wheel is taught with archetypes that signify each linear direction:

- South: Serpent
- West: Jaguar
- North: Hummingbird
- East: Eagle or Condor

Peruvian shamanism uses these directions as well as the energy of the heavens and earth to create a sacred space. The space is created before a healing session or on land. After many years, I learned that the space can also be created within or used to pray over a meal, a home, a car, or any other possession or being. The idea of creating a sacred space is really about coming into harmony with it, and I believe that any technique can be used as long as it's meaningful to you. Our American culture cannot always identify with what is not present within it. I suggest using what works for you. Once a sacred space is created, a healing can begin.

For a moment, I'd like you to think about what a sacred space looks like for you. What "archetypes" would work for you to call to? Many times we have animals or places in our lives that we

resonate with, and they can signify something important for us. This process is more in-line with Michael Harner's program of "core shamanism," which pulls the cultural influence out and helps you connect in your own way. You just need to know what you are calling on (what you are trying to be present with) and be in integrity with it. Otherwise, as I have found many times, when you don't know what you're calling, all kinds of things can show up. These lessons work in life outside of shamanism too.... What are you directing into your life? Many times we just call on help, but sometimes, help can come in and teach us the hard way.

Moving through the lessons of the South had me looking at everything I didn't like about myself and taught me techniques for changing that. It wasn't until many years later that I would fully understand the principles taught, and today, I still use them to rebalance my mind. The following principles not only aid in the work of a healer and shaman, but they also assist in many other "non-shamanic" incidents in life:

- Non-judgment
- Non-suffering
- Non-engagement
- Walk with beauty

NON-JUDGMENT

The principle of non-judgment is excellent in every avenue of life. What I found in every case where judgment was involved was that those doing the judging did so from a need for healing. Sometimes this need is more obvious than not. Imagine this principle being taught in schools or used in the workplace. What if we had these teachings as a part of our school systems or workplaces? I'd like you to take notice of where you judge someone and how that judgment resides within you.

EXERCISES:

1. What / who do you judge?______________________________

2. How would it make you feel to be judged this same way?

3. How does that judgment live within you? __________________

4. When do you find yourself saying the following statement with someone else? "You should…." __________________________

5. Where is your ego at when you are allowing judgment to stand in your way? ______________________________

____
____
____
____
____

6. Can you create sacred space, and if so, what does it look like, and how can you step out of its way? ______________________

____
____
____
____
____

7. Notice how the sacred space makes you feel and how the other person might feel. Write down those feelings. __________

____
____
____
____
____

NON-SUFFERING

Sometimes a painful event can bring on a thought that can bring on more thoughts until the thoughts become more painful than the event itself. So many times, I have thought about something painful to the point of losing sleep over it and I become exhausted and actually create the event I was fearing. This situation happened often in my career, but I kept wondering if I somehow created Tia's death too.

We can move from a place of suffering by knowing that the force and power that created us is watching out for us. That doesn't always mean we don't have to go through something to get the best lessons, but it does mean that no matter what we do or don't do, we are loved and will have another chance at whatever it is until we get it right. We are here to learn, and my prayer has always been a prayer to learn gracefully the lessons I need to understand in this lifetime.

When patterns continue to show up in our lives, we must understand these are great opportunities to grow and learn. But, it's not always easy to remove ourselves from the story taking place. Maybe death was an opportunity for growth in disguise?

EXERCISES:

1. Where in your life are you suffering? ____________________

____
____
____
____
____
____
____

2. Where do you notice patterns of suffering? (What is repeating in your life?) ______________________________________

____
____
____
____
____
____
____

3. Can you move into or shift these repeat patterns into gifts? How are these life lessons great gifts for you? ______________

____
____
____
____
____
____

4. What would a more positive spin on these life lessons sound like if you rewrote them? ______________________________

____
____
____
____
____

NON-ENGAGEMENT

Not getting attached to someone or something can sometimes be very hard to do. Often, we can be very empathetic or very controlling about a situation or event and not even know it. For example, I knew a young man who was born with a spinal deformity, and each time I saw him, I would pray for his healing so he no longer needed his crutches or wheelchair. Then one day, he told me he would go regularly to a certain bar, and each time he walked in, everyone knew who he was. He talked about "cutting a rug" on the dance floor and how all the girls liked to roll him around in his wheelchair and watch him do tricks. He was clearly the center of attention and loved it. If he had been just some guy with legs, he would not have stood out. I finally heard a little voice say to me, "What if he chose his deformity for his life experience and that choice was working out perfectly?" If that were true, then I realized I could no longer wish he would have functioning legs like mine. His legs were perfect!

Often when we get very involved or emotionally connected with people, we not only judge them and wish them to be more like us (because we are familiar with that), but we can become so close that we don't see they may represent our similarities. In a healing capacity, when one resonates with someone else so well, the person can actually miss the one thing that really does require healing. When we get attached, we also create expectations. The true meaning of creating sacred space is really standing in a place of complete non-judgment without expectation...allowing the individual to make a choice. The choice can come at that moment or later when the person has had more life experience, which creates comfort in knowing how to make a better choice. Engagement can also hinder another's growth. For example, when a mother is overprotective of her daughter, the daughter isn't able to learn on her own or have her own experiences and becomes reliant on the mother. Create the space and get out of the way. Many times, moving out of the way may feel as if we don't care or we are being lazy, but with a defined vision and simply one request or prayer for a better outcome, miracles can happen. Spirit works in mysterious ways.

EXERCISES:

1. What outcomes are you attached to? ____________________

____

____

____

____

____

____

____

____

____

2. What people, places, or events are you trying to control in your life? ____

____

____

____

____

3. If you let go of the need to control or engage, what do you think would happen? ______________________________

____

____

____

____

4. What "systems" can you put in place to create a neutral space of allowing and to ease your need for control? ______

____

____

____

____

____

WALKING WITH BEAUTY

Walking with beauty is very much the way of the aloha spirit, which basically says there really is no need to change any more than our mind. If there is nothing that needs fixing, can we truly see that, and if we do, can we be fully in joy and harmony and enjoy it? If everything were exactly perfect as it is, then what? Is there truly a need for changing it? Can you walk the lines between seeing the need for healing and creating harmony and accepting things as they are? Does that thought make you feel guilty or unbalanced? Does it seem unnatural to believe that everything could actually be perfect after all?

EXERCISES:

1. Identify those things that are beautiful in your life: _________

2. How do these things reside within and around you? _______

3. What "negative" things in your life have occurred that eventually worked out to be positive shifts for the better? _________

LEVELS OF ENGAGEMENT

Continuing the lessons of the South, one must gain a brief understanding of what are called the "Levels of Engagement." They can be described as:

1. Literal: the everyday tactile kind of "earthy stuff." Ask what's wrong and try to fix it.
2. Energetic: beyond earthly and what exists in the soul—karma.
3. Symbolic: from one thing, belief, emotion to another—shifting.
4. Mythic: spirit or connection to oneness.

Once the concept of non-engagement is fully understood, one begins to understand how to get in and do the work needed without becoming attached. The training would continue and we would learn how to use a pendulum and then a core function of healing the energetic body—called an "illumination." You can read more about the illumination process in Alberto Villoldo's book *Shaman, Healer, Sage*. In order to do the illumination process, we need to define further our wounds and begin to create our medicine bags. In the class, we would use crystals or stones to contain or stand for the main "issues" in our lives we wanted to heal. You can easily create a medicine bag yourself. Find a few stones and bring up all the emotions around each issue you have; then simply blow all the anxiety of the wounds, emotions, and physical pain into the stones one at a time. Each stone represents one issue. You can even do this exercise while outside gardening with your kids. Then bury the stones in the yard for the earth to heal the problems.

IDENTIFYING THE SHADOW SELF

The shadow self is the self that gets in the way and causes what comes in to be filtered so we see things differently and it becomes harder for us to see truly what is ours. It is very important to know what your shadow is so it is not imposed on

anyone else. It doesn't mean we always have to tell everyone what it is either! Following are some questions to help you identify your shadow self that you may want to ask while doing the illumination process above or any other healing process of yoga practice you are currently involved in. Whatever your spiritual background or daily practice is, I think you will find these to be great questions to answer as you walk through defining yourself. When you truly know yourself and open the wounds and look deeper into your soul, you will discover more of your truth.

EXERCISES:

1. What don't you want to see about yourself? ______________

2. What or whom can't you be with? ______________

3. What or whom do you avoid? ______________________________

4. What stalks you? ______________________________

5. What keeps you from your goals? ______________________________

6. What secrets do you keep from yourself? ______________________________

7. What did you not tell someone that harmed him or her? ___

8. Where in your body do you feel it? ___

9. What goals have you not achieved? ___

THE WEST CLASS

Moving into the West class was the most exciting moment in my training. I was nearly desperate for the class once I decided it might help me find Tia. I had many things that were beyond amazing happen in the first class, and I had high hopes for this one. We began talking about how we would be healing our relationships and also the pain of our ancestors within our body so our wounds wouldn't be passed to our offspring. We also talked about how we would eventually get comfort from our lineage when we couldn't sleep or needed help healing.

We discussed the psychological model of rescuer, victim, and perpetrator, and how we are trying to break out of this model and move into a more observatory position to watch the roles being played out—stepping away so we are no longer part of the story but merely an observer. We talked about how in the absence of fear there is only love and no anger. We learned to clear death's fear from our body by going through a death and dying ritual and coming into balance with what's around us. We would look at how our loved ones died, the lessons they gave us, what drained their life forces, what challenges they left us, and what their gifts were to us. We would revisit the concepts of the shadow self as well as move beyond losing a loved one. Here is where we began to honor them as they were, the lessons they gave, and to understand how we chose them as teachers. We learned that the gifts will be there if we allow them, and we can shift from being the wounded into being the healer.

We would also be taught in this class not to follow the masses, not to use backdoors or sacred cows (ways out of doing something), not to jump to conclusions, and to notice any affinity or similarity because it would teach you something about yourself. We also learned that we should walk with integrity, a solution to life's problems will bless you, and healing is a journey, not an

intervention. The final lesson we learned was how to extract energies from our energetic body that were not our own. This tool would prove to be very valuable for me later. We were told to "trust the process" because it would work every time. These words would also be put into my toolbox for later.

Finally, we were told that things are not always as they seem. I would learn that this work would become much like peeling the layers of an onion, and we would learn to correct issues in our lives by reliving them on many levels until we reached a kind of core understanding.

HELPING YOU DISCOVER YOUR TRUTH

When you find a strong core spiritual program to follow, you can use the guidelines of that program to help you heal. Shamanism may or may not be your thing, but there are some great lessons to build upon if you have no other spiritually-based program to help you heal. Many who have taken the shamanic journey have said that each of us has a shaman within. In other words, you have the power to heal yourself. Sometimes a helping hand to point you in the right direction is all you need. As you dive into any path, you will begin a journey into finding your inner truth.

SEEK. TRUST. BELIEVE. LOVE.

CHAPTER 3

HEALING *Your Grief*

"Death may be the greatest of
human blessings."
— Socrates

At this point in my training and despite my best efforts to hold onto her, I would lose sight of the idea that I was looking for Tia and get lost in my own healing (likely her plan all along). I barely accepted that Tia was gone, and now Mai Tai was distracting me with his health. When he had laid down on the trail that day, I knew his time was drawing near. Due to the training I had just gone through, I was much better prepared for his passing than I was with Tia. I was absolutely fascinated with it, in fact. Death was just meant to continue awakening me on my journey. It would keep happening and as it did I kept growing.

I was finally seeing the gifts Tia had brought me, and her dying sparked my interest on this path. I now knew that because I was aware they were my teachers, the lessons would be easier to see and understand. I knew she was holding space with me for Mai Tai. I knew how to hold him as he would prepare to depart. The last week that Mai Tai lived was so powerful. We had such amazing conversations in such deep silence. He would grow weaker each day, and I could see he was struggling with leaving me. He fought to stay cognizant and upright. At this

point, I had built a mandala in my yard under a big oak tree. I had landscaped in a beautiful flowing river and waterfall next to my mandala and planted healing herbs and flowers. I hung crystals from many of the oak tree's branches and called it my "fairy spot." Here is where Mai Tai and I would spend his last days.

Yes, by this point, I think my husband had started to wonder whether I had gone off the deep end. One day he asked me why I had all the crystals hanging there. I replied that I had hoped to meet a fairy and that it would be a healing spot in our garden. Another day, we were at the store when I told him I wanted to buy some chocolate and picked up a box of it. He looked at me kind of weird and asked "Why?" because he knew I didn't like chocolate. I told him it was for a project. His questions continued until I finally told him I had heard that fairies like chocolate. In response, he took the chocolate I had picked up and set it back on the shelf and instead chose a different box. When I asked him what he was doing, with a straight face he said, "Well, if the fairies don't come to eat it, then I'd like the kind with almonds!" I suppose now I see how funny that really was.

I knew Mai Tai could pass any day now, so I began to think of our past together and all the things he had taught me. As he was dying, he taught me even more. I originally attributed my knowledge of all things herbal and medicinal to him because he always responded better to natural medicine, but then as we sat there in our sacred spot, he began to teach me about reading the signs of nature as well. I started to take notice of the countless yellow butterflies in the garden. Today I see them as a sign of approaching death since they have always been present just before a loved one's passing. As I thought about these things, I began to realize what had also happened at the time Tia was about to pass. Our yard was overtaken with toads, frogs, and hungry snakes. It was like something out of *National*

Geographic. I began to see that nature does tell us what we need to know in more ways than we understand. I began to understand more about totem animals and their meanings, but I also began to have this kind of knowing that just showed up in my conscious awareness. Sitting in quiet with Mai Tai taught me to see the signs from Tia's death and now his. I watched very closely, as I was a keen observer of my teacher.

Then for the first time in my life, I called out to something greater than myself, asking that a sign be given to me about Mai Tai's passing. Within thirty seconds, over 1,000 brown sparrows flew into the yard. They were everywhere! Mai Tai looked up as if he had called them for me and it was part of his plan. He would watch them in such peace—breathing long and deeply with great content. I would sit under the tree in amazement that day as I watched the sparrows and burned a small fire in my chiminea to honor him and help release his soul. I sat clearing his chakras (small energy centers on the body accessed in the Illumination healing process) as I had been taught in class. I suddenly felt that all this was part of a plan, and a kind of peace came over me that day. I know Mai Tai felt it too.

The garden grew silent and still, and I could more easily accept his passing. He had lived ten years. I was okay with not taking him into a vet's office. I promised him we would do this calmly at home. I never actually knew what was ending his time (physically), but spiritually and emotionally, I knew it was time. He hated going to the vet, and I knew how hard it had been when near the end of her life, I had left Tia there for four days on IV fluids and how delirious she was when I saw her again. She even had "crate nose" because she had been trying for several days to get out. She had never been locked up in her life, so I felt a kind of guilt that she had spent some of her last days in a cage in a vet's office. This time with Mai Tai, I would hand things over to a Higher Source, and doing so made it just so peaceful...not easy, but peaceful.

A few days passed and Mai Tai was still with me. I was now officially playing the role of a massage therapist in our one office; sometimes when you own a business, you have to play roles you didn't initially intend to play. I would have to go to the office to do just one massage that day, and there was no doubt in my mind that this would be the day Mai Tai would pass. I was very close to canceling the session, but something told me I should honor the session since Mai Tai might prefer to pass when I was not with him. I fought back tears and rushed in to do the massage. Then I rushed home, all the while wondering why this massage had been put in the middle of his dying process. I may never fully understand. When I got home, I rushed into the house and looked everywhere inside for Mai Tai without finding him. I knew he might like to pass in the yard as Tia had done, so I looked there next. I found him trying to get into the house via his doggie door, but he had passed out just before he made it in. I saw that he was still breathing and had waited for me. I scooped him up and put him on his favorite doggie bed. I would then learn the most powerful lessons from him.

THE CHAKRAS & DEATH

In class, I had been taught to watch the chakras during the time of passing. If they were spinning correctly, they would be going clockwise. (Reference Alberto Villoldo's book *Shaman, Healer, Sage* for more details on this process.) I started to use my pendulum, as taught in class, to monitor Mai Tai's chakras. There are generally seven chakras in the body used in the healing process. Chakras are little spinning funnels of energies that can be manipulated for healing the energetic body. They are also a large part of the yogic principles and practices. There are so many theories about chakras I could write a book on the subject alone. But basically, here is a high-level view of the location of the chakras:

1. At the base of the spine (root)
2. At the navel point
3. Between the navel and the heart
4. At the heart
5. At the throat
6. Between the eyes (third eye)
7. At the top of the head

I checked Mai Tai's first chakra, which is associated with being on the earth, grounded, and connected. It was spinning clockwise. As I worked up through all the others, I could see that they were releasing and starting to spin counterclockwise, which was associated with death (or severe trauma). The only other chakra spinning clockwise was his third eye, which is the place of intuition; this meant the likelihood of his having a "white light" experience (a connection to spirit) was very real. I knew then that he was going to leave his body and was likely to have a connected experience with the angels. I grew very emotional trying to see what he was seeing as I kept praying that he would go peacefully. I kept unwinding and cleaning out and clearing his chakras that were already moving backwards; I figured if I kept them clean, it would somehow ease his passing. Then I began to see he had a bit of discomfort, so I raised my voice to what I now referred to as God and yelled out, "Don't you make him suffer! Let him go!"

At that very moment, I realized I was the one who needed to let him go. I not only knew that I was holding him back, but I somehow knew I could take myself over to the other side and call him into the light. I don't know how I knew it; my intuition just kicked in and I was never the same again. I just imagined what it might look like in the light, and suddenly, I was there! I called his name in my mind and I saw his physical body respond. I knew he could hear me without having to speak. I called him as I always did and said, "Good boy, good boy; come here, good boy!" I watched his physical body perk up and his

tail wag, and in one big deep breath, he came running to me in the light of what might be referred to as heaven, wagging his tail in trust and love. I felt an overwhelming kind of love consume me like I had never felt before. I immediately checked his physical body and saw that his root chakra was now beginning to spin backwards, and his third eye was still moving strongly. I knew he was being taken in by the angels and into the white light where I had just been. It was beautiful!

And then he just passed! Of course, after all of the excitement was over, I just fell onto him and cried and cried. My best friend, my solid for ten years, was gone! After ten years of constant familiarity, I reached down, pulled him into my arms, and just held and rocked him and cried. We had such a great long life together, but one thing I quickly realized right then and there was that I had spent so much time gone and at work and not with him. What I wouldn't have given to have had that time back to do it differently. And guess where my husband was? Again, he was at work. But for me, priorities began to change.

Within just a few months of this experience, I would suddenly quit being woke by one of our two little kittens. Previously every morning, she would be lying on my heart and licking my chin. But this day, she was not there, and then the next day, again not there. I knew something was wrong. She was found a few days later lying in the grass from an accident with my husband's two big outdoor Akita dogs. My husband told me he had buried her and just as quickly as she entered my life she was gone.

And if all of this wasn't enough, Sangria, my long-haired black Shar Pei, would also now become ill. Death just kept knocking on my door. As I mourned the loss of now three, I prepared to lose the fourth. Suddenly, life became exhausting and slow and I was absolutely drained. I wondered what was going on and why this was continuing to happen. Shortly after I rescued

her, Sangria had jumped out of a car and done major damage to her front leg. She had a permanent brace on as an effort to keep her leg, but it wasn't set properly and caused her much discomfort and pain. I couldn't talk my husband into taking her to a specialist; instead, a handful of times, he gave her a chiropractic adjustment and told me he wasn't going to pay for a specialist because vets just wanted to rip us off.

Meanwhile, Sangria, Sushi, and I had made a commitment to Tia that we would all walk in the park more, and when Mai Tai passed, we honored that with even more intent. One warm sunny, snowy winter day, we drove to our trail and went for quite a long (almost timeless) walk. As we approached the back side of the park where none of us had ever been before, we came across the most beautiful big Douglas Fir. Beneath it was a cleared out bed made of pine needles. I was exhausted, so I just fell under there and Sangria came and lay sandwiched right next to me to keep me warm. I just cried. Sushi ran in circles with a big smile on her face, which lightened my mood. I sat under that tree and watched the needles fall in the sun and the glistening snow crystals all around me. I took in the intoxicating fragrance as I prayed that Sangria would find a healer and I wouldn't lose another.

After some time, we got up and continued our walk. I would wonder why we were working so hard at our careers, and yet Sangria wasn't getting the care I felt she deserved. What was the point of all the hard work when those you loved were suffering? It wasn't like we didn't have the money; my husband just didn't believe in the value of most veterinarians' care, and he thought they overcharged for their services. I was exhausted and my heart hurt so badly I couldn't seem to make my own decisions. I just prayed. Hope was all I had left.

The dogs and I walked just a few feet on an uncharted trail before we turned a corner. Then I saw someone walking to-

ward us in the sunlight. I had been crying and praying, so I didn't pay much attention at first. She just appeared standing in front of us—Celeste…an animal healer. She asked me what was wrong with Sangria's leg and whether she could send her healing. I nearly started to cry, but I held it in and just said, "Of course." As quickly as Celeste appeared, she disappeared into the distance as we walked on. I was beginning to learn the power of prayer and the idea of manifestation. I like to think she extended Sangria's life just a bit longer.

That day, I had the idea that I wanted to get a Shar Pei puppy who would meet Sangria before she died. I wanted her to teach the puppy all the things I liked and didn't like before she left. I would start the research that day and begin to put a bug in my husband's ear.

LIFE SHIFTING

Many things were beginning to shift in my life. As I completed the last two shaman classes, I decided to sign up for a nine-month yoga certification program. I also sought out additional places to learn my shamanic work. I would involve myself in both Alberto Villoldo and Michael Harner's classes, but I never really found the right fit. I did have some fascinating experiences, though, before they ended.

In Massachusetts, I would arrive early for one of my first of Alberto's classes and decide to go for a walk outside. I had just been talking to my friend Jo that I met in the earlier shaman classes back in Michigan. Before I left, I told her about a dream I had about a bear chewing off my pinky finger and I wondered what it meant and whether there was something that could be inferred by it. At Mai Tai's death, I was learning about totem animals and was following up on how to work with them. I had a hard time seeing them or working with them in the beginning of my classes because the process seemed so odd to me. Yet I

had always loved animals. As I tried to interpret my dream, all I could think was that I had done something that caused my spirit bear to disrespect me or she was trying to get my attention in some way. It took me a ton of work to find her, and my teachers even had to do special ceremonies for me since they said we couldn't progress in the training without knowing our totem animal or spirit guide. Everyone in class had successfully found his or her spirit guide, but I was completely unable to let my mind go there. I thought I was hopeless and I'd never be a good shaman.

As I was walking, Jo called me and I talked to her as I walked. At the same time, I kept turning around because I heard footsteps behind me, but when I looked, nothing was ever there. Finally, I told Jo I was hearing footsteps crunching in the leaves directly behind me. I wondered whether it was a physical thing, or I was being paranoid, or it was something beyond my understanding. Finally, I turned around one more time, and there, four feet away, was a big black bear! My first reaction was not fear, but admiration for how beautiful it was. I saw the shine on its coat, the glistening in its eyes, and the shine of its teeth and tongue. I was not afraid at all. I said to Jo very calmly, "What do you do if you are face-to-face with a bear?" She gasped and said, "Ah…don't run?" Running wasn't even a thought in my mind. I was in awe of its beauty. And it was intrigued with me. We just looked at each other for a bit, and then a car approached and scared it up the hill.

The experience was odd. I don't think the man driving the car saw the bear, but he stopped to ask whether I needed a ride and I wasn't sure why. I told him, "No, I'm just out for a walk." After he left and I told Jo what had happened, she said she was glad nothing had happened to me since she couldn't do much from her living room in Indiana. We joked about what would have been more dangerous—the bear or a ride with a stranger?

I walked back to the building where class was going to be taught and decided to walk the trails near the building. I soon realized they didn't go far, so I sat down on the bench. Within a few minutes, I felt a magical kind of presence in the woods behind me. I swear I heard giggling. I looked around, saw nothing, and shrugged my shoulders, thinking I was making it up. I just sat there then, looking about and wondering about life when something suddenly flew into my face. It hit my nose and my cheekbone just below my eye. It felt like feathers, so I looked around, expecting to see a fallen bird, but nothing was there. I wondered whether my mind was getting the best of me, but I swear I heard another giggle and felt a presence behind me. I just smiled, knowing what it was but finding it hard to believe I was admitting it to myself—I believed I'd just had my first encounter with a fairy. I figured this event was something I might always have to keep to myself, so I just laughed, shrugged my shoulders, and went inside to prepare for class.

AN ANGEL'S GRACE

Once I reached the classroom, I was alarmed by the number of students present. It was a much larger group than I was used to. When it came time to find a partner to work with, I was overwhelmed. I also felt frustrated because I had paid money for the class, come all this way, and yet, I had already experienced these same teachings in Michigan. I finally approached the dean of the school, who told me if I went back and worked with another person and got nothing, I should come see her.

I partnered with someone one more time. He was a very sweet young man. He was there with his girlfriend, although she wasn't in the class. I saw everything so very clearly as I worked with him, and I told him everything I saw very quickly since all I wanted to do was talk with the teacher and get my money back. But the young man was in awe of my ability because I so quickly saw him. He asked me all kinds of ques-

tions about how I did it. I told him I didn't know really, but that I had been doing it for several months. He told me he had been doing it for quite some time as well. I could see his soul and all his wounds. I realized that when I became focused on something else and wasn't trying as hard, his wounds became transparent.

Our goal for the exercise was to discover the partner's soul wound that was ready to heal by moving into an altered state of consciousness, which was enhanced by the shaking of a rattle and drum and guided "tour" by the instructor. Generally it was taught the wound would appear through a series of events we were instructed to walk through. I never really used the guidance once I first learned it. I just jumped ahead on my own. It was as if the training wheels had come off and all of a sudden I could just see inconsistent energies within his energy body. I told him I could see a discrepancy between his schooling and his desired profession and he was quite bothered by it, among other things. He explained that his dad was very upset he didn't have higher aspirations for his career. It was causing much trauma in his being. He was shocked I could see this, but it seemed so elementary to me.

Then it was his turn to work with me. He told me he was confused and felt shy about telling me what he saw. He acted shocked as he told me he had never before seen so much light when working on someone, and he said he was in awe. I was actually shocked to hear that; I had expected just to hear some useless story from him. Then he asked, "Are you a…are you a…I know this will sound strange, but…are you…an angel?" I told him how I had been beginning to see so much light around me leading up to this event and I had wondered why, so maybe that explained what he saw. The funny thing was that I wanted wounds to appear to be healed. I wasn't ready to be told I might be an angel. I certainly didn't feel like one.

He and I finished earlier than the rest of the group and said goodbye. He didn't know how to take me, and I honestly didn't care. I knew I was different, and I was beginning to accept that I was now opening up to things very few people seem to know or experience.

During the break, I approached the teacher. I told her we were supposed to be finding wounds, but no one could find any on me. I had come to heal my wounds. I was actually upset that I had none! She laughed and said, "Wait a minute; let me look…." She closed her eyes and looked as if she might be peering into my soul or scanning my energetic blueprint. Then she told me she also saw none. She could see I was frustrated. Next, she told me she could see my soul from the beginning of time to the end of time, and I was a wise old soul who had walked this earth many times. She would tell me I was a bright light. I felt honored and realized I had needed this conversation. I started to see that when doing this work, it isn't really all about finding the bad in someone, and "bad" is just a matter of interpretation anyhow. I would gain great lessons from this understanding as the class ended for the day. I didn't go back for the rest of that class because I realized I would have to learn on my own now. I could see that my training wheels needed to come off and that was my expensive lesson for this trip. But I still had one more class in Michigan and I had already signed up for a shamanic class near Toronto with Michael Harner's program.

When I traveled for this class, I spent several hours driving and arrived later than expected. I reached my hotel, but despite all my phone calls and knocks on the door, I received no response and actually had to spend the night in my car. That entire night, I would wonder why I had created this experience. I hadn't always felt drawn to this program, but I wanted to know everything about shamanism in hopes of finding my Tia and learning more about what Mai Tai had tried to teach me with his

passing. And this class was a prerequisite to the class I really wanted to take on learning to talk with nature spirits.

I finally got into the front office just a few minutes before class started the next morning. The hotel staff quickly let me into my room, so I showered and headed to class late, only to realize I had no idea where I was going. I went into the office to ask whether anyone had left me an address or directions to get there as I had been told they would. There were none. I decided I would go for a drive and try to find the building where it might be hosted. I expected it to be in a large building. As I drove around, I became quite frustrated. I hadn't slept and I had no directions. The last thing I wanted to do was turn around and drive all the way back home again.

I'd finally had enough. I pulled into a driveway to turn around so I could go back to the hotel to sleep and figure out what to do later. Just as I was turning, I looked up and saw the mailbox... on it was the name of the woman arranging the training, so I realized it must be taught in her home. I pulled in, and sure enough, it was where I was supposed to be.

I didn't really seem to connect with the class, but it was a great experience to see another form and practice of shamanism. I think what I learned from the experience more than anything was that even when you don't think you are where you are supposed to be, you are exactly where you need to be!

Ask yourself: When in your life were you exactly where you needed to be even though you didn't think you were supposed to be there? Where did you meet your partner? Have you ever been in an accident with someone, only to find out that person would play a significant role in your life? Have you ever been stuck in a traffic jam or missed a flight, only to find that it saved you from an accident or a bad layover? Have you ever broken off a relationship with someone or had someone end one with

you only to find someone better? Did it all turn out for the best in the end, so that you were exactly where you needed to be?

This class would be the first of many times when I would confirm that I was always where I needed to be. We are never lost and nothing ever needs to be found.

A BIT OVERWHELMED

I would begin to go to yoga class once a week now to keep myself grounded with my shamanic work since it seemed to be making me very "floaty." The day I first walked into Valerie's class at Red Lotus Yoga Center and saw her in her beautiful white clothing and turban, I felt a bit out of my element. But with all the exhaustion I felt from all the deaths I'd experienced and all my recent traveling, I honestly didn't care. The hardest step was walking in the door and I had done that. It was the first time in my life when I just didn't care. I was working hard on myself, and I knew I was taking this class for me and I was there for all the right reasons, so I really began to love it.

I first took these Kundalini yoga classes to assist me in my shamanic work. I knew if I could find ways to connect to yoga, it would enhance my shamanic visions, which might help me find and talk to Tia. I found yoga helped my visual experiences in my own healings, as well as helped my shamanic clientele, which was now growing. I also discovered that I no longer needed all the chiropractic treatments for my bad back and neck. And I stopped getting so many massages for achy muscles. My body was feeling better. My mind was more at ease.

SELF EDUCATION

The massage work I was doing was now jumpstarting all of my visual and healing work. For a while, I felt as if I were in boot camp because when I first lay my hands on a client, I could see

everything instantaneously that was a disruption in the person's energetic body—causing limitations in his or her physical, emotional, and spiritual bodies. I was taking shamanic classes, yoga classes (which then turned into an entire nine-month certification program), master's classes in transpersonal psychology, doing massage, and running the offices. I wasn't really sure anymore how I was going to find Tia in all this self-discovery, but I plugged along.

My interest in all things metaphysical was piqued, and I couldn't learn or read enough. My book collection was growing like never before; previously, I had only read a handful of books for enjoyment over the course of my life, outside of books for formal education; now I had stacks and stacks of books beside my bed, next to my new altar in my meditation room, and in my car in case I was stuck in traffic. I began to read every shamanic healing book I could get my hands on, but somehow, I never remained focused enough to finish many of them. I suppose this might be called the "enlightenment phase" of my life.

What I was learning in school was boring and no longer interested me. I didn't just want to study things; I wanted to use the learning to make a difference in my life and other people's lives. My husband started to get frustrated with all the books next to the bed. Each morning he used to kiss me goodbye, but now, after tripping over the books, he decided it was too risky. (That was the excuse I made for him anyway.)

I did, however, finish my shamanic classes with a few fascinating observations and lessons. I noticed that as I did my yoga alongside my shamanic practice, I was really opening up psychically. I tried so hard for many months to connect to the many things I was told we could do in the shamanic work, but I just couldn't seem to understand how to see psychically. Now everything was about to change. My psychic vision just started opening up. We were told we had to do all these "journeys"

(guided meditations) to find certain things for our healing or the healing of others. We were told we would need spirit guides or gifts to make these healings happen. I felt most of the time I was making these things up as I moved through the guiding, and I just didn't resonate with these aspects of shamanism. But the moment I realized it doesn't always have to go the way it was taught, I really began to blossom.

THE NORTH CLASS

In the North class, we would learn to embark on self-empowerment and the importance of approaching each moment like it was the first. We would be taught to lose expectations and agendas; to clear the clutter from our lives, our minds, our bodies, and eventually our souls; to breathe life into our relationships; and to be translucent, but with nothing to hide. We would learn to be useful, valuable, and sweet, but to stop projections and to be open to possibilities, hope, and desire. We would be told to keep achieving what we were called to do. I would receive messages in my work that when I remained calm and I cleared the clutter out of my life, I would become aware of whom and what I would become. I would open spiritually and visually in one guided meditation. During one class visual experience, I was handed a ball of light. I was told the ball represented an idea or thought. Later, I would learn it was a gift from my ancestral parents. I had never just been given an intangible, I thought, but I had no proof that anything else really existed either. I was excited to see what this gift would evolve into later, but I also realized I would likely never know.

THE EAST CLASS

The East class would take me further along my path, teaching me to let go of my teachers and to become the teachings; this process would free me from the need to be perfect (making me more self-referencing). We would also learn to feed ourselves in

healthy ways (energetically, emotionally, physically). We would gain an understanding that we are our own artists, creating our own souls to embrace our destinies. The lessons would teach us to step beyond fear and ego and become a sacred space, rather than holding one. We were taught that at this stage we should be able to soar like an eagle and to facilitate change to dream the world into being. (But I may not have quite been there yet.) We would also learn the shaman is many times the seer and not the doer. Rather than calling on our lineage, we would become it.

We would be told that God is not external; God doesn't work through us, but as us—we are God! This same lesson would later be taught to me in my yoga training, and it was something that always seemed to come up as an issue with many around me (particularly those who practiced Christianity, for reasons I cannot always understand). I spent some time trying to understand this concept at various stages because I wanted to learn. Most of the argument I heard was that Jesus was the Son of God (so we were not sons and daughters of God), and that God was separate or outside—someone we prayed to outside of us. I personally don't think Jesus was trying to teach us that message. I think Jesus wanted us to study what he was studying and not idealize him, but I likely don't know enough to discuss it further. I didn't really care what was right or wrong for others because the way I looked at it was: Well, what if that were true? I might as well at least be open-minded to it, and then I can decide.

Yoga opened me up to understanding that we are to become the teachings as well. Both traditions seemed to be telling me that the message was to follow the teachings and either become them or become a teacher to master the teachings. I believe Jesus may have been a son of God and master teacher, and he wanted us to learn what he was learning—not to follow him, but to follow the teachings. When you are unable to find

enlightenment yourself, maybe you don't believe it can come through you, so you rely on others to help you find your way. And that's okay too, but it sure is fun when you can find it yourself! It becomes a bit more pliable and personal when you can get there using the teachings rather than the teacher. I have also been taught in both teachings not to put your teachers on a pedestal; they are human and learning just like the rest of us. If any of us had perfected the human experience, we wouldn't be here having it!

We would be taught in the East class to check ourselves and our strategies and to deconstruct what we perceived as real to take it to the mythic (spirit) level. Just about any issue or subject you move into this level of awareness will surely not be as it seems, and quite honestly, it can spin you in multiple circles from which you never find your way out. Try it with any subject—take it as big as you can go and then combust it! What you will find is that you end up back where you started, but you will also find that it's all from the same source anyway. You may find it is more useful just to dream the world into being and focus on the light rather than argue about what is "correct."

We would also be taught that where there is reluctance, we need to study what's not working and to discover what it would take to transcend or shift it. Where does this reluctance exist in the literal mind? When we become aware of the shadow side of ourselves, we can shift it so it no longer blocks the transformation process since fear can talk us out of everything. We would be taught that healers work with the known, shaman work with the knowable, and sages work with the unknown. And, finally, we would be told to surrender to our becoming. This message would nearly haunt me later as I tried to understand what my becoming was. I learned that surrendering is very challenging, but sometimes it's the most logical option.

EXERCISES:

1. Where is your reluctance? ______

2. What would it take to shift that reluctance? ______

3. How do aspects of your shadow self interfere and cause fear in your life? ______

4. What does your becoming look like? ______

FIRE CEREMONY

At certain points during our training, we were required to do fire ceremonies. One particular ceremony I performed (actually improvising over my gas fireplace on the lower level one cold winter) would become a very powerful moment. I was feeling sad and sorry for myself; I wanted Tia and Mai Tai with me to see the new person I was becoming, and for the first time in my life, I was authentically proud of that person, but I was very sad because no one wanted to share in the new me, and those who might have were gone. I wanted so badly for my husband to come downstairs and ask me what I was doing and how to do it. I wanted him to see what I was now opening to, and I wanted to help him transform any pain he had in his life. Instead, he remained upstairs as I rattled my rattle and sang my song very quietly so I didn't scare or disturb him. He was doing his normal Sunday routine of reading and marking his chiropractic X-rays. I just cried my eyes out and sang and rattled. Once my guard was down, I deeply connected to spirit. Suddenly, I felt a tap on my leg. I opened my teary eyes, but nothing was there. I figured it must have been a muscle twitch since I was used to getting those because of all the yoga I was doing. Again, I felt it and nothing was there. I continued to connect to the ceremony and the moment. When I was done, I took a picture of the room. I wanted to know whether anyone from the spirit world was present. I saw the most amazing orbs in one of my pictures. I began to study it closer.

ORBS AND THE UNKNOWN

I knew that orbs (usually seen as white balls or globes of light that look a bit like sunspots in pictures) were drawn to ceremonies and celebrations, and I knew they were starting to show up in people's pictures in class. Somewhere in my training, I had learned that my vision was not like everyone else's; the way I "saw" was through claircognizance (clear knowing), as

opposed to clairvoyance (a kind of seeing). Yes, I could see the orbs, but I also had a knowing. I've known things most of my life that most don't in this lifetime. During a fire ceremony I was doing at home I knew at that very moment that the spirit of my husband's father, Joe, was present. I could see a very clear face inside the orb...actually two faces. I tried to include this in the center insert, but the reprinted image didn't come through clearly. I would be visited regularly by Joe for several months and even started smelling his cologne. I asked my husband what cologne Joe had worn and bought a small sample of it just to be sure it was him. It most certainly was. I learned that seeing psychically comes in many forms—clairalience (smelling), clairsentience (feeling / touching), clairaudience (hearing / listening), clairgustance (tasting). I was beginning to learn that when I talked about my experiences with others, the first thing they would ask was, "What did it look like?" But I usually couldn't see anything. I just knew something. And I knew they were more than just balls of light.

Orbs started showing up in many of my pictures and I have included a few of them in the center insert. My understanding of orbs would grow deeper over time and I would learn there are many types. I believe what cameras catch is a spiritual presence that is always amongst us but is just now starting to be seen with newer, more powerful advanced photography cameras. These orbs are our lineage, our grandmothers and grandfathers, and I believe they can even be thought-forms or elementals, such as nature spirits or angels or other ascended masters. They can also be a collective consciousness of many beings. I believe this is much like multiple personalities within humans—some are more outwardly expressed than others. If you've ever met people who connect to and channel the voice of spirit you will also see they tend not just to connect to one being, but multiple beings. Orbs (or spiritual beings) are generally drawn to spiritual celebrations and weddings. I've included a photo of one time when I was out walking in nature, which

I did to connect with nature often after Tia died. I was told by my teachers that the size of the orb present that day meant I was very well-received. Nature really tries to help us and heal us and loves us so deeply. I wish humans would really learn to love and respect nature more fully. I encourage you to go out and be with nature; send love to the earth and ask for guidance and healing in return. Never take anything without giving something.

On another occasion during my training, we would do drumming circles in class or when there was a full moon. I enjoyed going to these events just as an excuse to see my new "weird" friends who were like my spiritual family now. They understood me better than anyone ever had, and many of them didn't pass judgment on my wounds or my other idiosyncrasies. This particular day when we gathered was not any different than any other and the same folks were there as usual. A request for a healing for Peru was made—an earthquake had occurred there the week prior. I never really seemed to connect to these drumming circles, but I certainly did this day. My friend Jo was drumming on the same large drum covered in glass that had been in the room the day I first met the shaman healer. Others were dancing around and playing musical instruments. The shaman healer handed me a rattle and asked whether I'd like to try it. She told me little about it, but as I took it from her hands, I studied it since I couldn't understand why she had handed it to me to begin with; I had a fine rattle already. It was some kind of horn that had been cut off and sealed on both ends. It was off-white with some faded black coloring in the center. The handle was wood. It appeared as if it were Native American in nature. It was a very solid instrument and well-constructed, but I paid no further attention to it as I began to rattle and dance around.

We were given no instructions for how to perform the healing on the land, so I mostly just danced around in a circle.

Each time I got to Jo, we caught each other's eyes and just giggled, beat, and rattled a bit louder. She was singing in her most amazing voice and nothing felt out of the ordinary. As the dancers started to slow down, the music began to slow as well. You can feel a certain kind of energy when the circle is about to close—a sense of completion and peace. But this time, I suddenly connected very, very deeply to something that visually appeared in my mind's eye like a heavy black energy over a solid structure. I assumed I was seeing the land of Peru. The black thick energy, almost like a volcanic smoke, was lifting up and away from the land. And then all of a sudden, it flew up and away and the music just stopped. I looked around and wondered whether anyone else had experienced it. It didn't appear as if anyone else had.

We started to gather our hands for the healing circle and song that was our way of saying, "Until we meet again." As I went to take the hand of the shaman healer, who was beside me, she noticed my hand was covered in black ash. Of course, I questioned the rattle; I inspected it in great detail. There was absolutely no possible way that rattle could have produced ash from the contents in it. There was no hole. I stood there for a moment before I asked the shaman healer what it was—even though it was obviously black ash. When I asked her how it got on my hand, she just smiled. I asked her, "What do I do with it?" She replied, "What are you called to do?" My first reaction was to rub it into my skin, but the shaman healer asked whether I was sure I wanted to do that; I might like to study it a bit more. I just wiped it into my arm and went on to hold hands and closed our circle.

At this point in my training, nothing really surprised me, and something in me knew this experience was a gift, but I also knew this was nothing new to me (even though it had never happened before). I remember thinking, "This must be normal." I wanted to know more about it, but I didn't want to stand

out or distract the group. This experience was something that would always stand out as a highlight in my work, but at the same time, fascinating as it was...it just was. After Mai Tai and Tia's deaths, all I could think was that many things happen I don't understand; I didn't understand their deaths any more than I understood this experience. I was blessed to have experienced it, and it never happened again. The shaman healer would tell me after class that she knew I was "a great earth healer." I was honored to know this, but this "just was" as well.

GOING DEEPER

That night when I got home, my husband asked me how the event went. I told him about the bizarre thing that had happened. He asked whether the ash was still there and whether he could see it. I told him it wasn't. I'm not sure how I expected him to respond, but he sort of shrugged his shoulders and said, "Well, that's nice." I felt that unless he had been there with me, there was no way he could understand what had happened. I realized then that I might be taking this journey alone. It saddened me, but I was not going to give up now. I was on a quest to understand what had happened to Tia, and now I was questioning what had just happened with the ash.

I only told a handful of people about this experience from fear I'd be ridiculed or I'd need to find a way to do it again. I backtracked to where I was at physically, spiritually, emotionally, and in my visions when the experience happened. I had been happy in my focus on healing the land. I had seen the heaviness of the land lifting, and just as it lifted, the drumming had ended and the ash had appeared. I hold this time as very sacred, and I'm thankful to have felt I made a difference in some way, yet I wasn't sure exactly what I had done. My husband and I were golfers, so I reasoned this experience was like hitting a hole in one. I had once gotten one and I understood that many pro golfers never did. This was definitely my hole in one.

A series of other events unfolded during the training: pictures taken at fire ceremonies in which orbs appeared, feeling taps on my shoulder when asking whether I had a spirit guide there to help, hearing the roar of jaguars outside the room during ceremonies, and watching my dogs and cats' reactions as I worked with my personal animal totems (they would chase them or sometimes cower in their presence). In one particular class, I was partnered up with my teacher. I was not really prepared for what I would be told about the healing that needed to occur for me. I was told that I had an "alien implant" located just under my eyebrow. I was very frightened by this and nearly shook as he explained it to me after the extraction. I took notice that during the healing, I saw a dark presence float up, out of, and over me, and then leave; it was rare for me to see that kind of visual during a session. Others in class would all talk matter-of-factly about how they'd also had one and had it removed. When I asked whether they had known that they had one, they explained that they knew they were being observed at night and / or had profuse shaking and convulsions prior to or at the time of extraction. I thought I was dreaming and said to myself, "Who are these people?" I tried to reason out what I was a part of and whether my involvement was the right choice. I had a few sleepless nights following this event. It would be months before I became settled and at peace with this occurrence, and several more before it started to make sense to me.

PRAYER

After months of racking my brain, I would come to understand that spirit does not judge or complicate—we do! Spirit also has no attachment, so we must be specific about what we are asking for or want to know. And I realized some inner personal asking must have happened for these events to have occurred. I started praying a lot. But I always seemed to pray as I was taught—outside myself...to something greater than me. Prayer contains energy that heals, and it creates a sacred space. I've

learned that when we release something, it must be replaced by something. For example, when we can release pain and replace it with love, we can step more gracefully into our becoming. I learned many amazing life lessons in these classes, but I also look at them as a bicycle waiting for the training wheels to be removed as I charge ahead beyond the training and lessons I was taught. I can see they are great lessons to revisit at any stage in life though.

By the time the classes were coming to an end, I had made some great friends. I honored and cherished my teachers for sharing some of the most life-changing information I had ever been privy to, and even though they told us not to put them on pedestals…I kinda did. I loved them deeply for helping me understand myself in ways I never could have dreamt. I still had many questions. Unfortunately, I suppose all good things must come to an end. Since then, they have moved on and no longer teach classes and I have only seen them once since. I was told they were unhappy with something I unknowingly did and it hurt me greatly, but I took that as part of the teaching as well. It was time to release my teachers, regardless of any misunderstandings. I will always feel great love toward them, but it's not likely we are meant to go through the next phases together. I was to be self-sourcing now.

Shamanism, for me, would play a very huge and integral role in transforming my life. I am thankful for all of the experiences. I will forever remember all who were involved in my classes and who helped me transform into a more whole person. I believe many of us are blessed to find something that helps us transform and develop a greater sense of self. For me, there would be a fire lit within me to continue seeking a greater understanding for my soul's purpose. This would not be the end of my journey, but simply the end of a formalized training, and the beginning of self-sourcing. I was still full of questions since I now knew that nothing is as it seems.

HELPING YOU DISCOVER YOUR TRUTH

Whatever your faith is—Christianity, Judaism, Islam, Buddhism, Hinduism, Sikhism, etc.—my goal is NOT to urge you to convert to another or to leave your existing realm of beliefs. My goal is simply to communicate that a deep spiritual world does exist, and a few (myself included) may never fully understand it. I started a spiritual path. You too may be at a crossroads on your journey. Just know that not all things make sense. Know it is perfectly normal to question, consider, seek, and explore for your inner truth. What you discover may surprise you, shock you, alarm you, or frighten you. And that is okay. Just know that you are not alone; many of us are out there also seeking for truth and understanding. We may never fully understand. Just have the experience; sometimes just the experience becomes your answer.

SEEK. TRUST. BELIEVE. LOVE.

CHAPTER 4

GOING IN *Different Directions*

"A dog is the only thing on earth that loves you more than he loves himself."
— Josh Billings

This was not the life I had envisioned living. And I kept hearing this voice in my head saying, "It's now time to step into your becoming!" But I had no idea what that meant. I had just spent all this time in my classes breaking down the barriers that kept me from love. I realized I had no idea what love looked like until Tia and Mai Tai's deaths had led me to removing my energetic blockages. Now I wanted a deeper connection with someone who also wanted one. What was familiar to me had just died, and I was left with a stranger. I had no idea who the man was whom I had married. I never saw him either. I was struggling with the concept of divorce. I was now a "spiritual person," and divorce wasn't something a spiritual person did! I was learning how to love differently, communicate differently, and everything was becoming more connected and meaningful...except my marriage. The therapists we had frequented for some time now suggested we spend time rekindling our relationship, but we began to discuss that neither of us knew what there was to rekindle. We were more like business partners than anything.

BIG CHANGES AHEAD

My husband would leave the house at 5 or 6 a.m. and come home around 6 or 7 p.m. He was a chiropractor, and he had an hour-long drive to his office in a small community in the "thumb" in northeast Michigan. He was a Canadian citizen who had been raised just across the border in Sarnia, Ontario. Up to this point, he had played a very important role in my life. He had pulled me away from the corporate world and taught me about new ways of living and healing. We would go to chiropractic seminars where I would hear about all kinds of unique alternative forms of healing, and he would enlighten me about chiropractic, massage, ultraviolet, ultrasonic, and natural herbal supplement healing. I was always intrigued with this world, but it wasn't until I married him that I became fully immersed in it. He taught me about business ownership and took me away from the materialist city life to a quieter country setting. He took me from a life of material competition and one-upping the neighbors to treating and caring for them. But somewhere along the way, it all shifted. I stepped away from my corporate job, only to become dedicated to growing not just one office (where he worked as an associate under another doctor's umbrella) but multiple offices with multiple employees.

Together, we developed a system that worked very well, and with my initial cash investment, time, energy, and business acumen, the business grew very quickly. Eventually, we bought out his partnership, he got a green card, we hired two doctors, and we owned three offices. We had over twenty-five employees and many bills to pay. We were extremely busy, and despite my best efforts to return to my career, I was needed to babysit the offices while he treated patients. He was seeing more than thirty patients a day in his primary office and was too busy ever to step foot in the other two offices. On average, we had revenue of about $400K per year in each office and were very successful. We even tried to create a consulting business at one

time, but we were too busy to promote it properly. He would advise the doctoring, I would manage the flow of the office (and pretty much everything else), and we had another employee who would monitor the billing for the insurance companies. As a result, to this day, I could walk into any chiropractic office and immediately tell you what works and what doesn't and how to be successful. But mostly I learned about the human-ness of patients. I heard their stories and watched them suffer in pain. I knew I could help people in ways I never knew before.

JACK OF ALL TRADES

In all this chaos, my husband would suddenly start getting home later and later, and he usually was so exhausted by the time he reached home that he just wanted to crash in front of the TV. We even set up the TV in the kitchen with oversized chairs so we could relax and eat while we watched programs. If we were lucky, he would get home by 7 p.m. and we would have three or four hours to catch up before bed. Most nights when he got home, I was already in my pajamas, my makeup scrubbed off, and ready to relax. There was nothing romantic about any of it, but we were both inspired to continue building and growing our offices.

After we built all three offices, we decided to do something unheard of and offer super-cheap, high quality massages in all of our offices. I built, remodeled, and decorated spa-like settings in the offices, and we offered full body one-hour massages for only $37, among other treatments. Insurance paid for the massages most of the time, and every teacher in a twenty-mile radius came in to see us. (Teachers usually have really great insurance, and if they like you, they tell others.) So, immediately, we were completely full. But being busy required more employees and more babysitting. We had a doctor with an attitude, and during a very busy time, he let go of our busiest massage therapist. I was the likely candidate to take on this

role in one of our offices, so I finally decided I would never put on a suit or high heels again and go back to the corporate rat race. I was doing very well financially, and the more I worked, the less I thought of Mai Tai and Tia.

Somewhere in all of it, however, I also forgot about my husband and he about me. I think he was turned off by the fact that I had now resigned my corporate job and was wearing scrubs because he loved to brag about the six-figure income I had once made. I was very happy to have left my career behind after I had tried a few times to go back. I wasn't a fit for the corporate world, and I wanted more freedom with my entrepreneurial spirit. The days would turn into nights and continue on at after-work parties. In advertising, it was all about who you know and what brand you were using. It was always stressful. I "borrowed" countless dresses from name brand department stores (wearing and returning) regularly in order to fit into that materialistic world. I was never a fit for it! In fact, on numerous occasions, I would find myself hiding in either my car or a bathroom stall crying—usually because I couldn't lie and I couldn't play games. I put in long hours and tried as hard as I could, with little to no respect. I'd stay and work late hours and work beyond the cleaning crews and sometimes be looked down on if I rolled in late the next morning because of it.

Just like I didn't fit into the corporate world, I didn't fit the stereotypical role of the doctor's wife. Instead, I was very hands-on in our practices and thankful for everything I learned in our offices. In fact, I became well-known in Michigan (by other chiropractic offices and the X-ray companies) for being "the doctor's wife who remodels offices." Because of my career income and home equity, I was able to be an initial investor. Because of my talent and education, I was a primary player in the creation of these offices. I did all the payroll and books as well. From 2003-2008, we were on fire with these offices. In five short years, we took them from conception to full-out birth and I began to love

it. Sure we had some hurdles; my husband was so busy in his office, one doctor was up and running in our newest clinic, and the office I worked in needed all kinds of babysitting.

Tia would die in 2006, and from 2006 until 2008, I remained involved in the office, but I now realized I needed to shift my ways. I had been (or maybe Tia had been) grooming myself for this change all along without really even knowing it. I was surrounded by healers and receiving regular weekly massages and chiropractic adjustments myself. Staff needed to be trained (and babysat on occasion) and patients needed the TLC that sometimes the doctor and other staff were not giving. I did everything I could to backfill where they fell short. I made chocolate chip cookies on occasion and left a fresh fruit basket in the waiting room. I figured if the staff fell short of the patients' expectations, they would feel loved as they grabbed a snack on the way out the door.

During those two years, I became a regular figure in one of the offices, which was located in a rural horse community. The office itself was in an old farmhouse with a rock wall basement. The paved parking lot had once been a horse pasture, and within the parking lot was another building that had once been the barn and now housed a natural herb store and computer design company. When the loud gravel trucks went by (they did so on a regular basis), the walls of the old farmhouse would shake and the dirt in the rock walls would fall. The whole staff hated processing X-rays in the creepy darkroom or doing laundry (massage sheets) in the "Michigan basement." Everyone could feel a certain energy about the house, which had a kind of old, dark history; however, it wasn't until I began my shamanic training that I understood what was really there. The more time I spent there, the more I slowly became sensitive to the energies, as I'll explain shortly.

It was a very busy time for me. I hardly saw my family and didn't have any real friends. I had already begun my yoga teacher training and was discovering a kind of light within my soul that I knew was special. The shamanic classes were something I wanted more of, so I continued to search for new teachers. But the yoga seemed to be coming into my life more strongly than I had intended. I had never wanted to be a teacher; I had just hoped yoga would teach me more about moving into transcendental states in my shamanic work. I continued to study my transpersonal psychology program too. My visual experiences also were growing stronger.

One sunny day when I finally had a day off, I was sitting outside on the back deck of our home, reading and studying, when I was suddenly overtaken by a flashing, shiny light in my consciousness. It was alarming, yet comforting at the same time. I would note the day and the time. I would go to bed that evening and again be overcome by the lights. Shortly thereafter, I would receive a call from my mom telling me that Aunt Cheryl's boyfriend (Abe) had passed away. I noted that these lights had kept appearing around the time of his death, and I wondered whether that was a coincidence or the opening or teaching of something, and of course, I wondered why it was happening. What could be the purpose of me knowing the time of death and that angels (or bright lights I believed to be angels) were there? I would table this experience for now, but again…another death. This would be the fifth death in just under two years since Tia's passing.

PUPPY FEVER

In February 2008, I was nervously pacing the floor at the Detroit Metro Airport as I waited to pick up a new addition to our family. I had saved up some money for a trip to Peru, but instead, I had finally talked my husband into getting a puppy. We had spent a few years in marriage counseling and it seemed

like he was willing to make some effort in our relationship. This puppy would be a new start.

Our counseling began with a rocky start—when the first therapist asked my husband about certain things in his childhood, he decided he no longer wanted to go. But, we did try two other therapists before he quit. I was really excited about going every week because I was fully on a self-improvement path by then. We'd bounce around from one therapist to another and finally another. Not much would get resolved and my husband would never go very deep emotionally. Although, it was an opportunity to have a date night in town after our session...though some sessions left us with more tension than others and date night wasn't always a good thing. If nothing else, we were able to get a nice meal those nights.

My husband began to stay out later and not come home from work right away, stopping at the bar to pick up dinner (and a few drinks I wasn't supposed to know about) on the way home. We were bringing home close to $300K per year now, and the offices were up and running and going strong, but at the sacrifice of our marriage. I was now involved in loving practices with school, yoga, and shamanism, and I was becoming jealous of watching others have the most amazing and beautiful relationships. I hoped my husband and I could have the same, but it was becoming more and more apparent that we wouldn't.

That day at the Detroit airport, I could hardly wait for the new puppy's arrival. I was pacing the floor and talking to the woman at the front counter just to make sure I was in the right place and I had the timing correct, and I must have asked her three times whether a puppy was on the flight. She was finally able to confirm for me that the puppy had arrived and would be in the baggage claim area in another thirty minutes. I walked away and just started crying. When I finally saw that little tiny cat-sized container come through on the baggage belt, my first

thought was, "Oh, my goodness, I forgot how small puppies are!" It had been eleven years since I had gotten a puppy.

The puppy was very nervous and had just taken a flight in from North Carolina with a layover stop in between. I couldn't believe she wasn't put on a direct flight, but I was so happy finally to be united with her. The minute I had her in my hands, I nearly shook her out of the crate in anticipation of meeting her. I practically dumped her out, and then I grabbed her up and squeezed her and cried. I would not have known if another human were anywhere in that airport that day! She would stay in my arms the whole way home. When we got home, I wanted her to meet Sangria and learn all the things I told Sangria I wanted her to teach her. And she taught her each one almost instantly as if she knew. The biggest thing was to make sure she never ran away and always stayed by my side. She always obeyed and was within an arm's reach. But the new puppy didn't even feel like a part of my life or our home.

She was very quiet, almost standoffish—not like a typical puppy. She had wise healing eyes and definitely was an old soul. She lay quietly on her bed next to Sushi as if to say, "Now is not my time." She was a Shar Pei, and in my experience knowing the breed, and others who owned them, there is one thing in common we all seem to notice: They aren't really dogs! They are wise old souls...teachers even.

At this point, it seemed as if I were a master of death since I had now lost Tia, Mai Tai, a kitty, my uncle (Abe), and soon Sangria also. This death would be even more graceful than the others. Sangria was obviously failing; my husband noticed this, and before we went to bed one night, he dragged her bed into the bedroom (with her riding on top) and closed the bedroom door. Sangria would ask to come up on our bed just after we pulled her into the bedroom and just before I crawled into bed. She looked at me with the most loving eyes, so I pulled her up

onto the bed. I was about to get in bed and turn off the light when she suddenly had a small heart attack and passed as quickly as I put her up on the end of the bed. I couldn't believe how quickly and easily it happened.

My husband said, "Oh shit! Now what do we do with her?" I said, "What other choice do we have but to bury her?" He actually asked me whether we could put her outside in the cold sleeting rain until he came home from work the next day! "WHAT?" I said. I told him that if he didn't want to help, that was fine, but I was going to go outside and bury her. It was around 10 p.m. and it was cold and dark. Death isn't always convenient; somehow, we can only accept inconvenience with new life.

My husband had finally been home with me for the first time for a death, and he watched her pass so easily. I had done so much shamanic work on her to prepare her for this moment. I told her well in advance that I was going to welcome her passing because I knew how much discomfort her leg gave her. It was always hard for me to accept that I couldn't help her leg and neither could the doctors, but I learned to accept that this was her path and to move out of the way. Watching her pass made me see that death could be simple and easy and I wanted everyone to see it could be that way. I was surprised that my husband didn't comment about how easily Sangria passed, but I realized he had never experienced the other animals' deaths to know any differently. I began to wonder whether my husband was afraid of death so he had simply chosen to avoid their passings; after all, he was not very in touch with his emotions and always kept quite a distance.

The morning after we buried Sangria, I woke in tears, rage, and anger. I was momentarily distracted by the visiting doves that landed on top of the tall thin trees in the front yard. They seemed to be multiplying upon each death. When Tia died,

there was one; another joined it after Mai Tai passed, and now I was watching a third nearby about to join them. At the time, I was so angry that everything that meant anything to me was being taken. I also could see my marriage was failing. I had left my career for our businesses, and I had tried so hard to build our life together, but it all felt wasted and pointless since my husband just didn't seem to care. I felt as if I had given up everything in my life for us and our offices. I was now past my prime reproductive years, so children were not likely to be part of my near future. My husband was also now embarrassed that I was working in the offices. He made a point of telling me he didn't like the "hippy look" I had going on—in my scrubs or scrub alternatives. Not only did I have all these deaths occurring, but my vision was opening, and my marriage was failing.

One Saturday, we were walking into Starbucks before we went into work, and after my husband remarked with distaste about my headband (required to keep hair back during massage work), I noticed a book for sale on the shelf that I picked up. After looking at it for a few seconds, I had tears in my eyes. My husband was embarrassed by my look and now my tears. His comments didn't bother me so much; it was that the book felt so sad and I told him so. When he asked how I knew it was sad, I said, "I don't know." He asked me what it was about and I told him it was about a father and son and their relationship issues; he suggested I must have read the back cover to know that, but he knew I hadn't. He then read it and said I was correct. I couldn't tell him how I knew; I just did.

I was always upstairs in a closed door massage room at our office, and I was the busiest massage therapist in all three of our offices, so I didn't have time to notice what was going on downstairs in the rest of the clinic. I also was still doing the bookwork, so I saw the numbers and knew we were successful, but not as successful as my husband would have liked. One day, he decided he didn't want to keep the doctor, so he

would himself work in the office on his off days of the week. It was not a good move for him, us, or the office. We had strange hours and he was exhausted. He would now only have Saturday afternoon and Sunday off, and he was really too tired to treat patients. The only benefit was that we could schedule our drive in and lunch together so we were able to spend more time with each other. The only problem was it gave us more time to notice how different we were from one another.

One day, we were planning to go to lunch after I finished a massage. Something happened to me that day. Just after I finished my massage, I took notice of a very loud screaming blue jay in the yard. There was just no way you couldn't hear this blue jay. As I finished up with my client and said goodbye, a strange feeling came over me. I suddenly felt this kind of opaque film lift from the space around me. It was suddenly no longer hazy and gray. I kept asking everyone else whether they saw or felt it too. I couldn't understand what it was or why no one else saw or felt it. I was very puzzled by it. I continued to talk about it at lunch with my husband, and finally, I could tell he was getting annoyed, so I stopped and just watched and wondered what I had foreseen. I would go on about my day and go to my weekly yoga class that Thursday night. When I got home, my husband told me my mom had left a message on the answering machine that my grandmother had passed that day around lunchtime. I was shocked, but not about her death; rather, because I had somehow known it. I started to realize that the light I was now regularly seeing was related to deaths that were occurring right then or shortly after. And so now, only two years after Tia's death, I was on death number six. I was near numb at this point.

In yoga training the weekend shortly after my grandmother's passing, I would be honored by my classmates taking a moment to honor my grandmother and another student's father by singing the Akal mantra (a way of releasing the soul at the

time of death), and just at the very time we had finished and I was wiping the tears from my eyes, I saw a blue jay in the yard. I then knew that my grandmother was there with me. I was still moving strongly forward in my shamanic work, with or without teachers, but what I was realizing now was that something happened somewhere to open the flood gates because now the experiences would really expand. I sometimes wondered whether my grandmother was on the other side assisting me with my visions since she had been quite intuitive. Following are just a few stories from the massage room...the place where everything really started to shift.

MASSAGE WITH THE ANGELS

I was working on a regular massage client, who always seemed to be one of my easier massages. She had told me she wore her diabetes monitor because once she had gone into a coma and almost died. She also told me how her Chinese Shar Pei whom she loved so dearly had died around that time, and how when she first woke from her coma, her young son was sitting there. The first words she heard were "Mom, I knew you'd come back because we need you more on this side than they need you on the other side." I had nearly forgotten about this until one of the last times I worked on her something very unique happened.

That day, the music was low and we were both very quiet and relaxed. As the massage was ending, I sat down on the stool as I had always done to finish up on her head, neck, and shoulders. Suddenly, the room got very "fuzzy" in a kind of cloud or white fog. I can't say for sure whether my eyes were closed or open, but I was very, very relaxed. She was, from what I could tell, nearly asleep. All of a sudden, the whole massage table (and me on my stool) seemed to be floating on a cloud. I knew I was still touching and rubbing her, but I couldn't feel my entire body. I knew I was still in the physical, but I was also

in what I like to think was heaven. We floated around and were held in this space with no need to go anywhere and no need to question where we were. I was simply observing. There was this feeling of oneness that came over me as well as this compassionate, loving holding that embraced me. Maybe we were in a womb of some sort since no one else appeared to be there, but I could feel something, many someones actually. Before I knew it, my mind was active and I was asking whether I was supposed to be there and how long I had been there because I was on a schedule and couldn't run long on the massage.

Just as quickly as I was there, I was back. My whole body was shaking in a very light tremble. All I could think was that I had spent a moment in the hands of angels. I finished the massage, and just before I headed out, I whispered to her that the massage was over. I hesitated, but told her, "All I can say is that your angels were very present with you today." Then I left the room and just started to bawl my eyes out! I knew something very special had just happened. I was trying to wash my hands, breathe, and get it together before she came out. I kept thinking and saying to myself, "Something really big just happened in there, but I don't know what to do!" I didn't know how to explain to her that I thought we had just been in heaven. A few minutes later, she came out, and in complete tears—a real mess.

I apologized to her and told her it was not my intention to upset her. She said she knew why her angels were so strong. She explained that she was in the room looking at the calendar and that exactly one year ago to the same day and time, she had come out of her coma. She and I hugged and cried, and I told her I had just known that when I started to open up to my shamanic vision, I would have a great experience with her. And at that moment, I wondered why I had said that since I had never thought much about it beforehand. I began realizing that none of my degrees or my career path up to that point ever

meant anything to me, and that moments like these were a gift. I would be asked by the few I shared the story with what the angels looked like. I said they had no form and you couldn't see them, but you simply knew they were there.

I started noticing that the more yoga I did, the greater my vision became. The more I saw and experienced, the more I would open up. I began to see pain around my clients. I could see a red color, as if a light were being beamed from above. When I would talk to people about the pain or discomfort, they actually didn't seem overly surprised that I knew it was there. Yet I was very uncomfortable with the knowing at first. It seemed to come and go, and I couldn't always rely on it being there, and I wasn't sure why.

MASSAGE MOMENTS

Word of what I had experienced must have gotten out because soon I had the most interesting clients filling our waiting room. It was actually quite comical, too. Our office was in a little farmhouse in a rural area, yet my clients were very diverse in character and location. I would sometimes laugh when I came down to the waiting room because of the diversity I was drawing; then I could truly experience the diversity of my own soul. I knew I was attracting the mirror of who I was. Here are a few of the characters that graced me with their beautiful presence:

There was Epinow, a nearly seven-foot tall African-American man who worked at Detroit Energy. His name meant "big mountain," and he would come in off his Harley, in all black leather and tall boots with aboriginal tattoos that had various meaning, and drape his large body over both ends of my massage table. His dreadlocks would flow off the table and onto the wood floor. He was a very sweet man, and I really enjoyed talking to him, except for the fact that he always felt he wasn't getting a good massage because he wasn't paying a lot for it.

"George from the Junkyard" was going to tell me exactly how I was going to do the massage and all the rules for what did and didn't get touched as he lay down in his peeled back Carheart overalls (never exposing his legs). He acted very tough and asked for a deep tissue massage of just his neck, shoulders, and back. When he realized my strength, he asked me to go lighter (under his tough guy breath, of course).

Then, there was "Gassy Guy," who despite his good upbringing, decided to pass gas each time he came into the room, so I would always enter to that horrible smell. One time I got so fed up that when I came into the room, I sprayed air freshener everywhere and I didn't even care whether he knew why. Otherwise, I had to spend an hour in there smelling it!

There was the "Finger Pointer," who went on about how everything was wrong with everyone else but her for the entire hour; I took notice during these sessions that my finger would start to swell up and was nearly inoperable after I finished. Then I just heard a voice say, "Point it at yourself and it will go away!" As I pointed at myself, I could actually see the swelling disappear. This was absolutely fascinating to me. I began to see where and how I was blaming others, and I learned that when I began to take full responsibility for my life by pointing the finger at myself, I was allowing for a great healing to occur. Again, I don't know how I knew to do this.

"Baby Poop"—she always smelled like baby poop. I don't know how I could tell it was baby poop and not some other kind, but it would permeate from her skin and her whole being. She would make me realize that when people were around babies, as she was for her career, or they were related to someone having a baby or having one themselves, I would smell the same thing. When I told another client I smelled baby poop, she told me her son and daughter-in-law had been trying to have a baby for months, and the next week I saw her, she told

me her daughter-in-law was pregnant. I was never wrong about it, but I learned to stop telling people they smelled like baby poop since it was not always taken so well, and I'd nearly hide in the corner after I said it. Not very tactful indeed. These were just some of the experiences that happened to me in the massage room, but then there was one last visit from my grandmother's spirit.

One day, about a month after her death, my grandmother came to me at the office and asked me for my forgiveness. I wasn't sure why she needed it, so I told her, "Grandma, I forgive you for whatever you need, but my guess is there are many more whom you need to visit because you were not a nice lady." That instant, she seemed to float away. She would return now and then (with the smell of her cigarettes) just to check up on me, but never to ask for anything else. I assume she was working on getting to the other side (while possibly sitting in Purgatory) and working to heal the wrong she did here on earth. This visit caused me no emotion; I had never been close to her, but I had loved her just the same. My mom later explained to me that my grandmother had suggested I was given more attention than my sister, and she blamed my mother for it. My mom thought maybe she was apologizing for those words.

EXERCISES:

1. Are you feeling distant from your partner? Many times we seek in our partner what we need to bring into our own lives. What aspects or longings in a partner do you think you may be looking to enhance or change within yourself? ________________

____

____

____

____

2. How many times have you just known something but couldn't explain how or why? Think into your past and identify what is common about each occurence. Does it happen with the same person, the same time of day. Is there a common smell? List your occurences and thoughts below: _________

____

____

____

____

____

3. Who is drawn to you and what lessons are they teaching you? Especially note how they really get under your skin and bother you—there is a golden nugget of healing there! ___________

____

____

____

____

____

HELPING YOU DISCOVER YOUR TRUTH

Sometimes in the process of pursuing your truth, you need to let go of the familiar and embrace change. The people with whom you are making this journey may support you or they may not. The reality is that everyone has mental "stuff" going on. Your challenge is to partner with someone on your journey who is growing just as you are. Often in relationships, one grows and the other does not. When this happens, you have to ask yourself whether you can let go of the familiar and embrace all life has to offer. To me, this is the true meaning of life. On your journey, make sure you match your passions with your gifts. In doing so, you can take full responsibility for your full life and begin a journey to seek your truth.

SEEK. TRUST. BELIEVE. LOVE.

CHAPTER 5

EMBRACING *Newfound Gifts*

"Wisdom begins in wonder."
— Socrates

When Sangria died, I was left with Sushi, my rescued girl, and the new pup. Her name would take some time to determine. I would go through all my copies of *Barker Magazine* (a Shar Pei breed specific magazine) to look for inspiration. The fascinating thing was that every page I had turned down eleven years prior (when I got Mai Tai) was a good-sized 4-color ad for the breeder I had gotten her from. I hadn't even realized it had been so long since I subscribed or that the kennel and breeder's names were somewhere in my subconscious. Eleven years earlier, I must have subconsciously known of my future plan.

The puppy would go to the office with my husband on occasion, and when he didn't take her, she would go with me. She was raised the first seven months of her life in our chiropractic offices. As a young pup, she would curl up in her bed and blankets and sleep most of the day except when I showed her off to the occasional visitor. She was such a sleepy girl most of the time. She would hardly ever wet herself, and never once did she chew anything she wasn't supposed to. Her eyes were magical, and many of my intuitive friends would remark what

a healer and magical being she was. Her eyes were absolutely intoxicating. At one point, she started to get a bit more energy, and soon after, my husband was finding it a bit challenging to take her into the office since she would end up in the treatment rooms bothering patients. It was sad for all of us when she had to start staying home with Sushi. And Sushi wasn't much happier because she was getting older and didn't really want to play with her. Sushi and she would run around in our newly landscaped yard on the days we were home. My husband still was never home much so the three of us would spend a lot of time together.

I was now running a business within our business—doing the occasional shaman session for anyone I could talk into it. I was not extremely confident in my work as a healer, and I had high expectations for myself because I was always thinking I had to one-up the last metaphysical phenomenon or tell people the story they expected to hear. This would cripple me a bit since I wanted to give the client a solid understanding of what had been accomplished in the session. But it was often hard for me to put into words the experiences that were happening. I enjoyed doing the massage because no expectation existed of having the experience explained. It allowed some of the pressure to fall away from having to give a performance or magic show, if you will. I knew I had the power to see and heal, but I couldn't understand how or why, or better yet, how to explain what was happening—I often didn't know myself.

WORKING WITH YOUR HANDS

When you work with your hands on people in any healing art, and you do it repeatedly or daily, after a while you start to know things on an intuitive level. For me, I started to see things: colors, images, and even disturbances in someone's energy field. The great thing is that I began to understand that the only reason I could see these things was because they were some-

how related to me. The work I needed to do on myself was right there in front of me in the other person. The trick was finding it—because it's harder sometimes to see our own "stuff." Our stuff is masked many times by our beliefs or a built-in human denial system. So it becomes a gift to place your hands on anyone...considering you are aware and ready to do your work! When you know you have a problem, but you can't see how to solve it, just start paying attention to the people and situations around you for clues—it's all there because it's a reflection. But do so with a completely open mind!

The way I see it, whatever Divine Light or God Source you follow would not put you here without taking care of you. I think, though, that a certain point comes where you have to step away from judgment—the idea that anything is wrong in the first place—and learn not so much to accept it, but to kind of roll with the punches. Learning grace, in my case through pure exhaustion, helps ease you through life's moments. It can turn challenges into opportunities. And when you step out of your way, that is when opportunity is easier to see. When you begin to take what life gives you as a lesson or a gift in whatever form it comes to you, you place yourself in the mindset of ease...and then grace. Getting out of your way means accepting you... moving into your truth.

VISITATION WITH PEARL SNOVER

There were times in our little farmhouse office when we knew we were not alone. For example, there was something funny about the earth and stone basement that gave us the creeps. I called on my shaman teacher to do a land and home clearing for me. It took some time, but she was able to remove three very negative energies she found in the home. Even then, none of the staff wanted to be there alone. I would find the building seemed almost to breathe, and doors would occasionally pop open and creak.

But I also discovered a kind and loving energy in the building with which I began to connect. As time went by, I almost befriended that energy. I would finally see a face in my mind, and with that face, I developed a theory. I sensed someone had died there related to some kind of relationship struggle between two men, possibly with or over a woman. I also had a strong sense that one of the men might have been gay. I just felt a softer kindness to him. After some time, we began to hear rumors that someone had been killed in the home. We weren't sure whether or not to believe that. Someone told me to go to the city offices and look into the house's history, but I just never had the time.

One sunny cool October day, I happened to be downstairs in the main clinic. I was preparing to go to lunch and much of the staff had already left. An older man and woman came in with many old picture frames and told me the house's whole story. Before they could tell me anything, I pointed out in one of the high school pictures they showed me the man who had owned the house. They asked how I knew who he was. I could only say I was sensitive to that kind of thing and I'd been talking to him for years. The woman told me his name was Pearl Snover, and she had been his niece. He had been a very kind and well-respected man, had often volunteered with the Girl Scouts, and had never married. One night, she and her family drove past the house late at night and thought it odd that a light was still on in it because Pearl usually didn't stay up late. She felt something was wrong, and her family followed up on it the next day. They found out Pearl had let someone in (presumably a man) who had killed him.

When she gave me the pictures of Pearl at various ages, I nearly started crying. I finally had a name and certain image to associate with the kind energy I felt in the home. I had felt tragedy, but I had always felt kindness over tragedy. I told her a bit about my visions and how I knew his spirit. I don't think

she thought any differently of me; in fact, she felt honored to have made the trip to present the images, and I told her I would immediately hang them on the wall so everyone could know the history of the home and land.

Pearl liked to sit in front of the fireplace in our waiting room and wander the halls upstairs in what became our massage room and spa. He was always around and showed himself to me as a young man in his twenties and an older man in his seventies. He never seemed to want anything other than simply to watch. This experience felt like a kind of homecoming for me, and from that day forward, I felt a kind of kinship and warmth in my heart for Pearl, and the building would always warm my heart upon entering and leaving it. Each night when I left, I would say, "Goodnight, Pearl. I'll see you tomorrow!" I tried to talk to Pearl afterwards to understand what had happened and how I could help him pass to the other side, but he never gave me an answer.

After several years of owning the office, we had an offer to sell it to the doctor who had just bought our other office less than a year prior. My husband wanted out because for some reason we always had a hard time keeping a good doctor on staff and it was stressful for him to manage. When were about to sell the office, I felt very sad to be leaving since I knew it would mean not only losing my job, my clients, and my friends, but also probably my husband. The last day we were open for business before selling the office, I was upstairs and had just said goodbye to my last massage client. I was changing the massage table sheets when I fell onto the table and started to cry. I was so sad about selling the office where I had grown so much, and I was scared about my future since I sensed a great change was coming.

Suddenly, I stopped crying as a deafening silence came over me. I could suddenly see the stairs in my mind's eye, and at

the top, I could make out a man. He seemed to be floating in a white light toward me. I was not afraid. I would lose sight of him and be present back in the room. Then as I lay there in my tears with my eyes closed, I felt a kind of indent on the massage table as if someone sat next to me. I didn't have to open my eyes. I felt his hand touch my back, and I felt a kind of warmth that I will never forget so long as I live. I realized very quickly that it was Pearl. He was rubbing my back as if to say, "It's okay" and "Thank you!" I felt pressure, but not warmth.

As soon as I realized it was him, he floated out through the wall, over the roof, and into the air. I believe his spirit was released after he had been somehow locked in the house all those years. I was in awe. I started to cry more, and then I realized he was saying that all things must end and yet, I knew this was not really the end. We'd had a kind of friendship I hadn't even realized until then. It will always warm my heart.

I'm not sure what happened exactly to release his spirit, but off he went. He had to have been trapped in that house for over fifty years, floating in a state of limbo. Now he was released and free to go home. Maybe he had gained clarity or simply made the choice, but either way, I stopped crying and thought maybe I had needed to leave myself in order for him to go. I think about Pearl often and say a little prayer for him when I do. I like to think that one day in heaven we will meet.

EXERCISES:

Some things in life just don't make sense! Pearl's story may seem unbelievable, but lots of people report being able to sense the passing of a loved one and to communicate with the person's spirit. Let's spend some time reflecting on this...

1. Have you ever lost a loved one and prayed to him or her and then somehow unexplainably felt the person's spirit with you? If so, write about your experiences here: ____________

____

____

____

____

____

____

____

THE MAYA CENTER

As we prepared to close our office, I started transitioning a few clients over to my new yoga and healing center. My parents let me temporarily borrow their second home; it had been up for sale for a long time, but the housing market and economy in Michigan was horrible, so it wasn't selling. I had always loved the land it was on. It was nestled back in on twenty-five wooded (and magical) acres in the trees. It had a long driveway and a large pond out front. It had been vacant for a while so it needed some TLC. I began working on it once we decided to sell our office.

I had hoped to continue doing a few massages, but I really hoped to do more healing work and begin teaching yoga. My husband assured me he would get me help and even indicated he might join me from time to time for an occasional chiropractic appointment or yoga class. Somehow I had it in my head that I would have some kind of support running my business there and maybe we would even hire a receptionist for me. It was very hard to be in session and answering the phone at the same time. But after some time, it became very obvious that he had never had any intention of helping me, much less joining me. Once our office was sold, I was shocked by how many people just disappeared. I had no clients.

I was suddenly out of work and all alone on twenty-five acres. I had changed a lot of people's lives. I had thought I was making a difference. I had thought I was loved. I had thought everyone liked the new person I had become. I had never thought after all the countless years of working so hard in my career and in our offices that I would end up on twenty-five acres in the woods all by myself!

My husband continued to be at work all the time, and I worked my tail off again to try to build my business one more time. This time I had no money and no help. I had never taught a yoga class before, and I didn't even have training in massage; technically, in Michigan I could be sponsored by a doctor (my husband) and still do massage, but now I was not under his umbrella in the offices and couldn't use his insurance due to an agreement we had with the buying doctor; plus, the laws for massage in Michigan were changing. After doing massage for two years, I would have to go back to school for a year to get certified, and I was already paying a fortune taking courses for my transpersonal psychology degree and hoping to move toward a Ph.D. I started to realize the cost of school and the time it would take, so I decided to take time off from continuing my education. I believed I could help people better as a shaman healer.

I wasn't happy in my marriage or that I had given up so much for my husband and our offices, only to have him sell them out from under me. I figured we'd have them for several more years. I had been making a nearly six-figure income again, but now I would have to go on unemployment. It was so humiliating. Everything I had worked so hard for was gone. In my mind, this loss was death number seven. I didn't know what normal was anymore, and I was exhausted. I figured I'd give it one more effort to try to grow a healing and yoga business, but I was three miles down a dirt road and far away from most large towns. I didn't see it working, but I marched ahead anyhow.

I put out some advertising, painted the walls, and bought some yoga blankets and mats. I put some chai tea on the stove and started my yoga music. I decorated and landscaped. I set up a few massage rooms and treated my existing one or two clients a week. I started off my yoga center with a Summer Solstice event and a few shamanic healing ceremonies. I had a pretty great turn-out. I was nearly in tears at the love that was shared that first day and night. I started yoga with full classes, but it dwindled from there. I had a few regulars each week and worked really hard to grow it.

Once everything was up and running, the energy was absolutely magical. Just magical—the smells of the tea, the people, the setting. Then I started making langar (community meals generally served in a yoga community) and everything was just perfect! New friendships were made and stories shared. It was hard for me to leave that amazing space each night and go back home. I just loved the energy. Something very magical was happening at what was now named the Maya Center.

HELPING YOU DISCOVER YOUR TRUTH

Some of the experiences you have in your life have no reasoning or scientific explanation. The key is to have an open mind and believe anything is possible. And some of your possibilities are not taught in school or in textbooks, hence leaving you in wonder. The key is to understand that none of us are just "normal" or "ordinary." In fact, if no one has told you before, I will tell you now: You are extraordinary! Accepting, embracing, and loving yourself and your many gifts is a key to finding your inner truth.

SEEK. TRUST. BELIEVE. LOVE.

CHAPTER 6

LETTING GO OF WHAT No Longer Serves

"Explanation by the tongue
makes most things clear, but
love unexplained is better."
— Rumi

I had what I viewed to be a problem—I wanted a deeper connection with everyone in my life, but my husband wouldn't go through marriage counseling any longer, and he wouldn't work on the marriage either. In an effort to get closer it seemed as if I had pushed him further away.

I had been doing visits with our therapist alone on occasion, and they were mostly not even related to our marriage, but my husband grew very suspicious that we had been talking about him behind his back. I was going through a phase of seeing world phenomena before they occurred (tidal waves, tsunamis, etc.), and I believed having someone to talk to about them would help. I was not able to talk to anyone in my life about them, and if I tried to talk to my husband, at best, he would just listen and let me cry. I was not able to sleep, and I was very bothered about these visions. The therapist and I hardly ever discussed my husband, but I really got a lot out of those sessions because I was able to get out what was weighing on my mind.

It was hard to keep my head above water when things seemed like they would inevitably change. After these sessions ended, when I called the therapist to tell him about our pending divorce, he told me he wasn't surprised at all since my husband never wanted to open up about his feelings. That saddened me to know he knew we would not work and didn't ever say anything to me about it or didn't seem to make any special effort on our behalf. I realized it was not up to him to make that effort though.

STEPPING INTO YOUR BECOMING

I wasn't sure why my husband was just content with everything as it was; maybe he was just afraid of change or the way he would be viewed if he were the one who left the marriage. Someone once told me I would know how much he loved me if I left him. When I began to consider divorce, I decided to do a yoga cleanse to clear my body and mind, to be still, to be sure no outside forces were causing me to make this decision. I had never believed in divorce and my husband had told me he didn't either. This would be the first "official" cleanse I would ever do.

One day during the cleanse, I was sitting on my yoga teacher's stand and taking notice of the feel of the sheepskin rug beneath me when, with tears in my eyes, I heard a voice in my head say, "You must leave him to step into your becoming!" That really scared me. I had stepped away from my career years before to run our businesses, and we had just finished selling the office. I had lost my job and a source of good income in the sale. I was scared what would happen to my husband and me if we stayed together, but I was more frightened by what would happen to me if we separated.

I had left my career in 2002 and it was now 2008. My career field had shifted and was nearly obsolete, or it would require

new training to compete and earn the six-figure income I had previously. I absolutely did not want to go back to what I was doing prior to 2002, but I didn't know anyone who was making a decent living teaching yoga or doing healing work. I was growing tired of healing people and hearing about their aches, pains, and problems all day, and I wanted to pursue other things, but I wasn't sure what those other things were. I also knew I could be more effective in front of larger audiences versus one-on-one in the treatment room. I also knew this might be the time to work on me and not on someone else.

MAKING A TOUGH DECISION

One day, I went to yoga and just decided I wasn't going to go home after that night. I was going to stay at the Maya Center. I wasn't sure what I was going to do for an income, and I had never intended to teach yoga, but it seemed silly not to teach something I had trained in for nearly a year, and I also knew it could help people (as well as myself). I felt bound to massage because I already had clients, and I didn't want to disappoint them. The truth was I was just in no position to be healing or teaching anyone since I needed to work on me. I didn't need anyone to reflect back to me what I already knew or to fill my mind with his or her opinions, and I began to lose clients and make a turn into a downward spiral of worry and depression.

Soon my now eight-month-old pup (appropriately now named Shiitake by her grandpa; I called her "Tak" for short), Sushi, and my "magic" cat Penelope would move in with me. (I was once told that "every witch needs a good cat" and she was quite a magical healing kitty.) My husband and I were never very good at communicating with one another; I was under the impression he would fight for me if I moved out, but he was under the impression we were, in his words, "trying some time apart." My entire world had suddenly flipped upside-down. Nothing I recognized was present in it.

When we had married, I had been earning more than my husband since he was just opening his own office. I had all the furniture, plates and dishes, sheets and towels. He was living out of a suitcase in a rental home. I had been in my career for nearly a decade while he was practically starting from scratch. He had an old rusted out Nissan Pathfinder (complete with melted candy and dog hair in the cup holders) and only the bare essentials. He was never home enough to notice how little he had. I had now walked out and left everything I had worked so hard for during the ten years prior to our marriage and now the six years of our marriage. I had sold the house I owned before our marriage and taken the equity to pay off bills and buy into our businesses.

Now I had little savings and no career. What hurt me most was leaving behind everything I had when he was the one most able to afford new things, but he thought nothing of it. Everything I'd ever owned—including furniture, cars, sentimental objects reminding me of all those I had lost, even the yard where my kiddos were buried—I now no longer had. Everything I ever owned or anything that was ever important to me I had just walked away from! I was very scared about what came next. I didn't even have a bed to sleep on. I spent the first nights on a massage table in my treatment room and just cried all night.

TIME FOR CHANGE

Very shortly after I left my husband, with no plans discussed about next steps, I realized it had been nearly five years since I had been intimate with a man and I was really craving any kind of attention. I kept wanting to connect with my husband, but he would barely talk to me, and not about our issues, so slowly we kept moving toward divorce.

Soon after I became open to the idea of dating again, I met "Mr. Florida," and then for the first time in my life, I understood

love. I understood connection. I had been craving a partner in my life who would open up emotionally and join me on the self-improvement and spiritual path. Mr. Florida was divorced and lived near St. Petersburg, Florida. He was in town for a Theta Healing class he was teaching. He would introduce his learned healing techniques to me and I would introduce Kundalini yoga and shamanism to him. He later introduced me to Matrix Energetics and spiritual leader Amma, and I taught him how to eat healthier. We learned a great deal from one another. We could look each other in the eyes and see deep into each other's souls in ways I had only imagined existed. Sadly, in the past I had only experienced that connection with my dogs. Over the course of several months, he often came to town and visited. We had so much fun going to every spiritual event in town, and I would even take a trip to Florida for a Kundalini yoga solstice event.

Mr. Florida and I would teach healing events and retreats here and there and do healings with clients on occasion. Neither of us was very focused. We really just wanted to play. We had great ideas, but neither of us was very good at implementing any of them and no one else could get us to focus on any of them long enough to help us out either. We were incredible manifestors. Somehow the magic we played with attracted more magic. I had spent my entire marriage never once going to a friend's house for dinner, but all of a sudden, Mr. Florida and I were having people over for spiritual dinners, potlucks, and healings, and going out and doing the same at others' homes. I really enjoyed having a kind of social life that I hadn't seen since the year 2000. So much time was spent growing my career and our businesses that I had forgotten about socializing. I was so enjoying doing things with Mr. Florida as a couple with common interests. Then one night we experienced the most amazing thing that has ever happened in my life—but I'll save that story for the next chapter.

EXERCISES:

If you are coming out of a relationship and / or in search of your soulmate, in the exercise lines below, write your "top ten" "must haves" in your partner. You could even call these your "non-negotiables." I encourage you not to settle for anyone, so be specific and firm about whom you want to make your journey with.

1. ______________________________
2. ______________________________
3. ______________________________
4. ______________________________
5. ______________________________
6. ______________________________
7. ______________________________
8. ______________________________
9. ______________________________
10. ______________________________

1. Ask yourself: How do these characteristics reside within me?

____

____

____

____

____

____

____

____

____

____

____

2. Remembering that the Law of Attraction says like attracts like, ask yourself: How would my partner complement me if I had these characteristics? ______________________

____

____

____

____

____

HELPING YOU DICOVER YOUR TRUTH

I once believed marriage should be forever and so did many of my spiritual friends (and they were sure to tell me their opinion). I have since learned that life is too short to spend the rest of your life with the wrong partner. We likely designed everything exactly as we did before we incarnated, and marriage problems are just another experience we chose to partner on for our next soul lesson. I once heard that many of us go through a "practice marriage" so we can find the one marriage that is for keeps. If you are going through a rough time in your relationship, don't lose hope; you are stronger than you realize, and will find true love on your journey in pursuit of your truth.

SEEK. TRUST. BELIEVE. LOVE.

CHAPTER 7

KNOWING We Are Not Alone

"The only true wisdom
is in knowing you know nothing."
— Socrates

I had just taught a very connected and peaceful yoga class, the fire was still burning in the fireplace, the room was warm and cozy, and the smells of langar, incense, and chai tea were permeating the air. It was snowing heavily and absolutely beautiful outside. The moon was full and glistening on the snowy crystals as they fell. The deer were walking through the yard, and Mr. Florida and I were enjoying watching them. I had no furniture in the house except for an old brass bed Mr. Florida had dragged up from the basement and placed in the kitchen. I had hung a curtain so no one knew it was there, and it became my bedroom for a while. It was a grand step up from the massage table I had been sleeping on previously. As we sat there, Mr. Florida was educating me about portals, Matrix Energetics, and various other healing modalities.

All of a sudden, we saw a light come up the driveway. We were so startled that we jumped up. Then we watched it pan the yard, much like a car would it if had pulled up and was now turning around to leave. The house was in the middle of twenty-five wooded acres, no neighbors were nearby, it was dark

out, our students had long since gone, and when we looked at the clock, it was 1:11 a.m. so it was a very unusual time for any car to pull up. Our only thought was that on this snowy night, one of our students might have been unable to get home.

I went to the front door and Mr. Florida followed. When I opened the door, I expected to see a car or someone walking to the door. Instead, I saw nothing! I walked out onto the porch and turned the light on. Almost a foot of fluffy glistening fresh snow had fallen so the driveway was entirely covered with it and there was not a trace of a tire track.

Suddenly, out of the corner of my eye, I saw something move in the back room so I went to see what it was. I caught the shadow of a tall being passing through the room's center. I will never forget that image. It was a very dark shadow, and it most certainly was not human! It was very tall with an arched upper back and shoulders, and its side profile resembled the grim reaper. Here is a picture I drew of it:

I wondered what we had done to invite in these visitors. I asked Mr. Florida, "Did you see that?" He said, "I don't know what it was, but the hairs on the back of my neck are standing

straight up! Something definitely went through here!" Nothing else happened that night, but I wondered why we'd had such a visitor. It felt as if something Mr. Florida and I had been doing had invited it.

This incident reminded me of an event my parents had experienced when they had lived in the same house. They were home one night when my sister and I, as teenagers, were out with friends. They saw a light come up the driveway and assumed one of us had come home. The light pulled up in a similar manner to what we had experienced this same night... panning the yard as if it were a car turning around in the driveway. But when no one ever entered the house, my mom and dad decided it must have just been the TV. Within a few more minutes, a huge flash of red light fell directly from the sky into the yard. Three times it flashed into the earth and through the wooded lot in the backyard. They both saw it! A few days later, their TV exploded. Then nothing more happened.

UNCERTAINTY

Not long after, Mr. Florida needed to get back to Florida. By that point, it appeared I would be moving in to the house permanently, so he was helping me paint a few walls on the lower level. I was so busy fixing up the house and enjoying the feeling of connection and the depth of intuition and insight Mr. Florida and I shared that time began to escape me and I barely knew my husband even existed. He never called or emailed me, and for the first time since we had been separated, I quit feeling like I needed him in my life. If it were that easy for him to let me go and not look back, I wasn't going to make any effort to meet with him. My friend had been correct—if I left him, I would learn how much he cared about me...and I guess he didn't.

I was swirling around from one spiritual phenomenon to the next with miracles in every moment. Mr. Florida and I would

play games with each other, and he once told me that I could manifest nearly anything in a shorter time than he had ever seen anyone else do. When he asked me to manifest something, I told him I would be given a gift by someone before the day was over, even though it was already 6 p.m. Not only did I receive that gift, but gifts kept coming for days thereafter, and in many forms. I was given several new outdoor garden plants, several yards of mulch to plant around them, and I would meet a woman named Tia Maria (my dog's name) and her husband Scott (the name of the guy I was dating when Tia came into my life).

I kept thinking the games would have to end, and sooner or later, I would have to focus on life. I had moments when Mr. Florida was gone back to Florida when I really missed my husband and wished he would just call or come over to visit. I also acknowledged that I needed his grounding energy. Although from that point on, whenever I communicated with him, it would go very badly. For example, one day he actually decided he wanted to meet me for lunch. We went to his choice location—the bar at Chili's restaurant, which was loud and had ball games blaring on television sets. He was obviously a regular there now since he introduced me to the bartender. When he asked whether I wanted a drink, I ordered a sparkling water. He laughed and said, "Just loosen up and have a drink!" He had always said I was "uptight." He knew I was not a big drinker, and never in our entire time together had he ever seen me drink more than a half glass of wine. I wasn't sure why he was trying to push something on me as he should have known I didn't like to drink alcohol. Another time when we met at a restaurant, he asked me whether I was happy, and I said, "No, actually I'm not, but I'm trying." Later, I realized what he was really saying was, "I want to commit to someone else if we are not going to work." But I would only find that out several months later.

Mr. Florida had now gone back to Florida, and I wasn't sure when or if I would see him again. By then, I had noticed he didn't have much of an income and he wasn't teaching classes any more. He had been a computer programmer, but he was no longer doing that. I would later find out his car, motorcycle, and home were about to be repossessed, and he had a roommate. I had never dated anyone who lived like that even in my more juvenile years. I realized I had left my successful doctor husband and been having the time of my life with a man who might never make enough to support us. I had gotten used to having nice things and a nice home, and for the last fifteen years, I had enjoyed a six-figure income. I had never experienced having to make choices of what to go without. I was very nervous, very sad, and confused about my future. And now I suspected my husband was dating very actively.

We had painted my bedroom and moved a bed into it before Mr. Florida left, so I finally had a place to sleep with walls and a door. The first night I slept in the room turned out to be another fascinating experience. As I lay there about to fall asleep, I started to see blue vine-like lights crawling up the walls. I started to see motion and movement in the room. It was pitch dark and I was all alone on twenty-five acres and nearly started to cry. Shiitake and Sushi were lying on their dog beds on the floor across the room. Neither seemed to be bothered by anything. I lay there frozen in my bed as I had done when I was a child and had these kinds of experiences. I felt so helpless and hopeless too.

I called Mr. Florida and told him I was mad at him for leaving me all alone after we painted the walls with the weird powder he had recommended putting on the walls. His roommate had been selling the white powder for about $150 a bottle; it had supposedly gone through some process so when it was painted on walls it would create a type of God-like (zero point) energy in the room. We had used it on the entire room, and we had

noticed that the room would get very silent as each wall was finished. In fact, when Mr. Florida was helping me, he was having quite an experience in the other bedroom as he drew sacred images on the floor and walls with the paint and then painted over them. We were tiling the floors so they would never be seen either. When I took pictures of him that day, they showed the most amazing lights surrounding him. They were golden in color and shining off his left shoulder. Something was captured in those pictures that was very divine. It appeared as if golden fairies were circling him. But on this night, the walls were all painted and he was not there. I was scared and very alone.

When I tried to go back to sleep, I began to see tall thin beings come into the room and stand around my bed. I could only see them as shadows, but they stood like posted soldiers watching me and never moving. I kept blinking my eyes and thinking I was making it up. Maybe my mind was getting the best of me. I continued to watch the wall light up, and then it just stopped. The room now felt very still yet very busy. It's very hard to put into words what was happening that night. I noticed a movement on the room's far end that later others would explain to me. I had no idea what was happening. I had many gifted healers in and out of that house and would later get many opinions about what had happened. All I know is I did not make up what I saw. I'll explain a bit more later as the experiences expanded further.

I would continue to teach yoga, now just one day a week, and nearly all my massage clients had quit coming. I would have the occasional shamanic healing client, but those would come to an end too. I had one massage client who was now more like a friend who would come to my Saturday yoga class, and then she and another student would stay after class for massages. While the massage was in session, she complained about her knee pain. We had done some work on her knee in the office and were continuing that work. But on this day, we would take

it to a whole new level. I suspected the incidents involving the visitors were somehow connected. I had been trained in my shamanic work that we would be able to ask for help from our lineage and spirit guides and that was a normal invocation when I began all of my sessions from then on. But I started to see beings that looked very human, but glowing in all white clothing and shining in white auras, coming into my treatment rooms to offer assistance and healing. This would later be explained to me as "The White Brotherhood." It took away any doubt about my healing abilities, and in fact, I would sometimes lay down myself and ask for healing, or crazy as it sounds, leave the room or step out of the way so they could do their work. I found others who were noticing the same phenomena. I didn't understand it, but I knew I had a team at my back to help if it got to be more than I could understand.

When I stopped the massage to work on her knee, all of a sudden I heard an odd kind of whirling noise. I had just placed my hands above her knee, and when I moved my hand away, I no longer heard the noise. When I moved my hand back, it got louder and made me jump back. It startled me because somehow I just knew it definitely wasn't from this planet! I told her I had heard something and had never picked that up from her before. I stepped back and called on the angels and guides for assistance. We had definitely fed on each other's energy on many past occasions, and our psychic nature was heightened when we were together. For example, one time in the chiropractic treatment room, she was not feeling well; as I tried to work on her, I kept telling her I felt as if I were going to vomit. As that feeling got stronger in me, it got stronger in her. She finally just yelled, "Don't touch me!" I was a bit shocked but happy to stop because I was about to toss my cookies and so was she. We fed on each other's energy like that each time we were together. So we were familiar with this kind of thing before this session had started.

Now, as I followed the energy I felt in her knee, it seemed to take me up her leg. I could nearly see the energy line or cord. I asked her whether she could feel it with me as I worked up from her knee through her leg and into her hip. From her hip, it would cross her pelvis and go up the opposite side of her body and into her neck and shoulders; then it dissipated as it entered her third eye. It was humming. I felt like her body had been transformed into a kind of container or antenna for another being to live within. I tried energetically to move the "structure" I had found inside her physical body, and each time I did, she would either start to shake or scream. I felt like I was doing a kind of exorcism. Her eyes were beginning to roll back, but in my head, I heard my teachers saying, "Trust the process. Trust the process." I played with loosening the energy until I found a place where it would exit. Traditionally, we are taught to do these kind of extractions using a Vogel crystal (uniquely cut and pointed at both ends), but the crystal was not proving to be powerful enough. I realized there was both a structure and a being, and the being had to come out first.

In shamanism, we would traditionally call this a "non-integrated energy," but in this case, I knew it was from outside of this planet and perhaps this galaxy. It would eventually come out, but not without a fight. Her body started to convulse and shake. I had never seen her (or anybody I treated) ever react like this. When I had gone to classes outside of Michigan, I had sometimes watched it happen when people were worked on. It was an alarming sight the first time I saw it, but I knew it to be the norm for the practice. I had just not personally seen it to such an extreme before. I told her we were going to remove another being's energy, and before we did, I needed her to take a moment and thank it for serving her and not to be afraid and that we would send it to the light and back home and it would be freed. As she came to grips with many childhood memories and a sense of knowing this being had aided her in many areas of her life, it was hard to release it but eventually, the being

was out. We finished the session because I could see it had taken a lot out of her. We would have to do another session to release the remaining structure.

When we finished, my next client was waiting in the other room, and she was open-minded enough to listen to our story; in fact, she said she'd had dark circles under her eyes before the session and now no longer did. I had heard of this happening when an energy was released and had seen it one other time, but clearly something very amazing happened in that treatment room that day.

A few days later, my friend came back with her mom. She said she'd had a hard time getting home after the last session, and I felt bad that I had sent her on her way. I assumed she would have used her best judgment about driving home since she seemed a bit dazed and confused, but so was I. I'd had no idea what had just happened, but I'd had to forget about it quickly to move onto my next session. Now, she was very quiet about the experience, so we just proceeded. When I asked her whether she had felt any metal in her mouth, she said she had tasted metal very strongly for the last few days and wanted to get it out of her. I sensed a kind of metal structure in her body, and it had seemed to cause her ovaries and female anatomy great issues in her young adult life. We removed the structure fairly easily by envisioning liquifying it and it released within just twenty or thirty minutes.

After the session, we had lots of time to talk, and I would hear from her mother about how in her childhood her headboard was scratched up and she would yell and scream, "I don't want to be taken" and "They are here!" I don't know much about alien abductions, but I think this conclusion was the only one we could make. Her mother and she went on to tell me she'd had her female parts removed, and how the doctors had been shocked to see the scarring she had internally. We all under-

stood something had been coexisting within her, and not very peacefully, but we couldn't understand much more at that time. We continued to work together, and she and her mother would become loyal regulars at the Maya Center. She was always a comfort to have around because if I saw or experienced something, she would do the same, and I needed the validation at that time. I was experiencing things few people on this planet ever do, so I felt blessed...and a bit scared, but blessed. We will forever have a special kind of bond from our experiences that so few will ever hear about, see, or experience.

MEETING CHARLIE

During this time of strange happenings, I counted on the system I had learned, and I knew not only that the system would not fail me, but that my faith in my spirit guides and lineage would "watch my back" and give me a strength outside of myself as I proceeded. The lineage would also now grow very familiar because my grandparents would come into the next healing I would do to offer their support and love.

I soon found out that my sister was not only six months pregnant, but she was having some trouble and was scheduled to go in for a follow-up with her doctor to determine the baby's health. When I told her and my mom about the work I was doing, I was shocked that she was even remotely interested, much less willing to give it a try. I sometimes question whether it was her willingness to try a shamanic healing session with me, or it was Charlie (her baby) pulling her in. The day she came for her session with me, I was a bit nervous about what I should share with her. I already had an idea about what was going on, but my sister had always been emotionally sensitive, so I was scared I would do or say something to upset her. But this day, I could see her guard was down because she was truly worried and scared. This wasn't a side of my sister I often saw. I knew we could make a shift, and I had told her to come see

me before she got her test results because we could shift the outcome. I was surprised that she didn't even find that idea odd. As soon as we started the session, I watched my paternal grandparents come into the room and stand by the massage table where she lay. I wasn't sure whether I should tell my sister about their presence, but eventually I did. As soon as I started to work, I was overwhelmed with emotion, and when I covered her in the sacred space we always begin our sessions with, I could sense her emotions bubbling, and I could see the most amazing pinkish purple light engulfing the room.

Later that night, I wrote the following description of what occurred during that healing session to allow Charlie to be born healthy and thriving:

The Color of the Sky Looks Like Charlie's Dragon Tonight

Not such a long time ago on a cold, quiet February night, a bright shooting star from a faraway land crossed the sky. This experience used to be a celebrated and rare occasion since it was a time when wishes were made. But now, the enlightened are coming and they are carrying our wishes with them! You see, many bright stars have been shooting through the sky lately, and this was a very special night for me. This night, a little boy named Charlie was riding on one of those stars as it shot across the dark black sky.

Charlie was a star seed—a special boy from way beyond this planet and from deeper beyond than even this galaxy. He came, like so many others of this new time, with special powers that would save all the people of the land.

Now Charlie was different in many ways from little boys who had come to this land before, yet he was also very much the same. Even before Charlie was born, he could be talked to in his mother's womb. One night, while he was in the womb, his mother was worried that something had gone wrong and Charlie had changed his mind about being born, but that night I really got to know how special this boy was going to be.

I am a medicine woman so his mother came to me for healing. She wanted to make sure Charlie was comfortable and ready to be born. Charlie talked to me from inside his mother's womb and told me he would be coming to this planet with a special friend. But his friend was lost, so he needed me to help him or he wouldn't come. As a medicine woman, I call this kind of friend a Spirit Guide. Each little boy and girl has at least one Spirit Guide of his or her very own. Charlie wanted to be sure his could come with him for the journey of his lifetime ahead. Charlie sent me looking for his Spirit Guide.

I looked under rocks, over cliffs, around corners, and finally, I went very high up into the sky. I went so high up that the blue sky turned to dark outer space, then into a bright white. This is the brightest white that you could imagine. We don't have as much of this bright light here on this planet as we once did, but Charlie and his Spirit Guide showed me where to go to find it. As I looked around, the light was so bright that I could hardly see. Then there came this smoky white cloud that filled all of the air. Beyond the cloud of white heavenly smoke was a pale pink and purple light. I could start to make it out—it was a very tall figure. I could see it was coming closer to me. I was not scared at all since the light was like heaven and I knew it was one of Charlie's best friends. I had not met Charlie or his friend yet, but

I was filled with so much love and light that I knew this reunion was going to be oh, so sweet!

The purple, white, and pink colors melted together in front of me to form the most beautiful and magical dragon in all of the heavens and earth combined. The air felt warm, comforting, and loving. I could feel the heat coming from the dragon's skin and breath. I could see why Charlie would not come to this planet without such a good friend.

I would ride down from the heavens on the dragon's back, then I would stand outside the womb as the dragon entered to be reunited with his best friend, and I watched the brightest lights unite once again. From that day forward, no matter where Charlie went, he would never be alone. Even as he grew into a little boy and later a man, he would always have his friend.

I cut a few energetic cords (known to bind one soul to another) and simply brought Charlie a friend (Spirit Guide) to help him come into the world. After this session, Charlie and I always could connect with one another through our thoughts. We would carry on conversations while he was in the womb, and there is no denying the special connection we still seem to have today. I don't see him as often as I'd like, but he never fails to respond with incredible love when he sees me. My mom and sister (even my dad) notice the bond we have. I'm not sure I always understand it, but it sure is nice to know how much I am loved. It's my hope that one day when he's older we can have a conversation about this magical time.

There are so many magical children that have come to the planet for a new awakening of humankind. I think perhaps Charlie was just giving me a glimpse into this magical world to show me what is possible.

EXERCISES:

1. Perhaps the experiences I shared of extraterrestrials coming into the house or removing energy from my client's body seem too unbelievable to you. If you feel that way, that's okay. Use the space below to journal about any experiences you have had or questioned in your life around concepts or theories that we are not alone. How would you behave differently if you knew we were not? ____________________

2. What in your life has caused you to question everything you ever believed? How has this event opened your awareness? __

3. What magical things have you noticed from children that you've never seen before? Are they healers, psychics, mystics? And, especially, have you noticed their diets? I've found a plant-based diet seems a bit more natural for them.) Make some notes here if you like: ______________________________

____

____

____

____

____

____

____

____

HELPING YOU DISCOVER YOUR TRUTH

It has taken me a number of years to find peace with these experiences, but I finally have. My knowledge base (and security in self) has grown well beyond these experiences as well. Not everything in your life makes sense. It doesn't have to. That is what makes life worth living. Life is like reading a novel; you continue turning the pages to see what unfolds next. The key is to keep an open mind and trust that all of your past experiences and any future mysteries will bring you closer to realizing your inner truth.

SEEK. TRUST. BELIEVE. LOVE.

CHAPTER 8

SEEKING ANSWERS ON YOUR *Spiritual Journey*

"Happiness consists in realizing
it is all a great strange dream."
— Jack Kerouac

My husband never could have understood what was happening in my new world, and I was happy not to explain it. I knew his father's spirit had tried to get his attention for months, but when I told him this, he had done nothing to pursue it. It was just too weird for him. (And he really didn't know what to do either.) He had his own agenda, and I was not part of it. For a period of time, he just seemed to vanish. As I was growing and experiencing these things, he was nowhere to be found. I would make trips over to our house with Sushi and Tak while he was at work and just sit and look around and ask myself, "Why?" and "What am I supposed to do now?" The girls didn't understand why we never stayed to play in the yard long. I'd look at my things and recall memories. The couch Tia sat on often was alone and abandoned in a lifeless room. There were still dog beds on the floors, but no one other than us to use them.

I'd also start to think that if the house were going to be sold or appraised, I would have to finish some of the projects that were started. My husband knew I was handy and fully capa-

ble, so when I talked to him about it, he offered to pay me the remaining money I needed to make my trip to Peru that fall if I would finish the work. I was appreciative, but again I wondered why he wouldn't talk to me to try to work out our problems. I was very confused. I still dreamt about him coming back to me.

I worked very hard on the house's final projects because I wanted to go to Peru so badly. I wasn't really sure what my husband's motive was for sending me to Peru. We hadn't been intimate for nearly five years, and I began to wonder whether he had a secret life or had been having an affair all along. He didn't have many friends, but all of a sudden, he was never around. Sure he worked a lot, but when he wasn't working after we separated, I had no idea where to find him.

Before we separated, he had also paid a lot of money for a cosmetic surgery and spent a lot of time on chat services talking about it. He told me he had joined Facebook and was hooking up with old friends, but I wondered who they were because I had met so few of them. had no idea who he was because all we had done during our marriage was work. I even began to wonder whether he really was at work all the hours he said he was. I wondered whether he had some kind of plan and he wanted me to go off to Peru so I wouldn't know about it.

We also had made a few attempts to work out money arrangements. On one occasion, he invited me over, lit my incense, put on my music, and set the stage like we always did when we had company. But this time I was the company! I was very bothered by this behavior. I was also very bothered by the short amounts of time he would schedule for our discussions, how he had this smug kind of look and attitude when we talked, and how he would be all dressed up to go out as soon as he got rid of me. I remember turning on my voice recorder when I realized he was lying to me because I could no longer hear him. All I could see was the cloud over his left shoulder. I could

only read it as lies or deceit. I even thought he might be under a negative influence. I sat and studied the cloud as words kept coming out of his mouth. I had been told we were moving into a time of seeing people's lies, so I wondered whether I was experiencing just that. So many words were coming out of his mouth, but all I heard was noise. I kept turning my head, trying to see the cloud of lies differently. I was confused why it was there and what I was supposed to do about it. It took me until today finally to understand that this was there for his experience and mine. I would see the lies and he would need to experience the influence they had over him.

My mind was spinning. But I finished up the projects so the house was ready for an appraisal and sale. I had thought if I did the work at the house, I might see more of him, but instead, he was always gone. I was starting to understand I was really just hired help and nothing more.

TRAVELING TO PERU

In August 2009, I flew to Peru, feeling full of wounds, but I was excited finally to meet the shaman of the Andes and be right at the source. Once there, I would be set up with a roommate I had met a few times before in Michigan. I liked her, but I sensed she wasn't sure about me. She would tell me about her ill mother back home in ICU and how she worried about her. I knew very little more about her and she didn't share much. I was with people I recognized from class, but I didn't really connect with anyone. Once I was settled in my room, I went to where everyone was gathering. There I was told the shaman would be joining us shortly. For me, the first time I laid eyes on the shaman and their bright smiles and clothing, I was home in my heart. I was in awe of the presence they held. I finally had followed my heart to my desires, and I couldn't believe I was standing right in front of them. I couldn't take my eyes off them. I was so excited to take this journey and heal my heart.

The journey through Peru would involve healings each day as we traveled around and saw all the sacred sites and performed sacred ceremonies. We would sit in circles and share and heal, and time just seemed to fly by. We went shopping and hiking and saw the most amazing sights. Most of the group enjoyed going out and drinking at night, which I didn't like to do. I was there to do lots of work and healing, not to party. I was actually shocked that others were not there for the same reason. I just accepted we were all on different paths. I would go to bed early and get up early. I ate healthy food and slept amazingly well, but shortly after we got there, I became very ill and couldn't keep anything down. I had to stay home for a few days while the rest of the group went touring, and I found it very interesting that within this group hardly a single healer asked me how I was or offered to do a healing. Finally after the second day, my roommate asked whether she could get me anything. I told her I would love any kind of juice. I waited all day for that juice, but when she came back, she didn't bring any or even ask me how I was. The next morning, she told me she couldn't find any the night before. The third morning, I was finally able to get up. I was starving, so I made it to breakfast and was able to keep down a bit of fruit.

We had to pack up our bags and relocate that day, but before we got onto the bus, the shaman was asked by our group leaders whether they would do a healing on me. They found me a chair and then they blew spiritual water all over my entire body. They circled me, rattling their bells and hitting me hard on the head with their medicine bags. I was soaking wet and covered in "Aqua de Florida" (spiritual water) and very nervous about getting on that bus and trekking off to our next location.

I was thankful when we finally arrived at the next location. I was given a room that overlooked the courtyard, which was full of hummingbirds and the most vibrant and brilliant flowers. It was such a relaxing room that I literally could have stayed there

until the end of my days. I was so hungry though, so I made my way out to find food. The staff was very accommodating since it was common for the tourists to have stomach issues from both the high altitude and levels of bacteria there. They offered to make me a very bland vegan meal and to give me some herbal heat packs and a healing session in my room later; they even walked me back to my room because I was so exhausted and could barely move. I must have looked really horrible considering the kind of attention I was getting. But by the end of the third day, I began to feel better. I was thankful to know we had a free day now with no planned activity before going to Machu Picchu the next day. We did do some shopping and it was an easy day for me, so I was finally feeling better.

Instead of looking at my health as a sickness, I looked at it as a healing. I was aware that the energy the shaman were creating with all the ceremonies, one after another, were likely shifting me more than my physical body was accustomed to. Even though the shaman and I didn't speak the same language, I could understand they were shifting idiosyncratic things in my being that were preventing me from standing in my fullness. I almost didn't care about what they were doing because it was likely that at this stage my mind, body, and soul were in better hands with them than with me. I was very unhappy about the turn of events in my life, so in a way, my being in Peru was like my taking a last chance on life. I was very unhappy because of the recent incidents with my husband, so I had known it was time to get some help seeking answers.

That night before we packed to leave, we did one more ceremony with the shaman. My roommate volunteered in a demonstration using one of the shaman's handmade ponchos. I noticed a strange kind of streak of gold-colored light following her as she went through the ceremony. I didn't know whether this light resulted from the ceremony or something else happening. When the ceremony ended, I slowly walked back to the room.

As I walked, I noted the amazing Southern Cross star formation in the sky. I had never seen anything like it before. When I reached my room, my roommate was crying and another girl was with her. Prior to this event, she had loosened her tongue with the aid of a few alcoholic drinks and told me she had dated one of the trip's organizers, so she had decided to come to Peru to make sure he knew how she felt; therefore, I figured something had backfired with this plan to make her upset. But much to my surprise, she had just gotten a phone call from home saying her mother had passed. Since I didn't know her very well, I wasn't sure how to handle this situation other than to say I was sorry for her loss. I was dealing with so many of my own issues and had just started to feel better myself. I didn't know what I could say or do to help her feel better, and since her friends were comforting her, I began to feel very alone on this journey.

Oddly enough, my traveling companions were composed of one core group of family and friends, and then there were others who were just running at a slower pace and either couldn't keep up or just wanted to take their time on every journey we had. I was somewhere between and generally walking or experiencing everything alone. Once while we were walking on the Inca trail, I all of a sudden realized no one else was around—half the group was behind me and the other half was in front. I could see neither group, and at a few points, I had no idea which way to turn and was using my intuition to make my choice—left or right. As I walked the locals were poking their heads out of homes that looked like they had been abandoned long ago and watched as I walked by. I could see the curtains being turned back as if they didn't see many large groups on a regular basis. There were stray cows and chickens running freely and people tending to farming fields below. I wasn't sure if I was safe all alone, but I held faith and continued to walk. Eventually I found the group ahead and re-joined them in a courtyard where our bus awaited to take us back to our hotel.

OFF TO MACHU PICCHU

The next day we journeyed to Machu Picchu by bus and train and settled in at our hotel so we could wake at 4 a.m. to hike up the gigantic mountain Huayna Picchu that rises over and divides Machu Picchu. Its elevation is nearly 9,000 ft compared to the highest point in Machu Picchu, of 8,000 ft. It's rarely climbed since there are so many other buildings to see, and unless you're there with a guide, you wouldn't even know that hiking up it would be an option. I really had no idea what I was getting myself into when I hiked there, but I knew Don Francisco, one of the shaman, was going so I wanted to be able to spend an entire day studying him.

We began the hike after being counted at the gate. Only a limited number of people are allowed to enter each day, and campers are discouraged by only allowing small day packs to be carried in. I had no idea what a long hike it was going to be, and I also hadn't taken into account my several days of not feeling well, but soon I realized I was severely dehydrated and struggling with the altitude. As we hiked up, I would become short of breath and questioned whether I could make it to the top. I would reach the 9,000-foot peak, but not without a struggle. The sun was very hot as we approached the summit, so that took a toll on me as well. The views were spectacular, and it felt like we could nearly reach up and touch God and the heavens. The top was covered in large black boulders, and it was hard to rest without falling between or off them. We watched as a condor flew in the distance (a sign of good luck for the shaman), and I took note of the quietness in the air.

We were told the hike down was actually more work than going up, so if we had struggled at all going up, we should consider going down the same way we came up. That made no sense to me so I continued on with the group. I became very thankful that I stayed with the group because, shortly after,

Don Francisco found a cave, and upon inspection, began to scream excitedly, "Meteor, meteor, meteor!" Then he began to count the meteors. "Uno, dos, tres..." and yelled when he got to twelve, "Doce, doce, doce...ceremony, ceremony, ceremony!" Immediately, he prepared for a ceremony. We were told via a translator that this was a kind of sacred space. I figured the twelve meteors might have something to do with the calendar, but I wasn't sure. Since I was born on 12/12, it was my favorite number nonetheless.

During the ceremony, the most beautiful thing occurred. I wondered whether anyone else could see it, but I observed that no one else did; they were just sitting in a circle smiling at one another and looking around. I wanted to scream, "Are you guys seeing this?" The sound of the cicadas in the background was intoxicating and seemed to harmonize with us as if calling out, "We are here!" Then this incredible beam of light went flying out through the cave's ceiling, and I could sense other beings picking it up. I wanted to tell everyone we were part of a communication to beings outside of our awareness. I wondered why we were calling out and to whom. (I sensed they were not of this planet.) I wanted to ask questions, but as I thought of the questions, they seemed to be answered with words such as, "It is simply an organized event in time that was scheduled to occur at this very time and place when we arrived." After the ceremony, the cicadas would quiet down and we would stop for lunch, where we would watch Don Francisco nod off in the hot sun. I studied his innocence and smiled.

Then we continued down. The path seemed very easy at first, but then we started to climb and I started to run low on water. It seemed as if the rest of the group would move gracefully ahead, and suddenly, I was behind, and it was just Don Francisco and me. I had my alone time with him, but I was unsure it was how I had expected it to go. I was struggling with the climb, but I didn't want anyone to know. As I started to slow

down, Don Francisco said to me, "Aqua," so I showed him I was very low. He kept motioning for me to drink the water and repeating, "Aqua, aqua, aqua!" Then something happened that had never once occurred in my life until now—I quit! I couldn't move! I gave up! It was rare to hear words like that come from my mouth or even to accept the idea in my head. But I just fell down and everything started to spin, and I felt as if I were going to pass out. I lay there unconscious for a few minutes, and then I heard Don Francisco yelling, "Aqua, aqua, agua, corazon, corazon, aqua, aqua rapido!" but no one came! He was getting nervous, but then he suddenly calmed as I began to sense help from the trees.

I began to see that the trees were sending me love; I could suddenly see (with my eyes closed) all the details of their branches and leaves and the way the light was shining on them—every detail; then I could see their molecular structure and the water that lay on or maybe was stored within them. But I didn't want to take the help. I didn't want to go on at first. I was happy being exhausted and giving in. Don Francisco just stood quietly and held the space as sacred, and suddenly, it was as if I could hear his thoughts and understand his actions as he stood back to let me process this moment and decide how I wanted to take it.

For a brief moment, I knew I had a choice. I knew that if I wanted to, I could choose the exit strategy of the failed heart and dehydration (and not return home), or I could find another solution that would allow me to move forward and step back into life. I thought about how I had nothing to return to at home. I watched Don Francisco hold the space and get out of the way so I could decide. He stood in complete non-judgment. He was aware that this was my moment, and I watched (more sensed) him as he watched (sensed) me. It was here that I found the magic. I started to tear up. It was his ability to hold a space of complete neutrality that allowed me to choose to take another step and move on. I had never experienced anything like this

before. Suddenly, I knew I needed to share this kind of neutrality, and I saw how it could be applied in the lives of everyone I knew. I sort of saw it as a kind of secret to life. We are all here for the experience each of our lives has to offer, and I knew if I could help others without judgment and stand in neutrality, I would be offering others the same gift of this experience.

I realized I would take the "energetic water" the trees had shown me and seemed to offer up in my healing. I asked nature to assist me in providing me with the strength and energy to go on. I assumed it would all happen energetically since nothing else seemed to make sense. I got up just in time for one of our group leaders to come over, not to check on me so much, but to check on Don Francisco and make sure he was still with the group. When the leader arrived, Don Francisco nearly grabbed the water right out of his hands and made him give it to me. The leader was completely unaware of what had just happened and why. It dawned on me then that everything I had done in my life to that point I had always made look easy. Nothing was easy, but I had just never let people know when I was struggling since I had never wanted to be a disappointment or inconvenience to anyone. As I got up, Don Francisco took my backpack and put it on his back to carry along with his own very heavy bag, all the rest of the way down. I began to tear up again in response to his unconditional love. It was never about getting to the top and down. It was most definitely about the journey in between! I was lightheaded and dizzy until I got to the bottom. The views were breathtaking (literally), and the sun slowly began to work its way down behind the big mountain.

I walked down wondering why I had chosen to go on, how I would share Don Francisco's actions, and whether anyone would really understand the power of standing in neutrality and allowing others to choose. As I walked, I sorted things out in my head with each step. I wondered why I had chosen life, and

what I could do to make my own or another's life better. What changes or improvements would I actually make? How had this experience really changed me?

The remainder of the trek down was actually down (rather than up as we had been doing…to get down). When we got down, we would walk through Machu Picchu and take a moment sitting on one of the impressive walls. As we sat there, I felt my body and heart, and I wanted to cry, but then some llamas started coming toward us, which excited Don Francisco so much he started yelling and smiling, "Yama, llama, llama, yama!" I was again in awe of his innocence. I spent the entire day with him and only saw him get mad the one time when no one gave me water, and then, he hadn't been so much mad as concerned. I had an energy healer crush on him, and on his power, grace, ease, and awareness—I didn't know humans could exist in that way. There was nothing mean or spiteful in him. He was here to help the entire planet…no…the universe. He understood his role in the universal plan. I was just simply in awe. Somewhere along the way, either up or down, I realized I was no longer seeking Tia—I was seeking awareness and truth.

EXERCISES:

1. Think of a time in your life when you wanted to quit, give up, or even take your own life. What circumstances brought you to that position? ______________________________________
____
____
____
____
____
____
____

2. You obviously persevered onwards in your journey. Below write why you continued on your path to find your truth. ______

______

______

______

______

______

RETURNING HOME

I don't remember much about the trip after Machu Picchu. We had one more land healing ceremony inside Machu Picchu despite the explicit instructions given by park officials upon entering that there would be none. But we happened to be located in an area where the patrols understood the need and allowed it to occur. Many tourists gathered around and watched. I began to connect to a kind of energy that was nothing I'd ever expected. It was as if I could see beings working within another dimension. I remembered a point on the Inca Trail that we had walked several days prior when I felt another energy presence there that was outside of this dimension. I would take note of it but nothing more on this visit. I will explain a vision later on that refers back to this location on the trail. I didn't know it had grabbed so much of my unconscious mind until later. Before I knew it, the ceremony was over, the bags were packed, and I was heading to the airport to go to the only place I knew as home. I was sad to leave and return to my former environment because I knew once there I would likely have to prepare for a divorce.

Many people would grow ill on the long trip back to the airport, so we needed to stop a few times. I was also starting not to feel well again, but then I realized how exciting it would be to get onto the plane and have food I could trust and finally eat. As I approached the plane, ham and cheese sandwiches were being handed out. I told the stewardess I was a vegan

and had stated that on my reservation and asked whether they had anything else. I was told to go to the back of the plane and ask when I got on. I was really looking forward to that meal too. They told me they had nothing else and asked me what my seat number was. After I told them, they said they would get back with me. I was not feeling well at all, but suddenly, a stewardess approached and asked me to follow her. I had no idea why, but she took me up to first class with her and pointed to a seat. Peru would grace me with one last gift as I took my seat. I felt, at this point, that I had earned it. I had a long flight with the best food I had seen in days. I had a great dinner that night and an even better breakfast in the morning. I also sat next to the sweetest man who wanted to know all about my trip. At the end of our conversation, he said, "Thank you for the gift." I asked, "The gift?" and he said, "The gift of our conversation," and I nearly cried. I guess the magic of Peru was carried within me and I must have just shared it. I wasn't even exactly sure what I had just said, but I suppose in some way it had helped him. And he, a complete stranger, made me understand that my husband's heart was closed, and that if a complete stranger could show me more love than he could, I would be better off moving on.

Once I arrived back in the States, I almost began to cry. I saw how much space there was between things and how clean things were and I was in awe. I could only imagine what people would think who had never seen that kind of living before. I was so grateful. The next day was a weekend and my mom would pick me up to join her while shopping at her usual haunt—Costco. As we walked in the doors, I was again in awe. I had forgotten how much choice we had in the United States. I watched as people basically either said, "Yes, I want that" or "No, that's not good enough for me!" after I had seen so many starving people in Peru. I was thankful but something felt unbalanced. I would cry for days as I appreciated the simple things like putting my toothbrush in the water under my faucet or having a healthy nutritious meal. I was so thankful!

EXERCISES:

1. What simple things in life are you thankful for?
    1. ______
    2. ______
    3. ______
    4. ______
    5. ______
    6. ______
    7. ______
    8. ______
    9. ______
    10. ______

2. Who do you believe opens his or her heart completely to you and to whom can you completely open yours? ______

3. Whom would you like to have this kind of relationship with?

4. What do you need to do to connect more deeply with this person? ____
____
____
____
____

HELPING YOU DISCOVER YOUR TRUTH

Many people wait until the end of their lives to travel and experience other cultures; then upon retirement, they lack the health to make such trips. That is not what I want for you. I want you to set your intention as to where you want to travel, and then save or create the resources to make it happen. Then go out there in the world. Explore. Experience. Embrace. Live life to the fullest and your inner truth will appear.

SEEK. TRUST. BELIEVE. LOVE.

"A dog has the soul of a philosopher."

Plato

ANGEL DOG PRODUCTIONS

WEBSITES - BOOK COVERS - IMAGES - PRESENTATIONS

Leilani 2014

Leilani and Patrick 2014

Leilani 2014

Vegan Dog Treats

Shiitake's legacy brand...

She hopes to help other dogs!

Leilani, 2014

NEW PUPPIES 2014

Shiitake 2007

2014 - Portabello ("Bella")
Kauai King Kennels Kauai, HI

2014 - LeiLani
Kotrys Kennels, Maui HI

My best friend "Tak" 2013 Maui

Our first ride in the car on Maui

Bamboo forest, Maui 2013

Shiitake's first Lei, Maui 2013

Maui 2013

Riding with Patrick

Makena Beach, Maui 2013

Bamboo Forest, Maui 2013

Watching Fish
Ahihi Bay, Maui

Alaska Airlines®

Welcome Aboard

Customer NICOLE GABRIEL

Flight # 8607 Seat # 11C

Relax, I'm onboard too!

On behalf of Alaska Airlines, we wish you and your pet a most enjoyable flight.

PROVIDE TO CUSTOMER AT ORIGIN STATION

The doctors said you wouldn't make it to Maui... But you got to see more things than most humans do in your lifetime!

Bless you my sweet girl... you will never leave my heart!

Meeting Japanese Water Healer
Masaru Emoto Peru 2010

Don Francisco, Peru 2009

Don Francisco

Despacho Ceremony

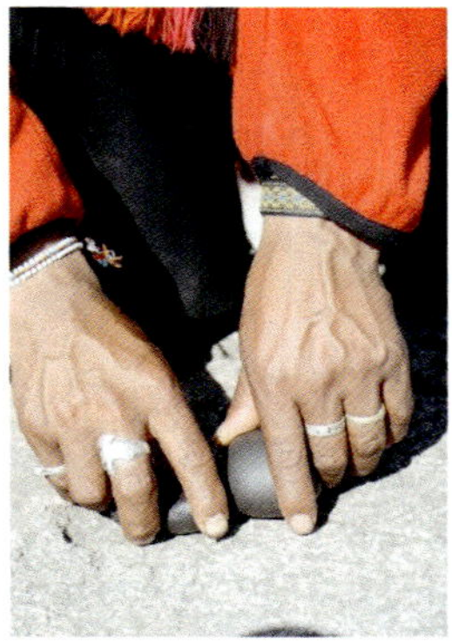

Encychu Knocking

My Happy Daisy Despacho
Peru 2010

Don Francisco Peru, 2010

Peru with Don Francisco, 2009

Don Francisco 2010

Puerta de Hayu Marka, Peru

Shaman couple

Huayna Picchu, Peru

Mount Shasta, California

Island of the Sun, Bolivia

Inca Trail Views

Belize Pyramid

Belize Caves

Lei Line, Peru

Meteor Ceremony

Inca Trail Farm

Healing Patrick's heart Victoria, BC 2012

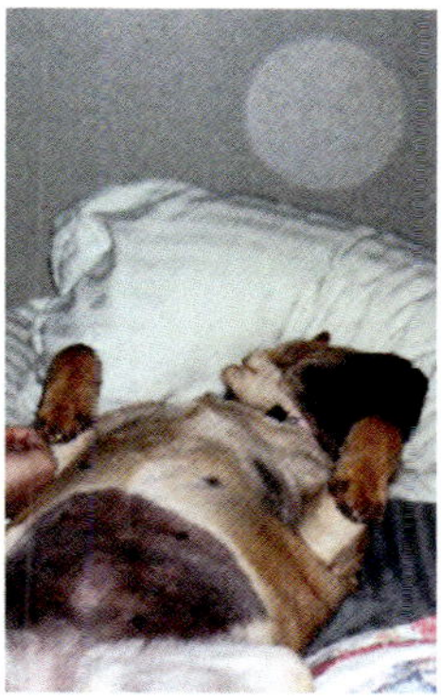

Tia's healing orb after spay 2001

The CWC, Metamora, MI

The Maya Center Lungar 2012

The Maya Center snowy driveway

What would you say to your daughter if she was this age and asked you what happened to her husband and kids?

Nicole 4 years old
Michigan

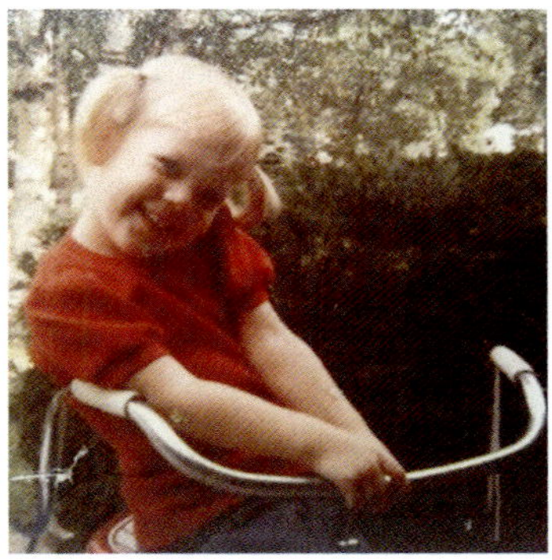

Welcome to the Maya Center

Nature Spirit

Nature Spirit Connection

Mai Tai & Tia 2001

Tia 2001

Sangria 2003

Shiitake "Tak" arriving on Bainbridge Island, WA

"Puppy Latte" from Starbucks, 2008

Sushi 2003 Michigan Trails

Sushi's Retirement on Maui 2013

Shiitake 9 weeks Feb 2008

"Hello cows, my name is Shiitake and I'm from Michigan!" Maui 2013

Shiitake's Grave Upcountry Maui

The Maya Center

Top of Huayna Picchu
Peru, 2009

The Maya Center 2012

Shamanic Healing Peru 2009

SEEK. TRUST. BELIEVE. LOVE.

CHAPTER 9

GRIPPING *Reality*

"Opportunities to find deeper powers within ourselves come when life seems most challenging."
— Joseph Campbell

My trip to Peru made me think twice about continuing my master's degree (and into my Ph.D.) in transpersonal psychology, but upon returning, I made one last trip to California to finish up the first year of my school program. I arrived a day early, but I had no idea I was early and had never planned it that way. The event would not start until the next evening with a kickoff banquet, so I decided to get up early that day and go to Mount Shasta and back, and if I got back too late, I would just miss the opening ceremony since I dreaded those kinds of events anyway. I had rented a cute little yellow VW Beetle and got up early to make the drive. I had heard all about the magical powers of the area back when all the chaos of the "visitation" first occurred at 1:11 a.m. that winter morning with Mr. Florida. Actually, a series of phenomena had led me to Mount Shasta that day, so let me back up....

One day, very shortly after the events of that winter morning, I received a phone call from a woman named Kathy who asked whether I had been associated with the chiropractic clinic in town. When I told her I had, she told me she had received a

channeled message that she needed to find me. She went to the clinic to ask about me, but it was closed so she went to the vitamin shop next door, which had one of my Maya Center advertising postcards so they gave her my contact information. She told me it was important for her to meet me, and she wanted to come over right away. Mr. Florida happened to be in town, so I told him about the situation and how I was curious to meet Kathy and know what she wanted.

When Mr. Florida and I met her, he told her about the incident with the light in the driveway, the being that had passed through the house, and the opening of what he (and several others now) called a "portal" or "stargate." We had begun to notice that as we stood in the bedroom near where I saw the blue vines light up and crawl up the wall, we could feel something passing through us or moving within the room. We even would light candles and watch the flame's direction, and sometimes, we'd feel something and the candles would nearly blow out. Mr. Florida would bring many people into the bedroom who were shaman, healers, and sensitives, and everyone felt something. People told me it was a portal, but I had no idea how they knew that. I would just listen and watch, but I knew something was happening there, and when Mr. Florida showed Kathy this space, she felt it too.

Kathy turned out to be a heavyset woman with auburn hair and quite an attitude. She would tell me from the beginning how it was going to be. Then she invited herself and two other friends over the next day and said she had been told that a ceremony needed to be performed there in the early morning of the spring equinox and she wanted me to perform and lead it. I had no idea why it was so important, but out of curiosity, I agreed. It was strange, but on the cold morning before they arrived, I knew I needed to trudge through the woods and swamps on the edge of the twenty-five acres and bury single-pointed quartz crystals. During my shaman training, I

had been taught that this would create additional sacred space and protections for the land and those on it. So I put on my winter wear and planted four crystals in the earth. Cold, wet, and winded, I returned just as they began to pull up the driveway. As we began the ceremony, I called to the spirits of south, west, north, east, the land, and then the heavens. As I did so, a strange sound started to come from the woods. It sounded like Native Americans preparing for war. We heard a kind of Indian chant. Kathy was sure to point it out and tell us exactly what it was: "The Native Americans on this side of the land are preparing to fight those on that side of the land." I felt a bit unsettled about continuing, but I called upon a Higher Power and placed my trust there that I would do what was of the highest and best order for all concerned.

Upon opening the space, I instructed the others how to sing a particular song we used in my shamanic training. We sang for a bit until Kathy interrupted to point out that an energy was coming in and we all needed to go into the woods deeper to receive a transmission. As we proceeded to walk into the woods, I found myself watching Kathy, her friends, and Mr. Florida spinning in the woods like surprised cockroaches blinded by the light. While they were struggling to find some kind of transmission, I was innocently overtaken by one. It was as if the sky opened up and an angelic code in another language was downloaded into my being. I saw the alphabet characters, but I didn't recognize them; they looked like the combination of a Middle Eastern script and a musical note. I received them quickly and then stood there wondering what the others were doing and whether they had also had an experience. I suddenly felt compassion and even sorrow for them since they had all come from great distances to be there that morning and not one of them seemed to get anything. I wondered why, if we were all God's children, that message seemed only for me. I was starting to see myself as gifted in some way, but I was not sure what to do with that.

After the ceremony was completed, Mr. Florida invited all the women into my bedroom to visit "The Portal." I was always uneasy about these visits because it felt as if I were not supposed to share it with just anyone. I learned my intuition was correct when I now experienced the most outrageous event I have ever had. This event and my involvement with these women would be the most negative experience of my awakening and haunt me for years.

When we entered the room, I started to feel some very heavy and negative energy, but my curiosity had gotten the best of me, causing me to be lured into what appeared to be a kind of game for them. Both of the other women ran counseling businesses, and one of them was a professional psychotherapist. Since they were helping people, I trusted that they were inherently good. As we became relaxed in the space, they started to transform their physical bodies into something else. I thought my eyes were playing tricks on me since we were in a partially darkened room. But Mr. Florida was there with me, so I relied on him to tell me what he was seeing as well.

Mr. Florida and I were talking to Kathy. The room was full of distraction with the others talking and playing with the energies of the portal. Then the Ph.D. (a gray-haired woman in her late fifties) leaned up against the wall where the portal was. Suddenly, it appeared as if her body had fallen into the wall and only her head remained. But her head was starting to shift into something that was not human. I grew very frightened, but then I eased my mind by thinking of the sacred space I had earlier created. I said to the other woman, "Oh my God, her head is shifting into an old wrinkly troll's!" She told me to keep it quiet because she was embarrassed to show her true self. I was shocked by what I was seeing, shocked that she could not only shift into something else, but that I also knew what it was. I was shocked that the others knew it too. I asked Mr. Florida quietly in a whisper whether he also saw her face. Then her

face turned into something that looked like an alligator. She grew large snake-like yellow eyes with long black pupils and an extended snout. Her skin grew scales and turned into a dark blackish green. It all happened so quickly, but they were reacting as if this experience were the norm and there was nothing to fear. I was nearly ready to pass out at the sight of what I was seeing, but I was trying not to be offensive, and I was also still not sure whether I had just made it all up.

I had seen something I could not wrap my head around. As the woman stood there coming back into the room and back into herself, I began to wonder whether she had done something negative to the portal or in my sacred space. I knew I would need to use every power in me to clean and clear everything in that space upon their departure. They would hover around a bit longer until eventually they decided it was time to leave. Several hours had passed in what felt like minutes, and after they left, I was speechless.

This event caused me to look at everything I ever knew and to question it as false. It was as if a curtain or veil had been pulled and nothing I had ever thought true was behind it. I trusted nothing and no one. I wanted to cry, but part of me also wanted to tell everyone that nothing is as it seems. No one is as he or she appears. But who would believe me, and had this experience really been real? Had I made it all up?

A few days later, I got a phone call from Kathy, inviting me over to one of their homes for lunch. I wasn't sure that going would make much sense, but again, my curiosity got the best of me. I wanted to know who or what these women were and what they wanted, so I went. After we ate, they asked me whether they could do a bit of a reading on me. After I consented, they told me things that gave credibility that they had gifts and were reading me. But then suddenly they were telling me how dangerous Mr. Florida was and that I should fear for my life. They

told me his intentions were not good, and they were worried he would physically abuse me. They nearly had me convinced. They continued to feed all kinds of negative energy at me, and when the reading was over, they told me they had a gun, so they suggested they go back to the house with me to threaten him and make him leave. I was shocked. I had begun by innocently seeking Tia and a greater connection to spirit, and now there was a gun involved! A gun! Really? Why? How? What had I done to deserve this?

By this point, I knew something was terribly wrong with these women, but I tried to play it cool. I would carefully change the conversation, lead them to believe I would do something about Mr. Florida, and ease myself out the front door and eventually right out of their lives! When I got home, I told Mr. Florida all about it and how they said they needed to remove me from the sacred land to get to me. They told me they were trying to lure me away from Mr. Florida and the property because they wanted to talk to me without him there, but I would sense they wanted me alone for darker reasons. I just wasn't sure exactly what those reasons were. They were trying to gain power by moving me into a place of fear, though. I told Mr. Florida I was worried about why they said what they had about him and how it had brought up doubt, but in my heart, I knew he was incapable of such behavior. I did realize, though, that our time together needed to end because I was becoming very exhausted and just needed peace to heal my heart. I so badly wished my husband would have seen that in marriage there was "for better or worse," and this was the time I needed him to be my husband the most. I needed to be held by someone who loved me.

After this event, people just started coming to my house and calling and saying they were drawn there and could they just walk the land or meet me. Everyone started showing up, and many of them wanted to spend time in my bedroom, so it was starting to get a little out of hand. All I ever wanted in all of this

was just to find my Tia. Before I knew it, I was inviting in all this energy and these people into the most intimate (and what should have been peaceful) room in my house. I needed some time to digest many things, and I wanted everyone in my life to go far away so I could. There was hardly anyone I could talk to about this event or the possible UFO experience, and if I tried, I'd likely be locked up in a psych ward.

SPENDING TIME ALONE

I knew I needed to spend time asking myself what was true. I would spend the next several months alone, and I didn't want to leave the house or entertain anyone. I found a local church to go to and waited for Mr. Florida to figure out his next steps. He would move in with a friend of mine temporarily while both he and this friend tried to convince me that he was the love of my life. Yes, we'd had some deep and meaningful times, but the change I was going through was way more than I had bargained for, so I needed to be alone. I knew I wasn't losing my mind; I knew what I had experienced, and I knew it was all for me and not to be shared (at least not now). I so badly wanted my old life back, and I so wished my husband would comfort me, but I knew the likelihood of that happening was just wishful thinking. In time, Mr. Florida would get on a plane and return to Florida, and I would never see him again.

MEETING JUDITH

Shortly after "surviving" the UFO and "Reptilian Women" experiences I would begin to search the Internet to see whether I could find out any additional information or connect with others having similar experiences. I was shocked to find so many others had experienced these types of phenomenon. It was all there right in front of me. Some experiences were pretty far out there, so it was hard to weed through what I deemed phonies and real cases.

At this time, I was absolutely fascinated with Egypt, and Mr. Florida had even remarked that he knew nothing else, other than dogs, that could hold my attention like anything related to Egypt. I would sit and read about and research Egypt for hours. Needless to say, when a healer from Egypt popped into my world, via Facebook, I took notice. I also took notice of some comments on his page, including from a woman who had written something about portals. I ended up connecting with her and we had a long phone conversation. It turned out that part of what she did was open stargates and portals. She told me everything I described to her sounded like a portal had opened, and it was normal to have a lot of activity around it when it opened. She assured me that things would calm down.

She recommended I connect and have a reading with a woman named Judith, who turned out to be one of the most unique women I have ever met. Judith had been doing channeling work (accepting the voice of spirit through her) for years, and she was drawn to work related to extraterrestrials and crop circles and had written a few books on the subject. Judith was said to be an "oracle," and she did mystical readings that were on a whole different level than any spiritual reading I had ever encountered. She worked as a light worker and channeled mystical messages. She told me I was likely being visited by Arcturians or Pleiadians, and there was nothing to be afraid of. She also told me the same thing about the portal as the other woman—it would be busy at first and then it would calm down. As strange as it sounded, I felt easier knowing someone else understood what was happening—two someones. If any of the below is true, then I believe I've tapped into some great spiritual masters to assist me along on my path and I'm grateful for their presence. There is uncertainty in many things in life, and if there is any chance they are here to help and are of the light, then why not hold out hope as our great planet is in dire need?

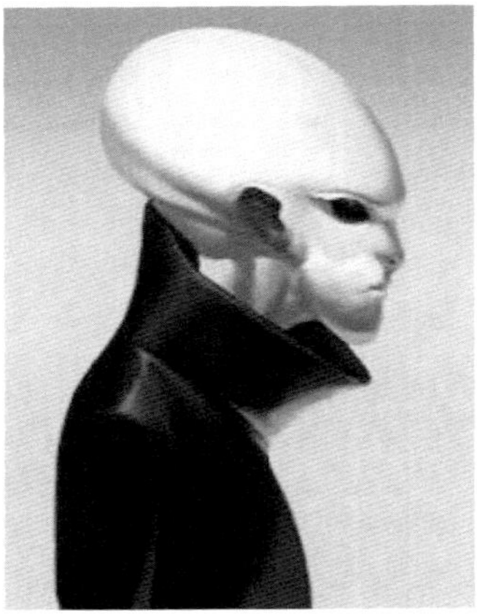

Image of Arcturian (Found on Internet, artist unknown)

ABOUT THE ARCTURIANS

Edgar Cayce has said in his teachings that Arcturus is one of the most advanced civilizations in this galaxy. *The Book of Knowledge—The Keys of Enoch* and *We, the Arcturians* are great books to read more about them, but there are so many others. It's said that the Arcturians work very closely with ascended masters called the Brotherhood of Light. They are said to be high vibrational frequencies—meaning closer to light, spirit, God. They are said to be benevolent beings from a blue planet orbiting the red giant star Arcturus in the Boötes constellation. The planet orbits at approximately thirty-six light years from our solar system. The Arcturians are said to be the most intellectually acute species known and one of the most caring. When I looked up the images I could find of these beings, I found a being that looked just like the beings I saw, and people all over the Internet were talking about them. I would learn that they are helping us to remember the memories of who we were and who we are. Raising your consciousness simply means allowing what is stored in your subconscious to rise to the conscious level for it is within the subconscious that all divine truths reside.

Image of Pleiadians (Found on Internet, artist unknown)

ABOUT THE PLEIADIANS

Pleiadians are also known as "Nordics" and are humanoid in appearance. They come from the star systems surrounding the Pleiades located in the constellation of Taurus, and they're said to be extremely concerned about Earth and our future and want to help us toward a higher spiritual destiny. The higher and lighter the frequency, the closer to the God source one becomes. They have come to help us gain wisdom and true understanding about our real essence—to open up more to love, and to feel our connection with one another and the universe. In the Earth realm, love is only experienced and known at a low level compared to all that truly exists. The God / Spirit frequency is beyond anything we know. It is Pure Love—it is Pure Light. Pleiadians are generally blonde-haired and light-skinned. In certain Cherokee legends, it is said that their people originated in the Pleiades long ago and they claim to have come to this world as "starseeds" to bring light and knowledge. If that is true, then many of us with Native American blood have Pleiadian genes. If you hear the terms "Lemurian" or "Atlantean," they would likely fall under the category of Pleiadians.

As Judith went through the reading, something was awakened in me. Suddenly, I was no longer listening to her but experiencing the story of her words. I was in Egypt with Jesus and Mary Magdalene, and there were ancient pharaohs and light bodies all present for this moment in time. Suddenly, a universal connection and plan were in front of me that seemed to tie all these experiences together in a way nothing else could. The mystical reading would go into great detail and last well over an hour. I felt so at home, as if I had been found, as I listened to her words. I would be reminded through our conversation that we are all seeking light, and no matter what, I needed to keep in mind that universal kind (not just mankind) cannot evolve to a higher vibration or God source unless all beings find their way to the light.

Judith also told me I was unique and my DNA was encoded with mystical knowledge, which was associated with her work to decode what she called "the records of creation." There was no doubt in my mind that we were very deeply connected. I would find out later that Judith would place me in her "soul group" that she called the "13.13.13." Each of us in her soul group had come to her within a few days of one another, and later, we would participate together in conference calls. She would tell us that our special DNA codes were important for integration of this material into the collective, and that we were also grounders for the intense energies that challenged her physical body. She explained this reading would even affect the Akashic Records (records of mystical knowledge encoded in the astral plane). I knew what she had done was way more than a reading. It was more like a synchronistic event, a coming together that was marked in time, that would unlock the keys of humanity and assist in all beings' divine enlightenment.

Judith and I were both very excited to meet each other. I wanted to spend time with her to learn so much more, but I also knew it was unlikely we would ever physically meet. She lived in

New Mexico and I in Michigan, and it seemed as if each time I moved in her direction, she would travel to another location on the globe.

Over the next few years, I would follow her recorded channelings that were passed to the whole group via email and I would call in to participate in the calls. It seemed as if whatever I did on my end would pop up in her channelings and messages. In the case of the reptilian women, I wanted to clean out the energy with which I felt they had contaminated the portal. I would place a large Vogel crystal (used for extracting negative energies) next to it overnight and ask that, as I slept, my most powerful spirit guides or masters would work to clean it. At that same time, Judith was awakened by a vision of Jesus standing in a portal with a large crystal. On occasions when I would travel (to Peru, for example) she would receive healing energies from Peru in her visions. Wherever I went, something would come into her vision directly related to my whereabouts.... I was very drawn to travel during this time. It was always about healing and I always knew that wherever I found myself, even if I didn't know I was doing anything, something within my DNA was helping or healing me and the planet just by my being there. I slowly began to see that no matter where I was, I was always in the right place.

LOSING TIME

When you work with higher energies, time gets manipulated so I would often lose track of it. But one event in particular would have me questioning where I went. One day, during the height of all the UFO and portal phenomena, I left the house for a holiday event at my parents' house. It was a cold and snowy late afternoon. I drove down the long wooded driveway, and as I approached the end at the street, it was as if time shifted and I suddenly blacked out, but I could feel myself still driving. I was not scared at all. I remember driving, but it felt as if I were

not going anywhere fast. I could feel the bumpy dirt road beneath me, and I felt a sensation as if I were there but I was not. I drove for about twenty minutes at least, and then suddenly, I felt lost and had no idea where I was. I came back into myself and called Mr. Florida (who was still visiting at the time). When I asked him how long it had been since I left, he said about twenty or thirty minutes. I told him I had driven down the driveway and started the ten-minute drive to my parents' house, but all this time later, I was back at the end of the driveway again. I told him I thought something had happened. All he said was "Cool!" I didn't know what to do and just continued on to my parents. I was deep in my thoughts, but not really as shaken up as I probably should have been. I felt as if I had gone somewhere, and I wondered where that somewhere was. In the back of my mind, I wondered whether I was abducted, but I could only share those thoughts with Mr. Florida since no one else in my world would have understood. I would read years later in Dolores Cannon's books of experiences time and time again where this kind of episode would most definitely turn into a visitation on another plane where great lessons and teachings would be gained. This time was very confusing for me, and it has taken years for me to come to grips with all of the experiences.

SEEING THE LIGHT WITHIN

After Mr. Florida left for good, I had this sweet little Catholic Mexican woman come to me, maybe more out of curiosity than anything else since her energy appeared to be very clean. She told me how she prayed the rosary daily, believed deeply in Jesus, and had regular conversations with God. I nearly fell to the floor when I saw the light within her. It was so bright! I had, just weeks prior to this session, heard how you can only see in others what you have within yourself. I thought people were coming to me to remove the bad things, but now I could see they were resonating with all aspects of me. I nearly fell over since I could only see this incredible light in her because it also

existed within me. I started to cry with her, and we hugged and cried some more. We were just somehow so overtaken by the acknowledgment of each other's light.

This experience reminded me of a time when I was out to lunch with Mr. Florida before he left to go back home and I asked him whether he could see the amazing light within and around the man who had just walked into the restaurant. The man was simply glowing. Mr. Florida told me he thought he could, but he trusted what I saw. When I got up and went to the restroom, he apparently went over and asked the man why his light was so bright. The man explained it was because of his deep relationship with Jesus Christ. When I returned to the table, Mr. Florida told me his response and part of my insides just sung from knowing I could see his light. Just before we left, we went over to his table so I could be introduced to him. I was in awe that I could see his light. It was brighter than that of any human I'd ever seen. And better yet, I knew my light was growing!

I began to wonder why if I could see this light in people, I didn't see it in all of them. I realized something must be unique about them or me. The concept of light stuck with me for quite some time. When I went to yoga events, people who appeared to be saint-like in my eyes (with bright lights of their own) were coming to me to ask me crazy questions like "Has your light always been so bright?" or "What did you do to get your light so bright?" or "Was it the tantric yoga we did today that brightened your light? It's amazingly bright!" I wasn't sure what was going on, but the way I saw it, I must have been doing something right. I recalled the shamanic training event where the person I was paired with had asked me whether I was an angel. He had told me he had worked on many people and he had never seen a light so bright and it was blinding. I wasn't sure what to make of it then, but something inside of me knew I was an angel. Now I started to question things; for example, if he could

see my light, he must be an angel as well. I began to wonder whether we are all angels but have been muddied by the physical and all our wounds and experiences. I wondered what set me aside from others and how I would live my life differently knowing I might be an angel. I wanted to talk to other people who were angels. I read many books by Doreen Virtue and especially related to her little book, *Realms of the Earth Angels*. It was a great place to start.

Then I went to a place of deep confusion and almost despair because I wasn't sure how to live life from here on out or whether I should do anything differently if I were an angel. Without any provoking, within a day of questioning my light, I had a very visual client come in for a massage and explain to me that today she could see my wings and that she knew I was an angel, but she had never seen one before. I felt like an alien or a freak! I didn't feel beautiful! I felt far from it. I would now feel obligated to live as an angel and wondered whether I was up for the challenge. It felt more like an obligation than a freedom. It felt heavy. I prayed for days after hearing these stories of my light. I never felt I received an answer. I wondered what truth looked like for me and for others, and if we were all blinded by some kind of veil.

At this point, I had little concept of time or interest in life. It's almost strange that this kind of light and beauty would cause me such distress. I would spend time studying the dark side of the experiences I had just witnessed and would begin to see the play of light versus dark and how the two could serve one another. Each required the other for growth. I knew the light would eventually pop through if I just bored through all the dark. I held on to all the faith I could.

My family would question what I was doing and when I'd step back into my career, but I was trying with everything in me to understand what was happening to me and to find ways not

just to reground myself but to find the will to live. How could anyone relate to what I was going through? For well over a year, I would only teach my yoga classes, and I realized I did so not so much from love of teaching them as to ensure I wasn't alone and to inspire myself to stay alive. My students literally kept me alive at one point. Also, Shiitake would become a kind of spiritual guard dog, and from here on out, she seemed to have my back. When energy would shift, she always seemed to know and come between me and any other person to tell me she felt it. It was almost as if she were asking, "Are you sure you want to proceed?" At the same time, I would go into the deepest depression of my life and realize that if nothing mattered to me, my guard and fear levels were way down. I was just surrendering to whatever God had in store for me. I suppose I just needed to exhaust myself.

I seemed to float into the most magical places when I stopped caring about life and the judgments of the self and others. In my visions, I would see many things. Once, I saw the skyline of Jerusalem. I didn't really know what it looked like, but upon researching it, I found my vision was right on. But I had no idea what to do with it. I just recalled a particular mosque-like building that seemed to call to me, but it wasn't like I could easily get there to inspect it and find out why. I wasn't sure how these visions were serving me.

In another vision, I would be introduced to a man with a long white beard, white hair, and wearing a long white gown and holding a white cane. I had seen him many times in my visions since I was a child. (I called him Noah as a child because he resembled the man on the Noah's Ark sheets on my bed.) He was the guardian of a special place that seemed to coexist in the same location that had caught my eye in Peru off the Inca trail—possibly another dimension. It was, but it wasn't. I saw that this place existed in the very same place as a farmer's land just off the Inca trail, and now I knew why it was captivating to

me as I walked it alone that day in Peru. I realized that multiple dimensions exist here on our planet at the same time as the one we are living in here and now. He would show me what he called the "Knowing Stone." As I approached it, I could see that the walls were made of crystals that were blinking, reading, and learning my energy, and soothing me as well as teaching me. The crystals were alive and sensing my energy, and as I entered into this circular room, the crystal walls emitted a soft sound (a hum almost) and blinked in a multitude of colors, but mostly green, which I knew to be the color of the heart and healing.

The man now asked in the most loving manner how he could help me. His speech was telepathic, and I understood he was there to help and serve me. He asked what I'd like to know from him or the stone. I told him that in all this work, the only thing I wished to know was "Where is my Tia?" As she walked out from around the stone, he asked whether there was anything else. I grew so emotional from learning that Tia was there that I didn't care to know more. I heard, "She has always been with you and always will be." I imagined reaching down and holding her, smelling her, feeling her and I became so emotional that I cried myself right out of the vision and back into this reality. This would be only the second time in several years that I had seen her in my dreams or visions.

DENNIS & THE CROW

I had some very powerful healing sessions that would be among the last I would do since I no longer felt the draw to do work as a healer. I wasn't sure whether I had fulfilled some karma or I was simply healing myself to the point where I no longer attracted those needing the healing, but nonetheless, I would fade away from the title of "healer" shortly after these sessions and almost take on the role of observer. I guess when I look back on it, I was learning from life experiences, and possibly, now I was moving toward what the shaman had talked about in

regards to stepping into that Master Shaman role. Life was my classroom, not an institution.

Before I had left the massage and chiropractic office, I'd had an experience with a sweet Parkinson's massage client. He was in his mid-fifties and came in regularly so every massage therapist there had worked on him at one time or another. He would walk slowly and shake heavily, but generally when he would get on the massage table, he would relax and shake less. One day, I was just about finished with his massage and he was very relaxed. All of a sudden, I heard the caw of a bird and saw an image in my mind's eye that alarmed me—a shadow was coming at him that actually made me duck. It was a large crow, and it flew into the room and straight into his back. I stopped for a moment to ask myself whether I had actually seen that, but as I watched him, I saw him take the biggest, clearest breath I had ever seen him take, and as he exhaled, he was no longer shaking. The massage was actually complete, but I kept going a bit longer just to make sure he was okay…and to reground myself from the experience. I exited the room and let his wife know he was done so she could go in and help him up. All of a sudden, we heard a loud crash in the room and she went running in. He had obviously tried to get up on his own and fallen.

I went downstairs to tell the staff he had fallen and to keep an eye on him. As I did so, I heard a little voice telling me he would not be around much longer, and it suddenly came out in my words with the staff. We would be selling the office soon after, so I didn't expect ever to see Dennis again. Actually, I would see him one last time at the Maya Center. Within a month of the crow flying into his back, I would see great bright lights one night that woke me from my sleep, and I knew those lights meant someone had passed. Even though we no longer owned the office, the next day, I would get a call from the girls in the office telling me Dennis had died.

Ironically, the day Dennis passed, his wife had a massage set up with me for herself. I was not expecting her to arrive, but just ten minutes late, there she was standing at my door with tears in her eyes! I couldn't believe she was there. We talked for a while and she told me how it had happened. I told her I would love to give her a massage and that she should just let out all her grief as I did so. I was honored beyond belief that she trusted me with her heart. When she asked me whether Dennis had ever told me he was dying, I told her he hadn't. I didn't tell her about the crow because it still seemed strange to me, but I thought it was a sign or way for Dennis to release any pain or sorrow and let go, and maybe it was how I knew he would pass. I really loved this couple and truly honored the time we shared together. I was beginning to understand how short the time is that we have here, and how much it matters in so many ways. I stood in love and observed.

THE BOY WITH THE GREEN GOO

I was now able to see and work with angels through death and dying experiences, and I began to wonder whether it was why I had experienced so many deaths to begin with. I was also opening up to seeing into the other side, and I was able to know the status of those who had passed over. I first went there with Mai Tai's death; then shortly after, I was contacted by an old client who told me her two preteen children were going through kidney failure. Ironically, Tia had died of kidney failure and I believe it also ended up claiming both Mai Tai and Sangria's lives. I had gone on a quiet but personal mission to understand kidney failure in the Shar Pei breed and initially started all this work not just to find Tia, but to find the source of the disease that took her life because I loved the breed and kidney failure was so common for it.

Not only would this woman contact me to tell me about the kidney failure in her home, but she also contacted me just days

after her fourteen-year-old son's death. She told me her whole house was unsettled after his death. She asked whether I could see or talk to him. I told her I could try if she wanted to stop by. Ten days after his death, she showed up at my healing center. I told her I wouldn't charge her and asked her to lie down on the massage table. She was exhausted and very angry and emotional, but after she took some deep breaths, she began to calm down. Then I began to see a little boy. I told her I could see a boy with a kind of bowl-style haircut and shiny brown hair. I told her he was full of energy and I couldn't get him to sit still long enough to talk to him. She confirmed it was likely him and told me that, before he got sick, he was very active and energetic and had a hard time sitting still. I told her he was playing with something green and stringy or sticky in his hands. She told me that on his last hospital visit, he kept hitting her with something green and stretchy. Again it was confirmed that I was actually seeing him, and I was in awe that I could even do so.

She wanted me to ask him whether he was okay and why he was showing up in his sister's dreams. She also asked why she could feel him around the house. I told her he seemed to be saying he was happier than ever before and finally home and finally free. I also told her she was merely his temporary guardian on earth and she was not at fault for anything. He died because his experience as a human was over. He seemed to be elated and celebrating that he had moved on, but he couldn't fully go until the family could release him. She told me she wanted to die to be with him. When I explained that her daughter needed her, she said that was the only reason why she didn't find a way to do it. I went on to tell her that he wanted her to know he was concerned about her and he continued to say he was fine and happier than ever! She and I talked afterwards about my visions, and I asked whether she had any other questions, but she was so distraught and even embarrassed that she had shown up crying that she simply said, "Thank you" and left.

I wondered whether I had given her what she was seeking, but I was told by my inner knowing that everything was perfect and she got what she needed. Several years have gone by now and I have not heard from her, but I still try to hold sacred space for her and her family. I know she came into my life to show me how silly it is to mourn the loss of a loved one because people (or pets) who have passed are generally happier once they arrive on the other side, but they cannot be completely free when they have to worry about those left behind. In our pain, we can keep them limited, and we must learn to let go because we love them so deeply. Standing in a place of deep love, we must move on, if not for ourselves, we must do it for them. I would know this now when the next loss came into my life and I took into account all these words to release them fully. I would be able to share these observations now in hopes of helping others.

TWO OLDER MEN

This very large older man, a farmer who looked a bit like Santa Claus, would come in for a massage on occasion. He would tell me how much pain he was in and all the muscle relaxers he needed to take to relieve his pain. I honestly didn't realize just how much pain he was in until his wife came for an appointment of her own. As she lay down on the table, she told me her husband used to be in so much pain until he had started to see me. I said, "Oh, that is so nice and I'm glad I could help." She said, "Oh, but you don't understand—he was literally in so much pain that he regularly talked of taking his life." She went on to say that he no longer talked that way. I started to cry and told her I was so thankful that I could help him. She told me when he talked so highly of me, she wanted to see whether I could also relieve her pain. I would never see either of them again after that day. I can only hope they both felt so well that they never again needed care. I was overwhelmed with gratitude for being able to help them since I really hadn't known what I was doing. I was just observing their pain.

On another occasion, I would clearly see that another older man who was a regular seemed to have something wrong in his brain. I would tell two of our different doctors at various times when he was coming into the clinic about this matter, but I was too shy to say anything to him. Neither doctor was able to see or diagnose anything, and in fact, the man stopped coming for chiropractic since he stated my massages were helping him much more, but when we sold the office, he followed me to the Maya Center for massage. I kept watching his head and wondering when there would be an opportunity for me to say anything to him. Maybe if he told me he had headaches, it would open the door, but he was generally very quiet. I had been going through a very hard time with my divorce at this point, so I wasn't giving full attention to my clients. But one day his son called to apologize that his father had missed his appointment; he'd had emergency brain surgery instead and was in ICU in the hospital. I suddenly felt very bad that I had said nothing, but I was just never sure how I could.

WHO'S TOP DOG?

It would come to my attention very early on that animals seemed to imitate what is "wrong" in our lives by showing similar symptoms to our human ailments. More times than not when a student or client would come to me asking questions about healing a pet, I would find indications of similar "problems" with the pet's human. If you ever want to know the best approach to self-improvement, I would tell you to get a dog. Dogs by nature are the most loyal companions. In that loyalty, they also vie for top or alpha dog in the family pack. They almost seem to take on the pain of their family members in an effort to own the top dog ranking. My theory is that they want to mimic what ails the human to stay on par with a learned human behavior or way of life because they naturally see us as alpha. Although, sometimes we fail to take the alpha role or life pulls us off center and dogs either just follow our lead...or

worse, they act out. When someone notices his or her dog is ill, the first question I ask is: "What's going on in your home that your dog is imitating?"

A student of mine once came to me about her dog and I asked her this question. She claimed to know exactly what was going on in her home and went home and made some changes. Within a few days of making this change in her home, she reported back to me that her dog was amazing all the doctors and no longer needed the diabetes meds or insulin shots and was near a full recovery. They began to ask her what she had done. In this case she clearly acknowledged a need for healing in her home, but it's not always that easy. If you use Louise Hay's book *How To Heal Your Life* and use the body parts of your animal as a guideline, you will find the human link. Usually the left side of the body relates to the female family member and the right to the male. Then follow other practices to cut energetic cords so that your pet is always freed from the ties to your life's traumas.

DISCOVERING CONTINUITY

Everything would magically start to fall into place as I finally took my trip to California and Mount Shasta. I wanted to see the mountain because of what Mr. Florida had told me about it, and I had been directed to a series of books that I had just completed—the *Telos* series by Aurelia Louise Jones. Resonating with these books and my portal experience ultimately drew me to Mount Shasta. People had told me they could see the portal in my room leading to Lemuria, a legendary lost continent in the Pacific Ocean. It is believed by some that survivors of Lemuria have lived at Mount Shasta, and the *Telos* series talks about Telos, the City of Light, beneath Mount Shasta. I needed to close the circle of knowledge by making this visit.

As I entered the town of Mount Shasta, I noticed some unique images in the store windows and I suddenly felt very at home.

I decided I needed to check out a crystal store before making my way to the mountain. In the store, I found a huge assortment of Aurelia Louise Jones' books and some CDs as well as a few crystals said to have been created by NASA to replicate the crystal found in the center of the spaceship discovered at Roswell; unexpectedly, here was an association that led me into UFO phenomenon. Of course I bought some of the stones, and then I stumbled upon a few laminated cards of beings called "Ascended Masters" that I had started to see in my visions. I hadn't heard of ascended masters before and wanted to know more about them so I bought nearly every card the store had. I also bought some of Aurelia's meditation CDs.

When I got back into the car, I immediately put the CDs in the player and starting listening to the meditations. I was really enjoying them because they felt so comforting and familiar. It was already starting to get dark and I knew I had a long drive back. If I went to see the mountain, I would get caught in the dark and the school administrator was calling me (nearly harassing me) that my things were in the wrong room and the Dean of the School was actually trying to get into that room. I told them I was driving and would not be back for several hours. They now knew I had no intention of making it to the opening ceremony and I was a bit embarrassed about it They called me back to let me know they needed to move my things so the dean could get into the room, and I said that would be fine. I wanted to hurry to get to my room before it became a further inconvenience, so I put the CD on and hit the road.

As I listened to the CD, I nearly flew off the road when I heard Aurelia describe nearly exactly my experience with the "Knowing Stone." I realized then that where I had been in my visions was a place others had also been. I wondered whether only a few special people could get there. I began to wonder whether there were others like me. I began to see a continuity existed in everything I was experiencing and that it all does find a way

to come together. I began to become hopeful that I had not lost my mind. When I arrived back at the seminar, I placed the ascended masters cards all over in the new gigantic beautiful room I had now been placed in (to make up for my supposed inconvenience). I put the crystal near me and slept until morning.

EXERCISES:

A reason exists for everything. When you let down your guard and trust and believe that you will find what you are seeking, guess what? You will! I had now found my Tia and knew she was safe—even if it were only for a short while in an amazing vision that others might not deem real. I had seen my girl, and in just that moment, we were both free!

1. Have you sought a spiritual path and become lost in what you were finding / experiencing? Explain. ____________________

____

____

____

____

____

2. Have you started down a path only years later to poke your head out, take a breath, and realize where you were and that everything you ever knew had changed? Explain. ____________

____

____

____

____

____

3. Did something keep driving you forward but you had no idea why? Explain: ______

4. What experiences have you had in your life that have frightened you to the core? ______

5. What resources, people, faith did you draw upon to put your fears aside to set your mind at peace and bring you comfort? ______

HELPING YOU DISCOVER YOUR TRUTH

Many times in your life, things just don't make sense. You will be bombarded with other people's issues, challenges, and drama as they attempt to suck you into their problems. When this happens, be firm, protect yourself, learn from their mistakes, and stay on your path so you can continuously seek your inner truth regardless of how bizarre the circumstances appear. When no one else understands what's going on in your world, unseen forces are at your side, routing you through this "challenging script" that you wrote with your divine masters and God. When all else fails, nothing is left but you and the divine (God). Stop for a moment and look at that car parked next to you at the next stoplight or the person standing next to you in line. Imagine what challenges that person is facing that you might or might not relate to. Bless the person and hold him or her in peace, love, and light. We are here together simply to follow through on our scripts. You can help yourself and another to find your inner truths by standing firmly in love with the divine at your back.

SEEK. TRUST. BELIEVE. LOVE.

CHAPTER 10

UNDERSTANDING LIMITATIONS WITH Psychology

"Don't grieve.
Anything you lose comes
around in another form."
— Rumi

I went through the motions of the seminar to finish up my first year—in and out of boring lectures—and then went to hear Charles Tart, the founder of transpersonal psychology, speak to an audience. He seemed to be a very calm and kind man. I was very curious to hear what he had to say. I respected him for his knowledge and experiences, and he shared his story and how he began down the path of what is now known as transpersonal psychology. Then he began to talk of a case where he was working with a woman during a sleep study and how she started to float out of her body at night. He gave her numbers in various different scenarios on pieces of paper next to her bed. Each time she guessed the right numbers (in her sleep and as she left her body), so he concluded she was indeed able to read the numbers accurately each time.

I began to think about how a shaman would look at this scenario; yes, her reading the numbers was phenomenal and very intriguing, but didn't anyone wonder why she was leaving her body? I got up enough nerve to raise my hand and ask what her mental state was at the time of the study. He told me

very explicitly that her mental state did not matter since she was asleep...and reading the correct numbers. When I asked whether anyone had considered that a trauma might have occurred as her reason for stepping out of her body, he didn't seem to want to discuss it and moved on to the next hand raised. He even seemed very bothered by my question. When Mr. Tart called on the next person, she caught his attention by stating, "I used to step out of my body on a regular basis." His eyes opened and his ears perked up. She continued, "I think it was because I was experiencing a trauma and it was not safe to be in my body" (the point I was trying to make). He didn't seem to have an answer.

I wondered whether we were simply going to study the occurrence or we were going to help heal the individual. As I worked through my seminar's remainder, I clearly saw that healing was not something we would be trained to do in this program. If I completed the master's degree and continued into a Ph.D., I would merely be studying phenomena. At this point, I was looking at things through a shaman's eyes. I couldn't see the point in spending another $100K to study something when I had already built an incredible foundation that was making drastic improvements in people's lives. I might have understood differently had I continued, but it seemed as if a certificate were all I needed.

I suppose this experience was when I first realized my power as a healer and the lacking integration of true societal methods of healing. I knew that if I followed my heart and my inner knowing, I would go beyond the institution. I found it hard to attend the remainder of the seminar once I made up my mind not to continue, and eventually, I would retreat to my room, lie in bed, and mostly just cry. I missed the familiarity of my dogs and my husband and knew he had likely met someone (or several someones) either before or shortly after our separation, so now I was a very distant memory from his past. While in

California, I met an old high school friend and we had a great time catching up. One thing he said was that it was not too out of character for me to have become a yoga teacher because I was always a "pretty cool chick" and always pretty "laid back." It made me glad to think I was not too far off base from what I was as a young child because at this phase in my life, I had been questioning everything.

I started to see my gifts as a yoga teacher were something I had been carrying all along. Stepping into yoga had initially felt awkward for me, but once I got comfortable with it, it became second nature. I never like to stand up in front of a crowd, but when I saw I could transform people, doing so didn't bother me in the least. In fact, I began to see how public speaking was a way to empower people, and when they showed up, they knew they were going to have to do the work themselves. Shamanism spoke to me in other ways because you had to give in for someone else to "fix" you. In yoga, you would take ownership of that. I started to see a strength in people who were willing to sacrifice themselves and their comfort for growth in yoga. I started to wonder whether I could ever achieve that same kind of understanding with shamanism.

And then I began teaching shamanism. I never would have started, but my clients were asking me when I would and whether I could teach some of its techniques to help them take ownership of their own healing. I was finding that things were naturally falling away that no longer served me. And shamanism was knocking on my door again...but this time as a teacher! I had learned in my yoga classes that to teach something was to master it; I had never thought I could teach shamanism, but I sure wanted to master it. I was still questioning what had happened with all the deaths I had experienced and why I had to go through all of them at once. I wasn't learning what I had hoped to learn in the school program either. In fact, all the money it was going to cost to go through the program just sickened me.

I could actually make money to teach and learn as a bonus. I thought I might learn more about what I hadn't found answers for as I stepped into teaching.

I offered my services for free to those who couldn't afford them because I felt they would be able to help themselves (and others) to do their own healing, versus continuing to come to me. That wasn't always good for business, but I taught them how to do the "fishing." I ran two sets of classes for more than a year, and eventually, we combined both groups and had one large graduating class. I would later hear of all the amazing things the group was doing with the new tools I had taught them. I would also learn they were not only helping others but helping and working with each other in times of need. I was so grateful to have taught these students, but it seemed as if I only needed to teach for this short period and move on. There never seemed to be any more demand, and I had grown tremendously as a result, so I stopped teaching until the students appeared or I was ready again. I had many things to prepare for in my future, and teaching shamanism was not currently going to be one of them.

HEADING TOWARD DIVORCE

Once I returned home from the school seminar, I decided it was time to start removing more items from our home and taking them to my new home on twenty-five acres—The Maya Center. I was hopeful that the seminar would have taught me new approaches for handling divorce in a spiritual manner or that my husband would have changed his mind while I was gone, but I suppose he didn't even know I had left. The school program had now cost me nearly $30K; I was even being billed for classes I didn't take, but there was no way to argue with such a large institution—especially when I was in a fragile emotional state. I just had no energy and decided I would just walk away. I hoped for support in the program for all the life events

I had going on, but none was offered. It was just a large institution trying to make a profit, and I was merely a means to an end. I needed to focus on what was coming. My husband was not coming back and I needed to get a clear head.

I started going over to our home during the day while he was at work to go through all the things that had been in my life for the prior thirty-seven years. It was an overwhelming process. Not to mention at times I would enter the house to find empty beer and wine bottles and multiple dining plates as if he had been having several dinner parties. While I was trying everything I could to heal myself and waiting for him to come back to me, he had already forgotten all about me and was having multiple "good times" with "friends." I didn't even know he had friends. I would sit in the house and just cry and lose focus on my tasks at hand and sit paralyzed and numb with the idea that he could so easily dispose of me. I wondered who had been sitting in the chair I was in and had once shared with Mai Tai, Tia, and Sangria. I wondered who was now sleeping in my bed. One day when I came over to clean out some of the remaining closets, I was crying while he was in another room doing his normal routine. I kept hoping he would stop me or come in to talk to me, but he never did. All of a sudden, I heard him approaching and thought maybe I was wrong, but instead, he told me he was going out and to turn everything off when I left. I couldn't believe how cold he was. He never asked me how my Peru trip went or anything. He always seemed to have somewhere better to be and would never discuss the separation.

But he did want to talk about money—how he would keep all of it, including many of my things, and I could take my personal items, my dogs and cat and go. So one day I went over to the house to make an asset list for our pending divorce since I had heard it was quite expensive to have someone else do it. I came into the house with my morning tea, a scone, a clipboard and paper and went to sit in the kitchen. When I noticed a card

and flowers on the kitchen counter, I remembered it was his birthday. There was a small part of me that thought (simply out of routine) that they were even left for me. I was so emotional that I had forgotten all about his special day. Someone had only half-filled out the card, including writing some words about sex—I couldn't even read it all because my eyes got blurry. I walked into the other room and saw a suitcase on the floor and makeup in the bathroom. On the bed we had shared was a very sexy black dress, and on the wood floor I had installed were a pair of size 9 black high-heeled shoes. Piles of cheap fake gold bracelets were on the bench at the end of the bed my mother had bought and I had upholstered. When I saw the box of condoms poking out of the nightstand drawer, my heart fell into my stomach. I walked back out to the kitchen to see whether a name was on the card. There was—his ex-girlfriend from before we had married, "Ms. Va-Va-Voom!" If you ever met Ms. Va-Va-Voom, you'd know why she was given that name. I had heard some stories about her, and later I would see pictures of her with her neckline on her dress down to her bellybutton and her hem line just below her rear end. And worse yet, she was cheating on her husband to be with mine! Then suddenly I heard a noise and water running in the upstairs bathroom. I knew she had seen me coming and run upstairs to hide in the bathroom. I immediately started to cry and shake as I walked toward the door through which I had entered and kissed my old life goodbye! There was nothing spiritually that could have been done or said; no miracle phenomena to get me out of the reality of this moment. I had been replaced! I got into the car and started to cry. That night my husband would get flowers and a card from the same person he had been with before he met me.

On the way home, I stopped to cry in my mom's arms. She thought I was dating and had moved on all this time. I told her I was keeping myself busy until he figured out he missed me and begged for me to come back. I now knew why he never

had. I didn't want to compete with Ms. Va-Va-Voom! The reality of divorce was upon us. We had been separated nearly two years and it looked like time would heal nothing between us. I tried to go to the most spiritual place in my head that I could. I tried so hard to forgive him, but I was angry, bitter, and sad. I tried to be okay with him seeing her because I had dated Mr. Florida, so it only seemed fair. But now it was all making sense. I wasn't sure how long I had been played and when they had started communicating, but since she happened to live in Florida, I knew the relationship must be serious for them to make such an effort to be together.

I was so angry and so sad. Other people had jobs, kids, spouses, homes, and their sanity, but I felt like I had lost all of that. I was so angry that I was even drawing angry people into my healing rooms. I would have a man show up one day to pay me for work I had done for his wife. He was obviously looking for healing himself, but when I placed him on the table to offer him a free healing, he was so mad he started punching the massage table. It was rather frightening, but eventually he cooled. I also attracted other depressed people, such as a young girl who was a cutter. I tried to help her, but until I could help myself, I couldn't really help anyone. She would teach me that. I needed someone or something to help me break my anger cycle.

I had studied more in my shamanic and yoga practices about healing my heart than I had in the nearly $40K psychology program I had attended, so now I was also mad that I had wasted so much time and money on it. I had a huge debt and nothing more than a promise that the words "certified" would be mailed to me on a piece of paper for credentials in case some day someone actually asked. I was upset about the cost of yet another master's level program that hadn't helped me, and upset that the shamanic and yoga work I had been doing that had made such an impact on my life was considered "alternative" and weird by everyone in my world.

EXERCISES:

1. Think back to the angriest and saddest times in your life. What were the circumstances that put you in that position?

2. What did you do that helped you escape that situation in your life?

3. What can you do at this moment in your life so you will never again find yourself in that situation?

HELPING YOU DISCOVER YOUR TRUTH

There is an old Jim Rohn quote that says, "Formal education will make you a living; self-education will make you a fortune." I just want you to know that it is your life experiences that put you on the path to finding your truth...not some degree or accreditation. I should know as I have more degrees than I know what to do with. Also know that you are human so you are bound to have ups and downs in your life. Remember, it is always darkest before the dawn. Finally, remember what the German philosopher Friedrich Nietzsche said, "That which does not kill us makes us stronger."

SEEK. TRUST. BELIEVE. LOVE.

CHAPTER 11

SURVIVING Divorce & Depression

"Change in all things is sweet."
— Aristotle

I was at home feeling sorry for myself and very alone. Shiitake and Sushi were looking at me as if to say, "Well, now what, Mom?" I decided to light a big fire in the fireplace and curl up on a blanket. Several months had gone by and I had signed up for an online dating service. All of a sudden, a chat window popped up on my computer. It was a lighthearted guy from Colorado who soon had me laughing. With each sentence we shared, I wondered more about who "Mr. Colorado" was. I was so lonely and sad, so on a whim, a week later I thought it would lighten my spirits to fly out to Colorado to meet him. At this point, nothing seemed too weird for me to do. I was toying with the idea of where I might live once I was divorced, and I realized if I looked at this situation as an opportunity rather than an obstacle, it would lift my spirits more. I had decided when I placed my dating ad that I had always liked Colorado so that's where my profile said I lived. I figured I would meet someone and move there. And now I had met Mr. Colorado.

After several months of back and forth visits, Mr. Colorado became my angel. When he heard about the kinds of offers my

husband was making me in the divorce settlement, he nearly erupted and suggested I borrow money from him (until I received a settlement) to hire a good lawyer. His brother was an attorney, so he provided me a contact in Michigan. I would meet with several attorneys when Mr. Colorado came to town. We picked one, but it didn't work out very well, and after much heartache, we picked another. After nearly $30K was spent, we finally found one last attorney to take the divorce to completion.

Mr. Colorado held me together during all of it. I would get very depressed and upset at the money being spent, but Mr. Colorado assured me it would all be okay. I was emotionally and physically exhausted, but he kept moving me forward. I would spend my days crying and depressed, but Mr. Colorado would pick me up, dust me off, and make me smile. Most nights I would cry while Mr. Colorado rubbed my back until I finally fell asleep. I had never met someone more focused on making sure I was okay. I honestly think if it weren't for him, I might have considered ending my life. If he hadn't cared for me, I wouldn't have eaten, I wouldn't have had moments of peace, or been able to smile. He would make sure my girls (Sushi and Shiitake) were well-loved and exercised and included in all decisions. I even had an agreement with him that if anything happened to me, he would care for them the way I did.

Mr. Colorado's family had a condo in Breckenridge, Colorado, so we would go there with the girls to relax and get away. We never skied as I never wanted to leave my girls alone, so we would just relax, eat well, walk, read, or watch movies. The condo was so peaceful, warm, and cozy inside that even the girls didn't like going out in the cold and snow. Once in awhile we would go to this little pizza shop and have breadsticks and salad. It was quite nostalgic of the innocence of childhood. I almost expected an ice cream freezer or candy counter and the smell was most heavenly. I would temporarily forget about the issues back in Michigan when we would escape there.

HEADING WESTWARD

At one point, Mr. Colorado worried so much about my mental state that he wanted me to pack up the girls and a small U-Haul and come live in Colorado with him until I got through the divorce. So one day I packed, got in the car with my girls, and drove solo across the country with our small U-Haul in tow. I found the drive so peaceful, and even though it was long, I loved having the time to clear my mind and take in the sites. A visit to a friend in Nebraska made for a nice stop along the way. The vast farm fields seemed to show me there was room for expansion and to remind me that all things in life are cyclical and continuous. When, on a whim, Mr. Colorado decided he would fly to meet me in Nebraska, I was shocked by how caring he was to make sure I was not alone on my trip. I was generally overwhelmed by how he constantly went above and beyond to care for me. I had never met anyone who was willing to sacrifice so much for someone whom he really didn't even know that well yet. He had got in the middle of my ugly divorce and held me all the way through it, and that is something I will never forget as long as I live.

I was finally divorced on 1/11/11 (quite a magical numerical date). My intuition was opened with all the spiritual work I had done, and I knew the exact amount of the settlement a year or two before it actually happened, but it was very hard for me to accept. I knew my husband was hiding money in his native Canada and in several safety deposit boxes in the States. I knew he told many lies and it had taken him several years to plan everything. He had a degree in finance and knew how to handle numbers well. He was the doctor and I was just "the wife," so he seemed to have a lot of credibility until people finally understood my side of the story. On that last day in court, I would see him for the first time in many months. After all was done and said, I left with my attorney, happy to have settled after all this time, but when I realized my husband would never fight

for me and never come back, I got into my car and just cried. On that day, I would be freed from all marriage-related karmic wounds...or would I?

FINALLY ON MY OWN

My settlement was quite large, although I honestly feel it should have been more, but I suspected my ex-husband had spent plenty of years hiding money and planning for the divorce. I suddenly felt guilty and wondered whether he hadn't lied and really didn't make as much money as I thought. I worried that karma was going to bite me in the ass, and I worried that I had misunderstood things. My parents and others who knew him supported me and said they knew something was always a bit fishy and there were untold truths. I hoped one day I would know all the truths, but I could see the lies in the gray clouds floating around him. I also physically saw extra safety deposit box keys and P.O. Box keys on his keychain that I had no part in, and I saw several inches thick of large dollar bills in the glove box of his car and envelopes of cash in his wallet, and I predicted or foresaw the final settlement well before it happened. I wanted to live my life as cleanly as possible, so that I didn't bind him to me financially. But I also wasn't stable enough mentally to move forward, and I needed the income to live on while I figured things out. I needed to release all of my concerns to a power greater than me and accept that this too was all part of the "script" and planned for me before entering this life.

Just before the settlement, I needed to drive back to Michigan because my vehicle would go to him in the settlement. Once I got home to my twenty-five acres and opened the doors, I suddenly felt so free and alive. The dogs ran in happy circles and chased my cat Penelope (who had been left behind and cared for by my "sangat" of family, friends, and students). They were so happy, and seeing their excitement made me realize

it was a much better fit for me than living in the beige neighborhood home in Colorado. I was happy to be reunited with the land, the memory of the odd experiences actually seemed to comfort me now, and again I could teach yoga. I really missed teaching yoga on the land. I missed sharing a meal, chai tea, warm fires, and like-minded conversation with my students and friends. I suddenly realized I was not going back to Colorado. I realized Mr. Colorado had also become a bit controlling and needed me to check in with him regularly. I was so enjoying my freedom that was just inherent with the land. I had connected so deeply with it and every ounce of me longed to stay. I felt as if the land knew me better than I knew myself. I would often look to my girls to show me how I felt since the transition had left me not knowing myself sometimes. They would smile, dance, and nearly sing in happiness, so I knew I must be happy too.

However, in time I realized everything around me had memories attached to my husband. I knew I would never truly be happy unless I could create new memories with someone else, somewhere else. Mr. Colorado and I were not likely to create the memories in Michigan since he had a full life, family, and job in Colorado. I didn't like Colorado enough to make the move, and it just didn't feel right within my being to be there. I started to understand I had been very angry when I met Mr. Colorado, and for some reason, he was very angry at life too. Anger attracted anger. We would eventually split.

Everything I took to Colorado in that U-Haul was returned to me by Mr. Colorado as cargo on a semi-truck. It included every single thing I had ever given him. He was bitter and angry over the time and money he had invested in me, and I felt horrible that he was so hurt. I felt like a disease from which he was purging himself, and so much aggression and anger was wrapped up in those boxes that I felt belittled. I felt ashamed for following and listening to my heart. It would take some time, but I needed to get over it and move on. I finally saw that the anger I had at

the onset of our relationship had faded, and so I was no longer attracted to it in Mr. Colorado.

I would take many months to repay Mr. Colorado for his kindness of the loan. I wished so badly that I could have loved him as he loved me, but I just didn't and couldn't. I realized he was sent to me as a kind of angel to keep me alive and get me through the divorce. He made me feel as if I were worth saving, and I wondered what great thing I would do in life for which he had saved me. I wondered about the karma between us, and I could only hope that I had saved him in another life because I couldn't wrap my head around why it had all occurred. I didn't think I was worthy of being saved or cared for. It seemed as if I were walking away from a good thing, but I realized when I saw his anger and control issues that it was time to take inventory of mine.

LESSONS FROM DIVORCE

During these years, I learned several things about divorce and how to get through it spiritually, emotionally, and financially. I'd like to share briefly these thoughts. First, and not the most spiritual of subjects, there is no need to hire an attorney to help you disagree with your partner until you're in front of a judge. All the expense usually happens before you see the judge, and it all comes down to "he said, she said." Next, no one else can prove trends in spending habits, who needs to have money or spend what to survive, who took what money out of what account when, etc. You need to be accountable and stand up for yourself. Finally, when you decide to split, there is no longer a "We." Draw up as many documents as you can on your own. And finally, the most important part is how you handle yourself spiritually. As you would imagine, I was told that I was not handling myself as a spiritual person should. But understand that yoga and shamanism are "practices," and whatever you are studying is simply a practice or a study until

you have become a master. You are bound to make mistakes and bound to fight for what you believe and what is important to you. Just like everything else in life, divorce is an opportunity to learn.

HEALING DEPRESSION

At first, as I started the divorce process, I didn't understand the karmic nature of things. I knew it was all part of a plan I had written before entering this life, but stepping into doing and understanding what I learned was difficult. My heartache had led to depression, and when you're depressed, it's hard to take the next step, but I learned that if I didn't take it, I would never change anything. Here are a few starting points I would learn to live by to help me beat my depression. I hope they can help you:

- Eat healthy foods.
- Exercise, even if it's just a walk.
- Forgive yourself and others.
- Release expectations, or at the very least, share them. You're not always going to get what you want, but when you don't openly communicate your visions, you can become withdrawn and upset and think no one sees you. Not getting what you want can cause depression...so don't set yourself up for it with expectations.
- Get a pet—pets teach us to live in the present.
- Live in the present moment. Each day is a new chance.
- Love yourself, but if that's too hard, love another.
- Devote some time or activity in your life to other people. If you can't live for you, live for them!
- Accept that change is inevitable.
- Know that we come from the same source and we are

more alike than we are different.

- Connect with the source that created you.
- Step out of the story that is your life and know that this source (and you) developed the plan you are living. Have faith in it.
- Remember that we are not designed to understand everything or we wouldn't be here to experience it.
- Unite with God.

It is also important to keep in mind the four principles of shamanism I mentioned in Chapter 2:

1. Non-judgment
2. Non-suffering
3. Non-engagement
4. Walk with beauty

Finally, understand the roles of The Drama Triangle often used as a psychological model in traditional psychology: The Drama Triangle: The Three Roles of Victimhood: perpetrator, victim, and rescuer. Understand these roles and then play NONE of them. Watch the roles and step outside of the story. This action is so important in any life crisis. Step out of the story and you will no longer be stuck in the drama. By stepping out of the drama, I was able to see the result nearly two years in advance. Come to grips with it as just another story that time heals.

EXERCISES:

1. If you are going through a divorce (or any other major crisis), ask yourself: What stories am I repeating? ______________

____

____

____

---

2. Who is playing each role of victimhood and how are those roles serving each of them?

Perpetrator: ______________________________
Victim: __________________________________
Rescuer: _________________________________

3. What is the end result you are expecting? ____________
____
____
____
____
____
____

Paint the picture of how it will end and visualize it. Define the outcome. Relationships hold a lot of karmic issues. See where the repeat patterns are showing up for you. The closest relationships are the greatest teachers.

HELPING YOU DISCOVER YOUR TRUTH

The end of a long relationship or marriage can be a devastating experience if you let it be. So don't let it get the better of you. Forgive your partner and yourself. This is the best gift you can give yourself. Don't be angry. Don't be bitter; get better! Don't be sad that your partner is gone; be happy that he or she lived! Remember the good times and focus on what you have learned, not what you have lost. There is an old saying that a relationship can last for a season, a reason, or forever. Discover the reason for your relationship and cherish that reason for a lifetime. Allow this reason to serve you on your journey as you search for your inner truth.

SEEK. TRUST. BELIEVE. LOVE.

CHAPTER 12

LEARNING TO Stand in Love

"He is the richest
who is content with the least,
for content is the wealth of nature."
— Socrates

I realized that my ex no longer served me, so to release him would mean I could better step into my becoming. I think it nearly killed me to do it, but I did. When Mr. Colorado no longer served my highest and best, I was able to move on as well. I was seeing that I was powerful, more powerful than I had thought. I had no idea where I would end up with all this "so called power," but I knew I had been through a lot and many changes were not easy.

OFF TO PERU AGAIN

Before Mr. Colorado and I split, I made one more trip to Peru to make up for the previous trip when I had not felt so well. The trip went off without a hitch, and I noticed how differently it went since I was in a more aligned place than the year before. I was becoming more sure of myself and more grounded in my spiritual and healing work. In fact, while I was there I would be told in countless ways that my path was that of a healer and master shaman. On this visit, the shaman seemed to notice my shift and I sensed a kind of intuitive conversation between

us. It was a kind of unspoken language that could go on coherently amid everything else. I would partake in a ceremony where I would pull "The Shaman" card from the deck, and later, I would be told by the shaman himself that I had good energy and was a master shaman in the making. When I asked how I would become one, I was told that life experiences were the only training I needed. My first thought, upon hearing his remarks from the translator, was, "Oh God! Not more change and heartache!" But I was told I had good and peaceful energy, a far cry from my previous visit just a year prior.

I found deeper connections this time in visiting the ancient sites and Machu Picchu. Instead of simply being in awe of the sites, I would study (and see) what was running beneath their appearances or facades. I would see where light entered and fed the ground and the ruins. I would see beings walking among the land that were within another dimension (although I couldn't hold the image for long). I would see other non-human races working the land, and I was unalarmed by their presence. It simply just was. The things I had seen up to this point prepared me for realizing that so much is bigger than us that we will never really know the answers to. There is no end to the wondering or questioning. I would sense, see, and feel the purposes for the significant markers placed on the land at ancient historical sites. I didn't know why it was—it just simply was.

As we toured around, our guide told me he could see my spirit within or floating over the land. He told me he could see my great connection to the land. I felt that connection on this visit, but I hadn't on the previous one. He would take us to ancient sites, and before he explained the purpose of certain markers, I would tell someone else about them. Then he would look at me with wide eyes and tell the same story, wondering how I knew it already. I would just shrug my shoulders, as if to say, "Good guess?" With one particular marker, the instant I touched it, I felt it call out to all the other sacred sites on the planet. It called

to Egypt, to the pyramids in Mexico, to Stonehenge, to pivotal points on the map. I saw ceremonies from long ago as if they were happening that day. I walked the land, nearly forgetting that I no longer had dark hair and skin from being here in a previous life. I knew the land and felt the energy.

I would meet a new shaman on this trip who used the song of the ayahuasca medicine, but not the plant concoction itself. Using the plant itself can create a psychedelic experience that it is said can teach you the purpose of life and help you heal when nothing else has worked. It has been said to have healed cancer and to have shown great images among other things. I have studied the song, but never the medicine of the vine ingested into my body. It would take me some time for that. It is said the plant will show you images (sometimes seen in cloths and painting) and teach you its vibration, which can be transitioned by gifted healers into song. It's a strange combination of notes that doesn't generally contain words, but mostly sound—heard by the human as grunts, groans, humming, and / or a whistle. It would be the most remarkable healing I have ever experienced.

HEALING WITH A MASTER

One very cold night, I was the second to last in the group to have my private session with the shaman. We would meet in a hotel room at the resort, and upon my entering, the shaman immediately said "Colorado." He didn't speak much English, and when I asked why he said that, he could not answer me. We caught each other's eye in a special way that I was beginning to notice between energy healers. It's a kind of eye sparkle and an inner acknowledgment: "Yes, I'm aware you are connected." I smiled, and then he asked for my medicine bag (messa) and motioned for me to lie down on the bed. Almost immediately when I lay down, I started shivering. Something had clearly shifted in me as soon as I gave in to the healing. I was so cold

that my lips had to be blue. I was sure of it. The room started to spin, and I fought to keep my eyes from rolling back in my head. The sun hadn't finished setting yet, so the room seemed to grow unusually dark.

The shaman was working on me in a way that felt familiar, yet different from how we had been trained. I knew in general what he was doing, but then I became lost and realized I was not in control but seemed to be mush in his hands. I finally just gave in and closed my eyes. I wanted to cry, but tears wouldn't come out. I just lay there and shook and came in and out of consciousness. When he pounded his hard medicine bag on my head, something came out of my feet…a kind of energy was released. I assumed it was an energy that was not mine or that no longer served me so it left. But then he started to sing, chant, and whistle, and I lost my ability to reason and think. Suddenly, I was floating in colors and shapes and so at peace. It felt as if I were being held by the angels in the massage room a few years before, but instead of angels, along came a spider….

I have never been fond of spiders and they have not turned up much in my healing work, but suddenly, I was being held in a soft white cocoon and rocked by a female spider. I felt so deeply loved like never before in my life. I didn't question how illogical it seemed to be loved or held by a spider; instead, I fell deeper into it and just relaxed. For the first time since I had started my shamanic work years before, I took a deep breath, completely let go, got out of my own way, and let God come into me. I expanded beyond allowing and just became all knowing and all that is, while still being held within that web.

Often when an animal comes into our awareness, whether it is physically or spiritually, it has a message for us. Here is, at a high level, what the spider means according to Ted Andrews' book *Animal Speak*: "The spider found within the web reminds us that we are the center of our own world. We are the keepers

and the writers of our own destiny, weaving it like a web by our thoughts, feelings and actions."

I stayed there in the cocoon for quite some time, and when I began to move from that vision, I opened my eyes to find the man who had been beating on my head with his bag of rocks was now leaning over and kissing my head as tears flowed down my face. The room was engulfed in so much love that my eyes burst with tears—tears not of joy or pain, but tears of release. For a moment, I could see the loving embrace of a power greater than me that was flowing into all things—from everything to everything. It was not coming from any one place but from everything. The energy I felt was much like that I had felt the very first time I'd had a shamanic healing session where everything was forgiven and my guard was down. I was in complete trust of what would come next at any future stage of my life; all the wrongs of the past were forgiven and seen now as lessons for my soul's growth, and I was forgiven for any misunderstandings. This experience would aid me in moving forward—forgiving myself, forgiving my ex, forgiving Mr. Colorado, forgiving my parents or teachers.

Although one more woman was supposed to have a session after me, the shaman informed us that he now had to leave. I joked that "I broke the shaman," but we knew his wife was ill at home, and although it seemed ironic that the wife of a healer was ill, I sensed more that I hadn't broken him, but broken his heart wide open so he wanted to return home to his love after that session. I so wished to curl up into bed with someone who loved me and be held all night into the morning—just as the spider had done. It saddened me to be alone now without my husband or anyone, but the remainder of the trip confirmed that my soul is here floating on a journey, and part of my lesson is to realize I have the power to do that alone. Alone is how I came into the world and how I will go out of it.

TRAVELING WITHIN PERU

As we traveled the countryside, I shared my views and experiences with others, but each of our perceptions was different and really only for ourselves. When we arrived at our next location, I roomed with another woman from Michigan who had joined our group late. She was a therapist who informed me of something I had been questioning for some time—that I had been whining and crying in my sleep several nights in a row. I wondered why I had been waking up so exhausted each morning for years; I knew my heart was very broken, but now I was aware that my heartache was on the subconscious level as well. I became aware of all the healing work to clear my past, but now was the time to clear the present and all that I created as "wrong" in this lifetime and just let it go.

We saw some more beautiful sights, but I was really ready now to go home. I had been away nearly a month, and I missed anything that was familiar, especially my girls. Returning from Peru is always a bit disorienting because of the differences in altitude, culture, and especially the standard of living. This time when I returned and placed my toothbrush under the faucet for the first time, I would just bawl and bawl. I wasn't really exactly sure why, but I think I was scared by the symbolism of the clean unpolluted water and returning home alone with a wide open future in front of me. I had less pain and heaviness in my body; it felt unusually light to the point that I almost wanted some heaviness back.

HIGH SCHOOL REUNION

Within a day of returning, I had a twenty-year class reunion to attend. I felt a bit disoriented and had an upset belly so I wasn't very excited to go. I was so worried I'd end up getting sick in front of all my classmates, but instead, they all got drunk and acted stupid in front of me. I had just returned from rocking in

a spider's web, so there was no one there I could relate to. I had never seemed to fit well into my class and now I again felt out of place. I only had two meaningful conversations with two very unlikely people, one of whom was an airline repairman (and never very popular in school) and the other an old neighbor. I found that those deemed as "nerds" were much more worthy of good conversation than those I had assumed were my friends. Everyone just seemed to want to be entertained and to laugh at everyone else, but I was really hoping for a deep and meaningful conversation. I wasn't sure how to approach anyone, and I began to see it was unlikely I'd rekindle an old friendship or start a new one. I felt very separated and alone. Many of my classmates had kids or spouses; I had a new last name but no spouse. I was the divorced girl without a job. At previous reunions, I'd had so many great materialistic things to talk about, but this time, I left unfulfilled.

I wondered whether I could only find the deep conversations I craved within my yoga or shaman communities—and whether others ever cared to have them or knew what they were. I wondered whether I had been privy to many love-filled moments of sharing in the communities I had become accustomed to and such relationships only existed there. I wondered whether people were holding back or knew any better. I wondered whether I asked for too much and my expectations were too high. I wondered whether anyone else thought the same way I did. I just felt so different. I didn't care about fitting in or standing out. I just wanted to share love and kindness with another. It brought such comfort to see so many familiar faces at my reunion, but without the interaction, it felt as if I were looking at a moving "hologram" in an old yearbook.

I went home alone, but knowing much more about myself and how to connect to my power. I let go of the need to fit in, and the concept of expectations and outcomes was examined.

I became upset that other people I knew were in happy marriages, having babies, and raising kids while I was having these eclectic and mind-blowing experiences. I wanted some sense of normalcy. I even began to dream of the beige house and white picket fence, and then I would laugh when I thought about what the neighbors might say when they saw flying saucers floating over it or my kids standing in the yard with magic wands.

AYAHUASCA CEREMONY

There is a difference between knowing intuitively how things will go and having expectations for them to go a certain way. I was very curious about the ayahuasca ceremony and had always wanted to do a session, but since I was a non-drinker and didn't like to be under the influence, it took me some time to come to grips with it. After much study, meditation, and thought, it had found me. They say, "When mother comes looking for you, you don't want to deny her." Well, she found me, followed me all the way home from Peru, and just happened to be only a few miles from the Maya Center right there in Michigan. I "stumbled" upon the group performing the ceremony in Peruvian tradition and paid attention to the calling.

It was a much more calm, peaceful, and loving ceremony than I had expected. I was a bit nervous when I read that it was likely I would spend the entire session vomiting. I was given a bed, a pillow, a bottle of water, a roll of paper towel, and my very own barf bucket. The session would start with smoke-blowing, chanting, and rattling by the lead shaman, and then we would be offered a series of three drinks. Almost immediately, people starting throwing up. I took my first drink and just sat there in a cross-legged position, happy to be there. I took notice that no one else was sitting. I would go for my second drink and continue sitting. Everyone all around me was throwing up. Then the girl next to me starting singing the most beautiful song. A moth

came into the room and danced over my head. The sun was shining right on me, and it was far more beautiful than it seems it should have been. The shaman asked whether anyone would like to take a third and final drink; many others were already barfing profusely, but I seemed to be having very little experience at all. He laughed and asked whether I'd like another, as if surprised I was handling it so gracefully. I took my third drink and sat back down. I decided that since it was the last drink, I would lie down and try to have an experience.

I had set my intention before the ceremony to clear all heartache left over from my divorce. I remained clear on my intentions until I lay down. After that third drink, the room started to spin just a bit. I was seeing some images starting to come in and felt no need to release myself. I listened to the beautiful voice of the girl next to me; it made everything so light and peaceful. I was so thankful for her voice. I started to bring myself back into my intention and began to see that the plant was indeed teaching me. It was showing me this vine where all life would always flow (it would never stop flowing), and then I saw the vine's leaves. I saw that each leaf was a life experience, and at any point, one could jump off and have that experience and stay as long as he liked or jump into the vine and ride the wave of constant motion and life. I began to see that my divorce was just one of those leaves. I saw it as heavy, so I didn't want to stay and simply left. I learned that life is always changing and nothing is more constant in life than change. I knew from that point forward I must accept that nothing will ever remain the same and it's not designed to. I saw death and divorce were just a part of that constant. I asked for happier leaves too!

It seemed that the session was wrapping up just as it was getting started, and before I knew it, I was in the car and driving home on all the back dirt roads just in case I was still in an altered state. The next morning, I felt as if I had just come out of the twenty-four-hour flu, but for the most part, I was just

at peace with it. When others asked why I hadn't thrown up, I explained that my "trick" was not to see myself as separate from the vine, but merged as a part of it. I realized a great motto to live my life by was: I am not separate but part of the vine of life. I learned to observe life without judgment and stand in love with each situation. The experience seemed to come more easily then. I realized that my way of letting go was by learning to stand in love, by forgiving, and by pure exhaustion of my judgments and expectations so I could simply move on to observations.

EXERCISES:

1. Where in your life have you held expectations and how have they let you down? ______________________________

____

____

____

____

2. Which people do you expect to behave certain ways? ________

____

____

____

____

____

3. How do they upset you when they don't behave the way you'd expect? ______________________________

____

____

____

4. How do you communicate your expectations? ___________

5. How would life look for you if you let go of those expectations?

HELPING YOU DISCOVER YOUR TRUTH

I challenge you to be an original! You are a unique, one in a million. In a world where you are taught to fit in, I encourage you to embrace your uniqueness and stand out. Don't let society's expectations of how people "should be" play a role in your life. Stand firm, stand alone (if necessary), and stand up for who you are and what you believe in. Let your uniqueness and passions shine, and allow them to be your beacon of light and brighten your way in your search for your inner truth.

SEEK. TRUST. BELIEVE. LOVE.

CHAPTER 13

OBSERVING The Dating Mirror

"Study without reflection is a waste of time;
reflection without study is dangerous."
— Confucius

Having just returned from Peru, I was in observation mode. I thought back to when I was eighteen and had decided to become a vegetarian. I had stomach issues that became more and more obviously related to diet as I aged, and I noticed that making healthier choices kept me from going to the ER cramped over in pain. When I met my husband, I would try to eat a few various fish options, but when I would find remnants of bones or skin, I would become aware of what I was eating and nearly vomit on the spot. He would try to get me to drink wine, thinking it was romantic I suppose, but I would nearly fall asleep on or under the table after a few sips and just wanted to go home and go to bed, which would make him angry. I would begin to cut out many sodas and sugars during our relationship, and by the time I was going through a divorce, I was well into being, not just a healthy eater, but a vegan. I was noticing how much healthier my body felt by also cutting out fried or cooked food. Eventually, I was nearly entirely a raw food vegan. I was now about twenty years free from meat. I felt better than I ever had, and then something would click in me during another cleanse.

I realized that God gave us food without having to kill for it, and if we ate what God gave us, we would live much closer to a God source. I also saw that altering it was like telling God it wasn't good enough just as it was. But I also saw great creations coming out of raw food kitchens where the food had been beaten, shaved, or whipped but not heated, and its general structure and nutrition were basically still intact. I saw the art in the creation and began to enjoy the fullness of the flavors. I was creating fabulous meals for my students and enjoying every minute of it. I bought nearly every raw food cookbook I could get my hands on. I was finding great joy in food. It had been some time since I had found joy in much of anything. I was noticing through my food choices my energy felt lighter and my depression was dissipating. I began to experiment with other styles of yoga and started leaving the house again. I was noticing people in my life who were inspired to introduce raw food into their lives. I realized I was helping people become healthier by demonstrating good healthy life (and food) choices myself. I was inspired when I saw I was inspiring others. I noticed heavier energies leaving my life and lighter energies coming in. This wasn't even about food anymore.

As I was cleaning up my diet, I was cleaning out my closets. I knew that when I was prepared to leave my life on twenty-five acres, I would need to release many things that were weighing me down. I had closets full of clothes and way too much furniture and other household items, and if I were moving forward to find a job and source of income, I would need to release many things. I just started giving away everything. After yoga, we would have giveaway parties, and when people came in the door, I had clothes bagged or hanging everywhere. I was so happy to release so much, and never have I looked back and said, "I wish I hadn't."

ONLINE DATING

What I began to observe was that as I moved and shifted through phases in myself, I was attracting others as potential partners who not only showed the qualities I was enjoying about myself but also the qualities I loathed about myself. I would meet "Dr. Beer Goggles," the eye doctor, and he would fill the same need as my ex for a period of time, but then I realized I had already lived that life and it was all too similar. He would show me that it truly was time to leave my ex and move on. Mr. Beer Goggles drank a bit too much and didn't eat well, which basically reflected his whole life—a bit disheveled and unorganized with many financial drains. I observed and altered my own life.

Then I met "Dr. Heart Attack," coincidentally, a heart surgeon. He loved his alcohol and oddly strange animal extremities for dinner that I didn't know were something people even ate. He was overworked, overweight, angry under the cool-guy exterior, and I couldn't find really much healthy about him, but I was interested in his mind and education. I knew he was brilliant, but he never shared his mind. Of course, I was evaluating my educational level and had questioned whether I should go back to school to kick off a new life. I imagined he had school debt up to his eyeballs based on his lifestyle, and I didn't want that for me, but I generally liked him. I was learning what I didn't want so I could figure out what I did want. There was just no way I could kiss a man who had just eaten pig or cow balls (or any other part for that matter)! It was good therapy for me to stay focused on my healthy lifestyle.

So again I would join another dating service, but this time one geared toward other vegans since that had become a very important factor for me in finding my mate. I understood it was more than a diet now—it was also a lifestyle—and it was about being conscious as well. Finding another vegan meant finding

someone who was shifting away from the karma in meat, loved animals, had likely moved through various stages of spirituality, was questioning "the system" we have been programmed to believe, and who studied or understood that optimal health was not found in packaged or processed foods. What I also realized was that someone who became vegan was also someone who wanted to live a clean life, was into self-improvement, and tended to be entrepreneurial in his pursuits. Why entrepreneurial? Because he would have to be crafty in the kitchen to feed himself, and he would need to be forward thinking to find solutions for meals out. If he went above and beyond in the kitchen, he would likely do so in other avenues in his life. Unfortunately, I didn't understand that his willingness to experiment might also include the bedroom!

I would meet "Mr. Smooth Voice," the most amazing man, via a vegan website. I was immediately taken by his handsome picture. When I first heard his voice, it sounded like a smooth jazz radio station host soothing you to sleep at night. In fact, he once worked in TV news broadcasting. Mr. Smooth Voice was a newly practicing Buddhist, a vegan, and physically fit. He seemed perfect! We spent a bit of time talking on the phone and then in person. He explained to me that he had suffered from various "events" in his life that he was in therapy to heal. I listened with an open heart and ears. I needed to be able to observe to hear / understand him fully. After all, I knew there were keys in there to heal my own life. But I had not always been good at listening. He was clearly working very hard on himself, and I honored that and his forthcoming personality. But, honestly, he seemed like a lot to handle when I was still dealing with healing my own life. Although, there wasn't much you couldn't like about Mr. Smooth Voice. He was genuinely fond of everyone. He cared deeply for those he let in. I sensed he was at a phase in his life where he was prepared to let in a special someone, but he needed to tell me who he was and what he needed first.

We would go out to some great meals and a few movies, and I even did a healing session with him, to which he was quite open. But I wasn't prepared to learn he had been bisexual his whole adult life. He was prepared to have a long-term relationship with a woman, but he still wanted to see men. He even wanted to have children. But he preferred to live in a separate home so he could continue with his lifestyle. Initially, I took this news very hard because I really liked him, but I wasn't sure about some of the instabilities in his life (regardless of his sexual choices). I was able to see many of the more obvious dark forces at work within him and gloriously released them from myself. I was thankful for the mirror.

One night, I went home and cried because I was so disturbed by the idea of dating and how different people were from me, and I missed the lifestyle I'd had with my ex. I wanted to have a healthy relationship with a man and even have the option to have kids if the timing and other things were right. But Mr. Smooth Voice had thrown me for a loop. I took a deep dive into myself when I met him. It turned out I was still holding onto a lot of judgment, some darkness, and I had expectations for how a marriage and relationship were supposed to look and be. I saw that I needed to define better who I was and what I wanted and needed. Again, I was learning what I didn't want. Sooner or later, that would turn into me finding out what it was I did want. I would later laugh at myself for how I seemed to have set up my life script before coming here, so I would learn through dating and dogs. And dogs with dates is even more telling! If they don't like each other, you just know it's not going to work! A pretty keen observation, I thought—I'd let my dogs pick my date!

Along came "Mr. Playboy French Canadian Vegan Sailor," a naturopathic doctor in a small town near Quebec City. He was very handsome, very physically fit, ran a fasting business out of his home, loved to cook, understood and prepared raw

vegan food, and was a fairly active sailor and pretty handy with gardening, home remodeling projects, and even had a degree in architecture (a passion of mine). He seemed a bit dreamy... well, on paper anyway!

He would talk me through what a fasting would look like and told me that he had even once had the willpower to fast for fourteen days on nothing but water after he split from his partner of fifteen years. I thought, "Wow! This guy is even more extreme than I am." Of course, I wanted to try it and I wanted him to talk me through it. So I would do it before we met just to be sure I was in tiptop shape when we did. I had such a hard time with it.

I planned to go a week partaking only of water, and I did quite well for the first three days, but when I went to have the colon hydrotherapy, I ended up pulling over and vomiting on my way home in rush hour traffic! Since there was nothing in me to come out, it was quite painful and my body was weak. I would get massages every other day as he said, and I even sheepishly did another colon hydrotherapy session just to make sure everything was clean. If I were going to do it, I was going to do it right. He told me I was likely having a kidney reaction when my low back was wrenching in pain. And the colon assistant told me I had a gallbladder flush as indicated by the green-colored liquid coming out. This was all so extreme and hard on my body. I thought I was going to die. It was funny really that I had spent so much time in a deep depression, and here I was finally nearly killing myself! It really made me decide that I didn't want to end my life after all, and I did enjoy parts of it enough to know that I did at least want to eat again. On day six, I'd had enough and could go no further. It was all very aggressive for my sensitive body. I knew I had a lot to purge and release from my past, but now my body and my bank account were in the line. Cleansing my body was hard, but it helped life fall more in balance in the end.

Mr. Playboy French Canadian Vegan Sailor would fly to Michigan for our first meeting shortly after I began to eat food again. He would see my home, meet my girls, and my kitty, Penelope. We ate very simple and clean uncooked vegan meals. We went for long walks outdoors, and we sat in front of the fireplace while he whispered to me in his native French language. (I had no idea what he was saying, but it sure sounded romantic.) He stayed for a few days, and we really seemed to hit it off. Before meeting, we would spend hours on the phone and talk all night and into the morning. I would go to visit him within a few weeks of his visit to see his clinic and meet his son. He asked whether I'd like to go on his annual sailing trip in the British Virgin Islands. I had never been sailing before and wasn't even very fond of water, but I was looking forward to the adventure and spending time with my sexy new vegan friend.

TIMELINE TRAVEL

Before I could go sailing, however, I had to make an emergency call and go through some fear therapy with Jeff, a healing friend of mine, to release my fear of water. I wasn't really sure where the fear came from and was hoping Jeff could help me figure that out. Much of our healing work together would have already started prior to my meeting Mr. Playboy French Canadian Vegan Sailor, and I'd had some simply awesome experiences. I didn't share many of the details of these sessions with Jeff since he kept me focused on the task at hand, but during one session in particular, I was shocked by what I was seeing. I seemed to be able to jump ahead of the tasks he was presenting to me and have visual experiences beyond the bounds of his instruction or time. This jumping ahead was something I realized I could do when the shamanic training wheels came off. I knew guided meditations and shamanic journeys tended to go too slowly for me, and I found it very hard to focus on the voice and stay with the story and would wander off. It seemed to become a kind of norm for me. I knew I could generally stay

with the story, but it usually served me better to float off into my own worlds. Any time an organized spiritual event happened, I became accustomed to understanding the general principle and just running with it. Jeff started to walk me through a new modality called Timeline Therapy. I started to get the gist of what it was, but I didn't want to offend him by not paying attention and wandering off into grand experiences.

We talked for a bit, and as we did, he took note of certain words I continued to repeat and wrote them down. I guess "judgment" was a repeat theme. When the issue of judgment came up, he would ask me to close my eyes, imagine a timeline, and figure out where on that timeline the issue first arose. He asked, "Where did you first see or feel judged?" If it were in the past, he would ask whether it were in another life. For me, judgment went so far back that I was actually physically turning my head to find it. I could have nearly turned my head in circles. It had been within me for so long that I didn't know much about living without it. I flashed through lifetimes like a virtual card catalog. Suddenly, it was dark and raining and I arrived at a scene—the first instance of judgment....

There I stood next to Jesus on the cross. He was on a hill and I was standing behind a rock wall at a lower elevation. I could see him mouthing something to me, but I couldn't understand it. I wanted to know what he was saying, but it was raining and dark and so hard to see. It was cold and we were physically and emotionally exhausted. It seemed as if the words were more a telepathic knowing. I sensed that I was very close to Jesus, a relative. Jesus kept appearing in my visions so I was curious who I had been in this lifetime, but that was not my task here. I was seeking judgment, but I was getting caught up in finding out anything about who I was and why and how I was with Jesus. Jeff was prompting me to move on. I told him it was raining and I was cold. I was trying to hear what Jesus was saying or to read his lips. Jeff was telling me to move on since it was dangerous

to get stuck in the story, but I was sticking there because I was so intrigued. Jeff asked whether judgment existed there, and I said, "Of course it does." He asked whether it was the first time I had seen it, and I said I didn't think so. He asked me to find it, and somehow, my subconscious redirected me away from the scene. Then I saw, in split seconds, what seemed to be every life Jesus had ever lived on every other planet and in every other form (and formless). I saw all lives and situations that were a part of his story, and I saw that the event (with him on the cross) had been carefully planned for many lifetimes. This event was the ultimate judgment, where Jesus himself was heard saying what was captured later in Scripture: "Father, forgive them for they know not what they do." I knew that even though it took much time to manifest and plan, this event was written well in advance. Jeff kept prodding me to move on. When he asked how this scene related to me, I said I didn't understand it; all I knew was that it was planned, and somehow just experiencing the story and seeing that whole experience helped me see and heal judgment.

We would work on fear of water next, but honestly, I was still so caught up in what had just happened that I don't even remember what we talked about. But something we talked about made me less nervous, and I actually felt prepared to go snorkeling and sailing. Go figure.

SAILING THE CARIBBEAN

Just before the trip, Mr. Playboy French Canadian Vegan Sailor seemed to be very sidetracked and kept forgetting his promise to call me. Sometimes the whole day would go by and he didn't call. I had a sneaking suspicion I was not the only woman in his life. I believed the fasting might have something to do with increasing my intuition since I had noticed also that I was much more connected when I did my yoga cleanses. After I fasted, I even began to taste chemicals and strong perfumes in my

mouth if they were put on my body. My body had never been so clean so any kind of chemical substance really bothered me. Mr. Playboy French Canadian Vegan Sailor and I originally had met on a vegan dating website, so I realized if I went back onto it and logged in, it would tell me when he was last active. I wasn't a sneaky or non-trusting type, but I was curious.

On those many long late night (and into early morning) phone calls, he would tell me he wanted to have kids and even have me move in, but he wasn't much into marriage. He said he would consider it, but he preferred his freedom. Red flag! I regularly wondered whether he felt this way because he had fidelity issues, but I figured if he were using me, I might use him right back and go on that sailing trip regardless because it sure sounded fun. Of course, when I defined these issues within him, I wondered where they existed within me. He would also teach me many things without even knowing he was. I learned to let go of so much since he was the master of fasting—I learned to go without what didn't serve me or bring me joy. I would begin to look at every aspect of my life where joy wasn't present since joy and love were the things I didn't want to go without. He would also challenge all of my visual experiences, and he taught me they were simply my experiences to be had. If someone really wanted to know me, he would care to listen to the story of how I became the person I am today.

Once I went online, I discovered he had been quite active. I started taking notes of each time he logged in, and while he was sailing, he had logged in nearly every day. I suspected he might be lonely sailing without his family, and the one time we went on Skype together, I could see he wasn't with another woman, but I was on my guard regardless. I wondered after everything I had gone through why this distrust had appeared in my life and how I would move through it. But I would figure that out after I took my first sailing trip.

Once I arrived, I met up with Mr. Playboy French Canadian Vegan Sailor's friends and later with him. He was suntanned, muscular, and wearing his little speedo with a bandanna tied around his neck. He looked like he was right in his element as he stood behind the wheel of his sailboat...with this kind of godly glow.

We would immediately take off to sea. I managed to get through the trip quite well with both the morning swims and the sometimes choppy waves. I would have really quite enjoyed the trip if I didn't notice that one night, while I was preparing to fall asleep below, he was not just surfing the waves on the deck of our sailboat but also surfing on the dating site. That was the last straw! This sort of put a kink in my romantic journey in a sailboat with Mr. Playboy French Canadian Vegan Sailor. I remained quiet and calm and didn't say anything right away since I wanted to enjoy the trip, but the last few days were very challenging for me, and I knew when I left I would never see him again. I called him out on his online escapades eventually, and it was quite funny to see him try to dance around the situation since he didn't know that I not only knew the truth but I could see his lies. He had been caught red-handed.

As we all returned to the airport, we couldn't understand why roads were blocked and travel was challenging; we finally caught the news of a storm coming in. I never expected to see him again after that trip so as I walked onto the plane, I don't think I even looked back for one final goodbye. I just smiled in my heart because I realized karma was in bed with nature that day; low and behold, each of our planes got out of the airport except for Mr. Playboy's. I wouldn't know until I was safely on the ground back in Michigan, but his flight was cancelled and he was held back for an additional three days in what was either called a tropical depression or, in my eyes, a not-so-fluke hurricane. Well...karma bites!

PLENTY OF FISH IN THE SEA

Again, I would go home alone, but this time with a plane full of very tanned, beautiful single men. Although I didn't meet anyone, I sure enjoyed looking, and ironically, the ocean I once had feared would now teach me there were plenty more fish in the sea. Getting on that plane and never communicating again was the easiest decision I ever made. I had learned some great techniques about diet, fasting, nutrition, and how to honor my body, mind, and spirit. I had learned how to listen to my inner voice and trust myself and how to trust in a Higher Source that seemed to have my back and was helping me simply to lift my feet and walk forward. If the script were already written, then that was all I needed to do. Yet another observation in dating....

I walked through dating as a student, but I knew sooner or later it might give me some level of mastery in my life so maybe I could teach others. I had been teaching yoga and shamanism, and I was struggling in those roles as I maneuvered my own life struggles and challenges. I knew the messages from the shaman in Peru about living my life and taking in the experiences was to make me some kind of a great shaman, but it was becoming harder to give myself that title. I was finding that titles were limiting me. I was circling back around to the beginning of my shamanic training…it's all circular. Back to the basics and core teachings. I would circle over and over, and as new things came up in my life, I would revisit the fundamentals of my teachings. As I revisited my teachings, I would draw new students. I put a group of fascinating people through a year-long shamanic healing program now and they were out changing lives. It brought me great joy. I watched as they started from where I ended. If only I could have started where they were, I thought. Wouldn't I then be that much wiser?

My shamanic work would now become a part of me and would soon lose its label. I would tell my students regularly that a few

weekend classes were not enough to give yourself the title of "shaman" and to be careful how they used it. I would learn that to be a true shaman was to know it in your heart. I would need to practice shamanism internally…a sacred space within would create a sacred space in my every step throughout life externally. I would begin to understand this process was no different than my yoga practice, and if I established a regular practice of both on my own, my students would become my mirror. How could I teach something if I were not practicing it outside of the teaching? I would find that for a period in my life, the Maya Center would serve as my learning grounds for all things yoga, shamanism, and diet. But it wouldn't be until later that I would understand the fullness of this.

EXERCISES:

1. Sit for a moment, close your eyes, and breathe deeply. Then write a paragraph below describing the characteristics of your ideal mate. ________________________________

____

____

____

____

____

2. Describe how this person is similar to you and how he or she is different. Are you really seeking these characteristics in yourself or are you looking for someone to help balance you? ______

____

____

____

____

____

---

3. What are you afraid of and how are those things mirrored in your relationships or life situations? How have you conquered the fear? ______________________________

4. Relationships can be hard and we see our ugly human qualities sometimes as we part and go separate ways. If you look back on all your relationships, is there a theme? ___________

5. Are there things that occurred in one relationship that you found happened over and over? Who was attracted to you, and most importantly, what qualities did you like or dislike about this person and how was that both present within you and how did you learn from it? ______________________________

HELPING YOU DISCOVER YOUR TRUTH

Whether or not you are dating, take a look at all relationships in your life and ask yourself what you think that person (or people) is there to guide you with. Who is the one who charges you up the most? Is he or she actually the brilliant teacher you called for? And the one who loves you the most—has he or she done so before in another lifetime? When you start to honor that each relationship serves you in many ways, you can simply say, "Thank you for helping me find my truth," and then decide who brings you the most joy to continue the journey with and how you can return the favor. When you find love, it's easy to say you will never take it for granted, but truth sometimes hides behind those who really shake up your whole foundation (unfortunately).

SEEK. TRUST. BELIEVE. LOVE.

CHAPTER 14

EATING Food As Medicine

"Let food be thy medicine
and medicine be thy food."
— Hippocrates

By this point, I knew that a healthy, primarily green, and most definitely vegan diet would be a key component of my life until the end of my days. The cleaner I got my body, the more I could put my pain and depression behind me, and the more intuitive I would become as well. Just as I could taste the chemicals applied to my body through non-natural topical body wash or shampoo, I could "taste" other negative energies in my life. I had spent over twenty years as a vegetarian, and switching to veganism was something that wasn't very hard for me since I had already mostly adopted that lifestyle. I was noticing when I met other non-animal-eating vegans, they seemed to be more open spiritually as well. I couldn't tell whether becoming a vegan made a person more spiritually open or whether more spiritually open people ended up becoming vegans—they just seemed to go hand-in-hand, but I would study this matter for some time. I found gentler souls and more like-minded people in relation to diet than I did in relation to shamanism and yoga combined. Shamanism seemed to attract many who needed help healing until they either were healed or stepped into healing, but this crowd was not always vegan. Yoga seemed to draw

someone who needed to eat healthily in order to move on the yoga mat more comfortably. Either way, I found both groups were, at minimal, sensitive to the animal's fear or karma. Many of the shaman would partake in eating meat, though they would pray over it first to release its fear or karma. I noticed, though, something unique seemed to evolve in yoga students. I noticed when the body moved more, the desire for healthier food options was more present.

HEALTHIER FOOD OPTIONS

It seemed to me that when people questioned their diet, they were also questioning "the system." The system might be the upside-down food pyramid regulated by government, or that we were falsely educated as children about how healthy animal protein and a good glass of milk were required for our growing bodies. Now it's understood in many vegan circles that all those animal proteins and dairy are causing all kinds of autoimmune diseases and a whole slew of other problems. If you haven't studied any of it, you must, at minimum, read the book *The China Study* by T. Colin Campbell and Thomas M. Campbell. I wondered why the government would present something not in our best interests. This book opened the door for me to questioning what other things the government is not telling us, supposedly for our own good. I began to question not just food, but my UFO encounters, spiritual experiences, healing gifts, psychic gifts, and the idea that school institutions would teach us to study people but not heal them, or better yet, not to allow spirituality into public schools. And what exactly are we teaching our kids in school if we are avoiding discussions on the concept of the source from which we were all born? I spent so many years seeking, and each time I uncovered answers, more questions arose.

As I studied one thing, it circled me around to another. I began to wonder whether Starbeings or ETs ate animals. My

guess was that eating meat might only be present in a heavier dimension such as our own. If we became truly evolved as humans, wouldn't killing an animal be the opposite of the most divine aspects of love? If we didn't have to take from a helpless being, why would we? As I cleaned my body and grew a deeper connection with plant food, I just couldn't understand, if there were no need to harm another to live, why we would. I have noticed more and more babies being born who struggle to take their mothers' milk if their mothers are on a high-protein animal-based diet. I would notice more and more children being born with issues of lactose intolerance, allergies, sinuses, digestion, and high body mucus issues. I would observe and pass no judgment on others, but simply take note. It's not our fault because unless we pay our own money to study health and nutrition, we don't know any better since, again, it's not taught in schools. Why?

I started to remove more and more toxic foods and / or unnatural topical skin or beauty products from my diet each time I would cleanse. I would notice that small toxins in the environment became very challenging for me. My senses were more heightened in every sense. I could smell and taste differently as well. I would take notice of others' body odors and become distinctly aware of toxins held in their bodies. The smell permeating from the skin or off the breath would quickly indicate potential for disease for me. Greens (especially kale) would become a daily part of my diet. Something magic happens when you cleanse your body that clicks deep within you where you no longer consciously have to choose whether "this is good for me and I should eat it," and where you just crave healthy, good green and live food. Besides, when was the last time you walked down the produce aisle and asked anyone how many calories were in an apple, carrot, or pear?

When we eat foods that closely resemble what God gave us in their natural form, we eat the healthiest. There are many

cleanses out there to try, but in my opinion, it's best either to go completely without and let your body heal or find simple green juices. When you go completely without, you allow your body to heal from allergies to specific foods that you might not even know you had. You know you're doing something right when you crave good foods. Craving good food leads to craving good people...craving and living a good life...craving new healthy habits, etc.

I'd love to give you some great recipes or books to read, but all you have to do is type in the word "vegan" on www.amazon.com and you will get over 8,000 results. You'll find some great things there. Type in "Sarma Melngailis" and you'll find one of my favorite authors and her great raw vegan cookbooks.

I'll leave you with some great advice I have learned over the years: Make food a first thought, not an afterthought, as healthy meals are planned. When you are starving, you tend to go for what is quick, easy, and satisfying right now. Three-quarters of the grocery store is processed food or animal products. Challenge yourself to stay only in the produce section as you shop. Don't eat two or three hours before bedtime. Eat your food slowly and chew thoroughly. After twenty minutes, stop eating to see whether you feel full; then stop for more than an hour. Don't drink water with food, but it's okay twenty minutes before or after. Drinking liquids during your meal dilutes your naturally occurring digestive enzymes and stomach acids, which makes it harder to break down food. Stomach acids are dissipated with the act of consuming liquids with solids because water is excreted faster than solids. If you are chewing adequately (creating saliva), you should be able to eat comfortably without lots of liquids. Allow your saliva naturally to help you swallow your food. Juice fresh fruit and veggies, eat fruits in the mornings to avoid sugar cravings throughout the day, avoid anything processed (including tofu), avoid sugar, do regular fasts or cleanses, and when in doubt—greens, greens, greens, and water,

water, water! Get as close to what God gave you in nature, not in a can or a boxed package! Although…a Vitamix and a food dehydrator sure are nice too!

EXERCISES:

- Challenge yourself with a new vegan recipe per week.
- Challenge yourself only to shop the produce section at your local grocery store.
- Watch a movie on veganism on YouTube once a week.
- Try a fast or cleanse. I have several I can recommend.

HELPING YOU DISCOVER YOUR TRUTH

When you clear out the toxic foods in your life, you are really and truly honoring yourself. It's a conscious effort of which only you are in control. No one makes you eat. You are in full control of your body (your temple). When the desire for healthier options becomes present in your diet, it makes its way into every other aspect of your life. Once the toxins are gone, then you are not sidetracked by body aches or pains and your true essence can come through. When you eat to live, rather than live to eat, you have more time for what is truly meaningful. Without the presence of food, there is no distraction to the open and loving conversations that result. Our culture makes it very challenging not to fall victim to sweet, salty, and fattening treats! The next time you get together with friends, I challenge you to do something that doesn't involve food, and I bet you will spend more time having quality conversations leading to the discovery of your truth!

SEEK. TRUST. BELIEVE. LOVE.

CHAPTER 15

ATTRACTING Love

"Love and faith are a mighty spell."
— Rumi

A lot of time had passed. It was July 2011 and my ex was now further from my mind. I had heard a woman he was dating had moved in with him. I would learn more about her over time, including that not only was she a "bigger presence" than me, but she was also very, very different from me. We were just two different people. I finally understood that I was just not a match for him, and after all this time, I learned that we were only meant to get each other to the point we did and move on. We were never meant to be long-term. Had I known that earlier, would I have continued ahead? But didn't we write our script? I was starting to understand the idea of a kind of "spiritual amnesia" that is necessary for us to complete our life mission. Despite all the heartache, I needed this relationship for growth.

FINDING MY MATCH

I had decided that the idea of dating was exciting, but I was becoming stronger and now really needed to start thinking about returning to a career or finding a new one and setting some goals for myself again. I had an MBA, had once made a

six-figure income, and was capable. I dreaded the thought of "punching the time clock" and wearing uncomfortable business clothing like I had in my past, but I was at a loss about what else I could do. I was making no money teaching yoga or shamanic healing, and even though I was certain I was very good at it (not something I could ever say in my career), I wasn't sure how to make an income on which I could support myself. I wondered even whether I was supposed to teach any of it for an income or whether I was simply meant to use the tools to work through and experience all the times I had been through. I had set goals and overachieved them my whole life. And I remembered how I had chosen to get up that day in Peru and continue on with my life. I had seen and experienced things that many couldn't even dream of doing. I had helped so many people heal. And I had lived to tell about it. What kind of career could I ever have that would give me the kind of freedom and gratification I had experienced for the last eight years, and how did all of this make me a better person?

I was starting to see that it was not so much the experiences that mattered but who I was becoming. The experiences helped me to heal anger, release judgment, grow spiritually, trust in myself, eat healthily, and narrow in on finding my truth. I was still suffering a bit of depression because now I had no one with whom to share my stories, and I was actually getting tired of trying to remember them, questioning their validity, or even continuing to tell them. I began to understand they were my "secrets" meant for me to experience so telling someone else about them would never really mean as much to another person as they did to me. But I was exhausted from holding on to them and trying to explain to people who I was as a result and why I was making the life choices I was. I figured the stories were ultimately for me in the end, but they seemed so unreal and like a once-in-a-lifetime thing. Maybe they would serve someone else so they needed to be shared. I knew that if I kept them in, they would haunt me, but I questioned whether

I could share them authentically. Would I be judged for having them (even though I couldn't help that I did), and who would want me as a partner if I told him everything? I decided I had to write them down, but I wasn't sure even where to start. It had been five years since Tia had died, but at this point, I still hadn't figured out that Tia was sending me on this journey to open my heart for what would happen next.

MEETING "MR. BUSINESS"

During all this time since 2006, I had been having a vision each day of a man I had still not met. I knew he lived in the Pacific Northwest and that where he lived were sea lions that could be heard from his house. I knew his name started with a "P," he had two sons, and there was some kind of law background or connection to the law (I thought he was likely to be an attorney). I was thinking of moving and wondered whether I should move to the Pacific Northwest in hopes of finding him.

When I was dating Mr. Playboy French Canadian Vegan Sailor, I had been contacted by Mr. Business (Patrick) on match.com, but we didn't get very far—just a few emails I think. Now that I had broken it off with Mr. Playboy, Patrick resurfaced via an email on the same dating service. When we first connected, Patrick seemed rather fast and abrupt, and I was so busy with so many other things that I honestly didn't pay much attention to him. I was being contacted regularly by various men, and I was trying to move out of a deep depression, gather myself, and figure out my life plan. I had mostly given up on finding anyone, and I just figured he'd make me a bunch of promises, or have hidden secrets, or turn into someone I didn't want to be with in the end. I honestly was not prepared for yet another relationship, and I was finally beginning to focus on me. I was scared about my future and needed to find a job. I didn't want once again to give up everything for yet another guy who would mess up my heart, my life, and question both my experiences

and who I had become as a result of them.

I didn't even notice that Patrick perfectly fit the mold of the person I had been wondering about since 2006. Honestly, I felt he was abrupt, fast, almost rude even, and he didn't appear to have an ounce of romance in him when he first approached me. He gave me a list of what he wanted, told me he was tired of dating, and said he'd sign a few books he was the author of and drop them in the mail. He told me to read them and contact him if I were interested. He went on to tell me that he didn't want to carry on long phone conversations or back and forth texts until we met. He was very particular and knew exactly what he wanted. I was completely turned off!

But the books arrived and I started to read them. I was not so much impressed about the content as the fact that they were well-organized, that he had made the effort to arrange his thoughts, and he had gone the extra mile to do something I had been called to do since 2006—write a book. I was nearly plagued with the idea of writing before I could move on with life, and I needed some help. I didn't know whether the universe was merely bringing me help (as had been happening in my dating experience up to now) or bringing me my soulmate. My first thought was "Well, if nothing else, maybe he can help me." I was exhausted, but I was a bit lonely too, and after a few Skype calls, I realized he was much more business-oriented than I had been used to for a while, but he reminded me a lot of myself when I was at the height of my career and also of my dad. I could see he was very compassionate, caring, focused, grounded, and outgoing. I could also see how he would be helpful in bringing me back into the world. I honestly didn't go into our relationship with any idea of it being long-lasting since nothing in my life to that point seemed to be. I figured he would come and go like everything else. But I also noticed that was not Patrick's style. He wanted something long-term and was immediately trying to decide whether I would be "the one." I

hadn't met anyone like that ever, and it sparked my interest. I knew having someone successful and grounded in my life would serve me well, and so I took a chance.

I told Patrick I was going to be in his general direction for a yoga class I was taking and maybe we could meet. I went on to tell him about the hot spring spa I was staying at in New Mexico, and after many conversations and Skype calls, we felt it was time we meet. Besides, we had discussions about how we felt it seemed odd to fall in love over the computer, but we both admitted we thought we might have. I told him I had to remain focused on my classes and I'd be gone to them all day. He told me he wanted to write his third book and could use the time while I was in classes to do that. It was a kind of test really because he would see the full picture of me in my white yoga clothing and full turban. He would see the teachers and other classmates, and if he didn't judge me or them, then we would already have one thing out of the way. I didn't think anyone would date me if he saw me in my yoga clothes (except for another yogi). Love would quickly be challenged by our faith in different belief systems. He, a Christian, and me, well... "spiritually interested" in all things. (You have now heard my story; how do you explain all that?) He did initially struggle a bit with some of it, but after a few long walks and deep thoughts, he decided to give it a chance. I even took him to the 11/11/11 event in New Mexico to celebrate the coming of the Aquarian Age (just ten months after my divorce was official). A whole group full of turban heads! He was impressed by the video of Yogi Bhajan (the man who brought Kundalini Yoga to North America from India), and he even enjoyed the food. I was actually quite surprised how well he handled it all because he clearly was out of his element.

After our week together, Patrick would go home to Bainbridge Island, WA and I would go back to Michigan. I had previously met another man in the D.C. area with whom I'd a very similar

meeting and I would never see him again, so I wasn't sure what would happen after we each went home to our own lives. We would plan for him to come out to visit (and meet my parents), and shortly thereafter, I would visit him on Bainbridge Island in Washington. I took it a day at a time, and I was very aware that this relationship would take some time to nurture and grow since we both had relationship wounds to heal.

It wasn't until I visited Patrick and heard the sea lions that first morning that I realized he was the man I had been seeing since 2006 (six years ago now). He lived in the Pacific Northwest, he had two sons, I heard the sea lions, and even though it was his ex-wife who was the lawyer, he had earned his bachelor's in political science. It didn't take long before we were talking about how to join our lives together. He told me his plan was to live on Bainbridge Island for another year and a half until his youngest son graduated from high school, and then he would go with him when he went to college in Hawaii. He asked me whether I'd like to move to Hawaii with him. I had never been to Hawaii, and I wasn't sure whether he was all wet or for real. It seemed a bit like a fairytale to me, and I wasn't going to hold my breath. It was strange, but he abruptly came into my life while many others came in much more gracefully, and just as gracefully as they came in, they left. I prepared for his abrupt departure from the very beginning. But then I started to see that Patrick was a very hard worker, a man of his word, very focused, determined, and the way he entered our relationship, knowing exactly what he wanted and not stopping until he found it, made me believe not only that he would make it happen, but he would make us happen.

I had so much stuff to get rid of and move, and I was now receiving a good amount of money from my divorce settlement, and I was talking about moving anyhow, so I did something totally crazy. I gave away nearly everything I had (I had been doing so for years anyway) and I packed up what was left, called

a moving company, found a rental house on Bainbridge Island, Washington, and just decided it was time and I was leaving. My entire life in Michigan I had never felt at home, and my entire being always needed to go west. Patrick would come in to visit one last time and we watched as everything got loaded into the moving truck. We were so anxious to start our new life together that we decided at 4 p.m. that day that we would pack up my little Honda Element with all our bags, two dogs, a cat, a few snacks, and hit the road as a snowstorm was starting.

Hardly anyone in my life felt I was making the best decision to go, but I knew that if I didn't, I would end up living a life meant for someone other than me. It was time for a change. Rumi once said, "Love puts reason to silence." It took us seven days to get to Bainbridge Island, Washington from Michigan, and we traveled in the cold and snow much like I had done those times back and forth to and from Colorado. I knew the trip well. But little did I know back then that I was in training for this experience. During this trip, it felt as if we had been together for much longer than we had. We had great conversations and got to know much more about each other. It was kind of crazy—I had just met Patrick in November and here it was only—January! It was very hard for me to leave Michigan as I had spent my whole life there. I realized nothing is as it seems, no one is as he or she seems, and no matter where I lived, the Divine and all my experiences would be alive within me. I left my ex with the idea I was going to be stepping into my becoming, and my becoming seemed much more romantic anywhere but where I was—especially if it would be in Hawaii. I had no idea how this was going to work out, but I stepped out of fear and took a chance.

ARRIVING ON BAINBRIDGE ISLAND

Once we arrived on Bainbridge Island, my pets and I would need to spend a few days living with Patrick until my things arrived. It was very cramped in his little condo, and there was

no yard for the dogs. It was actually nice because it forced us to take them for long walks outside. Patrick lived right on the beach and Shiitake loved the water. My things arrived after being delayed by the snowstorm we had just passed through, and they quickly overcrowded my small rental home. I spent days going through everything with only narrow aisles to walk through. I was absolutely overwhelmed with how much stuff I had. It hadn't looked like that much in my large home, and I had gotten rid of so much before the move and left more than half of it with my ex in our settlement.

Patrick was quickly back to work, and suddenly, I was all alone in a strange place. I was learning that my life was going to be very different in a smaller home for a while since I was experiencing a reality check on how this new life was going to go without the security of the dual ($300K) income I had become accustomed to when I was married. It also dawned on me that I had no friends, and if I wanted to go anywhere like the store, I had to look up directions on how to get there. I got lost every time I left the house. I wasn't teaching yoga or shamanic healing, so no one was coming and going in and out of the house. It was very quiet. Patrick was always working during the day so I started to get very sad. My relationships with my dogs seemed to be the only thing familiar, and Sushi was old and not able to interact with me as she once had; she spent most of her day lying outside. Shiitake was very involved and very active and hung on my every word. I'd spend my whole day talking to no one but Shiitake until Patrick's workday was done and he came over or I went to his cramped little condo.

As I went through my things, I had moments when I would cry because I began to realize I had already given up so much, lost so much, left so much behind, and now it seemed the only choice was to let more go. It was very, very scary for me. When everything is new and changes, it makes you want to hold onto everything that is familiar. My girls and I would get through all

of this together. They were my constants. I finally got up enough courage to start selling things on Craigslist, but with each item sold, I gave up another memory. The things I really liked were listed with higher price tags, so when they sold, at least it filled my bank account. I kept telling myself that releasing the old would only make room for the new, and that the new would be even better than I could realize. I said goodbye to each memory with each sale, and I said little prayers that my belongings would create even better memories for the new owners. I knew I had come into this life without these things, and I would be leaving without them too. While I had the rental home, it became my goal to release as much as I could. I spent a lot of time thinking about what was left—mostly anything that had nothing to do with my ex or reminded me of my past. If I had nothing, I told myself, then at least I had my girls, my stories and experiences, my newfound connection with myself, and my faith.

I tried to do familiar things with my girls when Patrick was busy working or traveling, but I realized I had to create new familiars. I tried to make chai tea on the stove like I used to do at the Maya Center, but I had no friends to come over to enjoy it with me. When the weather was cold, I wanted to sit in front of the fireplace and watch a movie, but I no longer had a fireplace. I wanted to go to dinner or go shopping, but everyone I knew was so far away. And added to the difficulty was that we were talking of moving to Hawaii, so if I did make friends, I would once again leave them behind. Making friends has never been easy for me so I made little to no effort. I was forty years old and this was my first time away from home. I began to think that falling in love shouldn't be this hard. I began to wonder whether I was trying too hard to create something or whether it was wrong for me to be giving up so much.

For the next year and a half, I would sell as much as I could and make many efforts to "reinvent myself," but my heart wasn't in it. Everyone close to me told me I needed to do something

and I was too talented and personable not to. Patrick encouraged me to try selling my photography, so I spent countless hours taking pictures, matting, and framing them. I entered them into art shows and got placed, but I hardly sold a thing. I opened my home up to try to sell my work, but I only seemed to attract lonely, elderly folks looking for someone to talk to. I got frustrated and gave up. I got a part-time job at a retail clothing store and ended up losing money because, yes, the clothes were just too desirable, but it kept me busy until I knew what my next step would be.

I was suddenly floundering as I tried to find my way back into the world. I started with what was familiar and opened my home to do yoga one night a week, but Shiitake saw to it that it didn't last long since she preferred to have me all to herself and made everyone feel very unwelcome by jumping all over them. I had learned to pay attention to her actions after all these years together, and I finally realized I really didn't want to teach yoga right then but simply needed to practice it myself.

Patrick would lose patience with me from time to time, and he wondered about my character since I was not interested in returning to a career; however, I was just starting to break free from years of spiritual transformation and deep depression, so I felt accomplished each day just for sticking my head out of my shell. But it seemed everyone else was pushing me for more.... Sure, I had proven I could make a six-figure income before, but it hadn't brought me the kind of happiness I gained from helping real people and working with mind-bending healing and energy. I just couldn't understand how I could ever get excited again about pushing meaningless deadlines on meaningless projects in the corporate world. And would it ever remotely bring me the kind of satisfaction that healing and helping people did? I wanted to stay with the magic and bend my mind some more, but I also knew that making money was more practical and prudent. I had met many on my path who

had given up everything to follow spirit, but life seemed so complicated for them. They would flounder from home to home and sleep wherever they could find a bed or wherever the next big spiritual event would take place. They were losing their homes, their cars, and their minds. I knew I needed the grounding of a home, a relationship, and an income, and yet my eyes had been opened to so many new things.

While I was separating from my husband, I was also watching my dad battle prostate cancer, and my sister had announced she was six months pregnant and now unsure of her future. I could feel the pain in my mom's heart from everything we were all going through. I didn't want to make anyone worry, but I couldn't get my head (or heart) in the game. I tried to be there for them, but I needed to be there for me. I did healings on my family members from afar and was able to shift many things, whether or not they believed I did. I never told them since I knew they wouldn't understand or believe. I could see I was containing my dad's cancer and had assisted in the healthy birth of my sister's baby.

I thought about how when my dad found out he had cancer, he began to make healthier choices, such as changing his diet and quitting smoking. He had read the signs and knew if he didn't make a change, it could cost him his life. I wondered how I could be any different. I'd had an opportunity to make a change, and I had gone through it and come out the other side. If my dad went back to smoking and eating poorly, then he was taking the risk of the cancer returning. If I went back to the way I was before my transformation, would I have learned anything? I thought long and hard about this. I realized I couldn't possibly go back to where I came from because everything had changed and nothing existed the way it once had. So the next question became—what do I do with all that I have learned and become? I would table this question for now and hope that Patrick could be patient with me as I figured it out.

GETTING ENGAGED

Nearly a year went by and my lease was about to come to an end. I intended once it ended to rent month-to-month until Patrick and I settled our plans for moving to Hawaii. Would we really make it become a reality?

On 12/12/12, Patrick took me to Cannon Beach, Oregon for a birthday weekend on the coast. We loaded up the girls in the car and off we went. It was always unbearably cold and rainy there, but it was one of Patrick's favorite places. There he would ask me to marry him. It was my forty-first birthday and amazingly ten years since my ex had asked me the same question. I couldn't believe how much had changed in my life in that time. I had suspected the question would be coming, and it was scary for me to consider saying, "Yes," but I did. I was so scared that life would fast-forward and Patrick and I would end the same way I had with my ex. I'd had no idea when asked the same question ten years prior that I would have been divorced. I knew my answer to Patrick would be "Yes," but I was very scared nevertheless. Patrick's heart had been broken also, and I knew it was not something he had planned either. Or was it? Again, who had written the script? Suppose our hearts had needed to be broken open for each other, and we had planned that before we met.

What I was learning this time around was that the kind of love I needed was not some fluffy romantic love (with the French language whispered into my ears by a man in a tight speedo), but a practical love, a grounded love, a love that would be forgiving of all things I wanted us to grow into, and a love that was understanding of what caused me pain and wanted to help me grow and learn from it. Patrick seemed to understand what I needed; he was on a self-help path too, although his path was more business-minded. For me, he would become a grounding force because he accepted me for who I was and loved

me deeply, and that just made me love him more. There really wasn't a lot of "fluff" or reading between the lines with Patrick. It was or it wasn't. It felt a bit cold and hard for me at first, but I realized within it was a lot of love and compassion. He just knew what he wanted.

The girls would have a great time walking and playing at the beach and were exhausted on the ride home and slept nearly the whole way. We shared our engagement with our family and friends. It was an exciting time, but we had a challenging road ahead of us before we could join our lives together.

MOVING IN TOGETHER

Back on Bainbridge Island one morning, I was sound asleep in my bed when I started hearing noise outside. It was yet another yucky, cold, dreary Washington day, and I had just worked a long shift in my retail job the night before, but I got out of bed to see what was going on. There were landscapers in the yard and I recalled the landlord mentioning they would be by. I crawled back into bed and dozed off again. I had the day off and was in no hurry to get up. Suddenly, I heard the voice of a woman who seemed to be approaching me. I opened my eyes and found a woman standing in my bedroom's doorway. I thought it might be the landlord's wife whom I had never met. She started yelling at me, asking me why I hadn't let her in and why I was still in bed at 10 a.m. She started telling me I couldn't run a business in my home or sell things, and she kept going on about countless other things. I was barely awake and shocked that she was in my house and making all these statements. I immediately called the police and Patrick. I told her to leave and go outside until I could get dressed. In all the commotion, Shiitake decided to bite Sushi, so I started to cry profusely since blood was dripping from her head. It was just a shock to all of our systems. We were used to the privacy of our own home and living on twenty-five acres in the woods. I had never paid my rent late

and was a very good tenant. My first thought was, "Oh, God, where am I am going to live now, and what am I going to do?"

I almost wanted to pack my bags and go back to Michigan, but I had nowhere to live since the Maya Center was no more and Patrick had no room for me. After all the dust settled, I knew I would leave there when the lease expired, although I had no other options. I looked for another place to rent, and I was even tempted to move to some other city or state altogether, thinking this situation was not meant to be and I just needed to go find a job and settle down by myself. I was tired of waiting—waiting to get a job, waiting to move, waiting for Patrick's son to graduate from high school so we could move to Hawaii—just tired of waiting! I wondered whether all the waiting would evolve into our moving to Hawaii and merging our lives, and if it did, would we just end up divorced anyway? Stepping into my becoming was hard!

Patrick was in a tiny condo, so there was just no way we could both live there. I had just finally unpacked and organized all my things. If I moved in with Patrick, I would not only have to get a storage unit, but I'd have to get rid of more stuff. I couldn't imagine getting rid of even more. I barely had anything left. Not knowing what else to do, I quit my job, started listing more things for sale, and packing once again.

Shiitake (and I) didn't take all the change very well, and with so much chaos around us, she became a barometer for my stress. My shamanic work had trained me to look for repeat stories. Now it seemed as if the "shit on me" pattern was continuing. I knew I needed to release it, so instead of being angry or emotional, I tried to move into being thankful for the awareness. The pattern had initially become evident when I watched how easy it was for my ex just to walk away. As I transitioned into a new person and went through change, many people in my life had just walked away. I kept healing myself, but I still

wasn't stable enough to handle all this change—nor was Shiitake. We had already been through so much that it was extremely hard to accept that we weren't stable yet. I think we were feeding off each other's energy. Shiitake could feel my fear and concern; whenever I got upset and showed tears or anger, Shiitake would react by beating up Sushi. It got so bad that Patrick told me he was afraid of Shiitake and something needed to change for us to remain together.

Patrick, however, didn't understand a few things: 1.) Shiitake was feeding off the instability in me and the threat to the stability of our home, and we had never before had much human drama in our home. 2.) I had made an agreement with my dogs a long time ago, as I was beginning to date, that if they didn't like my boyfriend or he didn't like them, we would end the relationship since they came first. 3.) I knew Patrick and I had met to help each other, so this would be one of the "tests" to see whether our love could withstand life's challenges. 4.) When life got very hard for me from experiencing so many things at once, it was Shiitake who had kept me alive. There were times I wanted to end my life as I progressed through my divorce and "dark nights of my soul," but I knew if I did, she would likely be put to sleep and not re-homed. She had an aggressive nature with strange dogs (and Sushi), and because I used to rescue the breed, I knew she would not be placed. I had stood up that day on the mountain in Peru and chosen life and everything it involved, including Shiitake. I promised my girls when I divorced my ex that no matter what happened, I would be sure always to feed them before I ate myself. What Patrick didn't know was that Shiitake had saved my life countless times, and if it weren't for her, I wouldn't even be alive as a choice for him now, but how do you tell someone that without appearing unstable, judgmental, or worried?

My depression had never come from a place of not loving myself but a place of questioning how to live with what I'd experienced. It took me some time to realize that what I was experi-

encing were my own gifts and who I was, and I needed to fall in love with myself. When I started accepting the experiences as gifts, I was able to love myself. When I accepted as opportunities what I originally had thought of as failures and mistakes, I began to love myself. And when I began to love myself, I began to step into my truth and become able to trust in myself. I knew Shiitake was a gift, not a mistake—not a hindrance, but an opportunity. I knew if Patrick could understand any part of this, he would understand that she and I had an unconditional love that was not going to be broken. It became clear to me that if he could not work through this hurdle, we were not meant to move forward. He would remain cautious of her and (truthfully now) I of him, but we continued ahead with the packing and moving. I would end up moving out of my rental house and spending the next five months living with him in his little cramped condo. Little did I know how hard it would be on all of us.

Challenged by our situation, I sought new ways to find a solution that was both grounded and practical as well as spiritually connected and loving. I knew Shiitake was more than a dog, but often words escaped me when I tried to share my knowing of this in the physical, three-dimensional world. I had faced this challenge most of my life, but now was different because it involved both of my loves and our futures together.

EXERCISES:

1. Why do you live where you live? ____________________________

____

____

____

____

____

2. Where have you always dreamed of living? ______________

3. What has kept you from moving there? ______________

4. What obstacles do you need to deal with or remove from your life to allow you the freedom to move (cut the cord) to where your heart desires? ______________

HELPING YOU DISCOVER YOUR TRUTH

Let's face it; often we live wherever our parents decided to settle. Desirable location or not, this is often the truth. You may be waiting for your ship to come and take you away, but…that is never going to happen! You need to take risks. You need to get out there. You need to listen to your heart and be willing to move; otherwise, love may allude you for a lifetime. I believe a better life is out there waiting for you. You need to develop the courage to lose sight of the shore and swim out to your ship. In doing so, you just may attract the love of your dreams and find your truth in the process.

SEEK. TRUST. BELIEVE. LOVE.

CHAPTER 16

LEARNING FROM Animals

"I care not much for a man's religion whose
dog and cat are not the better for it."
— Abraham Lincoln

Every animal is here to teach us as long as we're paying attention. Generally, silent observation is the best method for communication. Each dog in my life has come to me as a gift to teach me a very beautiful new skill or lesson. Upon her death, Tia would open me up to shamanism and continue walking me through my metaphysical and spiritual journeys as I would grow and learn. Mai Tai would teach me about herbs, tinctures, homeopathy, reading the signs of nature, all things natural medicine, and into food. He would also introduce me into holding death and the dying in a sacred way. Sangria would teach me about peaceful and easy death and our ability as humans to walk gracefully and lovingly over to the other side and back...seamlessly. Sushi has always taught me how to find peace and love in every situation, to keep a smile on my face, against all odds—wag my tail more, and to observe peacefully my surrounds. But Shiitake would now start vying for all of my attention. I realized she was trying to teach me something and was getting frustrated that I wasn't listening. Maybe I was listening, but I just wasn't acting.

DOG TRAINING OR NICOLE TRAINING?

Once we moved into Patrick's little condo, the fighting between the dogs heightened. I knew how stressful it was for me to be there, and Shiitake was not doing much better. I was trying to make it a home, but with limited space and most of my things in storage, I had to work with what I had. Patrick had the home decorated in his style and he had his ways of doing things, so it was very hard for me to come in and not want to change a few things to make it my home as well. His furniture was very dark, masculine, nautical-themed and it held his family's history. It was meaningful to him, but it only reminded me that he'd had another very rich and full life before me, and I had no part in that history. Creating a grounded and loving home had always been extremely important to me, but now I seemed to have little control over it. I had always been a huge home improvement guru and all my family and friends knew that about me. Now being in this condo felt like being in prison for me. I had no place to retreat to that was my own and no place to do my yoga.

All the change and Shiitake's temper turned out to be too much for Patrick, and it deeply challenged our relationship. We were at a crossroads. I suggested we opt for dog training as an interim solution. It would cost me a fortune, but it turned out to be the best thing I could have done, not only for Patrick and me, but because now Shiitake and I would finally be able to speak a common language and bond deeper than ever before.

For me, nothing was greater than being able to communicate with the one being I loved the most. Now after all these years together (mostly me following her), Shiitake would finally become my student. With most of my dogs, it had been the other way around because I had learned so much from them, but now I began to see that as part of the problem. I was not taking the alpha role—in this relationship or in any other area of my

life. I knew that dog behavior specialist Cesar Millan taught that most dogs' problems could be found, not in the dog, but in the dog's human. I had no idea what I was doing wrong, but now Shiitake would teach me a great lesson. As I began to take leadership over her, I watched as she followed me instead of me following her. She really counted on me telling her what to do, and she was thriving as a result. She was ultimately teaching me to be a leader.

When we met with the trainer, Shiitake was very excited to show off her new skills. She was progressing so well that even Patrick was impressed and said he was no longer worried about her behavior, so we began considering the Hawaii transition even more. We progressed with all the state import documentation, rabies shots, and got micro chips. I was so proud of Shiitake and loved taking her places to challenge her new skills; she excelled and we grew so close.

We would have a setback, however, when Shiitake nipped at Sushi in a moment of jealous excitement when I picked them up from their care. This time, the trainer said there was not much more he could do. Shiitake had learned some skills, but her aggression was not something we could change. We got kicked out of school! When I watched the trainer walk away, I felt I had been abandoned much as I had been in my divorce. I was so worried about how Patrick would take it, but he handled it quite well. By then, maybe he realized how much she meant to me, and I to him. We were both trying so hard.

LYMPHOMA

After a bit of time, we realized Shiitake was not feeling well. Her lymph glands were swollen. I had never felt them so swollen, so I knew something was very wrong. The vet's office did some tests and sent them to the lab, so we had to wait a few days for results. Almost immediately, I noticed Shiitake was feel-

ing worse. We were now just days away from relocating to our new home in Maui, Hawaii. Shiitake and I had been through so much together—the separation and divorce, moving out of our home and into the Maya Center, relocating to Colorado, traveling so far and long, all the nights of tears and wondering where we'd end up next, the late nights of yoga, all the growth from performing and teaching shamanic healing, the boyfriends I had dated, the long walks in the woods in Michigan, Colorado, and on the rocky beaches of the Pacific Northwest. We had come all the way across the country, and sacrificed having a yard for the last five months. To move to Hawaii, we had also gone through several rounds of shots and tests, filled out paperwork, and bought our plane tickets and dog crates. Shiitake and Sushi's names were decoratively placed on the sides of the crates, and I had even purchased therapeutic bedding, cooling fans, stuffed toys, chew bones, and a baby monitor to make sure my girls had a safe and easy flight.

And then the call came—Shiitake had cancer! Lymphoma! My heart fell into my stomach and I nearly passed out. After everything we had been through—this was going to be the move that would make up for it all and reward her with the most amazing ending. We were supposed to go on long walks on the beaches and put everything we had been through in the past. This was supposed to be the reward for surviving it all, for all the things I hadn't gotten right along the way that had caused her pain and suffering, for all the days I had made her sit and listen to me cry. After all that, there was just no way she wasn't going to make it through this. I was going to make sure she got better so I could finally show her joy and gratitude for sticking with me through it all. Now I began to fear I had killed her with all my poor choices; she was not quite six years old, so this was way too soon for me to lose her. The doctors advised that she be put down and not make the trip, but there was no way that was going to happen. We just needed to get her comfortably on that plane and let her enjoy a few days on the beach.

My bond with Shiitake now exceeded anything I had ever experienced with any other being. After everything we had gone through, when the dust cleared, we had been left standing...together! I knew there was something different and special about her. She had been sent to me as a gift from beyond to be my child, mentor, a friend, and trusted advisor who always listened and rarely passed judgment. I even dreamt one night that she was dressed in a silver spacesuit and was my co-pilot in my exploratory spacecraft. I sensed we had been partners in many lifetimes.

I tried to imagine life without her in hopes that by jumping ahead, I could gain the necessary lessons without her passing. I tried to learn as much and as quickly as I could so I could figure out a backdoor way to extend her life and release her eminent early departure. I would shake my rattle, dance with burning incense, pull out my medicine bag, pray, and meditate daily. But all I could discover was that she had served her purpose, played her role, and it was nearing her time of departure. I didn't know any other tricks. I hoped I hadn't done this to her, and I hoped that by stepping temporarily away from yoga and shamanic practices (at a time when I should have stepped more deeply into them), I hadn't made choices that were killing her. I prayed to release any bonds, cords, or ties I had created to cause this situation. And I wondered about all the vaccines she had been given prior to her departure. Were they the cause of her lymphoma?

MOVING TO MAUI

The day came when Patrick and Sushi flew to Maui to pick up the keys to the house and accept the forty-foot container of our household items we had previously shipped that would be delivered to our new house in Maui in a few more days. The next day Shiitake, Penelope, and I would fly to join them. I was so nervous about the trip and Shiitake's comfort. I cried all the way

as I drove to the airport with Patrick's son asleep in the backseat, waiting to take the car back home after my departure. I cried through the airport and onto the plane. I sat next to a nice woman who was sweet enough to ease my pain and tell me all about her and her husband's journey to their new home overseas a few years earlier. I had placed a wireless baby monitor in Shiitake's crate, and somehow it made it safely through all the security checks. The door to her crate closed and Shiitake peacefully lay down on her bed for her six-hour flight. I showed Shiitake to the woman on the monitor, and we both watched her for most of the trip until the battery ran out. Then I was a nervous wreck until she arrived in my sight on the ground. She actually did very well with her travels.

We would begin our new cancer treatment plan a few days after arriving. I had read everything about lymphoma in dogs that I could, and I found a veterinarian who helped me make natural choices since chemotherapy was known not to be a solution and would make her sick every day of what little life she likely had left. Shiitake would teach me about canine diet, nutrition, immunizations, and the horrors of the dog food industry. I found myself awake all hours researching and studying every source I could find. I was beginning to understand that I had done many things "wrong," even though I had been trying very hard to do everything right. Together, we created a new vegan food for her that led to new vegan treats, and of course, we needed a label for our brand, so she would inspire me to draw again. Together, we would create our brand: Vegan Dog Treats (www.Vegan-DogTreats.com), and it would become her legacy upon her passing if that were God's plan.

I never once questioned the ingredients when I made the treats. It was as if something greater than me came through and put things in a bowl, and "poof" they were made. I never even altered the original ingredients. Shiitake seemed to be inspiring me to help make changes in the care of our canine

companions by taking a look at ingredients in common dog foods and asking the question, “Is it right to kill one for another to survive?” I began to hear her needs and her thoughts to help other dogs heal and live healthy and happy lives. After we looked at foods that would aid in the fight against cancer in dogs, we wanted to share the most important detail we learned. We hope you hear it:

DON'T FEED YOUR DOG COMMERCIAL DRY DOG FOOD!

Why? There is no guarantee that what is in the food is actually good for your dog. There is no government regulation on what actually goes into the food. It can possibly contain strange meats or animal parts from sick or euthanized animals. In various materials I read there might even be other cats and dogs in the food. Also, when cooked at high temperatures, this dog food becomes damaged or denatured. If you would like to know more about the research we found, please contact me through my website. I would love to share that with you. It is very hard to cure cancer when it takes over the body, but there are things we learned together that can help to prevent it from occurring. This became a passion for both of us to share and I have included more details and a special report as an appendix to this book to discuss our findings further.

Shiitake was only expected to live about a month after her diagnosis, but she had now far surpassed her termination date and seemed to be thriving. We had time to enjoy the beaches and make daily trips into the cool clean air of the Haleakala National Park in upcountry Maui. She got to visit Hana and drink from the waterfalls in many locations on the island. She went for great walks and long car rides, and as I first became exposed to new areas in my new home, she would be there right alongside me, experiencing them too. There was nothing I wanted to do more than to absorb each moment I could with her.

LOSING MY BEST FRIEND

For a brief period, from November 2011 until April 2013, I had a break from past experiences when I met Patrick. But from April until October 2013, I was reliving my past again as if I were preparing to say goodbye to it along with Shiitake's passing.

On October 13th, 2013, Patrick would return from a flight after a speaking trip on the mainland and Shiitake and I would pick him up at the airport. I sensed she was holding on for him. When he arrived, I had never before seen her so excited to see another being as she was that day. She was not usually very affectionate in a physical sort of way, but that day she greeted Patrick with the biggest kiss right on his lips as if to say, "I'm so thankful you are here so I can finally go home. You were my momma's choice, and you are mine too." That night, I knew she would pass within a few hours. It was a hard night for her physically and me emotionally.

The next morning when Patrick got up (again she chose to be with him), she got out of her bed and struggled to reach the backyard. In the yard, she lay down and could no longer get up. I went in the house to fetch the blanket she and I would always lie on during our trips upcountry to the lavender farm so we could take in the fresh country air. Shiitake would watch cows, I would read, and we would carry on conversations as only best friends would. This would be the last time we would share that blanket together. I placed it on the grass in the backyard and pulled her tired body up onto it. I could tell she so wanted to get up and walk into the house as if nothing were wrong, but she could barely lift her head.

Patrick now came to join us and I informed him that she was on her way. I knew she wanted to teach Patrick about death and dying, and I could see it would be a great lesson for him

because death had never been so close to him before and he was a bit afraid. Death brings with it an immediate feeling of awe and humility, and once you experience it, you are forever changed.

Suddenly, I could see the light and that she was leaving her body. It was the most entrancing and mesmerizing light, and it had clearly captivated her in awe as her eyes glazed over and she heard the calling to come home. Suddenly, I was engulfed in a kind of love both paralyzing and so beautiful that words cannot describe it. What I saw next showed me how much she loved me. She actually had a choice between me and the light, and she questioned it at least five times as if trying to decide whether she should stay or go. But she knew she had to leave. From my past experiences, I knew I needed to give her permission to go so her spirit would be released, so I did so countless times. I kept coaxing her into the light, telling her to run into it like she had run all those times behind my car on country roads in Michigan. I said over and over, "Go, go, go, go, let's go" like I used to prompt her as she ran with a smile. I was her cheerleader, encouraging her to run into the light. But her love for me was as strong as it was for the light. I was reminded of a quote by Josh Billings: "A dog is the only thing on earth that loves you more than he loves himself."

I finally felt like I had to push her away since her physical body kept struggling to decide. One last breath, and ahhh... peace came over her body and...she was gone. I sat there with her and Patrick and thought, "Oh, my God...life is sure going to change." Patrick and I were both in tears and he was speechless. It was a bonding moment like I'd never had with anyone else. Patrick was so fully present with us and so attentive and loving. Through all I'd been in my life, this was the most meaningful event I had ever witnessed with another person. She was the love of my life, and I knew that if she left, it meant Patrick would take care of me now.

I had questioned whether Maui should be my home, but this morning, I knew Shiitake would need to be buried, and that would forever make Maui her home. Home is where the heart is, and now my heart and her body have found home. A few minutes after her passing, we got up to prepare to bury her, but I was suddenly stopped mid-stride and nearly taken to my knees by the most golden yellow and white bath of light and love I had ever witnessed. I knew it was a gift of her love and life. I knew she was fully present with me in a way she could not have been when merely a dog. She would show me now her full essence. She was always more than a dog to me, and now she was proving it to me, as if to say, "You were right." She was clearly an angel!

At that moment, I knew we all have choices when we come to earth and we choose what being will serve us best. Shiitake would come in the most trusting and loyal form that would impact me the most. If she had come as a person, I would not have had her constant companionship. Our disagreements would not have been so easily forgiven, and our love might not have been so pure or complete. She was an ascended master, a healer, a sage, an elder, and so much more than a dog. I knew I hadn't lost her; she had come to gain my trust and friendship and love so she could assist me now from the other side.

She knew she needed to teach Patrick about death so he could understand what I had been through so many times before. The golden love-filled glow of light I experienced was clearly her revealing her true self and expressing her love. I had never seen this truth so clearly with the passing of all the others, so I felt something special was occurring that would take away the last of my pain. Each loved one who passed had always offered to take some of my pain, but now Shiitake took what was left over, and she let me know she could now serve me better without the binding physical form.

Now each day when I wake, I can look into the mountains and see Shiitake looking over the land and watching over us. In every word I write and each step I take, I sense and feel her like I never could when she was alive. I breathe her now. She is in my everything. To carry that kind of love within and around with me is empowering. To be loved so deeply is humbling. I don't think it is often in this life we get to know a love like this, and when we get caught up in our expectations about where and who it should come from, we might miss it altogether.

I would finally see the innocence of all animals and how a greater power divinely created them for our comfort, companionship, and almost to test our level of compassion. Dogs in particular have an innate loyalty and love without judgment. They require or expect nothing in return. They live in the moment and forgive actions of the past and care not much about their future. Each day a dog forgives your actions from the day before and simply stands in love.

To me, dogs seem more like angels. Many times in my life I believe I have been mis-understood and looked at differently regarding my love for animals. Animals aren't dressed in white robes with a glowing light to fit into our human mold of what an angel might be, but what if they are angels? If you had angels in your presence, would you leave them outside in the cold, make them eat bad food, over-vaccinate them, or treat them poorly? What if God sent you your own little guardian angel? The gift of an animal is a sure sign God hasn't forgotten about you and really does love you. And maybe sometimes you just need a little guiding and / or help or just a new best friend.

EXERCISES:

1. Think for a moment about your favorite pet (whether he or she is still with you or passed). What are the five greatest lessons your pet has taught you about truth:

1. ____
____
2. ____
____
3. ____
____
4. ____
____
5. ____
____

2. Have you ever questioned the number of vaccines, antibiotics, or other pharmaceutical drugs your veterinarian supplies versus the number of natural and or homeopathic solutions he or she provides? How many times has your pet gotten worse after a vaccine instead of better? And have you ever been guilted into giving your pet the veterinarian recommended vaccines when you didn't think he or she needed them? Journal notes and dates of vaccines here: ______________________________
____
____
____
____
____
____
____
____
____

3. Are you aware there are many natural alternatives available for your pets and that very few veterinarians are trained in either this or nutritional supplementation and / or diet. God created your puppy to be strong to survive, so let me ask you: is it necessary to alter what God so brilliantly manufactured? Make note of where to find alternatives to puppy vaccines and start your pup off right with alternative options, not poisonous chemicals. ______________________________

____

____

____

____

____

(Note: Did you know that many vaccines are not needed and that a Titres test can actually show your pet's antibodies prior to considering the vaccine to determine whether or not it is needed in the first place?)

HELPING YOU DISCOVER YOUR TRUTH

Anatole France once said, "Until one has loved an animal, a part of one's soul remains unawakened." In the journey of finding your inner truth, you are bound to have many setbacks on your path. Some of them you see coming and some you don't. Some you can avoid and some you can't. Some of these experiences you can share, and other times you can't. Perhaps instead of seeking help from someone who does not understand, allow your pet to be your sounding board, your beam of light, and your strength during your time of weakness. Learn from your pet. Be still. Observe his or her level of joy and pure excitement just to "be" and live in the "now." Perhaps some of the answers you seek on your journey of truth can be found within your pet. Embrace him, love her, and enjoy the "now" because more times than not, you will outlive your pet.

SEEK. TRUST. BELIEVE. LOVE.

CHAPTER 17

EVOLVING Through Change

"The secret of change is to focus all of your energy, not on fighting the old, but on building the new."
— Socrates

I was now caught in a struggle of how to merge my journey and experiences into a financially rewarding livelihood, career, or source of income without losing the magic and knowledge that had been gained. Everyone around me was basically telling me, "Those experiences were memorable, but it's time to put them behind you and move on," but I didn't know how. Everything I had thought existed one way had turned out to exist another. I was also afraid that if I moved forward, I would forget so many things about those I lost and the experiences I'd had. For that reason, I wanted to capture these memories and experiences in a book. I still hadn't figured out what I was supposed to do with it all. It didn't feel right to have all these experiences and then just go back to what I was doing because nothing was the same any more. I'd often say to myself, "How do you make ash come off your hands and spend time with the angels and then go make a sale, write a report, or give a meaningless work presentation?" I could no longer understand how to take what was so meaningful and apply it to the practical world. I wanted the magic, but I also needed an income.

I thought back to all the times I had received slack for my choices. No one really knew what I had been through because I was afraid to talk about it. When I did get the courage to talk about my experiences, I was often judged and teased. I would learn they were simply made for me only, but I so wished I could share them. I had found that in some of the spiritual circles I belonged to people could be the most judgmental. What I failed to realize then was that others in those circles were going through their own awakenings and in the mode of analyzing the details of their own personal growth and development. Many times I tried to find what in the yoga community is called a "sangat" (spiritual group) where I could openly share, but it was not something that came easily. I knew it was something I needed to create—a safe space and a healthy environment where people could freely and openly share without judgment. When found, the integrity of such a "circle" is a true blessing because they are few and far between in my experience.

It's strange how competitive and judgmental people can be. If we are all here for the experience, wouldn't it make more sense to support one another as we go through life's challenges? Let's make this change together! I will open my heart and arms for you if you have been through something you need support with. If your community doesn't have an organization or group that you resonate with, then I challenge you to seize the need and create one. I'll even speak with you to get you started!

THE TEN OX HERDING PICTURES

On my path to enlightenment, I would study the *The Ten Ox Herding Pictures* from D.T. Suzuki's Zen Buddhist teachings which illustrate the stages of a Mahayana Buddhist practitioner's progression toward enlightenment. I felt my own journey had followed a similar set of stages. The stages are:

1. Searching
2. Discovering
3. Perceiving
4. Catching
5. Taming
6. Riding
7. Transcending concepts
8. Transcending concepts and self
9. Reaching the source
10. Returning to society

I supposed I was at that last phase of enlightenment and was now meant to "mingle in the marketplace." I was hoping for an eleventh stage that would tell me what to do next (in more detail). I understood that all that had happened...simply happened.

Stepping back, I would realize what the ayahuasca ceremony taught me—there is the vine of life and then there are all these little leaves of experience. They are all of the same source and there is no separation. All this time later, I would finally realize that if I were to see them as anything less than connected, I would always feel their separation. Change was constant in that little vine during my ceremony—flowing up and down and seeming to go nowhere but always with the possibility of going anywhere and everywhere. So just as the vines of life grew, rooted, and created more leaves, so I would create more experiences. I could get onto a leaf that was dying or infected and fall off, or I could stay a while on a healthy green leaf (possibly a metaphor for a vibrant new experience) for a while and then move on. I guess I just spent a while on the death and change leaves over the last couple of years. I figure if there is a leaf for every experience in life, I might choose more wisely in my future which ones I'd like to hang out on for a while...love, peace, contentment, etc. What leaves are you on and how long are you staying?

When going through so much change, there really is no other way through it than finding a way into self-love. We ultimately come into this lifetime alone, and our souls go out alone.... We didn't come with directions or a simple manual for how we would work, but when we find a way to shift our belief system into a connection with the source in which all these agreements were made, and we find peace in that relationship, we can be better guided on our soul's journey into truth. No matter the journey, we always have ourselves, our actions, our thoughts, our education, and our personal experiences. Everything changes, but you can't escape yourself. You might as well make a good friend in you.

EXERCISES:

Take a few moments to jot down the five major changes / challenges you are currently facing:

1. ______________________________
2. ______________________________
3. ______________________________
4. ______________________________
5. ______________________________

If you had a magic wand, what would be the best case scenario you would have each of these changes / challenges result in? Write down the best results for each of these growth opportunities.

1. ______________________________
2. ______________________________
3. ______________________________
4. ______________________________
5. ______________________________

(Note: When you pre-determine the results of the change in your mind, more times than not, your subconscious mind will instruct your body to deliver the results you desire.)

HELPING YOU DISCOVER YOUR TRUTH

Change is the only thing in life that you can count on. Things are not guaranteed to stay the way they are in your life. I challenge you to keep an open mind, embrace change, and become the change you wish to see in yourself and in others.

Gandhi said ""If we could change ourselves, the tendencies in the world would also change. As a man changes his own nature, so does the attitude of the world change towards him.... We need not wait to see what others do."

My challenge to you is to seek out ways in your community in which you can be the catalyst of change. In doing so, you will evolve and your inner truth may become more clear.

SEEK. TRUST. BELIEVE. LOVE.

CHAPTER 18

LEADING From Within

"There's nothing which can be more precious in you than your own relationship with your own consciousness."
— Yogi Bhajan

After every experience has been had and people and places have come and gone...there is nothing left but you. After all the bending and stretching to be someone else for someone else is done…there is nothing left but you. When you're done telling the stories of excuses, pointing fingers, and asking the why's… there is no one else but you. Whether you go for a run, a walk, or do errands, it's your shadow that is always next to you. You can't escape you!

For me, my experiences ultimately provided several years of growth and learning, and I know I am a better person for them today. I would also learn the power of the mind and would find myself years later finally able to step into my yoga practice… authentically. I would finally hear Yogi Bhajan (teacher of Kundalini yoga) say, "If you conquer your mind, you can conquer the world."

I would discover the link between leadership and truth and know that one cannot lead even oneself if he doesn't know his own personal truth. In Kundalini yoga, this personal truth is our

"Sat Nam." "Sat" means "Truth" and "Nam" means "Name." You could translate it as "True Name" or "Truth is my name." It is a way of acknowledging that at our essence is the Essence. The "Truth," which is bigger than any human truth, isn't a matter of right or wrong or even a concept that we can clearly articulate. It is simply an acknowledgment that the Great Mystery is who we are—the reality of our existence.

When the dust cleared, I was the one who had to stand in my essence, and it would be the practices of Kundalini yoga that would keep me grounded, connected, and break the business of my mind. I had been given the spiritual name "Nirankar Kaur" nearly a decade earlier. "Nirankar" means "the Formless One," or "God without form." It was explained to me as "one who sees God in all." "Kaur" is a name given to all women in this path, meaning "grace." You could say my full name means "One who sees God in all and does so with grace."

Years ago, the last thing I would have done during a trauma in my life would be to think about sitting in meditation. But, when everything else is in chaos, it really is the safest place to be. The day Shiitake died I would sit in my meditation and take a unique role of leadership in chanting the Akals to help her spirit pass over. "Akal" is a chant used to release the soul when someone dies. It means that there is no death, only liberation. Kundalini yoga would suddenly become something I could see as a constant amid so much change. It was like my shadow and always there. It cost me nothing but my time. Through the teachings of Yogi Bhajan, I would finally start finding peace of mind, awareness, and acceptance of universal truth. I would also see that reality would not be a mystery to me, nor would conflict disturb me, and fear would dissolve. And when fear lessens, you can walk a path of truth and the path toward peace is easier.

This wasn't the true essence of what I initially had in mind for how either my life would go or how I would view leadership, but I took faith in the fact that this script was written and everything was perfect exactly as it was. When we are authentic in ourselves, we can be very connected and powerful leaders of truth, of others, and most importantly, ourselves. Here are some of my favorite quotes about "truth" from "The Master":

"Life is a lie
if you do not find the eternal truth."

"The fundamental law of truth is that it
penetrates through all darkness."

"What is a lie? Truth spoken in fear. Just realize that truth spoken in fear is nothing but a lie. And how many of you lie? Everybody. Whoever speaks in fear, lies."

"Sat Nam. Sat is the truth, Nam is the identity, the noun, the personality, and your ego. Whenever your ego feels the light of God, you will be very humble. That is the test. You will be very compassionate. You will be very graceful. You will be very tolerant. You will not be rude. You can't be!"

"In the beginning you are you, in the middle you are you, in the end you are God. There's nothing else. If you can't close your eyes, you can't open your eyes, that's the end of the eyes. There's nothing to it. Nothing was, nothing is, nothing shall be."

"You speak truth to hurt each other. You are not honest. Truth doesn't hurt anybody. Truth uplifts you. Truth is a force...not to be used to hurt people."

— Yogi Bhajan (1929 - 2004)

EXERCISES

List five ways you are allowing others to take a leadership role in your life:

1. ____________________
2. ____________________
3. ____________________
4. ____________________
5. ____________________

Now list five actions you can take to claim your life back and become the leader of your heart, soul, and life.

1. ____________________
2. ____________________
3. ____________________
4. ____________________
5. ____________________

Journal on the quotes about truth from Yogi Bhajan. ____________________

HELPING YOU DISCOVER YOUR TRUTH

Patrick always tells me that "Leadership is not given; rather it is taken!" I am challenging you as you seek your inner truth to stand up for what you believe in, search for how you can apply it to your life, and finally take that leadership role in your life, think for yourself, become the captain of your own ship, and be the creator of your destiny. In the process, I am quite confident that you will discover your inner truth.

SEEK. TRUST. BELIEVE. LOVE.

A FINAL NOTE
ENJOYING THE *Best Days* OF YOUR LIFE

"This is love: to fly toward a secret sky, to cause a hundred veils to fall each moment. First to let go of life. Finally, to take a step without feet."
— Rumi

I believe there are certain laws of the universe that work like a big pendulum and that say when life swings in one direction, it must eventually swing in another. From negative to positive my pendulum had now swung, and now it was time for me to share fully what I had learned along the way.

Although I had always dreamed of writing a book, I never would have imagined doing so from my desk overlooking the Iao Valley mountains in Maui, Hawaii. I hear the beautiful songs of the common Myna bird, listen to the rustling sound of the tropical breezes as they brush though the large palms, and watch the butterflies circling around the pink Hong Kong orchid tree in our front yard. I wonder about the good karma that led me here to this tropical paradise. I deeply miss Shiitake, but I am thankful she is resting in her home in the Haleakala mountain range behind me. Next to me, out the side window, is a view of the large cruise ship that just came into port. I think of how these travelers save up a lifetime to come here once, or twice if they are lucky, and I now live here and have laid the foundation to spend the rest of my life here on Maui!

I reflect on what happened in my past and tear up with a warm heart. The confusion and chaos has passed, and today I am thankful...just thankful. Shiitake made it here to hand me off to my new home, where I just completed my daily yoga practice. I also just went for a four-mile walk / run in our neighborhood—with a more intimate view of the Iao Valley and the West Maui Mountains. My old girl Sushi lies here by my side now. She's not the same dog she once was and she sleeps most of her day away now. She has lived through it all with me and is still here holding the experiences and stories too. I sometimes think she fared better than I as each day she teaches me to be at peace, observe my surroundings, and stand against all odds in love. She is the oldest living Shar Pei I have ever known (more than thirteen years old). By the time you read this book, I am sure she will have passed. She's been through a lot. She is very empathic, just like me. She feels and senses everything. She even developed a permanent small white tear shape in her chocolate-colored fur near her right eye during those days I spent crying in Michigan. But she continues to smile. Her last day here is approaching all too soon, and we have been prepared for many years. She has taught me about non-attachment and unconditional love—showing me it's okay to release her to the divine when she is ready. She has many friends to greet her upon her arrival.

Years ago, I heard that voice in my head say, "It's time to step into your becoming!" If I had known then what was ahead in order for me to get where I am today, I honestly can say that I'm not real sure I would have done it...simply out of fear. I thought stepping into my becoming would always be a positive experience and one good experience would build upon another. But sometimes, shaking up those things that aren't serving you and learning to honor those that are is necessary for finding your inner truth—ultimately stepping into your becoming. In that shake up, you can find your passions and open to a greater love than otherwise you ever could have known existed.

When you can stand in—and follow—love, you can find your truth. First search within yourself. Once you find that love, commit to it. Others will be drawn to celebrate it with you.

I followed Tia as she led me into my truth, and as I did so, I would lose so much—my husband, Mai Tai, Sangria, two kitties, my grandmother, my uncle, several clients, my uncle's sister, my ex-mother-in-law, my Shiitake, my yoga center, my newly remodeled home, the car in the driveway, and my furniture. But Shiitake's passing taught me that death is never the end, and I am left behind because I am strong, still seeking mastery, and my work is far from complete. I have so much more to gain. We all have "experiences," and when they have been had, they simply just are. They are not wounds...but sometimes growing pains. Our attitudes and what happens in our mind is really the key to our success. I now know that because I got through everything I did, I can get through anything. You can too!

Whatever experiences you have in your life, when you develop great self-love and a connection to the divine, nothing can shake or break you. None of my experiences broke me. They only made me stronger. I was not left with guilt, fear, or confusion. Just love.

Dwell in the grace of God and the true sat nam of self feels no guilt or shame.... Forgiveness and love of self and other has no name or label—they just are. I wish for you the same. You can reach the state of just being and knowing that this is enough.

But how do you get there? Now that you have read this book, what's next for you? What has inspired you to find your inner truth? What actions are you going to take? What parts of the world are you going to visit? Whom are you going to love? What newfound passions are you going to pursue? What hobbies are you going to develop? What books are you going to read (or write)? What classes are you going to take?

I purposely titled this book *Finding Your Inner Truth* and my goal is to help you discover your truths! Therefore, I challenge you right now to write out ten action items that you commit to doing within the next ninety days. (Don't read any more until you fill in all ten exercises below.) I promise you that taking action on your list will result in your innermost truth being revealed, and you will have developed the skills to overcome any and all obstacles that come your way.

1. ____________________	6. ____________________
2. ____________________	7. ____________________
3. ____________________	8. ____________________
4. ____________________	9. ____________________
5. ____________________	10. ____________________

Now that you have written out your ten actions, you will see that the events of your past build your character and they are your truths. What is true for you and me may differ, but in the end, your opinions and beliefs are formed based on your experiences. They set the foundation for who you are. Only you can have your own unique experiences. When you begin to recognize your Self, you recognize your innocence and can form a more powerful relationship with your mind.

What if, just what if, you really did sit down with a powerful group of spiritual leaders before you incarnated here and wrote life all out just as it's occurring? Just so you could grow and learn. And what if you were performing really, really well as you simply go through it…one step after another…and instead of saying, "Oh, God, now what?" in horror, you say, "I'm fantastic for making it through that!" or "Gosh, I handled that well!" What if you simply changed your mind about the issues, and instead of having pain and discomfort, you just got a great lesson in how to grow and expand your soul?

So take a deep breath—you have done nothing wrong! That's the great thing…you are just taking the steps you designed with your angels and masters! What you set your mind to can create miracles. Learn to follow your heart and start with controlling your mind. Patrick once told me that happiness is a choice, but when I was losing so much, I couldn't see that. Your waters will sometimes muddy, but they do eventually clear. When times got to be the most challenging for me, I used this phrase to get through some very tough times: "Everything is perfect exactly as it is." Coincidentally, this is very similar to the Hawaiian "aloha" way of being…which, among many definitions, means love or acknowledging the divinity that dwells within and without. Both concepts must be experienced to be fully understood—again suggesting that truth is within the experience.

I've been asked by many how to start on a path of self-improvement or awareness. I often suggest that a three to ten-day cleanse is a great place to start. It will quiet your mind and "jolt" your system out of your old ways and give you some quiet time to readjust to new healthier ways and tune in to you. I challenge you to begin by finding a great green cleanse or going on a simple water diet for as many days as you can. I have a few I can recommend if you contact me. Build from there. Then find a group of spiritually minded people whom you resonate with and meditate or do yoga with them. They will support you until you are strong enough to do it yourself. It takes thirty days to break a habit, sixty to establish a new habit, and ninety to solidify it according to the Kundalini yoga belief system. So know it will take some time.

As I conclude this book, my hopes are to have shared with you stories of my life that have inspired you to search for and find your truths. My goal was to stretch your mind, to help you determine what is your potential, both in your present and future. So I will end with a series of "what if" questions to keep you thinking long after you put this book down:

- What if...your truth is your identity?
- What if...you are far more talented than you realize?
- What if...you could heal others with the touch of your hands?
- What if...we are not alone on planet earth?
- What if...you are truly one-in-a-million?
- What if...you forgave those who betrayed you?
- What if...God really loves you no matter what?
- What if...you no longer ate animals?
- What if...you could truly choose your destiny?
- What if...the answers you seek are within you?
- What if...your deceased loved ones can hear you speak?
- What if...what you are seeking is already present within you?
- What if...your pet is actually more than just an animal?
- What if...change actually makes you stronger?
- What if...you pursued your passions?
- What if...you dedicated your life to serving others?
- What if...there are thousands of other planets with life?
- What if...you became the change you wish to see in others?
- What if...love is the greatest joy or ultimate meaning to life?
- What if...your soulmate supported you in your dreams?
- What if...you embraced change?
- What if...you took the leadership role in your life?
- What if...you let go of your past wounds?
- What if...you lived in the now?
- What if...you stopped letting your mind rule you?
- What if...you stopped being a victim and became a victor?
- What if...you focused on what you have, not on what you don't?
- What if...you seized this moment and lived in the now?
- What if...you unconditionally believed in yourself?
- What if...you knew how much I believe in you?

I don't expect you to believe all the things you read in this book. I'm sorry, but it's the only story I've got! I understand that you too may have had experiences in your life which are unbelievable. This is where our lives and stories connect, leaving us both on the same journey in search of our inner truths.

I want you to write and tell me where you are in your life and how you need help or support. I can get you started in the right direction for your transformation. I'm also available to discuss and consult with you regarding cancer care or diet issues as they relate to your canine best friend. I am also available to coach you through the grieving process of losing your pet. Additionally, I can teach you shamanic healing, Kundalini yoga, and how to become a vegan or make a raw food transition. I can also participate in or perform retreats here on Maui or the mainland. Please also let me know whether you need a website, help writing your unique story, or any other creative work.

Please contact me via email at Nicole@FindingYourInnerTruth.com or call or text me at (808) 280-5559. I wish you a big Mahalo and Aloha on your path to finding inner truth! I wish you all the success possible as you discover and implement your inner truth into your life!

By the way, we are welcoming two new puppies into our home by the time this book is published—a bulldog named Leilani and another Chinese Shar Pei named Portabello (Bella) in honor of Shiitake. I am excited to practice everything Shiitake taught us. As you know, Patrick and I are engaged, and maybe I'll let him talk me into becoming his wife in our near future...after all, I hear Maui is a great place for a wedding!

I challenge you to seek the truth, trust in God, believe in yourself, and love unconditionally. I wish you the best of luck, happiness and the discovery of your inner truth.

Your Friend,

Nicole Gabriel

SEEK. TRUST. BELIEVE. LOVE.

APPENDICES

SEEK. TRUST. BELIEVE. LOVE.

APPENDIX A

DETOX *Kriya*

"Every man is the builder of a temple called his body.
We are all sculptors and painters, and our material
is our flesh and bones."
— Henry David Thoreau

I wouldn't be helping you at all if I didn't at least include one kriya (exercise set) for you to practice. We detoxify continuously throughout life. We process food, thoughts, and all forms of energy. When that flow is continuous and clear, we are steady and flexible. The trouble is that we accumulate more than we process. We become weighted down under the ash of metabolism and the remnants of old emotions. This set systematically moves the energy of the body and mind to keep you light and vitalized.

1. Lie down on your back with your legs straight. Your heels are together and your toes point upward. Keeping your heels together, spread your feet apart so they both point out to the sides. The right foot points to the right and the left foot points to the left. Then close your feet so they once again point straight upward. Continue quickly opening and closing your feet, keeping your heels together. Continue for 4 minutes.

2. Remain on your back and put your hands under your head. Raise your legs up about two feet and scissor the legs up and

down without letting the descending heel touch the ground. Keep your legs straight. Do not bend at the knees. This exercise clears up inner anger when done vigorously. Continue for 4 minutes.

3. Lie down on your stomach and stick out your tongue. Exhale through your mouth and push up into Cobra Pose. Inhale through your mouth as you lower yourself back to the ground. Continue, keeping your breath and movement strong. This exercise removes toxins from the body. Continue for 6 ½ minutes.

4. Turn over onto your back and bring your knees up to your chest. As the knees touch the chest, raise your arms up to 90 degrees (parallel to each other). Straighten your legs and lower your arms and legs back to the floor at the same time. Continue this movement vigorously for 3 minutes. This is a controlled movement. There should be no noise when the arms and legs touch the ground.

5. Sit in Easy Pose and revolve the torso around the base of the spine. This churning movement is done in a counter-clockwise direction. Continue for 3 minutes. Move as quickly as you can during the last minute.

6. Stand up. Bend over and grab your ankles. While holding onto your ankles, sit down in Crow Pose and come back up. Continue this movement for 2 minutes.

7. Sit comfortably in Easy Pose with your spine straight. Chant "Sat Nam, Sat Nam, Sat Nam, Sat Nam, Sat Nam, Sat Nam, Wahe Guru" (meaning: "Truth is my identity" and / or "Wow to the infinite truth"). One full repetition of the mantra takes 7-8 seconds. Continue for 11 minutes.

To finish: Inhale deeply and stretch your arms over your head with your palms touching. Hold your breath 20-40 seconds as

you stretch your spine upward. Exhale. Repeat this sequence two more times.

This set can be found in the manual *Self-Experience* by Yogi Bhajan.

SEEK. TRUST. BELIEVE. LOVE.

APPENDIX B

FEEDING YOUR Dog As A Vegan

"Nature does nothing uselessly."
— Aristotle

Many times in my healing work, students asked me whether I could help heal their pets. When we start asking about others, we are really just starting to see ourselves. As stated in Chapter 15, in nearly every case, I told them to look at what was going on in their home first. When a pet is not feeling well, many times it comes from disharmony in the home. Every once in awhile, a dog comes into your life and changes everything. If you have listened to the messages of what came through for Shiitake and me, and you apply any portion of it to your life, whether you have a pet or not, you will find renewed energy and vitality as well as release from anger and discomfort. Unhealthy food causes more negative shifts than just weight gain—that's for sure! If you want to be healthy physically, spiritually, or emotionally, having a pet will teach you so much about yourself... when you pay attention.

WHAT'S IN YOUR DOG'S FOOD?

You may not opt to feed your dog as a vegan, but did you know that dogs are fully able to thrive on a vegan diet? They are

omnivores just like humans! They are scavengers in nature and not dependent on meat-specific protein or a high level of protein to fulfill their basic dietary needs. Veggies and grains can be consumed very easily. Have you noticed how much healthier vegan humans are? If so, maybe it's time to start feeding your dog the same way.

Did you know that 50 percent of dogs will likely experience cancer by the time they reach their senior years? That's alarming! (That's way higher than the rates in humans.) According to recent statistics from VPI Pet Insurance, dogs are twice as likely to develop leukemia as humans, four times more likely to suffer from breast cancer, eight times more likely to develop bone cancer, and a whopping thirty-five times more likely to develop skin cancer! Dogs regularly inhale unseen cancer causing materials…in fact, they are in their food as preservatives. And 95 percent of pets derive their nutritional needs from processed foods! You might as well throw your dog a candy bar for dinner! And the FDA says there is NO requirement that pet food products have pre-market approval, yet it assures us the ingredients are safe. Pet food manufacturers fill their foods with some of the cheapest sources of protein they can find…and remember how we already discussed that this much protein isn't really needed anyway? So where do those cheap sources of protein come from? Well, that's what's so horrible! It's stated all over in various sources on the Internet, so imagine if it were found true, that euthanized cats, dogs, and other farm animals often end up in rendering vats to make meat meal and bone meal. If this is so, dogs might end up eating dogs! And the euthanasia drug—pentobarbital—has been found in the rendered byproducts. I'd be open to evidence one way or another if you'd like to share your knowledge. Of course, it's the norm to add chemical preservatives and artificial additives to food.

Not only are the "meats" an issue, but fungus in wheat, toxins in chemically treated corn, "healthy additives" (too many

of which cause death due to kidney and liver failure), paint enamel, and rat poisoning have been found in foods that are recalled. Imagine what didn't get caught. Basically, pet food provides a convenient income for slaughterhouses to dispose of and even make money for what is unfit for human consumption. And most pet food manufacturers don't test their products for bacterial toxins. The pet food industry is a $1.5 billion a year business. The rules on ingredients are the "With Rule" and the "Flavor Rule." The "With Rule" allows for ingredient names to appear on the label, such as "made with real chicken" as long as at least 3 percent of the food has that ingredient in it. The "Flavor Rule" allows for a food to be designed as a certain flavor as long as the ingredients are sufficient to "impart a distinctive characteristic" to the food, even if it contains none of the actual ingredient. Then there are the "natural" and "organic" claims. The "natural" term was adopted by the Association of American Feed Control Officials (AAFCO) and is very broad. It allows for artificially processed ingredients to be labeled as "natural." "Organic" has a much more strict legal definition under the USDA National Organic Program. However, the words can appear in the brand name even if the ingredients are not natural or organic. And beware—the term "organic" does not imply anything at all about the welfare of the animals it comes from, for example factory farming.

The pet food industry exists in a regulatory vacuum where it's hard to enforce laws. The small amount of meat left on the bones is the meat in the pet food. Cooking and other processing of meat and byproducts can greatly diminish nutritional value. To make pet food nutritious, it must be fortified with vitamins and minerals because the ingredients are not wholesome. Restaurant grease and biodiesel fuel are added to make it taste better. And when dry food is mixed with liquid, it can release bacteria that was picked up in the production process.

I was feeding my dogs a "human grade" dog food so I thought it was safe. But after doing some research, I found "human grade" to be a meaningless term. That's why the pet food companies often use it. It, along with "USDA inspected," implies that the ingredients have passed some kind of USDA human consumption standards, but there are ways around these standards. For example, the facility might have been USDA inspected during the day, but the pet food is made at night.

The year I lost Mai Tai and Sangria—2007—there were two large pet food recalls, one due to the high levels of melamine in wheat gluten and rice protein from China (added to increase falsely the protein content), and the other because of the rapid onset of kidney disease in dogs and cats as a reaction to the combination of melamine and cyanuric acid in their food.

I switched Sushi and Shiitake to a "bones and raw food" (BARF) diet a year before Shiitake died, but I also researched and found out that a raw food diet can be fatal to dogs with compromised immune systems. The bacteria levels can be quite high in this diet, and there is a potential for choking, teeth breaking, or internal punctures if whole bones are involved. This diet also needs to be supplemented with veggies. And, of course, we still might question where the ingredients come from—they could still be GMO and contain pharmaceuticals.

Cancer treatment can cost several thousands of dollars per patient. But cancer is only one of several nutrition-related diseases. Chronic digestive problems, dental disease, heart disease, hyperthyroidism, bloat, kidney disease, urinary tract infections, and obesity are some of the others. Veterinarians are busier than ever, and their industry will expand by 36 percent by 2020. The food industry's influence on veterinary practices is extreme. Many modern vet practices believe in the science behind the bags of food and have come to rely on the income provided by selling those foods provided.

So what can you do? Stop feeding your pets dry food! Most dry foods contain large amounts of cereal grain and starchy veggies. They are generally high in carbohydrates, full of corn gluten, wheat gluten, peas, potatoes, and high fat. What ends up coming off the pet food production line is processed, overheated, and completely non-nutritious.

VEGAN WONDER DOG

Many pet food companies are using veggies as cheap fillers, so if you are skeptical about going vegan, how can it be any worse? There are tons of scare tactics out there saying that being vegan is inappropriate for dogs. But it has been shown that a vegan dog can maintain a healthy body weight, has a healthier coat, increased health and vitality, clean eyes and ears, and a happier disposition. Did you know that giant gorillas are vegan? Aren't we in their family group? If you're still skeptical, read the story of Bramble, the vegan dog who lived to twenty-seven. It is possible to raise your dog vegan, and preventative good eating is worth the time and money…for both humans and dogs!

"Change is never painful, only the
resistance to change is painful."
— Buddha

"Nothing will benefit health and increase the
chances for survival of life on Earth as the
evolution to a vegetarian diet."
— Albert Einstein

You can find a SPECIAL REPORT (as a free downloadable PDF file) to help you prepare your dog's meal at www.Vegan-Dog-Treats.com. Yes, feeding your dog vegan food is not as easy as opening a bag of food, but if you love yourself and your pet, you will switch around a few things in life to make it happen…and who knows—you may learn a thing or two to help your diet too!

Finally, if I haven't convinced you yet, I recommend you go to YouTube, and in the search box, type in the following and watch these films / documentaries. By no means do I have any affiliation with them, and I warn you that they may alarm you.

1. *Food Inc.*
2. *Food Matters*
3. *Forks Over Knives*
4. *Vegucated*
5. *Super Size Me*
6. *The Ethics of What We Eat*
7. *Earthlings*
8. *Fast Food Nation*
9. *Food For Thought*
10. *May I Be Frank*
11. *Fat Sick And Nearly Dead*

Once you have viewed these films, ask yourself whether you will ever be a "flesh eater" again or eat "frozen body parts" moving forward. If you think a plant-based diet seems healthier, then please help your pets out by helping them become vegan too. If going vegan seems too extreme for you, then please consider a rotation of some of what I have provided in this book or my online special report.

In the process of finding your inner truth, look for areas in your life where you made a decision to think for yourself (and your pet) and do what is right to allow you, your body, and your pet to heal in a healthy way. Believe you me, your future self (and the animal's) will thank you for making these healthy choices now. And know that this extends beyond just food. Don't let scare tactics make you think immunizations and antibiotics are the answer or solution either because it's just what has always been done in the past. Break free of the "system" and see that there are many other options for your pet and for your health. Our pets are here to teach us something and it's time we listen!

I'll leave you with this thought-provoking quote by German philosopher, Arthur Schopenhauer:

> "Compassion for animals is
> intimately associated with
> goodness of character, and
> it may be confidently asserted
> that he who is cruel to animals
> cannot be a good man."

SEEK. TRUST. BELIEVE. LOVE.

ABOUT THE AUTHOR

NICOLE GABRIEL, MBA is an author, professional speaker, spiritual and life coach, animal loss and grief counsellor, student and teacher of Peruvian Shamanism and Kundalini yoga teacher (RYT500). She is a raw vegan food enthusiast and nutrition coach, seeker of truth, animal rights advocate, supporter of women in technology, and owner of Vegan Dog Treats and Angel Dog Productions. As a former Auto Executive from Detroit, she holds an MBA in Technology Management. She is Certified in Transpersonal Psychology at the Master's Level, has a BA in Communications, and a degree in Graphic Design and Commercial Art.

For more than twenty years, she has studied business, personal growth and development, spirituality, health, nutrition and wellness. She spent nearly a decade of her life traveling the world in search of herself after a series of life-changing events—spending time in Central and South America working with shamanic healers, and more locally, studying the yogic philosophies of, in particular, Kundalini yoga.

Prior to retiring from a six-figure income in corporate America at age thirty-two, Nicole spent a decade in web-related technology management, marketing, and advertising as a "Big 3" automotive executive in Detroit. She followed that experience by successfully building and growing $1.2 million per year chiropractic / spa offices in three locations throughout Michigan.

Today, She lives on Maui, Hawaii with her fiancé Patrick, their English Bulldog and Chinese Shar Peis. Among other things, she runs her businesses Vegan Dog Treats (a healthy dog snack alternative) and Angel Dog Productions (designing websites, book covers, speaker presentations, and logos for aspiring new business owners and new authors).

Let Nicole Help Guide You to Find Your Inner Truth!

SEEK. TRUST. BELIEVE. LOVE.

ABOUT PET GRIEF COUNSELING

Have you lost your best friend? Does it feel like no one can understand the pain of your loss? You and I know that we haven't just lost our pet! Our "hairy children" are not only our best friends, but are accepted into our lives sometimes as a substitute for a partner, a child, or other companion. They are solidly there during traumatic or emotional times in our lives. They are our loyal companions and sometimes the only ones there for us when everyone else walks away. And their loss can really break our hearts!

Whether you have lost a dog, cat, rabbit, or horse, Nicole would like to offer you a no-obligation, complimentary 30-60 minute consultation to help you heal from your grief. Please contact her (call or text). With her help, you will get through this grieving process and heal your pain.

Nicole has lost many of her companions, and after coping with the initial grief of the loss, she eventually found the strength she wants to share with you...to help you heal. Let her be someone to talk to during this time of great mourning and change.

Nicole@FindingYourInnerTruth.com
www.FindingYourInnerTruth.com
(808) 280-5559

SEEK. TRUST. BELIEVE. LOVE.

ABOUT ANGEL DOG PRODUCTIONS

Nicole Gabriel has spent twenty-plus years in the arts, doing advertising, marketing, and website development, among other things. She began her other business (Vegan Dog Treats) with the help of her canine companion Shiitake. The brand needed a label so Nicole started there. The logo was born with a cartoon image of Shiitake on the bag, website, and business cards. After a short period of time, people started asking who did the creative work. Angel Dog Productions was born.

Angel Dog Productions (ADP) designs book covers, interior book layout, websites, logos and images that are used for personal or corporate branding. Much of the focus for her clients is to get them set up with a "look" to launch their book, speaking, and marketing campaigns. Nicole also creates speaker presentations. ADP's goal in creating websites is to make the content simple and easy to manage for the owner. Nicole loves what she does and loves helping people so please look her up. She'd love to hear from you! Call or text for a no-obligation, complimentary 30-60 minute consultation.

www.AngelDogProductions.com
Nicole@AngelDogProductions.com
(808) 280-5559

SEEK. TRUST. BELIEVE. LOVE.

ABOUT VEGAN DOG TREATS

After nearly a decade of watching her dogs struggle with daily and terminal health issues, Nicole Gabriel successfully created a new way to feed pets that is not only good for them but a humane approach that leaves a smaller global footprint on the planet and doesn't require the taking of a life.

Dogs are classified as omnivores and are scavengers by nature. All the ingredients in Vegan Dog Treats are organic, natural, all vegan, and raw. The ingredients are kept primarily intact when they are not heated, which means they keep their nutrients. Flavors include: (Visit the website for the latest flavors.)

- Peanut Butter and Jelly: Made with Maui Kula Strawberries and fresh organic peanut butter.
- Coconut Banana: Great for bones, joints, skin, and hair.
- Pumpkin: High in antioxidants.
- Cheezy Veggie: Made with nutritional yeast and bell peppers, and also high in antioxidants.

If you're going to feed your dog a snack, why not make it a healthy alternative that doesn't require killing one to serve another? It just makes sense!

www.Vegan-DogTreats.com
Nicole@Vegan-DogTreats.com
(808) 280-5559

SEEK. TRUST. BELIEVE. LOVE.

ABOUT SHAMANIC HEALING & YOGA TEACHING

During her travels to Peru, Bolivia and other locations in Central and South America, while working with shamanic healers, Nicole was told she would be a great healer and teacher and through her life experiences she would excel. In her yoga, she would be told that to master something was to teach it. So you could say she's still seeking mastery.

If you have always wanted to know how to heal yourself or another through shamanic healing techniques, Nicole teaches a series of classes that will start you on your way.

She is also available (as Nirankar Kaur) to teach Kundalini yoga. She is available as a guest teacher, lecturer, meditation guide, or "humanology philosopher" for your organization, studio, or center. Call or text for a no-obligation, complimentary 30-60 minute consultation.

www.FindingYourInnerTruth.com
Nicole@FindingYourInnerTruth.com
(808) 280-5559

SEEK. TRUST. BELIEVE. LOVE.

ABOUT LIFE, NUTRITION & WELLNESS COACHING

Are you unhappy at work? Are you always tired and lacking energy? Have you put on a few pounds and your jeans no longer fit? Are you suffering from emotional or physical pain? Are you stressed and looking for both career and relationship solutions?

Personal growth and development has been a keen subject of interest for Nicole Gabriel her whole life. While others her age were out doing silly teenager things, she was sitting at home reading books from self-help authors. From there, her interests flowed into diet and then spirituality.

Let Nicole show you how to move from tragedy, loss, death, or change into a better you! With certification in Transpersonal Psychology and several years of alternative therapy practice and research, Nicole will listen and help hold you through whatever stage of life you are experiencing. We can discuss diet for you and / or your pet. The light is just around the corner so let's just find the switch! Your wellness is within reach. Call or text for a no-obligation, complimentary 30-60 minute consultation.

www.FindingYourInnerTruth.com
Nicole@FindingYourInnerTruth.com
(808) 280-5559

SEEK. TRUST. BELIEVE. LOVE.

BOOK NICOLE GABRIEL TO SPEAK AT YOUR NEXT EVENT

When it comes to choosing a compassionate speaker for your next event, you'll find no one more capable of transforming your audience than Nicole. She will take your hand and lead you on a transformational journey. Her stories are inspiring, comical, tragic, and mysterious—yet, at the same time, by having just a little faith, you will be transported into a magical sacred space where the big "ah-ha's" happen.

Whether your audience is 10 or 10,000, in North America or abroad, Nicole Gabriel will deliver a tailor-made message of inspiration for your meeting, conference, or classroom. Speaking topics include:

- Embracing Change
- Becoming a Leader from Within
- Transforming Your Life
- Letting Go and Having Faith
- Peruvian Shamanism Theories & Practice
- Kundalini Yoga Theories & Practice
- Becoming Vegan
- Eating Food As Medicine
- Learning From Animals
- Defining Self

www.FindingYourInnerTruth.com
Nicole@FindingYourInnerTruth.com
(808) 280-5559

SEEK

THE TRUTH

TRUST

IN GOD

BELIEVE

IN YOURSELF

LOVE

UNCONDITIONALLY

"All truth passes through three stages.
First, it is ridiculed.
Second, it is violently opposed.
Third, it is accepted as being self-evident."

— Arthur Schopenhauer, German philosopher
(1788 – 1860)

"Sometimes the dance of life has us taking new steps or causes us to forget "moves" we already know. Take Nicole's hand and let her gracefully lead you through an incredible journey as you reflect on your own life."

— Lyla B. Berg, Ph.D., Author of
Leaving the Guilded Cage

"Sometimes in life you get knocked down and feel that the world is against you. It is during these challenging times that your faith in God will be tested. In Nicole's book, she experienced such a test and her faith in God ultimately led her through her pain to a deeper connection to her truth. This book can do the same for you."

— Frank Reed, Author of
In *God We Trust Dollar$ & Sense*

"When you are silent, open your heart and listen to the animals. You may hear their subtle wisdom and guidance as Nicole did. When Nicole found a way to communicate with her animals, she began a journey of spiritual awakening that led her to her inner truth. Let Nicole and her animals inspire and guide you on your personal path of discovery."

— Wanda Buckner, EdD. Author of *Choosing Energy Therapy: A Practical Guide to Healing Options for People and Animals*

"Throughout life we all go through challenges that may feel like insurmountable obstacles. This book will help you avoid the land mines of emotions when everything seems to turn upside down. When you read it you'll get the feeling that Nicole is "just like you." This is a book you'll want to give as a gift to make a difference in someone's life."

— Kieran Murry, Author of *Go For Your Gold*, and
Co-Founder of Ignite-U

"Profound life changes are an opportunity to learn to live from your heart and trust your inner guide. Nicole's nurturing grace and healing words helped me to overcome tragic loss and channel my energy in a positive, healthy direction. I went from barely existing to THRIVING in every aspect of my life—love, health, business, and more! Let Nicole open your heart to your infinite possibilities for true happiness!"

— Camille Leinbach, Owner / Holistic Skin Care Therapist
Autumn Moon Aesthetics

"*Finding Your Inner Truth* is full of fascinating stories and transformative life changing experiences that will have you both amazed and comforted. As you walk through Nicole's experiences you understand the gifts of a greater source and how healing from trauma can take you into a place of mastery and magnificence. This book is a must read for all seekers of inner truth!"

— Nora Yolles-Young, C.Ht., Author of *Healing Effortlessly*

"What is fascinating to observe is how Nicole was true to the natural experiences of her astrological and numerological cycles. Even when life presents us with challenges (as we understand our personal timing) it is quite eye-opening how we can affirm when profound transformation finds us. It's amazing what she got through. This book is a must read if you too are going through a big shift as you seek your TRUTH, no matter how much it may even hurt."

— Sharita Star, Author of *It's All in the Name*

"Nicole's adventures take us beyond this dimension and into soft sweet places I know exist where answers can be found that extend beyond time and space. This is quite a journey into truth!"

— Ann Patrykus, Author of *Akashic What?*

"*Finding Your Inner Truth* is a life-changer. Nicole's process helps reveal what you may already know, but didn't actually believe. Learning to have the confidence and courage to trust provides a whole new way of living."

— Teri Citterman, Author of *From The CEOs' Perspective*

"In *Finding Your Inner Truth*, Nicole uses the challenges and triumphs of her personal experiences to assist readers through processing, defining, and creating the lives they want. With sensitivity she helps you sort out and make sense of your experiences, emotions, and dreams as you move through your journey."

— Dana E. Morrison, Author of *Transforming Your Life Now*

"This book reminds us that no matter how challenging the events of our life are, we will always have ourselves and our connection with a force greater than us. It's that connection that guides us to our inner truths."

— Helen Yoon, Author of *Daring to Change*

"I met Nicole between two major moves that most people would find too daunting and watched her fight for the best treatment of a beloved pet while developing a product line for other animals. I am in awe of her and what she can accomplish. This is a person I want to take advice from to fully embrace life."

— Sandra Hixson-Matthews, Author of *Kiss Your Food*

"If you are feeling overwhelmed by life's challenges, Nicole's book will take you by the hand and help you navigate the road. *Finding Your Inner Truth* reminds us that we are not alone, and illuminates a deeper purpose behind our journey."

— Suzan H. Proia, C. HT Personal Excellence Specialist,
EFT Practitioner, Certified Hypnotherapist

“We often treat the truth like an elusive ideal and stumble through life in an effort to capture it. In Nicole Gabriel’s *Finding Your Inner Truth* we discover that the truth is not elusive. It has always existed within us. Through “The Great Initiation” we learn that all of our experiences, good and bad, lead us to become the living embodiment of our Inner Truth.”

— Luis Fuentes, Author of *Life Lessons from the Lantern*

“*Finding Your Inner Truth* is a refreshing read. With loving insight, you will be inspired to reclaim your life. I was reminded that our lives are made up of equal parts of sorrow and joy and that it is impossible to have one without the other. Wise, warm, and gentle Nicole Gabriel will teach all of us how to let go of what no longer serves us and to stand in love.”

— Bonnie Marie Richter, Author of
The Best Places to Kiss in the Northwest

“Life is an adventure. What Nicole experienced is never easy to share. Yet this book is a candid and transparent journey through Nicole’s extraordinary experiences. She has opened up her heart to share the challenges and joys of her spiritual adventure. Her story is an invitation to grow, learn, and enjoy the journey as you seek your own truth and purpose.”

— Jorge Colon, Author of *Leveraging Social Capital*

“We each have our own adventure and sometimes it looks nothing like we thought it would. Nicole’s story shows us that the key to navigating our adventure, no matter how many twists and turns it offers, is in remembering that Love is our true North.”

— Kim Ann Curtin, Author of *Transforming Wall Street*

"*Finding Your Inner Truth* teaches how to clean up YOU by letting go of what no longer serves your life. This makes room for clean living of the mind, body, and soul! Get ready to step into a whole new way of being with this must-read book and learn to turn the messier things in life into your blissful truth!"

— Carol Paul, Author of *Team Clean*

"This book is a must-read if you are looking for direction on your life's path. *Finding Your Inner Truth* will open your eyes in many new ways you never imagined. It will have you crying, laughing, and feeling challenged to live within your truth, whatever that may be for you."

— Randall Broad, Author of *It's An Extraordinary Life*

"I loved learning how Nicole found peace through love, loss and self discovery. You too will benefit from this book!"

— Sue Mocker, Author of *The Hope Factor*

"Sometimes it takes a great shake up in our lives to live in our truth and to do on this planet what we were meant to do. If you've had a great change in your life, this book will walk you through how to start tackling it and ways to go about putting the pieces back together."

— Al Foxx, Author of *Achieving NO LIMITS—Embracing Change*

"I could have used this book many times as I learned the hard way some of these very lessons Nicole shares with us here in her book. What a powerful reminder of the lessons we learn and the life challenges we face. Nicole captures how we can overcome with some practical, down-to-earth and realistic ways that each of us can use to address things we face and to come out on the other side happier, healthier, and stronger than ever before!"

— Aaron D. Murphy, Author of *Aging in Place*

"Whether you are experiencing change, looking to redefine your familiar, or seeking answers on a spiritual path, this book takes you on an amazing journey of self-discovery and teaches you to stand in love no matter what life challenges come your way."

— Jeffery Bow, Author of *Stop Thinking, Start Believing*

"We each step into our becoming and our truth in our unique ways. This book teaches that when we open our mind to the idea that anything is possible, we can grow as a person and step into our truth."

— Lori Chaffin, Author of *Messages Straight From the Heart,*
Publisher of *Hawaii Wellness Directory* and
Your Health Hawaii Magazine

"Nicole Gabriel's book teaches you how to solve life's challenges, regardless of how unexpected and surprising they may be. She reminds you, in gentle and effective ways, that the answers you seek are always within yourself. Buy this book if you want to experience an amazing journey of self-discovery that awakens your Soul and changes your life."

— Jody Rose Helfand, Author of *Transforming Yourself*

"Nicole's book *Finding Your Inner Truth* shares how you can easily unlock the answers that you have been searching for all along. She will take you on a journey that leads to self-awareness, self-empowerment, and self-discovery!"

— Brandy Lokelani Sinoto, Author of *Stepping Into Your Greatness*
and #1 Earner PURIUM Health Products

"Nicole will awaken new passions in you. You owe it to yourself to live more, love more, and struggle less. Start here right now!"

— Michael Fulmore, Author of *Unleashing Your Ambition*

Praise for FINDING YOUR INNER TRUTH

"Each of us is profoundly unique and co-creative with reality. The specific events of our life are unpredictable. The miraculous capacity of the human heart and consciousness is to distill meaning, gather courage and gratitude in equal measure, and act with integrity no matter what happens. When we do that, our path is clear and we embrace the present as we create a future. Nicole shares her personal experiences of challenge and elevation and how that kindled an awakening. She asks us to ask our self what is true, unique, and real for our self. Then she gives tips and techniques to help us live that truth in each moment. A good way to live and love."

— Gurucharan Singh Khalsa Ph.D., Author of *The 21 Stages of Meditation*, *Breathwalk*, and *The Mind* (coauthored with Yogi Bhajan) Director of Training - Kundalini Yoga Research Institute

"*Finding Your Inner Truth* is the story of a woman seeking peace and answers to life's most difficult questions. When Nicole finds herself overcome by grief over the death of her dog, she begins a journey that would test anyone's beliefs. Imagine *Marley and Me* and *Eat, Pray, Love* combined and you'll understand the magic embodied in this very human, canine, and universal tale of soul-searching. Better yet, you'll resonate with it, be as surprised as Nicole was by some of her mystical experiences—ranging from speaking to the dead to discovering a portal to other worlds in her home—and come away with a new awareness and understanding about the meaning of your life."

— Tyler R. Tichelaar, Ph.D. and award-winning author of *Spirit of the North: A Paranormal Romance*

"Get ready to stretch your sense of possibilities. This book is full of love for animals, divorce, career challenges, death, energy healing, veganism, world travel, relationships, starting over again and even a few paranormal surprises! It's all here in this eye-opening book. If you are going through change and searching for answers this book will show you how to 'be' in your essence as you seek your inner truth. It will open and stretch your mind as to what is possible both in your life, and in the universe!"

— Patrick Snow, Professional Speaker, International Best-Selling Author of *Creating Your Own Destiny* and *The Affluent Entrepreneur*

Peu éloignée du mont du Chant de la grue, la région entre les districts de Xinjin 新津 et de Pi 郫 dans la plaine occidentale de Chengdu avait abrité la culture néolithique de Baodun 寶墩 (2700-1700 avant notre ère) ; des murs massifs de terre damée clôturaient son site principal à Xinjin. La haute civilisation Sanxingdui 三星堆 (1700-1150 avant notre ère) s'était quant à elle développée au nord de Chengdu ; les vestiges de la cité mise au jour à Guanghan 廣漢 en font l'un des plus remarquables sites de l'âge du bronze en Asie orientale. La découverte qui y fut faite en 1986 d'une importante cache d'artefacts, incluant des masques de bronze aux yeux extrêmement protubérants, donne une indication de la particularité de la culture ethnique du Sichuan[15]. Légende, archéologie et historiographie concourent pour souligner la singularité du pays qui fut le berceau du taoïsme du Maître céleste. Situé aux confins occidentaux de la civilisation Han, ce pays servait en outre d'interface avec les mondes tibéto-birman, indien et centre-asiatique.

Comme nous l'avons vu, au cours des dernières années de la dynastie Han la région du Sichuan entra en quasi-autonomie. Conjuguée à la composition pluriethnique de la plaine de Chengdu et des populations montagneuses environnantes, cette relative indépendance constitua un facteur décisif de l'essor du taoïsme du Maître céleste. Après son installation dans le Nord-Est, à Hanzhong, la communauté primitive des Maîtres célestes entra en relation avec le peuple Ba 巴 du Sichuan oriental[16]. Toute une mythologie se cristallisa progressivement autour des actes du fondateur Zhang Daoling, associée essentiellement à la géographie mythique du pays de Shu. Ce fut Ge Hong, bien qu'originaire de la région méridionale du Jiangnan 江南, qui en rapporta le récit le plus élaboré dans ses *Vies des transcendants* 神仙傳, interprétant la vocation originelle de Zhang à la lumière de sa propre quête alchimique de transcendance[17]. L'influente hagiographie par Ge Hong s'achève en apothéose avec l'ascension vers le ciel de Zhang Daoling depuis le mont de la Terrasse des nuages 雲臺山 au bord septentrional du bassin du Sichuan.

Héros et guérisseur

La Terrasse des nuages était située en territoire Ba, sur le fleuve Jialing 嘉陵江 entre Cangxi 蒼溪 et Langzhong 閬中. C'était le site de l'un des Vingt-quatre diocèses du mouvement du Maître céleste. Quand Zhang Daoling fut officiellement canonisé sous les Tang, une hagiographie nourrie associait les actes et miracles du fondateur aux lieux de culte diocésains[18], établissant des parallèles entre les travaux de Zhang et ceux des héros culturels des anciens Ba et Shu, spécialement les premiers civilisateurs et transformateurs de la topographie du Sichuan, Bieling et Li Bing. Comme ceux-ci, le créateur des Vingt-quatre diocèses en vint à être vénéré comme un héros du pays doté d'une connaissance intime de sa géographie naturelle et surnaturelle[19].

Dans la continuité des héros antérieurs producteurs de richesses, la création du puits de sel de Lingjing 陵井 dans la préfecture de Lingzhou 陵州 (aujourd'hui Renshou 仁壽, quatre-vingts kilomètres au sud de Chengdu) fut attribuée à Zhang. La production de sel était une source importante de prospérité dans le Sichuan des Han (voir fig. 2). Dans la préfecture de Ling, Zhang Ling devina l'emplacement d'une grande source de saumure et en subjugua les déités tutélaires du lieu-dit[20], soulignant combien les cultes locaux furent prompts à adopter les modèles mythiques et rituels des récits fondateurs des États et des identités culturelles[21]. La fondation requérait de subjuguer ou de bannir les puissances démoniaques en place, et de leur substituer un ordre nouveau sous l'autorité civilisatrice du héros fondateur, lequel provenait le plus souvent de l'extérieur du territoire[22]. Le paradigme *sujétion suivie d'allégeance et de conversion*, évoquant les rites féodaux de fondation étatique, servait aussi de modèle pour la consécration de l'autel taoïste. Habituellement, le processus impliquait de prêter un serment d'alliance, tel que le Pacte de l'Unité correcte.

Maints serments d'allégeance ponctuent la biographie de Zhang Daoling dans les *Vies des transcendants*, si bien qu'ils en devinrent un attribut régulier de sa fonction d'exorciste. Dans son rôle de répresseur des démons des Six cieux, le Maître céleste est dépeint comme un guérisseur combattant la propagation des miasmes et des épidémies

Fig. 2. Production de sel 制鹽. Brique funéraire Han du district de Pi 郫縣, Chengdu (IIe siècle de notre ère). Estampage appartenant à la collection de l'auteur, reproduit avec l'autorisation du Musée du district de Pi 郫縣文管所.

qui affligeaient le monde des Han orientaux[23]. La maladie était largement répandue dans les plaines paludéennes. Le *Mémoire de Shu* 蜀記 rapporte que Zhang Ling cherchait à gagner les terres montagneuses pour échapper à la malaria et y passa maître dans l'art d'expulser les démons[24]. La vocation guérisseuse des premières générations de meneurs du mouvement est soulignée dans la plupart des plus anciens comptes rendus, l'un d'eux suggérant sans ambages que Zhang Daoling profita de la prévalence de la peste et de l'insécurité à cette époque pour persuader ses adeptes d'adopter un comportement moral face à l'adversité[25].

Visions de l'apocalypse

Pour marquer le passage du temps et la révolution des époques, le calendrier chinois utilise deux cycles imbriqués de longueurs inégales, l'un divisé en dix « troncs célestes » 天干 et l'autre en douze « rameaux terrestres » 地支. L'appariement de troncs et de rameaux consécutifs génère un autre cycle de soixante binômes, utilisé pour désigner les heures, les jours et les années[26]. Quand un cycle sexagésimal prend fin, un nouveau commence, faisant écho au mouvement cyclique des corps célestes[27]. Ce système de mesure du temps se combinant à la cosmologie transformative du *Livre des mutations* 易經 – dualité du yin et du yang et succession des Cinq agents 五行 – produit davantage encore de cycles imbriqués. Voici comment Nathan Sivin a décrit le mécanisme qui en résulte, tel que l'expose un manuel astronomique des Han :

> Des cycles furent déterminés pour les phénomènes à représenter, et, par un processus qui revient à trouver les plus petits communs multiples, des cycles plus grands furent construits pour contenir et subsumer des séries de cycles plus petits. Quand ce processus fut fait, le système fut rendu intégral par un cycle de la « grande année », comme une roue immense actionnant une accumulation de roues graduées plus petites disposées en sous-systèmes. Il était donc nécessaire de trouver l'époque, pour déterminer depuis combien de temps exactement le cycle le plus grand avait commencé[28].

Quand les commencements de plusieurs cycles coïncidaient, il s'agissait d'une « conjonction » 會 signalant une crise. Le *Livre du centre du Seigneur Lao* 太上老君中經, un traité de cosmologie de la période des Han orientaux, explique que les conjonctions *jihai* 己亥 impliquant trois cycles se produisaient tous les trente-six ans. Dans ces années de triple jonction 三合之歲, des perturbations cosmiques affectaient le Ciel et la Terre, produisant inondations et sécheresse, guerre et famines, épidémies et invasions de sauterelles, ce qui causait de grands bouleversements parmi la population. Lors de jonctions encore plus critiques, avec des périodes plus longues, les effets étaient davantage amplifiés et finissaient par s'amalgamer dans un désastre cataclysmique.

Le *Livre du centre du Seigneur Lao* opposait à cette vision d'apocalypse la promesse messianique de la venue de sages 聖, saints 賢, hommes réels 真人 ou transcendants 仙人 taoïstes, qui restaureraient périodiquement l'ordre cosmique et sauveraient l'humanité. Les utopies millénaristes ne demandaient qu'à se répandre dans les temps de bouleversements sociaux et politiques. Les crises des empires sur le déclin, et Han et romain, provoquèrent des réponses similaires, il va de soi, dans le langage cosmologique propre à chacun[29]. Comme l'a remarqué Anna Seidel, sans la chute de la dynastie Han, la religion taoïste telle que nous la connaissons n'existerait pas. Ses premières communautés, suspectes – comme leurs homologues chrétiennes – de subversion politique, assumaient les attributs de la prérogative impériale à la place d'administrations locales défaillantes[30]. En Chine, l'influence du messianisme apocalyptique fut encore amplifiée par la croyance selon laquelle les institutions religieuses et politiques reposaient sur les mêmes principes cosmologiques. L'effondrement des unes causait chez les autres une crise existentielle, nécessitant son remplacement par des substituts symboliques.

Dans les dernières années des Han, le *Livre du centre du Seigneur Lao* annonçait la fin imminente d'un cycle majeur et l'avènement d'une nouvelle ère appelée « Jaune » où seuls les immortels et les initiés taoïstes échapperaient à la destruction du monde précédent[31]. Le mécanisme des cycles cosmiques était mû par des préoccupations politiques et morales parallèles : le déclin d'une époque et l'éclosion d'une autre se traduisaient par l'essor et la chute des dynasties, selon l'octroi ou la suppression du mandat céleste. Telle fut la base du programme idéologique de l'insurrection des Turbans jaunes 黃巾 qui surgit en 184 de notre ère, une année *jiazi* 甲子 de bon augure au début d'un nouveau cycle sexagésimal. Le chef des Turbans jaunes, Zhang Jue 張角, annonçait une ère nouvelle intitulée « Grande paix du Ciel jaune » 太平黃天 sous l'égide de l'Empereur jaune, Huangdi 黃帝, le souverain primordial parfait[32]. En se référant à Huangdi, la couleur jaune (*huang*) évoquait aussi l'enseignement Huang-Lao 黃老 du taoïsme des Han. Dans le système de la corrélation des Cinq agents, qui associait la succession de divers éléments à la révolution séquentielle de cinq agents universels, la couleur jaune correspondait au point cardinal « centre » et aussi à l'élément « terre ». Dans une lettre adressée à Cao Cao en 192, les rebelles Turbans jaunes proclamaient que la révolution du Grand cycle céleste 天之大運 avait sonné le glas de la dynastie Han et mis en branle l'essor de la Maison jaune 黃家[33]. Le slogan de Zhang Jue en 184 était « Ciel azur trépasse ; Ciel jaune se lève » 蒼天已死，黃天當立. Ciel azur était une divinité stellaire apparaissant au sein de la constellation du Boisseau du Nord[34]. Le slogan signifiait que le monde visible (le ciel bleu) allait céder au royaume des ténèbres (les Sources jaunes). La désagrégation de l'ordre politique semait déjà le chaos dans le monde des esprits. Infestation démoniaque et épidémies en étaient les messagers. La vision d'un empire autre naissait[35].

Le mouvement millénariste de la Voie de la Grande paix 太平道 prolongeait la vision d'un état idéalisé dans l'Antiquité mythique, thème confucéen fondé sur la notion que l'harmonie cosmique et sociale découlait de la force morale d'un souverain sage. En ces temps-là, le climat et la nature étaient propices, les moissons abondantes, et tous les humains atteignaient un âge vénérable. Le *Livre de la Grande paix*, dont la version originelle date de la dynastie des Han orientaux (25-220 de notre ère), prêchait une doctrine de responsabilité humaine qui façonna considérablement la pensée taoïste médiévale en matière de rédemption : à partir de la relation cosmologique entre Homme et Ciel, l'ouvrage dépeignait le fardeau humain des péchés et des infractions, les rétributions envoyées par le Ciel, dévoilait l'apocalypse prochaine et la promesse du salut[36]. À la fin du cycle cosmique, quand le monde serait visité par des hordes de démons apportant dévastation et maladies contagieuses, un petit nombre d'élus échapperait au carnage grâce à leur état de préparation par la prière et le jeûne, et grâce à la protection offerte par des textes sacrés et des talismans. La promesse sotériologique des Maîtres célestes à la première communauté était de devenir les membres consacrés du « peuple semence » 種民, ceux qui survivraient à la fin du monde et formeraient le germe des « générations à venir » 後世. Au IIIe siècle, les *Préceptes d'admonestation des maisonnées* 大道家令戒 proclamaient : « Ils contempleront la Grande paix et seront délivrés 度脫 du cataclysme, et ils deviendront le peuple semence des générations à venir. Même les calamités de la guerre, de la maladie et de l'inondation, ils les traverseront indemnes. Ainsi seront-ils appelés [la congrégation du] Tao[37]. » Le tract des *Transformations de Laozi* rapporte une manifestation du Seigneur Lao en 155 (voir « Le pays de la révélation » au chapitre premier), promettant la disparition des épidémies sous les derniers Han[38]. Là, le sauveur désigné était le prophète Li Hong 李弘, figure d'un culte local au Sichuan qui devait réapparaître ultérieurement à des moments critiques, durant la période des Six dynasties[39].

Le bouddhisme prédisait aussi des cycles temporels apocalyptiques menant à la dégénérescence et à la destruction périodiques du monde. Chaque ère cosmique ou *kalpa* 劫 se terminait par un cataclysme de feu, de déluge et de vent, suivi par un *kalpa* intermédiaire d'obscurité et de vide. Dans de tels moments, des bodhisattvas et des bouddhas sauveurs apparaîtraient, en particulier Maitreya 彌勒, le Bouddha à venir, après Śākyamuni 釋迦牟尼, le Bouddha de l'ère historique. Les vrais justes seraient alors séparés des pécheurs et renaîtraient dans des régions paradisiaques au-delà de ce monde. D'autres êtres sensibles renaîtraient dans les niveaux inférieurs d'un nouveau « monde réceptacle », en fonction de leur mérite karmique. Parallèlement au cycle de destruction et de renouveau cosmiques courait celui de l'essor et la chute du *dharma*. La disparition du *dharma* signalait la fin de la vraie doctrine 末法, jusqu'aux rares conjonctions où un bouddha ou un sage-roi tournant-la-roue-du-*dharma* (*cakravartin* 轉輪聖) apparaissait en ce monde, créant une fois encore les conditions de l'avancement spirituel et de la paix universelle[40].

Au IVe siècle, la doctrine bouddhiste vint enrichir les attentes eschatologiques et messianiques taoïstes, sans pourtant fondamentalement les altérer, tant et si bien que Maitreya en vint à être vénéré comme un sauveur et à faire l'objet d'un culte comparable à celui de Li Hong. L'apparition de l'un comme l'autre était redoutée en tant que signe annonciateur de subversion, puisque leur venue signifierait la fin de régimes politiques cruels, corrompus et plongés dans les ténèbres de l'ignorance. Comme les prophéties apocryphes chinoises, la doctrine de la fin du *dharma* reliait des processus cosmiques à la dépravation humaine. Une conséquence en fut l'émergence de pratiques dévotionnelles et d'écoles doctrinales nouvelles en Chine, cherchant des voies plus directes vers le salut[41]. La question du Mandat du ciel, critique à la fin des Han, devint dominée par sa dimension morale. La destruction du monde par un déluge, accompagnée par l'extinction du soleil et de la lune et l'attente d'un rédempteur, fut annoncée comme la rétribution de la dépravation des hommes. Dans *La conversion des barbares par Laozi* 老子化胡經, un Céleste vénérable 天尊 proclame la fin d'un grand *kalpa* avec l'envoi d'armées d'inspecteurs dans le monde pour séparer les justes des méchants suivant les registres du mont Tai 太[泰]山. Le Céleste vénérable révèle les voies du paradis et de l'enfer, avant de conclure par la promesse d'une ère de Grande paix, qui verra la terre être aplanie et un Seigneur véritable 真君 descendre avec Maitreya pour gouverner l'humanité[42].

De la même façon, le poème du IVe siècle *Les transformations illimitées du Seigneur Lao* 老君變化無極經 présentait la perspective de la Grande paix aux élus, reliant cette fois-ci le salut à l'ordination, et exhortant les adeptes à traiter les divinités protectrices de leurs registres d'ordination avec tout le respect qui leur était dû :

> Aussitôt que le Seigneur maître 師君 se fut manifesté, [les démons] furent entièrement exterminés.
> Alors la Grande paix prévalut, et le Seigneur véritable apparut.
> Les méritants rejoignirent l'autre rive et devinrent les élus.
> Leurs noms furent enregistrés et rapportés en haut au Très Haut Seigneur [Lao],
> Et il leur conféra des registres talismaniques pour protéger leurs personnes.
> Invoquez-les (les divinités inscrites) avec attention, et elles veilleront sur vous constamment !
> Servez-les respectueusement, et elles vous seront profondément attachées[43] !

L'instruction du Maître céleste à Zhao Sheng 正一天師告趙昇口訣, une apocalypse de la même période fondée sur la prophétie de départ de Zhang Daoling à ses principaux disciples, lie la promesse de salut à l'institution des diocèses. Zhang Daoling relate qu'après avoir été investi Seigneur de tous les démons en vertu du Pacte de l'Unité correcte, il établit les Vingt-quatre diocèses par correspondance avec les vingt-quatre énergies vitales 二十四氣. Le temps cosmique était structuré par vingt-quatre « nœuds énergétiques » 節氣 ou stations du soleil, qui divisaient l'année solaire en quatre saisons entourant les solstices d'hiver et d'été et les équinoxes vernal et automnal.

Six subdivisions dans chacun des quarts produisaient les vingt-quatre nœuds. Dans les diocèses correspondants, Zhang établit des hiérarchies cléricales et d'ordination pour convertir les adeptes de cultes hérétiques et profanes 邪俗, c'est-à-dire des cultes dédiés aux dieux et aux démons des Six cieux dépassés. Un peu comme dans la première attente judéo-chrétienne d'une résurrection communautaire après le Jugement dernier[44], cette humanité perdue échapperait au déluge annoncé en tant que congrégation des Vingt-quatre diocèses sous l'égide des Trois cieux. Les élus seraient ceux qui auraient été ordonnés dans les diocèses, ceux dont les noms d'ordination étaient inscrits dans le Registre pourpre 紫簿 du peuple semence[45].

La congrégation des élus

En prévision de la fin du monde concomitante de celle des Han, la carte des Vingt-quatre diocèses dessinait une terre de salut. Cet espace sacré, révélé au Maître céleste, y prit une forme communautaire et liturgique, offrant au Peuple du Tao un refuge politique et un havre salvifique pour échapper au sort funeste de l'humanité[46]. Sous les Han, le mot *zhi* 治, employé dans la nomenclature administrative depuis les Royaumes combattants et traduit ici par « diocèse », désignait le siège d'une administration locale. Il signifiait l'ordre, la sécurité et les effets civilisateurs du gouvernement, y compris le contrôle des forces de la nature et celui de la sphère surnaturelle par la mise à distance des démons et des influences mauvaises ; d'où les sens étendus de « guérir » et « sauver » du mot *zhi*. Déjà dans le Mohisme, *zhi* désignait, outre un ordre sociopolitique et moral, une attitude révérencieuse à l'égard des esprits[47]. Les diocèses du Maître céleste étaient administrés par des libateurs, titre porté sous les Han par les anciens du lieu ayant des fonctions administratives et sacrificielles[48]. Le mot *dioecesis*, dont les racines grecques et latines renvoient à des juridictions locales, fut de la même manière adopté par les administrateurs ecclésiastiques.

Anxiétés apocalyptiques et attentes messianiques favorisent l'ascendance d'empires de substitution. Aussi bien le langage que les institutions des Maîtres célestes suggèrent que le mouvement à ses débuts avalisait une forme d'amalgame avec le gouvernement temporel et que ses membres se considéraient comme une entité politique. L'espoir utopique de Grande paix sous le règne d'un Seigneur véritable nourrissait de semblables visées. Les Vingt-quatre diocèses constituaient un espace d'autorité alternative, administrativement structuré, à l'intérieur du territoire des Han sur le déclin. Pourtant, le royaume dont les diocèses traçaient la carte n'était en rien de ce monde. Les véritables circonscriptions des libateurs étaient inscrites dans les étoiles, et la carte réelle des diocèses était une constellation. De telles visions du ciel ici-bas résultaient de la « division des domaines » 分野, soit l'appariement de régions terrestres et célestes. La division des domaines avait été utilisée pour mettre en corrélation les Neuf provinces de la Chine ancienne avec les Neuf cieux, apparier douze états féodaux avec les douze stations de la planète Jupiter, et ainsi de suite[49]. Bien que les Vingt-quatre diocèses correspondissent originellement à vingt-quatre énergies cosmiques, grâce à une nouvelle révélation en 196, quatre diocèses complémentaires développèrent le système pour désormais refléter les Vingt-huit mansions 二十八宿, un zodiaque de constellations près de la ceinture écliptique de la sphère céleste. Chaque mansion avait une « étoile déterminative » 距星[50] qui servait à fixer les positions des corps célestes et suivre les stations de l'orbite sidérale de la lune.

La division des domaines visait surtout une finalité astrologique : la présence d'un astre funeste ou le mouvement propice d'un corps céleste dans un secteur donné du ciel avait des répercussions dans le domaine géopolitique correspondant sur Terre. Appliqué aux diocèses, ce procédé organisait l'espace, le temps et la « Destinée personnelle » des adeptes du Maître céleste en un unique système intégré. Grâce aux soixante binômes spatio-calendaires, l'année de naissance de tout individu et, par conséquent, sa destinée personnelle pouvaient être associées à un site diocésain et à la maison lunaire correspondante[51].

Avec l'implantation des lieux de culte de la communauté du Maître céleste à Hanzhong, la référence spatiale des diocèses se trouva détachée de l'ancrage géographique révélé à Zhang Daoling. Le déplacement de la communauté vers le nord en 215, et de nouveau sous les réformes de Kou Qianzhi, accentua plus avant la délocalisation des lieux de culte. Avec la diffusion du taoïsme du Maître céleste à toute la Chine, et la dispersion des communautés au-delà des sites originels au Sichuan, l'affiliation diocésaine des fidèles se tourna de plus en plus vers les homologues stellaires des diocèses. L'ascendant des Vingt-quatre diocèses du Ciel, comme celui de la Nouvelle Jérusalem ou de la Cité de Dieu, répondait à la désintégration de l'empire et à la dispersion des fidèles qui s'ensuivit. Tout au long des siècles de désunion après la chute des Han, le message messianique du mouvement du Maître céleste situait le lieu du salut et du renouveau dans un espace reliant la *civitas terrena* et la *civitas dei*, c'est-à-dire le présent communautaire des sanctuaires diocésains et le royaume des élus à venir.

Chaque siège diocésain abritait un sanctuaire où le libateur conservait les archives administratives, recevait les offrandes des fidèles et exécutait des rituels de requête en leur nom. Les premiers témoignages détaillés de l'ordre liturgique et administratif du système datent du Ve siècle. Le patriarche Shangqing Tao Hongjing 陶弘景 (456-536) codifia le rituel de la communauté sur la base des instructions révélées en son temps par Zhang Daoling et transmises dans l'*Hagiographie de Dame Wei de Nanyue* 南嶽魏夫人傳. Tao compléta cette description visionnaire par des sources anciennes alors encore à sa disposition, dont le *Rite de Hanzhong pour entrer dans le sanctuaire diocésain et assister aux audiences dans l'oratoire* 漢中入治朝靜法 (vers 200 de notre ère)[52]. Un autre témoignage fondamental nous vient de Lu Xiujing dans son *Ordre sommaire de la communauté taoïste par Maître Lu* 陸先生道門科略. À l'instar des admonitions du Maître céleste du IIIe siècle, ce traité réprimande le désordre et la déviance des pratiques contemporaines eu égard à l'idéal des normes de la communauté primitive de Hanzhong. Avec ces semonces, Lu Xiujing entend instruire en creux sur ce que devrait être l'ordre liturgique du Maître céleste :

> Mais les fidèles d'aujourd'hui mettent tout sens dessus dessous. Je propose solennellement d'exposer ces maux dans ce qui suit. Le Maître céleste établit les diocèses et en institua les fonctions de la titulature sur le modèle des commanderies, districts, municipalités et préfectures de la bureaucratie de ce monde 陽官 pour administrer la population. Les fidèles du Tao avaient tous leurs maisonnées enregistrées et leurs dossiers tenus ; chacun dépendait d'un lieu d'affiliation donné[53].

Lu poursuit en exposant les fonctions exercées par la prêtrise diocésaine, lesquelles se trouvaient curieusement ressembler à celles de l'administration du recensement et des impôts du gouvernement local des Han, avec la compilation de « registres de vie » 命籍 des maisonnées et la collecte de « riz de gage » 信米[54]. Les gages étaient appelés rituellement et les registres actualisés lors des Trois assemblées 三會 annuelles, jours durant lesquels « le Monarque céleste 天帝 et tous les grands saints descendaient ensemble et se réunissaient dans la grande salle du diocèse »[55]. Lu Xiujing, dans sa critique des déviations contemporaines, visait les domaines suivants :

Assemblées 會. Les adeptes choisissant de fréquenter les sanctuaires en fonction de leur proximité plutôt que de leur affiliation, mettaient à mal le bon fonctionnement des diocèses, lequel dépendait de la tenue rigoureuse des recensements de la population. En outre, ils négligeaient les règles alimentaires et ne respectaient ni les protocoles rituels ni les procédures de conservation des modèles de requêtes. Contrevenir aux règles communautaires portait atteinte aux relations et entraînait des conflits sociaux. Le vrai devenait faux et le bon était rendu mauvais. Mise sens dessus dessous, la société sombrait dans le trouble.

Enregistrement des maisonnées 宅錄. Quand l'enregistrement réglementaire était négligé lors des Trois assemblées annuelles, le désordre s'installait dans les dossiers. Les nouveau-nés n'étaient pas enregistrés et demeuraient laissés-pour-compte jusqu'au grand âge. Les morts continuaient à figurer parmi les vivants. Les mariages n'étant pas déclarés, les épouses conservaient un statut de célibataire au registre de leur famille de naissance. Lu dénonçait comment le désordre des registres menait à des méprises de catégories (voir « Mélanger les tuiles et les jades » au chapitre 5), mêlant vifs et trépassés et confondant l'existant et le non-existant. Pire, parce que les affligés faisaient appel à des prêtres quelconques qui n'avaient aucune connaissance des dossiers diocésains afférents, leurs requêtes contenaient des informations non identifiables, et par conséquent ne pouvaient être traitées par l'administration des Trois cieux. Pour éviter ces écueils, il convenait de déclarer tous les membres masculins et féminins de la famille avec rigueur. Les changements de situation familiale donnaient lieu à des « banquets de cuisine » 廚 communautaires, d'importance variable[56]. Seule la naissance des nourrissons survivant au-delà du premier mois devait être enregistrée, en spécifiant bien le sexe du nouveau-né. Les mariages imposaient l'échange de dossiers entre les deux diocèses concernés, l'inscription des renseignements identitaires de la mariée dans le registre de maisonnée de l'époux et l'annotation appropriée du registre familial de naissance de l'épouse.

Gages de foi 信. Les registres de vie 命籍 et les offrandes de gages constituaient les deux piliers de la relation prêtre-fidèle. Ces gages étaient dus annuellement le cinquième jour du dixième mois. À cette occasion, si la maisonnée n'avait connu aucune évolution, seul un banquet était requis. Si la maisonnée s'était réduite, le gage offert demeurait au même niveau mais nul banquet n'était requis. Faute de recevoir un paiement de gage, le diocèse bloquait les dossiers ici-bas. Nulle autre forme d'offrande ne pouvait se substituer aux gages réglementaires. Un défaut de paiement répété entraînait la suppression du dossier de la maisonnée par l'administration des Trois cieux. Les familles frappées de maladie et d'envahissement démoniaque ne pouvaient s'en prendre qu'à elles-mêmes.

Oratoires domestiques 靖室. Lu Xiujing rappelle les règles strictes qui s'appliquent à leur établissement et à leur tenue, à savoir une structure à part, nette, sans fioriture ni ornement intérieur, qui soit aspergée et balayée comme les demeures des dieux[57]. Seuls quatre éléments de mobilier étaient admis : un encensoir, une lampe, un autel de requête et un couteau à livre pour corriger les erreurs de rédaction[58]. Lu Xiujing s'insurge contre les arrangements profanes, autels ornés, bannières et icônes, qui prévalaient à son époque. Là encore, il dénonce une confusion des genres, entre recherche et simplicité, ostentatoire et ordinaire. Pire, nombre de maisonnées n'avaient point d'oratoire et s'en remettaient à des accommodements de fortune, à l'extérieur ou à l'intérieur, où des ouvertures laissaient s'égarer les animaux domestiques et la saleté s'accumuler. Parfois ces espaces servaient abusivement de débarras.

Vêtements rituels 法服. Ceux-ci étaient copiés sur l'habit de cour, avec des normes précises pour les turbans, bonnets, robes, pantalons, jupes et capes, indicatives de l'ordre hiérarchique[59]. Les vêtements constituaient aussi une catégorie distincte d'offrande de gages, avec des spécifications séparées pour les hommes et les femmes. Toujours attentif à la hiérarchie, Lu Xiujing blâmait la pratique des rangs inférieurs consistant à usurper les prérogatives vestimentaires des échelons supérieurs ou à mal assortir des types et classes disparates de vêtements, source de pagaille et de confusion. Les vêtements avaient des divinités tutélaires, prévenait-il. S'habiller à l'encontre du code offensait ces esprits et prêtait à de sérieuses conséquences.

Promotions au mérite et ordinations laïques 受籙. Pour les membres de la congrégation, trois « services » 勤 constituaient un « mérite » 功 et trois mérites, une « vertu » 德. Les détenteurs de trois vertus pouvaient se voir décerner un « registre » 籙, c'est-à-dire recevoir un certificat d'ordination laïque[60]. On pouvait alors, sur la base de mérites ultérieurs, progresser d'un « registre de dix généraux » à un « registre de cent cinquante ». Les novices ayant les qualifications requises pouvaient être ordonnés prêtres et progresser sur l'échelle hiérarchique diocésaine. Lu Xiujing dénonçait parmi les abus l'étude sans rattachement à un maître, « comme une herbe sans racine » 無根之草, l'octroi indu de registres ou de diocèses, l'absence de dossier ou de qualification, et l'acceptation d'un registre de la main d'un maître étranger au mépris de la séquence appropriée d'avancement. Les nominations abusives à des fonctions cléricales étaient cause de déclin institutionnel et de conduites répréhensibles, comme manger dans un oratoire ou y boire de l'alcool, ou bien encore faire du démarchage pour des requêtes dans des villages éloignés au lieu de recueillir, comme cela était prescrit, les demandes au sein de son sanctuaire attitré[61].

Signification du sacrifice

Le récit de la rédemption depuis le fond des âges peut se conter comme une histoire du sacrifice. L'instruction du Maître céleste d'implorer le Ciel par l'adresse de requêtes et des gages ne se matérialisa pas sur le mont du Chant de la grue *ex nihilo*. Pour en situer la portée, il convient de replacer le rituel d'imploration dans l'histoire des représentations chinoises de la dette et de la restitution. Comment le suppliant envisageait-il sa rançon ? Comment les ritualistes définissaient-ils ce qui constituait une juste offrande ? Depuis le second millénaire avant notre ère, les sacrificateurs chinois faisaient des offrandes aux ancêtres royaux déifiés, aux dieux des cieux (soleil, lune, étoiles, planètes), à la terre (sol et céréales, fleuves et lacs, vent et pluie, directions de l'espace). Les conceptions de ce qui constituait une offrande expiatoire variaient et évoluaient avec le temps, des premières victimes humaines et animales aux effigies et jades rituels. Selon que la divinité destinataire résidait dans les cieux, dans la terre ou dans l'eau, les victimes sacrificielles étaient brûlées, ensevelies ou immergées.

Au temps des Qin et des Han, les sacrificateurs concevaient leur relation avec le monde des esprits comme une obligation contractuelle en vertu de laquelle une dette sacrificielle était due aux esprits afin de les payer de retour pour leurs faveurs[62]. Quand le Maître céleste proclama l'Alliance pure pour administrer les offrandes de la congrégation aux esprits et au clergé, il institua un code sacrificiel réformé, composé à la fois d'éléments nouveaux et anciens. Nous devons l'un des premiers récits du contrat de l'Alliance pure une fois encore à Lu Xiujing, qui l'identifia comme ayant fait partie de la dispensation originelle. Lu rapporte que le Maître céleste purifia l'univers 蕩滌宇宙 pour endiguer un flot d'infestation démoniaque. Par la suite, « le firmament entier et toute la terre ne contenaient plus de démons déchaînés et funestes. [Le Maître céleste] abolit les nombreux tabous 諸禁 et forma une Alliance pure pour gouverner le peuple : les esprits ne mangent ni ne boivent 神不飲食 et les maîtres ne reçoivent pas de paie 師不受錢 »[63].

La recherche de la délivrance était motivée non seulement par l'expérience tangible de l'adversité, mais aussi par l'omniprésence d'interdits invisibles, les « nombreux tabous » dans le passage ci-dessus qui induisaient en erreur même le pratiquant le plus scrupuleux. Dans les temps de déclin dynastique et de mauvais présages, le malheur s'intensifiait en raison de la « promiscuité entre hommes et démons », des catégories bien séparées quand prévalait l'ordre cosmique. Dans les rituels de requête, les suppliants présentaient des offrandes aux esprits et au prêtre. L'*Explication interne des Trois cieux*, articulant l'Alliance pure à peu près dans les mêmes termes que Lu Xiujing, développait l'injonction aux maîtres de ne pas accepter de paiement pour les services rituels, ajoutant qu'il leur était interdit de « voler le peuple » et que la consommation de viande et d'alcool leur était défendue[64].

Si les esprits ne mangent ni ne boivent, en quoi devaient consister les offrandes ? L'*Almanach de requêtes de Maître Pin rouge* fournit des réponses détaillées à cette question. Dans le répertoire de l'*Almanach*, une liste particulière d'offrandes correspondait à chaque type de prière de requête. Les offrandes incluaient la fourniture, premièrement, d'objets utiles à l'exécution des rituels (huile pour lampe, encens, pinceaux, nattes pour s'asseoir, etc.) ; et deuxièmement, d'objets de nature contractuelle ou sacramentelle (anneaux, bracelets, effigies etc.). Ces derniers pouvaient être coûteux. De plus, il y avait des offrandes monétaires fournies sous la forme d'espèces, de riz et de soie. Les offrandes en espèces étaient appelées « argent de gage » 信錢. En fait, les différents types d'offrandes étaient tous définis comme des « gages rituels » 儀信[65], c'est-à-dire des gages de la sincérité du suppliant : « Avant de présenter une requête, on doit d'abord préparer des gages pour permettre aux dieux de vérifier que son objet et son caractère sont sincères. En l'absence de gages, les dieux n'accepteront pas [la requête] et réprouveront l'attitude mesquine et égoïste du requérant[66]. »

La valeur d'un objet traduisait la sincérité du requérant en tant que fidèle et partenaire contractuel (voir « La scène et l'offrande » au chapitre 3). Les offrandes de gages du Maître céleste relevaient d'un schéma rituel déjà observé dans les sacrifices de gages des Royaumes combattants, dans lesquels des offrandes de jade et de soie – servant principalement de support d'écriture – accompagnaient les prières, avec la promesse additionnelle d'un sacrifice animal d'action de grâce dans l'éventualité où la requête serait accordée. Ces gages étaient enregistrés par écrit sur bambou, sur soie ou sur jade, comme preuve supplémentaire de la sincérité du suppliant[67]. La première communauté de Hanzhong continuait de distinguer les offrandes servant de gages 信 de celles conçues comme dédommagement[68]. Car les dieux étaient d'abord incités à descendre vers l'autel par la promesse que l'on veillerait à leur récompense dès que le résultat désiré aurait été obtenu : « Les officiels célestes 天官 invités seront promus et récompensés conformément à l'annonce du mérite 言功 des Trois assemblées. Cette promesse sera honorée sans faute 不負效信. Puisse le Très Haut dans sa miséricorde résoudre l'affaire, *et cetera* 云云[69]. »

Matériel et supports d'écriture (pinceaux, papier, encre, grattoirs) étaient un attirail liturgique omniprésent. La charité bouddhiste accordait un mérite particulier à de tels dons, spécialement aux pinceaux pour copier les soutras. Étant donné la nature scribale du rituel du Maître céleste et la nature sacrale de l'écriture chinoise, les documents de la requête, en un sens, étaient eux-mêmes le sacrifice communiquant une prière et lui donnant force[70]. Dans l'*Almanach*, le rapport intrinsèque entre prière et sacrifice se reflète dans le binôme liturgique « Offrande de requête » 章醮[71].

Le terme pour « offrande » (*jiao* 醮) dans cette expression appelle un commentaire. Selon le compendium rituel antérieur aux Han *Cérémonies et rites* 儀禮, le mot *jiao* fut utilisé pour les sacrifices à partir de la période des Zhou occidentaux (1046-771 avant notre ère), initialement pour des offrandes de viande séchée et d'alcool faites à l'occasion de rites nuptiaux et d'imposition du bonnet viril[72]. À partir des Han, *jiao* désigna plus particulièrement la pratique sacrificielle des maîtres des méthodes, experts en prédiction politique, divination astro-calendaire et techniques d'immortalité[73]. Cette tradition a été identifiée comme l'ancêtre de l'offrande *jiao* taoïste[74]. Tandis que les fondateurs du mouvement des Maîtres célestes héritaient du savoir-faire des maîtres des méthodes principalement dans le domaine de la prophétie politique[75], les techniques d'immortalité de ces derniers, comprenant les sacrifices *jiao*, prirent de l'importance dans le taoïsme pratiqué par Ge Hong en Chine méridionale au début du IVe siècle. Le terme *jiao*, en grande partie débarrassé de sa connotation archaïque de sacrifice sanglant, entra plus tard dans le discours rituel taoïste dominant par le biais des écrits de Ge Hong et de son école (voir « Le retour du sacrifice » au chapitre 9).

Depuis les temps anciens, les offrandes aux morts, qu'il s'agisse de nourriture, d'argent, de biens funéraires ou de leurs répliques, mettaient l'accent sur la subsistance[76]. Sous les Han, le sacrifice aux ancêtres et le culte des esprits étaient mus par l'idée que les esprits souffraient d'un besoin irrépressible de provisions fournies par les vivants[77]. Les prières de requête indiquent que les ancêtres frustrés étaient responsables des infestations attribuées à la « promiscuité entre hommes et démons ». Par conséquent, la dispensation du Maître céleste s'opposait au culte des ancêtres fondé sur leur subsistance, rejetant non seulement les sacrifices sanglants et animaux, mais les offrandes alimentaires en général[78]. Comme d'autres réformes religieuses, le postulat de l'Alliance pure que les dieux ne mangent ni ne boivent combattait une pratique séculaire et ravivait l'idéal décrit comme la voie pure et austère du passé, ainsi que le soutenait avec emphase le liturgiste des Tang Zhang Wanfu 張萬福 (voir « Le retour du sacrifice » au chapitre 9). Le *Commentaire Xiang'er* interprétait une phrase dans *Laozi*, 7, « Le Ciel dure et la Terre vit longtemps » 天長地久, comme signifiant que le Ciel et la Terre, en conformité avec la Voie, étaient autosuffisants et par conséquent indifférents aux sacrifices : « Ceux qui pratiquent la Voie vivent ; ceux qui perdent la Voie meurent[79]. La méthode correcte du Ciel ne réside pas dans le sacrifice 祭餟, la prière 禱 et l'offrande 祠. La Voie interdit par conséquent les sacrifices, les prières et les offrandes[80]. »

Rompant avec la pratique du sacrifice, le taoïsme du Maître céleste conserva le langage du sacrifice, transformant la nature des offrandes, antérieurement destinées à subvenir aux besoins, en gages contractuels qui conféraient au suppliant des droits sur le monde des esprits. Ceci était la pierre angulaire de la dispensation du Maître céleste. Le taoïsme n'est certainement pas la seule des religions du monde à avoir fait de la réforme sacrificielle son fondement[81]. La rémission des péchés, non expiatoire, qu'enseignait le Christ rompait avec l'impératif ancien de verser le sang en réparation. « Donner sa vie en rançon pour la multitude » était le sacrifice mettant fin aux sacrifices[82]. Le bouddhisme s'opposait également à tout sacrifice impliquant d'ôter la vie[83]. La tradition védique postulait que la création était un acte de sacrifice de soi et qu'il était en principe impossible de restituer sa dette personnelle à la création et néanmoins vivre. Par conséquent, les *brāhmaṇa* imaginèrent le remplacement de la victime ultime – le soi – par des substituts de sublimation progressive. Frits Staal observa l'exécution d'un rituel védique de l'Autel de feu en 1975, pour lequel des gâteaux de riz remplaçaient les chèvres comme victimes sacrificielles. La difficulté qu'éprouvèrent les sacrificateurs tentant d'étrangler et d'abattre les gâteaux de riz, comme le prescrit l'ancien code sacrificiel, fut finalement résolue par la récitation d'un *mantra*[84].

Le contentieux qui motiva la réforme sacrificielle dans la Chine ancienne est résumé graphiquement par le terme « culte illicite » 淫祀. Cette étiquette s'appliqua aux pratiques considérées comme répréhensibles pour plusieurs motifs complémentaires : la nature du sacrifice (sang, viande ou alcool), une dépense ou un zèle excessif, la suspicion de desseins sectaires ou subversifs, ou le non-respect par le sacrificateur des convenances dans les relations hiérarchiques, de parenté ou communautaires avec l'objet du culte[85]. Que la puissance d'un être spirituel fût mobilisée avec des effets bénéfiques ou néfastes dépendait de sa relation avec le suppliant. Il se pouvait que l'ancêtre d'une personne fût un démon pour son prochain. Il était illégitime d'alimenter avec des offrandes sacrificielles un esprit sans lien de parenté ou étranger. L'aube de l'ère des Trois cieux fut annoncée par l'avènement du Maître céleste expulsant les démons. L'*Explication interne des Trois cieux* ordonnait : « Le peuple ne se livrera pas à tort aux cultes illicites d'autres démons et esprits » 民不妄淫祀他鬼神[86]. En d'autres termes, la congrégation des Maîtres célestes régulerait et purifierait sa pratique du sacrifice sur la base de l'Alliance pure avec les dieux des Trois cieux et *ne se prosternerait pas devant un autre dieu*[87].

CHAPITRE 2

CULPABILITÉ FATIDIQUE

> Au Ciel et sur la Terre, il y a des divinités chargées d'administrer les transgressions. En fonction de la gravité des violations commises par une personne, des années sont biffées sur le compte de son temps à vivre imparti par le destin. Au fur et à mesure que son compte décroît, la fortune de la personne décline ; elle devient sujette au malheur et à la maladie. Quand son lot est épuisé, elle meurt.
>
> *Baopu zi neipian jiaoshi*, 6.114,
> citant le *Livre de Maître Pin rouge* 赤松子經.

La notion de l'origine du mal est illustrée dans les *Préceptes supérieurs de sagesse sur les racines de la culpabilité* 智慧罪根上品戒, un des premiers livres sacrés du Lingbao qui dépeint le Très Haut Seigneur Tao 太上道君 arpentant toutes les directions de l'espace pour y inspecter les Prisons terrestres. Il y trouve les esprits d'hommes et de femmes peinant aux travaux forcés. Certains sont relégués aux Trois bourbiers 三塗, les trois chemins défavorables de la réincarnation comme détenu des enfers, animal ou fantôme affamé ; d'autres encore aux Cinq souffrances 五苦, les épreuves subies par ceux qui renaissent détenus des enfers, fantômes affamés, animaux, démons ou êtres humains. Le Seigneur Tao s'enquiert pour chacun à la fois des causes des châtiments, des conditions pour « extirper et rédimer les racines de leur culpabilité » afin d'obtenir la délivrance, ainsi que de la longueur des peines à purger[1].

Quand ils priaient pour les âmes des défunts, les suppliants avouaient être plus guidés par de sombres appréhensions que par une quelconque capacité à percer la cause spécifique d'un châtiment. Les rituels d'expiation envisageaient de ce fait tous les cas de figure. La « Requête de Fengdu » 酆都章 visait l'absolution des transgressions tant à la morale bouddhiste – violations contre les Trois conditions 三業 (legs karmique des actes, mots et pensées passés) et les Six sens 六情 (tentations des yeux, oreilles, nez, bouche, mains et cœur) – qu'aux préceptes du Maître céleste – violations contre les *Cent quatre-vingts préceptes* 一百八十條科[2] : « Nous implorons le pardon des Trois conditions et des Six sens reportés des vies antérieures 前身 du défunt, pour les cas où il aurait accumulé les transgressions, ou bien commis des péchés cardinaux ou encore violé les *Cent quatre-vingts préceptes* et été condamné au *samsāra* pour dix mille *kalpas* 輪迴萬劫 dans la nuit éternelle de l'obscurité[3]. »

Pour se frayer un chemin dans le dédale des interdictions, les almanachs étaient indispensables. La pratique de gérer la destinée par la divination calendaire des interdits journaliers 日禁 remontait à la période des Royaumes combattants[4]. Les Livres des jours 日書, tel le manuscrit sur lamelles de bambou du IIIe siècle avant notre ère découvert à Shuihudi 睡虎地 au Hubei, combinaient utilement des listes de tabous à observer au fil des jours avec des almanachs pour rites propitiatoires et d'exorcisme. Le mot « almanach » 曆, dans les titres des manuels médiévaux de requêtes comme l'*Almanach de requêtes de Maître Pin rouge*, situe les rituels de prière des Maîtres célestes pour la guérison et la délivrance dans l'orbite de la tradition antérieure des Livres des jours[5]. Maître Pin rouge se réfère au Céleste aîné 天老, un conseiller légendaire de l'Empereur jaune[6] :

> Maître Pin rouge demanda au Céleste aîné Pingzhang 平長 pourquoi les requêtes présentées un jour *jichou* 己丑 restaient sans réponse. Pingzhang répondit : « Quand les requêtes et offrandes respectueusement présentées

arrivent au Portail du ciel 天門 [ce jour-là], le portail est fermé. » Derechef [Pin rouge] demanda à quels moments du jour et de la nuit [le portail] s'ouvrait et se refermait. Pingzhang donna une réponse détaillée fondée sur le *Code* 科文[7].

Contrairement aux requêtes soumises en vain les jours *jichou*, les talismans présentés les jours *wuxu* 戊戌 étaient infailliblement efficaces. C'était parce que, ces jours-là, le Monarque céleste sortait par le Portail du ciel pour accorder les souhaits[8]. Les tables détaillées des heures d'ouverture et de fermeture du Portail du ciel étaient reproduites dans l'*Almanach de requêtes* pour consultation avant de fixer la date d'un rituel de requête[9]. Un autre facteur déterminant était l'horoscope de l'individu, tiré de deux binômes cycliques : la « Destinée personnelle » 本命, représentant son année de naissance, et la « Progression annuelle » 行年, l'âge horoscopique de l'individu en une année donnée. Sur la base d'une méthode de comptage remontant au temps des Han et codifiée au VIe siècle, deux procédures distinctes étaient utilisées pour calculer la Progression annuelle des hommes et des femmes : pour les hommes, le décompte était progressif depuis l'année de naissance à partir du binôme *bingyin* 丙寅 ; pour les femmes, le décompte se faisait à rebours à partir du binôme *renshen* 壬申[10]. Le binôme auquel on arrivait par cette méthode représentait alors l'âge horoscopique, ou Progression annuelle, de la personne pour l'année en cours.

Les racines du mal répertoriées dans le tableau « Rédimer sa destinée » distinguent trois types de responsabilité caractérisés par différents degrés de responsabilité personnelle : celle imputable à la volition personnelle (le salaire du péché), celle subie du fait de facteurs environnementaux ou d'influences malignes (les puissances du mal), et celle héritée du passé (culpabilité ancestrale).

Le salaire du péché

En termes freudiens, la Chine traditionnelle se range parmi les civilisations de la honte plutôt que de la culpabilité[11]. Cependant, l'utilité de cette distinction pour décrire le tort taoïste est limitée. Le terme habituel pour le péché était *zui* 罪, qui désignait les transgressions punissables tant de la loi sacrée que de la loi séculaire, soit les péchés et les crimes commis dans les mondes du yin, invisible, et du yang, visible, respectivement[12]. Les violations de la loi sacrée portaient le stigmate supplémentaire du sacrilège. Crimes et péchés n'étaient pas des actes isolés aux conséquences limitées. Ils altéraient les conditions de vie de ceux qui les perpétraient, provoquant la rétribution et assombrissant leur destinée potentielle. Sous la loi pénale des Han, les condamnés étaient tatoués ou mutilés pour exhiber leur casier judiciaire à vie[13]. De la même façon, l'état de péché, en tant qu'infraction à la loi sacrée et aux préceptes de la communauté religieuse, persistait comme une tache dans le Grand livre de la destinée de l'individu, aux yeux de la communauté et dans la propre conscience du pécheur. L'introspection scrupuleuse était un impératif moral aussi bien pour les taoïstes que pour les bouddhistes et les confucianistes[14]. Avec l'adoption grandissante de la morale bouddhiste dans la société chinoise, la notion taoïste du péché s'étendit pour inclure l'attachement, l'avidité, les appétences, les infractions aux Dix préceptes du bodhisattva 菩薩十戒 et même les méfaits involontaires motivés par l'altruisme (voir « La piété filiale » au chapitre 8). En principe, l'expiation permettait aux infractions au code moral d'être réparées et aux fardeaux personnels d'être annulés, semblablement à la relaxe dans la loi pénale[15]. Selon la section « Préceptes et interdits » 禁戒 de l'*Almanach de requêtes de Maître Pin rouge*, les transgressions étaient rachetables, sauf certains crimes odieux et péchés mortels qui dépassaient les bornes du pardon.

> Les *Ordonnances* 令 déclarent : ces scélérats et rebelles qui tuent de leur propre main, conspirent contre leur seigneur ou commettent le parricide ne peuvent pas être rédimés par le mérite [du renoncement] aux richesses matérielles. Ils doivent fouler la montagne des couteaux 刀山, plonger dans l'arbre des épées 劍樹 et subir l'ébouillantement et le rôtissage. Dans dix mille années ils ne seront pas pardonnés. Telle est la difficulté d'extirper leurs crimes et d'obtenir la rédemption[16].

Adresser une requête pour obtenir la délivrance était en soi sujet à des règles strictes, et les violations de ces règles étaient passibles de l'envoi de punitions nouvelles, sous la forme notamment de réductions du lot de vie du pécheur[17]. Le code de Maître Pin rouge fait référence aux « Statuts » pour interdire aux membres de la congrégation de pénétrer dans le diocèse en violation des jours de tabous et des règles régissant la présentation des Requêtes, les Offrandes, l'adresse aux départements des palais 宮曹 célestes et l'invitation des officiels 請官, c'est-à-dire le rite de convocation des divinités concernées[18]. De même, étaient aussi interdits d'entrer dans le sanctuaire diocésain ceux qui avaient subi une pollution de naissance ou de mort, ou avaient contrevenu aux codes comportemental et vestimentaire. Les requérants devaient observer certaines prescriptions Tapage domestique, mauvais temps, maladie et irrespect de règles alimentaires constituaient des infractions de tabous :

> *Tabous d'évitement* 避忌. Le *Code* déclare : Un disciple qui présente une Offrande de requête 章醮 ne peut ôter la vie. Les contrevenants ont leur compte de vie réduit de deux années[19]. Le tintamarre des jeunes ou des vieux, des poules ou des chiens dans une maisonnée où une requête est en train d'être présentée, n'est pas tolérable. L'infraction est punissable [de la réduction] d'une année de la durée de vie. En cas de grand vent ou de forte pluie, ou de vent et pluie continuels, la présentation de requêtes ne peut avoir lieu. Les contrevenants sont punis d'une année de maladie. Ceux qui souffrent des Six afflictions 六疾[20] ne peuvent participer à la présentation de requêtes. Les contrevenants ont leur durée de vie réduite de trois années. Ceux qui présentent une requête ne peuvent consommer du vin, de la viande ou des cinq légumes âcres 五辛[21]. Les contrevenants ont leur compte de vie réduit d'une année[22].

Les sphères des humains et des esprits interagissaient imperceptiblement, à l'instar de particules intriquées. Toute occurrence dans la nature était mystérieusement reliée au sort humain. Les cycles de la vie humaine étaient régis par les étoiles, la nature et d'obscures procédures au pays des morts. Des tabous étaient associés à la naissance, au mariage et à la mort ; à la grossesse, l'accouchement et la petite enfance ; à la pollution rituelle ; aux demeures et aux tombes ; au dérangement du sol par des travaux agricoles ou de construction ; à la configuration du terrain et aux directions cardinales de l'espace ; ainsi qu'aux heures, jours et années du calendrier[23]. Le taoïsme du Maître céleste divisait l'univers en une triple structure administrée par les Directoires du ciel 天府, de la terre 地府 et de l'eau 水府. Il s'agissait des domaines des Trois officiers 三官, les juges dans l'au-delà. Offenser ceux-ci ou bien les divinités de la nature présidant aux Cinq pics, aux Quatre cours d'eau, aux montagnes, torrents et forêts 五嶽四瀆山林孟長, entraînait des souffrances rétributives et des adversités émanant de l'environnement[24]. En devenant des esprits ou des démons, les corps des morts se dissolvaient dans les milieux respectifs tombant sous la domination des Trois officiers : le souffle dans l'air, la chair dans la terre, le sang dans l'eau. À côté des tabous des étoiles et du sol, l'eau était porteuse d'interdits particulièrement effrayants. Les prières pour l'absolution d'offenses faites aux divinités de l'eau étaient adressées au Directoire de l'eau, lieu d'enregistrement des péchés et de jugement[25]. La « Requête pour éradiquer les calamités causées par les dieux des fleuves », par exemple, visait à garantir au suppliant la traversée « d'années de déclin et de mois de crise » 衰年厄月 en le déchargeant des « épreuves dues à l'adversité des Trois fleuves 三河之厄 » :

> Nous prions humblement que les Empereurs de l'Eau et les autres dieux et seigneurs des Trois fleuves 三河, Quatre mers 四海 et Neuf rivières 九江 absolvent Untel d'années de déclin et de mois de crise[26]. Au Directoire de l'eau, où le registre des noms 名係 est tenu, puisse-t-on proclamer son passage et ne pas faire qu'il soit incarcéré dans les multiples prisons [de l'enfer…]. Nous supplions humblement les Trois officiers du Ciel, de la Terre et de l'Eau de publier un *Édit impérial de Nüqing* 女青詔書 pour lui épargner la souffrance et le préserver du mal à jamais[27].

L'*Almanach de requêtes* regroupe ce type d'édit sous l'appellation *Statuts et ordonnances des édits impériaux de Nüqing* 女青詔書律令. Dans la religion des Han, des édits pour la protection des occupants des tombes étaient publiés par le Monarque céleste, le dieu suprême et l'étoile la plus brillante du pôle nord céleste[28]. Vers la seconde moitié du IIIe siècle, un manuel, les *Statuts démoniques de Nüqing et de la Métropole sombre* 女青玄都鬼律令, prit forme à partir d'une longue tradition de démonologie[29]. Le texte stipule des préceptes et tabous pour les membres de la congrégation du Maître céleste, au côté de lois pour les démons. Les codes pour les humains et les démons étaient interconnectés, puisque la conduite morale d'un adepte et son observance des tabous étaient susceptibles de contrôler les démons et d'en repousser les infestations. Les préceptes pour les taoïstes étaient initialement promulgués pour endiguer le flot de mal démoniaque dans un temps de décadence et de déclin. Obéir aux préceptes préservait les initiés de la rétribution de la maladie et d'un compte de vie réduit[30].

La première étape vers l'expiation était de faire montre de remords et de repentir, ce qui s'accomplissait par une confession complète des péchés[31]. Selon l'*Abrégé des documents* 典略 du IIIe siècle, les prières du Maître céleste étaient originairement des confessions adressées aux Trois officiers pour obtenir la guérison :

> La méthode de prière consistait à écrire le nom et le patronyme de la personne malade et à déclarer son désir d'avouer le péché. Trois exemplaires étaient préparés, dont un était présenté au Ciel en étant exposé sur une montagne, un était enseveli dans la Terre et un était plongé dans l'Eau. Ils les appelaient les *Confessions autographes aux Trois officiers* 三官手書[32].

Le modèle d'une telle confession pour maîtres taoïstes (*daoshi* 道士), intitulée « Requête par un maître taoïste pour la déposition d'une confession autographe aux Trois officiers » 道士天地水三官手書籙狀章, est préservé parmi une collection de requêtes présentées au nom de prêtres : après lecture complète des informations identitaires et du rang d'ordination du clerc, le suppliant écrivait de sa propre main une confession complète de ses péchés[33]. Conformément à une procédure arrêtée, les fautes étaient détaillées une par une, dans un langage sobre, en évitant les fioritures ou les subterfuges tels que confesser une transgression moindre pour en dissimuler de plus sérieuses. Si une confession était incomplète, les officiers examinateurs n'en absoudraient aucune partie. L'âge du pécheur et le moment précis de l'offense étaient enregistrés. Si un suppliant violait les règles confessionnelles, des conséquences additionnelles s'accumulaient. Tenant l'acte dans ses mains, le repentant sollicitait le Très Haut Seigneur Lao, le seigneur du Ministère de la justice 都官, le seigneur examinateur des Registres de vie 考行狀 et les vingt-quatre officiers 二十四官, les trois Maîtres célestes fondateurs, les officiers militaires et civils de la Chancellerie de tous les districts, commanderies et administrations locales, et les quatre seigneurs inquisiteurs chargés de l'investigation 考召 des éthers miasmatiques dans les quatre directions de l'espace[34]. Le prêtre officiant annonçait alors : « Untel est tombé malade. Aujourd'hui, il a personnellement composé un témoignage confessant par écrit ses péchés 首寫過咎, les véniels comme les graves, citant ses bonnes et mauvaises actions, tous classés par type et comptés tel qu'exposé dans le document. Il implore pour sa vie, et supplie que sa maladie puisse être expulsée et guérie. »

Le maître faisait alors état des bonnes résolutions du suppliant et implorait le pardon des Trois officiers, suivi par une litanie d'invocations directionnelles. Si un incident passé n'était que lointainement remémoré, le suppliant jurait de persévérer dans l'introspection. À partir de ce jour, il se réformerait sans relâche et se soumettrait à la mortification, rompant définitivement avec son moi antérieur. Son corps était actuellement en proie à une maladie chronique calamiteuse. Inconscient, il peinait à respirer, sa vie ne tenant qu'à un fil. Réfléchissant à ses fautes, il en assumait le blâme mais ne pouvait pas s'absoudre lui-même. Ployant sous les difficultés et perclus de frustration, il n'avait nul lieu vers où se tourner pour demander du secours. Ainsi était-il venu au diocèse et exposait-il par confession écrite tous les péchés de sa vie et chaque faute commise depuis l'âge de sept ans. Il suppliait le Grand Tao de donner à sa vie un nouvel élan, les Officiers du Ciel, de la Terre et de l'Eau, et les cent vingt bureaux concernés, d'être indulgents, de revenir sur la diminution du nombre de ses années de vie et de les restaurer, d'oublier ce qui relevait du passé et de faire preuve d'indulgence à l'égard de ce qui était à venir. Finalement, il demandait respectueusement que les seigneurs examinateurs, gardes, soldats, etc., reçussent des promotions et des récompenses, et que leurs émoluments et grades augmentassent conformément aux statuts du Bureau du ciel 天曹 : « Que chacun d'eux retourne à son bureau et fasse le compte de son mérite[35]. »

À l'époque des Tang, la pratique primitive de confession du Maître céleste, augmentée de rites monastiques bouddhistes pour absoudre les violations des vœux, avait produit des écritures comprenant sermons et litanies d'expiation comme la *Litanie pour la délivrance miséricordieuse des Neuf ténèbres et la rémission des péchés par le Très Haut* 太上慈悲九幽拔罪懺[36]. Outre les confessions périodiques des moines, les confessions sur le lit de mort devinrent requises pour aplanir le chemin de la réincarnation et assurer une vie bienheureuse après la mort. Un manuscrit de Dunhuang comporte cette prescription :

> À l'approche de la mort, les frères et les sœurs doivent d'abord confesser les innombrables péchés 無量重罪 accumulés de leur vivant, puis recevoir les préceptes, faire une Retraite, entreprendre de fabriquer des icônes, de copier les écritures et autres actes méritoires, contribuer aux biens [monastiques] avec libéralité et subvenir aux besoins des moines et des nonnes [...]. Alors, quand leurs yeux se fermeront, ils renaîtront dans la Terre pure 淨土 le jour même sans passer à travers les Trois bourbiers[37].

Les puissances du mal

La distinction entre les dettes relevant de la responsabilité d'un individu (péchés, fautes, transgressions, infractions) et celles contractées passivement par exposition (miasme, pollution, astrologie, sorcellerie) n'était pas toujours nette. Lu Xiujing souligne cette ambiguïté dans son analyse de la volition morale d'un individu comme étant moitié « dotation », moitié « discernement » (voir chapitre 7, Sermon 9). Pour les besoins de cet ouvrage, nous emploierons le mot « mal » pour désigner les facteurs affectant la destinée d'une personne de manière délétère. Maladies et infortune résultaient de conjonctions défavorables, de « collisions » avec des astres funestes, de conflits horoscopiques et d'« emmêlement » dans des configurations astrologiques défavorables comme le Filet du ciel et la Nasse de la terre 天羅地網[38]. En jugeant du sort d'une personne, l'*Almanach de requêtes de Maître Pin rouge* considérait que le Filet du ciel était associé aux binômes spatio-temporels *xu* 戌 et *hai* 亥 et la Nasse de la terre à *chen* 辰 et *si* 巳[39]. La « Requête pour démêler le Filet du ciel et la Nasse de la terre » 解天羅地網章 explique :

> [Le bénéficiaire] Untel, son épouse et ses enfants ont rencontré l'adversité. Peut-être sont-ils pris au lacet 纏結 du Filet du ciel et de la Nasse de la terre[40]. Ils ont porté leur affaire devant votre serviteur [le prêtre] et ont demandé une requête. Avec son érudition superficielle, il a une compréhension limitée de la divination météorologique et n'a pas l'esprit des calculs. Pour prédire l'avenir [du bénéficiaire], il dépend entièrement des six

décades 六甲 [du cycle sexagésimal], des Cinq agents et de l'alternance [des trigrammes] *bo* 剝 et *fu* 復 [causant l'essor et le déclin de la fortune]. On considère généralement que *xuhai* 戌亥, la région du yang extrême, est le Filet du ciel, tandis que *chensi* 辰巳, le territoire du yin extrême, constitue la Nasse de la terre. Quand la destinée d'une personne dans une année donnée 年命 rencontre ceux-ci, il ou elle subit des désastres[41].

Une série complète de tabous était associée à la pollution rituelle due aux événements du cycle de la vie :

Pollution de mort et de naissance 殗穢. Le *Code* déclare : quand un décès survient dans une famille, indépendamment de l'avancement en âge [du défunt], quand une femme donne naissance, et lors d'un « grand deuil » 大喪 [c'est-à-dire la mort d'un père ou d'une mère], une pollution de cent jours s'ensuit. Quand une femme en couches ou son nourrisson subit malheur, une pollution de cent jours s'ensuit. Ceux qui entrent dans la salle de travail [où se déroule un accouchement] subissent une pollution qui dure trois jours. Quand un enfant ou un esclave meurt, une pollution d'un mois s'ensuit. Quand un animal domestique meurt, la pollution dure un jour. La pollution ne s'étend pas en dehors de la demeure. En cas de [perte d'un membre de la famille entraînant] une période de deuil d'un an 朞喪, une pollution de quarante jours s'ensuit. En cas de deuils de neuf mois 大功 et de trois mois 緦麻[42], la pollution reste en vigueur pendant le mois [du décès]. Une fois le mois écoulé, la pollution se dissipe. Ceux qui rendent visite à une famille en deuil sont pollués pour la durée de la journée. Les prolongements [volontaires] de deuil n'entraînent pas de pollution [additionnelle]. Les offrandes alimentaires d'une maisonnée en deuil et celle [offerte] le troisième jour puis un mois complet après une naissance sont toutes impropres à la consommation[43]. Dans toutes les occurrences de pollution ci-dessus, il est défendu de célébrer une Retraite, faire une Offrande ou présenter une requête. Quand on entre en contact [avec une pollution rituelle] dans d'autres endroits, on peut se contenter de la dissiper avec de l'eau lustrale 符水[44].

Il était interdit à quiconque étant impliqué dans telles situations de participer aux rituels de requête pour la durée stipulée de la pollution. Les prêtres avaient également interdiction de rédiger des documents de requête après contact avec une pollution de naissance ou de décès (voir ci-dessous). Bien que la sévérité de la pollution dépendît du degré de parenté entre le défunt et la personne portant le deuil, comme le reflètent les périodes de deuil différenciées, tous les membres de la maisonnée, y compris les dépendants, les enfants, les esclaves et les animaux domestiques, étaient soumis à ce genre de pollution. Les membres de la maisonnée en tant qu'entité rituelle comprenaient « les hommes et les femmes, jeunes et vieux, les bœufs, les chevaux et les six espèces d'animaux domestiques », ainsi qu'il est expliqué dans la « Requête pour éliminer les invasions de tigres » 收除虎灾章 (voir « Commanditaire et bénéficiaire » au chapitre 3). La « Requête pour purifier la demeure des pollutions de naissance et de mort » 生死解殗洗蕩宅舍章 prenait en charge cette exigence :

> Le commandant militaire de tel district dans telle préfecture, au nom de sa maisonnée comprenant tant de personnes, jeunes et vieilles, frappe le sol de sa tête ce jour et prend refuge 歸命 dans le Très Haut. En raison de naissances et de décès dans la résidence, ils craignent présentement qu'une pollution ne s'ensuive. Les exhalaisons nocives de tabous se rapportant aux douze divisions du temps, à la Destinée personnelle et à la Progression annuelle ont envahi la maison. [La maisonnée] ce jour fait appel à votre serviteur [le prêtre officiant] pour demander la présentation d'une requête pour la purification du logis et de la cour. Puisse la pollution de naissance et de mort être purifiée, et l'intérieur comme l'extérieur devenir éclatants de brillance. Que des dragons divins montent la garde pour la protection desdites personnes.

Le texte poursuit avec une invocation des officiers sauveurs sous la forme d'une litanie des « seigneurs dissipateurs de pollution de mort » 解殗君 sous l'autorité des Cinq empereurs des directions cardinales de l'espace et du centre. Comme dans de nombreux rituels exorcistes, l'agent pollueur devait être expulsé dans l'eau :

> Puissent-ils descendre, avec cent vingt officiers et généraux, baigner et laver ces hommes de chair 肉人 pour expulser leur pollution de naissance et de mort. Que des Filles de jade émissaires 玉女使者, chacune avec cent vingt officiers et généraux, fournissent l'eau de l'essence véritable 眞精之水 et l'encens des cinq harmonies 五和之香[45] pour purifier et asperger le puits, le fourneau, *et cetera*, de la maisonnée d'Untel. Que la [pollution de] mort majeure entre dans la mer et de mort mineure entre dans le fleuve,

que toutes les mille morts et dix mille pollutions soient éradiquées en temps voulu[46].

Les personnes frappées de la pollution de mort et de naissance avaient quant à elles interdiction d'entrer dans les cours d'eau. Leur présence dans un diocèse était comparable à des substances nauséabondes polluant le sanctuaire :

- Toute personne sujette à la pollution de mort et de naissance ne peut entrer dans les cours d'eau, les forêts et les marais.
- Un animal domestique qui a mis bas n'est pas autorisé à entrer dans un diocèse pendant sept jours.
- Un nourrisson n'est pas autorisé à entrer dans un diocèse pendant cent jours.
- Le nouveau-né d'un animal domestique n'est pas autorisé à entrer dans un diocèse pendant un mois.
- Les gages en vue d'une Offrande de requête ne doivent pas être empruntés à autrui. Il est interdit de brûler des substances nocives et impures, des plumes, des fourrures, des peaux animales ou des cornes dans un diocèse[47].

Si ce qui avait trait à la menace d'infestation démoniaque en général occupait une place importante au sein de l'*Almanach de requêtes de Maître Pin rouge*, les rédacteurs de requêtes se référaient pour les détails aux *Statuts démoniques de Nüqing et de la Métropole sombre*. Nüqing et la Métropole sombre étaient deux prisons situées dans les profondeurs du pays des morts Fengdu. Les *Statuts démoniques*, transmis sous une forme fragmentaire, s'attachent à décrire nombre des 36 000 démons statutaires et en nomment plus de trois cents, permettant aux adeptes de les expulser en récitant leurs noms et en reconnaissant leur apparence[48]. Bien que les catégories de démons et d'infestations fussent multiples et changeantes, un type fréquemment tenu pour responsable des maux des requérants était la corruption d'énergie vitale 氣 connue sous le nom de « souffle pervers » 邪氣, autrement dit les souffles vieux 故氣 des morts. Les âmes des morts, « tueuses » 煞, et les « cadavres » 尸 étaient de nature connexe. D'autres contenaient les « essences » 精 de plantes et d'animaux, d'éléments naturels comme les fleuves, ou d'objets comme les pierres et les arbres morts. L'influence néfaste la plus invasive était appelée « miasme » 注, une notion ayant cours aussi en médecine et en épidémiologie chincises traditionnelles[49]. La libération du mal dans le taoïsme médiéval se comprenait typiquement comme une « délivrance des miasmes » 解注. La terminologie des requêtes pour obtenir ce genre de relaxe dans l'*Almanach de requêtes de Maître Pin rouge* se retrouve dans les « Écrits de délivrance des miasmes » 解注文 accompagnant les défunts dans leurs sépultures. Des récipients en poterie comportant de tels écrits et nommés « vases de délivrance des miasmes » 解注瓶, ont été exhumés de tombes de la période des Han orientaux et d'après[50].

Le terme « miasme » (*zhu* 注) était apparenté à *zhu* 疰, qui signifiait maladie infectieuse ou chronique. En rapport avec l'idée de contagion 染疾, il pouvait s'appliquer tant aux émanations nocives se déployant de la matière organique putrescente qu'aux conjonctions astrologiques de mauvais augure polluant l'atmosphère. Le terme *zhu* apparaît dans de nombreux composés, tels que *yangzhu* 殃注 (miasme désastreux), *sizhu* 死注 (miasme mortifère), *shizhu* 尸注 (miasme cadavérique), *shangzhu* 傷注 (miasme délétère), *zhuqi* 注氣 (exhalaison miasmatique[51]), *zhusha* 注殺 (miasme tueur) et ainsi de suite. Les effets des miasmes *zhu* étaient tout aussi nébuleux, apportant ici tracas ou malheur, là maladie voire décès. Les effets relativement bénins étaient qualifiés par l'expression *kanke* 轗軻, dénotant le déplacement cahincaha et hasardeux d'un chariot le long d'un chemin défoncé. Employé pour décrire les aléas et contrariétés de la vie, *kanke* racontait les conditions précaires, les frustrations et les espoirs déçus ; rapportée aux états psychosomatiques, la formule évoquait la mauvaise humeur, la démoralisation ou encore le désarroi. Et le *Règlement de la Métropole sombre* 玄都律文 désigne la « débilité *kanke* » 轗軻衰耗 comme la rétribution frappant une personne coupable de « quarante vilenies » 人有四十惡 parmi les quatre cents existantes[52].

Tout comme les êtres humains étaient habités par un panthéon d'officiers protecteurs, ils étaient aussi en proie au travail destructif d'agents corporels parasitiques et pathogènes. La croyance traditionnelle voulait que toute créature fût un agrégat habité et animé par des esprits psychosomatiques. Ceux-ci comprenaient sept âmes *po* 魄 matérielles et trois *hun* 魂 éthérées, ressemblant aux composantes matérielles et immatérielles de l'âme grecque. Selon la physiologie taoïste, les âmes *po* étaient des démons qui recherchaient la destruction du corps. La mort était définie comme la séparation des âmes et du corps. En théorie, après la mort, les *po* devaient descendre dans la terre et les *hun* s'élever dans l'air. En pratique, toutefois, les suppliants pouvaient exprimer des espoirs et attentes disparates, par exemple : « Que leurs âmes *hun* et *po* soient acheminées en haut, et qu'elles retournent à la matrice et renaissent comme nourrissons » 反胎還嬰[53].

La métaphore chinoise de l'enfer était la « prison » 獄. Une catégorie de requêtes pour le salut des morts recherchait la « libération de la prison » 開牢獄 ou la relâche des « entraves et menottes de la prison » 牢獄桎梏 par lesquelles des hommes ou des démons, sur ordre des Trois officiers, attachaient les transgresseurs[54]. Que ce soit sous forme d'incarcération, d'envoûtement ou d'emmêlement dans les fils invisibles de l'astrologie, la captivité était une métaphore générique pour la rétribution dans ce monde comme dans l'autre. La délivrance était une libération de l'incarcération. Pour obtenir une renaissance favorable ou un transfert au paradis, le pécheur devait d'abord être relâché de prison, c'est-à-dire, tel Lazare délié, être libéré de toutes les entraves et empêchements. Dans la « Requête pour défaire les malédictions » 解咒詛章 qui suit, une victime de possession par sorcellerie est représentée comme étant prise dans une toile de sortilèges et de malédictions et saisie par des démons :

> Ces derniers temps le résident a rencontré des frustrations ; confus sont ses rêves et ses pensées, il est sujet à des hallucinations monstrueuses tandis que des présages diaboliques continuent à l'envahir. Ses quatre membres lui semblent lourds ; son teint est cireux. Ses esprits sont à la dérive et n'adhèrent plus à son corps. La divination 占筮 a établi qu'une personne maléfique 惡人 lui a jeté des sorts 厭禱 en prononçant cent malédictions 呪詛 impliquant le Ciel et la Terre, convoquant les démons et faisant appel aux esprits. Soit la personne maléfique a fait une gravure des nom et patronyme [de la victime], soit elle a dessiné son portrait, soit elle a percé le cœur [du portrait] avec un couteau, soit elle a coupé les cheveux et les ongles [de la victime][55], sollicitant les esprits et les dieux du sol. Nous craignons que la victime n'ait été saisie par les démons de cent pactes 百盟之鬼[56]. [Le bénéficiaire] ne sait pas par quels actes de mérite la relaxe peut être obtenue et son corps et sa destinée sauvegardés. Il ne peut que d'un cœur fidèle adhérer à la Retraite et se soucier des gages rituels 持齋儀信. Mettant

humblement sa confiance dans le Grand Tao, il a porté son cas devant votre serviteur, implorant la présentation d'une requête pour réviser et dénouer la malédiction 飜解呪詛. Me prosternant révérencieusement en son nom, je présente cette requête adressée au Bureau du ciel[57].

La culpabilité ancestrale

Un type particulier de pollution miasmatique émanait des tombes sous la forme de doléances des morts. Les « plaintes sépulcrales » 塚訟 donnaient lieu à des litiges pour obtenir réparation de ces doléances, contribuant à la pollution définie comme « préjudice résultant de procès 訴訟 dans les tombes : ces derniers courroucent le Ciel et la Terre, causent l'agitation des morts et leur font troubler les vivants »[58].

Dans la loi des Han, le terme *song* 訟 renvoyait à une doléance portée devant les autorités par la partie lésée afin d'obtenir la réparation d'un tort[59]. Les plaintes sépulcrales relevaient de la juridiction des Trois officiers en tant que juges dans l'autre monde[60]. Les litiges parmi les morts étaient tenus responsables des cauchemars, de la maladie et de la mort, ainsi que des malheurs et des frustrations, dans le monde des vivants. Pareils effets malheureux étaient les symptômes de la rétribution d'injustices subies par les morts, que ce soit durant leur vie ou comme habitants du monde souterrain. Un type spécial de requête, celle qui prenait en charge les plaintes sépulcrales, est représenté par deux formulaires dans l'*Almanach de requêtes de Maître Pin rouge*[61]. Les conséquences des poursuites judiciaires engagées dans le monde souterrain figurent aussi dans d'autres contextes. Dans la « Requête pour annoncer la repentance au vu de la Destinée personnelle » 本命謝過口啓章, par exemple, les esprits du suppliant sont troublés, lui faisant craindre la rétribution de ses méfaits et de ceux de ses ancêtres. Comme les requêtes originelles du Maître céleste, sa prière prend la forme d'une confession adressée aux Trois officiers :

Notre souffle vital 神氣 est troublé, nos trois âmes *hun* sont instables et nos sept âmes *po* agitées[62]. De crainte et d'appréhension, nous frappons révérencieusement le sol de notre tête devant l'Empereur de jade souverain 皇上玉帝. Votre serviteur et les autres présents, de par notre comportement depuis sept générations d'ancêtres, avons commis des crimes dans le monde du yin et des fautes dans le monde du yang. Nous sommes coupables des péchés accumulés, ainsi que d'avoir ôté la vie[63].

Comme les plaintes sépulcrales, les effets nocifs parmi les vivants de la culpabilité d'ancêtres défunts frappaient les descendants du coupable. Le risque judiciaire inhérent à l'hérédité était un principe inscrit dans la loi pénale des Han, dans laquelle la sanction la plus lourde pour des crimes commis par un individu impliquait sa parenté dans la rétribution. Cela pouvait conduire à la punition ou l'extermination de clans entiers, y compris les enfants du responsable condamné et ses descendants[64]. On croyait que la culpabilité héritée remontait à au moins sept ou neuf générations d'ancêtres. La doctrine millénaire du *Livre de la Grande paix* employait le terme « fardeau transmis » 承負[65] pour ce concept de mal – défini comme des violations contre le Ciel commises dans le passé et héritées par le présent – pour expliquer que l'humanité était de plus en plus condamnée par un fardeau de culpabilité collective en constante accumulation. Les problèmes du monde présent découlaient des fautes des trépassés[66]. La notion taoïste de fardeau transmis différait de celle du péché originel chrétien – bien que toutes deux pussent être décrites comme des ruptures de contrats avec le Ciel – en ce qu'elle était cumulative et transmise par les lignes de descendance et de parenté. Comme pour la pratique légitime des cultes aux esprits, le tort dépendait du lien de parenté. La notion de culpabilité ancestrale chinoise était analogue à celle de la faute ancestrale grecque, vue comme « un concept au cœur de la pensée grecque ancienne sur la théodicée, l'héritage, le privilège et la souffrance, les attaches de la richesse et de la moralité, la responsabilité individuelle, les liens qui unissent les générations et les grands mouvements de l'histoire »[67].

Le fardeau hérité ressemblait en apparence à la doctrine bouddhiste de causalité karmique 宿緣, c'est-à-dire les causes et conditions héritées des propres vies antérieures d'un individu 夙生. Comme nous le verrons ci-après, l'*Almanach de requêtes de Maître Pin rouge* porte témoignage de l'assimilation du fardeau hérité à la causalité karmique, et parfois de la confusion des deux doctrines. Inversement, les bouddhistes chinois considéraient que les effets karmiques pouvaient être infligés à la descendance[68]. En réalité, alors que les deux doctrines postulaient que les vivants étaient responsables des actions des morts, elles différaient fondamentalement quant à la responsabilité morale d'un souffrant sujet à la rétribution : le pénitent bouddhiste recherchait la rémission des péchés personnels commis dans ses existences antérieures, tandis que le taoïste priait pour être déchargé de toute implication dans les crimes de ses ancêtres[69]. Plus important, la rédemption personnelle du suppliant était considérée comme dépendant de l'acquittement et du salut préalables de plusieurs générations d'ancêtres défunts. Compliquant encore les choses, en Chine, le lien unissant les générations s'étendait telle une chaîne continuelle en amont et en aval de tout individu :

> Nous supplions les Trois officiers, les implorant d'ordonner que les dix mille fautes de votre serviteur Untel soient effacées à partir de maintenant, que les charges pesant sur lui soient levées et que le *qi* miasmatique soit extirpé. Que les neuf bénédictions et la paix éternelle soient sur ses sept générations d'ancêtres, ses père et mère, et ses descendants jusqu'à la cinquième génération[70].

CHAPITRE 3

LES PROTAGONISTES ET LA RANÇON

Les rituels d'« adresse de requête » étaient conçus pour fléchir les puissances du destin. La dramaturgie de la rédemption mettait en jeu trois groupes de protagonistes : le commanditaire et les bénéficiaires du rituel, le ou les prêtres officiants et les arbitres divins du destin. Stephen Teiser fait observer que les prières liturgiques impliquaient l'interaction ritualisée entre des acteurs qui n'appartenaient pas tous nécessairement au même plan spatio-temporel[1]. Il se pouvait que les bénéficiaires fussent des ancêtres défunts ou des communautés d'absents. Les commanditaires pouvaient être représentés par des mandataires. Un participant involontaire fréquemment présent était le « corps de substitution », une effigie. À la différence des dieux silencieux et invisibles, les prêtres officiants et les suppliants laïcs avaient des rôles écrits à l'avance et des voix audibles. La scène pour la transaction rédemptrice était l'espace de l'autel, sa devise l'offrande de gages, et son scénario le protocole liturgique.

Les requérants, par l'intermédiaire du prêtre, se reconnaissaient d'abord humblement simples « hommes de chair » 肉人, en employant pour eux-mêmes des qualificatifs tels que « progéniture de subalterne » 下官子孫 ou « créature ordinaire née d'un ventre » 素以胎生. Ce dernier qualificatif associait les êtres humains aux vivipares du point de vue de la quadruple classification des créatures 四生[2]. L'officiant prêtait sa voix au suppliant lorsqu'il personnifiait ce dernier et s'adressait aux dieux comme le ferait un ministre à son souverain :

> Je [le prêtre] me permets de rendre compte, en conformité avec les documents. Né tels jour et mois de telle année, dans tels préfecture, district et village, [le commanditaire] déclare et annonce personnellement ce jour : Homme de chair né d'un ventre et descendant de mortels, il lui fut accordé la rare fortune de servir le Grand Tao. À jamais gracieusement favorisé, son exultation est sans fin ! Mais étant un homme de chair, nombreuses sont les défaillances de sa foi. Ainsi s'est-il exposé au mal et a-t-il encouru moult adversités. En proie à des pensées et des rêves délirants, il a des visions impies[3].

La voix du prêtre se détachait plus nettement quand il informait les dieux qu'« Untel a abordé votre serviteur, formulant cette requête » et énumérait les offrandes fournies par le suppliant comme gages de sa bonne foi. Ayant assuré les dieux du repentir et des largesses du requérant, le prêtre pouvait alors amorcer le dénouement par l'« Invitation des officiers », une invocation des divinités enclines à accorder la demande.

Commanditaire et bénéficiaire

Le commanditaire 主 engageait la demande de rituel pour son compte ou celui d'un tiers, et en supportait le coût. Pour demander un rituel de requête, le commanditaire s'adressait à un prêtre, le maître des rites 法師 ou maître de l'Offrande de requête 章醮師. Généralement, le commanditaire était un membre enregistré de la congrégation, de bonne réputation et détenteur d'une ordination laïque, et le prêtre le libateur du diocèse. S'assurant qu'il était libre de pollution et d'autres injonctions de tabous, le commanditaire se rendait au sanctuaire diocésain « d'un pas diligent, le port droit et la tenue soignée »[4]. L'*Almanach de requêtes* exposait des règles additionnelles pour entrer dans le sanctuaire :

> Tous ceux qui entrent dans le diocèse doivent se comporter avec respect et sérieux et faire montre de révérence. Leur maintien ne doit être ni fier ni extravagant. Ceux qui pénètrent dans le sanctuaire diocésain ne doivent pas se donner l'air sévère, parler de façon vaine ou inappropriée, bavarder ni plaisanter. À l'intérieur du diocèse, il est interdit de découvrir son corps [...]. Ceux qui se rendent au diocèse afin de demander une requête pour être secourus d'épreuves et de maladies sont tenus d'être ceints et de porter des socques 履版. Ils doivent respectueusement se prosterner et faire une confession complète. Ils ne doivent être ni hautains ni rancuniers, ni se vanter effrontément. Les contrevenants encourent une sentence du troisième degré 三刑論[5].

L'amende pour cette sentence n'est pas connue. Le barème s'échelonnait de vingt jours de balayage de route pour une sentence du premier degré à la fourniture de deux mille tuiles de couverture pour une sentence du sixième degré. Le commanditaire faisait d'abord une déclaration quant à la crise à résoudre, fournissant les données personnelles du suppliant. Comme il était prévu que le rituel prît effet par la correction du Grand livre de la destinée du bénéficiaire, le commanditaire prêtait une attention particulière aux informations relatives à l'identité. La plus petite erreur d'enregistrement annulait toute chance d'efficacité pour le compte du bénéficiaire, tout en pouvant impliquer une autre personne dans des conséquences imprévues. Une attention spéciale était accordée à l'importance de la sincérité. Une demande sincère devait être faite avec naturel, sans élaboration :

> Quiconque souhaitant présenter une requête fait d'abord une déposition complète déclarant ses district de naissance, lieu de résidence, rang officiel, nom, patronyme et âge, ainsi que le nombre de membres de la maisonnée et de dépendants vivants, homme ou femme, jeune et vieux, etc. Conformément aux statuts du Tao, il ou elle fournit tels gages rituels à telle localité et fait appel au maître des rites Untel pour demander la présentation d'une requête. Demandant grâce, il ou elle soumet expressément un rapport. Il doit être substantiel, nullement artificieux ; naturel, en rien élaboré ; simple, point embelli ; vrai, pas faux ; droit, pas désordonné ; judicieux, aucunement alambiqué ; modeste, nullement péremptoire ; clair, pas opaque. S'il est franc et fidèle, il émouvra le Ciel et la Terre et diligentera les démons et les dieux. Quand il sera présenté au Bureau du ciel, la réponse sera

immédiate. Les contrevenants ont leur compte de vie réduit d'une année 奪算一紀[6].

Le commanditaire était souvent aussi le bénéficiaire du rituel. Dans leur étude classique de la nature et des fonctions du sacrifice, Henri Hubert et Marcel Mauss définirent le « sacrifiant » comme le sujet qui en recueillait les bénéfices ou en subissait les effets. Il pouvait s'agir d'un individu ou d'une communauté – une famille, un clan, une tribu ou une nation[7]. Cette définition, fondée sur les pratiques des Hindous et des Hébreux, s'applique aussi au rituel rédempteur taoïste dont le bénéficiaire pouvait être soit un individu, soit une communauté qui avait à répondre d'un passif collectif. L'*Almanach de requêtes* distingue différents types de requêtes en fonction de leurs bénéficiaires individuels ou collectifs, ainsi que des circonstances particulières : « Quand un laïc 世人 souhaite présenter une requête, que ce soit au nom du foyer et du pays 家國, de sa propre personne 己身, de dépendants 眷屬 ou d'ancêtres défunts 先亡, chaque sorte diffère suivant sa spécificité. » À l'évidence, un répertoire classifié comme l'*Almanach de requêtes de Maître Pin rouge* constituait pour un prêtre à la recherche d'un formulaire de requête approprié un outil essentiel, qui tenait compte de tous les critères ci-dessus tout en prenant en considération les circonstances qui déterminaient au cas par cas la destinée d'un individu donné. Le passage continue ainsi :

> Le nombre des années et la destinée de toute vie humaine sont sous la juridiction d'une constellation. Lorsque des événements fâcheux surviennent, le nom est enregistré dans le Registre noir 黑簿, faisant que les esprits de la personne deviennent confus et son sommeil agité. Bientôt il se déplace avec une difficulté croissante et la durée de sa vie est diminuée. Mais si un honnête homme au cœur pur et de bonne foi, qui place sa confiance dans la loi du Tao, présente ses prières par le biais d'un talisman de requête 章符, ses péchés sont instantanément effacés et des bénédictions viennent accroître sa prospérité et le nombre de ses années, tandis que ses ancêtres défunts se voient élevés et comblés[8].

Un type particulier de rituel de requête était conçu pour rédimer la « Destinée personnelle » des individus. La maladie, l'infortune et les crises cycliques de la vie résultaient d'« oppositions » 逆 astrologiques, de « collisions » 衝 ou de l'« obscurcissement » 暗 de l'étoile de vie de l'individu. La *Table d'almanach pour les offrandes de requête à l'Étoile primordiale* 元辰章醮立成曆 donnait le mode d'emploi pour se concilier les trois groupes de dieux de la destinée qui déterminaient le sort des individus : les soixante dieux de la Destinée personnelle 本命神 associés aux soixante binômes cycliques, les sept étoiles du Boisseau du Nord 北斗 et les soixante dieux des Étoiles primordiales 元辰神[9]. Ces derniers, répartis en deux séries distinctes, étaient les marqueurs horoscopiques et les étoiles de destinée des hommes d'un côté, et des femmes de l'autre. L'*Almanach du cycle sexagésimal de la Destinée personnelle et des Étoiles primordiales* 六十甲子本命元辰曆[10] était utilisé en même temps que la *Table d'almanach* pour pointer les corrélations entre ces divinités et leurs suites respectives, d'une part, et les individus en fonction de leur année de naissance 本命支干, d'autre part. La santé et le bien-être d'un individu étaient liés en outre à la luminosité de son étoile de destinée dans la constellation du Boisseau[11]. Dans l'*Almanach de requêtes de Maître Pin rouge*, les étoiles du Boisseau sont invoquées dans des contextes divers, telle cette litanie pour obtenir la guérison de maladies chroniques :

> Nous prions que les sept étoiles du Boisseau du Nord effacent Untel des noms des morts : Loup vorace 貪狼星 et Grande porte 巨門星 pour interrompre la source de la mort ; Préservation de l'honneur 祿存星 et Incorruptible 廉貞星 pour remplacer son corps de mort ; Air civil 文曲星 et Air martial 武曲星 pour expurger le registre de mort ; et Vainqueur des armées 破軍星 pour bloquer les assauts des vapeurs mortelles 殺氣不加 avec Trame céleste 天綱[12].

Les groupes de parenté formaient des entités rituelles solidaires. Ceci est corroboré par les ordonnances régissant les membres de la famille dans l'*Almanach de requêtes* : quand un père « endurait l'épreuve de la maladie », son fils présentait une requête en son nom. Tous deux étaient conjointement tenus responsables de toute infraction au code rituel. Le même principe de représentation de parenté s'appliquait au frère aîné et au frère cadet, à l'époux et à l'épouse, à l'oncle paternel et au neveu. Quand un oncle maternel, une tante paternelle ou une tante maternelle était gravement malade, il ou elle demandait à un descendant non spécifié de présenter une requête en son nom conformément à la règle qui s'appliquait aux oncles et aux neveux[13].

Les prières soulevaient communément des questions de parenté, qu'elles aient trait aux ancêtres ou aux dépendants, cités par de nombreux requérants dans leurs suppliques. Dans les exemples suivants, par contraste, le bénéficiaire du rituel était soit le groupe domestique tout entier 闔門 ou un seul membre de la maisonnée. Si le mot « famille » 家 était fréquemment employé dans les requêtes, il se référait plutôt à la communauté d'habitation, comprenant la famille, les dépendants, les serviteurs et même les animaux domestiques. Un groupe solidairement passible de rétribution, par exemple sous la forme de pollution rituelle ou de miasmes subis conjointement, pouvait constituer un bénéficiaire unique rachetable collectivement. La « Requête pour éliminer les invasions de tigres » 收除虎災章 donne un exemple de rituel qui était expressément commissionné au nom d'un tel groupe :

> En ce moment, nous traversons de funestes calamités ; des tigres et des loups sont entrés sur notre territoire, dévorant des hommes vivants et blessant les six espèces d'animaux domestiques. De jour en jour et mois après mois, [l'invasion] gagne en sévérité et nous n'avons aucun moyen d'y mettre un terme. Nous craignons pour les vies des membres de telle maisonnée, hommes et femmes [...]. Puissent les hommes et les femmes, les jeunes et les vieux, les bœufs, les chevaux et les six espèces d'animaux domestiques de telle maisonnée dans [tels] district et préfecture, aller et venir, et partir ou entrer, sans être confrontés aux épreuves des calamités des tigres et des loups, et puisse ce mal cruel être empêché d'en franchir les bornes[14].

Les modèles de requêtes figurant au début du recueil de Maître Pin rouge s'intéressaient aux crises dans la sphère publique au sens large. Ces prières répondaient aux soucis quotidiens d'une société rurale soumise aux caprices du climat, requérant la protection des cultures contre les insectes nuisibles. Gérer les ressources en eau et prier pour la pluie en temps de sécheresse étaient des devoirs incombant traditionnellement aux officiels locaux. Bien que les règles communautaires pour la congrégation du Maître céleste à ses débuts fissent une vertu d'éviter tout contact avec les autorités et les officiels de l'État, les requêtes pour le bien public et la protection civile suggèrent que le rôle des prêtres taoïstes dans la Chine médiévale se rapprocha des fonctions rituelles du gouvernement local, tel qu'il l'était jadis dans l'office de libateur sous les Han (voir « La congrégation des élus » au chapitre premier).

Un petit nombre de requêtes qui s'intéressaient aux offenses faites aux préceptes religieux et à la moralité publique, brosse implicitement le tableau des défis de la vie collective d'alors. L'inventaire de Maître Pin rouge contient les titres « Confession et repentance pour des offenses faites aux préceptes » 違犯科要首謝乞原章, « Propitiation des Cinq tombes pour les méfaits officiels et privés » 官私咎謫死病相連斷五墓殃注章 et « Séquestrer les querelles et la calomnie » 銷口舌誹謗章[15]. Le texte d'une « Requête pour mettre un terme aux querelles de tous côtés » 斷四面口舌章 est préservé dans un autre recueil. Adressée aux Trois officiers, cette requête demande la mobilisation de soldats spirituels pour appréhender les démons des disputes, des médisances, des malédictions, des jurons, des crimes capitaux, de l'insoumission, des intrigues, de la diffamation des maîtres et de la calomnie du Tao[16]. Des règles correspondantes de comportement et de moralité publique dans les *Cent quatre-vingts préceptes* et les *Statuts démoniques de Nüqing* visaient à prévenir la survenue de telles infractions.

D'autres requêtes, telles que « prévenir les blessures », « intercepter les officiels » et « empêcher les voleurs d'entrer », s'intéressaient aux questions de sécurité publique[17]. Les spécimens de ce genre de prières qui ont survécu montrent qu'elles visaient à protéger les communautés des tigres, des incendies et de la guerre De façon significative, une « Requête pour la prévention des présages de feu » 收除火殃章 n'était pas destinée à prévenir les risques d'incendie en tant que tels, mais à dissiper l'angoisse de leur prémonition. La prière rapporte que le requérant avait récemment été en proie à des visions. Subitement, il avait vu un « présage de feu » 火殃[18] descendre en tel lieu. Son éclat illuminait le sol, attisant une vision apocalyptique qui s'apparentait à la parabole de la Maison en feu dans le *Soutra du lotus* : « Nous craignons qu'une conflagration mortifère ne se propage dans le village, assaillant la population. Hommes et femmes vont succomber au désastre ; innombrables sont les cris angoissés des multitudes, laïcs et religieux[19] ! »

Une « Requête pour la protection en campagne militaire » 保護戎征章 était commanditée par les familles de soldats afin de prier pour leur sécurité (et pour dissiper l'anxiété partagée) :

> Longue est la route franchissant cours d'eau et montagnes, traversant les fleuves Huai 淮 et Si 泗[20]. Face à l'ennemi féroce, au milieu des sabres, il est aux prises avec la cruauté de la guerre [...]. Les hommes de chair ont peu de mérite, [il est] bien insuffisant pour repousser le désastre. Il est à craindre qu'Untel ne puisse pas sortir indemne de ce moment critique [...]. Qu'Untel ne soit pas atteint par l'épée, délivrez-le du péril 度脫厄難[21] !

Des prières analogues se trouvent dans des manuscrits des garnisons frontalières de Dunhuang, fréquemment engagées au combat, et dans des Oraisons vertes présentées au cours des guerres civiles à la fin des Tang[22]. Prières, sortilèges et diagrammes magiques pour la protection des soldats appartenaient à un ancien répertoire rituel, dont le *Dessin repoussant les armes* 辟兵圖, une peinture sur soie découverte à Mawangdui 馬王堆, au Hunan, dans une tombe des Han occidentaux (206 avant notre ère-9 de notre ère), constitue un spécimen[23].

À côté des individus en vie et des communautés de destinée collective, les morts formaient une circonscription rituelle à part. Dans l'*Almanach de requêtes de Maître Pin rouge*, la pensée des morts détenus dans les Prisons terrestres et subissant l'inquisition des Trois officiers constitue une source majeure d'anxiété faisant l'objet de rituels de requête. Les poursuites judiciaires dans l'au-delà, comme ici-bas, échafaudaient un dédale de procédures obscures :

> Incarcéré dans diverses prisons, il est tantôt dans la prison de Hebo 河伯, tantôt dans la prison de Nüqing 女青, ou encore auprès du dieu de la cité (le juge des enfers) ou bien dans le temple de l'esprit du sol 城隍社廟. Incapables de localiser les âmes *hun* et *po* du défunt, nous prions pour son transfert, afin qu'il puisse être en paix, s'élever jusqu'au Palais céleste 天堂, où il sera vêtu et nourri et pourra flâner sans soucis[24].

Le Palais céleste, aussi nommé Palais des bienheureux 福堂, était un lieu de pérégrination sans entraves et de réjouissance bienheureuse où la nourriture et le vêtement se matérialisaient spontanément 衣食自然 et où rien ne manquait. Si leur vocabulaire rappelait celui des écrits bouddhistes, les suppliants taoïstes de la congrégation des Maîtres célestes ne tendaient vers ces palais élyséens que dans l'intérêt des morts en souffrance. Et là, leur souci premier était qu'une fois les morts acquittés et apaisés, ils ne viendraient plus tourmenter les vivants. Les suppliants priaient comme suit pour un membre décédé de leur famille : « Libérez inconditionnellement le défunt, qu'à tout jamais il puisse quitter le Bourbier des ténèbres 幽塗 et s'élever au Palais des bienheureux, là où nourriture et vêtement ne sauraient manquer, et d'où il ne sera plus jamais à même d'entretenir des plaintes miasmatiques contre les vivants 不得注訟生人[25]. »

Ce paradis pouvait être atteint par un acte de transfert ou de promotion, à condition que le sujet ait obtenu préalablement d'être relâché de prison avec décharge complète. Le rituel de requête, véhiculant les prières et offrandes de la famille inquiète, était indispensable pour obtenir des autorités pénales de l'au-delà qu'elles « effacent les charges portées contre le défunt, annulent sa condamnation et le libèrent de prison, sa sentence entièrement purgée »[26]. Des documents de requête en appelaient au Bureau du ciel et au mont Tai 泰山 où péchés et mérites étaient enregistrés[27]. Car avant de devenir un complexe carcéral, le Pic de l'Est du mont Tai avait déjà été associé à l'assignation, à l'enregistrement et au jugement de la mort. Les noms de ceux destinés à la Longue nuit étaient inscrits dans le Registre noir qui y était tenu[28].

Le scribe

Les suppliants souhaitant engager les officiers de l'autre monde à modifier, à l'avantage d'un bénéficiaire, une entrée accablante dans les registres, s'assuraient de présenter, parmi leurs offrandes aux clercs de ce monde et de l'autre, du matériel d'écriture et des ustensiles de correction en abondance. L'écriture avait été le médium du rituel et de la divination en Chine depuis son apparition sur les plastrons de tortues et les os oraculaires[29]. Une communication écrite aux dieux était un symbole sacramentel investi de pouvoir et le prêtre officiant était au premier chef un scribe dont le rôle consistait à produire, dépêcher, archiver ou décharger rituellement les missives adressées à l'au-delà sous la forme de requêtes et de talismans. Les prières de requête adoptaient la langue des mémoriaux de cour. Les talismans et actes exorcistes se terminant par l'expression « à exécuter sur-le-champ, par ordre ayant force de loi » 急急如律令 revendiquaient l'autorité des édits impériaux. Certains écrits sacraux étaient confiés aux flammes. Et dans le cas de rituels de demande de guérison, la requête était expédiée aux dieux du corps malade via l'ingestion de cendres par le patient :

> Après que la requête a été présentée, la brûler dans le sanctuaire diocésain. En broyer [les cendres] avec deux centièmes d'once 分 de cinabre véritable 真朱. Mélanger avec du miel pour faire des pilules. Entrer dans l'oratoire à l'aube, faire révérence et les ingérer. Même [un patient] à l'article de la mort vivra immanquablement. Se garder de le faire savoir à quiconque. En entrant dans l'oratoire pour écrire une requête demandant la guérison d'une maladie, brûler de l'encens de tous côtés[30].

D'autres requêtes n'étaient pas rituellement livrées au feu. Pour leur mise en sûreté ou leur élimination, l'*Almanach de requêtes de Maître Pin rouge* fournissait des instructions particulières intitulées « Entrepôt d'anciennes versions de requêtes » 藏章故本 et « Cessation des requêtes » 斷章. Une fois présentées, les requêtes contenant des renseignements sur l'identité du bénéficiaire, et sur les noms et rangs des agents divins efficaces, devaient être préservées des dégâts, de la profanation et de l'usage non autorisé. L'élimination ultérieure de ces prières constituait elle-même un acte rituel augurant bénédictions et délivrance :

> Les requêtes destinées aux flammes sont incinérées[31]. Celles qui ne sont pas brûlées sont conservées, scellées et entreposées dans des boîtes, rouleaux et liasses s'accumulant toujours plus. Conformément aux rites, elles ne doivent pas être dispersées. Des pertes sont à craindre à cause de la profanation par des insectes ou des rats, ou des dégâts dus à l'humidité et à la décomposition. Bien révérencieusement, nous n'osons contrevenir aux consignes. Par conséquent, ce jour, conformément au Code, nous mettons au rebut et sacrifions tel nombre de pièces collectées depuis tels année, mois et jour, les transformant par le feu 火化 sur tel autel pur ou en tel lieu pur. Puisse la fumée s'élever jusqu'aux dieux et faire descendre leurs énergies-*qi*, répandant le bonheur et éloignant le malheur[32].

Dans la période des Shang tardifs (vers 1200-1045 avant notre ère), les os oraculaires étaient révérencieusement entreposés en tant qu'archives de divination. Incombustibles, ils finirent inhumés et oubliés au fil du temps pour n'être redécouverts qu'à la fin du XIXe siècle. Les prières de requêtes, par contraste, étaient destinées à partir en fumée tôt ou tard. Les historiens des religions doivent à l'obligation cléricale des prêtres de faire des copies des prières et de les archiver d'avoir pu accéder à ces sources inestimables :

> Le *Code des Grands véritables* déclare : Quand la présentation d'une requête au nom d'une personne est accomplie, les requêtes mineures sont roulées, placées dans une enveloppe et remises pour être copiées séparément après la fermeture de l'encensoir. Les requêtes majeures sont promptement copiées comme modèles [...]. Les requêtes contenant les rangs et titres de véritables officiers 真官, les noms et patronymes de démons et d'esprits, les instructions secrètes des dieux du ciel et de la terre 靈祇 ne doivent pas être profanées[33].

Les textes des prières les plus importantes étaient d'abord désacralisés par la suppression des éléments chargés de puissance et leur remplacement par le terme générique *moumou* 某某, « tel » ou « untel ». L'exemplaire « neutralisé » était alors conservé dans un répertoire comme modèle et devenait un formulaire pouvant servir de référence ultérieurement. Au fil des siècles, les prêtres qui consultaient le répertoire en complétaient et recyclaient le contenu, perpétuant une trace écrite jusqu'au temps présent. Un modèle, dit « version standard » 正本, servait de formulaire pour un type donné de requêtes, classé selon les catégories listées dans l'inventaire en tête du répertoire. La relation entre la version standard et les prières auxquelles elle servait de modèle était celle d'un contrat avec ses contremarques, garantissant l'authenticité et le pouvoir sacramental de la version dérivée :

> Toute requête est basée sur une version standard. Les transcriptions sont soigneusement collationnées et clairement présentées. En aucun cas une ancienne version ne peut être réutilisée. Les circonstances de l'affaire ne sont pas les mêmes et les officiers devant être invoqués[34] sont différents. Les familles laïques ne peuvent pas conserver copie

des requêtes. Les contrevenants sont passibles d'une sentence du cinquième degré 五刑論[35].

À la suite de la déposition du commanditaire, le prêtre sélectionnait dans l'inventaire de l'*Almanach de requêtes* la catégorie appropriée de rituel de requête. Ensuite, il recherchait dans le corps du texte un modèle de prière correspondant au rituel sélectionné. Comme l'a souligné Lu Xiujing, l'ameublement clairsemé d'un oratoire se limitait à quatre éléments, parmi lesquels un autel de requête et un grattoir (voir « La congrégation des élus » au chapitre premier). L'*Almanach* spécifie que l'autel de requête était une table basse aux dimensions, à la forme et au matériau prescrits :

> L'autel est long de deux pieds et quatre pouces, large d'un pied et deux pouces, et haut de huit pouces. Il doit invariablement avoir des pieds incurvés. Le bois de cyprès 柏, de *phoebe nanmu* 楠 ou de catalpa 梓 convient le mieux. De nos jours, nombreux sont ceux qui utilisent des tables hautes avec des pieds droits. Ceci est contraire aux rites. Les violations du code se paient en réductions de durée de vie[36].

L'inventaire de l'*Almanach de requêtes* fournissait aussi les listes des offrandes de gages correspondant à chaque type de rituel. Le commanditaire était responsable de la fourniture des quantités prescrites de riz, d'encens, d'huile, de matériel d'écriture, etc. Une date acceptable et de bon augure était choisie pour le rituel. Le prêtre transcrivait soigneusement son texte d'après le formulaire, en adaptait le contenu, en remplissait les blancs. La « Méthode pour écrire les requêtes » 書章法 donne des instructions détaillées pour produire le document, y compris la préparation rituelle de l'encre et la mise en page déférente du texte :

> Quand vous écrivez des requêtes, n'utilisez pas le pinceau et la pierre à encre n'importe comment. Pour broyer l'encre, tournez vers la gauche quarante-neuf fois et frottez [le pain d'encre contre la pierre à encre] à plusieurs reprises de cette façon[37]. Placez « je me permets de rapporter » 以聞 un pouce sous « respectueusement » 再拜 et séparez « votre serviteur nommé » 臣姓 de « je me permets de rapporter » de trois colonnes. Éloignez [ciel de] « Grande pureté » 太清 à trois colonnes de « votre

serviteur » et [étoile de la] « Grande année » 太歲 à trois colonnes de « Grande pureté ».

Nul caractère erroné ou mal écrit n'était admis, et le papier ne pouvait être déchiré. Le rédacteur rajustait sa coiffe et son habit, évitant d'exposer son corps, et adoptait une attitude soumise et respectueuse. Il ne devait pas s'accroupir. Quand le texte était fini, il était relu et vérifié :

> Ne suspendez pas [le caractère] « vie » [en bas d'une colonne] et n'exposez pas [le caractère] « mort » [en haut]. Le mot « démon » 鬼 ne peut pas occuper la tête d'une colonne. Ne détachez pas les noms des patronymes des personnes. Ne permettez pas à quiconque d'éveiller le ciel de la Grande pureté [en vain] en lisant [la requête] subrepticement. Le jour et le mois ne doivent pas être inscrits par avance, mais seulement quand ledit moment approche[38].

Comme les communications de la cour, les requêtes liturgiques respectaient des formats et des formulations prescrits. La langue sacrale de la prière accomplissait plus que la communication verbale : injonctive et performative, elle exécutait une action, à la manière d'un prononcé de jugement. Les instruments juridiques distinguent les préambules, qui exposent les circonstances d'une affaire, de la partie opérative, qui accomplit l'acte juridique[39]. De même, les prières de requête employaient différents registres rhétoriques, incluant des expressions d'humilité, de la prose descriptive et des ordres vernaculaires. Pour fléchir les dieux, une prière devait d'abord établir son honnêteté et sa sincérité. Le requérant était invité à écrire une prose franche et non alambiquée[40]. Imitant les mémoires adressés à l'empereur, le suppliant énonçait des formules comme « Avec crainte révérencielle » 誠惶誠恐[41]. Il se pouvait que la version servant de modèle abrégeât les expressions ou passages récurrents de ce genre avec *et cetera* 云云, laissant au rédacteur de la requête le soin d'insérer les formules appropriées. Les locutions liminaires et finales, notamment, étaient adaptées aux circonstances et au degré d'urgence :

> Le *Code* déclare : Quand vous présentez une requête en cas de maladie mineure ou pour une affaire insignifiante, il suffit de dire « votre serviteur Untel frappe le sol de sa tête et rend compte respectueusement » 臣某稽首再拜上言 [...]. Quand vous présentez une requête en cas de maladie grave ou pour une affaire urgente, déclarez « votre serviteur Untel, implorant le pardon de son crime capital, frappe le sol de sa tête et rend compte respectueusement » 頓首死罪稽首再拜上言. Idem à la fin de la requête. Les contrevenants subissent des diminutions de durée de vie[42].

En tête de toute requête, le prêtre déclarait son rang d'ordination complet 具法位, accompagné par les mots « En conformité avec les documents, j'annonce respectueusement » 上言謹按文書. Un préambule suivait, détaillant les renseignements fournis dans la déposition du suppliant, puis une déclaration du problème dont la requête était l'objet, et un diagnostic provisoire de la cause de la crise. Une déclaration générale de contrition couvrait toutes les offenses envisageables commises par les membres vivants ou décédés de la famille. Aux remords du bénéficiaire d'avoir appelé le malheur sur lui, le prêtre joignait l'expression personnelle de son propre rabaissement :

> Votre serviteur Untel et son disciple sont les descendants d'humbles rustres 草苗. Le travail à la ferme est son gagne-pain. Une chance rare lui a permis de servir le Grand Tao. Il a reçu des registres d'ordination multiples 賜佩重籙 et a été gratifié d'une charge diocésaine 治職. Des officiers et soldats célestes gardent sa personne. [Mais] il a amassé des montagnes et des océans de fautes, et pas une once de mérite. Responsable devant le Ciel et la Terre, il lui répugne d'avoir l'esprit tranquille[43].

Pour finir, la partie opérative articule le résultat souhaité, comme dans la phrase « Nous prions que les sept étoiles du Boisseau du Nord effacent Untel des noms des morts » (voir la requête citée *supra*, p. 77).

Les arbitres du destin

Les arbitres du destin résidaient dans les étoiles, le milieu naturel et les divisions du temps et de l'espace. Ils habitaient le temple et l'autel, logeaient dans les icônes, les rituels et les objets sacramentels. On pouvait établir leur présence grâce à des médiums spirituels, des manifestations et des miracles, et grâce aux prières exaucées. Le modèle de requête citait déjà le panthéon qu'il convenait d'invoquer en fonction de la catégorie de prière, mais il fallait que le prêtre adaptât le destinataire générique aux circonstances particulières. Pour cela, le *Protocole des Mille deux cents officiers*, un manuel répertorié comme ayant fait partie de la révélation originelle du Maître céleste, était à portée de main. Le *Protocole* était un registre de la bureaucratie divine, de ses départements et de ses services, des noms des seigneurs responsables, de leurs résidences et personnels subalternes. Comme les requêtes, les officiers concernés étaient classés par affliction et par type de problème. Leurs noms étaient copiés dans le texte de la requête en une litanie facilitant leur invocation. Dans de nombreux cas, on trouve une filiation entre le panthéon de l'*Almanach de requêtes de Maître Pin rouge* et différents éléments et fragments de la tradition du *Protocole*, dont n'a été transmis aucun texte intégral, s'il en exista jamais un[44].

Le panthéon était aussi hétérogène que la démonologie des *Statuts de Nüqing*, et incluait une variété de dieux populaires et de démons. L'*Almanach de requêtes de Maître Pin rouge* énumère les principaux seigneurs, officiers et généraux à convoquer dans une section intitulée « Invitation des officiers » 請官[45]. Nous verrons au chapitre suivant que le panthéon de Pin rouge était en fait plus conséquent et plus finement différencié que ne le suggère ce résumé, incluant notamment des divinités féminines spécialisées dans l'accouchement et l'éducation des enfants, la sériciculture et les ablutions purgatoriales. Une version plus détaillée de l'« Invitation » est préservée dans l'*Ascension à la perfection* 登真隱訣 par Tao Hongjing, laquelle cite le *Protocole* et inclut des commentaires de Tao[46]. Une autre version citant également le *Protocole* est préservée dans les *Grades des requêtes et des officiers* 正一法文經章官品[47]. Ces aperçus du panthéon ne nous renseignent guère sur l'identité de chaque entité divine inventoriée. En revanche, ils donnent une indication précieuse quant à la structuration des rituels de requête et ils ouvrent des perspectives quant aux domaines de préoccupation des suppliants.

La section « Urgences » 有急 faisait référence à toutes sortes d'infortunes critiques, souvent imputables à des doléances émanant des morts[48]. Dans l'« Invitation des officiers », les rétributions correspondaient en majorité pour de tels cas à des symptômes morbides, tels les troubles gastriques et intestinaux, les affections du visage et des yeux (voir Li Wan, « Trois prières » au chapitre 12), les abcès, les maladies chroniques, les « souffles vieux », les contagions d'origine démoniaque, l'exténuation, l'émaciation, l'atrophie mortelle ; une seconde catégorie d'urgences regroupait les symptômes psychosomatiques tels l'anxiété, le désarroi, les rêves confus et la volatilité des âmes *hun* and *po*.

Un autre domaine de préoccupation se rapportait au foyer et aux logis : les maladies causées par les démons du puits et du fourneau 井竈鬼, les « démons coercitifs » 強鬼 tenus responsables des possessions 精祟, les dommages corporels causés par les « miasmes de mort multiple » 多死喪注 s'abattant sur une seule famille, les fantômes envahissants et les esprits hanteurs, les perturbations du foyer dues aux litiges de démons réfractaires, ou les apparitions de revenants des tombes de cinq générations d'ancêtres 五墓 et les spectres errants des victimes de mort violente. Pour abolir les lieux de culte illégitimes, les idoles, l'adoration des démons et la sorcellerie, on faisait appel au Seigneur Pingtian 平天君 avec cent vingt officiers et généraux. Ceux qui souhaitaient progresser dans la voie de la transcendance, mais que frustraient les conditions de précarité et les maladies infectieuses, étaient sauvés par le Seigneur Tianjing de Xusu 虛素天精君 et ses cent mille guerriers revêtus de rouge[49].

Que ce soit à dessein ou du fait d'une transmission partielle, l'« Invitation des officiers » de Maître Pin rouge suggère que le panthéon des requêtes visait principalement l'exposition du souffrant aux tabous du milieu naturel et la culpabilité ancestrale, par opposition à la culpabilité personnelle, comme causes radicales de rétribution. Parmi les effets péjoratifs de ces dettes, l'accent portait sur la maladie, l'adversité et la perte de vitalité, par opposition aux tourments concernant la vie dans l'au-delà (voir les catégories listées dans le tableau « Rédimer sa destinée »).

Corps de substitution

Une conduite téméraire pour chercher à obtenir la délivrance consistait à expédier un « corps de substitution » 替身 aux arbitres du destin, en particulier aux juges des cinq directions, afin d'« échanger les noms et troquer les corps » 貿名易形 avec le bénéficiaire. La *dramatis personae* de la rédemption serait incomplète sans la mention de ces boucs émissaires. Aussi appelés « figurines de remplacement » 代形, ils prenaient la place d'une personne, vivante ou décédée, qui était passible d'inquisition, de conscription ou de punition. Le remplacement reposait sur le transfert coercitif du moi entaché du suppliant à un corps de substitution chargé de la rétribution et subissant le sort mal engagé du suppliant – l'inverse d'une usurpation d'identité. Le prêtre prenait soin de s'assurer que la permutation était enregistrée et promulguée dans les Grands livres du destin de toutes les directions de l'espace. Le rituel d'expédition du corps de substitution peut se décrire comme la mise en scène d'une métaphore, un « sacrifice de libération » performatif[50].

Le principe du sacrifice vicariant est bien connu de ceux qui étudient les religions du bassin méditerranéen, depuis l'expulsion hébraïque de boucs émissaires jusqu'au rite grec *pharmakos* de bannissement de pollution ou d'expiation de culpabilité par son transfert à un substitut[51]. En Chine, l'utilisation d'effigies funéraires 俑 à la place de victimes sacrificielles constitue un exemple ancien de substitution mortuaire. On retrouvait la notion de « châtiment vicariant » 代人受刑 dans le domaine juridique, bien que son application fût controversée[52]. Les obligations de corvée et de conscription militaire pouvaient de même être déléguées à un serviteur ou un esclave. Le *Laozi* emploie le terme « chien de paille » 芻狗 pour désigner une effigie. Aujourd'hui encore, les rituels chinois de guérison psychosomatique et de purification ont recours à l'expulsion de corps de substitution[53].

Les corps de substitution trouvés dans des tombes Han et Jin étaient des figurines de métal ou de bois. Les textes de pacification de tombe de la même période mentionnent fréquemment le fait que des effigies de plomb 鉛人 préservaient les défunts des châtiments et les affranchissaient des liens de la mort[54]. Un texte dans une tombe des Han orientaux suggérait plus avant qu'une figurine pût aussi prendre sur elle les devoirs statutaires de l'occupant de la tombe en matière de corvée et d'impôts dans l'autre monde ; un autre texte proposait que l'esclave de substitution se rendît utile dans la tombe pour la cuisine et les tâches ménagères[55]. La figurine, que montre la planche 1, est peinte sur une tablette en bois de pin datée du 6 décembre 340 de notre ère. Le personnage, en station verticale et dont la ceinture arbore le nom « Effigie de pin » 松人, est entouré par une prière qui continue au verso, faisant appel à l'émissaire du Monarque céleste 天帝使者, une divinité exorciste officiant lors des funérailles[56]. La prière indique à Effigie de pin de prendre la place du défunt Wang Luozi 王洛子, en association avec « Effigie de cyprès » 柏人, qui prend la place des membres survivants de la famille. Nous apprenons que Wang était décédé des suites d'une conjonction astrologique ou d'une exposition à des miasmes. On s'attendait à ce qu'après sa mort, il fût l'objet de poursuites démoniaques. Effigie de pin devait prendre sur elle la totalité des charges de l'accusation et des châtiments de Wang. Si les membres survivants de la famille devenaient impliqués dans les procédures de l'autre monde, alors Effigie de cyprès assumerait toutes *leurs* épreuves. Un exorcisme dans les cinq directions détournait toutes les poursuites possibles intentées de tous côtés par des démons revenants. La prière se termine par un appel à délivrer de tout mal les membres vivants de la famille[57].

Grâce aux sables secs du Gansu, cette mince tablette de pin a survécu 1 680 ans en parfaite condition. L'*Almanach de requêtes de Maître Pin rouge* recommande l'étain 錫 comme matériau de choix pour fabriquer des corps de substitution : un requérant envoya cinq effigies d'étain 錫人五身 se présenter aux Cinq directions au nom du bénéficiaire, afin de prendre sa place et son nom[58]. L'usage ancien ne faisait pas de distinction nette entre le plomb, l'étain et leur alliage. Peut-être ces substances argentées étaient-elles toutes considérées comme étant des répliques convenables de l'argent métal pour accompagner les morts dans la tombe. La feuille d'étain 錫箔, utilisée pour fabriquer la monnaie sacrificielle, était un autre substitut acceptable[59]. La liste d'offrandes de gages qui accompagnait une « Requête de l'Effigie d'argent » 銀人 suggère que ces effigies étaient en feuille d'argent 銀箔. La « Requête de l'effigie d'argent comme corps de substitution pour une maladie chronique et mortelle » 病死不絕銀人代形章 stipule : « Le nombre d'effigies en feuille d'argent 銀箔人 correspond au nombre de personnes dans la famille, une figurine par personne. Si l'argent est indisponible, utiliser l'étain, ou à défaut quatre-vingt-dix-neuf pièces de monnaie. Après la présentation de la requête, les jeter dans l'eau[60]. »

Pour la rançon de la destinée des vivants, on ne regardait pas à la dépense. La majorité des requêtes pour leur délivrance par des corps de substitution stipulaient des effigies en or : « Avec une effigie d'or 金人一軀, nous faisons appel au Boisseau du Nord pour sauver la vie [du bénéficiaire] et éradiquer l'épreuve de la mort[61]. » L'exemple suivant s'intitule « Requête de l'effigie d'or et de pourpre pour la détresse sévère et les maladies chroniques » 久病大厄金紫代形章[62]. Or et pourpre évoquaient un statut supérieur, comme dans le titre honorifique « Seigneur du sceau d'or et du ruban pourpre ». Ici, l'or renvoyait à la substance de l'effigie, et la pourpre à une longueur de soie en fil pourpre, matériau noble digne du gage d'un prince (voir « La scène et l'offrande » ci-après). Quarante pieds de ce tissu accompagnaient le rituel[63]. L'Invitation des officiers qui suit explique que la délivrance thérapeutique s'opérait par le transfert des identités civiles et physiques du patient vers son substitut :

> Au nom d'Untel, j'invite les seigneurs impériaux des Trente-deux cieux 三十二天帝君, les Contrôleurs de longévité 長生司馬[64], les Seigneurs primordiaux de Nanchang sauvant par effigie 代形度命南昌元君 et les émissaires du Surintendant de la vie 監生使者[65], trente-deux personnes chacun, à monter leurs dragons volants et leurs chars emplumés. Que les seigneurs des Trente-deux cieux descendent chacun avec neuf mille milliards de fantassins et de cavaliers. Offrant l'effigie d'or d'Untel 某金人 avec de la soie en fil pourpre 紫紋, je présente mes hommages aux départements du palais des régulateurs des mansions mesurant le cours des astres 曆星檢宿宮曹 dans les Trente-deux cieux : puissent-ils substituer les noms et échanger les corps 貿名易形 ! [...] Substituez le nom personnel d'Untel, échangez son corps et inscrivez son nom au Registre de vie dans le Calendrier de jade 玉曆之中[66].

S'ensuivait une litanie des dieux de l'horoscope et de la destinée du suppliant dans les constellations des Vingt-huit mansions, du Boisseau du Nord et des Trois terrasses 三台, ainsi que ceux des quatre saisons et des Cinq agents. Une série finale d'invocations appliquait le changement d'identité aux registres des quatre directions cardinales et du centre.

La scène et l'offrande

Durant la liturgie, ces invocations dans les cinq directions étaient prononcées devant les autels des Empereurs vert, rouge, blanc et noir situés aux quatre côtés de l'aire rituelle, et devant l'autel central de l'Empereur jaune. Pour nous représenter la scène, nous nous tournons vers la *Table d'almanach pour les offrandes de requête à l'Étoile primordiale*. Ce manuel contient un calendrier pour déterminer l'horoscope d'un individu, un protocole liturgique pour exécuter le rituel et un diagramme des préparatifs de l'autel pour le service (voir fig. 3). Cette aire rituelle, richement dotée et ressemblant à un mandala, était loin de la simplicité et du dépouillement de l'oratoire domestique[67].

L'espace rituel était installé dans une cour intérieure purifiée, avec quatre portails directionnels : le Portail du ciel 天門 (Nord-Ouest), la Porte terrestre 地戶 (Sud-Est), le Portail des démons 鬼門 (Nord-Est) et le Portail des hommes 人門 (Sud-Ouest). Au-dessus de chacun d'eux était fixé un « talisman des quatre portails ». Des encensoirs étaient placés sur les quatre côtés et au centre de l'aire de l'autel. De chaque côté, des lampes étaient suspendues, ainsi que des bannières de la couleur correspondant à la direction[68]. Huit des douze autels externes avaient des emplacements pour des lampes votives représentant les Vingt-huit mansions. À côté de l'autel central de l'Empereur jaune se trouvait la table du maître taoïste. Devant elle étaient placés trois autels supplémentaires : le pupitre pour rédiger les requêtes 章草 au milieu avec, d'un côté et de l'autre, les autels aux sept étoiles du Boisseau et aux Trois terrasses, représentant les deux principales constellations du destin dans Ursa Major. À l'ouest de l'aire rituelle principale, trois autels latéraux étaient dédiés aux ancêtres, au dieu du fourneau et aux dieux domestiques du sol et des céréales.

Les offrandes de gages étaient disposées devant l'autel central : exposer la rançon était essentiel à la transaction rédemptrice. Ce qui suit est la liste des offrandes de gages destinés à « pacifier l'autel » 鎮壇 du rituel de requête à l'Étoile primordiale :

1. Mille deux cents pièces de monnaie comme argent de gage 信錢
2. Douze boisseaux de riz blanchi 白米
3. Quarante pieds de soie brute blanche 白素
4. Cent vingt jetons de calcul 算子
5. Un demi-gallon (1,2 *dou* 斗) d'huile végétale 清油
6. Cent vingt pieds de fil de soie vert 青絲線
7. Une effigie en or 金人
8. Une paire d'anneaux en or 金環 [comme gages de bonne foi 劵]
9. Un couteau à livre 書刀
10. Cent feuilles de papier 紙
11. Deux pinceaux 筆
12. Un bâton d'encre 墨
13. Une natte immaculée 淨席
14. Un taël de cinabre 朱 [pour fabriquer les pilules et l'encre vermillon]
15. Une livre d'encens 香
16. Un bracelet en argent 銀條脫 [autre gage de bonne foi][69]

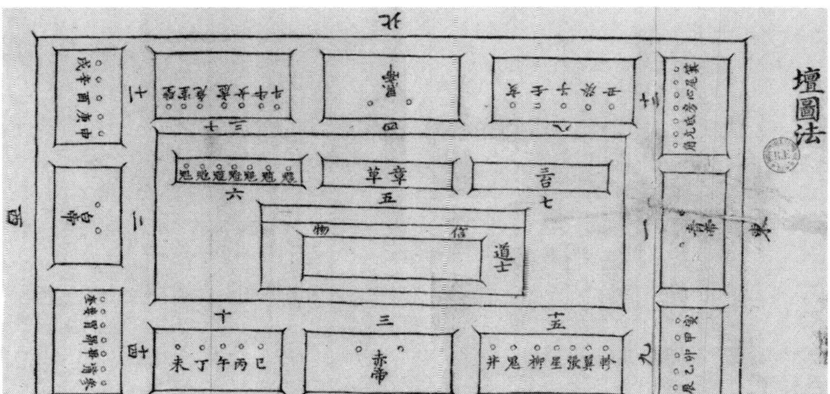

Fig. 3. Plan de l'aire rituelle pour le culte à l'étoile présidant à la destinée d'un individu. *Yuanchen zhangjiao licheng li*. A.1a-b. *Daozang*, édition des Ming de 1598. Reproduit avec l'autorisation de la Bibliothèque nationale de France.

L'item n° 6 de la liste d'offrandes servait de paiement de gage dans les ordinations et pour enfiler des perles ou des pièces de monnaie. Ce fil de soie vert était aussi utilisé pour ficeler les rouleaux de requêtes avant de les sceller pour envoi. La « Requête pour extirper la destinée avec du fil de soie vert » 青絲拔命章 illustre plus avant les intentions sacrificielles de plusieurs autres objets de la liste :

> Dernièrement, Untel est souffrant du fait de la Progression annuelle de cette année, *et cetera*. Aujourd'hui il présente révérencieusement quarante pieds de soie brute [item n° 3] comme gage rituel pour promouvoir sa destinée et traverser ce point critique ; douze boisseaux de riz de la destinée 命米 [item n° 2] pour accroître sa réserve, rallonger son compte de vie, ajouter au grenier et amasser des *hu* 斛 et des *dou* 鬥 (mesures de riz) ; mille deux cents pièces de monnaie [item n° 1] en gage de sa dévotion loyale, pour réguler les trois cent soixante souffles vitaux engendrés au fil des jours[70] et pour stabiliser les palais [des organes internes] ; des pinceaux, de l'encre, du papier et des jetons de calcul [items n°s 4 et 10-12] pour noter une entrée parmi les noms des vivants[71] ; cinq effigies en étain [item n° 7] pour demander qu'elles se présentent au nom de l'intéressé auprès des Cinq directions pour prendre sa place et échanger son nom ; de l'encens, de l'huile, des lampes et des bougies [items n°s 5 et 15] pour diffuser leur lumière continuellement. Il utilise les gages d'argent et de riz pour faire montre de sa sincérité loyale et racheter sa destinée 拔贖生命[72].

Le coût des offrandes normatives pour ce rituel de requête à l'Étoile primordiale représentait une dépense considérable. « La fortune d'un homme lui sert de rançon », dit Salomon, car donner sa fortune aux pauvres est la voie royale vers le Ciel[73]. Dans la Chine bouddhique et taoïste aussi, les libéralités caritatives étaient la grande source de mérite. Mais comment ceux qui étaient eux-mêmes dans l'indigence se procuraient-ils la rançon de leur destinée ? Puisque les offrandes étaient conçues comme des gages de sincérité, une question foncièrement personnelle, les emprunter à autrui n'était pas admis[74]. Heureusement, la largesse sacrificielle était définie comme relative et se mesurait au rang du suppliant et à ses moyens :

> En outre, dans le cas de requêtes sans gages normatifs[75], les gens aisés les accroissent, tandis que les pauvres les diminuent. Quand des familles prospères et de haut rang espèrent gagner du mérite mais sont parcimonieuses avec leur richesse et produisent des gages dignes d'indigents, alors

aucun bénéfice ne leur reviendra. Le *Code* déclare : « Quand des démunis ou nécessiteux demandent une Offrande de requête, le maître fournira les gages rituels à leur place. » Les anciennes requêtes 舊章 avaient chacune leur usage spécifique, mais il en existait trois grandes catégories : celles pour l'empereur, celles pour les seigneurs et les princes, et celles pour les gens du peuple. Leur classement n'était pas le même et les inventaires des objets [sacrificiels] différaient. Ceux-ci ne doivent pas être confondus, ni traités sans discernement[76].

Selon l'ancienne liturgie des *Mille deux cents officiers* et les Trois cents grandes requêtes, on distinguait trois degrés dans la hiérarchie des requêtes, celles qualifiées d'« éminentes » 疋數 pour les empereurs, de « supérieures » 丈數 pour les seigneurs et les princes, et de « populaires » 民數 pour les gens du peuple. Les distinctions entre les offrandes de gages correspondantes étaient qualitatives (couleur de la soie, métal des pièces de monnaie) et quantitatives (quantités de riz, d'huile, d'encens)[77]. L'*Almanach de requêtes de Maître Pin rouge* prononce une injonction sévère concernant la destination finale des offrandes, soulignant combien le détournement était un souci récurrent :

> Le *Code* déclare : Les biens offerts comme gages de requête doivent être donnés aux nécessiteux[78]. Il importe que les actions caritatives soient accomplies en secret. Il n'est pas permis au maître d'utiliser l'intégralité [des biens offerts en gage], ni d'en prendre plus de trois dixièmes comme honoraires[79]. Le code du Ciel est sévère ! Les contrevenants s'exposent au châtiment des Trois officiers, les épreuves affectant neuf générations d'ancêtres qui se verront relégués comme démons à jamais. Peut-on être oublieux de cela ? Ainsi la règle est donnée dans les moindres détails. Puissent les pratiquants en connaître les dispositions[80].

Le cadre rituel pour présenter la requête était un rite d'audience 朝禮 calqué sur le modèle des cérémonials relatifs aux visites rendues à une cour féodale[81]. Après la purification, le prêtre entrait dans l'aire de l'autel en prononçant des incantations adressées aux quatre directions. Venait ensuite le rite initial d'Activation de l'encensoir 發爐. La fumée qui s'élevait présageait le succès ou l'échec de la requête. Dans l'Extériorisation des officiers 出官, un exercice de visualisation, le prêtre invoquait son panthéon intérieur personnel. Puis il convoquait les Officiers du mérite 功曹, des messagers et des clercs pour expédier la requête à la cour céleste (voir fig. 4).

Avant de les envoyer, il lisait une fois la prière de requête à haute voix, puis dirigeait le cachetage rituel du document. Sur l'enveloppe étaient inscrits les mots « respectueusement soumis au Trône de jade du Portail d'or de la spontanéité du vide » 虛無自然金闕玉陛下, l'adresse de la cour du Saint des derniers jours 後聖 du Shangqing, Li Hongyuan 李弘元[82]. La requête était alors prête à être acheminée au Ciel. L'audience au Ciel était exécutée par l'œil intérieur du prêtre : prosterné devant l'autel, il visualisait un flot d'énergie *qi* rouge jaillissant depuis son cœur vers le haut. L'écliptique du soleil 黃道 s'offrait à la vue[83]. La traversant, il apercevait le Portail du ciel. S'étant assuré préalablement des heures d'ouverture, il était reçu et rendait hommage au Maître céleste Zhang Daoling. Un immortel apparaissait pour recueillir le mémorial de requête. Le prêtre était alors conduit en présence du Très Haut, qui parcourait le texte et y apposait la validation « Trône de jade de la Grande pureté » 太清玉陛下. De retour devant l'autel, le prêtre se lève et annonce « Je me permets de rapporter… », avant de conclure le rituel par une série de rites qui reproduisaient symétriquement les étapes initiales : le retour des Officiers, le congédiement et la récompense, la fermeture de l'encensoir et la sortie de l'aire de l'autel[84].

4a

4b

Fig. 4a. Escortes portant les bannières du Céleste vénérable rédempteur des Neuf ténèbres et du Sauveur du Ciel Zhuling. Fig. 4b. Messagers acheminant des requêtes au Ciel. *Wushang huanglu dazhai licheng yi*, 39.16b-17a. *Daozang*, édition des Ming de 1598. Reproduit avec l'autorisation de la Bibliothèque nationale de France.

Chapitre 4

Un dessein rédempteur

Nombre des préoccupations qui occasionnaient les prières de requête dans la Chine médiévale figuraient déjà parmi les interrogations inscrites sur les os oraculaires de la période tardive des Shang : inondations, sécheresses, guerres, maladies, rêves, tabous, accouchements, moissons, sauterelles, vers à soie, communications avec les esprits et les démons. Le *Règlement de la Métropole sombre* répond à la question « Pourquoi prions-nous ? » par son catalogue de rétributions subies pour des actions commises : accidents et infortune soudaine, infécondité, emprisonnement, pauvreté, épreuves, maladie, épidémie, mort prématurée, déluge et incendie, conflit armé, banditisme, calamités agricoles et séricicoles, disette, blocage d'avancement. C'étaient là les adversités pour lesquelles les prières de requête du Maître céleste cherchaient la délivrance[1]. Nous en classons les intentions sous cinq rubriques.

Guérison

Pour les adeptes des écoles taoïstes du Maître céleste et du Shangqing, la maladie était une manifestation primordiale du mal, que ce soit comme rétribution du péché ou brèche dans la séparation entre les royaumes des vivants et des morts[2]. La phrase « hommes et démons se mêlèrent dans la promiscuité et un mal spectral se répandit à travers le pays » (voir l'introduction de la Première partie) faisait référence à la propagation des miasmes de maladie dans les temps de dépravation et de décadence. Pour y remédier, les taoïstes médiévaux prescrivaient le remède de la confession et de la pénitence[3]. Selon le *Règlement de la Métropole sombre*, la meilleure prophylaxie était le « remède de sagesse » 慧藥, c'est-à-dire l'obéissance aux Préceptes de sagesse (voir « Les Dix préceptes » au chapitre 6 et la « Leçon 5 » au chapitre 7) qui promettaient la santé en récompense d'attitudes et de comportements moraux. Les « Cent préceptes médicinaux » 百藥律 étaient une litanie de bonnes actions dont chacune comptait pour un remède, comme l'illustrent les extraits suivants :

[1] Vénérer le Ciel et honorer la Terre vaut pour un remède	尊天敬地爲一藥
[5] Aimer la vie et détester tuer vaut pour un remède	好生惡殺爲一藥
[9] Ne pas brûler les forêts vaut pour un remède	不燒山林爲一藥
[21] Pratiquer la libéralité sans rien attendre en retour vaut pour un remède	施不望報爲一藥
[27] Souhaiter le bien pour autrui vaut pour un remède	爲人願福爲一藥
[41] Parler avec modestie vaut pour un remède	言語謙遜爲一藥
[43] Ne devoir aucune dette ancienne[4] vaut pour un remède	不負宿債爲一藥
[62] Faire l'aumône selon ses moyens vaut pour un remède	因富布施爲一藥
[64] Soutenir les personnes âgées vaut pour un remède	扶接老弱爲一藥
[100] Faire usage de la parole pour accomplir le bien vaut pour un remède	以言爲善爲一藥[5].

Vu sous ce jour, le recours à la médecine ou à la thérapie rituelle était non seulement vain, mais peccamineux, car, comme l'affirme l'introduction aux Cent préceptes médicinaux, « la vertu est votre médecin, la conduite votre remède. Une personne qui ne cultive pas sa conduite morale mais fait largement usage de traitements médicaux, qui accumule les péchés mais recourt grandement aux requêtes sans changer sa conduite, ne fait qu'aggraver son état de péché ».

Inversement, les « Cent préceptes morbides » 百病律 assimilaient les actions mauvaises à des maladies, avertissant que, en la matière, la prophylaxie était plus aisée que la thérapie curative :

> Être sauvé des calamités et délivré de la détresse est moins simple que la prévention. Guérir les maladies et soigner les maux est moins efficace que la bonne conduite [...]. Quant au méchant, même s'il désire se sauver par des requêtes et des offrandes, des prières et des remèdes, des talismans et des registres, tant qu'il n'est pas disposé à changer son cœur, ses péchés ne peuvent pas être vaincus. Il subit des diminutions de son compte de vie et son corps est envahi par la maladie [...]. Méditez sans faillir sur les péchés qui ont provoqué votre maladie [...]. C'est seulement quand vous aurez été entièrement absous de tous vos péchés et de tout le mal commis que la maladie sera éradiquée.

Certaines « maladies » des préceptes morbides étaient de simples antithèses de « remèdes » correspondants, par exemple la maladie [2] de ne pas prendre soin des personnes âgées, la maladie [79] de générosité dans l'espérance d'un retour et celle [80] de détester la vie et prendre plaisir à tuer. D'autres maladies étaient définies indépendamment :

[1] L'inconstance du fait de joie et de colère est une maladie	喜怒無常是一病
[10] Tenir un double langage et n'être pas digne de confiance est une maladie	兩舌無信是一病
[22] Chercher des nids et en casser les œufs est une maladie	探巢破卵是一病
[26] Pousser autrui à abandonner son épouse est une maladie	教人去婦是一病
[29] Prendre plaisir à faire observer les fautes d'autrui est une maladie	喜說人過是一病
[49] Utiliser la sorcellerie pour nuire à autrui est une maladie	蠱道厭人是一病
[65] Dénigrer les mérites d'autrui est une maladie	敗人成功是一病
[72] Mépriser beaucoup et aimer peu est une maladie	多憎少愛是一病
[92] Se moquer des aveugles, des sourds et des simples d'esprit est une maladie	笑盲聾暗是一病
[100] S'emparer des biens d'autrui est une maladie	強奪人物是一病[6].

Dans l'*Almanach de requêtes de Maître Pin rouge*, la maladie provient fréquemment de l'interface entre les vivants et les morts. Lors des assemblées rituelles, les bénéficiaires de ce type de prières sont tant des individus que leur groupe de parenté. Les troubles mentaux – pensées, rêves confus, cauchemars, divagations – apparaissent en conjonction avec les affections physiques. Les rêves, les visions et les présages étaient scrutés en tant qu'irruptions du monde invisible. On remarque l'attention particulière prêtée à l'évolution de la maladie caractérisée comme étant, par exemple, au stade initial, continue, prolongée, de longue durée ou chronique. De telles distinctions impliquent des fautes morales comme cause de l'absence de rétablissement parmi d'autres considérations. L'*Almanach de requêtes de Maître Pin rouge* associe les maladies incurables à d'obscurs litiges dans l'au-delà et à la transmission de culpabilité ancestrale, résultant de brèches ouvertes entre les mondes des vivants et des morts. Pour ces raisons, le mouvement du Maître céleste, à ses débuts, rejetait autant le culte ancestral qu'il dénigrait la médecine, le premier parce qu'il favorisait la perméabilité entre les deux mondes, la seconde comme n'étant pas conforme à la morale[7].

Même si diagnostic et divination avaient leur place dans la guérison rituelle et que les suppliants y avaient recours, de nombreuses requêtes suggèrent que la pratique de la divination était sommaire et ne pouvait donner au mieux que des résultats incertains. Couvrant un large éventail de causes possibles par des formules génériques de contrition, officiants et patients admettaient leur incapacité à connaître l'origine de la maladie et sa raison d'être. En pratique, le requérant procédait par tâtonnements ordonnés. Le passage suivant fournit le catalogue des requêtes et des stratégies de guérison :

> Le *Code des Grands véritables* énonce : Dans tous les cas de maladie, présenter d'abord une requête de plainte 首狀. À défaut de rétablissement, présenter une requête pour acquittement 解考[8]. Toujours à défaut de rétablissement, présenter une requête pour l'acquittement de l'inculpation des ancêtres défunts 解先亡罪謫. À défaut de rétablissement, présenter une requête de transfert[9]. En cas d'aggravation, présenter une requête pour l'élimination ou l'incarcération des démons miasmatiques. En cas d'échec, présenter une requête majeure pour la délivrance du malheur et du mal.

> À défaut d'amélioration, présenter une requête pour la relaxe des inculpations des Cinq tombes 五墓謫. À défaut d'amélioration, présenter une requête pour endurer l'affaiblissement et passer au travers des calamités. À défaut de rétablissement, présenter une requête pour faire revenir les âmes *hun* et rappeler les âmes *po*[10]. À défaut de rétablissement, présenter une requête pour l'apaisement des tombes et la dispersion des nuisances causées aux Cinq sols[11]. À défaut de rétablissement, présenter une requête pour pacifier le foyer, soumettre les esprits et éliminer les démons. À défaut de rétablissement, présenter une requête pour la levée des inculpations majeures en tous lieux 分解中外大考[12].

Le texte se poursuit en distinguant les requêtes pour les états aigus 危急, chroniques 進退 ou critiques 大危篤. Solliciter les dieux indûment avec une requête urgente était punissable de vingt jours de balayage des routes ou de réparation des ponts. Associant différentes maladies aux divinités responsables, la « Requête pour guérir les maladies » 疾病醫治章 offre un aperçu du panthéon guérisseur :

> Nous rendons compte respectueusement, *et cetera*. Ces derniers temps, [le patient] a contracté une maladie mettant ses jours en danger. Il a approché votre serviteur [le prêtre] pour demander la présentation d'une requête au Département des Trois cieux 三天曹 dans l'espoir de rachat. Depuis dix jours, il souffre d'accès de froid et de chaud tandis que sa circulation cutanée est déréglée. Soit il a attrapé cette maladie du fait d'avoir été exposé au vent ou de s'être couché dans le froid, ou bien il est puni par les Cinq supplices 五刑 et les Trois calamités 三災[13]. Nous ne le savons pas, plongés que nous sommes dans l'ignorance, et demandons que le cas soit entendu et fasse l'objet d'une investigation [...]. Respectueusement nous faisons appel aux seigneurs Céleste médecin 天醫 et Grand médecin 太醫 qui occupent des places d'honneur au Bureau du ciel, avec leurs douze officiers, pour qu'ils descendent dans son corps au siège de l'affection et administrent un traitement. Nous envoyons notre demande aux quinze Officiers du mérite guérisseurs 治病功曹 en son nom[14]. Nous faisons monter au Bureau du ciel notre demande d'expurger les causes [de la maladie] découlant des fautes et transgressions commises dans ses existences antérieures et en cette vie, et de rétablir ses Cinq viscères 五臟, ses quatre membres et ses cent artères [...]. Nous prions en outre chacun des seigneurs Sauveurs 度命君, Prolongateurs de vie 益算君 et des Acquittements 解考君, respectivement, [...] de soumettre

les démons des esprits hétérodoxes, souffles vieux et poisons pestilentiels, et de permettre au patient de se rétablir, *et cetera*[15].

Protection du foyer

Parmi les préoccupations du foyer, la protection des épouses et des jeunes enfants, spécialement la menée à bon terme de la grossesse, de l'accouchement et la traversée de la petite enfance, figuraient depuis l'Antiquité comme objet constant de rituels de protection et de divination. Ces thèmes occupent aussi une place importante dans la littérature médicale et dans les almanachs de requête médiévaux[16]. Le contexte rituel des requêtes transparaît dans le passage suivant d'un livre sacré dédié à la protection de l'enfant à naître et à la sauvegarde des influences maléfiques de la mère et de l'enfant, datant probablement des Tang :

> Du début de la grossesse jusqu'à la plénitude de dix mois [suivant le calendrier lunaire], il est juste d'accomplir des œuvres méritoires avant l'échéance, de faire célébrer des rituels, de copier ce livre et de faire des offrandes avec une dévotion pleine et entière. Quand arrive le mois de la naissance, inviter trois, cinq, sept ou dix maîtres taoïstes, soit dans le temple, soit au foyer, suspendre les bannières et attacher les dais, allumer les lampes en continu, brûler de l'encens et faire ses dévotions. Réciter en psalmodiant le *Livre merveilleux des dieux du cycle sexagésimal pour protéger le fœtus et préserver la vie* sept fois sept fois, ou cent fois, ou jusqu'à mille ou dix mille fois[17].

La présentation d'une « Requête pour protéger le fœtus » 保胎章, dans laquelle les futurs parents « Untel et son épouse Unetelle » priaient les gardiens des enfants à naître et des parturientes pour obtenir leur protection contre les attaques démoniaques, était l'un des rituels à exécuter avant la naissance :

> Nous invitons respectueusement deux seigneurs Pacificateurs du fœtus 安胎君, deux seigneurs Protecteurs du fœtus 護胎君, deux seigneurs Soutenant les fragiles à travers les calamités 扶衰度厄君[18] et deux seigneurs de Dix mille bénédictions pour résoudre les calamités 萬福

> 解厄君[19], avec mille deux cents officiers et généraux, à descendre au nom de l'épouse Unetelle pour sauvegarder sa vie et sa grossesse et veiller à un accouchement aisé. Nous invitons aussi deux dames Saintes mères protectrices du fœtus 保胎聖母君 avec mille deux cents officiers et généraux à garder et protéger le Champ de cinabre médian des Trois originels 三元丹田之中[20] de l'épouse Unetelle, à repousser les essences miasmatiques 邪精, les gobelins 魍魎 et les demons voleurs 鬼賊 et à protéger et sustenter le nouveau-né. Puissent-ils faire que la personne de l'épouse Unetelle soit sauve et que lui soient épargnées les complications, que sa grossesse soit protégée et que les Six Jia 六甲 [du terme] soient stabilisés, afin qu'à la plénitude de dix mois la mère et l'enfant puissent se contempler. Pour que la tranquillité soit accordée à tous deux, nous implorons la puissante protection des grands saints du Portail du ciel 天門大聖. Puisse le corps de la mère Unetelle être apaisé et que nulle contrariété ne survienne[21].

Ayant atteint son terme, l'épouse anxieuse présente une « Requête pour hâter l'enfantement » 催生章 au panthéon des sages-femmes et obstétriciens divins. Le titre *jun* 君, signifiant « seigneur » ou « dame », renvoie probablement ici à des divinités en majorité féminines : la dame Porte des enfants du Portail du ciel 天門子戶君, la dame Qui dépêche la parturition 速生君, la dame des Nourrices 乳母君, la dame Guidant la parturition 導生君, le Céleste médecin secondant la parturition 天醫助生君 et la dame Hâtant l'enfantement 催生君. À ceux-ci, l'épouse Unetelle confie son accouchement imminent :

> Puisse la naissance se faire en douceur, se passer de toute complication et suivre un cours normal, chassant toutes les offenses de tabou faites aux [démons] tueurs de l'année, du mois et de l'heure, et aux [démons astraux] Tigre blanc 白虎 et Étang vivier 咸池[22]. Puissent les mille miasmes et les dix mille esprits être annihilés, puissent la mère et l'enfant être saufs, et que tout aille selon leurs vœux et les désirs de leurs cœurs et soit sans péripétie aucune[23].

Cet obstacle franchi, les parents n'étaient pas au bout de leurs tourments. Dans la « Requête pour la protection des nouveau-nés et des enfants » 保嬰童章[24], Untel se repent de ses fautes et plaide l'innocence de l'enfant, dont il est craint qu'il soit en proie aux influences miasmatiques de la Nourrice 乳母 et du Comte du fleuve 河伯[25]. La « Requête pour le salut et la radiance supérieure des nourrissons » 小兒上光度化章 ci-dessous était de nature prophylactique. Au moment de la présentation de cette requête, l'enfant n'était qu'un peu indisposé, mais, craignant une détérioration, les parents Untel faisaient appel aux seigneurs resplendissants des Cinq radiances 五光君 du ciel, de la terre, des étoiles et des Cinq agents des directions cardinales et du centre pour protéger la santé de l'enfant :

> Dernièrement, leur fils Untel a eu des pensées et des rêves confus. Nous craignons que ceux-ci soient de mauvais augure. Ses quatre membres sont faibles et nous sommes inquiets de ce qu'il pourrait avoir contracté une maladie grave [...]. Nous prions pour qu'il retrouve son regard clair et son contentement. Nous demandons à l'Officier du ciel de biffer son nom du registre de mort, de purifier ses souffles vieux, d'entrer son nom parmi ceux des vivants, de faire que ses Six entrailles soient en harmonie et ses Cinq viscères stabilisés. Puisse sa radiance connaître la plénitude de la longue vie, que tous les spectres soient entièrement bannis, que ses pensées et ses rêves soient vrais et justes, sa nourriture et sa boisson savoureuses, et qu'il soit gardé sain et sauf à jamais[26].

Les habitations faisaient aussi l'objet de préoccupations rituelles multiples. Leurs résidents étaient passibles de rétribution pour avoir offensé les esprits de la terre par des travaux de construction, des altérations faites aux bâtiments ou aux terrains, et pour d'autres violations de tabous domestiques. Des citations de tabous à observer datant du IIIe siècle avant notre ère et se rapportant aux demeures 室忌 et aux violations du sol 土忌 ont été exhumées en 1975 à Shuihudi 睡虎地[27]. La « Requête [au sein d'un rituel] d'Annonce de mérite en vue de la suppression des registres de mort du mont Tai » 絕泰山死籍言功章 de Maître Pin rouge attribue le malaise d'une maisonnée perturbée aux Contrôleurs du destin 司命 :

> Année après année, nous avons subi des revers, notre trajectoire de vie est fâcheuse et la demeure est perturbée. La destinée dépend des douze seigneurs Contrôleurs du destin 十二司命君 sous l'Empereur d'En Haut du Ciel auguste 皇天上帝[28]. Conformément à l'ancienne liturgie du Maître céleste, puissent nos noms être biffés du registre de mort du mont Tai et

effacés de la liste des peines capitales sur la Contremarque de droite 右契 aux jours fastes des Trois assemblées[29].

Le requérant sollicite ensuite un transfert d'enregistrement au Palais de la longue vie 長生宮 et demande « que la détresse soit épargnée aux proches qui nous ont précédés dans la mort et que ces derniers reçoivent le mérite suprême [d'accéder au Palais des bienheureux] où nourriture et vêtement ne sauraient manquer ». La « Requête pour se concilier le sol » 謝土章 de Maître Pin rouge prie pour les habitants d'une résidence néfaste, invitant les cinq seigneurs de la Conciliation du sol 謝土君, du Contrôle de la terre 制地君, de l'Absolution du sol 解土君, de la Pacification du sol 安土君 et de la Stabilisation du foyer 定宅君, respectivement, à descendre et chasser l'ensemble des esprits des Cinq sols dans les Cinq directions[30]. Un recensement des causes possibles du dérangement fait suite, avec une litanie des dieux du sol potentiellement offensés et une énumération des tabous calendaires régissant les travaux de construction :

> Depuis que cette résidence a été construite, des excavations anciennes et nouvelles, des déplacements de cloisons et des remplacements de piliers, l'érection de bâtiments, des terrassements, de nouveaux ajouts, nivellements et comblements ainsi que l'altération des voies d'accès ont violé des interdits et tabous issus des [esprits des] Six Jia 六甲禁忌 [...] : Sols blanc, noir et jaune[31] ; l'empereur du sol, le roi du sol ; le ministre du sol, les généraux du Directoire du sol 土府, les dieux du sol, le seigneur marquis du sous-sol de deux mille boisseaux 土下君侯二千石[32] ; les sols yin et yang, les quatre saisons, les Cinq agents et le souverain suprême du centre ; les princes divins des Cinq sols, soit ceux de devant et derrière la demeure, à gauche et à droite de la demeure et le magistrat de la cour au centre [...], l'adjudant du portail 門丞 et le commandant de la porte 戶尉[33], les esprits du puits et du fourneau ; le dragon vert et le tigre blanc, l'oiseau vermillon et le guerrier sombre, le serpent volant 螣蛇 et le dragon tapi 伏龍, la Grande année, le Grand yin 太陰, le Grand yang 太陽, les Contrôleurs du destin, et les tabous relatifs aux douze divisions du jour 十二時辰[34].

À ce point, la conciliation du sol est engagée par une litanie directionnelle et des suppliques de pardon invoquant les secteurs des Neuf palais 九宮, soit les huit palais des directions cardinales et intercardinales, portant les noms des Huit trigrammes 八卦[35], et le palais du centre :

> Pour les dieux du sol de l'Est qui ont été offensés, [nous implorons] relaxe et pardon 解謝 du Palais Zhen 震宮 (Est), pour les dieux du sol du Sud qui ont été offensés, relaxe et pardon du Palais Li 離宮 (Sud), pour les dieux du sol de l'Ouest qui ont été offensés, relaxe et pardon du Palais Dui 兌宮 (Ouest), pour les dieux du sol du Nord qui ont été offensés, relaxe et pardon du Palais Kan 坎宮 (Nord), et pour les dieux du sol du centre qui ont été offensés, relaxe et pardon des palais Qian 乾 (Nord-Ouest), Kun 坤 (Sud-Ouest), Gen 艮 (Nord-Est), Xun 巽 (Sud-Est) et autres. Puissent-ils tous accorder leur pardon bienveillant, puissent les esprits mauvais et les souffles vieux de l'Est, de l'Ouest, du Nord et du Sud et leurs dommages maléfiques être expulsés sur-le-champ et la maisonnée d'Untel, jeunes comme vieux, connaître à jamais protection et bénédiction[36].

Agriculture et sériciculture

Découverte en 1993 à Zhoujiatai 周家臺 au Hubei, une prière inscrite sur lamelles de bambou dans les années 209 à 206 avant notre ère s'engageait à offrir un sacrifice au Divin laboureur 神農 en cas de récolte abondante[37]. Les requêtes pour la pluie et les moissons figurent parmi les plus anciennes prières enregistrées. Dans l'*Almanach de requêtes de Maître Pin rouge*, nous trouvons une solennelle « Requête pour [conjurer] la sécheresse » 天旱章 qui a les marques d'un document officiel de la période Tang. Au contraire de la plupart des requêtes qui identifiaient précisément la localité intéressée, celle-ci fait référence à la zone affectée en la nommant « le pays » 國境. Le prêtre endosse le rôle de suppliant, agissant vraisemblablement pour le compte d'un officiel. Aux faveurs reçues en tant que taoïste initié, il ajoute sa vocation d'être au service de l'État. L'expression « cette époque éclairée » 聖世 fait référence à la dynastie régnante.

> Humble et ignorant, [votre serviteur] Untel a eu l'heur de rencontrer la congrégation du Tao 道會 et le privilège d'être le témoin de cette

> époque éclairée. La causalité karmique l'a favorisé de pouvoir accéder aux grands rites. À l'abri du Très Haut, un maître l'a pris en pitié. Dénué de tout mérite, jour et nuit il s'inquiète – comme s'il marchait sur la glace ou au bord d'un ravin 如履冰谷[38] – de n'avoir aucun moyen de revaloir au Ciel et à la Terre leur bonté. Le jour de son ordination, votre serviteur jura d'embrasser fidèlement l'enseignement de son maître, de disséminer largement la Voie et la Vertu, de servir l'État et de protéger la vie, d'œuvrer au salut de tous et faire de l'aide à autrui sa priorité. Dernièrement, le ciel et la terre traversent une mauvaise passe, le yin et le yang se contrarient l'un l'autre et les quatre saisons sont déréglées. Le pays subit une grave sécheresse et les céréales ne sont pas récoltées. Nous voyons là un déferlement de troubles démoniaques. Le yang pur 純陽 en dessus, le yin condensé 凝陰 en dessous, les deux souffles n'interagissent plus et la pluie bienfaisante 玄澤 ne tombe pas. Vent sec et soleil de plomb éprouvent la population et brûlent semailles et récoltes. Voici qu'elle redoute le soleil comme le poisson dans l'ornière asséchée 涸魚[39].

Ceci est suivi par une réflexion philosophique sur les causes et les conséquences cosmiques et politiques de la sécheresse, et la nécessité de restaurer les Cinq agents. Sous la rhétorique officielle, on distingue sans doute aucun que l'orateur se situe dans la tradition liturgique du Maître céleste :

> Ne se risquant pas à ses propres conjectures, votre serviteur prend appui révérencieusement sur la liturgie du Maître céleste 天師科法. Puisse-t-il subir brûlure et ébouillantement pour ses fautes ! Respectueusement il soumet cette requête, frappant le sol de sa tête de crainte et d'appréhension, criminel qu'il est, méritant de mourir.

La partie injonctive des prières comme celle-ci était une litanie de divinités spécialisées invoquées pour résoudre la difficulté exposée dans la requête. Les « officiers » invités dans l'invocation ci-dessous correspondent, avec des variations mineures, à une rubrique du panthéon du Maître céleste dans les *Grades des requêtes et des officiers*. Leurs noms dérivent d'un registre correspondant dans le *Protocole des mille deux cents officiers*. Lü 呂 était le patronyme du Comte du Fleuve, les trente-six Empereurs de l'eau étaient ses fils, et les douze Filles des rivières ses filles, tous étant des divinités aquatiques chargées de la pluie, sous le commandement de la dame Ombre-Lumière[40] :

> Du Palais de Lingtai 靈臺宮, nous invitons respectueusement un seigneur Hanming 漢明君 avec mille deux cents officiers et généraux, y compris les officiers responsables en charge du Tonnerre céleste 主攝天雷 ; du Palais de Yuanming 元名宮, [nous invitons respectueusement] la dame Ombre-Lumière 小玄明君 avec cent vingt officiers et généraux, y compris les officiers responsables répondant au Comte du Fleuve 河伯, le jeune maître Lü 呂公子, les trente-six Empereurs de l'eau 水帝, les douze Filles des rivières 溪女, les Empereurs de l'eau des Neuf rivières 九江水帝, le Marquis du contrôle des crues 河平侯, avec des clercs assistants et les esprits de l'eau de la section médiane 中部水神 qui gonflent les nuages et provoquent les averses ; du Palais de Hetian 河天宮, [nous invitons respectueusement] un seigneur Beixuan des Neuf mers 九海北玄君 avec cent vingt officiers et généraux contrôlant l'envoi de vapeur d'eau et l'émission de vent et de tonnerre ; du Palais de Taishan 太山宮, les seigneurs des Neuf vallées de Sizhou 泗州九谷君 avec mille deux cents officiers et généraux chargés de soulever la vapeur d'eau[41].

L'invocation ci-dessus ayant ouvert les vannes, une autre requête était à disposition pour endiguer les dégâts potentiels : il s'agit de la « Requête pour faire cesser l'excès de pluie après avoir prié pour la pluie » 請雨得水過止雨章 dans laquelle la référence à « cour et peuple » 朝野 donne ici aussi à la prière un ton solennel ; les « vieux rites » 舊儀 renvoient à la liturgie de la communauté des Maîtres célestes de Hanzhong. Les divinités invitées relèvent du même panthéon de la pluie que celui donné dans les *Grades des requêtes et des officiers* :

> Parlant au nom du peuple en détresse, votre serviteur a respectueusement demandé que s'entrouvrent les nuages et que tombe la pluie. Votre vaste bienfaisance plut à verse de toute part et l'atmosphère yin est descendue tout alentour. Sur ce, la pluie ne cessa pas de tomber, abondamment et continuellement, jusqu'à ce que les cent rivières débordassent. Le labeur du peuple fut gâché, les champs inondés et les semis submergés. Cour

> et peuple éperdus ont prié votre serviteur de présenter respectueusement cette requête, conformément aux vieux rites. Nous communiquons humblement notre appel pour que les officiers des pluies et des sources 雨泉官 précédemment sollicités par votre serviteur retournent tous maintenant au Bureau du ciel, et que les officiers du Palais 中官 les inscrivent et prennent leurs dispositions en vue de leur récompense pour service méritoire. Nous demandons en outre qu'un Duc céleste seigneur Rectificateur atmosphérique 天公正氣君[42] avec cent vingt officiers et généraux, et Heshang 河上 avec mille deux cents Filles de jade 玉女, descendent tous ensemble[43]. Nous soumettons au Bureau du ciel notre demande que la pluie cesse et que le vent tourne. Puissent le Comte du vent 風伯 et le Maître de la pluie 雨師 se conformer aux quatre saisons et aux huit périodes 四時八節 [de l'année solaire] et ne pas provoquer d'erreur ni d'excès[44]. Rappelez les nuages et rameutez les brumes, que les Trois luminaires 三光 (soleil, lune et étoiles) rayonnent et fassent cesser la pluie en temps opportun. Que tous les officiers annoncent leur mérite et se présentent pour leurs récompenses[45].

Avec la « Requête pour empêcher les sauterelles et les rats de dévorer les semis » 卻蟲蝗鼠災食苗章 nous plongeons au plus profond des campagnes et des terres agricoles. Le texte est d'une tonalité plus rurale. Le commanditaire est une personne privée. Le panthéon spécialisé invoqué contre la vermine correspond à un autre sous-ensemble parmi les *Grades des requêtes et des officiers* :

> Ces dernières années, la culture des champs a été calamiteuse de toutes parts. Cette année, en tel lieu, les épis des champs ont été dévorés par une invasion fatale de sauterelles 災蝗 impossible à enrayer. Votre serviteur a été sollicité pour en implorer l'expulsion 禳辟. Se prosternant à terre, il soumet respectueusement cette requête. Au nom de la maisonnée Unetelle, nous demandons humblement au seigneur des Champs célestes 天田君 du Palais du portail nord 北門宮 avec cent vingt officiers et généraux[46] de se charger de la prévention des dommages aux cultures causés par les invasions de sauterelles, d'insectes et de souris, et d'ordonner que les dégradations dues aux insectes et aux souris soient entièrement éradiquées. Nous requérons en outre le seigneur des Champs célestes 天野君 du Palais du Bout de la Terre 地盡宮, avec cent vingt officiers et généraux, de descendre pour le bienfait du travail agricole et d'empêcher les cerfs, oiseaux,

> insectes et rats d'occasionner des nuisances[47]. Nous requérons en outre le seigneur de l'Origine yang des trois *qi* 三氣陽元君, avec cent vingt officiers et généraux, qui règne dans le Palais des nuages jaunes 黃雲宮, de contenir les fléaux d'oiseaux et de bêtes et de mettre hors d'état de nuire les esprits des céréales sur pied 穀稼[48]. Le Grand Tao souverain du vide 虛皇大道[49] commande les dieux du sol 土地 de la localité, les suzerains 孟長 des montagnes et forêts, les douze Filles des rivières 十二溪女 et les seigneurs du Sol et des Céréales du district 社稷邑君[50]. Ordonnez que les champs d'Untel procurent une moisson double et échappent à de nouveaux désastres[51] !

La « Requête pour contrôler les invasions de rats » 收鼠災章 fait appel au même panthéon pour contenir les dégradations causées par les rongeurs. Elle invite le Tigre blanc de Nanshan 南山白虎 avec ses généraux et ses troupes à « descendre en masse, se saisir des colonies de rats infestant les terres, les refouler en rase campagne où le grain ne manque pas et les tenir à l'extérieur des bornes »[52].

Un rituel impérial ouvrait chaque nouvelle saison de labour, associé à un sacrifice au Premier sériciculteur 先蠶. Puisque la production de soie représentait l'activité féminine par excellence, l'impératrice cueillait symboliquement quelques feuilles de mûrier pour les vers à soie impériaux à cette occasion[53]. Les lamelles de bambou de Zhoujiatai montrent des villageois présentant des requêtes au bénéfice des vers à soie vers 209-206 avant notre ère, comme ce fut le cas tout au long des périodes ancienne et médiévale en Chine[54]. Les vers à soie domestiqués étaient non seulement fragiles et sujets aux maladies, mais exposés à l'extermination méthodique inhérente au cycle de production de la soie : les précieux cocons filés par les larves de *bombyx mori* étaient obtenus en ébouillantant les animaux vivants avant que le processus de la mue n'endommageât les fibres de la soie[55]. Les bouddhistes chinois et indiens, perturbés par la mise à mort systématique des insectes, vénéraient le patriarche Aśvaghoṣa comme dieu des vers à soie[56]. Les taoïstes exécutaient des rituels et maniaient sceaux et talismans (fig. 5) pour obtenir la fertilité et la protection de la population des vers à soie, immanquablement en danger[57].

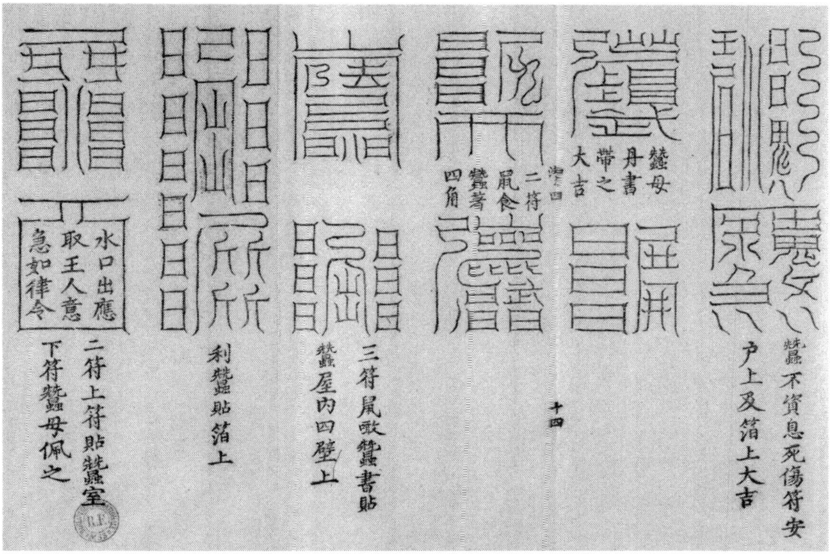

Fig. 5. « Talismans au bénéfice des vers à soie » 利蠶符, détail montrant des talismans à suspendre au-dessus de la porte, sur les murs dans la maison des vers à soie, aux claies des vers à soie et à la ceinture de la « mère des vers à soie ». *Taishang laojun hunyuan sanbu fu*, A.17b-18a. *Daozang*, édition des Ming de 1598. Reproduit avec l'autorisation de la Bibliothèque nationale de France.

Au Sichuan, patrie du mouvement du Maître céleste, le « ramasseur de vers à soie » Can Cong 蠶叢 était vénéré comme un ancêtre totémique, et des offrandes étaient faites à un panthéon complexe de déesses de la sériciculture dans des lieux saints dédiés[58]. L'*Almanach de requêtes* et les *Grades des requêtes et des officiers* incluent tous deux un panthéon séricicole du Maître céleste, avec des départements distincts présidant au sort des vers à soie, aux mûriers et à la culture des vers à soie[59]. Une « Requête pour la protection des vers à soie » 保蠶章 était prononcée dans le cadre d'un rituel de fertilité durant lequel le clan des vers à soie était adoré comme une famille divine prolifique. Le terme « maison des vers à soie » 蠶室 renvoyait à la pièce ou au bâtiment chauffé pour l'élevage des vers à soie, confié aux soins d'une « mère des vers à soie » 蠶母, et en leur temps aux établissements de sériciculture qui travaillaient pour les cours féodales de la Chine ancienne :

> Cela fait maintenant plusieurs années que la culture des vers à soie est improductive. Nous craignons qu'une offense ait été commise[60]. Par conséquent, ce mois, en un jour faste et à une heure propice, à l'intérieur de la résidence, nous demandons aux maisons des vers à soie de l'Empereur vert à l'Est, l'Empereur rouge au Sud, l'Empereur blanc à l'Ouest et l'Empereur noir au Nord, et de l'Empereur jaune au centre, au premier ancêtre, aux beaux-parents et aux descendants de la famille des vers à soie, aux maisons des vers à soie dans le Ciel en haut et en dessous de la Terre, à toutes les trente-six maisons des vers à soie, de mener une enquête. Jour et nuit, Untel se demande avec anxiété comment obtenir secours. Il ne peut que, de tout cœur, placer sa confiance dans le Grand Tao. Respectueusement, il offre ces gages de sa sincérité et sollicite votre serviteur pour soumettre cette requête en supplication.

Le commanditaire, et bénéficiaire, de ce rituel était manifestement le chef d'une maisonnée rurale, ou son éleveuse (« mère ») des vers à soie désignée, nonobstant le fait que le bénéficiaire déclaré était le clan étendu des vers à soie et leurs ancêtres. La production déclinante de l'élevage du commanditaire indique que la famille des vers à soie était en péril. D'où l'envoi de corps de substitution (voir « Corps de substitution » au chapitre 3) aux Cinq directions pour obtenir la délivrance :

> Nous invitons les beaux-pères de substitution, les belles-mères de substitution, les premiers ancêtres familiaux de substitution, les pères et mères de famille de substitution et les descendants familiaux de substitution des Cinq directions, ainsi que les guerriers de droite et de gauche des quatre directions. Nous demandons aux Seigneurs divins en haut de descendre et de stabiliser les jeunes filles et les jeunes mariées de l'élevage des vers à soie[61]. Que les vers à soie noirs soient comme des dragons, les vers à soie blancs comme des tigres, le son de leur rampement comme le vent, le son de leur dévorement comme la pluie, et puissent les sons retentir comme le tonnerre ! [...]. Puissent les papillons et larves [de *bombyx*] 蛾蠶 de la maisonnée d'Untel lui donner satisfaction cette année, qu'ils prolifèrent à foison et à jamais. Bannissez les maladies infectieuses et que les pertes dues aux insectes et aux rats soient entièrement effacées. Humblement nous

supplions qu'[Untel] puisse récolter dix mille boisseaux de cocons 繭 et obtenir mille livres de fil de soie[62].

La délivrance des morts

> Les vivants appartiennent au Ciel auguste 皇天 et les morts aux Sources jaunes 黄泉. Les vivants et les morts empruntent des chemins séparés 生死異路 ; Untel ne doit pas être dérangé en sa personne[63] !

Les rituels pour absoudre les défunts visaient aussi à prévenir le retour des morts contrariés parmi les vivants. Les vivants et les morts dépendaient les uns des autres pour leur délivrance : les morts pour échapper aux souffrances de l'inquisition *post mortem*, les vivants pour éviter les poursuites judiciaires d'outre-tombe. Pour le meilleur et pour le pire, les deux sphères communiquaient et étaient interdépendantes.

Le passage de ce monde à l'autre d'un parent récemment décédé, représenté par le cortège funèbre, était un moment de transition délicat[64]. De la mise en bière jusqu'à l'ensevelissement dans la tombe, le défunt comme les survivants étaient exposés aux démons agresseurs de cercueils. D'effrayantes créatures gardiennes étaient placées dans les tombes pour repousser le mal (voir planche 2). Le manuel des *Grades des requêtes et des officiers* comporte deux chapitres sur la protection de la dépouille du défunt, sous les titres « Soustraire au mal les personnes décédées » 收死人耗害 et « Sauvegarde contre les démons des cortèges funèbres et des tombes » 收葬送塚墓鬼[65]. La « Requête pour ouvrir la voie » 開通道路章 de Maître Pin rouge aborde la première étape de ce rite de passage, la mise en bière :

> La sépulture d'Untel, en déshérence et portant malheur, est envahie par des esprits et des démons. Pour le mal qui s'abat puis remonte aux défunts, on ne peut que s'en prendre à soi-même. À telle heure, tels jour, mois et année, en raison d'une maladie grave et incurable, [Untel] a trépassé. Dans la stricte observance de la cérémonie d'usage, il gît en bière dans la grande salle. De toujours et à jamais, les [chemins des] personnes défuntes sont insondables ; les âmes *hun* et *po* du récemment trépassé ignorent depuis lors en quelles voies elles doivent renaître[66].

La prière « Requête pour la procession funéraire et l'inhumation » 出喪下葬章 visait à protéger le corps d'influences astrologiques néfastes durant son transfert au lieu d'inhumation, comme celles des douze rameaux terrestres désignés 月建 tour à tour par le manche du Boisseau du Nord au cours de sa rotation annuelle autour de l'étoile polaire, ou d'une conjonction néfaste de l'étoile de la Grande année :

> Tels jour, mois et année, le défunt Untel a remis son âme aux Trois officiels. Le deuil a été observé en sa résidence en telle localité. L'inhumation n'a pas encore eu lieu. Tel moment de ces jour et mois verra le transit de la dépouille d'Untel dans son cercueil de telle localité vers tel lieu d'inhumation [...]. Il est à craindre qu'il subisse du mal du fait [de la violation] des mille interdits et dix mille tabous en rapport avec le Général de la Grande année, les douze rameaux terrestres désignés, les tueurs qui appréhendent et torturent 鉤刑破殺[67], les souffles vieux des subalternes 下官故氣[68].

L'invocation implore alors cinq seigneurs de la Grande candeur et du Grand commencement 太素太始君[69], avec cent vingt officiers et généraux et douze chargés d'inhumation 葬埋吏[70], d'envoyer un talisman de commandement et un *Édit impérial de Nüqing* au gouverneur du monde souterrain 地下二千石[71], au magistrat du tumulus 丘丞, au comte de la tombe 墓伯, au marquis des tombeaux 塚侯 et aux officiers en charge des interdits et tabous en relation avec les voies de communication, les limites des chemins et le terre-plein central des routes, afin que ceux-ci ne puissent pas porter atteinte à la famille d'Untel.

La « Requête pour ouvrir la voie » citée ci-dessus invoque le seigneur du Grand mystère 太玄君 avec ses subalternes[72] et le général en chef du Corbillard sans ornements [tiré par des] chevaux blancs 素車白馬大將軍, protecteur des cortèges funèbres[73]. Le requérant demande l'envoi d'un talisman aux Trois officiers et d'un *Édit de Nüqing* aux esprits de la tombe et aux administrateurs des geôles et diverses prisons 牢檻諸獄. Ensuite, vient la supplique du bain et de la purification qui précédaient l'ascension de l'âme au paradis. Ces procédures purgatoriales donnaient lieu lors des ablutions à des requêtes spéciales, notamment celle de transmettre les vêtements du défunt et ses effets à l'autre monde. Baigner, coiffer et ceindre une dépouille constituait un rituel d'investiture et d'initiation permettant le passage de l'âme tourmentée à un état de félicité[74]. Les effets personnels constituaient d'utiles accessoires outre-tombe en même temps que des offrandes rédemptrices. La « Requête pour l'envoi des habits et effets du défunt et pour obtenir le transfert par l'acquittement de l'inculpation » 齎亡人衣物解罪謫遷達章 considère les effets personnels comme une rançon pour l'âme du défunt :

> Nous offrons respectueusement les vêtements et les ornements d'Untel durant sa vie, consistant en tels types d'habits et d'effets, afin de racheter l'âme *hun* du défunt Untel d'une condamnation sévère [...]. Relaxez les âmes *hun* et *po* d'Untel, levez les accusations portées contre lui, annulez ses condamnations et relâchez-le de prison, sa sentence pleinement purgée. Baigné, coiffé et ceint 沐浴冠帶, qu'il soit promu au Palais des bienheureux. Qu'il retourne à la matrice pour se réincarner, et puisse-t-il revenir dans un foyer méritant[75] !

Les expressions « acquittement de l'inculpation » et « envoi des habits et effets » dans le titre de cette requête relient lesdites prières aux pratiques d'inhumation et aux documents funéraires. Les biens funéraires inhumés avec le défunt s'accompagnaient d'inventaires, appelés « Titre des habits et effets » 衣物券, qui étaient adressés à la bureaucratie du monde souterrain[76]. Un exemple de ce type de document, daté de 361, issu de la tombe de Zhou Fangming 周芳命, née Pan 潘, à Changsha, inventorie les habits et effets personnels qui la suivirent dans la tombe : « Ces vêtements et objets qui accompagnent son corps sont tout ce que Pan porta et utilisa comme ornements durant sa vie. Ils ne peuvent faire l'objet de revendications par quiconque ou servir de remise de dettes[77]. »

Les dispositions pour le bain des défunts étaient autant chargées de sens métaphorique que celles relatives à leur habillage. Le *Soutra sur les salles de bains et les ablutions pour le sangha* 佛說溫室洗浴衆僧經 bouddhique, traduit en chinois au IIe siècle de notre ère, préconisait l'hygiène personnelle autant pour prévenir la maladie que pour apaiser les morts, éliminer la pollution et écarter les périls[78]. Dans des adaptations bouddho-taoïstes postérieures, comme le *Livre du Lingbao sur le bain du corps et du cœur* 太上靈寶洗浴身心經,

l'aspect rédempteur des ablutions fut de plus en plus mis en avant[79]. On peut penser que la prière suivante, « Requête d'ablutions » 沐浴章, accompagnait les pratiques mortuaires consistant à laver et vêtir le corps du défunt en vue de l'inhumation. Mais en même temps, l'adresse métaphorique de la prière rejoignait une scène parallèle dans laquelle l'âme était jugée. On y plaidait la purification de ses souillures et l'acceptation de la rançon offerte :

> Nous soumettons respectueusement [le fait] que le défunt est gardé en détention par les Trois officiers depuis son trépas avec son fardeau de transgressions diverses durant sa vie. Soumis à des souffrances extrêmes, la délivrance ne lui a pas encore été accordée. Aujourd'hui nous ne pouvons que placer notre confiance dans la puissance du Grand Tao pour secourir ses âmes *hun* des ténèbres. Pour laver les péchés 愆尤 de son karma 宿業 antérieur, nous remettons présentement avec respect les habits et effets du défunt durant sa vie, ainsi que des gages de pacification 鎮信 incluant monnaie, riz, encens, huile, soieries directionnelles 方綵, pinceaux, encre et autres[80]. Nous demandons qu'une salle de bains 浴堂 soit installée dans une cour immaculée 淨庭. Que les ustensiles de bain soient tous purs et propres, et que [le défunt] échappe au Bourbier de ténèbres. Nous prosternant humblement jusqu'à terre, nous présentons cette requête et envoyons notre demande au seigneur des Ablutions et ses officiers 沐浴君吏, à la dame des Ablutions 沐浴夫人 et aux Filles de jade lavandières 洗浣玉女 – mille deux cents personnes – pour qu'ils procèdent au bain de la dépouille du défunt, lavent ses souillures et éliminent ses impuretés, ôtent ses fers 桎梏 et lui permettent de contempler la lumière radieuse et de flâner dans la félicité, là où vêtement et nourriture abondent et où rien ne saurait manquer. Puissent sa tombe être pacifiée et des bénédictions être accordées aux vivants[81].

Dans la topographie du salut taoïste, le bain était le lieu de passage où l'âme purifiée émergeait de l'obscurité du monde souterrain dans un palais de lumière. Alors que le Purgatoire chrétien était un « troisième lieu » distinct, situé entre le Ciel et l'Enfer[82], la rédemption taoïste n'était ni un lieu, ni un état, mais l'une des étapes au long cours du voyage perpétuel. La conception du salut n'était ni dualiste ni tripartite, et la délivrance des fautes, loin d'une évasion totale, ne constituait qu'une phase dans le sort des êtres sensibles. Que la trajectoire fût ordonnée comme la « transmutation incessante » chinoise ou le *samsāra* indien, nulle destination n'était définitive ou immuable.

Le pays sans retour

Que « les vivants et les morts empruntent des chemins séparés » 生死各異路, imploraient les actes servant à dissiper les miasmes et sécuriser la tombe trouvés dans certaines sépultures, et que « ne puisse se produire aucune irruption miasmatique, seulement des bénéfices pour les vivants » 不得相注仵，便利生人. Le mot *guǐ* 鬼, signifiant « démon », est apparenté à son proche homophone *guī* 歸, « revenir ». Les actes et rituels de pacification de la tombe étaient conçus pour prévenir le retour des morts parmi les vivants[83]. Une injonction rituelle récurrente était « Tu ne reviendras pas ! » 不得重復.

L'idée que les morts contrariés « appréhendaient les êtres humains » 逮累生人 et que leurs émanations « s'emparaient des vivants » 注逮生人 montre la perméabilité entre les deux mondes : si les vivants pouvaient toucher les morts par leurs prières et leurs offrandes, les morts de leur côté pouvaient atteindre les vivants et les contraindre à résoudre leurs litiges ou à partager leurs souffrances[84]. Selon Tao Hongjing, « dans les cas aggravés d'une kyrielle de morts dans la même famille impliquant parents, frères ou époux, il faut s'attendre à une réversion subséquente de miasmes, infusant le monde des vivants 後還注復生人 et les frappant dans leur chair »[85]. La « Requête pour asperger la maison d'un défunt récent » 新亡灑宅逐注却殺章 était prononcée dans un rituel pour purifier l'habitation de la pollution causée par le redouté retour miasmatique du pays des morts :

> Ces dernières années, les résidents de cette maisonnée ont été affligés par l'adversité. Il y a eu des décès et des deuils en série. Untel est tombé malade et il est mort tel jour de tel mois. Nous craignons que, le jour de la mort d'Untel, un retour miasmatique parmi les vivants 注復生人 ne se soit produit [...]. Nous, hommes de chair, tremblons d'effroi, incapables de recouvrer notre sang-froid. [Les gens de la maisonnée] ont porté l'affaire devant votre serviteur, lui demandant de refouler

les miasmes mortifères de la résidence, pacifier les esprits et stabiliser le *qi*. Respectueusement soumis comme indiqué.

La prière rapporte que lors d'un décès, les âmes *hun* et *po* du défunt se dispersent. Elles se transforment en huit âmes tueuses 八殺, en miasmes mâles et femelles funestes 雌雄咎注[86], en démons du corbillard et stellaires, qui, s'élevant, reviennent empêtrer 纏綿 les résidents et les frapper d'atteintes mortelles. Le prêtre demande l'aide d'émissaires de l'eau bénite 神水使者 pour assainir et purifier la résidence par le balayage et l'aspersion : « Puissent-ils voyager dix mille *li* à travers les nuages pour rafraîchir et purifier l'habitation et laver et éliminer la pollution du cadavre[87]. » À défaut d'une telle purification, une liaison avec des parents décédés subsisterait et il en résulterait une contagion chronique de la famille survivante. La prière pour un membre malade de la famille, intitulée « Requête pour prévenir la reconnexion avec les morts » 斷亡人復連章, fait état de ces affres :

> Nous cherchons à deviner si les morts provoquent le malheur en rétablissant le lien 更相復連, pérennisant ainsi l'affliction. Nous craignons que, tant que le contact avec les morts n'est pas rompu, la contagion ne puisse jamais être enrayée 死亡不絕注復不斷. La famille entière est anxieuse, craignant que le patient ne trépasse. Ce jour, s'exprimant avec sincérité du fond du cœur, ils se sont tournés vers votre serviteur pour demander qu'il soit sauvé.

Le requérant implore ensuite cent mille seigneurs de la Destinée personnelle 本命君 de dissoudre les exhalaisons *qi* des morts-vivants 亡人復連之氣 et prie pour leur « déconnexion » 斷絕 afin que, désormais, les âmes des trépassés demeurent rigoureusement écartées des vivants – « les vivants et les morts empruntent des chemins séparés ; Untel ne doit pas être dérangé en sa personne[88] ».

DEUXIÈME PARTIE

Le périple intérieur : la réforme de Lu Xiujing

Le thème du don rédempteur accorde la préférence tantôt au sacrifice, tantôt à l'abnégation de soi. Quand l'offrande se déplaça de l'effusion de sang vers le renoncement, le don devint sacrifice de soi[1]. L'évolution de la conception du moi fut la clef de ce processus. La liturgie réformée du patriarche du Lingbao Lu Xiujing (406-477) tourna résolument le regard du suppliant taoïste vers son moi intérieur, par contraste avec la métaphore de l'audience de cour, tournée vers l'extérieur, qui sous-tendait l'Offrande de requête des Maîtres célestes. « La quête de la vie commence par l'abdomen », enseignait le prêcheur Lu Xiujing. Pour Lu et ses disciples, le salut de sa destinée passait par la construction du regard intérieur, car « la destinée réside en moi » 命在於我 et « la vie qui ne finit pas demeure au fond de soi » 長生在己也[2]. Cette vision intérieure permettait à l'adepte non seulement d'accéder à la connaissance et à la préservation de sa propre personne, mais également d'intérioriser tout l'univers. L'aboutissement du périple intérieur était le retour à la Nature originelle. La quiétude, la pureté, la renonciation et un esprit de pénitence étaient les prérequis pour entreprendre ce voyage. On se devait aussi d'observer des injonctions morales, comme celle de mettre en congruence la vie intérieure et le comportement extérieur. Pour y parvenir, Lu Xiujing instruisit ses disciples dans la pratique du rituel de la Retraite 齋 – la discipline requise pour régler la conduite extérieure – et dans l'observance de préceptes 戒 comme tuteur pour fortifier le moi intérieur contre la tentation.

Alors que l'adresse de requêtes à la bureaucratie du monde invisible demeurait pour Lu Xiujing et les taoïstes des générations suivantes une voie vers la délivrance, le programme rituel gagna en variété et laissa plus de place à la culture morale personnelle. La méditation du Shangqing 上清 envisageait déjà une approche du salut par la pratique individuelle de la culture de soi[3]. La réforme de Lu Xiujing édicta la Retraite Lingbao 靈寶齋 comme liturgie du salut universel subordonnant la culture de soi au cadre du rituel collectif. La Retraite poursuivait en gros les mêmes visées rédemptrices et s'adressait aux mêmes communautés de fidèles que l'Offrande de requête : guérison et salut personnels, expiation et délivrance des parents et des ancêtres, préservation et bénédictions pour les collectivités désignées et l'État. Le rituel funéraire, cependant, vit l'intention des obligés se déplacer de la pacification des morts loin des vivants vers le désir filial de félicité pour les parents et ancêtres défunts comme une fin en soi. Les taoïstes du Lingbao, tout en pratiquant la culture morale personnelle, recherchaient la délivrance par le rituel communautaire de la Retraite, confiants que la plus haute récompense n'irait pas à ceux qui « voulaient seulement se sauver eux-mêmes, sans une pensée pour le salut d'autrui » (voir « Le salut pour tous » au chapitre 5). Ainsi, la doctrine de salut universel et l'idéal de compassion du bodhisattva avaient posé leur marque sur la sotériologie taoïste.

La Deuxième partie de ce livre porte essentiellement sur Lu Xiujing, sa réforme du rituel rédempteur taoïste, son programme de renouveau moral et son enseignement sur le sens et la pratique du rituel communautaire de Retraite nouvellement codifié par ses soins. Le chapitre 5 (« Le disciple des Trois cavernes ») situe la pensée de Lu Xiujing dans l'histoire religieuse et intellectuelle de son époque, la dynastie méridionale des Liu Song (420-479). Le chapitre 6 (« La Retraite du Joyau sacré ») examine la réforme du Lingbao sous l'angle de l'enseignement et la pratique de la Retraite. Dans les chapitres 7 et 8 (« Corrigez votre cœur, corrigez votre conduite ! » et « Gagner l'autre rive par le revaloir »), nous plongeons dans les deux collections subsistantes de méditations et sermons composés par le patriarche Lu pour ses disciples : *Lumière du rituel*, dix leçons tirées du *Laozi* sur la maîtrise de soi, la quiétude, l'alchimie physiologique et la méditation ; et *Cinq sentiments de gratitude*, la plus bouddhiste des exhortations pastorales de Lu Xiujing.

Dans le Jiangnan du Ve siècle, la région de naissance de Lu Xiujing au sud du bas Yangzi, plusieurs défis majeurs furent constitutifs de sa vocation comme patriarche « refondateur » de la religion taoïste : la diaspora du mouvement des Maîtres célestes après l'invasion de la Chine septentrionale, la compétition entre de multiples courants taoïstes en Chine du Sud, et l'expansion vigoureuse du bouddhisme. Les prédications de Lu Xiujing illustrent la double stratégie qu'il conçut pour réformer le taoïsme médiéval en réponse à ces défis : la première, un renouveau de l'ancienne sotériologie taoïste, et typiquement chinoise, du retour à la Nature originelle ; la seconde, une large assimilation de la doctrine mahayaniste au sein du premier canon consolidé d'écritures et de protocoles liturgiques taoïstes.

CHAPITRE 5

LE DISCIPLE DES TROIS CAVERNES

Le taoïsme médiéval prit un tour décisif avec les réformes de Lu Xiujing pour penser autrement la servitude et la libération, l'adversité et la préservation, la nature du rituel rédempteur. Conservateur en apparence, Lu défendit les institutions de la première communauté du Maître céleste pour mieux les réformer. Lu fut, en fait, un innovateur radical qui transforma fondamentalement le taoïsme. Il systématisa le corpus scripturaire du Lingbao ou Joyau sacré, dans lequel abondaient les idées et la terminologie bouddhistes, recodifia le rituel taoïste à partir de la nouvelle Retraite du Lingbao, et conçut le premier canon taoïste intégré, les *Écritures des Trois cavernes* 三洞經[1]. Le canon comprenait trois grandes divisions, ou « cavernes » : le corpus du Shangqing ou Caverne des véritables 洞真, celui du Lingbao ou Caverne du mystère 洞玄, suivis des textes talismaniques et tables ésotériques de la Chine du Sud dénommés « Écrits des Trois souverains » 三皇文 ou Caverne des divinités 洞神. Adoptant pour lui-même le titre de « disciple des Trois cavernes » 三洞弟子, Lu érigea cette structure tripartite sans inclure le corpus des Maîtres célestes, lequel continuera néanmoins à fournir l'ordre de base de l'ordination laïque et cléricale. Le *Livre de la Grande paix* et d'autres traditions textuelles majeures étaient pareillement omis, reflétant un parti pris en faveur des œuvres provenant des courants taoïstes du Jiangnan. Dans cette nouvelle structure intégrée et hiérarchique, le corpus du Shangqing, subséquemment systématisé par le disciple de seconde génération de Lu Xiujing, Tao Hongjing, à Maoshan 茅山 (Jiangsu), vint à représenter l'achèvement de l'ordre d'initiation.

Visionnaire, la réforme de Lu Xiujing dépassa la fragmentation et le déclin d'une communauté taoïste, disparate, qui s'était dispersée dans un empire divisé. Pour y parvenir, il fut nécessaire d'agir sur plusieurs fronts. Le premier consista à intégrer les différents courants des écoles méridionales du taoïsme qui prospéraient dans le Jiangnan natif de Lu, soit le territoire de la dynastie des Liu Song (420-479), d'ores et déjà le centre démographique et économique de la Chine[2]. Deuxièmement, il fallut que Lu Xiujing clarifiât comment la sotériologie taoïste réformée par le Lingbao se démarquait du bouddhisme populaire, en plein essor. La stratégie de Lu fut de réintégrer la vision contemplative et les techniques transcendantales anciennes de Laozi et de Zhuangzi 莊子 au cœur de la pratique taoïste. Troisièmement, Lu s'efforça de rétablir les fondements moraux du mouvement du Maître céleste à ses débuts, pour combattre la déliquescence des pratiques contemporaines (voir « La congrégation des élus » au chapitre premier)[3].

Préconiser un renouveau de l'ancienne communauté du Maître céleste était une affaire délicate, à cause de la propension à l'insurrection politique dont le mouvement était suspect. L'appel de Lu Xiujing à la réforme et au repentir visait une génération qui croyait une fois encore que la fin du monde était proche. Vers la fin des Jin orientaux (317-420), un culte messianique du Maître céleste produisit les *Incantations divines des grottes abyssales* 太上洞淵神咒經, offrant le salut face aux hordes démoniaques qui devaient engloutir et oblitérer l'âge de dépravation[4]. La rébellion taoïste de Sun En 孫恩 et Lu Xun 盧循, son beau-frère, qui balaya la région du bas Yangzi en 399-402, attisa des prophéties du même effet : les membres du clan Sun avaient été de fervents adeptes du taoïsme du Maître céleste depuis plusieurs générations. Leur soulèvement, menaçant la survie de la dynastie Jin orientale, suscita de nouvelles appréhensions quant au rôle d'arbitre du Mandat du ciel joué par le mouvement du Maître céleste[5]. Comme pour lever tout doute sur les visées politiques du mouvement, le tract du Maître céleste intitulé *Explication interne des Trois cieux* apparut opportunément pour couronner d'un halo de prophétie messianique la dynastie des Liu Song ascendante[6]. Le fondateur de la dynastie était Liu Yu 劉裕 (363-422), le général qui avait précédemment réprimé la rébellion de Sun En. Manière de réactiver le messianisme politique de la période des Han orientaux, Liu Yu fut proclamé le descendant et successeur légitime de la maison régnante des Han, également de patronyme Liu[7]. Son élévation faisait écho à la légende de Li Hong, la figure culte du Sichuan du Ier siècle vénérée comme une manifestation de Laozi divinisé[8]. Cette légende, propagée par les *Incantations divines*, soutenait qu'un sage nommé Li Hong avait migré au Jiangnan depuis le berceau historique du taoïsme au Sichuan. Exécuté à Jiankang pour sédition en 324 avec son frère puîné Li Tuo 李脫, un guérisseur religieux notoire, Li Hong fut canonisé plus tard comme Seigneur auguste du Portail d'or 金闕帝君, connu sous le nom de Li Hongyuan[9].

En 420, le moine bouddhiste Huiyi 慧義 (372-444) prédit que le renversement de la dynastie Jin par Liu Yu était décrété par le Mandat du ciel, et servit de médiateur pour que le *sangha* 僧伽, la communauté bouddhique, soutînt son ascension. Comme on pouvait s'y attendre, Liu Yu, devenu empereur Wudi 武帝 (r. 420-422), tint ce moine en haute estime et le couvrit de faveurs[10]. Dans la même veine que l'*Explication interne*, Lu Xiujing cita une prophétie apocalyptique tirée des écritures du Shangqing à la fin du IVe siècle pour annoncer l'ascension de Liu Yu. En tant que descendant supposé de la maison régnante des Han, Liu Yu allait rétablir la chaîne brisée de la succession légitime. Liant l'ascension de Liu et la révélation des écritures du Lingbao à la fin du IVe siècle à Jurong 句容 (Jiangsu), Lu Xiujing gratifia le monarque d'une alliance bouddho-taoïste qui vénérerait le fondateur dynastique comme un sauveur *cakravartin* venu restaurer la Grande paix consécutivement à une période de chaos de fin du *dharma*[11].

Lu Xiujing naquit en 406 au sein d'une famille aristocratique de l'est du Wuxing 吳興 (Zhejiang)[12]. La trajectoire de sa vie subit deux influences contraires : d'un côté, l'attrait de la cour impériale, de l'autre, le quiétisme et l'érémitisme typiquement professés par les élites de son temps et de sa classe sociale. Pour certains, le retrait était une stratégie d'autopromotion politique[13]. Lu passa ainsi les années décisives de sa carrière entre la capitale méridionale de Jiankang 建康 (la Nankin moderne) et le site sacré du mont Lu 廬山 (Lushan), près de Jiujiang 九江 au Jiangxi. Quand il céda aux convocations pressantes de l'empereur Mingdi 明帝 (r. 465-472), il invoqua comme modèles Laozi mais aussi Ge Xuan 葛玄 (164-244), l'oncle de Ge Hong et patriarche légendaire de la tradition textuelle du Lingbao, qui ni l'un ni l'autre ne s'étaient dérobés au service du souverain en tant que conseillers taoïstes[14].

Un monde séparait Jiankang du mont Lu. Pourtant, tous deux furent des lieux privilégiés de diffusion des idées, institutions et pratiques bouddhistes en Chine médiévale. Jiankang, la cité des palais, était l'ancienne capitale Jianye 建業 du royaume de Wu, restaurée et embellie de palais et de jardins élégants sous les Jin orientaux pour rivaliser de splendeur avec la capitale perdue du Nord, Luoyang 洛陽[15]. Elle devint l'un des plus importants centres d'érudition et de propagation du bouddhisme en Chine[16]. Lushan était un épicentre d'innovation religieuse, dominant la région où foisonnaient les cultes populaires qui furent au cœur des bouleversements politico-religieux du tournant du ve siècle[17]. Résidence de l'éminent moine bouddhiste Huiyuan 慧遠 (334-416) et de sa communauté florissante un demi-siècle avant l'arrivée de Lu Xiujing, le mont Lu se distinguait déjà comme un haut lieu pour le développement institutionnel du monachisme qui allait constituer la vocation de Lu Xiujing : collecte et catalogage des écritures, élaboration d'un canon, initiation et instruction dans la pratique du rituel de Retraite, rédaction des règles pour l'ordination et la consécration, de coutumiers pour la vie monacale. Huiyuan et Lu Xiujing avaient une culture intellectuelle commune : tous deux adeptes de l'Érudition du mystère, ils étaient profondément versés dans la lecture du *Laozi*, du *Zhuangzi* et du *Livre des mutations*[18]. Le maître de Huiyuan était Daoan 道安 (312-385), un éminent traducteur et compilateur du premier catalogue, partiel, des écritures bouddhistes en Chine. Après avoir entendu Daoan enseigner les soutras de la Sagesse du bouddhisme, Huiyuan connut une conversion radicale, déclarant le confucianisme, le taoïsme et les autres écoles chinoises de philosophie n'être « rien que de la menue paille »[19]. Lu Xiujing adopta lui aussi peu ou prou la vision bouddhiste du monde, mais il entreprit d'en incorporer les enseignements au sein de la sphère religieuse et philosophique taoïste.

Pour les générations ultérieures, le mont Lu figurerait le jaillissement de rivalité interreligieuse, mais aussi le dialogue. Le jeune Lu Xiujing n'était âgé que de dix ans lorsque Huiyuan mourut. Pourtant, la doctrine œcuménique des Trois enseignements 三教, si influente quatre siècles plus tard, à la fin des Tang, ferait remonter son origine à une rencontre, fictive, entre Lu Xiujing, Huiyuan et le poète Tao Yuanming 陶淵明 (365-427) sur le mont Lu[20]. Cette légende est mise en scène pour la première fois dans une peinture de Sun Wei 孫位 (fl. 876-936), dans le royaume de Shu, au temps des Cinq dynasties[21]. Une autre représentation, de Li Gonglin 李公麟 (vers 1041-1106), sous les Song du Nord, intitulée *Image de la Société du lotus* 蓮社圖, montre Huiyuan prenant congé de Lu Xiujing près du pont sur le Ruisseau du tigre (voir planche 3). Les deux personnages ont la mine rieuse et se saluent, par contraste avec la mine renfrognée de Tao Yuanming sur le départ et l'empressement du poète bouddhiste Xie Lingyun 謝靈運 (385-433) qui s'approche[22]. Dans l'esprit non sectaire des Trois enseignements, Huiyuan préférait le taoïste Lu et l'âpre Tao à son coreligionnaire et admirateur Xie. Bien que l'histoire ait surtout retenu ses excentricités taoïstes, Tao représente ici le confucianisme[23].

Comme nombre de familles de la noblesse locale, celle de Lu était de longue date adepte du taoïsme du Maître céleste. Lu Xiujing reçut son ordination à l'adolescence, à l'âge de quinze *sui*. Vers le même moment, son mariage fut arrangé et sa carrière engagée. Pourtant, Lu devait bientôt abandonner et son foyer et ses perspectives d'avancement. Fuyant les troubles du règne de Wudi, il passa les années suivantes comme ermite voyageur. Souffrant chroniquement d'une maladie respiratoire, il se souciait d'être toujours pourvu d'herbes médicinales[24]. Dans sa présentation du *Rituel de transmission pour les ordinations du Lingbao* 靈寶授度儀, Lu évoque sa propre ordination comme le point de départ d'une vie dédiée aux études scripturales :

> Après avoir reçu cette faveur imméritée, pendant dix-sept années, avec une sincérité sans réserve, j'ai obéi fidèlement, étudié avec diligence et lentement assimilé les écrits divins. Savourant leur signification profonde et concentrant toute mon attention, j'espérais les pénétrer. Avec une détermination inébranlable, je lisais et étudiais sans cesse, matin et soir[25].

L'intervalle de dix-sept années auquel renvoie le passage correspond à la période entre l'initiation de Lu et sa présentation du *Catalogue des écritures du Lingbao* 靈寶經目 à l'empereur Wendi 文帝 en 437, soit à l'étape de sa vie consacrée à la constitution systématique du corpus du Lingbao[26].

Vers l'an 451, tandis que Lu visitait la capitale pour se procurer des remèdes, l'empereur Wendi le convoqua au palais et en fit son instructeur[27]. Peu de temps après, au printemps 453, le règne long et stable de Wendi connut une fin violente avec l'assassinat de l'empereur par ses fils. Ce n'était pas le premier régicide, ou parricide, perpétré au sein de la famille Liu régnante. Mais quand il fut révélé que la médium Yan Daoyu 嚴道育, qui avait fourni le poison aux assassins, était une taoïste, qui plus est du Wuxing, la région natale de Lu Xiujing, le séjour de ce dernier dans la capitale se serait trouvé compromis[28]. Une autre famille aristocratique de ce district, le clan Shen 沈, adepte elle aussi des Maîtres célestes, fut mise en cause au fil de l'enquête sur l'assassinat[29]. Shen Yue 沈約 (441-513), le futur poète et historien dynastique de renom, perdit son père dans la purge, après l'exécution, un demi-siècle plus tôt, de son arrière-grand-père, commandant dans la rébellion de Sun En[30].

Pendant un temps, Lu Xiujing aurait erré çà et là en direction du sud avant de se fixer finalement au mont Lu. En 461, l'abbaye de la Simplicité et de la quiétude 簡寂觀 fut édifiée, dans un endroit reculé près de la Falaise de la cascade 瀑布巖, sur les pentes de l'adret de la montagne, pour héberger Lu et sa communauté[31]. En 515, Shen Xuan 沈旋, fils de Shen Yue, commémorera la fondation de l'abbaye dans une inscription sur stèle[32]. Au VIIIe siècle, le poète taoïste Wu Yun 吳筠 (mort en 778) se réfugia sur le mont Lu durant la rébellion d'An Lushan 安祿山 (755-757). Ému par la vue de la stèle érodée et les traces d'offrandes laissées par des générations de fidèles, Wu composa une nouvelle inscription, intitulée *Stèle pour le seigneur Lu, Maître de la simplicité et de la quiétude* 簡寂先生陸君碑[33]. Elle représentait Lu Xiujing menant une existence idyllique et retirée, s'appliquant aux arts de l'immortalité et pinçant les cordes de son luth[34]. Une génération plus tard, quand Li Bo 李渤 (773-831), l'hagiographe de la filiation Shangqing, séjourna à Lushan, il s'inspira du texte de Wu Yun pour composer une nouvelle inscription. Le texte de cette dernière allait constituer la biographie de Lu Xiujing en tant que patriarche du Shangqing dans le recueil intitulé *Filiation des Véritables* 真系 de Li Bo[35].

Il s'avère que, loin de la teneur conventionnelle des inscriptions sur stèles, le ministère de Lu Xiujing suscita une communauté florissante à l'abbaye de la Simplicité et de la quiétude, laquelle comptait encore cinq cents disciples après sa mort. Les sermons et exhortations du maître furent consignés par écrit pour guider la multitude des adeptes. Derrière la salle principale de l'abbaye, un bâtiment séparé abritait la plus importante bibliothèque taoïste de l'époque, dont le catalogue, gravé sur pierre, était exposé le long des murs. Le fonds comprenait mille deux cents rouleaux manuscrits conservés dans des coffrets de bambou, un ensemble de textes, livres sacrés, talismans et diagrammes collectés dans tout le Jiangnan ou conférés par la bibliothèque impériale[36]. Le Jiangnan du ve siècle vit les communautés bouddhistes et taoïstes entreprendre, parallèlement, de cataloguer et compiler des canons officiels[37]. Une polémique Tang, qui souligne le processus concurrentiel d'interaction de la formation des canons, prétendit que des moines bouddhistes de Lushan avaient volé des livres de l'abbaye de la Simplicité et de la quiétude et les avaient plagiés pour leurs besoins[38].

En 467, avant que la grande entreprise de construction canonique de Lu ne fût achevée, une nouvelle convocation l'appela à la cour de l'empereur Mingdi, qui était un fervent protecteur et du taoïsme et du bouddhisme. Au même moment, Mingdi ordonna pour Lu Xiujing la construction de l'abbaye pour la Vénération du vide 崇虛觀 au mont Tianyin 天印山, à la périphérie nord de Jiankang[39]. Accompagné par un disciple de Lushan nommé Chen Piaozhi 陳飄之, Lu atteignit la capitale l'année suivante[40]. En 471, il présenta à l'empereur le *Catalogue des écritures des Trois cavernes* 三洞經書目錄, l'inventaire du premier canon taoïste comprenant 1 228 rouleaux de manuscrits[41]. Ce total incluait un certain nombre de rouleaux « non encore révélés », une disposition qui laissait habilement la porte ouverte à de futurs ajouts mais qui suscita le dédain des bibliographes bouddhistes[42]. En réalité, Lu Xiujing avait plusieurs dizaines d'années d'avance sur la concurrence. Un projet de compilation d'un canon bouddhiste chinois ne vit le jour qu'à la fin du ve siècle, initié par le prince Xiao Ziliang 蕭子良 (460-494) des Qi du Sud. Le premier catalogue bouddhiste complet, héritant du travail antérieur de Daoan, fut présenté par l'érudit et moine Sengyou 僧祐 en l'année 515[43].

Toujours en 471, Lu célébra une Retraite des Trois originels à ciel ouvert 三元露齋 pour le rétablissement de l'empereur souffrant[44]. Il est rapporté qu'à la tombée de la nuit, des nuages s'amoncelèrent pour former un voile multicolore de bon augure, de la forme d'une voûte parsemée de joyaux, flottant au-dessus de l'abbaye pour la Vénération du vide[45], et qu'à l'accompagnement de ces signes, l'empereur fut miraculeusement guéri. Lu Xiujing passa à Jiankang les années qui lui restaient à vivre. Malgré sa réputation d'ermite, il devint une personnalité de cour célébrée et fut un ardent défenseur du taoïsme lors des confrontations publiques patronnées par l'empereur, à l'occasion desquelles les mérites comparés des deux religions étaient vivement débattus. Un banquet suivi d'un débat de ce genre fut donné en l'honneur de Lu Xiujing au Temple bouddhiste de l'ornement 莊嚴佛寺[46], puis un autre dans la Salle pour la réception des sages 延賢館 au Parc du beau bosquet 華林園 où l'empereur questionna en personne Lu Xiujing[47]. La communauté de Lu était florissante, attirant grand nombre de taoïstes, de courtisans et d'adeptes[48]. Lu décéda en 477 à l'abbaye pour la Vénération du vide et il fut inhumé sur le mont Lu (Lushan). Son héritier spirituel fut Sun Youyue 孫遊嶽[49].

Le faux mêlé au vrai : discerner les yeux de poissons des perles

Codes vestimentaires, règles comportementales marquant la distance entre lettrés et gens du peuple, séparation du sacré et du profane étaient autant de façons d'ordonner la société. Le monde selon Lu Xiujing était catégorisé comme « fin » 精 ou « grossier » 麤. Une société lucide et bien ordonnée se devait d'être différenciée par degrés de raffinement, notamment pour ce qui avait trait aux rangs de la noblesse sociale et à la perspicacité intellectuelle. Lu Xiujing déplorait que son époque « mêlât indistinctement le fin et le grossier » 精麤糅雜 et que « le moindre et l'important circulassent pêle-mêle » 小大混行[50]. L'enjeu du discernement était, pour Lu, essentiellement d'ordre moral : distinguer l'authentique du douteux, le vrai du faux, le bien du mal. Quand il s'agissait de défendre la vraie doctrine et de dénoncer les enseignements contrefaits répandus par des falsificateurs sans scrupules, c'était assurément le salut des fidèles qui était en jeu. La prolifération de soutras dits apocryphes constituait une source de préoccupation similaire pour les bibliographes bouddhistes : quels étaient les textes « authentiques » (c'est-à-dire traduits à partir d'originaux en sanskrit) et quels étaient les textes suspects ou faux (c'est-à-dire produits en Chine)[51] ? Lu Xiujing se fit fort d'authentifier l'ensemble des manuscrits qui véhiculaient la véritable révélation du Lingbao, cette grande synthèse doctrinale vouée à revitaliser le taoïsme et à fournir la riposte chinoise au bouddhisme. Dans sa préface du catalogue des écritures du Lingbao, Lu Xiujing s'adressait aux fidèles taoïstes en ces termes :

> Tel jour et tel mois de l'année Yuanjia 14 (437), le disciple des Trois cavernes Lu Xiujing enjoint solennellement à tous les adeptes qui se réclament du taoïsme de s'unir autour d'un code commun, de se vouer à la cause culturelle[52], d'exalter la transformation merveilleuse, de faire prospérer les temps présents et pleuvoir les bénédictions. Leur joie sera complète et ils connaîtront d'innombrables bienfaits. Quittez ces chemins-là de perdition 惡道[53] pour ce lieu-ci de salut 善場[54] ! Quelle plus grande récompense que le bonheur éternel pour ceux qui ne s'écartent pas du droit chemin[55] ?

Avant de disséminer la nouvelle doctrine du salut, il fallut faire la part entre les écritures et rituels authentiquement Lingbao et les imitations fabriquées avec l'intention de tromper et mystifier. La vérification de corpus scripturaires n'était pas une entreprise rare dans une société dont l'élite glorifiait la science bibliographique et le catalogage de livres[56]. Tao Hongjing poursuivra dans les traces de Lu Xiujing et son dessein, élevant l'art de l'analyse des manuscrits taoïstes vers de nouveaux sommets. L'objet des recherches de Tao était le corpus du Shangqing. En 468, les manuscrits de ce corpus avaient été confiés par ordre impérial à Lu Xiujing à l'abbaye pour la Vénération du vide, où ils constituèrent la première des trois divisions du canon des *Trois cavernes*, la Caverne des véritables. Après la mort de Lu, la collection passa entre de multiples mains avant d'atteindre Sun Youyue[57], qui les remit à Tao durant le séjour de ce dernier à Jiankang en 484-486[58].

Dans les *Déclarations des Véritables* 真誥, parues en 499, Tao relate les défis mémorables auxquels furent confrontés les dépositaires de telles révélations divines. Les manuscrits étaient fort recherchés par de fervents adeptes, en quête d'immortalité ou bien d'objets de valeur littéraire et calligraphique. Tao reconnut que les dépositaires des textes du Shangqing s'étaient laissé berner par de prétendus adeptes qui firent des copies non autorisées et les embellirent à leur façon. Des copistes et falsificateurs sans scrupules empochaient des « frais de transmission » pour de tels manuscrits, inspirés des gages rituels versés lors d'octrois légitimes. Un commerce lucratif de ces graphies naquit, en assurant dès lors la circulation grandissante. Certains rouleaux furent, à tort ou à raison, détruits en tant que faux présumés[59].

Lu Xiujing avait imputé à des dégradations comparables l'atteinte à l'intégrité du corpus du Lingbao, pareillement victime de son propre succès. Dans la préface du *Catalogue des écritures du Lingbao* de 437, il se plaignait que « ces derniers temps, les écritures avaient été dispersées, et les contrefaçons mélangées aux authentiques ». Des recherches extensives et prolongées lui permirent de prendre la mesure de la corruption subie : faux catalogage, altérations textuelles, réorganisation, substitution, ajouts, corrections fautives. Rappelant l'origine sacrée des textes, Lu Xiujing imputait ces offenses à des imposteurs sans scrupules :

> Après que le Céleste vénérable eut transmis ses enseignements, le grand *dharma* se répandit, d'innombrables sages en disséminèrent, éditèrent et réunirent les varia et points essentiels en dix sections et trente-six boîtes pour guider les futurs disciples et sauver les fidèles [...]. Ces derniers temps, les écritures ont été dispersées, et les contrefaçons mélangées aux authentiques [...]. Dans certains cas, une [filiation] Shangqing a été effacée ou d'autres livres ont été dérobés, certains ont forgé des préfaces et des explications, d'autres ont inversé chapitres et versets, ajouté des phrases, ou fabriqué des symboles et des diagrammes. Certains ont augmenté des corpus existants, tandis que d'autres établissaient des gages et des règles séparées. Des caractères non standards étaient utilisés ; les rimes ne correspondaient plus. La langue était triviale, la signification superficielle, et les sujets, sans queue ni tête, étaient présentés en désordre[60].

Lu Xiujing sépara les livres véritables des fabrications et conclut que l'amalgame avait été l'œuvre d'« adeptes téméraires 猖狂之徒

qui n'étaient pas disposés à s'appliquer à la pénétration du mystère et manquaient de résolution pour s'adonner à la recherche de la vérité ». Pauvrement instruits, impudemment avides et peu soucieux des conséquences, ils produisaient des fabrications destinées à impressionner les amateurs. Pour contraster pareille supercherie avec le vrai discernement, Lu Xiujing comparait leurs subterfuges à des tentatives légendaires de duper les possesseurs de trésors inestimables : « Ils ont l'impudence de glisser des yeux de poissons [parmi des perles] présentées au marquis de Sui 隋侯 et l'outrecuidance de faire passer de la pierraille [pour des jades] à la porte de Monsieur He 和氏[61]. » Lu se réfère à l'histoire de Sui, qui soigna un serpent blessé et en fut récompensé par une perle que le reptile reconnaissant lui apporta dans sa gueule depuis les profondeurs du fleuve. Bian He 卞和 découvrit une magnifique pierre de jade, qu'il offrit brute à trois princes successifs de l'État de Chu 楚. Les deux premiers faillirent à reconnaître la valeur de la pierre et, prenant He pour un escroc, le punirent l'un après l'autre de l'amputation d'un pied. Le troisième prince discerna finalement le joyau sous son apparence modeste et réhabilita le donateur estropié.

En tant que conservateur des rituels et des écritures Lingbao, soit du « Joyau sacré », Lu Xiujing comparait ces trésors spirituels à un amas d'or et de jade. « Ayant fait vœu de vénérer les écritures et les classiques dès son plus jeune âge »[62], il reçut l'accès au rite de salut du Lingbao avec désir et passion (voir « Le mérite du renoncement » au chapitre 8). Pour les clairvoyants, les écritures véritables étaient un trésor infiniment désirable : « Je chéris les écritures comme des perles et du jade » 愛經如珠玉, entonnaient les disciples quand ils se préparaient à la Retraite – non sans ironie, si l'on considère combien lucratif était le commerce des manuscrits du Lingbao[63]. Une prière retrouvée parmi les manuscrits de Dunhuang emploie des métaphores similaires quand elle compare les colonnes de caractères des livres sacrés à des « ligatures de jades » 行行貫玉 et leurs phrases à des « enfilades de perles » 句句連珠[64]. Lu Xiujing n'était pas le premier à lier l'histoire de la perle de Sui et celle du jade de He comme étant des paraboles de la découverte heureuse de trésors terrestres et spirituels[65]. Le *Prince de Huainan* 淮南子, un recueil taoïste composé à la cour de Liu An 劉安 (vers 179-122 avant notre ère), avait résumé la morale des deux anciennes fables d'une formule lapidaire : « C'est comme la perle du marquis de Sui ou le jade de Monsieur He. Celui qui l'acquiert détient tout ; celui qui le perd n'a plus rien[66]. »

Mélanger les tuiles et les jades

Le taoïsme occupait une place éminente dans la vie de la noblesse des dynasties méridionales dont étaient issus Lu Xiujing, son disciple de seconde génération Tao Hongjing, ainsi que Shen Yue de la génération intermédiaire[67]. Dans ce milieu social et intellectuel, certains se convertissaient franchement au bouddhisme. Devenu bouddhiste laïc, Shen Yue et, dans une moindre mesure, Tao Hongjing professaient une affinité avec les deux enseignements. Shen tenait même en grande estime Tao Hongjing, patriarche de la lignée Shangqing, et composa plusieurs poèmes en son honneur[68].

L'appartenance à la noblesse ne se traduisait pas toujours par la dotation d'un poste officiel mais, lustre des prouesses ancestrales aidant, elle conférait une souveraine conscience de soi. Les études généalogiques se développèrent au sein du Jiangnan de la fin du IVe siècle, encouragées par une agence impériale dédiée[69]. La famille de Lu Xiujing descendait de Lu Kai 陸凱 (198-269), un Premier ministre du royaume de Wu. La patrie ancestrale était l'est du Wuxing, une région fertile du bassin hydrographique du bas Yangzi située entre Hangzhou et Suzhou, sur la rive méridionale du lac Taihu 太湖. Avec la commanderie de Guiji 會稽 dans le nord du Zhejiang et la capitale Jiankang, elle formait un triangle qui avait constitué le cœur culturel et économique de la dynastie Jin orientale[70]. Quand les *Contes transmis et propos nouveaux* 世說新語 évoquaient le clan Lu parmi les quatre illustres patronymes cités – « Les Zhang étaient cultivés, les Zhu martiaux, les Lu loyaux et les Gu hospitaliers » 張文, 朱武, 陸忠, 顧厚[71] –, ils faisaient référence à la branche aînée de l'arbre généalogique, soit les Lu de la commanderie de Wujun 吳郡陸氏 (Suzhou). Cette branche du clan Lu descendait de l'homme d'État Lu Jia 陸賈 (vers 216-vers 172 avant notre ère) et comprenait le premier ministre Lu Xun 陸遜 (183-245). Elle produisit aussi plusieurs lettrés de renom, parmi lesquels Lu Ji 陸機 (261-303), dont Ge Hong assimilait les écrits au « jade du Kunlun luminescent dans la nuit »[72], et son frère Lu Yun 陸

雲 (262-303)[73]. Le critique littéraire Liu Xie 劉勰 (vers 465-522), dans *L'esprit littéraire et la gravure des dragons* 文心雕龍, tenait les deux frères pour « des esprits brillants qui se distinguaient par l'élégance de leur art »[74]. Les descendants du clan incluaient aussi Lu Na 陸納 (mort en 395), un haut dignitaire à la cour de l'empereur Xiaowu 孝武 des Jin[75], l'écrivain Lu Zhan 陸展 (mort en 454)[76], le peintre Lu Tanwei 陸探微 (mort vers 485)[77] et plusieurs érudits distingués.

L'exigence de Lu Xiujing pour le discernement moral et intellectuel était nourrie par une conscience de soi enracinée dans la distinction sociale et culturelle de son clan. Sous les Han orientaux, le penseur anticonformiste Wang Chong 王充 (27-97) déclarait intolérable que « la vacuité passât pour vérité, la substance devînt imposture, et les non-éclairés de ce monde ne distinguassent point un fait d'une invention, confondant pourpre et vermillon et assemblant pêle-mêle tuiles et jades 瓦玉集糅 »[78]. L'élite sociale du Ve siècle, spécialement les adeptes des Causeries pures 清談 engagés dans la spéculation philosophique et métaphysique taoïste, se piquait tout autant d'observer les distinctions les plus fines, y compris celles concernant les hiérarchies sociales. La mise en accusation publique par Shen Yue d'une mésalliance est un cas d'école : en tant qu'adjoint du palais au président de la Cour des censeurs, Shen adressa une pétition à l'empereur pour que soit mis en accusation le gentilhomme Wang Yuan 王源 qui avait accordé sa fille en mariage à un roturier. Shen se scandalisait du manque de discernement de Wang qui déshonorait les ancêtres du clan Wang de Donghai 東海[79]. L'établissement d'une distinction nette entre la classe sociale des lettrés et les gens du peuple n'émanait pas tant du mépris de classe que du devoir sacré touchant au culte ancestral et à l'ordre cosmique. Pour les taoïstes, la hiérarchie sociale était fondée sur rien de moins que la théologie des Trois cieux, instituée par les Maîtres célestes en vue de mettre un terme à la « promiscuité » de l'ère précédente des Six cieux. L'*Explication interne des Trois cieux* définissait trois types de conduites indiscriminées : (a) les rapports indus entre les sexes – à exclure par l'observance des règles de parenté dans le mariage ; (b) les sacrifices sanglants illicites, la consommation de viande et d'alcool, et les actes de dévotion dispendieux ou dédiés aux esprits illégitimes – à supplanter par la vénération du Tao pur et la pratique de visualisation ; et (c) l'amalgame des genres disparates, comme les hommes et les démons, les trois religions et les populations chinoise et étrangère[80].

Lorsque les conventions sociales sont considérées comme des impératifs rituels, le manquement à l'étiquette devient sacrilège. Lu Xiujing formula des règles de conduite pour les « frères et sœurs » 善男善女 (une expression bouddhiste renvoyant originellement aux fils et filles de bonne famille), afin qu'ils fussent admis à participer à la Retraite[81]. Il s'agissait de réguler les rapports entre les membres de sexe différent, entre les participants laïcs et les clercs, et entre des adeptes de statut social inégal. La sévérité de Lu Xiujing à l'encontre des chaussures rituelles inappropriées avoisine celle envers le scandaleux port de chaussures informelles lors d'une visite en société, dénoncé dans les *Contes transmis et propos nouveaux*[82]. Faisant écho au sentiment de Wang Chong au sujet du discernement, Lu enjoignait à ses disciples de maintenir une distance bienséante chaque fois que les observances rituelles rassemblaient des hommes et des femmes, des cercles de connaissances et des étrangers, ou des participants présentant « la disparité entre les tuiles et les jades » 瓦玉之殊. Et il ne souffrait pas non plus la venue des petits enfants :

> Quand les frères et les sœurs participent aux rites du Tao dans la félicité de la foi 信樂[83], ceignent leur ceinture, se recueillent pour recevoir [les esprits] et contemplent la transformation, il est convenable que debout ou assis, ils se tiennent à part, sans se mélanger[84]. Tous les commanditaires d'une Retraite 齋主, quel que soit leur rang, devront être ceints et porter les chaussures appropriées. Il n'est pas acceptable d'être négligent en matière de chaussures ; des punitions seront dûment appliquées[85]. Exprimez-vous toujours en harmonie et d'une voix douce. Il n'est pas permis de se héler les uns les autres. Élever la voix offense les Véritables célestes et viole les interdits liés aux esprits. En cas de deuil, les commanditaires et les invités [bénéficiaires] d'une Retraite doivent toujours conserver un maintien égal, même devant les inconnus, et ne pas faire étalage de leurs lamentations. Quand l'invité est humble et le commanditaire noble, vous avez la disparité entre les tuiles et les jades : leurs manières respectives doivent faire montre de retenue et la communication être rare[86]. Même en cas de recours répété aux rites du Tao, il n'est pas convenable d'adresser ses respects au maître taoïste. Car la Voie est incommensurablement vénérable et la Vertu noble, et même si le maître taoïste est humble, ses aspirations

sont élevées [...]. Les jeunes enfants non encore capables de participer à la Retraite ne sauraient être admis dans la grande salle du diocèse ni gêner le déroulement de la Retraite[87].

Les contrevenants étaient condamnés pour transgression à une amende en nature de quantités variables d'encens, d'huile ou de cinabre. Les punitions pour les offenses concernant le port désordonné des coiffes et des chaussures, les postures négligées et le bavardage s'appliquaient de la même manière à tous les participants, quels que fussent leur état civil et leur état de vie. Les officiants encouraient des punitions supplémentaires s'ils renversaient l'encens, répandaient l'huile de lampe ou manquaient de révérence dans leurs psalmodies, de même les commanditaires, s'ils fournissaient des ustensiles rituels défectueux ou offraient des provisions laissant à désirer[88].

Repentance et réforme

Prêcheur visionnaire, Lu Xiujing était animé par un sens aigu de sa mission. En écho à la phrase des *Sentences de Confucius* 孔子家語 disant que « tous les autres s'empressent vers cela, moi seul m'en tiens à ceci ; tous vacillent, moi seul tiens bon », il affirmait son rôle providentiel dans un âge de déclin et de confusion : « Ils vont jusqu'à embrouiller le Qi correct, souiller les Véritables purs et salir le Grand Tao. Déplorable ! Je suis né dans la période de déclin final du monde, durant laquelle la doctrine est dégénérée. Tandis que tous les autres poursuivent cela, je me risque à m'en tenir à ceci[89]. »

Les auteurs – contemporains – des *Incantations divines des grottes abyssales* et de l'*Explication interne des Trois cieux* exprimaient le même pressentiment de chanceler au bord d'une fin de cycle cosmique. De telles périodes, connues comme « fin du *dharma* », se voyaient condamnées par la disparition de la doctrine salvatrice. Lorsque Lu Xiujing pourfendait la dégénérescence de la doctrine, littéralement « l'écroulement de la discipline doctrinale » 教法綱頹, cela n'était pas une simple allusion conventionnelle à cette croyance. Dans l'*Ordre sommaire de la communauté taoïste par Maître Lu*, il présenta un tableau détaillé de sa vision de la société et de la condition des institutions taoïstes de son temps (voir « La congrégation des élus » au chapitre premier). Cet ouvrage rappelle en premier lieu que le taoïsme du Maître céleste avait été fondé pour sauver l'âge de dépravation qui avait succédé à la perfection de la haute Antiquité. Dans un contexte comparable de déclin et de corruption, Lu Xiujing considérait sa mission réformiste comme un retour à l'état de pureté restauré en son temps par Zhang Daoling après l'abomination du culte des démons des Six cieux.

Les historiens peinent à expliquer l'apparente incongruité de la vive défense par Lu Xiujing des institutions du taoïsme du Maître céleste dans l'*Ordre sommaire*, en même temps que sa promotion vigoureuse des écritures et des rituels du Lingbao. Comment le même individu a-t-il pu professer des croyances aussi disparates ? Selon une interprétation, Lu Xiujing s'employa à consolider l'ordre liturgique du Maître céleste à ses débuts dans le but de réformer ce qu'étaient devenus et le clergé et la société laïque taoïstes. Débarrassant le mouvement de son programme politique, il mit l'accent sur les valeurs confucéennes de parenté et de moralité sociale, l'influence civilisatrice du gouvernement et l'importance de soutenir l'État et d'œuvrer au bien commun. Ce faisant, il introduisit une forme distincte, élitiste et méridionale du taoïsme du Maître céleste[90].

L'historien Wang Chengwen considère plutôt que l'*Ordre sommaire* a correspondu à une première phase dans la carrière de Lu, avant sa conversion aux enseignements du Lingbao. L'appel de Lu Xiujing à une réforme du système diocésain des Maîtres célestes n'était pas nouveau. Les *Préceptes d'admonestation des maisonnées*, les *Incantations divines*, l'*Explication interne*, et l'*Ordre liturgique du Seigneur Lao* 老君音誦誡經 de Kou Qianzhi, répondaient déjà à des perceptions comparables de déclin et de désordre. Pour Wang Chengwen, la conversion de Lu fut mue par son inquiétude grandissante quant à l'état véritable de l'organisation du Maître céleste, et ceci au moment où le corpus du Lingbao offrait une vision alternative du renouveau[91].

Les preuves font défaut pour étayer formellement l'une ou l'autre hypothèse. D'une part, Lu soutint au contraire l'ascension politique de Liu Yu et critiqua la piété filiale confucéenne (voir « La piété filiale » au chapitre 8). D'autre part, quand Lu Xiujing écrivit l'*Ordre sommaire*, il avait déjà intégré la doctrine du Lingbao et élaboré le canon des Trois cavernes, mentionnant en particulier la codification rituelle des Trois cavernes 三洞之軌範 et le culte du Véritable Taiji 太極真人, divinité du Shangqing vénérée dans les écritures du Lingbao[92]. En outre, l'*Ordre sommaire* fait allusion au Lingbao quand il traite des préceptes et des vêtements rituels[93]. Enfin, le ton franc employé pour dénoncer les pratiques populaires et hétérodoxes, et exhorter à la réforme morale et institutionnelle, suggère l'autorité d'un chef religieux de rang élevé et non une œuvre de jeunesse.

Quelle que fût la motivation profonde de Lu Xiujing, sa réforme aboutit à structurer et faire du taoïsme un enseignement endogène qui puisse résister à l'expansion du bouddhisme, tout en intégrant les nouveaux mouvements méridionaux du Shangqing et du Lingbao. L'entreprise intégrative de Lu érigea sur les fondations du Maître céleste un édifice nouveau. Comme d'autres réformes religieuses, elle présenta son caractère novateur comme un retour aux origines. En matière de culte, la transformation du taoïsme médiéval par Lu reflétait l'évolution du panthéon et des pratiques sacrificielles vers la vénération « pure » des dieux et des écritures. Lu Xiujing poursuivit ainsi le processus de réforme sacrificielle initié par le mouvement du Maître céleste à ses débuts. Des communautés particulières, telle la secte des *Incantations divines des grottes abyssales*, continuèrent à se réclamer de l'héritage spécifique de Zhang Daoling, mais, à partir du ve siècle, le rituel du Maître céleste fut absorbé dans un large amalgame comprenant en outre des éléments du Lingbao et du Shangqing, comme l'illustre l'*Almanach de requêtes de Maître Pin rouge*. Le taoïsme était en passe de devenir l'organisation liturgique, hiérarchiquement intégrée, qui serait pleinement réalisée sous les auspices impériaux des Tang.

Le salut pour tous

Une innovation capitale du vivant de Lu Xiujing fut l'assimilation, dans la pensée rédemptrice taoïste, de la doctrine mahayaniste de salut universel, rehaussée du vœu du bodhisattva de s'efforcer d'atteindre la libération de tous les êtres sensibles. Les écritures du Lingbao reconnaissaient le mécanisme du transfert de mérite pour le salut d'autrui, déclarant que la Voie de la Grande compassion était le seul chemin vers l'immortalité. Un texte du corpus scriptural originel du Lingbao, le *Livre du salut* 度人經, éleva le plan de salut universel pour en faire un thème central du taoïsme médiéval, traduisant le vœu du bodhisattva en une aspiration à renoncer à son propre salut jusqu'à ce que toute l'humanité atteignît le Tao[94].

La piété de certains souverains médiévaux alla jusqu'à « renoncer à leur destinée » 捨命 (d'empereur) en faisant vœu d'entrer au monastère. Les dons considérables payés par l'État au *sangha* pour racheter la destinée des souverains constituaient des transferts pour le moins sensationnels, illustrant combien le transfert de mérite des offrandes et les actes de renoncement gagnaient du terrain en Chine. La perspective d'atteindre des bénéficiaires éloignés par transfert amplifiait grandement la portée de l'intercession précédemment envisagée par le rituel de requête du Maître céleste. Franchissant les frontières de parenté et de statut qui structuraient traditionnellement la société chinoise, la prise de conscience que profanes et religieux atteignaient le salut côte à côte conférait de la dignité aux congrégations laïques et introduisait un élément d'égalitarisme dans les associations de confraternité religieuse[95].

Les actes de renoncement et de libéralité étaient offerts comme un lot sacrificiel, avec les confessions, les jours du rituel de Jeûne 齋 bouddhiste. En dépit de son penchant élitiste et de sa passion pour les distinctions catégorielles, Lu Xiujing accordait une place centrale au concept mahayaniste de transfert de mérite par le biais d'offrandes pour le salut d'autrui dans le rituel de Retraite, l'équivalent taoïste du Jeûne bouddhiste. Le passage de la « culture de soi » individuelle, encore prépondérante dans les écrits du Shangqing et les pratiques des maîtres des méthodes, vers une vision de la rédemption universelle, exprimée dans des prières et des vœux pour sauver autrui par transfert de mérite, commença à être formulé de manière programmatique dans des textes du Lingbao comme le *Livre de la causalité karmique* 本行因緣經 :

> Ceux qui, dans des existences passées, ont étudié le Tao et reçu les écritures, mais qui ont seulement effectué quelques bonnes actions, ceux qui ont seulement voulu se sauver eux-mêmes sans une pensée pour le salut d'autrui, ceux qui ont recherché la Voie seulement pour leur propre compte sans jamais se soucier de savoir si les autres l'obtenaient, ceux qui ne croient pas à la portée profonde des enseignements des grandes écritures, ne pratiquent

pas la Retraite et les Préceptes et ne vénèrent pas les maîtres des Trois cavernes 三洞法師[96], ils se contentent tous du Petit véhicule. Par ce moyen, ils obtiendront seulement la Voie des immortels terrestres 地仙 : même s'ils peuvent atteindre la liberté d'aller et venir sans entraves[97], de vivre longtemps et ne jamais mourir, ils ne transcenderont pas les Trois mondes 三界[98], ne flâneront pas dans les dix directions 十方 ni ne contempleront le Portail d'or de la Capitale de jade d'En Haut 太上玉京金闕[99] !

Chapitre 6

La Retraite du Joyau sacré

« La Grande liturgie du Joyau sacré est descendue dans le monde pour sauver l'humanité » 靈寶大法下世度人, déclare Lu Xiujing dans le mémorial présentant son *Rituel de transmission pour les ordinations du Lingbao*[1]. « La Grande liturgie » établissait comme véhicule du salut le rituel de la Retraite (*zhai* 齋), institué par les sages « pour réguler toutes les affaires en fonction des circonstances ». La Retraite permettait aux pratiquants d'exercer le contrôle de soi et d'ériger un bouclier de pureté et de quiétude à l'encontre de la corruption et des contrariétés du monde. Le terme « retraite » renvoyait à une catégorie de pratiques ascétiques qui avaient été au centre du système sacrificiel chinois depuis l'Antiquité. Les réformes du Lingbao par Lu Xiujing rétablirent la Retraite *zhai* au cœur du programme rédempteur. Bien que présentée comme un renouveau de la tradition chinoise, l'approche de Lu fut paradoxalement aidée par le fait que le même terme *zhai* désignait aussi la pratique dévotionnelle principale du bouddhisme, le Jeûne ou « fête maigre » végétarienne, traduisant le mot sanskrit *poṣadha* 布薩 qui signifie abstinence et purification[2]. Le Jeûne bouddhiste combinait des rites de confession et de récitation avec les divers actes de renoncement que stipulaient les préceptes[3]. Le jeune contemporain de Lu Xiujing et maître de la loi *vinaya* 律師, Sengyou (445-518), mit en exergue pour les adeptes bouddhistes chinois la provenance indienne du Jeûne *zhai* dans un compendium rituel intitulé *Le jardin du dharma* 法苑[4].

Dans le Jiangnan du ve siècle, à l'époque où Lu Xiujing enseignait à ses disciples taoïstes l'exécution de la Retraite, une ferveur générale pour les pratiques du *zhai* s'était emparée des communautés religieuses bouddhistes et taoïstes. L'inspiration circulait dans les deux sens. Bouddhistes et taoïstes laïcs observaient des rites *poṣadha* ou *zhai* de purification de soi les jours de jeûne périodique et durant les mois réservés à l'abstinence. Dans la croyance chinoise, les jours et périodes calendaires de jeûne marquaient les dates auxquelles les inspections divines exigeaient des actes spéciaux de repentance. Le *Soutra des quatre Rois célestes* 四天王經, un apocryphe bouddhiste, et des livres similaires expliquant le système des inspections par les quatre divinités directionnelles, empruntaient leurs calendriers rituels au taoïsme[5]. Les bouddhistes observaient six ou dix jours de jeûne par mois, et trois mois de jeûne étendu dans l'année ; les taoïstes, dix jours et six mois, respectivement, sans compter les jours d'examen particuliers comme les Trois originels 三元. Ceux-ci étaient des jours de pleine lune – le quinzième jour des premier, septième et dixième mois – du calendrier lunaire, quand les Trois officiers effectuaient des inspections[6]. Sur fond de tels recoupements entre les logiques rituelles des bouddhistes et des taoïstes, Lu Xiujing s'efforçait d'étayer l'origine chinoise du *zhai*.

Les versions antérieures de la Retraite en Chine, celles du Shangqing et des maîtres des méthodes, mettaient l'accent sur la réclusion. Ce rituel-là se pratiquait individuellement ou auprès d'un maître[7]. Par contraste, la Retraite du Lingbao devint le véhicule principal de la nouvelle dynamique communautaire promue sous l'autorité de Lu Xiujing. Les célébrations publiques, appelées Assemblées de retraite 齋會, comptaient de nombreux participants. Certaines attiraient un public rivalisant avec les Réunions de jeûne 齋集 bouddhistes[8]. Plus de cent témoins assistèrent à la Retraite des Trois originels que Lu Xiujing célébra en 471 pour le compte de l'empereur Mingdi[9]. Le sens de la mission pastorale de Lu Xiujing n'apparaît nulle part plus clairement que dans les sermons et exhortations qu'il prononçait en préparation du rituel de la Retraite ou durant son exécution. Ses prédications exposaient le sens de la Retraite et la méthode correcte pour la pratiquer, et elles abordaient les sujets de préoccupation de la communauté naissante : approfondissement et guérison spirituels, comportement rituel, disposition mentale, préceptes moraux, actes de purification. Les sermons reprenaient aussi les enseignements de Lu Xiujing sur la sauvegarde de soi, la soustraction aux pièges de la mondanité, l'atteinte de la quiétude et la transcendance. En fournissant le code de conduite prôné par Lu pour réformer le taoïsme, ils dépeignent l'univers moral de cet âge de grands bouleversements.

Lumière du rituel

L'élément clef pour comprendre la mission pastorale de Lu Xiujing est le compendium de ses sermons liturgiques, *Lumière du rituel*. Le texte est organisé autour de l'exégèse de concepts mystiques et de termes philosophiques extraits de citations choisies du *Laozi*, ou *Livre de la Voie et de la Vertu* (*Daode jing* 道德經), le classique attribué au sage du même nom. Avant de traiter des sermons proprement dits au chapitre 7, il importe de s'interroger sur le sens du titre de l'ouvrage et sur la façon dont il éclaire la visée de l'enseignement de Lu Xiujing sur la Retraite. Lu est particulièrement attentif à fournir des définitions didactiques de termes clefs, expliquant que l'expression « lumière du rituel » se réfère au rôle simultané de l'illumination divine et de l'intelligence humaine dans l'œuvre du salut[10]. Il développe ces deux aspects dans un traité à part consacré aux rites et aux procédures liminaires, dont celle de la sélection des officiants, intitulé *Explications sur la Retraite du Lingbao : Protocole pour les illuminations rayonnantes, les préceptes et les punitions, les lampes et les prières* 靈寶齋說光燭戒罰燈祝願儀[11] : « L'élucidation (爝光) constitue ce que Zhuangzi appelle la flamme de la torche (爝火), qui renvoie au moindre luminaire. » Lu fait allusion à la modestie de l'empereur Yao quand il céda l'empire au reclus Xu You 許由, ainsi que le relate Zhuangzi : « Si le soleil ou la lune brille et la flamme de la torche n'est pas éteinte, cette dernière n'aura-t-elle pas du mal à répandre sa lumière[12] ? » En adoptant cette figure de rhétorique, Lu Xiujing confie humblement sa lanterne à l'illumination divine[13]. Les imperfections de l'humanité, poursuit-il dans son explication, étaient incorporées dans les Cinq impuretés 五濁 qui entravaient l'exécution idéale de la Retraite[14]. La quête du mystère par l'humanité ignorante était comparable à la condition de troglodytes confinés dans des cavernes tortueuses où les rayons du soleil ne pénétraient pas[15]. Plongés dans les ténèbres, ils comptaient sur la lumière d'une lampe pour se mettre à voir :

> Voici ce que veut dire la lumière de la torche ou « élucidation » : rendre claire l'idée maîtresse des textes sacrés de la Retraite et sélectionner les hauts officiants pour la liturgie. Le but est de parfaire ce qui est brut et quelconque pour révéler et éclairer la voie du mystère. Comme l'artisan qui a en main du bois tellement tordu ou gauchi qu'avant de pouvoir lui appliquer le fil à plomb, il doit d'abord en raboter l'extérieur et obtenir une forme droite[16]. Hélas, modeste et bon à rien, je manque tout autant de clarté[17] !

Les officiants à sélectionner étaient le maître des rites 法師, le chantre principal 都講 et le directeur de la Retraite 監齋, ainsi que les préposés aux livres sacrés 侍經, à l'encens 侍香 et aux lampes 侍燈[18]. Les *Explications sur la Retraite du Lingbao* contiennent des instructions pour l'octroi préliminaire des préceptes, la sélection et la consécration des officiants, et le barême des amendes pour les violations du code rituel et autres transgressions[19]. Outre les « Élucidations préliminaires », le livre comprend la « Présentation de la *Lumière du rituel* » 法燭敘, tirée du *Livre sur la Lumière du rituel* de Lu, incluant le premier des dix sermons précédé d'une introduction. Dans les deux rédactions, Lu explique l'expression « lumière du rituel » (*fazhu* 法燭) en définissant séparément ses composants *fa* et *zhu*. Là encore, Lu emploie les analogies du métier de charpentier et de la lumière de la torche du *Zhuangzi* pour illustrer son propos :

> *Fa* 法 veut dire « le compas et l'équerre du charpentier » 規矩, *fa* étant le terme général. Le compas est rond, l'équerre est rectangulaire. Tous les êtres se conforment à ces [standards] pour atteindre la rectitude 正. *Zhu* 燭 est un objet lumineux 有光之物 ; secondant la lune et succédant au soleil[20], il dissipe l'obscurité et illumine les ténèbres. Sa brillance nous permet de voir[21].

Le sinologue américain Albert Dien, dans son étude de l'illumination métaphorique à un âge où l'éclairage était un bien précieux, traduit *zhu* d'une façon très proche de la définition « objet lumineux » de Lu Xiujing :

> Le terme général pour l'éclairage *zhu* 燭 n'a aucun équivalent d'usage courant en anglais ; peut-être « luminant » (corps lumineux) s'en approche-t-il le plus. Il se pouvait qu'une lampe fût éclairée par une mèche en forme de bougie (*zhu*) plantée sur une pique, ou l'illumination pouvait s'obtenir d'une simple mèche flottant dans l'huile [voir planche 4] ; quand les lampes cessèrent de se présenter sous forme de bols avec une pique, on peut considérer que *zhu*, quel que soit son matériau, en était venu à renvoyer à ce que nous considérons être une sorte de bougie[22].

Dien souligne que les bougies étaient de précieux présents impériaux sous les dynasties du Sud, Liu Song, Qi et Liang. Tao Hongjing reçut un don de vingt bougies 燭二十鋌 de l'empereur Wudi des Liang[23]. Indépendamment de l'évolution technologique de l'éclairage, le caractère *zhu* avait depuis longtemps acquis le sens étendu de « rendre clair » ou « comprendre »[24]. Durant les Six dynasties, son emploi métaphorique était courant dans un contexte littéraire autant que religieux. Dans les textes sacrés du Lingbao, le Céleste vénérable du commencement primordial 元始天尊 est représenté utilisant un rai de lumière pour transmettre ses révélations, comme le rayon lumineux qui illumina l'univers quand le Bouddha commença à prêcher[25]. Le *Soutra de l'éloge de la lumière* 光讚經, traduit par Dharmaraksa en 268, était l'un des premiers textes de la Perfection de la Sagesse qui, un siècle plus tard, inspirèrent le développement des écritures et du rituel du Lingbao (voir « Les Dix préceptes » ci-dessous). Le mot *guang* dans l'expression *guangzan*, « éloge de la lumière », renvoie à l'émission de tels rais par le corps du Bouddha, et le mot *zan*, « éloge », est aussi employé dans le soutra pour signifier « expliquer » ou « illustrer ». Le Bouddha de la médecine, Bhaisajyaguru 藥師, fit le vœu de faire briller sa lumière sur tous les êtres pour dissiper la maladie de l'ignorance et les délivrer de la souffrance (voir planche 5)[26].

La définition par Lu de *fa* comme « le compas et l'équerre du charpentier », une expression qui voulait dire figurativement « le règlement », revient ailleurs dans l'énoncé « *fa* signifie modèle ou norme (法式) »[27]. On pouvait traduire *fazhu* alternativement par « la lumière de la loi / du *dharma* / de la religion », mais la classification des Retraites de Lu Xiujing (voir « Une Retraite pour toutes les circonstances » ci-dessous) indique qu'il entendait bien que le mot *fa* signifiât « rituel »[28]. Lu souligne d'un bout à l'autre des sermons que « rituel » signifiait « la conduite régulée par la discipline ». La pratique rituelle correcte réglait la conduite du pratiquant et servait de moyen d'illumination. Et les sermons de Lu Xiujing illuminaient cette pratique rituelle. Voici donc comment Lu explique l'objectif pastoral de ses sermons liturgiques :

> Sans rituel, la déviation ne peut pas se redresser d'elle-même. Si vous pratiquez le rituel sans comprendre, vous ne pouvez pas discerner vos mérites de vos démérites. Ceux qui aspirent à la droiture ne peuvent pas se passer du rituel. Ceux qui pratiquent le rituel ne peuvent pas se passer de la compréhension. Pour atteindre la maîtrise de soi[29], il est indispensable de pratiquer la Retraite. Pour pratiquer la Retraite, il est indispensable de lire ce livre. Ce livre sert par conséquent de lumière pour le rituel 此經故爲法之燭. Si vous le tenez en main pour avancer là où le Tao est caché, il vous permettra d'appréhender la vérité 秉之遊道藏, 故尅獲於真實也[30].

Dans la dernière phrase, « où le Tao est caché » peut aussi être compris comme « où la route est obscure ». Lu se sert d'une analogie similaire à celle de l'*Explication interne des Trois cieux* : « Étudier mais ne pas pratiquer la discipline de la Retraite, c'est être dans l'obscurité, comme marcher de nuit sans tenir de lampe » 冥冥如夜行不持火燭[31]. De fait, le rouleau des sermons de Lu était porté comme une lampe quand les cérémonies de la Retraite et des Préceptes étaient exécutées : « Ainsi le maître des rites doit le porter pour exécuter les cérémonies de la Retraite et de l'Initiation 行齋臨壇法, durant lesquelles la congrégation entière s'engage avec un cœur humble à recevoir [les préceptes] 眾皆虛心盟受者[32]. En conséquence, leur vision et leur ouïe deviennent claires et nettes, et l'enseignement de la grande Voie est limpide pour tous[33]. » Le mot « porter » 炳, utilisé ici pour transporter le livre, était couramment employé pour tenir une source de lumière portative.

Pareille illumination scripturale était d'autant plus indispensable dans un âge où même les instruits étaient aptes à ne pas voir plus loin que les troglodytes métaphoriques de Lu. Pour souligner les déviations contemporaines, Lu Xiujing cite Yan Zun 嚴遵, reclus de Chengdu au Ier siècle avant notre ère, l'un des pères de l'Érudition du mystère et un commentateur du *Laozi*[34] : « Videz votre esprit pour retourner à la Voie et à la Vertu ; calmez votre respiration pour visualiser les dieux » 虛心以原道德，靜氣以期 [存] 神明[35]. Par contraste avec cet idéal quiétiste et introspectif, Lu dit :

> Les érudits de ce temps dernier prisent l'éclat et méprisent la substance[36]. La félicité se trouve dans la quiétude, or ils s'agitent pour l'obtenir. La destinée réside en moi 命在於我, mais ils s'épuisent dans la quête des mondanités. De tels adeptes se contentent d'exécuter des Retraites et ne comprennent pas les rites de la Retraite 齋法 ou, s'ils comprennent les rites de la Retraite, ne connaissent pas la structure de la Retraite 齋體. Ou s'ils connaissent la structure de la Retraite, ils ne comprennent pas la signification de la Retraite 齋義. Ou s'ils comprennent la signification de la Retraite, ils n'en saisissent pas l'intention 齋意. Empêtrés dans la confusion et l'erreur, rien ne les arrête. Menant une vie déréglée, ils perdent tout principe et n'accéderont jamais au discernement. C'est comme présenter le dos au vent qui forcit ou suivre un fort courant : ne comprenant pas que c'est en allant à contre-courant que l'on retourne à la source, ils sombrent à jamais dans la Mer des malheurs 苦海[37]. Ne sont-ils pas à plaindre ? Cela n'est-il pas affligeant[38] !

Les Dix préceptes

Mengzi 孟子, le philosophe confucéen du IVe siècle avant notre ère, énonçait que « seulement après avoir observé la retraite, les interdits et les ablutions, est-il permis de sacrifier à l'Empereur d'En Haut » 齋戒沐浴則可以祀上帝[39]. Pour Lu Xiujing, *jie* 戒, traduit ci-dessus par « interdits », signifiait les préceptes ; se soumettre aux préceptes et à la purification était une double condition préalable à la participation à la Retraite du Lingbao. Les trois éléments – préceptes, purification et Retraite – représentaient différents aspects du renoncement personnel. L'accomplissement de ce renoncement par la Retraite était le nouveau sacrifice.

Dans la « Présentation » préfaçant ses sermons, Lu Xiujing retourne une fois encore aux visées de la Retraite, situant cette fois-ci l'origine du rituel dans un contexte prébouddhiste, indéniablement chinois : ce furent les sages, les héros culturels de l'Antiquité chinoise qui « instituèrent le rituel (*fa*) de la Retraite pour régler chaque affaire en fonction des circonstances » 故立齋法，因事息事. La phrase adapte celle du réformateur légiste Shang Yang 商鞅 (mort en 338 avant notre ère) qui dit des sages fondateurs de la dynastie Zhou occidentale (1046-771 avant notre ère) qu'« ils établirent des lois (*fa*) aux moments opportuns et ordonnèrent les rituels en fonction des circonstances » 當時而立法，因事而制禮[40]. Ce passage trouve un autre écho dans le classique de la tradition politique, les *Stratagèmes des Royaumes combattants*, dont Lu Xiujing emprunte le vocabulaire pour caractériser le double danger de la tentation, celle-ci naissant de l'intérieur, celle-là assaillant la personne de l'extérieur, comme « le bandit intérieur » et « le voleur extérieur »[41] :

> Les sages considéraient que les gens du commun, courant après la gloire et cédant aux Cinq désirs 五慾, étaient incapables d'eux-mêmes de se maîtriser[42]. En conséquence, ils établirent le rituel de la Retraite, réglant chaque affaire en fonction des circonstances. Les Préceptes 禁戒 protègent contre le bandit intérieur 內寇 et les rites solennels 威儀 contiennent le voleur extérieur 外賊. La récitation 禮誦 soumet le corps et la bouche : vous tirez avantage du mouvement 乘動 pour restaurer le repos 反靜. La méditation 思神 subjugue l'esprit et les pensées : vous résistez à l'être 禦有 pour retourner au vide 歸虛[43]. Qui est capable de calme et de vide s'unit au Tao : c'est comme faire retourner sur ses pas l'étalon fougueux 逸驥 et en faire la monture de votre retour à l'être véritable 歸真[44].

L'ironie veut que l'« étalon fougueux » prôné par Lu comme moyen du salut taoïste emprunte une métaphore bouddhiste qui décrit le cœur humain comme un cheval indomptable : « Comment serait-il possible de refréner ce cœur d'un pouce carré ? » 誰肯制此方寸心 demanda le prince Xiao Ziliang ; « l'étalon fougueux et l'impétueux rhinocéros vagabondent au large ; ils ne se laissent pas brider ! » 逸驥狂兕曠不禦[45]. L'allégorie bouddhiste du cœur-et-esprit 心 comme un cheval obstiné, à dompter par la méditation et l'observance des préceptes, s'imposa progressivement dans l'imaginaire de la discipline spirituelle taoïste (fig. 6)[46]. L'objet de la Retraite, selon Lu Xiujing, était de brider le cœur impétueux de l'adepte ; une fois discipliné, le cœur devenait une monture docile pour retourner au soi originel.

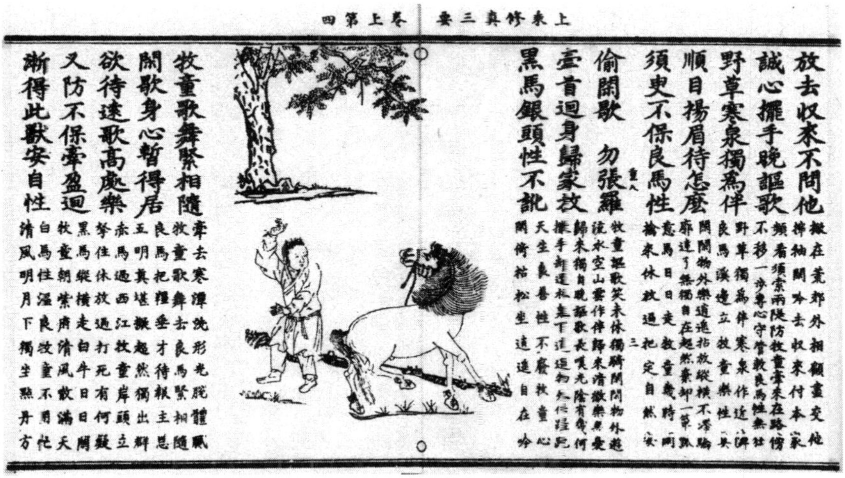

Fig. 6. Dompter le cheval de l'esprit. Illustration du Quanzhen dans *Shangcheng xiuzhen sanyao*, A.4a-b. Avec l'aimable autorisation de la Bibliothèque de l'Asie orientale et de la Collection Gest, Université de Princeton.

Lu Xiujing proposa que les Dix préceptes 十戒 du Lingbao agissent comme un harnachement pour protéger du « bandit intérieur »[47]. Ces préceptes remonteraient à une révélation consignée dans les *Instructions de jade sur l'écrit rouge* 赤書玉訣妙經[48]. Les mêmes préceptes figurent dans les *Grands préceptes supérieurs de sagesse* 智慧上品大戒, une collection de règles transmises aux candidats à l'ordination taoïste qui était courante au ve siècle[49]. Les *Instructions de jade* et les *Préceptes de sagesse* figurent tous deux parmi les écritures originales (datées d'environ 400 de notre ère) dont Lu Xiujing dressa la liste dans son catalogue des écritures du Lingbao[50]. En substance, les Dix préceptes de sagesse du Lingbao ressemblaient fort aux Dix préceptes du bodhisattva, qui de la même façon fournissaient le cadre disciplinaire du Jeûne bouddhiste *zhai* dans la Chine méridionale du ve siècle[51]. Pour les taoïstes, l'adoption de cette liste par le Lingbao marquait une rupture manifeste avec la pratique des Cinq préceptes, fondés sur des valeurs confucéennes et taoïstes, que prescrivaient les codes antérieurs du Maître céleste[52].

Les Préceptes du bodhisattva furent popularisés en Chine par le *Soutra du filet de Brahmā* 梵網經, un catéchisme laïc apocryphe pour bouddhistes chinois écrit du vivant de Lu Xiujing, et par sa suite, le *Soutra sur le collier karmique du bodhisattva* 菩薩瓔珞本業經[53]. L'enseignement indien sous-jacent, connu sous le nom de Perfection de la Sagesse ou *prajñāpāramitā*, figurait parmi les premières importations, et les plus déterminantes, du bouddhisme mahayana en Chine. Sa doctrine centrale affirmait que, bien que les choses phénoménales existassent, elles étaient vides de permanence et par conséquent non substantielles. Cette vision était en adéquation avec la philosophie ontologique des scoliastes de Laozi, comme Wang Bi 王弼 (226-249), et des adeptes du *Zhuangzi* et de l'Érudition du mystère. Daoan, Huiyuan et d'autres traducteurs de soutras en chinois recouraient à une stratégie appelée « concordance de sens » 格義 pour exploiter activement ces affinités, facilitant la pénétration de la pensée spéculative indienne en Chine[54]. Lu Xiujing était rompu à la littérature bouddhiste de la Sagesse, comme l'illustre la Leçon 5 (voir chapitre 7) dédiée aux préceptes de la Sagesse. Le sermon inclut la paraphrase d'une leçon intitulée « Qu'entendons-nous par Vaste sagesse ? » 何謂廣智慧, empruntée à l'une des premières écritures bouddhistes traduites en chinois, le *Soutra de méditation de la vive radiance* 光明定意經 (IIe siècle tardif)[55].

Le protocole du rituel de transmission de Lu Xiujing pour les Préceptes s'ouvre sur un « Hymne à la sagesse » 智慧頌, dont le dernier des trois vers relie explicitement les Préceptes à la Sagesse :

La Sagesse a engendré la racine des préceptes	智慧生戒根
Les Préceptes du vrai Tao sont suprêmes	真道戒爲主
Les Trois joyaux en émanent	三寶由是興
Les grands sages les reçoivent avec révérence	高聖所崇受
Voguez sur ce vaisseau d'immortalité	汎此不死舟
Pour gagner d'emblée [le paradis de] la Grande Abondance	倏欻濟大有
Quand les Élucidations des préceptes[56] ont cours	當此說戒時
Les esprits célestes viennent s'incliner	諸天來稽首[57].

Après avoir entonné cet hymne, les participants effectuaient des prosternements vers les dix directions de l'espace. Le maître des rites retournait alors du côté oriental de l'aire rituelle et, faisant face à l'ouest, exécutait le Rituel des préceptes solennels 戒威儀. En préambule à la déclaration des Préceptes, le maître des rites évoquait l'origine divine du rituel :

> Le Céleste vénérable déclara au Très Haut Seigneur Tao : Il est approprié de proclamer le son du *dharma* de toutes parts pour éclairer tous les êtres, afin qu'hommes et femmes puissent résoudre l'infortune, bannir l'anxiété, rechercher la bénédiction et le salut, et soient délivrés de toute souffrance 苦根[58], que les vivants puissent voir le Tao, que leurs personnes puissent être secourues des Huit conditions défavorables 八難[59] et que les morts puissent jouir de nourriture et de boisson dans le Palais céleste et obtenir une prompte réincarnation comme êtres humains ou sages rois *cakravartin* 轉輪聖王[60]. Pratiquez la Retraite pour obtenir la Voie ; que tous d'un même cœur demandent à recevoir respectueusement les Dix préceptes. Acceptez-les attentivement ; ne soyez pas oublieux ! D'un sentiment dévoué, méditez silencieusement et intégrez la Spontanéité 自然. Ne permettez pas que des pensées fugaces perturbent votre corps ou votre esprit. Ceux qui sont capables de respecter ceci, écoutez en silence :

1. Que votre cœur ne soit pas envieux 心不惡妒 et ne nourrisse aucune malveillance secrète. Examinez votre langage, gardez-vous de commettre une faute, et que votre pensée demeure dans la Loi.
2. Préservez la bienveillance et ne tuez pas 守仁不殺. Compatissez avec toutes les créatures vivantes et portez-leur secours. Que votre amour compatissant apporte soulagement de toute part et comble tous de bienfaits.
3. Préservez votre chasteté et obtempérez à la droiture 守貞讓義[61]. Ne vous livrez pas à luxure ; ne volez pas. Que votre conduite soit constante et vos pensées bonnes. Faites-vous violence et secourez autrui[62].
4. Évitez la convoitise et la volupté 不色不欲 ; libérez votre cœur de l'intempérance. Pur et consciencieux, que votre conduite soit sans souillure 無點污[63].
5. Abstenez-vous de calomnies 口無惡言. Que votre expression soit sans fioriture. Soyez juste et droit 中直[64] à l'intérieur et au-dehors, et ne commettez pas de transgression par des propos injurieux.

6. Abstenez-vous d'alcool[65], régulez votre conduite 斷酒節行 et tempérez vos dispositions. Sain et sauf d'esprit, vous ne perpétrez pas mille et un méfaits.
7. N'enviez pas ceux qui vous surpassent 不嫉人勝己[66], ne rivalisez pas pour le mérite et la gloire. En toutes choses cédez humblement. Effacez-vous et soyez prévenants envers autrui.
8. Ne contestez pas les enseignements des écritures 不得評論經教, ne dénigrez pas les écrits des sages[67]. Observez la Loi en votre cœur aussi fidèlement que si vous étiez en présence des dieux[68].
9. Ne vous battez pas, ne vous querellez pas 不得鬪 [鬥] 亂口舌, ne critiquez pas les quatre ordres 四輩[69], ne jugez pas les fautes des fidèles, ne nuisez pas au souffle vital.
10. Que vos conduites et agissements soient constants et entiers 舉動施爲平等一心 ; les hommes seront en harmonie et les dieux apaisés[70]. Comportez-vous ainsi sans faille[71] !

Les transgressions abordées dans ces Préceptes du Lingbao [PL] et celles des Préceptes du bodhisattva [PB], tels que le *Soutra du filet de Brahmā* les formule, sont presque identiques[72]. Les correspondances peuvent être schématisées comme suit :

1. Ôter la vie [PB 1 / PL 2]
2. Voler [PB 2 / PL 3]
3. Commettre des actes licencieux [PB 3 / PL 3 et 4]
4. Employer un langage faux ou offensant [PB 4 / PL 5]
5. Consommer ou vendre de l'alcool [PB 5 / PL 6]
6. Critiquer la communauté religieuse [PB 6 / PL 9]
7. Être envieux et parler mal d'autrui [PB 7 / PL 7]
8. Nourrir de la colère ou du ressentiment [PB 9 / PL 1]
9. Dénigrer la religion ou contester ses enseignements [PB 10 / PL 8]

Les préceptes concernant, respectivement, l'avarice [PB 8] et l'inconstance [PL 10] constituent la seule disparité entre les deux séries. Lu Xiujing croyait certainement dans la vertu indienne de la charité 布施 (sanskrit *dāna*) et au mérite de donner sans compter (voir « Lever les doutes » au chapitre 8) ; il se peut que l'injonction bouddhiste contre l'avarice fût si spécifique au rôle central du don d'aumône dans l'économie du *sangha* que son inclusion ne fut pas jugée essentielle dans les premiers préceptes du Lingbao[73]. Toutes les autres valeurs recouvraient parfaitement les codes moraux des communautés religieuses taoïste et bouddhiste.

La purification

L'attitude mentale adoptée par les participants au rituel devait être la suivante :

> Ceux qui pratiquent la Retraite joignent les mains et observent le silence dans une pièce retirée afin de dompter leurs états d'âme. Fermez résolument le portail des esprits 神關 pour ne laisser entrer aucun dérangement extérieur. Tenez-vous en aux Dix préceptes pour prévenir l'affleurement de pensées profanes. Renforcez votre courage, ayez le cœur résolu, et cultivez les dix conduites morales 十道行[74]. Plantez fermement votre détermination et ne vacillez jamais ! Fixez votre attention sur les mystères et attachez-vous à la vérité jusqu'à ce que chacune de vos pensées soit pure. C'est ainsi que la « Retraite » doit être comprise[75].

Le passage illustre le caractère préparatoire de la pratique des préceptes et de la purification avant le rituel de la Retraite. La formulation classique de Mengzi associait la Retraite à des actes d'ablution. En Inde, le sacrifice védique à Soma, *upavasatha*, était pareillement précédé par un rituel de purification, ancêtre lointain du Jeûne bouddhiste *poṣadha* pratiqué dans la Chine des Six dynasties[76]. Le jeûne comme abstention de nourriture figure également parmi les actes de purification préparatoires à la Retraite taoïste. Dans le registre courant, la signification de l'expression que nous traduisons ici par ablution 沐浴 est « se baigner ». Elle se compose de deux mots qui se réfèrent séparément à une aspersion de la tête 沐 et une immersion du corps 浴, soulignant les fonctions initiatrices et expiatoires de l'ablution. Dans les rituels mortuaires du Maître céleste, on faisait appel à la divine dame des Ablutions pour laver le défunt de ses péchés (voir « La délivrance des morts » au chapitre 4). Le bain d'eau chaude parfumée figure en tête de la liste des purifications de Lu Xiujing avant la performance de la Retraite. Par ailleurs, Lu explique en des termes quasi médicaux comment fabriquer le parfum pour ce bain et produire de l'encens tout en préparant des pilules aromatiques à ingérer : « Mélanger proportionnellement des aromates délicats assortis ; distiller à la vapeur en vue de faire des perles odorantes 香珠 ; les attacher avec un fil de soie verte et laisser sécher au soleil[77]. En outre, utiliser l'huile essentielle des aromates assortis pour fabriquer de l'encens, pour parfumer l'eau chaude du bain 香湯沐浴 ou pour préparer des pilules aromatiques 香丸 à ingérer, dans chaque cas selon le dosage prescrit[78]. »

Se tournant ainsi vers les principes purificatoires de la Retraite du Lingbao, Lu définit les impuretés à nettoyer comme relevant des « Trois barrières » 三關, à savoir le corps, la bouche et l'esprit. Ces barrières étaient les véhicules du péché et faisaient obstacle à l'illumination[79] :

> Le Très Haut Céleste vénérable 太上天尊 ouvrit le casier à livres de jade 玉笈 dans le Palais suprême de la Ténuité pourpre de la Métropole sombre 玄都上宮紫微 et en sortit la merveilleuse Retraite du Lingbao 靈寶妙齋 afin que l'humanité ne fût pas entravée par les perturbations dues aux Trois barrières : le *corps* est mû par la violence, l'avidité et la débauche ; par conséquent, nous le maîtrisons par la vénération rituelle. La *bouche* est susceptible de proférer l'injure, l'outrance et la duplicité ; par conséquent, nous la disciplinons par la récitation des écritures. L'*esprit* est sujet aux pensées de convoitise et à la colère ; par conséquent, nous l'employons à visualiser les dieux 思神. En appliquant ces trois méthodes, nous lavons notre cœur et purifions notre conduite. Purifier son cœur et sa conduite au plus haut point, c'est cela la signification de la Retraite[80].

Outre l'objectif d'ensemble de purification du rituel, les protocoles de la nouvelle Retraite du Lingbao se déclinaient selon plusieurs programmes spécifiques. Pour épouser cette diversification, Lu Xiujing réunit dix actes de purification, extraits du protocole de la cérémonie principale, comme préambule général à la performance de chaque sorte de Retraite. Ces dix actes de purification sont les suivants :

1. Baignez-vous dans de l'eau chaude parfumée 香湯沐浴 pour purifier votre souffle vital, que les cinq extrémités soient propres et les Neuf ouvertures 九孔 nettes[81]. Votre vêture immaculée, votre intérieur et votre

extérieur odorants et purs – telles sont les conditions pour accueillir la descente des Véritables exaltés et contempler l'approche des esprits sans forme.

2. Bannissez toutes les affaires du monde 廢棄世務 et détachez-vous des imbroglios profanes, protégez l'intérieur de l'extérieur. Sans entraves, pratiquez la non-action. Votre corps et votre cœur à l'aise, concentrez vos pensées sur leur seul objectif.
3. Jeûnez après la mi-journée et abstenez-vous de mets délicats 中食絕味[82]. Ceci émoussera les appétits, permettra à la plénitude et au vide d'atteindre la modération et harmonisera les organes internes. Votre souffle vital apaisé, nourrissez la source originelle.
4. Disciplinez votre corps et arrangez vos vêtements 謹身正服. Que l'ordre de la Retraite soit strict. Défaites-vous de l'impudence et évitez toute négligence. Vos actes de vénération et de contrition doivent dans tous les cas être parfaitement mesurés[83].
5. Scellez vos lèvres et cessez la conversation 閉口息語. Qu'il n'y ait nul propos déplacé. Les sons harmonieux rectifient le *qi*. La récitation des écritures éveille notre compréhension des hommes et des esprits et nous permet d'établir le contact avec les immortels et les sages.
6. Purifiez vos perceptions mentales 滌除心意. Il ne doit pas y avoir de pensée hétérodoxe. Maîtrisez les Six facultés 六根[84] et supprimez les Trois poisons 三毒[85]. Visualisez les dieux, méditez sur les Véritables, pénétrez la profondeur et la subtilité.
7. Brûlez de l'encens et présentez la fumée en offrande 燒香奏煙. Battez le tambour 鳴鼓 (c'est-à-dire grincez des dents) pour faire venir les dieux. Rapportez aux cieux des Trois puretés 三清 en haut et proclamez votre déclaration aux dix directions de l'espace.
8. Confessez vos fautes 懺謝罪咎 et implorez le pardon. D'un cœur pur et avec la plus grande sincérité, montrez une humble affliction et soyez tout à fait dans la désolation.
9. Faites preuve d'une grande compassion 發大慈悲 et prenez en pitié tout un chacun. Priez en tout lieu et en tout temps pour la délivrance de tous les maux et pour que la transmigration soit sereine et sans davantage de tourments.
10. Que votre conduite et vos actions soient entièrement calmes et dignes 進止俯仰每盡閑雅. Dans vos discussions avec autrui, limitez vos paroles au Tao et ne vous écartez pas de la Loi. Quand vous réalisez votre erreur ou transgression, prosternez-vous et faites une confession[86].

Les formes choisies de purification étaient ainsi conçues pour ôter les Trois barrières : purifier le corps par le bain, le jeûne, la discipline et par une tenue ordonnée ; la bouche, en s'abstenant de propos futiles et discordants ; et l'esprit, par le contrôle de la pensée, le détachement, la contrition et la compassion. Avec l'introduction de la Retraite, la purification rituelle devint une obligation constante de la vie monastique taoïste, se développant parallèlement à la nouvelle pratique liturgique[87].

Après avoir offert de l'encens et annoncé dans toutes les directions la performance du rituel, l'adepte, dans un état immaculé, était alors prêt à assister à la descente des divinités. Car, quand la Retraite se tenait, les dieux descendaient, par contraste notable avec le rituel de requête, durant lequel le prêtre officiant entreprenait le voyage inverse par son ascension chamanique au Portail du ciel[88]. Lu Xiujing appelle « Véritables exaltés » les divinités descendantes, et une recension ultérieure du texte fait référence à l'Empereur d'En Haut, retrouvant la déclaration classique de Mengzi : « Seulement après avoir observé la retraite, les interdits et les ablutions, est-il permis de sacrifier à l'Empereur d'En Haut[89]. »

Une Retraite pour toutes les circonstances

Les sages « établirent le rituel de la Retraite pour régler chaque affaire en fonction des circonstances ». Les protocoles rituels pouvaient servir pour de multiples intentions, et les réformes de Lu Xiujing introduisirent un degré de plasticité supplémentaire dans l'articulation du format de la Retraite. Le sens général du rituel était la purification, quel que soit le chemin emprunté, celui de la discipline, de l'observance des préceptes ou de la quiétude. À partir de cet objectif commun, Lu justifiait le besoin de différencier les types de Retraite du Lingbao selon leurs propos. Le premier était d'ordre pédagogique : en fonction des capacités inégales des adeptes et de leurs différents besoins spirituels, des niveaux gradués pour effectuer la Retraite et observer les préceptes étaient instaurés, soit une approche ressemblant fortement à la doctrine bouddhiste de l'*upāya* 方便 ou « moyens appropriés » pour atteindre l'illumination :

> La Voie estime que la Retraite et les Préceptes sont le début et la fin de l'établissement de la vertu et la porte de la recherche de la perfection. Mais nombre de personnes qui étudient la Voie et aspirent à l'immortalité, et de maisonnées qui prient pour la bénédiction et espèrent la bonne fortune, ne respectent pas [la Retraite ni les Préceptes]. Puisque l'intelligence d'un élève peut être brillante ou faible, la compréhension sera vive ou émoussée ; puisque ses capacités peuvent être supérieures ou inférieures, les devoirs seront plus ou moins nombreux. Par conséquent, les sages établirent des degrés de rusticité et de finesse, et distinguèrent des trajectoires séparées[90].

Un autre besoin tenait au calendrier liturgique : certaines observances, dont les confessions périodiques et les actes de pénitence, étaient reliées aux fêtes saisonnières ou à des conjonctures cycliques récurrentes. Le troisième était mû par des événements tels la mort ou un cas de maladie ou d'infortune. Comme le rituel de requête, les Retraites visaient des objectifs rédempteurs variés, dont le salut, l'expiation, la délivrance ou la préservation, et servaient des bénéficiaires divers – l'État, les ancêtres, soi-même ou le monde en général. Par conséquent, dans ses *Cinq sentiments*, sous la rubrique « Les divers rituels de Retraite » 眾齋法, Lu énuméra neuf Retraites du Lingbao distinctes qui étaient adaptées à des intentions particulières, chacune ayant en propre ses spécifications pour l'autel, son protocole et son calendrier liturgique. Leurs intentions respectives peuvent se résumer comme suit :

1. Harmoniser le yin et le yang et sauver le pays (Retraite du registre d'or 金籙齋),
2. Éradiquer les péchés des ancêtres défunts (Retraite du registre jaune 黃籙齋),
3. Sauver les âmes de myriades de générations d'ancêtres des Neuf ténèbres (Retraite de l'alliance avec les Véritables 明真齋),
4. Confesser trois fois par an ses violations des préceptes (Retraite des Trois originels 三元齋),
5. Solliciter huit fois par an le pardon des péchés des ascendants, ainsi que [le pardon des péchés] commis par soi-même dans les existences antérieures et dans la vie présente (Retraite des Huit périodes 八節齋),
6. S'améliorer et sauver autrui, éviter les désastres et obtenir la bénédiction (Retraite de la spontanéité 自然齋),

7. Rechercher la purification par des actes de dévotion et la prière (Retraite des Trois souverains [du canon] de la Caverne des divinités 洞神三皇之齋),
8. Exprimer la vénération par la purification de soi et en affirmant conjointement les principes de la pratique correcte conformément à l'enseignement unique (Retraite du Grand un[91] 太一之齋),
9. Honorer la pureté et la simplicité par les règles diététiques (Retraite de l'instruction 指教齋)[92].

Bien que la Retraite de l'instruction (9) fût attribuée à la tradition du Maître céleste et que la Retraite des Trois souverains (7) relevât de la section Caverne des divinités dans le canon taoïste, Lu Xiujing codifia l'ensemble de ces neuf rituels comme des Retraites du Lingbao[93]. Chacune de leurs intentions pouvait aussi être combinée avec des occasions ou des objectifs particuliers, élargissant davantage encore leur portée. En 471, par exemple, Lu Xiujing célébra la Retraite des Trois originels (4) comme un rite de confession périodique, servant à prier pour la santé de l'empereur[94]. Quant à la Retraite de la spontanéité (6), outre les bénéfices résumés ci-dessus, une version « suprême » 靈寶自然無上齋 procurait la délivrance des Cinq chemins 五道 de la réincarnation et oblitérait la transmigration, permettant aux pratiquants de transcender les Trois mondes du *samsāra* et d'accéder au salut universel[95].

CHAPITRE 7

CORRIGEZ VOTRE CŒUR, CORRIGEZ VOTRE CONDUITE !

La voie nouvelle pour atteindre le salut établie par Lu Xiujing liait la pratique du rituel de la Retraite avec le plan sotériologique du *Laozi* tel que l'avaient élaboré les scholiastes Han et les maîtres de l'Érudition du mystère. Dans cette vision de l'humanité que n'auraient désavouée ni la cosmologie du *Livre des mutations* ni la philosophie médicale du *Classique intérieur de l'Empereur jaune* 黃帝內經, l'univers et ses principes opératoires étaient en correspondance avec la physiologie humaine. Ce modèle présente des points communs avec l'enseignement hippocratique sur les conditions de la vie et de sa préservation, et avec les théories d'Aristote relatives à la vie intelligente, à l'âme et ses fonctions, au *pneuma* et aux émotions[1]. Mais si le corps matériel chinois était tout autant animé par des esprits et doté de vitalité, il était de surcroît, selon Lu Xiujing, soumis aux mécanismes corrélatifs et transformatifs ordonnés par les Cinq agents[2]. L'action combinée de la dotation vitale et des corrélations donnait au corps ses caractéristiques distinctives qui déterminaient la personnalité unique de l'individu (voir la Leçon 7 ci-dessous). Le corps était capable de sensation, de perception, de cognition et de discernement moral. En bref, il constituait une « personne », ainsi qu'un sujet de débats animés parmi les adeptes des Causeries pures par ailleurs férus de physiognomonie[3]. En voulant associer les spéculations intellectuelles en vogue à son dessein religieux et à sa quête de rédemption, Lu Xiujing ne visait rien de moins que le façonnement d'un « soi » taoïste par la pratique du rituel et de la méditation.

Les dix leçons de son compendium *Lumière du rituel* constituent un programme d'enseignement complet sur le sens et la méthode de la Retraite. Au mont Lu, le rituel de la Retraite, ou du Jeûne, *zhai* avait précédemment formé le cœur de la vie communautaire bouddhiste. Les sessions de « prédication du *zhai* » 齋講 faisaient partie du service liturgique ordinaire. Huiyuan avait développé ce type de prédication en s'inspirant de la pratique de son maître Daoan de ponctuer sa traduction des soutras d'exégèses scripturales impromptues[4]. En tant que chefs religieux, Huiyuan et Lu Xiujing se souciaient l'un comme l'autre d'expliquer le sens et la méthode du nouveau rituel *zhai* à la première génération de pratiquants. Les « Élucidations préliminaires sur la Retraite » de Lu Xiujing notent la pratique du Maître de délivrer un sermon introductif au commencement de la cérémonie, quand l'assemblée de la Retraite était réunie : « Les rites étaient expliqués dans les quartiers privés avant le début de la Retraite, pendant que l'on revêtait l'habit de cérémonie et brûlait de l'encens comme prescrit[5]. » L'habillage du prêtre, littéralement « ceindre la ceinture » 束帶, constituait un rite préliminaire.

Des prédications ultérieures marquaient les différentes phases de la Retraite. La liturgie des jours pour « pratiquer la Voie » 行道 était divisée en six périodes 六時, incluant trois offices diurnes et trois nocturnes, et des sessions dédiées aux offrandes, aux confessions et aux méditations[6]. Le rituel du Jeûne bouddhiste réservait un tiers de la journée aux exercices de méditation (*dhyāna* 禪)[7]. Une Retraite taoïste comprenait des audiences matutinales, méridiennes et vespérales. En outre, une Annonce nocturne 宿啓 se tenait la nuit précédant la Retraite durant l'installation rituelle de l'autel[8]. Lu Xiujing met en exergue le verset marquant l'intention liturgique de chacune de ses dix leçons en les fixant dans le protocole des offices :

> Par conséquent, j'énonçai dix versets du *Livre* [*de la Voie et de la Vertu*] 說經十章 pour déployer les offices de la Retraite. J'intitulai [le compendium des leçons] *Lumière du rituel*. Lors de l'Annonce nocturne, un verset était

énoncé ; lors de l'exécution des six offices, six versets étaient énoncés ; et au cours de la méditation en trois offices, les trois versets restants étaient énoncés[9].

Par ces dix leçons rattachées à dix versets extraits du *Laozi*, Lu professait les racines chinoises du *zhai*, nonobstant la popularité du Jeûne bouddhiste. Nous examinerons ci-après la teneur de chacune des dix leçons et verrons de quelle manière le compendium établit la Retraite du Lingbao, au sein de la religion taoïste, comme la nouvelle pratique toute intérieure pour nourrir le principe vital, conjurer une destinée mal engagée et obtenir la délivrance.

La Voie et la Vertu

En basant chaque leçon sur un verset extrait du *Livre de la Voie et de la Vertu* de Laozi (*Daode jing*), Lu Xiujing replaçait la Retraite au cœur de la sphère intellectuelle du taoïsme classique : l'enseignement mystique du *Laozi*, avec ses dimensions physiologiques et politiques, et le Jeûne du cœur 心齋 du *Zhuangzi*[10]. Le plus ancien exemplaire connu du *Daode jing*, le manuscrit sur lamelles de bambou de Guodian 郭店 au Hubei, date du milieu du IVe siècle avant notre ère. Pour les taoïstes des Six dynasties, c'était l'œuvre philosophique fondamentale et un important livre liturgique[11]. La transmission du *Laozi* correspondait à l'attribution d'un rang d'ordination initiatique[12]. À partir des Jin orientaux (317-420), un « engouement pour l'Érudition du mystère » 玄風 avait balayé la Chine méridionale, suscitant une vogue pour les études du *Laozi*, du *Zhuangzi* et du *Livre des mutations*[13]. Outre Lu Xiujing, ce courant intellectuel compta le taoïste Gu Huan 顧歡 (420-483), un autre aristocrate et philosophe méridional érudit, spécialiste de l'alchimie et des rituels, qui entra dans l'histoire comme commentateur du *Laozi* et comme l'un des pionniers de l'étude critique textuelle du canon du Shangqing[14].

La bibliographie de l'histoire dynastique des Song (960-1279) retiendra Lu Xiujing comme l'un de cinq scholiastes du *Laozi* pour la période des Han aux Tang, aux côtés dudit Vieillard du bord du fleuve, Heshang Gong 河上公, ainsi que Yan Zun 嚴遵, Wang Bi 王弼

et Fu Yi 傅奕. De toute évidence, son commentaire intitulé *Quelques éclaircissements sur le Daode jing de Laozi* 老子道德經雜說 jouissait d'une haute réputation parmi les premières œuvres exégétiques consacrées au *Laozi*[15]. Peut-être ces *Quelques éclaircissements*, perdus depuis, constituaient-ils un commentaire exhaustif similaire dans ses grandes lignes aux dix leçons expliquant un choix de passages qui intéressaient la pratique de la Retraite.

Pour Lu Xiujing, la portée centrale de la Retraite du Lingbao reposait sur la solidarité entre cosmologie, psychologie et physiologie. Au cœur de son analyse était le « souffle vital », ou « l'esprit et le souffle » 神氣, une notion à laquelle les préceptes du Lingbao et les actes de purification visant à préserver la vitalité de la personne accordaient une attention particulière (voir « Les Dix préceptes » et « La purification » au chapitre 6) :

> La parole du Tao : « Parmi les dix mille êtres, l'homme est le plus noble » 萬物人爲貴[16]. Les humains considèrent la vie comme la chose la plus précieuse. Les conditions nécessaires à la vie sont l'esprit 神 et le souffle 氣. Ce souffle vital réside dans le corps humain. Pour l'animation 命 de ses quatre membres 四體, l'être humain ne peut un seul moment être sans souffle, ni ne peut ne serait-ce qu'un instant perdre son esprit. Quand l'esprit se perd, les Cinq viscères se détraquent. Qui perd le souffle est entraîné vers la mort. L'esprit procède du souffle, tous deux s'engendrant mutuellement sans fin. Le souffle procède de l'esprit dont il tire sans trêve émulation et force. Quand l'esprit passe, le souffle périt. Quand la respiration cesse, le corps trépasse. Tout un chacun qui pourtant connaît la peur de mourir et la joie de vivre, néglige le fait que l'existence procède de l'esprit et du souffle. Ceux qui sans fin violentent leur cœur-et-esprit et malmènent leur souffle, qui encore et toujours vicient leur esprit et dissipent leur principe vital[17], qui jamais ne se soucient de quiétude ni ne prennent soin de leur être véritable, finissent éclopés ou mutilés. Comment peut-on ne pas chérir sa propre essence 精 ni entretenir son souffle pour les préserver, ni pratiquer la bonté et nourrir les autres créatures en vue de bénédictions à venir[18] ?

Le verset 42 du *Laozi*, qui sert de base à cette admonition introductive, s'achève par l'adage selon lequel les violents connaissent une fin calamiteuse[19]. Chacune des dix prédications qui suivent s'ouvre de la même manière avec l'intitulé « La parole du Tao » 道言, et chacune se termine sur une citation du *Laozi* introduite par les mots « Aussi est-il dit » 故曰. Le cadre métaphysique des dix leçons est la sotériologie taoïste classique du retour[20]. Lu construit cette vision par un exposé de psychophysiologie en corrélation avec les principes cosmiques, y compris la raison de l'agir moral et du discernement, les émotions et les facultés de perception – en d'autres termes, les composantes de la personne dans le taoïsme. Le même élan intellectuel embrassant le cosmos, l'humanité et le retour de l'adepte à ses racines ontologiques conduit alors l'auteur à travers la philosophie de quiétude de Laozi, vers l'alchimie physiologique et l'ultime libération accomplie par la méditation. Touchant aux techniques de respiration et de visualisation, les instructions finales abordent la concentration mentale et le voyage en esprit.

Maîtrise et quiétude

Les cinq premières leçons fondent la pratique de la Retraite sur les principes clefs du mysticisme du *Laozi* : la maîtrise de soi comme préalable nécessaire au gouvernement des autres, le non-agir comme fondement de direction du monde, le détachement comme source de la puissance. Énoncée au cours de l'Annonce nocturne préliminaire, la LEÇON 1 est consacrée à expliquer le titre *La Voie et la Vertu* et la relation entre la Voie, la Vertu et l'Homme[21]. Comme maints prédicateurs, Lu use de paraboles et de comparaisons. Ici, il établit la primauté de l'être humain comme le principe fructifiant de l'univers au moyen d'une série de questions rhétoriques émanant de comparaisons[22] :

> Si la loi du Tao 道法 existait sans les êtres humains, alors le principe ultime 至理 diminuerait et disparaîtrait, et [le Tao] retournerait à l'état de non-être 無有[23]. C'est comme semer du grain. Si l'on jette les graines au sol mais qu'il n'y a pas d'eau pour les humecter, alors comment peuvent-elles croître ? Si l'on a un seigneur et des ministres mais pas de peuple, alors comment peut-il y avoir de gouvernement ? Si l'on a le Ciel et la Terre mais pas l'Homme, alors comment la vie peut-elle apparaître et prospérer[24] ?

Dans la LEÇON 2, Lu Xiujing prend pour point de départ le verset 45 du *Laozi* : « Par la pureté et le calme le monde est rectifié » 清淨爲天下正, pour illustrer le pouvoir de la discipline et de la quiétude que génère la pratique de la Retraite :

> Qui veut gouverner les hommes doit d'abord se gouverner lui-même. Qui veut rectifier les autres doit d'abord se rectifier lui-même. Pour se gouverner soi-même et réguler ses pensées, rien ne vaut la discipline de la Retraite. « Retraite » 齋 veut dire mettre en ordre 齊. Elle sert à ordonner la conduite confuse de l'humanité. « Discipline » 直 est rectitude 正. Elle sert à corriger l'esprit du novice. Pureté des pensées et calme de l'esprit – c'est le sens de *zhai* et la raison pour entreprendre la Retraite.

La pureté et le calme sont aussi la défense qu'oppose le pratiquant aux soucis incessants, aux angoisses et aux envies insatiables de la vie quotidienne. Lu Xiujing les décrit de manière saisissante :

> La vie de l'homme connaît quatre grands tourments. Quand il a faim, il s'inquiète de la nourriture. Quand il a froid, il s'inquiète de se vêtir. Quand il a déjà atteint la suffisance vestimentaire et alimentaire, il s'inquiète d'amasser davantage. Ceux qui sont pauvres désirent la richesse. Ceux qui sont d'humble condition désirent la noblesse. Ainsi [les envies] d'honneurs, de goût, de musicalité, de beauté et tous les divers désirs s'engendrent les uns les autres. Quand on n'a pas encore gagné, on s'inquiète déjà de ne rien gagner. Quand on a déjà gagné, on s'inquiète de perdre. Les ambitions ne connaissent aucun moment de répit. Toute la vie, on ne s'inquiète que de peiner. Agité, on s'efforce de réussir, tandis que les affaires continuent de s'empiler. Le bon et le mauvais, le gain et la perte, le chagrin et la joie, le bonheur et la colère, un mental contrarié, un corps fatigué et un esprit amer – tout ceci éloigne du soi le *qi* de la Voie 道氣[25]. Quand les âmes *hun* et *po* quittent un être humain, le corps devient comme une ville vide. Les calamités se manifestent quotidiennement, les petits enfants pâtissent et périclitent, les gens meurent prématurément, ils sont ensevelis et se trouvent relégués aux Trois bourbiers, dérivant calamiteusement dans la vie après la mort 後世[26].

Des termes tout aussi concrets disent à l'adepte comment, en effectuant la Retraite, en calmant le corps et l'esprit, en pratiquant la modération et en concentrant ses pouvoirs mentaux sur la méditation, il ou elle peut se protéger de telles inquiétudes et tentations :

> C'est pour ces raisons que les sages ont institué la Retraite. Pureté et calme protègent des soucis de ce monde, refrènent pleinement les âmes *hun* et *po* 具錄魂魄[27] et reposent l'esprit essentiel. Vous devez la pratiquer avec la plus grande sincérité et la plus grande révérence, cesser de discourir et vous abstenir de faire du bruit, et ne pas parler en plaisantant. S'il y a des comportements répréhensibles, des pensées fugaces et un esprit distrait, alors l'œil ne peut discerner et ne perçoit ni le bon ni le mauvais, et l'oreille est sourde et n'entend ni les bonnes ni les mauvaises nouvelles. Qu'une vie simple soit votre but, le vide et le néant votre objectif. Faites de la modération votre principe et de manger peu votre fondement. Si vous focalisez vos pensées sur la Voie et visualisez les dieux, alors le Ciel et l'Homme seront consonants, les désastres seront évités, la bénédiction descendra et votre destinée originelle sera accomplie[28].

La Leçon 3 est succincte. Son thème est une phrase tirée du verset 48 du *Laozi*, sur le pouvoir de s'abstenir de tout agir intentionnel : « Pour gagner le monde, soyez sans cesse désengagé » 取天下常以無事[29]. Lu Xiujing applique la vision mystique de Laozi du pouvoir de la quiétude à la force que confère l'ordination dans le taoïsme du Maître céleste. Un adepte ordonné bénéficiait de la protection des esprits inscrits sur son registre d'ordination. Le registre des Généraux, officiels et soldats 將軍吏兵 correspondait à l'ordination de base pour hommes, femmes et enfants dans le taoïsme du Maître céleste[30]. Les agents mentionnés dans le titre du registre étaient les esprits gardiens du diocèse du Maître céleste délivrant le document et les garants de sa puissance[31]. Ils accordaient leur faveur au détenteur qualifié. Ce principe fut adopté par le système d'ordination du Lingbao et attirait également nombre de bouddhistes[32]. Mais, ainsi que Lu Xiujing chapitrait ses disciples, la protection des Généraux, officiels et soldats ne valait qu'en cas de comportement exemplaire de l'adepte et de sa pratique de la quiétude :

> La Retraite seule vous permet de servir et le Ciel et la Terre, en vous détachant calmement de vos pensées. Quand il ne subsiste plus une seule pensée, vous vous unissez au *qi* du Tao, qui circule et pénètre le genre humain 人道[33]. À la réception [de l'Ordination] des Généraux, officiels et

soldats, vous vous placez sous leur protection. Ceux-ci étant à vos ordres, chacune de vos aspirations est réalisée. Mais si vous êtes incapable de quiétude et vous abandonnez à l'agitation et à l'inquiétude, vous serez mal en point et ne serez soumis ni à vos supérieurs, ni à vos parents, ni aux autorités de l'autre monde. Quand la conduite vertueuse fait défaut au corps, quand le cœur est mauvais et ne s'est pas amendé, les officiels et soldats [spirituels] s'éloignent et ne viennent plus au secours des hommes. Ce qui vous échoit est fâcheux et les calamités s'accumulent. Aussi est-il dit : « Pour gagner le monde soyez sans cesse désengagé » 取天下常以無事[34].

La LEÇON 4 combine deux phrases du verset 57 du *Laozi* : « Je chéris la quiétude, le peuple se rectifie de lui-même » 我好靜人自正 et « Je suis sans désirs, le peuple revient de lui-même à la simplicité » 我無欲人自樸[35]. Ceci devient ici « Dans la quiétude, je suis sans désirs, et le monde se rectifie de lui-même » 無欲以靜天下自正. Lu Xiujing poursuit l'idée qui assimile la puissance à la non-intervention et au quiétisme mystique. Dans cette leçon, Dix capacités 十能 s'adjoignent aux Dix purifications et Dix préceptes exposés dans les *Explications sur la Retraite du Lingbao* comme prérequis à l'exécution de la Retraite[36]. Plusieurs de ces capacités ressemblent aux Dix perfections du bouddhisme mahayana, qui incluent de même générosité, patience, équanimité et renoncement par effacement de soi parmi les qualités requises pour la pratique du bodhisattva[37] :

> La *Retraite* consiste en la remise en ordre de toutes sortes de conduites et l'édification de toutes les vertus. Pour l'exécuter, vous devez être capable d'endurer l'humiliation, d'être docile, compatissant et charitable, de produire du mérite caché, de pratiquer la loyauté et la dévotion filiale, de faire montre de sincérité totale, d'être consciencieux et digne de confiance, de pratiquer la retenue, la révérence. C'est seulement après avoir acquis ces Dix capacités que l'on peut pratiquer la Retraite et apaiser son esprit, pratiquer l'examen de soi et l'introspection, et rediriger ses pensées vers le for intérieur. Votre bouche ne parlera pas sans raison, votre corps n'agira pas inconsidérément. Ainsi la couleur de l'incolore devient-elle visible, le son du silence audible, le goût de l'insipide délectable et le discours du mutisme communicable[38]. Ainsi les dieux descendront-ils et la bonne fortune surviendra-t-elle. Vous connaîtrez alors un changement de cœur et

vos intentions deviendront sages ; vous ferez de bons rêves annonciateurs de signes favorables et serez à même de voir des présages du futur[39].

Sans engagement intérieur, explique Lu Xiujing, on ne pouvait espérer le succès. L'efficacité du rituel était fondée sur la sincérité, et la mesure d'un « vrai » soi était la cohérence entre le dedans et le dehors[40]. Comme la « Présentation » introductive l'explique, l'adepte avait besoin d'être armé à la fois des préceptes pour contrôler sa volition interne (le bandit intérieur), et du rituel pour réguler son comportement externe (le voleur extérieur) :

> Si extérieurement vous n'exécutez pas les rites solennels et intérieurement ne gardez pas la règle des préceptes, vos faits et gestes passeront inaperçus et vos mérites ne seront pas consignés. Si vous êtes moins qu'absolument sincère, si vous doutez et hésitez, si l'intérieur et l'extérieur ne sont pas congruents et la bouche et le cœur ne s'accordent pas, si vos sentiments sont anxieux et votre disposition rétive, si vous êtes sujet à l'inconstance, maudissez en secret et éprouvez de l'envie, si vos pensées et vos intentions ne sont pas fidèles à vous-même, si votre essence est gaspillée en passions lascives, si vous convoitez la richesse et rêvez de sexe, si vous êtes incapable d'exercer le contrôle de soi, si en corps et en esprit vous êtes ainsi, alors, même si vous pratiquez la discipline de la Retraite, nulle bénédiction ne vous échoira tout au long de votre vie. Alors quoi ? Si vos pensées ne procurent pas la force intérieure et vos âmes *hun* et *po* subissent la servitude extérieure, votre *qi* harmonieux 和氣 s'éloignera, frappant votre résonance 感動 d'incapacité. Aussi est-il dit : « Dans la quiétude, je suis sans désirs, et le monde se rectifie de lui-même » 無欲以靜天下自正[41].

À la fin du cycle, la question de la congruence entre le dedans et le dehors sera revisitée sur le terrain de la visualisation intérieure du monde extérieur, où l'individu devient un avec l'univers.

Traitant d'abord de la force de la discipline des préceptes, la LEÇON 5 invoque les Préceptes de sagesse. Pour être sauvé, l'adepte doit prendre le « remède de sagesse » 慧藥, c'est-à-dire observer les préceptes qui constituent le cœur du programme rédempteur de la Retraite (voir les « Cent préceptes médicinaux » dans « Guérison » au chapitre 4). La section finale se présente comme un résumé. En fait, il s'agit d'une paraphrase de la leçon bouddhiste « Qu'entendons-nous par Vaste sagesse ? » 何謂廣智慧 du *Soutra de méditation de la vive radiance*[42]. Lu vise ici à expliquer une phrase trouvée dans les versets 4 et 56 du *Laozi* (« Émoussez le tranchant, dénouez ce qui est emmêlé » 挫其銳，解其紛), au moyen de l'enseignement bouddhiste sur le moyen approprié de la Sagesse 智慧之便[43] :

> Pour pratiquer la Voie et exécuter la Retraite, il est nécessaire d'observer la loi des préceptes 戒法. Le salut est sans bornes, les prescriptions rituelles subtiles. Refrénez vos attitudes et assujettissez votre cœur ; alors vous serez pur et vos penchants calamiteux seront éradiqués. Pratiquez le moyen approprié de la Sagesse (cf. « En résumé » ci-dessous) et extirpez [ainsi] le malheur de la transmigration 拔生死之難[44]. Interrompez toute pensée et rendez-vous au pays du non-agir. Étudiez en profondeur ce qui surgit[45], examinez avec soin ce qui s'abîme, observez ce qui pâtit et rétablissez-le avec le remède de Sagesse[46]. Si vous éprouvez de l'attrait pour la beauté et le profit, utilisez les préceptes pour vous couvrir les yeux[47] ; si la détestation et la rancœur vous parlent, utilisez les préceptes pour vous boucher les oreilles ; si vous avez du goût pour les mets savoureux et parfumés, utilisez les préceptes pour tempérer votre bouche ; si vous convoitez les richesses et les trésors, ou cédez à la tentation du désir, utilisez les préceptes pour émousser votre ardeur ; si vous avez une propension à la méchanceté ou aux mauvaises actions, utilisez les préceptes pour lui « casser un pied » 折足 (c'est-à-dire pour mettre votre inclination en incapacité)[48].
>
> En résumé[49] : Une personne qui n'enfreint pas les préceptes transcende les emmêlements du monde et ne s'enfoncera pas dans le bourbier. Séjournant au milieu d'attachements divers, son cœur demeure dans le réceptacle des préceptes du Tao 道誡[50] ; résidant en une maison de contrariétés, son cœur demeure dans le palais du salut béni 善救之堂[51] ; occupant une chambre obscure, son cœur demeure au foyer de la libération du *nirvāna* ; s'appuyant sur une maison peu sûre, son cœur demeure au portail des moyens appropriés 方便之門[52] ; assis dans un terrier de serpents, son cœur demeure sur le chemin de la renonciation 捨遠之逕[53] ; vivant dans l'antre de tigres et de léopards, son cœur demeure dans l'auberge de la bonne fortune ; confronté au danger d'embarquer sur un ouvrage flottant, son cœur projette une échappatoire[54]. Approchant d'une forêt en feu, son cœur contemple la paix de l'extinction 灌滅[55] ; se tenant sur un terrain de chardons et d'épines, son cœur demeure à l'abri d'une armure protectrice. Voilà ce que signifie observer les préceptes pour

pratiquer le moyen approprié de la Sagesse 智慧之便也[56]. Aussi est-il dit : « Émoussez le tranchant, dénouez ce qui est emmêlé » 挫其銳, 解其紛[57].

Alchimie et physiologie

Des démons destructeurs, appelés les Trois cadavres 三尸, assaillaient violemment le corps mortel des êtres humains. Ces agents pathogènes s'efforçaient de raccourcir la vie de leur hôte et de l'impliquer dans des frustrations, souffrances et infortunes croissantes[58]. À la moitié du cycle des prédications de Lu Xiujing, l'attention se déplace vers la dimension physiologique du *Laozi*, l'une des interprétations principales de ce classique. En fait, certains auteurs soutiennent que les plus anciennes strates du *Laozi* prônaient surtout des pratiques de culture physiologique connues sous le nom de « nourrir le principe vital » 養生 et les techniques de circulation du souffle, plutôt qu'elles ne portaient sur l'ascendant politique[59]. Les commentaires de l'époque Han allant dans ce sens incluent le *Xiang'er* 想爾 et le *Heshang gong*. Nourrir le principe vital impliquait de visualiser les Cinq viscères, les principaux organes internes, et les esprits correspondants. Le concept de Cinq viscères associait la théorie médicale à la dynamique de la cosmologie des Cinq agents et d'autres croyances populaires, comme l'atteste le *Traité sur les Cinq viscères* 五臟論 de la fin des Han (vers 200 de notre ère) dont circulaient un grand nombre de copies manuscrites produites à Dunhuang[60].

Dans la LEÇON 6, Lu Xiujing relie la théorie taoïste de physiologie humaine et les pratiques de nutrition du principe vital au verset 6 du *Laozi* : « L'Esprit de la vallée ne meurt jamais » 谷神不死[61]. L'Esprit de la vallée, également appelé la Femelle sombre 玄牝 et la racine du Ciel et de la Terre, était la matrice mystique de la création. L'exégèse de Lu se réfère à la trinité classique Ciel-Terre-Homme du *Livre des mutations*, l'ouvrage ancien de divination qui présentait les sphères physique, morale et humaine dans des états séquentiels de transformation[62]. L'étude des *Mutations* figurait parmi les quêtes intellectuelles prisées par les aristocrates du Sud et les taoïstes de cour, y compris les membres du clan Lu : Lu Ji 陸績 (188-219), ancêtre collatéral de Lu Xiujing, était l'auteur d'un commentaire du *Livre des mutations*, et les cousins de ce dernier, Lu Ji 陸機 (261-303) et Lu Yun 陸雲 (262-303), étaient des connaisseurs réputés des *Mutations*[63].

Tout hexagramme du *Livre des mutations* est conçu à partir des entités Ciel, Terre et Homme, chacune étant dotée d'aspects duels : yin ou yang pour la Voie du Ciel, faible ou fort pour la Voie de la Terre, bienveillant ou juste pour la Voie de l'Homme. Lu Xiujing, cependant, transforma la troisième paire antithétique, « Établissant la Voie de l'Homme sont la bienveillance et la justice » 立人之道曰仁與義, en quelque chose d'assez différent : « Établissant la Voie de l'Homme sont Trois causes et Cinq principes » 立人之道有三因五主[64]. Comme la leçon l'explique, les Trois causes et les Cinq principes renvoient aux composantes psychosomatiques de l'être humain, incluant les facultés mentales, les perceptions sensorielles et les émotions. Cette substitution permit à Lu Xiujing d'éloigner son discours de la haute cosmologie spéculative et de le ramener vers des questions pratiques de régulation morale, mentale et physique, jusqu'à donner de sages conseils comme ceux d'éviter le brouillard et la bruine et de s'abriter du vent et de la pluie :

> Que sont les Trois causes ? La première est *shen* 神 (esprit), la seconde *qi* 氣 (souffle) et la troisième *xing* 形 (forme corporelle). L'esprit dépend du souffle pour s'établir (cf. la discussion du « souffle vital » ci-dessus). Le souffle dépend de l'esprit pour circuler. Le corps dépend de l'esprit pour exister. L'esprit dépend du corps comme habitation. Quand l'esprit trépasse, le souffle se disperse ; quand le souffle se disperse, le corps meurt. Aussi les sages donnèrent-ils priorité à la nutrition de l'esprit ; ensuite, ils nourrirent le souffle ; enfin, ils nourrirent le corps. Quand les trois sont en harmonie et se profitent les uns aux autres, alors on peut vivre longtemps.
> Que sont les Cinq principes ? Le premier est *jing* 精 (essence), base de la vision des cinq couleurs ; le second est *shen* 神 (esprit), base de l'écoute des cinq sons ; le troisième est l'âme *hun*, base du discernement du bien et du mal ; le quatrième est l'âme *po*, base de la distinction du clair et du trouble ; et le cinquième est *qi* 氣 (souffle), base de la sensation de la souffrance et de la douleur.
> Ainsi, le corps est la demeure de l'âme spirituelle 神魂 ; les Cinq viscères sont la résidence de l'âme essentielle [physique] 精魂 ; les Neuf ouvertures sont les portes et fenêtres du souffle vital. Par conséquent, les êtres humains, dès la naissance, voient par les yeux, entendent par les oreilles, sentent par

le nez, parlent par la bouche et ressentent la douleur et la souffrance par le corps. Tout cela est l'œuvre de l'essence, de l'esprit, de l'âme *hun*, de l'âme *po* et du souffle. En l'absence de la première, il y a obtusion ; en l'absence du second, il y a confusion ; en l'absence de la troisième, il y a déclin ; en l'absence de la quatrième, la maladie survient ; en l'absence du cinquième, la mort s'ensuit. Quant aux morts, leurs yeux ne peuvent voir, leurs oreilles ne peuvent entendre, leur nez ne sent plus, leur bouche ne parle plus et leur corps ne connaît plus ni douleur ni souffrance. Serait-ce parce qu'ils n'ont plus ni oreilles, ni yeux, ni nez, ni bouche, ni corps ? C'est plutôt que leur essence, leur esprit, leur âme *hun* et leur âme *po* ont péri[65].

De la physiologie des perceptions sensorielles, Lu Xiujing se tourne ensuite vers l'effet des émotions et des appétits sur le corps et l'esprit :

La joie et la colère font que le discernement s'éparpille et n'est pas présent, les soucis et la tristesse font que l'esprit est bloqué et ne circule pas, la peur et l'anxiété font que les âmes s'envolent, et le manger et le boire excessifs font que le corps s'obstrue et que le souffle est empêché de circuler[66]. Par conséquent, les sages considéraient que la perte de l'esprit signifiait une mort prématurée ; la perte de discernement, la folie ; la perte de l'âme *hun*, le chagrin ; la perte de l'âme *po*, la pâleur ; la perte de la volonté, le chaos ; la perte de but, le manque de vitalité. En fait, dissipez le désir avec la vacuité du cœur, « émoussez le tranchant et dénouez ce qui est emmêlé » 挫其銳，解其紛 (cf. la Leçon 5) ; ne laissez pas l'attrait de la séduction et les excès endommager l'essence, ne laissez pas les idées noires, l'amour et la haine endommager l'esprit, ne laissez pas le désir du plaisir et l'importance des apparences endommager l'âme *hun*, ne laissez pas la colère et le franc-parler endommager l'âme *po*, ne laissez pas l'excès de nourriture ou de boisson endommager le corps, ne laissez pas les chagrins et les plaintes endommager le souffle ; alors seulement trouverez-vous le bonheur dans la solitude, l'union au *qi* du Ciel et de la Terre, la maîtrise de vous-même. Conformez-vous aux quatre saisons, adaptez-vous à l'hiver et à l'été, régulez le yin et le yang, harmonisez la joie et la colère, modérez le boire et le manger, tempérez la tristesse et l'affliction, évitez le brouillard et la bruine, abritez-vous du vent et de la pluie, chérissez le souffle et sustentez l'essence[67].

C'est alors que l'interprétation physiologique par Lu Xiujing de « l'Esprit de la vallée » du *Laozi* adopte la lecture prônée par le commentaire du *Heshang gong* : « Vallée signifie nourrir. Si l'homme peut nourrir son esprit, il ne meurt jamais. Esprit se réfère aux esprits des Cinq viscères[68]. » Le commentaire du *Heshang gong*, qui assimilait le *Laozi* aux enseignements relatifs à la longévité de l'ère des Han, figurait parmi les ouvrages vivement débattus entre Lu Xiujing et les *śramana* (ascètes) érudits du Temple bouddhiste de l'Ornement à Jiankang[69]. La Leçon 6 poursuit :

> L'Esprit de la vallée nourrit l'âme *hun*. Pratiquez l'introspection comme si vous étiez aveugle, pratiquez l'examen de soi (littéralement : « renversez l'écoute ») comme si vous étiez sourd. Vide et indifférent, vous n'habitez ni l'Est ni l'Ouest (les royaumes des morts et des vivants)[70]. En interne, visualisez 存 les Cinq viscères, distinguez leurs couleurs et leur apparence. Visualisez le cœur 心 pour sustenter l'essence 精, le foie 肝 pour l'intelligence. Visualisez les poumons 肺 pour obtenir l'aura 身光[71], la rate 脾 pour l'agilité du corps, les reins 腎 pour un *qi* durable. Si le souffle vital est préservé à l'intérieur, d'où la maladie surgirait-elle ? Aussi est-il dit : « L'Esprit de la vallée ne meurt jamais » 谷神不死[72].

La pratique ancienne consistant à visualiser les Cinq viscères est attestée dans des textes des Han comme le *Livre de la Grande paix* et le *Livre du Centre du Seigneur Lao*[73]. Plus près de la période de Lu Xiujing, elle figurait dans les textes de méditation du Shangqing[74]. Procédant des instructions ci-dessus, la LEÇON 7 transpose alors l'objet de l'exercice à la sphère de l'alchimie intérieure. Chaque personne venait au monde avec un ensemble de dotations : la vie, l'énergie, et les Cinq viscères comme « dépôts ». Ces organes étaient corrélés avec les Cinq agents, produisant une dynamique de transformation et d'agrégat qui déterminait les particularités physiques, la personnalité, le caractère et les dispositions morales de l'individu :

> L'homme est doté de Cinq viscères ; ils sont pourvus par les Cinq agents. Au-dehors, ils déterminent son corps physique 形體 ; au-dedans, ils déterminent sa personnalité 性情. Ses os sont corrélés avec le Bois, son sang avec l'Eau, sa chair avec la Terre, ses dents avec le Métal et la chaleur de son *qi* 氣煖 avec le Feu[75]. Le foie est [corrélé avec] la bienveillance 仁, les poumons avec la droiture 義, le cœur avec le comportement rituel 禮, les reins avec la fiabilité 信 et la rate avec la sagesse 智. La nature du

Bois est forte et droite ; la nature du Feu est féroce ; la nature de la Terre, tempérée ; la nature du Métal est sévère et cassante ; la nature de l'Eau, souple et déférente. Dès l'origine, la vitalité du *qi* dont chacun est doté est claire, trouble, dure ou tendre. Ceux qui sont dotés d'un *qi* clair sont intelligents et perspicaces, ceux dont le *qi* est tendre sont tolérants et aimables, ceux dont le *qi* est dur sont nobles et courageux, alors que ceux dont le *qi* est trouble sont obtus et méchants. Le caractère 情性 de chaque individu est fixé en fonction de ses corrélations et de ses dotations.

« Ce que le Ciel alloue s'appelle Nature » 天命之謂性[76]. Dans la poésie du ve siècle, on pensait que les mêmes dotations, avec leurs modulations des Cinq agents, donnaient lieu à l'expression versifiée et chantée des sentiments d'un individu[77]. La nature dont était dotée la personne, cependant, ne devait pas être considérée comme un acquis, ni n'était totalement prédéterminée. La nature humaine, pour être mise en accord avec le Tao, devait être soumise par une conduite disciplinée :

Le lot 命 de chacun, c'est sa nature 性[78]. Les insensés le dépensent imprudemment et le paient de leur vie. Les sages voient en profondeur et maîtrisent leur nature. Corrigez votre cœur, corrigez votre conduite ! Contemplez révérencieusement le Tao mystérieux. Examinez votre conscience et que chacun de vos actes soit en accord avec la Voie. Là où règne le besoin ou la discorde, servez-vous des statuts du Ciel 天科 et des codes rituels 法律 pour contenir vos émotions, changer votre nature et soumettre votre cœur. Suivez l'enseignement transmis par votre maître et prenez refuge auprès de vos instructeurs et vos anciens. Ne vous risquez pas à être négligent ni indolent !

Celui qui agit ainsi, les dieux du Ciel le garderont, les esprits de la Terre l'abriteront, les méchants le craindront, les instructeurs et les anciens le protégeront. Le Contrôleur du destin le sauvera, et il sera inscrit sur la Contremarque de gauche 左契 [de la vie]. Le Boisseau du Sud 南斗 portera son nom au Registre des naissances et le Boisseau du Nord le biffera du Registre de mort. Il deviendra un homme réel. C'est ce que veut dire « soumettez votre nature et protégez votre lot de vie ». Aussi est-il dit : « Faire retour à sa part allouée est devenir immuable. Celui qui ne connaît pas l'immuable agit imprudemment et va au-devant de l'infortune » 復命曰常，不知常，妄作凶[79].

La phrase thématique est une version abrégée du verset 16 du *Laozi* : « Faire retour à sa part allouée c'est devenir immuable. Connaître l'immuable, c'est être perspicace. Celui qui ne connaît pas l'immuable agit imprudemment et va au-devant de l'infortune » 復命曰常，知常曰明。不知常，妄作凶[80]. Ainsi, en se conformant au Tao, chacun retournait ultimement à sa nature originelle[81]. L'homme réel était celui qui incarnait le Tao et participait de la présence du Tao dans le monde. Atteindre cet état, c'était opérer le retour[82].

La méditation

Les trois derniers sermons de Lu Xiujing sur le *Laozi* accompagnaient les temps liturgiques réservés à la méditation. Inspirés par les enseignements du sage, ils offrent des réflexions sur la technique méditative et la dimension morale de la quiétude. Le lien entre le *Laozi* et le recours à la visualisation était déjà apparent dans les pratiques de « nutrition du principe vital » décrites ci-dessus. D'autres jonctions se font dans le domaine de la dévotion, avec la visualisation intérieure de Laozi en tant que divinité céleste, ou comme l'esprit occupant le « palais central » de la tête, et les récitations méditatives du *Laozi* comme une forme de vénération scripturale[83]. Pourtant, l'inspiration de Lu Xiujing pour les leçons sur la méditation et le *Laozi*, ci-après, se trouve ailleurs.

Après la philosophie de la sagesse *prajñā*, le second apport par ordre d'importance de la pensée bouddhique à la Chine par le biais des premières traductions de soutras fut dans le domaine de la méditation *dhyāna*[84]. Comme la doctrine de la vacuité *prajñāpāramitā*, la méditation *dhyāna*, avec son emphase sur la quiétude, la protection contre les stimuli intrusifs et la concentration profonde, n'était pas étrangère au monde conceptuel du *Laozi* et du *Zhuangzi*. Le sujet de la LEÇON 8 est la concentration méditative, *samādhi* 定. Ce texte paraît avoir inspiré la formulation du *Livre sur l'origine de la spontanéité du vide* 虛無自然本起經, un ouvrage des Tang qui reproduit *verbatim* plusieurs de ses énoncés[85]. La leçon est un développement du verset 52 du *Laozi* : « Bouchez les ouvertures, fermez les portes ; faites usage de votre lumière, inversez-en son éclairement » 塞其兌, 閉其門, 用其光, 復歸其明[86] :

> Pour être fidèle au Tao et calmer vos pensées, vous devez d'abord vous asseoir droit et fermer les portes, les oreilles et les yeux. Renvoyez la lumière de l'esprit pour éclairer le Palais écarlate 絳宮 (le cœur). Bannissez toute pensée. Vous ne devez pas forcer une vision. Vos pensées deviennent indistinctes. Pendant un long moment, respirez superficiellement. Vous entrez alors dans [un état] d'inconscience de soi 自然, dans lequel vous n'êtes plus conscient de votre propre respiration. Ignorant votre respiration, vous ne percevez plus l'existence de votre corps. Quand vous devenez capable d'oublier votre corps, vous avez atteint le *samādhi* 定. Vous faites face au Portail du Tao 道門[87]. À ce moment-là, votre esprit est dans le vide au-dessus des cieux. Tournant la tête pour regarder à gauche et à droite, vous ne voyez absolument rien. Comprenez cela comme le signe [que vous avez atteint le *samādhi*]. Aussi est-il dit : « Bouchez les ouvertures, fermez les portes ; faites usage de votre lumière, inversez-en son éclairement » 塞其兌, 閉其門, 用其光, 復歸其明[88].

En plus des traductions de soutras, les moines voyageurs contribuèrent à la dissémination en Chine d'idées et de techniques en provenance d'Inde. La cour de l'empereur Wendi, le premier protecteur de Lu Xiujing, accueillit le maître de *dhyāna* 禪師 d'Asie centrale, Kālayashas 畺良耶舍, en 424[89]. Cet expert étranger figure dans l'une des histoires de la collection du Ve siècle intitulée *Signes du monde invisible* 冥祥記 qui décrit avec précision l'expérience du *samādhi* : la nonne Tanhui 曇輝 (422-504), qui sera plus tard une connaissance de l'auteur des *Contes transmis et propos nouveaux*, avait un don naturel pour le *samādhi*. Alors qu'elle n'était qu'une enfant grandissant dans sa Chengdu natale, elle pratiquait déjà « l'assise » jusqu'à ce que sa conscience échappât à sa perception de soi. Tanhui pensait qu'il ne s'agissait là que de rêve. Une nuit, après qu'elle fût entrée en *samādhi*, on découvrit son corps inanimé, comme « du bois ou de la pierre », et qui avait cessé de respirer. La famille inquiète fit appel aux services d'un médium spirituel qui déclara la jeune fille possédée. En 432, quand Kālayashas visita Chengdu, Tanhui lui confia cette expérience. Reconnaissant le don de Tanhui, Kālayashas fortifia la résolution de la jeune fille d'embrasser la vocation religieuse, malgré les objections énergiques de sa famille[90].

La Leçon 9 qui suit s'intéresse à l'obstacle que constitue un esprit moralement instable pour atteindre le *samādhi*. Lu s'inspire du verset 10 du *Laozi* : « Mettez [votre âme] à l'abri et embrassez l'Un ; purifiez votre [champ de] perception mystique » 載營 [魄] 抱一, 滌除玄覽[91]. Il explique que l'agrégat d'éléments matériels et spirituels qui forme la personne acquiert la volition morale que lui assigne sa constitution cosmologique : le Qi primordial 元氣 cosmique a produit trois *qi* subordonnés, appelés Grand yang, Grand yin et Harmonie centrale 中和[92]. Similairement, trois Uns habitent l'être humain. Chacun des trois Uns est de même différencié par un *qi* distinct. Ces trois *qi* influent tour à tour sur l'esprit de la personne pour agir avec justesse (Harmonie centrale), pour faire le bien (Yang pur) ou pour commettre de mauvaises actions (Yin pur). La Leçon 6 nous enseignait dans son traitement des Cinq principes que le discernement du bien et du mal dépendait en premier ressort des âmes *hun* et *po*. Ici, nous apprenons plus avant que c'est en fonction de la nature de leur *qi* que les âmes exercent cette faculté :

> Dans le corps humain il y a trois Uns : l'esprit, l'âme *hun* et l'âme *po*. L'esprit est l'Un du centre, l'essence de l'Harmonie centrale ; son *qi* est juste. L'Un de gauche est l'âme *hun*, l'essence du Yang pur ; son *qi* est clair. L'Un de droite est l'âme *po*, l'essence du Yin pur ; son *qi* est trouble. L'Un du centre est mon esprit, la progéniture du Tao 道之子[93]. L'Un de gauche et l'Un de droite agissent en qualité de conseillers auprès de mon esprit. Parce que leur *qi* est [respectivement] clair et trouble, il y a une bonne et une mauvaise conduite. L'Un de gauche m'instruit avec constance de faire le bien ; mon mérite est chaque jour plus abondant, me permettant d'atteindre la vraie Voie. L'Un de droite m'enseigne à commettre de mauvaises actions et m'implique dans de mauvaises voies. Mon iniquité s'aggrave chaque jour et je m'enfonce dans la Citadelle du mal 邪城.

Voici établi comment l'action morale découle du discernement humain et de la volition. Mais Lu Xiujing, une fois de plus, ne saurait se satisfaire d'une vision déterministe de la personne à partir des dévolus cosmiques. Postuler les prédispositions d'un individu sert plutôt de point de départ pour exhorter les disciples à pratiquer la culture morale et la quiétude afin d'approfondir leur discernement :

> Ceux qui pratiquent le Tao, s'ils veulent comprendre les trois Uns, sont conscients du bien et du mal, distinguent le méchant du juste, se retirent du monde et calment leurs pensées. Ils deviennent profondément versés dans les écritures, retournent à leur soi et méditent. Alors la sagesse jaillit, les Cinq désirs sont soumis puis écartés, les Six sens[94] sont purifiés, la conduite devient droite et les bonnes actions s'accumulent ; elles obtiennent du mérite, et les esprits mauvais et démons de toute espèce de l'Un de droite capitulent de concert et ne peuvent m'assaillir. Mes pensées se préoccupent seulement de justice et d'être en communion 感通 [avec le divin et la nature][95].

Les préceptes visaient à contrôler les Cinq désirs et les Six sens (voir la Leçon 5). Un ensemble de six préceptes, les *Préceptes supérieurs de sagesse pour obturer les Six sens* 智慧閉塞六情上品誡, fut spécialement conçu à cette intention[96]. Ils permettaient à l'adepte qui les suivait d'obturer les yeux, les oreilles, le nez, la bouche, la main et le cœur. En conclusion de cette leçon, Lu va jusqu'à suggérer que ceux qui échouaient à accomplir la concentration méditative, malgré l'aide que leur apportaient les préceptes, étaient en mal de culture morale :

> Ceux qui ne discernent pas la méchanceté de la justice ne peuvent accumuler du mérite. Ils occluent fermement leurs oreilles et leurs yeux à la visualisation des dieux et [se ferment] à la pratique du Tao. De ce fait de multiples vices les assaillent conjointement, produisant de méchantes pensées. D'abord, leur esprit cède à la tentation, puis à la récidive. Sans cesse ils rechutent, sans pouvoir s'amender. Déjà [moralement] désorientés et fourvoyés, ils succombent à l'agitation mentale 不定 pendant dix mille *kalpas*. Aussi est-il dit : « Mettez [votre âme] à l'abri et embrassez l'Un ; purifiez votre [champ de] perception mystique »[97].

Succomber à l'agitation mentale et morale empêchait à jamais d'accomplir le *samādhi*. Comme le fit remarquer Erik Zürcher en référence au *Livre de l'entrée en samādhi* 入定經[98], alors que dans la pratique indienne le *samādhi* était essentiellement un exercice de discipline yogique, il glissa chez les taoïstes dans le domaine moral[99].

Cette observation vaut pour Lu Xiujing qui plaça sa leçon sur le discernement moral et la volition précisément dans le contexte de la méditation, faisant valoir que l'obstacle principal à l'atteinte du *samādhi* était de nature morale.

En contrepoint de la déclaration initiale « Parmi les dix mille êtres, l'homme est le plus noble » de la « Présentation », la LEÇON 10 referme le cycle sur une note d'un humanisme vibrant, la version taoïste de « Quel chef-d'œuvre que l'homme[100] ! » : « L'homme a l'essence, l'esprit, et les âmes *hun* et *po*. Sa forme le distingue parmi toutes les espèces. Sa Voie mérite le même respect que le Ciel et la Terre. En noblesse, il égale la Vertu des dieux. En intelligence, il atteint la perspicacité du soleil et de la lune[101]. » Pour les lettrés taoïstes du temps de Lu Xiujing, l'allusion au *Livre des mutations*, avec ses échos dans les commentaires et les classiques confucéens, était reconnaissable entre toutes : « L'homme supérieur s'accorde en vertu avec le Ciel et la Terre, en clarté avec le soleil et la lune, en régularité avec les saisons, en bonne et mauvaise fortune avec les dieux[102]. » Mais pour accomplir sa haute destinée, l'homme doit d'abord discipliner son esprit et son corps, et mettre en pratique les enseignements exposés dans les dix leçons :

> Il doit être capable de tranquilliser son corps et de fixer son esprit 定意, d'observer sérieusement les préceptes de la Retraite, d'honorer avec diligence les Trois joyaux[103], d'être rompu aux grades des fonctionnaires et soldats de l'Officier du ciel, de retourner sa lumière 復還光 pour pratiquer l'introspection 内觀[104] à partir des résidences 宮室 à l'intérieur du corps, de visualiser la source du rayonnement spirituel 神景[105], de rechercher avec constance le réel au milieu du vide et de pratiquer l'existence au cœur de la non-existence. C'est alors qu'il pourra gagner la lumière qui est au-dessus des Neuf cieux et accéder en deçà des Neuf terres. L'essence du Mystère 玄精[106] peut se révéler et le commencement primordial 元始 peut être transmis. C'est quand le Très Haut est vénéré complètement qu'il se manifeste dans sa plus grande vérité ; c'est quand la Voie de la vie 生道 est parfaitement chérie que les dieux répondent avec le plus de sincérité.

Le corps, à l'instar des grottes-cieux de la géographie mythique taoïste, était un microcosme[107]. C'est par l'introspection que la personne était en mesure de transcender ses limites et d'entrer, tel un chaman, en présence du divin. Lu invite son public à contempler la centralité cosmique de l'homme qui, devenant adepte, a la capacité mentale d'intérioriser le cosmos, à l'image du sage dont le corps physique fait un avec le Tao[108] :

> Par conséquent, la quête de la vie commence dans l'abdomen 故求生者,腹中而起. C'est au-dedans de notre propre corps que nous parvenons au fond du Ciel et de la Terre, parcourant les Quatre-vingt-une régions et arpentant les Quatre mers et les Cinq pics[109]. Ce sont mes souffles *chui* 吹 et *xu* 嘘 qui soulèvent les nuages et apportent la pluie, mes souffles *hu* 呼 et *xi* 吸 qui forment les marais et revigorent la sève[110].

Le passage se conclut sur une vision extatique du voyage en esprit[111]. Pour entamer sa dixième leçon et dépeindre les cimes vertigineuses atteintes par l'esprit qui s'adonne à la pratique solitaire de la méditation, Lu choisit le verset 47 du *Laozi* : « On peut discerner la Voie du Ciel sans regarder par la fenêtre ; on peut connaître le monde sans sortir de chez soi » 不窺牖, 見天道 ; 不出戶, 知天下[112]. Lu reformulait une phrase de Lu Jia 陸賈, l'homme d'État confucéen qui avait éprouvé une certaine attirance pour le taoïsme durant la période Han occidentale et qui, par ailleurs, était un ancêtre de l'une des branches du clan Lu de Wu. Décrivant la vision atteinte par le cuisinier Yi Yin 伊尹, avant qu'il ne soit fait conseiller du mythique roi Tang des Shang 商湯, Lu Jia écrit : « Son corps réside en une masure, mais son dessein franchit les confins de l'univers » 身在衡門之裏, 志圖八極之表[113]. Lu Xiujing entonne alors sa propre apologie de la puissance de la méditation :

> Le corps demeure tandis que l'esprit voyage comme dans la paume d'une main[114]. Méditant en son cœur, il récolte des bénédictions par-delà les confins de l'univers 坐修於胸心之裏，然臻福八極之表, la faveur des nuées et l'afflux des vapeurs, tout en gardant un calme immobile. En l'espace d'un instant, les [temps de] désastres sont dissipés et la longévité est atteinte. Car la vie qui ne finit pas demeure au fond de soi. Ainsi est-il dit : « On peut discerner la Voie du Ciel sans regarder par la fenêtre ; on peut connaître le monde sans sortir de chez soi » 不窺牖, 見天道 ; 不出戶, 知天下[115].

Les dix leçons guident, encouragent et fortifient l'adepte dans ses pérégrinations immobiles, cosmologiques, physiologiques et libératrices. Cette intériorisation par Lu Xiujing de la quête de la délivrance n'était pas à l'époque complètement nouvelle, comme en attestent le *Livre du centre du Seigneur Lao*, le commentaire de *Xiang'er* et la fusion des pratiques des *fangshi* et celles du Maître céleste opérée, au IVe siècle, par la visualisation intérieure du Shangqing. De plus, les écritures du Lingbao exploraient déjà la sotériologie du retour de Laozi d'une perspective alchimique toute intérieure : « L'élixir d'or réside en votre corps » 金丹在子形[116]. Le chapitre suivant examine les ressentis familiers, de gratitude filiale et de contrition, prônés par le Lingbao. Lu Xiujing en fait l'apologie et les prescrit comme « divin élixir pour sauver [ses parents] de la perdition » 神丹以濟沉溺 (voir « Lever les doutes » au chapitre 8). Après les dix leçons sur le *Laozi*, voici qu'avec les *Cinq sentiments de gratitude* nous assistons à la germination d'une nouvelle vision de la destinée et de la délivrance qui projette la physiologie et ses expressions dans le monde et le vocabulaire de l'alchimie. Au lieu d'adresser des requêtes aux dieux et de combattre les forces démoniaques du mal, cette approche nouvelle de la quête du salut, appelée Alchimie intérieure 內丹 sous les Tang, concoctait son élixir d'immortalité d'après les principes métaphysiques qui gouvernaient solidairement le cosmos, le corps humain et la personne[117].

Chapitre 8

Gagner l'autre rive par le revaloir

Avec Lu Xiujing, le Moyen Âge chinois voit naître une profonde réforme du taoïsme qui mise autant sur le renouveau de la sotériologie du retour de Laozi que sur une large assimilation des doctrines mahayanistes de la rétribution karmique et du salut. Si le compendium *Lumière du Rituel* de Lu s'attache à la première entreprise, ses *Cinq sentiments de gratitude* creusent plus avant la voie de la seconde[1]. Cet ouvrage déploie au sein de la même liturgie taoïste de la Retraite du Lingbao un parcours de contrition comprenant cinq méditations sur la dette filiale et la culpabilité et répondant à une logique rédemptrice, immanquablement d'inspiration karmique, différente de celle recherchée par *Lumière*, sans que son auteur ne se départe d'engager le dialogue avec la tradition chinoise.

Au dire de l'auteur, les *Cinq sentiments* furent originellement énoncés pour la consolation des disciples se soumettant à la Retraite de boue et de cendres 塗炭齋, un rite de pénitence rigoureux attribué aux premiers Maîtres célestes. L'occasion en fut une exécution du rite sous sa direction durant l'hiver 453[2]. Les *Cinq sentiments* caractérisent l'assimilation taoïste des méthodes rituelles bouddhiques pour racheter le sort des parents et des ancêtres défunts selon la moralité karmique indienne. Ces « sentiments » sont ceux de la gratitude et de la contrition : gratitude envers ses parents, ancêtres et maîtres ; contrition d'échouer à leur procurer la libération de la souffrance dans l'au-delà. Les *Cinq sentiments* rappellent la suite des Quatre gratitudes de l'Inde ancienne, des obligations contractées pour les bienfaits reçus de la mère, du père, des *brāhmana-śramana* et des maîtres[3].

En Chine, où la tradition confucéenne considérait le Fils du Ciel comme « père et mère du peuple », la vertu de piété filiale 孝 allait de pair avec la loyauté envers le souverain 忠. Le corps physique d'un être humain était conçu comme appartenant, au même titre, à ses parents naturels et au souverain. Le lien affectif entre parent et enfant cimentait tout l'édifice moral confucéen intégrant les relations de parenté, l'ordre social et le régime politique. Les taoïstes souscrivaient pour l'essentiel à cet ordre des choses. La dynastie Tang verra même émerger un culte taoïste consacré à la Voie de la piété filiale 孝道[4].

La piété filiale

Pour autant, les obligations et les sentiments associés à la piété filiale n'allaient pas de soi dans la morale sociale chinoise. Le *Laozi*, par exemple, était nettement en désaccord avec l'idée confucéenne de dévotion filiale. Tout d'abord, selon la cosmologie taoïste, les êtres humains, comme tous les autres phénomènes, descendaient du Tao primordial. Par conséquent, le corps humain n'était la propriété ni des géniteurs biologiques de la personne, ni du souverain[5]. Ensuite, le *Laozi* soutenait que la rhétorique de la piété filiale ne servait qu'à masquer la disharmonie sociale, une position qu'adopte Lu Xiujing dans le Troisième sentiment ci-dessous. Quant au bouddhisme, il considérait les liens d'affection au sein de la famille comme une forme de servitude dont il convenait de se libérer par la vie solitaire et la pratique du célibat.

Si la société traditionnelle chinoise ne voyait pas d'inconvénient à ce que l'un des siens opte pour une vie de réclusion ou s'en tienne à l'abstinence rituelle, le choix du célibat était une autre affaire. Le *Livre de la Grande paix* condamnait la continence comme étant néfaste pour la société et l'humanité[6]. Selon la philosophie confucéenne, le célibat menaçait la structure même du tissu social, soit le système de parenté et la continuité du culte des ancêtres. Puisque ce dernier dépendait de la fourniture d'offrandes par une chaîne continue de descendants, priver sciemment le lignage de progéniture équivalait à défier les ancêtres et renoncer à l'immortalité atavique. Pour Mengzi, « des trois manquements à la filialité, ne pas avoir de descendance est le plus grand »[7]. Mais le bouddhisme fut critiqué en Chine pour d'autres raisons encore. La tonsure du clergé bouddhique, faisant ressortir son communautarisme, était considérée comme un défi manifeste aux valeurs chinoises. Se raser la tête constituait un affront au devoir filial de préserver l'intégrité du corps, obligation sur laquelle les opinions taoïstes et confucéennes coïncidaient aussi[8].

En Chine, les bouddhistes cherchèrent naturellement à atténuer cette désapprobation. S'éloignant du modèle indien, les premiers bouddhistes chinois qui écrivirent sur les valeurs familiales jugèrent prudent d'adopter la piété filiale comme une vertu[9]. À tout le moins, les bouddhistes chinois pouvaient sans difficulté entériner le devoir d'un fils ou d'une fille de rechercher la relaxe d'ancêtres et de parents défunts dans l'au-delà, concept qui fit rapidement son chemin dans les écritures du Lingbao[10]. C'est bien naturellement que les bouddhistes transformèrent le devoir filial envers les ancêtres défunts à la lumière de la moralité et de la renaissance karmiques[11]. On peut voir l'une des premières tentatives de réconcilier le système de croyance bouddhiste avec les valeurs sociales chinoises dans la traduction, au IIe siècle de notre ère, d'un court texte sanskrit intitulé *Soutra de la difficulté de revaloir la bonté des parents* 父母恩難報經[12].

En Chine, la difficulté d'embrasser une lecture karmique de la piété filiale fut tempérée par l'attrait que suscita l'histoire de Maudgalyāyana, un moine bouddhiste indien connu en Chine sous le nom de Mulian 目連. La relation de Mulian secourant de l'enfer le fantôme affamé de sa mère servait de fondement à la Fête bouddhique pour le soulagement des âmes des défunts, nommée *ullambana* 盂蘭盆[13]. À quelle date cette fête se trouva établie en Chine n'est pas clair, mais on sait que l'histoire de Maudgalyāyana circulait du temps de Lu Xiujing sous la forme du *Soutra de l'ullambana* 盂蘭盆經, un texte apocryphe attribué au traducteur Dharmaraksa, et du *Soutra sur la récompense de la bonté parentale par des offrandes* 報恩奉盆經[14]. Circulait également le texte sacré qui prépara le terrain pour l'équivalent taoïste de ladite fête, le *Code des Trois originels* 三元品戒[15].

L'histoire de Maudgalyāyana décrit de manière saisissante la tragédie d'un Mulian incapable, malgré son ardente dévotion filiale, de réussir à secourir sa mère par ses seuls efforts. Pour nourrir le fantôme maternel affamé, il s'appuya sur le mérite de tout le clergé bouddhique, le *sangha* des dix directions. Le dispositif rituel pour le transfert du mérite collectif au profit de la mère de Mulian fut une grande offrande présentée par Mulian à la communauté le quinzième jour du septième mois lunaire au cours de la Fête pour le soulagement des âmes des défunts et de son rite de l'*ullambana*[16]. C'est alors que la communauté monastique et la société laïque bouddhistes pratiquaient des actes de don réciproque et d'échange. L'engouement du public chinois pour l'histoire de Mulian entraîna sa large diffusion via maints supports visuels et narratifs, retrouvés à Dunhuang, y compris des « récits de transformation » (*bianwen* 變文).

En outre, concevoir la manifestation du désir de salut pour ses parents dans un rite d'offrande alimentaire permit à la Fête bouddhique pour le soulagement des âmes des défunts de s'intégrer dans le paradigme rituel établi du culte ancestral chinois[17]. Comme parangon de piété filiale, cependant, Mulian défendait une conduite morale alternative selon laquelle la dévotion d'un fils ne devenait effective que par l'intercession rituelle du *sangha*, composé de célibataires. À l'imitation de Mulian, et avec le souvenir de la dette du Bouddha envers sa mère Māyā qui mourut en couches, la dévotion filiale bouddhique se concentra principalement sur le lien affectif entre fils et mères[18].

Malgré ces concessions bouddhistes à la sensibilité chinoise, la filialité demeura un sujet polémique. Une sérieuse pierre d'achoppement était l'injonction, dans le *Soutra de la difficulté de revaloir la bonté des parents*, d'instruire et de convertir les parents pécheurs ou ignorants afin de leur procurer le bonheur dans l'au-delà[19]. En dépit des intentions louables de l'injonction, elle était impossible à concilier avec la docilité respectueuse exigée des filles et des fils chinois. Au VIIe siècle, une réécriture apocryphe de ce texte, le *Soutra de la profonde bonté des parents* 父母恩重經, abandonna discrètement l'instruction séditieuse[20]. Cette seconde version aussi circula largement à Dunhuang, accompagnée d'un « texte d'explication de soutra » 講經文 qui en stimula la diffusion populaire[21].

Les *Cinq sentiments* de Lu Xiujing démontrent qu'il partageait implicitement la vision bouddhiste de la filialité. Dans sa vie personnelle, Lu fut l'un des premiers défenseurs du célibat taoïste et de l'abjuration aussi bien des liens de parenté que des aspirations séculières. Ces valeurs prenaient pour modèle la décision du Bouddha de s'éloigner de sa famille – princière – à l'âge de sept ans, une tradition popularisée dans le *Soutra du filet de Brahmā*[22]. L'engagement dans une renonciation si radicale, normalement associée à la prise des vœux monastiques, s'appelait « quitter la famille » (*chujia* 出家), par opposition à « demeurer chez soi » (*zaijia* 在家), la marque des croyants laïcs. Lu Xiujing et ceux de ses contemporains chinois qui empruntèrent la première voie rompaient visiblement avec les conventions, tout comme les premiers chrétiens choisissaient catégoriquement le changement d'état de vie quand ils « quittaient, à cause du royaume de Dieu, une maison, une femme, des frères, des parents, des enfants »[23].

Ayant embrassé si complètement la doctrine et la pratique bouddhiques dans sa vie, Lu Xiujing avait toutes les raisons de faire également sienne la rhétorique de défense bouddhique du célibat. On sait peu de choses de ses parents, excepté que son père Lu Lin 陸琳 paraît avoir été un ermite taoïste, puisque lui fut conféré le titre posthume de « Taoïste reclus éminent vivant retiré » 高道處士 après qu'il eut décliné neuf convocations à la cour[24]. La mère de Lu Xiujing était issue de la famille Yao 姚. Quand elle fut enceinte de lui, une vieille femme lui prédit que le corps de son fils serait marqué de signes surnaturels et qu'il serait Maître céleste. Lu Xiujing s'était marié et préparé à prendre un premier poste vers le moment de son ordination laïque[25]. Enfant, déjà, il menait une existence confinée. Le second des *Cinq sentiments* se réfère à la coutume des parents d'arranger le mariage et la carrière de leurs fils afin de leur assurer un statut et de leur fournir des moyens d'existence. Quand le canoniste et contemporain de Lu Xiujing, Sengyou (voir chapitre 5, introduction), avait lui-même appris à l'âge de quatorze ans que sa famille prenait des dispositions en vue de son mariage, il s'était enfui de la maison[26]. Bien qu'initialement Lu Xiujing ne se fût soustrait ni au mariage ni à la prise d'un poste officiel, on le décrivait volontiers comme « extérieurement impliqué dans les affaires du monde tout en s'en tenant intérieurement à la continence et à la simplicité, pratiquant l'abstinence des céréales, faisant chambre à part et logeant seul »[27]. Peu après, Lu Xiujing embrassait la vision du mariage du Lingbao, telle que la célèbre l'hymne :

Je me plais en la Loi comme en une épouse	樂法以爲妻
Je chéris les écritures comme des perles et du jade	愛經如珠玉
Respectant les Préceptes, je refrène les Six sens	持戒制六情
Observant la Voie, je bannis le désir[28].	念道遣所欲

Une pratique rhétorique efficace pour concilier les mœurs bouddhiques avec les attentes de la société chinoise consistait à emprunter l'expression des premiers écrits confucéens sur la dévotion filiale, spécialement le *Classique de la Piété filiale* 孝經 ou les formulations archétypales du *Livre des odes*. L'air « Kaifeng » 凱風 (*Airs de Bei* 邶風, 32) faisait l'éloge des mères et des bons fils pratiquant le sacrifice de soi[29]. L'ode « Liao e » 蓼莪 (*Ode mineure* 小雅, 202), une élégie à la mémoire des parents défunts, contenait les formules caractéristiques des sentiments d'amour filial en Chine[30] :

Mon père m'a engendré,	父兮生我
Ma mère m'a nourri,	母兮鞠我
M'a conduit, m'a élevé,	拊我畜我
Ils m'ont éduqué, m'ont instruit,	長我育我
Se sont occupés de moi, ont pris soin de moi,	顧我復我
À tout moment m'ont aidé.	出入腹我
Je souhaite leur revaloir leur bonté	欲報之德
Sans limite, comme le ciel[31].	昊天罔極

Les auteurs d'apologétiques bouddhiques tel le *Soutra de la difficulté de revaloir la bonté des parents* ou le *Soutra du bon fils* 孝子經 firent écho à ce langage, donnant à leur doctrine étrangère une consonance familière à l'oreille chinoise[32]. Les *Cinq sentiments* de Lu Xiujing recoururent au même moyen pour introduire la rédemption karmique bouddhique dans le rite de la Retraite taoïste. Ainsi le PREMIER SENTIMENT invoque d'abord la dette due aux parents pour leur anxiété et leur abnégation, en empruntant le langage et la cadence consacrés du « Liao e » :

> Père et mère m'ont engendré et instruit, m'ont nourri et formé[33]. Allant et venant, ils m'ont chéri et bercé en leurs bras, m'ont apaisé et consolé, m'ont dorloté et ont pris soin de moi[34]. Ils ont porté atteinte à leur propre santé par anxiété et se sont épuisés d'inquiétude. Quand j'étais indisposé ou tombais malade, ils étaient bouleversés et se préoccupaient de moi, leur cœur se consumant. Inquiets nuit et jour, ils oubliaient de se nourrir et renonçaient à dormir ; sombrant dans le trouble, ils se décharnaient[35]. Versant des pleurs incessants, ils languissaient après ma croissance et mon développement. Ayant pu parvenir à ce stade, je n'oublie pas leur grande et incommensurable bonté, et fais le vœu de la leur revaloir sans limite, comme le ciel[36] !

Ayant pris conscience de leur dette envers leurs parents, les disciples de Lu sont ensuite exhortés à méditer sur leur obligation à l'égard de leurs parents qui les lancèrent dans la vie au prix de leur propre salut. Le DEUXIÈME SENTIMENT commence avec le souvenir des rites de passage de l'enfance vers l'adolescence puis vers la vie adulte, prescrits par d'anxieux parents. Un texte de prière retrouvé à Dunhuang montre que des Retraites taoïstes étaient pratiquées lors des cérémonies d'imposition de bonnet pour jeunes gens et jeunes filles[37]. Ce rite ancien marquait le passage à l'âge adulte, théoriquement à vingt *sui*, voire plus tôt si la jeune personne était considérée comme nubile. Il est rapporté qu'en 463, à l'âge de 57 ans, Lu Xiujing fit cadeau à l'occasion d'une telle cérémonie d'un éventail en plumes d'aigrette, un accessoire prisé par les adeptes des Causeries pures, à un jeune compatriote de Wuxing nommé Zhang Rong 張融 (443-497)[38]. L'anxiété parentale se préoccupant notoirement d'aider les fils à fonder une famille et bâtir une carrière, on ne saurait s'étonner du mariage de jeunesse de Lu Xiujing et de sa formation en vue d'une carrière officielle.

Pourtant, l'enfer était pavé des meilleures intentions parentales. Mulian, « désirant sauver ses parents pour leur revaloir la bonté qu'ils avaient manifestée en le soignant et en le nourrissant », découvre que sa mère tourmentée s'est réincarnée aux enfers en un fantôme affamé[39]. L'adepte des *Cinq sentiments* se représentait ses parents défunts souffrant de punitions cruelles pour les torts collatéraux qu'ils avaient causés au nom de l'amour parental. Comme exemples de tels méfaits, le *Soutra du bon fils* mentionne le fait de soudoyer les enseignants et celui de courtiser les supérieurs[40]. Le sens de la culpabilité du suppliant est exacerbé par la conscience que c'est en vain que, jusqu'à présent, ses parents ont compté sur son aide pour échapper aux tortures infernales. Tourmenté par ces pensées et accablé par le remords, il fait vœu d'expier ses fautes par la pénitence « de boue et de cendres » :

> Père et mère ont pris des dispositions pour ma remise de bonnet et de ceinture et pour mon mariage. Ils ont accumulé des biens et assis les fondements de mes moyens d'existence. Désirant que je sois abondamment pourvu, ils ne se sont pas aperçus qu'ils étaient devenus avides. À force de se donner beaucoup de peine et d'être aux prises avec le monde extérieur, la rancœur et la parcimonie s'installent, menant au crime. Certains finissent par tomber dans l'indignité et commettent des offenses contre le Ciel et la Terre, ou causent des torts à autrui. Au-dehors, ils enfreignent la loi du pays ; au-dedans, ils contreviennent aux statuts de l'autre monde. Ils encourent des sanctions croissantes jusqu'à en perdre la vie. Et c'est moi qui suis à l'origine de tout cela, ayant déclenché ce désastre ! Les voici tombés dans les Trois bourbiers et frappés de nombreuses épreuves. Ils subissent l'arbre d'épées et se heurtent à la montagne des couteaux ; ils marchent dans les flammes ardentes et bouillent dans des chaudrons effervescents ; ils sont plongés dans la nuit des ténèbres et [subissent] le froid du gel glacial. Les voilà suspendus dans la cage de flagellation, sous le bâton à rosser, leurs douleurs par milliers et agonies par dizaines de milliers sont insupportables[41]. Mortifiés et misérables, et poussés à bout [par le fait de] de subir toujours plus, ils espèrent la relaxe mais ne peuvent pas se sauver par eux-mêmes[42]. Pensant à cela, je m'écroule et je suffoque, mon foie et mon cœur décompensent et mon corps entier est saisi de tremblements. Le corps et l'âme paralysés et accablés, je me prosterne anéanti et demande grâce avec de la boue et des cendres[43].

Les écrits confucéens sur la piété filiale exemplaire exaltaient le sacrifice de soi et le deuil emphatique pour les parents défunts[44]. Dans le dispositif rituel où Lu Xiujing prononça les *Cinq sentiments*, la version bouddho-taoïste de la piété filiale des participants s'exprimait en des termes d'une intensité comparable, leur ferveur éperdue passant de la contrition cuisante à l'évanouissement, du lâcher-prise à la perte de connaissance.

Lever les doutes

L'efficacité rituelle jointe au principe du transfert de mérite ouvrait la porte à l'intercession à distance des descendants en faveur de leurs parents, que ce fût lors de la Fête bouddhique pour le soulagement des âmes des défunts ou lors de la Retraite taoïste de boue et de cendres. Ce principe fournissait par ailleurs une exemption morale à l'obligation filiale chinoise d'engendrer une descendance et d'assumer les rôles conventionnels au sein des relations de parenté ou dans la hiérarchie sociale. La logique de ce retrait est présentée dans le TROISIÈME SENTIMENT. La formulation corrobore plus avant la méthode rhétorique de Lu Xiujing comme trouvant sa source d'inspiration dans un apologétique bouddhiste, en l'espèce *Comment Maître Mou lève nos doutes* 牟子理惑論. Cet écrit prend la forme d'un dialogue dans lequel Maître Mou réfute point par point les objections d'un interlocuteur anonyme. Il se présente comme l'œuvre d'un gentilhomme confucéen, réfugié à Jiaozhou 交州 (Hanoi) lors des bouleversements de la fin de la dynastie Han orientale. Bien que la date et la transmission de *Comment Maître Mou lève nos doutes* demeurent obscures, il est certain que l'ouvrage circulait à l'époque de Lu Xiujing et dans les lieux qu'il fréquenta[45]. De fait, c'est dans cet environnement qu'est attestée sa première apparition, conduisant certains auteurs à formuler l'hypothèse d'une origine aussi tardive que le ve siècle : un répertoire de livres bouddhiques compilé par Lu Cheng 陸澄 (425-494) pour le mécène de Lu Xiujing, Mingdi, contient une référence à *Maître Mou*[46]. Le célibataire résolu Sengyou édita le texte dans sa forme reçue et l'inclut dans son *Recueil pour magnifier et élucider* [*le bouddhisme*] 弘明集, un compendium de polémiques apologétiques[47]. *Comment Maître Mou lève nos doutes* est également cité dans le commentaire de Liu Jun 劉峻 (426-521) aux *Contes transmis et propos nouveaux*[48].

À propos du renoncement, dont traite le Troisième sentiment de Lu Xiujing, l'interlocuteur de Maître Mou avance cette objection :

> Parmi les hommes de ce monde, il n'en est aucun qui n'aime les richesses et les honneurs, haïssant la pauvreté et l'avarice. Aucun qui ne se réjouisse des plaisirs et de l'aisance, se dérobant devant le travail et la fatigue [...].

> Pourtant, les moines portent des robes rouges, mangent seulement une fois par jour, se coupent des Six sens et se retranchent du monde. En quoi cela peut-il être bien[49] ?

Dans les *Cinq sentiments*, Lu Xiujing défend la privation en prenant comme point de départ une observation similaire, mais la renverse alors en une admonition contre l'envie :

> Tous sous le Ciel, nobles et humbles, hommes et femmes, sont dotés d'un corps humain et du fardeau de prendre soin du corps et de la bouche[50]. En matière de nourriture, les humains font grand cas des cinq saveurs ; en matière de vêtement, des soies de cinq couleurs. Une fois rassasiés et réchauffés, ils ne peuvent toujours pas se contenir. Parés d'habits fastueux et d'objets précieux, ils s'amusent et s'en donnent à cœur joie avec leurs plans et projets. Jamais comblés, ils se gâtent l'esprit et font du mal à leurs corps sans même le savoir. Leur vitalité déjà dépérissante et leur corps décrépit, à la fin quel bien leur fera toute une vie affairée ? L'âme orpheline meurt seule et subit toutes sortes de souffrances. Ignorant en vérité, le monde ne comprend-il pas cela[51] ?

L'interlocuteur de Maître Mou, dûment chapitré, avance ensuite l'idée selon laquelle tout le monde attache « naturellement » du prix à la richesse, à l'aisance et aux honneurs. Cet argument prétendument « chinois » pouvait aisément être contré, comme le fait Maître Mou, en citant l'avertissement de Laozi contre les effets délétères des plaisirs des sens. Selon le verset 12 du *Laozi*, les cinq couleurs aveuglent l'œil, les cinq notes assourdissent l'oreille, les cinq saveurs endommagent le palais, et ainsi de suite[52]. Le Troisième sentiment de Lu Xiujing emprunte un raisonnement similaire : suivre ses penchants naturels conduit inévitablement aux périls de l'excès. Par ailleurs, l'acte parental ultime était la transmission de propriété à la descendance. Développant plus avant l'idée que l'amour parental poussait pères et mères à la faute et enfonçait leur progéniture dans la culpabilité, Lu soutient que, les parents ayant quitté ce monde, l'héritage qu'ils laissent devient un nouveau fardeau et une source de discorde :

> Le patrimoine du défunt est disséminé et devient le fléau de la postérité, engendrant la perfidie et provoquant le vol. Il est convoité par enfants et

petits-enfants, et les forts s'emparent de beaucoup tandis que les faibles obtiennent peu. Concéder et soustraire, perdre et gagner, tout cela nourrit la rancœur mutuelle. S'ils portent plainte devant le tribunal, ils subissent châtiments et exécutions ; s'ils en appellent aux esprits et aux démons, ils s'exposent à des calamités occultes. L'affinité avec [ceux qui partagent] les liens de chair et de sang est vouée à l'animosité réciproque. L'estime pour les proches est balayée comme de la poussière. L'amour fraternel dégénère fatalement en disputes pour des broutilles. Le corps périt et la famille est détruite. Ces querelles procèdent de la cupidité et des excès. Ils courent à leur perte, tous jusqu'au dernier. Sans jamais s'en rendre compte, ou bien, s'en rendant compte mais dans l'incapacité de renoncer. Les défunts s'y étaient résignés comme étant la norme ; ceux qui viendront feront de même, contents et sans regret[53].

Lu insiste ensuite sur le moyen radical pour se dégager des entraves inhérentes à la famille en prêchant la privation dans les sphères tant affective que matérielle. Premièrement, il convainc ses disciples de rompre avec les Six relations 六親 ; deuxièmement, il attaque le principe de l'héritage des biens. Selon Wang Bi, le scholiaste du *Laozi*, les Six relations étaient les rapports asymétriques entre pères et fils, frères aînés et cadets, époux et épouses[54]. Comme il a été mentionné plus haut, l'affirmation confucéenne selon laquelle les relations hiérarchiques promeuvent une société harmonieuse n'était pas universellement partagée. Le verset 18 du *Laozi* soutenait le paradoxe que « c'est quand les Six relations ne sont pas harmonieuses qu'il y a dévotion filiale et amour paternel » 六親不和有孝慈[55], suggérant que de tels idéaux ne faisaient que traduire une réalité plus laide, à savoir l'échec de l'harmonie familiale rêvée. Pour les contemporains de Lu Xiujing, l'effondrement des normes sociales et des valeurs familiales était un signe du désordre qui signalait une période de déclin terminal. L'année 453 durant laquelle Lu composa les *Cinq sentiments* connut le régicide de l'empereur Wendi, dont le successeur, Mingdi, allait éliminer des pans entiers de la dynastie impériale. On conçoit sans mal comment insécurité, régime instable et parricides, fratricides et régicides routiniers contribuèrent au sentiment d'alors :

Je vois ces maux et tourne en conséquence le dos au monde. Renonçant aux Six relations et abandonnant les honneurs et les engagements, je recherche le Tao et aspire à la vie, accumule toujours plus d'érudition et m'en vais quérir mon salut. Si je puis atteindre quelque utilité, je revaudrai d'abord leur bonté à mes parents qui m'ont élevé et éduqué jour après jour. Si je leur obtiens maintenant l'élixir divin qui les sauve de la perdition, qu'ils gravissent le pont de la Loi 法橋 et gagnent la rive inaccessible. Bondissant de joie mêlée de douleur, les cinq sens 五情[56] transportés, mon cœur plane et mon esprit vagabonde. Soudain je deviens oublieux de mes quatre membres. Inconscient, je lâche prise et prends refuge dans les Trois joyaux.

La seconde attaque de Lu cible alors la question de l'héritage. Maître Mou évoquait de manière saisissante l'histoire du prince indien Sudāna 須大拏, un souverain d'une parfaite générosité, cité en exemple dans le *Vessantara jātaka*, qui ne se contenta pas d'abandonner son héritage royal, mais renonça aussi à sa femme et à ses enfants[57]. Vers 400 de notre ère, le récit fut transposé dans le *Livre de sagesse du Lingbao pour fixer la résolution et comprendre le subtil* 靈寶智慧定志通微經[58]. Dans le *jātaka* tel que le restitue Maître Mou, l'épouse et les enfants abandonnés de Sudāna sont, comme Isaac, rachetés une fois que la détermination du père a été prouvée. Dans les *Cinq sentiments*, Lu Xiujing offre sa propre vision bienheureuse de la relaxe karmique par le don zélé et le transfert de mérite provenant de l'abandon de son héritage :

> J'étale mes possessions et renonce à tout au nom de la religion, ma seule peur étant de ne pas m'être débarrassé tout à fait de la pusillanimité. Je souhaite que mon père et ma mère puissent gagner le Palais des bienheureux, échapper à jamais aux Huit conditions défavorables et ne plus jamais connaître la détresse. Que ma petite sincérité puisse subvenir à tous leurs besoins[59].

En Chine médiévale, le célibat monastique faisait scandale non pas de par la *fuga mundi*, tourner le dos au monde séculier, mais à cause du *chujia*, quitter la famille et renoncer aux relations de parenté, la pierre d'angle de l'ordre social et des liens affectifs. Pour contrer de telles objections, Lu Xiujing fit bien comprendre à ses disciples que les fils et filles qui quittaient leur famille pouvaient maintenir des sentiments filiaux, non en dépit, mais au moyen, de leur renoncement.

Le mérite du renoncement

> Un jour, [Lu Xiujing] dit à un collègue fonctionnaire : « L'occasion se présente rarement deux fois. » Sur quoi il laissa aller son épouse et ses enfants, remisa ambition et devoirs, se dévoua entièrement à la religion, constamment et sans relâche, le jour comme la nuit[60].

Un récit du renoncement à sa famille par Lu Xiujing lui attribue le rôle d'un sauveur taoïste dont le secours s'inscrit explicitement en dehors des relations de parenté établies : ayant quitté sa maison pour un ermitage de montagne, Lu traversa le village à la recherche d'herbes médicinales. Alors qu'il séjournait brièvement dans son ancien foyer, sa fille tomba gravement malade. La famille craignit pour la vie de l'enfant et supplia Lu de la sauver. Mais Lu Xiujing ne se laissa pas émouvoir et refusa âprement de venir en aide à sa fille :

> Le Maître soupira et dit : « Si j'ai renoncé à mon épouse et à mon enfant pour me dévouer au mystère ultime, en passant par ma maison aujourd'hui, c'est comme si je logeais dans une auberge. Comment l'attachement de l'amour peut-il se renouer[61] ? » Sur ce, il secoua son habit et partit abruptement sans se retourner. Pourtant, un jour plus tard, sa fille était guérie de sa maladie[62].

Ainsi, après la secousse initiale causée par le rejet par Lu Xiujing de son propre enfant, à l'instar de Sudāna, pour finir, celle-ci est miraculeusement secourue à distance. En d'autres termes, les taoïstes pouvaient jouer un rôle au sein de la société comparable à celui du *sangha* bouddhique, qui procurait le salut aux parents non pas en se livrant à des actes conventionnels de piété filiale, mais en méditant et en exécutant des rituels dans la réclusion du monastère.

Le QUATRIÈME SENTIMENT montre que remplir ses obligations filiales et obtenir la relaxe de ses ancêtres constituaient un préalable à sa propre rédemption et à celle de ses descendants :

> Le Très Haut, les nombreux vénérables, les grands sages et les Véritables ont mis en branle cette vaste transformation[63] et ont produit les merveilleux rites pour nous délivrer des Trois bourbiers et nous sauver des Cinq chemins.

> Une fois que les griefs calamiteux de myriades de générations d'ancêtres accumulés au fil des *kalpas* sont complètement redressés, les âmes perdues des défunts s'élancent vers le Palais des bienheureux. Les élus de la causalité karmique reçoivent leur récompense tous jusqu'au dernier. C'est moi qui atteins la Voie, et ce sont les générations suivantes qui se voient conférer la félicité. Pareille grâce se produit rarement, apparaissant une fois tous les dix mille *kalpas*. Je me consacrerai à pratiquer fidèlement, de tout cœur et avec la plus grande dévotion, résolu à n'être négligent en rien[64].

L'amalgame ici encore entre le karma bouddhique dont on hérite et le fardeau taoïste de la culpabilité ancestrale brouille la distinction entre la culpabilité acquise au cours de ses propres existences antérieures et celle héritée des générations successives de ses ancêtres[65]. Le fait est que l'accès au salut du suppliant dépendait des deux. Les rites enseignés par Lu Xiujing obtenaient la décharge des parents décédés pourvu que l'on se repentît et expiât expressément soi-même au cours des Retraites de boue et de cendres et des Huit périodes[66]. L'objet de ces dernières était « huit fois par an de faire acte de contrition pour les péchés de ses ancêtres, ainsi que pour ceux commis par soi-même dans la vie présente ou au cours de ses existences antérieures »[67].

Le CINQUIÈME SENTIMENT est la reconnaissance due aux maîtres. La vénération des maîtres spirituels remontait au début du mouvement du Maître céleste. Comme on peut le voir dans la méditation finale, le culte rendu aux maîtres occupait une place comparable à celle du culte aux ancêtres. L'assimilation des deux était fondée sur l'idée que, alors que les parents conféraient la vie, les maîtres ouvraient le chemin de la vie après la mort[68]. Par conséquent, les enseignements d'un maître occupaient une place primordiale dans le plan rédempteur de la causalité karmique :

> Si j'obtiens cette bénédiction, ce sera pour une raison. La loi de la causalité procure la délivrance. Et c'est la bonté de mon maître qui m'a permis de voir clair[69]. Ma reconnaissance révérencielle est sans limite, débordant le ciel et la terre. Par conséquent, chaque jour que nous pratiquons la Voie, je prie avec la plus grande sincérité, espérant pouvoir posséder quelque petit mérite avec lequel lui redevoir sa bienveillance. Traversant les épreuves corporelles et la fatigue physique, je ne saurais m'épargner[70].

Repentance et expiation

Pour les premiers chrétiens, une discipline monastique stricte était « plus douce que le miel aux nécessiteux »[71]. Lu Xiujing écrivait à propos de la discipline de la Retraite du Lingbao qui relâchait de leur prison les âmes damnées des parents, qu'elle était un trésor inestimable qui devait être convoité joyeusement et jalousement : « En me soumettant à ce rituel, j'exulte sans fin – comme l'avaricieux tombant sur un amas d'or et de jade. La multitude ne le sait pas. Et moi seul je puis voir[72] ! » L'introduction des *Cinq sentiments* décrit les épreuves poignantes endurées par les participants à la Retraite de boue et de cendres, longue et à ciel ouvert, pour laquelle le texte fut originellement écrit. La conclusion reprend ce thème, faisant métaphoriquement allusion aux rudes exigences auxquelles devaient se soumettre les fidèles dans l'exécution du rite : jour après jour et durant des mois, dans l'épuisement croissant, les disciples peinent sans broncher, « pataugeant dans l'eau et foulant la glace, le froid leur glaçant le corps jusqu'à l'os ». Finissant par s'abstraire de leur environnement austère et de leur pénible contrition, ils « vainquent tous les obstacles », le cœur joyeux et apaisé. Colomban (540-615), enseignant à ses disciples la pénitence comme l'un des remèdes contre le péché, écrivit : « Car bien que cette discipline puisse sembler dure à des hommes endurcis […], ceux qui sont déterminés dans la crainte de Dieu la trouveront agréable et sûre[73]. »

Dans la vision programmatique de Lu Xiujing, le parcours de pénitence prescrit dans les *Cinq sentiments* était indispensable pour que s'accomplisse l'œuvre rédemptrice de la Retraite de boue et de cendres. La délivrance des parents et des ancêtres dépendait de la sincérité de la contrition de l'adepte. L'avertissement de Lu était catégorique : la méditation des *Cinq sentiments* s'imposait à tous comme préparation essentielle pour la Retraite de boue et de cendres. Il écrivait :

> Celui qui pratique la Retraite de boue et de cendres en manquant à l'esprit des *Cinq sentiments* n'accomplit pas le dessein de s'exhorter soi-même : premièrement, il gaspille de l'encens et produit un effort futile ; deuxièmement, il se livre à une imposture ; troisièmement, il manque de

respect envers les prescriptions rituelles ; quatrièmement, il salit l'enseignement de son maître ; et cinquièmement, il est passible de rétribution[74].

Non seulement l'expiation « de boue et de cendres », mais le projet rédempteur tout entier du rite de la Retraite était tributaire du parcours de repentance exposé dans les *Cinq sentiments* : « Les *Cinq sentiments* constituent la règle pour les maîtres taoïstes pratiquant les Six retraites 六齋. Ces dernières tirent toutes leur origine des grandes *Écritures des Trois cavernes*[75]. »

Les textes canoniques véhiculant l'instrument du salut devaient être traités avec le plus grand respect : « Vénérables et profonds, ils ne doivent pas être souillés ! Pour les lire, vous devez vous laver les mains et poser [les textes] sur une pièce de tissu propre ; pour les entreposer, vous devez les placer à l'intérieur d'un contenant. Vous ne pouvez pas leur manquer de respect. Ceux qui leur manquent de respect subissent inévitablement la calamité envoyée par le Ciel[76]. » Le type de calamité guettant les mécréants qui désacralisaient les rites du Lingbao et ses écritures est décrit en détail dans une histoire au sujet du bouddhiste laïc Xiao Ziliang, le prince érudit et dévot, également connu sous le nom de Poṣadha 淨住子, qui commandita la compilation du canon de Sengyou (voir chapitre 5, introduction)[77]. La narration rapporte comment le prince tomba sur un texte sacré du Lingbao. Après l'avoir parcouru, il le jeta au sol sans scrupule. Ses mains furent instantanément frappées d'abcès et de plaies qui lui causèrent une douleur insoutenable. Finalement, après une confession complète et la pénitence requise, le prince obtint le soulagement de ses souffrances avec l'aide d'un maître taoïste[78]. Ironie de l'histoire, l'*Initiation à la purification de Maître Poṣadha* 淨住子淨行法門, attribuée à Xiao Ziliang, était le texte utilisé par les bouddhistes pour inviter à la confession monastique et souligner la nécessité de la pénitence et de la contrition[79].

Dans ses instructions, Lu plaçait l'anxiété filiale énoncée dans les *Cinq sentiments* au cœur de l'exécution de la Retraite, ce qui marquait un changement radical par rapport à la priorité antérieurement accordée à l'exorcisme des défunts perturbés comme source de contagion et d'infortune pour les vivants. Désormais, le programme liturgique taoïste englobait le salut des parents, des ancêtres et des maîtres décédés. La séparation des royaumes des vivants et des morts visée dans les rites du Maître céleste, cédait la place à l'accent neuf mis sur la dévotion filiale, le renouveau du culte des ancêtres et l'assimilation de rites bouddhistes populaires pour les défunts. Avec le renouvellement du rite mortuaire taoïste opéré par le Lingbao, la rédemption ne vise plus tant la protection des vivants que la félicité des défunts parents. Le revaloir de la bonté des parents devient le préalable à sa propre libération et au salut de tous.

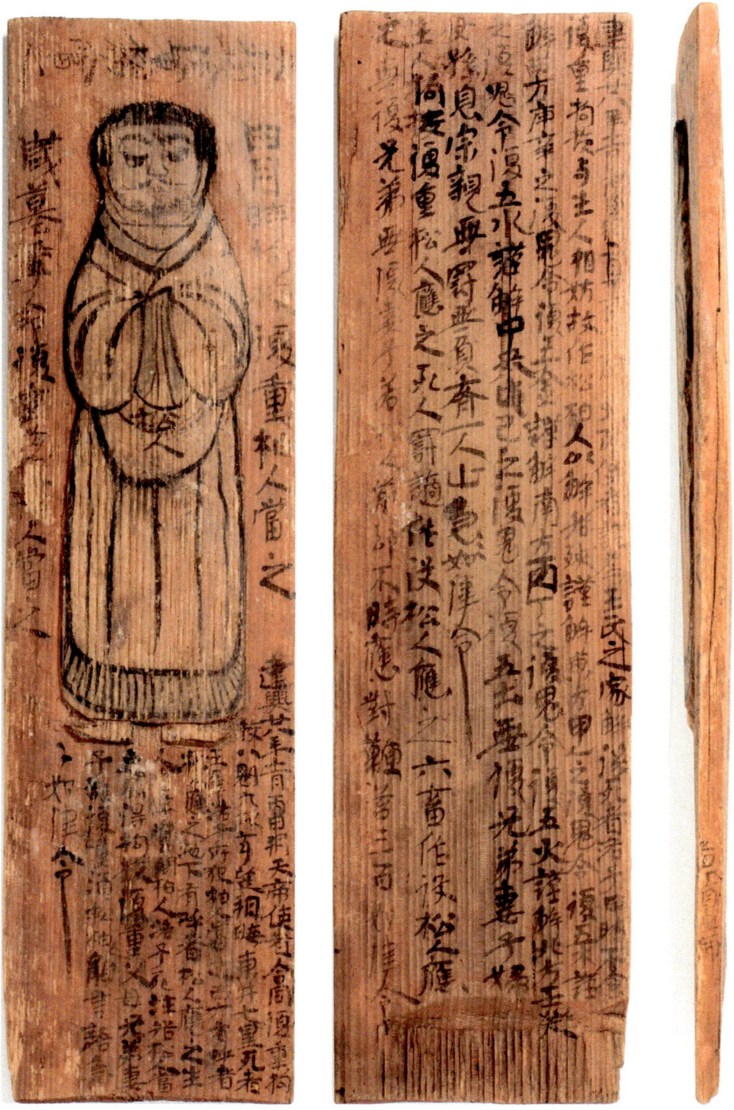

a. b. c.

Planche 1 : Effigie de pin 松人, tablette d'expulsion en bois 解除木牘 (340 de notre ère). Wuwei 武威, Gansu (a, recto ; b, verso ; c, vue latérale). Avec l'aimable autorisation du Chinese University of Hong Kong Art Museum.

Planche 2 : Gardien de tombe 鎮墓獸. Créature prodigieuse pour repousser le mal 辟邪神獸 du cimetière d'Astana 阿斯塔那古墓 à Turfan, Gansu. Période de la préfecture de Xizhou 西州 (640-791) des Tang. Avec l'aimable autorisation du Musée de Turfan 吐魯番博物館.

Planche 3 : Le pont sur le Ruisseau du tigre : rouleau suspendu des Song méridionaux (1127-1279), encre et couleur sur soie, 92 × 53,8 cm, d'après *La Société du Lotus* (1080) de Li Gonglin. Détail montrant, à droite du pont : Huiyuan présentant ses adieux à Lu, sous le regard de serviteurs ; dans le registre inférieur : Xie Lingyun arrivant à cheval et Tao Yuanming prenant congé dans une chaise à porteurs. Avec l'aimable autorisation du Musée de Nankin 南京博物院.

Planche 4 : Lampe en céladon 青瓷燈 des Liu Song (421 de notre ère). Avec l'aimable autorisation du Musée municipal de Nankin 南京市博物館.

Planche 5 : Bodhisattvas allumant des lampes dans le paradis du Bouddha de la médecine. Détail, peinture murale du mur nord de la Grotte de Mogao 莫高窟 n° 220 représentant des scènes du *Bhaisajyaguru sūtra* 藥師經變 (début des Tang). Avec l'aimable autorisation de l'Académie de Dunhuang 敦煌研究院.

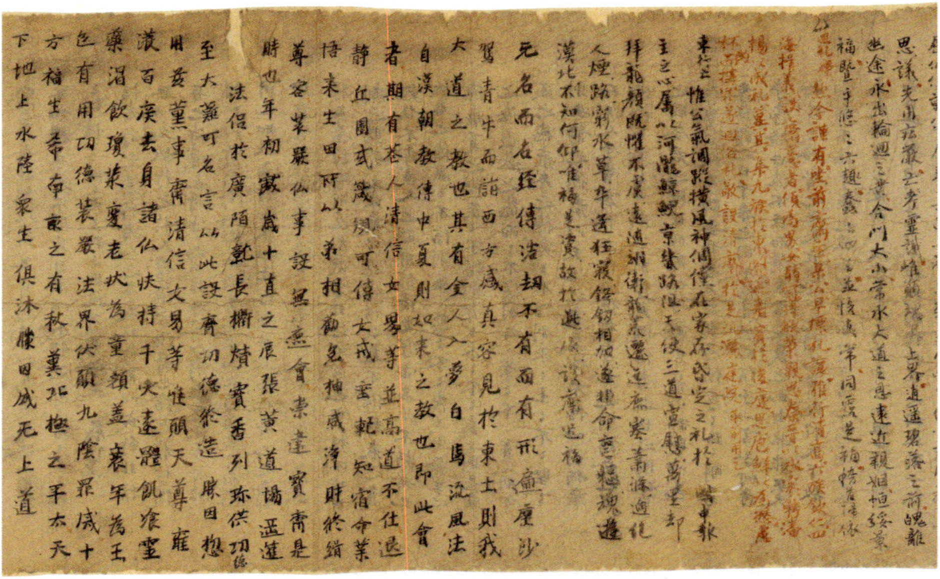

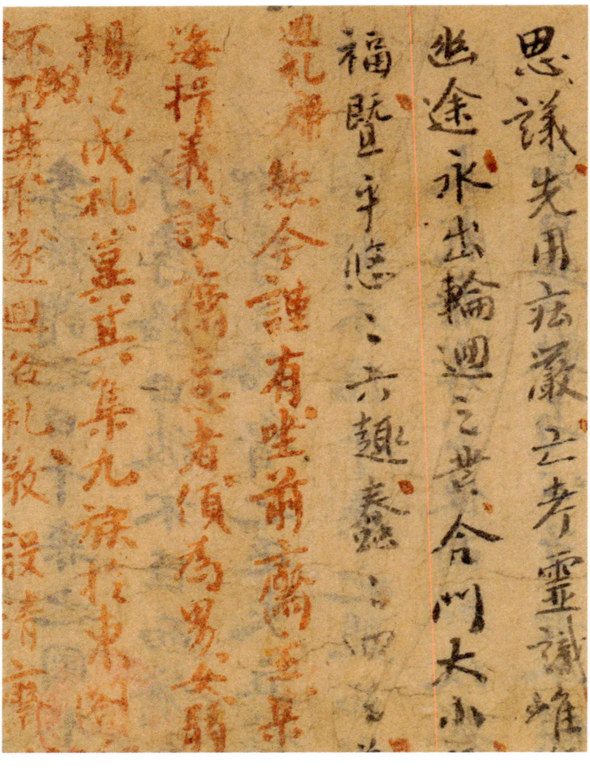

Planche 6 : *Recueil de prières taoïstes pour les Retraites et Offrandes pour le salut des morts*. Manuscrit P. 3562v de Dunhuang, détails montrant les colonnes 168 à 196 (ci-dessus) et 168 à 174 (ci-contre). Reproduit avec l'autorisation de la Bibliothèque nationale de France.

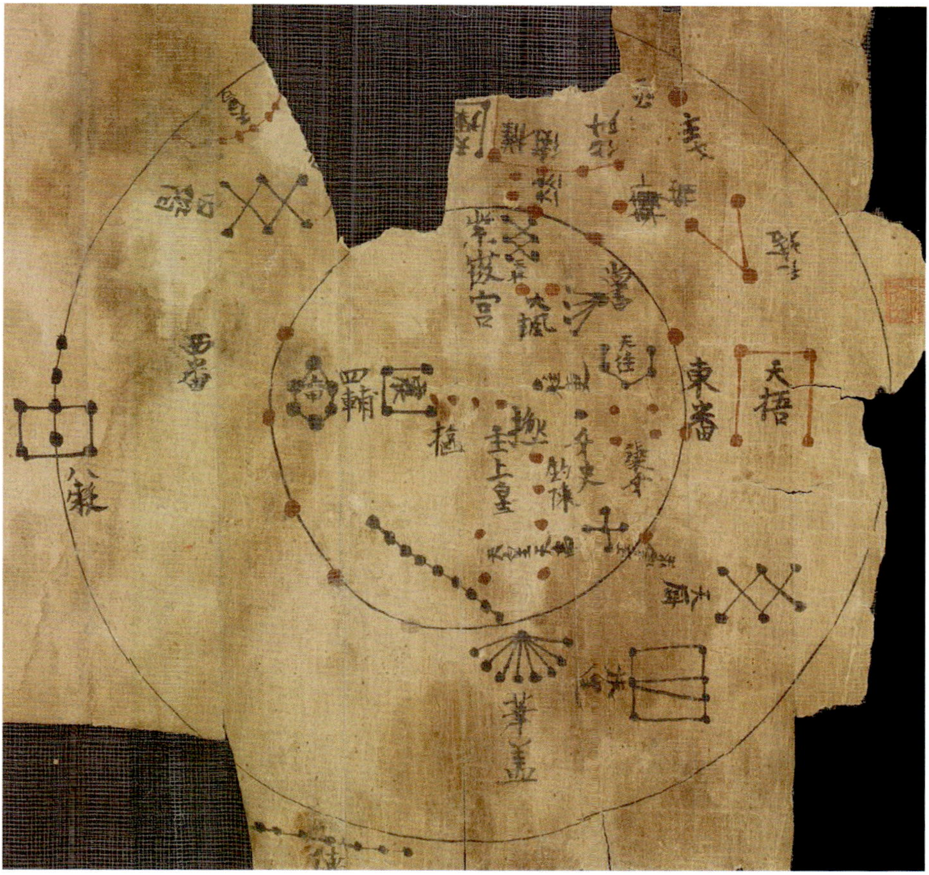

Planche 7 : Carte des étoiles du Palais de la Ténuité pourpre 紫微宮星圖. Manuscrit DB 076 de Dunhuang. Avec l'aimable autorisation du Musée de Dunhuang 敦煌博物館.

Planche 8 : Talisman *dhāranī* procurant protection, pouvoirs surhumains et rémission des péchés (xe siècle). Détail montrant l'Étoile polaire 北方神星 (à gauche) et la planète Ketu 計都星 (à droite). Dunhuang, grottes de Mogao 莫高窟. Peinture Stein 170. Avec l'aimable autorisation du British Museum.

TROISIÈME PARTIE

Tout sous un même ciel : la synthèse des Tang

Au fur et à mesure que le nombre des conversions au bouddhisme croissait au sein de la classe sociale et intellectuelle de Lu Xiujing au ve siècle, le patronage officiel du bouddhisme s'étendait en Chine du Sud. Après l'accession de Wudi 武帝 (r. 502-549) des Liang, fervent bouddhiste et connu comme « l'empereur bodhisattva », la pression officielle s'exerça sur l'élite méridionale pour qu'elle se conformât à sa vision de la souveraineté et de l'État bouddhistes. Durant un débat de cour au début de 504, Tao Hongjing s'opposa à l'historien Shen Yue en défendant le taoïsme, mais en vain : le jour de l'anniversaire du Bouddha cette année-là, le huitième jour du quatrième mois lunaire, l'empereur Wudi répudia publiquement le taoïsme. Peu après, un édit exigea que courtisans et membres de la famille royale se convertissent au bouddhisme. Quarante-huit mille convertis auraient suivi l'exemple de Wudi et reçu les préceptes bouddhistes[1]. Avant la fin de son règne, l'empereur devait à quatre reprises « abandonner sa personne » 捨身 et prendre refuge auprès des Trois joyaux afin que sa rançon fût payée au *sangha* par des sommes importantes prélevées dans les coffres de l'État[2].

Dans le même temps, Wudi adopta une vue conciliante des Trois enseignements, écrivit un commentaire du *Laozi* et entretint une relation ambiguë avec la communauté taoïste de Maoshan, le siège du mouvement du Shangqing, à soixante kilomètres au sud-est de Jiankang[3]. L'empereur estimait Tao Hongjing en tant que métallurgiste et alchimiste et favorisa par son patronage la fonderie de Tao, à Maoshan, qui produisit des épées précieuses pour l'usage personnel du souverain[4]. Cependant, cette relation n'offrait qu'une protection limitée à la communauté, comme en témoigne le *Mémoire des communications de Monsieur Zhou avec le monde invisible* 周氏冥通記 que Tao présenta à l'empereur en 518. Cet ouvrage était une biographie spirituelle de Zhou Ziliang 周子良 (497-516), l'un des disciples de Tao, laquelle mentionne la laïcisation forcée, un an auparavant, de la tante de Zhou, une médium taoïste célibataire nommée Xu Baoguang 徐寶光[5].

L'interdiction du taoïsme par l'empereur Wudi des Liang conduisit des taoïstes de Maoshan à migrer au Nord au début du VIe siècle, contribuant à la dissémination des traditions scripturales et rituelles méridionales[6]. En Chine septentrionale, ce qui restait de la diaspora du Maître céleste au IIIe siècle avait perduré sous les Wei du Nord. La tentative par Kou Qianzhi 寇謙之 (365-448) d'établir le taoïsme du Maître céleste comme religion d'État sous cette dynastie avait offert une alternative aux souverains ouverts à de nouvelles formes de patronage religieux. En 424, l'empereur Taiwu 太武 des Tuoba 拓拔 avait adopté le titre de Seigneur véritable de la Grande paix 太平真君 et en 442, il reçut l'ordination selon le rite du Maître céleste. Mais nombreux avaient été ceux qui avaient méprisé l'appropriation théocratique du taoïsme du Maître céleste par Kou, n'y ayant vu qu'une caricature du mouvement originel[7].

Le modèle imaginé par Kou ne survécut pas à la dynastie Wei des Tuoba. La dynastie des Qi du Nord transféra emphatiquement son patronage religieux au bouddhisme. Quant à la dynastie des Zhou du Nord, l'empereur Wudi 武帝 (r. 560-578) est connu pour avoir tergiversé avant d'engager sa politique religieuse. D'abord bouddhiste dévot, Wudi reçut ensuite une ordination taoïste en 567. L'empereur encouragea de vigoureux débats religieux à sa cour, mais il brida les clergés du bouddhisme et du taoïsme tout en prônant l'unité des Trois enseignements. Finalement, l'aspiration du souverain à réunifier l'empire divisé fit pencher la balance idéologique en faveur du taoïsme comme la religion la plus apte à incarner un héritage indubitablement chinois[8].

En 574, Wudi des Zhou fonda l'académie taoïste du Tongdao guan 通道觀 avec pour mission d'y compiler une collection encyclopédique des écritures taoïstes en abrégé. *L'Essentiel des secrets suprêmes* 無上秘要, un compendium ayant adopté les rubriques des *Écritures des Trois cavernes* de Lu Xiujing, parut peu de temps après la victoire des Zhou du Nord sur leurs rivaux, les Qi du Nord, en 577[9]. Wudi des Zhou mourut l'année suivant cette victoire, mais déjà l'*Essentiel* avait parachevé la standardisation des systèmes rituels taoïstes septentrionaux et méridionaux[10]. Après le court règne de l'empereur Xuandi 宣帝 (r. 578-580), il incomba au régent Yang Jian 楊堅 (541-604) de mener à bien le projet d'unification de Wudi des Zhou. Yang Jian fonda la dynastie Sui comme empereur Wendi 文帝 (r. 581-604). Ayant vaincu la dynastie Chen au Sud et dévasté la capitale méridionale de Jiankang en 589, il fut le premier souverain à régner sur l'ensemble de la Chine depuis 317.

Ironie du sort, eu égard aux desseins politico-religieux de Wudi des Zhou, Wendi était un bouddhiste fervent. Pour les siècles à venir, la politique à la cour allait être marquée par la rivalité entre les deux religions pour le patronage impérial. Au cours de ce processus, l'une et l'autre jouèrent un rôle grandissant en tant que fournisseurs de rituels pour le bénéfice et la protection de l'État. À la suite de l'éphémère dynastie Sui (581-618), l'empire unifié fut consolidé par la dynastie Tang (618-907) qui faisait remonter son ascendance au sage divinisé Laozi, dont le nom de famille était Li comme celui de la famille régnante. Cette alliance eut pour effet de fusionner le culte ancestral impérial avec la vénération populaire de Laozi. Le soulèvement qui porta au pouvoir le fondateur des Tang, Li Yuan 李淵, comme empereur Gaozu 高祖 (r. 618-626) traduisait des prophéties de salut messianique comparables à celles de l'ère Jaune à la fin des Han (voir « Visions de l'apocalypse » au chapitre premier) et à celles ayant marqué l'ascension des Liu Song (voir chapitre 5, introduction) :

> Durant les quatre cents années de division politique, de troubles sociaux et de fermentation culturelle qui s'écoulèrent [depuis la fin des Han en 220], ce fut précisément le rêve messianique de Taiping qui garda intacte la vision d'un empire chinois unifié et contribua de manière significative à son rétablissement sous les Tang. Encore et toujours, d'un bout à

l'autre de la période de désunion, la prophétie messianique « Les Han se relèveront ! » retentissait comme le cri de guerre des rebelles ; plus d'un empereur fut flatté du titre de Seigneur de Taiping, successeur des Han ; et quand les fondateurs de la dynastie Tang se posèrent consciemment en accomplissement de l'attente populaire spécifique d'un roi sauveur, ils agissaient selon un mode séculaire[11].

Le bouddhisme n'était pas moins disposé que le taoïsme à revêtir rebelles et souverains de l'habit messianique. L'attrait du bouddhisme gagna toutes les strates de la société sous les Tang, incluant la famille régnante. Dans l'ensemble, le patronage officiel des Tang profita autant aux deux religions. Les rares exceptions furent des épisodes d'hostilité à l'égard du bouddhisme en tant qu'enseignement étranger, accompagnés d'interdictions sporadiques bien que brutales, pour des raisons principalement économiques et fiscales[12]. Le même nativisme qui suscita périodiquement des polémiques anti-bouddhiques favorisait le taoïsme comme religion « ancestrale » de la famille impériale[13].

Comme le pouvoir politique et les réalisations culturelles de la dynastie des Tang s'étendaient au point de rivaliser avec ceux des Han, les souverains Tang pouvaient prétendre avoir rétabli la continuation avec la civilisation de l'Antiquité chinoise, interrompue par des siècles d'intrusion étrangère et de division territoriale. Cette revendication conduisit aussi à un regain d'intérêt pour le taoïsme ancien et les institutions religieuses des Han, plus particulièrement pour l'organisation de la première communauté du Maître céleste sous Zhang Daoling. L'affirmation qu'un lignage continu de Maîtres célestes reliait les Han orientaux aux Tang devint un symbole puissant de ce rétablissement de succession[14]. Dans un décret daté de 747, l'empereur Xuanzong 玄宗 (r. 712-756) canonisa le premier Maître céleste Zhang Daoling en lui conférant le titre de Grand précepteur 太師 qui désignait les conseillers suprêmes des souverains. Le même décret éleva le patriarche du Shangqing, Tao Hongjing, à la dignité de Grand protecteur 太保[15]. D'un bout à l'autre de la dynastie Tang, une succession de patriarches du Shangqing reçurent de grands honneurs impériaux. En accord avec la hiérarchie canonique et liturgique établie sous les Six dynasties, le Shangqing occupait le rang le plus élevé. L'empereur Xuanzong fut ordonné avec un *Registre précieux des Trois cavernes*

三洞寶籙 par le sixième patriarche du Shangqing, Sima Chengzhen 司馬承禎 (647-735). La poésie et la calligraphie du Shangqing faisaient l'admiration des cercles littéraires. Sur la base des comptes rendus de Tao Hongjing relatifs à la révélation et la transmission des écritures du Shangqing, l'érudit et ermite Li Bo établit une ligne de succession des premiers patriarches du Shangqing, intitulée la *Filiation des Véritables* 真系[16]. Embrassant les traditions du Maître céleste, du Shangqing et du Lingbao, les Tang épousèrent la vision intégrative de Lu Xiujing et en promurent une synthèse générale dans laquelle tous les principaux courants du taoïsme médiéval pouvaient se retrouver[17].

Après le fils de Zhang Daoling, Zhang Heng, et son petit-fils Zhang Lu, peu de prétendants à une succession linéaire sont attestés historiquement. L'un d'entre eux fut Zhang Bian 張辯 (actif en 552), auteur du *Protocole des diocèses du Maître céleste* 天師治儀, qu'il signa en tant que « Maître céleste à la treizième génération »[18]. Peu de temps après la canonisation de Zhang Daoling par Xuanzong, vers l'année 770, une famille Zhang apparue sur la Montagne du dragon et du tigre (Longhu shan 龍虎山), au Jiangxi, établit un nouveau lignage continu de Maîtres célestes[19]. Dans la troisième partie de ce livre, le chapitre 9 (« Les voies de l'initiation ») expose comment les Tang transformèrent le rituel du Lingbao et l'organisation liturgique de la communauté taoïste, réformés par Lu Xiujing, en un ordre hiérarchique intégré fondé sur, et rattaché à, l'enseignement de l'Unité correcte des Maîtres célestes. La pratique laïque et le rituel populaire fournirent des techniques rédemptrices complémentaires qui sont creusées aux chapitres 10 et 11 (« Sacramentalité et pratique religieuse laïque » et « Les instruments de la délivrance »). Enfin, le chapitre 12 (« Prières pour une nouvelle ère ») examine l'essor de l'« Oraison verte » comme véhicule prépondérant d'intercession rituelle pour le compte de l'État, sur fond de défis croissants à la maison régnante prise dans la tourmente politique et militaire de la transition des Tang aux Cinq dynasties.

Chapitre 9

Les voies de l'initiation

La Grande liturgie du Lingbao codifiée par Lu Xiujing devint la norme rituelle de la religion taoïste pour les Tang et les époques ultérieures. Cela ne signifie pas que le rituel du Lingbao ne continua pas à évoluer ou à assimiler de nouvelles influences. Comprenant à l'origine neuf catégories, la classification des Retraites connut des modifications au fil du temps. Le compendium institutionnel du VIIIe siècle, intitulé les *Six statuts des Tang* 唐六典, cite une septuple nomenclature : Retraites du Grand registre d'or, du Registre jaune, de l'Alliance avec les Véritables, des Trois originels, des Huit périodes, de la Spontanéité et, enfin, de Boue et de cendres[1]. Ces sept titres correspondent aux six premiers rituels dans le répertoire de Lu Xiujing, plus la Retraite de boue et de cendres que Lu avait classée à part (voir « Une Retraite pour toutes les circonstances » au chapitre 6). Les trois titres omis parmi les neuf de la liste de Lu étaient la Retraite de l'instruction, celle des Trois souverains et celle du Grand un. On verra dans « L'Unité correcte » ci-dessous que l'authenticité de la Retraite de l'instruction était contestée. Quant aux rituels des Trois souverains et du Grand un, on continuait à les pratiquer à la fin de l'époque des Tang, mais plus à la manière des Retraites. Ils s'étaient transformés en offrandes *jiao*, lesquelles finirent par être intégrées dans le rituel polyvalent de l'« Offrande à tous les cieux » 羅天醮 (voir « Une liturgie au service d'un dessein » au chapitre 12)[2]. Les *Six statuts des Tang* poursuivent : « En plus [des sept Retraites], il y a trois pratiques pour la délivrance et l'expiation : la première est la requête (*zhang* 章), la seconde, l'offrande (*jiao* 醮) et la troisième, le bain de sable (*maisha* 埋沙). »

Le retour du sacrifice

La dernière des trois pratiques, le bain de sable, faisait sans doute référence, génériquement parlant, aux rites de guérison[3]. La première et la seconde, le rituel de requête du Maître céleste et l'offrande *jiao*, se retrouvaient parfois associées dans l'*Almanach des requêtes* ou dans la *Table d'almanach pour les offrandes de requête* dans une séquence « offrande de requête » 章醮, c'est-à-dire un rituel de requête suivi d'une offrande cérémonielle. Dans les funérailles des époques Han et antérieures, des offrandes sacrificielles concluaient communément les prières pour remercier les esprits de leurs faveurs[4]. Comme il en a été question au chapitre premier, dans « Signification du sacrifice », les offrandes *jiao* de la Chine ancienne avaient été rejetées par les Maîtres célestes parce qu'elles requéraient des sacrifices sanglants ; mais, sous les Tang, une nomenclature réhabilitant l'ancienne séquence *zhai-jiao* (chapitre 6) s'établit graduellement.

Comment le sacrifice s'immisça-t-il dans la structure et le vocabulaire des rituels rédempteurs taoïstes dits « purs », soit non sanglants ? Lü Pengzhi montre, dans son étude du *jiao* dans le taoïsme médiéval, que la tradition distinguait trois filiations rituelles séparées qui comptèrent, outre celle du Maître céleste et celle du Lingbao, celle des *fangshi*[5]. Les *fangshi* étaient adeptes de méthodes pour atteindre l'immortalité qui comprenaient des rituels sacrificiels et exorcistes. Par contraste avec les deux autres filiations, les méthodes des *fangshi* étaient ésotériques, pratiquées individuellement et transmises de maître à disciple. Héritage des Royaumes combattants, ces méthodes intégrèrent le taoïsme sous les Han orientaux et survécurent dans des compendiums rituels méridionaux comme les *Cinq talismans du Lingbao* et les écrits de Ge Hong. Les sacrifices que les maîtres *fangshi* offraient aux dieux, après avoir reçu les Cinq talismans sacrés du Lingbao, étaient précédés par des rites de purification directionnels et la combustion de cinq sortes d'encens pour inviter les Cinq empereurs à descendre de leurs directions cardinales respectives et du centre. Les offrandes incluaient de l'alcool, de la viande, des fruits, « une volaille engraissée et plus d'un gallon et demi de vin, le tout pur, de choix et de qualité agréable »[6]. Les maîtres *fangshi* élevaient et sacrifiaient des oies au lieu de grues – la monture classique des immortels – pour transporter les dieux lors de leur descente[7].

Dans la quête alchimique de transcendance de Ge Hong, les sacrifices faisaient partie intégrante de la procédure pour préparer l'élixir. Le serment de transmission entre maître et disciple était scellé par un sacrifice, des sacrifices additionnels étaient présentés aux divinités tutélaires avant et après la préparation de l'élixir, et des sacrifices *jiao* appelaient à la descente des dieux, y compris les Cinq empereurs. Bien que Ge Hong exprimât son opposition aux sacrifices impurs, ses écrits témoignent de la pratique continue d'offrir de la viande et de l'alcool, et d'utiliser du sang dans les cérémonies de serment 盟[8]. Les offrandes *jiaoji* 醮祭 auxquelles Ge Hong fait référence soulignent sa proximité avec l'ancienne tradition des *fangshi*[9]. Lu Xiujing devait intégrer tous les courants de rituels pratiqués dans le Sud de la Chine au sein de la trame liturgique du Lingbao.

Entre les réformes de Lu Xiujing et celles de Du Guangting, il y eut Zhang Wanfu 張萬福, l'éminent liturgiste taoïste du milieu de l'époque Tang, actif à la cour de l'empereur Xuanzong et de ses deux prédécesseurs[10]. Zhang a laissé plusieurs œuvres, dont des protocoles pour les rituels d'ordination et la transmission des écritures, ainsi que des instructions sur les vêtements, les accessoires et les pratiques. Voici comment Zhang Wanfu définit le *jiao* dans son *Protocole pour les Offrandes aux dieux des registres d'ordination* 醮三洞真文五法正一盟威籙立成儀 :

> Le *jiao* est ce par quoi nous offrons notre sincérité au Ciel et à la Terre et implorons les dieux invisibles pour leurs grâces. Être moins qu'entièrement dévoué ne saurait gagner leurs faveurs. Que quelqu'un soit totalement sincère et pourtant que les bénédictions ne répondent pas – cela ne s'est jamais produit. Pas plus que l'on ait entendu dire que quelqu'un qui ne soit pas sincère ait néanmoins vu ses attentes comblées.

Tout adepte devrait dans sa pratique consacrer le meilleur de lui-même à cet égard.

En d'autres termes, pour Zhang Wanfu, l'offrande *jiao* était tout ce qui permettait d'adresser une prière sincère. Zhang donne ensuite des instructions pour la préparation d'un autel convenant à l'offrande : le cadre de prédilection était une grotte de montagne, mais, à défaut, les récipients et ustensiles cérémoniels pouvaient être disposés en tout endroit propre et retiré, libre d'animaux, de saleté et d'aliments impurs. On n'y pouvait tolérer ni profanation ni désordre. Zhang conclut en opérant une distinction claire entre les offrandes pures taoïstes et les sacrifices profanes :

> Fruits saisonniers et mets parfumés doivent être en abondance et frais [...]. Copieuse chère est requise comme pour un rituel de Retraite. Les ignorants de cet âge, qui ne sont portés ni vers le pénétrant ni vers le subtil, envisagent [pour offrandes] vin et viande séchée. [Ces hommes] ne viennent en ce monde que pour demeurer incroyants ! Or les rites du Tao sont purs et vides : ils écartent singulièrement la pollution de mort [...]. Ce sur quoi un homme de bien et de discernement est scrupuleux, suscite la moquerie de l'inculte[11] !

Dans l'*Almanach pour la transmission des écritures, préceptes et registres*, Zhang mentionne plus spécifiquement l'Offrande aux Neuf souverains 九皇醮儀[12]. D'autres rituels d'Offrande spécialisés, pour la plupart attribués à la tradition de l'Unité correcte, étaient courants durant la période des Tang : l'*Offrande aux dieux de la demeure* 正一醮宅儀, présentant thé, vin et nourriture au dieu du fourneau et aux gardiens de la maison pour prévenir l'infortune et les influences maléfiques[13] ; l'*Offrande aux dieux de la tombe* 正一醮墓儀, consistant en des libations aux dieux protégeant les sépultures[14] ; et l'*Offrande pour la délivrance de l'adversité* 正一解厄醮儀, destinée aux étoiles du Boisseau et aux dieux du destin pour détourner l'infortune et la maladie[15].

Ces protocoles orchestraient des cérémonies d'Offrande dédiées à des divinités particulières. Comme dans les liturgies taoïstes des Six dynasties, Retraite et Offrande se pratiquèrent séparément durant le plus clair de la période des Tang. Trois siècles plus tard, écrivant du point de vue des Song du Sud, le liturgiste du Lingbao Jiang Shuyu 蔣叔輿 (1162-1223) observa que le rituel de Zhang Wanfu ne comprenait pas encore d'offrandes *jiao* d'actions de grâce, une pratique qui n'apparut, selon Jiang, qu'avec la liturgie de Du Guangting. Voici comment il explique la logique de l'innovation de Du : « Quand on pratique la Retraite, [le prêtre] fait venir des divinités pour surveiller et garder l'aire rituelle. Une déclaration est publiquement proclamée selon laquelle, pour leurs allées et venues, [les dieux] se sont donné beaucoup de peine. C'est pourquoi une Annonce de mérite 言功 est faite, et un banquet d'Offrande est déployé pour régler leur récompense[16]. »

Avant cette innovation, de simples déclarations de mérite concluaient déjà les rituels du Maître céleste sous la forme de « requêtes d'annonce »[17]. L'Annonce de mérite intégra la liturgie de la Retraite avant la fin des Six dynasties. Dans l'*Essentiel des secrets suprêmes*, un protocole pour une Retraite des Trois souverains associait déjà l'« exposition d'offrandes *jiao* en face de l'autel » 對壇設醮 à une Annonce de mérite en vue de la récompense des divinités et de leur avancement. L'offrande prescrite dans le rituel des Trois souverains était un sacrifice de style *fangshi* constitué de jujubes, viande séchée et vin[18]. Le protocole général établi par Du Guangting pour la conclusion du rite combiné s'intitulait « Offrande présentée lors du renvoi » 散壇設醮[19].

Associer les rituels taoïstes de l'Offrande et de la Retraite dans une unique séquence liturgique réhabilita l'ancienne logique sacrificielle du concept de *jiao* des *fangshi*, à défaut de la réalité de leur contenu. Cette association fut le signe d'un retour de la structure archétypale qu'évoquait Mengzi lorsqu'il affirmait que « seulement après avoir observé la retraite, les interdits et les ablutions, est-il permis de sacrifier à l'Empereur d'En Haut ». La codification de Lu Xiujing plaçait les Préceptes (les interdits) et la Purification (les ablutions) en préambule de la Retraite (voir « La purification » au chapitre 6). Insistant sur la signification nouvelle du *jiao*, Zhang Wanfu opéra une démarcation nette entre le sacrifice profane et les offrandes pures introduites par les Maîtres célestes. La réforme de Du Guangting restaura alors la séquence rituelle complète pour conclure la Retraite par une Offrande d'action de grâce et de récompense. Ceci demeura le motif structurel sous-jacent du rituel taoïste aux périodes subséquentes[20]. L'intention rédemptrice s'était déplacée au sein de la structure et de l'ordre sacro-saints, préservés. Et comme Zhang Wanfu le rappelait aux adeptes des pratiques révolues, le changement le plus profond était que la rançon sanglante soit sublimée en une offrande nouvelle qui « écartait la pollution de mort » et avait pour unique raison d'être d'engager la sincérité du suppliant.

L'Unité correcte

Le terme *zhengyi* 正一 (Unité correcte) apparut au IIe siècle pour désigner l'ordre cosmologique sous-jacent à la doctrine de Zhang Daoling[21]. Le renouveau du taoïsme du Maître céleste sous les dynasties méridionales des Qi et des Liang maintint cette désignation comme un encouragement à l'orthodoxie au cours de la période précédant la réunification politique à la fin du Ve et au début du VIe siècles[22]. En tant que précurseur commun aux diverses écoles et traditions textuelles du taoïsme médiéval, l'Unité correcte devint la pierre angulaire de l'édifice ecclésiastique qui devait servir de structure à l'ordre liturgique des Tang, comprenant la hiérarchie de l'ordination et le canon scriptural, et embrassant tous les courants doctrinaux majeurs, le clergé comme les laïcs.

Le *Traité de l'Unité correcte* 正一論 reflète cet esprit de renouveau. Il se présente sous la forme d'un dialogue entre un invité candide, qui pose des questions sur l'hétérodoxie et la pureté doctrinale, et une autorité, implicitement en position d'hôte, qui fournit les réponses. Le problème central pour toute réforme s'efforçant d'accomplir l'unité doctrinale était d'expliquer la réalité stratifiée de la révélation qui produisait, de façon continue au fil de l'histoire, des modifications aux enseignements originels du Maître céleste. Les nouvelles révélations remplaçaient-elles les rituels et panthéons préexistants, coexistaient-elles avec ceux-ci ou les dénaturaient-elles ? Un important cas d'espèce était le statut doctrinal de la révélation du Lingbao, en particulier la place du rituel de Retraite du Lingbao, par rapport au système liturgique du taoïsme du Maître céleste.

Lu Xiujing avait utilisé le terme « correct » (*zheng* 正) pour marquer la fonction du rituel comme critère pour rectifier ou réguler les déviations. Le nombre « un » (*yi* 一) signifiait aussi unir, unifier ou systématiser. Le *Traité* explique la notion d'Unité correcte en l'assimilant à l'Unicité primordiale indifférenciée :

> L'Un est l'Unité correcte. Le seigneur Zhang [Daoling] unifia le monde au moyen de l'Unité correcte. L'univers n'est pas deux, la Trame céleste agit comme un, et les confins de l'espace se conforment au même modèle[23]. Le Ciel couvre et la Terre porte. Dans l'instruction et la pratique religieuses, si l'on n'a pas l'Unité correcte, alors comment peut-on distinguer le bien du mal[24] ?

Ce court *Traité* date peut-être de la période des Qi du Sud ou du début des Tang[25]. Au VIIe siècle, la traduction du traité philosophique de l'école Sarvāstivāda du Cachemire, l'*Abhidharma mahāvibhāsā śāstra* 阿毗達磨大毗婆沙論, scrutait, à une plus grande échelle, l'étendue de la divergence doctrinale dans une étude comparable, présentée elle aussi sous le format question-réponse. Concernant la bataille entre les écoles de pensée dans le sous-continent indien, le *śāstra* déclarait que le bouddhisme à ses débuts connut « quatre-vingt-seize sortes d'enseignements hétérodoxes »[26]. Dans le *Traité de l'Unité correcte*, le candide emploie la même expression pour désigner le degré de divergence doctrinale en Chine :

> Qui plus est, les enseignements transmis par les sages se réfèrent à des périodes précises. Comment se fait-il que les doctrines d'un âge donné divergent entre nouvelles et anciennes[27] et quatre-vingt-seize variétés, chacune se réclamant de [l'autorité de] la transformation mystérieuse[28] ? Aussi, comment les taoïstes peuvent-ils considérer l'Instruction 旨教 et le Lingbao comme étant deux mises à exécution d'un même rituel ? Si on les conserve et observe [toutes les deux], on risque de contrevenir à la pratique rituelle des souverains anciens. Un écart d'un seul instant comptera à jamais comme une grave infraction[29] !

En d'autres termes, comment la Retraite de l'instruction attribuée à Zhang Daoling pouvait-elle en même temps faire partie de la révélation du Lingbao ? La question était peut-être plus pertinente que l'auteur du

Traité ne le comprenait : la recherche moderne a établi que la Retraite de l'instruction n'apparut qu'au Ve siècle, comme un prétendu héritage du premier Maître céleste[30]. Lu Xiujing lui-même se départit momentanément de sa rigueur en matière de critique textuelle pour brouiller cette question, revendiquant l'ascendance au mouvement du « Maître céleste » de la Retraite de l'instruction, tout en la classifiant comme « Lingbao » (voir « Une Retraite pour toutes les circonstances » au chapitre 6). C'est plus particulièrement l'antinomie entre l'expiation selon les anciens rites et selon les innovations introduites par la réforme du Lingbao qui rendait perplexe le candide du *Traité* : comment les sages pouvaient-ils permettre à des pratiques aussi disparates d'exister côte à côte[31] ? L'auteur contre cette question avec l'aide de Zhuangzi. Dans le chapitre « Pieds palmés » 駢拇, Zhuangzi se moque du vice de raisonnement consistant à comparer des entités sans commune mesure : « Si quelque chose est long, cela ne veut pas dire que c'est excessif ; et si c'est court, cela n'implique pas que c'est déficient. C'est pourquoi, bien que les pattes du canard soient courtes, les rallonger ne ferait que lui causer du tort ; et bien que les pattes de la grue soient longues, les couper ne lui procurerait que de la souffrance[32]. » Zhuangzi permet ainsi au *Traité de l'Unité correcte* d'éluder le problème de la réconciliation de traditions rituelles disparates comme étant pareillement sans rapport :

> Considérer que la Retraite [de l'instruction] peut être réduite, ou l'Expiation [de boue et de cendres] peut suppléer les lacunes du Lingbao, non seulement n'est pas admis par le Maître céleste, mais contrevient aussi fondamentalement aux intentions du seigneur Ge 葛 [Xuan, patriarche du Lingbao]. Les érudits de ce monde raccourciraient volontiers la grue et distendraient le canard, mais quelle que soit la sincérité de leur souhait d'égaliser le long et le court, l'un ne peut en aucune façon compenser l'autre[33].

L'auteur du *Traité* soutenait que la Retraite de boue et de cendres était le rituel expiatoire par excellence. Bien que cette Retraite dût sa réputation à l'approbation de Lu Xiujing (voir « Repentance et expiation » au chapitre 8), le *Traité* nous rappelle que ce fut le Maître céleste, agissant au nom de Laozi, qui révéla ce rituel au monde : « Le Grand sage Maître céleste a [d'ores et déjà] donné ses préceptes pour sauver tous les êtres ; comment les gens d'aujourd'hui peuvent-ils les rejeter et ne pas les suivre[34] ? »

> Concernant le rituel de Boue et de cendres, les péchés du monde sont profondément enracinés. Sans un grand mérite, les péchés passés ne peuvent être expiés. Sans la Boue et les cendres, il est impossible d'obtenir la relaxe de l'inculpation, et sans relaxe, la quête de l'immortalité ne peut aboutir ni le monde de la souffrance être transcendé. Le quinzième jour du dixième mois de la première année de Han'an (le 20 novembre 142 de notre ère) au mont Yangping 陽平山, le Maître céleste transmit [le rituel de] l'Instruction pour enseigner aux divers officiers comment intégrer les rangs des immortels. [Ses principaux disciples] Wang 王 [Chang 長] et Zhao 趙 [Sheng 昇] le pratiquèrent et, avec le temps, s'élevèrent jusqu'à la Voie supérieure [des immortels][35]. En ce temps-là, le rite d'expiation de Boue et de cendres était déjà courant, alors que les rituels de la Retraite du Lingbao ne s'étaient pas encore répandus[36].

Par suite des révélations du Lingbao, les voies du salut qui s'offraient aux taoïstes vivant sous les Tang s'étaient multipliées. Elles comprenaient l'ordination cléricale ou laïque, les vœux monastiques et une large gamme de rituels spécialisés. L'accès à chacune d'elles passait par un programme unifié d'initiation scripturale progressive, avec la transmission des préceptes correspondants. Comme leur promulgateur Zhang Daoling, les textes de l'Unité correcte bénéficiaient de la sanction officielle sous les Tang. À un moment donné, entre la compilation de l'*Essentiel des secrets suprêmes* à la fin du VIe siècle et l'émergence des Tang au début du septième, on assigna à ces textes une place dans le Canon taoïste. L'ajout d'un nouvel ensemble de Quatre auxiliaires 四輔 aux Trois cavernes de Lu Xiujing développa le canon taoïste en une septuple structure. Les divisions supplémentaires remédiaient à plusieurs omissions majeures dans la compilation originelle de Lu : le *Classique de la Voie et de la vertu*, le *Livre de la Grande paix* et les *Incantations divines des grottes abyssales* ; le quatrième auxiliaire, la *Division de l'Unité correcte* 正一部, devint le répertoire des textes du Maître céleste. L'héritage scriptural du taoïsme forma dès lors une structure complète. Au VIIe siècle, Meng Anpai 孟安排, l'érudit taoïste à la cour de l'impératrice Wu Zetian 武則天 (r. 684-705), en dressa un nouveau catalogue. Le canon des Tang fut compilé sur ordre de l'empereur Xuanzong et promulgué en 748. Dans la septième division de ce canon (soit le quatrième Auxiliaire) étaient rassemblés les *Textes statutaires de l'Unité correcte* 正一法文[37].

L'ordination

En l'an 735, Xuanzong promulgua un *Commentaire impérial du Livre de la Voie et de la vertu* 唐玄宗御註道德真經[38]. Comme les textes de l'Unité correcte, le *Livre de la Voie et de la vertu*, avec ses commentaires et les textes associés, représentait un degré séparé d'initiation au canon et une étape dans la hiérarchie de l'ordination, attestée par un « registre » 籙. Ces registres conféraient au porteur les pouvoirs d'un grade et d'un commandement d'officiers subalternes dans le monde des esprits. Au cours des premières années du règne de Xuanzong, Zhang Wanfu clarifia l'ordre rituel nouveau avec sa hiérarchie d'ordination, développé d'après l'enseignement doctrinal de Lu Xiujing. Dans son *Almanach pour la transmission des écritures, préceptes et registres* 道士受三洞經誡法籙擇日曆, Zhang détailla le mode progressif d'initiation scripturaire avec les remises graduelles de chaque groupe de textes, accompagnés par des listes de préceptes à observer de plus en plus volumineuses[39]. Une cérémonie de transmission, accompagnée de l'acquittement de gages correspondant au nouveau degré d'ordination, marquait chaque avancement. Des manuscrits de cette époque, retrouvés à Dunhuang, montrent que la hiérarchie d'ordination qui prévalait à la périphérie nord-ouest de la Chine était essentiellement la même qu'à la capitale Chang'an.

Les manuscrits de Dunhuang spécifient que les registres de l'Unité correcte étaient inscrits sur des bandes de tissu destinées à être portées autour des reins lors de la cérémonie de transmission durant laquelle le disciple était consacré avec l'attribution d'un nom rituel et des aspersions d'eau. Un individu obtenait le rang de « disciple de la Foi pure » 淸信弟子 du Lingbao à la réception des Dix préceptes, suivi par deux degrés successifs d'initiation au *Livre de la Voie et de la vertu*. Ceux-ci ouvraient la voie à une éventuelle vocation de maître taoïste. Des « attestations » 狀 de l'ordination laïque de disciples de la Foi pure, préservées à Dunhuang, montrent que les récipiendaires étaient des adolescents ou de jeunes adultes des deux sexes, vivant dans un monastère ou non. Les rituels du Lingbao pouvaient être exécutés dans l'un ou l'autre de ces contextes, et l'initiation à la Foi pure semble avoir été une étape intermédiaire vers la prise des ordres religieux[40]. À partir de ce grade, recevant consécutivement les *Incantations divines* et d'autres groupes de textes, les ordinands avaient le rang de membres du clergé ou « maîtres des rites » 法師. Lors de l'initiation finale aux écritures du Shangqing, le clerc ou maître des rites obtenait le titre de « maître des rites des Trois cavernes » 三洞法師. De la même façon que le rituel de cour et les rites de passage dans la Chine ancienne (rites de prise de bonnet, de deuil et d'audience) étaient classés selon le statut social et l'ancienneté, les échelons d'ordination taoïstes déterminaient les classes de rituel que leur détenteur était autorisé à exécuter[41].

Un manuel monastique du début des Tang distingue six grades de taoïstes, depuis les hommes réels divins et immortels transcendants jusqu'aux quatre classes de pratiquants mortels ici-bas : les ermites de la montagne, les moines et nonnes, les adeptes laïcs vivant en famille et les prêtres libateurs. Le rang de libateur, réservé initialement aux chefs des diocèses dans la première communauté du Maître céleste, fut par la suite le propre des initiés laïcs détenant un registre du Zhengyi[42]. Après s'être soumis à cette ordination première, un taoïste pouvait ainsi choisir parmi trois vocations comme cadre de pratique : la société laïque, la communauté monastique ou la réclusion dans un ermitage de montagne.

Les vœux monastiques

Pour les taoïstes des Tang, l'option de quitter son foyer pour vivre dans une communauté monastique 住觀, fort débattue aux siècles précédents (voir « La piété filiale » au chapitre 8), était devenue un choix accepté[43]. Non seulement le monachisme promettait la délivrance et la protection à ceux qui le pratiquaient, mais il contribuait aussi au salut universel en engendrant pour tous des « champs de mérite » 福田 (en sanskrit *punyaksetra*) et en produisant des sphères karmiques de bénédiction générées par la prière, l'exécution de rituels et les bonnes actions. L'essor du monachisme dans la Chine des Tang, comme dans l'Europe chrétienne du VIIe siècle, fut soutenu par la monétisation croissante de la rédemption, parallèle au développement économique[44]. En Chine, les monastères bouddhiques bénéficièrent d'une accumulation de biens à grande échelle, comprenant propriétés foncières, serfs, moulins à eau, pressoirs à huile et institutions de prêt. Le caractère salvateur du don pour le donateur conférait une sanctification des biens monastiques et protégeait la pureté des communautés monastiques de la souillure de la possession matérielle. Faire don de sa fortune à un monastère procurait un mérite immense. Tout ce qui intégrait les « biens inaliénables » 常住 du *sangha* par le biais de la charité était « propriété pure » 淨財. Des adeptes laïcs appelés « hommes purs » 淨人 géraient ces actifs pour le compte des moines et des nonnes. Les biens inaliénables constituaient une forme de dotation sociale perpétuelle. Ces concepts économiques et juridiques nouveaux arrivaient en Chine via les traités *vinaya* bouddhiques sur la discipline monastique[45]. L'adaptation taoïste de l'une des règles *vinaya* de ce type, intitulée « Rites du monachisme » 住觀威儀 et faisant partie du code *Liturgie solennelle de l'Unité correcte* 正一威儀經, affirmait que les monastères taoïstes étaient pareillement dotés de biens inaliénables incluant encens, huile, riz, blé, combustible et légumes, et qu'ils possédaient des domaines, des moulins, des serviteurs, des animaux et des outils et instruments[46].

Comme en Europe, toutes les strates de la société chinoise, aristocratie, classes dirigeantes et autres laïcs, étaient saisies d'un grand élan caritatif. Bien que les abbayes taoïstes ne soient pas réputées pour avoir atteint un niveau de richesse comparable à celui de nombreux monastères bouddhiques, le lien entre renoncement, bonnes œuvres et salut, dont Lu Xiujing s'était fait l'avocat constant et fervent, allait maintenant de soi dans les milieux taoïstes. Des contes miraculeux des Tang illustrent tant l'abondance que la nature sacramentelle des biens inaliénables de certains monastères taoïstes[47]. Comme les chrétiens se voyaient promettre les plus grandes récompenses au Ciel pour avoir soulagé la souffrance des pauvres, les bouddhistes professaient que le don caritatif, tel que l'exemplifiait le prince Sudāna, était la vertu suprême[48]. Parmi tous les agents de la loi karmique, la charité était le plus efficace. L'attrait que suscitait cette doctrine chez les taoïstes transparaît dans le *Livre du Lingbao sur la causalité karmique de la rétribution* 靈寶業報因緣經, qui daterait de la fin du VIe siècle ou du début du VIIe, dans lequel le Seigneur Tao enseigne à l'homme réel du Salut universel 普濟真人 les cinq types d'actes méritoires apportant secours et délivrance de l'adversité : (1) la confection d'images du Seigneur Tao ; (2) la copie des écritures ; (3) la fondation d'un monastère et l'ordination comme moine (un seul individu quittant son foyer pour prendre une charge de préposé aux écritures et aux icônes pouvait éveiller des aspirations spirituelles chez de nombreux laïcs) ; (4) la pratique de Retraites, confessions et dévotions ; et (5) les actes de charité envers tous. Ces derniers engendraient « de vastes champs de mérite et portaient les récompenses à leur comble »[49]. C'est de la générosité que jaillissait par ailleurs l'ensemble des autres actions méritoires, et la communauté monastique en était la principale bénéficiaire. Au niveau le plus élémentaire, le don quotidien de nourriture aux moines procurait un mérite considérable (voir « Les rituels » au chapitre 11).

Un autre livre sacré du Lingbao du VIIe siècle, intitulé *Récompense karmique de quitter sa famille* 出家因緣經, exposait les gains de ceux qui prenaient les vœux monastiques. Un soutra bouddhique de la fin du VIe siècle portant le même titre lui servit peut-être de modèle[50]. Le lecteur est conduit devant une assemblée de deux cents princes et épouses, ministres d'État et hommes et femmes du peuple, unis dans une même aspiration à l'illumination. Se prosternant devant le Très Haut Céleste vénérable 太上天尊, ils déclarent leur désir d'« abandonner la capitale, conjoints, enfants et foyer, [ils] font solennellement le vœu de recevoir les *Écritures des Trois cavernes*, et consacrent leur vie entière à des actes méritoires qui, dans les temps à venir, produiront des bénédictions pour les générations passées, présentes et futures ». Le Céleste vénérable, qui avait convoqué cette assemblée dans le dessein d'en instruire les participants, se met alors à prêcher « les lourdes conséquences karmiques de quitter sa famille ». Les fruits des vœux monastiques incluaient la grâce de « racheter le sort des générations passées et de porter secours aux indigents, aux prisonniers, aux vieillards et aux malades, aux oiseaux et aux bêtes, aux aveugles et aux sourds, aux malades des Six afflictions et à tous les êtres sensibles »[51]. Inversement, rompre les vœux et enfreindre le code monastique – y compris les règles rituelles, diététiques et matérielles – entraînaient une rétribution proportionnellement élevée. Le *Code pour la vénération de la Voie* 奉道科戒, un manuel pour moines et nonnes taoïstes de la période des Sui ou du début des Tang, s'ouvre par deux chapitres entiers détaillant les récompenses et les rétributions, y compris les punitions des contrevenants à la règle monastique[52].

Comment un novice prenait-il les vœux monastiques ? Zhang Wanfu a laissé un compte rendu sommaire des rites d'ordination pour deux princesses impériales, Jinxian 金仙 et Yuzhen 玉真, qui devinrent nonnes taoïstes en 711, l'année précédant la prise du pouvoir de leur frère Longji 隆基 comme empereur Xuanzong[53]. Prêtre officiant lors de cette cérémonie, Zhang inventoria soigneusement les accessoires rituels, y compris les fastueuses offrandes de gages, le mobilier, les récipients et les ustensiles, mais il n'en décrivit pas le déroulement. En revanche, le protocole d'une cérémonie de vœux plus ordinaire se trouve dans le *Code pour la vénération de la Voie*. Il s'intitule « Cérémonie pour gagner l'autre rive » 度人儀, parce que le vœu avait pour effet de rendre l'ordinand à même de gagner la rive tant convoitée du salut.

Au cœur de la célébration figurait la remise des Dix préceptes, que précédait une incantation de l'« Hymne à la sagesse » extrait du rituel de transmission de Lu Xiujing. En effet, la cérémonie des vœux monastiques suivait de près le rituel de transmission des préceptes de Lu Xiujing (voir « Les Dix préceptes » au chapitre 6). La différence était que l'ordination monastique avait des conséquences bien plus radicales : l'action de « quitter le foyer » remplaçait littéralement la famille biologique par la communauté religieuse. Les moines et nonnes bouddhistes marquaient cette étape par l'adoption du nom de clan Śākya (Shi 釋) du Bouddha, comme une mariée le faisait lorsqu'elle intégrait la lignée de son époux. Les taoïstes exprimaient le poids symbolique du départ du foyer différemment, en prenant congé de leur père, de leur mère, de leurs ancêtres et du souverain par des prosternements successifs. Le protocole commente que, une fois revêtus de l'habit monastique, ils ne s'inclineraient plus jamais devant père, mère ou empereur, d'où cet adieu « sur le seuil, à l'entrée du Tao ». Ensuite, l'ordinand prononçait le vœu du triple refuge 三歸, la version taoïste du refuge dans les Trois joyaux bouddhiques, le *triśarana*. Pour les taoïstes, livrer leur personne aux Trois joyaux signifiait abandonner leur corps à la Voie, leur esprit aux écritures et leur vie au maître. Après avoir prononcé ce vœu, ils étaient revêtus des trois habits monastiques. Enfin, s'étant coiffés de la coiffe rituelle, ils étaient prêts à recevoir les préceptes[54].

Moines et nonnes ordonnés détenaient les mêmes qualifications liturgiques et grade clérical que les maîtres taoïstes non monastiques. Ensemble, ils étaient appelés « maîtres et nonnes taoïstes » 道士女冠[55]. Sous les Tang, les monastères étaient désignés par le terme *guan* 觀 (abbaye), un dérivé du mot *guan* 館 (auberge) utilisé dans ce contexte sous les Six dynasties. Résider au sein d'une communauté monastique offrait un degré de réclusion intermédiaire entre la société laïque et l'ermitage de montagne. Les codes pour l'agencement d'un monastère et ses bâtiments auxiliaires, sous les Tang, évoquent des complexes architecturaux élaborés comprenant des salles pour le culte, les prédications et les assemblées, des cabinets de méditation, des resserres pour les écritures, des réfectoires, des quartiers séparés pour les moines résidents et de passage, plus des ateliers, des moulins, des terrasses, des tours, des corps de garde et des jardins[56]. Cette vision était sans doute plus prescriptive que descriptive, modelée sur les livres de règles monastiques bouddhiques, lesquels dérivaient quant à eux des codes du *vinaya* indien, traduits en chinois aux IVe et Ve siècles. Dans le même temps, les règles présidant au mode de vie des moines et des nonnes prévoyaient des cellules individuelles simples, meublées avec parcimonie, avec un nombre limité d'ustensiles pour le couvert et la toilette, seule propriété personnelle autorisée[57]. La vie quotidienne monastique obéissait à la règle des observances, offices, dévotions, récitations, leçons et confessions, rythmée par les rituels accomplis au nom de la communauté, de commanditaires laïcs ou de l'État. À leur décès, moines et nonnes étaient inhumés suivant les règles prescrites pour les corps et les possessions, telles que les exposait la *Liturgie de l'Unité correcte* sous la rubrique « Rites mortuaires solennels » 死亡威儀 :

> Quand meurt un condisciple ou maître respectable, son décès est annoncé par trois cent soixante coups de cloche. Après que tous les frères se sont rassemblés, ils poussent des gémissements par trois fois, brûlent de l'encens et récitent les écritures. Puis ils apprêtent le corps pour l'inhumation selon les rites. Après que le corps a été couché dans un sac de toile et mis dans

un cercueil, il est conduit dans une forêt ou un marécage pour y être enterré simplement. Il n'est pas permis d'ériger une tombe ni de marquer la sépulture avec un arbre ou un monticule de terre. Les talismans et registres de l'Unité correcte [du défunt], ses certificats d'ordination, ses anneaux de gage et son épée sont empaquetés dans un sac et inhumés avec le corps. Écrire soixante-douze talismans et revêtir le corps conformément aux rites ; présenter une *Requête de pacification de la terre* 戊己章 et une *Requête de mise en bière* 棺殮章[58] ; placer les costumes rituels avec le corps. Ce qui reste des vêtements et effets personnels, literie et ustensiles en possession du maître défunt, après les dons et le règlement des droits, est intégré après cession aux biens inaliénables[59]. Ni la famille proche ou lointaine, ni les relations internes ou externes ne peuvent interférer[60].

Chapitre 10

Sacramentalité et pratique religieuse laïque

La pratique religieuse laïque et les rituels populaires ouvraient des voies de salut et de protection comparables à celles de l'initiation cléricale et complémentaires, que ce soit par les ordinations laïques, la vénération personnelle des livres sacrés et des icônes, l'incantation de formules sacrées, l'usage de sceaux et de talismans, ou la pratique de rites d'exorcismes pour l'expulsion des esprits et d'autres maux. On peut dire que ces méthodes revêtaient un caractère sacramentel en ce sens qu'elles recourraient à des symboles religieux investis de la puissance divine ou spirituelle que véhiculaient des objets matériels ou des actes rituels. Bien que les pratiques sacramentelles touchent tous les domaines d'activité taoïstes, ce chapitre et le suivant s'intéresseront plus particulièrement à leur usage par les pratiquants laïcs ou pour leur compte. Notre guide sera les *Divines manifestations du taoïsme* de Du Guangting, un recueil de miracles dont des croyants firent l'expérience et qui manifestaient la puissance occulte des divinités, rituels, objets et pratiques[1]. Les récits de témoignage de ces corroborations miraculeuses offrent un aperçu unique de la foi et de l'imaginaire religieux de la fin des Tang.

Une partie substantielle des *Divines manifestations*, consacrée au sacramentaire, relate les effets des méthodes sacramentelles et décrit leur mode opératoire. Typiquement, les sacramentaux taoïstes étaient des objets inscrits : des écritures 經, des registres 籙, des talismans 符 et des sceaux 印. Le fondement de leur puissance se rattachait aux symboles féodaux de l'autorité, aux attributs du pouvoir et aux instruments contractuels de la Chine ancienne. À cet égard, un sacrement taoïste ressemble à un *sacramentum* romain et à un *symbolon* grec. Dans une étude remarquable, Anna Seidel a montré les continuités idéologiques entre, d'un côté, les anciens écrits « apocryphes » 讖緯 de prédiction politique, les talismans de type *fu* et les écritures révélées du Lingbao, et de l'autre, entre les trésors impériaux chinois et les objets sacrés taoïstes[2]. Les instruments sacramentels conféraient au croyant le pouvoir de communiquer avec le monde invisible, sommer dieux et démons et mobiliser soldats et officiers spirituels. Les sacrements taoïstes comprenaient diverses formes d'écriture, de représentation visuelle ou mentale (icônes 像, visualisation 思), d'actes (rituels 法, récitation 誦) et d'incantations (formules sacrées 呪). Les sacramentaux pouvaient être des objets portés sur soi ou pendus à la ceinture, comme des insignes ou des amulettes. Les sanctuaires et les accessoires rituels étaient des entités sacramentelles à part entière : cloches 鐘, tambours 鼓, pierres sonores 磬, encensoirs 爐 et vêtements 法服. Toutes étaient investies de la puissance des divinités tutélaires qui les habitaient.

Les effets des sacrements taoïstes étaient multiples. D'abord, on pouvait manier lesdits objets sacramentaux comme des instruments puissants, d'aucuns diraient « magiques »[3]. Comme le bouddhisme, le taoïsme prônait la délivrance par des actes de dévotion, et chaque sacrement offrait un moment efficace de dévotion à son dieu ou à ses esprits tutélaires. En tant que fournisseurs d'instruments sacramentaux pour la vénération et la protection, les monastères servaient d'interface entre le clergé et la société laïque. En accomplissant les rituels, en copiant les écritures et les talismans et en produisant les icônes et les sceaux, moines et nonnes participaient au salut des fidèles laïcs.

Le *Livre miraculeux pour redresser les torts et obtenir la délivrance* 解冤拔度妙經 était un opuscule fournissant aux fidèles laïcs un court texte pour la méditation personnelle et la vénération dans leur oratoire domestique. À ces frères et sœurs, le Très Haut Seigneur Lao promettait bénédiction et protection. Ils seraient absous et autorisés à accéder à la félicité et au salut. Les âmes égarées dans le monde souterrain monteraient au Ciel[4]. Dans les *Divines manifestations*, des narrations dévotionnelles corroboraient les textes sacrés populaires en inculquant la peur de la captivité et des tortures infernales tout en offrant l'espérance d'une délivrance au paradis. Dans cet esprit, la « Manifestation du pouvoir du registre porté par Liu Tu » 劉圖佩籙靈驗 égrène les châtiments horribles de l'enfer qui attendaient ceux qui dénigraient les Trois joyaux, tout en soulignant que les hôtes bienheureux du paradis étaient des initiés taoïstes. Un enseignement concomitant de l'histoire est que la destinée de chaque individu était déterminée par le solde des « causes », c'est-à-dire les bonnes et les mauvaises actions, méritantes ou punissables, qui étaient dûment enregistrées et vérifiées par les comptables en charge du Grand livre de la destinée[5].

L'histoire de Liu Tu – un Mulian aux traits chinois qui sauve son père plutôt que sa mère – est à dessein située en des temps prébouddhiques, sous les Han orientaux. Liu Tu est un clerc de district à Jiangxia 江夏 au Hubei, qui, adolescent, a reçu l'ordination taoïste laïque. Enfant, il a montré une aptitude précoce pour l'arithmétique. Le dixième jour du second mois de l'année 109 de notre ère, à minuit, le seigneur du mont Tai, gouverneur du royaume des morts sous le Pic de l'Est, dépêche un émissaire dénommé Ailes gracieuses 雅羽 chez Liu Tu pour le convoquer. Ailes gracieuses a la prévenance de rassurer la famille de Tu que celui-ci reviendra. Suivant son guide, Tu parvient au Ciel et paraît devant une assemblée de cinq seigneurs. Siégeant au nord, le Très Haut Seigneur Lao préside, tandis que Taishan est assis sur le trône oriental en tant que seigneur du Pic de l'Est :

> Une fois que [Liu] Tu eut porté révérence aux cinq seigneurs, le Seigneur Lao lui commanda en ces termes : « Vous êtes mort en dépit du fait que vous êtes connu pour vénérer la Voie, croire aux Véritables et promouvoir la bonté. Je vous ai fait venir parce que vous êtes bon en arithmétique et que je souhaite que vous vérifiiez le Grand livre de toutes les multitudes sous le ciel. » Le seigneur Taishan ordonna à Ailes gracieuses d'escorter Tu afin qu'il rencontrât les aides et officiers de droite et de gauche. Ils durent alors vérifier ensemble le Grand livre de tous sous le ciel.

Le moment de la mort de chaque individu était arrêté dans le Registre des vivants. Le risque d'erreur nourrissait naturellement l'anxiété, comme le démontre cette ordonnance sépulcrale remise aux esprits du monde souterrain pour le compte d'une femme qui mourut en l'an 147 de notre ère : « Vérifiez vos registres de noms, calculez si l'année et le mois concordent, vérifiez, comparez et contrôlez encore le jour de la mort ! Si le jour et l'heure concordent, comparez et vérifiez encore le jour de la mort[6] ! »

Après que Tu et les aides et officiers ont terminé leur travail de vérification, les enregistrements des trépassés en bonne et due forme sont transférés à une archive distincte :

> Le deuxième jour, à minuit, tous les documents étaient en ordre, les [noms des] morts avaient été enlevés et ceux des vivants corrigés. Quand l'enregistrement fut achevé, [Liu Tu] demanda la permission de retourner chez lui. Le Très Haut Seigneur Lao dit : « Que l'émissaire emmène Tu pour lui montrer les lieux de punition et de bénédiction. »

Ailes gracieuses conduit alors Liu Tu au premier niveau de l'enfer, où ils voient trois mille femmes sous la torture, pendues à un grand arbre par la tête et avec des fers de cent livres aux pieds. Au deuxième niveau, des hommes subissent le même châtiment. Poursuivant jusqu'au dixième niveau de l'enfer, ils voient des gens endurant des interrogatoires, menottés, battus avec les mains liées derrière le dos, ébouillantés dans des chaudrons, portant de lourdes pierres sur la tête, leurs corps brisés percés de piques de fer, certains brûlant dans les flammes, d'autres se fouettant mutuellement, tous souffrant d'insupportables agonies.

> Ailes [gracieuses] dit : « La raison de cela est le dénigrement des Trois joyaux et la tromperie du peuple. » Puis ils entrèrent au onzième niveau. Là, ils virent le père défunt de [Liu] Tu parmi trois cents hommes se fouettant les uns les autres. Sur le seuil de la prison de Pingkang 平康獄 au Ciel, Tu s'exclama amèrement en ces termes, frappant le sol de la tête : « Quel fut le crime de mon père pour qu'il connaisse pareille souffrance dans la mort ? » Ailes dit : « De son vivant, le père de Monsieur était le gardien d'une prison qui exécuta des personnes innocentes et accusa faussement des hommes bons. Cela fait maintenant sept années, depuis

sa mort, qu'il endure ce châtiment. Il devrait être possible d'obtenir qu'il renaisse. J'enverrai à l'Officier du ciel une requête de votre part pour que votre père soit relâché[7]. » [Liu] Tu se présenta alors de nouveau au Très Haut Seigneur Lao, frappant le sol de sa tête un million de fois. Le Très Haut Seigneur Lao dit : « Grâce à vous, votre père sera libéré sans plus tarder. Ne vous affligez plus. » Derechef, il ordonna à Ailes gracieuses d'amener Tu au Palais de la Grande pureté 太清宮 où il vit trente-six mille individus arborant l'habit noir et serrant des tablettes d'or[8]. Ils psalmodiaient les écritures tandis que nourriture et boisson étaient copieusement fournies et que la musique faisait trembler les cieux. Ailes dit : « De leur vivant, ces gens ont été ordonnés avec les registres de l'Officier du ciel 天官符籙. Ils se sont employés inlassablement à faire le bien, leurs noms ont été entrés dans [le ciel de] la Grande pureté et ils ont atteint cette félicité[9]. »

Les chrétiens du Moyen Âge croyaient que seule une infime fraction de l'humanité monterait au Ciel. Par contraste, le paradis des taoïstes pouvait accueillir une confortable majorité, du moins parmi ceux qui s'étaient soumis à l'ordination laïque. À la fin de l'histoire, Liu Tu paraît une nouvelle fois devant le Seigneur Lao qui le laisse enfin retourner dans le monde des mortels en l'enjoignant d'annoncer à tous, laïcs et religieux, la rétribution, et d'exhorter ses semblables mortels à se confesser chaque mois pour requérir le pardon de leurs péchés et l'absolution de leurs fautes. En guise de conclusion, une « Discussion » citant l'*Hagiographie de Maître Wenshi* 文始先生內傳, le disciple de Laozi et gardien de la passe à travers laquelle le sage partit pour l'Ouest, dépeint la cosmologie sotériologique aperçue dans la vision de Liu Tu[10]. La « Discussion » explique qu'une fois enregistrés, les péchés et les mérites de tous ceux qui venaient au monde et mouraient étaient examinés par le Bureau du ciel et l'Officier de la terre. Pas un cheveu de leur tête n'échappait à l'examen minutieux, car le [*Daode*] *jing* dit : « Le Filet du ciel est vaste [et son maillage] est large, mais rien ne lui échappe[11]. » Dans ce panorama de l'au-delà, le mont Luofeng 羅酆山 occupe le quadrant nord et abrite les Six palais des dieux démoniaques des Six cieux[12]. Ceux qui mouraient traversaient les Six palais et y recevaient leur châtiment en fonction de la loi de causalité karmique. Vingt-quatre prisons étaient disposées par groupes de huit au-dessus, en dessous et dans les entrailles de Luofeng[13]. Il y avait en outre des Prisons terrestres sous le mont Tai, et toutes les autres montagnes, rivières et mers renfermaient elles aussi des prisons, chacune avec des administrateurs, des assistants et des examinateurs. Les bons montaient au Palais céleste tandis que les méchants échouaient dans les Prisons terrestres. Tous les condamnés à des châtiments passaient d'abord par les Trois bourbiers et les Cinq souffrances ; puis ils étaient soumis à des travaux forcés, halant des pierres du mont Meng 蒙山 pour le mont Tai ou puisant de l'eau au Gué occidental 西津 pour l'envoyer à la Mer orientale 東海[14], ou bien ils renaissaient dans les Trois destinées mauvaises ou dans les Quatre tribus, comme domestiques, ou comme victimes des Six afflictions, ou bien encore ils payaient pour des péchés commis dans des vies antérieures.

Les pécheurs cherchant à échapper aux châtiments infernaux n'avaient pas tous la chance d'avoir une progéniture aussi disposée et apte à faire fléchir l'Officier du ciel que Liu Tu. Dans les années 870, quand Wu Xinglu 吳行魯 servait comme gouverneur militaire du Xichuan 西川, la province du Sichuan occidental sous les Tang, il donna l'ordre que le porche imposant et finement ouvragé de l'abbaye de Longxing 龍興觀, près de Chengdu, fût démantelé et emporté dans un monastère bouddhique[15]. (Nous retrouverons ce porche plus loin, en compagnie d'une mère pratiquante taoïste et d'un jeune enfant.) Aggravant davantage son geste sacrilège, le gouverneur fit aussi démanteler le clocher de l'abbaye, endommageant l'enceinte du sanctuaire. Il s'agissait là précisément du dénigrement des Trois joyaux dont Liu Tu avait appris qu'il causait les pires souffrances en enfer. Et effectivement, c'est là que l'on découvre ensuite le gouverneur en proie à des tourments perpétuels. On sait que l'auteur, Du Guangting, entretenait de bonnes relations avec la partie lésée dans cette histoire, c'est-à-dire la communauté taoïste de l'abbaye de Longxing[16]. C'est peut-être avec ce public à l'esprit que Du observe ironiquement les vaines tentatives de Wu pour se soustraire à son châtiment : quelques années après le vol du porche, un collègue de Du, nommé Yin Sixuan 尹嗣玄[17], rapporta qu'un ancien membre du personnel au service du gouverneur était passé dans l'autre monde après avoir succombé à la maladie, mais était revenu à la vie pour décrire ce qu'il avait vu :

[Wu] Xinglu était prisonnier de chaînes de fer et d'entraves, poussé par des officiers démoniaques à haler des matériaux de construction de Longxing. Il ne connaissait, jour et nuit, aucun repit, car à peine avait-il empilé le bois de construction que celui-ci repartait en s'envolant. Il continuait à le déplacer ainsi, sans savoir dans combien d'années lui serait accordée la permission de cesser. [Xinglu] voulut demander à ses descendants d'ériger un porche pour racheter son péché. Mais parce que les descendants étaient appauvris et dans le besoin, ils n'en eurent simplement pas les moyens[18] !

Les registres d'ordination

Le succès de l'intercession de Liu Tu en faveur de son père et son témoignage salutaire à propos du système des Grands livres du destin et du jugement dans l'autre monde furent rendus possibles par son ordination laïque. À l'âge de quinze ans, Tu avait reçu le Registre des soixante-quinze généraux 七十五將軍符籙 édictant le fait que ce nombre précis d'officiers célestes étaient désormais à son service.

Selon l'usage, un adepte laïc atteignait ce niveau d'ordination douze années après la première initiation de l'enfance[19]. Les ordinations de l'Unité correcte apportaient protection, absolution et guérison aux enfants et adultes laïcs[20]. Les ordinands recevaient d'abord l'ancien titre de libateur des Maîtres célestes qui leur conférait la puissance dudit office et l'attribution de subordonnés spirituels. Nous avons vu que les registres de Dunhuang étaient consignés sur des bandes de tissu (voir « L'ordination » au chapitre 9). Le Registre de l'inspecteur du mérite 都功籙, initialement légué par Zhang Daoling à ses descendants pour secourir le peuple, était à l'origine inscrit sur une tablette de bois et pendait à la ceinture. Comme dans d'autres sphères de la vie quotidienne des Tang, l'emploi du papier permit d'innover : au VIIIe siècle, des certificats sur papier étaient délivrés couramment pour répondre à la demande croissante de registres et réduire les coûts de fabrication, tout comme la soie avait précédemment remplacé comme support d'écriture le bois et le bambou, matériaux moins maniables[21].

Les registres étaient des instruments sacramentaux qui conféraient aux membres des congrégations et à leurs maisonnées contrôle et autorité sur les officiers spirituels du diocèse. Un registre identifiait son porteur et lui donnait pouvoir[22]. Un maître de maison, par exemple, pouvait être ordonné d'un Registre efficace pour sécuriser la demeure 鎮宅靈籙. Ceci plaçait les membres de la maisonnée sous la protection des armées spirituelles des dix directions de l'espace, repoussait les influences démoniaques et délivrait les habitants du mal[23]. Les registres comportaient le nom des officiers spirituels, ainsi que parfois leur image, comme aide à la visualisation. Lu Xiujing avait mis en garde les pratiquants : s'ils négligeaient de vénérer ces esprits, ils perdraient leur protection (voir « Maîtrise et quiétude » au chapitre 7). L'expérience de Zhao Ye 趙業 en apporte une illustration : au cours de l'ère de règne Kaicheng 開成 (836-840), quand Zhao était un jeune garçon, il avait été promis au dieu stellaire Grand un 太一 en étant soumis à une ordination Zhengyi du huitième grade 正一八階籙[24]. Plus tard, Zhao devint magistrat du district de Jin'an 晉安縣, près de la ville-préfecture moderne de Guangyuan 廣元 au Sichuan. Pris par ses devoirs séculiers, Zhao oublia l'engagement religieux de son enfance. Le jour vint où l'écart entre ses obligations envers le monde spirituel et celles dues à César lui fut brusquement rappelé. La vision liminaire vint à Zhao lors d'une expérience extracorporelle au seuil de la mort. Étant tombé malade, il décéda d'abord brusquement, tandis que ses mains et ses pieds demeuraient souples et son cœur tiède. Trois jours plus tard, Zhao Ye revint à la vie pour raconter ce qui suit :

> Je fus poursuivi par un officier du monde souterrain et entraîné de force. Quand j'en demandai la raison, il dit seulement que c'était une affaire concernant une dette due pour un reniement. Pour ma part, j'étais convaincu de n'avoir pas commis ce délit et conclus qu'il devait s'agir d'une arrestation indue. Après trente à cinquante lieues, nous arrivâmes sur une crête montagneuse où se dressait un palais magnifique. Là se trouvait une foule nombreuse. Un acolyte s'avança et me dit : « N'es-tu pas Zhao Taixuan 趙太玄 ? » Je répondis : « Je suis Zhao Ye, magistrat du district de Jin'an. » L'acolyte rit et dit : « Comment as-tu pu oublier ? » Un autre acolyte vint après le premier et dit[25] : « Le Grand un ordonne la convocation de Zhao Taixuan. » Le gendarme me lâcha aussitôt et j'entrai dans le palais avec les acolytes. Le Grand un n'était pas visible ; je ne vis qu'un taoïste qui dit : « À l'âge de six *sui*, tu fus malade et reçus un registre d'ordination

> Zhengyi du huitième grade. Ton nom [d'ordination] fut Taixuan. Quand tu te permis de prendre une fonction profane, oublias-tu également cela ? Le Grand un a ordonné que tu sois relâché et repartes. Tu devras ceindre un registre 佩籙 et t'entraîner à la perfection, pratiquer des actes méritoires au profit de tous les êtres, occuper ton poste et exercer ta charge sans convoiter de gains indus ni faire peu de cas de la vie des gens ! » Quand il eut fini de parler, il disparut[26].

Zhao avait déjà recouvré la santé. Il reçut révérencieusement une nouvelle ordination, pratiqua les rituels infatigablement et se dévoua à faire le bien, reprenant son nom d'ordination, Taixuan.

L'histoire du révérend maître Pan prend le contre-pied de l'épisode vécu par Zhao : Pan est un homme de bien charitable qui n'a jamais recherché ni promotion ni distinction en ce monde ou dans l'autre. Pourtant, un immortel en visite le récompense de sa bonté avec une ordination du Registre de magistrat du dieu du sol des neuf provinces du Zhengyi 正一九州社令籙. Ceci a pour effet de conférer à Pan le pouvoir d'un magistrat dans le monde invisible, à la tête d'un personnel civil et militaire nombreux[27]. Submergé par les innombrables rapports portés à son attention, Pan ne tarde pas à trouver ingrates ses tâches officielles. Il se résout à enfreindre la seule injonction que lui avait adressée l'immortel, à savoir s'abstenir de viande et de légumes à saveur alliacée. À l'instant où Pan avale de la viande et de l'ail, il se voit relever de ses fonctions. Cependant, le répit longtemps espéré cesse bientôt quand l'immortel revient avec de terribles avertissements de rétribution et remet à Pan un jeu de talismans avec lesquels se racheter. Le révérend maître Pan passe alors le reste de ses jours à rédimer sa destinée confisquée en aidant autrui par l'exécution de rituels, la dispensation de talismans et l'accomplissement de bonnes œuvres[28].

La coutume voulait qu'une famille taoïste pratiquante demandât la première ordination Zhengyi pour leur enfant quand celui-ci était âgé de sept ans[29]. Cependant, les parents pouvaient implorer la guérison et la protection de leur enfant par l'ordination quand cela s'avérait pressant. Zhao Ye reçut son ordination du huitième grade dès l'âge de six ans parce qu'il était souffrant. Et un tout jeune enfant de deux ans, dénommé Jia Qiong 賈瓊, reçut son registre pour la seule raison que lui et sa mère passèrent devant un temple où une cérémonie d'ordination était en cours. Cette histoire-là nous conduit aux abords de Chengdu, le troisième jour du troisième mois lunaire, le jour de la Fête du printemps. C'était la période pour se soumettre à des rituels de purification, et celle des excursions dans les faubourgs. À Chang'an, le poète Du Fu 杜甫 (712-770) était connu pour avoir apprécié la vue d'élégantes dames du palais déambulant sur les berges de la Rivière serpentine lors de la Fête du printemps de 753[30]. Les résidents de Chengdu fréquentaient volontiers les marchés aux vers à soie animés qui jouxtaient les temples taoïstes importants et les sites de pèlerinage[31]. Le marché le plus proche se trouvait juste à l'extérieur de la ville, près de l'abbaye de Longxing au mont Xueshe 學射山 (aujourd'hui Fenghuan shan 鳳凰山), celle dont l'admirable porche avait été profané par le gouverneur Wu Xinglu dans les années 870. Refondée sous la dynastie Sui, l'abbaye de Zhizhen 至真觀 des Zhou du Nord faisait partie, sous les Tang, du réseau des abbayes préfectorales nommées Longxing à partir de 707. Du Guangting, faisant parfois usage de l'ancien nom du temple, aimait à en décrire le terrain spacieux et les caractéristiques architecturales[32]. Après la chute des Tang, les anciens bâtiments furent restaurés en 916. À cette occasion comme en d'autres, Du y célébra des rituels d'Offrande et y accomplit des Retraites pour le compte du souverain de Shu[33].

Les visiteurs arrivant de Chengdu franchissaient l'enceinte septentrionale de la ville par la porte de Taixuan 太玄門, empruntaient le pont de l'Ascension des immortels 昇仙橋 et atteignaient l'abbaye après un trajet de six kilomètres :

> Jia Qiong de Chengdu était âgé de trois *sui*. Parce que sa mère était en route pour aller visiter le marché aux vers à soie le troisième jour de la troisième lunaison, ils passèrent devant le portail de l'abbaye de Longxing, où une foule participait à une Retraite d'ordination. Sur ce, ils allèrent voir et [Jia Qiong] reçut une ordination du Registre pour enfants 童子籙.
> Une dizaine d'années plus tard, la sœur aînée [de Qiong] étant souffrante, sa mère pria l'érudit retraité Wu Taixuan 吳太玄 d'entrer dans l'autre monde pour son compte afin d'enquêter sur la cause de la maladie. Pendant qu'il y était, il devait aussi vérifier la destinée de vie de [Jia Qiong]. Le jour suivant, Taixuan s'en revint et dit : « La cause de la maladie est [le dieu]

des rivières et des rigoles 江瀆 [神][34]. Adressez-lui vos prières et elle se rétablira aussitôt[35]. Le nom de Jia Qiong n'apparaît pas dans les archives. » Très inquiets, père et mère demandèrent à Taixuan d'enquêter plus avant. Pour accéder à l'autre monde afin d'y mener une enquête pour le compte d'autrui, Taixuan devait se faire enfermer à l'intérieur d'une pièce où il s'endormait profondément et partait [en songe]. Il ne tolérait pas qu'on le dérangeât par des cris. [La maisonnée] attendait jusqu'à ce qu'il s'éveillât de lui-même et les appelât pour qu'ils ouvrissent la porte. Quand ils l'ouvrirent après son retour, une nuit ou deux plus tard, il fit une relation des affaires de l'autre monde aussi précise que s'ils en avaient été eux-mêmes les témoins oculaires, et ses paroles étaient confortées par des preuves vérifiables.

Ayant été derechef requis de vérifier le nom de [Jia] Qiong, il dit : « Quand il était âgé de trois *sui*, le troisième jour de la troisième lunaison, il reçut un Registre Zhengyi à l'abbaye de Longxing. Dès lors, son nom fut rattaché au Directoire du ciel et ne dépendit pas de l'administration de la terre. Après avoir échoué à voir son nom dans les dossiers terrestres, je l'ai déniché dans le Cahier jaune 黃簿 du Bureau du ciel »[36].

La réprimande de Zhao Ye et le dossier manquant de Jia Qiong sont des allégories de la consécration d'un enfant par l'acte de le nommer, et de sa renaissance par le rituel de son initiation. Ils illustrent comment le rituel d'ordination déterminait l'identité d'une personne et la sauvegarde de sa destinée. Le nom d'ordination reliait l'énergie vitale de l'initié aux divinités figurant dans le registre[37]. Comme dans le rite baptismal chrétien, c'était le nom conféré lors de l'initiation qui était inscrit dans les cieux. Les *Préceptes d'admonestation des maisonnées* montrent que, pour les taoïstes, ce principe s'enracinait dans l'institution d'enregistrement des élus de la première congrégation du Maître céleste : « Le taoïste est pur et correct ; son nom appartient au plus haut du Ciel. Les profanes sont impurs et souillés ; quand ils meurent, ils relèvent du Bureau de la terre[38]. »

Les écritures sacrées

Les *Divines manifestations* rapportent nombre de témoignages poignants d'épisodes de famine, de guerre, de maladie et de cataclysmes soudains qui accablèrent la société chinoise à la fin des Tang. Pour la génération de Du, l'emblématique mise à sac de la capitale Chang'an par l'armée rebelle de Huang Chao 黃巢, le 8 janvier 881, jeta une lumière crue sur la violence et l'insécurité qui dominaient alors. L'empereur Xizong 僖宗 (r. 873-888), à la cour duquel Du Guangting servait comme maître taoïste, dut fuir vers l'ouest à Chengdu tandis que l'armée rebelle pénétrait dans la capitale par l'est. Le sort de la population urbaine, estimée à un million d'individus au IXe siècle, était déjà scellé le 6 janvier, quand les rebelles franchirent la passe de Tongguan 潼關, dernière ligne de défense le long des abords orientaux de la ville[39]. Au cours des mois suivants, la capitale fut brûlée et pillée, ses habitants massacrés, déplacés, détenus ou contraints aux travaux forcés. Mort, exil, captivité et corvée : les termes figurant littéralement la réalité d'alors servaient de métaphores à la servitude et à la rétribution envisagées pour le monde invisible, dont les laïcs cherchaient à se protéger et à se libérer par le rituel. Les deux mondes se reflétaient l'un l'autre et se rejoignaient dans l'expérience humaine. Empruntant aux relations de témoins oculaires du pillage de Chang'an, les récits de témoignage de délivrance miraculeuse dans les *Divines manifestations* reliaient fermement les deux réalités[40].

De façon typique, les laïcs recouraient à des actes méritoires de dévotion pour implorer la délivrance. La vénération des textes sacrés et des icônes était accessible à tous en toutes circonstances. Le fait de copier les écritures et de fabriquer ou restaurer des icônes conférait des bénédictions en tous genres, tandis que la récitation des écritures procurait le soulagement d'innombrables maux[41]. Le *Livre pour écarter les fléaux et préserver la vie* 消災護命經 était un texte prophylactique populaire. Il est fréquemment mentionné dans la littérature taoïste, et deux exemplaires manuscrits ainsi qu'une édition imprimée de Dunhuang datée de 868 attestent de sa large circulation[42]. Les *Divines manifestations* montrent comment la récitation de ce court texte sauva Li Xuanli 李玄禮 de la captivité durant le sac de la capitale. Cette source fait valoir au passage que la brièveté du texte en facilitait la dissémination. Résident de Chang'an, Li avait auparavant entendu un sermon sur le *Livre pour écarter les fléaux et préserver la vie* à l'abbaye des Tang ascendants 興唐觀, l'un des grands sanctuaires taoïstes de la capitale, sis près du mur nord-est de la ville, où il avait obtenu une copie du texte sacré[43]. Le lecteur des *Divines manifestations* découvre la puissante protection que procura le *Livre pour écarter les fléaux et préserver la vie* à Li Xuanli, à son insu, grâce au témoignage de l'ennemi :

> [Li Xuanli] le récita assidûment et sembla être capable de prévoir tout événement, bon ou mauvais. Quand Huang Chao franchit la passe, [Xuanli] partit avec la foule en fuite. Il fut fait prisonnier et entraîné avec quelque trente ou cinquante personnes au [quartier] Changhua 昌化 (en face du palais impérial). Quand le commandant des rebelles vit [Xuanli], il descendit les marches et l'accueillit cérémonieusement, demandant[44] : « Qui a amené cette personne ici ? » Et il s'inclina pour [inviter Xuanli à] s'asseoir. Xuanli était terrifié et se retint d'abord de gravir l'escalier, mais après [son] insistance répétée, il s'assit avec [le commandant, qui lui] demanda quels actes méritoires il avait accomplis pour être gratifié d'un tel effet. [Xuanli] répondit : « Autrefois, j'ai reçu un texte taoïste, le *Livre pour écarter les fléaux et préserver la vie*, au cours d'une prédication. Je l'ai récité dix mille fois. » Le commandant dit : « Quand je vous ai vu arriver, Monsieur, précédé de quatre jeunes [gardiens], votre personne flanquée de deux grands immortels et de divinités gardiennes en armure, de guerriers Vajra 金剛 et de bêtes spirituelles léonines remplissant la cour derrière vous, j'ai pensé qu'il devait s'agir du cortège de garde d'un empereur ou d'un sage ! Étant donné que c'est dû à un texte sacré taoïste, je souhaiterais en recevoir copie. » Xuanli dit : « Ce texte sacré compte quelque trois cents caractères et tient sur une seule feuille de papier[45]. Il est très commode à transmettre. » Il brûla de l'encens et le récita une fois, puis en écrivit un exemplaire qu'il remit [au commandant]. Le commandant ordonna à dix soldats d'escorter [Xuanli] hors de la ville, d'où ce dernier parvint à rattraper la cour en exil[46].

Les jeunes gardiens que le commandant rebelle avait observés au-devant de Xuanli étaient des envoyés des étoiles gouvernant la destinée humaine. Le *Livre des jeunes gardiens* 護諸童子經, un autre opuscule qui circulait sous les Tang, était récité pour appeler pareilles créatures célestes à descendre sur des chars de nuages volants, « nombreux comme des grains de sable », et à se hâter de venir en aide à un adepte en détresse[47]. La fin de cette histoire relate comment Li Xuanli rejoignit la cour impériale à Chengdu.

La maladie était endémique dans la région durant les années d'exil de l'empereur (881-885) du fait des combats incessants qui s'y livraient. La préfecture de Lianzhou 連州, près de la moderne Yibin dans la partie méridionale du bassin du Sichuan, était quant à elle en proie à la famine et aux épidémies. Du Guangting, qui avait lui-même suivi la cour à Chengdu, rapporte qu'un laïc assidu à la récitation du *Livre des incantations divines*, nommé Wang Qingyuan 王清遠, put venir au secours de nombreuses victimes dans la région grâce à ce livre sacré[48]. Wang refusait toute récompense pour sa sollicitude, hormis de modestes quantités d'huile et d'encens qu'il utilisait pour la vénération de son exemplaire du *Livre des incantations divines*[49].

Le *Livre d'oreiller du Seigneur Lao* 老君枕中經, autre opuscule saint populaire sous les Tang, produisit un miracle comparable pour le vieux Deng 鄧老[50]. Deng était un paysan prospère de Suizhou 遂州, l'actuelle Suining 遂寧 dans le bassin oriental du Sichuan. À la suite de la guerre, sa famille fut réduite à la misère et frappée de maladie. Un beau jour, Deng se rendit au temple abandonné qui se trouvait au milieu de ses champs. Alors qu'il était en train d'y ramasser des rouleaux d'écritures se trouvant dispersés sur le sol, un vieil homme mystérieux apparut et, pointant le *Livre d'oreiller du Seigneur Lao*, l'enjoignit de le vénérer, lui disant que cela procurerait de grandes bénédictions et la délivrance des désastres. Deng prit le mince rouleau et s'en alla le réciter et le méditer avec assiduité. Après trois ou quatre années, sa famille avait recouvré la santé et retrouvé ses moyens d'existence. L'auteur ajoute que Deng transmit une copie du texte à un visiteur de Chengdu dont la famille bénéficia pareillement de sa vénération[51].

L'archétype du texte sacré rédempteur était le *Livre du salut*[52]. Il avait le pouvoir de délivrer les fidèles des périls les plus graves, et apportait de surcroît des secours inattendus :

> Chen Taiqing 陳太清 était un maître taoïste de l'abbaye Tiantai 天台觀 (sur le mont Tiantai 天台山 au Zhejiang[53]). Quand il eut dépassé l'âge de cinquante ans, il renonça à sa famille et entra en religion. Il récitait inlassablement le *Livre du salut* de jour comme de nuit. Qu'il marchât ou fût assis, quoi qu'il fût en train de faire, ses lèvres ne cessaient jamais [leur récitation]. Taiqing était d'un naturel rustre et fourbe. Les gens de son village natal l'abominaient. Quand il entra en religion, il perdait déjà ses

cheveux et ses dents. Après avoir récité le texte pendant dix années, ses cheveux blancs redevinrent noirs et ses dents tombées repoussèrent. Sa force physique fut revigorée et son pas redevint alerte. Même de robustes jeunes gens ne parvenaient pas à le suivre quand ils escaladaient les montagnes en sa compagnie[54].

Décrit d'abord sous un jour peu flatteur, Taiqing n'avait rien du candidat désigné pour bénéficier d'une destinée heureuse selon la justice de rétribution. Le lecteur saisit ainsi d'autant mieux que le pouvoir du *Livre du salut* et l'efficacité de sa récitation assidue permettent de passer outre aux conséquences karmiques des pires tares. Ce pouvoir est explicite dans l'histoire de Zhang Renbiao 張仁表, un prédicateur taoïste discoureur et hypocrite qui est emporté aux enfers pour y être châtié. Devant le portail, il lui revient à la mémoire comment il ne cessait d'exhorter ses ouailles à prononcer le nom du Sauveur de tous les maux 救苦. C'est ce qu'il s'emploie alors à faire, persistant malgré les moqueries de ses tourmenteurs, jusqu'à ce qu'il obtienne la relaxe[55]. Si les anthropologues qualifient de « magie » les procédures rituelles dont l'efficacité visée est perçue comme étant automatique[56], les histoires qui précèdent peuvent se comprendre différemment, lorsqu'on se place à un niveau de lecture religieux. La notion selon laquelle même les pécheurs invétérés pouvaient être rachetés faisait partie intégrante des doctrines de salut universel par les « moyens appropriés », dans le Mahayana puis dans le Lingbao. Le *Soutra du lotus*, inspiration probable de l'histoire de Zhang Renbiao, enseignait qu'il suffisait à un prisonnier d'invoquer le nom de Guanyin 觀音 pour être libéré de ses chaînes, « qu'il soit coupable ou innocent » 若有罪，若無罪[57].

Les icônes

Quand le pèlerin chinois Yijing 義淨 (635-713) revint d'Inde en 685, il rapporta que, là-bas, les moines et les laïcs imprimaient des images du Bouddha sur de la soie ou du papier et les vénéraient avec des offrandes où qu'ils allassent[58]. Au temps de Yijing, la vénération des icônes dans les temples, plaçant les fidèles sous la protection des divinités représentées, était déjà répandue en Chine, mais cela n'avait pas toujours été le cas dans l'une et l'autre civilisation. En Inde, les théories sur l'essence des icônes remontaient aux spéculations védiques sur les mérites respectifs des mots et des images à incarner le divin[59]. À l'origine, l'hindouisme et le taoïsme étaient tous deux sceptiques quant à la possibilité ou la pertinence de représenter matériellement des divinités que l'on pensait être immatérielles[60]. Pourtant, avec le temps, la pratique consistant à livrer les dieux au regard spectateur de celui qui médite – et qui s'y laisse voir en retour – créa une demande en représentations physiques, ne serait-ce qu'à titre d'aide pour le regard invisible. La ferveur populaire bouddhique finit par embrasser l'adoration des images, établissant la pratique dans la Chine d'avant les Tang, et les taoïstes se laissèrent gagner par cette ferveur. Les *Divines manifestations* illustrent l'attrait que les icônes portatives, qui avaient autrefois retenu l'attention de Yijing en Inde, suscitaient dans la Chine de la fin des Tang auprès des taoïstes itinérants, fussent-ils religieux, réfugiés, soldats, diplomates ou marchands.

L'histoire suivante se déroule dans le même cadre que celle de Li Xuanli, au début de 881, quand la capitale tomba aux mains des rebelles de Huang Chao. Son héros, Liu Cunxi 劉存希, était un initié du culte du Maître céleste de l'« abbaye de l'Ascension des Tang » 唐興觀, peut-être une erreur de copiste pour « abbaye des Tang ascendants », le sanctuaire où Li Xuanli avait reçu son exemplaire du livre sacré[61]. Après la canonisation de Zhang Daoling, le culte du Maître céleste prospéra tant et si bien que les *Divines manifestations* consacrèrent un volume entier aux « Miracles du Maître céleste » 天師靈驗. Liu, originaire de Pengcheng 彭城 (Xuzhou 徐州 au Jiangsu), était un officier du palais de Chang'an qui servit d'envoyé aux régions éloignées de l'empire. Quelques années après avoir échappé aux rebelles, il se retrouva à Chengdu où il rapporta à Du Guangting l'épisode suivant :

> Depuis l'enfance, [Liu Cunxi] vénérait [l'image du] Maître céleste à l'abbaye de l'Ascension des Tang. Ayant fait le vœu de faire dupliquer une icône pour ses dévotions, il en obtint une peinture sur un rouleau de soie. Dans ses allées et venues, il la gardait précieusement. Même quand

> il recevait l'ordre de voyager loin au nord et au sud en mission, jamais, même un seul jour, il ne négligeait de déposer [devant l'icône] des offrandes d'encens. Au moment où Huang Chao se rebella, [Liu] était de service au palais. Dans la confusion qui s'ensuivit, il ne put rattraper la suite impériale. Tout ce qu'il put faire fut d'enrouler sa peinture sur soie du Maître céleste et d'aller de l'avant en la tenant révérencieusement. Il suivit une compagnie d'une trentaine de ses semblables qui furent tous faits prisonniers, tués ou blessés. Lui seul en réchappa.

Liu fut alors miraculeusement réuni avec son épouse. Après avoir survécu à d'autres périls, ils arrivèrent en lieu sûr. Du Guangting note l'avoir connu plusieurs années après au Xichuan, rencontre qui mena à la transmission à la fois de l'histoire et de l'icône : « Il vint portant sur lui le rouleau du Maître céleste, et [m']en transmit une copie », écrit Du[62].

L'expression « fabriquer une icône pour ses dévotions » 圖寫供養 renvoyait à la reproduction fidèle d'une image pour sa vénération personnelle par des offrandes. On pouvait alors faire appel à la divinité représentée pour la protection et la délivrance. Un manuscrit de Dunhuang glorifie une icône, commissionnée au nom d'un maître souffrant, qui dépeignait le Véritable sauveur à l'écoute des cris du monde 尋聲救苦眞人, le même qui était venu au secours de Zhang Renbiao[63]. Ce sauveur miséricordieux prenait pour les taoïstes la place de Guanyin, le bodhisattva de la compassion Avalokiteśvara dont les épithètes étaient « sauveur » et « qui écoute les cris du monde ». La section du *Soutra du lotus* intitulée « la Porte universelle » 普門品 énumère, parmi les maux dont on pouvait obtenir la délivrance, l'incendie, l'inondation, la captivité et le banditisme – des dangers qui évoquent précisément les situations périlleuses rapportées par les *Divines manifestations*[64]. Dans la vision narrée de façon pittoresque par Du Guangting, le Sauveur de tous les maux met en scène une épiphanie, clairement à l'intention des iconographes. Les attributs qu'il expose sont ceux de Guanyin, prolongeant la doctrine bouddhique selon laquelle Guanyin était capable d'adopter tout moyen opportun pour soustraire les victimes à un danger[65].

Réaliser la copie d'une icône constituait en soi un acte méritoire. Le pouvoir sacramentel de la copie supposait l'existence d'un original garantissant l'authenticité de l'image. La reproduction de Liu Cunxi se fondait sur l'autorité d'une image dans un temple. À son tour, l'efficacité de la nouvelle copie effectuée pour Du Guangting était fondée sur les miracles réalisés par la copie de Liu Cunxi. Une autre icône de la même divinité était vénérée par Zhao Keyan 趙可言. Dans son cas, l'authentification initiale avait été obtenue dans un songe :

> Le révérend maître Zhao Keyan de Qiongzhou 邛州 (Qionglai 邛崍, à soixante-dix kilomètres au sud-ouest de Chengdu) entra en religion à un jeune âge. En ce temps-là, il ne pratiquait encore aucune dévotion. Mais quand il vit en songe le Maître céleste, il [en] fit une icône et la vénéra. [Zhao] était d'un naturel droit et simple, franc dans ses propos. Quand il présentait des suppliques au nom de tiers, concernant leur bonne ou mauvaise fortune ou priant pour le soulagement de leurs épreuves, il s'en remettait toujours au Maître céleste et procédait en jetant des blocs de divination. Si c'était affirmatif, il continuait ; si c'était négatif, il cessait. Ainsi, chaque fois qu'il venait au secours de gens affligés de maladie ou intercédait pour eux par la prière, des miracles ne manquaient pas de se produire[66].

L'icône, fixant et authentifiant la représentation picturale de la vision du monde invisible, pouvait ouvrir le regard intérieur du fidèle[67]. En variation de ce thème, un songe intervient après la visualisation de l'image. L'action décrite est une mise en scène du *jintan* 禁壇, un rite de purification et d'exorcisme que l'on exécute encore de nos jours pour protéger et consacrer l'autel taoïste selon le modèle de la Méthode de l'épée du Maître céleste 天師劍法[68]. Ce manuel des Tang pour l'exécution du rite montre comment le prêtre établit son contrôle sur les esprits malins dans toutes les directions de l'espace en brandissant son épée d'exorciste et en pulvérisant de l'eau lustrale par la bouche : l'eau « crachée par les cinq dragons [directionnels] lave le ciel et la terre »[69]. L'épée descendait de « la précieuse épée héréditaire du Maître céleste », léguée par le Très Haut à Zhang Daoling qui, avant de monter au ciel, la confia à ses successeurs « pour le secours des multitudes » (voir fig. 7)[70].

Fig. 7. Exorciste avec épée et eau lustrale. *Taishang zhengyi jie wuyin zhouzu bilu*, 2b. *Daozang*, édition des Ming de 1598. Reproduit avec l'autorisation de la Bibliothèque nationale de France.

Le récipiendaire de cette vision fut le dénommé Huangfu Qia 皇甫洽, un fervent et pieux fidèle de Chengdu qui avait plusieurs fois visité le puits de sel de Lingjing à Lingzhou (Sichuan), ce lieu saint cité dans la légende de Zhang Daoling où se trouvait un portrait du Maître céleste (voir « Héros et guérisseur » au chapitre premier)[71]. Qia en fit faire une icône pour sa vénération privée. Un jour, une épidémie se déclara dans le voisinage, et dix des domestiques de Qia furent frappés par la maladie :

[Huangfu Qia] en personne leur administra des bouillons médicinaux et leur présenta nourriture et boisson de ses propres mains. Son anxiété croissant, et comme il ne ménageait pas ses efforts, il devint somnolent et s'assoupit

> au milieu de la journée. Dans son rêve, une jeune personne entra et dit : « Le Maître céleste est arrivé. » Et, de fait, il vit entrer le Maître céleste, en habit blanc et coiffe en forme de fleur, brandissant une épée. Il prit un bol rempli d'eau de l'emplacement des offrandes [devant l'icône], l'éleva et en aspergea d'abord le corps [de Qia, qui] éprouva une sensation soudaine de bien-être. Ensuite, [le Maître céleste] fit le tour des quartiers d'habitation, à l'intérieur et à l'extérieur, les aspergeant d'eau. Puis il plaça le bol sur l'autel et s'en fut. Sur ce, les dix [patients] se rétablirent tous aussitôt. Les familles du voisinage aussi allèrent mieux. La maisonnée [de Qia] vénère révérencieusement [le Maître céleste] encore à ce jour.

La scène finale donne à voir sous quelle forme Huangfu Qia perçut la présence de la contagion puis son expulsion :

> Au moment de la descente du Maître céleste, ce dernier resta trois jours. Il dit à Qia : « Du fait de votre grande sincérité, j'ai obtenu du Ciel un congé de trois quarts d'heure, qui correspond à trois jours dans le monde des hommes, pour vous sauver. » [Qia] fut aussi témoin que le Maître céleste ordonna à des assistants de s'emparer de deux démons dans le fourneau, sous l'empilement de bois de chauffage et dans le tas de fumier. Sur le faîte de la maison était assis un grand démon dont les pieds pendaient jusqu'aux corniches. Le Maître céleste les fit saisir et envoyer au mont Qingcheng 青城山 (au nord-ouest de Chengdu) pour y être incarcérés. Le Maître céleste émit ces instructions avec un pinceau vermillon, sur quoi les démons déguerpirent à la vitesse de l'éclair. Toute la maisonnée en fut témoin[72].

L'encre vermillon servait pour la rédaction des mandats d'arrêt contre les démons des maladies miasmatiques[73].

Avec notre dernier exemple, l'iconographie des songes prend un tour nouveau. L'histoire renverse la séquence qui conduisit Huangfu Qia de la vénération d'une icône à la guérison. Ici, une vision due à la fièvre est à l'origine de la délivrance et ce n'est que subséquemment que le fidèle est guidé vers la découverte du portrait d'origine dans un sanctuaire. L'abbaye de Zhaocheng 昭成觀 se trouvait dans le quartier de Banzheng 頒政坊 de la capitale, face au flanc occidental du palais impérial[74]. Initialement construit en 670, ce sanctuaire fut consacré de nouveau en 739 pour commémorer l'impératrice Zhaocheng 昭成太后 (morte en 693), feu la mère de l'empereur Xuanzong[75]. Ainsi, au moment des événements relatés dans l'histoire suivante, le temple avait plus de deux cents ans. À l'intérieur, longtemps laissée à l'abandon, sa peinture murale du Maître céleste se décolorait et s'écaillait. Les visites des fidèles avaient diminué et les offrandes avaient cessé peu à peu. Pour remédier à cette situation, la divinité fit appel au secours d'un résident local :

> La peinture murale du Maître céleste de l'abbaye de Zhaocheng : avec le passage d'innombrables mois et années, ses couleurs avaient foncé et la peinture s'écaillait. Plus aucun encens n'était offert en contrebas des galeries. Un résident du quartier de Banzheng, nommé Li, souffrait d'une fièvre paludéenne depuis plus d'un an. Les médecins étaient incapables de le guérir. Chaque jour plus émacié, il attendait son heure. Et voici qu'en songe il eut la vision d'un taoïste, grand de huit ou neuf pieds, qui venait au-devant de lui. Sa robe d'étoffe frôla le visage [de Li] de sa large manche[76]. Ce dernier goûta instantanément une sensation de fraîcheur. [Le taoïste] lui dit : « Tu es maintenant guéri et n'as plus de souci à te faire[77]. » Sur ce, Li s'éveilla, guéri, et put prendre un peu de nourriture et de boisson. Jusqu'à tard, il déambula dans sa maison avec une canne sans éprouver aucune fatigue. Mais frappé par la sensation que le taoïste de son rêve se trouvait devant lui, il fut soudain saisi de l'envie d'entrer dans l'abbaye de Zhaocheng. Sa famille, inquiète du fait de son asthénie, fit de son mieux pour l'en dissuader, mais il n'écouta pas et s'en alla à l'intérieur du temple. Debout face au portrait du Maître céleste, il l'étudia minutieusement et pendant longtemps. Puis il dit : « C'est celui que j'ai vu en rêve », et il se prosterna plusieurs fois. Il ordonna à un sculpteur utilisant la technique de laque sèche 夾紵, le lettré retiré Liu 劉處士, de modeler le portrait du Maître céleste, et fit réparer la salle[78]. Matin et soir, il y fit des offrandes. Les prières des gens étaient immédiatement suivies de bénédictions.

Les sculpteurs en laque sèche utilisent la technique dite « en couches de toile de chanvre » 夾紵, consistant à placer sur un modèle en argile des couches successives de matériau, à les imbiber de laque et à les laisser à sécher. Le modèle est ensuite retiré, laissant un noyau creux[79]. L'auteur achève sa relation sur une note technique et iconographique qui pourrait servir de guide pratique pour la fabrication de statues, incluant la représentation des organes vitaux et de symboles de longévité à l'intérieur du noyau creux. Des techniques similaires se pratiquaient en Inde ancienne pour transformer les icônes en dieux vivants[80].

> Concernant le portrait sculpté en laque sèche : à l'intérieur de la sculpture se trouvait une toile de séparation en soie peinte de couleur chair ; des tissus cousus en soie cramoisie formaient les Cinq viscères, les intestins et l'estomac. La trachée comptait douze nœuds et douze anneaux, et se raccordait à la base de la langue. L'intérieur des viscères était rempli d'encens de cinq couleurs, chacune corrélée à l'organe correspondant des Cinq viscères[81]. À l'intérieur du cœur était placé un miroir de mercure[82]. Le tout était d'une extrême finesse, différent des sculptures ordinaires. Le modèle d'argile à l'intérieur de la sculpture fut emporté à l'abbaye de Tianchang 天長觀 (proche de la porte occidentale Yanping 延平門 de la ville). Doré avec faste et somptueusement paré, [le modèle] produisit à son tour des manifestations divines[83].

Chapitre 11

Les instruments de la délivrance

Les instruments de la délivrance dont il va être question dans ce chapitre étaient, d'une façon analogue, des objets sacramentels conférant pouvoir et autorité. Les talismans et les sceaux avaient d'emblée pour qualité d'être des dispositifs contractuels. La puissance de commandement des incantations et des rituels, quant à elle, dérivait d'actes et d'énoncés performatifs. En tout état de cause, lorsque la délivrance était fondée sur un transfert de mérite ou une remise de dette, une monnaie d'échange était requise[1]. Ce qui était en jeu était considérable : on se souvient que lorsque le gouverneur Wu Xinglu demanda secours à ses descendants pour payer la rançon de sa relaxe, ceux-ci n'en eurent pas les moyens. Même si cela put donner satisfaction à la partie lésée, cette issue ignorait le principe du Maître céleste selon lequel la pauvreté ne devait pas faire obstacle à la rédemption et les offrandes devaient être proportionnées aux moyens du requérant (voir « La scène et l'offrande » au chapitre 3).

La monnaie d'échange

Se peut-il que Du Guangting rapportât l'histoire de la rétribution de Wu Xinglu à dessein ? Quoi qu'il en soit, le même auteur proposa une solution ingénieuse au problème de la remise effective d'une rançon abordable. L'usage des offrandes en papier s'était progressivement imposé au cours de l'ère des Tang. Dans la longue histoire de la substitution sacrificielle, il s'agissait d'une innovation capitale. En Chine, depuis l'Antiquité, on déposait dans les sépultures des répliques de divers moyens de paiement, incluant l'argent. Attestée dès la fin des Sui, la substitution du papier aux monnaies en bandes de soie est un procédé qui s'inspira certainement du remplacement antérieur de la soie par le papier comme support pour l'écriture[2]. Au début des Tang, des découpes de « papier-monnaie » 紙錢 commencent à être mentionnées comme répliques des pièces de cuivre[3]. Au départ décrié par les officiels lettrés comme une pratique employée par les médiums spirituels – une observation exacte, comme nous le verrons dans les histoires des deux femmes nommées Zhang –, cet usage gagna en respectabilité après que l'empereur Xuanzong l'eut approuvé[4].

Une source de la fin du VIIIe siècle explique comment le papier-monnaie était ficelé à l'imitation des ligatures de pièces. D'autres relations dans la littérature narrative des Tang témoignent de l'utilisation du papier-monnaie comme devise du monde souterrain, tout en expliquant les modalités de transaction et le taux de change[5]. Du Guangting mentionne l'emploi de monnaie et de chevaux [de papier] sacrificiels 奏獻錢馬 dans un rituel funéraire et recommande de brûler cent ou deux cents billets de papier comme offrande idéale au dieu du sol 燒錢一二百紙極佳矣 à la fin de la Retraite du registre jaune[6]. Un autre texte de la fin des Tang décrit la combustion de vêtements et de monnaie [de papier] 燒衣服及錢財 après une requête pour résoudre une plainte sépulcrale[7]. Les offrandes de papier-monnaie disposées au pied de l'autel dans les rituels de Retraite étaient ensuite « transformées par combustion » 燒化. Le fait d'être combustible n'était pas le moindre des avantages du papier-monnaie sacrificiel, puisqu'il permettait que la transaction et le transit de l'offrande entre les mondes visible et invisible fussent opérés par le feu.

Mais il semble que Du ait eu à l'esprit un degré supplémentaire de substitution et d'abstraction. Le type de papier-monnaie qu'il décrivit n'impliquait pas l'imitation de pièces ou de ligatures[8]. Dans les histoires suivantes, Du veille à expliquer la convertibilité et le taux de change entre ligatures de sapèques et papiers-monnaies. Une ligature 貫 (ou 千) de monnaie consistait en une unité de mille sapèques de cuivre 銅錢. Selon Du, une ligature de monnaie dans le monde ici-bas avait valeur d'un billet de papier dans l'autre monde. En tant qu'instrument d'échange, la monnaie sacrificielle de Du Guangting s'apparentait au système de lettre de change des Tang, connu sous le nom de « monnaie volante » 飛錢, qui précéda l'introduction de la monnaie fiduciaire sous les Song. La monnaie volante apparut au Sichuan, région connue à l'époque pour être à la pointe de la production de papier, de l'imprimerie et du commerce. À l'origine, les marchands de thé du Sichuan échangeaient des ligatures de sapèques de cuivre contre des lettres de change au taux d'une pour une. Une lettre de change était payable au porteur, éliminant ainsi la nécessité pour les marchands de transporter de la monnaie encombrante et simplifiant l'acheminement des taxes provinciales dues à la capitale[9]. Pour faciliter les transactions en « monnaie volante », les gouvernements provinciaux maintenaient un réseau de dépôts locaux ainsi qu'une chancellerie à la capitale fonctionnant comme une chambre de compensation pour les fonds collectés[10].

Se référant à la fin du IXe siècle, les *Divines manifestations* décrivent une procédure analogue pour les transactions avec le monde des esprits. Un comptoir de la Trésorerie du Bureau céleste 天曹庫 était établi à la cour de l'Empereur du Nord 北帝院 dans le temple du diocèse du Siège de jade 玉局化 à Chengdu[11]. Dans les histoires ci-après, le personnel de cette branche de l'Agence comptable du Bureau céleste 天曹計會 comptait un « préposé à la trésorerie » 庫子, faisant du sanctuaire une agence pour le commerce entre le monde des vivants et celui des esprits. Du Guangting était depuis longtemps associé au sanctuaire du diocèse du Siège de jade, où il avait résidé et célébré des rituels pendant de nombreuses années[12]. Ici l'on doit imaginer l'auteur parlant de ses paroissiens et les sermonnant, leur rappelant que les dettes, spécialement celles dues aux défunts, devaient être réglées avant le Nouvel an et que les gratifications accordées aux clercs et aux subalternes n'étaient pas moins obligatoires dans l'autre monde que dans celui-ci. Plus important, il leur faisait comprendre que les transactions effectuées en monnaie spirituelle accomplissaient métaphoriquement la rédemption des âmes et la délivrance des vivants :

> Trois années après que l'épouse de Zhang He 張郃 de Chengdu fut décédée, elle revint chez elle et parla par l'intermédiaire d'un médium : « Quand la suite impériale séjournait à Shu (881-885), le Xichuan expédia des troupes au Fort de la pacification du pays 安國寨 à Xingping 興平 (Shaanxi) pour soumettre [le rebelle] Huang Chao[13]. En ce temps-là, deux hommes de la famille voisine, celle du vieux Feng 馮老, père et fils, reçurent l'ordre de s'engager avec l'avant-garde[14]. À leur départ, ils mirent en lieu sûr chez nous des biens d'une valeur de trente ligatures de sapèques 三十千[15]. Le père et le fils Feng tombèrent tous deux au combat et n'en revinrent pas. Leurs possessions ont depuis été épuisées.
> Ces derniers temps, l'affaire a soudain refait surface dans l'autre monde. Mon esprit a été arrêté et des comptes lui ont été demandés. Après un délai de six années, la décision du Bureau céleste venait de tomber. Elle stipulait que puisque [les deux Feng] étaient morts au combat et n'en étaient pas revenus, cela ne constituait pas un cas de spoliation sévère. En conséquence, le litige pouvait être réglé par [la] remise d'un paiement de trente ligatures de sapèques[16].
> Les officiels étant réaffectés après le vingt-cinquième jour du dernier mois lunaire de l'année, et comme il faut clôturer les comptes de l'année en cours, l'argent doit être remis avant le vingt-cinq du mois courant. Contactez le préposé à la Trésorerie du Bureau céleste 天曹庫子 à la cour de l'Empereur du Nord du diocèse du Siège de jade pour procéder au paiement[17]. Un billet de papier équivaut à une ligature de sapèques 一張紙作一貫. En outre, le préposé à la Trésorerie, l'huissier et le commis au dossier sont à récompenser chacun séparément. Ce n'est pas différent du monde humain. »
> Le vingt-troisième jour du dernier mois de la troisième année de Guanghua 光化 (16 janvier 901), [l'époux] se rendit à la cour de l'Empereur du Nord et régla le dû pour l'affaire en souffrance. Cette nuit-là, en rêve, son épouse l'en remercia et s'en alla.

Honorer les dettes anciennes et les droits prioritaires était un principe inscrit dans les populaires « Cent préceptes médicinaux » (voir « Guérison » au chapitre 4) et dans les règles monastiques pour la passation des effets personnels des moines et nonnes défunts (voir « Les vœux monastiques » au chapitre 9) – d'où l'importance de régler les dettes en souffrance avant le début d'une nouvelle année comptable. La narration ci-dessus montre comment la dette comptable et métaphorique contractée en ce monde affectait la tranquillité des esprits dans l'autre, une source constante d'anxiété dans la religion chinoise. On lit dans un document funéraire des Han orientaux : « Que les esprits reconnaissent que nous, les vivants, nous nous acquittons de nos dettes envers eux comme le prouvent ces documents contractuels, et puissent les esprits ne pas pénaliser ceux d'entre nous qui ont trépassé. » Dans les contrats sépulcraux, cette formule était fréquemment jointe aux inventaires d'offrandes et de biens devant être remis aux officiers célestes. Les accusations de vol et de détournement étaient communément l'objet de plaintes d'outre-tombe[18].

L'histoire de Zhang He connaît deux courtes suites qui confirment la localisation de l'agence de la Trésorerie du Bureau céleste et corroborent son mode de règlement. La seconde de ces suites fournit une illustration remarquable à la fois du poids des obligations humaines et de la fluidité de la procédure d'acquittement par-delà le fossé séparant le monde des morts de celui des vivants. Dans cette histoire, une dénommée Zhang 張 de Qiongzhou a récemment perdu son époux. Elle craint maintenant pour son fils, lequel s'est fait incarcérer à la suite du décès du père. Ce dernier avait fait partie de l'état-major de Zhang Lin 張琳, commissaire adjoint de l'armée de Yongping 永平軍[19]. À ce point du récit, le défunt descend par l'intermédiaire d'un médium pour parler à son épouse et lui demander de soumettre une requête au commissaire adjoint :

> « En cours de route, rends d'abord visite à la cour de l'Empereur du Nord au diocèse du Siège de jade et paie deux cents ligatures en monnaie du Boisseau du Nord 北斗錢. Je devrais être en mesure d'obtenir la relâche [de notre fils] par l'Agence comptable du Bureau céleste. Deux cents ligatures de sapèques équivalent à deux cents [billets de] papier, et ce sera tout. » L'épouse fit ce qui lui avait été dit et paya l'argent. Sur ce, son époux lui apparut en rêve et lui dit : « L'affaire est résolue. » Le jour suivant, elle rendit visite au commissaire adjoint qui accepta effectivement sa demande. Ainsi elle se rendit compte que la fonction du papier-monnaie

était incontestable et que les affaires de l'autre monde ne différaient en rien de celles de ce monde-ci[20].

L'âme de l'épouse de Zhang He avait été rachetée dans le monde souterrain par le remboursement d'une dette en souffrance. Dans l'autre histoire, un captif dans le monde des vivants est relâché au moyen d'un transfert de fonds vers le Boisseau du Nord[21]. Après en avoir reçu la double confirmation du monde des morts et de celui des vivants, la mère du prisonnier ne peut que conclure que « la fonction du papier-monnaie était incontestable », en d'autres termes, que les métaphores fonctionnent. La doctrine bouddhique du transfert de mérite et la primauté de la charité comme source de mérite avaient déjà révolutionné les procédures rédemptrices du taoïsme médiéval. Maintenant, la commodité des lettres de change sacrificielles ouvrait des perspectives pour satisfaire le Contrôleur du destin à une échelle véritablement astronomique. À partir des Song, la monnaie de papier devint la norme pour les transactions importantes, aussi bien comptables que sacrificielles. On n'arrête pas le progrès : en 2017, un temple à Taiwan rapportait que l'introduction de chèques sacrificiels, certifiés compensables dans l'autre monde, avait cette année-là, à l'occasion de la Fête des âmes, diminué la pollution atmosphérique en réduisant de cinq tonnes la quantité de papier brûlé[22].

Les talismans

Les talismans 符 étaient des injonctions adressées au monde invisible. Leur fonction dérivait d'une pratique de la Chine ancienne consistant à faire correspondre les moitiés d'une tessère d'accréditation pour établir l'identité et la légitimité des parties contractantes. Pour des besoins militaires et administratifs, les tessères servaient à authentifier la transmission d'instructions, par exemple pour lever des troupes en quelque lieu éloigné. Comme les sceaux, les tessères certifiaient le crédit du porteur[23]. Dans cet esprit, les talismans accompagnaient habituellement les prières, les performances rituelles et les actes sacramentaux.

Des maîtres spécialisés utilisaient des talismans comme une technique rituelle à part entière. L'*Almanach de requêtes de Maître Pin rouge* contient des instructions pour la production des talismans. Les invocations et la visualisation ci-dessous devaient être exécutées pendant que l'on traçait les signes talismaniques en maniant l'encre des différentes couleurs prescrites :

> Quiconque souhaitant écrire un talisman grince d'abord des dents 叩齒 [pour appeler les dieux et repousser les démons] face à la direction royale 向王方, consacre [l'aire rituelle] avec l'épée et l'eau 敕劍水, visualise les sept étoiles [du Boisseau du Nord], prononce une incantation et rejette en crachant [de l'eau lustrale][24]. Puis il procède à une annonce [...]. La méthode pour écrire un talisman consiste à tracer d'abord la bordure extérieure avec de l'encre verte 青墨. À l'intérieur de celle-ci, le motif du talisman 符文 est dessiné en vermillon 丹. Si l'encre verte est indisponible, le vermillon peut aussi être utilisé [pour la bordure]. Quand un talisman pour soigner les maladies démoniaques 邪病 est écrit, on doit utiliser du cinabre véritable 眞朱, pilé avec de l'os de tigre. Après le pilage, humecter le pinceau et écrire le talisman. Réciter l'incantation[25].

Le commentaire d'un passage correspondant dans l'*Ascension à la perfection* explique :

> L'encre verte est une pâte épaisse de malachite 空青 finement pilée. La malaxer et confectionner des pastilles ; les mettre à sécher au soleil. Piler juste avant usage, de la même façon que pour fabriquer de l'encre [...]. L'os de tigre doit d'abord être broyé en fines particules. En tamiser trois *fen* 分 à travers une double épaisseur de soie et y incorporer deux *fen* de cinabre ; amalgamer avec la pâte purifiée. À utiliser pour écrire les talismans[26].

Les adeptes des talismans avaient pour maître Ge Hong, dépositaire de plusieurs traditions talismaniques méridionales comprenant les Trois talismans 三部符 et les Écrits des Trois souverains, dont Ge louait le pouvoir de délivrer du mal 辟邪[27]. Cette tradition donna son nom au texte sacré intitulé les *Trois talismans du Seigneur Lao Hunyuan* 老君混元三部符, populaire sous les Tang. Ce recueil contenait des modèles de talismans à confectionner pour soigner, pour décontaminer la pollution rituelle et pour protéger les demeures, les champs, les cultures et les vers à soie. D'autres étaient proposés pour exorciser les fantômes et les démons, chasser les rats ou délivrer un pratiquant de la détresse et du danger[28]. Mais Ge mettait en garde contre la prolifération désordonnée de méthodes de guérison par exorcisme fondées sur les Trois talismans en Chine du Sud, à laquelle se livraient des pratiquants sans scrupules[29]. Du Guangting notait de manière analogue qu'à cause des vicissitudes de la transmission informelle, les erreurs textuelles abondaient, entraînant la perte d'efficacité des talismans. Au cours de la période Xiantong 咸通 (860-874), rapporte-t-il, un certain Shi Deyi 史得一 sauva un exemplaire des *Trois talismans du Seigneur Lao* des eaux de crue se retirant de la berge d'une rivière. Le rouleau flottant sur la rivière était demeuré sec. Perplexe, Shi le rapporta chez lui. Cette nuit-là, deux jeunes gens lui apparurent et dirent :

> Nous sommes les préposés aux talismans [du Seigneur Lao] 侍符童子[30]. Les précieux talismans du Très Haut circulent depuis longtemps parmi le peuple. Quand on les recopie, des erreurs se produisent, au point que leur fonction se perd. Quand les caractères sont incorrectement écrits, les démons et esprits n'ont rien à exécuter ou subir. C'est pour cela que leur utilisation a peu d'effet. Maintenant, ce texte faisant autorité peut être communiqué aux praticiens taoïstes pour soulager les souffrances du peuple. Les réponses se manifesteront infailliblement[31].

La dissémination incontrôlée des instruments sacramentels entraînait des défauts d'authenticité et de transmission sur lesquels on pouvait rejeter la faute s'ils ne produisaient pas le résultat attendu. Du Guangting entra en possession d'un talisman du haut Moyen Âge provenant des mêmes cercles méridionaux. Il s'intitulait « Talisman de l'Esprit pur » 素靈符, d'après le dépôt céleste où avait été promulgué le *Livre de l'Esprit pur* 素靈經 d'origine[32]. Dans la préface de l'édition qu'il en fit, laquelle identifie Maître Lu (Lu Xiujing) comme le transmetteur des deux premiers chapitres, Du explique comment la version authentifiée en sa possession fit son apparition au milieu de la période des Tang : le seigneur Zhai Qianyou 翟君乾祐, adepte des talismans, remontant le fleuve vers Shu, fit halte et rôda par les bois et le long des cours d'eau près de la gorge de Wushan 巫山峽[33]. Suivant une directive reçue en songe qui le mena à la falaise du Céleste vénérable 天尊峰, il tomba sur un homme réel qui lui transmit un rouleau d'« écrit de cinabre » 丹書. Ce rouleau contenait le Talisman de l'Esprit pur[34]. Capable de guérir les maladies, de contrôler les esprits malins, de chasser les démons, de commander aux éléments, vent et eau, et de dompter les loups et les tigres, il fit grandement bénéficier de sa puissance la population de la région des Trois gorges. Durant l'ère Tianbao (742-756), Xuanzong ne manqua pas de convoquer Zhai au palais. Un siècle plus tard, l'écrivain Duan Chengshi 段成式 (vers 803-863) devint adepte de ce talisman[35]. Un exemplaire se retrouva dans la bibliothèque de l'abbaye de Xiandu 仙都觀 sur le mont Pingdu 平都山 (Fengdu), un sanctuaire restauré par le Premier ministre Duan Wenchang 段文昌 (773-835), le père de Duan Chengshi[36]. C'est là que Du Guangting redécouvrit le texte. Il explique dans la préface à son édition intitulée *Véritables talismans de l'Esprit pur du Lingbao* 靈寶素靈真符 : « En l'an 906, alors que je recherchais des écrits au mont Pingdu, je reçus à mon tour cet exemplaire. Je l'ai édité pour l'intégrer dans le Canon des Trois cavernes 三洞藏, dans l'espoir que les adeptes puissent dans le futur connaître aussi son usage salvateur[37]. »

Du voyait dans l'histoire de cette transmission un enjeu qui dépassait l'intérêt bibliographique. Chaque transmetteur de talisman, y compris lui-même, contribuait à l'œuvre salvifique. Quand le révérend maître Pan saisit l'opportunité de sauver autrui et de se racheter au moyen de talismans (voir « Les registres d'ordination » au chapitre 10), il obéissait à l'injonction d'un immortel : « Quand des gens malades ou dans le besoin viennent quérir le soulagement, enquêtez sur les causes de l'affliction […] et délivrez-les par mes talismans. Vous-même, ne recherchez pas des ligatures de sapèques, mais appliquez-vous à la seule accumulation de mérite afin de racheter votre faute. » Malades et souffrants vinrent en masse trouver Pan, qui leur porta « secours avec de l'écriture sigillaire vermillon »[38]. Refuser les récompenses matérielles était une condition préalable au succès de la guérison par les talismans :

> Dans le traitement de la maladie, il est nécessaire de mépriser les récompenses matérielles. Si vous agissez dans un esprit de secours et de charité, les esprits vous aideront certainement et le souffle vital du Tao répondra sans aucun doute. Si, en revanche, vous agissez dans l'espérance du gain et sans esprit de secours, vos actes n'auront aucune efficacité ; au contraire, ils vous causeront du dommage à vous-même. Les talismans et les incantations des rites du Tao sont là pour aider les gens dans la maladie et la souffrance[39].

Comment s'administrait un remède talismanique ? Les *Divines manifestations* fournissent la démonstration pittoresque d'un talisman thérapeutique à l'œuvre. Le talisman appartient au répertoire de Ye Zangzhi 葉藏質, le révérend maître Ye de Yuxiao 玉霄葉尊師, actif en 860-874 au temple du Palais de Yuxiao 玉霄宮 sur le mont Tiantai, au Zhejiang, dont Du Guangting était natif[40]. Du écrit : « En dehors des périodes de dévotions, [Ye Zangzhi] portait secours aux gens au moyen de la technique talismanique » 符術. L'incident raconté ci-après concerne un patient également nommé Ye 葉氏. Sa famille immensément riche résidait à Wuzhou 婺州 (l'actuelle Jinhua 金華), cent cinquante kilomètres à l'ouest du Tiantai. Ye avait des antécédents de « démence » 癲狂 chronique, un terme couvrant divers désordres mentaux et neurologiques, dont la maladie maniaco-dépressive et l'épilepsie. On le voyait périodiquement se dévêtir en public, courir dans tous les sens et tomber à terre[41]. Se moquer des gens affligés de démence était une faute morale énumérée parmi les « Cent préceptes morbides »[42]. La narration attire l'attention du lecteur sur la façon dont les troubles étaient perçus et ressentis par l'entourage du malade, en l'occurrence par des parents inquiets et des fonctionnaires prévenants de la municipalité, faisant tout pour contenir les irruptions d'un comportement inadapté et anxiogène :

> À la suite d'une crise particulièrement grave ayant duré plusieurs mois, [Ye] geignait ou ricanait, courant de-ci de-là, dévêtu, déployant une force égale à celle de plusieurs personnes. D'abord, on le ligota avec des liens de soie, mais il s'échappa et sortit dans la rue, où il commit des saccages dans l'enceinte officielle. On ne pouvait ni le maîtriser ni le ramener. Les fonctionnaires considéraient que le fils d'une riche maisonnée ne pouvait être soumis à des punitions sévères mais, puisqu'il avait déjà commis des délits répétés, sa famille eut l'obligation de le maintenir sous bonne garde. [La maisonnée] multiplia rites bouddhiques, exorcismes, offrandes aux moines, prières de bénédiction et sacrifices aux dieux et aux démons, et fit appel à des médiums des deux sexes. Tout fut tenté, mais nul n'obtint de résultat. À l'origine, les membres de la famille n'étaient pas des croyants taoïstes mais, fortuitement, ils rencontrèrent quelqu'un qui les incita à se rendre au [mont] Tiantai pour demander un talisman au révérend maître de Yuxiao, car la maladie était sensible à l'expulsion. Sur ce, ils préparèrent des soieries, des ustensiles et des récipients avant

de pénétrer dans la montagne et de quérir un talisman. Le révérend maître dit à leur émissaire : « La maladie devrait être guérie dès que ce talisman atteindra la résidence. » Il n'avait que faire des soieries et des ustensiles et les rendit dans leur totalité.
Trois jours avant le retour de l'émissaire, le malade se montrait agressif, rompant des cordes et jetant des pierres. Toute la famille avait barricadé les portes pour le repousser, mais il brisait les verrous et arrachait les loquets. Nulle force ne pouvait lui résister ; la fureur de son insanité était humainement irrépressible. Quand tout d'un coup, il retrouva son calme, regagna de lui-même ses quartiers, se lava les mains et le visage, utilisa serviette et peigne, noua sa ceinture et se chaussa. Tenant une tablette [d'audience], le visage serein, il exécuta une profonde révérence au bord de la route sous le portail. Ravis, les membres de la famille rivalisèrent les uns avec les autres pour s'enquérir de ce qui s'était passé. Il souriait, mais ne répondait pas, sauf pour dire qu'un envoyé céleste allait arriver. Oubliant de boire et de manger et sans prendre le temps de dormir la nuit, il se tenait là diligemment, faisant le pied de grue et dressant le cou, dans une attente impatiente et à l'affût. Ruisselant de transpiration, il faisait tout pour ne pas succomber à l'épuisement. Deux jours et trois nuits plus tard, le messager arriva, tenant le talisman[43]. Comme il franchissait le portail, [Ye] s'inclina, lui souhaita joyeusement la bienvenue et s'empressa d'ouvrir la marche. Dès qu'il obtint le talisman, il l'avala. [Ye] ferma les yeux et la maladie fut aussitôt guérie. Plus tard, il se présenta respectueusement en personne au portail du monastère et fit une donation substantielle d'or et de soie pour la rénovation des bâtiments du sanctuaire. Toute la famille vénéra désormais le Tao. Elle fit ériger un oratoire et une salle de prédication. Matin et soir, tous y présentaient des offrandes d'encens et y faisaient leurs dévotions[44].

Michel Strickmann a comparé la procédure d'ingestion des talismans (voir « Le scribe » au chapitre 3) à la consommation d'une ordonnance médicale : en remettant ainsi la prescription aux divinités du corps responsables de la maladie, les talismans ingérés avaient une portée inatteignable par d'autres remèdes[45]. Cette thérapie suscita le scepticisme des rationalistes dès le début du taoïsme du Maître céleste. Au IIIe siècle, un historien commentait :

Le maître [...] disait à ceux qui souffraient de maladie de se prosterner et de réfléchir à leurs transgressions, puis leur donnait à boire de l'eau infusée

> de talisman. De celui qui n'avait souffert de maladie que pendant quelques jours et s'était rétabli, il disait : « Cette personne a foi dans le Tao. » Ceux qui ne guérissaient pas étaient donc ceux qui n'avaient pas foi dans le Tao[46].

Cet auteur se référait à la méthode d'ingestion d'un talisman de papier sous forme liquide, après combustion du papier servant de support et mélange des cendres obtenues avec de l'eau. Plus étrange encore paraît être la façon dont Ye avala le talisman entier. Dans les *Contes transmis et propos nouveaux*, une histoire dénonce cette méthode comme présentant des risques pour la santé, et cite le cas d'un pratiquant qui tomba malade après avoir consommé des liasses de talismans en papier[47]. Mais l'utilisation des talismans ne se limitait pas à leur ingestion. Dans un épilogue à l'histoire ci-dessus, Du Guangting décrit l'action différente d'un second talisman envoyé par le maître de Yuxiao à la même occasion, destiné celui-là à être fixé au-dessus du portail de la résidence des Ye. On constate son activation dans deux incidents impliquant du personnel de maison. Dans le premier, une domestique, qui a bu du vin dérobé dans la cuisine, vomit juste en dessous du talisman. Un esprit indigné, haut de trois ou quatre pouces, ayant l'apparence d'un général en armure et brandissant une épée, est aperçu s'enfuyant du talisman. La famille se hâte de brûler de l'encens à titre d'apaisement. Dans le second incident, une servante d'une maisonnée du voisinage apparentée à la famille Ye, souffre de « folie démoniaque » 風魔. Alors qu'elle passe devant la résidence des Ye, on la voit hésiter devant le portail, puis soudain pousser un cri. Le même général du talisman est aperçu brandissant son épée au-dessus de la tête de la femme. Interrogée, elle rapporte que, quelques moments plus tôt, un esprit a fauché une créature au milieu des airs, laquelle est tombée dans le col de son habit. Avec l'aide d'autres servantes appelées sur les lieux par Ye, on découvre une tête de serpent encore sanguinolente à l'intérieur du col de la servante. Sa possession est ainsi levée[48].

Les modèles de talismans fournis par les *Véritables talismans de l'Esprit pur du Lingbao* s'accompagnent de consignes variées quant à leur mode d'application : avaler, brûler puis avaler, avaler dans de l'eau, ingérer par avalements successifs, écrire sur une porte, attacher à la ceinture, écrire sur papier pour faire des boulettes à avaler, et ainsi de suite. Un talisman pour dissiper la mélancolie (fig. 8) porte les instructions suivantes :

> Le talisman ci-dessus soigne les gens atteints de dépression et de mélancolie, ceux qui souffrent d'irrépressibles pulsions ou de morosité viscérale, et ceux qui poussent des hurlements ou souffrent de manie obsessionnelle. Utiliser de la soie jaune et écrire [le talisman] en rouge, puis le faire avaler [au patient]. L'écrire ensuite au-dessus du cœur [du patient]. L'écrire encore sur cinq pouces de soie cramoisie et le placer sur le bras gauche [du patient]. Le coucher sur le côté. Se conformer aux indications et la guérison s'ensuivra[49].

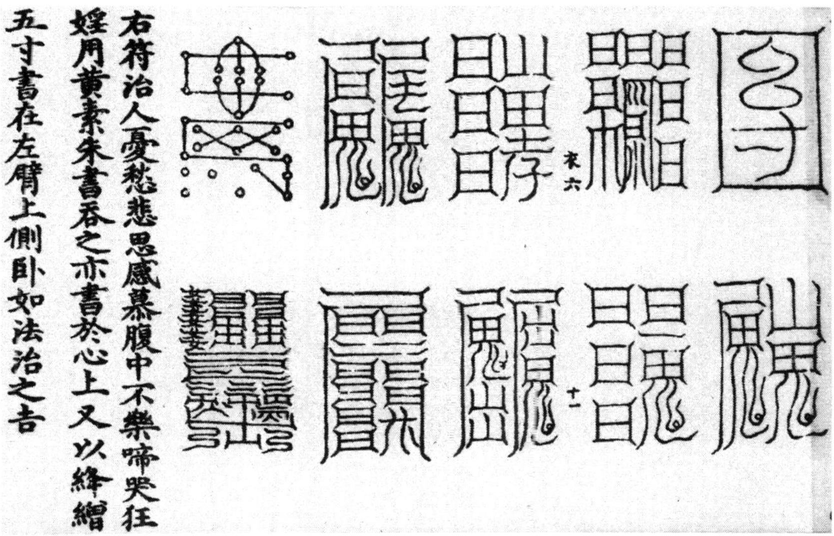

Fig. 8. Talisman pour « Dissiper les pensées mélancoliques » 解悲思. *Taishang dongxuan lingbao suling zhenfu*, C.13b-14a. Avec l'aimable autorisation de la Bibliothèque de l'Asie orientale et de la Collection Gest, Université de Princeton.

Dans la même section, le « traitement de la fièvre paludéenne » 治瘧疾 associe un talisman à des incantations et à une requête. D'autres instructions spécifient que l'écriture ou l'usage de talismans devaient s'accompagner d'incantations. Ces différentes méthodes étaient toutes basées sur des principes apparentés, et elles étaient utilisées conjointement, ou combinées avec d'autres instruments sacramentels comme les épées et l'eau lustrale. Une instruction donne : « Écrire à l'encre rouge sur le ventre du patient », soulignant l'affinité des talismans avec les sceaux qui étaient couramment imprimés sur la partie souffrante du corps du malade.

Les sceaux

L'auteur et ami de Ge Hong, Gan Bao 干寶 (mort en 336), prône la supériorité des sceaux sur d'autres méthodes pour exercer le pouvoir sur le monde invisible dans le récit suivant :

> He Yu 賀瑀 de Guiji 會稽 (Zhejiang) tomba un jour malade et perdit connaissance. Seul son cœur demeurait tiède. Il décéda, mais revint à la vie trois jours plus tard. He raconta qu'un officier l'avait emmené au Ciel où il fut introduit dans une pièce secrète du Bureau de l'administration. Un rayonnage occupait la pièce. Sur l'étagère supérieure se trouvait un sceau et sur l'étagère du milieu, une épée. [He Yu] fut autorisé à prendre ce qu'il voulait. Ne pouvant atteindre l'étagère supérieure du fait de sa petite taille, il prit l'épée et s'en fut. L'officier lui demanda : « Qu'avez-vous pris ? » Il dit : « J'ai pris l'épée. » L'autre dit : « Dommage que vous n'ayez pas pris le sceau. Le sceau peut contrôler les cent esprits, l'épée ne confère que le commandement du dieu du sol local 社公 »[50].

L'Essentiel pour pratiquer la perfection du Canon de l'Unité correcte 正一法文修真旨要 du début des Tang décrit ainsi la puissance extraordinaire des sceaux (voir fig. 9) pour soigner les maladies :

> Pour sauver des vies, en péril de mort, rien ne vaut les sceaux. Dans les temps anciens, Fan Li 范蠡 en usa et provoqua l'écroulement de montagnes, le reflux des rivières et des mers, fit trembler de peur les puissances spirituelles et retentir le tonnerre[51]. Avec les sceaux, on peut fondre le métal et polir le jade, restaurer le souffle vital et faire revenir les âmes *hun* [pour réanimer les cadavres] ; combien plus facilement alors peut-on guérir les malades au moyen de ceux-ci[52] !

Fig. 9. « Sceau spirituel du Monarque céleste » 天帝神印 pour guérir les maladies. *Zhengyi fawen xiuzhen zhiyao*, 19b. *Daozang*, édition des Ming de 1598. Reproduit avec l'autorisation de la Bibliothèque nationale de France.

Les découvertes archéologiques récentes font écho à ce que l'on peut lire sur l'emploi des sceaux dans la littérature narrative médiévale, de Gan Bao à Du Guangting[53]. On trouve des descriptions de sceaux taoïstes dans les manuscrits de Dunhuang et des manuels comme les *Méthodes de visualisation, de sceaux, de souffles et d'incantations* 思印氣訣法, un guide pour contrôler les esprits de la nature et les épidémies, sceller les portes aux démons, se soustraire à l'adversité astrale, empêcher les morts de revenir et dissiper les calamités s'abattant sur la maisonnée[54]. L'instrument de choix était le sceau du Dieu jaune – c'est-à-dire le Monarque céleste – de Yue 黃神越章, un sceau connu par des spécimens archéologiques datant des Han orientaux[55]. Il fut utilisé par Ge Hong, qui le décrivit comme un gros objet de quatre pouces carrés porteur de cent vingt caractères gravés ; les anciens, expliqua-t-il, le suspendaient à leur ceinture quand ils pénétraient dans des régions montagneuses reculées[56].

Ici encore, les *Divines manifestations* révèlent avec à propos la face cachée de l'un des mystères sacramentaux. Les maladies mentales faisaient couramment l'objet de soins sacramentels, sans nul doute à cause de leur nature irréductible aux époques prémodernes et parce qu'elles évoquaient la possession par des esprits. Particulièrement efficaces étaient les sceaux nouvellement gravés. Prenons le cas de Zhang Rang 張讓, qui fut sauvé par le sceau de Yue. Zhang, dont le foyer était à Guizhou 桂州, région multiethnique de Longsheng 龍勝 dans l'actuel Guangxi, voyageait dans les comtés de Xiang 湘 et d'E 鄂 (Hunan et Hubei) lorsqu'il fut atteint de « troubles mentaux », l'une des Six afflictions. Voici comment Du en décrit les symptômes :

> Au début, [Zhang Rang] souffrit de désorientation et de perte de mémoire : en chemin, il se perdait, confondant l'est et l'ouest ; à l'intérieur, il était assis, absorbé, prenant le matin pour le soir. Quelques mois plus tard, il contracta une colère furieuse, tançant démons et esprits tout en insultant ses frères en humanité. Après quoi, il courait nu çà et là, complètement désinhibé. Il pénétrait dans l'eau ou les flammes et s'exposait aux lances et aux lames, sans redouter les blessures. À maintes reprises il endura brûlures, entailles et contusions.

À la différence du fils Ye, Zhang Rang était loin des siens, sans parents attentifs ni agents de l'autorité publique à ses côtés. Mais voilà qu'un prêtre taoïste du nom de Yuan Guizhen 袁歸真 prit l'initiative de soigner Zhang et d'expulser son mal. Du Guangting insiste sur le fait que Yuan grava et activa l'instrument sacramentel spécialement pour cette occasion. La fabrication et l'activation des sceaux, en particulier dans le cas du sceau de Yue, constituaient des étapes essentielles de la procédure rituelle. Était-ce en raison du développement de la xylographie ou pour des raisons de commodité ? Les fabricants de sceaux taoïstes sous les Tang utilisèrent, en tout état de cause, de plus en plus le bois au lieu des matériaux durs traditionnellement employés comme support pour les sceaux[57] :

> Le *daoshi* Yuan Guizhen grava un sceau neuf du Dieu jaune de Yue. Après avoir fait des offrandes, il le mit à l'épreuve. Il brûla de l'encens et appliqua le sceau, comme prescrit, sur le cœur et le dos [du patient]. Rang était alors en train de déambuler, l'esprit dérangé. Quand [Guizhen] l'attrapa et apposa le sceau, [Rang] fut pris de vertige et s'évanouit. Guizhen sut alors que le sceau était efficace. Derechef il employa du cinabre (pour faire une empreinte vermillon), brûla de l'encens et apposa le sceau sur le cœur une fois de plus. [Rang] fut instantanément guéri. Une créature

semblable à un pigeon s'échappa de sa bouche et percuta le sol plusieurs dizaines de pieds plus loin. Les gens s'avancèrent pour l'examiner. Ils découvrirent qu'il s'agissait d'une simple chauve-souris de grande taille portant apparemment l'empreinte de caractères sigillaires sur son dos. Rang revint alors à lui et retrouva son état d'antan. De toute part Guizhen porta secours aux malades et, usant de ce sceau, il obtint de nombreux signes de sa puissance[58].

Un autre sceau figurant dans les *Divines manifestations* appartenait au répertoire d'exorcismes de l'Empereur du Nord 北帝, le souverain du monde des morts : c'était le sceau de Tianpeng 天蓬印, nommé d'après les généraux Tianpeng des esprits stellaires qui étaient les maréchaux de l'Empereur du Nord[59]. Dans l'histoire suivante, le sceau manifeste son pouvoir en venant à bout d'une grave sécheresse dans la plaine de Chengdu en 880. Les eaux en crue qui en résultèrent noyèrent diverses espèces de chenilles et de sauterelles, deux fléaux que les taoïstes combattaient en même temps que les inondations et la sécheresse au moyen de rituels de requête et de la Retraite du registre d'or[60].

Fan Xiyue 范希越 de Chengdu était un adepte versé dans les techniques du culte de l'Empereur du Nord 北帝修奉之術[61]. Il relata en personne cette histoire à Du Guangting, en même temps que celle d'un miracle antérieur, accompli avec le même type de sceau, survenu au cours de l'attaque de la ville de Chengdu par le royaume voisin de Nanzhao 南詔, probable référence à l'incursion de tribus de Nanzhao, collectivement appelées Man 蠻, durant l'hiver 874-875[62]. Tandis que tous les habitants du voisinage s'enfuyaient face à l'envahisseur Man, Xiyue entreprit de protéger sa résidence de l'allée des Bouilleurs de colle 煮膠巷 en dissimulant un sceau de Tianpeng entre les tuiles du toit de la salle principale. Quand les Man battirent finalement en retraite, la maison de Xiyue était la seule à être encore debout.

En l'an 880, la sécheresse avait duré dans la plaine de Chengdu du troisième au cinquième mois lunaire. La population anxieuse était sur le point de se résigner à la perte des récoltes quand Fan Xiyue grava un sceau de Tianpeng et fit des offrandes. Ses offrandes – condition requise pour l'activation du sceau – étaient irréprochables. Xiyue entreprit au nom du peuple de mettre le sceau à l'épreuve et il pria pour la pluie depuis les rives du lac Wansui 萬歲池. Cette étendue d'eau, près de l'abbaye de Longxing (Zhizhen) et du mont Xueshe[63], s'était formée sur le site d'une carrière utilisée, en 311 avant notre ère, pour extraire les matériaux de construction des premiers remparts de Chengdu[64]. Au IIIe siècle avant notre ère, quand Li Bing avait créé le système d'irrigation et de prévention des inondations de la plaine de Chengdu, il avait canalisé deux des cours d'eau pour remplir les douves de la ville. Il avait également édifié plusieurs ponts, dont le pont de l'Ascension des immortels que traversaient les voyageurs de Chengdu qui se rendaient au mont Xueshe[65] :

> Sur ce, [Xiyue] se rendit à l'abbaye de Zhizhen et accomplit une Retraite. Le même jour *gengchen* 庚辰 (8 juillet) à l'heure *xu* 戌時 (19-21 heures), il jeta le sceau dans le lac. Un vent spectral survint et une tempête se leva tandis que des nuages sinistres s'amoncelaient de toutes parts. À l'heure *hai* 亥時 (21-23 heures), une pluie torrentielle éclata qui dura jusqu'au point du jour et au petit matin. Puissants éclairs et coups de tonnerre se succédaient sans discontinuer avec de terrifiantes réverbérations. [Xiyue] ne parvint à retourner à la préfecture [de Chengdu] que lorsque la pluie se calma. Sur le pont de l'Ascension des immortels, l'eau atteignait le ventre de son cheval. Les quatre douves extérieures le long du mur d'enceinte avaient débordé et submergé les berges. Toutes les espèces de chenilles et de sauterelles furent noyées et anéanties pour de nombreuses années.

La fin de cette narration illustre comment le sceau de Tianpeng de Fan Xiyue connut un usage annexe : l'empereur Xizong, qui dut fuir en exil à Chengdu l'année suivante, enjoignit Xiyue de recourir au pouvoir extraordinaire du sceau pour prédire la fin de l'occupation de la capitale par Huang Chao. L'offrande *jiao* qui fut exécutée au palais autour du sceau de Tianpeng produisit un oracle sûr quant à la défaite des rebelles[66].

Les incantations

Dans l'arsenal de l'Empereur du Nord, l'incantation de Tianpeng 天蓬呪 n'était pas moins redoutable que le sceau du même nom[67]. Une version datant du IVe siècle de cette incantation est préservée dans les *Déclarations des Véritables* de Tao Hongjing. L'incantation avait le pouvoir de mettre impérieusement en demeure l'escouade de destructeurs de démons de Tianpeng, et les esprits astraux du même acabit, d'attaquer, d'anéantir et de disperser tous les spectres cadavériques et démons nocifs susceptibles de sévir du nord au sud[68]. Un livre des Tang intitulé *Divine incantation de Tianpeng pour préserver la vie et dissiper les calamités* 天蓬護命消災神咒 recommandait cette incantation pour prévenir les désastres et subsister à la fin du *kalpa*[69]. Les *Divines manifestations* décrivent un adepte se soustrayant aux travaux forcés durant l'occupation de Chang'an par Huang Chao, en s'élevant d'un bond en l'air après avoir récité l'incantation de Tianpeng[70].

Pouvoirs surnaturels et libération physique ou sotériologique faisaient l'objet d'incantations dans les religions de l'Asie depuis l'époque des mantras védiques. La rencontre des traditions indigènes chinoises en matière d'écriture et d'énonciation d'incantations avec les mantras *dhāranī* et les pratiques rituelles associées du bouddhisme engendra de nouvelles techniques taoïstes[71]. Les incantations pouvaient se combiner avec d'autres instruments sacramentels, de même que la fabrication de talismans et de sceaux et leur activation pouvaient s'accompagner d'incantations. Le dosage de ces différents remèdes dépendait de la gravité du cas, ou bien procédait par tâtonnement :

> Avant d'aller pratiquer le soin d'une maladie par une incantation, vous devez faire exécuter par tous les membres de la famille du patient les dévotions du petit matin au Tao et les rites de purification. Toute la maison doit être silencieuse ; tout bruit ou trouble doit être écarté. Il convient qu'alors le maître taoïste s'approche du patient, brûle de l'encens et examine son état avec le plus grand soin. Si les symptômes physiques sont graves voire péjoratifs, le maître doit toute affaire cessante visualiser pour son compte les esprits et faire circuler les souffles dans son propre corps, puis appliquer le sceau trois fois [au patient]. À la mi-journée, il doit retourner examiner la condition du patient pour voir si elle s'est ou non un peu améliorée. S'il n'y a pas d'amélioration, il doit prononcer l'incantation une fois encore. Au cours de la nuit, il doit de nouveau examiner [le patient, évaluer] si quelque changement est intervenu, et dans la négative, il doit derechef proférer l'incantation[72].

Quel était l'effet de l'incantation de Tianpeng sur le récipiendaire ? Ici encore, les *Divines manifestations* nous fournissent un aperçu de l'empreinte simultanée transférée par l'incantation vers les mondes visible et invisible. Relatant un nouvel incident impliquant l'abbaye de Zhizhen, Du Guangting rapporte d'abord la version selon la perspective yang de ce monde, puis dévoile au lecteur la scène yin correspondante dans le monde des ténèbres, telle qu'un patient à l'article de la mort, sauvé par l'énoncé de l'incantation de Tianpeng, en fit l'expérience. Tout commença avec un jeune homme qui décéda subitement, sans prodrome. Alors que son corps était encore tiède, sa famille bouleversée fit venir des médecins, des médiums et des exorcistes. Nul n'eut de remède. Pour finir, elle manda un maître taoïste de l'abbaye de Zhizhen, Zhang Qianyao 張乾曜. Celui-ci, constatant l'urgence de la situation, demanda une épée, aspergea de l'eau lustrale, brûla de l'encens et prononça l'incantation de Tianpeng cent fois. Le défunt remua soudain, puis revint à la vie. Interrogé sur ce qu'il avait vu, il dit :

> Il y avait quatre envoyés en habit jaune 黃衣使[73]. Ils menaient un étalon à la main et me dirent de le monter. Une fois sur le cheval, je fus emporté. Devant, la route était sombre, comme envahie de fumée ou de brouillard. Soudain, je vis le révérend maître Zhang, coiffé d'une capuche de soie écarlate, tenant une épée affûtée à la main. Il commandait à plusieurs milliers de soldats en habit noir qui s'avançaient en formation. Comme ces derniers pressaient l'allure, les envoyés et le cheval disparurent soudain. Je tombai au sol et demeurai étourdi un long moment. Ce n'est que grâce au secours des acolytes du révérend maître que je fus capable de revenir[74].

Quand un adepte se rendait coupable de négligence, le sceau de Tianpeng perdait son pouvoir, comme les autres sacrements taoïstes. En référence aux registres d'ordination, Lu Xiujing prévenait que « quand la conduite vertueuse fait défaut au corps, quand le cœur est mauvais et ne s'est pas amendé, les officiels et soldats [spirituels] s'éloignent et ne viennent plus au secours des hommes » (voir « Maîtrise et quiétude » au chapitre 7). L'esprit du talisman du portail de la résidence des Ye partit précipitamment, indigné, quand le sol en dessous de lui fut souillé. Les *Divines manifestations* relatent un exemple de même type impliquant l'incantation de Tianpeng. Wang Daoke 王道珂 était un résident de Nanba 南笆 dans le district de Shuangliu 雙流 (près de l'aéroport de l'actuelle Chengdu, seize kilomètres à l'ouest de la ville). Au temps de l'exil de l'empereur Xizong, Daoke gagnait sa vie comme diseur de bonne aventure au marché du district, utilisant des plastrons de tortue, des tiges d'achillée et des techniques talismaniques. Daoke ne manquait jamais, à son habitude, de réciter l'incantation de Tianpeng. Mais tous les soirs, il troquait les gains de la journée contre de la nourriture et du vin et ne rentrait chez lui qu'une fois ivre. Un matin, entre son village et le marché, il fit route avec un colporteur d'ail. Sur le chemin du retour cette nuit-là, un démon vulpin aux yeux incandescents le terrassa. Daoke comprit que les esprits gardiens de Tianpeng avaient abandonné sa personne qui empestait l'ail et le vin. Il se hâta de rentrer chez lui. Après avoir exécuté des ablutions et des purifications, il revint sur la scène de sa défaite et parvint à exorciser le démon[75].

Les rituels

Les rituels de requête, les Retraites et les Offrandes, étaient répertoriés en tant que tels comme sacrements efficaces dans les *Divines manifestations*, occupant une catégorie à part (les *juan* 14-15). Nombre des miracles qui y sont rapportés comme faisant foi, étaient considérés comme des réponses aux rituels commandités par les empereurs ou des hauts fonctionnaires, dans lesquels les manifestations prenaient la forme de présages de bon augure et de bénédictions pour le peuple tout entier. D'autres rituels mentionnés secoururent des participants laïcs ordinaires, par exemple la Grande offrande 大醮 que célébra Ye Fashan 葉法善 (mort en 720), maître taoïste de troisième génération et ancêtre du Ye Zangzhi adepte de talismans cité précédemment, durant ses années de pratique à l'abbaye de Lingkong 陵空觀 à Luoyang, en 656-661[76]. Fashan était réputé pour sa capacité à démasquer les esprits démoniaques[77]. Dans le miracle rapporté, il résolut un cas d'« envoûtement démoniaque » 魅病 collectif, une condition comparable à la démence, tandis qu'il exécutait un « autel de feu » 火壇, un rituel manifestement inspiré des rites du feu védiques ou iraniens[78]. Le spectacle du rituel captiva la ville tout entière :

> Les hommes et les femmes de la ville vinrent tous en spectateur. Soudain, des dizaines de personnes se précipitèrent dans les flammes, mais quand

la foule alarmée vola à leur rescousse, les premiers émergèrent totalement indemnes. Fashan dit : « Tous ces gens subissaient un envoûtement démoniaque. C'est grâce à ma méthode qu'ils furent sauvés. » Quand on les interrogea, on découvrit que c'était bien le cas. [Le démon] fut confondu et tous étaient guéris[79].

Les protocoles des Tang pour les Offrandes et requêtes d'exorcisme populaire montrent que les taoïstes laïcs recouraient à des rituels pour protéger les cultures agricoles, les habitations et les sépultures, pour guérir les enfants malades et pour obtenir le soulagement des effets de la magie noire et des ensorcellements. Des manuels des Tang, comme les *Rites d'extériorisation des officiers et de requête* 出官章儀 et le *Livre pour défaire les malédictions* 解釋咒詛經, donnent l'exemple de telles pratiques[80]. Des aperçus instructifs d'usage de rituels de délivrance et de protection dans la société laïque peuvent s'observer dans les prières votives préservées dans les manuscrits de Dunhuang. La majorité d'entre elles concernait des rituels bouddhiques, exécutés par des moines de rang inférieur pour le compte de laïcs[81]. Un nombre plus réduit était utilisé par la communauté taoïste locale[82].

La principale collection de prières votives taoïstes se rattache à un formulaire manuscrit conservé à la Bibliothèque nationale de France (voir planche 6). Le début du texte manquant, l'éditeur moderne lui a donné pour titre *Recueil de prières taoïstes pour les Retraites et Offrandes en vue du salut des morts* 道教齋醮度亡祈願文集[83]. En fait, seulement la moitié des vingt-quatre prières concernait les morts. Le reste concernait diverses communautés, familles et habitations locales. On y discerne trois types d'intentions : l'absolution des membres de la famille et des maîtres défunts de toute rétribution dans l'autre monde, la préservation des influences mauvaises et l'obtention de bénédictions. Les bénéficiaires étaient le commanditaire, des membres de sa famille, la communauté, l'État ou encore tous les êtres sensibles. Une prière supplémentaire visait à obtenir la guérison des maladies 病差文 (col. 124-130), une autre le retour indemne d'une expédition militaire 征迴平安文 (col. 131-140) et une autre, enfin, était offerte en action de grâce pour les prières exaucées 報願文 (col. 243-252)[84].

Les prières, qui datent du milieu du VIIIe au début du Xe siècle, ont une couleur locale certaine. Les rituels qui leur sont associés n'ont pas encore été touchés par les réformes de Du Guangting. Plusieurs prières évoquent la vie militaire sous le régime de l'Armée du retour à l'allégeance 歸義軍, qui sécurisa la frontière occidentale de la fin du IXe au début du Xe siècle, alors que la famille Zhang 張 dominait à Dunhuang[85]. Reflet de la culture religieuse de cette région servant de point de passage entre la Chine et l'Asie centrale, les prières taoïstes sont singulièrement imprégnées d'idées et de pratiques bouddhiques, montrant une affinité étroite entre la communauté bouddhique qui y dominait et la minorité taoïste. Une oraison taoïste prie pour qu'une nonne bouddhiste défunte, une instructrice *ācārya* 闍梨, « puisse atteindre le *nirvāna* » (col. 96-103). Dans le même registre, une prière de Nouvel an 歲初願文 pour une « cérémonie sans restriction » 無遮會, c'est-à-dire ouverte à tous, était conjointement commanditée par les communautés taoïste et bouddhique, l'officiant utilisant la tribune pour prêcher un message d'œcuménisme bouddho-taoïste (col. 180-196). Les prières explicitent remarquablement le rôle, rarement précisé, dévolu aux commanditaires et aux participants laïcs dans l'exécution des rituels : balayer la cour, offrir de l'encens et des fleurs, requérir les services d'officiants, disposer les icônes, faire des offrandes de nourriture et d'autres offrandes sacrificielles, porter révérence, faire ses dévotions et réciter les écritures. Parmi les intentions répétées des commanditaires de la Retraite figuraient l'obtention de mérite par les actions charitables, la confection de bannières et d'images des Célestes vénérables, la copie des écritures, la restauration d'icônes et la fourniture de lampes votives pour « illuminer les Neuf ténèbres » 九幽, le séjour des morts.

Le repas rituel de la mi-journée 午齋 était le principal moment d'interaction entre les communautés monastiques et la société laïque. Le protocole intitulé « Rituels de fête maigre » 凡齋法 (col. 220-240) prescrivait le déroulement et les adresses pour le repas monastique de midi, après lequel on ne consommait plus aucun aliment pendant le reste de la journée. Des donateurs laïcs fournissaient le repas. En échange, moines et nonnes exécutaient un rituel lors du repas de la mi-journée en l'honneur du donateur et pour exalter le mérite de la charité. Le repas se tenait dans le monastère ou à la résidence du donateur. Le principe de réciprocité prévalait : on rendait visite ou on recevait chez soi, on échangeait des dons et on priait pour la large circulation du mérite acquis. La séquence liturgique dudit rituel du repas de la mi-journée comprenait plusieurs étapes. À leur arrivée à la résidence de la fête maigre 齋家, les participants prennent place, se lavent les mains et récitent les écritures. On guide le donateur pour effectuer les gestes ritualistes : s'agenouiller, s'asseoir, chanter et exécuter les dévotions. Quand le moment du repas arrive, tous rendent hommage et touchent le sol de la tête devant le Très Haut grand Tao suprême et les Trois joyaux. Le commanditaire de la « fête maigre » se prosterne et fait l'éloge du mérite des actions charitables. La communauté répond par une prière appelant un « ornement » 莊嚴 de cent mérites pour le commanditaire. Cette expression bouddhique renvoie au mérite revenant au bénéficiaire pour une bonne action[86]. De nouvelles prières – pour l'ornement de sagesse du donateur, le salut des morts, le bonheur des vivants, la paix dans le monde et la délivrance de tous les êtres – élargissent le cercle des bénéficiaires du mérite devant être transféré. Après d'autres chants, le commanditaire adresse une prière dédicatoire aux aliments. Le maître des rites proclame : « De tous les mérites, l'offrande de nourriture a la primauté : dans la vie, elle procure la joie ; dans l'au-delà, elle fait gagner la renaissance au Ciel. Dans le monde à venir, [le donateur] demeurera en la Terre pure, où nourriture et vêtement abondent spontanément. C'est pourquoi l'offrande de nourriture d'aujourd'hui est universellement présentée à tous les cieux. »

Tandis que circule la nourriture, un chant énonce : « En haut, la nourriture est offerte aux Célestes vénérables ; au milieu, aux anciens maîtres ; et en bas, elle atteint les multitudes du royaume du *dharma* 法界眾生. Que tous soient rassasiés ensemble. » Après le repas, le maître des rites derechef exalte l'aumône comme l'action méritoire par excellence et fait acte de contrition pour toute faute commise au cours de l'accomplissement du rituel. Le donateur exprime ses remords de n'être pas allé jusqu'à se dépouiller de toutes ses possessions : « L'offrande est achevée. Craignant que le mérite en soit déficient, les dons librement consentis de biens purs aux Trois joyaux seront multipliés » (voir « Les vœux monastiques » au chapitre 9).

Les assemblées périodiques des associations de district 邑 de Dunhuang donnaient également l'occasion aux fidèles laïcs d'interagir avec le clergé monastique[87]. Des Retraites étaient commanditées chaque mois tour à tour. Selon les ressources combinées de la localité – village ou communauté urbaine –, ces Retraites pouvaient rassembler des offrandes plus ou moins abondantes. La première de deux « Prières d'association de district » 邑願文 rattachées au formulaire de la Bibliothèque nationale de France (col. 15-33 et 104-115 respectivement) énonce l'intention des rituels. On entame la prière par le recensement des Trois joyaux taoïstes – Tao, écritures et maître :

> Le Tao est la mère de toutes choses, les écritures le vaisseau pour véhiculer les quatre classes de créatures (voir chapitre 3, introduction), tandis que le maître est apte à assurer le passage de tous les êtres vers l'autre rive. Grands sont les Trois joyaux ! Insondables ! Tout le monde est converti et nul ne faillit à répondre. Ainsi aujourd'hui le commanditaire de la Retraite, avec l'entière association de district 合邑人 et d'autres[88], grâce au miroir de sagesse suspendu en permanence, connaissent la fugacité du corps matériel ; grâce à la lampe de la connaissance brillant constamment, ils comprennent l'impermanence d'une destinée fragile. Ensemble, ils ordonnent des causes méritoires et accomplissent des actes de vénération pour que leurs prières soient entendues. Le pont érigé autrefois s'accomplit aujourd'hui. Chaque mois [des commanditaires] offrent tour à tour une Retraite pour garantir la protection de leurs familles. Anxieux de ne pas gagner suffisamment de mérite, ils multiplient les actions charitables et font don de biens purs pour atteindre tels ou tels mérites 厶功德.

Les termes « tels ou tels mérites »[89], écrits en caractères de taille réduite, invitaient le prêtre à énumérer à cet emplacement les offrandes présentées. Ici, la liste des offrandes débute par les accessoires rituels – icônes, écritures et bannières – et une explication de leur efficacité dévotionnelle. Le premier groupe, les icônes, fait explicitement le lien entre offrande et mérite, car les marques de sainteté visibles sur les icônes offertes étaient la preuve du mérite acquis. Voici cette liste :

> *Icônes*, avec soixante-douze marques primaires 七十二相, immaculées et sans défaut, et quatre-vingt marques secondaires 八十一好, entièrement rares et belles[90] – ceux qui les contemplent révérencieusement oblitèrent

les Neuf ténèbres et ceux qui les vénèrent transcendent les Trois mondes. *Écritures*, avec des colonnes comme des ligatures de jades 灌 [貫] 玉 et des phrases comme des enfilades de perles 連珠 – ceux qui les récitent reçoivent de hautes protections dans le monde des morts comme dans celui des vivants ; ceux qui les révèrent par des offrandes obtiennent la bénédiction de l'Homme et du Ciel. *Bannières*, en dix segments 十絕, en élégante profusion[91], de couleurs bariolées et aux neuf radiances, tourbillonnant librement au vent, effrayant l'oiseau qui passe.
La cour est alors aspergée et balayée ; encens et fleurs sont solennellement offerts, les disciples déférents déroulent les portraits des hommes réels, disposent d'exquises offrandes des neuf cuisines et brûlent le délicat encens de cent mélanges. Mérite imposant, inépuisablement admirable !

Des commanditaires organisaient des Retraites d'association pour le compte de divers bénéficiaires, dont l'État, la communauté locale et leurs familles respectives. D'autres rituels étaient consacrés à la famille tout entière, ou à un membre de celle-ci, vivant ou mort. Le cadre de ces rituels était généralement familial. L'officiant de la « Prière de retraite » 齋願文 qui débute le formulaire (col. 1-14) annonce : « Nous sommes venus dans cette maison pour tenir une Retraite [d'action de grâce] pour prières exaucées » 就此家庭，設齋報願 (col. 9). Une prière pour ce type d'occasion 報願文 (col. 243-252) rend grâce pour la bénédiction reçue par une famille au cours de l'année révolue et prie pour que l'armée en campagne à la frontière revienne sauve. La « Cérémonie de banquet de retour » 回禮席 (col. 171-174) est une prière familiale pour une Retraite d'action de grâce à l'occasion d'une cérémonie d'imposition de bonnet[92]. D'autres prières dans un état fragmentaire concernent l'habitation familiale, par exemple « Entrer dans une demeure » 入宅 (col. 212-213) et « Construire une demeure » 造宅 (col. 214-219).

Un type courant de prière à Dunhuang était les « oraisons funèbres » 東行亡 (col. 175-179) et les prières pour les funérailles et la commémoration du défunt aux jours prescrits après la mort d'un membre de la famille. On marquait les dates des sept premiers intervalles de sept jours puis le centième jour après le décès[93]. Le formulaire fournit des modèles de prière pour le décès d'un frère 兄弟亡 (col. 141-148), d'un époux ou d'une épouse 夫妻亡 (col. 149-154), d'un fils ou d'une fille 亡男女 (col. 155-158) ou d'un père 亡考 (col. 159-170 et 197-209). D'autres étaient énoncées à des dates non spécifiées pour des pères ou mères défunts 亡考妣文 (col. 34-51, 52-65) ou un enfant décédé 亡孩子 (col. 210-211). Des prières pour des membres défunts du clergé évoquent « tel maître des rites des Trois cavernes 三洞某法師 de l'abbaye de la Grue blanche 白鶴觀 » (col. 66-81) et une femme, « maître des rites Zhang de l'ordre Dongxuan (Lingbao) à l'abbaye de Xuanzhong » 玄中觀洞玄張法師 (col. 82-95)[94]. L'intention des rites de commémoration était d'aider et d'accompagner les âmes des défunts récemment trépassés sur la route incertaine menant à la renaissance. En chemin, les défunts passeraient par des moments critiques, des phases d'examen et de jugement qui détermineraient leur destinée dans l'autre monde. Les laïcs en deuil, taoïstes ou bouddhistes, disposaient le portrait du défunt, invitaient des maîtres à exécuter des rituels, se livraient à la récitation diurne et nocturne des écritures et priaient pour que le défunt puisse ne pas « sombrer dans les Trois bourbiers, mais renaître sur un chemin favorable »[95]. Les Retraites du double sept 七七齋 marquaient lesdits jours par des prières particulières. Le centième jour après le décès, une prière finale concluait la période de deuil.

Chapitre 12

Prières pour une nouvelle ère

Au milieu de l'ère des Tang apparut à la cour un nouveau type de prière taoïste appelé Oraison verte 青詞. Initialement, les auteurs de ces prières étaient les rédacteurs officiels des édits impériaux, mais la charge de les écrire incomba de plus en plus à d'éminents taoïstes et hommes de lettres séculiers. Au fil du temps, la nouvelle élite adopta l'Oraison verte comme prière de prédilection, laquelle nous renseigne sur la quintessence des intentions de l'époque pour les Retraites-Offrandes. À la base de ce mouvement, on retrouve une fois encore Du Guangting, qui ouvrit la voie au développement de la prière d'Oraison verte en tant que genre littéraire et qui enrichit le répertoire rituel taoïste de cultes stellaires protecteurs et rédempteurs nouvellement importés de l'Asie du Sud et de l'Asie centrale[1].

L'Oraison verte

L'institution officielle des Oraisons vertes date de la veille de la rébellion d'An Lushan (755-757) et revient en force au cours du soulèvement de Huang Chao (874-884). Le parallèle entre les deux crises dynastiques qui avaient valu l'exil aux gouvernements des empereurs

Xuanzong et Xizong, à Chengdu, respectivement en 756 et 881, ne pouvait échapper aux courtisans de la fin du IXe siècle. Une prière commanditée par Xizong en 881, examinée ci-dessous, se réfère explicitement au précédent constitué par l'exil antérieur. La période entre les deux règnes avait connu une progression constante de l'autonomie régionale qui finira par disloquer l'empire Tang et engendrer la configuration multipolaire des Cinq dynasties au nord et des Dix royaumes au sud. Les Oraisons vertes attestent de l'importance croissante dans ce contexte des Retraites, Offrandes et prières taoïstes commanditées par les puissances en lutte : la dynastie aux abois et les militaires, mais aussi les nouveaux dirigeants et leurs clans, et les potentats locaux cherchant à s'établir. De part et d'autre, la religion taoïste n'était jamais loin du pouvoir temporel, et le culte ancestral rendu à Laozi par les souverains des Tang avait contribué à approfondir la relation symbiotique de la religion et de l'État. Les grandioses Offrandes « au firmament » 周天醮 et « à tous les cieux » 羅天醮 commanditées par l'État, que Wang Qinruo 王欽若 (962-1025) devait plus tard revendiquer comme faisant partie d'une révélation à l'empereur Taizong 太宗 (r. 976-997) des Song, firent leur apparition au cours de la transition des Tang aux Cinq dynasties[2]. Documents de cour à l'origine, les Oraisons vertes devinrent le modèle de prière de la nouvelle classe dirigeante qui émergea des bouleversements politiques à la fin des Tang.

La plus riche collection de prières d'Oraison verte est le recueil fragmentaire des *Œuvres de Guangcheng* 廣成集 de Du Guangting, qui en compte 282. Le titre « Maître Guangcheng », qui fait écho à l'épithète de Laozi comme conseiller légendaire de l'Empereur jaune, fut conféré à Du Guangting en 913 par Wang Jian 王建 (847-918), le fondateur du royaume de Shu. Dans les *Œuvres de Guangcheng*, les Oraisons vertes les plus anciennes datent du début de l'exil de Xizong en 881, et les plus récentes de 917, l'année précédant la mort de Wang Jian[3]. En tant qu'ancien officiant du palais sous Xizong, Du Guangting joua un rôle prépondérant dans le développement du genre. Lettré et auteur prolifique, prêtre éminent, autorité incontestée en matière de liturgie et expert en astrologie, Du fut un rédacteur d'Oraisons vertes distingué et fort prisé.

Le genre de l'Oraison verte combine des fonctions liturgiques et des critères stylistiques d'un grand perfectionnement. Les passages descriptifs sont souvent écrits en prose parallèle 駢文[4]. Dans les *Œuvres de Guangcheng*, les vers parallèles sont des couplets en vers tétrasyllabiques ou bien en vers de longueur inégale alternée[5]. Par exemple, le couplet ci-dessous se compose de paires de tétrasyllabes et d'hexasyllabes se correspondant en alternance :

Cloches baleines et pierres sonores phœnix	鯨鍾鳳磬
Font flotter leur carillon jusqu'aux Neuf cieux ;	飄逸響於九天
Flammes grues et fumée dragon	鶴焔龍煙
Transportent notre sincérité aux Trois domaines[5].	達精誠於三境

L'expression recourt fréquemment à des figures de rhétorique et à des locutions faisant écho aux textes sacrés et aux classiques[7]. Les *Œuvres de Guangcheng* dépeignent finement les difficultés psychologiques du suppliant et sa motivation pour rechercher l'intercession rituelle :

> Inquiétée par la fumée des feux d'alarme, elle était sans nouvelles. Portant son regard vers Bao 褒 et la rivière Mian 沔, elle s'y envola en esprit. Elle scruta les montagnes et les rivières, mais sa vue était barrée. Sa prémonition anxieuse refoulée, elle ne savait où adresser ses supplications. Alors elle se rendit révérencieusement au temple du Tao et implora qu'on soumît une requête en son nom[8].

En plus d'exprimer l'intention votive du commanditaire, la locution accomplissait un acte rituel. Comme les requêtes *zhang* antérieures, les Oraisons vertes suivaient des règles de composition et des motifs structurels employant un langage modulaire à des moments prédéfinis. Dans le style d'un mémorial, le module initial commence par « Votre serviteur a appris » ou « Nous considérons humblement ». Il évoque ensuite, en des termes élevés, les principes cosmiques responsables de la destinée humaine et l'action du rituel taoïste dans le monde invisible. Par exemple, la prière pour une Offrande aux Neuf luminaires célébrée par le conseiller impérial Yan 嚴常侍 au mont Qingcheng, introduit la situation astrologique particulière du conseiller Yan par une observation générale, en prose parallèle, sur le système intégré de gouvernance présidant aux mondes naturel et humain et à l'inéluctabilité de la juste rétribution :

> Nous considérons humblement que le Ciel et la Terre dispensent les pouvoirs spirituels et que les Trois officiers fixent les critères de la vie et de la mort ; que le yin et le yang exposent les signes astronomiques et que les Neuf luminaires accordent le bénéfice de la lumière ; que le Palais du Sud 南宮 délivre les talismans de la longévité et que le Bureau du Nord 北府 produit les tablettes pour redresser les transgressions ; que les étoiles en orbite, les pics montagneux et les cours d'eau jugent impartialement ; et que l'entièreté du royaume des hommes est gouvernée au sens le plus étendu[9].

Le cœur des oraisons comprend une partie descriptive et une partie votive. La première expose l'occasion du rituel et la situation du suppliant. Les commanditaires, y compris les souverains, assument humblement la pleine responsabilité de la conjoncture défavorable dans laquelle ils se trouvent et offrent leur contrition. Après une expression comme « se prosternant » 伏惟 ou « désirant humblement » 伏冀 vient la partie votive. Elle contient l'exposé de l'objet de la prière et la résolution espérée. Un court épilogue atteste de la sincérité des participants ou tire une leçon de la démarche rituelle qui les anime.

Les Oraisons vertes intercèdent pour la protection et la bénédiction des commanditaires ou du bénéficiaire du rituel, rendent grâce, offrent des récompenses pour la résolution de situations difficiles, recherchent l'expiation des fautes et transgressions passées, le salut des parents et ancêtres et la délivrance des morts. Les voix que l'on peut distinguer dans les prières appartiennent aux mêmes catégories de protagonistes que pour les rituels de requête : le maître taoïste en qualité de prêtre officiant (souvent accompagné d'autres prêtres et d'assistants), le commanditaire, et le (ou les) bénéficiaire(s) du rituel. Lorsqu'il ne fait pas qu'un avec le commanditaire, le bénéficiaire est fréquemment introduit par « pour le compte de », comme dans l'« Offrande au firmament par Mo Tingyi pour le compte du commissaire adjoint à la pacification Zhang [Lin] à l'occasion de son anniversaire » 莫庭乂爲安撫張副使生日周天醮[10]. Le lieu de la performance rituelle pouvait être un temple, un palais, une résidence privée ou un sanctuaire en quelque lieu saint reculé. Typiquement, les commanditaires collectifs étaient les familles régnantes, les officiels et les militaires, mais aussi des taoïstes et des congrégations de temples, mêlant clercs et laïcs[11]. Le taoïste laïc Li Xuanjing 李玄儆, endeuillé par la mort de sa fille, pria pour sa délivrance et le salut de son âme. L'Oraison verte qui a consigné les circonstances du rituel indique que, veuve, la fille était entrée en religion et devenue une nonne taoïste pieuse, tandis que son père menait à bien une mission militaire pour le compte du souverain. Ses devoirs l'empêchaient de s'acquitter de son propre vœu de se dévouer entièrement au Tao, quand sa fille tomba soudain malade et trépassa. À la fin de la prière, Li Xuanjing, devant l'autel, confie les registres d'ordination et les vêtements de sa fille aux flammes[12].

Les adeptes taoïstes commanditaient et exécutaient couramment des rituels pour exorciser les demeures ou les sites de construction (voir aussi « Protection du foyer » au chapitre 4). Une Oraison pour un rituel de ce type cherchait à pacifier une demeure par une Offrande aux Cinq empereurs 五帝大醮 représentant les directions de l'espace :

> Votre serviteur, ignare et quelconque, comprend peu les principes mystérieux. Il réalise des modifications en fonction des circonstances et se lance dans des travaux au gré de ses forces. Quand on entreprend des constructions, il est inévitable d'enfreindre des tabous. Là où des forages et des excavations ont lieu, le dérangement est grave. Soit on entre en conflit avec la loi du pays[13], soit on viole la Voie du Ciel, faisant abandonner leur garde aux esprits dragons et rendant les habitations impropres. Redoutant la perdition et l'accumulation des calamités [...][14].

La prière se conclut par une confession des fautes de l'auteur et l'aveu de sa contrition dans l'espoir d'apaiser les esprits offensés. Les travaux de construction pour la rénovation d'un temple inquiétaient particulièrement le clergé, puisque les résidents contrariés n'étaient autres que les dieux vénérés dans le sanctuaire concerné. En pareilles occasions, des Oraisons vertes annonçaient que les travaux de rénovation allaient commencer ou venaient de s'achever. Un soin particulier était pris pour signifier la réalisation de travaux de restauration d'icônes et de peintures murales, la principale demeure d'un dieu dans un temple. Ces rituels invitaient les divinités à revenir au sanctuaire, reprendre leur résidence et pacifier le site. L'abbaye de l'Aîné 丈人觀 au mont Qingcheng était le sanctuaire de l'immortel Ning Fengzi 甯封子, Aîné de Qingcheng 青城丈人. Sur décision de l'empereur Xuanzong, cette divinité prit un rang supérieur à tous les dieux des Cinq pics sacrés de la Chine[15]. C'est pourquoi son temple devint le centre des rituels effectués au nom de l'empereur Xizong quand celui-ci chercha refuge au Sichuan et, plus tard, de Wang Jian qui y consolida son régime indépendant[16]. Xizong conféra à la divinité un nouveau titre et ordonna la rénovation du temple[17]. Les travaux de construction s'accompagnèrent d'Offrandes d'annonce et de pacification au début et à la fin de la restauration[18]. Du Guangting revisita alors le site afin de prier pour le retour de l'Aîné[19]. Une Offrande séparée annonça l'achèvement des peintures à l'intérieur de l'abbaye, en particulier un *Panthéon des Cinq pics* 五嶽諸神 par le peintre taoïste Zhang Suqing 張素卿 (vers 845-vers 927) qui exaltait Qingcheng au-dessus des Cinq pics[20]. Achevant la chronique de son patronage officiel, Du Guangting fit l'éloge du magistrat de district local Mo Tingyi, qui avait commissionné les travaux, dans une inscription sur stèle datée de 895 et intitulée *Sur la restauration méritoire des sanctuaires du mont Qingcheng* 修青城山諸觀功德記[21].

Une liturgie au service d'un dessein

La plupart des Oraisons vertes étaient occasionnelles, c'est-à-dire composées en réponse à des événements isolés. L'occasion pouvait en être le décès d'un parent, une conjonction astrologique défavorable, une maladie, un cas de sécheresse ou un conflit armé. Ces intentions spécifiques pouvaient notamment s'inscrire dans le cadre liturgique général des Offrandes périodiques ou saisonnières. Par exemple, une prière pour la guérison ou le salut pouvait être énoncée les jours d'inspection des Trois originels. Comme d'autres prières liturgiques, les Oraisons vertes déclaraient l'intention du rituel associé, fournissaient les détails de l'infortune du bénéficiaire et plaidaient pour sa résolution. Les rituels associés étaient les Retraites *zhai* instituées par Lu Xiujing au Ve siècle, avec l'ajout plus récent des Offrandes *jiao*. Par conséquent, les prières de Du Guangting s'intitulent « Oraison de Retraite » 齋詞, « Oraison d'Offrande » 醮詞 ou simplement « Oraison » 詞 avec un qualificatif facultatif[22]. La plupart des rituels avaient de multiples finalités : la rédemption des morts dépendait de l'expiation des péchés du suppliant, et les prières pour résoudre les difficultés des vivants comportaient habituellement des demandes de bénédiction et l'expression d'actions de grâce.

La pluralité des intentions rend hasardeuse toute tentative de classement des Oraisons vertes dans les *Œuvres de Guangcheng* par type d'objectifs. Par ordre décroissant d'importance, on pourrait recourir aux rubriques suivantes : le temps et le destin, les étoiles de la destinée, et l'au-delà. Le plus grand nombre de prières tombent dans les deux premières catégories. Les fidèles taoïstes faisaient régulièrement des offrandes aux dieux stellaires et adressaient leurs supplications pour la délivrance ou la divination à des esprits astro-calendaires[23]. En plus des procédés astrologiques traditionnels, les prières de Du Guangting font état de nouveautés de l'astrologie gréco-indienne importées par les Sogdiens via l'Asie centrale, et des prescriptions tantriques du sous-continent indien qui atteignaient la Chine dans les traductions des moines itinérants. Un sous-groupe était formé par les Offrandes de destinée personnelle et les rites apotropaïques pour prévenir les conjonctions néfastes affectant le « palais personnel » 身宮 d'un individu, et les Offrandes aux dieux du destin lors de l'anniversaire du jour de la naissance. Des commanditaires de tout rang social étaient susceptibles de parrainer des rituels de destinée personnelle. Compte tenu du statut quasi officiel des Oraisons vertes, les figures publiques prédominaient.

Le cas du fondateur du royaume de Shu offre une bonne illustration de la logique des rituels de destinée personnelle. Wang Jian était né en 847, une année *dingmao* 丁卯. Ces caractères cycliques représentaient ainsi sa Destinée originelle 元命. À la fin d'un cycle de soixante années, l'année *dingmao* suivante intervint en 907, l'année de la fin des Tang et de la fondation du royaume indépendant à Shu. La destinée *dingmao* de Wang pouvait s'interpréter comme la preuve astrologique que le destin le désignait comme souverain de Shu. Dans l'ordre spatial, le binôme *dingmao* correspondait à Gegui 葛璝, associant ainsi la destinée de Wang à ce diocèse, conformément à la tradition d'affiliation diocésaine des adeptes des Maîtres célestes[24].

En 907, Wang Jian ordonna la restauration du sanctuaire de Gegui, et des rituels de destinée personnelle y furent exécutés en son nom[25]. Ces rituels, cependant, n'avaient pas tous valeur de célébration : au printemps de 907, l'astronome de cour rapporta une conjonction de mauvais augure pour la région terrestre de Shu, juste au moment où Wang Jian y lançait son entreprise fondatrice. Des rituels furent frénétiquement commandités pour éviter un désastre imminent, comme nous le verrons.

Les fêtes taoïstes annuelles étaient l'occasion de rituels de confession et d'expiation. Les Trois primordiaux marquaient les jours d'inspection des Trois officiers. Les Retraites des Trois primordiaux, que Lu Xiujing avait instituées ces jours-là, servaient de plus en plus de rites mortuaires. Le censeur en chef Feng Juan 馮涓, un conseiller militaire et diplomatique de Wang Jian, tint un cycle complet de Retraites des Trois primordiaux pour le salut de sa défunte mère, Madame Li, grande dame de la commanderie de Longxi 隴西郡太夫人李氏[26]. La prière présentée le jour du Primordial supérieur (quinzième du premier mois) indique l'anniversaire de sa mort comme étant le vingt-sixième jour du premier mois lunaire[27]. Les Retraites et Offrandes célébrées les jours des Trois originels à l'intention de mères défuntes, de membres de la famille décédés et des ancêtres soulignent l'affinité de cette pratique taoïste avec le rituel *ullambana* bouddhique, le Primordial médian coïncidant avec la Fête pour le soulagement des âmes des défunts. Les fêtes des Trois assemblées marquaient aussi l'observance des jours d'inspection et de commémoration des assemblées de la congrégation du Maître céleste avec confessions, offrandes et enregistrement des maisonnées. D'après Lu Xiujing, les Huit périodes 八節 étaient des fêtes calendaires où l'on demandait pardon pour les péchés des ancêtres et pour ceux commis par soi-même dans cette vie et les précédentes[28]. Du Guangting explique que lesdits jours étaient propices pour pronostiquer la bonne et la mauvaise fortune et prédire les rétributions bienfaisantes et punitives. En une occasion, il fait une Offrande pour obtenir le pardon de ses péchés et le salut de ses ancêtres[29]. D'autres dates cycliques, comme *liujia* 六甲, *jiazi* 甲子 ou *gengshen* 庚申, signalaient d'autres conjonctions lors desquelles se tenaient des inspections et s'appliquaient des interdits de tabou spéciaux sous le regard des dieux vigilants[30].

Les Offrandes aux dieux stellaires pour résoudre des questions en litige d'ordre astrologique rivalisent en importance avec les rituels calendaires. Les Oraisons vertes de Du laissent transparaître toute son expertise astrologique telle qu'il l'exerce comme érudit de cour au service du pouvoir, ou pour le compte de commanditaires privés[31]. La constellation taoïste essentielle du destin était le Boisseau du Nord, le groupe d'étoiles le plus distinctif près du pôle céleste ou Faîte du Nord 北極. Cette constellation revêtait une importance particulière pour les taoïstes. La divinité du Grand un résidait au centre du Palais de la Ténuité pourpre 紫微宮 circumpolaire (voir planche 7), siège du Tao et lieu de retour ultime dans les exercices de méditation et l'alchimie physiologique[32].

Les découvertes archéologiques montrent que le Boisseau du Nord jouait un rôle primordial dans les pratiques funéraires chinoises depuis les temps néolithiques[33]. La rotation du Boisseau autour du Faîte du Nord, pivot cosmique, mesurait les heures et les saisons. En tant que gardien du temps et régulateur, le Boisseau du Nord était le siège céleste de l'administration de la destinée. En plus des sept étoiles d'Ursa major, l'astérisme de Neuf étoiles 九星 comprenait deux « ministres » invisibles appelés Étoile assistante 輔星 et Étoile subordonnée 弼星. Le Registre de mort était conservé au Boisseau du Nord, tandis que le Boisseau du Sud 南斗, une mansion, détenait le Registre des naissances[34]. Les Oraisons vertes pour racheter la destinée s'adressaient diversement au Boisseau du Nord et/ou au Boisseau du Sud, et pouvaient en outre se combiner avec des Offrandes à la destinée personnelle ou aux esprits de la date de naissance. En 913, Wang Jian célébra en action de grâce une telle Offrande au Boisseau du Sud parce que les éclipses lunaires et solaires attendues lui avaient été épargnées. Une éclipse solaire présageait l'ascension d'un sujet qui ferait de l'ombre au souverain[35]. À cette occasion, la cour poussa un soupir de soulagement collectif quand les phases de la nouvelle et de la pleine lune, conjonctions durant lesquelles les éclipses solaires et lunaires sont susceptibles de se produire, furent toutes deux passées[36] :

> Selon les livres de l'*Origine céleste* 天元[37], du Shangqing et d'autres [écoles], quand le cinquième jour du cinquième mois lunaire tombe un jour *bingwu* 丙午, cela présage des bénédictions qui portent secours aux êtres

> vivants et procurent des bienfaits à toutes les créatures, apportent l'harmonie aux diverses espèces et la paix à la nation. Cela diffuse largement les faveurs que procure la vertu du yang[38]. Cette année, les quatre planètes Mars, Mercure, Vénus et Saturne se sont rassemblées dans [la station de Jupiter] Shi Chen 實沈之墟 [correspondant à la région terrestre de Shu[39]]. En outre, ceci s'est produit alors que les degrés de progression du soleil tombaient dans la saison la plus chaude. Le jour de la nouvelle lune du cinquième mois 合朔 (7 juin 913), une éclipse solaire était attendue, mais elle ne se produisit pas[40]. Le jour suivant la pleine lune 既望 (22 juin 913), une éclipse lunaire était attendue, mais elle ne se produisit pas. Or, le cinquième jour [du cinquième mois] est effectivement tombé un jour *bingwu* (11 juin 913)[41].

Le répertoire de l'astrologie horoscopique incluait également des Offrandes aux Cinq planètes 五星 et aux Neuf palais. Le vice-directeur Cui Yin 崔隱, qui souffrait de maladie chronique, observa que des phénomènes astrologiques mystérieux avaient pénétré le palais de sa destinée et mettaient ses cycles majeur et mineur de destin en « collision » 大運與小運衝破. Il s'agissait des cycles de Destinée personnelle de dix années d'une part, et d'une année de l'autre[42]. Cui présenta une Offrande de contrition et de repentance aux Neuf palais pour recouvrer la santé, prolonger ses jours et obtenir l'absolution[43]. Le dispositif des Neuf palais, un carré magique ancien divisé en neuf champs, servait à cartographier la position et la dynamique des corps célestes « volant » à travers les Palais 飛宮, et à suivre leurs trajectoires dextrogyres ou lévogyres[44]. De la même façon, le Filet du ciel et la Nasse de la terre constituaient des grilles servant à localiser les « emmêlements » dans les configurations astrologiques défavorables. En 896-897, quand la cour impériale dut abandonner la capitale pour la seconde fois et alors que Wang Jian menait sa guerre de conquête à Shu, Du composa une Oraison verte pour une Offrande au Filet du ciel et à la Nasse de la terre, commanditée par Wang, pour obtenir sa relaxe d'une conjoncture présageant un désastre[45].

Parmi les Oraisons vertes adressées aux divinités stellaires, les prières pour les Offrandes aux Neuf luminaires 九曜醮 constituent une catégorie à part entière. Les Neuf luminaires formaient une entité astrologique distincte des Neuf étoiles du Boisseau du Nord, comprenant les Cinq planètes, le soleil et la lune, plus deux autres planètes invisibles, Rāhu 羅睺 et Ketu 計都 (voir planche 8)[46]. Coupant les orbites imaginaires du soleil et de la lune dans la sphère céleste, ces planètes de l'ombre étaient tenues pour responsables des éclipses solaires et lunaires. L'oraison présentant un rituel de guérison pour la vue de Li Wan 李綰 (voir « Trois prières » ci-dessous) était de ce type. Héritée de l'Inde védique, avec des ajouts helléniques et iraniens, l'astrologie des Neuf luminaires fut popularisée en Chine au IXe siècle par un manuel de bouddhisme tantrique incorporant des éléments du culte taoïste du Boisseau du Nord, et faussement attribué à l'éminent astronome et traducteur Yixing 一行 (683-727)[47]. Dunhuang, le principal carrefour de tels échanges, a préservé de nombreuses traces de la popularité de la technique des Neuf luminaires, sous forme de traités manuscrits, d'images, d'horoscopes et d'amulettes.

L'un de ces manuscrits explique la méthode horoscopique fondée sur le culte des Neuf luminaires[48]. Il s'agit de la méthode de Progression annuelle des Neuf luminaires 九曜行年 pour déterminer les influences nocives. La Progression annuelle représentait la destinée d'un individu dans une année donnée, en fonction de son âge horoscopique (voir le début du chapitre 2). Selon la Progression annuelle des Neuf luminaires, la destinée d'une personne avançait par cycles de neuf ans, à l'intérieur desquels chaque année était gouvernée par l'un des Neuf luminaires successivement. Sur la base de ce système, le manuscrit regroupe ses pronostics sous neuf rubriques, chacune corrélant la Progression annuelle d'une personne dans une année donnée avec l'un des luminaires[49].

Du Guangting était non seulement réceptif à ces nouveaux apports, il était lui-même à l'avant-garde de l'innovation. Bien que Du prétendît que son Offrande au firmament se fondait sur l'ancienne liturgie du Lingbao, on ne trouve aucune trace de quelque antécédent que ce soit de ce rituel, ni de l'Offrande à tous les cieux qui lui est apparentée, avant les *Œuvres de Guangcheng*[50]. Ces dernières incluent huit prières dans la première catégorie, et six dans la seconde. Les Offrandes étaient présentées, respectivement, aux constellations de l'horizon céleste (Offrande au firmament) et à toutes les étoiles dans les cieux étagés au-dessus de la sphère céleste, lesquels étaient également appelés « l'univers » 普天 (Offrande à tous les cieux)[51]. Les deux types d'Offrande, originellement sans claire différentiation, étaient pour le bénéfice du règne[52]. Dans les *Œuvres de Guangcheng*, les Offrandes au firmament comprennent une série de rituels au nom de l'empereur Xizong en exil et pour le souverain de Shu en pleine ascension, Wang Jian, afin de dissiper les effets de conjonctions astronomiques défavorables sur le plan politique[53].

Dans une prière commandée par l'officiel du Trésor Li Yanfu 李延福 pour une « Offrande à tous les cieux au nom du prince de Shu » 爲蜀王修羅天醮, Du Guangting fait humblement informer les dieux par Wang Jian de sa conquête récemment réalisée en 907, la dix-septième année depuis sa première occupation de Chengdu en 891 :

> Dans le passé, votre serviteur fut favorisé de bénédictions sublimes et autorisé à hériter de la bonne fortune du Tao. De peu de mérite, il est indigne d'endosser le fardeau d'un homme d'État. À travers des milliers de *li* de montagnes et de rivières, il a guerroyé dans six commanderies militaires ; au cours de dix-sept années de pacification, il a établi sa domination sur le territoire[54].

Dans les *Œuvres de Guangcheng*, notre troisième et dernier groupe d'Oraisons vertes concerne l'au-delà. Selon l'ordre rituel de Lu Xiujing, les Retraites du registre jaune servaient à « éradiquer les péchés des ascendants défunts ». La codification amplifiée par Du Guangting dans la *Liturgie de la Retraite du registre jaune* 太上黃籙齋儀, achevée vers 901, transforma le rituel originel en un dessein programmatique général de délivrance à la fois des vivants et des morts[55]. Ainsi l'Oraison verte de Du pour une Retraite du registre jaune, conjointement parrainée par Liu Yin 劉殷 et Fei Shun 費順 de Xipu 犀浦 (dans le district de Pi 郫縣 à l'ouest de Chengdu), dédiait le rituel à la prospérité de l'État, à la longévité et au bien-être du peuple, au salut des ancêtres et à la fin de la guerre[56]. Wang Chengxiu 王承休 (mort en 926), qui devait devenir notoire comme eunuque dépravé jouissant de la faveur du second souverain de Shu, tint une Retraite du registre jaune afin de prier pour que sa mère, Madame Dou 竇, se rétablît d'un mal incurable que l'on attribuait à des doléances dans l'autre monde et à une conjonction astrologique défavorable[57]. Dans une version privée du même rituel, exécuté à sa résidence, la grande dame Zhang 張 pria pour les membres défunts de sa famille, afin de les délivrer des litiges d'outre-tombe et leur permettre de gagner l'autre rive[58]. Pour le vice-général Huang Qi 黃齊, endeuillé, Du Guangting écrivit :

> En l'espace d'un mois seulement, [Huang Qi] a perdu successivement deux fils. Vies gâchées en leur milieu, ce sont des ombres affligées et orphelines. Lugubre saison des sacrifices d'automne et d'hiver, crépuscule désolé de l'espoir abandonné ! De peur que leurs âmes captives ne soient toujours en détention 懼彼營魂，尙爲拘滯, nous croyons humblement que leur délivrance dépend entièrement d'actes de dévotion[59].

Le père des deux garçons, Huang Qi, était un taoïste laïc pieux et une connaissance familière de Du Guangting[60]. Le jour de toutes les âmes du Primordial médian, ils célébrèrent un rituel dédié à l'allumage de lampes votives. C'était l'ouverture d'une Retraite du registre jaune pour le repos des deux fils de Huang, réalisée pour illuminer le royaume sombre de la Longue nuit et pour rétablir la paix dans la famille. Du Guangting en rédigea l'Oraison verte :

> Votre serviteur a appris qu'un grand pardon intervient les jours des Trois originels, durant lesquels les cieux déversent leurs bénédictions. L'obscurité éternelle des Neuf nuits 九夜 est le royaume du double yin, au plus profond de la terre[61]. Pour dissiper ses ténèbres accumulées, nous empruntons les lampes spirituelles. En haut, elles reçoivent [la clarté] des Trois luminaires (soleil, lune et étoiles) ; en bas, elles illuminent les âmes égarées. Les écritures et les rituels donnent la primauté à la délivrance de ceux qui nous précèdent. En ce jour du Primordial médian nous entamons une [Retraite du] registre jaune, exécutant audiences et confessions dans et selon l'ordre prescrit, avec les trois offices quotidiens, pour l'absolution de myriades de fautes. Dûment pourvus d'encens et d'huile [pour les lampes], nous présentons nos offrandes. Nous désirons humblement que la brillance ardente de l'oiseau *luan* 鸞 et la splendeur flamboyante du phœnix diffusent leurs rayons jusqu'au Bureau de la terre, et que la lumière stellaire et l'éclat des [flambeaux de] lotus dispersent les ombres du monde souterrain[62]. Élevez-vous entièrement au-dessus des chemins de l'amertume 苦趣 et quittez à jamais le gué lugubre 冥津 ! Que les neuf générations d'ancêtres renaissent au Ciel, que de grandes bénédictions soient accordées aux six parentèles, que les désastres soient dissipés sans présages, et que la bonté

se répande sans limite. Nous demandons respectueusement la paix pour cette famille et attendons de recevoir de grandes bénédictions[63].

À la différence de la Retraite du registre jaune dont les intentions pouvaient être plurielles, la Retraite de l'alliance avec les Véritables était exclusivement dédiée au salut des ascendants, frères et sœurs, conjoints et enfants défunts[64]. Selon les propres termes de Lu Xiujing, ce rituel « sauve des Neuf ténèbres les âmes de myriades de générations d'ancêtres ». Du Guangting compléta la liturgie ordinaire de ce rituel par des services dédiés au salut d'un souverain décédé commissionnés par des membres de la famille impériale[65]. La prière de son Oraison verte pour un rituel commandité par Wang Chengyan 王承鄢 explique que la Liturgie de l'alliance avec les Véritables du coffret de jade 明真玉匱之科 avait la capacité d'arracher les défunts aux portes des ténèbres, leur permettant de trouver l'expiation et leur procurant la relaxe. L'intention de cette prière était de rechercher l'absolution des péchés du père défunt de Wang, qui avait été un taoïste dévot, afin d'obtenir sa délivrance, l'ascension de neuf générations d'ancêtres et la protection des parents proches et éloignés[66]. La première des trois prières examinées de plus près ci-dessous est une Oraison verte de ce type pour une Retraite de l'alliance avec les Véritables commanditée par un homme d'État de Shu.

Trois prières

Les traductions suivantes visent à transmettre la saveur de la langue des Oraisons vertes de Du Guangting et à reconstituer les contextes historiques et personnels des prières sur la base des informations qui peuvent être glanées dans d'autres sources quant à leurs circonstances, commanditaires et bénéficiaires. Les trois oraisons sélectionnées sont associées, respectivement, à une liturgie pour le salut de parents défunts, à un rite d'action de grâce pour la protection d'un époux et d'un fils lors d'une campagne militaire, et à un rituel de guérison.

DU GRAND CONSEILLER ZHANG POUR LE REPOS DES ÂMES DE SES PARENTS

L'« Oraison pour une Retraite de l'alliance avec les Véritables pour le salut des défunts, célébrée par le grand conseiller Zhang du ministère des finances » met en évidence le patronage d'élite des Oraisons vertes[67]. Bien que, par déférence envers le rang du commanditaire et des bénéficiaires, le texte évite tout nom personnel, des indices circonstanciels permettent d'identifier le grand conseiller Zhang 張, sans aucun doute, comme étant Zhang Ge 張格 (mort en 926), un ministre d'État du royaume de Shu[68]. Du Guangting servit Zhang à la fois comme rédacteur d'Oraisons vertes et comme conseiller en matière de documents officiels[69]. Zhang a laissé suffisamment de traces dans l'historiographie pour nous permettre de reconstituer avec précision les circonstances personnelles ayant conduit au rituel. Il se trouve que les événements qui suscitèrent la prière étaient liés de façon poignante au drame de la chute de la dynastie des Tang en cours. Le père de Zhang Ge était Zhang Jun 張濬, homme d'État et acteur de premier plan sur la scène politique et militaire des dernières années des Tang. Bien que Zhang Jun eût prudemment renoncé à ses fonctions, son prestige suscitait encore la jalousie et fit naître le soupçon dans l'esprit de l'usurpateur Zhu Wen 朱溫 (852-912), futur empereur Taizu des Liang 梁太祖. Sa défiance conduisit Zhu à ordonner l'assassinat de Zhang Jun. L'acte fut commis la dernière nuit de la troisième année de l'ère Tianfu 天復 (20 janvier 904), dans le domaine rural du Henan où Zhang s'était retiré. Quand un officier loyal nommé Ye Yan 葉彥 avertit la famille de l'approche des tueurs, Zhang Jun enjoignit à son fils de s'échapper et d'assurer la continuité de la lignée. Après avoir, en pleurs, dit adieu à ses parents, Zhang Ge fut escorté en lieu sûr par Ye. Il changea de nom et se rendit à Shu, où Wang Jian le nomma ministre. En 925, quand le royaume de Shu antérieur tomba aux mains des Tang postérieurs, Zhang Ge fut capturé et emmené à Luoyang. Se remémorant la bonté de Ye Yan, Ge rechercha la famille Ye. Yan était déjà décédé, mais l'ancien grand conseiller récompensa généreusement les membres survivants de sa famille[70].

Quant à la mère de Ge, après le meurtre de Zhang Jun, elle se dissimula parmi le peuple. Elle se rasa la tête et se fit nonne, errant entre les capitales Chang'an et Luoyang. Quand Wang Jian l'apprit, il la fit appeler en secret et l'accueillit à Shu, l'honorant du titre religieux de « Grande maîtresse à la bénédiction compatissante » 慈福大師. Après la mort de Wang Jian, la carrière de Zhang Ge connut un coup d'arrêt. Au cours de la lutte pour la succession, il fut critiqué et rétrogradé dans un poste éloigné. Au même moment, une réprimande, considérée par les loyalistes comme ayant été inventée de toutes pièces, accusa Zhang d'avoir fait preuve de négligence dans sa loyauté en se dérobant au destin funeste de son père, et dans sa dévotion filiale, en faisant le deuil de sa mère en privé[71]. L'accusation, portant sur les deux points de la loyauté et de la piété filiale, illustre parfaitement le dilemme moral auquel faisaient face de nombreux fils et acteurs politiques de cette époque, contraints de choisir leur camp et de tenter de survivre alors que s'effondrait l'empire des Tang. À moins de mourir loyalement au côté de son père, comme la réprimande le préconisait, la piété filiale exigeait de Zhang Ge, premièrement, qu'il vengeât la mort de son père, et deuxièmement, qu'il démissionnât de son poste durant la période consacrée au deuil de sa mère.

L'oraison verte fut probablement commanditée avant que Zhang Ge ne tombât en disgrâce en 918. C'est ce que suggère la déférence du ton – en outre, aucune des Oraisons vertes datables dans les *Œuvres de Guangcheng* n'est postérieure à 917. La prière accompagnait une Retraite de l'alliance avec les Véritables pour la délivrance des parents de Zhang du royaume des morts et leur transfert au paradis. Cette retraite fut exécutée vers la fin de l'année pour l'anniversaire de la mort des deux parents, à la cour de l'Empereur du Nord du diocèse du Siège de jade. Le texte est traduit ci-dessous *in extenso* afin de faire ressortir la structure des prières des Oraisons vertes : une déclaration introductive, qui commence par les mots « Votre serviteur a appris », rappelle en prose parallèle solennelle l'origine et la dissémination de la doctrine taoïste et le bienfait salvateur du rituel. Le paragraphe commençant par « Le vingt-cinquième jour de ce mois » inaugure la partie principale du texte, exposant les circonstances du rituel et son intention. La phrase de conclusion, « Le cœur fervent et révérencieux, nous revalons leur faveur aux vrais dieux », commente, un peu comme un chœur grec, la démarche rituelle accomplie :

Votre serviteur a appris que le Très Haut initia la révélation et que le Souverain primordial répandit la doctrine. Les Trois registres[72] fixèrent le corpus du Jinming[73], dont le mérite s'étend à l'Homme et au Ciel. Les Neuf ténèbres révélèrent la Liturgie du coffret de jade, dont les bénéfices englobent les vivants et les morts[74]. Respectueusement, nous demandons des instructions aux écritures, et nous observons avec obéissance les écrits mystérieux. Révérencieusement, nous prions pour la miséricorde de la délivrance ; avec zèle, nous affichons le sérieux de notre repentance.
Le vingt-cinquième jour de ce mois fut l'anniversaire de la mort de la défunte mère [du grand conseiller Zhang] Madame Liu 劉, dame de Chu 楚國 sous les Tang, citée grande dame de Song 宋國 à titre posthume, sous les Shu. Le trentième jour de ce mois est l'anniversaire de la mort de son défunt père, grand conseiller et grand précepteur de l'héritier présomptif sous les Tang. Il se retira de ses fonctions et fut nommé à titre posthume Grand défenseur, sous les Shu[75]. Respectueusement, nous présentons des offrandes d'huile, de chandelles, d'encens, de fleurs et de nourriture à la cour de l'Empereur du Nord du diocèse du Siège de jade dans la préfecture de Chengdu, et révérencieusement, nous accomplissons une cérémonie du Lingbao de l'Alliance avec les Véritables d'un jour et d'une nuit. Quatorze maîtres taoïstes exécutent le rituel d'audience trois fois par jour et récitent les écritures. Faisant face aux corps célestes, nos cœurs à nu, nous dépêchons les dragons d'encens pour remettre notre rapport en haut. Alors que nous gisons prosternés, les Hauts vénérables nous considèrent avec pitié, tandis que la pléiade des sages déverse sa radiance. [Les vénérables] font une large proclamation aux Quatre bureaux et verrouillent la porte des Trois mondes[76]. Ils envoient le commandement du Talisman des neuf dragons qui ouvre la cour glaciale de la longue nuit, purifie par le feu et le bain les corps et les âmes, délivre les esprits et les relève. Ces derniers, quittant la résidence du fond des ténèbres, entrent au palais de l'apogée du soleil[77]. Leurs péchés sont effacés et les doléances dissipées. Leurs noms sont supprimés du registre des défunts et enregistrés selon les échelons du Tao. La roue [de la transmigration] tourne vers une contrée de bénédiction, où ils peuvent se lever et rejoindre les rangs des transcendants[78]. Les neuf mystères accomplis et l'insondable connaissance atteinte, tous gagnent le salut.
Le cœur fervent et révérencieux, nous revalons leur faveur aux vrais dieux.

L'abandon par Zhang Ge de son père et la fin tragique de ce dernier, la séparation précipitée d'avec ses deux parents, le conflit de loyauté entre ses responsabilités publiques et les obligations filiales durant le deuil de sa mère suggèrent toute une souffrance morale. Que la réprimande contre le grand conseiller Zhang fût fabriquée ou pas, ou de date postérieure, le sentiment de culpabilité d'avoir failli à ses parents devait habiter l'esprit de Zhang lorsqu'il commémora leur mort et pria pour leur délivrance.

Dame Yue rédime un vœu

La dame de la principauté de Yue 越國 (859-922), née Zhang 張, était l'épouse principale de Wang Zongkan 王宗侃 (858-923), un fils adoptif de Wang Jian. Le nom de famille originel de Zongkan était Tian 田[79]. Du Guangting se réfère à dame Yue par son titre ou, lorsqu'il parle à sa place en tant que commanditaire de la prière, par « votre servante » 妾. Il s'agissait là d'un terme de modestie que les femmes mariées employaient pour se référer à elles-mêmes. Le fils cadet du couple, Wang Chengzhao 王承肇, était, comme son père, connu pour ses capacités militaires.

L'« Oraison votive d'action de grâce de dame Yue pour le compte du commandant de la campagne Zongkan » peut être datée de l'an 912[80]. Les événements auxquels la prière se réfère comme s'étant déroulés « l'année précédente » eurent lieu entre le troisième et le douzième mois lunaire de 911. L'adversaire non nommé de Wang Zongkan était Li Maozhen 李茂貞 (856-924), gouverneur militaire et seigneur de guerre redoutable durant les dernières années de la dynastie des Tang. En tant que prince de Qi 岐, Li occupait la principauté située dans la région de Hanzhong, entre le Sichuan et la capitale, berceau de l'ancienne communauté du Maître céleste et zone frontière stratégique pour Wang Jian durant la guerre menée en vue de consolider les frontières du royaume de Shu. En 904, Wang accorda sa fille en mariage au neveu de Li Maozhen, dans le but de cimenter une alliance délicate avec un voisin intraitable. Après que les Liang postérieurs 後梁 (907-923) eurent succédé à la dynastie des Tang dans le territoire de la capitale, Li Maozhen déclara l'indépendance de Qi en 908. En 909, les relations entre Qi et Shu se dégradèrent. En 910, Wang Jian rappela sa fille à Shu[81], et au printemps de 911, on rapporta que Qi massait des troupes près de la frontière de Shu. Le chef du secrétariat Wang Zongkan, conseiller de confiance de Wang Jian et par ailleurs général chevronné, se porta volontaire pour prendre la tête d'un corps expéditionnaire de cent vingt mille hommes contre Qi. Nommé commandant de l'armée en campagne du Territoire du Nord 北路行營都統, Zongkan emprunta la route pour Xingzhou 興州, qui était ornée de bannières et de drapeaux, le 9 avril 911[82]. Xingzhou se trouvait à plus de cinq cents kilomètres au nord-est de Chengdu, dans le district moderne de Lüeyang 略陽 au-delà de la limite actuelle du Shaanxi.

Le 19 septembre 911, Wang Zongkan subit une sévère défaite au Col de la glaise noire 青泥嶺, à Lüeyang. Des pluies torrentielles firent déborder la rivière Han 漢江, forçant Zongkan à battre en retraite vers le district voisin de Baoxi 保西[83]. Encerclé par l'ennemi, le reste de ses troupes fut au bout du compte sauvé par une armée de secours commandée par Wang Jian en personne. Les forces conjuguées de Shu eurent raison des Qi à la bataille du Méandre des perles 明珠曲 de la Rivière du cheval blanc 白馬河, un affluent nord de la Han, à l'ouest du district de Mian 勉. Après être passées par Xingyuan 興元 (Hanzhong), les troupes victorieuses revinrent à Chengdu, qu'elles atteignirent le 30 décembre 911, après huit mois et trois semaines d'une campagne ardue[84]. L'Oraison verte composée par Du Guangting contient l'extrait suivant :

> L'année dernière, Wang Zongkan, l'époux de votre servante, leur fils Chengzhao et d'autres ont mené une campagne militaire pour réprimer l'insurrection, servir l'État et se mettre au service du souverain. Alors qu'ils étaient sur le point de prendre la ville reculée [de Xingzhou], ils furent submergés par les eaux en crue des mois durant. Inquiétée par la fumée des feux d'alarme, [dame Yue] était sans nouvelles. Portant son regard vers Bao[85] et la Mian[86], elle s'y envola en esprit. Elle scruta les montagnes et les rivières, mais sa vision était barrée. Sa prémonition anxieuse refoulée, elle ne savait où adresser ses supplications. Alors elle se rendit révérencieusement au temple du Tao et implora qu'on soumît une requête en son nom. Une assemblée rituelle fut solennellement ordonnancée, requérant en réponse le déploiement des soldats célestes et l'apport de la protection des esprits véritables. Soudain, le robuste rempart s'ouvrit et [les forces de Shu] écrasèrent l'ennemi féroce. En parachevant la débâcle, ils gagnèrent

la récompense du souverain. Les armées s'en revinrent triomphales et les familles furent réunies.
Assurément si la conquête procède d'une stratégie judicieuse, la protection vient du mérite de la pratique religieuse. Observant les jours fastes, [dame Yue] revaut la bonne fortune que lui a accordée le ciel. Ayant présenté à plusieurs reprises des rituels de Requête et d'Offrande[87], nous offrons cérémonieusement ce rite d'action de grâce. D'un cœur scrupuleux, nous présentons des gages ; nous mettant à genoux, nous brûlons de l'encens.

Le retour triomphal de Wang Jian à la tête de l'armée fut l'occasion de son élévation à la dignité d'« Empereur splendidement martial profondément sagace et radieusement filial du Grand Shu » 大蜀英武睿聖光孝皇帝[88]. Rendant grâce pour ces événements et priant pour l'empereur et le royaume, Du Guangting rédigea une autre Oraison verte, celle-là pour accompagner une « Offrande au Grand un par la communauté taoïste au nom de l'empereur, avec allumage des lampes du registre d'or »[89]. Une troisième prière, commanditée par le prince héritier Yuanying 元膺 pour la même occasion, porte la date du 14 juin 912[90].

Du Guangting conclut la prière de dame Yue par la leçon « Assurément si la conquête procède… », associée à une déclaration de sincérité. Les prêtres et les poètes chinois pouvaient prendre des voix d'emprunt avec des effets singuliers. Nous avons déjà relevé le langage imagé décrivant la souffrance morale de l'épouse ainsi que la promesse cathartique de délivrance par le rituel. Le vécu féminin de la guerre et la réponse religieuse à l'anxiété du requérant sont ici finement observés : réduite par l'absence de nouvelles à imaginer par procuration les périls du combat en de lointaines et sauvages contrées, dame Yue est paralysée par des peurs indicibles. Ce n'est que lorsqu'elle dirige ses pas vers le temple taoïste et place sa confiance dans le rituel, la prière et les offrandes, pour qu'ils agissent sur les ressorts cachés de la destinée de son époux et son fils, que ses supplications parviennent à leur fin et la délivre de la souffrance[91].

De Li Wan pour la vue

Li Wan figurait lui aussi au nombre des hauts dignitaires militaires, sous le règne de Wang Jian. Au cours de la campagne de 911 contre Qi, il servit comme commandant en chef de l'infanterie dans l'armée en campagne du Territoire du Nord sous le haut commandement de Zongkan[92]. À cette époque, Li Wan était connu sous le nom de Wang Zongwan 王宗綰. Le changement de nom avait eu lieu en 894 après que Li, un officiel des Tang avec trente années de service à son actif, avait capitulé face à Wang Jian avec d'autres officiers pris au piège à Pengzhou 彭州, assiégée pendant deux années. La chute de cette importante ville préfectorale, située à trente-six kilomètres au nord-ouest de Chengdu, acheva la conquête de la province de Xichuan par Wang Jian[93]. Wang Jian adopta Li Wan, lui donnant pour nom Wang Zongwan[94]. Nommé successivement gouverneur de plusieurs régions frontalières importantes, Zongwan servit comme administrateur de Shuzhou 蜀州 dans le nord-ouest du Sichuan (l'actuel Maoxian 茂縣) à partir de 896, comme gouverneur de la région militaire de Wuding 武定軍 dans l'est du Sichuan à partir de 897, ainsi qu'à d'autres postes dans le Nord et le Nord-Ouest[95].

À l'heure de la mort de l'empereur Zhaozong 昭宗, avant-dernier occupant du trône des Tang assassiné par Zhu Wen à l'automne 904, Zongwan était gouverneur militaire de Xingyuan, à mi-chemin entre Chengdu et Chang'an. À ce moment critique, Zongwan servit d'intermédiaire diplomatique entre Wang Jian et la cour, transmettant à Chengdu la proclamation de la mort de l'empereur et rapportant la réponse qui cherchait à établir la neutralité de Shu à l'égard du souverain des Liang postérieurs alors en pleine ascension[96]. Après la campagne de 911 contre Qi, Zongwan conduisit en 915 une incursion profonde à l'intérieur du Gansu comme commissaire militaire de l'armée du Territoire du Nord. En 916, il mena une nouvelle campagne contre Qi, cette fois-ci en tant que commissaire en chef de la région Nord-Est. Surgissant par la passe de Dasan 大散 dans le Shaanxi, Zongwan infligea une lourde défaite à l'armée de Qi, qui entraîna l'occupation de Baoji 寶雞 et le siège de Fengxiang 鳳翔 au dixième mois. On rapporte que, terrifiés par Wang Zongwan, le peuple de Fengxiang et l'armée de Qi refusèrent alors de quitter la ville pour aller le combattre. Il fallut d'abondantes chutes de neige pour que les soldats de Shu fussent rappelés à Chengdu[97]. En 918, après la mort de Wang Jian, un édit posthume conféra à Zongwan le titre de Gardien de l'État et le second souverain de Shu le fit prince de Lintao 臨洮. Confident intime des deux souverains, Zongwan s'attira les éloges de ses contemporains pour sa générosité, sa prévenance et sa modestie, nonobstant ses mérites et son rang élevé à la cour[98].

Cependant, l'histoire officielle ne releva pas que Wang Zongwan/ Li Wan remporta ces succès alors qu'il était en proie à une maladie chronique lui provoquant douleurs et détresse intenses. Une affection oculaire le fit commanditer à maintes reprises des rituels taoïstes de délivrance. C'est à cette occasion que la prière ci-dessous fut présentée par Du Guangting pour le compte de Li Wan. Ce dernier était un taoïste laïc ayant reçu l'ordination. Du et Li se connaissaient probablement depuis qu'ils avaient tous deux servi à la cour des Tang. En ses jeunes années, Li Wan avait été gouverneur civil de Zhedong 浙東, la région native de Du dans la province du Zhejiang. Du note que c'est au cours de l'ère Xiantong 咸通 (860-874) que Li reçut son ordination du révérend maître Ye Zangzhi, alors abbé du temple du Palais de Yuxiao au mont Tiantai (voir également « Les talismans » au chapitre 11)[99]. Le titre de la prière, « Oraison pour une Offrande aux Neuf luminaires commanditée par le censeur Li Wan », suggère que le rituel eut lieu avant que Li changeât de nom en 894[100]. Voici comment y est décrite la maladie de Li Wan :

> Année après année, [Li Wan] souffre d'une affection oculaire. Même le recours à l'acupuncture et l'augmentation de prises médicamenteuses assidues ont failli à le rétablir, accroissant d'autant son inquiétude. Il craint que le cycle du yin et du yang ne soit la cause de l'occurrence de cette calamité grave, et que la progression des mansions et des luminaires ne produise sa détresse. Il a présenté des prières et des offrandes dans l'espoir d'obtenir le soulagement. Aujourd'hui, la trajectoire d'une éclipse lunaire dans le palais de sa destinée personnelle est la présente [cause du] mal persistant. À ce stade critique, il ne sait vers où adresser ses requêtes ; flanchant, il se retrouve démuni. Il a appris que la véritable liturgie fournit une tradition textuelle ainsi qu'un protocole d'offrandes et de libations. Le cœur ferme et avec une sincérité entière, il implore l'inspection divine, exécute scrupuleusement les offrandes et les rites, et invite les vénérables esprits à descendre. Gisant prosterné devant les dieux imposants des Neuf luminaires, il baigne dans leur éclat et recueille leur illumination. Puissent ses fautes passées être absoutes et puisse-t-il être relaxé de sa culpabilité. Que ce mal calamiteux soit anéanti et qu'il soit soulagé de ses misères. Faites que l'Adolescent pourpre [de l'Est] le garde, que son Palais oculaire

soit débarrassé des douleurs lancinantes et de l'irritation[101]. Puisse l'Empereur vert [de l'Est] le protéger et le soutenir, et son foie marquer des signes de rémission. Puisse cette déchéance morbide céder pour de bon, sa bonne fortune reprendre le dessus et sa durée de vie se régénérer.

La médecine conventionnelle avait fait défaut et on considérait que la cause profonde du mal de Li Wan était d'ordre astrologique et moral. Dans cette prière, le siège de l'organe malade est identifié comme le « Palais oculaire » 眼宮. Selon le *Livre du centre du Seigneur Lao*, la tête héberge trois paires de cavités dans trois palais distincts, dont l'un, également appelé le « Palais écarlate », abrite les yeux[102]. Il est intéressant de noter que Li prie aussi pour la santé de son foie. Les médecins chinois connaissaient depuis l'Antiquité la relation entre le foie et les maladies oculaires : le *Classique intérieur de l'Empereur jaune* dit que « le foie gouverne les yeux » 肝主目[103]. Yin-yang et les Cinq agents gouvernaient le flux de *qi* par lequel le foie s'ouvrait aux yeux. Dans la configuration des Cinq viscères, le foie était corrélé avec la couleur verte et avec l'Est, d'où l'invocation de l'Adolescent pourpre et de l'Empereur vert, tous deux orientaux.

Confronté à une affection incurable d'origine obscure, Li se trouvait dans un état mental voisin de l'anxiété de dame Yue et du remords affligé de Zhang Ge. Comme eux, il ressentait ce sentiment d'impasse, cette impression d'être pris au piège, un ébranlement certain et, comme pour dame Yue, l'épreuve de l'horizon bouché et des implorations sans suite – du moins jusqu'à ce qu'il se souvînt du pouvoir du rituel. Ces trois suppliants firent appel à l'intercession salvatrice du rituel taoïste et eurent recours à ses célébrations « solennellement ordonnancées » comme ultime remède pour obtenir la délivrance et l'apaisement de leurs tourments.

Épilogue

Perspectives

Ce livre s'est attaché à retracer, sur une période de huit siècles, l'évolution des croyances taoïstes relatives à la dette et au rachat, et à relater les procédés dont disposaient les Chinois du Moyen Âge pour conjurer une destinée fâcheuse. La période médiévale chinoise s'ouvre avec l'établissement du taoïsme en tant qu'ordre liturgique communautaire, la propagation du bouddhisme à tous les niveaux de la société et l'interaction des deux religions entre elles, ainsi qu'avec les croyances et pratiques issues de l'Antiquité. Le système religieux qui naît de ces rencontres partage certains traits avec d'autres religions du monde, notamment celles des pays d'Asie qui ont embrassé le bouddhisme, mais il prend une configuration propre à la Chine médiévale. Ce système réforme et remplace le régime sacrificiel de la Chine ancienne et, à son tour, connaît une transformation marquante à l'aube de l'ère moderne. Si ce récit trouve un point de départ naturel avec l'émergence parallèle du taoïsme et du bouddhisme sous les Han Orientaux, le passage vers la modernité est plus difficile à situer. L'historien Naitō Konan 内藤湖南 (1866-1934) fut le premier à le placer entre le milieu du VIIIe et la fin du Xe siècle, durant la longue transition Tang-Song. La périodisation de Naitō se fonde sur des critères de transformations sociales, démographiques, économiques et culturelles. Suscitant un regain d'intérêt ces dernières années, elle est corroborée par des mutations concomitantes de la sphère religieuse et des rapports entre État et société[1].

Le chapitre 12 vient d'illustrer comment l'État Tang récupère et intègre des bénéfices croissants du rituel taoïste, y puisant protection divine et sanction liturgique, alors que les Oraisons vertes deviennent la prière de choix pour les élites nouvelles qui émergent à la fin des Tang. La rébellion de Huang Chao précipite le déclin des familles aristocratiques de la Chine médiévale et sonne le glas de l'ancienne capitale Chang'an, mettant un terme à des siècles de domination politique et culturelle de la métropole sur les provinces et rompant la dernière digue face à la montée des régimes régionaux[2]. Régionalisme et mutations sociales transforment les modèles traditionnels de patronage religieux à partir des Cinq dynasties. Une nouvelle structure de pouvoir polycentrique engendre des pratiques rituelles nouvelles, conduisant à l'absorption croissante des cultes locaux dans la religion canonique[3]. Le recours aux rituels taoïstes par les chefs régionaux rivaux pour asseoir la protection et la légitimation de leur pouvoir devient la pratique normative des premiers souverains de l'empire Song réunifié. Cette fonction liturgique essentielle du taoïsme de la fin des Tang est entérinée sous la dynastie Song, par le truchement des révélations attribuées à leur divinité tutélaire, Yisheng baode 翊聲保德, durant les années 960-994[4]. Ainsi s'accomplit le cycle des médiations taoïstes du mandat politique mis en branle par l'intervention du Seigneur Lao à la fin des Han.

La chute des Tang marque un tournant dans l'histoire des religions chinoises, décisif bien au-delà de leurs rapports avec le pouvoir de l'État. Le mouvement du taoïsme des Maîtres célestes, ou de l'Unité correcte, change de fond en comble, bien qu'il conserve son nom. Le modèle ancien des congrégations diocésaines se réorganise en de nouvelles formes de vie religieuse, reproduisant comme précédemment les structures du gouvernement local mais désormais réorganisées en « associations de temple » 會. Ces dernières, au lieu de constituer des enclaves d'élus parmi les profanes, font désormais partie intégrante du tissu associatif de la société locale. On peut faire remonter le début de ce changement au milieu de la période des Tang[5]. Un culte laïc à Zhang Daoling se répand à la suite de la canonisation du premier Maître céleste sous le règne de l'empereur Xuanzong. Le lieu de pèlerinage et de culte à Zhang Daoling établi sur la Montagne du dragon et du tigre, au Jiangxi, et situé le long de la route commerciale reliant la région du bas Yangzi à la Chine du Sud et du Sud-Est, se développe et devient le siège du nouveau lignage héréditaire de Maîtres célestes, qui monte en puissance dans la seconde moitié des Tang et porte le même patronyme Zhang que le fondateur originel[6]. L'organisation quasi ecclésiale des Zhang de la Montagne du dragon et du tigre évolue en une autorité centrale pour les ordinations taoïstes, fournissant des services liturgiques de plus en plus élaborés[7]. De nouveaux rituels apparaissent pour rappeler les âmes des morts des enfers, offrir guérison et protection, pratiquer des exorcismes et rechercher la délivrance de la sécheresse, des incendies et d'autres infortunes.

Mais le renouveau religieux de la transition Tang-Song ne s'achève pas avec la refonte du taoïsme de l'Unité correcte. Les liturgistes Song des XIIe et XIIIe siècles produisent de nouveaux compendiums de rituels Lingbao, amplifiant plus avant les codes médiévaux de Lu Xiujing, Zhang Wanfu et Du Guangting. À partir des Tang, l'école Chan 禪宗 du bouddhisme apporte une dimension authentiquement chinoise à la religion indienne qui gagne une large influence dans l'Asie orientale tout entière. La pénétration du tantrisme en Chine transforme peu à peu le rituel bouddhiste mais aussi le rituel taoïste. Un nouvel ordre taoïste nommé Véracité parfaite 全真, qui met l'accent sur la conversion radicale, l'ascétisme moral et l'alchimie intérieure, émerge comme le modèle communautaire dominant de la Chine du Nord au XIIe siècle. Véracité parfaite et Unité correcte continuent à former les deux piliers de l'édifice liturgique taoïste durant la période moderne. De la fin des Han aux Cinq dynasties, la vie spirituelle et intellectuelle de la Chine avait été dominée par le taoïsme et le bouddhisme. Le confucianisme, relégué à l'arrière-plan, fait un retour à partir de la fin des Tang. L'enseignement revivifié nommé Érudition du Tao 道學 ou néoconfucianisme, devient à partir du XIe siècle l'orthodoxie d'État et le reste pendant la majeure partie de la période impériale tardive. Le paysage religieux et spirituel en Chine au début de l'ère moderne s'est fondamentalement métamorphosé au contact de ces interactions ; les perceptions de la condition humaine et les aspirations à la transcendance aussi. La transition des Tang aux Song fournit ainsi un terme pertinent au cadre chronologique de ce livre.

Tout au long de la période examinée, les croyances relatives à la nature du mal, la souffrance et le salut se diffusent à une allure inégale à travers des sociétés hétérogènes occupant de vastes espaces, souvent fragmentés. Les données de l'archéologie suggèrent un développement multiforme découlant de sources variées et se propageant le long de filières diverses – un rappel pour les historiens de la difficulté de relier tous les points sur la carte religieuse de la Chine médiévale. Les résultats de cette étude rejoignent les observations faites par Peter Brown quant au rythme variable du changement et à l'absence d'un récit dominant au début de l'histoire du christianisme, celles de Stanley Tambiah concernant la divergence entre les représentations majoritaires et minoritaires, ou encore celles de Jacques Le Goff au sujet de la lente gestation des croyances dans les coulisses de l'histoire avant qu'elles ne se fondent dans le courant dominant[8]. Le lecteur aura perçu en l'espèce le déploiement inégal des principes sacrificiels dans la Chine médiévale, l'intériorisation concomitante de la quête taoïste de la délivrance, l'adoption graduelle de la moralité karmique par la société chinoise, le retrait puis le renouveau du confucianisme.

Dès l'avènement de l'ordre taoïste des Maîtres célestes, l'emploi de la désignation « Unité correcte » traduit le souci de lutter contre les divisions et les pratiques hétérodoxes. Le disciple des Maîtres célestes et le réformateur du Lingbao, Lu Xiujing, dénoncera pareillement l'hétérogénéité comme une abomination, au même titre que la promiscuité et le mélange des genres. Si, en dépit de sa diffusion inégale et disparate, nous pouvons retracer l'histoire de la quête taoïste de la délivrance avec quelque assurance, c'est largement grâce au témoignage des exécutants des rituels chinois, transmis au fil des siècles par une foule de récits, requêtes et tracts. Les voix des protagonistes d'alors nous parviennent distinctement. Les angoisses existentielles, confiées aux prières écrites, prononcées et archivées par les scribes sacerdotaux, expriment tant les peurs et aspirations des fidèles que les enseignements du clergé quant aux afflictions présentées, les causes et les remèdes, et les réparations à payer. À la fin de la période étudiée, le prêtre et érudit Du Guangting traduit en prières liturgiques et récits de dévotion les plaintes dont il est saisi. Dans les *Divines manifestations*, il diagnostique l'infortune, la maladie, l'anxiété et les désordres mentaux tels qu'ils sont vécus par les affligés, par leur entourage et par les guérisseurs religieux. Au seuil de la période moderne, la somme de témoignages rapportés par cet auteur représente l'apogée médiéval d'une longue tradition d'écrits taoïstes, depuis les ordonnances sépulcrales des Han orientaux, les premières confessions des Maîtres célestes, maints formulaires de requête tirés d'almanachs usagés, les sermons liturgiques de Lu Xiujing, jusqu'aux compendiums de rituels et aux narrations des Tang.

Ces traces écrites de la période médiévale dépeignent une humanité chargée dès la naissance de dettes et d'obligations, d'un fardeau qui ne pouvait que s'alourdir au contact du monde. La liste des dettes continuait à s'allonger du fait des offenses aux vivants et aux morts, et des infractions à la loi et aux préceptes. Un Monde de l'ombre était habité par les dieux, les esprits et les âmes sans repos. Ils étaient à la fois les arbitres de la destinée et du châtiment, les pourvoyeurs de maux, les pouvoirs offrant protection, les juges émettant les inculpations ou les acquittements qui apportaient détresse, maladie et mort, ou bonne fortune, bonheur et longévité.

L'intérêt pour le monde invisible n'est certainement pas l'apanage de la Chine médiévale ni des sociétés prémodernes. Le raisonnement scientifique s'accorde avec l'intuition religieuse sur le fait que la réalité se déploie largement hors de portée de la perception humaine directe ou en des lieux où l'observateur ne peut pas être présent. La conscience de l'imperceptible est une faculté cognitive humaine développée tôt dans la vie quand l'enfant saisit le fait que des pensées et des événements se produisent dans des espaces autres que celui qu'il occupe. Dans la prière « Dame Yue rédime un vœu », le protagoniste se projette en esprit vers le lieu inatteignable de la souffrance des membres de sa famille (voir « Trois prières » au chapitre 12). Voyage en songe et projection mentale faisaient partie du répertoire habituel des médiums et des adeptes de la méditation. La capacité humaine à visiter le monde invisible et à le conceptualiser par la métaphore ou l'abstraction produisait les types de témoignages dans lesquels puise cette étude.

Les métaphores utilisées pour concevoir et représenter l'univers mental du taoïsme médiéval ont conservé toute leur couleur et leur effectivité. La décharge déliant une destinée mal engagée était obtenue par une rémission rituelle de dette, et la première et dernière des dettes humaines était celle due pour le crédit de vie. Si cette dette était proprement remboursée par le sacrifice de soi, l'offrande du soi – sujette à interprétation, substitution et sublimation – pouvait prendre différentes formes, allant du gage ou du renoncement à l'action de grâce[9]. De manière analogue, le rachat et la délivrance étaient diversement représentés : guérison, purification, retour à la source, libération de servitude, soulagement du manque et de l'anxiété, passage de l'obscurité à la lumière.

Les prières appelées Oraisons vertes font état du fait que les suppliants souffrent d'angoisse, comme s'ils perdaient pied ou se voyaient pris dans une impasse. Une confession du mouvement des Maîtres célestes à ses débuts l'exprimait déjà ainsi : « Ployant sous les difficultés et perclus de frustration, il n'avait nul lieu vers où se tourner pour demander du secours » (voir « Le salaire du péché » au chapitre 2). Quand il ne restait nulle autre voie, la religion était le recours ultime pour agir sur une destinée fâcheuse. Dans un article peu connu publié il y a plus de trente ans, Michel Strickmann proposait de lire le rituel taoïste médiéval comme une thérapie contre les émanations néfastes du monde invisible et de concevoir le salut comme la guérison des maux de ce monde et de l'autre[10]. Le neuropsychiatre Boris Cyrulnik observe que la religion fournit une thérapie efficace pour apaiser l'angoisse mentale du type de celle qui résulte des appréhensions du mal. En conséquence de quoi, Cyrulnik situe l'effet thérapeutique de la religion principalement dans la sphère des perceptions[11]. Dans le contexte de la religion chinoise médiévale, l'*Almanach de requêtes de Maître Pin rouge* va dans ce sens, présentant des modèles de prières, par exemple, pour prévenir la survenue de présages et de pressentiments. L'objet déclaré de telles prières n'était pas de prévenir les désastres, mais d'apaiser l'anxiété résultant de leur appréhension (voir « Commanditaire et bénéficiaire » au chapitre 3). Avec les cauchemars et les divagations, les prémonitions angoissées étaient comprises comme des irruptions néfastes de l'au-delà, tels les procès intentés par les morts se sentant lésés : « Confus sont ses rêves et ses pensées, il est sujet à des hallucinations monstrueuses tandis que des présages diaboliques continuent à l'envahir » (cf. « Les puissances du mal » au chapitre 2).

Un appel à la protection divine pouvait atténuer le stress mental dû à de telles appréhensions et restaurer un sentiment de sécurité. Saint Ignace de Loyola (1491-1556), le fondateur de la Société de Jésus, écrivait : « Cette anxiété qui afflige l'âme ne plaît point à Dieu, car Il veut que nos limites et nos faiblesses prennent appui en Sa force et en Sa toute-puissance[12]. » En tant que protection contre l'insécurité et les écueils de l'existence humaine, la pratique taoïste cherchait à restaurer l'intégrité première du soi endommagé. Préconisant des exercices spirituels, Lu Xiujing enseignait que cultiver la pureté et la quiétude offrait une défense contre les soucis incessants, les tribulations et les appétences impulsives de la vie quotidienne (voir « Maîtrise et quiétude » au chapitre 7). Outre les offrandes et les actes de repentance, le rituel thérapeutique taoïste mettait en œuvre des substituts pour procurer la délivrance. Transformant la conceptualisation métaphorique en performance, les souffrants transféraient leur infortune vers des effigies à usage unique destinées à être bannies avec leur fardeau (voir « Corps de substitution » au chapitre 3).

L'analyse de Cyrulnik fait le lien entre l'extase religieuse – l'autre face d'une appréhension anxieuse du mal – et les effets de la thérapie spirituelle. Une formule de requête des Maîtres célestes met en exergue l'allégresse qui découlait de la libération de telles appréhensions : « À jamais gracieusement favorisé, son exultation est sans fin ! » Lu Xiujing compara la félicité d'accéder aux rites de salut au ravissement de l'avare tombant sur un trésor caché, et décrivit l'euphorie induite par les rites de pénitence comme suit : « Bondissant de joie mêlée de douleur, les cinq sens transportés, mon cœur plane et mon esprit vagabonde » (cf. « Lever les doutes » au chapitre 8). Les disciples « épousaient » la Loi et « adoraient » les écritures comme des joyaux, un langage que l'on trouve dans les écrits extatiques des mystiques, du Cantique des cantiques aux poèmes soufis.

La technique thérapeutique traverse la pratique religieuse, sans considération de dogme et de croyance. La méthode de méditation de Lu Xiujing devait beaucoup à la pratique indienne. Étonnamment, ses prescriptions relatives au voyage en esprit et au *samādhi* ont aussi une affinité avec les techniques de visualisation de saint Ignace, dont les *Exercices spirituels*, pour leur part, provenaient de diverses pratiques antérieures. Moshe Sluhovsky a remarqué : « Plus vieille que l'Église elle-même, la tradition des exercices spirituels, de prendre soin de son soi (*cura sui ipsius*) au moyen du développement personnel, intellectuel ou spirituel, était constitutive de l'éducation et de l'autoformation des élites grecques et romaines[13]. » Quant à Lu Xiujing, il s'appropriait volontiers le réceptacle de la thérapie rituelle du yoga et du bouddhisme pour le remplir de contenu chinois et taoïste (voir chapitre 7).

Dans ses études magistrales d'un paradis presque inatteignable et de la perspective quasi certaine d'une punition infernale, en Europe médiévale, Jean Delumeau a peint un panorama des peurs et des espoirs qui étreignaient la société occidentale jusqu'à atteindre un état d'anxiété proche de la psychose[14]. Une prière taoïste médiévale est ainsi rédigée : « Nous, hommes de chair, tremblons d'effroi, incapables de recouvrer notre sang-froid » (voir « Le pays sans retour » au chapitre 4). Delumeau observe que, sous toutes les différentes appréhensions du mal, qu'elles soient articulées en référence à la maladie, la possession, la guerre, les récoltes avariées, le manque ou la perte, se trouvait la peur de la mort et de ses conséquences. Si la dette fondamentale d'un être humain était l'emprunt de la vie, l'inévitabilité de sa restitution concentrait aussi les peurs innées du débiteur. Comme le formule une étude récente, « la vie et la mort ne sont que les formes les plus radicales de l'économie du don du destin »[15].

Les premiers chrétiens avaient cette consolation que le germe de la vie éternelle était comme un grain qui devait d'abord tomber en terre et mourir pour porter beaucoup de fruit[16]. Anna Seidel observait que les espoirs taoïstes d'immortalité aussi étaient surtout *post mortem*[17]. « Nous ne savons pas par quels actes méritoires nous pouvons être rançonnés de la porte des ténèbres », reconnaissait la prière citée au début de ce livre où, pour avoir prise sur sa destinée, le suppliant met sa foi dans l'efficacité du rituel. D'autres requérants croyaient au pouvoir salvateur des instruments sacramentaux ou des actes de dévotion. Le scrupule pressait les fidèles à confesser leur dette, donnait de l'urgence à la contrition du débiteur et à son désir de rachat et de délivrance. Les espoirs et les peurs de la société chinoise médiévale qui transpirent des sources taoïstes résonnent des appréhensions décrites par Delumeau. Ils témoignent assurément de l'aspiration au salut, compris comme une libération de la servitude dans ce monde et dans l'autre, fondée sur l'effacement rituel des dettes.

Repères chronologiques

Périodes d'unité :	*Périodes de fragmentation :*	*Chine du Nord*	*Chine du Sud*	
Han orientaux 東漢 **(25-220)**				
	Trois royaumes 三國 *(220-280)*	*Wei* 魏 *(220-265)*	*Shu* 蜀 *(221-263)*	
			Wu 吳 *(222-280)*	*Six dynasties* 六朝 *(220-589)*
Jin occidentaux 西晉 **(265-316)**				
		Seize royaumes 十六國 *(304-439)*	*Jin orientaux* 東晉 *(317-420)*	
	Dynasties du Nord et du Sud 南北朝 *(386-589)*	*Wei du Nord* 北魏 ou *Tuoba Wei* 拓跋魏 *(386-534)*	*Liu Song* 劉宋 *(420-479)*	
		Wei orientaux 東魏 *(534-550)* et *Wei occidentaux* 西魏 *(535-557)*	*Qi du Sud* 南齊 *(479-502)*	
		Qi du Nord 北齊 *(550-577)* et *Zhou du Nord* 北周 *(557-581)*	*Liang* 梁 *(502-557)* *Chen* 陳 *(557-589)*	
Sui 隋 **(581–619)**				
Tang 唐 **(618–907)**				
	Cinq dynasties et Dix royaumes 五代十國 *(907-979)*	*Cinq dynasties* *(907-960)* dont *Liang postérieurs* 後梁 *(907-923)*	*Dix royaumes* *(907-979)* dont *Shu antérieurs* 前蜀 *(907-925)*	

Notes

Introduction

1. Pour le contexte de cette prière, voir « La délivrance des morts » au chapitre 4.
2. Voir Brown, *Ransom of the soul*, p. 16-24.
3. Strickmann, « Therapeutische Rituale », p. 198-199 ; Mollier, « Visions of evil », p. 76-82.
4. Sur le crédit de vie initial, voir Wagner, « Fate's gift economy », p. 197-198.
5. Brown, *Ransom of the soul*, p. 23.
6. Voir Hulmes, « Semantics of sacrifice ».
7. Voir "Le symbole donne à penser", dans Ricœur, « La symbolique du mal », p. 323-332.
8. Anderson, *Sin*, p. 4-6, et chapitres 2 à 5.
9. Voir Granoff et Shinohara (dir.), *Sins and sinners*.
10. Sur la traduction et l'incommensurabilité des cultures, voir Tambiah, *Magic, science, religion*, chapitre 6.
11. Voir Hulsewé, *Remnants of Han law*, p. 17.
12. Voir Hou Ching-lang, *Monnaies d'offrande*, p. 101-102, et chapitre 10. Cf. le « trésor au Ciel » chrétien, Brown, *Ransom of the soul*, p. 25-33 ; Anderson, *Charity*, p. 113-135.
13. Voir Hulsewé, *Remnants of Han law*, p. 71-101 (administration de la justice, livres de comptes), 102-155 (châtiments), 205-224 (rédemption), 225-250 (amnistie).
14. Voir Seidel, « Traces of Han religion », p. 42-43 et 45-46.
15. Cf. von Hagen et Welker, *Money as God ?*, spécialement le chapitre 5.
16. Hou Ching-lang, *Monnaies d'offrande* ; Wagner, « Fate's gift economy », p. 211-212. Sur le concept chrétien de transfert de mérite, voir Anderson, *Charity*, p. 113-122. Cf. Brown, *Ransom of the soul*, p. 92, citant les *Sermons* d'Augustin :

« Le Seigneur notre Dieu veut faire de nous des espèces de commerçants ; Il nous propose une transaction à distance. »

17. Voir Harper, « Chinese demonology », p. 472-479.

18. Voir *Taishang zhengyi fawen jing*, 6a. Sur *jiechu*, voir Lian Shaoming, « Han-Jin jiechu wen », et Espesset, « Criminalized abnormality », p. 40.

19. Fraser, *Philosophy of the Mòzǐ*, p. 40-48, 104-128.

20. Kleeman, *Celestial Masters*, p. 85-86.

21. Cf. Hubert et Mauss, « Essai sur la nature et la fonction du sacrifice », p. 36-47.

22. Voir Lin et Radich, *A distant mirror*.

23. Voir Barrett, « Advent of the Buddhist conception of religion ».

24. Voir Lai Guolong, *Excavating the afterlife*, p. 137-138 ; Venture, « Écriture et communication ». Cf. Pollock, *Language of the gods*, p. 39-74, sur les origines rituelles du sanskrit.

25. Voir respectivement *Chisong zi zhangli* et *Guangcheng ji*, *juan* 4 à 17.

26. *Taishang xuanci zhuhua zhang* (désormais *Zhuhua zhang*) et P. 3562v (voir *Daojiao zhaijiao duwang qiyuan wen ji*).

27. Sur les genres de prières liturgiques taoïstes, voir Maruyama Hiroshi, *Dōkyō girei monjo*.

28. *Taishang dongxuan lingbao fazhu jing* et *Dongxuan lingbao wugan wen* (désormais cité comme *Wugan wen*).

29. Voir *Daojiao lingyan ji* ; Verellen, « Evidential miracles ».

Première partie
Un remède pour sauver l'humanité : adresser une requête au Ciel

1. Voir *Chisong zi zhangli* et Verellen, « Heavenly Master liturgical agenda ». Sur l'histoire de ce texte, voir Wang Zongyu, « *Chisong zi zhangli* de chengshu niandai ». Voir aussi « Le scribe » au chapitre 3 pour le processus d'accrétion de l'ouvrage.

2. Le *Code* était le *Taizhen ke* (vers 420), une collection aujourd'hui perdue de rituels surtout du Maître céleste. Pour une autre citation approximative du même passage du *Code*, voir Kleeman, *Celestial Masters*, p. 73. L'*Almanach de Maître Pin rouge* était un précurseur de l'*Almanach de requêtes de Maître Pin rouge*.

3. Cf. *Da daojia lingjie*, 14a-b ; Ōfuchi Ninji, *Shoki no dōkyō*, p. 143-149.

4. Voir Cedzich, « Organon ».

5. *Chisong zi zhangli*, 1.1a ; cf. *Santian neijie jing*, 1.5a : « À partir du règne de Guangwu des Han (25-57 de notre ère), les voies du monde déclinèrent progressivement et hommes et démons se mêlèrent. »

6. Voir Sterckx, « Religious practices », p. 415-417.

7. Zhang Xunliao et Bai Bin (dir.), *Zhongguo daojiao kaogu*, vol. 1, p. 306.

8. *Yangping zhi*, 20b et *Da daojia lingjie*, 14a. Pour une histoire détaillée, voir Kleeman, *Celestial Masters*, p. 21-110.

9. Voir *Da daojia lingjie*, 14a, et l'hagiographie de Zhang dans le *Shenxian zhuan* 神仙傳, citée dans le *Taiping guangji*, 8.55-58. Voir aussi Liu Ts'un-yan, « Was Celestial Master Zhang a historical figure ? ».

10. Voir Chen Yuan *et al.* (dir.), *Daojia jinshi lüe*, p. 4 ; Kleeman, *Celestial Masters*, p. 74-78.

11. *Sanguo zhi* (*Wei shu* 魏書), 8.263-264, citant le *Dianlüe* 典略 par Yu Huan 魚豢 (actif 220-232) dans son commentaire ; voir aussi Kleeman, *Celestial Masters*, p. 23-30.

12. *Yangping zhi* (voir Kleeman, *Celestial Masters*, p. 113-116) ; *Da daojia lingjie* (voir Bokenkamp, *Early Daoist scriptures*, p. 149-185). Sur la date Wei de ces textes, voir Wang Jing, « *Zhengyi fawen tianshi jiaojie kejing* ».

13. Voir Zürcher, *Buddhist conquest*, chap. 3.

Chapitre premier
Postulats rituels

1. Sur l'Alliance pure, voir Schipper, *La religion de la Chine*, chapitre 3.

2. Wang Zongyu, « Daojiao de "liutian" shuo », p. 22-49 ; Wang Haoyue, *Xijing qiuzhen*, p. 51-53.

3. Voir *Taishang lingbao wufu xu*, C.8b-9a. Sur ce texte, voir Raz, « Creation of tradition ».

4. *Laozi jiaoshi*, p. 174.

5. Voir *Santian neijie jing* ; Bokenkamp, *Early Daoist scriptures*, p. 188-194 ; et Raz, *Emergence of Daoism*, p. 232-245.

6. Voir Lü Pengzhi, « Jade instructions », p. 47-48 ; Zhao Yi, « Nanchao daojing *Santian neijie jing* zaitan », p. 43-45 ; Stein, « Religious Taoism », p. 62-65.

7. Voir Seidel, *Divinisation de Lao Tseu*, p. 84-91.

8. Seidel, « Image of the perfect ruler », p. 225. Liu Yi, *Jingtian yu chongdao*, p. 409-415, argumente en faveur du VIe siècle sur la base d'indices circonstanciels.

9. *Laozi bianhua jing*, col. 91-95 ; traduction adaptée de Seidel, « Image of the perfect ruler », p. 225.

10. Voir Seidel, « Taoist messianism », p. 167. Le titre « nouvellement manifesté » est attesté pour la première fois dans le *Da daojia lingjie*, 14a.

11. Voir Yoshikawa Tadao, « Shoku ni okeru shin'i no gaku no dentō ».

12. Voir Sage, *Ancient Sichuan*, p. 147-156, 174-181.

13. Voir Nylan, « The legacies of the Chengdu plain », p. 312-321.

14. Voir Peng Bangben, « In search of the Shu kingdom », p. 75-91.

15. Voir Flad et Chen, *Ancient central China*, p. 71-107.

16. Voir Stein, « Quelques remarques », p. 22-27 ; Kleeman, « Ethnic identity », p. 24-32, et *Great perfection*, p. 11-60.

17. *Shenxian zhuan*, cité dans *Taiping guangji*, 8.55-58 ; traduit dans Campany, *To live as long*, p. 349-356.

18. Voir Verellen, « Twenty-four Dioceses », p. 29-34.

19. Cf. *Huayang guo zhi jiaobu tuzhu*, 3.132 : « Bing avait de bonnes connaissances en astronomie et en géographie » 冰能知天文、地理.

20. Voir Verellen, « Zhang Ling and the Lingjing ».

21. Voir Schipper, *La religion de la Chine*, p. 305-327.

22. Duyu 杜宇 descendit du ciel et Bieling fit surface dans le Yangzi ; voir *Shuwang benji* 蜀王本紀, cité dans *Taiping yulan*, 888.2b.

23. Voir Lin Fushi, *Zhongguo zhonggu shiqi de zongjiao yu yiliao*, p. 62-69, et son tableau chronologique des épidémies sous les Han orientaux (p. 26).

24. Cité dans *Xiao dao lun*, 146b ; attribué ailleurs à l'officiel des Han orientaux Li Ying 李膺 (mort en 169).

25. Cf. *Dianlüe* 典略, cité dans *Sanguo zhi*, 8.264 ; traduit dans Kleeman, *Celestial Masters*, p. 29-30.

26. Soixante, le plus petit commun multiple de dix et de douze, est la période du cycle combiné.

27. Needham, « Astronomy », dans Needham *et al.*, *Science and civilisation*, vol. 3, p. 396-408.

28. Sivin, « Cosmos and computation », p. 9.

29. Puett, « Forming spirits », p. 2-7 ; Auyang, *Dragon and the eagle*, p. 267-310.

30. Seidel, « Imperial treasures », p. 294.

31. *Taishang laojun zhongjing*, B.15b-16b, dans *Yunji qiqian*, 19.450-452 ; Schipper, « Inner world », p. 128-130.

32. Voir Levy, « Yellow Turban religion and rebellion » ; Michaud, « Yellow Turbans ».

33. *Sanguo zhi* (*Weishu*), 1.9 ; cf. Seidel, « Das neue Testament des Tao », p. 152.

34. Sterckx, « Religious practices », p. 419.

35. Barrett, « Religious change », p. 438-440.

36. Voir Hendrischke, *Scripture on Great Peace*, p. 1-66 ; Seidel, « Sûtra merveilleux », p. 320-324, et « Taoist messianism ».

37. *Da daojia lingjie*, 15a.

38. *Laozi bianhua jing*. Voir Seidel, *Divinisation de Lao Tseu*, et « Image of the perfect ruler », p. 217-221 ; Liu Xianglan, « Dunhuang ben *Laozi bianhua jing* ».

39. Voir Seidel, « Image of the perfect ruler », p. 236-245.

40. Pour une vue d'ensemble des idées eschatologiques et messianiques taoïstes et bouddhistes, voir Zürcher, « Prince Moonlight », p. 2-10. Sur le concept bouddhiste de la fin de la doctrine, voir Nattier, *Once upon a future time*, p. 90-118.

41. Zürcher, « Prince Moonlight », p. 10-22.

42. *Taishang laozi huahu miaojing* ; Seidel, « Sûtra merveilleux », p. 309-310, 323-337.

43. *Laojun bianhua wuji jing*, 3a-b ; traduction adaptée de Dudink, « The poem *Laojun bianhua wuji jing* », p. 114-115.

44. Cf. Madigan et Levenson, *Resurrection*, p. 2-8.

45. *Zhengyi tianshi gao Zhao Sheng koujue*, 1a-2a.

46. Voir Verellen, « Twenty-four Dioceses ».

47. Fraser, *The philosophy of the Mòzi*, p. 27-31, 106-107.

48. Voir Bielenstein, *Bureaucracy of Han times*, p. 98 et 102 ; Kleeman, *Celestial Masters*, p. 325-326.

49. Voir Pankenier, *Astrology and cosmology*, p. 265-276.

50. Voir Verellen, « Twenty-four Dioceses », p. 18.

51. Voir l'exemple de Wang Jian sous « Une liturgie au service d'un dessein » au chapitre 12 et le tableau des correspondances dans Verellen, « Twenty-four Dioceses », p. 27-28.

52. Voir *Dengzhen yinjue*, 3.5b-27a ; traduit dans Cedzich, « Ritual der Himmelsmeister », p. 107-158.

53. *Lu xiansheng daomen kelüe*, 2a. Pour une traduction complète, voir Nickerson, « Abridged codes of Master Lu ».

54. Les détracteurs interprétaient largement ceci comme une usurpation de l'imposition de l'État ; voir *Hou Han shu*, 75.2435 ; *Huayang guo zhi jiaobu tuzhu*, 2.72 ; Ōfuchi Ninji, *Shoki no dōkyō*, p. 374-379.

55. Voir « Sanhui ri » 三會日, *Chisong zi zhangli*, 2.5a.

56. Sur ces banquets rituels, voir Kleeman, « Feasting without the victuals », p. 149-157.

57. Sur les débuts de l'histoire de cette institution qui occupait une place importante dans les pratiques confucéennes, taoïstes et bouddhistes, voir Wang Chengwen, *Han-Jin daojiao yishi*, p. 3-171.

58. Sur le couteau à livre servant de grattoir, voir Tsien Tsuen-hsuin, *Written on bamboo and silk*, p. 194-198.

59. Voir Kleeman, *Celestial Masters*, p. 233-239, et Bokenkamp, « Early Lingbao scriptures », p. 104-108, sur les vêtements rituels. Voir Dien, *Six Dynasties civilization*, p. 319-330, sur les normes correspondantes de l'habillement séculier.

60. Sur les mérites et les vertus, cf. Kleeman, « Cultivating conduct ».

61. Sur les assemblées, diocèses, oratoires, ordinations, le rattachement à un maître, le paiement des gages et les banquets, voir aussi *Xuandu lüwen*, 11a-17a.

62. Sterckx, « Religious practices », p. 429.

63. *Lu xiansheng daomen kelüe*, 1b (voir aussi 8a) ; voir aussi Schipper, *La religion de la Chine*, p. 127-160.

64. *Santian neijie jing*, A.6a.

65. Pour ce terme, cf. *Chisong zi zhangli*, 3.8b, 24b.

66. *Chisong zi zhangli*, 1.1b-2a.

67. Voir Lai Guolong, *Excavating the afterlife*, p. 137-138.

68. Voir Cedzich, « Ritual der Himmelsmeister », p. 58.

69. *Chisong zi zhangli*, 3.21b. Cf. la variante « ce serment de loyauté ne sera pas rompu » 不負丹誓 (5.34a), une formule se trouvant aussi dans *Shangqing huangshu guodu yi*, 4a.

70. Cf. Strickmann, *Chinese poetry and prophecy*, p. 93-94, et Hubert et Mauss, « Essai sur la nature et la fonction du sacrifice », p. 42, sur les « sacrifices-demandes » (*Bittopfer*).

71. Voir *Chisong zi zhangli*, *juan* 1, 2 et 5.

72. *Yili zhushu*, 3.42-59.

73. Sur les maîtres des méthodes en Chine ancienne, voir Ngo Van Xuyet, *Divination, magie et politique*.

74. Voir Lü Pengzhi, « Zaoqi daojiao jiaoyi », p. 20-25, 69-83.
75. Seidel, « Imperial treasures », p. 370-371.
76. Sterckx, « Religious practices », p. 415-417.
77. Voir Bumbacher, *Empowered writing*, p. 59.
78. Voir Strickmann, « Therapeutische Rituale », p. 197 ; Chan et Tan (dir.), *Filial piety*, p. 44-70.
79. *Laozi jiaoshi*, p. 29.
80. *Xiang'er zhu*, col. 374-375 ; traduit dans Puett, « Forming spirits », p. 18.
81. Voir Stroumsa, *Making of the Abrahamic religions*, chap. 2, « The end of sacrifice ».
82. Matthieu 20, 28.
83. Krishan, « To what extent Buddhism repudiated Vedic religion ? ».
84. Staal, *Agni*, p. 113-125.
85. Voir Kleeman, « Licentious cults » ; Lai Chi Tim, « Opposition of Celestial Master ».
86. *Santian neijie jing*, A.6a.
87. Exode 34, 14.

Chapitre 2
Culpabilité fatidique

1. *Taishang dongxuan lingbao zhihui zuigen shangpin dajie jing*, B.7b-8a ; cf. Kamitsuka Yoshiko, *Dōkyō kyōten*, p. 61-71.
2. Voir Hendrischke et Penny, *« The 180 precepts »*. Il s'agit de l'une des premières et plus complètes collections de règles pour les taoïstes du Maître céleste.
3. *Chisong zi zhangli*, 5.10b.
4. Voir Harper et Kalinowski (dir.), *Books of fate*.
5. Voir Kalinowski, « La littérature divinatoire », p. 96-99 ; Chen Hao, « Yishi, shenti, zuizhe », p. 249-252, et Zhou Yanping, « *Chisong zi zhangli* ».
6. Voir Zhu Yueli, *Daojiao kaoxin ji*, p. 429-441.
7. *Chisong zi zhangli*, 1.1a-b.
8. « Tianlao wen sanhuang » 天老問三皇, *Chisong zi zhangli*, 2.27b-28a.
9. *Chisong zi zhangli*, 1.19a-20a.
10. Voir Kalinowski, *Cosmologie et divination*, p. 425-426.
11. Nylan, « Living without sin », examine cette question ; voir aussi Eberhard, *Guilt and sin*.
12. Voir Wang Tianlin, « Tianshi dao jiaotuan de zuiguan ».
13. Voir Hulsewé, *Remnants of Han law*, p. 124-128.
14. Voir Wu Pei-Yi, « Self-examination and confession », p. 6-16.
15. Cf. Espesset, « Criminalized abnormality », p. 38-43, sur la culpabilité et la rédemption dans le *Taiping jing*.
16. « Jinjie », *Chisong zi zhangli*, 2.29b.
17. Voir Csikszentmihalyi, « Allotment and death » ; Campany, « Living off the books », p. 131-134.

18. Dans le *Chisong zi zhangli*, l'autorité à laquelle on s'adresse est indiquée sous la forme « tel département du palais » 某宮曹. Voir aussi *Yuanchen zhangjiao licheng li*, 2.12a.

19. L'unité *ji* 紀, « cycle », définie par ailleurs comme 300 jours (voir *Baopu zi neipian jiaoshi*, 6.114), correspond dans ce contexte à une année ; voir *Chisong zi zhangli*, 2.19a.

20. Les Six afflictions étaient le froid 寒疾, la fièvre 熱疾, les afflictions des extrémités 末疾, les afflictions gastriques ou intestinales 腹疾, les divagations 惑疾 et les troubles mentaux 心疾. Une autre explication les associe aux six *qi* 六氣 saisonniers : yin 陰, yang 陽, vent 風, pluie 雨, obscurité 晦 et lumière 明.

21. C'est-à-dire les cinq légumes à saveur alliacée 五葷, considérés comme impurs ; voir Wang Chengwen, *Han-Jin daojiao yishi*, p. 176-199 ; Strickmann, *Chinese magical medicine*, p. 54-55.

22. « Biji », *Chisong zi zhangli*, 2.28a.

23. Voir Liu Tseng-kuei, « Taboos » ; Wu Yakui, « Daojiao jinji chuyi ». Cf. Brown, *The body and society*, p. 59 : « Dans l'ancien monde, l'usage considérait les relations sexuelles, l'accouchement et la mort comme les sujets propres du tabou. »

24. *Chisong zi zhangli*, 3.22b ; voir aussi 3.5a et 6a, et *Zhuhua zhang*, 2.7b ; Lai Chi Tim, « Tian di shui sanguan ».

25. Voir *Wushang biyao*, 9.8a et 54.19a ; *Chisong zi zhangli*, 3.20b.

26. Ce groupe de divinités figure dans le *Nüqing guilü*, 2.4b, où un « démon des quatre cours d'eau » 四瀆鬼 prend la place du seigneur des Quatre mers.

27. « Bahe zhang » 拔河章, *Chisong zi zhangli*, 5.15a-16a ; Verellen, « Heavenly Master liturgical agenda », p. 323-324.

28. Voir *Chisong zi zhangli*, 5.33b ; Seidel, « Traces of Han religion », p. 39-42 ; Liu Yi, *Jingtian yu chongdao*, p. 267-283.

29. Pour le titre complet de l'ouvrage, voir *Nüqing guilü*, 3.1a ; voir aussi *Xuandu lüwen* et Harper, « Chinese demonology ».

30. Voir Kleeman, *Celestial Masters*, p. 146-189 ; Lai Chi Tim, « Demon statutes of *Nüqing* ».

31. Voir Tsuchiya Masaaki, « Confession of sins », p. 39-43.

32. *Dianlüe*, par Yu Huan 魚豢 (actif 220-232), cité dans *Sanguo zhi* (*Wei shu*), 8.264 ; voir aussi Ōfuchi Ninji, *Shoki no dōkyō*, p. 151-156 ; Lai Chi Tim, « Tian di shui sanguan », p. 1-30 ; et Kleeman, *Celestial Masters*, p. 188.

33. *Zhuhua zhang*, 2.12a-15a.

34. Cf. Cedzich, « Organon », p. 19-21.

35. « Daoshi tian di shui sanguan shoushu lu zhuang zhang », *Zhuhua zhang*, 2.12a-15a.

36. *Taishang cibei jiuyou bazui chan* ; cf. Kuo Li-ying *Confession et contrition*.

37. *Taishang dongxuan lingbao jingtu shengshen jing*, 199b.

38. Voir Kalinowski, « La littérature divinatoire », p. 100.

39. « Tianluo diwang », *Chisong zi zhangli*, 2.8b.

40. Cf. *Chisong zi zhangli*, 3.18a : « Il est à craindre qu'ils soient emmêlés dans le Filet du ciel et la Nasse de la terre » 恐天羅地網所見纏綿.

41. « Jie tianluo diwang zhang », *Chisong zi zhangli*, 4.2b-4b.

42. Allusion aux degrés de deuil via les vêtements correspondants prescrits par le code vestimentaire 服制.

43. Cf. *Yunji qiqian*, 41.11b, 45.5a-b. Cf. *Xuandu lüwen*, 5a, et Hou Ching-lang, « Chinese belief in baleful stars », p. 200, sur le tabou moderne contre la consommation d'offrandes alimentaires aux démons par opposition aux dieux ou aux ancêtres.

44. « Yanhui », *Chisong zi zhangli*, 2.23a-b. Sur l'héritage de la Chine ancienne quant aux règles concernant les tabous liés à la mort dans la pratique du Maître céleste, voir Wang Chengwen, *Han-Jin daojiao yishi*, p. 206-214.

45. Cf. *Wushang biyao*, 49.2a.

46. « Shengsi jieyan xidang zhaishe zhang », *Chisong zi zhangli*, 5.11a-12a.

47. « Jinjie » 禁戒, *Chisong zi zhangli*, 2.28b. Cf. *Xuandu lüwen*, 19b.

48. Pour Nüqing et Xuandu, voir *Taizhen yudi siji mingke jing*, 1.6a-b. Pour un résumé succinct de cette compilation, voir Strickmann, *Chinese magical medicine*, p. 80-88.

49. Voir Strickmann, *Chinese magical medicine*, p. 23-39.

50. Voir les exemples illustrés et la discussion dans Liu Zhaorui, *Kaogu faxian*, p. 12-38.

51. Traduit par « injection de *pneuma* » dans Kleeman, *Celestial Masters*, p. 346-347, renvoyant aux châtiments appliqués par les officiers de l'autre monde en rétribution d'actes spécifiques.

52. *Xuandu lüwen*, 2b.

53. *Chisong zi zhangli*, 3.14b.

54. *Zhengyi chuguan zhang yi*, 10a-12a. Cf. *Zhengyi fawen jing zhangguan pin*, 2.7b (désormais cité comme *Zhangguan pin*). Sur les entraves et les menottes, cf. *Zhen'gao*, 6.8b ; sur les prisons démoniaques, *Zhuhua zhang*, 1.15b, 5.11a ; sur la rétribution des Trois officiers, *Lu xiansheng daomen kelüe*, 9a.

55. Cf. Sterckx, « Religious practices », p. 426-427 ; sur les tabous liés aux cheveux et aux ongles, voir Liu Tseng-kuei, « Taboos », p. 919-923.

56. C'est-à-dire en dehors du Pacte de l'Unité correcte 正一盟威 du Maître céleste.

57. « Jie zhouzu zhang », *Chisong zi zhangli*, 3.8a-10a.

58. *Chisong zi zhangli*, 4.7a.

59. Voir Hulsewé, *Remnants of Han law*, p. 90-91.

60. Strickmann, « Therapeutische Rituale », p. 193-196 ; Cedzich, « Ritual der Himmelsmeister », p. 52-54.

61. « Da zhongsong zhang » 大塚訟章 et « You da zhongsong zhang » 又大塚訟章, *Chisong zi zhangli*, 5.19a-34b ; sur le premier, voir Nickerson, « The Great petition for sepulchral plaints », dans Bokenkamp, *Early Daoist scriptures*, p. 230-274 ; et Maruyama Hiroshi, « Sei'itsu dōkyō no jōshō girei ni tsuite », p. 52-60. Voir aussi Jiang Shoucheng, « Zhongsong kao ».

62. Cf. la « Requête pour défaire les malédictions » discutée ci-dessus (*Chisong zi zhangli*, 3.8a-10a). Sur le souffle vital, voir le chapitre 7.

63. « Benming xieguo kouqi zhang », *Chisong zi zhangli*, 3.14a-16b.

64. Voir Hulsewé, *Remnants of Han law*, p. 112-122.

65. Liu Xiaomin, « Qiantan daojiao de chengfu shuo » ; Liu Zhaorui, « "Chengfu shuo" yuanqi lun ».

66. Voir *Taiping jing hejiao*, 48.57-61 ; Hendrischke, *Scripture on Great Peace*, p. 141-152.

67. Gagné, *Ancestral fault in ancient Greece*, p. 3.

68. Voir Maeda Shigeki, « Between karmic retribution », p. 101-102 et 106-117.

69. Zürcher, « Buddhist influence », p. 136-141.

70. *Chisong zi zhangli*, 3.14b.

Chapitre 3
Les protagonistes et la rançon

1. Teiser, « Ornamenting the departed », p. 229.

2. Nées respectivement d'un œuf, d'un ventre, de l'humidité ou par transformation spontanée.

3. *Chisong zi zhangli*, 5.15a-b.

4. *Xuandu lüwen*, 19b.

5. *Chisong zi zhangli*, 2.28b-29a ; cf. le barème des sanctions en 2.19a.

6. « Zhangci » 章辭, *Chisong zi zhangli*, 1.18b-19a. L'unité *ji* 紀, qui signifie « cycle », correspond ici à une année ; voir *Chisong zi zhangli*, 2.19a.

7. Hubert et Mauss, « Essai sur la nature et la fonction du sacrifice », p. 37-38 ; cf. Teiser, « Ornamenting the departed », p. 229.

8. *Chisong zi zhangli*, 1.1a-b.

9. Voir Verellen, « Tianshi dao shangzhang », et Cheng Lesong, « *Yuanchen zhangjiao licheng li* suo jian de zhengyi zhangyi ».

10. *Yuanchen zhangjiao licheng li* et *Liushi jiazi benming yuanchen li*. Voir le tableau de correspondances dans Verellen, « Tianshi dao shangzhang », p. 61-63 ; voir aussi Lü Pengzhi, « Zaoqi daojiao jiaoyi », p. 77-79.

11. Cf. Hou Ching-lang, « Chinese belief in baleful stars », p. 228.

12. « Jiubing dae jinzi daixing zhang » 久病大厄金紫代形章, *Chisong zi zhangli*, 6.5b-6a ; cf. la requête pour démêler le Filet du ciel et la Nasse de la terre (*Chisong zi zhangli*, 4.4a). « Bloquer les assauts des vapeurs mortelles » : cf. « Bannir les hordes de démons et les empêcher d'assaillir les hommes » 斥却妖群使不加人 (*Zhuhua zhang*, 1.5a-6b).

13. *Chisong zi zhangli*, 2.29a-b.

14. « Shouchu huzai zhang », *Chisong zi zhangli*, 3.6b-8a.

15. Les titres sont inventoriés dans *Chisong zi zhangli*, 1.8a, 1.10b et 1.13b. Sur le mal de la calomnie, voir aussi *Taishang shangqing rangzai yanshou baochan*, 1a.

16. *Zhuhua zhang*, 2.9a-10a.

17. Les titres sont inventoriés dans *Chisong zi zhangli*, 1.6b et 1.10a.

18. Sur ce sens du terme, cf. *Chaoye qianzai*, « Supplément » 補輯, p. 177.

19. « Shouchu huoyang zhang », *Chisong zi zhangli*, 4.18b-20a.

20. Un confluent du Yangzi, provenant du Henan, et un fleuve au Shandong, respectivement.

21. « Baohu rongzheng zhang », *Chisong zi zhangli*, 6.26a-27a.

22. Voir Liu Yongming, « P. 3562v » (2), p. 16-17 ; Teiser, « Ornamenting the departed », p. 203 ; et les prières pour le compte de militaires dans le *Guangcheng ji* dont traite le chapitre 12.

23. Voir Huang Ruxuan, « Mawangdui “pibing tu” yanjiu ».

24. *Chisong zi zhangli*, 4.17b. Dans le système à trois niveaux du mont Fengdu, Hebo et Nüqing étaient deux des huit prisons situées en dessous de la montagne. Les dieux de la cité et du sol remplissaient dans l'autre monde les fonctions judiciaires du magistrat local.

25. *Chisong zi zhangli*, 6.2b.

26. Voir *Chisong zi zhangli*, 6.14a ; cf. Teiser, « Ornamenting the departed », p. 232.

27. Voir, par exemple, *Xiang'er zhu*, col. 327-328, 372-373 ; *Ziyang zhenren neizhuan*, 1.5b-6a ; *Dengzhen yinjue*, 3.14a.

28. *Taishang dongxuan lingbao sanyuan pinjie gongde qingzhong jing*, 7a-b.

29. Voir Strickmann, *Chinese poetry and prophecy*, p. 87-97 ; Bumbacher, *Empowered writing*.

30. « Shuzhang fa » 書章法, *Chisong zi zhangli*, 2.3a-4b. Sur la préparation des requêtes de guérison et leur usage thérapeutique, voir aussi *Dengzhen yinjue*, 3.11b-12b.

31. Corrigé d'après *Yaoxiu keyi jielü chao*, 11.16b.

32. « Duanzhang », *Chisong zi zhangli*, 2.26b-27b.

33. « Zangzhang guben », *Chisong zi zhangli*, 2.26a-b.

34. « Transcriptions », « réutilisée » et « officiers » ont été corrigés d'après *Yaoxiu keyi jielü chao*, 11.16a-b.

35. *Chisong zi zhangli*, 2.26b ; cf. Cedzich, « Organon », p. 27-28. L'amende pour une sentence du cinquième degré était de trois mille ligatures de chaume pour le toit du sanctuaire diocésain ; voir *Chisong zi zhangli*, 2.19a.

36. « Zouzhang an » 奏章案, *Chisong zi zhangli*, 2.27b.

37. Cf. *Dengzhen yinjue*, 3.12b : « Le mouvement vers la gauche (lévogyre) est celui des étoiles [pivotant autour de l'étoile polaire]. Prenez position face à l'est. Le frottement répété est appelé les quarante-neuf passages de la composition… »

38. « Shuzhang fa », *Chisong zi zhangli*, 2.3a-4b. L'auteur est redevable à Grégoire Espesset d'avoir amendé ce passage.

39. Voir Austin, « Performative utterances », dans *Philosophical papers*, p. 235-236. Sur les actes expressifs et le langage performatif, voir aussi Tambiah, *Magic, science, religion*, p. 24, 58 ; Teiser, « Literary style », p. 365-370.

40. *Xuandu lüwen*, 12a.

41. « Chenghuang chengkong », *Chisong zi zhangli*, 2.18a.

42. « Qishou zaibai » 稽首再拜 et « Dunshou sizui qishou zaibai » 頓首死罪稽首再拜, *Chisong zi zhangli*, 2.18a-b.

43. *Chisong zi zhangli*, 3.5b-6a.

44. Voir Cedzich, « Organon ».

45. « Qingguan », *Chisong zi zhangli*, 2.18b-22a.

46. *Dengzhen yinjue*, 3.14b-23b ; traduit dans Cedzich, « Ritual der Himmelsmeister », p. 131-147.

47. *Zhangguan pin* ; voir Wang Zongyu, « *Zhengyi fawen jing zhangguan pin* jiaokan ».

48. *Dengzhen yinjue*, 3.14b.

49. *Chisong zi zhangli*, 2.18b-22a.

50. Cf. Tambiah, *Magic, science, religion*, p. 58-59, sur les « actes expressifs » impliquant des effigies. Voir aussi Cedzich, « Corpse deliverance ».

51. Voir Lévitique, 16 : 22 ; Lyonnet et Sabourin, *Sin, redemption and sacrifice*, p. 269-289 ; Girard, *Scapegoat*, p. 112-124.

52. Fang Xiao, « Caoyu "tishen" ».

53. Voir *Laozi*, 5 (*Laozi jiaoshi*, p. 22-23) et Schipper, *La religion de la Chine*, p. 219-234.

54. Zhang Xunliao et Bai Bin, *Zhongguo daojiao kaogu*, vol. 1, p. 229-244.

55. Poo Mu-chou, « Preparation for the afterlife », p. 27.

56. Seidel, « Traces of Han religion », p. 34-39 ; Liu Yi, *Jingtian yu chongdao*, p. 199-258.

57. Zhang Xunliao et Bai Bin, *Zhongguo daojiao kaogu*, vol. 5, p. 1420-1434 ; Lian Shaoming, « Jianxing nianba nian », p. 116.

58. *Chisong zi zhangli*, 3.20a.

59. Hou Ching-lang, *Monnaies d'offrande*, p. 6.

60. « Bingsi bujue yinren daixing zhang », *Chisong zi zhangli*, 1.11b. Certaines des pièces de monnaie trouvées dans des tombes ont pu répondre au même besoin ; voir Liu Weipeng et Cheng Yi, « Han-Jin muzang zhong suizang taoping », p. 81.

61. « Yima zhang yi yun kaidu zhang » 驛馬章亦云開度章, *Chisong zi zhangli*, 4.5b ; cf. Chen Guofu, *Daozang yuanliu kao*, p. 283-284.

62. « Jiubing dae jinzi daixing zhang », *Chisong zi zhangli*, 6.2b-9b.

63. Voir aussi *Chisong zi zhangli*, 1.18a, 1.17a et 6.3a.

64. Cf. *Wushang biyao*, 9.7a-b.

65. Cf. les Sauveurs surintendants de la vie 監生度命君 ci-dessous (*Chisong zi zhangli*, 6.6a-7a).

66. *Chisong zi zhangli*, 6.4b-5b. Le Calendrier de jade était le registre des immortels ; voir Schipper, « Inner world », p. 116-117.

67. Cf. les autels du bouddhisme ésotérique introduits en Chine durant la période des Six dynasties ; Shinohara Koichi, *Spells, images, and mandalas*, p. 206.

68. Voir *Yuanchen zhangjiao licheng li*, 1.3b, commentaire.

69. *Yuanchen zhangjiao licheng li*, 1.2b-3a.

70. Les 360 *qi* correspondent aux jours de l'année.

71. Les jetons de calcul étaient utilisés pour calculer le solde du compte de vie. Quand le compte alloué à un individu était épuisé, son nom était transféré au registre des morts ; voir l'histoire de Liu Tu au chapitre 10.

72. « Qingsi baming zhang » 青絲拔余 [命] 章, *Chisong zi zhangli*, 3.19b-20b. Le caractère 余 dans le titre est une erreur graphique pour 命 ; cf. l'inventaire, *Chisong zi zhangli*, 1.3b.

73. Proverbes 13, 8 ; voir Brown, *Ransom of the soul*, p. 22. Sur la charité rédemptrice dans le judaïsme et le christianisme, voir Anderson, *Charity*.

74. Voir l'interdiction dans *Chisong zi zhangli*, 2.28b.

75. « Requêtes sans gages normatifs » 章無的信 : lire *zhundi* 準的 pour *di* 的 ; cf. *Chisong zi zhangli*, 1.18a.

76. *Chisong zi zhangli*, 1.1b-2a.

77. « Lun sandeng zhang » 論三等章, *Chisong zi zhangli*, 1.18a-b ; voir aussi Hou Ching-lang, *Monnaies d'offrande*, p. 108-109.

78. Cf. *Chisong zi zhangli*, 2.29a : « Les offrandes et gages sacrificiels 贐信 doivent être distribués parmi le Peuple du Tao. »

79. Sur les implications économiques du système de gages, voir Schipper, *La religion de la Chine*, p. 146-157.

80. *Chisong zi zhangli*, 1.1b-2a.

81. Voir Verellen, « Tianshi dao shangzhang », p. 50-54, et l'illustration dans *Taishang laojun da cunsi tu zhujue*, 20b-21a.

82. Voir *Shangqing housheng daojun lieji* ; traduit dans Strickmann, *Le taoïsme du Mao Chan*, p. 209-224.

83. Voir Sun Weijie et Gai Jianmin, « Huangdao shier gong ». Sur les représentations picturales de ce voyage, voir Gesterkamp, *The heavenly court*.

84. « Cunsi » 存思, *Chisong zi zhangli*, 2.23b-24b, citant le *Code des Grands véritables* ; traduit dans Cedzich, « Ritual der Himmelsmeister », p. 95-97.

Chapitre 4
Un dessein rédempteur

1. Voir *Xuandu lüwen*, 18a-b.

2. Sur ce qui concerne la tradition Shangqing, voir Stanley-Baker, « Drugs, destiny, and disease ».

3. Cf. Brown, *Rise of Western Christendom*, chap. 11, sur les *medicamenta paenitentiae*.

4. « Dette ancienne » : littéralement, l'endettement karmique transféré des incarnations antérieures. La référence renvoie ici à la vertu du règlement de sa dette dans les délais (voir « La monnaie d'échange » au chapitre 11).

5. *Xuandu lüwen*, 5b-7b.

6. *Xuandu lüwen*, 8a-11a.

7. Cf. Strickmann, « Therapeutische Rituale », p. 189-192.

8. Littéralement, une « décharge d'enquête ». La « Requête pour guérir les maladies » ci-dessous en appelle au seigneur des Acquittements.

9. C'est-à-dire la promotion au paradis d'ancêtres défunts poursuivis et condamnés.

10. Voir la « Requête pour défaire les malédictions », dans « Les puissances du mal » au chapitre 2.

11. Les Cinq sols sont les cinq types d'esprits de la terre, ici spécifiquement dans leur capacité à déstabiliser les tombes. Cf. ci-dessous et *Zhen'gao*, 10.16b.

12. « Qingguan », *Chisong zi zhangli*, 2.18b-19a.

13. Les Cinq supplices sont les punitions de la Chine ancienne : tatouage 墨, amputation du nez 劓, amputation des pieds 剕, castration 宮 et peine de mort 大辟 ;

voir *Shangshu zhengyi*, 3.75. Les Trois calamités prédites par l'apocalypse bouddhiste étaient : épée, peste et famine ; ou incendie, inondation et vent.

14. Pour le Céleste médecin et le Grand médecin, leurs subalternes et la formule pour leur descente dans le corps du patient, voir *Zhangguan pin*, 1.12a. Pour les Officiers du mérite guérisseurs, cf. *Shangqing huangshu guodu yi*, 2a.

15. « Jibing yizhi zhang », *Chisong zi zhangli*, 3.20b-21b.

16. Voir Zheng Zhiming, « *Chisong zi zhangli* yu shengsi », p. 88-91, et le manuscrit *Taichan shu* 胎產書 de Mawangdui ; Harper, *Early Chinese medical literature*, p. 27-28.

17. *Taishang shuo liujia zhifu baotai huming miaojing*, 2a.

18. Ce dieu est aussi invoqué dans *Chisong zi zhangli*, 5 18a. « Soutenir les fragiles à travers les calamités » était l'objet de rituels de requête distincts. Voir « Fushuai due baohu zhang » 扶衰度厄保護章, *Chisong zi zhangli*, 3.23a-25a, et les titres connexes en 1.6b, 14b et 15a.

19. Cf. la requête intitulée « Jiee yanming » 解厄延命章, *Chisong zi zhangli*, 1.14a.

20. Les Trois originels sont les esprits des trois divisions du corps, les Champs de cinabre.

21. « Baotai zhang », *Chisong zi zhangli*, 4.12a-13a.

22. Étang vivier, une étoile néfaste pour qui était né sous son signe. Tigre blanc était redouté pour son attaque du fœtus ; voir Hou Ching-lang, « Chinese belief in baleful stars », p. 197, n. 10, et p. 209-219. Voir aussi Strickmann, *Chinese magical medicine*, p. 67, sur les démons astraux indiens ravisseurs de nourrissons.

23. « Cuisheng zhang », *Chisong zi zhangli*, 4.13a-14a. Cf. « Sauvegarder les accouchements et les grossesses » 保產生胎妊, *Zhangguan pin*, 2.13b-14a.

24. « Bao yingtong zhang », *Chisong zi zhangli*, 4.15b-16b.

25. La Nourrice, associée aux miasmes des fleuves, apportait les maladies infantiles ; voir *Zhuhua zhang*, 3.1b-3b. Le Comte du fleuve était un démon et une prison dans le niveau inférieur de Fengdu ; voir Cedzich, « Organon », p. 67 ; Sterckx, « Religious practices », p. 421.

26. « Xiaoer shangguang duhua zhang », *Chisong zi zhangli*, 4.14a-15b ; cf. *Zhuhua zhang*, 5.1a.

27. Voir le catalogue dans Kalinowski, « Les traités de Shuihudi », p. 225-227.

28. Sur les Seigneurs du destin, cf. Sterckx, « Religious practices », p. 419 ; Bumbacher, *Empowered writing*, p. 64.

29. « Jue Taishan siji yangong zhang », *Chisong zi zhangli*, 4.23b-24b. Sur le Taishan, voir Sterckx, « Religious practices », p. 421-423. La Contremarque de droite était un registre tenu au Département du ciel ; voir *Laozi Xiang'er zhu*, col. 372-373. Sur les rectifications des registres aux jours des assemblées, cf. Verellen, « Twenty-four Dioceses », p. 41-42.

30. Cf. *Zhangguan pin*, 3.4a-b (Contrôle de la terre) et 3.2b (Absolution du sol).

31. Pour ces divinités du sol, voir *Nüqing guilü*, 2.4a.

32. Le salaire annuel en grain d'un gouverneur de commanderie sous les Han ; cf. le titre « gouverneur du monde souterrain » dans « La délivrance des morts » au chapitre 4.

33. Pour ces dieux des portes, voir aussi *Yuanchen zhangjiao licheng li*, 1.20b.

34. Des divinités supervisant les tabous calendaires et de la maisonnée ; cf. *Chisong zi zhangli*, 2.2a, 5.13a et 2.10b-11a.

35. Cf. Kalinowski, « Transmission du dispositif », p. 774 ; Wu Liyu, « Lun jiugong jisi », p. 289.

36. « Xietu zhang », *Chisong zi zhangli*, 3.25a-26b.

37. Sterckx, « Religious practices », p. 419.

38. Voir *Maoshi zhengyi*, 12.747 : « Tremblant comme sur le bord d'un ravin, prudent comme foulant la glace fine » 惴惴小心, 如臨于谷。戰戰兢兢, 如履薄冰.

39. Une allusion à la carpe dans une ornière asséchée de Zhuangzi ; voir *Zhuangzi jishi*, 26.924.

40. Voir « Zhu qingyu » 主請雨, *Zhangguan pin*, 4.11b-12b ; et Cedzich, « Organon », p. 66-67, n. 183.

41. « Tianhan zhang », *Chisong zi zhangli*, 3.1a-3b.

42. Sur le Duc céleste, voir Harper, « Contracts with the spirit world », p. 233 et 236, n. 28.

43. Pour ces divinités, voir *Zhangguan pin*, 4.11b-13a.

44. Le Comte du vent et le Maître de la pluie étaient des divinités de la nature mentionnées dans le *Classique des montagnes et des mers* 山海經 du IVe siècle avant notre ère.

45. « Qingyu de shuiguo zhiyu zhang », *Chisong zi zhangli*, 3.3b-4b.

46. Voir « Zhu tianzhong » 主田種, *Zhangguan pin*, 4.2a-b. Cf. « Labour et gourdes » 田作瓜瓠 (*ibid.*, 1.17a-b).

47. Voir *Zhangguan pin*, 1.17a, dans lequel le nom de ce dieu est donné comme « seigneur des Neuf champs » 九野君 ; 3.10b répertorie un « Seigneur sans terre » 無野君, également du Bout de la Terre, en relation avec les invasions de rats.

48. Voir *Zhangguan pin*, 4.2b. Cf. « Sanqi yang wuyuan jun » 三氣陽無元君, *Zhangguan pin*, 2.6b.

49. Un des Trois vénérables 三尊 du panthéon du Shangqing.

50. Les dieux du sol et des céréales avaient un autel dédié dans l'aire rituelle (voir texte *supra*, p. 92).

51. « Que chonghuang shuzai shimiao zhang », *Chisong zi zhangli*, 3.4b-5b.

52. « Shou shuzai zhang », *Chisong zi zhangli*, 3.5b-6b ; cf. « Zhu jie chongshu jingguai » 主解蟲鼠精怪, *Zhangguan pin*, 2.6b.

53. Voir Bodde, *Festivals in classical China*, p. 263-272 ; Kuhn, « Textile technology », p. 247-272.

54. Voir Sterckx, « Religious practices », p. 425 ; Huang Zheng et Wu Wei, *Dunhuang yuanwen ji*, p. 208 ; *Daojiao lingyan ji*, 7.218-219.

55. Sur la production de la soie, voir Kuhn, « Textile technology », p. 285-433.

56. Voir Young, « For a compassionate killing », p. 29-36, et *Conceiving the Indian Buddhist patriarchs*, p. 186-216.

57. *Si yin qi juefa*, 5a ; *Taishang laojun hunyuan sanbu fu*, 1.17a-20a.

58. Voir Verellen, « Zhang Ling and the Lingjing », p. 261, et Kuhn, « Textile technology », p. 257-272.

59. Voir « Zhu can sang » 主蠶桑 et « Hu can zi hao » 護蠶滋好, dans le *Zhangguan pin*, 4.1a-2a et 1.16b-17a, respectivement ; *Zhuhua zhang*, 1.9b, 5.1a. Cf. Cedzich, « Organon », p. 61-62.

60. *Fancu* 犯犓 corrigé en *fanchu* 犯觸.

61. Cf. *Zhangguan pin*, 1.16b-17a.

62. « Baocan zhang », *Chisong zi zhangli*, 5.16a-17b.

63. « Duan wangren fulian zhang » 斷亡人復連章, *Chisong zi zhangli*, 4.17b.

64. Cf. Zheng Zhiming, « *Chisong zi zhangli* yu shengsi », p. 95-100 ; Nickerson, « "Opening the Way" », p. 64-66.

65. *Zhangguan pin*, 1.13a-15a et 3.1a-3b.

66. « Kaitong daolu zhang », *Chisong zi zhangli*, 5.14a-b. La suite de ce passage est citée dans l'introduction du présent ouvrage.

67. Pour *gou* 鉤, lire *ju* 拘 : voir *Chisong zi zhangli*, 3.26a et 6.10a.

68. « Chusang xiazang zhang », *Chisong zi zhangli*, 6.17a-18a.

69. Cf. *Zhangguan pin*, 3.4a.

70. Cf. *Zhangguan pin*, 1.14b (« dieux du sol de l'inhumation » 葬埋土公), 3.1b (« démons d'inhumation » 葬埋之鬼).

71. Littéralement, « deux mille boisseaux de grain », le salaire annuel d'un gouverneur de commanderie sous les Han.

72. *Zhangguan pin*, 3.2a ; *Chisong zi zhangli*, 6.1b-2b.

73. Cf. *Zhangguan pin*, 1.13a, 3.2a-3a ; Cedzich, « Organon », p. 71.

74. Voir Huang Shih-shan, *Picturing the true form*, p. 265-266.

75. « Ji wangren yiwu jie zuizhe qianda zhang », *Chisong zi zhangli*, 6.12b-14b.

76. Voir Zhang Xunliao et Bai Bin, *Zhongguo daojiao kaogu*, vol. 3, p. 805-1002 ; Lai Guolong, *Excavating the afterlife*, p. 137-159 ; Dien, *Six Dynasties civilization*, p. 322-326 ; Ikeda On, « Chūgoku kodai bosō ».

77. Dien, « Turfan funereal documents », p. 31-32.

78. Voir *Fo shuo wenshi xiyu zhongseng jing*, 802c.

79. Voir *Taishang lingbao xiyu shenxin jing* ; Kamitsuka Yoshiko, *Dōkyō kyōten*, p. 291-320 ; Cheng Cunjie, « Dunhuang ben *Taishang lingbao xiyu shenxin jing* yanjiu ».

80. Les « soieries directionnelles » étaient aux couleurs correspondant aux Cinq directions ; voir *Chisong zi zhangli*, 1.2b-3a : « cinq soies directionnelles suivant les couleurs directionnelles » 五方綵隨方色.

81. « Muyu zhang », *Chisong zi zhangli*, 6.1a-b.

82. Cf. Le Goff, *La naissance du Purgatoire*, p. 9-27.

83. Voir Zhang Xunliao et Bai Bin, *Zhongguo daojiao kaogu*, vol. 2, p. 351-574 ; Nickerson, « "Let living and dead take separate paths" » ; Bokenkamp, *Ancestors and anxiety*, p. 56-58.

84. *Chisong zi zhangli*, 6.11b, 13a.

85. Voir le commentaire de Tao dans le *Dengzhen yinjue*, 3.20b.

86. Cf. *Zhuhua zhang*, 3.11a, « miasmes mâles et femelles des trépassés récents et des défunts d'antan » 新死故亡雄雌注.

87. « Xinwang sazhai zhuzhu quesha zhang », *Chisong zi zhangli*, 6.20a-21b. Sur l'eau bénite, voir « Shenshui pin » 神水品, *Wushang biyao*, 4.14b-15b.

88. « Duan wangren fulian zhang » 斷亡人復連章, *Chisong zi zhangli*, 4.16b-18a.

Deuxième partie
LE PÉRIPLE INTÉRIEUR : LA RÉFORME DE LU XIUJING

1. Voir Hubert et Mauss, « Essai sur la nature et la fonction du sacrifice », p. 30 ; Hulmes, « Semantics of sacrifice », p. 279 ; et Stroumsa, *Making of the Abrahamic religions*, chapitre 2.

2. *Taishang dongxuan lingbao fazhu jing*, 10a et 2a (désormais *Fazhu jing*). Voir « Lumière du rituel » au chapitre 6 (destinée) et la Leçon 10 au chapitre 7 (quête de la vie, longévité).

3. Voir Robinet, *Méditation taoïste*.

Chapitre 5
LE DISCIPLE DES TROIS CAVERNES

1. Sur les connotations religieuses du terme « Joyau sacré » et les antécédents du corpus du Lingbao, voir Kaltenmark, « Ling-pao » et « Quelques remarques sur le *T'ai-chang Ling-pao wou-fu siu* ».

2. Voir Liu Shufen, « Jiankang and the commercial empire ».

3. Kobayashi Masayoshi, *Rikuchō dōkyōshi*, p. 189-216, défend la conclusion excessive selon laquelle l'ordre du Maître céleste naquit seulement au ve siècle comme une idéalisation rétrospective de la communauté de Hanzhong.

4. *Taishang dongyuan shenzhou jing* (désormais cité comme *Shenzhou jing*) ; voir Mollier, *Apocalypse taoïste*, p. 170-187.

5. Voir Miyakawa Hisayuki, *Chūgoku shūkyōshi*, vol. 1, p. 193-270.

6. *Santian neijie jing*, 1.9a-b ; traduit dans Bokenkamp, *Early Daoist scriptures*, p. 221-222.

7. Voir Seidel, « Taoist messianism », p. 168, et « Imperial treasures », p. 349-351.

8. Ainsi que consigné dans le *Livre sur les transformations de Laozi*. Voir *Laozi bianhua jing* ; Seidel, *Divinisation de Lao Tseu*, p. 98.

9. Seidel, « Image of the perfect ruler », p. 237-238.

10. Voir Tsukamoto Zenryū, *History of early Chinese Buddhism*, p. 892 ; Tang Yongtong, *Han Wei liang Jin Nanbei chao fojiao shi*, p. 415-486.

11. Voir la *Préface du Catalogue des écritures du Lingbao* de Lu Xiujing, présenté en 437 au successeur de Liu Yu, l'empereur Wendi, *Lingbao jingmu xu*, dans *Yunji qiqian*, 4.52 ; Bokenkamp, « Scriptures new and old », p. 465-467.

12. Voir le fragment de la biographie de Lu dans l'ouvrage perdu *Daoxue zhuan* 道學傳 de Ma Shu 馬樞 (522-581), cité dans *Sandong qunxian lu*, 2.16b-17a (Bumbacher, *Fragments*, p. 218). Pour une vue d'ensemble des sources biographiques dispersées sur Lu Xiujing, voir Chen Guofu, *Daozang yuanliu kao*, p. 38-44 et 466-468 ; Vitiello, « Studio sul taoista Lu Xiujing » ; et De Meyer, *Wu Yun*, p. 385-403.

13. Holcombe, *In the shadow of the Han*, p. 128.

14. *Daoxue zhuan*, cité dans *Sandong qunxian lu*, 2.5a-b (Bumbacher, *Fragments*, p. 210-211).

15. Voir Dien, *Six Dynasties civilization*, p. 37-45 ; Liu Shufen, *Liuchao de chengshi*, p. 111-134 ; Steinhardt, *Chinese architecture*, p. 132-137.

16. Voir Zürcher, *Buddhist conquest*, p. 81-159.

17. Voir Miyakawa Hisayuki, « Local cults around Mount Lu ».

18. Sur Huiyuan, voir Tsukamoto Zenryū, *History of early Chinese Buddhism*, p. 805-999 ; Zürcher, *Buddhist conquest*, p. 230-231, 240-253 ; Tang Yongtong, *Han Wei liang Jin Nanbei chao fojiao shi*, p. 346-347.

19. *Gaoseng zhuan*, 6.211 ; traduit dans Zürcher, *Buddhist conquest*, p. 240.

20. Voir *Lushan ji*, 1.1028a, et *Fozu tongji*, 26.269c.

21. Sur l'histoire des représentations picturales de la scène, voir Nelson, « The bridge at Tiger Brook ».

22. Sur la rencontre de Xie Lingyun avec Huiyuan sur le mont Lu en 413, voir Li Tian, « Lushan zhumu huahui wenhua », p. 226.

23. La scène représentée dans la peinture est expliquée dans l'inscription par l'ami du peintre, Li Chongyuan 李沖元 ; voir Nelson, « The bridge at Tiger Brook », p. 264-265. Le titre du tableau de Li Gonglin fait référence aux communautés populaires de la Terre pure de son époque.

24. *Daoxue zhuan*, cité dans *Sandong zhunan*, 1.16a (Bumbacher, *Fragments*, p. 208). Les voyages de Lu s'étendirent jusqu'à la gorge Wuxia 巫峽 et au mont Emei 峨眉 au Sichuan ; voir *Zhenxi*, 5.74.

25. *Taishang dongxuan lingbao shoudu yi*, 1a (désormais cité comme *Shoudu yi*).

26. *Lingbao jingmu*. Voir les reconstitutions dans Bokenkamp, « Sources of the Ling-pao scriptures », p. 479-485, et Wang Chengwen, *Han-Jin daojiao yishi*, 2e partie.

27. *Zhenxi*, 5.74 ; *Daoxue zhuan*, cité dans *Sandong zhunang*, 1.2a (Bumbacher, *Fragments*, p. 204-205).

28. *Song shu*, 99.2424 ; *Zizhi tongjian*, 126.3976-3978. La région était connue pour ses chamans ; voir Wiles, « Daoist aunt », p. 265-272 ; Vitiello, « Studio sul taoista Lu Xiujing », p. 296.

29. Voir Liu Yi, « Jin-Song tianshi dao shi », p. 226-229.

30. Voir Mather, *The poet Shen Yüeh*, p. 5-11, 85, 115-120 ; De Meyer, *Wu Yun*, p. 394.

31. *Lushan zhi*, 4.50b-51a ; Chen Guofu, *Daozang yuanliu kao*, p. 39-40 ; *Daoxue zhuan* (Bumbacher, *Fragments*, p. 217). Voir aussi Li Tian, « Lushan zhumu huahui wenhua », p. 226-227 ; Wu Guofu, *Lushan daojiao shi*, p. 43-66 ; Ouyang Zhen, « Lushan daojiao wenhua chuyi », p. 114.

32. *Liang shu*, 13.243 ; pour l'inscription, voir *Lushan Jianji guan zhi bei* 廬山簡寂觀之碑, dans *Lushan shiwen jinshi guangcun*, p. 551 ; traduit dans De Meyer, *Wu Yun*, p. 392-398.

33. *Jianji xiansheng Lu jun bei*.

34. Voir De Meyer, *Wu Yun*, p. 394.

35. *Zhenxi*, 5.74-75.

36. Voir Ji Bin et Hua Hongbin, « Qiantan Lushan daojiao cangshu », p. 164. Cf. *Lushan zhi*, 4.49b, et *Lushan ji*, 2.1033c. Sur la conservation des écritures dans les bibliothèques monastiques, voir *Dongxuan lingbao sandong fengdao kejie yingshi*,

2.5b-7a (désormais cité comme *Fengdao kejie*) ; traduit dans Kohn, *Daoist monastic manual*, p. 117.

37. Voir Zacchetti, « Notions and visions of the canon », p. 85-96, et Bokenkamp, « Lu Xiujing, Buddhism ».

38. Verellen, « Evidential miracles », p. 248-250.

39. Chen Guofu, *Daozang yuanliu kao*, p. 41, 328 ; *Maoshan zhi*, 1.11b ; pour la date, voir *Fozu tongji*, 36.346b.

40. *Daoxue zhuan*, cité dans *Sandong zhunang*, 2.5a-b (Bumbacher, *Fragments*, p. 208-111).

41. Voir Schipper et Verellen (dir.), *The Taoist canon*, vol. 1, p. 14-17 ; Chen Guofu, *Daozang yuanliu kao*, p. 282-283.

42. Voir Kohn (trad.), *Laughing at the Tao*, p. 136-138, 151-153, 156.

43. Cf. Zacchetti, « Notions and visions of the canon », p. 93.

44. *Daoxue zhuan*. Voir Bumbacher, *Fragments*, p. 205, et *Taiping yulan*, 667.6b.

45. *Song shu*, 29.836-837 ; traduit dans De Meyer, *Wu Yun*, p. 385.

46. Chen Guofu, *Daozang yuanliu kao*, p. 40-41.

47. Cette salle était également connue comme le Palais pour la réception des sages 延賢堂 ; voir *Song shu*, 29.856 et *passim* ; cf. Dien, *Six Dynasties civilization*, p. 41 ; et la carte dans Steinhardt, *Chinese architecture*, p. 134 (33).

48. *Daoxue zhuan*, cité dans *Sandong zhunang*, 2.6b (Bumbacher, *Fragments*, p. 209, 214).

49. Voir *Zhen'gao*, 20.2b, et Strickmann, « On the alchemy of T'ao Hung-ching », p. 139 ; Chen Guofu, *Daozang yuanliu kao*, p. 44-46.

50. *Shoudu yi*, 2a.

51. Voir Zacchetti, « Notions and visions of the canon », p. 99, n. 17.

52. Un écho possible du poète Sun Chuo 孫綽 (314-371) ; voir Bokenkamp, « Scriptures new and old », p. 454, n. 11.

53. Les mauvais *gati* ou chemins de déchéance, équivalents des Trois bourbiers. Ils pouvaient aussi être au nombre de quatre ou cinq. Cf. « Les Cinq chemins » dans « Une Retraite pour toutes les circonstances » au chapitre 6.

54. La construction de la phrase 離彼 X 入此 Y fait écho à *Laozi*, 12 : « Conséquemment [le sage] rejette l'un en faveur de l'autre » 故去彼取此. Voir *Laozi jiaoshi*, p. 46.

55. *Lingbao jingmu xu*, dans *Yunji qiqian*, 4.51.

56. Voir Drège, *Les bibliothèques en Chine*, p. 177-193.

57. « Song Lushan Jianji Lu xiansheng » 宋廬山簡寂陸先生, dans *Zhenxi* 5.75 ; Chen Guofu, *Daozang yuanliu kao*, p. 43 ; Strickmann, « Mao Shan revelations », p. 53 ; Bokenkamp, « Sources of the Ling-pao scriptures », p. 434.

58. Strickmann, « On the alchemy of T'ao Hung-ching », p. 139.

59. Voir *Zhen'gao*, 19.9b-20.4b ; traduit dans Strickmann, « Mao Shan revelations », p. 41-62.

60. *Lingbao jingmu xu*, dans *Yunji qiqian*, 4.51-53 ; voir la traduction intégrale dans Bokenkamp, « Scriptures new and old », p. 454-459.

61. *Lingbao jingmu xu*, dans *Yunji qiqian*, 4.52 ; Bokenkamp, « Scriptures new and old », p. 467-468.

62. *Lingbao jingmu xu*, dans *Yunji qiqian*, 4.53.

63. *Wugan wen*, 4b, et *Shoudu yi*, 41a.

64. P. 3562v, col. 23 ; voir Liu Yongming, « P. 3562v » (1), p. 18, et sous « Les rituels » au chapitre 11.

65. Cf. Matthieu 13, 45-46 : « Le royaume des cieux est comparable à un négociant qui recherche des perles fines. Ayant trouvé une perle de grande valeur, il va vendre tout ce qu'il possède, et il achète la perle. »

66. « Scruter l'obscur » 覽冥訓, *Huainan honglie jijie*, 6.198. Les deux histoires étaient couramment citées dans la poésie et la prose des Six dynasties.

67. Voir Liu Yi, « Jin-Song tianshi dao shi » ; Strickmann, « Mao Shan revelations ». Cf. Brown, *Ransom of the soul*, p. 127-129, sur la noblesse comme vecteur de recrutement pour les premières communautés monastiques chrétiennes.

68. Mather, *The poet Shen Yüeh*, p. 115-120.

69. Voir Tian Xiaofei, *Beacon fire*, p. 35, 37 ; Li Chuanyin, « Nanchao puxue yu zhengzhi ».

70. Holcombe, *In the shadow of the Han*, p. 25-28.

71. Voir *Shishuo xinyu jianshu*, 8/142.490-491 ; Mather, *New account*, p. 261.

72. *Jin shu*, 54.1472, 1481.

73. Voir la table 62 dans Wang Yi-t'ung, *Wuchao mendi*, vol. 2. Sur Lu Xun et d'autres membres de la famille Lu à la cour de Sun Quan 孫權 (r. 229-252), voir De Crespigny, *Generals of the South*, p. 334-339, 502-503.

74. Voir Sujane Wu, « The biography of Lu Yun », p. 1-2.

75. Voir la table 62 dans Wang Yi-t'ung, *Wuchao mendi*, vol. 2 ; Strickmann, « Mao Shan revelations », p. 16, 38 ; Mather, *New account*, p. 75. Lu Na a une biographie dans *Jin shu*, 77.2026-2027.

76. Zhang Zhenjun, « Observations », p. 89-90.

77. *Lidai minghua ji*, 6.143.

78. *Lunheng jiaoshi*, 29.1179. L'expression « confondre pourpre et vermillon » voulait dire manquer de discernement ; voir *Hou Han shu*, 36.1231.

79. *Zou tan Wang Yuan* 奏彈王源, dans *Wenxuan* 文選, 40. Voir Knechtges, « Marriage and social status » ; Mather, *The poet Shen Yüeh*, p. 159-160.

80. Voir *Santian neijie jing*, A.1b-2a ; Schipper, « Purity and strangers », p. 71 ; Stein, « Religious Taoism », p. 64.

81. Voir Zürcher, « Buddhist influence », p. 106.

82. *Shishuo xinyu jianshu*, 24/15.775 ; Qian, *Spirit and self*, p. 164. Cf. les remarques de Lu au sujet du vêtement dans l'*Ordre sommaire de Maître Lu* (dans « La congrégation des élus » au chapitre premier).

83. « Félicité de la foi » était une expression bouddhiste renvoyant à la confiance joyeuse des croyants.

84. Cf. *Pusa shouzhai jing*, 1116a : « Les jours de jeûne du bodhisattva, il n'est pas convenable [pour les hommes] de plaisanter avec les femmes ou de s'asseoir [avec elles]. Il en va de même pour les femmes. »

85. Dans les rituels de requête, les socques en bois étaient obligatoires (voir « Commanditaire et bénéficiaire » au chapitre 3) ; cependant, le *Shishuo xinyu* (voir n. 82) désapprouvait les socques 屐 sauf pour les tenues informelles ; cf. Dien, *Six Dynasties civilization*, p. 315-317.

86. Voir ci-dessus l'observation de Wang Chong au sujet de l'incorrection de mélanger les tuiles et les jades.

87. *Zhuyuan yi*, 17b-18b.

88. *Zhuyuan yi*, 14b-16a.

89. Voir *Kongzi jiayu yizhu*, 3.129-130 et *Wugan wen*, 1a-b.

90. Voir Sun Ruixue, « Lu Xiujing yu tianshi dao ».

91. Voir Wang Chengwen, « Lu Xiujing daojiao xinyang » (2), p. 29-30 ; et *Han-Jin daojiao yishi*, p. 653-706.

92. *Lu xiansheng daomen kelüe*, 5a-b ; Schipper et Verellen, *Taoist canon*, vol. 1, p. 127.

93. Wang Chengwen, « Lu Xiujing daojiao xinyang » (1), p. 1-2.

94. Voir *Lingbao wuliang duren shangpin miaojing* ; Verellen, « Evidential miracles », p. 237.

95. Gernet, *Buddhism in Chinese society*, p. 243-244, 274-777.

96. Les maîtres qualifiés pour conférer l'ordination ; voir Schipper, « Ordination ranks », p. 136-143.

97. La liberté des contraintes matérielles ou mentales dont jouit un être éclairé.

98. Les trois domaines du *samsāra* : les mondes du désir, de la forme et du sans-forme.

99. *Taishang dongxuan lingbao benxing yinyuan jing*, 1b-2a. Voir aussi Bokenkamp, « The Silkworm and the bodhi tree », p. 326-331.

Chapitre 6
La Retraite du Joyau sacré

1. *Shoudu yi*, « Biao », 1a.

2. Voir Wang Chengwen, « Cong zhaijie guifan lun ».

3. Hureau, « Buddhist rituals », p. 1213-1230 ; Gernet, *Buddhism in Chinese society*, p. 257-259.

4. Le *Fayuan zayuan yuanshi ji* 法苑雜緣原始集 disparut ultérieurement, mais la préface de Sengyou a été préservée dans son *Chu sanzang jiji*, 12.90b ; traduit dans Schmidt-Glintzer, *Hung-ming chi*, p. 141.

5. *Si tianwang jing*, 118b ; traduit dans Soymié, « Les dix jours de jeûne », p. 9-10.

6. Voir Soymié, « Les dix jours de jeûne », p. 5 ; Wang Haoyue, *Xijing qiuzhen*, p. 126-139 ; et Lü Pengzhi, « Lingbao fast of the Three Primes ».

7. Voir *Wugan wen*, 4b, et ci-après.

8. Voir Hureau, « Buddhist rituals », p. 1221-1222 ; Mather, *The poet Shen Yüeh*, p. 156.

9. Voir ci-dessus et Chen Guofu, *Daozang yuanliu kao*, p. 41 ; Lü Pengzhi, *Tang qian daojiao yishi*, p. 169.

10. Cf. Johnston, « *Fiat lux, fiat ritus* », p. 17.

11. *Dongxuan lingbao zhai shuo guangzhu jie fa deng zhuyuan yi*, 1a-b (désormais cité comme *Zhuyuan yi*), surtout développé d'après les prolégomènes de la *Lumière du rituel*. Cf. la recompilation dans *Wushang huanglu dazhai licheng yi*, 16.18a (désormais

cité comme *Licheng yi*). En fait, aucune des versions reçues ne se réfère aux lampes ni aux prières.

12. « Xiaoyao you » 逍遙遊, *Zhuangzi jishi*, 1.22-23 ; cf. Michael, *Pristine Dao*, p. 46-47. Sur l'usage du *Zhuangzi* par Lu Xiujing, voir Kamitsuka Yoshiko, *Dōkyō kyōten*, p. 130-142.

13. Cf. Colomban (540-615), *Instruction* (« Ainsi enrichis-tu ma lanterne de ta lumière ») ; voir Brown, *Rise of Western Christendom*, p. 251.

14. Le désir, la convoitise, les vues erronées, l'illusion et les afflictions. Une définition bouddhiste comprend le *kalpa* des derniers jours, les vues erronées, l'illusion, les afflictions et l'abrègement de la durée de vie.

15. Paraphrase possible de Ge Hong : « Le soleil et la lune ne peuvent pas répandre leur lumière dans des cavernes tortueuses. » Voir *Baopu zi waipian jiaojian*, 17.453.

16. Paraphrase du *Zhuangzi jishi*, 1.39. Le fil à plomb servait à marquer une ligne droite avec de l'encre. Voir Needham, *Science and civilisation*, vol. 4, 2e partie, p. 60.

17. *Zhuyuan yi*, 1a-b.

18. *Zhuyuan yi*, 13a-14b. Sur ces catégories d'officiants du Lingbao et leur provenance, voir Wang Chengwen, « Gu lingbao jing de zhaiguan ».

19. Sur le Rituel des préceptes, voir 7b-12b et ci-dessous ; sur les officiants, 12b-14a ; sur les amendes, de 14a à la fin du texte.

20. *Zhuyuan yi*, 5a, donne *fu* 輔 (assister) au lieu de *si* 嗣 (succéder à).

21. Ces définitions apparaissent sous la forme d'une note dans *Taishang dongxuan lingbao fazhu jing* (désormais cité comme *Fazhu jing*), 1a ; dans le corps du texte dans *Zhuyuan yi*, 5a.

22. Dien, « Lighting », p. 1. Voir aussi Dien, « Light after dark », pour des exemples archéologiques. Je suis redevable à Albert Dien pour les informations fournies à ce sujet.

23. Voir *Huayang yinju xiansheng benqi lu* 華陽隱居先生本起錄, dans *Yunji qiqian*, 107.2325. Le quantificateur *ting* 鋌 est ambigu. Dien cite des occurrences des variantes *ting* 挺 et 梃 (signifiant « vertical », « droit ») qui suggèrent des bougies (Dien, « Lighting », p. 5-6, 29-30).

24. Dien, « Lighting », p. 2.

25. Voir Seidel, « Sûtra merveilleux », p. 314.

26. Voir Zacchetti, *In praise of the light*, p. 3, n. 5. Sur l'emploi de la lumière dans le contexte religieux sous les Six dynasties et les Tang, voir aussi Dien, « Light after dark », p. 318-319.

27. *Fazhu jing*, 2b.

28. Sur les sens pertinents de *fa*, voir Strickmann, *Chinese poetry and prophecy*, p. 95-96.

29. Voir chapitre 7. Au sermon 1, ce terme renvoie spécifiquement au contrôle des appétits sensoriels.

30. *Fazhu jing*, 1a-b. Cf. le sermon 2 ci-dessous, sur la gouvernance de soi et la correction de ses pensées.

31. *Santian neijie jing*, B.2b. Cf. les *Instructions familiales de Monsieur Yan* du VIe siècle, qui comparent l'étude à un âge avancé à « marcher de nuit en tenant une lumière » 如秉燭夜行 ; *Yanshi jiaxun jijie*, 3.166.

32. Corrigé sur la base de variantes dans *Zhuyuan yi*, 6b.

33. *Fazhu jing*, 2b.

34. C'est-à-dire Zhuang Zun 莊遵, également connu comme Yan Junping 嚴君平. Le caractère *zhuang* devint tabou après le règne de Mingdi des Han (57-75 de notre ère) ; voir Alan K. L. Chan, « Essential meaning », p. 106-117. Sur Yan et l'Érudition du mystère, voir Nylan, « The legacies of the Chengdu plain », p. 314-315.

35. *Fazhu jing*, 2a. Voir *Laozi zhigui*, p. 22. L'original donne *cun* 存 à la place de *qi* 期.

36. Voir « Repentance et réforme » au chapitre 5, où Lu déplore d'être né dans la période de déclin final.

37. Sur l'utilisation de ce terme bouddhiste par Lu Xiujing en référence aux souffrances sans bornes qui sont le lot des mortels, voir Tang Yijie, *Wei Jin Nanbei chao shiqi de daojiao*, p. 280.

38. *Fazhu jing*, 2a-b.

39. *Mengzi zhushu*, 8b.230.

40. *Shang jun shu jinzhu jinyi*, 1.6 ; cf. Pines, *Book of Lord Shang*, p. 122.

41. Voir respectivement *Zhanguo ce*, 119.663 et 29.1058 : « Tant que le bandit intérieur n'est pas pacifié, vous ne pouvez pas repousser l'ennemi extérieur » 內寇不與，外敵不可距.

42. Les Cinq désirs 五慾, également 五欲, les désirs nés des cinq sens : son, vue, odeur, goût et esprit. Sur le contrôle de soi, cf. « Lumière du rituel » ci-dessus et chapitre 7, sermon 1, où il est fait référence au contrôle des appétits sensoriels.

43. L'Un, en se différenciant, engendra le repos et le mouvement, et l'être à partir du vide ; voir Michael, *Pristine Dao*, p. 65. Protéger 關 : le *Zhuyuan yi* donne « arrêter » 閑.

44. *Fazhu jing*, 2a ; *Zhuyuan yi*, 6a.

45. *Jingzhu zi jingxing famen*, 30.317a.

46. Voir Komjathy, *Taming the wild horse*.

47. À propos des séries de Dix préceptes dans le taoïsme, voir Kusuyama Haruki, « Dōkyō ni okeru jikkai ».

48. *Taishang dongxuan lingbao chishu yujue miaojing*, A.2b-3a (désormais cité comme *Yujue miaojing*) ; voir Lü Pengzhi, « Jade instructions ».

49. *Taishang dongzhen zhihui shangpin dajie*, 1b-2b (désormais cité comme *Shangpin dajie*).

50. Voir Bokenkamp, « Sources of the Ling-pao scriptures », p. 479, 481.

51. Funayama Tōru, « Rikuchō jidai ni okeru bosatsukai », p. 52-106.

52. Voir Kleeman, « Cultivating conduct », p. 159-164.

53. Voir *Fanwang jing*, B.1004c-1005a, et *Pusa yingluo benye jing*, A.1012b ; Funayama Tōru, « Acceptance of Buddhist precepts », p. 103-104, 110-113, et « Bodhisattva practice », p. 15-33.

54. Liu Jiahe, « Early Buddhism and Taoism », p. 38-41.

55. *Fo shuo chengju guangming dingyi jing*. Voir Nattier, *Guide*, p. 94-101 ; Pu Chengzhong, « Notes ».

56. Les Élucidations des préceptes étaient des assemblées monastiques se déroulant au milieu et à la fin du mois lunaire pour expliquer les préceptes et confesser les transgressions.

57. *Zhuyuan yi*, 8a.

58. Sanskrit *duhkhin*, la faculté de souffrir.

59. Les huit conditions de renaissance (comme habitant de l'enfer, fantôme affamé, animal, etc.) qui faisaient obstacle à l'illumination.

60. Les sages rois tournant la roue du *dharma* 法輪.

61. Le *Shangpin dajie* donne « soyez déférent » 推讓 au lieu de « obtempérez à la droiture ».

62. Voir Kleeman, « Cultivating conduct », p. 161.

63. Le *Shangpin dajie* donne 無玷汙.

64. Le *Yujue miaojing* donne « loyal et droit » 忠直. Cf. *Zhengyi lun*, 4a : « Concernant les paroles dignes de foi, elles ne sont pas embellies ; il en a toujours été ainsi. Et les belles paroles ne sont pas dignes de foi, maintenant comme toujours. »

65. Le *Shangpin dajie* donne « modérez l'alcool » 減酒 ; les Préceptes du bodhisattva interdisaient « le commerce d'alcool » 酤酒

66. Le *Yujue miaojing* et le *Shangpin dajie* donnent 不得 à la place de 不.

67. Cf. le *Soutra du lotus* au sujet de calomnier les écritures ou le *dharma* dans le bouddhisme. *Miaofa lianhua jing*, 9.15b.

68. Cf. *Lunyu zhushu*, 3.35 : « Sacrifiez aux dieux comme s'ils étaient présents » 祭神如神在.

69. Terme bouddhiste désignant les moines, les nonnes et les pratiquants laïcs des deux sexes ; cf. Zürcher, « Buddhist influence », p. 116.

70. Le *Yujue miaojing* donne « les hommes seront en harmonie et les dieux apaisés » 人和神睦.

71. *Zhuyuan yi*, 8a-9b.

72. Voir *Fanwang jing*, B.1004c-1005a.

73. Gernet, *Buddhism in Chinese society*, p. 195-228.

74. Les écrits de Lu qui ont subsisté ne s'étendent pas sur cette expression, en rapport avec les dix bonnes et dix mauvaises actions 十善十惡 diversement définies dans le bouddhisme et le taoïsme dans le cadre des préceptes.

75. *Zhuyuan yi*, 1b.

76. Voir Wang Chengwen, *Han-Jin daojiao yishi*, p. 172-176 (ablutions) et 318-365 (*poṣadha*).

77. Un fil de soie verte (ou noire) était utilisé pour les offrandes rituelles (voir « La scène et l'offrande » au chapitre 3) et pour constituer des ligatures de pièces de monnaie (voir « Kongque dongnan fei » 孔雀東南飛, dans *Xian Qin Han Wei Jin Nanbei chao shi*, 10.285).

78. *Wugan wen*, 7a. Je suis redevable à Liu Yan 劉焱 pour ses commentaires avisés à propos de cette traduction. « Huile essentielle », littéralement « huile précédente » 前油, renvoie au produit initial obtenu par distillation à la vapeur et utilisé pour fabriquer les arômes et parfums.

79. Cf. *Licheng yi*, 16.11b-12a.

80. *Zhuyuan yi*, 3a-b ; cf. *Licheng yi*, 16.19b-20a.

81. Les neuf ouvertures corporelles ; également écrit 九竅. Sur le souffle vital, voir « La Voie et la Vertu » au chapitre 7.

82. Terminologie bouddhiste. Après le repas de la mi-journée, également appelé « repas de l'abstention » 齋食, aucune nourriture n'était consommée durant le reste

de la journée. Cf. le traité sur le repas unique, de Shen Yue ; Tian Xiaofei, *Beacon fire*, p. 65.

83. Actes de contrition : littéralement, « se prosterner et se claquer la joue » 叩搏.

84. Les Six facultés sont les perceptions sensorielles des yeux, des oreilles, du nez, de la langue, de la peau et de l'esprit ; selon la moralité bouddhiste, elles engendraient le péché et l'affliction.

85. Concept bouddhiste, les Trois poisons renvoient aux effets délétères de l'envie, de la colère et de l'ignorance.

86. *Zhuyuan yi*, 1b-2a ; cf. *Licheng yi*, 13.4b-5b.

87. Voir *Fengdao kejie*, 1.16a.

88. Voir l'« Hymne à la sagesse » cité ci-dessus. Sur la descente des esprits, voir aussi *Zhuyuan yi*, 10a-b, et *Shangpin dajie*, 5b-6a.

89. *Licheng yi*, 13.4b.

90. *Wugan wen*, 4b.

91. Sur le Grand un, voir Pankenier, *Astrology and cosmology*, p. 90.

92. *Wugan wen*, 5b-7a. Voir aussi Lagerwey, « Canonical fasts » ; Lü Pengzhi, *Tang qian daojiao yishi*, p. 182-192.

93. Voir Lü Pengzhi, « Tianshi dao zhijiao zhai ». La Retraite de boue et de cendres 塗炭齋, énumérée séparément par Lu Xiujing, remontait selon la tradition à Zhang Lu ; voir Chen Guofu, *Daozang yuanliu kao*, p. 328.

94. Voir l'introduction du chapitre 5 et Lü Pengzhi, « Lingbao fast of the Three Primes ». Servir l'État était l'une des fonctions explicites de la Retraite du Lingbao ; voir Seidel, « Imperial treasures », p. 352.

95. *Zhuyuan yi*, 2b-3a. Les Cinq chemins renvoyaient à la renaissance d'un individu comme divinité, être humain, animal, fantôme affamé ou détenu des enfers.

Chapitre 7

Corrigez votre cœur, corrigez votre conduite !

1. Voir Polanski, *Aristotle's* De anima.

2. Cf. Nylan, « *Yin-yang*, Five Phases, and *qi* ».

3. Voir Qian Nanxiu, *Spirit and self*, chapitre 5.

4. Cf. Hureau, « Buddhist rituals », p. 1222-1225. Sur la technique de prédication de Huiyuan, voir Cao Ling, « Guanyu Nanchao de changdao », p. 27-30.

5. *Zhuyuan yi*, 1a-b ; voir aussi l'annotation sous le titre du texte. « Retraite » 齋 est une correction de « Retraite et Offrande » 齋醮, probablement une corruption textuelle ; voir Lü Pengzhi, « Zaoqi daojiao jiaoyi », p. 139, n. 247.

6. *Shenzhou jing*, 7.12b, 17.5a.

7. Voir *Pusa shouzhai jing*, 1116b.

8. Pour le rituel de l'Annonce nocturne de Lu Xiujing, voir *Licheng yi*, 16.

9. *Fazhu jing*, 2b.

10. Sur le Jeûne du cœur, voir Schipper, *Taoist body*, p. 195-208.

11. Sur la pratique rituelle consistant à réciter le *Laozi*, voir Ōfuchi Ninji, *Shoki no dōkyō*, p. 170-174.

12. Voir *Wushang biyao*, 35.1a-2a ; Schipper, « Taoist ordination ranks », p. 137-142.

13. Voir *Song shu*, 67.1778 ; Mather, *The poet Shen Yüeh*, p. 42.

14. Voir Strickmann, « Mao shan revelations », p. 31-32.

15. Voir *Laozi Daode jing zashuo*, catalogué dans *Song shi*, 205.5177.

16. Cf. *Taishang lingbao wufu xu*, A.19b. La noblesse de l'homme parmi toute la création est un thème récurrent dans la cosmologie chinoise ; cf. *Shangshu zhengyi*, 11.270, et *Xiaojing zhushu*, 5.28.

17. « Dissipent leur principe vital » : le *Zhuyuan yi* donne 凋其命.

18. *Fazhu jing*, 1b-2a ; *Zhuyuan yi*, 5b-6b.

19. Voir *Laozi jiaoshi*, p. 176.

20. Cf. Michael, *Pristine Dao*, p. 95.

21. Voir Verellen, « Lu Xiujing (406-77) on Daoist practice », p. 181-182.

22. Cf. *Santian neijie jing*, A.1a-b. Sur la « mutualité du Ciel et de l'Homme » confucéenne, voir Tu Wei-ming, *Centrality and commonality*, p. 9.

23. Cf. *Lunyu zhushu*, 15.216 : « L'Homme est capable de magnifier la Voie, ce n'est pas la Voie qui magnifie l'Homme » 人能弘道，非道弘人.

24. *Fazhu jing*, 3a ; *Zhuyuan yi*, 7a.

25. Cf. la Leçon 3 : « Quand il ne subsiste plus une seule pensée, vous vous unissez au *qi* du Tao. »

26. *Houshi* : comme *laishi* 來世, un terme bouddhiste pour le monde après la mort.

27. Selon Ge Hong, pour prévenir la dispersion des âmes, les pratiquants taoïstes exécutaient un « rituel de rétention » 拘錄之法. Le terme *julu* 拘錄 s'écrivait aussi *luju* 錄具 ; voir *Baopu zi neipian jiaoshi*, 2.19-20.

28. *Fazhu jing*, 3b-4a ; *Laozi jiaoshi*, p. 184. Ce dernier donne « quiétude » 淸靜 au lieu de « pureté et calme » 淸淨.

29. *Laozi jiaoshi*, p. 193.

30. Voir *Zhengyi fawen taishang wailu yi*, 7b et suivantes.

31. Voir *Chisong zi zhangli*, 4.21b-22a.

32. Voir *Shoudu yi*, 7a ; Schipper, « Taoist ordination ranks », p. 131-134 ; Lü Pengzhi, « Tianshi dao shoulu keyi », p. 113 ; Hureau, « Buddhist rituals », p. 1220.

33. La circulation et la perfusion du *qi* du Tao dans le corps de l'adepte sont mentionnées dans le *Rite de Hanzhong* cité dans *Dengzhen yinjue*, 3.11a.

34. *Fazhu jing*, 4a-b.

35. *Laozi jiaoshi*, p. 232.

36. Voir ci-dessus et *Zhuyuan yi*, 1b-2b.

37. Durt, « On gratitude », p. 239 ; Funayama Tōru, « Buddhist theories of bodhisattva practice », p. 15-18.

38. Cf. *Laozi*, 14 (*Laozi jiaoshi*, p. 52).

39. Une recension approximative du passage final, à partir de « pratiquer l'examen de soi », se trouve dans *Taishang hunyuan zhenlu*, 25a, et plusieurs autres textes postérieurs.

40. Cf. *Zhuyuan yi*, 9a, n° 5 des Dix préceptes : « Que votre expression soit sans ornement. Soyez juste et droit à l'intérieur et au-dehors. » Cf., également, J. S. Bach, Cantate BWV 179 : « Wer so von innen wie von außen ist, der heißt ein wahrer Christ. »

41. *Fazhu jing*, 4b-5a.

42. *Fo shuo chengju guangming dingyi jing* (désormais cité comme *Dingyi jing*).

43. Voir *Laozi jiaoshi*, p. 19 et 228. Lu cite la variante *dissipez votre rancœur* 解其忿 à la place de *dénouez ce qui est emmêlé*.

44. Il s'agit d'une phrase du *Dingyi jing*, 453b.

45. Cette séquence, jusqu'à « remède », est une paraphrase du *Dingyi jing*, 453b : 觀其所起，察其所滅。視其所病，選以何藥。

46. Remède de Sagesse 慧藥 : correction de « remède de bonté » 惠藥 ; cf. *Licheng yi*, 16.23a.

47. La séquence jusqu'à « casser un pied » est reprise dans (ou dérive de la même source commune que) *Yaoxiu keyi jielü chao*, 4.2a.

48. L'expression « pied cassé, nourriture renversée » 折足覆餗 signifie incapacité ; voir *Livre des mutations*, 94 : « quand un pied du chaudron [à trois pieds] *ding* 鼎 se casse, la nourriture est renversée » 鼎折足，覆公餗 (*Zhou Yi zhengyi*, 5.208).

49. Ce qui suit est une paraphrase de *Dingyi jing*, 453b.13. Le dernier élément (terrain de chardons et d'épines), cependant, manque dans la version reçue du *Dingyi jing*.

50. Le *Dingyi jing* donne « facteurs d'illumination » 道品.

51. *Dingyi jing* : « maison des Six périls » 六患之舍 ; « palais des Six puretés » 六淨之堂.

52. *Dingyi jing* : « chambre des Cinq dissimulations » 五蔽之室 ; « abri des moyens appropriés » 方便之護.

53. *Dingy jing* : 捨遠之徑.

54. On adopte la variante 壞船 du *Dingyi jing* au lieu de « bateau dérivant » 浮船 et celle 圖 du *Dingyi jing* au lieu de 固.

55. On adopte la variante 安 du *Dingyi jing* au lieu de 要.

56. *Dingy jing* : « Ainsi le lettré éclairé pratique-t-il le moyen approprié de la Sagesse pour se dégager du cycle des renaissances » 是以明士行智慧之便，拔出生死之難.

57. *Fazhu jing*, 5b-6a.

58. *Zhuyuan yi*, 2b-3a. Voir aussi « Les puissances du mal » au chapitre 2.

59. Voir Michael, *In the shadows of the Dao*, p. 10-12, et chapitre 5.

60. Voir Harper, « Précis de connaissance médicale », p. 70-106.

61. *Laozi jiaoshi*, p. 25.

62. Voir Shaughnessy, *Unearthing the Changes*, p. 1-36, pour l'histoire ancienne de cet ouvrage.

63. Voir Strickmann, « On the alchemy of T'ao Hung-ching », p. 187 ; *Sanguo zhi*, 57.1328 ; Vitiello, « Studio sul taoista Lu Xiujing », p. 302-303 ; *Jin shu*, 54.1472 et 1481 ; et Sujane Wu, « Biography of Lu Yun », p. 1-2, 11-22.

64. Comparer *Zhou Yi zhengyi*, 9.326, et *Fazhu jing*, 6a. La bienveillance et la justice reviennent néanmoins dans la Leçon 7 de Lu, en référence au foie et aux poumons.

65. Sur ces catégories binomiales, cf. Despeux, « Âmes et animation », p. 75.

66. Référence aux sept passions 七情 : la joie, la colère, le chagrin, la peur, l'amour, la haine et le désir 喜怒哀懼愛惡欲.

67. Sur les étiologies liées au vent, voir Unschuld, *Medicine in China*, p. 67-73.

68. *Laozi Daode jing Heshang gong zhangju*, 1.21-22 Sur les liens du *Heshang gong* avec le *Huangting neijing*, voir Despeux, « Âmes et animation », p. 77-79.

69. Voir *Daoxue zhuan*, cité dans *Sandong zhunang*, 2.6a (Bumbacher, *Fragments*, p. 209 et 212).

70. Selon les textes de pacification des tombes d'époque Han, « les vivants étaient placés sous [la juridiction de la capitale] Chang'an à l'Ouest, les morts sous [celle du] mont Tai à l'Est » 生人屬西長安，死人屬東太山 ; voir Wu Rongceng, « Zhenmu zhi wen », p. 58.

71. La lumière entourant le corps dans les images bouddhistes. Par contraste, une maladie des poumons était cause de pâleur et d'une langue blanche ; voir *Taishang wuji dadao ziran zhenyi wucheng fu shangjing*, A.7b.

72. *Fazhu jing*, 6a-7b.

73. Voir Puett, « Becoming Laozi », p. 223-252, et Schipper, « Inner world », p. 114-131.

74. Voir Robinet, *Méditation taoïste*, p. 94-129.

75. Le *qi* était le régulateur de la température corporelle. Le *qi* chaud, par exemple, provoquait une « maladie de chaleur sévère » 大熱病 ; voir *Huangdi neijing suwen yijie*, 28.236. Dans le système d'Aristote, c'était le *pneuma* qui régulait la chaleur corporelle ; voir Polansky, *Aristotle's* De anima, p. 221.

76. *Zhongyong* 中庸, in *Liji zhengyi*, 12.399 ; Tu Wei-ming, *Centrality and commonality*, p. 5-6.

77. Mather, *The poet Shen Yüeh*, p. 40.

78. Sur les notions taoïstes et pré-taoïstes de *ming* 命 (vie, lot, part allouée, destinée) en rapport avec le corps, voir Bokenkamp, « Simple twists of fate », p. 151-168.

79. *Fazhu jing*, 7b-8a.

80. *Laozi jiaoshi*, p. 66.

81. Cf. Xiang Shiling, « Study on the theory of "returning to the original" », p. 503-504.

82. Ainsi que l'a décrit Zhuangzi ; voir Michael, *Pristine Dao*, p. 140-141.

83. Voir Kohn, « The *Tao-te-ching* in ritual », p. 150-153.

84. Voir Liu Jiahe, « Early Buddhism and Taoism », p. 38.

85. *Taishang laojun xuwu ziran benqi jing*.

86. *Laozi jiaoshi*, p. 206-207.

87. *Taishang laojun xuwu ziran benqi jing*, 9a, commente « le Tao » comme étant « le Vide » 道者虛也.

88. *Fazhu jing*, 8b. Cf. la Leçon 10 ci-dessous : « retourner sa lumière 復還光 pour pratiquer l'introspection. »

89. Voir *Gaoseng zhuan*, 3.128-130.

90. *Mingxiang ji*, cité dans *Fayuan zhulin*, 22.453a ; traduit dans Campany, *Signs from the unseen realm*, p. 223-224.

91. *Laozi jiaoshi*, p. 37, 40.

92. Voir *Taiping jing hejiao*, 18.19 : « 元氣有三名，太陽，太陰，中和 » ; Espesset, « À vau-l'eau », p. 66. Cf. *Renwu zhi*, 1.14, et la représentation grecque de l'âme comme *harmonia* ou « harmonisation » du corps, Polansky, *Aristotle's* De anima, p. 103-112.

93. Référence à l'Un primordial en cosmogonie ; cf. *Laozi*, 42 (*Laozi jiaoshi*, p. 174, et la Leçon 1) : « Le Tao produisit l'Un » ; sur la trinité Ciel-Homme-Terre produisant toutes les choses phénoménales, voir Michael, *Pristine Dao*, p. 56-57 ; et sur le Tao comme ancêtre ultime de l'humanité, voir Michael, *Pristine Dao*, p. 98.

94. Les organes des sens et la perception sensorielle comme partie prenante de la composition et du fonctionnement de l'être humain en tant qu'agrégat de matériel et d'immatériel ; voir Zürcher, « Buddhist influence », p. 112-113.

95. Un principe d'éducation morale confucéenne ; cf. *Zhou Yi zhengyi*, 7.284 : 感而遂通天下之故.

96. Voir *Shangpin dajie*, 6a-b.

97. *Fazhu jing*, 8b-9b.

98. *Taishang xuanyi zhenren shuo miaotong zhuanshen ruding jing*.

99. Voir Zürcher, « Buddhist influence », p. 112.

100. *Hamlet*, acte II, scène 2.

101. *Fazhu jing*, 9b.

102. *Zhou Yi zhengyi*, 1.23.

103. Une adaptation du triple refuge 三歸 dans les Trois joyaux (*triśarana*) bouddhistes : le Bouddha, la doctrine et le *sangha* ; pour les taoïstes, il s'agissait de la Voie, des écritures et du maître ; voir Zürcher, « Buddhist influence », p. 115.

104. Cf. le thème de la Leçon 8, tiré de *Laozi*, 52 : « Faites usage de votre lumière, inversez-en son éclairement. »

105. Des esprits à demeure ; cf. Strickmann, « On the alchemy of T'ao Hung-ching », p. 173-175.

106. Voir *Zhen'gao*, 10.18b.

107. Voir Verellen, « The beyond within ».

108. Michael, *Pristine Dao*, p. 61.

109. Le royaume du milieu (la Chine) était délimité par cinq montagnes sacrées et entouré par quatre mers et quatre-vingt-une régions barbares.

110. Ces souffles correspondent à quatre des six façons différentes d'expulser l'air ; voir Maspero, *Le taoïsme*, p. 532-535. Cf. le *Classique des montagnes et des mers* (IVe s. avant notre ère), à propos de Zhuyin 燭陰, l'esprit dragon du mont Zhong 鍾山 : « Son [âpre] exhalation *chui* fait l'hiver, sa [douce] exhalation *hu* fait l'été » 吹爲冬，呼爲夏 (*Shanhai jing jiaozhu*, 3.230). Sur l'inhalation et l'exhalation cosmique du yin et du yang, voir Michael, *Pristine Dao*, p. 57-58.

111. Sur le voyage en esprit dans le bouddhisme, le taoïsme et la peinture de paysage chinoise, voir Tian Xiaofei, « Seeing with the mind's eye ».

112. *Laozi jiaoshi*, p. 189. Voir aussi Schipper, « Inner world ».

113. *Xinyu jiaozhu*, A.89.

114. Cf. la phrase « L'esprit voyage, le corps reste » 神往形留 dans « Pour Xi Kang » 贈嵇康, de Guo Xiashu 郭遐叔 (époque Wei), *Xian Qin Han Wei Jin Nanbei chao shi*, 8.476.

115. *Fazhu jing*, 9b-10a.

116. *Taishang dongxuan lingbao bawei zhaolong miaojing*, 2.13a.

117. Cf. Pregadio, « Early Daoist meditation », p. 123.

Chapitre 8
Gagner l'autre rive par le revaloir

1. *Wugan wen*.

2. *Wugan wen*, 1b. Sur la Retraite de boue et de cendres, voir Bokenkamp, « Sackcloth and ashes » ; Yamada Akihiro, « Totansai kō » ; Wang Guiping, « Daojiao tutan zhai fa » ; Lagerwey, « Canonical fasts », p. 66-76.

3. Durt, « On gratitude », p. 239-240.

4. Voir *Xiaodao Wu Xu er zhenjun zhuan* ; Schipper, « Taoist ritual and local cults », p. 826-828.

5. Michael, *Pristine Dao*, p. 96-97. Cf. 1 Corinthiens 6, 20 : « Vous ne vous appartenez plus à vous-mêmes, car vous avez été achetés à grand prix. »

6. Voir Strickmann, « Taoist confirmation », p. 473 ; et *Taiping jing hejiao*, 42.37-38 ; Hendrischke, *Scripture on Great Peace*, p. 96-97, 100-101.

7. *Mengzi zhushu*, 7B.210, paraphrasé avec approbation par Maître Mou (cf. la section « Lever les doutes » ci-dessous) : « des manquements à la filialité, nul ne dépasse l'absence d'enfant » 不孝莫過於無後 (*Mouzi lihuo lun*, 1.3a).

8. Voir Michael, *Pristine Dao*, p. 96-97 ; et *Xiaojing zhushu*, 1.3, cité dans *Mouzi lihuo lun*, 1.2c, ainsi que d'autres écrits polémiques.

9. Voir Ch'en, « Filial piety in Chinese Buddhism ».

10. Voir, par exemple, *Taishang dongxuan lingbao benxing suyuan jing*, 12b.

11. Cf. Bokenkamp, *Ancestors and anxiety*, p. 1-32.

12. *Fumu en nanbao jing*.

13. Voir l'étude phare de Teiser, *Ghost Festival*.

14. Tous deux datent du ve siècle ; voir *Yulanpen jing* (cf. *Chu sanzang jiji*, 4.28c) et *Baoen fengpen jing*.

15. Voir *Taishang dongxuan lingbao sanyuan pinjie gongde qingzhong jing*, et Lü Pengzhi, « Lingbao fast of the Three Primes », p. 37-38.

16. Teiser, *Ghost Festival*, p. 48-56.

17. Cf., chez les premiers chrétiens, la pratique familiale du repas de fête pris à proximité de leurs morts ; Brown, *Ransom of the soul*, p. 36.

18. Voir Durt, « On gratitude », p. 241-242 ; Cole, *Mothers and sons*, p. 41-55.

19. *Fumu en nanbao jing*, 779a ; Cole, *Mothers and sons*, p. 43-44.

20. *Fumu en zhong jing* ; voir aussi Akizuki Kan'ei, « Dōkyō to bukkyō no *Fubo enchō kyō* ». Pour une comparaison des deux textes, voir Guang Xing, « *Fumu en nanbao jing* yu *Fumu en zhong jing* ».

21. Voir Makita Tairyō, *Gikyō kenkyū*, p. 55-60.

22. *Fanwang jing*, B.1003c ; Durt, « On gratitude », p. 241.

23. Brown, *Body and society*, p. 34 et 42, citant Luc 18, 29.

24. Voir *Maoshan zhi*, 10.11a.

25. *Daoxue zhuan*, cité dans *Sandong qunxian lu*, 2.16b-17a (Bumbacher, *Fragments*, p. 218).

26. *Gaoseng zhuan*, 11.140 ; Link, « Shih Seng-Yu and his writings », p. 22.

27. *Daoxue zhuan*, cité dans *Sandong qunxian lu*, 3.2a (Bumbacher, *Fragments*, p. 214-215).

28. Premier verset de l'« Hymne de la triple annonce » 三啓頌 ; voir *Shoudu yi*, 41a.

29. *Maoshi zhengyi*, 2.133-135.

30. Voir Holzman, « Place of filial piety », p. 187, et Cole, *Mothers and sons*, p. 111.

31. *Maoshi zhengyi*, 13.778-779 ; traduction adaptée de Waley, *Book of songs*, p. 185.

32. Voir *Fumu en nanbao jing*, 779a, et *Xiaozi jing*, 780b.

33. Le *Fumu en nanbao jing* (loc. cit.) distinguait, à la suite du « Liao e », les rôles respectifs du père et de la mère comme étant d'« engendrer » 生 et d'« élever » 養. Cf. Cole, *Mothers and sons*, p. 44-45 ; Bokenkamp, *Ancestors and anxiety*, p. 3-4. La formulation dans *Fumu en zhong jing*, 1403b, « Sans père, je ne serais pas engendré, sans mère, je n'aurais pas été élevé » 非父不生，非母不育, fait écho à un autre verset du « Liao e » : « En l'absence de père, qui me soutiendrait ? En l'absence de mère, qui m'appuierait ? » 無父何怙，無母何恃 (*Maoshi zhengyi*, 13.777). Cf. la réécriture taoïste : « Sans père je ne serais pas engendré, sans mère je n'aurais pas été élevé » 非父不生，非母不養, dans *Taishang laojun shuo bao fumu en zhong jing*, 2b.

34. Cf. *Xiaozi jing*, 780b.

35. Oublièrent de se nourrir : corriger *wangjin* 忘金, « oublieux de la dépense », en *wangshi* 忘食.

36. *Wugan wen*, 2a. Une première version de cette traduction et des suivantes du *Wugan wen* parut dans Verellen, « Five sentiments », p. 404-406.

37. Liu Yongming, « P. 3562v », (1), p. 24 ; (2), p. 16-17.

38. Voir *Nan Qi shu*, 41.721, et *Nan shi*, 32.833. Éventail en plumes d'aigrette : voir Liu Yang, « Origins of Daoist iconography », p. 34-52.

39. *Yulanpen jing*, 779a, et *Baoen fengpen jing*, 780a ; traduit dans Teiser, *Ghost Festival*, p. 49.

40. Cf. *Xiaozi jing*, 780b.

41. Cf. *Taizhen yudi siji mingke jing*, *passim*. Sur l'ébouillantement, le bûcher et la flagellation dans la loi des Han, voir Hulsewé, *Remnants*, p. 122-124, 129. Voir aussi Teiser, « Having once died », sur les représentations de l'enfer dans le bouddhisme des Tang.

42. Cf. *Xiaozi jing*, 780b : « Dans l'eau bouillante, les flammes et dix mille afflictions, leurs cris solitaires ne sont d'aucun secours. »

43. *Wugan wen*, 2b.

44. Voir les exemples dans le *Hou Han shu* que cite Holzman, « Place of filial piety », p. 193-199.

45. Voir un résumé des hypothèses sur la question dans Keenan, *How Master Mou*, p. 3-7.

46. Voir *Falun mulu* 法輪目錄, dans *Chu sanzang jiji*, 12.93c.

47. Voir *Mouzi lihuo lun*.

48. Voir *Shishuo xinyu*, 4/23.214 ; traduit dans Mather, *New account*, p. 110.

49. *Mouzi lihuo lun*, 1.4c ; traduit dans Keenan, *How Master Mou*, p. 119.

50. Cf. *Anan wenshi fo jixiong jing*, 753c : les disciples des Derniers jours, nés en ce monde de démons (*māra* 魔界) et soumis à la chaîne de causalité (*nidāna* 因緣), prenaient part aux occupations de la vie familiale et au « fardeau de prendre soin du corps et de la bouche ».

51. *Wugan wen*, 3a.

52. Voir *Laozi jiaoshi*, p. 46.

53. *Wugan wen*, 3a-b.

54. Voir Wagner, *Chinese reading*, p. 177.

55. Voir *Laozi jiaoshi*, p. 72.

56. Les cinq sens (vue, ouïe, odorat, goût et toucher) dont résultent les Cinq désirs.

57. *Mouzi lihuo lun*, 1.3c ; Keenan, *How Master Mou*, p. 105-109. Sur la réception de cette histoire en Chine, voir Bokenkamp, « The Viśvantara-jātaka ».

58. *Taishang dongxuan lingbao zhihui dingzhi tongwei jing*, 9a-16a ; cf. Zürcher, « Buddhist influence », p. 103.

59. *Wugan wen*, 3a-b. Cf. *Xiaozi jing*, 780b : « Que dorénavant mes deux parents résident à jamais en paix en ce monde ; à la fin de leurs jours, que leurs âmes renaissent au Ciel » 於是二親處世常安，壽終魂靈往生天上.

60. *Daoxue zhuan*, cité dans *Sandong qunxian lu*, 2.16b-17a (Bumbacher, *Fragments*, p. 218).

61. Un des six attachements 六著 du bouddhisme : avidité, amour, haine, doute, luxure et orgueil.

62. *Daoxue zhuan*, cité dans *Sandong qunxian lu*, 1.15b-16a (Bumbacher, *Fragments*, p. 207).

63. Les principes cosmiques transformant la vie, ainsi que la sagesse professée par les sages.

64. *Wugan wen*, 4a.

65. Voir « La culpabilité ancestrale » au chapitre 2 et Bokenkamp, *Ancestors and anxiety*.

66. Voir Zürcher, « Buddhist influence », p. 136-138 ; *Wugan wen*, 7b.

67. *Wugan wen*, 4b. Sur l'histoire du rite des Huit périodes, voir Wang Chengwen, « Gudai guojia jisi ».

68. Cf. Verellen, *Du Guangting*, p. 18-19.

69. Dans le *Shoudu yi*, 1a et 42b, les Trois maîtres ouvrent le chemin de la délivrance 三師開度. Voir aussi *Wushang biyao*, 34.6b et 50.1a (ce dernier passage porte sur la Retraite de boue et de cendres).

70. *Wugan wen*, 4a.

71. Brown, *Rise of Western Christendom*, p. 248.

72. *Wugan wen*, 4b.

73. *Wugan wen*, 1b, 4b ; *Règle pour les moines*, citée dans Brown, *Rise of Western Christendom*, p. 250-251.

74. *Wugan wen*, 2a.

75. Sur le terme générique de Six retraites, voir Lü Pengzhi, *Tang qian daojiao yishi*, p. 187.

76. *Wugan wen*, 1a.

77. Voir sa biographie dans *Nan Qi shu*, 40.692-701 ; voir aussi Tang Yongtong, *Han Wei liang Jin Nanbei chao fojiao*, p. 457-461 ; et Tian Xiaofei, *Beacon fire*, p. 19.

78. *Daoxue zhuan*, cité dans *Sandong zhunang*, 1.8a-b (Bumbacher, *Fragments*, p. 219-220).

79. Voir *Jingzhu zi jingxing famen* et Kuo Li-ying, *Confession et contrition*, p. 111.

Troisième partie
Tout sous un même ciel : la synthèse des Tang

1. Voir Tian Xiaofei, *Beacon fire*, p. 52-67.
2. En 527, 529, 546 et 547 ; voir Gernet, *Buddhism in Chinese society*, p. 243-244.
3. Tian Xiaofei, *Beacon fire*, p. 47 et 56-58 ; Strickmann, *Le taoïsme du Mao Chan*.
4. Strickmann, « On the alchemy of T'ao Hung-ching », p. 155-159. Sur les épées de Tao, voir aussi Fukunaga Mitsuji, « Daojiao de jing yu jian », p. 419-423 et *passim*.
5. Voir *Zhou shi mingtong ji*, 3.8b ; Mugitani et Yoshikawa (dir.), *Shūshi meitsūki*, p. 159, 164-165 ; cf. Strickmann, « Taoist confirmation », p. 469, et Wiles, « Daoist aunt », p. 274-275.
6. Voir Lü Pengzhi, *Tang qian daojiao yishi*, p. 264-265.
7. Voir Kleeman, *Celestial Masters*, p. 196-209.
8. Voir Kohn, *Laughing at the Tao*, p. 29-32.
9. *Wushang biyao* ; voir Lagerwey, *Wu-shang pi-yao*, p. 1-21 ; Cheng Lesong, *Zhonggu daojiao leishu*, p. 73-120.
10. Lü Pengzhi, « Daoist rituals », p. 1344.
11. Seidel, « Taoist messianism », p. 162 ; voir aussi Bokenkamp, « Time after time ».
12. Gernet, *Buddhism in Chinese society*, p. 30-62.
13. Cf. Barrett, *Taoism under the T'ang*.
14. Voir Barrett, « Emergence of the Taoist papacy », p. 89-90 ; Chen Guofu, *Daozang yuanliu kao*, p. 309.
15. *Tang huiyao*, 50.1031 ; Barrett, « Emergence of the Taoist papacy », p. 96.
16. *Zhenxi* ; voir Strickmann, « On the alchemy of T'ao Hung-ching », p. 190-191 ; sur l'ordre Shangqing sous les Tang, voir Kamitsuka Yoshiko, *Dōkyō kyōten*, p. 410-496.
17. Sur la formation d'une orthodoxie taoïste à partir du Vᵉ siècle, voir Raz, *Emergence of Daoism*, p. 210-256.
18. Voir *Tianshi zhi yi*, dans *Shoulu cidi faxin yi*, 19b.
19. Schipper et Verellen, *Taoist canon*, vol. 1, p. 467-468.

Chapitre 9
Les voies de l'initiation

1. *Tang liudian*, 4.125.
2. Voir, par exemple, *Guangcheng ji*, 9.127-128 (Trois souverains) et 9.128, 13.185-188 (Grand un).

3. *Maisha* (correction de la lecture *lisha* 理沙 ; voir *Tang liudian*, 4.125, n. 112) était une thérapie exorciste du Turkestan durant laquelle le corps était recouvert de sable chaud ; voir Saidura, « Maisha liaofa », p. 54.

4. Voir Harper, « Contracts with the spirit world », p. 242-248.

5. Lü Pengzhi, « Zaoqi daojiao jiaoyi » ; voir aussi Raz, *Emergence of Daoism*, p. 91-126.

6. *Taishang lingbao wufu xu*, C.4b.

7. *Taishang lingbao wufu xu*, C.3b ; Kaltenmark, « Quelques remarques », p. 8.

8. Voir Raz, *Emergence of Daoism*, p. 98-101.

9. Voir *Baopu zi neipian jiaoshi*, 11.179 et 16.268.

10. Sur Zhang Wanfu, voir Maruyama Hiroshi, *Dōkyō girei monjo*, p. 420-457.

11. *Jiao sandong zhenwen wufu zhengyi mengwei lu licheng yi*, 1a-b.

12. *Dongxuan lingbao daoshi shou sandong jingjie falu zeri li*, 5b.

13. Voir *Zhengyi jiaozhai yi* ; pour la requête, voir *Chisong zi zhangli*, 5.12a-14a (gages, 1.16a).

14. *Zhengyi jiaomu yi*.

15. *Zhengyi jiee jiaoyi* ; cf. Lü Pengzhi, « Zaoqi daojiao jiaoyi », p. 77-79.

16. *Licheng yi*, 15.3b.

17. Voir Cedzich, « Ritual der Himmelsmeister », p. 101-102.

18. Voir *Wushang biyao*, 49.1a et 18a-b ; Lagerwey, *Wu-shang pi-yao*, p. 152-156 ; Steavu, *Writ of the Three Sovereigns*, p. 168.

19. *Taishang huanglu zhai yi*, 50.1a-11a ; cf. Zhang Zehong, *Daojiao zhaijiao fuzhou*, p. 44-45 ; Sun Yiping, « Lun Du Guangting dui daojiao zhaijiao », p. 22 ; Zhou Xibo, *Du Guangting daojiao yifan*, p. 177-179.

20. Voir Zhou Xibo, *Du Guangting daojiao yifan*, p. 47-70.

21. Par exemple dans l'inscription sur la stèle de Zhang Pu datée de 173 de notre ère.

22. Voir Raz, *Emergence of Daoism*, p. 210-256 ; Kobayashi Masayoshi, *Tōdai no dōkyō*, p. 67-100.

23. Afin de rester dans le registre des entités cosmiques, je lis « Trame céleste » 天綱 au lieu de « Trame mystique » 玄綱. Ce dernier terme renvoie aux points essentiels de la philosophie et de la doctrine taoïstes ; voir De Meyer, *Wu Yun*, p. 40-43.

24. *Zhengyi lun*, 2a.

25. Le *Nan Qi shu*, 54.934-935, l'attribue au taoïste du Wuxing, Meng Jingyi 孟景翼. Des indices suggèrent une origine remontant aux Tang. Voir Lü Pengzhi, « Tianshi dao zhijiao zhai » (1), p. 361.

26. *Abhidharma mahāvibhāsā śāstra*, 66.342b. Un emploi analogue du nombre 96 figure également dans l'une des premières traductions, l'*Abhidharma vibhāsā* 鞞婆沙論 (383), T.1547, 4.439a.

27. Lu Xiujing et Tao Hongjing émettaient de semblables doléances ; cf. Bokenkamp, « Scriptures new and old », et *Zhen'gao*, 19.12a.

28. Au Ve siècle, le nombre 96 signifiait plus généralement le chaos de la diversité ; voir *Shenzhou jing*, 7.5b.

29. *Zhengyi lun*, 1a.

30. Voir Lü Pengzhi, « Tianshi dao zhijiao zhai ».

31. Cf. Lü Pengzhi, « Tianshi dao zhijiao zhai » (2), p. 518-520.

32. *Zhuangzi jishi*, 8.317.

33. *Zhengyi lun*, 2b-3a ; cf. Wang Haoyue, *Xijing qiuzhen*, p. 122-126.

34. *Zhengyi lun*, 5b. Cf. *Laozi*, 27 : « Le sage excelle toujours à sauver l'humanité et par conséquent ne rejette jamais un humain ; il excelle toujours à sauver les êtres et par conséquent n'en rejette aucun » (*Laozi jiaoshi*, p. 109).

35. Cf. *Zhen'gao*, 4.2a-b.

36. *Zhengyi lun*, 3a.

37. Voir Schipper et Verellen, *Taoist canon*, vol. 1, p. 17-27.

38. Voir *Tang Xuanzong yuzhu Daode zhenjing.*

39. *Dongxuan lingbao daoshi shou sandong jingjie falu zeri li.*

40. Voir Schipper, « Taoist ordination ranks », p. 131-142.

41. Voir Lü Pengzhi, « Ordination ranks », p. 97-99.

42. *Sandong fengdao kejie* 三洞奉道科誡 (voir *Fengdao kejie*), cité dans *Yiqie daojing yinyi miaomen youqi*, 17b-18a ; traduit dans Kohn, *Daoist monastic manual*, p. 175-177.

43. Sur le développement du monachisme en Chine, voir Schipper, *La religion de la Chine*, chapitre 5.

44. Voir Anderson, *Charity*, chapitres 5 et 11 ; Gernet, *Buddhism in Chinese society*, chapitre 7 ; Brown, *Ransom of the soul*, p. 21-23.

45. Gernet, *Buddhism in Chinese society*, p. 66-73.

46. « Zhengyi zhuguan weiyi », dans *Zhengyi weiyi jing*, 18a-b.

47. Voir *Daojiao lingyan ji*, 17.330-333.

48. Voir Anderson, *Charity*, chapitre 9, et « Lever les doutes » au chapitre 8 ci-dessus.

49. *Taishang dongxuan lingbao yebao yinyuan jing*, 6.12a-13a.

50. Voir l'entrée *Fo shuo chujia yinyuan jing* 佛說出家因緣經 dans *Lidai sanbao ji*, 4.51a.

51. *Taishang dongxuan lingbao chujia yinyuan jing*, 1a-3a.

52. Voir *Fengdao kejie.*

53. Sur ces princesses, voir *Jiu Tang shu*, 51.2176 ; sur leur ordination, *Chuanshou sandong jingjie falu lüeshuo*, B.18a-20b (traduit dans Benn, *Cavern-mystery transmission*, p. 115-120).

54. *Fengdao kejie*, 6.9b-10a ; traduit dans Kohn, *Daoist monastic manual*, p. 167.

55. Voir Kohn, *Daoist monastic manual*, p. 65.

56. Cf. la prescription pour un sanctuaire diocésain du Maître céleste 治屋 dans *Yaoxiu keyi jielü chao*, 10.1a-2b ; traduit dans Kleeman, *Celestial Masters*, p. 228-230.

57. *Fengdao kejie*, 3.8b-9b ; traduit dans Kohn, *Daoist monastic manual*, p. 122-123.

58. Cf. « La délivrance des morts » au chapitre 4 ; au sujet de la « pacification de la terre » : voir *Yushi jing*, 4a.

59. Le *vinaya* bouddhique prescrivait d'honorer en priorité les dettes en souffrance et les promesses de dons ; voir Gernet, *Buddhism in Chinese society*, p. 85-93.

60. « Zhengyi siwang weiyi », dans *Zhengyi weiyi jing*, 19a-b.

Chapitre 10
Sacramentalité et pratique religieuse laïque

1. *Daojiao lingyan ji.*

2. Seidel, « Imperial treasures ». Voir aussi Bumbacher, *Empowered writing.*

3. La notion de « magie sacramentelle » est partisane ; voir Thomas, *Religion and the decline of magic*, p. 47 et 55 ; et Tambiah, *Magic, science, religion*, p. 18-21.

4. *Taishang daojun shuo jieyuan badu miaojing*, 1b. Dans son contenu, ce texte fait référence à l'« expiation des péchés » 拔罪 plutôt qu'à la « délivrance » 拔度 qu'évoque son titre.

5. Cf. Campany, « Living off the books », p. 138-140.

6. Voir Seidel, « Traces of Han religion », p. 32-33.

7. Cf. *Chisong zi zhangli*, 4.15a : « Nous faisons appel à l'Officier du ciel 天官 pour le biffer du registre des morts, pour purifier son vieux *qi* et pour l'enregistrer parmi les noms des vivants. »

8. Soit l'habit des fonctionnaires de grade inférieur et l'insigne des immortels se rendant à la cour céleste.

9. « Liu Tu peilu lingyan », dans *Daojiao lingyan ji*, 14.296-298.

10. Le titre complet de l'ouvrage était *Hagiographie de Yin Xi, le gardien de la passe et homme réel suprême, maître Wenshi* 文始先生無上真人關令尹喜内傳 ; cf. le fragment dans *Sandong zhunang*, 9.8b-14b.

11. *Laozi*, 73 ; voir *Laozi jiaoshi*, p. 288, et Wagner, *Chinese reading*, p. 367.

12. Le pays des morts ; cf. Mollier, « La méthode de l'Empereur du Nord », p. 337-339. Cf. *Baopu zi neipian jiaoshi*, 3.46. La description de Luofeng qui suit s'inspire librement du *Zhen'gao*, 15.1a-b. Voir aussi Bokenkamp, *Ancestors and anxiety*, p. 33-59.

13. Cf. *Taizhen yudi siji mingke jing*, 1.6b.

14. Le mont Meng était une montagne « dévolue » au service du mont Tai ; voir *Dongtian fudi yuedu mingshan ji*, 386 ; pour sa localisation dans les environs du mont Tai, voir *Shangshu zhengyi*, 6.143. Le Gué occidental était proche de l'embouchure de la rivière Zhe 浙江 (aujourd'hui Qiantang 錢塘) dans la baie de Hangzhou dans la province du Zhejiang ; voir *Shuijing zhushu*, 40.3301. La Zhe renversait sa course sous l'effet du mascaret remontant son embouchure depuis la baie. Les deux phrases précédentes se trouvent aussi, avec des variantes, dans le *Taiwei lingshu ziwen langgan shenzhen shangjing*, 8b, et le *Taizhen yudi siji mingke jing*, 1.5b.

15. Sur la nomination de Wu comme gouverneur, voir *Zizhi tongjian*, 252.8160, et Wu Tingxie, *Tang fangzhen nianbiao*, 6.984.

16. Voir aussi ci-dessous et Verellen, « Green memorials », p. 16. Au début du XIe siècle, l'extrait d'une anecdote des *Conversations du pavillon de chaume* 茅亭客話 reflète leur relation familière : « Le maître taoïste Tang Dongqing 唐洞卿 de l'abbaye de Longxing fit porter par un novice un bol de navets au Maître céleste Du Guangting » (*Maoting kehua*, 2.15).

17. Voir Verellen, *Du Guangting*, p. 42-43. Cette histoire explique que Yin était venu à Shu parmi la suite de l'empereur Xizong, en référence au gouvernement en exil (881-885).

18. « Yizhou Longxing guan qutu yan » 益州龍興觀取土驗, dans *Daojiao lingyan ji*, 2.172-173.

19. Voir les degrés successifs dans le *Zhengyi fawen taishang wailu yi*, 11a.

20. *Yaoxiu keyi jielü chao*, 10.5a-8a. Kobayashi Masayoshi, *Tōdai no dōkyō*, p. 13-63, surestime leur importance en réduisant tout le système d'ordination des Tang à l'ordre de l'Unité correcte ; voir la discussion dans Liu Zhongyu, *Daojiao shoulu zhidu*, p. 60-180, et Lü Pengzhi, « Ordination ranks ».

21. *Daojiao lingyan ji*, 11.258-259 ; Tsien Tsuen-hsuin, *Written on bamboo and silk*, p. 129-131.

22. Voir Bumbacher, *Empowered writing*, p. 97-109.

23. *Wushang sanyuan zhenzhai jinglu*, 4a-13a.

24. Sur cette divinité, voir Pankenier, *Astrology and cosmology*, p. 90, et chapitre 12. Sur l'association de l'ordination du huitième grade avec le Grand un, cf. *Yaoxiu keyi jielü chao*, 10.7a-b.

25. Suivant *Yunji qiqian*, 119.1632.

26. « Zhao Ye shou zhengyi bajie lu yan » 趙業授正一八階籙驗, dans *Daojiao lingyan ji*, 11.264-265.

27. Voir *Taishang zhengyi yuelu yi*, 5b.

28. *Shenxian ganyu zhuan*, 3.464-465 ; traduit dans Verellen, « Encounter as revelation », p. 382-383.

29. Schipper, « Taoist ordination ranks », p. 131.

30. Voir la ballade de Du, « Les belles dames » 麗人行.

31. Les nuits de la Fête du printemps, le marché aux vers à soie du diocèse de Gegui 葛璝 attirait une foule de dix mille personnes ; voir *Daojiao lingyan ji*, 17.340-341. Autre destination populaire, le marché aux vers à soie du diocèse de Changli 昌利 était fréquenté par des pèlerins de la Fête du printemps priant pour une descendance (*Daojiao lingyan ji*, 17.341).

32. Voir *Shenxian ganyu zhuan*, 1.432, et *Daojiao lingyan ji*, 2.172.

33. *Guangcheng ji*, 1.14, 2.19, 13.187-188 et 15.214.

34. Sur cette divinité, cf. *Luyi ji*, 4.53.

35. « Se rétablira » : lire *chai* 差 comme 瘥.

36. « Jia Qiong shou zhengyi lu yan » 賈瓊受正一籙驗, dans *Daojiao lingyan ji*, 11.261-262, reproduit avec des variantes dans le *Yunji qiqian*, 119.2630-2631.

37. Schipper, « Taoist ordination ranks », p. 132.

38. *Da daojia lingjie*, 11a ; cf. Kleeman, *Celestial Masters*, p. 4. Voir aussi *Zhou shi mingtong ji*, 2.4b-3.11b et, sur l'opposition entre enregistrement céleste et terrestre, *Daojiao lingyan ji*, 11.258-260.

39. Schafer, « Last years of Ch'ang-an », p. 145.

40. Voir les chapitres 10-12, « Preuves de l'efficacité des écritures, rituels, talismans et registres » 經法符籙靈驗, dans *Daojiao lingyan ji* et Verellen, « Evidential miracles », p. 233-255.

41. Sur les récompenses de la récitation, voir Bumbacher, *Empowered writing*, p. 126-131.

42. Voir *Taishang shengxuan xiaozai huming miaojing*, P. 2471 et S. 3747. Sur l'édition imprimée, voir Twitchett, *Printing and publishing*, p. 20-22.

43. Ce temple avait été édifié en 730, sous le règne de l'empereur Xuanzong ; voir *Tang huiyao*, 50.1027.

44. « Commandant » : l'édition citée corrige tacitement le caractère *shi* 師 de l'édition canonique en *shuai* 帥.

45. Le *Taishang shengxuan xiaozai huming miaojing* transmis compte 305 caractères.

46. « Li Xuanli *Huming jing* yan » 李玄禮護命經驗, dans *Daojiao lingyan ji*, 11.262 ; Verellen, « Evidential miracles », p. 237.

47. Voir *Taishang dongxuan lingbao hu zhu tongzi jing*.

48. Voir *Shenzhou jing*. Sur l'expérience de l'exil de Du, voir Verellen, *Du Guangting*, p. 63-100.

49. « Wang Qingyuan *Shenzhou jing* yan » 王清遠神呪經驗, dans *Daojiao lingyan ji*, 10.253-254.

50. Voir *Taishang laojun xuanmiao zhenzhong neide shenzhou jing*.

51. « Deng lao *Zhenzhong jing* yan » 鄧老枕中經驗, dans *Daojiao lingyan ji*, 12.272-273 ; voir aussi la version intitulée « Deng lao » 鄧老 dans *Shenxian ganyu zhuan*, 1.440-441.

52. Voir chapitre 5 et le *Lingbao wuliang duren shangpin miaojing*.

53. Pour cette localisation, voir *Daojiao lingyan ji*, 7.223.

54. « Chen Taiqing *Duren jing* yan » 陳太清度人經驗, dans *Daojiao lingyan ji*, 12.273-274.

55. « Zhang Renbiao Taiyi tianzun yan » 張仁表太一天尊驗, dans *Daojiao lingyan ji*, 5.197-199 ; Verellen, « Evidential miracles », p. 240-242.

56. Voir par exemple Tambiah, *Magic, science, religion*, p. 7.

57. *Miaofa lianhua jing*, 7.56c.

58. Voir Strickmann, *Chinese magical medicine*, p. 124 ; cf. Copp, *Body incantatory*, p. 47 et p. 257, n. 82.

59. Voir Colas, *Penser l'icône*, p. 19-40 et 67-107.

60. Colas, « Competing hermeneutics », p. 151-155 ; Verellen, « The dynamic design », p. 165-166.

61. Si c'est bien le cas, l'erreur survint tôt dans l'histoire du texte, car le même nom apparaît dans la version de 1028 dans *Yunji qiqian*, 119.262.

62. « Liu Cunxi tianshi zheng yan » 劉存希天師幀驗, dans *Daojiao lingyan ji*, 8.227-228 ; Verellen, *Du Guangting*, p. 76.

63. P. 4053.

64. Voir *Miaofa lianhua jing*, 7.

65. Voir *Daojiao lingyan ji*, 1.162 ; Verellen, « Evidential miracles », p. 239-243.

66. « Qiongzhou Zhao Keyan shi tianshi yan » 邛州趙可言事天師驗, dans *Daojiao lingyan ji*, 8.233.

67. Cf. Teiser, « Having once died », p. 447-450.

68. Cf. *Daojiao lingyan ji*, 8.234- 235 ; Verellen, *Du Guangting*, p. 15-16.

69. *Zhengyi chitan yi*, 3.a-b.

70. « Tianshi jian yan » 天師劍驗, dans *Daojiao lingyan ji*, 13.285-286, 11.258 ; Wu Zhen, *Wei shenxing*, p. 132-138 ; Barrett, « Emergence of the Taoist papacy », p. 99.

71. Verellen, « Zhang Ling and the Lingjing », p. 253.

72. « Huangfu Qia shi tianshi yan » 皇甫洽事天師驗, dans *Daojiao lingyan ji*, 8.231.

73. Voir « Shuzhang fa », *Chisong zi zhangli*, 2.4b.

74. Voir Thilo, *Chang'an*, vol. 1, p. 162.

75. *Tang huiyao*, 50.1027.

76. « Manche » : par erreur, l'édition de Luo Zhengming a remplacé 袖 par 神. La robe d'étoffe est un habit ordinaire, fait de laine ou de chanvre et non de soie.

77. « Guéri » : corriger 差 (à lire comme 瘥) au lieu de 較, suivant le *Yunji qiqian*, 119.2610 (cf. le texte relatif à Jia Qiong ci-dessus).

78. « Ordonna » : lire 命 au lieu de 召善, d'après le *Yunji qiqian*, 119.2611. « Réparer » : par erreur, l'édition citée a remplacé 改 par 必.

79. Voir Pelliot, « Les statues en "laque sèche" », p. 186-191.

80. Voir Colas, « Competing hermeneutics », p. 166-167.

81. Les Cinq viscères et leurs couleurs étaient appariés selon les corrélations des Cinq agents.

82. Sur les miroirs dans les statues, y compris celle-ci, cf. Huang Shih-shan, *Picturing the true form*, p. 77-78.

83. « Zhaocheng guan tianshi yan » 昭成觀天師驗, dans *Daojiao lingyan ji*, 8.226-227.

Chapitre 11
Les instruments de la délivrance

1. Cf. Anderson, *Charity*, chapitre 8.

2. Voir « Sui Renqian » 睢仁蒨, dans *Mingbao ji*, B.27. Le *Fengshi wenjian ji jiaozhu*, 6.55, prétend, sans preuve, que la pratique commença durant la période des Wei et des Jin. L'utilisation du papier comme support pour l'écriture se généralisa au IIe siècle de notre ère ; voir Tsien Tsuen-hsuin, *Written on bamboo and silk*, p. 148-152.

3. Voir « Wang Shu » 王璹, dans *Mingbao ji*, C.71.

4. Voir Hou Ching-lang, *Monnaies d'offrande*, p. 3-15.

5. Voir Dudbridge, *Religious experience and lay society*, p. 54-55.

6. *Taishang lingbao yugui mingzhen dazhai yangong yi*, 16a (les chevaux servaient à raccompagner les esprits) ; *Taishang huanglu zhai yi*, 55.15b.

7. « You da zhongsong zhang » 又大塚訟章, dans *Chisong zi zhangli*, 5.24a.

8. Des textes antérieurs comptaient déjà la monnaie sacrificielle en billets (plutôt qu'en pièces), probablement en référence à des représentations sur soie ; voir, par exemple, le *Taiping guangji*, 100.670 (première moitié du VIIIe siècle), 334.2656 (seconde moitié du VIIIe siècle) et 310.2454 (IXe siècle).

9. Voir von Glahn, « Re-examining the authenticity », p. 80-82 ; Carlen, *Brief history of entrepreneurship*, p. 98-99 ; Vogel, « Mothers and children ».

10. Voir Twitchett, *Financial administration*, p. 72-73.

11. Pour « diocèse », par déférence pour le nom personnel de l'empereur Gaozong (r. 649-683), Li Zhi 李治, Du substitue le caractère *hua* 化 au caractère tabou *zhi* 治.

12. C'est notamment là qu'il signa la préface, datée de 891, de son compendium rituel intitulé *Taishang huanglu zhaiyi*. Sur ses activités liturgiques dans ce temple, voir « Trois prières » au chapitre 12 et Verellen, *Du Guangting*, p. 116-120.

13. Cf. *Xin Tang shu*, 224B.6404, qui donne 砦 pour « fort » et date cette campagne de 881.

14. On corrige 馮老人 suivant le *Yunji qiqian*, 121.2667-2668.

15. « Chez nous » 某處 : l'édition citée donne par erreur « chez eux » 其處.

16. « Trente ligatures de sapèques » 三十千 corrige 三千貫 suivant le *Yunji qiqian*.

17. « Préposé à la Trésorerie » 庫子 corrige 庫中, suivant le *Yunji qiqian*.

18. Voir Harper, « Contracts with the spirit world », p. 236-237 et 257 ; Strickmann, « Therapeutische Rituale », p. 194.

19. Zhang Lin (corriger 霖 en 琳) figure dans les pages des *Divines manifestations* et des *Œuvres de Guangcheng* comme commanditaire assidu de rituels auprès de Du Guangting. Selon la biographie de Zhang dans le *Shiguo chunqiu*, 40.597, il fit campagne avec l'armée de Yongping à Qiongzhou en 890.

20. « Zhang He zou tiancao qian yan » 張郃奏天曹錢驗, dans *Daojiao lingyan ji*, 15.300-301.

21. La monnaie du Boisseau du Nord était payée à l'Administration du destin pour résoudre les crises ; voir Hou Ching-lang, *Monnaies d'offrande*, p. 109.

22. *Taipei Times*, en ligne : http://www.taipeitimes.com/News/taiwan/archives/2017/09/20/2003678796.

23. Voir Raz, *Emergence of Daoism*, p. 127-176 ; Bumbacher, *Empowered writing*, p. 13-80.

24. « Direction royale » : la direction saisonnière ou astrologique dominante ; cf. *Yunji qiqian*, 68.5a, qui prescrit « un prosternement dans la direction royale [de l'étoile] de la Grande année » 向太歲王方再拜.

25. « Shufu shi » 書符式, *Chisong zi zhangli*, 2.1b-3a.

26. Voir *Dengzhen yinjue*, 3.14a. Le *fen* est un centième d'once.

27. Voir *Baopu zi neipian jiaoshi*, 19.309 ; Steavu, *Writ of the Three Sovereigns*, p. 22-33 ; cf. Seidel, « Imperial treasures », p. 310-316 et 325-327.

28. Voir les titres des divers talismans représentés dans le *Taishang laojun hunyuan sanbu fu*.

29. Voir *Baopu zi neipian jiaoshi*, 9.159 ; Lü Pengzhi, *Tang qian daojiao yishi*, p. 46.

30. De tels jeunes gens et préposés étaient parfois représentés dans la suite du Seigneur Lao ; cf. *Daojiao lingyan ji*, 10.249.

31. *Xianzhuan shiyi*, 4.866 ; cf. Schipper et Verellen, *Taoist canon*, vol. 1, p. 484.

32. Voir *Dongzhen taishang suling dongyuan dayou miaojing*, 1b.

33. Dans le *Lishi zhenxian tidao tongjian*, 42.1a-3b, Zhai Qianyou figure également dans la lignée de transmission d'un autre écrit ésotérique, le *Zhenyuan celing shu* 鎮元策靈書.

34. « Écrit de cinabre » : voir Seidel, « Imperial treasures », p. 298-299.

35. Voir *Youyang zazu*, 5.57-58, pour l'exploit surnaturel par lequel Zhai rendit sûre la navigation des dangereuses Trois gorges du fleuve Yangzi pour les marchands. Du Guangting intégra une version légèrement modifiée de cette histoire dans son

Xianzhuan shiyi, 2.801-803. La citation dans le *Taiping guangji*, 30.194-195, a une double attribution.

36. Voir Verellen, *Du Guangting*, p. 124-125.

37. *Taishang dongxuan lingbao suling zhenfu*, « Préface » 序, 1a-b.

38. *Shenxian ganyu zhuan*, 3.465 ; Verellen, « Encounter as revelation », p. 383.

39. *Zhengyi fawen xiuzhen zhiyao*, 16a ; cf. Strickmann, *Chinese magical medicine*, p. 126.

40. Voir Verellen, *Du Guangting*, p. 13-14 ; pour les dates, voir *Daojiao lingyan ji*, 13.281.

41. Voir Unschuld *et al.*, *Huang di nei jing su wen*, p. 721, n. 13. Sur la « démence » dans la tradition taoïste, voir Strickmann, *Chinese magical medicine*, p. 240-244.

42. *Xuandu lüwen*, 10b.

43. L'édition de Luo Zhengming répète ici par erreur les quatre dernières phrases.

44. « Yuxiao Ye zunshi fu yan » 玉霄葉尊師符驗, dans *Daojiao lingyan ji*, 11.260-261 ; *Yunji qiqian*, 119.2629-2630.

45. Strickmann, « Therapeutische Rituale », p. 191-192.

46. *Sanguo zhi* (*Wei shu*), 8.264, citant le *Dianlüe* 典略 de Yu Huan 魚豢 (actif vers 220-232) ; traduit dans Kleeman, *Celestial Masters*, p. 29.

47. *Shishuo xinyu jianshu*, 20/10.708.

48. *Daojiao lingyan ji*, 11.261.

49. *Taishang dongxuan lingbao suling zhenfu*, C.14a-20b.

50. *Soushen yi*, 15.182-183.

51. Pour l'immortel Fan Li (actif vers 496-465 avant notre ère), commanditaire de la méthode du sceau, voir les références dans Campany, *To live as long*, p. 196, n. 218.

52. *Zhengyi fawen xiuzhen zhiyao*, 16a-b ; cf. Strickmann, *Chinese magical medicine*, p. 126-127.

53. Voir Liu Zhaorui, *Kaogu faxian*, p. 131-174 ; Strickmann, *Chinese magical medicine*, p. 123-193.

54. Voir P. 3810, P. 3853, P. 3874 et *Si yin qi jue fa*, 1a-6a.

55. Wang Yucheng, *Daojiao fayin lingpai tan'ao*, p. 37-53. Sur le Dieu jaune, voir Liu Yi, *Jingtian yu chongdao*, p. 267-283.

56. *Baopu zi neipian jiaoshi*, 17.287 ; Strickmann, *Chinese magical medicine*, p. 140-143. Voir aussi *Taishang laojun hunyuan sanbu fu*, A.22b-23a.

57. Voir les illustrations et la discussion dans Huang Shih-shan, « Daoist seals » (1), p. 75-76 et 85-88.

58. « Zhang Rang huangshen yuezhang yin yan » 張讓黃神越章印驗, dans *Daojiao lingyan ji*, 13.286.

59. Voir Strickmann, « History, anthropology, and Chinese religion », p. 228-229, n. 32.

60. Voir *Guangcheng ji*, 4.55.

61. Sur celles-ci, voir Mollier, « La méthode de l'Empereur du Nord ».

62. Voir *Zizhi tongjian* 252.8171-8173.

63. Dans *Luyi ji*, 1.20, un prêtre de ce temple bâtit un nouveau sanctuaire sur le mont Xueshe avec du bois de construction miraculeusement récupéré du fond du lac Wansui.

64. Voir *Huayang guo zhi jiaobu tuzhu*, 3.128-129.

65. Aujourd'hui le pont Sima 駟馬橋 sur la rivière Pi 郫江 ; voir *Huayang guo zhi jiaobu tuzhu*, 3.152, et annexe 2, p. 226-227.

66. « Fan Xiyue tianpeng yin yan » 范希越天蓬印驗, dans *Daojiao lingyan ji*, 13.287.

67. Voir Liu Zhiwan, « Tempōshin to Tempōju ni tsuite ».

68. Voir *Zhen'gao*, 10.10b ; traduit dans Strickmann, « History, anthropology, and Chinese religion », p. 228.

69. *Taishang dongyuan beidi Tianpeng huming xiaozai shenzhou miaojing*, 2a-4b. Voir aussi le *Taishang zhengyi zhougui jing*, un compendium de l'Unité correcte qui présente des incantations similaires pour éloigner le malheur.

70. « Cao Kui Tianpeng zhou yan » 曹戣天蓬咒驗, dans *Daojiao lingyan ji*, 12.271-272 ; Verellen, *Du Guangting*, p. 76-77.

71. Sur les traductions chinoises de la littérature *dhāraṇī*, voir Shinohara, *Spells, images, and mandalas* ; sur leur interaction avec le taoïsme, voir Copp, *Body incantatory*, p. 44-57.

72. *Zhengyi fawen xiuzhen zhiyao*, 15b ; traduit dans Strickmann, *Chinese magical medicine*, p. 126.

73. Des messagers de la mort ; cf. *Daojiao lingyan ji*, 11.259, *Luyi ji*, 5.72, et *Xianzhuan shiyi*, 3.821.

74. « Zhang Qianyao Tianpeng zhou yan » 張乾曜天蓬呪驗, dans *Daojiao lingyan ji*, 11.264.

75. « Wang Daoke Tianpeng zhou yan » 王道珂天蓬呪驗, dans *Daojiao lingyan ji*, 10.252-253.

76. Voir *Chaoye qianzai*, 3.64.

77. Voir Wu Zhen, *Wei shenxing jiazhu*, p. 124-127.

78. Cf. Staal *et al.*, *Agni*, p. 93-94 et 125-139. Sur l'envoûtement démoniaque, voir Strickmann, *Chinese magical medicine*, p. 245.

79. « Ye Fashan jiao lingyan » 葉法善醮靈驗, dans *Daojiao lingyan ji*, 14.295-296.

80. Voir *Zhengyi chuguan zhang yi* et *Taishang laojun shuo jieshi zhouzu jing* ; voir aussi les Offrandes présentées au chapitre 9 (demeures et tombes) et *Zhuhua zhang*, 3.1a-4b (enfants).

81. Voir Teiser, « Ornamenting the departed », p. 204 ; Huang Zheng et Wu Wei, *Dunhuang yuanwen ji*.

82. Wang Ka, *Dunhuang daojiao wenxian*, p. 39-48.

83. Voir *Daojiao zhaijiao duwang qiyuan wen ji*. Les références aux colonnes du texte ci-après (col.) citent cette édition. Cf. l'édition antérieure dans Ma De, « Dunhuang wenshu *Daojia zazhai wenfan ji* », p. 226-242, et la reproduction du manuscrit dans Ōfuchi Ninji, *Tonkō dōkyō*, vol. 2, p. 893-898.

84. Cf. Liu Yongming, « P. 3562v » (2), p. 15-19, et Soymié, « Ikutsu ka no Tonkō bunken », p. 1-14. Les catégories correspondent généralement à celles identifiées par Teiser pour les prières bouddhiques dans « Ornamenting the departed », p. 203.

85. Voir Rong Xinjiang, *Eighteen lectures*, p. 40-47 ; Liu Yongming, « P. 3562v » (1), p. 12-17.

86. Voir Teiser, « Ornamenting the departed », p. 201.

87. Voir Gernet, *Buddhism in Chinese society*, p. 259-277.

88. La seconde « Prière d'association de district » donne ici « les frères et sœurs de l'association locale unifiée et autres » 合邑善男子善女子等 (col. 106).

89. La seconde prière donne ici « divers actes méritoires » 諸功德.

90. Les marques physiques de sainteté du Seigneur Lao ; voir *Xuanyuan huangdi shengji*, dans *Yunji qiqian*, 102.2208 ; cf. les trente-deux marques primaires 三十二相 et quatre-vingt marques secondaires 八十種好 sur le corps du Bouddha. Celles-ci constituaient l'ornement externe 外莊嚴 d'un adepte ayant accompli un mérite parfait, l'ornement interne étant le fruit de la dévotion contemplative ; voir *Taishang yicheng haikong zhizang jing*, 2.19b.

91. C'est-à-dire constituée de dix segments de tissus de différentes couleurs ; voir *Huangting neiwai yujing jingjie*, 4a. Cf. les bannières de huit ou neuf carrés de tissu coloré dans Jera-Bezard et Maillard, « Origine et montage », p. 88.

92. Cf. Liu Yongming, « P. 3562v » (2), p. 16-17.

93. Voir *Taishang dongxuan lingbao zhihui zuigen shangpin dajie jing*, B.7b-8a.

94. Sur ces abbayes, voir Ma De, « Dunhuang wenshu *Daojia zazhai wenfan ji* », p. 245-246.

95. Voir *Taishang dongxuan lingbao zhuanshen duming jing*, 10b, et Teiser, *Scripture on the Ten Kings*, p. 20-30. Sur les prières pour les morts *yuanwen* de Dunhuang, voir Teiser, « Wei wangzhe yuan ». Des prières additionnelles marquant le premier anniversaire de la mort, et le troisième, portent à dix le nombre total de services commémoratifs.

Chapitre 12
Prières pour une nouvelle ère

1. Sur l'origine et les premiers développements du genre, voir Verellen, « Green memorials », p. 51-59.

2. Sur la révélation revendiquée, voir *Yisheng baode zhuan*, A.3a.

3. Cf. Mitamura Keiko, « Tōdai zengo ni mieru seishi », p. 136. Dans le *Guangcheng ji*, les plus tardifs des mémoriaux *biao* 表, relatifs à la mort de Wang Jian et ses funérailles, datent de 918.

4. Cf. Teiser, « Literary style », sur les prières *yuanwen* 願文.

5. La métrique des vers alternés était 4-5, 4-6, 4-7, 4-8, 6-4, 7-4 et 8-4 ; cf. Zhou Xibo, « Du Guangting qingci », p. 15-18.

6. Voir « Feilong shi Tang Yi wei huang taizi jiangdan xiuzhai ci » 飛龍使唐裔爲皇太子降誕修齋詞, dans *Guangcheng ji*, 5.69-70. Le battant d'une « cloche baleine » était sculpté en forme de baleine.

7. Sur les caractéristiques stylistiques des Oraisons vertes, cf. Zhang Haiou et Zhang Zhenqian, « Tang-Song qingci » ; Mitamura Keiko, « Tōdai zengo ni mieru seishi » ; Zhou Xibo, « Du Guangting qingci » ; Cheng Juanyang et Liu Xianglan, « Lun Du Guangting de zhaijiao ci ».

8. Voir *Guangcheng ji*, 12.173 ; voir aussi « Trois prières » ci-dessous.

9. « Yan changshi Zhangren shan jiuyao jiao ci » 嚴常侍丈人山九曜醮詞, dans *Guangcheng ji*, 6.87.

10. *Guangcheng ji*, 13.179. Le magistrat Mo Tingyi et Zhang Lin (voir « La monnaie d'échange » au chapitre 11) étaient deux officiels de premier plan et les patrons réguliers de rituels exécutés par Du Guangting ; voir Verellen, « Liturgy and sovereignty ».

11. Sur les changements du mode de patronage religieux que reflète la commission des Oraisons vertes, voir Verellen, « Green memorials », p. 59-67.

12. « Li Xuanjing wei wangnü xiuzhai ci » 李玄儆爲亡女修齋詞, dans *Guangcheng ji*, 5.72. Selon la *Liturgie solennelle de l'Unité correcte*, les registres et les vêtements étaient inhumés avec les moines et nonnes défunts ; voir « Les vœux monastiques » au chapitre 9.

13. Corriger 王方 en 王法 ; cf. *Wugan wen*, 2b : 或外犯王法，內犯冥科.

14. « Anzhai jiao ci » 安宅醮詞, dans *Guangcheng ji*, 11.155.

15. Voir « Jiutian shizhe » 九天使者, dans *Luyi ji*, 1.17.

16. Voir Verellen, *Du Guangting*, p. 126-128.

17. Voir le mémorial de cour de Du dans *Guangcheng ji*, 2.23.

18. « Gao xiu Qingcheng shan Zhangren guan jiao ci » 告修青城山丈人觀醮詞 et « Qingcheng shan Zhangren dian gongbi an tudi jiao ci » 青城山丈人殿功畢安土地醮詞, dans *Guangcheng ji*, 6.86 et 17.233-234.

19. Voir « Xuan zaiwang Qingcheng anfu zhenling jiao ci » 宣再往青城安復真靈醮詞, dans *Guangcheng ji*, 17.234, et les mémoriaux de cour de Du dans *Guangcheng ji*, 2.27-28.

20. Voir « Zhangren guan hua gongde bi gaozhen jiao ci » 丈人觀畫功德畢告真醮詞 et « Hua wuyue zhushen jiao ci » 畫五嶽諸神醮詞, dans *Guangcheng ji*, 6.91-92 ; Mesnil, « Zhang Suqing », p. 138-139 ; Gesterkamp, *The heavenly court*, p. 27-28.

21. Voir Verellen, « Liturgy and sovereignty », p. 66-68.

22. Sur *zhaici* et *jiaoci*, cf. Zhang Haiou et Zhang Zhenqian, « Tang-Song qingci », p. 47.

23. Sur les précédents à l'époque des Royaumes combattants, voir Harper, « Warring States natural philosophy », p. 831-852.

24. Pour l'appariement de Gegui avec *dingmao*, voir Verellen, « Twenty-four Dioceses », p. 27.

25. Voir, par exemple, « Shu wang benming jiao Gexian hua ci » 蜀王本命醮葛仙化詞, dans *Guangcheng ji*, 9.131-132, et Verellen, « Liturgy and sovereignty », p. 68-73 ; Wu Zhen, « Cong Du Guangting liupian Luotian jiao ci », p. 20.

26. Sur Feng Juan, voir *Shiguo chunxiu*, 40.589-591 ; Wang Hongjie, *Power and politics*, p. 150-152.

27. « Feng Juan dafu zhu shangyuan zhai ci » 馮涓大夫助上元齋詞, dans *Guangcheng ji*, 4.60-61.

28. *Wugan wen*, 6b.

29. « Bajie jiao ci » 八節醮詞, dans *Guangcheng ji*, 11.155-156.

30. Sur les rituels calendaires et la destinée, voir Liu Yongming, « P. 3562v » (2), p. 12-15 ; Stein, « Religious Taoism », p. 70-71 ; Ho Peng Yoke, *Chinese mathematical astrology*, p. 30-33.

31. Voir Sun Weijie et Gai Jianmin, « Zhaijiao yu xingming ».

32. Voir Liu Yi, *Jingtian yu chongdao*, p. 147-161, et Deng Wenkuan, *Dunhuang tianwen*, p. 94-98.

33. Voir Pankenier, *Astrology and cosmology*, p. 88-102 et 337.

34. *Fazhu jing*, 8a ; Pankenier, *Astrology and cosmology*, p. 331. Sur les registres de naissance et de mort, voir aussi « Alchimie et physiologie » au chapitre 7.

35. Voir Xiong, « Astronomical divination », p. 186-190.

36. Cf. le mémorial de félicitations de Du pour une non-occurrence similaire en 917 dans le *Guangcheng ji*, 2.26-27.

37. Le *Livre de l'Origine céleste* contenait les conjonctures fatidiques divulguées au Céleste aîné par le Seigneur Lao ; voir *Taishang huanglu zhai yi*, 52.15a, et *Chisong zi zhangli*, 1.1a-b.

38. Une date proche du solstice d'été, le cinquième jour du cinquième mois correspondait au Yang pur 純陽.

39. Voir Pankenier, *Astrology and cosmology*, p. 269.

40. Zhang Peiyu, *Sanqian wubai nian*, p. 1024, enregistre néanmoins une éclipse solaire à la date du 7 juin 913.

41. L'unique occurrence d'un jour *bingwu* lors du cinquième jour du cinquième mois sous les Shu antérieurs tomba en 913 ; cf. Wu Yu, « Du Guangting *Guangcheng ji* », p. 248.

42. Ho Peng Yoke, *Chinese mathematical astrology*, p. 160-162.

43. « Cui Yin shilang xuanxiang jiugong jiao ci » 崔隱侍郎玄象九宮醮詞, dans *Guangcheng ji*, 15.205-206.

44. Ho Peng Yoke, *Chinese mathematical astrology*, p. 23-30.

45. « Chuanzhu tianluo diwang jiao ci » 川主天羅地網醮詞, dans *Guangcheng ji*, 7.103.

46. Voir Kalinowski (dir.), *Divination et société*, p. 238-240.

47. Le *Fantian huoluo jiuyao* ; voir Kotyk, « Yixing and pseudo-Yixing », p. 16-20.

48. P. 3779r ; voir Kalinowski, *Divination et société*, p. 268. La méthode composite de Du Guangting faisait appel à plusieurs modèles ; voir Zhao Zhen, « "Jiuyao xingnian" lüeshuo », p. 31-33.

49. Voir Zhao Zhen, « "Jiuyao xingnian" lüeshuo », p. 25-27, qui montre les correspondances avec le *Fantian huoluo jiuyao*.

50. Pour l'origine présumée Lingbao, voir « Mo Tingyi zhoutian jiao ci » 莫庭乂周天醮詞, dans *Guangcheng ji*, 6.90.

51. Luotian : Da Luo 大羅 était le ciel le plus élevé ; voir *Dongtian fudi yuedu mingshan ji*, 385 ; *Yunji qiqian*, 21.486.

52. Wu Zhen, « Cong Du Guangting liupian Luotian jiao ci », p. 19-20 et 22, n. 12.

53. Voir Verellen, « Green memorials », p. 73-76.

54. « Li Yanfu wei Shu wang xiu Luotian jiao ci » 李延福爲蜀王修羅天醮詞, dans *Guangcheng ji*, 9.126-127. Pour la fonction de Li Yanfu à Shu, voir *Jingjie lu* 儆戒錄 (xe siècle), cité dans le *Taiping guangji*, 467.3853.

55. Voir *Taishang huanglu zhai yi*.

56. « Xipu Liu Yin Fei Shun huanglu zhai ci » 犀浦劉殷費順黃籙齋詞, dans *Guangcheng ji*, 5.68-69.

57. « Xingzhou Wang Chengxiu tejin wei mu xiu huanglu zhai ci » 興州王承休特進爲母修黃籙齋詞, dans *Guangcheng ji*, 5.70-71. Sur Wang Chengxiu, voir Dudbridge, *Portrait of Five Dynasties*, p. 124-143.

58. « Zhang shi guo tai furen jiu zhai xiu huanglu zhai ci » 張氏國太夫人就宅修黃籙齋詞, dans *Guangcheng ji*, 4.47-48.

59. « Huang Qi wei er wangnan zhu huanglu zhai ci » 黃齊爲二亡男助黃籙齋詞, dans *Guangcheng ji*, 4.57-58.

60. Voir *Luyi ji*, 2.32-33 ; Verellen, « Shu as hallowed land », p. 253-254.

61. L'endroit où descendent les âmes tourmentées 苦魂 ; voir *Wushang biyao*, 28.1b.

62. Lotus : des flambeaux ayant la forme d'un lotus ; cf. « Zhongyuan zhong xiu jinlu zhai ci » 中元衆修金籙齋詞, dans *Guangcheng ji*, 4.55 : « Que la flamme des flambeaux de lotus 蓮炬 des neuf radiances éclaire le gué lugubre en bas ! »

63. « Huang Qi zhu zhongyuan huanglu zhai ci ershou, zhu randeng ci » 黃齊助中元黃籙齋詞二首，助然燈詞, dans *Guangcheng ji*, 4.57.

64. Voir *Dongxuan lingbao changye zhi fu jiuyou yugui mingzhen ke* ; Zhou Xibo, *Du Guangting daojiao yifan*, p. 185-205.

65. Voir Schipper et Verellen, *Taoist canon*, vol. 1, p. 582-583.

66. « Wang Chengyan wei wangkao xiu mingzhen zhai ci » 王承鄴爲亡考修明真齋詞, dans *Guangcheng ji*, 5.74-76.

67. « Hubu Zhang xianggong xiu qianba mingzhen zhai ci » 戶部張相公修遷拔明真齋詞, dans *Guangcheng ji*, 4.46.

68. Voir *Shiguo chunqiu*, 41.602-604 ; Verellen, *Du Guangting*, p. 154-155.

69. Voir *Lishi zhenxian tidao tongjian*, 40.12a-b, passage dérivé d'un texte perdu de la fin du XIe siècle, le *Gaodao zhuan* 高道傳, par Jia Shanxiang 賈善翔.

70. *Jiu Tang shu*, 179.4661.

71. *Jiu Wudai shi*, 71.944.

72. Les Trois registres : les registres d'ordination jaune 黃籙, d'or 金籙 et de jade 玉籙 ; voir *Taishang dongxuan lingbao zhihui dingzhi tongwei jing*, 8b.

73. Corpus Jinming : des écritures et rituels révélés au mont Jinming ; voir *Taishang dongxuan lingbao yebao yinyuan jing*, 6.1b.

74. Par référence à l'*Alliance avec les Véritables du coffret de jade dans les Neuf ténèbres* ; voir *Dongxuan lingbao changye zhi fu jiuyou yugui mingzhen ke*.

75. Voir *Sizhi tongjian*, 262.8540.

76. Quatre bureaux : constellation comprenant les groupes stellaires Siming 司命, Silu 司祿, Siwei 司危 et Sizhong 司中, en charge de la supervision des « officiers démons » 鬼官 ; voir *Liji zhengyi*, 17.599. Verrouillent la porte : à la place de 關明, lire 關門. Le texte de l'édition citée 開明 est erroné.

77. Le soleil entre dans son « logis supérieur » au début de l'été, après avoir fondu son âme *hun* en or liquide ; voir *Wushang biyao*, 3.1b.

78. Les rayons de cette roue la divisaient en segments représentant les chemins de la réincarnation ; voir Teiser, *Reinventing the wheel*, p. 3-49.

79. *Shiguo chunqiu*, 39.572-573 ; Liu Yumao *et al.*, « Chengdu shi Longquan yi », p. 41-43.

80. « Yueguo furen wei dutong Zongkan linggong huanyuan xieen jiao ci » 越國夫人爲都統宗侃令公還願謝恩醮詞, dans *Guangcheng ji*, 12.173-174 ; cf. Mitamura Keiko, « Tō-matsu Godai ni okeru shūkyō », p. 10-11.

81. Wang Hongjie, *Power and politics*, p. 128-132.

82. *Zizhi tongjian*, 268.8740.

83. *Zizhi tongjian*, 268.8745-8746 et *Xin Wudai shi*, 63.788.

84. *Zizhi tongjian*, 268.8749.

85. À l'ouest de Hanzhong.

86. Un affluent de la Han, dont la course traverse les districts de Lüeyang et de Mian.

87. Cf. la « Requête pour la protection en campagne militaire », dans « Commanditaire et bénéficiaire » au chapitre 3, présentée par les familles de soldats pour leur sécurité.

88. Voir Wang Hongjie, *Power and politics*, p. 132.

89. « Daomen wei huangdi jiao taiyi bing dian jinlu deng ci » 道門爲皇帝醮太一并點金籙燈詞, dans *Guangcheng ji*, 12.185-186.

90. « Taizi wei huangdi jiao taiyi ji dian jinlu deng ci » 太子爲皇帝醮太一及點金籙燈詞, dans *Guangcheng ji*, 12.186-187.

91. La qualité littéraire de ce passage a été notée dans Zhou Xibo, « Du Guangting qingci », p. 21.

92. *Zizhi tongjian*, 268.8745.

93. Voir Verellen, *Du Guangting*, p. 145-146.

94. *Zizhi tongjian*, 259.8455.

95. *Zizhi tongjian*, 260.8488 et 8509.

96. *Shu Taowu jiaojian*, 1.104.

97. *Zizhi tongjian*, 269.8796, 8798, 8804 et 8807.

98. Voir sa biographie dans *Shiguo chunqiu*, 39.579-580.

99. Sur le poste de Li Wan à Zhedong et son ordination, voir *Daojiao lingyan ji*, 13.281-282.

100. « Li Wan changshi jiuyao jiao ci » 李綰常侍九曜醮詞, dans *Guangcheng ji*, 6.83-84.

101. L'Adolescent pourpre : cf. *Zhen'gao*, 1.16a. Le *Maoshan zhi*, 10.3a, explique que le grand seigneur Adolescent vert 青童大君, également appelé Adolescent pourpre de la canopée verte 青蓋紫童 et homme réel dans le Boisseau 斗中真人, régnait sur les palais de la Mer orientale.

102. *Taishang laojun zhongjing*, B.8a ; *Yunji qiqian*, 19.443. Les deux oreilles occupaient le Palais de la salle de jade 玉堂宮 ; nez et bouche, le Palais de la salle de lumière 明堂宮. « Palais écarlate » désigne par ailleurs le cœur (cf. « La méditation » au chapitre 7).

103. Voir Unschuld *et al.*, *Huang di nei jing su wen*, p. 106. Voir aussi Harper, « Warring States natural philosophy », p. 860-866 ; Needham, *Science and civilisation*, vol. 6, 6e partie, p. 109.

Épilogue
PERSPECTIVES

1. Voir l'article bibliographique de Chen Song, « The state, the gentry, and local institutions ».

2. Tackett, *Destruction*, p. 187-234.

3. Voir Schipper et Verellen, *Taoist canon*, vol. 2, p. 633-639.

4. Voir *Yisheng baode zhuan.*

5. Schipper, « Taoist ritual and local cults », p. 832-834.

6. Barrett, « Emergence of the Taoist papacy » ; Amato, « Rebirth of a lineage ».

7. Voir Wang Jianchuan, *Zhang tianshi zhi yanjiu*, et l'étude complète de Vincent Goossaert, *Heavenly Masters : two thousand years of the Daoist state*, à paraître.

8. Brown, *Ransom of the soul*, p. XIII-XV ; Tambiah, *Magic, science, religion*, p. 20 et *passim* ; Le Goff, *La naissance du Purgatoire*, p. 13.

9. Voir le tableau « Rédimer sa destinée », p. 21, et Hulmes, « Semantics of sacrifice », p. 279.

10. Strickmann, « Therapeutische Rituale », p. 185-188.

11. Cyrulnik, *Psychothérapie de Dieu*, p. 11-43.

12. Young, *Letters of St. Ignatius*, p. 404-405.

13. Sluhovsky, *Becoming a new self*, p. 71-76.

14. Voir les résumés dans Delumeau, *De la peur à l'espérance.*

15. Wagner, « Fate's gift economy », p. 197.

16. Jean 12, 24 ; sur cette image, cf. le mythe grec de Déméter et Perséphone.

17. Seidel, « Post-mortem immortality », p. 225-226. Pour un résumé des destinées posthumes envisagées dans la religion chinoise, voir Goossaert, *Bureaucratie et salut*, p. 9-30.

Ouvrages cités

Abréviations

D. : *Zhengtong daozang* 正統道藏 (1445), éd. facsimilé Shanghai, Commercial Press, 1924-1926. Numérotation des textes selon Schipper et Verellen, *Taoist canon*, vol. 3, p. 1393-1440.

T. : *Taishō shinshū Daizōkyō* 大正新修大藏經. Tokyo, Taishō issaikyō kankōkai, 1924-1932.

Sources primaires

Abhidharma mahāvibhāṣā śāstra 阿毗達磨大毗婆沙論 (vers IIe s. de notre ère), trad. Xuanzang 玄奘 (656). T. 1545.

Anan wenshi fo jixiong jing 阿難問事佛吉凶經, trad. An Shigao 安世高 (actif vers 148 de notre ère). T. 492.

Baoen fengpen jing 報恩奉盆經 (ve s. ?), soutra apocryphe. T. 686.

Baopu zi neipian jiaoshi 抱朴子內篇校釋, par Ge Hong 葛洪 (283-343), éd. Wang Ming 王明, Pékin, Zhonghua, 1980.

Baopu zi waipian jiaojian 抱朴子外篇校箋, par Ge Hong 葛洪 (283-343), éd. Yang Mingzhao 楊明照, Pékin, Zhonghua, 1991.

Chaoye qianzai 朝野僉載, par Zhang Zhuo 張鷟 (vers 660-vers 740), éd. Zhao Shouyan 趙守儼 ; avec *Sui Tang jiahua* 隋唐嘉話, Pékin, Zhonghua, 1979.

Chisong zi zhangli 赤松子章曆 (Six dynasties et Tang). D. 615.

Chu sanzang jiji 出三藏記集 (515), comp. Sengyou 僧祐. T. 2145.

Chuanshou sandong jingjie falu lüeshuo 傳授三洞經戒法籙略說 (713), par Zhang Wanfu 張萬福. D. 1241.

Da daojia lingjie 大道家令戒 (vers 255 de notre ère), dans *Zhengyi fawen tianshi jiaojie kejing*, 12a-19b.

Daojiao lingyan ji 道教靈驗記 (vers 905), par Du Guangting 杜光庭, dans *Du Guangting jizhuan shizhong jijiao*, vol. 1, p. 139-351.

Daojiao zhaijiao duwang qiyuan wen ji 道教齋醮度亡祈願文集, ms Dunhuang P. 3562v, éd. Liu Yongming, « P. 3562v » (1), p. 17-26.

Dengzhen yinjue 登真隱訣 (entre 492 et 514), comp. Tao Hongjing 陶弘景. D. 421.

Dingyi jing : voir *Fo shuo chengju guangming dingyi jing.*

Dongtian fudi yuedu mingshan ji 洞天福地嶽瀆名山記 (901), par Du Guangting 杜光庭, dans *Du Guangting jizhuan shizhong jijiao*, vol. 1, p. 377-399.

Dongxuan lingbao changye zhi fu jiuyou yugui mingzhen ke 洞玄靈寶長夜之府九幽玉匱明真科 (vers 400). D. 1411.

Dongxuan lingbao daoshi shou sandong jingjie falu zeri li 洞玄靈寶道士受三洞經誡法籙擇日曆, par Zhang Wanfu 張萬福 (actif vers 711-713). D. 1240.

Dongxuan lingbao sandong fengdao kejie yingshi 洞玄靈寶三洞奉道科戒營始, attrib. Jinming qizhen 金明七真 (début Tang). D. 1125.

Dongxuan lingbao wugan wen 洞玄靈寶五感文 (453), par Lu Xiujing 陸修靜. D. 1278.

Dongxuan lingbao zhai shuo guangzhu jie fa deng zhuyuan yi 洞玄靈寶齋說光燭戒罰燈祝願儀, attrib. Lu Xiujing 陸修靜 (406-477). D. 524.

Dongzhen taishang suling dongyuan dayou miaojing 洞真太上素靈洞元大有妙經 (Six dynasties). D. 1314.

Du Guangting jizhuan shizhong jijiao 杜光庭記傳十種輯校, par Du Guangting 杜光庭 (850-933), éd. Luo Zhengming 羅爭鳴, 2 vol., Pékin, Zhonghua, 2013.

Fantian huoluo jiuyao 梵天火羅九曜, attrib. Yixing 一行 (683-727). T. 1311.

Fanwang jing 梵網經 (vers 420), soutra apocryphe, attrib. Kumārajīva 鳩摩羅什 (334-413). T. 1484.

Fayuan zhulin 法苑珠林, comp. Daoshi 道世 (mort en 683). T. 2122.

Fazhu jing : voir *Taishang dongxuan lingbao fazhu jing.*

Fengdao kejie : voir *Dongxuan lingbao sandong fengdao kejie yingshi.*

Fengshi wenjian ji jiaozhu 封氏聞見記校註 (entre 780 et 805), par Feng Yan 封演, éd. Zhao Zhenxin 趙貞信, Pékin, Zhonghua, 1958.

Fo shuo chengju guangming dingyi jing 佛說成具光明定意經, trad. Zhi Yao 支曜 (actif vers 185 de notre ère). T. 630.

Fo shuo wenshi xiyu zhongseng jing 佛說溫室洗浴衆僧經, trad. An Shigao 安世高 (actif vers 148 de notre ère). T. 701.

Fozu tongji 佛祖統紀 (1269), par Zhi Pan 志磐. T. 2035.

Fumu en nanbao jing 父母恩難報經, trad. An Shigao 安世高 (actif vers 148 de notre ère). T. 684.

Fumu en zhong jing 父母恩重經 (Tang), soutra apocryphe. T. 2887 ; mss Dunhuang.

Gaoseng zhuan 高僧傳, par Huijiao 慧皎 (497-554), éd. Tang Yongtong 湯用彤, Pékin, Zhonghua, 1992.

Guang hongming ji 廣弘明集, comp. Daoxuan 道宣 (596-667). T. 2103.

Guangcheng ji 廣成集, par Du Guangting 杜光庭 (850-933), éd. Dong Enlin 董恩林, Pékin, Zhonghua, 2011.
Guangzan jing 光讚經 (286), trad. Dharmarakṣa 竺法護. T. 222.

Hongming ji 弘明集, comp. Sengyou 僧祐 (435-518). T. 2102.
Hou Han shu 後漢書, par Fan Ye 范曄 (398-445), Pékin, Zhonghua, 1963.
Huainan honglie jijie 淮南鴻烈集解, éd. Liu Wendian 劉文典 *et al.*, Pékin, Zhonghua, 1989.
Huangdi neijing suwen yijie 黃帝內經素問譯解, éd. Yang Weijie 楊維傑, Taipei, Tailian guofeng chuban she, 1984.
Huangting neiwai yujing jingjie 黃庭內外玉景經解, par Jiang Shenxiu 蔣慎修 (Tang). D. 403.
Huayang guo zhi jiaobu tuzhu 華陽國志校補圖注, par Chang Qu 常璩 (actif vers 350), éd. Ren Naiqiang 任乃強, Shanghai, Guji, 1987.

Jianji xiansheng Lu jun bei 簡寂先生陸君碑 (761), par Wu Yun 吳筠, dans *Quan Tang wen* 全唐文 (éd. Pékin, 2001), 926.9659-9660.
Jiao sandong zhenwen wufa zhengyi mengwei lu licheng yi 醮三洞真文五法正一盟威籙立成儀, par Zhang Wanfu 張萬福 (actif vers 711-713). D. 1212.
Jin shu 晉書, par Fang Xuanling 房玄齡 (578-648), Pékin, Zhonghua, 1974.
Jingzhu zi jingxing famen 淨住子淨行法門, attrib. Xiao Ziliang 蕭子良 (460-494), résumé dans *Guang hongming ji*, 27.306a-321b.
Jiu Tang shu 舊唐書 (945), par Liu Xu 劉昫 (887-946) *et al.*, Pékin, Zhonghua, 1975.
Jiu Wudai shi 舊五代史, par Xue Juzheng 薛居正 (912-981), Pékin, Zhonghua, 1976.

Kongzi jiayu yizhu 孔子家語譯注, annot. Wang Su 王肅 (195-256), éd. Wang Deming 王德明, Guilin, Guangxi shifan daxue chuban she, 1998.

Laojun bianhua wuji jing 老君變化無極經 (IVe s.). D. 1195.
Laojun yinsong jiejing 老君音誦誡經, par Kou Qianzhi 寇謙之 (365-448). D. 785.
Laozi bianhua jing 老子變化經 (vers 185 de notre ère), mss Dunhuang S. 2295. Facsimilé dans Seidel, *Divinisation de Lao Tseu*, p. 131-136.
Laozi Daode jing Heshang gong zhangju 老子道德經河上公章句, éd. Wang Ka 王卡, Pékin, Zhonghua, 1993.
Laozi jiaoshi 老子校釋, éd. Zhu Qianzhi 朱謙之, Pékin, Zhonghua, 1984.
Laozi xiang'er zhu jiaojian 老子想爾注校箋, éd. Jao Tsung-I 饒宗頤, réimpr. Shanghai, Guji, 1991.
Laozi zhigui 老子指歸, par Yan Zun 嚴遵 (Ier s. av. notre ère), éd. Wang Deyou 王德有, Pékin, Zhonghua, 1994.
Licheng yi : voir *Wushang huanglu dazhai licheng yi*.
Lidai minghua ji 歷代名畫記, par Zhang Yanyuan 張彥遠 (vers 820-876), dans *Zhongguo shuhua quanshu* 中國書畫全書, vol. 1, Shanghai, Shanghai shuhua chuban she, 1993.
Lidai sanbao ji 歷代三寶紀 (597), par Fei Changfang 費長房. T. 2034.
Liji zhengyi 禮記正義, dans *Shisan jing zhushu*.
Lingbao jingmu 靈寶經目 (préface 437), mss Dunhuang P. 2256 et P. 2861.

Lingbao jingmu xu 靈寶經目序, par Lu Xiujing 陸修靜 (406-477), dans *Yunji qiqian*, 4.51-53.
Lingbao wuliang duren shangpin miaojing 靈寶無量度人上品妙經. D. 1.
Lishi zhenxian tidao tongjian 歷世真仙體道通鑑 (préface 1294), par Zhao Daoyi 趙道一. D. 296.
Liushi jiazi benming yuanchen li 六十甲子本命元辰曆 (Six dynasties). D. 1289.
Lu xiansheng daomen kelüe 陸先生道門科略, par Lu Xiujing 陸修靜 (406-477). D. 1127.
Lunheng jiaoshi 論衡校釋, par Wang Chong 王充 (27-97), éd. Huang Hui 黃暉, Pékin, Zhonghua, 1990.
Lunyu zhushu 論語注疏, dans *Shisan jing zhushu*.
Lushan ji 廬山記, par Chen Shunyu 陳舜俞 (mort en 1076). T. 2095.
Lushan shiwen jinshi guangcun 廬山詩文金石廣存, comp. Wu Zongci 吳宗慈 (1879-1951), éd. Hu Yingjian 胡迎建 *et al.*, Nanchang, Jiangxi renmin chuban she, 1996.
Lushan zhi 廬山志, par Mao Deqi 毛德琦 (XVIIIe s.), Jinan, Qi Lu shushe, 1996.
Luyi ji 錄異記 (comp. entre 921 et 925), par Du Guangting 杜光庭, dans *Du Guangting jizhuan shizhong jijiao*, vol. 1, p. 1-135.

Maoshan zhi 茅山志 (vers 1330), comp. Liu Dabin 劉大彬. D. 304.
Maoshi zhengyi 毛詩正義, dans *Shisan jing zhushu*.
Maoting kehua 茅亭客話 (après 1006), par Huang Xiufu 黃休複, dans *Quan Song biji* 全宋筆記, vol. 2, 1re partie, Zhengzhou, Daxiang chuban she, 2006.
Mengzi zhushu 孟子注疏, dans *Shisan jing zhushu*.
Miaofa lianhua jing 妙法蓮華經, trad. Kumārajīva 鳩摩羅什 (334-413). T. 262.
Mingbao ji 冥報記, par Tang Lin 唐臨 (vers 601-vers 660), éd. Fang Shiming 方詩銘, Pékin, Zhonghua, 1992.
Mouzi lihuo lun 牟子理惑論 (Ve s. ?), dans Sengyou 僧祐 (comp.), *Hongming ji* 弘明集, 1.1a-7a. T. 2102.

Nan Qi shu 南齊書, par Xiao Zixian 蕭子顯 (489-537), Pékin, Zhonghua, 1984.
Nan shi 南史, par Li Yanshou 李延壽 (actif vers 618-676), Pékin, Zhonghua, 1975.
Nüqing guilü 女青鬼律 (IIIe s.). D. 790.

Pusa shouzhai jing 菩薩受齋經, soutra apocryphe, attrib. Nie Daozhen 聶道真 (IIIe s.). T. 1502.
Pusa yingluo benye jing 菩薩瓔珞本業經 (Ve s.), soutra apocryphe. T. 1485.

Renwu zhi 人物志, par Liu Shao 劉邵 (vers 180-vers 245), trad. Luo Yinghuan 羅英換 et Fu Junlian 伏俊璉, Pékin, Zhonghua, 2007.

Sandong qunxian lu 三洞群仙錄 (préface 1154), comp. Chen Baoguang 陳葆光. D. 1248.
Sandong zhunang 三洞珠囊, comp. Wang Xuanhe 王懸河 (actif vers 683). D. 1139.
Sanguo zhi 三國志 (297), par Chen Shou 陳壽, Pékin, Zhonghua, 1985.
Santian neijie jing 三天內解經, par Xu *shi* 徐氏 (actif vers 421-478). D. 1205.

Shang jun shu jinzhu jinyi 商君書今註今譯, attrib. Shang Yang 商鞅 (mort en 338 av. notre ère), éd. et trad. He Lingxu 賀淩虛, Taipei, Taiwan shangwu, 1987.
Shangcheng xiuzhen sanyao 上乘修真三要, par Gao Daokuan 高道寬 (1195-1277). D. 267.
Shangpin dajie : voir *Taishang dongzhen zhihui shangpin dajie*.
Shangqing huangshu guodu yi 上清黃書過度儀 (IIIe s. ?). D. 1294.
Shangshu zhengyi 尙書正義, dans *Shisan jing zhushu*.
Shanhai jing jiaozhu 山海經校注, éd. Yuan Ke 袁珂, Chengdu, Ba Shu, 1992.
Shenxian ganyu zhuan 神仙感遇傳 (après 904), par Du Guangting 杜光庭, dans *Du Guangting jizhuan shizhong jijiao*, vol. 2, p. 417-555.
Shenzhou jing : voir *Taishang dongyuan shenzhou jing*.
Shiguo chunqiu 十國春秋 (1669), par Wu Renchen 吳任臣, Pékin, Zhonghua, 1983.
Shisan jing zhushu 十三經注疏, éd. Song, réimpr. (1815) Ruan Yuan 阮元, éd. Li Xueqin 李學勤, 26 vol., Pékin, Beijing daxue chuban she, 1999-2001.
Shishuo xinyu jianshu 世說新語箋疏, par Liu Yiqing 劉義慶 (403-444), éd. Yu Jiaxi 餘嘉錫 *et al.*, Shanghai, Guji, 1993.
Shoudu yi : voir *Taishang dongxuan lingbao shoudu yi*.
Shu Taowu jiaojian 蜀檮杌校箋, par Zhang Tangying 張唐英 (1029-1071), éd. Wang Wencai 王文才 et Wang Yan 王炎, Chengdu, Ba Shu, 1999.
Shuijing zhushu 水經注疏, par Li Daoyuan 酈道元 (mort en 527), comm. Yang Shoujing 楊守敬 et Xiong Huizhen 熊會貞, éd. Duan Xizhong 段熙仲 et Chen Qiaoyi 陳橋驛, Nankin, Jiangsu guji, 1989.
Si tianwang jing 四天王經 (ve s.), soutra apocryphe, attrib. Zhiyan 智嚴 et Baoyun 寶雲. T. 590.
Si yin qi jue fa 思印氣訣法 (Tang). D. 869.
Song shi 宋史 (1346), par Toghto 脫脫, Pékin, Zhonghua, 1977.
Song shu 宋書 (493), par Shen Yue 沈約, Pékin, Zhonghua, 1974.
Soushen ji 搜神記, par Gan Bao 干寶 (mort en 336), éd. Jiang Shaoying 江紹楹, Pékin, Zhonghua, 1979.

Taiping guangji 太平廣記 (987), comp. Li Fang 李昉 *et al.*, Pékin, Zhonghua, 1961.
Taiping jing hejiao 太平經合校, éd. Wang Ming 王明, Pékin, Zhonghua, 1960.
Taiping yulan 太平御覽 (983), comp. Li Fang 李昉 *et al.*, Pékin, Zhonghua, 1960.
Taishang cibei jiuyou bazui chan 太上慈悲九幽拔罪懺 (Tang). D. 544.
Taishang daojun shuo jieyuan badu miaojing 太上道君說解冤拔度妙經 (Tang). D. 372.
Taishang dongxuan lingbao bawei zhaolong miaojing 太上洞玄靈寶八威召龍妙經 (ve s.). D. 361.
Taishang dongxuan lingbao benxing suyuan jing 太上洞玄靈寶本行宿緣經 (Six dynasties). D. 1114.
Taishang dongxuan lingbao benxing yinyuan jing 太上洞玄靈寶本行因緣經 (vers 400). D. 1115.
Taishang dongxuan lingbao chishu yujue miaojing 太上洞玄靈寶赤書玉訣妙經 (vers 400). D. 352.
Taishang dongxuan lingbao chujia yinyuan jing 太上洞玄靈寶出家因緣經 (VIIe s.). D. 339.

Taishang dongxuan lingbao fazhu jing 太上洞玄靈寶法燭經, par Lu Xiujing 陸修靜 (406-477). D. 349.
Taishang dongxuan lingbao hu zhu tongzi jing 太上洞玄靈寶護諸童子經 (Tang). D. 328.
Taishang dongxuan lingbao jingtu shengshen jing 太上洞玄靈寶淨土生神經, mss Dunhuang P. 2383, P. 2401v et P. 2703 ; éd. *Zhonghua daozang* 中華道藏, vol. 4, p. 197-206.
Taishang dongxuan lingbao sanyuan pinjie gongde qingzhong jing 太上洞玄靈寶三元品戒功德輕重經 (vers 400). D. 456.
Taishang dongxuan lingbao shoudu yi 太上洞玄靈寶授度儀, par Lu Xiujing 陸修靜 (406-477). D. 528.
Taishang dongxuan lingbao suling zhenfu 太上洞玄靈寶素靈真符 (préface entre 913 et 933), attrib. Lu Xiujing 陸修靜 (406-477) et Du Guangting 杜光庭 (850-933). D. 389.
Taishang dongxuan lingbao yebao yinyuan jing 太上洞玄靈寶業報因緣經 (VIe-VIIe s.). D. 336.
Taishang dongxuan lingbao zhihui dingzhi tongwei jing 太上洞玄靈寶智慧定志通微經 (vers 400). D. 325.
Taishang dongxuan lingbao zhihui zuigen shangpin dajie jing 太上洞玄靈寶智慧罪根上品大戒經 (vers 400). D. 457.
Taishang dongxuan lingbao zhuanshen duming jing 太上洞玄靈寶轉神度命經 (Sui ou Tang). D. 340.
Taishang dongyuan beidi Tianpeng huming xiaozai shenzhou miaojing 太上洞淵北帝天蓬護命消災神咒妙經 (Tang). D. 53.
Taishang dongyuan shenzhou jing 太上洞淵神咒經 (vers 400-420), éd. Du Guangting 杜光庭 (850-933). D. 335.
Taishang dongzhen zhihui shangpin dajie 太上洞真智慧上品大戒 (vers 400). D. 177.
Taishang huanglu zhai yi 太上黃籙齋儀 (vers 901), par Du Guangting 杜光庭. D. 507.
Taishang hunyuan zhenlu 太上混元真錄 (VIIe-VIIIe s.). D. 954.
Taishang laojun da cunsi tu zhujue 太上老君大存思圖注訣 (Tang). D. 875.
Taishang laojun hunyuan sanbu fu 太上老君混元三部符 (Tang). D. 673.
Taishang laojun shuo bao fumu en zhong jing 太上老君說報父母恩重經 (Tang). D. 662.
Taishang laojun shuo jieshi zhouzu jing 太上老君說解釋咒詛經 (Tang). D. 652.
Taishang laojun xuanmiao zhenzhong neide shenzhou jing 太上老君玄妙枕中內德神咒經 (Tang). D. 872.
Taishang laojun xuwu ziran benqi jing 太上老君虛無自然本起經 (Tang). D. 1438.
Taishang laojun zhongjing 太上老君中經 (Han orientaux ?). D. 1168 et *Yunji qiqian*, 18-19.
Taishang laozi huahu miaojing 太上老子化胡妙經, ms Dunhuang S. 2081.
Taishang lingbao wufu xu 太上靈寶五符序 (Jin orientaux). D. 388.
Taishang lingbao xiyu shenxin jing 太上靈寶洗浴身心經 (Tang), mss Dunhuang S. 3380 et P. 2402.
Taishang lingbao yugui mingzhen dazhai yangong yi 太上靈寶玉匱明真大齋言功儀, par Du Guangting 杜光庭 (850-933). D. 521.
Taishang shangqing rangzai yanshou baochan 太上上清禳災延壽寶懺. D. 191.

Taishang shengxuan xiaozai huming miaojing 太上昇玄消災護命妙經 (Tang). D. 19.
Taishang shuo liujia zhifu baotai huming miaojing 太上說六甲直符保胎護命妙經 (Tang ?). D. 50.
Taishang wuji dadao ziran zhenyi wucheng fu shangjing 太上無極大道自然真一五稱符上經 (vers 400). D. 671.
Taishang xuanci zhuhua zhang 太上宣慈助化章, éd. Du Guangting 杜光庭 (850-933). D. 617.
Taishang xuanyi zhenren shuo miaotong zhuanshen ruding jing 太上玄一真人說妙通轉神入定經 (Six dynasties). D. 347.
Taishang yicheng haikong zhizang jing 太上一乘海空智藏經 (début Tang). D. 9.
Taishang zhengyi fawen jing 太上正一法文經 (Tang ?). D. 1204.
Taishang zhengyi jie wuyin zhouzu bilu 太上正一解五音咒詛祕籙 (vers 1400). D. 1217.
Taishang zhengyi yuelu yi 太上正一閱籙儀, comp. Du Guangting 杜光庭 (850-933). D. 797.
Taishang zhengyi zhougui jing 太上正一咒鬼經 (Tang). D. 1193.
Taiwei lingshu ziwen langgan huadan shenzhen shangjing 太微靈書紫文琅玕華丹神真上經 (Jin orientaux). D. 255.
Taizhen yudi siji mingke jing 太真玉帝四極明科經 (Six dynasties). D. 184.
Tang huiyao 唐會要, par Wang Pu 王溥 (922-982), Shanghai, Guji, 2006.
Tang liudian 唐六典 (738), par Li Linfu 李林甫 *et al.*, éd. Chen Zhongfu 陳仲夫, Pékin, Zhonghua, 1992.
Tang Xuanzong yuzhu Daode zhenjing 唐玄宗御註道德真經 (entre 732 et 735), attrib. empereur Xuanzong 玄宗. D. 677.
Tianshi zhi yi 天師治儀 (vers 552), par Zhang Bian 張辯, première partie (上) conservée dans *Shoulu cidi faxin yi* 受籙次第法信儀 (D. 1244), 19b-30a.

Wugan wen : voir *Dongxuan lingbao wugan wen*.
Wushang biyao 無上祕要 (après 577). D. 1138.
Wushang huanglu dazhai licheng yi 無上黃籙大齋立成儀 (postface 1223), comp. Jiang Shuyu 蔣叔輿 *et al.*. D. 508.
Wushang sanyuan zhenzhai linglu 無上三元鎮宅靈籙 (VIe-VIIe s.), attrib. Jinming qizhen 金明七真. D. 674.

Xian Qin Han Wei Jin Nanbei chao shi 先秦漢魏晉南北朝詩, éd. Lu Qinli 逯欽立, Pékin, Zhonghua, 1983.
Xiang'er zhu 想爾注 (IIe s. de notre ère ?), attrib. Zhang Lu 張魯, ms Dunhuang S. 6825 (facsimilé Ōfuchi Ninji, *Tonkō dōkyō*, vol. 2, p. 421-434) ; éd. *Laozi xiang'er zhu jiaojian*.
Xianzhuan shiyi 仙傳拾遺, par Du Guangting 杜光庭 (850-933), éd. Luo Zhengming, *Du Guangting jizhuan shizhong jijiao*, vol. 2, p. 741-878.
Xiao dao lun 笑道論 (570), par Zhen Luan 甄鸞, dans *Guang hongming ji*, 9.143c-152c.
Xiaodao Wu Xu er zhenjun zhuan 孝道吳許二真君傳 (Tang). D. 449.
Xiaojing zhushu 孝經注疏, dans *Shisan jing zhushu*.
Xiaozi jing 孝子經 (IVe s. ?). T. 687.

Xin Tang shu 新唐書 (1060), par Ouyang Xiu 歐陽修 et Song Qi 宋祁, Pékin, Zhonghua, 1975.

Xin Wudai shi 新五代史 (1073), par Ouyang Xiu 歐陽修, Shanghai, Zhonghua, 1975.

Xinyu jiaozhu 新語校注, par Lu Jia 陸賈 (vers 216-vers 172 av. notre ère), éd. Wang Liqi 王利器, Pékin, Zhonghua, 1986.

Xuandu lüwen 玄都律文 (vers 500). D. 188.

Xuanpin lu 玄品錄 (1335), par Zhang Tianyu 張天雨. D. 781.

Xuanyuan huangdi shengji 混元皇帝聖紀, par Yin Wencao 尹文操 (622-688), dans *Yunji qiqian*, 102.2204-2208.

Yan shi jiaxun jijie 顔氏家訓集解, par Yan Zhitui 顔之推 (531-591), éd. Wang Liqi 王利器, Pékin, Zhonghua, 1993.

Yaoxiu keyi jielü chao 要修科儀戒律鈔, par Zhu Faman 朱法滿 (début VIIIe s.). D. 463.

Yili zhushu 儀禮注疏, dans *Shisan jing zhushu*.

Yiqie daojing yinyi miaomen youqi 一切道經音義妙門由起 (713), par Shi Chong 史崇 *et al.*, D. 1123.

Yisheng baode zhuan 翊聖保德傳 (1016), par Wang Qinruo 王欽若. D. 1285.

Youyang zazu 酉陽雜俎, par Duan Chengshi 段成式 (vers 803-863), éd. Fang Nansheng 方南生, Pékin, Zhonghua, 1981.

Yuanchen zhangjiao licheng li 元辰章醮立成曆 (Six dynasties). D. 1288.

Yujue miaojing : voir *Taishang dongxuan lingbao chishu yujue miaojing.*

Yulanpen jing 盂蘭盆經 (Ve s. ?), soutra apocryphe, attrib. Dharmarakṣa 竺法護. T. 685.

Yunji qiqian 雲笈七籤 (vers 1028), comp. Zhang Junfang 張君房, éd. Li Yongsheng 李永晟, Pékin, Zhonghua, 2003.

Yushi jing 玉室經, par Li Chengzhi 李成之 (Yuan). D. 1078.

Zhangguan pin : voir *Zhengyi fawen jing zhangguan pin.*

Zhanguo ce 戰國策, comp. Liu Xiang 劉向 (79-8 av. notre ère), Shanghai, Guji, 1978.

Zhen'gao 真誥 (499), comp. Tao Hongjing 陶弘景. D. 1016.

Zhengyi chitan yi 正一敕壇儀 (Tang). D. 800.

Zhengyi chuguan zhang yi 正一出官章儀 (Tang). D. 795.

Zhengyi fawen jing zhangguan pin 正一法文經章官品 (Six dynasties). D. 1218.

Zhengyi fawen taishang wailu yi 正一法文太上外籙儀 (Six dynasties). D. 1243.

Zhengyi fawen tianshi jiaojie kejing 正一法文天師教戒科經 (vers 255 de notre ère). D. 789.

Zhengyi fawen xiuzhen zhiyao 正一法文修真旨要 (début Tang). D. 1270.

Zhengyi jiaomu yi 正一醮墓儀 (Tang). D. 802.

Zhengyi jiaozhai yi 正一醮宅儀 (Tang). D. 801.

Zhengyi jiee jiaoyi 正一解厄醮儀 (Sui-Tang). D. 794.

Zhengyi lun 正一論 (fin Six dynasties à début Tang). D. 1228.

Zhengyi tianshi gao Zhao Sheng koujue 正一天師告趙昇口訣 (IVe s.). D. 1273.

Zhengyi weiyi jing 正一威儀經 (début Tang). D. 791.

Zhenxi 真系 (805), par Li Bo 李渤, dans *Yunji qiqian*, 5.69-85.

Zhou shi mingtong ji 周氏冥通記 (517), par Zhou Ziliang 周子良, éd. Tao Hongjing 陶弘景 (517). D. 302.

Zhou Yi zhengyi 周易正義, dans *Shisan jing zhushu*.
Zhuangzi jishi 莊子集釋, éd. Guo Qingfan 郭慶藩, Pékin, Zhonghua, 1961.
Zhuhua zhang : voir *Taishang xuanci zhuhua zhang*.
Zhuyuan yi : voir *Dongxuan lingbao zhai shuo guangzhu jie fa deng zhuyuan yi*.
Ziyang zhenren neizhuan 紫陽眞人內傳 (Six dynasties). D. 303.
Zizhi tongjian 資治通鑑, par Sima Guang 司馬光 (1019-1085), Pékin, Zhonghua, 1956.

Sources secondaires

Akizuki Kan'ei 秋月觀暎, « Dōkyō to bukkyō no *Fubo enchō kyō* » 道教と佛教の父母恩重經, *Shūkyō kenkyū* 39, n° 4, 1966, p. 23-54.

Amato, Paul, « Rebirth of a lineage : the hereditary household of the Han Celestial Master and Celestial Masters Daoism at Dragon and Tiger Mountain », thèse de doctorat, Arizona State University, 2016.

Anderson, Gary A., *Charity : the place of the poor in the biblical tradition*, New Haven, Yale University Press, 2013.

–, *Sin : a history*, New Haven, Yale University Press, 2009.

Austin, John Langshaw, *Philosophical papers*, éd. J. O. Urmson et G. J. Warnock, Oxford, Oxford University Press, 1979.

Auyang, Sunny Y., *The dragon and the eagle : the rise and fall of the Chinese and Roman empires*, Armonk, Sharpe, 2014.

Barrett, Timothy H., « The advent of the Buddhist conception of religion in China and its consequences for the analysis of Daoism », *Sungkyun Journal of East Asian Studies* 9, n° 2, 2009, p. 149-165.

–, « The emergence of the Taoist papacy in the T'ang dynasty », *Asia major* 3e série 7, n° 1, 1994, p. 89-106.

–, « Religious change under Eastern Han and its successors : some current perspectives and problems », dans Nylan et Loewe (dir.), *China's early empires*, p. 430-448.

–, *Taoism under the T'ang : religion and empire during the Golden Age of Chinese history*, Londres, Wellsweep, 1996.

Benn, Charles D., *The Cavern-mystery transmission : a Taoist ordination rite of A.D. 711*, Honolulu, University of Hawai'i Press, 1991.

Bielenstein, Hans, *The bureaucracy of Han times*, réimpr. Cambridge, Cambridge University Press, 2008.

Bodde, Derk, *Festivals in classical China : New Year and other annual observances during the Han dynasty, 206 B.C.-A.D. 220*, Princeton (NJ), Princeton University Press, 1975.

Bokenkamp, Stephen R., *Ancestors and anxiety : Daoism and the birth of rebirth in China*, Berkeley, University of California Press, 2007.

–, « The early Lingbao scriptures and the origins of Daoist monasticism », *Cahiers d'Extrême-Asie* 20, 2011, p. 95-124.

–, « Lu Xiujing, Buddhism, and the first Daoist canon », dans Pearce, Spiro et Ebrey (dir.), *Culture and power*, p. 181-199.

–, « Sackcloth and ashes : self and family in the *tutan zhai* », dans Poul Andersen et Florian Reiter (dir.), *Scriptures, schools, and forms of practice in Daoism*, Wiesbaden, Harrassowitz, 2005, p. 33-48.

–, « Scriptures new and old : Lu Xiujing and mastery », dans Paul Katz 康豹 et Liu Shufen 劉淑芬 (dir.), *Xinyang, shijian yu wenhua tiaoshi : di sijie guoji Hanxue huiyi lunwen ji* 信仰、實踐與文化調適 – 第四屆國際漢學會議論文集, Taipei, Academia sinica, Institute of history and philology, 2013, p. 449-474.

–, « The silkworm and the bodhi tree : the Lingbao attempt to replace Buddhism in China and our attempt to place Lingbao Daoism », dans John Lagerwey (dir.), *Religion and Chinese society*, Hong Kong, Chinese University of Hong Kong et École française d'Extrême-Orient, 2004, p. 317-339.

–, « Simple twists of fate : the Daoist body and its *ming* », dans Lupke (dir.), *Magnitude of ming*, p. 151-168.

–, « Sources of the *Ling-pao* scriptures », dans Strickmann (dir.), *Tantric and Taoist studies,* vol. 2, p. 434-485.

–, « Time after time : Taoist apocalyptic history and the founding of the T'ang dynasty », *Asia major* 3e série 7, no 2, 1994, p. 59-88.

–, « The Viśvantara-jātaka in Buddhist and Daoist translation », dans Penny (dir.), *Daoism in history*, p. 56-73.

Bokenkamp, Stephen R., avec une contribution de Peter Nickerson, *Early Daoist scriptures*, Berkeley, University of California Press, 1997.

Brown, Peter, *The body and society : men, women and sexual renunciation in early Christianity*, New York, Columbia University Press, 2008.

–, *The ransom of the soul : afterlife and wealth in early Western Christianity*, Cambridge (MA), Harvard University Press, 2015.

–, *The rise of Western Christendom : triumph and diversity, A.D. 200-1000*, éd. rév., Malden (MA), Wiley-Blackwell, 2013.

Bumbacher, Stephan P., *Empowered writing : exorcistic and apotropaic rituals in medieval China*, St. Petersburg, Three Pines Press, 2012.

–, *The fragments of the* Daoxue zhuan *: critical edition, translation and analysis of a medieval collection of Daoist biographies*, Francfort-sur-le-Main, Peter Lang, 2000.

Campany, Robert Ford, « Living off the books : fifty ways to dodge *ming* in early medieval China », dans Lupke (dir.), *Magnitude of ming*, p. 129-150.

– (trad.), *Signs from the unseen realm : Buddhist miracle tales from early medieval China*, Honolulu, University of Hawai'i Press, 2012.

–, *To live as long as heaven and earth : a translation and study of Ge Hong's Traditions of divine transcendents*, Berkeley, University of California Press, 2002.

Cao Ling 曹淩, « Guanyu Nanchao de changdao » 關於南朝的唱導, *Dunhuang Tulufan yanjiu* 16, 2016, p. 20-33.

Carlen, Joe, *A brief history of entrepreneurship : the pioneers, profiteers, and racketeers who shaped our world*, New York, Columbia University Press, 2016.

Cedzich, Ursula-Angelika, « Corpse deliverance, substitute bodies, name change, and feigned death : aspects of metamorphosis and immortality in early medieval China », *Journal of Chinese Religions* 29, 2001, p. 1-68.

–, « The Organon of the twelve hundred officials and its gods ». *Daoism : Religion, History and Society* 1, 2009, p. 1-93.

–, « Das Ritual der Himmelsmeister im Spiegel früher Quellen : Übersetzung und Untersuchung des liturgischen Materials im 3. *chüan* des *Teng-chen yin-chüeh* », Thèse de doctorat, Université de Wurzbourg, 1987.

Chan, Alan K. L., « The essential meaning of the Way and Virtue : Yan Zun and "Laozi learning" in early Han China », *Monumenta serica* 46, 1998, p. 105-127.

Chan, Alan K. L., et Tan, Sor-hoon (dir.), *Filial piety in Chinese thought and history*, Londres, Routledge Curzon, 2004.

Chan, Shirley, Hendrischke, Barbara, et Wiles, Sue (dir.). *Willow catkins : festschrift for Dr. Lily Xiao Hong Lee on the occasion of her 75th birthday*, Sydney, The Oriental Society of Australia, 2014.

Chen Guofu 陳國符, *Daozang yuanliu kao* 道藏源流考 (1949), 2 vol., Pékin, Zhonghua, 1963.

Chen Hao 陳昊, « Yishi, shenti, zuizhe : Han-Tang jian tianshi dao de shangzhang yishi yu jibing » 儀式、身體、罪謫 – 漢唐間天師道的上章儀式與疾病, dans Cheng Gongrang 程恭讓 (dir.), *Tianwen* 天問, vol. 2, Nankin, Jiangsu chuban she, 2008, p. 241-264.

Chen Song. « The state, the gentry, and local institutions : the Song dynasty and long-term trends from Tang to Qing (review essay) », *Journal of Chinese History* 1, 2017, p. 141-182.

Chen Yuan 陳垣 *et al.* (dir.), *Daojia jinshi lüe* 道家金石略, Pékin, Wenwu, 1988.

Ch'en, Kenneth, « Filial piety in Chinese Buddhism », *Harvard Journal of Asiatic Studies* 28, 1968, p. 81-97.

Cheng Cunjie 程存潔, « Dunhuang ben *Taishang lingbao xiyu shenxin jing* yanjiu » 敦煌本《太上靈寶洗浴身心經》研究, *Daojia wenhua yanjiu* 13, 1998, p. 295-309.

Cheng Juanyang 成娟陽 et Liu Xianglan 劉湘蘭, « Lun Du Guangting de zhaijiao ci » 論杜光庭的齋醮詞, *Zhongguo wenhua yanjiu*, 2006/4, p. 148-155.

Cheng Lesong 程樂松, « *Yuanchen zhangjiao licheng li* suo jian de zhengyi zhangyi » 《元辰章醮立成曆》所見的正一章儀. *Zongjiao xue yanjiu*, 2011/3, p. 51-56.

–, *Zhonggu daojiao leishu yu daojiao sixiang* 中古道教類書與道教思想, Pékin, Zongjiao wenhua chuban she, 2017.

Colas, Gérard, « The competing hermeneutics of image worship in Hinduism (fifth to eleventh century AD) », dans Granoff et Shinohara (dir.), *Images in Asian religions*, p. 149-179.

–, *Penser l'icône en Inde ancienne*, Turnhout, Brepols, 2012.

Cole, Alan, *Mothers and sons in Chinese Buddhism*, Stanford (CA), Stanford University Press, 1998.

Copp, Paul, *The body incantatory : spells and the ritual imagination in medieval Chinese Buddhism*, New York, Columbia University Press, 2014.

Csikszentmihalyi, Mark, « Allotment and death in early China », dans Amy Olberding et Philip J. Ivanhoe (dir.), *Mortality in traditional Chinese thought*, Albany, State University of New York Press, 2011, p. 177-190.

Cyrulnik, Boris, *Psychothérapie de Dieu*, Paris, Odile Jacob, 2017.

De Crespigny, Rafe, *Generals of the South : the foundation and early history of the Three Kingdoms state of Wu*, Canberra, Australian National University, Faculty of Asian Studies, 1990.

De Meyer, Jan A. M., *Wu Yun, life and works of an eighth-century Daoist master*, Leyde, Brill, 2006.

Delumeau, Jean, *De la peur à l'espérance*, Paris, Robert Laffont, 2013.

Deng Wenkuan 鄧文寬 (éd.), *Dunhuang tianwen lifa wenxian jijiao* 敦煌天文曆法文獻輯校, Nankin, Jiangsu guji, 1996.

Despeux, Catherine, « Âmes et animation du corps : la notion de *shen* dans la médecine chinoise antique », *Extrême-Orient Extrême-Occident* 29, 2007, p. 71-94.

Dien, Albert E., « Light after dark : artificial illumination in the Six Dynasties period », dans Chan *et al.* (dir.), *Willow catkins*, p. 285-322.

–, « Lighting in the Six Dynasties period : "To make a light to seek clarity" 造燭求明 », *Early Medieval China* 13-14, 2007, p. 1-32.

–, *Six Dynasties civilization*, New Haven (CT), Yale University Press, 2007.

–, « Turfan funereal documents », *Journal of Chinese Religions* 30, 2002, p. 23-48.

Drège, Jean-Pierre, *Les bibliothèques en Chine au temps des manuscrits : jusqu'au xe siècle*, Paris, École française d'Extrême-Orient, 1991.

Dudbridge, Glen, *A portrait of Five Dynasties China : from the memoirs of Wang Renyu (880-956)*, Oxford, Oxford University Press, 2013.

–, *Religious experience and lay society in T'ang China : a reading of Tai Fu's* Kuang-i chi, Cambridge, Cambridge University Press, 1995.

Dudink, Adrianus, « The poem *Laojun bianhua wuji* : introduction, summary, text and translation », dans Jan A. M. De Meyer et Peter M. Engelfriet (dir.), *Linked faiths : essays on Chinese religions and traditional culture in honour of Kristofer Schipper*, Leyde, Brill, 1999, p. 53-147.

Durt, Hubert, « On gratitude in Japanese Buddhism », *The Japan mission journal* 60, n° 4, 2006, p. 238-242.

Eberhard, Wolfram, *Guilt and sin in traditional China*, Berkeley, University of California Press, 1967.

Espesset, Grégoire. « À vau-l'eau, à rebours, ou l'ambivalence de la logique triadique dans l'idéologie du *Taiping jing* ». *Cahiers d'Extrême-Asie* 14, 2004, p. 61-94.

–, « Criminalized abnormality, moral etiology, and redemptive suffering in the secondary strata of the *Taiping jing* », *Asia major* 3e série 15, n° 2, 2002, p. 1-50.

Fang Xiao 方瀟, « Caoyu "tishen" : dairen shouxing xianxiang de lishi xilun » 遭遇「替身」– 代人受刑現象的歷史析論, *Faxue jia*, 2014/3, p. 85-103.

Flad, Rowan K., et Chen, Pochan, *Ancient central China : centers and peripheries along the Yangzi River*, Cambridge, Cambridge University Press, 2013.

Fraser, Chris, *The philosophy of the Mòzi : the first consequentialists*, New York, Columbia University Press, 2016.

Fukunaga Mitsuji 福永光司, « Daojiao de jing yu jian : qi sixiang de yuanliu » 道教的鏡與劍 – 其思想的源流, dans Liu Junwen 劉俊文 *et al.* (dir.), *Riben xuezhe yanjiu Zhongguo shi lunzhu xuanyi* 日本學者研究中國史論著選譯, vol. 7, Pékin, Zhonghua, 1993, p. 386-445.

Funayama Tōru 船山徹, « The acceptance of Buddhist precepts by the Chinese in the fifth century », *Journal of Asian History* 38, 2004, p. 97-120.

–, « Buddhist theories of bodhisattva practice as adopted by Daoists », *Cahiers d'Extrême-Asie* 20, 2011, p. 15-35.

–, « Rikuchō jidai ni okeru bosatsukai no juyō katei : Ryū Sō-Nanseiki o chūshin ni » 六朝時代における菩薩戒の受容過程 – 劉宋·南斉期を中心に, *Tōhō gakuhō* 67, 1995, p. 1-135.

Gagné, Renaud, *Ancestral fault in ancient Greece*, Cambridge, Cambridge University Press, 2013.

Gernet, Jacques, *Buddhism in Chinese society : an economic history from the fifth to the tenth centuries*, trad. Franciscus Verellen, New York, Columbia University Press, 1995.

Gesterkamp, Lennert, *The heavenly court : Daoist temple painting in China, 1200-1400*, Leyde, Brill, 2011.

Girard, René, *The scapegoat*, trad. Yvonne Freccero, Baltimore, Johns Hopkins University Press, 1986.

Goossaert, Vincent, *Bureaucratie et salut : devenir un dieu en Chine*, Genève, Labor et Fides, 2017.

Granoff, Phyllis, et Shinohara, Koichi (dir.), *Images in Asian religions : texts and contexts*, Vancouver, University of British Columbia Press, 2004.

– (dir.), *Sins and sinners : perspectives from Asian religions*, Leyde, Brill, 2012.

Guang Xing 廣興, « *Fumu en nanbao jing* yu *Fumu en zhong jing* de yanjiu » 《父母恩難報經》與《父母恩重經》的研究, *Zongjiao yanjiu* 2014 (2015 秋), p. 13-50.

Harper, Donald. « A Chinese demonology of the third century B.C. » *Harvard Journal of Asiatic Studies* 45, 1985, p. 459-498.

–, « Contracts with the spirit world in Han common religion : the Xuning prayer and sacrifice documents of A.D. 79 », *Cahiers d'Extrême-Asie* 14, 2004, p. 227-267.

–, *Early Chinese medical literature : the Mawangdui medical manuscripts*, Londres, Kegan Paul, 1997.

–, « Précis de connaissance médicale : le *Shanghan lun* 傷寒論 (Traité des atteintes par le Froid) et le *Wuzang lun* 五臟論 (Traité des cinq viscères) », dans Catherine Despeux (dir.), *Médecine, religion et société dans la Chine médiévale : étude de manuscrits chinois de Dunhuang et de Turfan*, Paris, Collège de France, 2010, p. 65-106.

–, « Warring States natural philosophy and occult thought », dans Michael Loewe et Edward L. Shaughnessy (dir.), *The Cambridge history of ancient China : from the origins of civilization to 221 B.C.*, Cambridge, Cambridge University Press, 1999, p. 813-884.

Harper, Donald, et Kalinowski, Marc (dir.). *Books of fate and popular culture in early China*, Leyde, Brill, 2017.

Hendrischke, Barbara, *The Scripture on Great Peace : the* Taiping jing *and the beginnings of Daoism*, Berkeley, University of California Press, 2006.

Hendrischke, Barbara, et Penny, Benjamin, « The 180 precepts spoken by Lord Lao : a translation and textual study », *Taoist Resources* 6, n° 2, 1996, p. 17-29.

Ho Peng Yoke, *Chinese mathematical astrology : reaching out to the stars*, Londres, Routledge, 2003.

Holcombe, Charles, *In the shadow of the Han : literati thought and society at the beginning of the Southern dynasties*, Honolulu, University of Hawai'i Press, 1994.

Holzman, Donald, « The place of filial piety in ancient China », *Journal of the American Oriental Society* 118, nº 2, 1998, p. 185-199.

Hou Ching-lang. « The Chinese belief in baleful stars », dans Welch et Seidel (dir.), *Facets of Taoism*, p. 193-228.

–, *Monnaies d'offrande et la notion de trésorerie dans la religion chinoise*, Paris, Collège de France, 1975.

Huang Ruxuan 黃儒宣, « Mawangdui "pibing tu" yanjiu » 馬王堆《辟兵圖》研究, *Bulletin of the Institute of History and Philology, Academia sinica* 85, nº 2, 2014, p. 167-207.

Huang, Shih-shan Susan. « Daoist seals : activation and fashioning », *Journal of Daoist studies* 10, 2017, p. 70-103, et 11, 2018, p. 46-82.

–, *Picturing the true form : Daoist visual culture in traditional China*, Cambridge (MA), Harvard University Asia Center, 2012.

Huang Zheng 黃徵 et Wu Wei 吳偉 (dir.), *Dunhuang yuanwen ji* 敦煌願文集, Changsha, Yuelu shushe, 1995.

Hubert, Henri, et Mauss, Marcel, « Essai sur la nature et la fonction du sacrifice », *L'année sociologique* 2, 1898, p. 29-138.

Hulmes, Edward, « The semantics of sacrifice », dans S. W. Sykes (dir.), *Sacrifice and redemption : Durham essays in theology*, Cambridge, Cambridge University Press, 1991, p. 265-281.

Hulsewé, Anthony F. P., *Remnants of Han law*, Leyde, Brill, 1955.

Hureau, Sylvie. « Buddhist rituals », dans Lagerwey et Lü (dir.), *Early Chinese religion*, p. 1207-1244.

Ikeda On 池田溫, « Chūgoku kodai bosō no ikkōsatsu : zuizō ibutsuken ni tsuite » 中國古代墓葬の一考察 – 隨葬衣物券について, *Kokusai tōhōgakusha kaigi kiyo* 6, 1961, p. 51-60.

Jera-Bezard, Robert, et Maillard, Monique, « Origine et montage des bannières peintes de Dunhuang », *Arts asiatiques* 40, 1985, p. 83-91.

Ji Bin 計斌 et Hua Hongbin 滑紅彬, « Qiantan Lushan daojiao cangshu » 淺談廬山道教藏書, *Lantai shijie* 2015/9, p. 164-165.

Jiang Shoucheng 姜守誠, « Zhongsong kao » 冢訟考, *Dongfang luntan* 2010/5, p. 6-11.

Johnston, Sarah Iles, « *Fiat lux, fiat ritus* : divine light and the late antique defense of ritual », dans Matthew T. Kapstein (dir.), *The presence of light : divine radiance and religious experience*, Chicago, University of Chicago Press, 2004, p. 5-24.

Kalinowski, Marc (trad.), *Cosmologie et divination dans la Chine ancienne : le Compendium des cinq agents (*Wuxing dayi, *VI*[e] *s.)*, Paris, École française d'Extrême-Orient, 1991.

– (dir.), *Divination et société dans la Chine médiévale : étude des manuscrits de Dunhuang de la Bibliothèque nationale de France et de la British Library*, Paris, Bibliothèque nationale de France, 2003.

–, « La littérature divinatoire dans le *Daozang* », *Cahiers d'Extrême-Asie* 5, 1990, p. 85-114.

–, « Les traités de Shuihudi et l'hémérologie chinoise à la fin des Royaumes combattants », *T'oung pao* 72, 1986, p. 175-228.

–, « La transmission du dispositif des Neuf palais sous les Six dynasties », dans Strickmann (dir.), *Tantric and Taoist studies*, vol. 3, p. 773-811.

Kaltenmark, Max, « Ling-pao 靈寶 : note sur un terme du taoïsme religieux », dans *Mélanges publiés par l'Institut des hautes études chinoises*, vol. 2, Paris, Presses universitaires de France, 1968, p. 559-588.

–, « Quelques remarques sur le *T'ai-chang Ling-pao wou-fu siu* », *Zinbun* 18, 1982, p. 1-10.

Kamitsuka Yoshiko 神塚淑子, *Dōkyō kyōten no keisei to bukkyō* 道教経典の形成と仏教, Nagoya, Nagoya daigaku shuppankai, 2017.

Keenan, John P., *How Master Mou removes our doubts : a reader-response study and translation of the* Mou-tzu li-huo lun, Albany, State University of New York Press, 1994.

Kleeman, Terry F., *Celestial Masters : history and ritual in early Daoist communities*, Cambridge (MA), Harvard University Asia Center, 2016.

–, « Cultivating conduct and establishing merit 修行立功 : pursuing the good life in early Daoism », *Daoism : Religion, History and Society* 8, 2016, p. 151-167.

–, « Ethnic identity and Taoist identity in traditional China », dans Kohn et Roth (dir.), *Daoist identity*, p. 23-38.

–, « Feasting without the victuals : the evolution of the Daoist communal kitchen », dans Roel Sterckx (dir.), *Of tripod and palate : food, politics and religion in traditional China*, New York, Palgrave Macmillan, 2005, p. 140-162.

–, *Great perfection : religion and ethnicity in a Chinese millennial kingdom*, Honolulu, University of Hawai'i Press, 1998.

–, « Licentious cults and bloody victuals : sacrifice, reciprocity, and violence in traditional China », *Asia major* 3e série 7, n° 1, 1994, p. 185-211.

Knechtges, David R., « Marriage and social status : Shen Yue's impeaching Wang Yuan », dans Wendy Swartz *et al.* (dir.), *Early medieval China : a sourcebook*, New York, Columbia University Press, 2014, p. 166-175.

Kobayashi Masayoshi 小林正美, *Rikuchō dōkyōshi kenkyū* 六朝道教史研究, Tokyo, Sōbunsha, 1990.

–, *Tōdai no dōkyō to tenshidō* 唐代の道教と天師道, Tokyo, Chisen shokan, 2003.

Kohn, Livia, *The Daoist monastic manual : a translation of the* Fengdao kejie, New York, Oxford University Press, 2004.

– (trad.), *Laughing at the Tao : debates among Buddhists and Taoists in medieval China*, Princeton (NJ), Princeton University Press, 1995.

–, « The *Tao-te-ching* in ritual », dans Livia Kohn et Michael LaFargue (dir.), *Lao-tzu and the Tao-te-ching*, Albany, State University of New York Press, 1998, p. 143-161.

Kohn, Livia et Roth, Harold D. (dir.), *Daoist identity : history, lineage, and ritual*, Honolulu, University of Hawai'i Press, 2002.

Komjathy, Louis, *Taming the wild horse : an annotated translation and study of the Daoist horse taming pictures*, New York, Columbia University Press, 2017.

Krishan, Yuvraj, « To what extent Buddhism repudiated Vedic religion ? », *East and West* 43, 1993, p. 237-240.

Kuhn, Dieter, « Textile technology : spinning and reeling », dans Needham, *Science and civilisation*, vol. 5, 9e partie, 1988.

Kuo Li-ying, *Confession et contrition dans le bouddhisme chinois du Ve au Xe siècle*, Paris, École française d'Extrême-Orient, 1994.

Kusuyama Haruki 楠山春樹, « Dōkyō ni okeru jikkai » 道教における十戒, *Waseda daigaku daigakuin bungaku kenkyūka kiyō* 28, 1982, p. 15-32.

Lagerwey, John, « Canonical fasts according to Lu Xiujing », dans Reiter (dir.), *Affiliation and transmission in Daoism*, p. 41-79.

–, *Wu-shang pi-yao : somme taoïste du VIe siècle*, Paris, École française d'Extrême-Orient, 1981.

Lagerwey, John, et Kalinowski, Marc (dir.), *Early Chinese religion. Part one : Shang through Han (1250 BC-220 AD)*, Leyde, Brill, 2009.

Lagerwey, John, et Lü, Pengzhi (dir.), *Early Chinese religion. Part two : the period of division (220-589 AD)*, Leyde, Brill, 2010.

Lai Chi Tim 黎志添, « The *Demon statutes of Nüqing* and the problem of the bureaucratization of the netherworld in early Heavenly Master Taoism », *T'oung pao* 88, 2002, p. 251-281.

–, « The opposition of Celestial Master Taoism to popular cults during the Six Dynasties », *Asia major* 3e série 11, 1998, p. 1-20.

–, « Tian di shui sanguan xinyang yu zaoqi tianshi dao zhibing jiezui yishi » 天地水三官信仰與早期天師道治病解罪儀式, *Taiwan Journal of Religious Studies* 2, 2002, p. 1-30.

Lai Guolong, *Excavating the afterlife : the archaeology of early Chinese religion*, Seattle, University of Washington Press, 2015.

Le Goff, Jacques, *La naissance du Purgatoire*, Paris, Gallimard, 1981.

Levy, Howard S., « Yellow Turban religion and rebellion at the End of Han », *Journal of the American Oriental Society* 76, 1956, p. 214-227.

Li Chuanyin 李傳印, « Nanchao de puxue yu zhengzhi » 南朝的譜學與政治, *Shixue lilun yanjiu* 2003/2, p. 75-85.

Li Tian 李田, « Lushan zhumu huahui wenhua de ru shi dao yinsu gaishuo » 廬山竹木花卉文化的儒釋道因素概說, *Jiangxi shehui kexue* 2010/3, p. 223-227.

Lian Shaoming 連劭名, « Han-Jin jiechu wen yu daojia fangshu » 漢晉解除文與道家方術, *Hanxia kaogu* 1998/4, p. 75-86.

–, « Jianxing nianba nian *songren* jiechu jian kaoshu » 建興廿八年「松人」解除簡考述, *Shijie zongjiao yanjiu* 1996/3, p. 116-119.

Lin Chen-kuo et Radich, Michael, *A distant mirror : articulating Indic ideas in sixth and seventh century Chinese Buddhism*, Hambourg, Hamburg University Press, 2014.

Lin Fushi 林富士, *Zhongguo zhonggu shiqi de zongjiao yu yiliao* 中國中古時期的宗教與醫療, Taipei, Lianjing, 2008.

Link, Arthur E., « Shih Seng-Yu and his writings », *Journal of the American Oriental Society* 80, n° 1, 1960, p. 17-43.

Liu Jiahe, « Early Buddhism and Taoism in China (A.D. 65-420) », trad. Dongfang Shao, *Buddhist-Christian Studies* 12, 1992, p. 35-41.

Liu Shufen 劉淑芬, « Jiankang and the commercial empire of the Southern dynasties : change and continuity in medieval Chinese economic history », dans Pearce *et al.* (dir.), *Culture and power*, p. 35-52.

–, *Liuchao de chengshi yu shehui* 六朝的城市與社會, Taipei, Taiwan xuesheng shuju, 1992.

Liu Tseng-kuei, « Taboos : an aspect of belief in the Qin and Han », dans Lagerwey et Kalinowski (dir.), *Early Chinese religion*, p. 881-948.

Liu Ts'un-yan, « Was Celestial Master Zhang a historical figure ? », dans Penny (dir.), *Daoism in history*, p. 189-253.

Liu Weipeng 劉衛鵬 et Cheng Yi 程義, « Han-Jin muzang zhong suizang taoping nei shengwu de chubu yanjiu » 漢晉墓葬中隨葬陶瓶內盛物的初步研究, *Jianghan kaogu* 108, n° 3, 2008, p. 78-85.

Liu Xianglan 劉湘蘭, « Dunhuang ben *Laozi bianhua jing* yu Laozi shenhua zhi jiangou » 敦煌本《老子變化經》與老子神話之建構. *Wuhan daxue xuebao* (*renwen kexue ban*) 67, n° 3, 2014, p. 80-85.

Liu Xiaomin 劉曉民, « Qiantan daojiao de *chengfu* shuo » 淺談道教的「承負」說, *Yichun xueyuan xuebao* 35, n° 4, 2013, p. 37-39.

Liu Yang, « Origins of Daoist iconography », *Ars orientalis* 31, 2001, p. 31-64.

Liu Yi 劉屹, « Jin-Song tianshi dao shi yanjiu zhiyi : yi dui "fengdao shijia" kaocha wei zhongxin » 晉宋天師道史研究之一 – 以對「奉道世家」考察爲中心, dans Cheng Gongrang 程恭讓 (dir.), *Tianwen* 天問, vol. 1 [*bingxu* 丙戌], Nankin, Jiangsu chuban she, 2006, p. 213-240.

–, *Jingtian yu chongdao : zhonggu jingjiao daojiao xingcheng de sixiang shi beijing* 敬天與崇道 – 中古經教道教形成的思想史背景, Pékin, Zhonghua, 2005.

Liu Yongming 劉永明, « P. 3562v *Daojiao zhaijiao duwang qiyuan wen ji* yu Tang dai de Dunhuang daojiao » (1) et (2) P. 3562V《道教齋醮度亡祈願文集》與唐代的敦煌道教 (一、二). *Dunhuang xue jikan* 2013/4, p. 10-26, et 2014/1, p. 12-23.

Liu Yumao 劉雨茂, Xue Deng 薛登, Mao Qiuxue 毛求學 et Zhu Zhangyi 朱章義, « Chengdu shi Longquan yi Wudai Qian Shu Wang Zongkan fufu mu » 成都市龍泉驛五代前蜀王宗侃夫婦墓, *Kaogu* 考古 2011/6, p. 33-44.

Liu Zhaorui 劉昭瑞, « "Chengfu shuo" yuanqi lun » 「承負說」緣起論, *Shijie zongjiao yanjiu* 1995/4, p. 100-107.

–, *Kaogu faxian yu zaoqi daojiao yanjiu* 考古發現與早期道教研究, Pékin, Wenwu, 2007.

Liu Zhiwan 劉知萬, « Tempōshin to Tempōju ni tsuite » 天蓬神と天蓬咒について, dans Akizuki Kan'ei 秋月觀映 (dir.), *Dōkyō to shūkyō bunka* 道教と宗教文化, Tokyo, Hirakawa, 1987, p. 403-424.

Liu Zhongyu 劉仲宇, *Daojiao shoulu zhidu yanjiu* 道教授籙制度研究, Pékin, Zhongguo shehui kexue chuban she, 2014.

Lü Pengzhi 呂鵬志, « Daoist rituals », dans Lagerwey et Kalinowski (dir.), *Early Chinese religion*, p. 1245-1349.

–, « The Jade instructions on the Red Writings for summoning ghosts and demons of the Northern Feng mountain and the five Lingbao True Writs », dans Florian C. Reiter (dir.), *Exorcism in Daoism : a Berlin symposium*, Wiesbaden, Harrossowitz, 2011, p. 31-49.

–, « The Lingbao fast of the Three Primes and the Daoist Middle Prime festival : a critical study of the *Taishang dongxuan lingbao sanyuan pinjie jing* », *Cahiers d'Extrême-Asie* 20, 2011, p. 35-61.

–, « Lingbao liuzhai kao » 靈寶六齋考. *Wenshi* 96, n° 3, 2011, p. 85-125.

–, « Ordination ranks in medieval Daoism and the classification of Daoist rituals », dans Reiter (dir.), *Affiliation and transmission in Daoism*, p. 81-107.

–, *Tang qian daojiao yishi shigang* 唐前道教儀式史綱, Pékin, Zhonghua, 2008.

–, « Tianshi dao shoulu keyi : Dunhuang xieben S. 203 kaolun » 天師道授籙科儀 – 敦煌寫本 S. 203 考論, *Bulletin of the Institute of History and Philology, Academia sinica* 77, 2006, p. 79-166.

–, « Tianshi dao zhijiao zhai kao » (1, 2) 天師道指教齋考 (上/下), *Bulletin of the Institute of History and Philology, Academia sinica* 80, 2009, p. 355-402 et 507-533.

–, « Zaoqi daojiao jiaoyi ji qi liubian kaosuo » 早期道教醮儀及其流變考索, dans Tam Wai Lun 譚偉倫 (dir.), *Zhongguo difang zongjiao yishi lunji* 中國地方宗教儀式論集, Hong Kong, Centre for the Study of Religion and Chinese Society, Chinese University of Hong Kong, 2011, p. 19-145.

Lupke, Christopher (dir.), *The magnitude of* ming *: command, allotment, and fate in Chinese culture*, Honolulu, University of Hawai'i Press, 2005.

Lyonnet, Stanislas, et Sabourin, Léopold, *Sin, redemption and sacrifice : a biblical and patristic study*, Rome, Biblical Institute, 1970.

Ma De 馬德, « Dunhuang wenshu *Daojia zazhai wenfan ji* ji youguan wenti shulüe » 敦煌文書《道家雜齋文範集》及有關問題述略. *Daojia wenhua yanjiu* 13, 1998, p. 226-248.

Madigan, Kevin J., et Levenson, Jon D., *Resurrection : the power of God for Christians and Jews*, New Haven (CT), Yale University Press, 2008.

Maeda Shigeki, « Between karmic retribution and entwining infusion », dans Penny (dir.), *Daoism in history*, p. 101-120.

Makita Tairyō 牧田諦亮, *Gikyō kenkyū* 疑經研究, Kyoto, Rinsen shōden, 1989.

Maruyama Hiroshi 丸山宏, *Dōkyō girei monjo no rekishiteki kenkyū* 道教儀禮文書の歷史的研究, Tokyo, Kyūko shoin, 2004.

–, « Sei'itsu dōkyō no jōshō girei ni tsuite » 正一道教の上章儀禮につ いて, *Tōhō shūkyō* 68, 1986, p. 44-64.

Maspero, Henri, *Le taoïsme et les religions chinoises*, Paris, Gallimard, 1971.

Mather, Richard B. (trad.), *A New account of tales of the world by Liu I-ch'ing with commentary by Liu Chün*, 2e éd., Ann Arbor, University of Michigan, 2002.

–, *The poet Shen Yüeh (441-513) : the reticent marquis*, Princeton (NJ), Princeton University Press, 1988.

Mesnil, Evelyne, « Zhang Suqing et la peinture taoïste à Shu », *Cahiers d'Extrême-Asie* 9, 1996-1997, p. 131-158.
Michael, Thomas, *In the shadows of the Dao : Laozi, the sage, and the* Daodejing, Albany, State University of New York Press, 2015.
–, *The pristine Dao : metaphysics in early Daoist discourse*, Albany, State University of New York Press, 2005.
Michaud, Paul, « The Yellow Turbans », *Monumenta serica* 17, 1958, p. 47-127.
Mitamura Keiko 三田村圭子, « Tōdai zengo ni mieru seishi : *Kōsei-shū* shoshū no jirei o chūshin ni » 唐代前後に見える青詞 – 『広成集』所収の事例を中心に, *Komazawa daigaku gaikoku-go ronshū* 11, 2011, p. 131-150.
–, « Tō-matsu Godai ni okeru shūkyō katsudō to setsudo-shi : *Kōsei-shū* o chūshin to shite » 唐末五代における宗教活動と節度使 – 『廣成集』を中心として, *Tōhō shūkyō* 120, 2012, p. 1-21.
Miyakawa Hisayuki 宮川尚志, *Chūgoku shūkyōshi kenkyū* 中國宗教史研究, Kyoto, Dōhōsha, 1983.
–, « Local cults around Mount Lu at the time of Sun En's rebellion », dans Welch et Seidel (dir.), *Facets of Taoism*, p. 83-101.
Mollier, Christine, *Une apocalypse taoïste du* V*e* *s. : le Livre des incantations divines des grottes abyssales*, Paris, Collège de France, 1990.
–, *Buddhism and Taoism face to face : scripture, ritual and iconographic exchange in medieval China*, Honolulu, University of Hawai'i Press, 2008.
–, « La méthode de l'Empereur du Nord du mont Fengdu : une tradition exorciste du taoïsme médiéval », *T'oung pao* 83, 1997, p. 329-385.
–, « Visions of evil : demonology and orthodoxy in early Daoism », dans Penny (dir.), *Daoism in history*, p. 74-100.
Mugitani Kunio 麥谷邦夫 et Tadao Yoshikawa 吉川忠夫 (dir.), *Shūshi meitsūki kenkyū (yakuchū hen)* 周氏冥通記研究 (譯注篇), Kyoto, Kyōto daigaku jinbun kagaku kenkyūjo, 2003.

Nattier, Jan, *A guide to the earliest Chinese Buddhist translations : texts from the Eastern Han and Three Kingdoms periods*, Tokyo, International Research Institute for Advanced Buddhology, Soka University, 2008.
–, *Once upon a future time : studies in a Buddhist prophecy of decline*, Berkeley, Asian Humanities Press, 1991.
Naundorf, Gert, Pohl, Karl-Heinz, et Schmidt, Hans-Hermann (dir.), *Religion und Philosophie in Ostasien : Festschrift für Hans Steininger*, Würzburg, Königshausen und Neumann, 1985.
Needham, Joseph, *et al.*, *Science and civilisation in China*, Cambridge, Cambridge University Press, 1954-.
Nelson, Susan E., « The bridge at Tiger Brook : Tao Qian and the Three Teachings in Chinese art », *Monumenta serica* 50, 2002, p. 257-294.
Ngo Van Xuyet, *Divination, magie et politique dans la Chine ancienne : essai*, Paris, Presses universitaires de France, 1976.
Nickerson, Peter (trad.), « Abridged codes of Master Lu for the Daoist community », dans Donald S. Lopez (dir.), *Religions of China in practice*, Princeton (NJ), Princeton University Press, 1996, p. 347-359.

–, « “Let living and dead take separate paths” : bureaucratization and textualization in early Chinese mortuary ritual », dans Penny (dir.), *Daoism in history*, p. 10-40.

–, « “Opening the way” : exorcism, travel, and soteriology in early Daoist mortuary practice and its antecedents », dans Kohn et Roth (dir.), *Daoist identity*, p. 58-77.

Nylan, Michael. « The legacies of the Chengdu plain », dans Robert Bagley (dir.), *Ancient Sichuan : treasures from a lost civilization*, Seattle et Princeton, Seattle Art Museum et Princeton University Press, 2001, p. 309-325.

–, « “Living without sin” : reflections on the pre-Buddhist world of early China », dans Granoff et Shinohara (dir.), *Sins and sinners*, p. 57-72.

–, « *Yin-yang*, Five Phases, and *qi* », dans Nylan et Loewe (dir.), *China's early empires*, p. 398-414.

Nylan, Michael, et Loewe, Michael (dir.), *China's early empires : a re-appraisal*, Cambridge, Cambridge University Press, 2010.

Ōfuchi Ninji 大淵忍爾, *Shoki no dōkyō : dōkyōshi no kenkyū, sono ichi* 初期の道教 – 道教史の研究，其の一, Tokyo, Sōbunsha, 1991.

–, *Tonkō dōkyō* 敦煌道經, 2 vol., *Mokuroku hen* 目錄編 (1) et *Zuroku hen* 圖錄編 (2), Tokyo, Fukutake shoten, 1978 et 1979.

Ouyang Zhen 歐陽鎮, « Lushan daojiao wenhua chuyi » 廬山道教文化芻議, *Shijie zongjiao wenhua* 2013/6, p. 114-116.

Pankenier, David W., *Astrology and cosmology in early China : conforming earth to heaven*, Cambridge, Cambridge University Press, 2013.

Pearce, Scott, Spiro, Audrey, et Ebrey, Patricia (dir.), *Culture and power in the reconstitution of the Chinese realm, 200-600*, Cambridge (MA), Harvard University Press, 2001.

Pelliot, Paul, « Les statues en “laque sèche” dans l'ancien art chinois », *Journal asiatique* avril-juin 1923, p. 181-207.

Peng Bangben, « In search of the Shu kingdom : ancient legends and new archaeological discoveries in Sichuan », *Journal of East Asian Archaeology* 4, 2002, p. 75-99.

Penny, Benjamin (dir.), *Daoism in history : essays in honour of Liu Ts'un-yan*, Londres, Routledge, 2006.

Pines, Yuri (trad.), *The Book of Lord Shang : apologetics of state power in early China*, New York, Columbia University Press, 2017.

Polansky, Ronald M., *Aristotle's* De anima, Cambridge, Cambridge University Press, 2007.

Pollock, Sheldon I., *The language of the gods in the world of men : Sanskrit, culture, and power in premodern India*, Berkeley, University of California Press, 2006.

Poo Mu-chou, « Preparation for the afterlife in ancient China », dans Amy Olberding et Philip J. Ivanhoe (dir.), *Mortality in traditional Chinese thought*, Albany, State University of New York Press, 2011, p. 13-36.

Pregadio, Fabrizio, « Early Daoist meditation and the origins of Inner Alchemy », dans Penny (dir.), *Daoism in history*, p. 121-158.

Pu Chengzhong, « Notes on the *Chengju guangming jing*, “Sūtra of achieving the bright light concentration” », *Buddhist Studies Review* 25, n° 1, 2008, p. 27-53.

Puett, Michael, « Becoming Laozi : cultivating and visualizing spirits in early-medieval China », *Asia major* 3e série 23, n° 1, 2010, p. 223-252.
–, « Forming Spirits for the Way : the cosmology of the *Xiang'er* commentary to the Laozi », *Journal of Chinese Religions* 32, 2004, p. 1-27.

Qian Nanxiu, *Spirit and self in medieval China : the* Shih-shuo hsin-yü and *its legacy*, Honolulu, University of Hawai'i Press, 2001.

Raz, Gil, « Creation of tradition : the Five Numinous Treasure talismans and the formation of early Daoism », thèse de doctorat, Indiana University, 2004.
–, *The emergence of Daoism : creation of tradition*, Londres, Routledge, 2012.
Reiter, Florian C. (dir.), *Affiliation and transmission in Daoism : a Berlin symposium*, Wiesbaden, Harrassowitz, 2012.
Ricœur, Paul, « La symbolique du mal », *Finitude et culpabilité*, vol. 2, Paris, Aubier, 1960.
Robinet, Isabelle, *Méditation taoïste*, Paris, Albin Michel, 1979.
Robson, James, « Sin, sinification, sinology : on the notion of sin in Buddhism and Chinese religions », dans Granoff et Shinohara (dir.), *Sins and sinners*, p. 73-92.
Rong Xinjiang, *Eighteen lectures on Dunhuang*, trad. Imre Galambos, Leyde, Brill, 2013.

Sage, Steven F., *Ancient Sichuan and the unification of China*, Albany, State University of New York Press, 1992.
Saidura, Abdullah Salamu 阿不都沙拉木・賽都拉 *et al.*, « Maisha liaofa de tedian he jili » 埋沙療法的特點和機理, *Zhongguo minzu yiyao zazhi* 9, 2011, p. 54-56.
Schafer, Edward H., « The last years of Ch'ang-an ». *Oriens extremus* 10, n° 2, 1963, p. 133-179.
Schipper, Kristofer M., « The inner world of the *Lao-tzu chung-ching* », dans Chun-chieh Huang et Erik Zürcher (dir.), *Time and space in Chinese culture*, Leyde, Brill, 1995, p. 114-131.
–, « Purity and strangers : shifting boundaries in medieval Taoism », *T'oung pao* 80, 1994, p. 61-81.
–, *La religion de la Chine : la tradition vivante*, Paris, Fayard, 2008.
–, *The Taoist body*, trad. Karen C. Duval, Berkeley, University of California Press, 1993.
–, « Taoist ordination ranks in the Tunhuang manuscripts », dans Naundorf *et al.* (dir.), *Religion und Philosophie*, p. 127-148.
–, « Taoist ritual and local cults of the T'ang dynasty », dans Strickmann (dir.), *Tantric and Taoist studies*, vol. 3, p. 812-834.
Schipper, Kristofer, et Verellen, Franciscus (dir.), *The Taoist canon : a historical companion to the Daozang*, 3 vol., Chicago, University of Chicago Press, 2004.
Schmidt-Glintzer, Helwig, *Das* Hung-ming chi *und die Aufnahme des Buddhismus in China*, Wiesbaden, Steiner, 1976.
Seidel, Anna, *La divinisation de Lao tseu dans le taoïsme des Han*, Paris, École française d'Extrême-Orient, 1969.

–, « The image of the perfect ruler in early Taoist messianism : Lao-tzu and Li Hung », *History of Religions* 9, 1969-1970, p. 216-247.

–, « Imperial treasures and Taoist sacraments : Taoist roots in the apocrypha », dans Strickmann (dir.), *Tantric and Taoist studies*, vol. 2, p. 291-371.

–, « Das neue Testament des Tao. Lao tzu und die Entstehung der taoistischen Religion am Ende der Han-Zeit », *Saeculum* 29, 1978, p. 147-172.

–, « Post-mortem immortality or the Taoist resurrection of the body », dans S. Shaked *et al.* (dir.), *Gilgul : essays on transformation, revolution and permanence in the history of religions*, Leyde, Brill, 1987, p. 223-237.

–, « Le Sûtra merveilleux du Ling-pao suprême, traitant de Lao tseu qui convertit les barbares (le manuscrit S. 2081) », dans Michel Soymié (dir.), *Contributions aux études de Touen-houang*, vol. 3, Paris, École française d'Extrême-Orient, 1984, p. 305-352.

–, « Taoist messianism », *Numen* 31, nº 2, 1984, p. 161-174.

–, « Traces of Han religion in funeral texts found in tombs », dans Akizuki Kan'ei 秋月觀暎 (dir.), *Dōkyō to shūkyō bunka* 道教と宗教文化, Tokyo, Hirakawa, 1987, p. 21-57.

Shaughnessy, Edward L., *Unearthing the Changes : recently discovered manuscripts of the Yi jing (I ching) and related texts*, New York, Columbia University Press, 2014.

Shinohara Koichi, *Spells, images, and mandalas : tracing the evolution of esoteric Buddhist rituals*, New York, Columbia University Press, 2014.

Sivin, Nathan, « Cosmos and computation in early Chinese mathematical astronomy », *T'oung pao* 55, 1969, p. 1-73.

Sluhovsky, Moshe, *Becoming a new self : practices of belief in early modern Catholicism*, Chicago, University of Chicago Press, 2017.

Soymié, Michel, « Les dix jours de jeûne du taoïsme », dans Yoshioka Yoshitoyo hakushi kanreki kinen ronshū kankōkai 吉岡義豐博士還曆記念論集刊行會 (dir.), *Dōkyō kenkyū ronshū : Dōkyō no shisō to bunka* 道教研究論集 — 道教の思想と文化, Tokyo, Kokusho kankōkai, 1977, p. 1-21.

– [Misheru Suwamie ミシェル・スワミエ], « Ikutsu ka no Tonkō bunken ni motodzuku kōki dōkyō no shosō » いくつかの敦煌文獻にもとづく後期道教の諸相, *Chūgoku bungakuhō* 40, 1989, p. 1-15.

Staal, Frits, *et al.*, *Agni : the Vedic ritual of the Fire altar*, Delhi, Motilal Banarsidass, 1986.

Stanley-Baker, Michael, « Drugs, destiny, and disease in medieval China : situating knowledge in context », *Daoism : Religion, History and Society* 6, 2014, p. 113-156.

Steavu, Dominic, *The Writ of the Three Sovereigns : from local lore to institutional Daoism*, Honolulu, University of Hawai'i Press, 2019.

Stein, Rolf A., « Religious Taoism and popular religion from the second to the seventh centuries », dans Welch et Seidel (dir.), *Facets of Taoism*, p. 53-81.

–, « Remarques sur quelques mouvements du taoïsme politico-religieux au IIe s. ap. J.-C », *T'oung pao* 50, 1963, p. 1-78.

Steinhardt, Nancy Shatzman, *Chinese architecture in an age of turmoil, 200-600*, Honolulu, University of Hawai'i Press, 2014.

Sterckx, Roel, « Religious practices in Qin and Han », dans Nylan et Loewe (dir.), *China's early empires*, p. 415-429.

Strickmann, Michel, *Chinese magical medicine*, éd. Bernard Faure, Stanford (CA), Stanford University Press, 2002.

–, *Chinese poetry and prophecy : the written oracle in East Asia*, éd. Bernard Faure, Stanford (CA), Stanford University Press, 2005.

–, « History, anthropology, and Chinese religion », *Harvard Journal of Asiatic Studies* 40, 1980, p. 201-248.

–, « The Mao shan revelations : Taoism and the chinese aristocracy », *T'oung pao* 63, 1977, p. 1-64.

–, « On the alchemy of T'ao Hung-ching », dans Welch et Seidel (dir.), *Facets of Taoism*, p. 123-192.

–, *Le taoïsme du Mao Chan : chronique d'une révélation*, Paris, Collège de France, 1981.

–, « A Taoist confirmation of Liang Wu Ti's suppression of Taoism », *Journal of the American Oriental Society* 98, 1978, p. 467-475.

–, « Therapeutische Rituale und das Problem des Bösen im frühen Taoismus », dans Naundorf *et al.* (dir.), *Religion und Philosophie*, p. 185-200.

Strickmann, Michel (dir.). *Tantric and Taoist studies in honour of R. A. Stein*, 3 vol., Bruxelles, Institut belge des hautes études chinoises, 1981, 1983 et 1985.

Stroumsa, Guy G., *The making of the Abrahamic religions in late antiquity*, Oxford, Oxford University Press, 2015.

Sun Ruixue 孫瑞雪, « Lu Xiujing yu tianshi dao gaige : yi *Lu xiansheng daomen ke lüe* wei zhongxin » 陸修靜與天師道改革 – 以《陸先生道門科略》爲中心, *Zhonghua wenhua luntan* 2011/5, p. 138-141.

Sun Weijie 孫偉杰 et Gai Jianmin 蓋建民, « Huangdao shier gong yu daojiao guanxi kaolun » 黃道十二宮與道教關係考論, *Zhongguo zhexue shi* 2015/3, p. 74-82.

–, « Zhaijiao yu xingming : Du Guangting *Guangcheng ji* suo jian tianwen xingzhan wenhua shulun » 齋醮與星命 – 杜光庭《廣成集》所見天文星占文化述論, *Hunan daxue xuebao* 30, n° 3, 2016, p. 70-76.

Sun Yiping 孫亦平, « Lun Du Guangting dui daojiao zhaijiao keyi de fazhan yu gongxian » 論杜光庭對道教齋醮科儀的發展與貢獻, *Zongjiao xue yanjiu* 2006/4, p. 19-23.

Tackett, Nicolas, *The destruction of the medieval Chinese aristocracy*, Cambridge (MA), Harvard University Asia Center, 2014.

Tambiah, Stanley Jeyaraja, *Magic, science, religion, and the scope of rationality*, Cambridge, Cambridge University Press, 1990.

Tang Yongtong 湯用彤, *Han Wei liang Jin Nanbei chao fojiao shi* 漢魏兩晉南北朝佛教史, Pékin, Zhonghua, 1955.

Teiser, Stephen F., *The Ghost Festival in medieval China*. Princeton (NJ), Princeton University Press, 1988.

–, « Having once died and returned to life : representations of hell in medieval China », *Harvard Journal of Asiatic Studies* 48, 1988, p. 433-464.

–, « The literary style of Dunhuang healing liturgies (患文) », *Dunhuang Tulufan yanjiu* 14, 2014, p. 355-377.

–, « Ornamenting the departed : notes on the language of Chinese Buddhist ritual texts », *Asia major* 3e série 22, 2009, p. 201-237.

–, *Reinventing the wheel : paintings of rebirth in medieval Buddhist temples*, Seattle, University of Washington Press, 2006.

–, *The scripture on the Ten Kings and the making of purgatory in medieval Chinese Buddhism*, Honolulu, University of Hawai'i Press, 1994.

– [Tai Shiwen 太史文], « Wei wangzhe yuan : Dunhuang yishi wenlei dingyi chutan » 爲亡者願 – 敦煌儀式文類定義初探, trad. Xie Huiying 謝惠英, dans Li Fengmao 李豐楙 et Liao Zhaoheng 廖肇亨 (dir.), *Shengchuan yu shichan : Zhongguo wenxue yu zongjiao lunji* 聖傳與詩禪 – 中國文學與宗教論集, Taipei, Zhongyang yanjiu yuan Zhongguo wenzhe yanjiu suo, 2007, p. 284-307.

Thilo, Thomas, *Chang'an : Metropole Ostasiens und Weltstadt des Mittelalters 583-904*, 2 vol., Wiesbaden, Harrassowitz, 1997 et 2006.

Thomas, Keith, *Religion and the decline of magic : studies in popular beliefs in sixteenth and seventeenth century England*, Londres, Weidenfeld and Nicolson, 1971.

Tian Xiaofei, *Beacon fire and shooting star : the literary culture of the Liang (502-57)*, Cambridge (MA), Harvard University Asia Center, 2007.

–, « Seeing with the mind's eye : the Eastern Jin discourse of visualization and imagination », *Asia major* 3e série 18, 2006, p. 67-102.

Tsien Tsuen-hsuin, *Written on bamboo and silk : the beginnings of Chinese books and inscriptions*, 2e éd., Chicago, University of Chicago Press, 2004.

Tsuchiya Masaaki, « Confession of sins and awareness of self in the *Taiping jing* », dans Kohn et Roth (dir.), *Daoist identity*, p. 39-57.

Tsukamoto Zenryū, *A history of early Chinese Buddhism : from its introduction to the death of Hui-yüan*, trad. Leon Hurvitz, Tokyo, Kodansha, 1985.

Tu Wei-ming, *Centrality and commonality : an essay on Confucian religiousness*, Albany, State University of New York Press, 1989.

Twitchett, Denis C., *Financial administration under the T'ang dynasty*, Cambridge, Cambridge University Press, 1970.

–, *Printing and publishing in medieval China*, New York, Frederic C. Beil, 1983.

Unschuld, Paul U., *Medicine in China : a history of ideas*, Berkeley, University of California Press, 1985.

Unschuld, Paul U., et Tessenow, Hermann, en collaboration avec Jinsheng, Zheng, *Huang di nei jing su wen : an annotated translation of Huang Di's Inner classic – Basic questions*, Berkeley, University of California Press, 2011.

Venture, Olivier, « L'écriture et la communication avec les esprits en Chine ancienne », *Bulletin of the Museum of Far Eastern antiquities* 74, 2004, p. 34-65.

Verellen, Franciscus, « The beyond within : grotto-heavens in Taoist ritual and cosmology », *Cahiers d'Extrême-Asie* 8, 1995, p. 265-290.

–, *Du Guangting (850-933) : taoïste de cour à la fin de la Chine médiévale*, Paris, Collège de France, 1989.

–, « The dynamic design : ritual and contemplative graphics in Taoist scriptures », dans Penny (dir.), *Daoism in history*, p. 159-186.

–, « Encounter as revelation : a Taoist hagiographic theme in medieval China », *Bulletin de l'École française d'Extrême-Orient* 85, 1998, p. 363-384.

–, « Evidential miracles in support of Taoism : the inversion of a Buddhist apologetic tradition in late T'ang China », *T'oung pao* 78, 1992, p. 217-263.

–, « Five sentiments of gratitude », dans William Theodore de Bary et Irene Bloom (dir.), *Sources of Chinese Tradition*, vol. 1, New York, Columbia University Press, 1999, p. 404-406.

–, « A forgotten T'ang restoration : the Taoist dispensation after Huang Ch'ao », *Asia major* 3e série 7, 1994, p. 107-153.

–, « Green memorials : Daoist ritual prayers in the Tang-Five dynasties transition », *Tang studies* 35, 2017, p. 51-86.

–, « The Heavenly Master liturgical agenda according to Chisong zi's petition almanac », *Cahiers d'Extrême-Asie* 14, 2004, p. 291-343.

–, « Liturgy and sovereignty : the role of Taoist ritual in the foundation of the Shu kingdom (906-25) », *Asia major* 3e série 2, 1989, p. 59-78.

–, « Lu Xiujing (406-77) on Daoist practice : ten lessons in *The Way and its virtue* », *Daoism : Religion, History and Society* 8, 2016, p. 169-206.

–, « Shu as a hallowed land : Du Guangting's *Record of marvels* », *Cahiers d'Extrême-Asie* 10, 1998, p. 213-254.

– [Fu Feilan 傅飛嵐], « Tianshi dao shangzhang keyi : *Chisong zi zhangli* he *Yuanchen zhangjiao licheng li* yanjiu » 天師道上章科儀 – 《赤松子章曆》和《元辰章醮立成曆》研究, dans Lai Chi Tim 黎志添 (dir.), *Daojiao jingdian yu Zhongguo zongjiao wenhua* 道教經典與中國宗教文化, Hong Kong, Zhonghua, 2003, p. 37-71.

–, « The Twenty-four Dioceses and Zhang Daoling : spatio-liturgical organization in early Heavenly Master Taoism », dans Phyllis Granoff et Koichi Shinohara (dir.), *Pilgrims, patrons, and place : localizing sanctity in Asian religions*, Vancouver, University of British Columbia Press, 2003, p. 15-67.

–, « Zhang Ling and the Lingjing salt well », dans Jacques Gernet et Marc Kalinowski (dir.), *En suivant la voie royale : mélanges en hommage à Léon Vandermeersch*, Paris, École française d'Extrême-Orient, 1997, p. 249-265.

Vitiello, Giovanni, « Studio sul taoista Lu Xiujing (406-477) », *Annali dell'Istituto universitario orientale di Napoli* 47, nº 3, 1987, p. 293-332.

Vogel, Hans-Ulrich, « Mothers and children : discourses on paper money during the Song period », dans Von Hagen et Welker (dir.), *Money as God ?*, p. 219-232.

Von Glahn, Richard, « Re-examining the authenticity of Song paper money specimens », *Journal of Song-Yuan studies* 36, 2006, p. 79-106.

Von Hagen, Jürgen, et Welker, Michael (dir.), *Money as God ? The monetization of the market and its impact on religion, politics, law, and ethics*, Cambridge, Cambridge University Press, 2014.

Wagner, Rudolf G., *A Chinese reading of the* Daodejing *: Wang Bi's commentary on the* Laozi *with critical text and translation*, Albany, State University of New York Press, 2003.

–, « Fate's gift economy : the Chinese case of coping with the asymmetry between man and fate », dans von Hagen et Welker (dir.), *Money as God ?*, p. 184-218.

Waley, Arthur (trad.), *The Book of songs*, éd. Joseph R. Allen, New York, Grove Press, 1996.

Wang Chengwen 王承文, « Cong zhaijie guifan lun gudai guojia jisi dui Han-Jin daojiao de yinxiang : jian dui Lü Pengzhi boshi yi xilie lunzhu de shangque » 從齋戒規範論古代國家祭祀對漢晉道教的影響 – 兼對呂鵬志博士一系列論著的商榷, *Zhongnan daxue xuebao* 56, nº 2, 2016, p. 77-102.

–, « Gu lingbao jing de zhaiguan zhidu yu tianshi dao ji fojiao de guanxi » 古靈寶經的齋官制度與天師道及佛教的關係, *Dunhuang Tulufan yanjiu* 6, 2002, p. 55-80.

–, « Gudai guojia jisi yu Han-Tang daojiao *bajie zhai* yuanyuan lunkao (1, 2) : jian dui Lü Pengzhi boshi yi xilie zhiyi de dafu » 古代國家祭祀與漢唐道教「八節齋」淵源論考 (上/下) – 兼對呂鵬志博士一系列質疑的答復, *Zongjiao xue yanjiu* 2016/2, p. 1-15, et 2016/3, p. 10-21.

–, *Han-Jin daojiao yishi yu gu Lingbao jing yanjiu* 漢晉道教儀式與古靈寶經研究, Pékin, Zhongguo shehui kexue chuban she, 2017.

–, « Lu Xiujing daojiao xinyang cong tianshi dao xiang lingbao jing zhuanbian lunkao (1, 2) : yi Lu Xiujing suo zhuan *Daomen kelüe* wei qidian de kaocha » 陸修靜道教信仰從天師道向靈寶經轉變論考 (上/下) – 以陸修靜所撰《道門科略》爲起點的考察, *Zongjiao xue yanjiu* 2014/2, p. 1-10, et 2014/3, p. 20-32.

Wang Guiping 汪桂平, « Daojiao tutan zhai fa chutan » 道教塗炭齋法初探, *Shijie zongjiao yanjiu* 2002/4, p. 46-55.

Wang Haoyue 王皓月, *Xijing qiuzhen : Lu Xiujing yu lingbao jing guanxi xintan* 析經求真 – 陸修靜與靈寶經關係新探, Pékin, Zhonghua, 2017.

Wang Hongjie, *Power and politics in tenth-century China : the Former Shu regime*, Amherst (NY), Cambria Press, 2011.

Wang Jianchuan 王見川, *Zhang tianshi zhi yanjiu : yi Longhu shan yixi wei kaocha zhongxin* 張天師之研究 – 以龍虎山一系爲考察中心, Taipei, Boyang wenhua shiye youxian gongsi, 2015.

Wang Jing 王璟, « *Zhengyi fawen tianshi jiaojie kejing* chengshu niandai kaobian » 《正一法文天師教戒科經》成書年代考辨, *Chengda zhongwen xuebao* 46, 2014, p. 69-98.

Wang Ka 王卡, *Dunhuang daojiao wenxian yanjiu : zongshu, mulu, suoyin* 敦煌道教文獻研究 – 綜述、目錄、索引, Pékin, Zhongguo shehui kexue chuban she, 2004.

Wang Tianlin 王天麟, « Tianshi dao jiaotuan de zuiguan ji qi xiande sixiang » 天師道教團的罪觀及其仙德思想, dans Li Fengmao 李豐楙 et Zhu Ronggui 朱榮貴 (dir.), *Yishi, miaohui yu shequ : daojiao, minjian xinyang yu minjian wenhua* 儀式、廟會與社區 – 道教、民間信仰與民間文化, Taipei, Zhongyang yanjiu yuan 1996, p. 511-545.

Wang Yi-t'ung 王伊同, *Wuchao mendi : fu gaomen quanmen shixi hunyin biao* 五朝門第 – 附高門權門世系婚姻表, 2 vol., Hong Kong, Zhongwen daxue chuban she, 1978.

Wang Yucheng 王育成 (éd.), *Daojiao fayin lingpai tan'ao* 道教法印令牌探奧, Pékin, Zongjiao wenhua chuban she, 2000.

Wang Zongyu 王宗昱, « Daojiao de "liutian" shuo » 道教的「六天」說, *Daojiao wenhua yanjiu* 16, 1999, p. 22-49.

–, « *Chisong zi zhangli* de chengshu niandai » 《赤松子章曆》的成書年代, dans Liu Zhongyu 劉仲宇 et Ji Hongzhong 吉宏忠 (dir.), *Zhengyi daojiao yanjiu* 正一道教研究, Pékin, Zongjiao wenhua chuban she, 2012, p 148-161.

–, « *Zhengyi fawen jing zhangguan pin* jiaokan » 《正一法文經章官品》校勘, dans Zheng Kai 鄭開 (dir.), *Shui qiong yunqi ji : daojiao wenxian yanjiu de jiuxue xinzhi* 水窮雲起集 – 道教文獻研究的舊學新知, Pékin, Shehui kexue wenxian chuban she, 2009, p. 51-100.

Welch, Holmes, et Seidel, Anna (dir.), *Facets of Taoism*, New Haven (CT), Yale University Press, 1979.

Wells, Matthew, « Self as historical artifact : Ge Hong and early Chinese autobiographical writing », *Early Medieval China* 9, 2003, p. 71-103.

Wiles, Sue, « The Daoist aunt : Xu Baoguang », dans Chan *et al.* (dir.), *Willow catkins*, p. 261-284.

Wu Guofu 吳國富, *Lushan daojiao shi* 廬山道教史, Nanchang, Jiangxi renmin chuban she, 2011.

Wu Liyu 吳麗娛, « Lun jiugong jisi yu daojiao chongbai » 論九宮祭祀與道教崇拜, *Tang yanjiu* 9, 2003, p. 283-314.

Wu Pei-Yi, « Self-examination and confession of sins in traditional China », *Harvard Journal of Asiatic Studies* 39, 1979, p. 5-38.

Wu Rongceng 吳榮曾, « Zhenmu zhi wen zhong suo jiandao de Dong Han dao wu guanxi » 鎮墓之文中所見到的東漢道巫關係, *Wenwu* 1981/3, p. 56-63.

Wu, Sujane, « The biography of Lu Yun (262-303) in *Jin shu* 54 », *Early Medieval China* 7, 2001, p. 1-38.

Wu Tingxie 吳廷燮, *Tang fangzhen nianbiao* 唐方鎮年表, Pékin, Zhonghua, 1980.

Wu Yakui 吳亞魁, « Daojiao jinji chuyi » 道教禁忌芻議, dans Chen Guying 陳鼓應 et Feng Dawen 馮達文 (dir.), *Daojia yu daojiao : di er jie guoji xueshu yantao hui lunwen ji* 道家與道教 – 第二屆國際學術研討會論文集, vol. 2, Guangzhou, Guangdong renmin chuban she, 2001, p. 559-568.

Wu Yu 吳羽, « Du Guangting *Guangcheng ji* suo zai biao, jiao ci xiezuo niandai congkao » 杜光庭《廣成集》所載表、醮詞寫作年代叢考, *Wei Jin Nanbei chao Sui Tang shi ziliao* 28, 2012, p. 243-248.

Wu Zhen 吳真, « Cong Du Guangting liupian Luotian jiao ci kan zaoqi Luotian dajiao » 從杜光庭六篇羅天醮詞看早期羅天大醮, *Zhongguo daojiao* 2008/2, p. 19-23.

–, *Wei shenxing jiazhu : Tang-Song Ye Fashan chongbai de zaocheng shi* 爲神性加注 – 唐宋葉法善崇拜的造成史, Pékin, Zhongguo shehui kexue chuban she, 2012.

Xiang Shiling, « A study on the theory of “returning to the original” and “recovering nature” in Chinese philosophy », *Frontiers of Philosophy in China* 3, 2008, p. 502-519.

Xiong, Victor, « Astrological divination at the Tang court », *Early Medieval China* 13-14, 2007, p. 185-231.

–, « Ritual innovations and Taoism under Tang Xuanzong », *T'oung pao* 82, 1996, p. 259-316.

Yamada Akihiro 山田明廣, « Totansai kō : Riku Shūsei no Sangen totansai o jiku to shite » 塗炭齋考 – 陸修靜の三元塗炭齋を軸として, *Tōhō shūkyō* 100, 2002, p. 47-67.

Yoshikawa Tadao 吉川忠夫, « Shoku ni okeru shin'i no gaku no dentō » 蜀における讖緯の學の傳統, dans Yasui Kōzan 安居香山 (dir.), *Shin'i shisō no sōgōteki kenkyū* 讖緯思想の綜合的研究, Tokyo, Kokusho kankōkai, 1984, p. 105-135.

Young, Stuart H., *Conceiving the Indian Buddhist patriarchs in China*, Honolulu, University of Hawai'i Press, 2015.

–, « For a compassionate killing : Chinese Buddhism, sericulture, and the silkworm god Aśvaghoṣa », *Journal of Chinese Religions* 41, 2013, p. 25-58.

Young, William J. (éd.), *Letters of St. Ignatius of Loyola*, Chicago, Loyola University Press, 1959.

Zacchetti, Stefano, *In praise of the light : a critical synoptic edition with an annotated translation of chapters 1-3 of Dharmarakṣa's* Guang zan jing 光讚經*, being the earliest Chinese translation of the larger Prajñāpāramitā*, Tokyo, The International Research Institute for Advanced Buddhology, Soka University, 2005.

–, « Notions and visions of the canon in early Chinese Buddhism », dans Jiang Wu et Lucille Chia (dir.), *Spreading Buddha's word in East Asia : the formation and transformation of the Chinese Buddhist canon*, New York, Columbia University Press, 2016, p. 81-108.

Zhang Haiou 張海鷗 et Zhang Zhenqian 張振謙, « Tang-Song qingci de wenti xingtai he wenxue xing » 唐宋青詞的文體形態和文學性, *Wenxue yichan* 2009/2, p. 46-53.

Zhang Peiyu 張培瑜, *Sanqian wubai nian liri tianxiang* 三千五百年曆日天象, Zhengzhou, Daxiang chuban she, 1997.

Zhang Xunliao 張勛燎 et Bai Bin 白彬 (dir.), *Zhongguo daojiao kaogu* 中國道教考古, 6 vol., Pékin, Xianzhuang shuju, 2006.

Zhang Zehong 張澤洪, *Daojiao zhaijiao fuzhou yishi* 道教齋醮符咒儀式, Chengdu, Ba Shu, 1999.

–, « Daojiao zhaijiao shishang de qingci » 道教齋醮史上的青詞, *Shijie zongjiao yanjiu*, 2005/2, p. 112-122.

Zhang Zhenjun, « Observations on the life and works of Liu Yiqing », *Early Medieval China* 20, 2014, p. 83-104.

Zhao Yi 趙益, « Nanchao daojing *Santian neijie jing* zaitan » 南朝道經《三天內解經》再探, *Nanjing Xiaozhuang xueyuan xuebao*, 2006/3, p. 43-48.

Zhao Zhen 趙貞, « "Jiuyao xingnian" lüeshuo : yi P. 3779 wei zhongxin » 「九曜行年」略說 – 以 P. 3779 爲中心, *Dunhuang xue jikan* 2005/3, p. 21-35.

Zheng Zhiming 鄭志明, « *Chisong zi zhangli* yu shengsi de yishi zhiliao » 赤松子章曆與生死的儀式治療, *Zongjiao xue yanjiu* 2010 (supplément 增刊), p. 84-101.

Zhou Xibo 周西波, *Du Guangting daojiao yifan zhi yanjiu* 杜光庭道教儀範之研究, Taipei, Xin Wenfeng, 2003.

–, « Du Guangting qingci zuopin chutan » 杜光庭青詞作品初探, dans Zheng Zhiming 鄭志明 (dir.), *Daojiao de lishi yu wenxue* 道教的歷史與文學, Chiayi, Nanhua daxue zongjiao wenhua yanjiu zhongxin, 2000, p. 1-25.

Zhou Yanping 周艷萍, « *Chisong zi zhangli* zeri biji yanjiu » 《赤松子章曆》擇日避忌研究, mémoire de master, Université de Pékin, 2007.

Zhu Yueli 朱越利, *Daojiao kaoxin ji* 道教考信集, Jinan, Qi Lu shu she, 2014.

Zürcher, Erik, *The Buddhist conquest of China : the spread and adaptation of Buddhism in early medieval China*, 3e éd., Leyde, Brill, 2007.

–, « Buddhist influence on early Taoism : a survey of scriptural evidence », *T'oung pao* 66, 1980, p. 84-147.

–, « Prince Moonlight : messianism and eschatology in early medieval Chinese Buddhism », *T'oung pao* 68, 1982, p. 1-75.

Index

Liste des illustrations

Planches

Figures

Table des matières

COLLECTION HISTOIRE

CLASSEMENT CHRONOLOGIQUE

[Généralités sur l'Histoire]

[H 142] Alain BOUREAU, *Kantorowicz. Histoires d'un historien*

[H 128] Gérard DELILLE, *L'Économie de Dieu. Famille et marché entre christianisme, hébraïsme et islam*

[H 88] Kurt FLASH, *Prendre congé de Dilthey. Que serait un néohistorisme en histoire de la philosophie?* suivi de *Congé à Dilthey*

[H 137] David. S. LANDES, *L'Heure qu'il est. Les Horloges, la mesure du temps et la formation du monde moderne*

[H 8] Daniel Shabetaï MILO, *Trahir le temps (Histoire)*

[H 10] Daniel Shabetaï MILO & Alain BOURREAU, *Alter Histoire. Essais d'histoire expérimentale*

[Généralités sur l'Antiquité]

[H 102] Polymnia ATHANASSIADI, *Vers la pensée unique. La montée de l'intolérance dans l'Antiquité classique*

[H 7] Jérôme CARCOPINO, *Les Bonnes Leçons*

[H 3] Moses Immanuel FINLEY, *On a perdu la guerre de Troie. Propos et polémiques sur l'Antiquité*

[H 33] Peter GARNSEY, *Famine et approvisionnement dans le monde gréco-romain. Réactions aux risques et aux crises*

[H 68] Peter GARNSEY, *Conceptions de l'esclavage d'Aristote à saint Augustin*

[H 118] Peter GARNSEY, *Penser la propriété. De l'Antiquité jusqu'à l'ère des révolutions*

[H 28] Fritz GRAF, *La Magie dans l'Antiquité gréco-romaine. Idéologie et pratique*

[H 1] Pierre GRIMAL, *Les Erreurs de la liberté*

[H 114] Alfredo LÓPEZ AUSTIN & Leonardo LÓPEZ LUJÁN, *Le Passé indigène. Histoire pré-coloniale du Mexique*

[H 31] Einar MÁR JÓNSSON, *Le Miroir. Naissance d'un genre littéraire*

[H 64] Ramsay MACMULLEN, *Les Émotions dans l'Histoire, ancienne et moderne*

[H 15] Arnaldo MOMIGLIANO, *Les Fondations du savoir historique*

[H 135] Vivian NUTTON, *La Médecine antique*

[H 84] Louis ROBERT, *Choix d'écrits*

[H 66] Youval ROTMAN, *Les Esclaves et l'esclavage. De la Méditerranée antique à la Méditerranée médiévale (VIe-XIe siècles)*

[H 39] Aline ROUSSELLE, *La Contamination spirituelle. Science, droit et religion dans l'Antiquité*

[H 17] Édouard WILL & Claude ORRIEUX, *« Prosélytisme juif » ? Histoire d'une erreur*

[L'Extrême Orient]

[H 104] Damien CHAUSSENDE, *Des Trois royaumes aux Jin. La légitimation du pouvoir impérial en Chine au IIIe siècle*

[H 129] Cédric FERRIER, *L'Inde des Gupta (IVe-VIe siècle)*

[H 109] Pierre MARSONE, *La Steppe et l'Empire. La formation de la dynastie Khitan (Liao). IVe-Xe siècles*

[H 119] Yuri PINES, *L'Invention de la Chine éternelle. Comment les maîtres-penseurs des Royaumes combattants ont construit l'empire le plus long de l'histoire (Vᵉ-IIIᵉ siècles avant J.-C .)*

[H 136] Michèle PIRAZZOLI-T'SERSTEVENS & Marianne BUJARD, *Les Dynasties Qin et Han. Histoire générale de la Chine (221 av. J.-C. - 220 apr. J.-C.)*

[H 151] Franciscus VERELLEN, *Conjurer la destinée. Rétribution et délivrance dans le taoïsme médiéval*

[Histoire Grecque]

[H 77] Alain DUPLOUY, *Le Prestige des élites. Recherches sur les modes de reconnaissance sociale en Grèce entre les Xᵉ et Vᵉ siècles avant J.-C.*

[H 74] Pierre ELLINGER, *La Fin des maux. D'un Pausanias à l'autre. Essai de mythologie et d'histoire*

[H 76] Christian HABICHT, *Athènes hellénistique. Histoire de la cité d'Alexandre le Grand à Marc Antoine*

[H 25] Mogens Herman HANSEN, *La Démocratie athénienne à l'époque de Démosthène. Structures, principes et idéologie*

[H 50] Mogens Herman HANSEN, Polis *et cité-État. Un concept antique et son équivalent moderne*

[H 92] Mogens Herman HANSEN, Polis. *Une introduction à la cité grecque*

[H 5] Victor Davis HANSON, *Le Modèle occidental de la guerre. La bataille d'infanterie dans la Grèce classique*

[H 36] Jean IRIGOIN, *Tradition et critique des textes grecs*

[H 148] Donald KAGAN, *Le Déclenchement de la guerre du Péloponnèse. Nouvelle histoire de la guerre du Péloponnèse, I.*

[H 57] Nicole LORAUX (dir.), *La Grèce au féminin*

[H 63] John MA, *Antiochos III et les cités de l'Asie Mineure occidentale*

[H 42] Irad MALKIN, *La Méditerranée spartiate. Mythe et territoire*

[H 9] Christian MEIER, *De la tragédie grecque comme art politique*

[H 79] Charalampos ORFANOS, *Les Sauvageons d'Athènes ou la didactique du rire chez Aristophane*

[H 147] Robert PARKER, *Miasma. Souillure et purification dans la religion grecque archaïque et classique*

[H 112] Stéphane RATTI, *Polémiques entre païens et chrétiens*

[H 113] Nicolas RICHER, *La Religion des Spartiates. Croyances et cultes dans l'Antiquité*

[H 53] Annie SCHNAPP-GOURBEILLON, *Aux origines de la Grèce (XIIIᵉ-VIIIᵉ siècles avant J.-C.). La genèse du politique*

[H 70] Pierre VIDAL-NAQUET, *Le Miroir brisé. Tragédie athénienne et politique*

[H 72] Pierre VIDAL-NAQUET, *L'Atlantide. Petite histoire d'un mythe platonicien*

[Histoire Romaine]

[H 95] Maria Grazia BAJONI, *Les Grammairiens lascifs. La grammaire à la fin de l'Empire romain*

[H 117] Véronique BOUDON-MILLOT, *Galien de Pergame. Un médecin grec à Rome*

[H 19] André CHASTAGNOL, *Le Sénat romain à l'époque impériale. Recherches sur la composition de l'Assemblée et le statut de ses membres*

[H 97] Pierre CHUVIN, *Chronique des derniers païens. La disparition du paganisme dans l'Empire romain, du règne de Constantin à celui de Justinien*

[H 27] Eugen CIZEK, *L'Empereur Aurélien et son temps*

[H 153] Jérôme FRANCE, *Tribut. Une histoire fiscale de la conquête romaine*

[H 11] Alexandre GRANDAZZI, *La Fondation de Rome. Réflexion sur l'Histoire*

[H 14] Ramsay MACMULLEN, *Le Déclin de Rome et la corruption du pouvoir*

[H 58] Ramsay MacMullen, *La Romanisation à l'époque d'Auguste*

[H 13] Régis François Martin, *Les Douze Césars. Du mythe à la réalité*

[H 32] Jean-Marie Pailler, *Bacchus. Figures et pouvoirs*

[H 101] Rose Mary Sheldon, *Renseignement et espionnage dans la Rome antique*

[H 110] Giusto Traina, *Carrhes, 9 juin 53 avant J.-C. Anatomie d'une défaite*

[H 2] Robert Turcan, *Les Cultes orientaux dans le monde romain*

[H 24] Robert Turcan, *Mithra et le mithriacisme*

[H 6] Zvi Yavetz, *César et son image. Des limites du charisme en politique*

[Antiquité tardive]

[H 134] Peter Brown, *À travers un trou d'aiguille. La richesse, la chute de Rome et la formation du christianisme*

[H 40] Ramsay MacMullen, *Christianisme et paganisme du IVe au VIIIe siècle*

[H 89] Ramsay MacMullen, *Voter pour définir Dieu. Trois siècles de conciles (253-553)*

[H 127] Éric Rebillard, *Les Chrétiens de l'Antiquité tardive et leurs identités multiples*

[H 108] Suzanne Teillet, *Des Goths à la nation gothique. Les origines de l'idée de Nation en Occident du Ve au VIIe siècle*

[H 99] Giusto Traina, *428. Une année ordinaire à la fin de l'Empire romain*

[Histoire Médiévale]

[H 126] Thomas N. Bisson, *La Crise du XIIe siècle. Pouvoir et seigneurie à l'aube du gouvernement européen*

[H 22] Alain Boureau, *L'Événement sans fin. Récit et christianisme au Moyen Âge*

[H 62] Alain Boureau, *La Loi du royaume. Les moines, le droit et la construction de la nation anglaise (XIe-XIIIe siècles)*

[H 80] Alain Boureau, *La Religion de l'État. La construction de la République étatique dans le discours théologique de l'Occident médiéval (1250-1350)*

[H 85] Alain Boureau, *L'Empire du livre. Pour une histoire du savoir scolastique (1200-1380)*

[H 93] Alain Boureau, *De vagues individus. La condition humaine dans la pensée scolastique*

[H 94] Alain Boureau, *Théologie, science et censure au XIIIe siècle. Le cas de Jean Peckham*

[H 103] Alain Boureau, *L'Inconnu dans la maison. Richard de Mediavilla, les franciscains et la vierge Marie à la fin du XIIIe siècle*

[H 125] Alain Boureau, *Le Désir dicté. Histoire du vœu religieux dans l'Occident médiéval*

[H 133] Alain Boureau, *L'Errance des normes. Éléments d'éthique scolastique (1220-1320)*

[H 132] Gianluca Briguglia, *Le Pouvoir mis à la question. Théologiens et théorie politique à l'époque du conflit entre Boniface VIII et Philippe le Bel*

[H 152] Julie Claustre, *Faire ses comptes au Moyen Âge*

[H 121] Arsenio Frugoni, *Arnaud de Brescia dans les sources du XIIe siècle*

[H 123] Arsenio Frugoni & Chiara Frugoni, *Une journée au Moyen Âge*

[H 111] Chiara Frugoni, *Le Moyen Âge sur le bout du nez. Lunettes, boutons et autres inventions médiévales*

[H 131] Chiara Frugoni, *Le Moyen Âge par ses images*

[H 105] Joseph Goering, *La Vierge et le Graal. Les origines d'une légende*

[H 122] Christophe Grellard, *Jean de Salisbury et la renaissance médiévale du scepticisme*

[H 31] Einar Már JÓNSSON, *Le Miroir. Naissance d'un genre littéraire*

[H 138] Joel KAYE, *Histoire de l'équilibre (1250-1375). L'apparition d'un nouveau modèle d'équilibre et son impact sur la pensée*

[H 38] Peter LINEHAN, *Les Dames de Zamora. Secrets, stupre et pouvoirs dans l'Église espagnole du XIIIe siècle*

[H 81] Elsa MARMURSZTEJN, *L'Autorité des maîtres. Scolastique, normes et société au XIIIe siècle*

[H 12] Robert Ian MOORE, *La Persécution. Sa formation en Europe (Xe-XIIIe siècles)*

[H 75] Donald MacGillivray NICOL, *Les Derniers Siècles de Byzance (1261-1453)*

[H 145] Agostino PARAVICINI BAGLIANI, *Le Bestiaire du pape*

[H 143] Gian Luca POTESTÀ, *Le Dernier Messie. Prophétie et souveraineté au Moyen Âge*

[H 66] Youval ROTMAN, *Les Esclaves et l'esclavage. De la Méditerranée antique à la Méditerranée médiévale (VIe-XIe siècles)*

[H 73] Steven RUNCIMAN, *Le schisme d'Orient. La papauté et les Églises d'Orient (XIe-XIIe siècles)*

[H 90] Steven RUNCIMAN, *Les Vêpres siciliennes. Une histoire du monde méditerranéen à la fin du XIIIe siècle*

[H 45] Joseph SHATZMILLER, *Shylock revu et corrigé. Les juifs, les chrétiens et le prêt d'argent dans la société médiévale*

[H 45] Joseph SHATZMILLER, *Shylock revu et corrigé. Les juifs, les chrétiens et le prêt d'argent dans la société médiévale*

[H 140] Catherine VERNA, *L'Industrie au village. Essai de micro-histoire (Arles-sur-Tech, XIVe et XVe siècles)*

[H 120] Nicolas WEILL-PAROT, *Points aveugles de la nature. La rationalité scientifique médiévale face à l'occulte, l'attraction magnétique et l'horreur du vide*

[H 150] Nicolas WEILL-PAROT, *Le vol dans les airs au Moyen Âge. Essai historique sur une utopie scientifique*

[H 17] Édouard WILL & Claude ORRIEUX, *« Prosélytisme juif » ? Histoire d'une erreur*

[Histoire Moderne]

[H 87] Florin AFTALION, *L'Économie de la Révolution française*

[H 96] Marcel BATAILLON, *Les Jésuites dans l'Espagne du XVIe siècle*

[H 106] Robert Descimon & Élie Haddad (sous la direction de), *Épreuves de noblesse. Les expériences nobiliaires de la haute robe parisienne (XVIe-XVIIIe siècle)*

[H 82] Ralph GIESEY, *Le Rôle méconnu de la loi salique. La succession royale XIVe-XVIe siècles*

[H 23] Anthony GRAFTON, *Faussaires et critiques. Créativité et duplicité chez les érudits occidentaux*

[H 91] Sophie HOUDARD, *Les invasions mystiques. Spiritualités, hétérodoxies et censures au début de l'époque moderne*

[H 65] Annick LEMPÉRIÈRE, *Entre Dieu et le roi, la République. Mexico, XVIe-XIXe siècles*

[H 83] Sabrina LORIGA, *Soldats. Un laboratoire disciplinaire : l'armée piémontaise au XVIIIe siècle*

[H 98] Evyatar MARIENBERG, *Niddah. Lorsque les juifs conceptualisent la menstruation*

[H 29] Hélène MERLIN-KAJMAN, *Public et littérature en France au XVIIe siècle*

[H 49] Hélène MERLIN-KAJMAN, *L'Excentricité académique. Littérature, institution, société*

[H 139] Robert MUCHEMBLED, *La Civilisation des odeurs (XVIe-début XIXe siècle)*

[H 47] Jean-Christophe SALADIN, *La Bataille du grec à la Renaissance*

[Histoire Contemporaine]

[H 60] Gilles BATAILLON, *Genèse des guerres internes en Amérique centrale (1960-1983)*

[H 55] Delphine BECHTEL *et alii* (sous la direction de), *Écriture de l'histoire et identité juive. L'Europe ashkénaze (XIX*e*-XX*e *siècles)*

[H 51] Christopher Robert BROWNING, *Politique nazie, travailleurs juifs, bourreaux allemands*

[H 69] Christopher Robert BROWNING, *Des hommes ordinaires. Le 101*e *bataillon de réserve de la police allemande et la Solution finale en Pologne*

[H 86] Christopher Robert BROWNING, *Les Origines de la Solution finale. L'évolution de la politique antijuive des nazis (septembre 1939-mars 1942)*

[H 107] Christopher Robert BROWNING, *À l'intérieur d'un camp de travail nazi. Récits des survivants : mémoire et histoire*

[H 78] Giuliana, Marisa, Gabriella CARDOSI, *À la frontière. La question des mariages mixtes durant la persécution antijuive en Italie et en Europe (1935-1945)*

[H 61] Renée DRAY-BENSOUSAN, *Les Juifs à Marseille (1940-1944)*

[H 44] Gabriel GORODETSKY, *Le Grand Jeu de dupes. Staline et l'invasion allemande*

[H 144] Gilles GUIHEUX, *La République populaire de Chine. Histoire générale de la Chine (1949 à nos jours)*

[H 46] Katy HAZAN, *Les Orphelins de la Shoah. Les maisons de l'espoir (1944-1960)*

[H 100] Maury KLEIN, *Le Krach de 1929*

[H 52] Tamara KONDRATIEVA, *Gouverner et nourrir. Du pouvoir en Russie (XVI*e*-XX*e *siècles)*

[H 141] Tamara KONDRATIEVA, *Bolcheviks et Jacobins. Itinéraire des analogies*

[H 59] Guenter LEWY, *La Persécution des Tziganes par les nazis*

[H 98] Evyatar MARIENBERG, *Niddah. Lorsque les juifs conceptualisent la menstruation*

[H 54] Mark MAZOWER, *Dans la Grèce d'Hitler (1941-1944)*

[H 124] Hervé MAZUREL, *Vertiges de la guerre. Byron, les philhellènes et le mirage grec*

[H 146] Xavier PAULÈS, *La République de Chine. Histoire générale de la Chine (1912-1949)*

[H 48] Robert Neel PROCTOR, *La Guerre des nazis contre le cancer*

[H 18] Claude SINGER, *Vichy, l'Université et les Juifs. Les silences et la mémoire*

[H 37] Claude SINGER, *L'Université libérée. L'Université épurée (1943-1947)*

[H 56] Claude SINGER, *Le Juif Süss et la propagande nazie. L'Histoire confisquée*

[H 149] Benn STEIL, *Le Plan Marshall. À l'aube de la Guerre Froide*

[H 116] Adam TOOZE, *Le Salaire de la destruction. Formation et ruine de l'économie nazie*

[H 130] Adam TOOZE, *Le Déluge. 1916-1931. Un nouvel ordre mondial*

[H 115] Sylvain VENAYRE, *Panorama du voyage (1780-1920). Mots, figures, pratiques*

Composition et mise en pages
Nord Compo à Villeneuve-d'Ascq

Ce volume,
le cent cinquante et unième
de la collection « Histoire »
publié aux Éditions Les Belles Lettres,
a été achevé d'imprimer
en février 2021
sur les presses
de La Manufacture imprimeur
52200 Langres

N° d'éditeur : 9780
N° d'imprimeur : 210193
Dépôt légal : mars 2021